MOON HANDBOOKS®

ALASKA

© DON PITCHER

Russian Church in Ninilchik

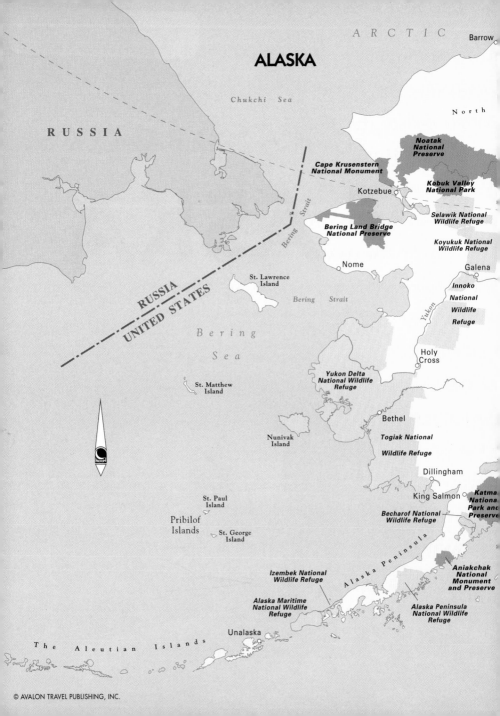

ALASKA

ARCTIC

Barrow

Chukchi Sea

North

RUSSIA

Noatak National Preserve

Cape Krusenstern National Monument

Kobuk Valley National Park

Kotzebue

Selawik National Wildlife Refuge

Bering Strait

Bering Land Bridge National Preserve

Koyukuk National Wildlife Refuge

Nome

Galena

RUSSIA

UNITED STATES

St. Lawrence Island

Innoko National Wildlife Refuge

Bering Strait

Yukon

Bering Sea

Holy Cross

St. Matthew Island

Yukon Delta National Wildlife Refuge

Nunivak Island

Bethel

Togiak National Wildlife Refuge

Dillingham

St. Paul Island

King Salmon

Katmai National Park and Preserve

Pribilof Islands

St. George Island

Becharof National Wildlife Refuge

Alaska Peninsula

Aniakchak National Monument and Preserve

Izembek National Wildlife Refuge

Alaska Maritime National Wildlife Refuge

Alaska Peninsula National Wildlife Refuge

Unalaska

The Aleutian Islands

O C E A N

Beaufort Sea

Prudhoe Bay

S l o p e

NORTHWEST TERRITORIES

Inuvik

Arctic National Wildlife Refuge

Vuntut National Park

UNITED STATES

CANADA

Gates of the Arctic National Park and Preserve

PIPELINE

DALTON HWY

TRANS-ALASKA

River

Arctic   Circle

Porcupine

Mackenzie

River

Kanuti National Wildlife Refuge

Yukon Flats National Wildlife Refuge

DEMPSTER HWY

River

Nowitna National Wildlife Refuge

White Mts. Nat. Rec. Area

Circle

YUKON TERRITORY

Fairbanks

Yukon

Yukon–Charley Rivers National Preserve

TOP OF THE WORLD HWY

②

Denali National Park and Preserve

②

Delta Junction

Dawson City

⑥

River

DENALI HWY

④

⑤

KLONDIKE HWY

⑧

Tok

Beaver Creek

④

③

Glennallen

①

TOK CUTOFF

②

ALASKA HWY

④

Watson Lake

Kenai National Wildlife Refuge

McCarthy

⑥

Whitehorse

Lake Clark National Park and Preserve

Wrangell–St Elias National Park and Preserve

①

Haines Jct.

①

Anchorage

Valdez

Kluane National Park

③

②

Skagway

CASSIAR

③

Cordova

BRITISH COLUMBIA

HWY

①

Seward

Chugash National Forest

Haines

Homer

Kenai Peninsula

Yakutat

JUNEAU

Cook Inlet

Kenai Fjords National Park

Glacier Bay National Park and Preserve

Gulf of Alaska

Chichagof Island

Petersburg

Kodiak

Admiralty Island National Monument

Sitka

Tongass National Forest

Wrangell

Misty Fiords National Monument

Hyder

Kodiak Island

Baronof Island

Stewart

Kodiak National Wildlife Refuge

Ketchikan

PACIFIC

Prince of Wales Island

Prince Rupert

OCEAN

0   100 mi

0   100 km

Queen Charlotte Islands

tundra pond near Kotzebue

© DON PITCHER

MOON HANDBOOKS®
ALASKA

EIGHTH EDITION

DON PITCHER

AVALON
TRAVEL

MAPS

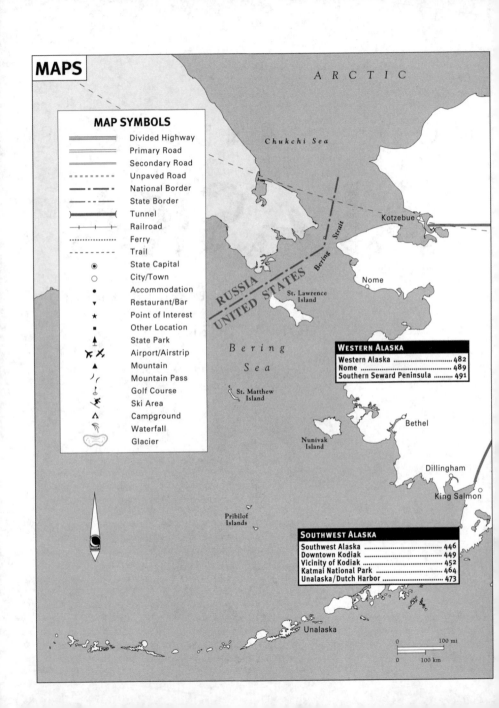

MAP SYMBOLS

Divided Highway	
Primary Road	
Secondary Road	
Unpaved Road	
National Border	
State Border	
Tunnel	
Railroad	
Ferry	
Trail	
State Capital	
City/Town	
Accommodation	
Restaurant/Bar	
Point of Interest	
Other Location	
State Park	
Airport/Airstrip	
Mountain	
Mountain Pass	
Golf Course	
Ski Area	
Campground	
Waterfall	
Glacier	

A R C T I C

Chukchi Sea

Kotzebue

RUSSIA
UNITED STATES

Bering Strait

Nome

St. Lawrence Island

B e r i n g

S e a

St. Matthew Island

Bethel

Nunivak Island

Dillingham

King Salmon

Pribilof Islands

Unalaska

0	100 mi
0	100 km

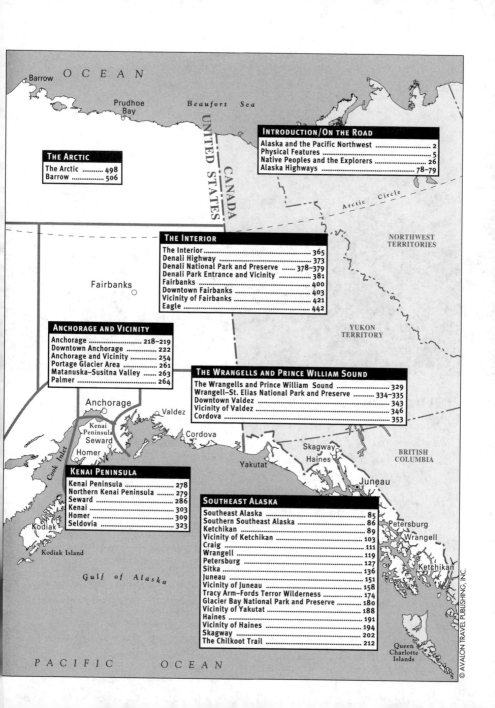

Barrow

OCEAN

Prudhoe
Bay

Beaufort Sea

UNITED STATES / CANADA

Arctic Circle

NORTHWEST
TERRITORIES

Fairbanks

YUKON
TERRITORY

Anchorage

Valdez

Kenai
Peninsula
Seward

Cordova

Homer

Skagway
Haines

BRITISH
COLUMBIA

Yakutat

Juneau

Cook Inlet

Kodiak

Kodiak Island

Gulf of Alaska

Petersburg

Wrangell

Ketchikan

Queen
Charlotte
Islands

PACIFIC   OCEAN

© AVALON TRAVEL PUBLISHING, INC.

Contents

Introduction 1

Dramatic mountains and immense glaciers. Lush forested islands draped in mist and mystery. Rivers thick with migrating salmon. Days of endless summer sun. Northern lights dancing across a dark winter sky. This is Alaska: a place apart, a last frontier that stirs the imagination of people the world over.

On the Road 47

The range of activities in the Great Land is mind-boggling: hiking, skiing, dog-sledding, snowmobiling, mountain biking, hunting, fishing, kayaking, canoeing, flightseeing.... Where to begin? Start planning your adventure here.

Southeast Alaska 84

Waiting beyond some 500 miles of rugged, rocky coastline, this is Alaska's Eden. Gray-blue clouds play a constant game of hide-and-seek with verdant islands, deep fjords drive up between snow-covered summits, waterfalls plummet hundreds of feet through evergreen forests, and brown bears prowl rivers rich in salmon.

Anchorage and Vicinity 216

The state's largest urban center offers all of the pleasures of city life, including good restaurants, hip coffeehouses, hopping bars, world-class museums, and a flower-filled downtown. But with Mt. McKinley and the Alaska Range looming above the skyline, you'll never forget you're in the last frontier.

The Kenai Peninsula

*The ever-popular Kenai is Alaska in microcosm, with
mountains and glaciers, fjords and offshore islands, and
large fish-filled rivers and lakes. Set off from Seward to
explore the Harding Icefield, or spend a day enjoying the
arts—man-made and otherwise—in Homer, Cosmic
Hamlet by the Sea.*

The Wrangells and Prince William Sound

*The glacial waters of Prince William Sound invite
visitors to cruise in the company of orcas and sea lions.
Meanwhile, the Wrangells include some of North
America's tallest mountains in a park that's less
accessible—and less crowded—than Denali.*

The Interior

Denali National Park is the most accessible wilderness in the world, marked by tundra vistas and drunken forests, snowcapped mountains and attending glaciers, high passes along adrenaline-pumping drops, abundant wildlife ... and above it all, 20,000-foot Mt. McKinley. Continue north to discover Fairbanks, a city on the edge of the arctic.

Southwest Alaska

This incredible sweep of wild and stormy coastline teems with marinelife, including walruses and sea lions. Kodiak Island is famous for its brown bears, while the windswept Aleutian and Pribilof Islands are a bird-watcher's paradise.

Western Alaska 481

This is Alaska's true outback, with scattered settlements far from the reach of "civilization." Dillingham, on the southern end of the Bering Sea, is considered the world's most productive red salmon fishery. Visitors to Nome will find that the legacy of the Gold Rush lives on.

The Arctic 498

Here, nature truly dominates, and human habitation is rare. The rugged Brooks Range parallels the Arctic Circle in a long arc, descending on its northern margin to the treeless tundra of the North Slope. The threatened but still pristine Arctic National Wildlife Refuge is home to a surprising diversity of wildlife—most notably the Porcupine caribou herd.

Resources 509

ABOUT THE AUTHOR
Don Pitcher

© DON PITCHER

Perhaps Don Pitcher's love of travel came about because he moved so much as a child; by age 15 he had lived in six states and two dozen East Coast and Midwestern towns. Don's family hails from Maine, but being born in Atlanta made him a southerner with New England blood. He moved west for college, receiving a master's degree from the University of California, Berkeley, where his thesis examined wildfires in Sequoia National Park. When his first scientific paper was published, he appeared headed into the world of ecological research.

Shortly after grad school Don landed what seemed the coolest job on the planet: being flown around Alaska's massive Wrangell–St. Elias National Park in a helicopter while conducting fire research. Wild places continued to beckon, and over the next 15 years Don built backcountry trails, worked as a wilderness ranger, mapped grizzly habitat, and operated salmon weirs—anything to avoid an office job. After that first season in Alaska, Don spent three months in the South Pacific, and quickly found himself addicted to travel. These explorations eventually took him to all 50 states and 35 countries.

During his first summer season, Don bought a copy of *Moon Handbooks Alaska-Yukon* and made notes in the margins. He later wrote the author, asking if he needed help on the next edition. That contact eventually led Don to become a travel writer, and he is now the author of this book, along with Moon Handbooks to Wyoming, Yellowstone and Grand Teton National Parks, Washington, and the San Juan Islands. He has photographed two popular travel books, and his images have appeared in a multitude of other publications and advertisements, and can be found in galleries across Alaska.

Don Pitcher now works full-time as a travel writer and photographer, basing his travels from Homer, Alaska, where he lives with his wife, Karen Shemet, and their children, Aziza and Rio. Find details on his latest projects at www.donpitcher.com.

In memory of Mary Ellen Fogarty
1957—1997

Your spirit lives in the land you loved
and in the people whose lives you touched.

Introduction

There is something about Alaska that has always stirred the imagination. From the first migrants who crossed the Bering land bridge during the ice ages, to today's travelers escaping the madness of city life, Alaska draws people from the world over to see its wonders: dramatic mountains and immense glaciers, rivers thick with migrating salmon, lush forested islands draped in mist and mystery, northern lights dancing across a dark winter sky. Here you can still find Native peoples following their subsistence way of life, and view wildlife that is truly wild—foraging brown bears, herds of caribou stretching to the horizon, or a cliff alive with thousands of nesting seabirds. This is still a place where crabbers risk their lives in wild Bering Sea storms; where you can en-counter dog teams on remote winter trails, fly by floatplane to places unchanged since primeval times, kayak in pristine inlets with eagles and whales as your companions, hike in the foot-steps of Klondike gold-rush miners, or hear the cry of a wolf as dusk falls.

Alaska is a place apart—both physically and culturally—from the rest of the United States. In Alaska, the term *wilderness* does not refer to a small enclave of the natural world surrounded by shopping malls, traffic jams, and suburban sprawl. The Great Land is so huge, so wild, so underpop-ulated, that it's almost incomprehensible: It falls right off the edge of your imagination. Here, like nowhere else on earth, human developments will always be dwarfed by the vastness of the land.

© DON PITCHER

Mt. Verstovia, Sitka

INTRODUCTION

EIGHT STATES IN ONE

This book divides Alaska into eight regions: Southeast, Anchorage and Vicinity, Kenai Peninsula, the Wrangells and Prince William Sound, Interior, Southwest, Western, and Arctic. (The term **Southcentral Alaska** is often applied to a broad middle portion of the state that includes Anchorage, the Kenai Peninsula, Prince William Sound, and the Wrangells.)

Southeast is Alaska's "Panhandle," a coastal region dissected by the Inside Passage. This intricate network of narrow waterways, where rugged, forested mountains rise from the water's edge, extends along the western edge of Canada from south of Ketchikan up to Skagway. The climate is cool, with very high precipitation. With few exceptions, transportation is limited to ferries and planes.

Anchorage and Vicinity is the state's economic and transportation fulcrum, possessing half the population of Alaska, the biggest airport, biggest malls, tallest buildings, and a diversity of lodging places, restaurants, and other cultural amenities. But the Chugach Mountains are nearby, and it's only a few hours' drive or a

ALASKA AND THE PACIFIC NORTHWEST

SIBERIA

RUSSIA
UNITED STATES

Bering Sea

ARCTIC OCEAN

Beaufort Sea

Fairbanks

Arctic Circle

NUNAVUT

ALASKA

Anchorage

NORTHWEST TERRITORIES

YUKON TERRITORY

PACIFIC OCEAN

Juneau

ALBERTA

Ketchikan

BRITISH COLUMBIA

Edmonton

Calgary

Vancouver CANADA

Seattle   MT

WA

Frankfurt

4,678 mi

3,434 mi

3,385 mi

Tokyo

2,846 mi

Anchorage

1,448 mi

Chicago

New York

Seattle

Portland

OR   ID

2,343 mi

Los Angeles

0   300 mi
0   300 km

CA   UT

NV

San Francisco

short flight to a multitude of wilderness destinations. This chapter also includes the fast-growing Matanuska–Susitna Valley to the north and the ski town of Girdwood to the south.

Kenai Peninsula is Anchorage's playground. Here you'll find world-famous salmon and halibut fishing, along with wildlife and glacier cruises, the trails, campgrounds, and cabins of Chugach National Forest, and fun small towns such as Homer and Seward.

The Wrangells and Prince William Sound encompasses the Copper River Valley and rugged Wrangell Mountains on the eastern edge of the state, along with the picturesque and island-filled Prince William Sound, which arcs across the Gulf of Alaska. The chapter includes the towns of Valdez, Cordova, Whittier, and Glennallen, but the high point is Wrangell–St. Elias National Park, the largest in America.

Interior includes Denali National Park, capped by the tallest mountain in North America—Mt. McKinley—along with the rest of the towering Alaska Range and hundreds of miles of hilly and forested country in all directions. Large rivers drain this vast region—the Yukon, Tanana, and Kuskokwim—home to a smattering of small towns and one mid-sized city (Alaska's second largest), Fairbanks. The region has short, warm summers and long, cold winters, with little precipitation, but lots of mosquitoes.

Southwest includes Kodiak, the Alaska Peninsula, the Aleutian Islands, and the Pribilof Islands. It's rugged and mostly treeless, with a population largely composed of Native Aleut and Eskimo. The climate is particularly disagreeable: foggy summers, wind-chilled winters, very stormy, and little sun. This area is also one of the world's most active volcano-and-earthquake zones: 4 out of 10 of the world's earthquakes occur here, and 40 active volcanoes mark the line where the Pacific tectonic plate bumps up against the North American plate. Transportation is mostly by plane, though limited ferry service exists.

Western is true bush Alaska, with a few mid-sized towns (Nome, Bethel, and Dillingham), along with a host of tiny Native villages. Much of this land is treeless tundra, but there are also majestic mountains and forests (notably at Wood-Tikchik State Park) and the richest salmon fishery in the world, at Bristol Bay. The gold-rush town of Nome has a rich history and many miles of roads to explore.

The **Arctic** region occupies a huge expanse of sparsely populated country dotted with very modest population centers at Kotzebue and Barrow, along with numerous Native villages and the sprawling oil complex around Prudhoe Bay. The rugged Brooks Range parallels the Arctic Circle across Alaska, but the northern edge of the state is vast, treeless tundra that extends all the way to the Arctic Ocean. The climate is an extreme version of the Interior's: long, cold winters and brief, cool summers, with a tiny amount of precipitation. Access is almost entirely by plane.

The Land

The major physical features of western North America continue unbroken into that giant head of land that is Alaska. The Great Plains of the U.S. Midwest extend to become the Mackenzie Lowlands and the North Slope, while the Rocky Mountains form an inland spine from deep in Mexico to the Brooks Range. West of the Rockies, a high plateau runs from British Columbia north through the interiors of Yukon and Alaska, then west to the delta of the Yukon River, where it dips into the Bering Sea.

To the west of this plateau, two parallel chains and an intervening depression can be traced all the way from Mexico to Alaska. The Sierra Nevada of California become in turn the Cascades of Oregon and Washington, the Coast Mountains of British Columbia, the St. Elias and Wrangell Mountains, the Alaska Range, and finally the Aleutian Range, which then sinks into the Pacific just short of Asia. Closer to the ocean, California's Coast Range becomes the Olympic Mountains of Washington. Farther north, a string of islands from Vancouver to the Queen Charlottes and the Alexander Archipelago runs into the St.

Elias Mountains, where the two chains unite into a jagged, ice-capped knot. In Alaska they divide again as the Chugach and Kenai Mountains swing southwest toward Kodiak Island. Between these parallel chains is a 3,000-mile-long depression starting with California's Central Valley, then continuing with Puget Sound, the Inside Passage, the Susitna Basin in Southcentral Alaska, Cook Inlet, and Southwest Alaska's Shelikof Strait. Only four low-level breaks occur in the coastal mountains: the valleys of the Columbia, Fraser, Skeena, and Stikine Rivers. Most of the places described in this book are within or near this mighty barrier, which contains the highest peaks, the largest glaciers, and most of the active volcanoes in North America.

GEOLOGY

Plate Tectonics

Briefly, the huge Pacific plate (the ocean floor) is drifting slowly northeast. It collides with the North American plate, on which the continent rests, along an arc that stretches from the western Aleutians in the Gulf of Alaska to the Inside Passage—defining one section of the famous Pacific "Ring of Fire." This meeting of plates jams the ocean floor under the continental landmass and gives rise to violent geologic forces: upthrusting mountains, extensive and large earthquakes, volcanic rumblings and eruptions, and movement along fault lines.

Somewhere in the mists of early geologic time, a particularly persistent and powerful collision between the two plates caused the Brooks Range to rise; erosion has whittled its highest peaks to 8,000 feet, half their original height. Later, a similar episode thrust the Alaska Range into shape. The Pacific plate even today continues to nose under the continental plate in the vicinity of Yakutat (near where Southeast meets Southcentral). The force of it pushes Mt. Logan—Canada's highest peak—slowly upward. Learn more about the geological forces that shape Alaska at the University of Alaska Fairbanks **Geophysical Institute** website: www.gi.alaska.edu.

Earthquakes

One of the world's most seismically active regions, Alaska has withstood some of the most

LAND OF SUPERLATIVES

Alaska boasts more superlative statistics than any other state in the country (itself a superlative). Consider: Alaska's total land area—591,000 square miles (375 million acres)—is more than twice that of the next-largest state, Texas. A little more than four Alaskas could be jammed into the continental United States, while almost 300 Delawares could be jigsaw-puzzled into the 49th state. Mt. McKinley (also known as Denali), at 20,306 feet, is the highest point in North America; the Aleutian Trench, plunging to 25,000 feet below sea level, is one of the Pacific's deepest ocean troughs. Sitka, with more than 4,700 square miles within its boundaries, has the largest area of any North American city, and the North Slope Borough, at 88,000 square miles (slightly larger than Idaho), is the largest municipally governed entity in the world. Alaska's 45,000-mile coastline is longer than the rest of the country's combined. Though only 3 percent of the state is covered in glaciers and icefields (debunking the "frozen wasteland" myth—the most common misconception about Alaska), it still has more than 100 times more glacial area than the rest of North America. With all of 635,000 people, Alaska ranks third to last among the states in population, behind only Wyoming and Vermont. If Manhattan had the same population density, 17 people would live there. And if all the Manhattanites were transplanted to Alaska, they'd each have 125 acres.

violent earthquakes and largest tidal waves ever recorded. In the last century, more than 80 Alaskan earthquakes have registered higher than 7 on the Richter scale. The most destructive occurred at 5:35 P.M. on Good Friday, March 27, 1964, when the most powerful earthquake ever recorded in North America rocked Southcentral Alaska. This 9.2 magnitude quake (80 times bigger than the famous 1906 San Francisco earthquake, which is estimated at around 7.8) had a devastating impact on the region, flattening 75 homes and businesses in Anchorage, creating tsunamis that wiped out nearly every coastal village in Southcentral Alaska, and wreaking havoc all the way to California. The quake and its tsunamis killed 131 people. It was the second strongest in the 20th century; only a 9.5 magnitude 1960 quake in Chile was larger.

Anyone who spends more than a few months in Southwest or Southcentral Alaska will probably feel at least one earthquake, and residents of the Aleutian Islands barely take notice of anything with a magnitude less than 6. The **U.S. Geological Survey's** website (http://neic.usgs.gov/neis/states/alaska) provides detailed information on Alaskan earthquakes, including this week's activity.

Tsunamis

An earthquake deep below the ocean floor in the Gulf of Alaska or the open Pacific is especially dangerous to the coasts of Alaska and Hawaii, along with the west coast of Canada and the United States. The activity creates enormous tidal waves (tsunamis), which, though only 3–5 feet high in open ocean, can travel at speeds exceeding 500 miles an hour. Contrary to popular fears, a tsunami does not slam into the coast with 20 or 30 feet of water, washing away everything in its path like a flash flood. Instead, the water slowly inundates the land to a depth of four or five feet. Then, after a brief and chilling calm, the wave is sucked back out to sea in one vast undertow. Most of the destruction caused by the great Good Friday earthquake was of this nature, attested to by hair-raising pictures that you'll see in places like Valdez, Seward, and Kodiak. If you hear a tsunami warning, get to higher ground immediately. The **West Coast & Alaska Tsunami Warning Center** (www.wcatwc.gov)is based in Palmer, and its website provides information on recent and historical tsunamis.

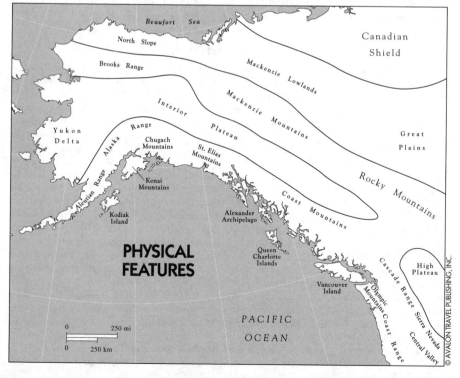

PHYSICAL FEATURES

Beaufort Sea

North Slope

Brooks Range

Interior

Mackenzie Lowlands

Mackenzie Mountains

Canadian Shield

Yukon Delta

Alaska Range

Chugach Mountains

St. Elias Mountains

Plateau

Great Plains

Aleutian Range

Kenai Mountains

Rocky Mountains

Kodiak Island

Alexander Archipelago

Coast Mountains

Queen Charlotte Islands

Vancouver Island

Cascade Range

High Plateau

Olympic Mountains

Coast Range

Sierra Nevada

Central Valley

PACIFIC OCEAN

0   250 mi

0   250 km

© AVALON TRAVEL PUBLISHING, INC.

tourists overlooking Exit Glacier at Kenai Fjords National Park, near Seward

Volcanoes

Like its earthquakes, Alaska's major volcanoes are located along the Aleutian chain. In fact, 57 active volcanoes stretch along this arc, and most have been active in the last 300 years. The largest recorded eruption occurred when Novarupta blew its top in 1912 (see Katmai National Park in the *Southwest Alaska* chapter), the most cataclysmic natural disaster since Krakatoa cracked 30 years earlier.

In the summer of 1992, Mt. Spurr, an active volcano 78 miles west of Anchorage, erupted with dramatic effects. It threw a cloud of ash nearly 50,000 feet into the air, coating Anchorage with an eighth-inch-thick layer of ash and closing Anchorage International Airport for 20 hours. If a mere eighth of an inch doesn't sound like much, imagine living inside a fireplace that hasn't been cleaned lately and you'll get an idea of how it felt. The University of Alaska Fairbanks' **Alaska Volcano Observatory** keeps track of volcanic activity, and its website at www.avo.alaska.edu has details on current and historic eruptions.

GLACIATION

A glacier forms in areas of high precipitation and elevation where the snow is allowed to pile up to great depths, compacting the bottom layers into solid ice. The great weight above the bottom ice (along with the force of gravity) pushes it slowly downward like a giant frozen river, scooping out huge valleys and shearing off entire mountainsides. When the rate of advance is balanced by melt-off, the face of the glacier remains more or less stationary. If the glacier flows more quickly than its face melts, it advances; if it melts faster than it flows, the glacier recedes. All air bubbles are squeezed out of the glacier by this tremendous pressure, which makes glacial ice extremely dense. It's so compact that the higher frequencies of light cannot escape or penetrate it, which explains the dark-blue tinge. And because of its density, it also melts at fantastically slow rates; a small chunk or two will keep a beer in a cooler chilled for a day or two.

Signs of the Glaciers

As you travel up the coast or hike in the national

parks of the Interior, you'll soon start to recognize and identify glacial landforms. While rivers typically erode V-shaped valleys, glaciers gouge out distinctly U-shaped **glacial troughs.** Valleys and ridges branching from the main valley are sliced off to create **hanging valleys** and **truncated spurs.** A side valley that once carried a tributary glacier may be left as a **hanging trough;** from these hanging valleys and troughs waterfalls often tumble. Alpine glaciers scoop out the headwalls of their accumulation basins to form **cirques.** Bare, jagged ridges between cirques are known as **arêtes.**

As a glacier moves down a valley it bulldozes a load of rock, sand, and gravel—known as **glacial till**—ahead of it, or carries it on top. Glacial till that has been dumped is called a **moraine. Lateral moraines** are pushed to the sides of glaciers, while a **terminal moraine** is deposited at the farthest point of the face's advance. A **medial moraine** is formed when two glaciers unite. These ribbonlike strips of rubble can be followed back to the point where the lateral moraines converge between the glaciers.

When looking at a glaciated landscape, watch for gouges and scrape marks on the bedrock, which indicate the direction of glacial flow. Watch, too, for *erratics,* huge boulders carried long distances and deposited by the glacier, which often differ from the surrounding rock. Glacial runoff is often suffused with finely powdered till or *glacial flour,* which gives it a distinctive milky-white color; the abundance of this silt in glacial streams creates a twisting, braided course. With a little practice, you'll soon learn to recognize glacial features at a glance. Learn more about glaciers and ongoing Alaska research at the **U.S. Geological Survey's** glacier and snow website, http://ak.water.usgs.gov/glaciology.

Permafrost

To picture permafrost, imagine a veneer of mud atop a slab of ice. In the colder places of the Lower 48, soil ecologists measure how much surface soil freezes in winter. In Alaska, they measure how much surface soil thaws in summer. True permafrost is ground that has stayed frozen for more than two years. To create and maintain permafrost, the annual average temperature must

remain below freezing. The topsoil above the permafrost that thaws in the summer is known as the **active layer.** With the proper conditions, permafrost will penetrate downward until it meets heat from the earth's mantle. In the Arctic, permafrost begins a few feet below the surface and can extend 2,000–5,000 feet deep. This is known as **continuous permafrost,** which almost completely underlies the ground above the Arctic Circle. **Discontinuous permafrost,** with permafrost in scattered patches, covers extensive parts of Alaska, particularly boggy areas covered by black spruce forests.

Frozen ground is no problem—until you need to dig in it. Russian engineers were the first to encounter industrial-scale problems with permafrost during the construction of the Trans-Siberian Railroad. In Alaska, gold mining, especially in deep-placer operations, often required up to two years of thawing hundreds of feet of permafrost before dredging could proceed. Today, houses frequently undermine their own permafrost foundations: Heat from the house thaws the ground, causing it—and the house above it—to sink. Similarly, road-building clears the insulating vegetation layer and focuses heat on the frozen layer, causing severe "frost heaving," the roller-coaster effect common to roads in Interior Alaska. In the 1970s, pipeline engineers had to contend with the possibility that the 145°F oil flowing through the pipe would have similarly detrimental effects on the permafrost, with potentially disastrous financial and ecological consequences. That's why more than half of the Trans-Alaska Pipeline is aboveground, supported by a specially designed and elaborate system of heat-reducing pipes and radiators. Today, there is increasing concern that warming global temperatures could have a devastating impact in the Arctic, causing permafrost to melt and greatly altering the ecosystem.

CLIMATE

Granted, over the course of a year, in any given location, Alaska's weather can be extreme and unpredictable. Because of the harshness of the winters, comfortable travel to many popular destinations is difficult from early October to late April. Contrary to popular perception, however, the weather can also be quite pleasant. Alaska's spring, summer, and fall are not unlike these seasons in Minnesota. It's cool, it's warm; it's wet and dry; sometimes it's windy, sometimes it's muggy, sometimes it's foggy. Maybe it's the worst weather in the world outside, but you're snuggling with your girlfriend in your large new tent after the most exciting raft ride of your life. Maybe it's the crispest, clearest day of your trip, but your camera got soaked in the river and your boyfriend ran off with the raft company bus driver. The weather, here as everywhere, has as much to do with the internal climate as the external. Be happy in the sun. Try to stay happy in the rain. Just keep happy. You're in Alaska. For the latest outdoor forecast, visit the **National Weather Service's** Alaska website, www.arh.noaa.gov.

Extremes and Trends

It hit 100°F in the state once, in Fort Yukon in 1915. Fairbanks regularly breaks 90°F in July. It gets cold in Fort Yukon too, dropping as low as -78°F (Alaska's record low is -82°F, recorded in aptly named Coldfoot in 1989). *Any* wind at all at that temperature would make you feel even colder, if that's possible. Thompson Pass near Valdez gets quite a bit of snow, holding the records for the most in 24 hours (5 feet), a month (25 feet), and a year (81 feet). But Barrow, at the tip of the proverbial "frozen wasteland," got just three inches of snow in 1936–1937. An average of almost 13 feet of rain falls in Ketchikan every year—what they call "liquid sunshine." But again, one year Barrow squeaked by with only an inch.

Though Alaska retains the reputation of the Great Frozen North, a distinct warming trend has had a noticeable effect on the state. Temperatures warmed abruptly in the summer of 1977 and have remained unusually warm ever since, throughout all the seasons. For example, meteorologists report that in the Interior, only on rare occasions over the past 20 years has the mercury dropped much below -40°F. Also, the temperature of the permafrost has risen several degrees. These and other indications of the greenhouse effect have been partially attributed to the thinning

ozone layer above the Arctic, similar to the "hole" that appears over the Antarctic every spring. Chlorofluorocarbons (CFCs) are considered the main culprit; Halon, a CFC found in fire extinguishers, is particularly prevalent in the fire-fighting systems of oil and gas developers. The ozone depletion in the Northern Hemisphere is thought to have much more dire consequences than in the Southern, since the north is much more populated. For the latest research, visit the website of the University of Alaska Fairbanks' **International Arctic Research Center:** www.iarc.uaf.edu.

Climatic Zones

It's possible to generalize about Alaskan weather and distinguish three climatic zones: coastal maritime, Interior, and Arctic. The main factor affecting the southern coasts is the warm Japanese Current, which causes temperatures to be much milder than the norm at those latitudes. This current also brings continuous rain as the humid Pacific air is forced up over the coastal mountains. For example, it rains in Juneau two out of three days. However, these mountains shield the Interior plateaus from the maritime air streams, so yearly precipitation there is low—a mere 15 inches. The Interior experiences great temperature extremes, from biting cold in winter to summer heat waves. The mountains also protect the coastal areas from cold—and hot!—Interior air masses. The Arctic Zone is characterized by cool, cloudy, and windy summers (averaging 50°F) and cold, windy winters—though not as cold as in the Interior.

Based at the University of Alaska Fairbanks, the **Alaska Climate Research Center** has detailed information on the state's climate, along with current weather conditions; find it on the web at http://climate.gi.alaska.edu.

THE LIGHT AND THE DARK

If you plan to be in Alaska from late May to late July, you can leave the flashlight at home. If you camped at the North Pole for a week on either side of summer solstice, the sun would barely appear to move in the sky, frying you to a crisp from the same spot overhead as if stuck in space. The Arctic Circle, at 67° latitude, is usually defined as

THE PINEAL GLAND

Most Alaskan life-forms pack a year's worth of living into five months of light, then hibernate through seven months of dark and cold. This is not only a cliché; it's also a fact based on physiology—the physiology of the pineal gland, to be specific. This gland (shaped like a *pine*cone) sits on a short stem in the oldest and most mysterious section of the human brain. It's a lonely gland—a unique, asymmetrical neuro-nub, surrounded by large masses of advanced symmetrical tissue. Until recently, it was among the most obscure structures on the human neurological frontier; in fact, only a couple of decades ago it wasn't even considered a gland but was known only as the pineal "body."

This is somewhat surprising, since its function in other vertebrates has been understood for a hundred years. In fish, reptiles, and birds, the pineal "eye" sits on a long stalk close to the brain's outer frontal section, right between the two regular eyes, where a third eye would be. However, it's not connected to the eyes or any other sensory pathways. Rather, the pineal gland is a simple, efficient photoreceptor, which senses and interprets the relative duration, intensity, and polarizing angles of light in the environment—making it the primary organ responsible for regulating internal circadian and seasonal rhythms. It tells fish how to navigate, birds when to migrate, and mammals when to sleep and reproduce.

How it works in other mammals is the key to understanding the gland's function in humans. Our gland produces a single (that we know of) hormone: melatonin. Melatonin circulates through the body and triggers two known reactions: drowsiness and reduced sex drive. What inhibits melatonin production? Light! The more sunlight—the higher its intensity and the steeper its angle—the less drowsiness and the stronger sex drive we feel. This helps explain many interesting general phenomena, such as why we sleep less deeply when it's not dark, the physiology of "spring fever," and why sex is better during the day. It also explains specific northern occurrences, such as why over two-thirds of Alaskan babies are conceived between May and September (as opposed to November and February as is commonly believed), and why you can do with a lot less sleep in Alaska in the summer.

---

the line above which the sun doesn't set on June 21, nor rise on December 21.

Barrow lies at 71° latitude, 4° and roughly 270 miles north of the Arctic Circle. Here the sun doesn't dip below the horizon for 84 days, from May 10 to August 2. (You'll definitely see, and probably buy, the famous postcard with the time-lapse photograph showing the sun tracing a very mild curve: "going down" in the north-northwest, hovering above the horizon, and "coming up" in the north-northeast.)

Fairbanks, 140 miles south of the Circle, has 22 hours of direct sunlight on summer solstice, with the sky (if it's clear) going from a bright orange-blue to a sunset purple to a sunrise pink and back to bright orange-blue. Even Ketchikan, at around 55° latitude, and probably the southernmost point on most Alaskan itineraries, enjoys more than 18 hours of daylight, with the starless dusk a paler shade of twilight. Similarly, in December Ketchikan receives six hours of pale daylight and Fairbanks only three, but at Barrow you wouldn't see the sun at all for nine weeks.

Why?

The explanation for the "midnight sun" lies in the tilted angle of the Earth's axis. Because the planet rotates off-center, the Arctic Circle leans toward the sun in summer, so a complete 24-hour rotation makes little difference in the angle at which the sun's rays strike the North Country. However, the rays do have to travel farther, and they strike Alaska at a lower angle, which you'll notice: The sun never gets nearly as high in the sky here as you're probably used to. Because of the low angle, the rays are diffused over a larger area, thus losing some intensity, which accounts for the cooler air temperatures. And since the sun seems to move across the sky at a low angle, it takes longer to "set" and "rise." In addition, the atmosphere refracts (bends) the sunbeams more dramatically closer to the poles, which causes the low light to linger even after the sun is down. This soft, slanting light is often magical, with sharp shadows, muted colors, and silky silhouettes—a photographer's dream.

Northern Lights

The continual light is a trippy novelty if you're traveling around Alaska for just a few weeks, but when you're there all summer, to paraphrase the commercial, "D-A-R-K spells relief." Stars? What a concept! Headlights? Oy vey! From early August on, though, you start losing daylight quickly, to the tune of an hour a week in Fairbanks. Temperatures drop, berries and rose hips ripen, mushrooms sprout, and there's the possibility of experiencing one of life's all-time great thrills: God's light show, the aurora borealis.

The far-flung Eskimo had a variety of mythical explanations for the lights. Many believed that they represented the spirits of ancestors or animals, while others relegated the lights to malevolent forces. Prospectors preferred to think of them as vapors from rich ore deposits. The Japanese, however, have attributed the most romance to them: A marriage consummated under the lights will be especially fulfilling. Scientists have lately raised some controversy over particular aspects of the aurora, such as that the lights never dip below 40 miles above the earth (though many northerners swear they've seen the lights dancing along the ground); whether or not the lights manifest an electric sound is still a matter of some dissension, and even the experts who believe it don't know why. But these days everyone agrees that the sun, again, is responsible for the show.

When the solar surface sparks, the energy propels a wave of ionized particles (known as the "solar wind") through space. When these anxious ions encounter the gases in the Earth's atmosphere, a madcap night of oxygen-nitrogen couples dancing begins. The sun's particles and the Earth's gases pair off, with the fastest ions grabbing the highest gases. The ensuing friction causes a red or yellow afterglow. The slower ions infiltrate the lower regions, and those encounters glow green and violet. The waving, shimmering, writhing ribbons of color cannot fail to excite your own ions and gases. For detailed information on northern lights and predictions of upcoming aurora activity, visit the website of the University of Alaska's **Geophysical Institute:** www.gi.alaska.edu. A number of lodges in the Fairbanks area have geared their winter season for people who come to view and photograph the northern lights. Many Fairbanks hotels will provide aurora wake-up calls upon request.

Flora

VEGETATION ZONES

The vegetation of the Alaska Interior falls into four main categories: rainforest, boreal forest, taiga, and tundra. The lush coastal **rainforests** of Southeast Alaska are dominated by hemlock, spruce, and cedar. The Sitka spruce, Alaska's state tree, rivals California redwoods in height, age, beauty—and commercial value, of course. Sparser forests stretch across Southcentral Alaska, with spruce continuing through northern Kodiak Island but not farther west than the adjacent mainland. Dense thickets of alder and willow grow in the higher, subalpine areas near the coast.

The **boreal forest** of the Interior lowlands consists primarily of scattered open stands of white spruce, paper birch, alpine fir, lodgepole pine, and balsam poplar (cottonwood). **Taiga,** the transition zone between boreal forest and tundra, is characterized by sparse and stunted black spruce, dwarf shrubbery (mostly the ubiquitous willow), and swampy areas known as "muskegs."

The lower-elevation **tundra,** also known as the "moist tundra," starts at treeline, around 2,500 feet. There you find undergrowth similar to that of the taiga, without the trees. The higher-elevation alpine tundra consists of grasses, clinging mosses and lichens, and an abundance of tiny, psychedelically bright wildflowers, including the unforgettable forget-me-not (state flower), with gaze-catching petals of light blue.

TREELINE

There are actually two treelines in Alaska: One is determined by elevation, the other by latitude. Generally, treeline descends in elevation as the latitude ascends. Although alder and poplar do survive in isolated stands near the Brooks Range, the Arctic region on the North Slope is mostly treeless tundra. Dwarf willow, alder, grasses, and moss give the tundra here the appearance of a shag carpet. This tundra belt continues along the shores of the Bering Sea to the Alaska Peninsula and Aleutian Islands. Southward, the Arctic vegetation is gradually replaced by Pacific coastal varieties.

FLOWERS

While you're hiking, an excellent book to have along is *Field Guide to Alaskan Wildflowers* by Verna E. Pratt. The photographs are good, the descriptions are usable, and the flowers are conveniently arranged by color.

Fireweed is a wildflower you'll come to know intimately during your travels in the North. It enjoys sunlight and grows profusely in open areas along roads and rivers. Given proper conditions, tall fireweed can grow to seven feet high. Its long stalk of pink flowers blossoms from bottom to top; sourdoughs claim they can predict the arrival and severity of winter by the speed with which fireweed finishes blooming.

In Southcentral and Interior Alaska, **prickly rose** is a common sight. The plant grows stems up to four feet high, with sharp stickers. The flowers have five pink petals; the bright-red rose hips ripen in mid-August and contain highly concentrated vitamin C. Pop 'em in your mouth, suck off the slightly tart flesh, spit out the pips, and climb a mountain.

Three kinds of **primrose,** also a pinkish red, are another common sight on the tundra. Other red wildflowers of the tundra include **purple mountain saxifrage, moss campion,** and large, bright-pink **poppies.**

White flowers include the **narcissus-flowered anemone,** similar to a **buttercup,** which also grows on the tundra. **Mountain avens** are easily recognizable—they look like white roses. A half-dozen different kinds of white **saxifrage** are widespread throughout the state. Be careful of the local **water hemlock,** which is deadly poisonous. Similar is the **yarrow,** a medicinal herb with a disk of small white flowers and lacelike leaves. As soon as you identify **Labrador tea,** you'll notice it everywhere in the forest and taiga. **Cotton grass** looks exactly like its name. **Daisies** and **fleabane** complete this group of plants with white flowers.

Larkspur looks similar to fireweed, only it's a dark purple. It grows on a long stalk and a dwarf bush. **Monkshood** is a beautiful dark-blue flower of the buttercup family; **harebells** and **bluebells** are easily identified around Denali. Three kinds of **violets** grow in the boreal forest. Light-purple **lupine** flowers grow in 20-inch clusters. **Asters,** resembling purple daisies, bloom all over the Interior.

BERRIES

Berries are the only fruits that grow naturally in Alaska, and luckily the many varieties are abundant, several are edible, a few even taste good, and only one is poisonous. If you're into berry collecting, get to know poisonous **baneberry** immediately. A member of the crowfoot family, it grows mostly in the Southeast and central Interior. The white berries look like black-eyed peas; they ripen to a scarlet red. **Juniper berries** grow throughout Alaska, but the **bog blueberries, Alaska blueberries,** and **huckleberries** are much tastier. Blueberries also grow on poorly drained, shady alpine slopes and are generally the first to ripen. **Salmonberries** turn a dark salmon-red in late summer, and are quite similar to raspberries.

Bunchberries and **elderberries** are good tasting but have been known to upset a stomach or two. **Bog cranberries** are best after the first frost, especially when they're a deep purple—deliciously tart. **High-bush cranberries** are common but are best just before they're completely ripe. **Wild strawberries** are even better, if you can get to them before the birds and rodents. The several kinds of **bearberries** (blue and red) are tasteless except to bears, and the **soapberry** will remind you of getting caught saying a dirty word as a kid. Pick up *Alaska Wild Berry Guide and Cookbook,* for the complete lowdown on Alaska's berries.

MUSHROOMS

Approximately 500 species of mushrooms are found in Alaska, thrusting up from the fecund forests from Ketchikan to Katmai and the rich tundra from Kantishna to Kotzebue. Most of the mushrooms are harmless to humans, and often edible; a handful are poisonous, such as varieties of **amanita** (especially the *muscaria,* or fly agaric) and **poison pax.** But if you learn to identify such common species as **hedgehogs** and **shaggy manes,** you'll enjoy happy hunting, mostly in July and August. For more information, see *Alaska's Mushrooms* by Harriette Parker.

FRANKENSTEIN CABBAGES

In 1941, the managers of the Alaska Railroad offered a $25 prize to the grower of the largest cabbage in the state, and since then cabbage growers have been competing. Usually, the largest cabbages at the Tanana Valley State Fair (in Fairbanks in mid-August) weigh in at 65–70 pounds, but the state record-holding cabbage is a 105-pounder, grown near Wasilla in 2000. It's an American, but not a world, record. Ten-pound celery, three-pound beets, two-pound turnips, and one-pound carrots are also blue-ribbon earners. Find them and more at the Alaska State Fair in Palmer at the end of August.

Fauna

If any aspect of Alaska embodies the image of the "last frontier," it's the state's animal kingdom. For millennia, Native hunters, with their small-scale weapons and limited needs, had little impact on wildlife populations. Eskimo and Aleut villages subsisted comfortably on fish, small mammals, and one or two whales a year; the interior Athabascan bands did well on a handful of moose and caribou. This all changed in the mid-1700s with the coming of the Russians and Americans. Sea otters, fur seals, and gray whales were quickly hunted to the verge of extinction. By the 1850s, the Alaskan musk ox had been annihilated. Wolves, in part because they preyed on the same game as humans, were ruthlessly hunted.

Conservation measures have nurtured their numbers and today Alaska boasts one of the largest concentrations of animal populations remaining on earth. For example, there are nearly twice as many caribou in Alaska as there are people. There's a moose and a Sitka black-tailed deer for every three people. If 80,000 sheep strikes you as an impressive number, consider 40,000 grizzly bears. Bald and golden eagles are commonplace, and while the magnificent trumpeter swan was believed near extinction in the Lower 48, it was thriving in Alaska. Marine mammals, from orcas to the recovering otters, are common (though they have recently experienced major declines in the Aleutians and western Alaska), and Alaskan waters also contain fish and other sea creatures in unimaginable quantities.

Wildlife Viewing

Alaska's wildlife is a major draw for both visitors and residents. The state's vast stretches of wilderness contain abundant mammals, birds, and fish, including some of the largest and most magnificent animals in the world. Land mammals such as brown (grizzly) and black bears, caribou, moose, Dall sheep, wolves, and musk ox are the main attractions, but the state also has incomparable populations of birds, including such favorites as bald eagles, puffins, loons, and sandhill cranes. Marine mammals include seals, Steller sea lions, and sea otters, along with beluga whales, orca (killer) whales, humpback whales, gray whales, and others.

A useful small guide to finding wild animals is the *Alaska Wildlife Viewing Guide* by Michelle Sydeman and Annabel Lund. If you're surfing the Web, visit the Alaska Department of Fish & Game's website at www.wildlife.alaska.gov, for details on dozens of species of Alaskan animals in their "Wildlife Notebook."

In Alaska, wildlife may be encountered up close almost anywhere outdoors. Many animals are well prepared to defend their territories against intruders (you), and even the smallest can bite. Never attempt to feed or touch wildlife. It is seldom good for it, you, or those who follow. Any animal that appears unafraid or "tame" can be quite unpredictable, so keep your distance. One thing you don't have to worry about is snakes; there are none in Alaska. Surprisingly, however, there *are* frogs, even above the Arctic Circle.

LAND MAMMALS

Brown Bears

The brown bear (also called grizzly) is the symbol of the wild country, and a measure of its wildness. Grizzlies once roamed all over North America. In 1800, there were over 100,000 of them; today, around a thousand survive in the Lower 48. Ironically, the grizzly is the state animal of California, where it is now extinct. Things are very different in Alaska, where 40,000 of these magnificent creatures still inhabit the land.

Denali National Park offers some of the most accessible bear-viewing in the state. The estimated 200 Denali grizzlies are still wild, mostly in their natural state. This is especially important for the continued education of the cubs, who are taught how to dig roots, find berries, catch ground squirrels, and take moose calves. However, Denali grizzlies are not afraid of people, and are extremely curious; some have tasted

canned beans, veggie burgers, and Oreo cookies. While no one has been killed by a grizzly at Denali, maulings have occurred, usually because of the foolishness of novice hikers and photographers or as a result of improper food storage. Take care, but don't be afraid to go hiking.

The natural grizzly diet is 80 percent vegetarian. They eat berries, willows, and roots, as well as preying on anything they can take: from ground squirrels to caribou, from foxes to small black bears. And they're challenged by nothing, except humans with high-powered weapons. Grizzlies are racehorse-fast and have surprising endurance; they need about 50 square miles for home territory and travel several miles a night. During the day they like to eat, sleep in the sun—often on snow patches—and entertain tourists on the shuttle buses.

Grizzlies are solitary creatures. Full-grown boars and sows are seen together only during mating season, in early summer. The gestation period is a little over five months, and the sows give birth in December to one to three cubs. The cubs are hairless, weigh one pound each, and remain blind for a week. They stay with the mother for over two and a half years—two full summers. They're then chased away sometime before July of the third summer, when the sow is ready to mate again.

Contrary to popular belief, bears do not hibernate. They do sleep deeply in dens during

BEAR PRINTS

black bear

grizzly bear

polar bear

brown bear

BOB RACE

the winter, sometimes for weeks. But they often get hungry, lonely, or restless, and step outside to forage for frozen roots, berries, and meat. Sometimes a bear will stay out all winter; that's the one that the Natives fear the most: the winter bear. Its fur tends to build up a thick layer of ice, rendering it nearly impenetrable, almost bulletproof. And of course, sows give birth in the deep winter, which they're certainly awake for.

Grizzlies and brown bears were once thought to be different species, but now are considered the same. Their basic difference is size, which is due to habitat. Grizzlies themselves are the world's largest land omnivores, growing to heights of 6–7 feet and weighing in at 500–600 pounds. However, they're the smaller of the two, because they live in the Interior and feed mostly on vegetation. Brown bears are coastal, and with a rich source of fish protein, they have achieved near mythical sizes. Kodiak brown bears retain a reputation for being the largest, reaching heights of over 10 feet and weights of up to 1,400 pounds. On Admiralty Island in Southeast Alaska the brown bears are a bit smaller, but population densities are the highest anywhere: around one bear per square mile!

Hiking in bear country requires special precautions; see "Coexisting with the Bears" in the *Interior* chapter. A number of areas offer outstanding brown-bear-viewing around Alaska. Read "Bear-Watching" in the *Southwest Alaska* chapter for details on seeing these wonderful animals. The most famous places are McNeil River, Katmai National Park, Pack Creek, and Kodiak Island.

Black Bears

Black bears are found in most forested parts of Alaska, though not on certain Southeast Alaskan islands. They are distinguished from grizzlies and brown bears by their size (much smaller), the shape of their face (much narrower), and the lack of a shoulder hump. Black bears are actually more dangerous to people than grizzlies: There have been more attacks and maulings in Alaska by black bears than by brown. Two places on Tongass National Forest offer a fine opportunity to watch black bears as they catch salmon: Anan Creek Bear Observatory near Wrangell and Fish Creek Wildlife Observation Site near Hyder.

Polar Bears

Polar bears dwell in northern and western Alaska, spending their lives wandering on pack ice (extensive areas of drifting ice) or along the coast. In winter, they wander south on the ice, sometimes even reaching the Kuskokwim River delta, but in the summer they are found out in the Chukchi Sea and Arctic Ocean. Visitors to Alaska are highly unlikely to see a polar bear in the wild; your best bet would probably be near Kaktovik, on the edge of Arctic National Wildlife Refuge (but even there only infrequently in the summer). The Alaska Zoo in Anchorage has a polar bear. The best place to see and photograph polar bears in the wild is around Churchill in Manitoba, Canada. Learn more at the U.S. Fish & Wildlife Service website: www.r7.fws.gov/mmm.

Moose

The moose is the largest member of the deer family, and Alaska has the largest moose. A bull moose in his prime gets to be about seven feet tall and weighs around 1,200 pounds, all from eating willow stems—about 30 pounds a day of them. They also eat aspen and birch, but willow is the staple of choice. The antlers, which are bone, are shed and renewed every year. Full-size antlers can weigh up to 70 pounds—that's mostly in September during the rut, or mating time. Bulls of near-equal rank and size butt their heads together to vie for dominance. You want to be real careful of bulls then. Touchy. The cows have one or two calves, rarely three, in May, and that's when you want to be real careful of the cows, too. The calves stay with the cow exactly a year; then she chases away the yearlings. Sometimes at the start of the summer season you'll spot a huge pregnant cow with a frisky yearling on her heels, and you've never seen a more hassled-looking expression on an animal's face. But that's family life.

Moose don't cover too much territory—about 30 miles a year, mostly in the forest, which provides natural defense against predators. The word *moose* comes from the Massachusetts Algonquian dialect and means "muncher of little twigs." By the way, the little flap of hair under the moose's chin is known as the "moostache." (Just kidding, it's really called the "dewlap.")

Harsh winters are deadly to moose. Deep snow and bitter cold can cause one in three moose in central Alaska to perish. Annually, hundreds of moose make their last stand along the snowless railroad tracks between Seward and Fairbanks and are killed by trains that don't stop for them. Other hundreds starve to death. Those hit by cars along roadways are butchered and distributed to the local people.

If Alaska moose are the world's largest, Kenai Peninsula moose are Alaska's largest. A Kenai moose holds the Alaskan record: at 10–11 years old, his antlers were just under 75 inches wide, he weighed 1,500–1,600 pounds, and he gave his life for Guinness.

Kenai National Wildlife Refuge was specifically established to protect moose, and these massive animals are common sights along Kenai Peninsula roads at dusk. Other places to watch for moose are within the Anchorage bowl and in the Matanuska–Susitna Valley northeast of Anchorage. Drive with care, since moose can suddenly step onto the road without warning, and their massive bulk means that a collision could be fatal to both the moose and people in the vehicle.

Moose can be very aggressive, particularly in the winter months when food is scarce. A number of people have been killed by moose attacks, even in Anchorage. Always give moose a wide berth, especially if you're walking, on a bike or skis, or with a dog. If a moose appears ready to attack, quickly hide behind a tree, car, or other obstruction. Pepper spray may be effective if all else fails, or you can try to outrun a moose if you have no other options; they generally don't run far. If the moose knocks you down, curl up in a ball, protect your head with your hands, hold still, and say a few thousand Hail Marys.

Caribou

Caribou are travelin' fools. They're extremely flighty animals—restless, tireless, fast, and graceful. Run and eat, run and eat, is pretty much all they do—oh yeah, and reproduce. Reindeer, although the same species, are smaller and often domesticated. Caribou are peaceful critters and they'll outrun and outdistance their predators, mostly wolves, rather than fight. They like to travel in groups, unlike moose, which are loners. And they cover 10 times as much territory. Their herding and migrating imperatives are similar to those of the plains bison; they gather in large numbers and think nothing of running 50 miles, almost on a lark.

Caribou are extremely well adapted to their winter environment. They have huge nasal passages and respiratory systems in order to breathe the bitterly cold winter air. Thick fur covers almost every inch of their bodies; the fur itself is protected by large, hollow, oily guard hairs. This tends to make caribou look much larger than they really are; a good-sized bull weighs 400–500 pounds, a cow about half that. Caribou have the richest milk in the animal kingdom: 20 percent fat. They've also got huge prancing hooves, immortalized in the Santa Claus myth, which are excellent for running, swimming, disco dancing, and pawing at the snow to uncover the moss and lichens on which they subsist all through the harsh Arctic winter. The word *caribou* comes from the Maine Algonquian dialect and means "scraping hooves."

The caribou is the only member of the deer family whose females grow antlers. Babies are on their feet and nursing within an hour of birth, and at one week they can run 20 miles. If they can't, they'll most likely die, since the herd won't wait. But this helps to keep the herd healthy, controls population growth, and provides food for the carnivores.

Alaskan Natives are among the caribou's natural predators. Historically, Natives ate the meat raw, roasted, and stewed. They ate all the organs, even the half-digested greens from the stomach. The little gobs of fat from behind the eyes were considered a delicacy. They used almost exclusively caribou hide for clothes, rugs, blankets, and tents. The leg skins were used to make mukluks; the long strands of stringy sinew provided sewing thread.

Nearly a million caribou roam across Alaska, with the largest herds in the Arctic, including within Arctic National Wildlife Refuge. Caribou are commonly seen within Denali National Park and Preserve and along Interior and South-central Alaskan roads, including the Glenn

Highway near Eureka, the Alaska Highway east of Tok, the Denali Highway, the Dalton Highway, and the Richardson Highway near Paxson.

Dall Sheep

Named for William H. Dall, one of the first men to survey the lower Yukon (1866), Dall sheep are sometimes called "Alaska bighorn sheep," because the Rocky Mountain bighorn is a closely related species. Distinguished by their brilliant white color, the rams grow large, curved horns, formed from a specialized skin structure made up of a compacted mass of hair and oil. The horns aren't shed; instead the sheep add another ring to them yearly, so the longer the horns, the older the ram, and the more dominant within the herd. The rams can weigh as much as 175 pounds; the ewes have small spiked horns and average 120 pounds.

Their habitat is the high alpine tundra, and they subsist on grasses, mosses, lichens, and flowers. Their bird's-eye view provides an excellent defense. They're also magnificent mountain climbers. Roughly 70,000 Dall sheep reside in the Chugach, Kenai, Alaska, and Wrangell mountain ranges in Alaska. During summer, the rams migrate high into the ranges, leaving the prime lower grazing grounds for the ewes and lambs. It's natural that they migrate, the same way it's natural that they have predators. Their alpine tundra habitat is very fragile, and it can take decades to regenerate after overgrazing. Migration and predation thus keep the flock healthy, control population growth, and guarantee the survival of the habitat.

Dall sheep inhabit mountain hillsides throughout much of Alaska. They are frequently seen on rocky slopes in Denali National Park, near Atigun Pass on the Dalton Highway, near Cooper Landing on the Kenai Peninsula, and along Turnagain Arm 20 miles south of Anchorage.

wolf

BOB RACE

Wolves

Wolves have traditionally been one of the most misunderstood, misrepresented, and maligned mammals, in both fact and fable. We've come a long way from the days when it was believed that wolves were innately evil, with the visage of the devil himself, eating their hapless prey—or little girls in red hoods—alive. But it wasn't until the mid-1940s, when wildlife biologist Adolph Murie began a long-term and systematic study of the wolves in Mt. McKinley National Park, that all the misconceptions comprising the accepted lore about wolves began to change.

For three years Murie tramped mainly on the plains below Polychrome Pass and became extremely intimate with several wolf families. (His book, *The Wolves of Mount McKinley*, published in 1944, is still considered a classic natural history text.) Though Murie concluded that a delicate balance is established between predator and prey to their mutual advantage, declining Dall sheep populations, political pressure, and, indeed, tradition forced the park service to kill wolves, which were considered, against Murie's conclusions, to be the cause of the sheep decline. Typically, though, the wolf population was in just as dire straits as the sheep, and for several years no wolves were killed in the feds' traps *because of their scarcity.*

Since then, many researchers and writers have come to incisive conclusions about the wolf. It's been determined that their social systems—within the pack and with the prey—are amazingly complex and sophisticated. The alpha male and female are the central players in the pack, surrounded by four to seven pups, yearlings, and other adults. The dominant female receives a long, involved courtship from the dominant male (though he might not necessarily be the biological father of the pups). Territories can be as small as 200 square miles and as large as 800 square miles, depending on a host of influences.

Perhaps the most complex and fascinating aspect of wolf activity is the hunt. Barry Lopez, author of the brilliant *Of Wolves and Men,* argues persuasively that the individual prey is as responsible as the wolf for its own killing, in effect "giving itself to the wolf in ritual suicide." Lopez maintains that the eye contact between the wolf and its prey "is probably a complex exchange of information regarding the appropriateness of a chase and a kill." Lopez calls this the "conversation of death."

With the advent of radio collaring and tracking from airplanes, the movements of individual wolves and packs have continually surprised wildlife biologists. Wolves often travel 5–10 miles an hour for hours at a time. In a matter of days, an individual cut loose from a pack can wind up 500 miles away. Thus wolves are able to select and populate suitable habitats quickly.

Alaska's 7,500–10,000 wolves are thriving, even though roughly 15 percent of them are harvested yearly by trappers. They can be found all the way from the Southeastern panhandle to the Arctic slope, but are most common in Interior Alaska. Denali National Park offers travelers the best chance to see a wolf from the road system, but wolves may also be seen in other parts of the Alaska Range, in Brooks Range foothills, and in Wrangell–St. Elias National Park.

Captive wolves can be seen at the Alaska Zoo (www.alaskazoo.com) in Anchorage. A nonprofit organization, Wolf Song of Alaska (www.wolfsongalaska.org), has an education center in downtown Anchorage.

Elk

Elk—a relatively common sight in the western Lower 48—were also prevalent in Alaska 10,000 years ago but disappeared during the last ice age. In the mid-1920s, Alaskans decided that elk would be an attractive addition to the territory's big-game species, and a handful of Roosevelt elk were imported from Washington state. After a few years of island-hopping, the cervids (deer) were finally transplanted to their permanent home, Afognak Island off the north coast of Ko-diak, and from there they apparently swam to Raspberry Island and Kodiak. Though the country was rugged—wet, windy, and choked with alder—the elk thrived in their new home, and some grew to 1,000 pounds. Within only 20 years (1950), 27 bulls were culled from the herd by resident hunters. Hunting continued up until the late 1960s, when a series of severe winters decimated the herds. Ten years of protection and mild winters allowed the herds to regenerate; today 1,200 elk live on Afognak and Raspberry Islands, with a second small population on Etolin Island near Petersburg.

Musk Ox

The musk ox is a stocky, long-haired animal with a slight shoulder hump and a very short tail. Despite their name, musk oxen have no musk glands and are not oxen. The largest member of the sheep family, this shaggy, prehistoric-looking creature was abundant in the North Country until it was hunted into extinction by the mid-1800s. In the 1930s, several dozen musk ox were transplanted from Greenland to Nunivak Island in the Bering Sea. Like the elk on Afognak, the musk ox on Nunivak thrived, and the resident Natives used the soft underwool to establish a small cottage industry knitting sweaters, scarves, and caps. And that's what it would have remained, a small cottage industry, if it hadn't been for Dr. John J. Teal, Jr., a student of Arctic explorer Vilhjalmur Stefansson. Stefansson recognized the potential of musk ox wool and inspired Teal to experiment with domesticating them. After spending 10 years with musk ox on his farm in Vermont, Teal concluded that they were amiable, hardy, and easy to domesticate. So in 1964, he started the Musk Ox Project at the University of Alaska in Fairbanks.

In 1984, the project moved to a farm in the Matanuska Valley, where musk ox are bred to produce *qiviut* (KEE-vee-ute), the soft underwool, which is renowned in Alaska for its insulation (eight times warmer by weight than sheep wool) and tactile (softer than the finest cashmere) properties. The *qiviut* is collected from the animals in the spring. The raw wool is sent to a mill in Rhode Island and then sold to Oomingmak (the Native word for musk ox, meaning "bearded one"; www.qiviut.com), a co-op consisting of 200 members in villages spread throughout western Alaska. Here the *qiviut* is knitted into garments, which are sold at retail outlets in Anchorage and at the farm near Palmer.

Today, wild musk ox can be found on the Seward Peninsula near Nome, on Nunivak and Nelson islands, the Yukon-Kuskokwim Delta, on the north slope near Prudhoe Bay, and in Arctic National Wildlife Refuge. The best places to see them up close are the Musk-Ox Farm in Palmer (www.muskoxfarm.org) and the Large Animal Research Station (www.uaf.edu/lars) at the University of Alaska in Fairbanks.

Lynx

Alaska's only native cat, the lynx is the northern version of the bobcat. Weighing around 20–30 pounds, these extremely secretive animals prey primarily on snowshoe hare, a species that undergoes an 8–11 year cycle of abundance. Lynx numbers fluctuate with those of hares, but lag one or two years behind. When a hare population crashes, lynx numbers soon decline, and they sometimes travel up to 400 miles in search of food. Although snowshoe hares are an important prey for lynx, when they are scarce lynx hunt grouse, ptarmigan, squirrels, and rodents, and may even take larger animals such as caribou or Dall sheep.

Lynx are sometimes seen during long periods of summer daylight, especially in years when they are abundant. Lynx have large, broad feet that function as snowshoes for winter hunting and traveling.

Mountain Goats

These members of the antelope family number between 13,000 and 15,000 in Alaska. They have snow-white coats, shaggy heads, and black, spiked horns up to a foot long, and weigh in at 150–300 pounds. They mostly inhabit the coastal ranges and eastern Alaska Range and are frequently seen high on cliffs so precipitous that they would probably scare even Dall sheep.

Sitka Black-Tailed Deer

These small deer are found throughout Southeast Alaska, in Prince William Sound, and on Ko-

diak and Afognak Islands. Visitors to all these areas may occasionally see deer, but some of the largest populations are on Kodiak Island. The deer population averages more than 300,000 individuals, but fluctuates widely, depending upon the severity of the winter. They're the second-most-prevalent game animal in Alaska behind caribou. They prefer a forest environment, but also roam high into the mountains for young shrubs and ripe berries in the late summer months. Males weigh 120 pounds, females 80 pounds.

Rodents

Ground Squirrels and Marmots are true hibernators: Unlike other mammals such as brown, grizzly, and polar bears, they sleep for six months straight, in a deep coma. This separation between life and death is one of the thinnest lines in the animal world. A ground squirrel's heart slows to about six beats a minute, and its body temperature lowers to just above freezing, around 38°F. (In fact, a zoologist at the University of Alaska Fairbanks has found that the core temperature of the arctic ground squirrel, the northernmost hibernator, can drop to as low as 26°F—six degrees below freezing! Of course, the squirrels don't "freeze" but "supercool.")

The hibernating squirrel takes a breath every couple of minutes. It uses up half its body weight, since it isn't eating. If you stuck a needle in a hibernating ground squirrel's paw, it would take the animal about 10 minutes to begin to feel it.

Ground squirrels provide a large part of the grizzly and wolf diet, and of scavenger birds' as well, since they're a common type of roadkill.

Marmots, similar to woodchucks, are sometimes mistaken for wolverines. They live in large rock outcroppings for protection and have a piercing whistle, which warns of approaching predators or other possible danger. Look for marmots around Polychrome Pass at Denali Park; ask the driver where exactly.

Alaska has a number of other members of the rodent family: shrews, mice, voles, lemmings, and porcupines). Long-tailed and least weasels occupy a wide habitat in the taiga and tundra. Martens are another member of the weasel family, similar to, though much more aggressive than, mink; the pine marten is one of Alaska's most valuable fur-bearers. Wolverines are in attendance, though you'd be very lucky to see one. Red fox are common in the Interior and South-central, and you're likely to see one at Denali Park; the white Arctic fox is a gorgeous animal, though you'll only see one in pictures.

MARINE MAMMALS

Marine mammals are found all along the Alaskan coast, from Ketchikan in the Southeast to Barrow on the Arctic Ocean. Sea otters are frequently found in harbors, bays, and inlets, particularly around kelp beds. Good places to look for whales, seals, sea otters, sea lions, porpoises, and other marine mammals are the Inside Passage, Prince William Sound, Kodiak Island, Kachemak Bay, and Kenai Fjords. The Pribilof Islands serve as rearing and resting areas for thousands of northern fur seals, harbor seals, Steller sea lions, and walruses in the summer. Only Native Alaskans have the legal right to hunt marine mammals.

An Endangered Ecosystem?

In the last several decades, scientists have watched with increasing alarm as marine mammal populations plummeted in the North Pacific and Bering Sea, particularly around the Aleutian Islands. Environmentalists blamed overfishing of pollock, while fisherman pointed the finger at long-term changes in ocean currents and temperatures. But the latest evidence points in a totally different direction—whaling. After World War II, Japanese and Russian whalers developed lethal ways to hunt bowhead, sperm, and humpback whales, killing at least a half-million of them before commercial whaling ended in the 1970s. These giant whales formed an important part of the diet for killer whales, and without this, the orcas turned to other food sources. As top predator in the ocean, killer whales apparently worked their way across the food chain, attacking fur and harbor seals in the 1970s, Steller sea lions in the 1980s and '90s, and most recently an animal with very little meat, sea otters. If this is indeed the cause for the decline of these marine mammals, there is little that can be done to halt the damage. Overfishing (or in this

case overwhaling) can have disastrous consequences for the oceans, and for animals and humans that depend upon the fish.

Sea Otters

A marine member of the weasel family, the sea otter had one characteristic that would seal its doom: a long, wide, beautiful pelt, that's one of the warmest, most luxurious, and durable furs in existence. Otter fur catalyzed the Russian *promyshleniki* to begin overrunning the Aleutians in the mid- to late-18th century, sealing the doom of the Aleuts as well as the otters. In 1803, Aleksandr Baranov (Alexander Baranof) shipped 15,000 pelts back to eastern Russia. Up until the 1840s, otter hunting was the primary industry in the Pacific, and when the Americans bought Alaska in 1867, nearly a million otters had been killed in the northern Pacific.

During the extreme lawless period in the last quarter of the 19th century, the otters were annihilated. In 1906, schooners cruised the north Pacific for months without taking a single pelt. In 1910, a crack crew of 40 Aleut hunters managed to harvest 16 otters. In 1911, otters were added to the International Fur Seal Treaty, giving them complete protection from everybody. Small, isolated populations of otters had managed to survive in the western Aleutians, and their numbers have increased over the past century to roughly 100,000 today. Approximately 90 percent of the world's sea otter population can be found in coastal Alaska. The otters are doing fine in Southeast Alaska, and slowly recovering from the 1989 *Exxon Valdez* oil spill in Prince William Sound, but in the Aleutians they have declined precipitously over the last decade, partly because of predation from killer whales. For more on the current situation, visit the Fish & Wildlife Service's website: www.r7.fws.gov/mmm.

Steller Sea Lions

George Wilhelm Steller was the naturalist aboard Vitus Bering's 1742 exploration of Alaska, and the first white man to step on Alaskan soil. Two marine mammals ended up with his name: the Steller's sea cow, a cold-water relative of the manatee; and the Steller sea lion. The sea cow was

INTRODUCTION

driven to extinction just 26 years later, a casualty of its not being afraid of humans and the tasty flavor of its flesh. Today, the sea lion in much of Alaska is equally endangered.

Steller sea lions are pinnipeds—marine mammals with flippers, not feet. Males can weigh up to 2,000 pounds; females peak at 600 pounds. Sea lions eat several kinds of fish, but mostly pollock. They range across the North Pacific from northern Japan and Siberia all the way to California. These playful but powerful animals were abundant in western Alaskan waters until quite recently. In the 1960s, for example, an estimated 177,000 sea lions lived in the Gulf of Alaska and along the Aleutians. Commercial hunting was halted in the mid-1970s, but the population continued to drop by more than 80 percent. By 2000, a mere 34,000 survived. The western Alaska population was officially listed as endangered in 1997, while sea lion populations in Southeast Alaska and farther south to California are considered threatened.

Researchers are unsure why Steller sea lions are disappearing at such an alarming rate, and there are a multitude of possible causes—including overfishing, toxic chemicals, and predation by sharks and killer whales. Most likely is some combination of factors, but if something isn't done, the Southwest Alaska population could be headed for extinction. Learn more about these fascinating animals—including the latest research—at the National Marine Fisheries Service's website: www.state.ak.us/adfg/notebook/notehome.htm.

Whales

The largest summer marine visitors to Alaska are the whales. Each spring **gray whales** are seen migrating north from Baja California; in the fall they return south. Also in the spring **humpback whales** move north from Hawaii. The humpback is easily distinguished by its hump-like dorsal fin, large flippers, and huge tail, which shows as it dives. These 50-foot-long creatures often breach (jump) or beat the surface of the water with their tails, as if trying to send messages. Smaller (30-foot) **minke whales** are also common.

The **killer whale (orca),** which is not actually a whale but the largest of the dolphins (up to 24 feet long), travels in groups hunting fish and marine mammals. Its six-foot-high, triangular dorsal fin and its black-and-white piebald pattern make it easily identifiable.

Whales can be spotted all along Alaska's thousands of miles of shoreline, but commercial whale-watching ventures are only found in Southeast Alaska, Prince William Sound, and the Kenai Peninsula. Larger towns in these areas all have charter boat operators that lead trips combining whale-watching with other activities such as fishing, sea kayaking, photography, glacier viewing, or bird-watching. The Inside Passage's protected waterways are favorite haunts of humpback and killer whales during the summer months, particularly around Admiralty Island, within Glacier Bay National Park and Preserve, and near Sitka. Look for beluga whales in Turnagain Arm along the Seward Highway south of Anchorage. Boat tours of Prince William Sound depart from both Valdez and Whittier, providing a good opportunity to see occasional killer, minke, and humpback whales. Kenai Fjords National Park and Resurrection Bay—both accessible by boat tour from Seward—are popular places to spot killer whales and humpbacks, along with sea otters, seals, sea lions, and colonies of puffins. There's also a fair chance of seeing whales on the Kachemak Bay wildlife boat trips that depart from Homer.

For more information on whales in Alaska, visit the National Marine Fisheries Service's website: www.fakr.noaa.gov/protectedresources.

orca

BOB RACE

Fur Seals

The Alaska species of fur seal *(Callorhinus ursinus)* is a kind of "seal bear," as its Latin name suggests. The bulls grow up to seven feet long and can weigh 400 pounds. Tens of thousands of these caterwauling creatures return to the Pribilof Islands yearly to breed. The dominant bulls arrive after eight months at sea in early June, the noisy fight for the prime beach real estate often results in bloody bulls. The cows show up a couple of weeks later—small (80 pounds), submissive, and steeling themselves for a bloody bounce on the beach. A big stud bull might accumulate 60–70 cows in his harem, and it's exactly as debilitatingly profligate a scene as it sounds. The bulls don't eat, living only off their own fat all summer, and look like skid row derelicts by mid-August when they take off to the North Pacific to eat, sleep, and regain their strength.

The gestation period is one year, and the cows return to the same rookery to give birth. The pups swim away in late October and return after a couple of years as "bachelors." Between two and seven years old, they play in the sand and surf, until the young males have grown big and bad enough to have their way with the cows. For more information on fur seals, visit the National Marine Fisheries Service's website: www.fakr.noaa.gov/protectedresources.

Walrus

What the Pribilofs are to the fur seal, Round Island in northern Bristol Bay is to the Pacific walrus. (See the *Western Alaska* chapter for details on Round Island.) Except here, it's a boys-only beach club; the females and babies remain in the northern Bering and Chukchi Seas, where they feed at the relatively shallow bottoms. Thousands of these giant 3,000-pound bulls cram themselves onto narrow beaches at the bottom of steep cliffs around the 1- by 2-mile island. It's an amazing sight, with the scrappy bulls ready to fight at the slightest affront; most of them are scarred from a multitude of old attacks, and broken or missing tusks are common. On the beach, walruses are ungainly, akin to Subaru-sized slugs. But in the water, these big fat fatties are slo-mo smooth. As with other marine mammals in the Bering Sea, walrus popula-

tions have declined in recent years, though they have not suffered the precipitous declines of Steller sea lions and otters. Learn more about these fascinating animals at the U.S. Fish & Wildlife Service's website (www.r7.fws.gov/mmm).

BIRDS

More than 400 species of birds can be found within Alaska, from tiny rufous hummingbirds to the nation's national emblem, the bald eagle. Because of Alaska's proximity to Siberia, many unusual species are sometimes seen, making islands in the Aleutians and within the Bering Sea of great interest to serious birders.

One of the rarest is the bristle-thighed curlew, with a population of a mere 5,000 worldwide—and its only breeding grounds are in Alaska. Eight of the curlews were banded in the Yukon Delta Wildlife Refuge in 1988, and one was subsequently seen on Caysan Island in the South Pacific, over 2,000 miles away. Many Asian species, such as the greenshank and the Siberian ruby-throat, only foray into the Americas as far as western Alaska.

Bird-Watching

Nome, the Pribilofs, and the Aleutians are popular destinations for birders looking to add to their life list. Excellent places to see nesting colonies of seabirds such as **puffins** and **kittiwakes** include Glacier Bay National Park and Preserve, Kachemak Bay near Homer, Kenai Fjords National Park near Seward, Fort Abercrombie State Park on Kodiak Island, Prince William Sound, the Pribilof Islands, and St. Lawrence Island.

Located on the edge of Fairbanks, **Creamer's Field** is a good place to view sandhill cranes, ducks, and geese during the spring and fall migrations. Also at Creamer's Field is the **Alaska Bird Observatory** (www.alaskabird.org), which conducts songbird research, and offers educational programs and birding reports for the area. For additional information, contact the Alaska State office of the **Audubon Society** (907/276-7034, www.audubon.org/chapter/ak) or call the regional birding hotlines for the Anchorage area (907/338-2473), Interior Alaska (907/451-9213), and the Homer area (907/235-7337).

Eagles

As many eagles are found in Alaska as in the rest of the United States combined. **Bald eagles** are common sights along the coasts, but with their unmistakable white heads, seven-foot wingspans, and dive-bombing, salmon-snatching performances, the thrill of watching them is not quickly lost.

The highest concentrations of bald eagles can be found on Admiralty Island, in Prince William Sound, and along the Copper River Delta near Cordova. Admiralty has the largest nesting population of bald eagles in the world, and is a great place to find them during the summer months. Over the winter you'll find upward of 3,000 eagles at the famous **Chilkat Bald Eagle Preserve,** along with several hundred of them on the Homer Spit (where they are fed). In spring, a good place to look for eagles is the Stikine River near Wrangell.

Golden eagles, found throughout the Interior, come without the distinctive "baldness" but are no less magnificent for their size. Plentiful around Denali Park, golden eagles perched on the tundra, standing more than three feet tall, have been mistaken for everything from grizzly cubs to adolescent hikers.

The **white-tailed eagle** is an Asian raptor; Attu Island in the western Aleutians is its only North American habitat.

Trumpeter Swans

The world's largest waterfowl, these swans boast wingspans as wide as eagles (seven feet) and can weigh up to 40 pounds! They're pure white, and so have figured prominently over the centuries in legends, drama, music, and metaphor. They fly as fast as 60 mph and as high as 10,000 feet on their migrations from Alaska to the Pacific Northwest for the winter (though a group of 500 overwinter in Alaska). They live to be 30

bald eagle

years old and have a hornlike call, which accounts for their common name.

In 1933, trumpeter populations hit an all-time low of 33 individuals in the Lower 48—having been hunted for their meat, down, and quills. But several thousand swans were seen by Alaskan bush plane biologists in the early 1950s, and by the early '70s, trumpeters were removed from the Endangered Species list.

Today, of the nearly 12,000 swans in North America, about 10,000 spend their summers in Alaska, 2,000 of them in the Copper River delta. (A great place to see them is on the road from Cordova to the Million Dollar Bridge.)

Geese

The **Aleutian Canada goose** has made a remarkable comeback from the edge of extinction over the past several decades. Smaller than Canada geese, Aleutian geese were common throughout the islands up until the 20th century, when decades of fox farming nearly wiped out the geese. Only a few hundred were left alive by the late 1960s, on one fox-free island. Feral foxes were removed from a number of other Aleutians and the geese were reintroduced; by 1990, their numbers had regenerated to the point (7,000) where they were removed from the ranks of the endangered and upgraded to "threatened."

Emperor geese are a distinctive black-throated bird, and nearly the entire population of 70,000 nest in Southwest Alaska, from the Aleutians to Kodiak.

Snow geese, on the other hand, are plentiful. Huge flocks totaling up to 100,000 birds migrate roughly 5,000 miles each year from central California through Alaska to their nesting grounds on Wrangel Island (in Russia).

Ptarmigan

The **willow ptarmigan** is the state bird, and one of the most popular targets of small-game hunters. Ptarmigan—willow, rock, and white-tailed—are similar to pheasant, quail, and partridge in the Lower 48. They reproduce in large quantities, molt from winter white to summer brown, and have a poor sense of self-preservation. The various Alaskan place-names containing "Chicken" usually refer to ptarmigan, which the namers had difficulty spelling.

MOSQUITOES

The mosquito, contrary to popular belief, is not Alaska's state bird. But skeeters are nearly as much a symbol of the Great North as glaciers, totem poles, and the aurora borealis. Mosquito eggs hatch in water, so the boggy, muskegy, marshy forests and tundra, plus all the ponds, lakes, creeks, sloughs, and braided rivers of Alaska, provide the ideal habitat for these bothersome creatures. Alaska hosts around three dozen varieties of mosquitoes.

Mosquitoes hibernate in the winter and emerge starting in March and April. Peak season is in late June and early July. The males don't alight or bite, but they do buzz around people's eyes, noses, and ears, which can be as, if not more, annoying than the bites. The males live 6–8 weeks, feeding on plant juices; their sole purpose in life is to fertilize the eggs the females produce. They also feed birds and larger insects.

The females live long lives, producing batches of eggs, up to 500 at a time. To nourish the eggs they feed on the blood of mammals, using a piercing and sucking mouth tube. The tube also injects an anticoagulant, which causes the itch and swelling from a bite. No Alaskan mosquitoes carry the diseases that tropical mosquitoes are known to, such as malaria, yellow fever, encephalitis, and elephantiasis.

Mosquitoes are most active at dawn and dusk. Windy conditions and low temperatures depress mosquito feeding and breeding. Mosquitoes are attracted to dark colors, carbon dioxide, warmth, and moisture. Mosquito repellent containing DEET (diethylmetatoluamide) is the most effective. A headnet helps keep mosquitoes and other buggy critters away from your face, and is a wise investment for anyone heading into remote parts of Interior Alaska or Kodiak Island. If you wear light-colored, heavy clothing (the stinger can pierce light materials), camp in high and dry places that are apt to be breezy, and rub repellent on all exposed skin, you should be able to weather mosquito season without too much difficulty.

FISH

Get someone going on fishing in Alaska and you won't be able to shut him or her up or get a word in edgewise for the whole afternoon, guaranteed. The fisheries program in Alaska is extensive, because commercial, sport, and recreational fishing are important to almost every state resident. Commercial fishing is Alaska's second-largest industry, and Alaska accounts for more than half of the nation's total seafood production. Sportfishing has always been popular, but is playing a more important role in Alaska's economy as tourism increases. Below is a brief survey of the most popular fish in Alaska's three million lakes, 3,000 rivers, and 45,000 miles of coastline.

coho salmon

BOB RACE

Salmon

Five kinds of salmon—king, red, pink, silver, and chum—all return to the same bend in the same little creek where they hatched, to spawn and die, ending one of the most remarkable life cycles and feats of migration and single-minded endurance of any living creature. You'll be steeped in salmon lore if only by osmosis by the end of your trip, and you'll get more than your fill of this most delicious and pretty fish.

The **kings** (also known as chinooks) are the

INTRODUCTION

world's largest salmon, and the world's largest kings spawn in Alaskan waters. The average size for a king is 40–50 pounds. The world sportfish record is 97 pounds, and a few 100-pounders have been caught in commercial nets. Kings generally spend five or six years in saltwater before returning to fresh to spawn: The more years spent in the ocean, the larger the fish. They run mostly between mid-May and mid-July.

Reds (sockeye) are the best-tasting salmon and the mainstay of the commercial fishing industry. They average 6–10 pounds and run in June and July.

Pinks (humpback) are the most plentiful, with massive runs of more than 150 million fish between late June and early September. They're smallish, 3–4 pounds, with soft flesh and a mild taste; they're mostly canned (or caught by tourists).

Silvers (coho) seem to be the most legendary of the salmon, for their speed, agility, and sixth sense. Their spawning growth rate is no less than fantastic, more than doubling their weight in the last 90 days of their lives. Silvers grow 7–10 pounds and run late, from late July all the way to November.

Chum (dog) are the least valued of the five Pacific salmon, even though they average 10–20 pounds, are extremely feisty, and are the most far-ranging, running way above the Arctic Circle. They're known as dog salmon because they've traditionally sustained working huskies, but chums remain popular with a hard-core group of sport anglers, who consider them terribly underrated. Surprisingly, they make some of the finest smoked fish.

Halibut

Halibut are Alaska's favorite monster fish and can grow so huge and strong that many anglers have an unsurpassed religious experience while catching one. "Chicken halibut" are the common 25–40 pounders, but 100- and 200-pounders are frequent sights in some ports; even 300-pounders are occasionally reeled in. The state-record halibut was a 464-pounder, more than eight feet long, caught near Dutch Harbor in 1996. Even though halibut are huge and require 80-pound test line with 20-ounce lead sinkers, they're not the fiercest fighting fish, and just about anyone can catch one on a good day's charter from Homer, Seward, Kodiak, Whittier, Sitka, or Dutch Harbor. It has a very white flesh, with a fine texture—many Alaskans regard it as the most flavorful (and least fishy-tasting) fish.

Smelt

The fattiest fish in northern waters is the Pacific Coast eulachon, also known as smelt, hooligans, and candlefish (legend claims that the dried fish are so fatty they can be wicked and lit like candles). These silver and white fish are roughly as long and slender as pencils, and run in monumental numbers for three weeks in early summer from Northern California to the Pribilofs. A traditional source of oil, the females are dumped into pits or vats by the ton and left to rot for two weeks. Then freshwater is added and the whole mess is boiled, during which the oil rises to the surface. After skimming, straining, filtering, and sterilizing, roughly 20 gallons of oil (reminiscent of cod-liver oil) can be processed from a ton of female smelt. The early males, in addition, are good tasting whether cooked, smoked, dried, or salted.

History

PREHISTORY

The Athabascan Indians of Canada have a legend that tells how, in the misty past, one of their ancestors helped a giant in Siberia slay a rival. The defeated giant fell into the sea, forming a bridge to North America. The forefathers of the Athabascans then crossed this bridge, bringing the caribou with them. Eventually the giant's body decomposed, but parts of his skeleton were left sticking above the ocean to form the Aleutian Islands.

In less fanciful terms, what probably happened was that low ocean levels during the Pleistocene epoch (some 30,000–40,000 years ago) offered the nomadic peoples of northeastern Asia a 50-mile-long, 600-mile-wide land "bridge" over the Bering Sea. One of the earliest records of humans in the Americas is a caribou bone with a serrated edge found at Old Crow in northern Yukon. Almost certainly used as a tool, the bone has been placed at 27,000 years old by carbon dating. The interior lowlands of Alaska and the Yukon Valley, which were never glaciated, provided an ice-free migration route. As the climate warmed and the great ice sheets receded toward the Rocky Mountains and Canadian Shield, a corridor opened down the middle of the Great Plains, allowing movement farther south. (Recent scientific evidence suggests that ancient peoples also sailed or paddled along the coast from Asia to North America.)

The Athabascans

The Athabascans (or Dene) were the first Native group to cross the Bering land bridge. Their language is spoken today from Interior Alaska to the American Southwest (among Navajos and Apaches). Way back when (anywhere from 40,000 to 12,000 years ago), these Natives of the Interior followed the mastodon, mammoth, and caribou herds that supplied them with most of their necessities. Agriculture was unknown to them, but they did fashion crude implements from the raw copper found in the region. Eventually, certain tribes found their way to the coast.

The Athabascan-related Tlingits, for example, migrated down the Nass River near Prince Rupert and then spread north through Southeast Alaska. The rich environment provided them with abundant fish and shellfish, as well as with the great cedar logs from which they fashioned community houses, totem poles, and long dugout canoes.

The Eskimo

Eskimos arrived from Asia probably some 10,000 years ago, near the end of the last ice age. Today they are found in Siberia and across Alaska and Arctic Canada to Greenland. Their language, which in Alaska is divided into the Inupiak dialect in the north and the Yup'ik and Alutiiq dialects in the south, is unrelated to any other in North America except that of the Aleuts. Like the Tlingits, they too lived near the coast, along the migratory routes of the marine mammals they hunted in kayaks and umiaks. They also relied upon caribou, birds, and fish. Their homes were partly underground and constructed of driftwood, antlers, whale bones, and sod. (The well-known snow-and-ice igloo was exclusive to Canadian Natives.) In the summer, skin tents were used at fish camps. The Eskimo did not use dogsleds until the coming of the white people.

The Aleut

Marine mammals and fish provided the Eskimo-related Aleuts with food, clothing, and household materials. The Aleut were famous for their tightly woven baskets. Before the arrival of the Russians in the 1740s, 25,000 Aleut inhabited almost all of the Aleutian Islands, but by the year 1800 only about 2,000 survived. The ruthless Russian fur traders murdered and kidnapped the men, enslaved or abandoned the women, and passed on their genes and diseases so successfully that today only 1,000 full-blooded Aleuts remain. The rest intermarried with the Russians, and scattered groups of their descendants are now found in the eastern Aleutians and the Pribilofs to the north.

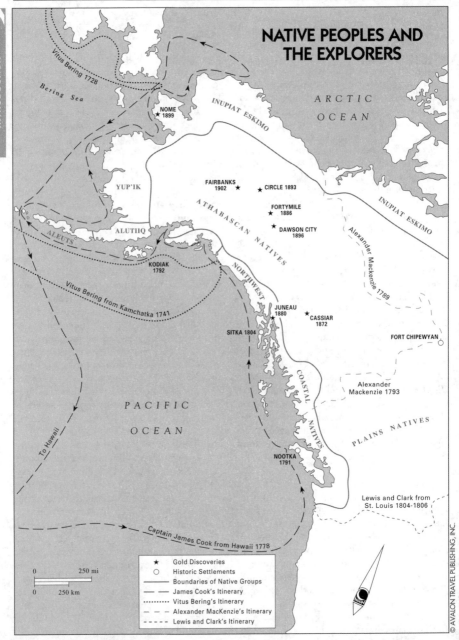

NATIVE PEOPLES AND THE EXPLORERS

Vitus Bering 1728

Bering Sea

ARCTIC OCEAN

NOME 1899

INUPIAT ESKIMO

YUP'IK

INUPIAT ESKIMO

FAIRBANKS 1902

CIRCLE 1893

ATHABASCAN NATIVES

FORTYMILE 1886

DAWSON CITY 1896

Alexander Mackenzie 1789

ALUTIIQ

ALEUTS

KODIAK 1792

NORTHWEST

Vitus Bering from Kamchatka 1741

JUNEAU 1880

CASSIAR 1872

SITKA 1804

FORT CHIPEWYAN

COASTAL NATIVES

Alexander Mackenzie 1793

PACIFIC OCEAN

PLAINS NATIVES

To Hawaii

NOOTKA 1791

Lewis and Clark from St. Louis 1804-1806

Captain James Cook from Hawaii 1778

0   250 mi
0   250 km

★ Gold Discoveries
○ Historic Settlements
── Boundaries of Native Groups
── James Cook's Itinerary
········ Vitus Bering's Itinerary
── ── Alexander MacKenzie's Itinerary
── ─ ─ Lewis and Clark's Itinerary

© AVALON TRAVEL PUBLISHING, INC.

EUROPEAN EXPLORATION

Vitus Bering

In the early 1700s, long before the New World colonists began manifesting their destiny by pushing the American frontier west to the Pacific coast, Russian *promyshleniki* (explorers and traders) were already busy pushing their own frontier east to the Pacific. After these land conquerors had delineated Russia's inhospitable northeastern edges, they were followed by indomitable sea explorers who cast off from the coasts in search of answers to questions that had intrigued Europeans since Marco Polo's *Travels*—mainly, whether or not Asia was joined with America, the mysterious land to the east that was vaguely outlined on then-contemporary maps.

Danish-born Vitus Bering, a sailor in the Russian navy for nearly 20 years, set out in 1725 for Kamchatka Peninsula, Siberia, on orders from Peter the Great. It took him and his crew three years, dragging rigging, cable, and anchors 2,000 miles over trackless wilderness and suffering innumerable deprivations to reach the coast, where their real journey into the uncharted waters of the North Pacific would begin. Bering built his first boat, *Gabriel,* and sailed past St. Lawrence Island (south of present-day Nome) and the Diomedes, but fog prevented him from glimpsing North America. He returned and wintered in Kamchatka, sailed again in the spring, and charted most of the Kamchatka coast, but foul weather and short provisions again precluded exploring farther east.

Over the next 10 years, Bering shuttled between Moscow and his beloved coast, submitting patiently to royal politics and ridicule from the leading scientists and cartographers, while planning and outfitting (though not commanding) a series of expeditions that charted the rest of the Siberian coast and Japan.

Finally, in 1741, at the age of 60, Bering undertook his remarkable voyage to America. Commanding the *St. Peter,* he sailed southeast from Kamchatka, came up south of the Aleutians, passed Kodiak, and sighted Mt. St. Elias on the mainland. By that time Bering, along with 31 members of his crew, was in the final throes of ter-minal scurvy. He died in December 1741 and was buried on what is now Bering Island, the westernmost of the Aleutians. Meanwhile, his lieutenant, Alexis Chirikof, commanding the *St. Paul,* had reached all the way to the site of Sitka. After much hardship, survivors from both ships made it back to Siberia—with a load of sea otter pelts. This bounty from the New World prompted a rush of Russian hunters and traders to Alaska.

Conflicting Claims

Reports of Russian advances alarmed the Spanish, who considered the entire west coast of North America theirs. Juan Perez and Bruno Hecata were ordered north from Mexico in 1774 and 1775. Spanish explorer Juan Francisco Quadra sailed as far north as Sitka in 1775 and 1779, but in the end, Spain failed to back up its claim with any permanent settlement north of San Francisco. It was Englishmen James Cook (in 1776–1780) and George Vancouver (in 1791–1792) who first carefully explored and charted this northern coast. In 1778, Cook landed on Vancouver Island, then sailed north all the way to what is now called Cook Inlet in Southcentral Alaska, in search of the Northwest Passage from the Atlantic. He continued to the Aleutians and entered the Bering Sea and the

Captain James Cook

Arctic Ocean. A decade and a half later, Vancouver, aboard his ship HMS *Discovery*, charted the coast from California to Southeast Alaska and claimed the region for England. His was the first extensive exploration of Puget Sound and circumnavigation of Vancouver Island; his maps and charts of this confounding coast were so accurate that they were used for another 100 years.

Exploration by Land

Meanwhile, explorers were reaching the Pacific overland from bases in eastern Canada and the United States. In 1789 a Northwest Company trader, Alexander Mackenzie, paddled down the Mackenzie River to the Arctic Ocean. Four years later, in 1793, he became the first person to cross the entire continent by land, reaching the Pacific at Bella Coola, British Columbia. Other employees of the same aggressive Montreal-based company explored farther south. In 1808, Simon Fraser followed the Fraser River, stopping near the present site of the city of Vancouver; in 1810–1811 David Thompson traveled from the headwaters of the North Saskatchewan River to the mouth of the Columbia, near present-day Portland. In 1803, after the United States purchased 827,000 square miles of territory west of the Mississippi River from France, President Thomas Jefferson ordered a military fact-finding mission into the area. Led by Lewis and Clark, a group of explorers paddled up the Missouri River to its headwaters and crossed to the Columbia, which they followed to the Pacific (1804–1806), helping to open vast expanses of western North America. American fur traders followed close behind. (The Alaskan interior, however, was not properly explored until the gold rush at the end of the 19th century.)

The Fur Trade

The excesses of the *promyshleniki*, who had massacred and enslaved the Aleut, prompted the czar in 1789 to create the Russian America Company, headed by Gregor Shelikof, a fur trader and merchant who in 1784 had established the first permanent settlement in Alaska at Three Saints Bay on Kodiak Island. Alexander Baranof, a salesman in Siberia, was the first director of the company;

he moved the settlement up to present-day Kodiak town, and for the next 20 years, Baranof *was* the law. One of the most powerful men in Alaskan history, he enslaved the remaining Aleuts, warred with the Panhandle Indians, initiated trade with the English, Spanish, and Americans, and sent his trading vessels as far away as Hawaii, Japan, and Mexico. Exhausting the resources of Kodiak and its neighborhood, he moved the company to Sitka, where, according to Merle Colby in his classic 1939 WPA *Guide to Alaska,* "from his wooden 'castle' on the hill surmounting the harbor he made Sitka the most brilliant capital in the new world. Yankee sailors, thrashing around the Horn, beating their way up the California coast, anchored at last in Sitka harbor and found the city an American Paris, its streets crowded with adventurers from half the world away, its nights gay with balls illuminated by brilliant uniforms and the evening dresses of Russian ladies." Except for the Tlingit Indians, who fought bitterly against Russian imperialism, Baranof's rule, extending from Bristol Bay in western Alaska to Fort Ross, California, was complete. His one last dream, of returning to Russia, was never fulfilled—on the voyage back to the homeland, Baranof died at the age of 72.

THE 19TH CENTURY
Political Units Form

In 1824 and 1825, Russia signed agreements with the United States and Britain, fixing the southern limit of Russian America at 54° 40' north latitude, near present-day Ketchikan. But the vast territory south of this line was left up for grabs. The American claim to the Oregon Territory around the Columbia River was based on its discovery by Robert Gray in 1792, and on the first overland exploration by Lewis and Clark. Britain based its claim to the region on its effective occupation of the land by the Northwest Company, which in 1821 merged with the Hudson's Bay Company. As American settlers began to inhabit the area, feelings ran high—President Polk was elected in 1846 on the slogan, "Fifty-four Forty or Fight," referring to the proposed northern boundary between American and

British territory in the Pacific Northwest. War between Britain and the United States was averted when both agreed to draw the boundary line to the Pacific along the 49th parallel, which remains to this day the Canadian/American border. Vancouver Island went to Britain, and the new Canadian nation purchased all the territorial holdings of the Hudson's Bay Company (Rupert's Land) in 1870. In 1871, British Columbia joined the Canadian Confederation on a promise from the leaders of the infant country of a railroad to extend there from the east.

The Russians Bail Out

The year 1863 was a one for the Russian America Company. Back in the motherland, Russia's feudal society was breaking down, threatening the aristocracy's privileged status. In Alaska, competition from English and American whalers and traders was intensifying. Food was scarce and supply ships from California were unreliable and infrequent. Worst, perhaps, was the dwindled numbers of fur seals and sea otters, hunted nearly to extinction over the past century. In addition, bad relations with Britain in the aftermath of the Crimean War (1853–1856) prompted Czar Alexander the First to fear losing his far-flung Alaskan possessions to the British by force. Finally, the czar did not renew the company's charter, and the Russian America Company officially closed up shop.

Meanwhile, American technology was performing miracles. Western Union had laid two cables under the Atlantic Ocean from the United States to Europe, but neither had yet worked. So they figured, let's go the other way around the world: They proposed laying a cable overland through British Columbia, along the Yukon River, across the Bering Strait into Siberia, then east and south into Europe. In 1865, the Western Union Telegraph Expedition to Alaska, led by William Dall, surveyed the interior of Alaska for the first time, revealing its vast land and resources.

> *Secretary of State William H. Seward purchased Alaska on March 30, 1867, for the all-time bargain-basement price of $7.2 million—two cents an acre. Subsequently, Alaska faded into official oblivion for the next 15 years—universally regarded as a frozen wasteland and a colossal waste of money.*

This stimulated considerable interest in frontier-minded Washington, D.C. In addition, Czar Alexander's Alaska salesman, Baron Edward de Stoeckl, was spending $200,000 of his own money to make a positive impression on influential politicians and journalists.

Secretary of State William H. Seward purchased Alaska on March 30, 1867, for the all-time bargain-basement price of $7.2 million—*two cents* an acre. The American flag was hoisted over Sitka on October 18, 1867. According to Ernest Gruening, first U.S. senator to Alaska, "a year later when the House of Representatives was called upon to pay the bill, skeptical congressmen scornfully labeled Alaska 'Icebergia,' 'Walrussia,' 'Seward's Icebox,' and '[President] Johnson's Polar Bear Garden.' If American forces had not already raised the Stars and Stripes in Sitka, the House might have refused to pick up the tab." (Stoeckl, meanwhile, reimbursed himself the $200,000 he'd invested and sent the other $7 million home to Alexander.) Subsequently, Alaska faded into official oblivion for the next 15 years—universally regarded as a frozen wasteland and a colossal waste of money.

Organic Act of 1884

This act organized Alaska for the first time, providing a territorial governor and law enforcement (though not a local legislature or representation in Washington). President Chester Arthur appointed federal district court judges, U.S. attorneys, and marshals. From 1884 to 1900, only one U.S. judge, attorney, and marshal managed the whole territory, all residing in the capital, Sitka. The first three appointees to the court in Sitka were removed in disgrace amidst charges of "incompetence, wickedness, unfairness, and drunkenness." A succession of scandals dogged other federal appointees—and that was only in Sitka; the vast Interior had no law at all until 1900, when Congress divided the territory into three legal districts, with courts at Sitka, Nome, and Eagle.

William H. Dall wrote of Alaska at that time as a place where "no man could make a legal will, own a homestead or transfer it, or so much as cut wood for his fire without defying a Congressional prohibition; where polygamy and slavery and the lynching of witches prevailed, with no legal authority to stay or punish criminals." Kipling's line, "There's never law of God or man runs north of 53," also refers to the young territory of Alaska. In contrast, Colby in his WPA guide commented that the gold-rush stampeders, "although technically without civil authority, created their own form of self-government. The miners organized 'miners meetings' to enforce order, settle boundary disputes, and administer rough and ready justice. Too often this form of government failed to cope with [serious problems] . . . yet the profound instinct of the American people for self-government and their tradition of democracy made local self-govern-

ment effective until the creation of the Alaska Legislature in 1912."

Gold!

Alaska's gold rush changed everything. After the California stampede of 1849, the search moved north. In 1858 there was a rush up the Fraser River to the Cariboo gold fields. In 1872, gold was found in British Columbia's Cassiar region. Strikes in Alaska and the Yukon followed one another in quick succession: at Juneau (1880), Fortymile (1886), Circle (1893), Dawson City (1896), Nome (1899), Fairbanks (1902), and Iditarod (1908).

A mobile group of men and women followed these discoveries on riverboats, dogsleds, and foot, creating instant outposts of civilization near the gold strikes. Gold also caused the Canadian and American governments to take a serious look at their northernmost possessions for the first time; the beginnings of Alaska's administrative infrastructure dates from those times. Still, in 1896, when Siwash George Carmack and his two

PANNING FOR GOLD

Panning for gold is not only great fun, it's also a good way to get involved in the history of Alaska. Besides, there's the chance you'll find a nugget that will become a lifelong souvenir. You might even strike it rich! The amount of equipment required is minimal: an 18-inch plastic gravity-trap gold pan (buy one at any local surplus or sporting-goods store for a couple of dollars), tweezers and an eyedropper to pick out the gold flakes, and a small vial to hold them. Ordinary rubber gloves will protect your hands from icy creek water. An automobile oil dipstick bent at one end is handy for poking into crevices, and a small garden trowel helps dig out the dirt under rocks. Look for a gravel bar where the creek takes a turn, for larger rocks forming eddies during high water, for crevices in the bedrock, or for exposed tree roots growing near the waterline. These are places where gold will lodge. Try your luck on any of the old gold-rush creeks; tourist offices can often suggest likely areas. Stay away from commercial mining operations and always ask permission if you're on someone's claim.

The principle behind panning is that gold, twice as heavy as lead, will settle to the bottom of your pan. Fill the pan half full of pay dirt you've scooped up from a likely spot and cover it with water. Hit the rim of the pan seven or eight times, or shake it back and forth. Break up lumps of dirt or clay with your hands and discard any rocks after rinsing them in the pan. Shake the pan again, moving it in a circular motion. Dip the front edge of the pan into the stream and carefully wash off excess sand and gravel until only a small amount of black sand remains. If you see gold specks too small to remove with tweezers, take the black sand out and let it dry. Later dump it on a clean sheet of paper and gently blow away the sand. The gold will remain. That's the basic procedure, though there are many ways to do it. It does take practice; ask a friendly sourdough for advice. Also, many spiked gold-panning facilities are found along the roads in Alaska—commercial, but good places to refine your technique.

Athabascan brothers-in-law discovered gold where Bonanza Creek flowed into the Klondike River in Yukon Territory, this vast northern wilderness could barely be called "settled." Only a handful of tiny non-Native villages existed along the Yukon River from Ogilvie and Fortymile in western Yukon to Circle and Fort Yukon in eastern Alaska, and a single unoccupied cabin sat on a beach at the mouth of the Skagway River at the terminus of the Inside Passage.

But by the end of 1897, perhaps 20,000 stampeders had skirted the lone cabin on their way to the headwaters of the Yukon and the sure fortunes in gold that awaited them on the Klondike. The two trails from Skagway over the coastal mountains and onto the interior rivers proved to be the most "civilized" and successful routes to Dawson. But the fortune-frenzied hordes proceeded north, uninformed, aiming at Dawson from every direction on the compass. They suffered every conceivable hardship and misery, from which death (often by suicide) was sometimes the only relief. And those who finally burst through the barrier and landed at the Klondike and Dawson were already two years too late to partake of the "ready" gold.

But the North had been conquered by whites. And by the time the gold rush had spread to Nome, Fairbanks, Kantishna, Hatcher Pass, and Hope, Alaska could finally be called settled (if not civilized).

The consequences of this Anglo invasion were devastating for the people who had lived in this harsh land for thousands of years. Epidemics of measles, influenza, and pneumonia swept through the Native communities, particularly in 1900 and 1918, sometimes killing every person in a village. Rescuers found entire families who had frozen to death because they did not have enough strength to keep the fire going. The impact of these deaths, combined with the sudden arrival of whites who introduced alcohol, depleted game and other food sources, and then brought Christianity as a replacement for indigenous beliefs, was profound. The consequences still ripple across Alaska, most notably in the form of rampant alcoholism, which is a factor in many Native accidents and suicides.

THE 20TH CENTURY

In the first decade of the 20th century, the sprawling wilderness was starting to be tamed. The military set up shop at Valdez and Eagle to maintain law and order, telegraph cables were laid across the Interior, the Northwest Passage had been found, railroads were begun at several locations, vast copper deposits were being mined, and thousands of independent pioneer-types were surviving on their own wits and the country's resources. Footpaths widened into wagon trails. Mail deliveries were regularized. Limited self-government was initiated: The capital moved to Juneau from Sitka in 1905; Alaska's first congressional delegate arrived in Washington in 1906; and a territorial legislature convened in 1912. A year later, the first men stood atop the south peak of Mt. McKinley, and the surrounding area was set aside as a national park in 1917. At that time, Alaska's white and Native populations had reached equivalency, at around 35,000 each. Judge James Wickersham introduced the first statehood bill to the U.S. Congress in 1916, but Alaska drifted along in federal obscurity until the Japanese bombed Pearl Harbor.

War

It's been said that war is good for one thing: the rapid expansion of communications and mobility technology. Alaska proves that rule. In the early 1940s, military bases were established at Anchorage, Whittier, Fairbanks, Nome, Sitka, Delta, Kodiak, Dutch Harbor, and the tip of the Aleutians, which brought an immediate influx of military and support personnel and services. In addition, in 1942 alone, thousands of miles of road were punched through the trackless wilderness, finally connecting Alaska to the rest of the world: the 1,440-mile Alaska Highway from Dawson Creek, B.C., to Delta, Alaska; the 50 miles of the Klondike Highway from Whitehorse to Carcross; the 151-mile Haines Highway; and the 328-mile Glenn Highway from Tok to Anchorage, among others. At the war's peak, 150,000 troops were stationed in the territory; all told, the U.S. government spent almost a billion dollars there during the war. (For a description of the actual fighting, see "War in the Aleutians" in the *Southwest Alaska* chapter.) After the war, as after the gold rush, Alaska's population increased dramatically, with servicemen remaining or returning. The number of residents nearly doubled between 1940 and 1950.

Statehood

The 1950s brought a boom in construction, logging, fishing, and bureaucracy to Alaska. The decade also saw the discovery of a large oil reserve off the western Kenai Peninsula in the Cook Inlet. The population continued to grow, yet Alaskans still felt like residents of a second-class colony of the United States and repeatedly asked for statehood status throughout the decade. Finally, on July 7, 1958, Congress voted to admit Alaska into the Union as the 49th state. President Dwight D. Eisenhower signed the official proclamation on January 3, 1959—43 years after Judge James Wickersham had first introduced the idea.

In the 92 years between Alaska's becoming a U.S. territory and its becoming a state, much of the land was split up into Navy petroleum reserves, Bureau of Land Management parcels, national wildlife refuges, power projects, and the like, to be administered by separate federal agencies, including national park, forest, and military services. By the time Alaska gained its statehood in 1959, only 0.003 percent of the land was privately owned—mostly homesteads and mining operations—and just 0.01 percent had been set aside for Native reservations, administered by the Bureau of Indian Affairs. The Statehood Act allowed Alaska to choose 104 million acres, but the issue of Native land ownership was not considered, and it would take oil discoveries in the late 1960s to force a redress for that injustice.

A little over five years after statehood, the Good Friday earthquake struck Southcentral Alaska; at 9.2 on the Richter scale, it remains the largest earthquake ever recorded in North America. But Alaskans quickly recovered and rebuilt with the plucky determination and optimism that still characterize the young state.

Oil Changes Everything

Alaska entered the big time, experiencing its most recent boom, in 1968, when Atlantic Richfield discovered a 10-billion-barrel oil reserve at Prudhoe Bay. The following year, Alaska auctioned off leases to almost half a million acres of oil-rich country on the North Slope for $900 million, 10 times more money than all its previous leases combined. A consortium of oil company leaseholders immediately began planning the Trans-Alaska Pipeline to carry the crude from Prudhoe Bay to Valdez. But conservationists, worried about its environmental impact, and Native groups, concerned about land-use compensation, filed suit, delaying construction for four years.

This impasse was resolved in 1971, when Congress passed the **Alaska Native Claims Settlement Act** (ANCSA), the most extensive compensation to any Native people in the history of the United States. It gave Alaska's aboriginal groups title to 44 million acres of traditional-use lands, plus a billion dollars to be divided among all American citizens with at least 25 percent Athabascan, Eskimo, or Aleut blood. The act also created a dozen regional Native corporations, a "13th Corporation" for Alaskan Natives in the Lower 48, plus more than 200 village and urban Native corporations.

The pipeline was built in 1974–1977. Again, after years of uncertainty, Alaska boomed, both in revenues and population. Since then, the state's economic fortunes have risen and fallen with the volatile price of oil. See *The Wrangells and Prince William Sound* chapter for more on one of Alaska's most infamous incidents, the 1989 grounding of the *Exxon Valdez,* which poured 11 million barrels of crude into the pristine waters of Prince William Sound.

Preserving the Wild Places

The ANCSA of 1971 had designated 80 million acres to be withdrawn from the public domain and set aside as national parks, wildlife refuges, and other preserves by 1978. In the mid- to late 1970s, in the wake of the completion of the pipeline, this was the raging land issue, generally divided between fiercely independent Alaskans who protested the further "locking-up" of their lands by Washington bureaucrats, and conservationists who lobbied to preserve Alaska's wildlife and wilderness. When Congress failed to act, President Jimmy Carter took a bold move that forever changed the way Alaskan lands are managed; he withdrew 114 million acres of Alaskan lands as national monuments on December 1, 1978. The withdrawal still rankles the state's right-wing politicians who regard it as a criminal act that should be prosecuted.

Two years later, with the anti-environment Ronald Reagan waiting to take over the reins of power, Carter signed into law one of the most significant pieces of environmental legislation ever enacted, the **Alaska National Interest Lands Conservation Act** (ANILCA). The act set aside 106 million acres of federal property as "public-interest lands," to be managed by the National Park and National Forest services, the Fish and Wildlife Service, and other agencies. These "d2 lands" (from section 17:d-2 of ANCSA) included the expansion of Mt. McKinley National Park (renamed Denali); the expansion of Glacier Bay and Katmai national monuments, which became national parks; and the creation of Gates of the Arctic, Kobuk Valley, Wrangell–St. Elias, Kenai Fjords, and Lake Clark National Parks, plus the designation of numerous national monuments and preserves, scenic and wild rivers, and new wildlife refuges.

INTO A NEW CENTURY

The last decade has not been especially kind to Alaska as oil prices dropped (they later rebounded), pulp mills closed down, logging decreased, and commercial fishing suffered from low prices and a market flooded with cheap farmed salmon from Chile, Norway, and British Columbia. Tourism has been one of the few bright spots, as travel to Alaska (particularly aboard cruise ships) rose dramatically. But even this is not without controversy, as locals complain of crowds at their fishing holes, RVs clogging the summertime highways, and thousands of cruise-ship passengers overwhelming small Southeast towns, along with water and air pollution from these enormous vessels.

Arctic National Wildlife Refuge

An ongoing battle between developers and conservationists is whether to allow exploration and drilling for black gold within the 1.5-million-acre Arctic National Wildlife Refuge (ANWR). In a political compromise in 1980, the Alaska National Interest Lands Conservation Act called for a federal study to determine if oil and gas could be safely recovered within ANWR. Oil companies are concerned about the day when the North Slope reserves finally run dry, and claim that the pipeline's many years of operation have proven oil development and environmental protection to be compatible on the North Slope. Also, improved technology has greatly refined development techniques, which further safeguard the wilderness. A poll of Alaskans would come down strongly in favor of opening the wildlife refuge to development, and there probably isn't one elected state politician who would dare stand up to the oil companies, which can pour many thousands of dollars into their (or an opponent's) campaigns. Oil money doesn't talk in Alaska politics—it yells.

Conservationists—along with a number of vocal Inupiat people from the tiny settlement of Arctic Village—have taken a strong stand against the development of ANWR, noting that any such development could imperil the 150,000-strong Porcupine caribou herd, a vital food source in their subsistence culture. In addition, they argue that this refuge is one of the few places on earth that protect a complete spectrum of Arctic ecosystems. The battle to open ANWR to drilling flares up every few years, and the man our Supreme Court deemed president—George W. Bush—is a vocal proponent of its development. I for one am hoping that he fails in this effort, and that ANWR remains one of America's last great wilderness.

Who Owns Alaska?

The vast majority of Alaska's 375 million acres is publicly owned, with less than one percent in private hands. Some 60 percent of this land is under federal management, with most of the rest in state or Native corporation hands. Get complete details on Alaska's public lands from **Alaska Public Lands Information Centers** (www.nps .gov/aplic/center) in Anchorage (907/271-2737), Ketchikan, Tok, and Fairbanks.

NATIONAL PARK SERVICE

In the federal scheme of things, the National Park Service gets all the glory. The national parks are the country's scenic showcases, and visitors come by the millions, usually to look, occasionally to experience. **Denali National Park and Preserve**—home to North America's highest mountain—is Alaska's most famous and overloved park, attracting well over a million tourists each year. Other well-known Alaskan national parks—**Glacier Bay National Park and Preserve, Katmai National Park and Preserve, Kenai Fjords National Park, Klondike Gold Rush National Historical Park, Sitka National Historical Park,** and **Wrangell–St. Elias National Park and Preserve**—are high on the list for travelers, and offer both visitor centers and various park activities. The other eight national parks and preserves (**Aniakchak, Bering Land Bridge, Cape Krusenstern, Gates of the Arctic, Kobuk Valley, Lake Clark, Noatak,** and **Yukon–Charley Rivers**) are so inaccessible that those with any facilities at all are prohibitively expensive for the average traveler, and the others are really no more than a name and a set of boundaries on the map.

People accustomed to national parks in the Lower 48 are surprised to find that very few trails run through Alaska's 15 parks. Most of the 54 million acres of national parkland are unforested and in the moist alpine tundra, where trails are not only unnecessary but largely detrimental to the ecology: As soon as the insulating ground cover is removed, the melting permafrost turns the trail into a muddy, impassable quagmire. Even in Denali, the only trails are around the park entrance and hotel area. Some parks (such as Denali, Glacier Bay, and Katmai) require backpacking permits; in the rest you're on your own. Several of the more accessible parks (Denali, Kenai Fjords, Klondike Gold Rush, Katmai, and Glacier Bay) have designated camping areas, but in the others you can pitch your tent on any level patch. For details on national parks in Alaska, request brochures from the National Park Service in Anchorage (907/271-2737, www.nps.gov/alaska).

FOREST SERVICE

In Alaska, the U.S. Forest Service manages the nation's two largest national forests: **Tongass National Forest** in Southeast Alaska, and **Chugach National Forest** in Southcentral Alaska. These forests cover 23 million acres of land, much of which is forested, but also comprising high mountains, glaciers, lakes, large rivers, and wild coastlines. Two national monuments within the Tongass—Admiralty Island and Misty Fiords—are popular with travelers, and 19 wilderness areas cover 5.7 million acres in the Tongass.

Both Tongass and Chugach are popular recreation destinations, with hundreds of miles of hiking trails and a number of campgrounds (free to $16) and visitor centers. Also within these forests are more than 180 wilderness cabins ($35–45/night), a few of which are reachable by road or trail, with the others accessible only by floatplane or boat. You must reserve them well in advance through **ReserveUSA** (518/885-3639 or 877/444-6777, www.reserveusa.com). Brochures describing the cabins are available from Forest Service offices or from Alaska Public Lands Information Centers in Anchorage, Fairbanks, Tok, and Ketchikan.

For additional information, contact Tongass National Forest (907/586-7928, www.fs.fed.us /r10/tongass) and Chugach National Forest (907/271-3992, www.fs.fed.us/r10/chugach).

FISH & WILDLIFE SERVICE

The Fish & Wildlife Service manages 16 different refuges covering more than 75 million acres in Alaska. Most of these are in remote regions that see little visitation (other than local subsistence hunters and fishermen), but they provide vital habitat for birds and other animals. The best-known Alaskan refuges are **Arctic National Wildlife Refuge** on the North Slope, **Kenai National Wildlife Refuge** on the Kenai Peninsula, and **Kodiak National Wildlife Refuge** on Kodiak Island. Kenai sees the most tourists and has a visitor center, hiking trails, canoe routes, and campgrounds. Kodiak has a visitor center, plus a number of public-use cabins available for rent. A large new visitor center in Homer provides a great introduction to the **Alaska Maritime National Wildlife Refuge,** which sprawls across 2,500 Alaskan islands. The nation's largest refuge (20 million acres) is **Yukon Delta National Wildlife Refuge** in Western Alaska. For details on all 16 refuges, contact the F&WS (907/786-3909; www.r7.fws.gov).

BUREAU OF LAND MANAGEMENT

Alaska's largest land-management agency (over 90 million acres) is the Bureau of Land Management (907/271-5960, www.ak.blm.gov). Most BLM land is undeveloped, but three popular recreation sites—**White Mountains National Recreation Area, Chena River State Recreation Area,** and **Steese Natural Conservation Area**—feature a handful of hiking trails, campgrounds, and public cabins in the vicinity of Fairbanks.

STATE LANDS

State Parks

The State of Alaska owns 89 million acres—almost a quarter of the state—and manages this land for a variety of purposes, from mineral and oil development to state forests. The state manages more than 110 state parks and recreation areas spread over three million acres. Located in Western Alaska, **Wood-Tikchik State Park** is the largest state park in America, encompassing 1.5 million acres. More accessible—it's the most popular state park in Alaska—is **Chugach State Park** which covers nearly a half-million acres bordering on Anchorage. Most of these state parks and recreation sites have trails and campgrounds. Camping fees are typically $10–15 per night, with some parks charging a $5 day-use fee. A number of state parks have public-use cabins for $25–65 per night.

For additional state park information call 907/269-8400 to request brochures and a statewide park map, or browse over to www.alaskastateparks.org. You can also use this website to check cabin availability; reservations are made at Department of Natural Resources public information offices in Anchorage or Fairbanks or state park offices.

Fish & Game

The Alaska Department of Fish & Game manages more than 30 state refuges, critical habitat areas, and wildlife sanctuaries, including the world-famous bear-viewing area at **McNeil River** and the **Walrus Islands** near Dillingham. It also jointly manages (with the Forest Service) the Pack Creek brown bear-viewing area on Admiralty Island. Also popular is **Creamer's Field Migratory Waterfowl Refuge** in Fairbanks. The agency issues sportfishing and hunting permits. For details on all its activities, contact the ADF&G (907/465-4180, www.state.ak.us/adfg).

NATIVE LANDS

Today, the 12 regional Native corporations and more than 200 village and urban corporations created in 1971 by the ANCSA own some 37 million acres in Alaska. Much of this is closed to public access except with special permits; fees are commonly charged.

The ANCSA attempted to bring Natives into the mainstream of society, and has succeeded in some ways, while failing in others. Surprisingly, the corporations created by the act have become primary forces in logging, mining, and other developments around the state, in sharp contrast to the preserve-the-land policies that might have been anticipated. In parts of Southeast and Southcentral Alaska the Native lands have been nearly all logged over; I know of one place where they logged almost within spitting distance of a Native cemetery and historic clan house. (Of course, these developments are driven by money, since corporations need profits to survive and to pay dividends to their Native shareholders.)

Economy and Government

COST OF LIVING

No doubt about it—this place is expensive. Alaska ranks near the top in cost of living for all the states. Numerous factors conspire to keep prices high. Most consumer goods must be imported from the Lower 48, and the transportation costs are tacked on along the way. In addition, the transportation and shipping rates within Alaska are similarly high, further inflating the cost of goods and services. In more remote regions especially, lack of competition, coupled with steady demand, ensures top-dollar prices. And let's not forget how long and cold and dark Alaskan winters are: the cost of heat and utilities is a hardship. Alaska ranks first in per-capita energy consumption in the United States.

Visitors to Anchorage and Fairbanks will be pleased to find that prices are not totally out of line with the Lower 48. Typical food prices in these two largest cities are around 25 percent higher than those in Portland, Oregon. Both cities have large discount-chain stores that help keep prices more reasonable. The big chains have also spread to Wasilla, Juneau, and Ketchikan, driving down prices in those areas (and squeezing local businesses).

Beyond these exceptions, the prices in the North are much higher than Outside, and are generally the worst in the most remote bush communities. Food costs in places such as Galena or Fort Yukon are more than twice those in Anchorage. Even in Homer—which is on the road system—food is 40 percent more expensive than in Anchorage. These financial realities apply to residents much more than to short-term visitors: If you're well prepared and you provision yourself adequately in the major commercial centers, any time spent in the bush shouldn't be too painful to the pocketbook.

MONEY FOR NOTHIN'

In 1976, with oil wealth about to come gushing out of the south end of the pipeline, voters approved a constitutional amendment calling for a percentage of all oil and mineral revenues to be placed in a **Permanent Fund** (www.apfc.org). Money from this account can only be used for investment, not for state operating expenses, which explains why during recent Alaskan recessions, when hundreds of state workers were laid off and state funds were severely cut back, billions of surplus dollars sat untouched in the fund. It's the only one of its kind in the country: The only state fund that pays dividends to residents, and the largest pool of public money in the country. In 2003 it totaled more than $25 *billion*—and this is after two years of stock market losses.

A portion of the interest and capital gains income from these assets are distributed to all Alaska residents—even children—in a yearly Permanent Fund Dividend check sent out each October. In 1982, the first year of the dividend, each Alaskan received $1,000, but it didn't reach that level again until the stock market boom of the late 1990s—when it topped out at nearly $2,000. The 2003 payout was $1,100 per person. All this sudden cash doesn't go unnoticed by local businesses, especially car dealers, furniture stores, and airlines, who put out a plethora of special deals as soon as the money hits the banks.

MAKING A LIVING
Employment
Anyone thinking of moving to Alaska to get rich is in for a rude awakening. For a number of years after the oil boom, Alaskans earned the most per capita of any state, but now Alaska ranks 33rd for income—and near the top for

cost of living. The state's unemployment figures are usually several percentage points above the national average, even during the peak summer season.

Despite this, you can still come to Alaska and make a decent living; after all, most Alaskans came from somewhere else (only a third of Alaskans were born in the state—the second-lowest such percentage in the country). But the opportunities, it should be stressed, are limited. For example, almost a third of the people collecting a paycheck in Alaska work for federal, state, or local government. And the industry that accounts for 87 percent of state revenues (oil and gas) accounts for just 3 percent of employment. The real growth of late has come at the bottom end, in service jobs and retail sales, where your income would probably leave you officially listed at poverty status. So if a job as a Wal-Mart stocker is your dream, hop on the next flight to Anchorage.

For employment information, visit the **Alaska Department of Labor's** website: www.labor .state.ak.us. Here you'll find details on jobs in all sectors, including seasonal cannery work, state positions, and relocation information. The site's **Job Bank** provides an up-to-date listing of openings around the state.

Fishing

Alaska's fisheries account for over half of America's commercial fish production. Three-quarters of the value is in groundfish (pollock and cod) and salmon, the rest in shellfish, halibut, herring, and others. Alaska produces almost all of the U.S. canned-salmon stock (200 million pounds), and eight Alaskan ports are among the country's top 50 producers, with Dutch Harbor/Unalaska almost always in the top three, and Kodiak not far behind.

Alaska's fisheries are probably the most carefully managed in America, with healthy stocks of wild salmon and halibut. Fish farming is illegal in Alaska, but farmed salmon from other areas have lowered demand and prices for wild salmon, forcing many Alaskan fishermen out of business. (See the sidebar *Alaska Salmon* in the *On the Road* chapter for details on the controversy.)

Learn more about Alaska's seafood industry (and get some good salmon and halibut recipes) from the **Alaska Seafood Marketing Institute** in Juneau: 907/465-5560 or 800/478-2903, and www.alaskaseafood.org.

© DON PITCHER

purse seiner catching salmon near Valdez

Agriculture

The percentage of Alaska's land used for farming is as minuscule as the percentage of Alaska's total economy that is accounted for by agriculture. Of the state's 375 million acres (17 million of it suitable for farming), only 910,000 acres are considered cultivable; of those, only 31,000 acres are occupied by crops. The Matanuska Valley (Palmer/Wasilla) and the Tanana Valley (Fairbanks/Delta) contain almost 90 percent of Alaska's usable farmland. Hay, potatoes, barley, and oats are the state's top ag products.

In addition to legal crops, Alaska is famous for marijuana, and that crop is widely regarded as the state's biggest money-maker. Cannabis-growing operations (most are now indoor operations) are especially big in the Matanuska Valley, where the potent Matanuska Thunder gains the favor of potheads everywhere. A measure to legalize pot failed in 2000, but medical marijuana was approved by the voters several years earlier.

Gold and Minerals

From 1880 to 1980, 30 million ounces of gold were taken from Alaska. Today, the Fort Knox Mine near Fairbanks is Alaska's biggest gold producer, extracting 1,000 ounces of gold per day. Another major gold mine is scheduled to open near Delta Junction in 2005, and other large hardrock mines are near Galena and McGrath, while small placer mines are common across Alaska.

Zinc is the state's most valuable mineral, mined at the enormous Red Dog Mine, 90 miles north of Kotzebue. The largest zinc mine in the world, it produces 575,000 tons of zinc and 100 million tons of lead a year. Coal is mined at Usibelli, near Denali National Park, and deposits of jade, molybdenum, chromite, nickel, platinum, and uranium are known, though the cost of mining in remote Alaska limits these ventures.

Oil and Gas

Everything that moves in Alaska is lubricated with oil, primarily North Slope crude. Without oil, the Alaskan economy would stiffen, shatter, and disappear into thin air. Oil and gas revenues account for 87 percent of the state's tax revenue. Alaska is so addicted to oil revenue that when the price of a barrel of oil drops by $1, the budget must be adjusted by $150 million. Though the industry accounts for just 3 percent of the total workforce, the average annual salary for these workers is $96,000. Few elected officials would dare speak out against the oil companies; they all know who pays the tab when election bills come in, and don't want that cash going to their opponents.

At more than 350 million barrels of oil a year, Alaska accounts for around 17 percent of the nation's oil production, second only to Texas. Peak production was in 1988, when 738 million barrels of Prudhoe crude flowed through the pipeline. The Prudhoe Bay oilfield, largest in North America and 18th in the world, had produced 14 billion barrels by 2003, but production continues to decline.

Enormous quantities of natural gas lie beneath the North Slope, and proposals have been made to build a gas pipeline paralleling the existing oil line, or to develop a gas-to-liquids technology so that the gas can be sent down the existing oil pipeline. Higher gas prices and increased demand may finally lead to its development within the next decade. In addition to the North Slope, both oil and gas are produced from offshore wells in Cook Inlet. The natural gas is used in Anchorage and Kenai, and at a fertilizer plant near Kenai.

Tourism

Tourism is Alaska's third-largest industry, behind petroleum production and commercial fishing. It's also the second-largest employer, accounting for thousands of seasonal jobs. More than a million visitors travel to Alaska each year, 90 percent of them arriving May–Sept. from the continental United States and Canada. Approximately half of all visitors (including business travelers) travel independently; the rest come up on cruise ships and package tours.

Native Corporations

Native corporations are major players in Alaska's economy, and they also have large investments (we're talking billions of dollars) spread all over the nation. The most financially successful of the regional corporations, **Arctic Slope Regional**

Corporation (www.asrc.com), had profits in 2001 topping $1 billion for its 9,000 shareholders. Other top companies include **Cook Inlet Regional Corporation (CIRI)** (www.ciri.com), **Chugach Alaska Corporation** (www.chugach-ak.com), **Doyon, Limited** (www.doyon.com), and **NANA Regional Corporation** (www.nana.com). Doyon, with more than 12 million acres, is the largest corporate landholder in the nation.

All of these companies are involved in tourism ventures around Alaska, but CIRI and NANA especially have major investments in tour companies, hotels, and other facilities. Another company that travelers to Southeast Alaska will certainly contact is the Juneau-based village **Goldbelt Corporation** (www.goldbelt.com) which runs the Mt. Roberts Tram, Glacier Bay National Park concessionaires, tour boats and buses, kayak trips, a hotel, and various other operations. If you travel in the North, you'll probably spend time in a Native-owned facility or on one of their tour boats or buses.

GOVERNMENT

Like Delaware, Wyoming, Vermont, and North Dakota, Alaska has only one representative to the U.S. Congress, along with two senators.

There are 20 state senators elected to four-year terms and 40 state representatives elected to two-year terms. They meet in the capitol in Juneau Jan.–April. Local government is a mishmash: 16 first- and second-class boroughs, first- and second-class unincorporated villages, and tribal governments.

Alaskan politics start on the conservative end of the spectrum, and head from there to I'll-pull-my-gun-out-to-show-you-how-right-wing-I-am. As of this writing, Republicans have the governorship (Frank Murkowski), a veto-proof majority in both houses, and all three congressional seats. After being elected governor in 2002, Murkowski appointed Lisa Murkowski, a relatively inexperienced legislator who happened to be his own daughter to take over his seat in the U.S. Senate. She stands for election in 2004, so things might change, especially given the presence of popular former-governor Democrat Tony Knowles on the ballot. Senator Ted Stevens and Representative Don Young have enormous political clout, and are so entrenched in power that only death will loosen their grip, and even that could be in doubt, since Stevens' son is also a politician. Stevens in particular is considered a king of pork-barrel politics, and his largesse makes Alaska the highest recipient of federal spending of any state, more than $11,540 per resident in 2003! Oink.

The People

In 2002, Alaska's population was 644,000. Of this, roughly 16 percent were of Native descent. The non-Native population is predominately white, with a small percentage of black, Hispanic, Asian, and Pacific Islanders. The Hispanic and Asian populations are growing rapidly in Alaska, and visitors to bush towns are often surprised to find that many of the restaurants are owned by Korean Americans, while the cab drivers may be from the former Yugoslavia and the cannery workers came from the Philippines or Mexico. Of course, the cruise ships that ply Inside Passage waters are staffed by workers from all over the globe. Anchorage has by far the most diverse population; by 2010 more than a third of its residents will be Hispanic, Asian, black, or Native.

Joe Average

According to statistics, the "typical" Alaskan is a 32-year-old white male; I think I know him: He's single, has a college degree, lives in Anchorage, works for Federal Express, hunts caribou with his buddies each fall, and is likely to be seen at Chilkoot Charlie's most Friday nights! The state has the second-highest percentage of kids under 18 of any state; only Utah (not surprisingly) is higher.

In Anchorage and the other large Alaskan cities, the ratio of men to women is almost equal, but the state as a whole has one of the highest male-to-female ratios in the nation: 104 males to 100 females (compared with 95 males to 100 females Outside). Of course, you should also know the old and all-too-accurate adage: Alaska, where the odds are good, but the goods are odd.

Alaska is the largest state but the third-least-populous (behind Wyoming and Vermont), resulting in the lowest population density—1.0 per square mile (compare this to Wyoming, which has the second smallest at 4.7, or New Jersey, which is the most crowded at 1,042). It's also second to last in the number of people born in-state (34 percent); Florida is last at 31 percent. Alaska takes last place in its percentage of farm workers (0.1 percent).

ALASKAN NATIVES

Southeast Natives

One of Alaska's only Indian reservations is at Metlakatla, near Ketchikan. A group of nearly 1,000 **Tsimshian** Natives relocated here in 1887 from their traditional homeland, slightly south near Prince Rupert, as a result of disagreements between William Duncan, the tribe's missionary, and his church superiors (see "Metlakatla" in the *Southeast Alaska* chapter for the complete story). These Natives are thus the only ones not included in the ANCSA. Similarly, about 800 **Haida** natives live on southern Prince of Wales Island at the southeastern tip of Alaska, and the northern extent of the Haida homeland.

The **Tlingit** (KLINK-it) Indians are the traditional dwellers of Southeast Alaska, related to the Interior Athabascans. Blessed with an incredible abundance of food, fuel, furs, and tools, the Tlingits evolved a sophisticated and complex society, religion, and artistry. The primary social unit was the community house, which typically sheltered 50–100 people. Huge trunks of cedar and spruce provided the house posts, often carved and painted with the clan's totemic symbols; slaves were put in the post holes to cushion the connection between totem and earth. One had to stoop to pass through the single door; no windows punctuated the long structure. Ten or so of these clan houses made up a village, and a number of neighboring villages made

© DON PITCHER

blanket toss, Barrow

up a tribe. But these distinctions held little importance to the Tlingits, who felt connected genetically only to members of the same clan.

All marriages occurred between clans; marrying within the clan was considered incestuous. Descent was matrilineal: Children belonged to the mother's clan, and a man's heirs were his sisters' children. Therefore the pivotal male relationship was between uncle and nephews. At the age of 10, boys went to live with an uncle, who taught them the ways of the world. The uncle arranged the boy's marriage to a girl of another clan, who remained with her mother until the wedding. The dowry price was usually a number of blankets; the Tlingits were famous for their weaving and embroidery. Feasts known as "potlatch" honored the dead while feting the living. The Tlingits knew how to party. Often the potlatch continued for days or even weeks, during which the host fed, clothed, and entertained a neighboring, usually wealthier, clan, then "gave away" the clan's most valuable possessions to them. It was understood that the hosted clan would reciprocate eventually, with an even greater degree of festivity and generosity.

The Tlingits had an intensely animistic belief system, in which everything, from glaciers to fish hooks, had a spirit. Tlingit shamans were virtually omnipotent, alternately controlling and beseeching *yek,* or karma, on behalf of the tribe. They also professed a complete understanding of the afterlife, "on authority of men who died and came back." Tlingit arts were expressed by men who carved totems for house posts, through the potlatch and other important events, and by women who wove exquisite blankets. Unlike the Aleut, the Tlingits were fierce warriors who were never completely conquered by invading Russians, going head-to-head and hand-to-hand every inch of the way, until they settled into an uneasy coexistence.

Athabascans

Nomadic hunters and migrants, the Athabascans are related to the Tlingit of Southeast Alaska and the Navajo and Apache of the American Southwest. They subsisted on salmon and the Interior's mammals, mostly caribou and moose. They passed the cruel winters in tiny villages of no more than six houses, with a *kashim,* or community center, as the focal point. They ice-fished and trapped in the dark, using dogsleds as transportation. Their arts were expressed primarily in beautifully embroidered clothing and beadwork. The men remained constantly occupied with survival tasks—finding food, building houses, maintaining gear. When the first white explorers and traders arrived in the early 19th century, the Athabascans immediately began to trade with them, learning the new cultures and in turn educating the newcomers in local customs and skills, not the least of which was dogsledding.

A tiny separate group of Native people, the **Eyaks** are found on the coast of Alaska between Cordova and Yakutat, and have distinct links to both the Athabascans to the north and Tlingits to the east.

Aleuts

As the Athabascans were almost entirely land-based people, the Aleuts were almost entirely dependent on the sea. Clinging to the edge of tiny, treeless, windswept Aleutian Islands, they lived in small dwellings made of sealskin-covered frames, with fireplaces in the middle and steam baths attached on the sides. They made sea otter skins into clothing and processed walrus and seal intestines into parkas. Their kayaks (called *bidarka*) were made of marine mammal skins stretched over a wooden or whalebone frame. Basketry was their highest artistic achievement, and their dances were distinctly martial, with masks, rattles, and knives.

When the Russians invaded the Aleutians in the mid-1700s like furies from hell, around 25,000 Aleuts inhabited almost all the Aleutian Islands and the southern portion of the Alaska Peninsula. Within 50 years, over half had died through violence, starvation, or disease. Most of the rest became slaves and were dispersed around the New World to hunt the sea otter and fight for the Russians. In fact, Aleuts traveled as far south as Catalina Island off the Southern California coast, wiping out the Gabrielino Indians there, along with the entire otter population, in 1810. Many of the women served as concubines to the Russian overlords, further diluting the Aleut lineage. Today, most Aleuts carry only half or a quarter Aleut blood; only 1,000 are considered full-blooded.

Eskimo

The term "Eskimo" comes from the French-Canadian *Esquimau,* which in turn is derived from the Algonquin *askimowew,* which means "eaters of raw fish." Although the term is not at all derogatory, the Natives of these regions often prefer to use more specific titles: the **Yup'ik** peoples of Southwest Alaska, the **Inupiat** peoples of the Arctic and circumpolar region, and the **Alutiiq** peoples of Kodiak Island, the Alaska Peninsula, and parts of Kenai Peninsula and Prince William Sound. In addition, remote St. Lawrence Island contains **Siberian Yup'ik** peoples. All four groups speak distinct dialects of the same basic language.

In traditional Eskimo culture there was a strong sense of community; their society was mostly leaderless, with every able member responsible for contributing to the struggle for survival. The

CAPSULE ALASKAN GLOSSARY

A type of pidgin called "Chinook" evolved in the Pacific Northwest in the 18th century. The language first developed in interactions between the large, powerful Chinook tribe of the Columbia River, which did business with white traders, and the Nootka tribe, which held a monopoly on the shells from which the shell money of the Pacific was manufactured. (Hence the name, "Chinook.") After Europeans arrived, Chinook adopted words from English and French; it became indispensable to traders in Alaska during the entire 19th century. Of the 500 words in the Chinook vocabulary, a few are still used today.

Some of the Alaskan words below have been borrowed from the Native tongues; the rest derive from the colorful frontier slang of explorers, traders, trappers, prospectors, fishermen, roughnecks, and travel writers.

akutak—Yup'ik Native word for Native ice cream: a combination of whipped berries, seal oil, and snow

Alaskan malamute—a particular breed of working dog used to pull sleds

Alcan—nickname for the Alaska Highway

Arctic Circle—an imaginary line, roughly corresponding to 67° north latitude, which the sun remains entirely above on summer solstice and entirely below on winter solstice

Aurora—goddess of dawn

aurora borealis—the scientific term for the northern lights

baleen—also known as whalebone, these stiff, flexible whale's "teeth" are woven into baskets by Eskimo men

banya—Russian in origin, a small sauna in which rocks surround a wood stove, and are sprinkled with water for a steam bath; common on Kodiak Island and along the Bering Sea

barabara—traditional Aleut or Eskimo shelter, made of driftwood and a sod roof

baidarka—an Aleut kayak covered with animal skins

blanket toss—originally a means of spotting game on the tundra, this Native event, where 6–8 people use a large blanket to toss the "spotter" high in the air and catch him; now part of most festivals and is demonstrated for tourists in Barrow and Kotzebue

break-up—the period in late April or early May when the river ice suddenly fractures and begins to flow downstream; a particularly muddy, slushy time of year

bunny boot—see vapor-barrier boots

bush—Borrowed from Africa and Australia, this term generally designates remote areas off the road system, particularly in Interior, Western, and Arctic Alaska

cabin fever—Alaskan-size claustrophobia due to the extreme cold and dark of winter

cache—pronounced "cash," a log hut built on tin-wrapped stilts used to store food and supplies beyond the reach of animals

Chain, The—nickname for the Aleutian Islands

cheechako—meaning "just arrived," used to describe newcomers and visitors, especially those who haven't spent a winter in Alaska or received a dividend check; some sourdoughs view anyone not born in the state as a cheechako

chinook—a strong warm wind originating in Prince William Sound; can be particularly destructive in hillside sections of Anchorage

chum—a kind of salmon; also known as dog salmon, after its primary consumers

d2—from the section of that name in the Alaska Native Claims Settlement Act; refers to the national-interest lands set aside for national parks and forests, wildlife refuges, preserves, and wild and scenic rivers

Eskimo—from French Canadian *Esquimau,* a word derived originally from northern Algonquin *askimoweu,* which means "eater of raw fish"

fish wheel—an ingenious mechanism that uses the current of a river or stream for power to scoop fish into a tank

freeze-up—the time of year, mostly in Northwest and Arctic regions, during which bodies of water are frozen and seaports are icebound

gussuk—derogatory Eskimo term for white person

honey bucket—in much of bush Alaska, the local sewage system: a five-gallon plastic bucket used as a toilet. The untreated waste is often dumped into rivers in the summer or onto river ice in winter (for natural "flushing" when the ice breaks up in the spring). Because of the obvious health hazards—not to mention the smell—the state has been trying to bring sewage-treatment facilities to small villages.

hootch—shortened version of the Chinook word "hootchenoo," meaning home-distilled spirits

husky—The generic term for sled dog. A toy poodle hooked up to a sled is technically a husky—for the brief moment before it's eaten by a large **Siberian husky.** Like the malamute, the Siberian husky is a singular breed famous for strength and intelligence.

icefog—caused by an inversion in which warm air traps cold air near the surface, which keeps getting colder and colder . . . until the water vapor in the air freezes, creating floating ice crystals; Fairbanks is notorious for its wintertime icefog

iceworm—originally a joke by sourdoughs on cheechakos, the joke was ultimately on the sourdoughs—iceworms actually exist, and you can see specimens in the museum in Juneau and at the Portage Glacier visitor center

Iditarod—Famous 1,000-mile dogsled race from Anchorage to Nome in February. One explanation of the name comes from the term "rod," a measurement of work accomplished in the gold fields; thus the word is actually a sentence: "I did a rod." Another holds that the name evolved from the name of an Ingalik Indian village reported as "Khadilotden." It was then reported by the USGS as "Haidilatna," and finally anglicized as Iditarod.

igloo—Alaskan Natives' shelters are never igloos made of ice (see *barabara*), except in extreme emergencies

Inside Passage—another name for Southeast Alaska; it refers to the many protected waterways of this island archipelago

Inupiak—a northern Eskimo dialect used by Inupiat peoples

iron dog—snowmobile

iron ranger—collection boxes at state and federal campgrounds

kuspuk—parka worn by Eskimo women, often with a small backpack-like pouch for carrying babies

liquid sunshine—Ketchikan's euphemism for rain

Lower 48—an Alaskan term used to refer to the contiguous continental United States

moose nuggets—small, round, brown turds, bravely made into jewelry by enterprising (usually bankrupt) local artisans

mukluk—boot made by Eskimo women, with tough sealskin soles, reindeer-hide uppers, fur and yarn trim, sewn together with caribou sinew

muktuk—an Eskimo delicacy of the rubbery outer layer of whale skin and fat; very chewy, served raw or pickled

mush—popularized by Sgt. Preston of the Yukon, this command means "Let's go!" to anxious dog teams everywhere; originally a Chinook term adapted from the French *marchons*

muskeg—swampy areas covered by moss and scrub

Native—the preferred term for Alaska's original inhabitants

no-see-ums—tiny biting flies that plague Alaska after mosquito season

nunatak—lonely rock peak jutting out above icefields

Outside—anywhere other than Alaska, primarily used in reference to the Lower 48

Panhandle—nickname for Southeast Alaska

permafrost—permanently frozen ground, with a layer of topsoil that thaws during the summer

petroglyphs—stone-age carvings on rock faces

poke—a miner's moosehide bag full of gold dust and nuggets

potlatch—A Native party to celebrate any occasion. Often the hosts would give away all their possessions to their guests. This exercise in the detachment from all worldly goods was also an exercise in gaining more, as the event conferred upon the guests the obligation to host a bigger potlatch with better gifts.

promyshleniki—early Russian explorers and traders

continued on next page

CAPSULE ALASKAN GLOSSARY (cont'd)

pushky—from Russian, the colloquial term for cow parsnip, a common plant that can cause caustic skin burns, particularly on a sunny day; most commonly used on Kodiak Island and in Southcentral Alaska

qiviut—underwool of musk ox, supposedly eight times lighter, warmer, and more expensive than wool

ruff—fur edge on a parka hood, often of wolf guard hairs

salt chuck—a narrow constriction at the end of a lagoon, where the direction of the water flow depends on the tides (out at low, in at high); mainly used in Southeast Alaska.

shit icicle—the pile of excrement that gathers in bush outhouses each winter in the form of an inverted icicle; when it gets too close to the top, someone has the unpleasant job of knocking it down

skookum—Chinook, meaning "strong" or "worthy"

skookum **house**—jail

Slope—The gently sloping tundra around Prudhoe Bay; also known as the North Slope; Slope workers are almost always employed by the oil companies

snowmachine—snowmobile

solstice—first day of summer (June 21) or winter (December 21)

sourdough—a mixture of flour, water, sugar, and yeast, allowed to ferment before being used to make bread or hotcakes; an old-timer

squaw candy—dried or smoked salmon

surimi—processed seafood product manufactured from bottom fish (usually pollock) in Kodiak, Unalaska, and other Alaskan ports; used in "crab" salads and cocktails, as well as in less expensive sushi

taiga—from Russian word meaning "land of little sticks," which describes the transition zone between the boreal forest and treeless tundra

Taku wind—sudden gusts of up to 100 mph that sweep down on Juneau from the nearby icefields

termination dust—the first snowfall that coats mountaintops at the end of summer, a sign that Alaska's many seasonal workers are about to be terminated

treeline—the elevation (in Alaska, 2,500 feet) and latitude (generally following the Arctic Circle) above which no trees grow

tundra—from another Russian word, meaning "vast treeless plain"; used to describe nearly 30 percent of Alaska's land area

ulu—a shell-shaped Eskimo knife that tourists buy in record numbers and airlines disallow in hand luggage

umiak—an open skin-covered Eskimo boat used in the hunting of whales and other sea mammals

visqueen—thin clear plastic sheeting

XtraTufs—high-top rubber boots ubiquitous on Southeast Alaskan feet

Yup'ik— dialect of the Bering Coast Eskimo

---

borderline between personal and communal property was fuzzy at best, and theft did not exist. Everything was shared, including (claim some anthropologists) wives. All justice was determined by what was deemed best for the community. Marriages, too, were so determined.

A boy entered adulthood after his first kill, and the event was celebrated by a large feast. A girl was considered grown as soon as she began menstruating, which was accompanied by a two-week ritual. The man-child selected a bride, paid a minimal price, and unceremoniously set up house in a hut similar to the Aleuts'—a bone-and-brush framework covered with moss and grass. "Igloos" made of snow and ice were used only as temporary shelters on the trail (and mostly by central Canadian Natives). Fuel was derived from whale oil and driftwood. They ate meat almost exclusively: fish, whale, walrus, caribou, birds. Also like their relatives the Aleut, they used skin and hides for clothing and boating. Masks are the most visible form of Eskimo art, but their aesthetic touch marks almost everything they make.

The Russians had little impact on the remote Eskimo, but their introduction to Western ways by the Boston whalers around the 1850s was swift and brutal. Many Eskimos quickly succumbed to whiskey, and Native men were shanghaied while unconscious to labor on the white whalers' ships. They learned about prostitution (renting the women) and slavery (selling them). They learned how to use firearms and casually kill each other, usually in a drunken fit. They acquired syphilis, white sugar, canned food, and money.

An encounter between the Eskimo of St. Lawrence Island and a single whaling vessel in 1880, described by Colby in his classic *Guide to Alaska* (1939), sums up the scene: "The master sent members of his crew ashore with bottles of grain alcohol, [for which] the Natives traded ivory, whalebone, and furs. The officers and crew selected a harem from the young women of the village, and paid them in alcohol. When the whaling vessel left, the entire village of 450 Natives was dead-drunk and beggared, for they had even cut up their skin boats to trade for liquor. Around them were plenty of hair seal and walrus, but by the time the village had sobered and collected weapons the game was gone. Only about twenty-five villagers survived."

The whaling years ended just before the gold rush began. But the ruin of the Eskimo culture was almost total. Gradually, with the help of missionaries and legislators, the Eskimo in the late 19th century turned to reindeer herding, which began to provide income, food, and skins. Today, an estimated 34,000 Eskimo live in Alaska, having doubled their number over the past 50 years. The Eskimo people live in an arc stretching from Siberia to Greenland.

NATIVE ARTS AND CRAFTS

Not unlike most other aboriginal cultures, Native Alaskan arts and crafts were intricately intertwined with animism, religious ceremony, and utility. Each group worked with its abundant natural resources to produce all the necessities of a lifestyle in which subsistence, religion, and artistic expression were inseparable.

Alaskan tourism and Native crafts have gone hand in hand since the first Russian stepped ashore. When John Muir arrived in Wrangell by steamer in 1890, he wrote, "There was a grand rush on shore to buy curiosities and see totem poles. The shops were jammed and mobbed, high prices paid for shabby stuff manufactured expressly for tourist trade. Silver bracelets hammered out of dollars and half dollars by Indian smiths are the most popular articles, then baskets, yellow cedar toy canoes, paddles, etc. Most people who travel look only at what they are directed to look at. Great is the power of the guidebook-maker, however ignorant."

A similar advice holds today, especially in the shops selling made-in-China Alaskan trinkets or carved-in-Bali totem poles and masks. When buying Native handicrafts from anyone other than the artist, always look for the **Silver Hand** logo that identifies the work as an authentic Native piece. Get details from the Alaska State Council on the Arts (907/269-6610 or 888/278-7424, www.eed.state.ak/akca). Good places to buy Native crafts are the various museum gift shops or directly from the artisans, if you visit remote villages.

Ivory

The Inupiat Eskimo of northern coastal Alaska are renowned for their use of ivory, harvested (only) by Natives from the tusks and teeth of walruses, as well as ivory from woolly mammoths and giant mastodons uncovered by miners or erosion. The ivory is carved, also known as "scrimshawed," and made into various implements. Today you'll see ivory jewelry, *ulu* handles, cribbage boards, and the like. The use of ivory for handicrafts is severely restricted by federal regulations established to protect the walrus. Native carvers can carve on ivory obtained from walrus killed for subsistence food, and non-Natives can legally carve on fossilized ivory (darker-colored ivory that was buried in the ground). But don't make the mistake of buying an ivory piece and then taking it through Canada, unless you have a written permit from the Convention on Trade in Endangered Species (www.cites.org). Avoid border confiscations and other legal problems by mailing your pieces home. You won't have any problems carrying them onboard an aircraft, unless your plane lands outside the United States.

Baskets

All Alaskan Native groups used available resources to fashion baskets for storage, carrying, and cooking. Birch-bark baskets, often lashed with spruce roots, were made by the forest Athabascans. The coastal Haida, Tlingit, and Tsimshian Indians used the bark of big cedar trees. They also made entire baskets of spruce roots, occasionally weaving in maidenhead ferns for decoration. The Yup'ik and Aleut Natives of Western Alaska are known for small, delicate baskets fashioned from coastal rye grass. They also process baleen, the long strips of cartilage-like teeth that hang from the upper jaw of whales, and weave the strips into baskets.

The finest examples of the different baskets are displayed in the largest Alaskan museums; commercial baskets sell for anywhere from $30 for simple birch-bark trays to several thousand dollars for large baleen baskets.

Masks

Each Native culture had its traditional mask-making technology and its complex ceremonial uses for masks. Eskimo mask art and ritual were among the most highly developed in the world. Masks, like totems, represented the individual animals and birds that were worshipped, and each mask was believed to embody the spirit, or *inua,* of the animal. The masks of the Athabascans were worn by dancers, accompanied by a tribal choir, to dramatize the tribe's relationship to animal spirits, as well as to entertain guests at feasts. Some believe Aleut masks symbolized the faces of ancient inhabitants of the western Alaska archipelago, though these people were only distantly related to the Aleut, if at all.

The use of masks has declined in Alaskan Native cultures, and the art of mask-making isn't as prevalent today as it's said to have been before contact with the Western world. But you will see commercial masks in Native galleries and gift shops around the North; these bear a close resemblance to those of long ago.

Totems

Totem poles were the largest and most dramatic of the Native arts and social images, though today, totemic images are reproduced in every medium and size. Typical totemic characterizations include highly stylized wolves, whales, bears, ravens, eagles, and beavers, as well as mythological monsters, human ancestors, and religious spirits. These images are a common sight in gift shops all over Alaska. A further description of totem poles is found under "Ketchikan" in the *Southeast Alaska* chapter.

Other Pieces

Fur parkas are the quintessential Eskimo garment, and are available in remote villages and at shops in Anchorage and Fairbanks. The finest of these are custom-made and cost a small fortune; ask locally for the best seamstresses. Beautifully crafted **dolls** are a hallmark of Eskimo artists who typically use furs and other local materials. Other distinctively Alaskan items include **dance fans, beadwork,** and handcrafted silver or jade **jewelry.**

On the Road

Alaska is the largest state in the union, with the third-smallest population (after Wyoming and Vermont), so it stands to reason that it also has the most landscape waiting to be explored. Because the Great Land is so vast, so rugged and diverse, and so anything-goes, the range, breadth, and depth of outdoor sports are mind-boggling. And Alaska has sufficient public transportation—by ground, water, and air—to get you to whatever outdoor location you've chosen for your recreation. If you're experienced and well prepared, you can catch a ride from, say, Glennallen to Kennicott in Wrangell–St. Elias National Park and backpack for a month without seeing another soul. Or start in Bettles and walk west across four

national parks in the Brooks Range clear to the Chukchi Sea on the west Arctic Coast. Or put your kayak into Resurrection Bay at Seward and paddle around Kenai Fjords National Park for 10 days. Or put a canoe into the Kobuk River at Ambler and float down to Kotzebue.

Hiking, backpacking, climbing, skiing, dogsledding, mountain biking, river rafting, sea kayaking, skiing, snowmobiling, snowshoeing, fishing, hunting, kayaking, canoeing, flightseeing, and photography are among the more common activities. And for the extremists among you, some of the wilder opportunities for recreation include paragliding, winter camping, and scuba diving. The possibilities, as they say, are truly limitless.

© DON PITCHER

Mount Drum and Glenn Highway west of Glennallen

Planning Your Trip

Readers of this book willing to expend a little energy will certainly be able to set up a travel itinerary that covers their own interests, but if you want to leave the arranging to others, you may want to contact one of the many itinerary planners who specialize in Alaska. These could be as close as your local travel agent, or one of the online information sources such as www.alaska.com, www.alaskaone.com, www.adn .com/visitor, www.everythingalaska.com, or www.inalaska.com. For a human touch from those in the know, try **Alaska Rainforest Tours** in Juneau (907/463-3466, www.alaskarainforesttours.com), **Viking Travel** in Petersburg (907/772-3818 or 800/327-2571, www.alaskaferry.com), or **Alaska Tours** in Anchorage (907/277-3000, www.alaskatours.com).

Hundreds of adventure-travel package operators offer everything from helicopter skiing on icefields and scuba diving off Kodiak Island to ice-climbing on Mt. McKinley and parasailing over Turnagain Arm. The best compilation of guides and outfitters appears in the annual *Alaska State Vacation Planner.*

INFORMATION SOURCES

A great starting point when planning a trip to Alaska is the official *Alaska State Vacation Planner,* produced annually through a joint partnership between the state and private businesses. It's distributed by the Alaska Travel Industry Association (907/929-2200 or 800/862-5275, www.travelalaska.com).

You may also want to contact the Alaska Division of Business and Community Development's **Office of Tourism** (907/465-2012, www.dced.state.ak.us/tourism), though it primarily deals with tourism development and planning. The website features a complete listing of Alaska chambers of commerce and visitors bureaus, including clickable links. You can also find state chambers of commerce at www.alaskachamber.com.

If you're a member of the American Automobile Association (AAA), get their *TourBook* and *CampBook* covering Alaska, plus detailed maps. Overseas visitors who belong to an affiliated club in their home country can obtain this material free by showing their membership card at an AAA office in any large city.

SUGGESTED ITINERARIES
One Week
If you only have a week, one option is to take the ferry ride from Bellingham to Juneau or Skagway round-trip (takes six days); or ride the ferry one way, tour Juneau, Glacier Bay, or Skagway, for example, then fly back from Juneau. The other option is to fly to and from Anchorage, see the city briefly, then head up to Denali National Park (what most people would do), down to the Kenai Peninsula, or over to Prince William Sound.

Two Weeks
Two weeks is the length of the average package tour to Alaska. In two weeks you can ride the ferry from Bellingham to Skagway, stopping off at, say, Juneau overnight. Spend a night in Skagway, a night in Whitehorse, then go overland to Fairbanks. A few nights in Fairbanks and Denali will get you ready for Anchorage; from there you can choose between the Kenai Peninsula and Prince William Sound as described above.

Alternatively, you could ride the ferry to Juneau, fly to Cordova and connect up with the Southwest ferry system, and do Prince William Sound and the Kenai Peninsula that way, then wind up in Anchorage. If your planning is tight and your timing is right, you might even be able to jam in Denali. That's starting to border on hysteria, though.

Three Weeks
Three weeks is about the minimum required to drive at least one way. It's a long three days from anywhere in the Pacific Northwest up the Alaska Highway or Cassiar Highway. But with your own car, you can cover as much ground as you like, as fast as you like. It's light most of the sum-

mer, so you don't have to worry about missing the scenery if you drive at "night." You can sleep when you're dead. If you really want to crank up the mileage (and don't mind being on the road the entire time), drive to Whitehorse, then Dawson, then Eagle, then Tok. From Fairbanks, you can get out there, going to hot springs at Manley or Central. Head down to Denali and Anchorage, then take in the whole Kenai Peninsula, and/or put your car on the *Chenega* to do the whole Prince William Sound excursion. Riding back on the ferry will save a lot of wear and tear on your wheels and your lower back.

Four Weeks or More

If you have all this time, and the big bucks, you can get as far out there as you want. Head up to Coldfoot above the Arctic Circle on the Dalton outside of Fairbanks. Or get to Cordova or Kodiak on the ferry system. You could also take the *Tustumena* for a week's ride to Dutch Harbor in the Aleutians. Or pay the price and go to McNeil River, Katmai, Nome, Barrow, or the Pribilofs. At the end of four weeks you'll either be very anxious to get back home, or anxious to get back home so you can pack your bags for the permanent move north to the Great Land.

PACK THE ESSENTIALS

The following items assume that your trip to Alaska takes place in the summer months. If you plan to travel before May or after September, additional winter supplies will certainly be needed. Even if you aren't planning to do much camping or backpacking, it's always smart to carry a sleeping bag—unless your idea of roughing it is staying at local bed-and-breakfasts. In general, plan on cool and wet weather for your trip, but also throw in a pair of short pants for those warm Fairbanks days.

Even if you arrive in Alaska without the correct gear, almost anything you need is available in the larger towns, and in Anchorage the prices are really not much higher than in Lower 48 cities. In addition, the larger cities typically have at least one place that rents outdoor gear such as tents and stoves.

In addition to the items listed below, travelers to Southeast Alaska and other rainy parts of the state should bring rubber boots and heavy-duty raingear. A **cell phone** can be especially useful if you want to stay in contact with friends and family while traveling, but coverage varies, so check with your phone company for specifics, and make sure your service plan doesn't hit you with stiff fees for calls from or within Alaska.

Clothing Essentials
- light, water-resistant coat (Goretex works well)
- sweater or windblock jacket
- lightweight gloves
- longjohns
- walking shoes
- hiking boots
- hiking socks
- liner socks
- rain pants
- warm cap
- swimsuit
- sunglasses

Camping Essentials
- internal-frame backpack
- day pack
- tent and ground cloth
- sleeping bag
- Thermarest pad
- water filter
- 50 feet of line
- jackknife or Leatherman (a better option)
- camp stove and fuel bottle
- water bottle
- fishing tackle
- plastic bags
- plate, cup, spoon, and fork
- cooking pot
- waterproof matches and lighter
- compass
- small towel
- first-aid kit
- sewing kit
- padlock
- insect repellent
- sunscreen

WHAT TO TAKE

Clothing

Wearing your clothing in layers allows you to add or remove items, depending on the temperature or your level of exertion. Start out with a T-shirt, thermal, or polypropylene top (and bottom). Summer visitors will want to bring a light, waterproof jacket and rain pants, plus a sweater or polypro pullover for warmth. Hiking boots are recommended if you plan to spend any time away from town, but hikers in Southeast Alaska will need rubber boots (wait to buy them there to find the right kind). Bring a warm cap and gloves. A hooded parka comes in handy, though a poncho is adequate and light, and can double as a ground cloth or awning. Very few restaurants expect dressy attire, but bring a sport coat, suit, dress, or skirt if you plan to hobnob with the nabobs. A new pair of pants, rather than the usual scruffy jeans, goes a long way toward looking casually presentable.

Camping Gear

Even in summer, weather conditions in Alaska can change suddenly, and you must be well prepared for rain and cold at any time. Water resistance and warmth (in addition to weight) should be your main criteria when buying camping equipment. Categorize and separate all your things in plastic bags or stuff sacks; pack it that way for convenient access and protection from moisture. If you're planning on hiking and traveling by public transportation, your loaded pack should not weigh more than one-quarter your body weight. Walk around the block with it a few times. Next imagine hiking 10 miles uphill into the rain with that load on your back. Now pack again—lighter this time.

Practice putting up your tent, cooking on your camp stove, and so on, before you set out. A Thermarest pad provides comfort, insulation, and protection from moisture—essential qualities in the North. Down sleeping bags are useless when wet, which is especially problematic in Southeast and Southcentral. Synthetic fiber is warmer when wet, less expensive, but heavier and bulkier.

A small camp stove is the only way to ensure hot food and drink on the trail. Firewood is often wet or unavailable; other times campfires are prohibited. Remember, camping fuel is not allowed on commercial aircraft. Dried or freeze-dried foods are light, easy to prepare, and less attractive to animals. Take some high protein/energy foods for hiking. A plastic water bottle is essential to have along; but you'll need a water filter even in remote backcountry areas.

The Great Outdoors

Respecting the Land

As you enjoy the recreational opportunities provided by the Alaskan landscape, make it your objective to leave no trace of your passing. Litter is pollution. Whenever you're tempted to leave garbage behind, think of how you feel when you find other people's plastic bags, tin cans, or aluminum foil in *your* yard. If you packed it in, you can pack it out. Burying garbage is useless, as animals soon dig it up. Be a caretaker by picking up trash left by less conscientious visitors. In this way, in part, you thank the land for the experiences it has given you.

Along shorelines, the intertidal zone is the best for campfires and human excrement. Human wastes in other areas should be disposed of at least 100 feet from any trail or water source. Bury wastes and carefully burn the toilet paper, if possible. Try to build your fire on sand or gravel and keep it small and under control. Extreme care should be taken during dry periods and in the forest. Refrain from doing anything that might cause even the smallest of accidental fires. Even in rainy Southeast, fires can get started that are difficult to extinguish, especially once they burn into the deep peat material on the forest floor.

Local People

As you explore, remember that Northerners are fiercely independent people who value their privacy. They can also be overwhelmingly hospitable if you treat them with respect. Never put up your tent in or near a village without first asking permission. When visiting a Native village or any small, isolated community, look people straight in the eye and be the first to say hello. Remember, you are the intruder, so you should be the one to make the effort to put them at ease.

Under no circumstances should you walk into a small settlement, fish camp, or other personal area and immediately start photographing people. This is rude and may well get folks angry. Most people are happy to pose for a photo if you simply take the time to talk, and express a genuine interest in them and their lives. But if they say no, just move on. There may also be times when it is best simply to leave before tempers flare, particularly when people have been drinking heavily (an all-too-common experience in some villages), or when their politics stray to the don't-tread-on-me fringe.

EXPLORING THE LAND

Hiking and Camping

Hiking and camping are the preferred outdoor recreations for the majority of Alaskans and visitors. These pastimes are available to practically anybody, from three-month-old infants to 93-year-old great-grannies. Here, you don't have to be in particularly good shape, you don't need a big bank balance, and you don't have to have the latest high-tech equipment. Most public land is open to free camping, though there are restrictions in the more populous areas.

For the size of the Alaskan outdoors, there are very few trails, but it's easy just to pick a direction, especially in the vast taiga and tundra, and go. Also, the perpetual daylight during hiking season allows for additional deviation from normal hiking-camping cycles, providing further freedom. And the definite possibility of encountering a variety and abundance of wildlife is an incalculable bonus. The few trails that do exist are covered in

ON THE ROAD

PHOTOGRAPHY

Hand in hand with hiking and camping goes photography—of the gorgeous scenery, the fauna and flora, and the special light. Professional photographers can have a literal field day in Alaska, because the ideal light conditions—at dawn and sunset everywhere else—continue throughout the long days of low light and long angles in the boreal region. Casual photographers are satisfied with automatic point-and-shoot, disposable, and cheap digital cameras, though none of these do justice to the grandness of Alaska.

A good starting setup would include a 28–105 zoom and a 100–300 zoom; longer and more expensive lenses (400 or 500 mm) are needed for serious wildlife work. A flash helps to fill in shadow areas on sunny days. A tripod is a must for wildlife, and slower films provide the tightest film grain. But also take some faster film (ISO 200–400) for those inevitable gray days. Amateurs typically shoot print film (an ISO 200 speed is fine for many purposes) since they want photos to show their friends, while pros shoot slides for reproduction in publications (especially films with heightened color saturation such as Fuji Velvia or Kodak Ektachrome 100VS). Don't be afraid to blow off as much film as your budget can stand, to get those few special shots.

Digital cameras are increasingly used by photographers at all levels, but here again, you should come with a backup device (or laptop computer) to store your images, especially if you're using one of the higher-end cameras that quickly fill storage cards.

A couple of caveats are in order. A common cause of wildlife incidents is foolish photographers either getting too close or having a false sense of security behind the camera. Your backcountry common sense should remain intact with or without a camera in front of you. Besides, there are times and places to not use a camera—mostly in order not to separate you from a given experience, but also in Native villages without permission. In addition, many museums prohibit the use of flash or tripods, and Russian Orthodox churches don't allow cameras or video.

their respective travel chapters. For more information about hiking, contact the **Alaska Public Lands Information Centers** (www.nps.gov/aplic) in Anchorage, Fairbanks, Ketchikan, and Tok.

Mountaineering

A number of organizations guide mountaineering expeditions in Alaska. For specific destinations, visit the Park Service or Forest Service websites for a list of permitted guides. Good wilderness guiding companies include **Alaska Mountaineering School** (907/733-1016, www.climbalaska.org) in Talkeetna, **Alaska Mountain Guides & Climbing School** (907/766-3366 or 800/766-3396, www.alaskamountainguides.com) in Haines, **Alaska Discovery** (907/780-6226 or 800/586-1911, www.akdiscovery.com) in Juneau, **N.O.L.S.** (907/745-4047, www.nols.edu) in Palmer, and **Alaska Wilderness Journeys** (907/733-2230 or 800/349-0064, www.alaskajourneys.com) in Talkeetna.

Mountain Biking

The most popular mountain biking trails are in the Anchorage area, and include many miles of paths (both paved and unpaved) along the shore and within a couple of city parks. Paved biking paths can also be found paralleling portions of the Seward Highway south of Anchorage, and in Fairbanks, Homer, Valdez, Juneau, and other cities. Many Forest Service trails are open to mountain biking, but some of these are muddy and challenging to ride. Especially popular is the Resurrection Pass Trail on the Kenai Peninsula.

The Anchorage-based **Arctic Bicycle Club** (907/566-0177, www.arcticbike.org) organizes road races, mountain bike races, and tours. Its website is an excellent source for anyone interested in cycling in Alaska, with links to bike shops and references to helpful books. Bike tours are described near the end of this chapter in "Specialty Tours."

Flightseeing

Even if you don't go backpacking while you're in Alaska, treat yourself at least once to a small plane or helicopter ride over some spectacular country. The flight from Talkeetna to Denali National Park is always a highlight—particularly with a landing on the Ruth Glacier. Flights over Glacier Bay from Juneau, Haines, or Skagway will leave you hyperventilating for two days. And you won't believe how grand Columbia Glacier really is on the flight over it from Anchorage or Valdez. For more tips on flightseeing—including safety precautions—see "Air Travel" later in this chapter.

FISHING

Alaska is world famous for its fish and fishing. More than half of America's commercial seafood production comes from the state, and sportfishing is a favorite activity of both Alaskan residents and visitors. Fishing options are equally vast in Alaska, where undeveloped areas stretch for hundreds of miles, and the population is clustered onto a tiny portion of the land. The state is speckled with more than a million lakes—including some of the largest in the nation—along with 34,000 miles of pristine coastline and 42 wild and scenic rivers.

The **Alaska Department of Fish and Game's** website (www.state.ak.us/adfg) has details on sportfishing, including descriptions of the various species, fishing regulations, news, and an abundance of other fish facts.

The *Anchorage Daily News* (www.adn.com) puts out an excellent free fishing guide describing the best spots in Southcentral Alaska, along with fishing tips and trends. It's available in visitors centers, or the website provides a weekly fishing forecast in the summer.

Alaska Fishing, by Rene Limeres and Gunnar Pedersen, is a comprehensive guide to fishing in Alaska, with detailed information on the when, where, and how to catch fish, along with natural history and other details. Locals, as always, are the best advice-givers about fishing technique, spots, and regulations, and might even share some secrets.

Popular Alaskan Fish

Salmon are the primary attraction for many sport anglers, and all five species of Pacific salmon are found in Alaska. Steelhead and rainbow trout, which are also salmonid, are famous for their beautiful coloration and fighting spirit. Rainbows are found in many streams and lakes around the state; the larger steelhead are the sea-run form.

Dolly Varden (also known as Arctic char) are a sea-run trout that flourish in many Alaska rivers. Arctic grayling occur in lakes and streams across the state, particularly in Interior Alaska and the Alaska Peninsula. The fish have a large and distinctive saillike dorsal fin, and put up a big fight when hooked. Other important freshwater fish species include lake trout, brook trout (an introduced species), northern pike, sheefish, and whitefish.

Pacific halibut is a large flatfish that is commonly caught in saltwater, particularly in Southeast and Southcentral Alaska. Halibut sometimes reach the proverbial barn-door size, and it isn't uncommon to see ones that weigh in excess of 200 pounds. Many Alaskans consider halibut the best-tasting fish in the state. In addition to salmon caught in saltwater, other popular ocean-caught sport fish include rockfish and lingcod.

Catching 'Em

Fishing is not only great fun, but the way to bag some super meals. All you need are a break-down or retractable rod, a variety of hooks, flies, spinners, spoons, sinkers, line (4- to 8-pound for freshwater, 12- to 30-pound for saltwater—depending on what you're after), and a reel. All but the rod will fit in a small plastic case. For bait, get a small bottle of salmon eggs for freshwater, shrimp for saltwater. Have a filet knife to clean the fish. While fishing, watch for protected areas with deadfalls or rocks where fish like to hide. You'll have the best luck in the early morning or late evening, or on cloudy days when the sun leaks out to shimmer on the water. So as not to attract bears, keep your catch on a stringer well downstream.

Fishing Regulations

Fishing licenses are required. In Alaska, 1-day nonresident sportfishing licenses cost $10, 3-day $20, and 14-day $50. If you plan to catch king salmon, all these fees are doubled. The Alaskan license is valid in national parks.

Fishing licenses are sold in most outdoor stores and by charter fishing operators. Ask for brochures outlining local fishing regulations when you buy your license. Check open and closed seasons, bag limits, and the like, to avoid trouble with the law. For the whole thing—spelled out in minute bureaucratic detail—request a copy of the regulations booklet from the **Alaska Department of Fish and Game** (907/465-4180, www.sf.adfg.state.ak.us).

Fishing Derbies

Many Alaskan towns have salmon or halibut fishing derbies in the summer. If one is going on when you visit, it may be worth your while to buy a derby ticket before heading out on the water. The prize money gets into the thousands of dollars for some of these, and more than a few anglers tell of the big one that would have made them rich if they'd only bought a derby ticket first. Some of the biggest fishing derbies are in Seward, Homer, and Juneau.

Guided Fishing

Local knowledge is one of the best ways to be assured of a successful Alaska fishing trip. By using a charter or guide service, you're likely to have a more productive sportfishing trip. Fishing guides can be found in most Alaskan communities, some offering float trips accessible by car and others going to more remote fly-in destinations. Charter fishing boats are available at coastal locations, particularly in Southeast and Southcentral Alaska and along the Kenai Peninsula.

Particularly important charter boat fishing towns include Homer, Seward, Kodiak, Valdez, Cordova, Juneau, Sitka, and Ketchikan. Charter boat trips typically last either a half-day or all day. Remote fishing lodges are widespread throughout the state, offering top-quality sportfishing with all of the amenities; find them in the *Alaska State Vacation Planner*, or online at www.travelalaska.com. Note that it's common to tip fishing guides, particularly if they're especially helpful or if you land a big one. There's no standard amount, but a 10 percent tip would certainly be appreciated.

ALASKA SALMON

Five species of wild Pacific salmon are found in Alaskan waters. All are anadromous—spending time in both fresh and salt water—and all five species also have at least two common names, making them confusing to newcomers. The yearly return of adult salmon is a major event for wildlife in many parts of Alaska, as quiet little streams suddenly erupt in a frenzy of life and death. Commercial fishermen search out the migrating schools in the ocean as they prepare to head up rivers and creeks to spawn. Anglers line the riverbanks, hoping to catch a big king or coho. Bears pace the creeks, ready to pounce on salmon in the shallow water. Foxes, eagles, ravens, gulls, and magpies wait for the salmon to weaken or die before feeding on them. Mergansers and smaller birds such as dippers eat the eggs, as do such fish as Dolly Varden and rainbow trout. Crab and halibut move into the areas near creek mouths, eating salmon carcasses that wash downstream.

Female salmon spawn in creeks and rivers during late summer throughout much of Alaska, digging holes ("redds") in the gravel with their tails before laying hundreds of small red eggs. The males fight for position to fertilize the eggs as soon as they are laid. Shortly after spawning, the salmon die, and their carcasses create a stench that permeates late-summer evenings. But these carcasses also add important nutrients to the system, nutrients that are used by the plankton that form the basis of the food chain. The plankton in turn are eaten by the young salmon fry that emerge from the eggs, thus helping to complete this never-ending cycle of life and death.

King (Chinook) Salmon
The largest of all Pacific salmon, the king commonly exceeds 30 pounds (the sport-caught record is 126 pounds), and is the most highly prized and one of the best-tasting sport fish in Alaska. The most famous place to catch kings is the Kenai River in Southcentral Alaska, but some of the finest kings head up the Copper River near Cordova.

Sockeye (Red) Salmon
Much smaller (6–10 pounds), and difficult to catch on spinning rods, sockeye are considered the best-tasting salmon. They turn bright red with an olive-green head when ready to spawn. Sockeye are the most important fish in the Bristol Bay and Kodiak areas, but for sport anglers, the most famous sockeye river is the Kenai, where "combat fishing" reigns in mid-summer.

Coho (Silver) Salmon
The silvery cohos generally weigh 7–10 pounds and are a beautiful and powerful fish that can be caught in both fresh and saltwater. They are another favorite of anglers, and have a more delicate flavor.

Chum (Dog) Salmon
Chum are also quite large (5–15 pounds) but are not considered as tasty as kings, sockeye, or coho. Spawning time turns them into grotesque monsters with huge dog-like teeth. The name dog salmon may also refer to their use as food for dogsled teams in central Alaska. Chum are a very important food source in villages along the Yukon River.

Pink (Humpback) Salmon
The smallest (3–4 pounds) and most abundant salmon in Alaska are the pinks. "Humpie" runs sometimes turn creeks into a seething mass of spawning fish. They are considered a "trash fish" by many Alaskans, but are fine to eat when caught in saltwater before they have started to change. Once they reach freshwater, however, they develop prominently humped backs and grotesque jaws.

Pinks are the major commercial fish in Southeast and Prince William Sound, and are the mainstay of many canneries.

Catching Salmon

When salmon move from the ocean into their spawning streams, their bodies undergo rapid changes that reduce the quality of the meat. The freshest and brightest salmon are found in the ocean or lower reaches of the rivers, rather than farther upstream. If you want to try your luck at fishing, purchase a 14-day nonresident fishing license for $50, or a 3-day nonresident license for $20. Licenses are available in sporting goods stores throughout Alaska. Before heading out, pick up a copy of the latest fishing regulations, or visit the Alaska Department of Fish & Game website: www.state.ak.us/adfg.

Many travelers carry a small collapsible fishing pole to save on space. These work well with trout and smaller salmon, but may not survive an encounter with a 10-pound silver, and certainly won't handle a 35-pound king.

Wild or Farmed?

Alaska is world renowned for its wild salmon, and careful management ensures that the fish will still be there for future generations. Unfortunately, fishermen are not faring so well. Many struggle to make their boat payments, while others have simply given up on their life work, and are now back in school learning a new trade or flipping burgers to make ends meet. In the last decade, the price of salmon has dropped by more than 50 percent, and the worldwide market share of wild-caught salmon went from 99 percent in 1980 to less than 40 percent today.

The reason for this abrupt change is the rise of salmon farming, primarily in Chile, Norway, the United Kingdom, and British Columbia. The state of Alaska prohibits salmon aquaculture to protect both its wild fish stocks and the 10 percent of state jobs coming from fishing. Unfortunately, the British Columbia government was considerably less far-sighted, and more than 120 fish farms dot their waters, along with another nine in the state of Washington.

Pen-raised fish are cheap, available year-round, and of a consistent quality, making them perfect for corporations feeding a global market. But they have had a disastrous impact on both commercial fishermen and the environment. Farmed salmon are more susceptible to diseases such as sea lice (which can then spread to wild fish), the huge concentrations of fish pollute local areas with waste, and they are a non-native species: Atlantic salmon. This last becomes a real problem when they escape, and hundreds of thousands of them have done so over the years, competing with the five species of wild Pacific salmon, spawning in the region's streams, and showing up in fishing nets across Alaska. Nobody knows what impact this will have on the wild Pacific salmon.

And what about the fish? Pen-raised fish are fed pellets of fishmeal, fish oil, and vitamins, plus antibiotics, not to mention the coloring added to their diet to make their meat pink instead of gray. Wild salmon taste far better, are not dyed, and have more of the omega-3 fatty acids that help protect your health. So the next time you see salmon at your local grocery store, ask if it's farmed Atlantic salmon or wild Pacific salmon. The farmed version will be cheaper, but what is the real price?

Learn more about Alaska's wild salmon and other fish from the **Alaska Seafood Marketing Institute,** 907/465-5560 or 800/478-2903, www.alaska seafood.org. For details on commercial fishing in Alaska, head to www.alaskareport.com.

© DON PITCHER

sea kayakers on Glacier Island, Prince William Sound

For information on fishing charters, available from every seaport in the state, check the local chamber of commerce websites or pick up brochures when you get into town.

ON AND ALONG THE WATER

Boating

Alaska's waters offer an endless range of boating opportunities, and in many coastal towns (particularly in Southeast) there are almost as many boats as cars. Boats are also important in inland parts of Alaska, particularly along major waterways such as the Yukon and Kuskokwim Rivers, where they provide a vital means of traversing undeveloped country. Skiff rentals are available in the larger coastal towns for those who want to head out on their own to explore or fish. Dozens of companies offer boat tours or charter boat fishing trips throughout the state, in vessels ranging from 13-foot aluminum skiffs to luxury motor yachts offering multiday ecotours.

Rafting

White-water rafting trips are offered by numerous adventure-travel outfitters around the state. Several of the more reasonable, short, and accessible trips include floats down the Sixmile Creek south of Anchorage, Nenana River at Denali, Kenai River at Sterling, Susitna River near Talkeetna, Mendenhall River near Juneau, Sheridan River near Cordova, and the Lowe River outside of Valdez. A large number of float-trip companies and wilderness outfitters offer overnight, several day, and up to three-week-long trips, particularly within Wrangell–St. Elias National Park. Check the list in the state's *Alaska Vacation Planner* (www.travelalaska.com) for names and addresses. Those looking to do it by themselves should buy Karen Jettmar's excellent *Alaska River Guide*.

Sea Kayaking

Sea kayaks are quiet and fairly stable, providing an outstanding way to explore hidden Alaskan coves or to watch wildlife. Because of this, kayaking has increased in popularity in recent years, both for independent travelers who rent a kayak and for those who choose a package trip with a professional guiding company.

Kayaks originated as skin-covered boats crafted by the Eskimos of Alaska and Siberia, but today's versions are built from more modern materials. Most sea kayaks have a hard outer shell of plastic or fiberglass, but folding kayaks (made with wooden or aluminum supports and waterproof covers) are also available. The latter can be folded into relatively compact packages, making them useful for travelers heading into remote areas accessible only by floatplane.

Companies offering sea kayak rentals and tours are in Southeast Alaska (Glacier Bay, Gustavus, Haines, Juneau, Ketchikan, Petersburg, Sitka, Skagway, and Wrangell), Kenai Peninsula (Homer, Seldovia, and Seward), Prince William Sound (Cordova, Valdez, and Whittier), Southwest Alaska (Kodiak, King Salmon, and Unalaska), and Western Alaska (Dillingham). All of these are described elsewhere in this book.

Two companies are particularly noteworthy. **Alaska Discovery** in Juneau (907/780-6226 or 800/586-1911, www.akdiscovery.com) is a long-established firm with kayaking trips throughout the Inside Passage and other outdoor adventures around the state. In business since 1977, **Baidarka Boats** in Sitka (907/747-8996, www.kayaksite.com) is a great place not only for tours, but also to buy quality equipment. Jim Howard's *Guide to Sea Kayaking in Southeast Alaska* describes 41 Inside Passage kayak trips.

Canoeing

Canoeing is a common activity on lakes and rivers in Alaska. Two canoe routes (Swanson River Route and Swan Lake Route) connect lakes within the Kenai National Wildlife Refuge, and another route links lakes across Admiralty Island National Monument. The Yukon River is a popular float trip, with many people starting in either Whitehorse or Dawson City and floating to the town of Eagle (or beyond). The country around Fairbanks is also very popular with canoeists who enjoy the relatively gentle Chena River. Canoe rentals are available in all these areas.

Sailing

Alaska has a small but active community of sailing enthusiasts, with sailboats in coastal towns from Ketchikan to Kodiak. Resurrection Bay near Seward generally offers the state's top wind conditions, and companies there offer day trips, sailing lessons, and bareboat charters. Other popular sailing areas (they have relatively dependable winds) are around Prince William Sound and in Kachemak Bay near Homer.

Surfing

Surprisingly, surfing is growing in popularity in Alaska. It will never be a particularly common sight, but many coastal towns—including Yakutat, Kodiak, Sitka, Homer, and Unalaska—have a few hard-core souls who head out when conditions are right. The state's best-known area is Yakutat in Southeast Alaska, where miles of uncrowded black-sand beaches attract surfers. Surfing supplies can be found in Yakutat and Kodiak.

Beachcombing

A treasure-trove of flotsam and jetsam awaits the savvy and the lucky along the thousands of miles of Alaskan coastline. Prizes include glass-ball floats (still used by Asian fishermen; the biggest ones can be worth thousands of dollars), life preservers, lantern buoys, whale teeth, ambergris, and even notes in bottles—I actually know a single woman who met a single fisherman that way. Beachcombing can be developed into a fine art, consisting of weather and tide patterns, wind and storm conditions, beach accessibility and topography. Experts advise that the best beachcombing is in early May, after the snow cover and before the competition from other beachcombers. Just for fun, check out www.beachcombers.org to see how all this floating debris has been used to track ocean currents.

Hot Springs

Alaska is a thermally active region, a fact attested to by its more than 100 hot spring sites, of which roughly a dozen are accessible and developed. Accessible, in Alaska, is a relative term: Possibly the most accessible hot spring in the state is at Chena, 60 miles east of Fairbanks on a paved road. Also accessible near Fairbanks is Manley Hot Springs, over 150 hard dirt-road miles. Circle Hot Springs, a similar distance from Fairbanks, is no longer open to the public. Other popular hot springs are in Southeast: White Sulphur and Tenakee on Chichagof Island west of

Juneau, Chief Shakes near Wrangell, and Baranof on Baranof Island. Contact the Alaska Department of Natural Resources for its map of thermally active areas in Alaska.

WINTER SPORTS
Skiing and Snowboarding

Downhill ski and snowboard areas are near Anchorage (Alyeska Resort, Hilltop Ski Area, and Alpenglow), Juneau (Eaglecrest), and Fairbanks (Moose Mountain and Skiland). The largest of these is **Alyeska** (907/754-1111 or 800/880-3880, www.alyeskaresort.com), with 500 skiable acres, 60 trails, a 60-passenger aerial tram, eight chair lifts, and two pony lifts.

Cross-country skiing (both classic and skate) is very popular in Alaska, particularly in Anchorage where many miles of lighted and groomed trails are available throughout the winter. Anchorage may well have the finest cross-country skiing of any American city, and a number of the nation's best Olympic skiers come from here. The city's main cross-country ski areas are in Kincaid Park, Hillside Ski Area, and the Tony Knowles Coastal Trail. Additional groomed ski trails can be found around Fairbanks, Homer, Juneau, Palmer, Eagle River, Seward, and Valdez. The **Nordic Skiing Association of Anchorage,** 907/276-7609, www.anchoragenordicski.com, is Alaska's largest cross-country association, and its website has links to other Nordic skiing groups in the state.

Dog Mushing

Dogsledding has a rich history in Alaska, and sled dog races are a major winter staple across much of the state. The most famous are the **Iditarod Trail Sled Dog Race** from Anchorage to Nome in March and the **Yukon Quest International Sled Dog Race** between Fairbanks and Whitehorse in

FESTIVALS AND EVENTS

The biggest events in Alaska revolve around the sun and snow. A number of Alaskans, especially those who live in the Interior and the north, believe that the purpose of summer solstice is to compress all the partying encouraged by the light and heat of summer into a single 24-hour period. Fairbanks has at least three "Midnight Sun" activities on solstice. The summer is also the time for town and citywide celebrations, such as Golden Days in Fairbanks, Little Norway Festival in Petersburg, and Colony Days in Palmer. There are fishing derbies in the waters off the coastal towns and athletic competitions, such as triathlons and mountain races, everywhere.

The most famous winter festivals are Anchorage's Fur Rendezvous and the Iditarod. Every town has some sort of winter carnival that frequently includes dog mushing, a snow sports competition, and accompanying arts and crafts fairs.

Typically, the major public holidays are also a cause for celebration, including Memorial Day (last Monday in May), July 4th (Independence Day), Labor Day (last Monday in September), Thanksgiving Day (last Thursday in November), Christmas, and New Year's Eve. The happiest days of the year, though, are in mid-October when the big Permanent Fund dividend checks show up in the mailboxes of state residents.

January
Kodiak—Russian Orthodox Starring Ceremony; Bethel—Kuskokwim 300; Seward—Polar Bear Jump Off; Anchorage Folk Festival

February
Anchorage—Fur Rendezvous; Cordova—Iceworm Festival; Fairbanks—Yukon Quest Sled Dog Race; Wrangell—Tent City Festival

March
Anchorage, Nome, and Wasilla—Iditarod Trail Sled Dog Race; Dillingham—Beaver Roundup Festival; Fairbanks—World Ice Art Championships and Winter Carnival; Kodiak—Pillar Mountain Golf Classic; Nome—Bering Sea Ice Golf Classic

April
Bethel—Camai Dance Festival; Girdwood—Alyeska Spring Carnival; Juneau—Alaska Folk Festival; Valdez—World Free Skiing Championship

February. A number of companies offer wintertime dogsled tours, some of which are timed to coincide with the Iditarod or Yukon Quest.

During the summer months, visitors can ride on wheeled sleds behind teams of dogs, providing a chance to get the feel of the real thing. These very popular rides—some led by Iditarod mushers—are offered in Girdwood, Fairbanks, Seward, Wasilla, and Denali. In addition, summertime dogsled tours take place on glaciers near Juneau, Skagway, and Seward. Tourists are flown up to the glacier by helicopter, and given a chance to ride along as the dogs head across the ice and snow. It's a unique—but very expensive—experience.

SPECTATOR SPORTS

The **Alaska Baseball League** consists of six semi-professional teams: Mat-Su Miners, Kenai Peninsula Oilers, Fairbanks Goldpanners, Anchorage Bucs, Anchorage Glacier Pilots, and Athletes in Action. The teams include talented college players from throughout the country who come to Alaska to play in June and July. Alaska Baseball League teams play each other, along with Outside teams from the West Coast and Hawaii, with the top teams ending up at the National Baseball Congress World Series in Wichita, Kansas. Alaskan teams have won these world series many times, and quite a few famous players have spent a summer on Alaska turf, including Mark McGwire, Tom Seaver, Greg Nettles, and Dave Winfield.

Hockey is very big in Alaska, especially in Anchorage and Fairbanks where overachiever dads push their kids onto the ice by age four. The **Alaska Aces** play professional hockey in the minor-league West Coast Hockey League, and both the University of Alaska Anchorage (UAA) and the University of Alaska Fairbanks (UAF) have nationally competitive hockey teams.

May
Cordova—Copper River Delta Shorebird Festival; Haines—Great Alaska Craftbeer & Homebrew Festival; Homer—Kachemak Bay Shorebird Festival; Kodiak—Crab Festival; Nome—Memorial Day Polar Bear Swim; Petersburg—Little Norway Festival

June
Anchorage—Mayor's Midnight Sun Marathon, Elmendorf Open House and Air Show, and Taste of Anchorage; Fairbanks—Midnight Sun Baseball Game and Yukon 800 Boat Race; Haines—Kluane to Chilkat International Bike Relay; Palmer—Colony Days; Sitka—Summer Music Festival

July
Kodiak—Bear Country Music Festival; Delta Junction—Deltana Fair; Eagle River—Bear Paw Festival; Fairbanks—Golden Days, World Eskimo-Indian Olympics; Girdwood—Girdwood Forest Fair; Homer—KBBI Concert on the Lawn; Seward—Mt. Marathon Race; Talkeetna—Moose Dropping Festival

August
Fairbanks—Tanana Valley Fair; Haines—Southeast Alaska State Fair; Ketchikan—Blueberry Arts Festival; Ninilchik—Kenai Peninsula State Fair; Palmer—Alaska State Fair; Seward—Silver Salmon Derby; Talkeetna—Bluegrass Festival; Valdez—Gold Rush Days

September
Kodiak—State Fair and Rodeo; Kenai, Valdez, Whittier, Wrangell—Silver Salmon Derby

October
Anchorage—Alaska Federation of Natives Convention; Sitka—Alaska Day Festival

November
Anchorage—Great Alaska Shootout; Fairbanks—Athabascan Fiddling Festival; Haines—Alaska Bald Eagle Festival; Sitka—Whalefest

December
Kodiak—Harbor Stars Boat Parade; Talkeetna—Winterfest

In bush Alaska, no sport is bigger than basketball, and any visitor who can play well stands a good chance of immediately being accepted by locals. There's intense competition among high school teams at the state level, and both UAA and UAF have their own basketball squads.

The state's biggest basketball event is the **Great Alaska Shootout** (www.goseawolves.com/shootout) held in Anchorage each November, and featuring seven top college teams and the lowly UAA Seawolves. This one gets national media attention because it's so early in the season.

Accommodations

HOTELS AND MOTELS

Within these pages you'll find hotels and motels in all price ranges. Prices are high in Alaska, so come prepared with a high limit on your credit card. In the major package-tour stops and off-the-beaten-track places with limited lodging, what's available is often booked way in advance. Unless you've made reservations, don't count on getting any rooms, especially the good cheap ones, at most Alaskan destinations. Fortunately, bed-and-breakfasts often offer a cheaper alternative. A good overall source for Alaskan lodging places is the official *Alaska State Vacation Planner.*

Throughout this book I have typically listed only two prices for most lodging places: **single, or s (one person), and double, or d (two people).** Prices listed are the mid-summer rates—which are the highest of the year. These prices do not include local taxes, which can sometimes reach 10 percent. Prices, of course, are not set in stone and will certainly head up over time. Always ask to see the room before deciding to stay at one of the less expensive motels, since places that I consider more than adequate may be beneath your standards.

If in doubt about where to stay, you may want to choose somewhere that gets the American Automobile Association seal of approval. The annual ***AAA TourBook*** for Alaska (free to AAA members) is a helpful guide to the better hotels and motels, offering current prices and relatively accurate ratings. Members can find the same info at www.aaa.com.

If you're staying in the more expensive hotel chains, always be sure to ask about the sometimes-substantial discounts such as AAA-member rates, senior discounts, corporate or government rates, business travel fares, military rates, or other special deals. Try not to take the first rate quoted at these places, especially if you're calling their 800 numbers; these "rack rates" are what they charge if they can get away with it. Ask if they have any promotional rates. You may also get better prices by speaking directly to desk clerks who are more likely to be able to dicker over price than the 800 number operators who probably work out of a room in a Texas prison.

If you don't smoke and can't stand the stench of tobacco in motel rooms, be sure to ask about nonsmoking rooms; many motels—particularly the newer ones—have them.

I've discovered that the best chain-hotel rates can often be found online through such sites as Travelocity (www.travelocity.com) and Priceline (www.priceline.com). Using Priceline, I once booked a room at the Anchorage Sheraton for $35 when the official price was $159! Of course, this was early May, when rooms are more plentiful. But even in mid-summer you can get rooms in Anchorage for half-off the going rate.

BED-AND-BREAKFASTS

Bed-and-breakfasts are popular all across Alaska, and are a great way to spend time with local residents in showcase homes, save a little money on accommodations, and get breakfast thrown in for the price of a night.

The Internet is the best place to get fast B&B information. Start with the **Bed & Breakfast Association of Alaska** (www.alaskabba.com), or one of the regional groups such as **Anchorage Alaska B&B Association** (www.anchorage-bnb.com), **Alaska's Mat-Su Bed & Breakfast Association** (www.alaskabnbhosts.com), **Fairbanks Association of B&Bs** (www.ptialaska.net/~fabb), **B&B Association of Alaska INNside Passage Chapter** (www.accommodations-alaska.com), and **Kenai Peninsula B&B Association** (www.kenaipeninsulabba.com). Local **chamber of commerce** websites also have links to local B&Bs; find a complete listing of these at www.alaskachamber.com.

A few of Alaska's B&Bs don't allow kids and almost none allow pets or inside smoking. Not all B&Bs take credit cards or out-of-state checks, so call ahead to make sure you don't arrive without cash. Many guest rooms have private baths, and if they don't, one is probably just a few steps away. Bed-and-breakfasts—favorites of 40-something professional couples—are a fine way to get acquainted with a new area, since you'll have opportunities to meet fellow travelers and the owners. Note, however, that often the single person rate differs little if at all from the price for couples.

One problem with B&Bs is that they sometimes get a bit too homey and lack the privacy afforded by motels. I've been in some where the owner sits by your table in the morning, feeling it his duty to hold a conversation. This may be fine sometimes, especially if you want to learn more about the local area, but it's not so great if you're looking for a romantic place or you just want to read the newspaper in peace.

HOSTELS

Hostels offer the least expensive *indoor* lodging options in Alaska, with bunk accommodations for $15–20 per person. They're a good choice for single travelers on a budget, or anyone who wants to meet fellow travelers. Although commonly called "youth hostels," these really are not just for high school and college folks—you'll meet adventurous people of all ages.

At last count Alaska had two dozen places offering hostel-type accommodations, in all the major towns, along with such surprising places as Girdwood, McCarthy, Sterling, Tok, and Ninilchik. Reservations are a good idea, particularly in mid-summer.

Hostellers stay in dormitory-style rooms (sep-

arate for men and women), and have access to showers, a communal kitchen, and laundry facilities. You should bring your own sleeping bag or linen (though these can be rented), and a variety of restrictions may put a crimp in things, including that the hostels generally close during the day, that no alcohol is allowed, and that most have a curfew. A room or two are typically saved for couples or small families. You'll find a complete listing of Alaskan hostels at **www.hostels.com.**

FISHING AND HUNTING LODGES

Alaska is world famous for its many wilderness fishing and hunting lodges, most of which offer multinight packages. These can be booked through your travel agent or directly with the lodge. A number of the better-known lodges are described briefly in this book, but see the *Alaska State Vacation Planner* for a more complete listing, or head to www.travelalaska.com. Also check the latest issue of *Alaska Magazine* for ads from many of these lodges.

HOME SWAPS

Several companies list Alaskan homeowners who are interested in a trade. If you live in Hawaii or California and want to see Fairbanks in midwinter, your home will be a hot property. If you live in North Dakota, good luck. Companies worth investigating include **Home Exchange** (310/798-3864 or 800/877-8723, www.home-exchange.com), **Home Link** (813/975-9825 or 800/638-3841, www.swapnow.com), **Intervac** (800/756-4663, www.intervacus.com), and **Holi-Swaps** (www.holi-swaps.com).

CAMPING

Tent camping is cheap (or free) in most parts of Alaska, and public showers are available in nearly every town. Any self-supporting dome tent will do: They're lightweight, and a cinch to erect, they don't need to be staked into the often rocky or frozen ground, and you can sit up in them during those long inclement stretches. For peace of mind and dryness of body in those wild and woolly nights in Southeast and Southcentral, make sure the tent is as waterproof as it can be. (Even so, bring a sponge.) A Thermarest inflatable pad will put a wonderful cushion of air between you and the ground; on top of it you can sleep on gravel, rocks, dead porcupines . . . . If you plan to camp for extended periods or in ultra-windy places such as Southwest Alaska, get a tent that will hold up to the weather. These cost more, and are available from better outdoor stores.

In Alaska, camping is allowed on most state lands and within the national forests (except close to towns). Some national parks require a backcountry-use permit. Camping on public property within city limits, however, is prohibited.

Campgrounds and RV Parks

Generally, two distinct types of campgrounds are available. State and federal government-operated campgrounds all offer a basic outdoor experience with a minimum of facilities, usually just pit toilets and water from pumps. Private RV park/campgrounds typically offer hot showers, washers and driers, dump stations, and plug-ins. A few of the nicest even have cable modems for your computer and TV. Private parks are far less natural—some are little more than gravel parking lots—and cater primarily to RV drivers, but most welcome tenters.

Government campgrounds are usually cheaper (rarely more than $12 nightly) than the commercial variety (typically $22–26). The showers ($3–5) at the commercial sites are generally open to noncampers, and are sometimes the only place in town to rinse off.

PUBLIC CABINS

For indoor sleeping in the great outdoors, check into the many wonderful Forest Service cabins in Southeast and Southcentral Alaska. At $35–45 a night, you get bunks for 4–6 people,

a woodstove, firewood, a table, and an outhouse. Of the more than 180 cabins in the Tongass and Chugach National Forests, however, only a few are accessible by road or trail; the rest require flying or boating in. These cabins are very popular, and reservations are accepted up to six months in advance. Reservations for some of the most-used cabins, especially during hunting and fishing season, are determined by lottery. All Forest Service cabin reservations are made through **ReserveUSA** (518/885-3639 or 877/444-6777, www.reserveusa.com). No extra charge for cabin reservations. This website has complete details on the cabins, including photos and access info.

Other public-use cabins are available through the Alaska Division of State Parks (various parks), the Bureau of Land Management (near Fairbanks), the National Park Service (Kenai Fjords National Park and Yukon-Charley Rivers) and the U.S. Fish & Wildlife Service (Kodiak National Wildlife Refuge). They're described in appropriate sections of this book.

LIGHTHOUSES

Alaska has more than a dozen lighthouses, 10 of which are still active. Preservation groups are working to open these to the public in one form or another, including three near Juneau: Sentinel Island Lighthouse, Point Retreat Lighthouse, and Five Fingers Lighthouse. In addition, Cape Decision Lighthouse near Wrangell is being renovated, along with the very remote Cape St. Elias Lighthouse southeast of Cordova on Kayak Island. You can also stay in an upscale faux-lighthouse in Sitka; it's called Rockwell Lighthouse, and operates as a guesthouse. Homer has another fun little fake lighthouse for lodging, along with a famous bar (Salty Dawg) built to resemble one. All of these are described in appropriate sections of this book.

The Coast Guard in Juneau (907/463-2267, www.unc.edu/~rowlett/lighthouse/ak.htm) has additional information on Alaskan lighthouses.

Food and Drink

The cheapest and healthiest way to eat is to buy groceries and prepare your own meals. This works fine for campers who bring a cookstove and dishes, and is also an option if you choose your lodging places carefully. Quite a few include kitchenettes with at least a minifridge and microwave. Hostels, of course, have full kitchens, and at a B&B you can leave the breakfast to the experts.

RESTAURANTS

Alaskan restaurants vary greatly in quality, but are much improved in recent years. True, many of the coffee shops, roadhouses, and cafés still serve pretty standard fare, and sometimes it seems they use the same menu, the same ingredients, the same grill and fryolator, and the same short-order cooks. But you'll also find a few surprises along the way, and all the larger towns have standout eateries. Anchorage—perhaps because it is home to almost half of all Alaskans—has the best selection of menu options and some of the finest restaurants in Alaska. It also has a great diversity of restaurants: bustling brewpubs, steak-

houses, Thai food, fine restaurants serving gourmet Italian or seafood, and cheap taco joints. You'll also find fine meals in Juneau, Fairbanks, Haines, Homer, Ketchikan, Seward, and Skagway, to mention but a few.

Seafood is the primary Alaskan specialty, particularly salmon, halibut, and crab. You'll find good seafood restaurants in all the coastal towns, and surprisingly even in Interior Alaska. Of course, nearly all of the larger Alaskan towns now also have at least one café or drive-through stand selling lattes and mochas. Unfortunately, in Alaska—as in the rest of the nation—the real dining-out kings are McDonald's, Burger King, Taco Bell, Domino's, and all the other fast-food outlets that are turning regional differences into a bland mediocrity of frozen burgers and whipped-shortening "milk shakes." No wonder Alaskans are becoming increasingly obese.

Basic Alaskan breakfasts cost $6–9, with lunches running $7–10. Dinner prices show a greater range, from simple $6 burgers to steak, prime rib, chicken, or seafood entrées going for $12–25.

ALASKA'S BEST DINING

Here are a few of my favorite Alaskan restaurants; they're all described in appropriate chapters of this book.

Anchorage
Marx Bros. Cafe
Ristorante Orso
Jens'
Moose's Tooth Pub and Pizzeria
F Street Station
L'Aroma Bakery & Deli
Saturday Market

Southeast Alaska
New York Hotel Cafe, Ketchikan
Ludvig's Bistro, Sitka
Fiddlehead Restaurant and Bakery, Juneau
Fireweed Bakery and Cafe, Haines
Haven Cafe, Skagway
Stowaway Cafe, Skagway

Kenai Peninsula
Christo's Palace, Seward
Ray's Waterfront, Seward
Cafe Cups, Homer
Fritz Creek General Store, Homer
Fat Olives Restaurant, Homer
The Homestead, Homer
Saltry Restaurant, Halibut Cove

The Interior
Cafe Michele, Talkeetna
Cafe Alex, Fairbanks
Alaska Salmon Bake, Fairbanks
Thai House Restaurant, Fairbanks

ON THE ROAD

Salmon Bakes

Splurge on these once or twice. The salmon—always wild Alaskan fish—is usually fresh, thick, and delicious, and it comes with the requisite macaroni, potato, and infernal three-bean salads, carrot and celery sticks, black olives for every finger, and sourdough rolls. Blueberry cake often tops off the meal. Different bakes have different takes on second helpings, and soft drinks or lemonade are usually included, but beer and wine are extra. The one at Pioneer Park in Fairbanks is Alaska's best; the two places in Juneau are a close second, and the one at Tok is right up there.

ALCOHOL

Alcohol is readily available in the larger Alaskan cities, along with most small towns on the road network or along the Inside Passage. Because of alcoholism problems in Native communities, many of the remote bush villages have banned its sale or importation. "Dry" communities prohibit alcohol, while "damp" towns allow limited amounts for personal use only. Before flying out to any remote village, be sure to ask about the local rules.

In the last few years breweries and brewpubs have begun to spread across Alaska, and several excellent ones are found in Anchorage. Other towns where you can buy locally made beers include Haines, Homer, and Wasilla. The state's most famous microbrewery is the Alaskan Brewing Company in Juneau, which produces a number of award-winning beers available both on draught and in six-packs throughout the Pacific Northwest.

© DON PITCHER

Many restaurants in Alaska have fish and chips made with fresh halibut.

Tips for Travelers

BORDER CROSSINGS

Immigration officials are trained to be suspicious, particularly in this post–September 11 world. Never argue or get angry with an official—it doesn't help, and they have the law on their side. The best approach is just to be as polite as possible. By the way, Alaska is part of the United States. Don't laugh: More than a few cruise ship tourists have stepped off the ship in Ketchikan and asked locals if they take American dollars!

Entry into the U.S.

Everyone other than Canadians must possess a passport and visa to enter the United States. Most Western Europeans and Commonwealth residents can usually obtain a six-month travel visa easily from American consulates, and citizens of some countries can get visas at the border. You must have an onward or return ticket. No vaccinations are required, and you can bring an unlimited amount of money (over US$5,000 must be registered). Be aware that you can wind up crossing a Canadian/U.S. border four times

ON THE ROAD

in each direction (Lower 48 into British Columbia or Alberta, back into Southeast Alaska, then into Yukon, then back into mainland Alaska). If you're an overseas visitor, make sure you understand the requirements for *re-entering* the United States. Get U.S. Customs info at www.customs.gov.

European and other international travelers need to be aware that many fruits, vegetables, and meats are not allowed into the United States. This is particularly true of meats that could harbor such diseases as foot-and-mouth disease or mad cow disease. For details on prohibited items, visit www.aphis.usda.gov/travel.

Entry into Canada

No visa is required of visitors from Western Europe, most Commonwealth countries, or the United States. Americans can enter Canada by showing a birth certificate, passport, or voter-registration card, along with a driver's license or other form of photo identification. For children, bring a birth certificate, baptismal certificate, passport, or immigration document. Everyone else must have a passport. Travelers under 18 must be accompanied by or have written permission from a parent or guardian to enter Canada. Handguns and automatic weapons are not allowed into Canada, even if you're simply driving through to Alaska or the Lower 48. A U.S. driver's license is acceptable in Canada, but international licenses are required for residents of other countries. Get details at the **Canada Customs and Revenue Agency** website (www.ccra-adrc.gc.ca).

Time Zones

Alaska is divided into two time zones, but nearly all of the state—from Southeast to the western tip of the mainland—is on Alaska time, one hour earlier than Pacific time or four hours earlier than the East Coast. The western Aleutians are on Hawaii time, two hours behind Pacific time. British Columbia and the Yukon are on Pacific time. So when you go from Prince Rupert to Ketchikan, Dawson to Eagle, or Beaver Creek to Tok you gain an hour; from Skagway to Whitehorse you lose an hour.

MONEY

Unless otherwise stated, all prices in this handbook are in U.S. dollars. Tipping (usually 15 percent of the bill) is expected at most sit-down eating places fancier than snack bars or takeaway counters. Tourism employees, fishing guides, and others providing personal service often depend on tips for their real income.

I travel almost exclusively using credit cards and an automated teller machine (ATM) card, but some people still prefer traveler's checks. The major **credit cards**—especially Visa and MasterCard—are accepted almost everywhere in the larger towns. This is probably the easiest way to travel, especially if you can get airline mileage credit at the same time. Note, however, that credit cards may not be accepted by businesses in bush Alaska, so call ahead if you aren't traveling with cash or traveler's checks.

You'll find **ATMs** in all the larger towns and increasingly in even the more remote settlements. Note that ATMs tack on a charge—usually $1.50 per transaction—to your own bank's fees. One way to avoid this charge is to make a purchase at a grocery store that takes ATM cards and simply ask to get cash back over the amount. For ATM locations, head to www.mastercard.com and www.visa.com/atms.

Traveler's checks from American Express, Bank of America, or Visa are accepted in most businesses; but don't arrive with traveler's checks in non-U.S. currency since they're only accepted at a few banks. In some remote villages, even traveler's checks may not be accepted.

Some Canadian and U.S. cash will make your first few hours in the neighboring country less of a hassle. Note that there are no exchange facilities at the borders; Canadians take U.S. dollars at a poor rate, while Alaskan businesses often refuse Canadian dollars (they do, however, take the coins at an equal value with U.S. ones!). Most Wells Fargo offices in Anchorage (and some other cities) will exchange Canadian dollars, Japanese yen, and euros for U.S. dollars.

Traveling on a Budget

Prices are high in Alaska, but that doesn't mean

you have to pay them. You can get away without spending a lot of money if you try. Planning is half the battle; budgeting is the other half. If you're driving up, take a friend or rider (or two), and your transportation expenses are immediately slashed. A credit card will give you security and extra time to pay when you get back home.

If you're on a very tight budget, do not even *think* of going to Alaska without a sleeping bag and tent. Two nights not spent in a hotel will pay for the tent. Definitely make reservations for the hostels in the big towns. Bring a backpacking stove and cook as much food as you can, and use the salad bars at supermarkets. With the money you save, you can splurge on an occasional restaurant meal and salmon bake.

HEALTH AND SAFETY

Hypothermia

Anyone who spends much time in the outdoors will discover the dangers of exposure to cold, wet, and windy conditions. Even at temperatures well above freezing, hypothermia—the reduction of the body's inner core temperature—can prove fatal.

In the early stages, hypothermia causes uncontrollable shivering, followed by a loss of coordination, slurred speech, and then a rapid descent into unconsciousness and death. Always travel prepared for sudden changes in the weather. Wear clothing that insulates well and that holds its heat when wet. Wool and polypro are far better than cotton, and clothes should be worn in layers to provide better trapping of heat and a chance to adjust to conditions more easily. Always carry a wool hat, since your head loses more heat than any other part of your body. Bring a waterproof shell to cut the wind. Put on rain gear *before* it starts raining; head back or set up camp when the weather looks threatening; eat candy bars, keep active, or snuggle with a friend in a down bag to generate warmth.

If someone in your party begins to show signs of hypothermia, don't take any chances, even if the person denies needing help. Get the victim out of the wind, strip off his clothes, and put him in a dry sleeping bag on an insulating pad. Skin-to-skin contact is the best way to warm a hypothermic person, and that means you'll also need to strip and climb in the sleeping bag. If you weren't friends before, this should heat up the relationship! Do not give the victim alcohol or hot drinks, and do not try to warm the person too quickly since it could lead to heart failure. Once the victim has recovered, get medical help as soon as possible. Actually, you're far better off keeping close tabs on everyone in the group and seeking shelter *before* exhaustion and hypothermia set in.

Frostbite

Frostbite is a less serious but quite painful problem for the cold-weather hiker; it is caused by direct exposure or by heat loss because of wet socks and boots. Frostbitten areas will look white or gray and feel hard on the surface, softer underneath. The best way to warm the area is with other skin: Put your hand under your arm, your feet on your friend's belly. Don't rub it with snow or warm it near a fire. In cases of severe frostbite, in which the skin is white, quite hard, and numb, immerse the frozen area in water warmed to 99–104°F until it's thawed. Avoid refreezing the frostbitten area. If you're a long way from medical assistance and the frostbite is extensive, it's better to keep the area frozen and get out of the woods for help; thawing is very painful, and it would be nearly impossible to walk on a thawed foot.

Beaver Fever

Although lakes and streams in Alaska may appear clean, you could be risking a debilitating sickness by drinking the water without treating it first. The protozoan *Giardia lambia* is found throughout the state, spread by both humans and animals (including beaver). The disease is curable with drugs, but it's always best to carry safe drinking water on any trip, or to boil any water taken from creeks or lakes. Bringing water to a full boil for one minute is sufficient to kill Giardia and other harmful organisms. Another option—most folks choose this one—is to use a water filter (available in camping stores). Note, however, that these may not filter out other organisms such as *Campylobactor jejuni*, bacteria that are just 0.2

microns in size. Chlorine and iodine are not always reliable, taste foul, and can be unhealthy.

Other Wilderness Safety Tips

Dealing with bears is discussed in "Coexisting with Bears" in the *Interior* chapter. The most important part of enjoying—and surviving—the backcountry is to be prepared. Know where you're going; get maps, camping information, weather, and trail conditions from a ranger before setting out. Don't hike alone. Two are better than one, and three are better than two; if one gets hurt, one person can stay with the injured party and one can go for help. Bring more than enough food, so hunger won't cause you to continue when weather conditions say stop. Tell someone where you're going and when you'll be back.

Always carry the **essentials:** map, compass, water bottle, first-aid kit, flashlight, matches (or lighter) and fire starter (Vaseline and cotton balls work great), knife, extra clothing (a full set, in case you fall in a stream), rain gear, extra food, and sunglasses—especially if you're hiking on snow. Many travelers now also carry along a GPS unit to stay oriented. Cell phones are popular, but often don't work in remote areas. Satellite phones are the ultimate safety toy, but are a pricey addition to your trip.

Check your ego at the trailhead; stop for the night when the weather gets bad, even if it's 2 P.M., or head back, and don't press on when you're exhausted—tired hikers are sloppy hikers, and even a small injury can be disastrous in the woods.

Crime

Alaska has a surprisingly high violent-crime rate; the most recent figures put the state at 10th in the nation in terms of violent crimes, with 588 such crimes per 100,000 residents. Part of this is due to simple demographics, since Alaska has the second-highest percentage of young people in the nation, but it is also a reflection of the impact of alcohol abuse. Alaska has a rape rate two-and-a-half times the national average, and the child sexual assault rate is a shocking six times the national average.

The good news is that crime has dropped in recent years, especially in Anchorage, where many of the worst incidents have taken place. In general you're quite safe traveling in Alaska, though you should take the standard precautions, such as not leaving belongings in an unlocked vehicle and not walking around certain Anchorage neighborhoods after dark. Also, it's wise to avoid situations where people have been drinking heavily, even in bush Alaska. To be honest, after 20 years in the North, my one personal experience with crime took place when gear was stolen from me in Prince Rupert, British Columbia! I'm not saying crime doesn't exist, but many Alaskan towns (particularly those off the road system) are so safe that folks leave their doors unlocked and their keys in the car.

ACCESSIBLE ALASKA

Because of the undeveloped character of Alaska, much of the state is not readily accessible to those with disabilities. This is particularly true in parts of bush Alaska, where even having a flush toilet may be a luxury, and climbing into small aircraft is a major challenge. Despite this, many towns and cities—particularly those that see an influx of elderly cruise ship passengers each summer—have made great strides in recent years. Even in remote areas, some Forest Service and State of Alaska cabins have wheelchair ramps, out-sized outhouses, and fishing platforms. In addition, quite a few trails around Alaska have been built for wheelchairs, including popular ones in Ketchikan, Juneau, and Anchorage. Hotels, buses, trains, cruise ships, tour boats, and ferries throughout the state all have some sort of accommodation for travelers in wheelchairs or with limited mobility.

A good one-stop place for disabled travelers is **Access Alaska** (907/248-4777 or 800/770-4488, www.accessalaska.org), a nonprofit independent-living center in Anchorage. They produce a useful, free listing of travel sources specifically directed to those with disabilities, including everything from wheelchair-accessible B&Bs and restaurants to tours for families where someone has limited mobility. Independent-living centers can also be found in Fairbanks (907/479-7940 or 800/770-7940) and Juneau (907/586-4920).

ON THE ROAD

In Anchorage, **Hertz** (800/654-3131, www.hertz.com) has rental cars with hand controls, **Alaska Cab** (907/563-5353) offers lift-equipped van service, and **JBR Transportation** (907/441-7714), rents a lift-equipped van.

Alaska Welcomes You (907/349-6301 or 800/349-6301, www.accessiblealaska.com) is a travel agency that specializes in setting up cruises, tours, and other trips for seniors, families with young kids, and travelers with special needs. They also have a database listing accessible facilities, accommodations, attractions, and tours around the state.

Akcess Eco-Tours (907/789-2090, www.akcess .org) in Juneau offers accessible van tours, plus boating and backcountry trips.

ALASKA FOR GAY AND LESBIAN TRAVELERS

Openly gay individuals may feel uncomfortable in politically conservative Alaska, so discretion may be wise, especially in rural areas such as Glennallen where Rush Limbaugh is regarded as a liberal. Anchorage is—not surprisingly—the primary center for gays and lesbians in Alaska. The nonprofit group Identity Inc. runs a **Gay and Lesbian Community Center** (2110 E. Northern Lights Blvd., 907/929-4528, www.identityinc.org), and also produces a monthly magazine, promotes the PrideFest event (www.anchoragepride.com) each June, and operates a help line. Two Anchorage bars—**Mad Myrna's** (530 E. 5th Ave., 907/276-9762, www.alaska.net/~madmyrna) and **The Raven** (708 E. 4th Ave., 907/276-9672)—are favorite meeting places. **Out North Contemporary Art House** (1325 Primrose St., 907/279-8200, www.outnorth.org) sometimes presents plays with a gay and lesbian slant, and several Anchorage B&Bs promote themselves for gay travelers and couples.

MEDIA AND COMMUNICATIONS

Newspapers

Alaska's unofficial state newspaper is the *Anchorage Daily News* (907/257-4200). The paper does a good job of covering world and regional news, and has a reputation for balanced reporting. Its website, www.adn.com, contains current stories, classified ads, upcoming events, weather, video and sound clips, plus Mike Doogan's insightful and biting commentary. It also produces a thick and free *Alaska Visitors Guide* (www.adn.com/visitors) that can be found in the larger visitor centers or online.

The state's other two large-circulation daily papers are the *Fairbanks Daily News-Miner* (907/456-6661, www.newsminer.com) and the *Juneau Empire* (907/586-3740, www.juneauempire.com).

The *Anchorage Press* (907/561-7737, www.anchoragepress.com) is a free weekly newspaper available from racks all around Anchorage. The paper takes a rough-edged anti-establishment, pro-marijuana stance and the articles tend to focus on local scandals that the *Anchorage Daily News* avoids. Its night-life coverage is also strong. Weekly newspapers come out in most of the state's mid-sized towns.

Alaska Magazine

This magazine is available at grocery checkouts and magazine racks across Alaska, and in many Lower 48 magazine shops. Like the *Milepost* and *Juneau Empire*, *Alaska Magazine* is owned by a Georgia-based media conglomerate, Morris Communications. The magazine has gone downhill since it was bought by Morris, but still offers glossy articles about the state. Don't expect any muckraking journalism here; the magazine is geared to Outsiders looking for taste-of-Alaska stories. Someday, perhaps, the editors will actually give in-depth coverage to such issues as alcoholism, the decline of marine mammal populations, how the oil companies keep a stranglehold on state politics, how tourism is hurting (and helping) small Alaskan towns, or other controversial topics. Don't hold your breath. Contact *Alaska Magazine* (907/272-6070, www.alaskamagazine.com).

On the Radio

Commercial radio stations are in all the larger towns, and the state is blessed to have the **Alaska Public Radio Network** (www.aprn.org), one of the finest public radio networks in America. Anchorage's **KSKA** (91.1 FM, www.kska.org) is the flagship station, but many Alaskan towns have their own versions, from Ketchikan's KRBD (www.krbd.org) to Barrow's KBRW (www.kbrw.org). Anchorage's noncommercial **KNBA** (FM 90.3, www.knba.org) is one of the only Native-owned radio stations in the nation, and broadcasts some of the best music programming in Alaska. Two other great ones are **KBBI** (890 AM, www.kbbi.org) in Homer and **KTNA** (88.5 FM, www.ktna.org) in Talkeetna.

Post Offices

Post offices are generally open Mon.–Fri. 9 A.M.–5 P.M., though a few open their doors on Saturdays. Anchorage's airport post office is open 24 hours a day year-round. When post offices are closed, their outer doors usually remain open, so you can go in to buy stamps from the machines. Many grocery store checkout counters also sell books of stamps at no markup.

To receive mail on the road (does anyone really do this in this era of email?), have it addressed to yourself c/o General Delivery. Convenient general delivery addresses are: Juneau, AK 99801; Fairbanks, AK 99701; Anchorage, AK 99501. General delivery mail is held 10 days.

Phones and Email

Telephone service is excellent to all the major towns and cities in Alaska, though you may experience a delay in some remote areas, and the wilderness lodges often depend upon radio or satellite phones. Cellular phone coverage is variable, and not all systems work even when services exist, so contact your carrier for a coverage map ahead of your trip.

Alaska is surprisingly well wired, and even the most remote towns now have some sort of online connection. Nearly every library in Alaska (except Ketchikan) has at least one computer where you can check your email or surf the Web for free, though you may need to wait in line or sign up ahead of time. In addition, nearly all towns now have commercial businesses where you can rent computers by the hour for the same purpose.

Getting There by Air

Alaska Airlines

The state's flagship carrier, Alaska Airlines (800/426-0333, www.alaskaair.com), is actually based in Seattle. The company has jet service to all the larger cities and towns in Alaska, as well as throughout the United States and all the way to Mexico. Their **Web specials** come out every week, and are good deals if you're able to travel at the last minute and only want to stay for a week or less.

The **Alaska Airlines Mileage Plan** is one of the best in the business—especially if you use one of its credit cards to amass additional miles. The miles are good on a host of partners, including American, British Airways, Continental, Horizon, KLM, LanChile, Northwest, TWA, Qantas, and even Amtrak. The airline miles are an especially good deal if you're traveling to remote (and expensive) towns where Alaska flies, such as Adak, Barrow, Nome, or Unalaska. You can also use miles for open-jaw trips that start in one city and end in another.

Other U.S. Carriers

Anchorage is the hub for air travel into Alaska, though there are direct flights into Fairbanks, Juneau, and Ketchikan from the Lower 48 states. Six of the big domestic carriers fly into and out of Anchorage International Airport: **Alaska Airlines** (800/426-0333, www.alaskaair.com), **American** (800/433-7300, www.aa.com), **Continental** (800/523-3273, www.continental.com), **Delta** (800/221-1212, www.delta.com), **Frontier** (800/432-1359, www.frontierairlines.com) **Northwest** (800/225-2525, www.nwa.com), and **United** (800/241-6522, www.ual.com).

Most of these flights arrive via Seattle, but Alaska Airlines also has year-round nonstop flights to Chicago, Los Angeles, and Portland, Oregon, with connecting service via Seattle to most Western cities and all the way to Boston, Denver, Miami, Newark, Orlando, Washington, D.C., and a number of Mexican cities. Northwest has year-round nonstop service to Minneapolis-St. Paul and Detroit, while Delta flies nonstop year-round to Salt Lake City and Cincinnati. In addition, **Hawaiian Vacations** (907/261-2700 or 800/770-2700, www.hawaiianvacations.com) offers charter flights between Anchorage and Honolulu or Maui, while **Sun Country Airlines** (800/359-6786, www.suncountry.com) has summertime charters connecting Anchorage and Minneapolis.

Summer-only nonstop Anchorage flights arrive from Atlanta (Delta), Chicago (United), Cleveland (Continental), Dallas (American), Denver (United, Alaska and Frontier), Houston (Continental), Los Angeles (Continental), Newark (Continental), Portland (Continental), San Francisco (Alaska and United), and St. Louis (American). Most of these are seasonal, though flights to Seattle, Chicago, and Minneapolis-St. Paul are year-round.

If you're looking to save money on airfares, check the "Travel-Transportation" section of the classifieds in the *Anchorage Daily News;* several local travel agencies list discount fares here, sometimes with rates lower than you might find from Lower 48 travel agents. Good ones include **One Stop Travel** (907/565-7877 or 800/770-4440, www.onestoptravel.net). **Easy Travel** (907/562-3279 or 800/383-3279 outside Alaska, www.easytravel.nu), **Thrifty Travel** (907/279-4312), and **Navigant International** (907/786-3232 or 800/478-2829, www.navigant.com).

International Flights to Anchorage

Anchorage is a major refueling stop for air cargo jets heading between Asia and North America, and the airport also has a number of international passenger flights. The following companies offer nonstop service into Anchorage: Alaska Air and **Air Canada** (888/247-2262, www.aircanada.ca) from Vancouver; **Korean Air** (800/438-5000, www.koreanair.com) from Seoul; **China Airlines** (800/227-5118, www.china-airlines.com) from Taipei; and **Thomas Cook Airlines** (800/524-6975, www.thomascook.us) from Frankfurt. **Magadan Airlines** (907/248-2994)

flies to Petropavlovsk on Russia's Kamchatka Peninsula from Anchorage. Two companies offer seasonal flights to Tokyo in the summer: **Japan Airlines** (800/525-3663, www.jal.com) and **Alaskan Vacations** (907/261-2700 or 800/770-2700, www.hawaiianvacations.com), a subsidiary of Hawaiian Vacations.

International Flights to Fairbanks

Most flights into Fairbanks include a stop in Anchorage, but Alaska Airlines does have one nonstop flight daily between Fairbanks and Seattle year-round. Northwest flies to Minneapolis-St. Paul in the summer, and Thomas Cook Airlines has seasonal service from Frankfurt to Fairbanks, with a stop in Whitehorse, Yukon. **Hawaiian Vacations** (907/261-2700 or 800/770-2700, www.hawaiianvacations.com) also offers charter flights between Fairbanks and Maui during the winter.

Air North (867/668-2228, 800/661-0407 in Canada, or 800/764-0407 in the U.S., www.flyairnorth.com) flies between Fairbanks, Juneau, Whitehorse, and Dawson City, year-round. Other Fairbanks air connections include a stop in Anchorage.

Regional Airlines

Alaska Airlines serves most larger towns around the state, including such far-flung places as Barrow, Nome, Bethel, Kodiak, and Dutch Harbor. **Era Aviation** (907/266-8394 or 800/866-8394, www.flyera.com) has daily service from Anchorage to Cordova, Homer, Kenai, Kodiak, and Valdez. **PenAir** (907/243-2323 or 800/448-4226, www.penair.com) flies from Anchorage to Aniak, Cold Bay, Dillingham, Dutch Harbor, Iliamna, King Salmon, McGrath, Pribilof Islands, Sand Point, and Unalakleet. **Hageland Aviation** (907/245-0119 or 866/239-0119, www.hageland.com) serves northern and western Alaska towns and villages, including Aniak, Barrow, Bethel, Dillingham, Pribilof Islands, and Nome. **Frontier Flying Service** (907/450-7200 or 800/478-6779, www.frontierflying.com) has hubs in both Anchorage and Fairbanks, with service between the two cities several times a day, plus flights to Aniak, Barrow, Bethel, Dillingham, and many bush villages from Allakaket to Wainwright.

GETTING AROUND BY BUSH PLANE

Flying in a real live Alaska bush plane is a spectacular way to see the state, and it's also the only practical way to access the vast majority of Alaska's roadless areas. You will never forget your first flight over Alaska, whether it's a floatplane heading to Misty Fiords National Monument or a tiny Super Cub taking you to a remote Arctic camp. These airlines have regularly scheduled, though expensive, flights to towns and attractions that either have no public ground transportation or simply can't be reached overland—which accounts for over three-quarters of the state. For many people who live in Alaska's bush, these planes provide a lifeline of mail, food, and supplies. The planes seat 2–12 passengers, and they fly no matter how many passengers are along, for the regular fare (if the weather's cooperating).

But if you're heading to a really remote cabin, fjord, river, glacier, or park, that's when you'll encounter the famous Alaskan bush pilots, with their equally famous charter rates, which can make Alaska Airlines' fares look like the bargain of the century. Still, you'll have quite a ride—landing on tiny lakes with pontoons, on snow or ice with skis, on gravel bars with big fat tires; and loaded to the gills with people, equipment, extra fuel, tools, mail, supplies, and anything else under the sun. Make sure you agree on all the details beforehand—charges, drop-off and pickup times and locations, emergency and alternative procedures, and tidal considerations. Never be in much of a hurry; time is told differently up here, and many variables come into play, especially weather. If you're well prepared for complications, and have a flexible schedule and a loose attitude, one of these bush hops will no doubt be among your most memorable experiences in Alaska, worth every penny and minute that you spend.

As far as what you can expect to pay, most flightseeing operations have preset itineraries and prices. Some companies flying out of the larger towns also have set rates to some of the more popular destinations. However, for most drop-off trips, you pay for the ride according to engine hours, both coming and going. So if your destination is a spot that's an hour from the airstrip, you pay for four hours of engine time (an hour out and an hour back, twice). Expect to pay around $310/hour for a three-passenger Cessna 185, or $515/hour for a six-passenger DeHavilland Beaver, the workhorse of Alaska.

Floatplanes are a common way to get to the rural parts of Alaska—and often the *only* way.

ON THE ROAD

Safety in the Air

Before you head out into the wild blue yonder, there are a few things you should know. Alaska has far more than its share of fatal airplane crashes every year, generally three to four times the national average for small planes. These have happened to even the best pilots flying for even the most conscientious companies, but certain operators cut corners in safety and allow their pilots to fly under risky weather conditions. You can't avoid all risks, of course, but you can improve your odds by taking a few precautions on your own.

First and foremost, you should choose your pilot and/or flight service with care. Just because someone has a pilot's license and is flying in Alaska doesn't mean that he or she is a seasoned bush pilot. You're well within your rights to ask about the pilot's qualifications, and about time spent flying *in Alaska*. The oft-repeated saying is, "There are old pilots and there are bold pilots, but there are no old bold pilots." Given a choice, you want an "old" one—not so much in chronological years, but one that's been flying in and out of the bush for a good long time. Ask locally about the air safety record of the various companies. Also ask which companies have the contracts with the Forest Service or other Federal agencies, since they tend to be ones that aren't allowed to take chances. You can also search the Internet for accident statistics for a specific company at the **National Transportation Safety Board's** website: www.ntsb.gov.

Even if you're just going on a 30-minute flightseeing tour, wear clothing appropriate for the ground conditions. Unplanned stops because of weather or mechanical problems aren't unusual. Warm, comfortable hiking clothes, raingear, and lightweight boots or sturdy shoes make reasonable bush plane apparel.

Weather is a major limiting factor in aviation. Small planes don't operate on airline-type schedules, with arrivals and departures down to the minute. Leave yourself plenty of leeway when

Flying in a real live Alaska bush plane is a spectacular way to see the state. You will never forget your first flight over Alaska, whether it's a floatplane heading to Misty Fiords National Monument or a tiny Super Cub taking you to a remote Arctic camp.

scheduling trips, and don't pressure your pilot to get you back to the airstrip so you won't miss your bus, boat, train, dogsled ride, or salmon bake. More than one crash has been the result of subtle or not-so-subtle pressure by clients to fly when it was against the pilot's better judgment. Never pressure a pilot to fly, and always try to act as a second pair of eyes to look for any signs of danger, such as other aircraft in the vicinity.

Before taking off, your pilot should brief all passengers on the location of safety and survival equipment and airsickness bags, how to exit during an emergency landing (or crash), and the location and function of the Emergency Locator Transmitter (ELT) and survival kit. Ear protection may also be supplied, as most small planes are quite noisy. Just in case, buy a set of foam earplugs at a sporting goods store before you go to the airport. They cost under a buck, weigh nothing, and are perfectly adequate for aircraft noise levels.

You'll probably be asked how much you weigh (don't be coy here—lives are at stake!) and told where you should sit. Weight and balance are critical in little planes, so don't whine about not getting to sit up front if you're told otherwise. Many companies place severe restrictions on how much gear they carry, charging excess baggage fees over a certain limit (sometimes less than 50 pounds).

Gear stowage can be a challenge in small planes, especially when transporting people who are heading out on long expeditions. Don't even think of showing up at the airfield with hard-sided luggage. Internal-frame backpacks, duffel bags, and other soft, easily compressed and stowed items are much easier to handle. Don't strap sleeping bags and other gear onto the outside of a pack. Lots of small items are much easier to arrange and find homes for than a few bulky things. Also, if you're carrying a canister of red pepper spray to deter bears, tell the pilot beforehand and follow directions for stowage. Pilots don't want the stuff inside the cabin (imagine what might happen if it went off in this enclosed space!), but they'll store it in a float if the plane is so equipped, or you may be able to strap it to a strut with duct tape.

Whenever you fly, leave a flight route, destination, expected departure and arrival times, and a contact number for the flight service with a reliable friend. Then relax and enjoy the scenery. Flying in Alaska is a tremendous experience, one that relatively few people get to enjoy, and, in spite of all the cautionary notes listed above, is still a generally safe and reliable way to get to and see the wilderness.

Getting There by Sea

FERRY

Ferries plying the Inside Passage from Bellingham to Skagway cruise up an inland waterway and through fjords far wilder than Norway's, surpassing even a trip down the coast of Chile to Punta Arenas. One difference is that the North American journey is cheaper and more easily arranged than its South American or Scandinavian counterparts. Another difference is the variety of services, routes, and destinations for this 1,000-mile historic cruise. Ferries operated by the **Alaska Marine Highway** (907/465-3941 or 800/642-0066, www.ferryalaska.com) are the core of travel in Southeast Alaska.

There are two primary state ferry networks: one from Bellingham, Washington, or Prince Rupert, British Columbia, and throughout Southeast Alaska; the other through Southcentral Alaska from Cordova all the way to Dutch Harbor in the Aleutians. In addition, a ferry sails between Whittier and Juneau twice monthly in the summer, linking the two regions together.

British Columbia Ferries (250/386-3431 or 888/223-3779 in B.C., www.bcferries.bc.ca) sails Canada's Inside Passage from Port Hardy at the northern tip of Vancouver Island to Prince Rupert on the B.C. mainland's north coast.

Alaska Marine Highway

One of the first actions of the newly created Alaska State government in 1959 was to establish a state ferry system. Originally it consisted of just a single boat, but after passage of a 1960 state bond, three new ships were built and more have been added over the years. The newest additions are two high-speed ferries, the *Fairweather,* which began service from Juneau to surrounding towns in 2004, and the *Chenega,* for Prince William Sound in 2005, along with a smaller traditional ferry, the *Lituya,* connecting Ketchikan and Metlakatla in 2004. All state ferries carry both passengers and vehicles, and offer food service. The larger ferries also have cabins, showers, storage lockers, gift shops, pay phones, and cocktail lounges.

Ferries generally stop for one or two hours in the larger towns, but less than an hour in the smaller villages. You can usually go ashore while the vessel is in port. Most ferry terminals open only an hour or two before ship arrivals, closing upon their departure. A baggage cart transports luggage from the terminal to the ship if you want to save your back a bit. There is a limit of 100 pounds of luggage per person, but this is only enforced if you are way over and the ship is full.

Life on Board

The ferries have a relaxed and slow-paced atmosphere; it's impossible to be in a hurry here! Many travelers think of the ferry as a floating motel—a place to dry off, wash up, rest up, sleep, and meet other travelers while at the same time moving on to new sights and new adventures. Ferry food is reasonably priced and quite good, but many budget travelers stock up on groceries before they board. The hot water is free in the cafeteria if you're trying to save bucks by bringing along cup-o-noodles and instant oatmeal.

For a bit of entertainment, try flying a kite from the back deck. Be sure it's a cheap one, however, since you can't chase it if it gets away. Another popular toy is a hackey sack. And if you bring a musical instrument along, *you'll* provide the entertainment. Light sleepers should bring earplugs since things can get pretty noisy sometimes, especially in the solarium.

Staterooms or Solarium?

Staterooms offer privacy, as well as a chance to get away from the hectic crowding of midsummer. These cabins have two or four bunk beds, and some also include private baths; other folks use the baths and showers down the hall.

If you don't mind hearing others snoring nearby, you can save a bundle and make new friends with fellow voyagers. There's generally space to stretch out a sleeping bag in the recliner lounge (an inside area with airline-type seats), as well as in the **solarium**—a covered and heated area high atop the ship's rear deck. The solarium has several dozen deck chairs to sit and sleep on, making it a favorite hangout for backpackers, budget travelers, cannery workers, and high school basketball teams. It's also a great place to enjoy the passing panorama and to make new friends. The solarium is so popular that at some embarkation points, there's often a mad dash up the stairs to grab a place before all the chairs are taken. To be assured of a deck chair, get in line five hours ahead of time if you're coming aboard in Bellingham in midsummer. When the weather is good you're also likely to see the rapid development of a tent city on the rear deck, often held down with duct tape (usually sold in gift shops on board).

Show Time

Between early June and Labor Day, the larger ferries have Forest Service interpreters on board. They provide videos and slide shows, give talks, answer questions about trails and campgrounds, and generally spoon-feed the Forest Service line. Be sure to pick up a forest map from them, and take a look at their "Opportunity Guide" for information on each town.

In addition to these naturalist-types, ferry passengers are often given the chance to watch or work with various artists and performers in the **Arts on Board** programs. These include concerts, Native crafts, and more. Feature movies are shown on the video monitors every day.

Getting Tickets

The ferries operate year-round. Get schedules and make reservations by calling 907/465-3941 or 800/642-0066, or online at www.ferryalaska.com. Reservations for the summer can be made as early as December, and travelers taking a vehicle should book as early as possible to be sure of a space. Before you get ready to board, it's always a good idea to call the local ferry terminal to make sure the ferry is on schedule; often they are running behind, and sometimes unforeseen events can totally change departure times.

Although there is usually space for walk-on passengers, it's a smart idea to make advance reservations for ferries out of Bellingham. This is especially true for cabins. Reservations are required for anyone with a vehicle, and are generally available six months in advance. The ferry system charges an extra fee to carry bicycles, canoes, kayaks, and inflatable boats aboard.

Discounts

Those driving a car to Alaska may be able to save money by riding the ferry during the off-season (Oct.–April). These typically include discounts for drivers (summertime drivers must pay for both their car and themselves) and for children in the winter holiday season.

Seniors over 65 can take advantage of bargain fares in the off-season when travel between most Alaskan ports is just 50 percent of the regular full fare. The discounts do not apply to vehicles or staterooms, or to certain ports, but you don't need to be an Alaskan to obtain them. Contact the ferry system for the fine print. Substantial discounts are also available for people with disabilities.

CRUISE SHIPS

For many people (particularly retirees), cruise ships offer the luxury way to see Alaska. A multitude of ships ply the Inside Passage and Gulf of Alaska waters, carrying some 800,000 people each summer—nearly half of all travelers to the state. Cruises make it easy for travelers to explore the Inside Passage while enjoying good food and cozy accommodations, and while leaving all the planning to someone else.

cruise ship and floatplane in Ketchikan

Cruise ship tourism has proven to be a mixed blessing for Alaska. True, it does bring in millions of dollars to the state, and towns such as Skagway are almost totally given over to cruise ships, but the ships also dump hundreds of thousands of gallons of wastewater into Alaska's pristine waterways, pollute the air, and cause major disruptions in local communities.

The Ships

Most ships depart from Vancouver, British Columbia, but some cruises also leave from Seattle or San Francisco. The largest vessel can hold 2,600 passengers, and some ships offer impressive buffets, luxurious atrium lobbies, private stateroom verandas, health spas, and lounges with live music and casinos. Not all ships are large and glitzy, however. The smallest "expedition" ships may hold just a few dozen passengers. On these, the emphasis is on education and ecotourism. Many of the smaller ships also have professional naturalists on board and act as "motherships" for short sea kayaking or hiking trips. Not surprisingly, expedition ships are considerably more expensive than the giant cruise liners.

Costs and Itineraries

Prices for cruises have dropped in recent years as more and larger ships have moved into the Alaskan market. The bargain deals are typically early or late in the summer season, and can be amazingly cheap at times. Cruises typically last 7–12 days, and are either taken as a round-trip tour of the Inside Passage or a one-way cruise that encompasses both the Inside Passage and towns along the Gulf of Alaska. It is also possible to add in a land tour, either as part of a hurried seven-day ship-and-bus package or as an add-on to the cruise. The add-on option often includes time in Southcentral and Interior Alaska, and might start with a trip through the Inside Passage followed by a bus tour from Skagway to Fairbanks, and a train trip to Denali National Park and then on to Anchorage where you fly home. Many other cruise options exist; contact the individual companies for details.

Two tips: It's preferable to take a "southbound" tour, which means you fly into Anchorage, see the mainland first, then finish off with your luxury cruise down to Vancouver. That's because the ground portion can be grueling, but then you can just relax on board the ship for the final leg. Also, be aware that the tour companies mostly target the retired market. This can be fun for those who can get into the spirit, but it isn't exactly a *Love Boat*-type experience for swinging singles. The average age has, however, dropped a bit as the prices have become more reasonable in the last few years. (Still, it isn't uncommon to have someone die on board of a heart attack; what do you expect when half the travelers are over age 70?)

The Big Ships

Any good travel agent—and many online travel sites—can set up an Alaska cruise, or you can book your own by contacting the companies directly. A good overall place to begin an exploration of cruise ship travel is the website of the **Cruise Lines International Association,** www.cruising.org. It has links to all the major players, plus general information.

The large ships that visit Alaska are operated by **Carnival Cruise Lines** (800/327-9501, www.carnival.com), **Celebrity Cruises** (800/437-3111, www.celebrity-cruises.com), **Crystal Cruises** (800/446-6620, www.crystalcruises.com), **Hapag-Lloyd** (www.hapag-lloyd.com), **Holland America Line** (800/426-0327, www.hollandamerica.com), **Princess Cruises** (800/568-3262, www.princesscruises.com), **Norwegian Cruise Lines** (800/327-7030, www.ncl.com), **Radisson Seven Seas** (877/505-5370, www.rssc.com), and **Royal Caribbean International** (800/327-6700, www.rccl.com).

Smaller Cruise Ships

You don't have to join these mega-ships to see Alaska by sea. A number of companies offer smaller ships (less than 100 passengers) for a more intimate look at the state. Of course, these are also considerably more expensive than ships that pack folks into every nook and cranny. Companies with small cruise ships include **Cruise West** (206/441-4757 or 800/580-0072, www.cruisewest.com), **Clipper Cruise Line** (314/727-2929 or 800/325-0010, www.clippercruise.com), **Glacier Bay Cruiselines** (206/623-2417 or 800/451-5952, www.glacierbaytours.com), **Lindblad Special Expeditions** (212/765-7740 or 800/397-3348, www.lindblad.com), **Society Expeditions** (800/548-8669, www.societyexpeditions.com), and **Alaska Sternwheeler Cruises** (800/434-1232, www.alaskacruisetour.com).

Even smaller boats provide the ultimate in luxury for groups of 6–8 people. Good expedition companies include **Alaska Sea Adventures** (907/772-4700 or 888/772-8588, www.yachtalaska.com), **Admiralty Tours** (907/790-3253, www.admiraltytours.com), **Midnight Sun Cruises** (800/939-2477, www.aipr.com/midnightsun), and **AK-Natural Offshore Adventures** (907/489-2233).

Getting There by Land

BUS

There is no regular bus service between the Lower 48 and Alaska, but you *can* get there from here. **Greyhound Canada** (604/482-8747 or 800/661-8747, www.greyhound.ca) covers much of Canada, reaching north to Whitehorse. From there, you'll need to hop aboard an **Alaska Direct Bus Line** (867/668-4833 or 800/770-6652) van for the rest of your trip to Anchorage, Fairbanks, Haines, or Skagway. Service is year-round.

Alaska Trails (907/479-3065 or 888/600-6001, www.alaskashuttle.com) has year-round service between Anchorage and Fairbanks, and seasonal service connecting Fairbanks with Dawson City, Yukon.

Several other companies have van service in Southcentral and Interior Alaska: **Denali Overland Transportation** (907/733-2384 or 800/651-5221, www.denalioverland.com), **Alaska Park Connection** (907/245-0200 or 800/208-0200, www.alaskacoach.com), **RC Shuttles** (907/479-

0079 or 877/479-0079, www.rcshuttles.com), **Seward Bus Lines** (907/563-0800, www.sewardbuslines.com), and **Homer Stage Line** (907/883-3914, www.homerstageline.com).

Green Tortoise

This is more than just a bus ride—it's a vacation and a cultural experience in itself. The ancient buses have foam mattresses, a lounge area with seats and tables, and communal meals. One of the best things about these trips is the people—alternative travel attracts good company. This is a friendly, unprivate way to travel, though not inexpensive.

Green Tortoise (415/956-7500 or 800/867-8647, www.greentortoise.com) has two or three trips each summer to Alaska, and each bus holds 32 passengers and two drivers. Book no later than March to ensure a space. Some trips leave from San Francisco and wind up in Anchorage, others start and end in Anchorage.

Despite the casual approach, Green Tortoise buses are reliable and have a good safety record. Green Tortoise also runs bus trips all over the country, and even to Central America.

CAR

Getting to Alaska by car is probably the cheapest and most flexible means of mobility. Its advantages over public transportation are manifold, so to speak. You can start anywhere, and once there, you can go anywhere there's a road, anytime you feel like it, stopping along the way for however long you decide. The roads in the North Country are especially fun, and you have some of them almost to yourself. On a few roads you'll rarely see another car. It's very open, unconfined, uninhibiting—a large part of the spell of the North. It's best to bring the car with you; trying to buy one at inflated Alaskan prices is not recommended and selling it at the end of your stay is problematic.

One essential for Alaskan drivers of all types is *The Milepost,* a fat annual book that's packed with mile-by-mile descriptions for virtually every road within or to Alaska (including, of course, the Alcan). The book is sold everywhere in Alaska—even Costco—and is easy to find in Lower 48 bookstores, or online at www.themilepost.com. Warning: Don't believe everything you read in *The Milepost;* some of the text is paid ads for specific businesses—watch for the small notice.

The Alaska Highway

You can drive all the way up and back, or put the car on the ferry one way. The Alaska Highway (nicknamed the **Alcan**) has been dramatically upgraded from the early days when you had to carry extra fuel and four spare tires, when you had to protect your headlights and windshield with chicken wire, and when facilities were spaced 250 miles apart. Today, the entire road is paved, gas stations are about every 50 miles, and roadhouses and hotels are numerous. Still, this road passes through 1,442 miles of somewhat inhospitable wilderness. Frost heaves and potholes are not uncommon. Mechanics are few and far between and parts are even scarcer. Gas prices are no laughing matter, especially on the Canadian side where they're typically almost double those in the Lower 48 states. If you're coming from anywhere east of Idaho or Alberta, you can hit Mile 0 of the Alaska Highway through Edmonton without having to backtrack east at all. But if you're heading north from the West Coast, or through the Canadian Rockies, you'll probably wind up in Prince George and have to head east a bit to Dawson Creek (the starting point).

Although official signage along the Alaska Highway is in kilometers, many services are marked in miles, a legacy of imperial measurement and the large number of Americans who travel this road. This only becomes confusing when you consider that highway improvements have shortened the original route. For example, Liard River Hot Springs is still marked as Mile 496, though it's now only 754 km (462 miles) from Dawson Creek.

You can also head west out of Prince George on the Yellowhead and take the **Cassiar Highway** north from Meziadin Junction to just west of Watson Lake in Yukon Territory. This 458-mile paved road is scenically stunning, but services are a little less frequent than on the Alaska Highway.

ON THE ROAD

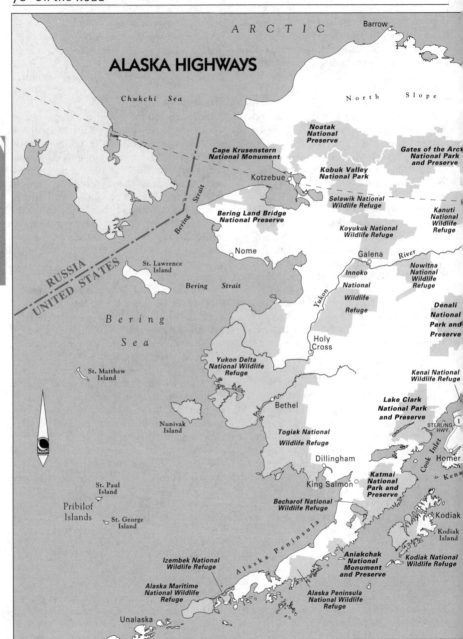

ALASKA HIGHWAYS

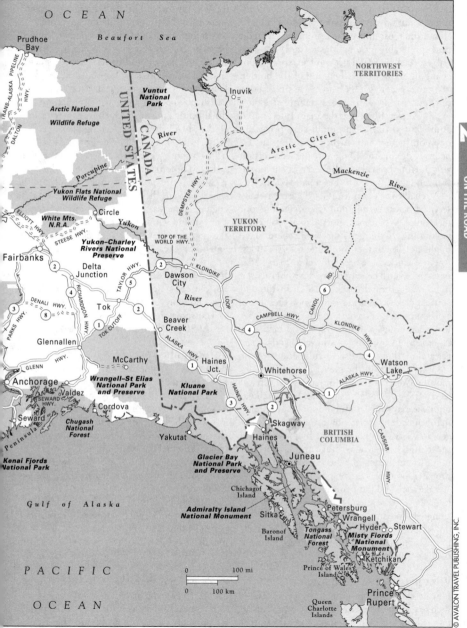

© AVALON TRAVEL PUBLISHING, INC.

ON THE ROAD

Go Prepared

A few common-sense preparations can eliminate all but the most unexpected problems. A credit card (preferably Visa or MasterCard) is essential, especially if you don't want to worry about changing money on either side of the border. You can expect to get hit hard by gas prices along the Alcan and in the more remote stretches within Alaska. But along the main Interior and Southcentral Alaska thoroughfares, prices are often only a few cents higher than Outside. Finally, by driving the whole way in one direction and putting the car on the ferry in the other, you can take different routes up and back.

A reliable car is a must. Get the car carefully serviced before setting out; when you ask your mechanic, "Will it make it to Alaska?" you won't be kidding. If you get stuck somewhere, there might not be another mechanic for 100 miles. And tow trucks have been known to charge $5 *a mile*. Since you'll be tempted to drive hundreds of miles off the beaten track, the best investment you can make in your car is five good tires. Bring a pressure gauge and check the tires frequently. A few spare hoses (and hose tape) and belts take up little room and can come in very handy. Spare gas and oil filters are also useful, because of the amount of dust on the gravel roads in the dry months. Water is an absolute necessity; carry at least a five-gallon jug. Also, if you have a cellular phone it may prove useful, not only for keeping in touch with friends at home, but also for emergencies. Service is good in the major cities and most mid-sized towns, but can be spotty or nonexistent elsewhere. Check with your service provider for a coverage map.

Take tools and jumper cables even if you don't know how to use them. Someone usually comes along who doesn't have tools but knows what to do. A lot of salt is laid down on the roads, especially in the mountains, so wash the car thoroughly at the first opportunity to minimize the rust.

Winter Travel Around Alaska

During the winter months, travelers to Alaska need to take special precautions. Always call ahead for road and avalanche conditions (see the sidebar "Safety in Avalanche Country" in the *Anchorage and Vicinity* chapter) before heading out. Studded snow tires and proper antifreeze levels are a necessity, but you should also have on hand a number of emergency supplies including tire chains, a shovel and bag of sand in case you get stuck, a first-aid kit, booster cables, signal flares, flashlight, lighter and candle, transistor radio, nonperishable foods (granola bars, canned nuts, or dried fruit), a jug of water, an ice scraper, winter clothes, blankets, and a sleeping bag. The most valuable tool may well be a **cell phone** to call for help—assuming you're in an area with reception.

If you become stranded in a blizzard, stay in your car. You're more likely to be found, and the vehicle provides shelter from the weather. Run the engine and heater sparingly, occasionally opening a downwind window for ventilation. Don't run the engine if the tailpipe is blocked by snow, or you may risk carbon monoxide poisoning.

Road Updates

For current road conditions, construction delays, and more, contact the **Alaska Department of Transportation** online at www.511.alaska.gov, or dial 511 toll-free anywhere in Alaska.

Car Rentals

An increasingly popular way to see Alaska is by flying into the state and renting a car. This provides travelers with flexibility, and the costs have dropped in recent years. Rental cars are available in all the larger towns, but they are generally cheapest out of Anchorage, where most of the major car rental companies have airport booths. Rates start around $45/day or $290/week for an economy car with unlimited mileage; the big chains may be higher. Note also that if you rent at the Anchorage airport, you'll have to add on an extra 10 percent airport concession fee, plus an 8 percent municipal tax, to these rates. For long rentals, it's always best to get a car away from the airport. In the peak summer season you should reserve up to two months in advance to get the best rates, and to be assured of finding any car at all when you arrive.

If you plan to rent a car for an extended period, it's probably worth your while to check travel websites such as www.travelocity.com to see which company offers the best rates. When reserving a car, be sure to mention if you have an AAA card or are a member of Costco; you can often save substantially on the rates. Also be sure to ask about driving restrictions, since most car rental companies prohibit their use on gravel roads such as the one to McCarthy; the exception is **Affordable New Car Rental** (907/243-3370 or 800/248-3765, www.ancr.com).

RV and Camper Rentals

Recreational vehicles are among the most despised sights on Alaskan roads, but they seem to proliferate like rabbits as soon as the snow melts each spring. Motor homes are infamous for cruising slowly down the Seward Highway south of Anchorage, wagging a tail of impatient cars for a mile or more behind. Many "snowbirds" drive up to Alaska for the summer in their RVs, fleeing to Arizona for the winters. Other folks fly into Anchorage, Fairbanks, or Whitehorse and rent one of these land yachts.

Despite these criticisms, RVs can be a decent choice if the gas price is not out of sight and if you can cram enough folks inside to cut your costs. But for just two people they are a profligate and environmentally disastrous investment. See the *Anchorage and Vicinity* chapter for RV and camper rental companies. Mid-summer RV rental rates are $165–195/day (depending upon the size), with 100 free miles daily.

TRAIN

Except for the White Pass & Yukon Route excursion between Skagway and Fraser, and the kids' choo-choos around Pioneer Park in Fairbanks and Alaska Live Steamers in Wasilla, Alaska's only train is the **Alaska Railroad.** The railroad runs 470 miles between Seward and Fairbanks, with a seven-mile spur between Portage and Whittier, and is the only state-owned railroad in America. The train—historic and a bit exotic—is also much roomier and slower than the tour buses but is about the same price (and occasionally even on time). Dining service is available, and helpful tour guides are on board in the summer months. In addition, some of the

trains will make flag stops to pick up hikers or people living in the Alaskan bush.

Two daily expresses (mid-May to mid-Sept.), one northbound and one southbound, run between Anchorage and Fairbanks for $175 (12 hours). Anchorage to Denali costs $125, Fairbanks to Denali $50. The train also connects Seward with Anchorage ($59) and Anchorage with Whittier ($45) daily in the summer. Contact Alaska Railroad (907/265-2494 or 800/544-0552, www.alaskarailroad.com) for details on these runs plus a variety of package tours that combine train rides with boat trips and other activities.

Princess Tours and Holland America Tours/Gray Line of Alaska hook double-decker superdome coaches to the end of the express trains in the summer, but these are a pricey option.

PACKAGE TOURS

A 7- to 21-day whirlwind around Alaska is available from dozens of tour packagers. All will book you onto one of a variety of cruise ships up the Inside Passage, reserve your hotel rooms, roll you between them on motorcoaches and railcars, and offer options for local and overnight side trips. Many are escorted by tour guides, and some even include all meals in the price. Many people choose this route for convenience, comfort, and security, though they certainly pay for what they get. The companies change, and their offerings also vary from year to year, so your best bet is to work through a travel agent who specializes in Alaska tours.

The two largest Alaska tour companies are **Holland America Tours/Gray Line of Alaska** (907/277-5581 or 800/544-2206, www.graylineofalaska.com) and **Princess Tours** (206/336-6000 or 800/835-8907, www.princess.com). Both of these are also major players in the cruise travel industry, and many cruise ship travelers simply add on a land segment to their voyage. **Alaska Sightseeing/Cruise West** (206/441-8687 or 800/580-0072, www.cruisewest.com) also sets up a wide variety of trips that include small-ship cruises and tours. A few other tour options include **Alaska Airlines Vacations** (800/468-2248, www.alaskaair.com), **Alaska**

Bound (231/439-3000 or 888/252-7527, www.alaskabound.com), **Alaska Travel Adventures** (907/783-2928 or 800/334-8730, www.alaskawildlandadventures.com), **Knightly Tours** (206/938-8567 or 800/426-2123, www.knightlytours.com), and **Tauck Tours** (203/226-6911 or 800/468-2825, www.tauck.com).

Specialty Tours

Contact **CampAlaska Tours** (907/376-9438 or 800/376-9438, www.campalaska.com) for tent camping tours of the state.

Birdwatchers should point their binoculars toward **Wilderness Birding Adventures** (907/694-7442, www.wildernessbirding.com) for extended trips to remote parts of the state, **St. Paul Island Tours** (907/278-2318 or 877/424-5637, www.alaskabirding.com) for trips to the Pribilofs, and **Bird Watching Tours of Anchorage** (907/248-7282 or 888/334-7282, www.anchoragebirding.com) for Anchorage-area trips. Other recommended companies include **Victor Emanuel Nature Tours** (512/328-5221 or 800/328-8368, www.ventbird.com) and **Wings Birding Tours** (520/320-9868 or 888/293-6443, www.wingsbirds.com).

For bicycle tours around Alaska, contact **Alaskan Bicycle Adventures** (907/243-2329 or 800/770-7242, www.alaskabike.com), **Alaska 2Wheel Tours** (907/522-1430, www.alaskamtbike.com), or **Backroads** (510/527-1555 or 800/462-2848, www.backroads.com).

Talkeetna-based **Alaska Photo Tours** (907/733-3051 or 800/799-3051, www.alaskaphototours.com) is recommended for budding wildlife photographers. Also of note is the Washington-based **Joseph Van Os Photo Safaris** (206/463-5383, www.photosafaris.com).

On-Your-Own vs. Package Tours

In Alaska, often the only way to get from here to there is through the air. To find the best-value fares, always compare the airlines to the big tour companies. You can usually get a better deal from the tour companies, which charge wholesale airfares and then add on the conveniences to compete with the regular coach fare. For example,

the best fare between Anchorage and Nome is generally only a few dollars more expensive than the entire Alaska Airlines Vacations price, which also includes one night's lodging, two city tours, and transfers. Also, always check the ads in the daily newspapers, where the tour companies sometimes advertise substantial reductions in their local package-tour prices. And of course, check such websites as www.travelocity.com and www.expedia.com for tour deals.

Even when the airfare alone seems substantially cheaper, by the time you add the airporter van both ways and rent a car to see the sights, you might as well take the tour. Besides, the tours themselves can be a good value. All this is contingent, of course, on short time; if you have unlimited days to explore, say, Kodiak, and lots of planning leeway, take the ferry and save your cash for other adventures.

BICYCLE

Inveterate cyclists have a love affair with bike riding that makes the relationship between car and driver look like a one-night stand. If you're indifferent to or can overcome the hardships (hills, trucks, rain and wind, bugs, time, security considerations, and sore muscles), the advantages of bikes are unassailable. They're free to operate, nonpolluting, easy to maintain, and great exercise. They also slow down the world and attract the immediate friendly and curious attention of the locals.

Almost all of the bus companies, ferries, and railways will carry your bike as accompanied baggage for a nominal amount, although a few want you to have it in a box. Most airlines also accept bicycles as luggage, as long as they're boxed before check-in (you may pay an extra charge). Before you buy a ticket, compare prices, then ask each airline about taking a bicycle.

Alaska can be just as hard on bikes as on cars, however, if not harder. Fifteen-speed mountain bikes are recommended to better handle the rough roads. Know how to fix your own bike, and take along a good repair kit, as bicycle shops are few and far between. At the minimum, you should have spare tubes and tires, a patch kit, a pump, extra cables, a spare chain, and a chain tool. Carry your gear in saddlebag panniers lined with plastic bags. Fenders are nice in wet weather. Warm, waterproof clothing is essential, particularly rain pants, poncho, rain hat, wool shirt, wool socks, and waterproof shoes. Bicycling gloves, shorts, and clear goggles are also necessary. You could buy everything you need in Anchorage.

Short-distance bicycles are available for rent in every major town and are an excellent way to see the local sights, especially in fair weather.

Cycling Information Sources

The Anchorage-based **Arctic Bicycle Club** (907/566-0177, www.arcticbike.org) organizes road races, mountain bike races, and tours, and its website is an excellent source for anyone interested in cycling in Alaska. Useful books are *Alaska Bicycle Touring Guide,* by Pete Praetorius and Alys Culhane, and *Mountain Bike Alaska: 49 Trails in the 49th State,* by Richard Larson. A few companies offer guided cycling trips around Alaska.

ALASKA PASS

The Alaska Pass (206/463-6777 or 800/248-7598, www.alaskapass.com) is a good option if you plan to travel using a combination of ferries, trains, and buses. The pass allows unlimited travel on cooperating carriers throughout Alaska, Yukon, and British Columbia. The passes are available for varying lengths of time, and you can either buy one that allows travel every day (not a good idea if you want to do something more than sit on a bus or ferry) or one that lets you travel a certain number of days out of the total. The latter cost $600 ($300 kids) for a 12-day pass that includes eight travel days; or $750 ($375 kids) for a 21-day pass that includes 12 travel days.

ON THE ROAD

Southeast Alaska

For many people, the name Alaska conjures up images of bitterly cold winters and sunshine-packed summers, of great rivers, enormous snowcapped mountains, and open tundra reaching to the horizon. If that's your vision of the state, you've missed its Garden of Eden, the Southeast. Almost entirely boxed in by British Columbia, Southeast Alaska's "Panhandle" stretches 500 miles along the North American coast. Everything about this beautiful, lush country is water-based: the rain that falls on the land, the glaciers that drop from giant ice-fields, and the ocean that surrounds it all. Gray-blue clouds play a constant game of hide-and-seek with the verdant islands; deep fjords drive up between snow-covered summits; waterfalls plummet hundreds of feet through the evergreen forests to feed rivers rich in salmon; brown bears prowl the creeks in search of fish; bald eagles perch on treetops beside the rugged, rocky coastline; and great blue glaciers press down toward the sea.

© DON PITCHER

Ketchikan's Creek Street

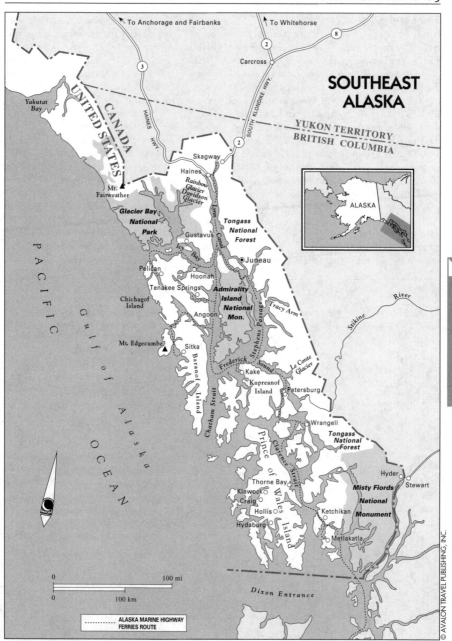

To Anchorage and Fairbanks

To Whitehorse

Carcross

SOUTHEAST ALASKA

YUKON TERRITORY
BRITISH COLUMBIA

ALASKA

CANADA
UNITED STATES

Yakutat Bay

HAINES HWY.

SOUTH KLONDIKE HWY.

Skagway

Haines

Mt. Fairweather

Rainbow Glacier
Davidson Glacier

Glacier Bay National Park

Tongass National Forest

Gustavus

Ice Bay

Juneau

Pelican

Hoonah

Tenakee Springs

Chichagof Island

Admirality Island National Mon.

Angoon

Tracy Arm

Mt. Edgecumbe

Sitka

Baranof Island

Chatham Strait

Frederick Sound

Stephens Passage

Stikine River

Le Conte Glacier

Kake

Kupreanof Island

Petersburg

Wrangell

Prince of Wales Island

Clarence Strait

Tongass National Forest

Hyder

Stewart

Thorne Bay

Klawock

Craig

Hollis

Misty Fiords National Monument

Ketchikan

Hydaburg

Metlakatla

PACIFIC

Gulf of Alaska

OCEAN

Dixon Entrance

MOON

0   100 mi
0   100 km

- - - - - - ALASKA MARINE HIGHWAY
FERRIES ROUTE

SOUTHEAST ALASKA

© AVALON TRAVEL PUBLISHING, INC.

The Land

Nearly 95 percent of the Southeast is federal property, most of it within Tongass National Forest and Glacier Bay National Park. The Panhandle is composed of a mountainous mainland and hundreds of islands, varying from rocky reefs that barely jut out of the sea at low tide to some of the largest islands in North America. Collectively, these islands are called the Alexander Archipelago. This ragged shoreline stretches for more than 11,000 miles and includes over 1,000 named islands, the largest being Prince of Wales, Chichagof, Baranof, Admiralty, Revillagigedo, and Kupreanof—names that reflect the English, Russians, and Spaniards who explored the area.

The Rainforest

Much of the Southeast is covered with dense rainforests of Sitka spruce (the state tree), western hemlock, Alaska yellow cedar, and western red cedar. Interspersed through these rainforests are open boggy areas known as "muskegs," with a scattering of stunted lodgepole pines and cedars. Above the treeline (approx. 2,500 feet) are rocky peaks covered with fragile flowers and other alpine vegetation. Shorelines often sport a fringe of grass dotted with flowers during the summer.

The rainforests here are choked with a dense, ankle-grabbing understory of huckleberry, devil's club, and other shrubs. Berry lovers will enjoy a feast in late summer as the salmonberries, red and blue huckleberries, and thimbleberries all ripen. If you're planning a hike, learn to recognize **devil's club,** a lovely, abundant plant with large maple-shaped leaves and red berries. Barbed spines cover the plants, and when touched they feel like a bee sting. The spines become embed-

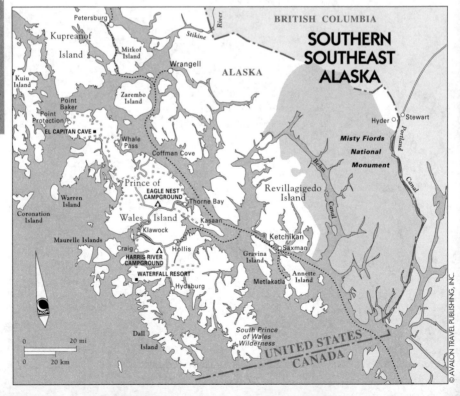

ded in your fingers and are difficult to remove, often leaving a nasty sting for several days. If you're planning a cross-country hike, wear leather gloves to protect your hands. Surprisingly, mosquitoes and other biting insects are not nearly as abundant in the Southeast as they are, for example, in Alaska's Interior. They can, however, make your life miserable some of the time, especially during no-see-um season.

Climate

Tourist brochures invariably show happy folks cavorting around gleaming glaciers under a brilliant blue sky. Photographers often wait weeks to capture all three elements: Southeast Alaska is rain country! Expect rain or mist at least half of the time. In much of the region, blue-sky days come once a week, if that. The cool maritime climate brings rain in summer, and rain and snow in winter. Most towns in the Southeast get 80 inches or more of precipitation, and of the major towns, Ketchikan takes top honors with 162 inches per year. The tiny fishing settlement of Port Alexander on the south end of Baranof Island drowns in 220 inches per year!

Weather patterns vary greatly in the Southeast; Skagway gets just 22 inches a year, but only a few miles away, precipitation tops 160 inches annually on the peaks bordering Canada. Fortunately, the driest months are generally June–August.

Residents learn to tolerate the rain, which they call "liquid sunshine." You won't see many umbrellas, but heavy raingear and red rubber boots are appropriate dress for almost any occasion. (Not surprisingly, the best raingear is sold in the Southeast.) If you ask, locals will admit to a grudging appreciation for the rain; it not only creates the lush, green countryside and provides ample streamflow for the vital salmon runs, it also keeps the region safe from overcrowding by the drier-minded set.

The People

Southeast Alaska has only 70,000 people. Nearly half live in Juneau, with the rest spread over nearly two dozen isolated towns and settlements strung along the Inside Passage. Much of the economy is based upon fishing, logging, governing, and

tourism. The towns are dependent upon the sea for their survival, not only for the fish it provides, but also as a way to transport huge log rafts to the mills. Fully 95 percent of the goods brought to the Southeast arrive by barge or ship, and most of the visitors arrive aboard cruise ships or state ferries.

The Southeast corresponds almost exactly to the ancestral homeland of the Tlingit (KLINK-it) Indians, and signs of their culture—both authentic and visitor-oriented—are common. Almost every town has at least one totem pole, and some have a dozen or more. Tlingit artwork generally includes carvings, beadwork, sealskin moccasins, and silver jewelry. It *doesn't* include the *ulus,* Eskimo dolls, and other paraphernalia frequently sold in local tourist shops.

GETTING THERE

Visitors come to the Southeast by three primary means: cruise ship, jet, and ferry (the Alaska Marine Highway). Cruise ships are easily the most popular method—more than 800,000 people travel this way each year—but also the most expensive and the least personal. See the *On the Road* chapter for various cruise options, including the more expensive small-ship voyages that take you to less-traveled spots.

The second option, air, is more popular with independent travelers. **Alaska Airlines** (800/426-0333, www.alaskaair.com) has daily flights from Seattle, with service to Juneau, Ketchikan, Wrangell, Petersburg, Sitka, Gustavus, and other Alaskan cities. Floatplanes connect these towns to smaller places and provide access to even the most remote corners of the Inside Passage, such as Elfin Cove, Tokeen, and Port Alexander.

Alaska Marine Highway

Only three Southeast towns (Haines, Skagway, and Hyder) are connected by road to the rest of the continent. All the others, including Juneau, the state capital, are accessible only by boat or plane. This lack of roads—hopefully they will never be built—has led to an efficient public ferry system, the best in the Western Hemisphere and the longest in the world. Most ferries sail between Prince Rupert, B.C., and Skagway, stopping along the way in the major towns. There is also weekly service from Bellingham, Washington, all the way to Skagway, a three-day voyage. In the larger towns, summer service is almost daily, but in the smallest settlements, ferries may be up to two weeks apart. Get schedules and make reservations at 907/465-3941 or 800/642-0066, or on-line at www.ferryalaska.com. Since most travel in the Southeast centers around the ferry schedules, it's a good idea to check the ferry schedule before making any solid travel plans. Reservations for the summer can be made as early as December, and travelers taking a vehicle should book as early as possible to be sure of space.

Ketchikan

After the 36-hour ferry ride up from Bellingham, Ketchikan is many first-timers' introduction to Alaska. Along the way they've heard tales from sourdoughs (and those who claim to be), talked to Forest Service naturalists, and watched the logging towns and lush, green islands of British Columbia float past. As the ferry pulls into busy Tongass Narrows, an air of expectancy grows among the newcomers who are about to take their first steps in Alaska.

The state's fourth-largest city (pop. 8,000, plus another 6,000 in nearby areas), Ketchikan bills itself as "Alaska's First City," and even its zip code, 99901, seems to bear this out. Quite a few ferry passengers don't bother to stop here, instead hurrying on toward Juneau and points north. Because downtown is two miles away, they only have time for a superficial bus tour or a walk to the grocery store for provisions. But with its great scenery, fine local trails, the world's largest collection of totem poles, a bustling downtown, and the famous Misty Fiords nearby, Ketchikan certainly deserves a longer stay.

The Setting
Located 90 miles north of Prince Rupert, Ketchikan clings to a steep slope along Tongass Narrows, on Revillagigedo (ruh-VEE-ya-he-HAY-do) Island; locals shorten the name to "Revilla." Fortunately, it doesn't bear the one-time viceroy of Mexico's full name: Don Juan Vicente de Guemes Pacheco de Pedilla y Horcasitas, Count of Revilla Gigedo! Locals call the town "three miles long and three blocks wide." It forms a continuous strip of development along the waterfront from the ferry terminal to beyond Thomas Basin. Because of this, Tongass Av-

enue—the only through street—has long been one of the busiest in the entire state. A hilltop bypass opened a few years back, but traffic is still very heavy on Tongass Avenue.

Much of Ketchikan is built on fill, on pilings over the water, or on hillsides with steep, winding ramps for streets. Fishing boats jam the three boat harbors (there are almost as many boats as cars in Ketchikan), and the canneries and cold-storage plants run at full throttle during the summer. Floatplanes are constantly taking off from the narrows, cruise ships crowd the docks, and tourists explore the downtown shops and attractions.

Ketchikan is one of the rainiest places in Alaska, getting upward of 13 feet a year, or an average of half an inch per day. Luckily, May–August are the driest months, but expect to get wet nevertheless. Locals adapt with "Ketchikan sneakers" (red rubber boots) and Helley Hanson raingear; umbrellas are the mark of a tourist. Residents pride themselves on almost never canceling baseball games, and enjoy weekend picnics at Ward Lake in a downpour. Weather predicting is easy in Ketchikan: If you can't see the top of Deer Mountain, it's raining; if you can, it's *going* to rain. For an only-in-Ketchikan sight, check out the Valley Park Grade School on Schoenbar Road. This unique school was built atop its own playground, creating an escape from the rain.

History
The name Ketchikan comes from *Kitcxan,* a Tlingit word meaning "where the eagles' wings are," a reference to the shape of a sandspit at the creek mouth. The sandspit was dredged in the 1930s to create Thomas Basin Boat Harbor. Rumor has it that several bodies were found then, and sus-

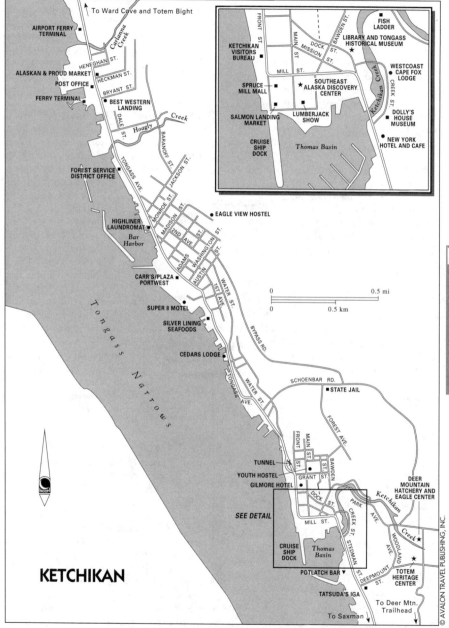

To Ward Cove and Totem Bight

AIRPORT FERRY TERMINAL

Carlanna Creek

HENEGHAN ST.

ALASKAN & PROUD MARKET
HECKMAN ST.
POST OFFICE
BRYANT ST.
FERRY TERMINAL
BEST WESTERN LANDING

DALE ST.
Hoagly Creek

FOREST SERVICE DISTRICT OFFICE

TONGASS AVE.
BARANOFF ST.
JACKSON ST.

HIGHLINER LAUNDROMAT
Bar Harbor

MONROE ST.
MADISON ST.
2ND AVE.
WASHINGTON ST.
ADAMS ST.
AUSTIN ST.

EAGLE VIEW HOSTEL

CARR'S/PLAZA PORTWEST

WATER ST.
1ST AVE.

SUPER 8 MOTEL

SILVER LINING SEAFOODS

CEDARS LODGE

BYPASS RD.

Tongass Narrows

0   0.5 mi
0   0.5 km

TONGASS AVE.
WATER ST.

SCHOENBAR RD.
STATE JAIL

FOREST AVE.

MAIN ST.
FRONT ST.
BAWDEN ST.
GRANT ST.

TUNNEL
YOUTH HOSTEL
GILMORE HOTEL

DOCK ST.
PARK AVE.
Ketchikan Creek

DEER MOUNTAIN HATCHERY AND EAGLE CENTER

SEE DETAIL

MILL ST.
CREEK ST.
STEDMAN ST.
WOODLAND AVE.
DEEPMOUNT ST.
Creek

CRUISE SHIP DOCK
Thomas Basin

TOTEM HERITAGE CENTER

POTLATCH BAR ▼

TATSUDA'S IGA

To Deer Mtn. Trailhead

To Saxman

KETCHIKAN

MOON

Detail inset:

FRONT ST.
MAIN ST.
DOCK ST.
MISSION ST.
BAWDEN ST.

FISH LADDER

KETCHIKAN VISITORS BUREAU

LIBRARY AND TONGASS HISTORICAL MUSEUM

MILL ST.

WESTCOAST CAPE FOX LODGE

CREEK ST.
Ketchikan Creek

SPRUCE MILL MALL

SOUTHEAST ALASKA DISCOVERY CENTER

SALMON LANDING MARKET

LUMBERJACK SHOW

DOLLY'S HOUSE MUSEUM

CRUISE SHIP DOCK

Thomas Basin

NEW YORK HOTEL AND CAFE

SOUTHEAST ALASKA

picious fingers were pointed toward the denizens of nearby Creek Street, the local red-light district.

One of Southeast Alaska's youngest major towns, Ketchikan began when the first of many salmon canneries at the mouth of Ketchikan Creek opened in 1885. By the 1930s it had become the "Salmon Capital of the World" (13 canneries), and Alaska's largest town. Overfishing caused salmon populations to crash in the 1940s, and the fishing industry was supplanted in the 1950s by a new pulp mill that turned the town into a major logging center.

For several decades Ketchikan's pulp mill was the biggest employer in Southeast Alaska, processing spruce and hemlock for the production of rayon and cellophane. The pulp mill closed in 1997, just as Ketchikan's economy shifted full-bore into tourism.

The big story today for Ketchikan—as in Juneau and Skagway—is cruise ships. More than 650,000 cruise ship folks step onto the docks here annually, and you'll see four or five ships tied up along Tongass Narrows most summer days. The rough old downtown with its flophouses and bars has been transformed into a collection of jewelry stores (38 at last count!), restaurants, espresso stands, and curio shops. Crossing guards, horse-drawn wagon rides, amphibious tours, a pseudo-logging show, and thousands of befuddled cruise shippies add to what Edward Abbey labeled "industrial tourism." Sad, but it makes the cash registers ring. Fortunately, the ships often depart by early evening, allowing locals and overnight visitors to rediscover this fascinating town. The town fathers must be spinning in their graves!

Ketchikan is one of the rainiest places in Alaska, getting upward of 13 feet a year, or an average of half an inch per day. Residents pride themselves on almost never canceling baseball games, and enjoy weekend picnics at Ward Lake in a downpour.

SIGHTS

Information Center
The **Ketchikan Visitors Bureau** (131 Front St., 907/225-6166 or 800/770-3300, www.visit-ketchikan.com) is right on the downtown dock.

It's open Monday–Friday 8 A.M.–5 P.M., Saturday–Sunday 7 A.M.–4 P.M. (longer when the cruise ships are docked) May–September; and Monday–Friday 8 A.M.–5 P.M. the rest of the year. Pick up their free map with a walking tour of local sites. The building also houses booths for local tour companies.

Southeast Alaska Discovery Center
A great place to start your exploration of Ketchikan is the Southeast Alaska Discovery Center (50 Main St., 907/228-6220, www.fs.fed.us). Operated by the U.S. Forest Service, this is one of four interagency public-land information centers in Alaska. It's filled with impressive exhibits—including a full-scale rainforest—that offer an educational portrait of the land and people of the Southeast. The 13-minute multimedia show "Mystical Southeast Alaska" is a must-see. The staff will help you with information on the outdoors, and the big gift shop features books, trail guides, and maps. The center is open daily 8:30 A.M.–5 P.M. May–September, and Tuesday–Saturday 10 A.M.–4:30 P.M. the rest of the year. Entrance to the exhibits and audiovisual show costs $5 (free for children under six, and for everyone in winter).

Logging Show
Located on Mill Street next to the cruise ship dock, the **Spruce Mill Complex** is the shopping center for downtown Ketchikan, with retail stores, souvenir shops, and restaurants. Ketchikan's old spruce mill stood on this site for many years, so it is perhaps fitting to find that the latest attraction is **The Great Alaskan Lumberjack Show** (907/225-9050 or 888/320-9049, www.lumberjackshows.com), a cornball 90-minute exhibition of old-time logging skills. Featured events include ax throwing, bucksawing, springboard chopping, logrolling, and a speedy 50-foot tree climb. Covered grandstands protect the audience from the inevitable rain. Since the pulp mill closed in 1997, logging has

© DON PITCHER

Creek Street

seen hard times in the Southeast, so it's a bit ironic that once logging is on the skids a Disneyesque version arises to entertain the cruise ship crowds. Shows take place three times daily, rain or shine, May–September, and cost $31 for adults, $15 for kids.

Tongass Historical Museum

The small Tongass Historical Museum (629 Dock St., 907/225-5600, admission $2) shares the library building, and is open daily 8 A.M.–5 P.M. mid-May–September; and Wednesday–Friday 1–5 P.M., Saturday–Sunday 1–4 P.M. the rest of the year. The museum contains local historical items—including the skull of a brown bear known as "Old Groaner"—plus exhibits on Native culture and commercial fishing. Look around for the model of a clan house, the 200-year-old Chilkat blanket, the dance paddle inlaid with abalone shell, the bentwood boxes, and the amusing totem pole with President Truman's features.

Creek Street

Ketchikan's best-known and most-photographed section features wooden houses on pilings along Ketchikan Creek. A boardwalk connects the buildings and affords views of salmon and steelhead in the creek. Now a collection of tourist shops, Creek Street once housed the red-light district; during Prohibition it was the only place to buy booze. Jokesters call it "the only place where both salmon and men came up from the sea to spawn." By 1946 more than 30 "female boardinghouses" operated here. Prostitution on Creek Street was stopped in 1954, and the house of Dolly Arthur was eventually turned into the **Dolly's House Museum** (907/225-2279, open daily all summer, $4). Inside are antiques, liquor caches, and risqué photos. Born in 1888, Dolly moved to Ketchikan in 1919, and worked at the world's oldest profession for many decades. When she died in 1975, her obituary was featured in newspapers across the West. Dolly's is fun to tour with grandmothers who would never otherwise step foot in such a place, and the fascinating collection of memorabilia makes it well worth a visit.

A **funicular car** ($2; free if you hike up and ride down) connects Creek Street with WestCoast Cape Fox Lodge, where you'll discover impressive vistas over Ketchikan and Tongass Narrows.

Other Downtown Sights

Outside the library/museum is **Raven Stealing the Sun Totem,** and not far away stands the **Chief Johnson Pole** (an older version is inside the Totem Heritage Center). Tiny Whale Park occupies the intersection across from the Forest Service office and is home to the **Chief Kyan Totem,** raised in 1993 to replace an older version. The older one was reputed to reward those who touched it by bringing money within a day. It's worth a try on the new one, but don't head immediately to Las Vegas on the basis of this claim.

Check out some of Ketchikan's many long aerobic **stairways** up to hillside homes and outstanding vistas. The best ones start from the tunnel at Front and Grant streets, and from the intersection of Main and Pine streets. If you have a bike (or better yet, a skateboard), you may want to test your mettle on Schoenbar Road, the route blasted out of a steep hillside behind town. By the way, the Front Street **tunnel** is said to be the only one in the world that you can drive through, around, and over! Or so claims the *Guinness Book of World Records.*

Meet Iditarod musher Ray Redington Jr. at **Redington's Mush Alaska** (619 Mission St., 907/225-6874, www.teamredington.com), where his family has exhibits on dog mushing, a video on the race (established by his late grandfather Joe Redington), and at least one of his dogs with cute puppies.

Get to picturesque **Thomas Basin Boat Harbor** on the south end of town by turning right on Thomas Street, just beyond the Salvation Army building. While there, head to the Potlatch Bar for a game of pool or a beer with local fishermen.

Totem Heritage Center

One of the highlights of the Ketchikan area, the Totem Heritage Center (907/225-5900, www.city.ketchikan.ak.us), is a quarter-mile walk up Deermount Street. It's open daily 8 A.M.–5 P.M. May–September, and Monday–Friday 1–5 P.M. the rest of the year, admission $5, or free for children under 12. The center was established in 1976 to preserve a collection of 33 original totem poles and house posts retrieved from abandoned village sites. Unlike other totems in the area, these works

are not brightly painted copies or restorations, but were carved more than a century ago to record Tlingit and Haida events and legends. Guides answer your questions and put on a short video about the totem recovery program. Surrounding the building is a short trail with signs identifying local plants. Out front is the Fog-Woman pole, by noted carver Nathan Jackson.

Deer Mountain Hatchery and Eagle Center

This small hatchery along Ketchikan Creek is just across a footbridge from the Totem Heritage Center. Signboards illustrate the process of breeding and rearing king and coho salmon, and visitors can feed the young fish. The hatchery is run by the Ketchikan Indian Council (907/225-5158, www.kictribe.com, open daily 8 A.M.–4:30 P.M. May–Sept., $8), with educational tours and a video on the life cycle of salmon. A large enclosure houses two eagles with permanent injuries—you might even see them catching salmon. Combination tickets to the hatchery and totem center are $11.

King salmon arrive from the Pacific Ocean to spawn at the hatchery late in the summer; look for them in the creek. A **fish ladder** to help them get past the falls is visible from the Park Avenue bridge. If too many fish return to spawn, the state opens Ketchikan Creek to dipnet fishing by locals, creating an astounding scene. Thousands of pink (humpback, or "humpies") salmon also spawn in the creek each summer. Another good place to see spawning humpies is **Hoadly Creek,** a half-mile south of the ferry terminal.

Totem Bight State Historical Park

Totem Bight (8 miles northwest of ferry terminal, 907/247-8574, www.alaskastateparks.org, no charge) has 15 Haida and Tlingit totems and a realistic replica of a clan house, complete with a brightly painted facade and cedar-scented interior. Be sure to pick up the fine brochure describing the poles and their meanings. The totems, carved 1938–1941, are replicas of older poles. They are surrounded by a stand of young hemlock trees and a view across Tongass Narrows. Although hundreds of tour buses come here each summer,

TOTEM POLES

These largest of all wooden sculptures were carved in cedar by the Tlingit, Haida, Tsimshian, Kwakiutl, and Bella Bella peoples of the Pacific Northwest. Their history is not completely known, but early explorers found poles in villages throughout Southeast Alaska. Apparently, totem-pole carving reached its heyday in the late 19th century with the arrival of metal woodworking tools. The animals, birds, fish, and marine mammals on the poles were totems that represented a clan, and in combination, conveyed a message.

Totem poles were very expensive and time-consuming to produce; a clan's status could be determined in part by the size and elaborateness of its poles. In a society without written words to commemorate people or events, the poles served a variety of purposes. Some totem poles told a family's history, others told local legends, and still others served to ridicule an enemy or debtor. In addition, totems were used to commemorate the dead, with a special niche at the back to hold the ashes of a revered ancestor.

Totem poles were never associated with religion, yet early missionaries destroyed many, and as recently as 1922, the Canadian government outlawed the art in an attempt to make the Natives more submissive. Realizing that a rich heritage was being lost because of neglect, skilled Native carvers worked with the Civilian Conservation Corps during the 1930s to restore older totems and create new ones. Today, active carving and restoration programs are taking place in Saxman, Ketchikan, Sitka, and Haines. Other good places to find totems include the Southeast towns of Hydaburg, Klawock, Kasaan, Juneau, Wrangell, and Kake.

totem poles and clan house, Saxman

© DON PITCHER

no city buses reach Totem Bight, so you'll have to walk or hitch here unless you have wheels. Just south of Totem Bight are a number of floating houses (locally called "wanigans").

Saxman

This Native village (ironically named for a white schoolteacher) is a 2.5-mile walk, $1.50 city bus ride, or $10 taxi ride south of Ketchikan. Saxman (pop. 400) is crowded with the largest collection of standing totem poles in the world—more than two dozen. Most were brought from their original sites in the 1930s and restored by Native Civilian Conservation Corps (CCC) workers; others came from a second restoration project in 1982. The oddest pole is topped with a figure of Abraham Lincoln, and commemorates the settlement of a war begun by the U.S. revenue cutter *Lincoln*. Probably the most photographed is the Rock Oyster Pole, which tells the story of a man who drowned after his hand became caught in a large oyster.

Adjacent to the totem park is a **carving shed** (free admission) where you'll find local artisans completing totems, masks, and other pieces. You're welcome to drop in whenever a carver is at work, which is most weekdays in the summer. Alaska's best-known carver, Nathan Jackson, can often be found working here. Interested in having one carved? You'll pay at least $2,000 a linear foot.

Also in Saxman is a cedar **Beaver Clan House** open only for tours. These two-hour tours by

Cape Fox Tours (907/225-4846, www.capefox-tours.com, $35) include a visit to the carving shed, a video on Tlingit culture, and a performance by the Cape Fox Dancers. Get tickets at the Ketchikan Visitor's Center.

The **Saxman Village Store** (907/225-4421) sells a mix of wares, including some locally made totems, masks, carved pieces, and even a few of the famous Tlingit button blankets. Two blocks downhill is the **Saxman Arts Co-op** (907/225-4166), with historic photos and additional locally made works.

Tours

Tour buses meet most ferries and provide two-hour city tours for $25. If you're staying in town, head to the visitor bureau, where a number of tour operators have booths for the cruise ship crowd. Rates start at $15 for an hour-long tour. Also popular are two-hour waterfront cruises offered by **Alaska Cruises** (907/225-6044 or 800/228-1905, www.mistyfjord.net, $50 adults/$25 kids) and visits to Saxman village from **Cape Fox Tours** (907/225-4846, www.capefoxtours.com).

HIKING

The Ketchikan area is blessed with an abundance of hiking trails and remote wilderness cabins maintained by the U.S. Forest Service. If you arrive in Ketchikan unprepared for a cabin stay, **Alaskan Wilderness Outfitting** (907/225-8886, www.latitude56.com) rents outboard motors, coolers, stoves, and dishes (but not sleeping bags). It even has a "cabin outfit" set up with the supplies you'll need at a Forest Service cabin.

Deer Mountain

The best hike from Ketchikan is up to the 3,000-foot summit of Deer Mountain (6 miles round-trip). Begin by heading a half-mile uphill from Deermount and Fair streets. Take the first left—the road to Ketchikan Lakes, source of the city's drinking water—and then an immediate right to the trailhead. The trail climbs along an excellent but strenuous path through dense Sitka spruce and western hemlock forests. There's an in-

credible view in all directions from the top of Deer Mountain, but right into July you'll have to cross snowbanks to reach the summit. (Raingear works fine for sledding down again.)

Just before the final climb to the peak, a trail to the left leads around the north slope and on to tiny **Blue Lake** and **John Mountain** (3,238 feet). Entirely above the timberline, this portion can be hazardous for inexperienced hikers. Carry a map and compass since it's easy to become disoriented if the clouds drop down. Ambitious hikers can do a 12-mile trek over the top, ending at Beaver Falls powerhouse, at the end of South Tongass Highway. One **shelter cabin** ($25) is atop Deer Mountain, and a second one (free) is at Blue Lake (cabin reservations: 518/885-3639 or 877/444-6777, www.reserveusa.com). Get current trail and cabin info from the Discovery Center.

Ward Lake Area

Several good trails are near the Forest Service campground at Ward Lake, eight miles north of downtown via Revilla Road. The 1.3-mile **Ward Lake Nature Trail** is an easy loop with interpretive signs and good summertime fishing for steelhead and salmon. **Ward Creek Trail** starts across from the day-use area and follows the creek 2.5 miles to Last Chance Campground. It's built for wheelchairs, with a couple of short spur paths leading to platforms over this beautiful creek.

Perseverance Trail climbs two miles to Perseverance Lake following a "stairway-to-heaven" boardwalk, passing through several muskegs along the way. Beyond this, you can take the **Minerva Mountain Trail** all the way to Carlanna Lake. Contact the Forest Service for details on the latter since this is a newly built trail.

Settler's Cove State Park, 16 miles north of Ketchikan, has a one-mile trail through the rainforest, with a pretty waterfall and spawning pink salmon in mid-summer.

Nearby Cabins

The Naha River watershed, 20 miles north of Ketchikan, contains one of the finest trail and cabin systems in the Southeast. The river once supported astounding runs of sockeye salmon and is still a popular salmon, steelhead, and trout fishing area for locals. At one time the town of **Loring** (established 1888) at its mouth had the world's largest fish cannery and was the main point of entry into Alaska. Today, it's a tiny settlement of retirees and vacation homes. **Heckman Lake,** six miles upriver, supported the world's largest and most costly salmon hatchery at the turn of the century. The hatchery failed, however, and all that remains are the overgrown ruins.

The pleasant six-mile **Naha River Trail** begins at Naha Bay, follows the shore of Roosevelt Lagoon, then climbs gently up to Jordon and Heckman Lakes. At the mouth of Roosevelt Lagoon is an interesting salt chuck where the direction of water flow changes with the tides. Covered picnic tables are nearby. More picnic tables are two miles up the trail at a small waterfall—a good place to watch black bears catching salmon late in the summer. There's a Forest Service cabin on Jordan Lake and two cabins on Heckman Lake (one wheelchair accessible); all three have rowboats and cost $45. Reservations at 518/885-3639 or 877/444-6777, www.reserveusa.com. Access to the Naha area is by sea kayak, floatplane, or skiff. Contact Knudsen Cove Marina (907/225-8500 or 800/528-2486; www.knudsoncovemarina.com), for skiff rentals or dropoffs.

Lake Shelokum, 40 miles north of Ketchikan, has a free three-sided shelter near a hot springs. A two-mile trail stretches from the shelter to Bailey Bay, passing the scenic lake and an impressive waterfall. Other cabins well worth visiting include **Lake McDonald, Reflection Lake, Helm Creek,** and **Blind Pass.** Get details at the Discovery Center in Ketchikan.

ON THE WATER
Sea Kayaking and Canoeing
The Discovery Center has detailed information on sea kayaking in the waters near Ketchikan, including Misty Fiords and a circumnavigation of Revilla Island. Greg Thomas and Kim Kirby of **Southeast Sea Kayaks** (907/225-1258 or 800/287-1067, www.kayakketchikan.com) lead a variety of kayak trips, including a 2.5-hour paddle along Tongass Narrows for $76 and all-day trips for $160. Contact them about guided

trips to Misty Fiords, or kayak rentals and transportation to do it yourself.

Southeast Exposure (515 Water St., 907/225-8829, www.southeastexposure.com), is mainly for the cruise ship crowd, offering a 2.5-hour waterfront tour ($50), and a 4-hour trip to Tatoosh Islands (by bus, boat, and kayak) for $85. Multi-day trips to Misty Fiords and kayak rentals are also available.

Ketchikan Parks and Recreation Department (2721 7th Ave., 907/225-9579) rents canoes and sports equipment, as well as skis and snowshoes in the winter.

Fishing, Boating, and Diving
Many Ketchikan companies offer charter fishing trips in search of salmon or halibut; see the visitors bureau for a complete listing. Rent skiffs ($85/day) and fishing gear to head out on your own from **Knudsen Cove Marina** (13 miles north of town, 907/247-8500 or 800/528-2486). If you're just looking to try your luck with all the locals who fish from the Creek Street bridge, rent a pole a block away from the little stand across from the Federal Building. **Mountain Point,** 5.5 miles south of Ketchikan, is a good spot to try your luck at salmon fishing from the shore.

The **Ketchikan Yacht Club** (907/225-3262, www.ketchikanyachtclub.org) sponsors low-key races on Wednesdays at 5:30 P.M. in the summer, and the skippers are always looking for volunteer crew members. It's a fun way to sail with the locals for free.

Alaska Deep Six (5 miles north of town, 907/225-4667) leads dive charters in the area.

ACCOMMODATIONS
For an up-to-date listing of local lodging places (with Web links), browse over to the Ketchikan Visitors Bureau website, www.visit-ketchikan.com.

Hostels
The **Ketchikan Youth Hostel** (907/225-3319, open only June–Aug.), downtown in the basement of the Methodist church at Grant and Main, costs $12 for Hostelling International members or $15 for nonmembers. It's open

6 P.M.–9 A.M., and the doors are locked at 11 P.M. If your ferry gets in after that, call the hostel promptly upon arrival and they'll open for you. The hostel isn't fancy—we're talking cots or foam mattresses on the floor—but is friendly and clean, with kitchen facilities and showers. It's a great place to meet other travelers. There's a four-night maximum stay.

Ketchikan's other budget option is **Eagle View Hostel** (2305 5th Ave., 907/225-5461, www.eagleviewhostel.com, open April–Oct.). The name tells something about its location—five blocks up a steep hill above Plaza Mall, with two wraparound decks from which to take in the view across Tongass Narrows. There are separate dorms for men and women (sheets and blankets provided), plus a couple's room, commons area, kitchen, baths, and laundry, all for $25 per person. No curfew or lockout times, so you can sleep in, and late ferry arrivals are welcome ($6 taxi ride). Owner Dale Rogers can provide boat access to remote campsites.

Hotels and Motels

Built in the 1930s and now on the National Register of Historic Places, the centrally located **Gilmore Hotel** (326 Front St., 907/225-9423 or 800/275-9423, www.gilmorehotel.com), exudes an old-fashioned ambience, but has been updated with modern furnishings. Rates are reasonable: $80–110 d for cramped rooms, $120 d for larger rooms with two beds and a harbor view, or $137 d for the suite, including courtesy van service and a light breakfast. Rooms over the bar may get noisy at night.

New York Hotel (207 Stedman St., 907/225-0246 or 866/225-0246, www.thenewyorkhotel.com), is a cozy hotel that has been painstakingly restored to its Roaring '20s heyday. It's a great location—facing the harbor and just a few steps off Creek Street—and the downstairs cafe is one of the best in town. Free airport and ferry shuttles, too. Rooms in the historic main building are small but nicely furnished: $94 s or $104 d with private baths and queen beds. Also available are three luxury suites with covered waterside decks along Creek Street for $149 d. The latter units feature lofts with spiral stairs, full kitchens, and jetted tubs. Highly recommended, but book early for the suites.

Super 8 Motel (2151 Sea Level Dr., 907/225-9088 or 800/800-8000, www.super8.com, $100–110 d) has typical chain lodging, including a courtesy van to the ferry or airport.

The Narrows Inn (907/247-2600 or 888/686-2600, www.narrowsinn.com, $125–135 d, including shuttle to town) sits four miles north of Ketchikan along Tongass Narrows. Rooms are small, but modern, bright, and nicely appointed. Waterside rooms (ask for room 1209) have small balconies where you can watch the parade of boats and planes, and three larger suites are available. A steak and seafood restaurant is also on the premises.

Cedars Lodge (1471 Tongass Ave., 907/225-1900 or 800/813-4363, www.cedarslodge.com, $110 s or d for standard rooms, up to $215 d for waterfront suites) has comfortable accommodations, some of which contain full kitchens and hot tubs. Most guests come here as part of a multinight fishing package. Open mid-May–September; courtesy van provided.

Best Western Landing (3434 Tongass Ave., 907/225-5166 or 800/428-8304, www.bestwestern.com) sits right across from the ferry terminal. The rooms are up-to-date and include microwaves and fridges; $138–160 d in standard rooms, $172 d in suites, or $210 for a two-bedroom apartment with full kitchen. Also on the premises are two restaurants and a fitness center to work off the weight you gain in the restaurants. A courtesy van is provided.

At the top end of Ketchikan's lodging spectrum is the elaborate **WestCoast Cape Fox Lodge** (800 Venetia Way, 907/225-8001 or 866/225-8001, www.westcoasthotels.com, $169–179 d, $250 d for a two-room suite). This large hilltop hotel looks over Tongass Narrows, and has spacious, modern rooms. A funicular car takes guests to the Cape Fox from Creek Street.

Fishing Lodges

Many fishing lodges can be found in the Ketchikan area, particularly on nearby Prince of Wales Island; see www.visit-ketchikan.com for a complete listing. **George Inlet Lodge** (907/225-

6077 or 888/550-6077, www.georgeinlet-lodge.com), 12 miles south of Ketchikan, was built in the 1940s as a bunkhouse for cannery workers at Hidden Inlet Cannery. After it closed in 1968, the building was barged to this site and transformed into a 10-room fishing lodge. Lodging and food are $1,080 d for three nights and two days, or $2,570 d for a fully guided three-night package.

Located 17 miles north of Ketchikan, **Salmon Falls Resort** (907/225-2752 or 800/247-9059, www.salmonfallsresort.net, open mid-May–mid-Sept.), has modern rooms and a dramatic shoreside setting. Fishing packages start at $950 per person for three nights, or $1,350 with a guide.

Yes Bay Lodge (907/225-7906 or 800/999-0784, www.yesbay.com) is a remote fishing lodge near Lake McDonald on the Cleveland Peninsula north of Ketchikan. The setting is wonderful, and the fishing is great; a famous steelhead stream is adjacent. Rates start at $5,500 d for a four-night all-inclusive package.

Also check out **Naha Bay Outdoor Adventures** (907/247-4453, www.nahabayoutdooradventures.com), a 20-minute boat ride from Knudson Cove Marina. Good fishing, hiking, sea kayaking, and more, starting at $1,200 d for three nights.

B&Bs and Vacation Rentals

You'll find links to Ketchikan B&Bs at www.visit-ketchikan.com, or let the reservation agency experts help you find a place: Contact **Ketchikan Reservation Service** (907/247-5337 or 800/987-5337, www.ketchikan-lodging.com) or **Alaska Travelers Accommodations** (907/247-7117 or 800/928-3308, www.alaskatravelers.com).

The Classic Stop B&B (907/225-3607), has a simple but comfortable private apartment for $98 d, including a make-it-yourself breakfast.

Captain's Quarters B&B (325 Lund St., 907/225-4912, www.ptialaska.net/~captbnb), has three rooms with private baths and harbor views for $80–85 d with continental breakfast; no kids.

Blueberry Hill B&B (500 Front St., 907/247-2583 or 877/449-2583, www.blueberry-hillbb.com), is a historic hillside home in a prime location atop the tunnel. Four rooms all have private baths and cost $110–145 d, including a full breakfast.

Lundberg's South Shore Inn (907/225-0909 or 888/732-0220, $125 d with continental breakfast), has a private two-bedroom apartment with kitchenette, woodstove, large deck, and private beach. The very comfortable home is seven miles southeast of town near Mountain Point.

Located four miles south of town, and right on the water, **Anchor Inn by the Sea** (907/247-7117 or 800/928-3308, www.alaskatravelers.com/anchor.htm), is a fine option for families, with a guest room ($85 d), plus three large suites ($115–125 d) with kitchenettes. All of these feature private baths and entrances.

Madame's Manor (324 Cedar St., 907/247-2774 or 877/531-8159, ext. 2484, www.madamesmanor.com) is a hilltop Victorian-style B&B with three lavishly decorated suites ($149–175 d with gourmet breakfast) and a separate apartment with a full kitchen ($95 d; three-night minimum). The deck overlooks Tongass Narrows, and is a wonderful place to sip your coffee in the morning. Highly recommended.

Nantucket House (907/247-3731, www.nantuckethousebb.com, $185 d) is a charming historic home (not a B&B) close to downtown, with a luxurious private suite, large deck, and full kitchen. The unit rents is perfect for honeymooners. Two other recommended vacation rentals are **Waypoint Inn at Herring Bay** (907/225-8605, www.waypointinn.com) and **Alaska's Hidden Cove Vacation Rentals** (907/225-7934 or 866/822-2683, www.akhiddencove.com).

Camping

There are no campsites in town, but the Forest Service operates two summer-only campgrounds ($10) in the scenic Ward Lake area—a world away from the craziness of downtown Ketchikan when the cruise ships are in port. Get there by heading five miles north from the ferry terminal and turning right up Revilla Road. Ward Cove is a good place to see eagles, so stop for a look before heading to the lake. The most popular camping area is scenic **Signal Creek Campground,** along Ward Lake. Another mile and a half north is **Last Chance Campground.** Both campgrounds have running water, and can be reserved ($9 extra) at 518/885-3639 or 877/444-6777, www.reserveusa.com.

Settler's Cove State Park, 16 miles north of the ferry, charges $10 for campsites in the trees. The beach is a popular spot for summer picnics, and a trail takes you through the rainforest to a small waterfall.

Clover Pass Resort (907/247-2234 or 800/410-2234, www.cloverpassresort.com), 15 miles north of Ketchikan, has RV hookups for $28. Open mid-April–September.

FOOD

Breakfast and Lunch

New York Hotel Cafe (207 Stedman St., 907/225-0246), is the first place I'd head for a meal. Great atmosphere (historic building with a classic back bar and tall windows facing the harbor) and excellent food—including a smoked salmon scramble for breakfast and chowder, burgers, or burritos for lunch. Dinners are available on Friday and Saturday evenings, and feature fresh seafood and pasta for $12–22. Decadent desserts too.

Dockside Diner (1287 Tongass Ave., 907/247-7787), is a hometown place with burgers, halibut and chips, hot beef sandwiches, liver and onions, and fried chicken, plus a big selection of pies. Breakfast is available all day, and the covered deck provides a view of busy Tongass Narrows.

Located right across from the ferry terminal, **The Landing Restaurant** (3434 Tongass Ave., 907/225-5166), fills with locals and travelers in search of a dependably filling breakfast. Jeremiah's Fine Food and Spirits is upstairs.

On Sundays, the **VFW Hall** (311 Tongass, 9 A.M.–2 P.M.), a half mile south of the ferry, serves up cheap and filling all-American breakfasts.

Dinner

Upstairs in the Spruce Mill Mall, **Steamers** (907/225-9420, closed Jan.–March, dinners $15–27) is a large and noisy tourist restaurant where you'll find fresh seafood, pasta, and steaks, along with two-dozen brews on draft. The featured attraction is steamer clams (hence the name), but all the seafood is good, and the serv-

ings are ample. Try the crab-stuffed oysters, chicken pasta, or baby back ribs. Make reservations for a window seat facing Tongass Narrows, though the view is usually blocked by one of those honking cruise ships.

Linnie's Red Anchor Cafe & Deli (1935 Tongass Ave., 907/247-5287) occupies a large building near Plaza Mall, and has cheap breakfasts, great chowders, and best-in-town, two-fisted sandwiches.

Head upstairs inside the Best Western Landing across from the ferry terminal to **Jeremiah's Fine Food and Spirits** (3434 Tongass Ave., 907/225-5166), a relaxing place for lunch and dinner. The Friday lunch buffet is also worth a try.

Ocean View Restaurant (1831 Tongass Ave., 907/225-7566, dinner entrées $9–16) is a favorite of locals, and with good reason. The food is varied and nicely prepared, the atmosphere is classy, prices are reasonable, and delivery is free. The menu encompasses pasta (including halibut fettuccine), steaks, seafood, burgers, and best-in-town pizzas, but Mexican dishes are the real attraction, and all meals come with chips and a dose of Mexican tunes over the speakers.

Good Fortune Chinese Restaurant (907/225-1818) is near the library on the north end of Creek Street. It's authentically Chinese, but also reasonable, including a $6 lunch of sweet and sour pork or spicy Kung Pao chicken. A la carte dinners are $12–14. Service is quick and friendly and the setting is unpretentious.

On's Thai House (127 Stedman St., 907/225-8424) overlooks Creek Street, and claims authentic Thai cuisine. I've had far better, but locals like it.

The best local chicken sandwiches, salmon burgers, and hamburgers can be found at the tiny **Burger Queen** (907/225-6060) just north of the Front Street tunnel. **McDonald's** is in the Plaza Mall .75 miles south of the ferry, and the local **Subway** (415 Dock St.) is downtown.

Fine Dining

With its 1920s-style decor, **Annabelle's Keg and Chowder House** (326 Front St., 907/225-6009) wins the "best atmosphere" prize among Ketchikan restaurants. The menu features seafood (including four kinds of chowders), salads, and sandwiches, along with prime rib on weekends. There are daily specials, plus cocktails and espresso. Located in the historic Gilmore Hotel, this is a good place to impress a friend. A summer-only ice cream parlor is also here, and the lounge has a jukebox.

Héen Kahídi Restaurant and Lounge (800 Venetia Way, 907/225-8001, entrées $20), inside Cape Fox Lodge, serves superb seafood and steak dinners in a romantic setting. Reserve ahead to get a window seat for an evening sunset over town.

Located 17 miles north of Ketchikan, **Salmon Falls Resort** (907/225-2752 or 800/247-9059, www.salmonfallsresort.net, dinners May–Sept. only) is a large octagonal restaurant specializing in steaks and seafood, with blackened halibut, king crab, steaks, lobster, and other filling fare for $20–35. The building vaults 40 feet overhead, with an impressive waterfall and dramatic views across Clover Passage.

Clover Pass Resort (907/247-2234 or 800/410-2234, entrées $17–30), 14 miles north of town, is another out-of-the-way place with white-linen dining along the water. The menu includes all the surf and turf standards, along with nightly specials.

The New York Hotel also serves weekend dinners, and has folk music most Saturday nights.

Coffee and Sweets

If you just want to relax and enjoy looking over busy Tongass Narrows, stop by **Coffee Connections** (521 Water St., 907/247-0521), for a cup of espresso or a pastry. **KetchiCandies** (315 Mission St., 907/225-0900 or 800/225-0970, www.ketchicandies.com) makes hand-dipped chocolates, and will ship your purchases.

Groceries and Seafood

The closest grocery store to the ferry (.25 miles north) is **Alaskan & Proud Market** (907/225-1279 or 800/770-8258, daily until 11 P.M.). **Carrs**, .75 miles south of the ferry, has a salad bar and the best selection of groceries in town. **Tatsuda's IGA** (633 Stedman, 907/225-4125) is on the south end of town.

Silver Lining Seafoods (1705 S. Tongass, 907/225-9865 or 800/478-9865, www.silver-liningseafoods.com) has quality local seafood—both fresh and smoked—and will also smoke, freeze, or can fish that you bring in.

Salmon Etc. (907/225-6008 or 800/354-7256 outside Alaska, www.salmonetc.com), has two locations: on Creek Street, and downtown at 322 Mission Street. It sells high-quality canned, smoked, or frozen salmon, halibut, crab, clams, and other sea critters.

ENTERTAINMENT AND EVENTS

A local theater group, First City Players (1716 Totem Way, 907/225-4792), puts on the light-hearted melodrama, ***Fish Pirate's Daughter*** Saturday evenings in July. The show has been going on since 1966, and tickets are only $13, or $30 with dinner. The Players produce more serious stuff in the winter months. Catch a movie downtown at the **Coliseum Twin Theater** (405 Mission St., 907/225-2294).

Ketchikan's live music scene changes each year, but something is always happening downtown; just follow your ears. **First City Saloon** (830 Water St., 907/225-1494) tends to bring in the better bands, and is the main dance spot in town. More rock at the **Arctic Bar** (907/225-4709), near the Front St. tunnel, where a pleasant patio hangs over Tongass Narrows. Surprise your friends back home with one of its risqué baseball caps. If Dave Rubin and his rockin' Potlatch Band are playing at the **Potlatch Bar** (907/225-4855), next to Thomas Basin, make tracks in that direction. You won't regret it. The **Alaska Bar** (114 Front St., 907/225-4600) has a motto worth putting into practice: "Celebrating the repeal of Prohibition every day!" The finest bar views are from **Cape Fox Lodge,** overlooking town above Creek Street. It's a nice place to get romantic.

Ketchikan's fun **July Fourth** celebration includes the usual parade and fireworks, plus a **Timber Carnival** with ax throwing, pole climbing, and a variety of chainsaw contests, ending with a dramatic pole-felling event. In the first week of August, check out the **Blueberry Arts Festival,** complete with slug races, pie-eating contests, a fun run, arts and crafts exhibitions, and folk music. Ketchikan also has king and silver salmon

SOUTHEAST ALASKA

fishing derbies and a halibut derby each summer. The **Winter Arts Faire** on the weekend after Thanksgiving is a good time to buy local arts and crafts. **Festival of the North** arrives in February, complete with music, art shows (including edible art!), and various workshops for the entire month.

INFORMATION AND SERVICES

The two primary information centers are the Ketchikan Visitors Bureau and the Southeast Alaska Discovery Center, described in *Sights*. Forest Service offices for **Ketchikan and Misty Fiords** ranger districts (3031 Tongass Ave., 907/225-2148) are a half-mile south of the ferry terminal.

Showers are available at **Highliner Laundromat** (2703 Tongass Ave.) and **The Mat** (989 Stedman St.). A better option is to head up Madison Street to the **high school swimming pool** (2610 4th Ave., 907/225-2010), where a swim, sauna, and shower cost $5.

Get fast cash from ATMs at First Bank and Wells Fargo downtown, and at the Carrs and A&P grocery stores.

Check your email at **Surf City** (907/225-3260) inside Sockeye Sams next to the tunnel. Only locals can use the computer terminals at the library for Internet access.

The main post office is next to the ferry terminal on the north end of town, and a branch post office is downtown in the Great Alaskan Clothing Company (422 Mission St.).

Ketchikan General Hospital (3100 Tongass Ave., 907/225-5171) is the largest in southern Southeast Alaska. **Ketchikan Medical Clinic** (3612 Tongass Ave., 907/225-5144) is out near the ferry terminal.

Shopping

The Spruce Mill Mall is the primary focal point for shopping in downtown Ketchikan. Cruise ships dock directly in front, disgorging their passengers to feed the hungry cash registers of such places as Caribbean Gems or Tanzanite International. Needless to say, locals would never step foot in these jewelry stores owned and staffed by Outsiders cashing in on the tourists. Fortunately, many of the other downtown shops—including a

number of places in Salmon Landing Marketplace—are locally owned and worth a visit.

Locals do much of their shopping at **Plaza Mall,** centering around Carrs and McDonald's, and the **Wal-Mart** (907/247-2156) five miles north of town. There's even a free summertime shuttle from downtown to Wal-Mart; it's mainly for cruise ship workers, but is also popular with cheapskate travelers.

Books

Ketchikan's too-small **public library** (629 Dock St., 907/225-3331, www.firstcitylibraries.org), is open daily and houses an excellent collection of Alaskana. An afternoon of reading at the tables along the big windows overlooking Ketchikan Creek is a pleasant alternative to soaking in the rain. Unfortunately, this may be the only Alaskan library where the computer terminals are off-limits to nonresidents.

A book-lover's bookstore, **Parnassus Bookstore** (907/225-7690) is upstairs above Soho Coho on Creek Street. Sit down and talk with the friendly owner, Lillian Ference, about the latest Ketchikan news. Parnassus stocks an especially impressive collection of women's books. The other bookstore in town is **Waldenbooks** (907/225-8120) in Plaza Mall.

Arts and Crafts

A surprisingly creative town, Ketchikan is home to a number of fine artists. The center of Ketchikan's art action is the historic 5-Star building on Creek Street, where artist Ray Troll holds down the fort at **Soho Coho** (907/225-5954 or 800/888-4070, www.trollart.com), with his weird and fishy T-shirts and prints. Other artists—including the wonderfully prolific Evon Zerbetz—also display their works here. The same building houses **Alaska Eagle Arts** (907/225-8365), with Tlingit designs and jewelry.

Herring Cove Originals Studio and Gallery (229 Stedman St., 907/247-2693, www.sharronhuffman.com), has fish-print T-shirts and distinctive linocuts and block prints. Other downtown galleries worth a visit include **Exploration Gallery** (633 Mission St., 907/225-4278, www.explorationgallery.com), **The Blue Heron**

(123 Stedman St., 907/225-1982, www.blue-heronalaska.com), **Eagle Spirit Gallery** (310 Mission St., 907/225-6626 or 866/867-0976, www.eaglespiritalaska.com), **Crazy Wolf Studio** (607 Mission St., 907/225-9653 or 888/331-9653, www.crazywolfstudio.com), and **Dockside Gallery** (907/225-2858, www.alaskanart.net) inside Salmon Landing.

For additional artwork, visit the gallery of the **Ketchikan Area Arts & Humanities Council** (716 Totem Way, 907/225-2211, www.ketchikanarts.org) near Creek Street. Exhibits change monthly, and they produce the *Ketchikan Arts Guide* with brief bios of local artists, plus descriptions of galleries, museums, and other places to find creative works.

TRANSPORTATION

Ferry
Ketchikan's ferry terminal (907/225-6182, or 907/225-6181 for recorded arrival and departure times) is two miles northwest of downtown. It's open Monday–Friday 9 A.M.–4:30 P.M., and when ships are in port. During the summer, **Alaska Marine Highway** ferries (907/465-3941 or 800/642-0066, www.ferryalaska.com) provide almost-daily runs to Prince Rupert, Hollis, Metlakatla, Wrangell, and points north. Ferry service to Bellingham is once a week.

The **Inter-Island Ferry Authority** (907/826-4848 or 866/308-4848, www.interislandferry.com) has daily service from here to Hollis on Prince of Whales Island.

Air
Ketchikan Airport is on Gravina Island, directly across Tongass Narrows from the ferry terminal. The **airport ferry** (907/225-6800, $4 round-trip) operates every half-hour daily 6:15 A.M.–9:30 P.M. **Airporter Shuttle** (907/225-5429) has service into town from the airport for an exorbitant $18 each way. The price does, however, include the ferry fare, and they meet all jets. If you're heading downtown and don't have a rental car, a better option is the **Tongass Water Taxi** (907/209-8294); Rich Schuerger takes you directly from the airport

to Thomas Basin in the heart of Ketchikan for $15 s or $19 d. Recommended.

Alaska Airlines (800/426-0333, www.alaskaair.com) has flights from Ketchikan to Juneau, Petersburg, Sitka, Wrangell, and other cities in Alaska and the Lower 48.

Two air taxi operators, **ProMech Air** (907/225-3845 or 800/860-3845, www.promechair.com) and **Pacific Airways** (907/225-3500 or 877/360-3500, www.flypacificairways.com), have daily service from Ketchikan to Prince of Wales Island and Metlakatla. **L.A.B. Flying Service** (907/772-4300 or 800/426-0543, www.labflying.com) flies from Ketchikan airport to Klawock. **Taquan Air** (907/225-8800 or 800/770-8800, www.taquanair.com) has scheduled flights to Hyder and Hydaburg.

ProMech, Pacific Airways, and Taquan also do flightseeing trips around Ketchikan. Other air taxi operators that offering flightseeing include **Carlin Air** (907/225-3036 or 888/594-3036, www.carlinair.com), **Family Air Tours** (907/247-1305 or 800/380-1305, www.familyairtours.com), **Island Wings Air Service** (907/225-2444 or 888/854-2444, www.islandwings.com), **Misty Fjords Air and Outfitting** (1285 Tongass Ave., 907/225-5155, www.mistyfjordsair.com), and **Southeast Aviation** (907/225-2900 or 888/359-6478, www.southeastaviation.com). Especially popular is a two-hour flightseeing trip to Misty Fiords National Monument that includes a landing on a lake for $200. All of these companies also do charters to nearby Forest Service cabins.

Car and Bike Rentals
Because Ketchikan's sights are so spread out, renting a car is a good idea. Rental rates (with unlimited miles) start around $40 from **Southeast Auto Rental** (7480 N. Tongass Ave., 907/225-8778 or 800/770-8778), **Alaska Car Rental** (2828 N. Tongass Ave., 907/225-5000 or 800/478-0007, www.akcarrental.com), and **Budget** (4950 N. Tongass Ave., 907/225-6004 or 800/478-2438, www.budget.com). Budget and Alaska Car Rental have cars both at the airport and on the Ketchikan side of Tongass Narrows; it's a $10 ferry ride each way to transport

the vehicles. Rent mountain bikes from **Southeast Exposure** (515 Water St., 907/225-8829, www.southeastexposure.com).

Getting Around
The **city bus** (907/225-6800, $1.50 each direction) runs throughout Ketchikan (including from the ferry terminal to town) every 15 minutes Monday–Saturday 5:15 A.M.–9:45 P.M. and hourly on Sundays 8:45 A.M.–3:45 P.M. Schedules are available at the visitor bureau. In town, catch it at the library or near the tunnel at Front and Grant streets.

The local taxi companies are **Alaska Cab Co.** (907/225-2133), **Sourdough Cab** (907/225-5544), and **Yellow Taxi** (907/225-5555). They charge about $10 from the ferry to downtown, $10 from downtown to Saxman, or $50/hour for tours (up to six people).

Vicinity of Ketchikan

MISTY FIORDS NATIONAL MONUMENT

The 2.2-million-acre Misty Fiords National Monument is the largest national forest wilderness in the United States, covering the east side of Revillagigedo Island, the adjacent mainland all the way to the Canadian border, and the long narrow Behm Canal that separates island and mainland. Misty contains a diversity of gorgeous scenery—glaciers, rainforests, narrow fjords, and rugged mountains—but is best known for the spectacular cliffs that rise as much as 3,000 feet from the ocean. Almost unknown until its establishment in 1978, Misty Fiords is today one of the highlights of an Alaskan trip for many visitors. Be forewarned, however, it's an expensive highlight.

The name "Misty" comes from the wet and cloudy conditions that predominate throughout the summer. Rainfall averages almost 160 inches per year, so be sure to bring rubber boots and raingear. Because of all this rain the land exhibits a verdant beauty, even when clouds drape the mountain slopes.

© DON PITCHER

Nooya Lake, Misty Fiords National Monument

Flightseeing and Boat Tours
On any given summer day, flightseeing planes constantly take off from Tongass Narrows for trips over the monument. Two-hour flightseeing trips cost $200 (including a water landing) and are offered by all the local air taxis.

Another excellent way to see Misty is by boat. **Alaska Cruises** (220 Front St., 907/225-6044 or 800/228-1905, www.mistyfjord.net) runs catamaran cruises into Misty Fiords in the summer. Along the way, the boats pass towering cliffs, peaceful coves, and dramatic New Eddystone Rock, which juts straight out of the water from a tiny island in the midst of Behm Canal. The tours turn around in Rudyerd Bay before returning to Ketchikan. Rates are $150 ($125 kids) for a 6-hour cruise or $240 ($200 kids) for a faster 3.5-hour trip—most folks choose this version—that in-

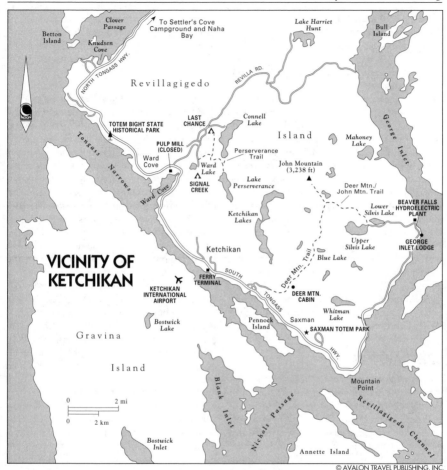

VICINITY OF KETCHIKAN

Betton Island
Clover Passage
Knudsen Cove
To Settler's Cove Campground and Naha Bay
Lake Harriet Hunt
Bull Island

NORTH TONGASS HWY.
Revillagigedo
REVILLA RD.

George Inlet

TOTEM BIGHT STATE HISTORICAL PARK
LAST CHANCE
Connell Lake
Island
Mahoney Lake
Tongass Narrows
PULP MILL (CLOSED)
Ward Cove
Ward Lake
Perserverance Trail
John Mountain (3,238 ft)
SIGNAL CREEK
Lake Perserverance
Deer Mtn./ John Mtn. Trail
BEAVER FALLS HYDROELECTRIC PLANT
Lower Silvis Lake
Ward Cove
Ketchikan Lakes
Upper Silvis Lake
GEORGE INLET LODGE
Ketchikan
Deer Mtn. Trail
Blue Lake
FERRY TERMINAL
SOUTH
KETCHIKAN INTERNATIONAL AIRPORT
TONGASS
DEER MTN. CABIN
Whitman Lake
Bostwick Lake
Pennock Island
Saxman
SAXMAN TOTEM PARK
Gravina
HWY.
Island
Mountain Point
0   2 mi
0   2 km
Blank Inlet
Nichols Passage
Revillagigedo Channel
Bostwick Inlet
Annette Island

© AVALON TRAVEL PUBLISHING, INC.

cludes a flightseeing return to Ketchikan (or vice versa). A delicious and filling lunch is included, and the on-board naturalist is exceptionally knowledgeable. When the weather cooperates, this is one of the best side trips you can take anywhere in Alaska.

Sea Kayaking Tours

The best way to see Misty Fiords is from a kayak. You can paddle there from Ketchikan, but only if you're experienced and adequately prepared. For $225 round-trip, Alaska Cruises does drop-offs and pickups at the head of Rudyerd Bay.

Two Ketchikan companies offer extended sea kayaking trips in Misty Fiords: **Southeast Sea Kayaks** (907-225-1258 or 800/287-1067, www.kayakketchikan.com) and **Southeast Exposure** (907/225-8829, www.southeastexposure.com). Expect to pay around $900 for a four-day trip. Both companies also rent kayaks and set up transportation into Misty for those who prefer to paddle independently. Kayakers should be warned that flightseeing planes and cruise ships may impact your wilderness experience in Rudyerd Bay, but other areas get far less use.

Hiking and Cabins

Misty Fiords National Monument has 14 recreation cabins (reservations 518/885-3639 or 877/444-6777, www.reserveusa.com, $35). Those near magnificent **Rudyerd Bay** are very popular, and reservations must be made months in advance. There are also 10 trails that take you from saltwater to scenic lakes, most with cabins or free three-sided shelters. Two of the best trails lead up to shelters at Punchbowl and Nooya Lakes. The three-quarter-mile **Punchbowl Lake Trail** switchbacks up from Rudyerd Bay, passing spectacular Punchbowl Creek Waterfall on the way. Punchbowl is one of the finest short hikes in Southeast Alaska, and there's a canoe and skiff at the lake. Both brown and black bears may be encountered on any of these trails, so be certain to make plenty of noise and to hang all food.

Before heading out on any overnight trips into Misty, talk with staff at the District Office (1817 Tongass, 907/225-2148). They can provide information on trail conditions, campsites, and what to expect. Be sure to request a copy of their Misty Fiords map.

METLAKATLA

Twelve miles southwest of Ketchikan on the western shore of Annette Island is the community of Metlakatla (pop. 1,500). Metlakatla (it means "saltwater channel" in Tsimshian) is Alaska's only Indian reservation, a status that was reaffirmed in 1971 when its residents refused to join other Native groups under the Alaska Native Claims Settlement Act. It is the only predominantly Tsimshian settlement in Alaska and the only place in the United States where fish traps are still legal. The quiet, conservative town has a strong religious heritage and the air of a pioneer village. Large frame houses occupy big corner lots, while vacant lots yield abundant berry crops. There seems to be a church on every corner—eight in all, none of them Catholic. Metlakatla boasts a flourishing cannery, cold-storage facility, fish hatchery, rock quarry, and a sawmill. Most of Annette Island is wooded, mountainous terrain reaching up to 3,500 feet, but the town of Metlakatla spreads out across a large, relatively flat portion of the island that contains many muskegs and lakes. Although Metlakatla is only a dozen miles away from Ketchikan, it gets 118 inches of precipitation per year, 44 inches less than Ketchikan.

History

In 1887, a Tsimshian Indian group left Canada in search of religious freedom in Alaska. They discovered an abandoned Tlingit settlement on Annette Island offering a sheltered bay, gently sloping beaches, and a beautiful nearby waterfall. Under the direction of Anglican missionary William Duncan (who established a similar community in Metlakatla, Canada), 823 Tsimshian followers began clearing a town site. The converts took new Christian names, dressed in suits, and abandoned much of their cultural heritage. At Metlakatla, Alaska, the settlers established a sawmill to produce lumber for the construction of houses and the first cannery.

The most ambitious building erected was a 1,000-seat church, "The Westminster Abbey of Alaska." It burned in 1948 but was replaced by a replica six years later. In 1891, the U.S. Congress granted the Tsimshians the entire 86,000-acre island as a reservation, a right they jealously guard to this day. Duncan maintained his hold over most aspects of life here until 1913 when a government school opened. (Duncan's paternalism extended in other directions, too: Rumors persist that the bachelor fathered many Metlakatla children.) He opposed the school, preferring that education remain in the hands of his church. The ensuing conflict led to intervention by the U.S. Department of the Interior in 1915, which seized the sawmill, cannery, and other facilities that had been under his personal control. Duncan died three years later, but his memory is still revered by many, and his influence can still be seen in the healthy little Indian settlement of today. For a fascinating account of Father Duncan and the two Metlakatlas, read Peter Murray's *The Devil and Mr. Duncan* (Sono Nis Press, Victoria, B.C.).

During World War II, the U.S. Army constructed a major military base seven miles from Metlakatla on Annette Island. The base included observation towers (to search for Japanese subs), a large airfield, hangars, communications towers, shore batteries, and housing for 10,000 men. At the time the airport was built, it was the most expensive one ever constructed by the government—everything kept sinking out of sight into the muskeg. Until construction of an airport on Gravina Island in 1973, this airfield was used for jet service to Ketchikan, forcing passengers to land on Annette and fly by floatplane to Ketchikan. With the area's notorious weather, delays were common; many times it took longer to get the last dozen miles to Ketchikan than the 600 miles from Seattle to Annette Island. Today, the Air Force is slowly constructing a 14-mile road across the northern end of the island to what will eventually become a new dock for the ferry to Ketchikan.

Sights

Father Duncan's Cottage (907/886-8687)—where the missionary lived from 1894 until his death in 1918—is open as a museum when cruise ships are in port or by appointment. The old photographs of Metlakatla and the fascinating assortment of personal items owned by Duncan make a stop here a must. The rather run-down **William Duncan Memorial Church** (built in 1954) stands at the corner of 4th Avenue and Church Street. Duncan's grave is on the left side.

A traditional **longhouse** (open Mon.–Fri. afternoons in summer) has been erected on the waterfront to stimulate local arts and crafts and to help recover the cultural traditions lost because of Duncan's missionary zeal. The back of the building has three totem poles, and the front is decorated with Tsimshian designs. Native dance performances take place when cruise ships are in port. Inside is a small library and a model of one of the floating fish traps that were used on the island for many years.

An adjacent **Artists' Village** has booths selling locally made crafts, and is open Wednesday and Friday in the summer, and when cruise ships are in port.

Metlakatla Tours (907/886-8687, http://tours.metlakatla.net) leads tours that include the Duncan house, cold-storage plant, artist village, and a dance performance at the longhouse. These often fill up quickly with cruise ship folks, but space may be available if you call ahead.

Hiking

Unlike almost everywhere else in Alaska, there are no bears on Annette Island, a relief to those who fear encounters with bruins. A short hiking trail runs from the corner of Milton Street and Airport Road on the southeast edge of town along **Skaters Lake,** a large pond where native plants and ducks can be observed. **Yellow Hill,** a 540-foot tall fragment of 150-million-year-old sandstone, is unique in Southeast Alaska. The rock is rich in iron and magnesium, giving it a lovely desert-like yellow color set off by gnarled old lodgepole pines. An easy boardwalk trail (20 minutes each way) leads up to its summit where you get panoramic vistas of the western side of Annette, along with the snowcapped peaks of nearby Prince of Wales Island. Get there by walking or hitching 1.5 miles south from town on Airport Road to the signed trailhead on the right side. Some people claim to see George Washington's profile in Yellow Hill.

Two trails access alpine lakes in the mountains east of Metlakatla. The **Chester Lake Trail** starts at the end of the road, .25 miles beyond the ferry terminal. From the trail you get views over the impressive **Chester Lake Falls,** which first attracted Duncan's flock to Annette Island. The trail climbs steeply up steps and a slippery path along a waterline used for power generation. Plan on 45 minutes to reach beautiful Chester Lake, where there's a small dam. From this point, the country is above timberline and it's possible to climb along several nearby ridges for even better views. Good camping sites are available, but be careful coming up the steep, slippery path with a pack.

Farther afield and not quite as scenic is the **Purple Lake Trail.** Take Airport Road four miles south of town and turn left near the Quonset huts at the unmarked Purple Mt. Road. Follow it two miles to the power plant. The unmarked trail heads directly up a steep jeep road. After a 30-minute climb, you reach a saddle and from there you can head up adjacent ridges into the alpine or drop down to Purple Lake (10 minutes). Another place worth a look is the aptly named **Sand Dollar Beach** on the southwest end of the island. Ask locally for directions.

Biking

The flat country around Metlakatla contains a labyrinth of dirt roads built during World War II, and if you have a mountain bike or car, they're well worth exploring. You'll find abandoned structures of all types: huge communications towers, strangely quiet empty hangars, old gun emplacements, and a major airport with no planes. From the south end of the road network are excellent views of Prince of Wales and Duke Islands, as well as the open sea beyond Dixon Entrance. This is the southernmost road in Alaska.

Accommodations and Food

Metlakatla Hotel and Restaurant (3rd Ave. and Lower Milton St., 907/886-3456, $88 d) has standard motel rooms with microwaves, fridges, and VCRs. Breakfast is only for guests, but lunch and dinner are open to the public, with fresh halibut and shrimp the featured attractions. Entrées run $6–13.

Tuck'em Inn B&B (907/886-6611, www.alaskanow.com/tuckem-inn, $75 d with continental breakfast) has six comfortable bedrooms in two houses on the same street.

Simple meals can be found at a couple of burger joints in town, or head to **Leask's Market** for groceries. Check the bulletin board here for such items as hand-carved fossil ivory or fresh Ooligan grease (if you don't know what it is, you probably won't like it). Metlakatla is a dry town, so alcoholic beverages are not allowed.

Events

Locals celebrate the establishment of Metlakatla each year on **Founder's Day,** August 7. As with most other American towns, Metlakatla also has a parade and other events on July Fourth.

Information and Services

Drop by the **municipal building** (907/886-4868), for local information. Camping is discouraged, and visitors who want to stay on Annette Island more than five days must obtain a special permit from the city. A local sponsor is required, and fishing is not allowed.

The **Lepquinum Wellness Center,** next to the high school, houses an Olympic-size swimming pool, plus a weight room, racquetball, sauna, and showers. Out front is **Raven and the Tide Woman Totem,** with a descriptive plaque.

Transportation

Metlakatla's **ferry terminal** (907/465-3941 or 800/642-0066, www.alaska.gov/ferry) is a mile east of town. During the summer, the *Lituya* connects Metlakatla with Ketchikan; this new boat just started service in 2004.

ProMech Air (907/225-3845 or 800/860-3845, www.promechair.com) and **Pacific Airways** (907/225-3500 or 877/360-3500, www.flypacificairways.com) have daily floatplane service between Ketchikan and Metlakatla.

HYDER AND STEWART

The twin towns of Hyder, Alaska, and Stewart, British Columbia, lie at the head of the long, narrow Portland Canal that separates Canada and the United States. The area's remoteness has kept it one of the relatively undiscovered gems of the entire Pacific Northwest coast. Most people arrive via the stunning 41-mile drive down Highway 37A from Meziadin Junction into Stewart, passing beautiful lakes, majestic glaciers, high waterfalls, spectacular mountain peaks, the narrow Bear River Canyon, and finally the mountain-rimmed, water-trimmed towns.

The town of Stewart (pop. 800), lies at the mouth of the Bear River, while tiny Hyder (pop. 90), is two miles down the road next to the mouth of the Salmon River. They are as different as two towns could possibly be. Stewart is the "real" town, with a hospital, churches, schools, a museum, a pharmacy, a bank, and the other necessities of life; it bills itself as Canada's northernmost ice-free port. In contrast, Hyder, "the friendliest ghost town in Alaska," makes the most of its flaky reputation. Between the two settlements lies an international boundary that seems of little importance; border checks are only made when re-entering Canada. Residents send their kids to school in British Columbia. Everyone uses Canadian currency and the Canadian phone system (area code 250). You can, however, mail letters from a post office in either country, saving postage and the hassles of shipping parcels internationally. Hyder is officially on Alaska Time, but everyone except the postmaster sets their watches one hour later, to Pacific Standard Time.

History

In 1793, Captain George Vancouver, searching for the fabled Northwest Passage, turned into Portland Canal. For days his men worked their boats up the narrow fjord, but when they reached its end after so many miles he was "mortified with having devoted so much time to so little purpose." Over a century later the area finally began to develop. In 1896, Captain David Gilliard of the Army Corps of Engineers (for whom Gilliard Cut in the Panama Canal was later named) explored the region and left behind four stone storehouses, Alaska's first masonry buildings. Prospectors soon arrived and found an incredible wealth of gold, silver, and other minerals in the nearby mountains. Stewart received its name from two of its earliest settlers, Robert and John Stewart. The adjacent Alaskan town was initially named Portland City, but postal authorities, wary of yet another Portland, vetoed it. Instead, the town was named after Frederick B. Hyder, a Canadian mining engineer.

Gold fever and the prospect of a transcontinental Canadian railway terminus attracted more than 10,000 newcomers to the area. The steep, mountainous terrain was difficult to build on; much of Hyder was constructed on pilings driven into the mudflats. The planned railroad made it only a few miles out of town, but in 1919 prospectors struck it rich. The Premier Gold and Silver Mine was, until its 1948 closure, the largest gold mine in North America. After it shut down, the local population dwindled to less than a thou-

The twin towns of Hyder, Alaska, and Stewart, British Columbia, lie at the head of the long, narrow Portland Canal that separates Canada and the United States. The area's remoteness has kept it one of the relatively undiscovered gems of the Pacific Northwest coast.

sand until development of the Granduc copper mine in the 1960s. To reach the rich Leduc ore vein, workers dug the longest tunnel ever built from one end—10 miles. A devastating avalanche in 1965 buried 40 men in a tunnel entrance, killing 27 of them. The mine operated until 1984 when it was closed down and dismantled, and the site was restored to a relatively natural condition.

The spectacular Stewart/Hyder area has served as the location for several Hollywood movies: *Insomnia, Bear Island, The Thing, Iceman,* and *Leaving Normal.* Recent years have also seen sporadic promises of new gold, silver, coal, or asbestos mines, but times have been hard of late. As one local told me, "The Moose Park Graveyard is full of people still waiting for Hyder to boom."

Sights

Housed in a Fire Hall from 1910, **Stewart Historical Society Museum** (Columbia and 6th, 250/636-2568, www.stewartmuseum.homestead.com, C$2) has wildlife specimens on the first floor as well as numerous historical items both upstairs and out front. Many of the items are from the region's rich mining history. It's open daily in July and August, and weekdays the rest of the summer.

On the U.S. side of the international border stands a tiny **stone storehouse** built in 1896 by Captain Gilliard. The building looks like an old jail and once served that purpose, but for much of its life it was a shoe repair shop. On the mudflats in front of Hyder are hundreds of old pilings, remnants of what was once a town of 1,000 people. The straight row of pilings in front of Stewart is all that remains of the aborted transcontinental railroad.

About eight km (five miles) out of Hyder (turn right at the end of the main drag) is **Fish Creek Wildlife Viewing Area.** From late July to mid-Sept. the creek is filled with pink salmon, along with some of the world's largest chum salmon—some weighing as much as 35 pounds. A viewing

SOUTHEAST ALASKA

FISH TRAPS

The floating fish trap was developed in 1907 and quickly proved an amazingly efficient way to catch salmon. The traps were constructed with heavy wire netting that directed migrating salmon into progressively smaller enclosures. All one had to do was wait. The traps were hated by most Alaskans because they were owned by "Outsiders" who could afford the high construction and maintenance costs, and because their efficiency took jobs from local fishermen. Their efficiency also robbed many streams of needed brood stock.

For many years these traps brought in over half of Southeast Alaska's salmon catch. Locals got even by stealing fish from the traps, and those who did often became folk heroes. As a territory, Alaska had no say in its own affairs, but when statehood came in 1959, the first act of the state legislature was to outlaw all fish traps. Only the Annette Island Reservation (which manages all waters within 3,000 feet of the island, and sets its own fish and game regulations) was allowed to continue operating the floating fish traps after statehood. The last of these was closed in the 1990s.

platform here provides an excellent vantage point for watching the black and brown bears that feast on the salmon. Forest Service (250/636-2367) staff are on hand to ensure the safety of bear-watchers and to answer questions; see bear photos at www.fishcreek.org.

The road beyond Fish Creek is well worth driving, but before heading out, be sure to ask about road conditions and snow levels; travel by RV is not recommended. Just a .25 miles beyond Fish Creek are remains of an old brothel operated by Dolly, Ketchikan's best-known madam. Continuing north, the road follows the Salmon River, passes the remains of a covered bridge that once provided access to a remote mine, then begins a torturous climb, re-entering Canada along the way. The first glimpses of stunning **Salmon Glacier** come into view 17 miles from Hyder, but the views improve as the ever-narrowing road climbs

above the treeline to a lookout point 23 miles from town. Beyond the glacier is **Tide Lake,** site of the world's greatest yearly snowfall: 88 feet in 1971.

Gorgeous **Bear Glacier,** 20 miles east of Stewart on Highway 37A, should not be missed. Like its more famous cousin, Juneau's Mendenhall, it is a "drive-up glacier" with the highway passing close to its base. The small lake in front is often filled with icebergs.

Hiking

The easiest local trail, **Rainey Creek Nature Walk,** takes off from the Rainey Creek Campground and follows the creek 1.5 miles to the north end of town. The mountains around Stewart and Hyder are crisscrossed with old mining roads, great both for day hikes and camping. The short and scenic **Barneys Gulch/Sluice Box Trail** begins near the dump, just across the Bear River north of Stewart. It starts along a disused railbed then climbs to a low viewpoint above town. A longer hike, but with much better views, is the trail to the abandoned **United Empire Loyalist Mine.** From the trailhead on Quarry Road, at the north end of Stewart just before Highway 37A crosses the Bear River, the trail climbs to a viewpoint overlooking the valley and Portland Canal. **Ore Mountain Trail** originates eight miles northeast of Stewart at Clements Lake (take the first right turn after Highway 37A crosses Bitter Creek). The 2.2-mile trail gains 3,500 feet as it climbs an old mining road above the tree line. Plan on four hours for the round-trip. Clements Lake itself is an attractive spot, with canoeing, swimming, and camping. The **Titan Trail** starts a half-mile beyond the Fish Creek Wildlife Site and climbs 4.4 miles up to the alpine and the remains of a 1920s mine.

For maps and more information on these and other local hikes, head to the field office of the **British Columbia Ministry of Forests** (corner Brightwell St. and 6th Ave., 250/636-2336).

Accommodations

Ripley Creek Inn (on 5th Ave., 250/636-2344, www.ripleycreekinn.homestead.com,

C$100–110 s, C$110–120 d) in Stewart is the finest local lodging choice, with a dozen large and nicely furnished rooms, including access to the sauna and exercise room. The lobby houses **Toastworks Museum,** an off-beat collection of some 600 antique kitchen appliances, some of which date to the 19th century. The owners also run Bitter Creek Cafe, which has a pair of simple but pleasant upstairs rooms for C$60.

In the center of Hyder, **Kathy's Korner B&B** (250/636-2393, $50–75 s, $60–85 d), has rooms in a new home with a large deck. Other options include **King Edward Hotel/Motel** (250/636-9160 or 800/663-3126, www.kingedwardhotel.com) in Stewart, and two Hyder places: **Grandview Inn** (250/636-9174, www.grandviewinn.net) and **Sealaska Inn** (250/636-9006 or 888/393-1199, www.sealaskainn.com).

Camping

Camp Run-A-Muck (250/636-9006 or 888/393-1199, www.sealaskainn.com), in Hyder, has tent and RV sites, as does **Bear River Campground** (250/636-9205, www.stewartbc.com) in Stewart. Stewart's city-run **Rainey Creek Campground** (250/636-2537, open May–Sept.) is quietly situated on the edge of town and has a cookhouse, free firewood, and pay showers.

Food and Drink

Several places serve meals in Stewart, but your best bet is **Bitter Creek Cafe** (5th Ave., 250/636-2166, open May–Sept.), an upscale place in this otherwise rough-at-the-edges town. The always-fresh food includes gourmet pizzas, pasta, seafood, Mexican, burgers, and home-made breads and desserts, along with espresso and nightly specials. An outside deck is a good place for a beer on a summer day. Inside, a 1930 Pontiac is the centerpiece for an eccentric collection of antiques. A computer is available to check your email.

Hyder has three bars for fewer than a hundred inhabitants, and getting "Hyderized" at the **Glacier Inn** (250/636-9243), is an experience that attracts folks from all over the world. It's cheap and lasts a lifetime (you even get an official

card), but could also prove expensive if you fail the test. Warning: It involves Everclear. The walls of the Glacier Inn are papered with thousands of dollars in signed bills left by drinkers, creating the "world's most expensive wallpaper." The tradition began when prospectors would tack up a dollar bill on the wall, in case they were broke next trip into town.

Information and Services

Stewart/Hyder International Chamber of Commerce operates the **Stewart Visitor Information Centre** (250/636-9224 or 888/366-5999, www.stewart-hyder.com, or www.stewartbchyderak.homestead.com) in Stewart, at the west end of 5th Avenue. It's open daily 8:30 A.M.–7 P.M. mid-May–mid-September.

The U.S. Forest Service has a summertime office/information center in Hyder; stop here for details on bear-viewing up the road.

For swimming, showers, and a weight room, head to **Stewart High School pool** on 9th Avenue. The public library is also at the high school. Wash clothes at **Shoreline Laundromat** in Stewart or Camp-Run-A-Muck in Hyder. There are no U.S. banks in the area, but Stewart has a branch of the Canadian Imperial Bank of Commerce with an ATM.

Canada Day (July 1) and the American Independence Day (July 4) provide the opportunity for a four-day party in Stewart and Hyder. **International Days,** as it's called, features a parade of pets, daily pancake breakfasts, and culminates in a fireworks display in Hyder as darkness falls on the fourth.

Transportation

There is no ferry service to Hyder. **Taquan Air Service** (250/636-9150 or 907/225-8800, www.taquanair.com) flies every Monday and Thursday between Ketchikan and Hyder. This is also the only time mail goes in or out of the Hyder post office.

Seaport Limousine (250/636-2622, www.tkp-biz.com/seaportlimousine) offers transportation between Terrace and Stewart, as well as guided tours of the area, including to Fish Creek and Salmon Glacier.

Prince of Wales Island

With more miles of roads than the rest of Southeast Alaska combined, a beautifully wild coastline, deep U-shaped valleys, rugged snow-topped mountains, hidden caves, and a wealth of wildlife, you might expect America's third-largest island (after Kodiak and Hawaii) to be a major tourist attraction. But Prince of Wales Island (POW) has thus far remained off the tourist path for a number of reasons, the primary one being logging. Much of the land has been heavily logged, with huge clear-cuts gouged out of the hillsides, particularly along the extensive road network. Logging has slowed markedly in recent years as the Forest Service shifts to a more diverse land-management policy, and as the Native corporations run out of trees to cut.

Actually, POW's notoriety is its saving grace as well: The towns are authentically Alaskan, with no pretext of civility for the tourists. The 7,000 or so people who live here are friendly, and the roads offer good opportunities for a variety of recreation—including mountain biking—not available elsewhere in the Southeast. The island is very popular with hunters, and the roads provide easy access to many bays for fishing. Black bears and deer are common sights, and wolves are occasionally seen. As logging has declined on POW, tourism—especially from those looking to catch halibut and salmon—has increased. Most of the main roads are now paved, and a ferry provides daily service between Ketchikan and Hollis.

Prince of Wales Island's largest settlement is Craig, on the west coast, but Klawock, Thorne Bay, and Hydaburg each have several hundred people. Rainfall on POW ranges 60–200 inches per year, depending upon local topographic conditions. As an aside, this is one of four Prince of Wales Islands on the planet. The others are in Canada's Northwest Territories, in Queensland, Australia, and in Malaysia.

Located in Klawock, the **Prince of Wales Chamber of Commerce** (907/826-3870, www.princeofwalescoc.org, Tues.–Fri. 10 A.M.–3 P.M. year-round) is a good source for local info.

CRAIG

Just across a short bridge from the western shore of POW Island, the town of Craig (pop. 1,500) overflows Craig Island. Named after Craig Miller—founder of an early fish cannery here—it was originally even more prosaically called "Fish Egg," for the herring eggs that are considered a Tlingit delicacy. Fishing and logging are the mainstays of Craig's economy, giving it a likable feeling. The town has two fish-processing plants and a number of sportfishing lodges. No real "sights" in town, but as you enter Craig you pass the **Healing Heart Totem Pole.** Black bears and bald eagles are often seen at the dump, a mile north of town.

Accommodations

Visit the local chamber of commerce website for descriptions and links to local lodging places. Very basic rooms with bath down the hall can be found above **TLC Laundromat** (on Cold Storage Rd., 907/826-2488, $40 s, $50 d).

Find quaint and cozy rooms at **Ruth Ann's Motel** (907/826-3378); $85 d in the main building, $120 for up to four guests in rooms with kitchenettes and decks, or $125 for the suite that includes a private hot tub. Nearby is **Haida Way Lodge** (907/826-3268 or 800/347-4625), which charges $90–100 d in standard rooms, or $110 d in rooms with jacuzzi tubs.

Inn of the Little Blue Heron (907/826-3608, $89–99 s, $99–109 d), facing the south boat harbor, has three rooms with private baths. A continental breakfast is served downstairs in TK's Cafe.

Dream Catchers B&B (907/826-2238 or 888/897-8167, www.alaskaone.com/dreambb, $95 s, $105 d) is a recently built home with three very attractive rooms, all with private baths, and including a continental breakfast.

If you have the money and like to fish, **Waterfall Resort** (907/225-9461 or 800/544-5125, www.waterfallresort.com), will put you in seventh heaven. Located on the south end of POW in a beautifully refurbished fish cannery, Waterfall is extremely popular with the elite crowd.

Pampered guests stay in Cape Cod–style cottages along a remote stretch of coast, and are treated to great fishing with a personal fishing guide, plus three sumptuous meals daily. It's not cheap: Two people should be ready to drop $6,400 for three nights, but this does include floatplane fare from Ketchikan and all expenses.

Right in Craig, **Shelter Cove Lodge** (907/826-2939 or 888/826-3474, www.sheltercovelodge.com) has package lodging-and-fishing trips, three days for $3,500–4,700 d, all inclusive. The lodge is modern and comfortable. Nearby is **Sunnahae Lodge** (907/826-4000, www.sunnahaelodge.com), an apartment-style building where a three-day fishing package costs $2,500 d.

Travelers can camp for free under the trees near Craig's ball field. Outhouses are nearby, with showers at TLC Laundromat or the Craig pool. **RainCountry RV Park** (on JS Dr., 907/826-3632), has RV hookups.

Food

Meal prices are high on POW; your best bet may be to stock up in Ketchikan or at the grocery store in Craig, **Thompson House** (907/826-3394), which has a deli and bakery. The historic **J.T. Brown's General Store** (907/826-3290) is a classic heart-of-town place with groceries, fishing gear, and other supplies. Right next door in another historic structure is **Ruth Ann's Restaurant** (907/826-3377), a classy place with an old-time atmosphere. You'll find good food three meals a day with a front-row view of the harbor from the dining room. The diverse menu includes seafood, chicken, and steaks for dinner ($20–26 entrées), plus burgers, salads, halibut, fish and chips, and sandwiches for lunch. Dinner reservations are advised if you want a window seat. The building also houses a popular but minuscule bar.

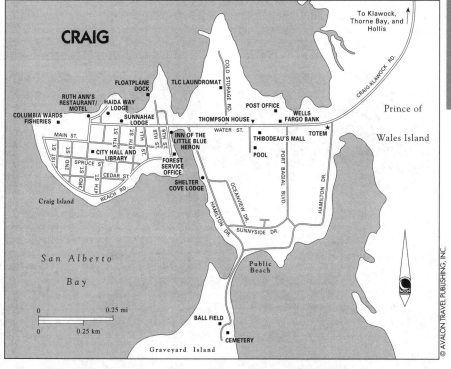

Also downtown is **Dockside Cafe,** with reasonable breakfasts—available all day—and great pies.

Get sandwiches, homemade soups, salads, espresso, and smoothies at **TK's Cafe** (907/826-3354), on the south side of the boat harbor. On the other side of the harbor is **Shelter Cove Lodge** (703 Hamilton Dr., 907/826-2939 or 888/826-3474, www.sheltercovelodge.com), with tall windows facing the water. The restaurant is open seasonally for lunch and dinner (entrées $18–24) with fine seafood, Caesar salads, burgers, fajitas, and steaks, along with homemade desserts. It fills with locals on Friday and Saturday nights for prime rib dinners.

Very good pizzas—including a pesto and artichoke version—can be had at **Papa's Pizza** (907/826-2244), which also serves chicken and lasagna.

Services

Located along the south boat harbor, the Forest Service's **Craig District Office** (907/826-3271) has maps and recreational information, including a listing of more charter fishing operators. ATMs can be found at the Wells Fargo and First Bank offices in Craig, and at the Thompson House grocery store.

Voyageur Bookstore (907/826-2333), across from the Thompson House grocery store, is a pleasant spot to hang out: books, espresso, gifts, and CDs all in one place.

Craig has a fine indoor **swimming pool** (907/826-2794), complete with water slide, hot tub, sauna, and weight room.

Log Cabin Sporting Goods (1 Easy St., 907/826-2205 or 888/265-0375), sells outdoor gear, and rents canoes and kayaks. Its sister company, **Alaska Sea Tours** (www.seatoursalaska.com), offers multiday kayak and canoe trips.

KLAWOCK

Six miles from Craig is the Tlingit village of Klawock (pop. 700), home to the oldest cannery in Alaska (1878), along with a bustling sawmill, state fish hatchery, and POW's only airport; all other POW settlements have floatplane service. Klawock is best known for its 21-pole **Totem Park** which dominates the center of town. These brightly painted poles—all originals—were moved from the old abandoned village of Tuxekan (20

the old docks at Klawock

© DON PITCHER

miles north) in the 1930s and restored. The **Prince of Wales Hatchery** (907/755-2231, www.powhasalmon.org) in Klawock raises coho and sockeye salmon, and has a 250-gallon aquarium filled with coho fry. Free tours are offered Monday–Saturday 1–5 P.M. in the summer.

Practicalities

Log Cabin Resort (907/755-2205 or 800/544-2205, www.logcabinresortandrvpark.com) has a variety of lodging options, starting with basic cabins that share a bathhouse for $55 d. Three suites with kitchenettes in the modern main lodge are $120 d, and a separate log house with a full kitchen is $120 d or $150 for five. RV ($21–24) and tent ($7 per person) sites are also available, along with canoe and skiff rentals, and charter fishing.

Although primarily geared to weekly fishing packages, **Southeast Retreat** (907/755-2994, www.aptalaska.net/~seretret), has a furnished two-bedroom apartment for $150 d, including use of a vehicle.

Other Klawock lodging places include **Columbine Inn** (907/755-2287), **Fireweed Lodge** (907/755-2930, www.fireweedlodge.com), **Forget Me Not Inn** (907/755-2340), **Klawock Bay Inn** (907/755-2959, www.ptialaska.net/~bonomi), and **Changing Tides Inn** (907/755-2305).

Dave's Diner (907/755-2986) has pretty good meals, or buy groceries at **Klawock IGA** (907/755-2722).

OTHER TOWNS
Thorne Bay

The settlement of Thorne Bay (pop. 600) was for many years the world's largest logging camp, and there's still some logging going on, but the focus is shifting to fishing and tourism. Thorne Bay isn't the most beautiful place, but it does have all the basics, including a grocery store, gas, lodging, and a Forest Service district office (907/828-3304).

McFarland's Floatel B&B (907/828-3335 or 888/828-3335, www.mcfarlandsfloatel.com) has deluxe two-bedroom log cabins that sleep four for $240. Car and skiff rentals are also available. **Boardwalk Lodge** (907/828-3918 or

800/764-3918, www.boardwalklodge.com) is a luxurious fishing lodge near Thorne Bay, with access by boat or air. **The Landing at Otter Cove** (907/247-3528 or 888/424-5445, www.otterinlet.com) has cabins for $155 per person, including lodging, a skiff, and fishing gear. Other accommodation options include **Welcome Inn B&B** (907/828-3940 or 888/828-3940) and **Adventure Alaska Southeast** (907/828-3907 or 877/499-3474, www.alaskasoutheast.com).

Ten miles north of town on Forest Highway 30 is **Sandy Beach Picnic Area,** an attractive sandy beach (rare in the Southeast) where you can pitch a tent.

Get very good pizzas from **Dale's Pizza** (907/828-8222), groceries from **Thorne Bay Market** (907/828-3306), and booze from **Riptide Bar** (907/828-3353). **Some Place to Go** has burgers and other fast food.

Thorne Bay's **Prince of Wales Island Logging Show and Fair** takes place the last weekend of July, with logging contests, a fair, and vendor booths. It's the island's biggest annual event.

Hydaburg

Hydaburg (pop. 400), 42 miles south of Craig, is the largest Haida settlement in Alaska. The Haida Indians are relative newcomers to the state, arriving in this Tlingit land around 1700. Originally from Canada's Queen Charlotte Islands, they were given parts of POW in compensation for the accidental killing of a Haida chief by the Tlingits. Hydaburg was established in 1911 when three nearby Haida villages combined into one. Hydaburg has the prettiest setting on POW, situated along scenic Sukkwan Strait. Most of the houses, however, are very plain BIA-style boxes. The newly paved road to Hydaburg was only completed in 1983, opening the town to the outside world. In town is a nice collection of totems restored by the CCC in the 1930s, along with a new one erected in 1991. For food, head to **Do Drop In Groceries** (907/285-3311). Ask locally for rooms to rent.

Kasaan

The Tlingit village of Kasaan (pop. 50) is a

rough 16-mile drive off the main road between Klawock and Thorne Bay. This is a wonderful out-of-the-way settlement, and just a 15-minute walk from the community hall are a beautiful **clan house** and a dozen totem poles set in the woods. The poles were mostly carved in the 1930s and '40s, and the clan house belonged to Chief Son-i-hat, who is buried nearby. (Try to ignore the logging that has been allowed almost right up to the graves.) Older totems are in the abandoned village of Old Kasaan, accessible only by boat.

Karta Lodge (208/754-0078 or 877/465-2782, www.kartalodge.com) is a fishing lodge near Kasaan.

Logging and Fishing Villages

Several tiny communities (mostly former logging camps) are along the road network on the north end of POW Island. The little settlement of **Coffman Cove** (pop. 200) is 53 miles north of Klawock. Visitors will find a restaurant and a general store (The Riggin Shack) with groceries, gas, and other essentials. Coffman Cove boasts several lodging options, all on the Web at www.coffmancove.org. They include **Coffman Cove Bunkhouse** (907/329-2219), **Coffman Cove Cabins** (907/329-2251), and **Oceanview RV Park/Campground** (907/329-2226), which has beach-front campsites, a laundromat, and showers.

TONGASS NATIONAL FOREST

Three times larger than any other national forest in the country, Southeast Alaska's Tongass National Forest is America's rainforest masterpiece. Within these 17 million acres are magnificent coastal forests, dozens of glaciers, snowcapped peaks, an abundance of wildlife, hundreds of verdant islands, and a wild beauty that has long since been lost elsewhere.

Originally named Alexander Archipelago Forest Reserve in 1902, the area became Tongass National Forest in 1907 by proclamation of President Theodore Roosevelt. It was later enlarged to include most of the Panhandle. For more information, visit the Forest Service Tongass website (www.fs.fed.us/r10/tongass), or contact the Southeast Alaska Discovery Center (907/228-6220) in Ketchikan.

Recreation

The Tongass is a paradise for those who love the outdoors. It has dozens of scenic hiking trails and over 1,000 miles of logging roads accessible by mountain bike (if you don't mind the clear-cuts and can avoid the logging trucks and flying gravel). The islands contain hundreds of crystal-clear lakes, many with Forest Service cabins on them. Fishing enthusiasts will enjoy catching salmon, cutthroat trout, and other fish from these lakes, the ocean, and the thousands of streams that empty into bays. The Inside Passage is composed of a

wonderful maze of semiprotected waterways, a sea kayaker's dream come true. Particularly popular with kayakers are Misty Fiords National Monument, Admiralty Island National Monument, Glacier Bay National Park, and the waters around Sitka and Juneau, but outstanding sea kayaking opportunities can be found throughout the Southeast. If you have a sea kayak, access is easy, since they can be carried on the ferries (extra charge). Ask the Forest Service recreation staff in the local district offices for information on nearby routes and conditions.

Wilderness Areas

Less than 5 percent of the Tongass has been logged or otherwise developed, so it isn't necessary to visit an official wilderness area to see truly wild country. However, 21 wilderness areas total well over five million acres in the national forest, offering outstanding recreational opportunities. The largest are **Misty Fiords National Monument** (2.1 million acres) near Ketchikan and **Admiralty Island National Monument** (956,000 acres) near Juneau. Other major wildernesses include **Tracy Arm–Ford's Terror** (653,000 acres) south of Juneau, **Stikine–Le Conte** (449,000 acres) near Wrangell, **Russell Fiord** (349,000 acres) near Yakutat, **South Baranof** (320,000 acres) south of Sitka, and **West Chichagof–Yakobi** (265,000 acres) near Pelican.

Several wilderness areas, such as the remote islands off the west coast of Prince of Wales (Coro-

Sixty-five miles north of Klawock is **Whale Pass** (pop. 60), with a general store and gas. Find lodging at **Northend Cabin** (907/846-5315), **Donna's Place** (907/846-5202), and **Bear Valley Lodge** (907/247-8512 or 800/936-9600, www.bearvalleylodge.com).

On the far northern end of POW are a couple of minuscule fishing/retirement villages. A long boardwalk connects the homes of **Port Protection** (pop. 50), where **Wooden Wheel Cove Lodge** (907/489-2288 or 888/489-9288, www.woodenwheellodge.com) has fishing-lodge accommodations by the week. **Point Baker** (pop. 50) has a small general store and the nation's only floating post office.

RECREATION

Hiking, Camping, and Cabins

There are only a few trails on POW. One of the best and most accessible is the 1.5-mile **One Duck Trail** southwest of Hollis. The trailhead is on the east side of the Hydaburg Road, two miles south of the junction with the Craig–Hollis Road. The path climbs sharply to an Adirondack shelter (free) on the edge of the alpine where the scenery is grand and the hiking is easy. Be sure to wear rubber boots since the trail can be mucky.

The **Soda Lake Trail** (marked) begins approximately 14 miles south of the junction along the Hydaburg Road. This 2.5-mile trail leads to

nation, Maurelle, and Warren Islands) are exposed to the open ocean and are inaccessible for much of the year, even by floatplane. Others, such as the Stikine–Le Conte, Admiralty Island, Russell Fiord, and Petersburg Creek–Duncan Salt Chuck wilderness areas are relatively accessible. There are developed trails or canoe/kayak routes within the Misty Fiords, Admiralty Island, Stikine–Le Conte, Tebenkof Bay, and Petersburg Creek–Duncan Salt Chuck wilderness areas.

Forest Service Cabins

Tongass National Forest has 150 public recreation cabins scattered throughout Southeast, providing a wonderful way to see the *real* Alaska. Most cabins are rustic, one-room Pan-Adobe log structures 12 by 14 feet in size, with bunk space for 4–6 people. They generally have a woodstove with cut firewood (some have oil stoves), an outhouse, and rowboats at cabins along lakes. You'll need to bring your own bedding, cookstove, cooking and eating utensils, Leatherman or Swiss Army knife, food, playing cards, candles, flashlight, matches, and mousetraps. (Some of this will probably be there, but it's better to be sure by bringing your own.) No cell phone coverage, so you're generally on your own when it comes to emergencies.

Many Forest Service cabins can only be reached by floatplane. These flights can be very expensive, averaging approximately $390/hour in a Cessna

185 (two people with gear) or $490/hour in a Beaver (up to five people with gear), but even those on a tight budget should plan to spend some time at one of these cabins. A few can be reached by hiking from towns (Ketchikan, Petersburg, Juneau, and Skagway), cutting out the expensive flight. If you're considering a flightseeing trip anyway, make it to one of these remote cabins where you get to see what the country is really like. This is one splurge you won't regret!

Cabin Reservations

The Forest Service charges $35–45/night for these cabins, with all fees going toward their maintenance. Reservations are on a first-come, first-served basis up to six months in advance; some of the most popular cabins are even chosen by lottery. The Forest Service publishes brochures describing recreation facilities, and can also supply Tongass National Forest maps showing cabin locations. Both the **Forest Service Information Center** (907/586-8751) at Centennial Hall in Juneau and the **Southeast Alaska Discovery Center** (907/228-6220) in Ketchikan, can provide cabin information, as can the ranger district offices scattered around the Southeast. All cabin rentals are made through **ReserveUSA**, (518/885-3639 or 877/444-6777, www.reserveusa.com.) There is no extra charge for cabin reservations.

a pungent collection of bubbling soda springs covering several acres. There are colorful tufa deposits (calcium carbonate, primarily) similar to those in Yellowstone, but on a vastly smaller scale. **Control Lake,** at the junction of the Thorne Bay and Big Salt Lake Roads, has a nice cabin ($45) with a rowboat. There are 20 other Forest Service cabins (reservations: 518/885-3639 or 877/444-6777, www.reserveusa.com) scattered around POW, most accessible only by floatplane or boat.

For world-class steelhead and salmon fishing, reserve one of the four cabins in the Karta River area north of Hollis. The five-mile-long **Karta River Trail** connects Karta Bay to the **Salmon Lake Cabin** ($35) and provides panoramic views of surrounding mountains. This is part of the 40,000-acre **Karta Wilderness.**

You can camp almost anywhere on POW's National Forest land, but avoid trespassing on Native lands (these are generally quite easy to identify since the trees have been scalped for miles in all directions). **Eagle's Nest Campground** ($8) is just east of the intersection of the Klawock–Thorne Bay Road and Coffman Cove Road. These campsites can be reserved ($9 extra) at 518/885-3639 or 877/444-6777, www.reserveusa.com. Also here is a pleasant pair of lakes (Balls Lakes—named for, well, you figure it out) with a short path down to tent platforms overlooking the water. This is a good place for canoeing. **Harris River Campground** ($8) is 19 miles west of Hollis on the road to Klawock.

Spelunking

Prince of Wales Island has the best-known and probably the most extensive system of caves in Alaska, and spelunkers keep discovering more.

In **El Capitan Cave** explorers found a treasure trove of bones from black bears, brown bears, river otters, and other mammals, the oldest dating back over 12,000 years. The cave is located on the north end of the island at Mile 51 near Whale Pass. Free Forest Service tours (907/828-3304) are offered Thursday–Saturday in the summer. Bring flashlights, warm clothing, and hiking boots; hard hats are provided.

Reservations are required at least two days in advance; no kids under seven.

Three miles south of El Capitan is another underground wonder. A stream flows out of Cavern Lake, and then underground for a few hundred feet before emerging from **Cavern Lake Cave.** You can wade up the waters into the cave for 150 feet or so.

Canoeing

The **Sarkar Canoe Trail** is an easy 15-mile loop route with boardwalk portages connecting seven lakes. The trailhead is at the south end of Sarkar Lake, on the northwest side of Prince of Wales, off Forest Road 20.

A more strenuous route is the 34-mile-long **Honker Divide Canoe Route.** This paddle-and-portage route begins near Coffman Cove at the bridge over Hatchery Creek on Forest Road 30, and works up Hatchery Creek to Honker Lake, which has a Forest Service cabin ($25). You may need to pull the canoe up shallow sections of the creek. The route then continues over Honker Divide on a mile-long portage to the upper Thorne River before heading downstream all the way to Thorne Bay. There is a two-mile portage to avoid dangerous rapids and falls. The route is strenuous and should only be attempted by experienced canoeists. For more information on either of these routes, contact the Thorne Bay Ranger District (907/828-3304).

Sea Kayaking

With its hundreds of miles of rugged coastline, and numerous small islands, inlets, and bays, POW offers tremendous opportunities for sea kayakers. One of the wildest areas is the 98,000-acre **South Prince of Wales Wilderness,** but access is difficult and much of the area is exposed to fierce ocean storms. Nearby **Dall Island** has exploring possibilities, but parts of it have been logged. On beaches exposed to the open sea, you'll occasionally find beautiful Japanese glass fishing floats that have washed ashore.

Three other wilderness areas along POW's outer coast—**Maurelle Islands, Warren Island,** and **Coronation Island**—offer remote and rarely visited places to see whales, sea otters, and nesting colonies of seabirds. You're likely to see a few fishermen, but nobody else.

In Craig, rent sea kayaks and canoes from **Log Cabin Sporting Goods** (907/826-2205 or 800/949-2205); its sister company, **Alaska Sea Tours** (www.seatoursalaska.com), offers multi-day kayak and canoe trips.

TRANSPORTATION
Ferry
The **Inter-Island Ferry Authority's** (907/826-4848 or 866/308-4848, www.interislandferry.com) *Prince of Wales* provides daily vehicle and passenger service between Ketchikan and the tiny spot called Hollis (no services other than phones and toilets). It's 25 miles from Hollis to Klawock, the nearest town. Reservations for vehicles on the ferry are highly recommended. A second ferry connecting Coffman Cove on the north end of Prince of Wales with Wrangell and Petersburg should be running by 2005.

TLC Cab (907/826-2966) has taxi and shuttle service all over the island, and meets all ferries at Hollis. They charge $12 per person from Hollis to Craig (or vice versa), or $24/hour for their nine-passenger van if you're heading elsewhere. **My Cab** (907/826-3077) is the other POW taxi company.

Air
On a rainy midsummer day when the clouds were almost to the water, I sat in Craig waiting to fly back to Ketchikan. The weather didn't look promising to me, but when I asked at the air taxi counter if they were flying, the woman took a glance outside and responded nonchalantly, "Oh sure, it looks pretty good today." We flew. Two air taxi operators, **ProMech Air** (907/225-3845 or 800/860-3845, www.promechair.com) and **Pacific Airways** (907/225-3500 or 877/360-3500, www.flypacificairways.com), have daily floatplane service from Ketchikan to Craig, Hollis, and Thorne Bay. In addition, both also offer mail-plane flights two or three times a week to the many logging camps and fishing communities that dot the island. **Taquan Air** (907/225-8800 or 800/770-8800, www.taquanair.com) has scheduled service to Hydaburg three times a week. All three of these also offer charter flights to remote areas. **L.A.B. Flying Service** (907/826-5220 or 800/426-0543, www.labflying.com) flies planes from the Ketchikan airport to Klawock.

The Road System
For a good road map, pick up the *Prince of Wales Road Guide* at Forest Service offices in Ketchikan, Craig, or Thorne Bay. In the last few years the roads have improved dramatically, and the most-used sections are now paved and in good condition, including roads connecting Hollis, Craig, Klawock, and Thorne Bay. The road to Coffman Cove will be paved by 2005. Some 1,500 miles of rough gravel roads, most built for logging operations, remain on POW, providing lots of interesting mountain bike rides—if you don't mind the old clearcuts and soggy weather.

Rent cars in Craig from **Wilderness Car Rental** (907/755-2691 or 800/949-2205, www.wildernesscarrental.com) or **Shaub-Ellison Tire & Fuel** (907/826-3450).

SOUTHEAST ALASKA

Wrangell

The quiet, friendly, and conservative settlement of Wrangell (pop. 2,000) sits near the mouth of the Stikine River. The streets are full of folks in pickup trucks, with their dogs hanging out the back and country tunes on the radio. Wrangell is quite unlike its neighbor, prim and proper Petersburg. Wrangell's inner harbor resonates with salmon- and shrimp-processing plants, fishing boats, and seaplanes, while totem poles guard historic Chief Shakes Island. Surrounding the harbor are old buildings on piles, wooded hillsides, and snowcapped mountains. Wrangell is compact enough that visitors can hoof it around to the most interesting sites in an hour or two and still have time to buy beer for the ferry. To see the area right, however, you should spend a couple of days, or longer if you're interested in exploring the mighty Stikine River.

HISTORY
Redoubt St. Dionysius
Third-oldest community in Alaska, Wrangell is the only one to have been governed by four nations: Tlingit, Russia, Britain, and America. Tlingit legends tell of an ancient time when advancing glaciers forced them to abandon their coastal life and move to what is now British Columbia. As the ice retreated after the last ice age, the Stikine River was their entryway back to the newly reborn land. When the Tlingits discovered that the river suddenly disappeared under a glacier, they sent old women to explore, expecting never to see them again. One can only imagine their astonishment when the women returned to lead canoes full of people out to the coast.

For many centuries the Tlingits lived in the Stikine River area, paddling canoes upstream to catch salmon and trade with interior tribes. Similarly, the river figured strongly in Wrangell's founding. Russians began trading with Stikine Indians in 1811; by 1834 the British were trying to move in on their lucrative fur-trading monopoly. To prevent this, Lieutenant Dionysius Zarembo and a band of men left New Archangel (present-

day Sitka) to establish a Russian fort near the Stikine River mouth. The settlement, later to become Wrangell, was originally named Redoubt St. Dionysius. When the British ship *Dryad* anchored near the river, the Russians boarded the vessel and refused to allow access to the Stikine. The *Dryad* was forced to return south, but a wedge had been driven in Russia's Alaskan empire. Five years later, the Hudson's Bay Company acquired a long-term lease to the coastline from the Russian government. Redoubt St. Dionysius became Fort Stikine, and the Union Jack flew from town flagpoles.

Gold Fever
The discovery of gold on Stikine River gravel bars in 1861 brought a boom to Fort Stikine. Hundreds of gold-seekers arrived, but the deposit proved relatively small and most prospectors soon drifted on to other areas. With the transfer of Alaska to American hands in 1867, Fort Stikine was renamed Wrangell, after Baron Ferdinand Petrovich von Wrangel, governor of the Russian-American Company. Its population dwindled until 1872 when gold was again discovered in the Cassiar region of British Columbia. Thousands of miners quickly flooded the area, traveling on steamboats up the Stikine. Wrangell achieved notoriety as a town filled with harddrinking rabble-rousers, gamblers, and shady ladies. When the naturalist John Muir visited in 1879 he called it "the most inhospitable place at first sight I had ever seen . . . a lawless draggle of wooden huts and houses, built in crooked lines, wrangling around the boggy shore of the island for a mile or so in the general form of the letter *S*, without the slightest subordination to points of the compass or to building laws of any kind."

By the late 1880s, the second gold rush had subsided and lumbering and fishing were getting started as local industries. The Klondike gold rush of the late 1890s brought another short-lived boom to Wrangell as the Stikine was again tapped for access to interior Canada, but Skagway's

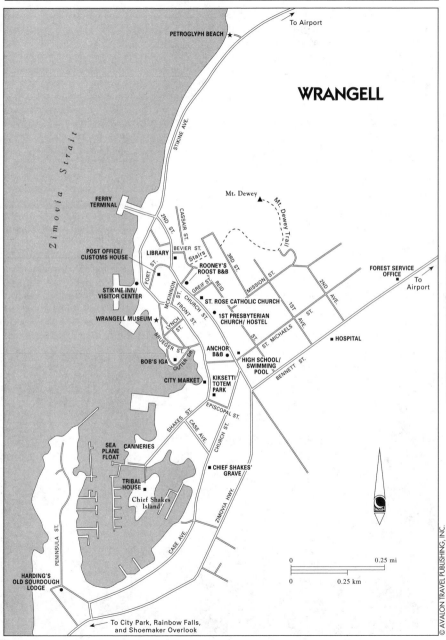

WRANGELL

To Airport

PETROGLYPH BEACH ★

Zimovia Strait

Mt. Dewey ▲
Mt. Dewey Trail

FERRY TERMINAL

STIKINE AVE.

2ND ST.

CASSAIR ST.

BEVIER ST.

3RD ST.

POST OFFICE/
CUSTOMS HOUSE

LIBRARY

ROONEY'S
ROOST B&B

Stairs

FOREST SERVICE
OFFICE

To
Airport

MISSION ST.

FORT ST.

GREIF ST.

REID

2ND AVE.

STIKINE INN/
VISITOR CENTER

MCKINNON ST.

CHURCH ST.

ST. ROSE CATHOLIC CHURCH

1ST PRESBYTERIAN
CHURCH/ HOSTEL

1ST AVE.

WRANGELL MUSEUM ★

FRONT ST.

LYNCH ST.

ST. MICHAELS

HOSPITAL

BRUEGER ST.

OUTER DR.

ANCHOR
B&B

BOB'S IGA

HIGH SCHOOL/
SWIMMING
POOL

BENNETT ST.

CITY MARKET

KIKSETTI
TOTEM
PARK

EPISCOPAL ST.

SHAKES ST.

CASE AVE.

CHURCH ST.

SEA
PLANE
FLOAT

CANNERIES

TRIBAL
HOUSE

CHIEF SHAKES'
GRAVE

Chief Shakes
Island

ZIMOVIA HWY.

PENINSULA ST.

CASE AVE.

HARDING'S
OLD SOURDOUGH
LODGE

0   0.25 mi

0   0.25 km

MooN

To City Park, Rainbow Falls,
and Shoemaker Overlook

SOUTHEAST ALASKA

Chilkoot Trail became the preferred route. With its rowdy days behind, Wrangell settled into the 20th century as a home to logging and fishing operations, still mainstays of the local economy. Rebuilt after destructive fires in 1906 and 1952, much of downtown is now on rock-fill and pilings. Today, Wrangell is searching for a more prosperous future—and tourism is right at the forefront of that quest—while getting by on the remaining industries: fishing, construction, and small timber operations. It's an easy-going, slow-paced, and friendly town, and a good place to unwind.

SIGHTS

Chief Shakes Island

This is the centerpiece of picturesque Wrangell harbor. A footbridge at the bottom of Front Street near Wrangell's cannery and cold-storage plant gives access to the island. Here you'll find the Tribal House of the Bear (907/874-3747, $2), an old-style Native log house built in 1939–1940 by the CCC. Inside are various artifacts, including beautifully carved houseposts. The house is only open when cruise ships are in port or by appointment. Surrounding the house are seven totems, reproductions of older poles from the area. Shakes Island is especially beautiful at night, surrounded by the town and harbor.

The Shakes lineage was established more than three centuries ago, after the Stikine Tlingits defeated Niska invaders and then forced the vanquished chief, We-Shakes, to give away his name in exchange for peace. **Chief Shakes V's grave** is on Case Avenue opposite the Hansen Boat Shop. A white fence surrounds it, and two carved killer whales watch silently.

Several impressive totem poles, carved by the CCC, stand in front of the Library on 2nd Street. Wrangell's small **Kiksetti Totem Park,** next to the City Market along Front Street, has four poles that were carved without the aid of power tools.

Petroglyphs

Hundreds of ancient petroglyphs (rock carvings) are found on Wrangell Island, but precisely who carved them or when is uncertain. They may date back more than 8,000 years. The best nearby carvings are only a 20-minute walk from town. To get there, turn left (north) from the ferry terminal

totem pole and clan house, Chief Shakes Island

THE PETROGLYPH MYSTERY

Petroglyphs (ancient rock carvings) are found along the coast from Kodiak to the Columbia River, although the greatest concentration is between Sitka and Puget Sound. The coastal type is very different from the petroglyphs of the interior plateau and central Oregon, but has similarities to carvings in the Amur River region of Siberia. Although a single style can be followed down the coast, no one knows who carved the petroglyphs, when they were carved, or why. Contemporary Natives have no knowledge of them. Many petroglyphs—such as those in Wrangell—face west and were carved on rocks below the high-tide mark. Were they territorial boundary signs? Greetings to returning salmon? Sacred places? As with Stonehenge, we can only speculate. Some have posited that the petroglyphs were just the idle doodles of some ancient graffiti artist. This is unlikely not only from a cultural perspective, but also because of the difficulty of pecking out a design in these hard, fine-grained rocks using only stone tools.

and walk two-thirds of a mile to a small parking area on the left. A newly built boardwalk provides access to the beach, where you will find a dozen petroglyph rocks along upper parts of the beach, especially those on the right side (facing the water). One of the best, a killer whale, lies on the edge of a grassy lawn to the right of the path. Most petroglyphs face seaward and are near the high-tide line. They may be covered by water if the tide is over 10 feet. To protect the originals, the state has set up several stone reproductions of the petroglyphs along the boardwalk for those who want to make rubbings. These can be created by placing rice paper—available in local stores—over the copies and rubbing with crayons, ferns, or charcoal. Other petroglyphs are in the Wrangell Museum and in front of the library. Do not make rubbings of the originals.

Wrangell Museum
Given the size of Wrangell, its museum (2906 Outer Dr., 907/874-3770) is a pleasant surprise.

Housed in the newly completed civic center, it's open Tuesday–Saturday 10 A.M.–5 P.M. May–September, and when cruise ships or ferries are in port. The rest of the year, hours are Tuesday–Saturday 1–5 P.M. Admission is $4 adults, $3 seniors, $2 ages 7–16, free for younger children. Professional exhibits take you through Wrangell's past with an in-depth look at the Tlingit, Russian, English, and American peoples who all called this place home. Petroglyphs, old photographs, Native artifacts, and local relics are crowded into this provocative museum. Of particular interest are the original houseposts from the Chief Shakes house. Carved in the 1740s—before contact with whites—they are the oldest Tlingit houseposts in existence. The museum staff is a good source of information about the town, and the gift shop has books on local history.

Mt. Dewey
A half-mile path winds up Mt. Dewey (actually more of a hill) from 3rd Street behind the high school. It's a steep 15-minute climb up to this viewpoint over Wrangell. You could probably find a place to camp up here in a pinch. On a wild stormy night in 1879, John Muir did just that. He, however, also decided to build a huge bonfire atop the hill, its flames dancing off the clouds. Muir later wrote, "Of all the thousands of campfires I have elsewhere built none was just like this one, rejoicing in triumphant strength and beauty in the heart of the rain-laden gale." To the Native people below, however, the fire ignited fears of evil spirits, and as Muir's partner noted, "the Tlingits ever afterward eyed Muir askance, as a mysterious being whose ways and motives were beyond all conjecture." During the 1920s, a dance pavilion crowned the top of Mt. Dewey; nothing remains of it today.

Other Sights
Wrangell is home to the oldest Protestant church building in Alaska, the **First Presbyterian Church,** as well as the oldest Roman Catholic parish, **St. Rose of Lima Catholic Church.** Appropriately located on Church Street, both were founded in 1879. The large, red neon cross atop the Presbyterian church is

one of only two in the world used as a navigational aid (the other is in Rio).

As you step off the ferry you will be greeted by local kids selling **garnets** for 25 cents to $10 depending upon the size. These imperfect but attractive stones come from a nearby garnet ledge along the Stikine River, deeded to the Boy Scouts in 1962 by a former mayor. Local children may collect the stones for free, but adults must pay $10 for a permit (available at the museum). At one time the mine was owned by the Alaska Garnet Mining and Manufacturing Company, the world's first women-only corporation.

ANAN CREEK WILDLIFE VIEWING SITE

Anan Creek, 30 miles south of Wrangell on the mainland, is a fine place to watch black and brown bears catching salmon and steelhead. A half-mile boardwalk leads from saltwater to an observation platform above the creek, and a three-sided blind sits closer to the falls where most of the action takes place. The best time to visit is the peak of the pink salmon run, mid-July–mid-August. Forest Service personnel are at the trailhead and observation area to provide information. No food is allowed along these trails, and flash photography is discouraged. The creek is shaded by tall trees and it's often raining, making photography a challenge.

Because of Anan Creek's popularity, permits ($10) are required, and a maximum of 64 visitors are allowed per day in July and August. If you're traveling on your own, get the permit from the Forest Service office in Wrangell (907/874-2323). If you're in a guided group, the guide will get your permit.

The Forest Service's **Anan Bay Cabin** (reservations: 518/885-3639 or 877/444-6777, www.reserveusa.com, $35) is just a mile away on a good trail, but is often booked months in advance; reserve early.

Many visitors to Anan Creek arrive on flights by **Sunrise Aviation** (907/874-2319 or 800/874-2311, www.sunriseflights.com), in Wrangell. The charter cost is $520 round-trip for a Cessna 206 (room for up to five people), or $99 per person

with a minimum of three. **Taquan Air** (907/225-8800 or 800/770-8800, www.taquanair.com) flies to Anan from Ketchikan. Several companies offer guided boat trips to Anan Creek: **Alaska Waters** (907/874-2378 or 800/347-4462, www.alaskawaters.com), **Alaska Charters and Adventures** (888/993-2750, www.alaskaupclose.com), **Breakaway Adventures** (907/874-2488 or 888/385-2488, www.breakaway adventures.com), and **Alaska Vistas** (907/874-3006 or 866/874-3006, www.alaskavistas.com). Expect to pay $170 per person for a trip that includes four hours on the ground at Anan.

Those with a sea kayak may want to paddle along the east side of Wrangell Island to Anan Bay. En route, be sure to visit scenic **Berg Bay,** an area rich in moose, mountain goats, grizzlies, deer, geese, and other wildlife. A Forest Service cabin ($35) is available here, and a trail leads from the cabin along Berg Creek for several miles into a cirque basin with old mine ruins.

RECREATION
Hiking

Scenic **Rainbow Falls Trail,** a moderately steep .75-mile hike, begins across the road from Shoemaker Bay Campground, five miles south of town. More ambitious bodies can continue three miles up the trail to **Shoemaker Overlook** (1,500 feet). The trail accesses large ridge-top muskeg areas and ends at a three-sided Adirondack-style shelter offering a panoramic vista of Zimovia Strait. The trail and shelter provide an excellent opportunity for an overnight camping trip. The trail is steep and often muddy, but has boardwalk in places.

Logging roads crisscross most of Wrangell Island, providing cycling opportunities for mountain bike enthusiasts—if you enjoy seeing cut-over land. Those with wheels may want to visit several areas on the island. **Long Lake Trail,** 28 miles southeast of Wrangell along Forest Road 6271, is a half-mile boardwalk that ends at an Adirondack shelter complete with a rowboat, fire grill, and outhouse. In the same vicinity is a 300-foot path to **Highbrush Lake,** where you'll find a small boat in which to practice your rowing skills. Individuals with disabilities may want to try fishing at **Salamander Creek,** 23 miles south of town on Forest Road 6265, where ramps lead right up to a pad along the creek. Good fishing for king salmon here, along with three campsites. For information on cabins and other trails around Wrangell, visit the Forest Service's **Wrangell Ranger District Office** (525 Bennett St., 907/874-2323).

Cabins

There are 21 different Forest Service cabins (info: 907/874-2323; reservations: 518/885-3639 or 877/444-6777, www.reserveusa.com; $35) near Wrangell, including several described in the *Stikine River* section. The closest is at **Virginia Lake,** accessible by floatplane—and another nearby cabin is at **Kunk Lake,** across Zimovia Strait from the south end of the Wrangell Island road system. Access is by kayak, or skiff if you can get someone to run you across. A 1.5-mile trail climbs to a three-sided shelter at the lake. From here, it's a relatively easy climb into high-elevation muskeg and alpine areas that cross Etolin Island.

Other Recreation

Rain Walker Expeditions (907/874-2549, www.rainwalkerexpeditions.com) rents bikes, canoes, and kayaks, plus a floating cabin near Anan Creek, from its office across from Stikine Inn. Rain Walker's Marie Oboczky leads informative nature hikes and bus tours, from two hours to all day. They're fun and geared to your area of interest, whether it's petroglyphs or rainforests.

Alaska Tugboat Tours (907/874-3101 or 888/488-4386, www.alaskatugtours.com) has one-day or multiday trips aboard a refurbished 1967 wooden tugboat. This is a fine way to watch whales and other wildlife.

A paved **walking/biking path** runs from Wrangell for six miles to the trailhead for Rainbow Falls at Shoemaker Bay.

Alaska Vistas (907/874-3006 or 866/874-3006, www.alaskavistas.com) guides sea kayaking day trips and multiday adventures in the Wrangell area.

Muskeg Meadows Golf Course (907/874-3443) is a nine-hole course with fairways covered in wood chips, artificial greens, and a driving range. Golf clubs are available for rent.

Wrangell has a fine **swimming pool** (907/874-2444) at the high school. Fishing and sightseeing **charters** are available through a number of local outfits; get brochures from the visitors center.

PRACTICALITIES

Accommodations

As you'd expect in this blue-collar town, Wrangell's accommodations are nothing fancy; local B&Bs are probably your best choice.

Wrangell's **Youth Hostel** (220 Church St., 907/874-3534, $18) is inside the Presbyterian church, and it's open all day mid-June–Labor Day. This is nothing fancy, with mats for sleeping, along with a kitchen and shower facilities. Space for families, too.

Anchor B&B (325 Church St., 907/874-2078, www.seapac.net/~anchorbb, $66 s, $76 d) is a historic 1912 home in the heart of town. The flower garden out front is easily the most beautiful in Wrangell, and the two guest rooms share a private upstairs living room and bath. Rates include a full breakfast.

Zimovia B&B (319 Webber St., 907/874-2626, www.zimoviabnb.com, $70 d), has one guest room in a new home with a private entrance, kitchenette, and sauna; continental breakfast included.

Rooney's Roost B&B (206 McKinnon, 907/874-2026, www.rooneysroost.com), has six comfortable guest rooms for just $75 d with shared bath, or $95 d with private baths. The nicely remodeled home contains collectibles, and a gourmet breakfast is included. Friendly owners, too.

Located two miles south of town, **Grand View B&B** (907/874-3225, www.grandviewbnb.com, $85–100 d) is a fine hillside home facing Zimovia Straits. The three guest rooms have private baths and the filling breakfast includes home-baked goods.

Guests at **Harding's Old Sourdough Lodge** (1104 Peninsula Ave., 907/874-3613 or 800/874-3613, www.akgetaway.com, $85 s, $95 d) stay in comfortable rooms with handmade quilts, Native art, and private baths. Family rooms sleep four for $135, and a six-person room with hot tub is $195. A continental breakfast is included, and lunch and dinner are available; local seafood is the house specialty. Guests can use the sauna and take the courtesy van around town.

Stikine Inn (107 Stikine Ave., 907/874-3388 or 888/874-3388, www.stikine.com, $85–95 s, $90–105 d) has a central location and aging furnishings; $110 for a suite with fridge and microwave.

Wrangell's most unique lodging option is **Rain Haven Houseboat** (907/874-2549, www.rainwalkerexpeditions.com), a surprisingly cozy place with room for five, plus cooking and bath facilities. During July and August it's located in remote Bradfield Canal, southwest of Wrangell. Take the canoe to nearby Berg Bay for a hike, or it's an hour paddle to the bears at Anan Creek. Three-day stays are $700 d, including transportation from Wrangell and a Stikine River jetboat trip. The rest of the year the houseboat is docked at Shoemaker Bay, five miles south of Wrangell, where it rents for $85 d, including transportation from town.

For something different, the extremely remote **Cape Decision Lighthouse** (907/790-3339) on the south end of Kuiu Island (75 miles southwest of Wrangell) is being renovated by a local preservation group. It isn't open yet, but summer caretakers may be needed.

Camping

Free tent camping is allowed (no RVs) at **City Park** just beyond the ball field, two miles south of the ferry on the water side of Zimovia Highway. The official limit is 24 hours, but this is not strictly enforced. Showers are available at a laundromat near Chief Shakes Island, and at the high school swimming pool.

You'll find additional camping at the city-run **Shoemaker Bay RV Park** (907/874-2444, tents free, RVs $10), five miles south of town and right alongside the highway. Open all year. One advantage of this campsite is its proximity to the Rainbow Falls and Shoemaker Overlook Trails. The Forest Service's free **Nemo Campground** is 14 miles south of town and up Forest Roads 16 and 6267; impressive views across Zimovia Strait.

Alaska Waters RV Park (241 Berger St., 907/874-2378 or 800/347-4462, www.alaskawaters.com, RVs $19) is on the south side of the harbor.

Food

Wrangell eating places leave much to be desired. The **Diamond C Cafe** (223 Front St., 907/874-3677), has standard American fare, good breakfasts, and homemade soups for lunch. **Waterfront Grill** (907/874-2353), inside the Stikine Inn, has Zimovia Strait views from the dining room, and a menu that includes pizzas, burgers, pasta, and chicken. A short distance up Front Street is **J & W's Fast Food** (907/874-2120, open summers only), with halibut burgers and shrimp.

Zak's Cafe (316 Front St., 907/874-3355) has good food, reasonable prices, and fast service. Across the street is **Jitterbug's** (907/874-3350), the local espresso place.

Bob's IGA (on Outer Dr., 907/874-2341) has a deli with inexpensive sandwiches. **City Market** (on Front St., 907/874-3336) is Wrangell's other grocery store. Both are closed on Sundays.

Locals hang out in **Marine Lounge** (274 Shakes St., 907/874-3005)—a.k.a. the Hungry Beaver—which has the best pizzas in town. Other popular drinking establishments are **Totem Bar** (116 Front St., 907/874-3533) and **Brig Bar** (532 Front St., 907/874-3442), which has live music some nights.

Events

Wrangell's big winter event is **Tent City Festival,** held the first weekend of February to commemorate the gold rush up the Stikine River in the 1860s. Featured activities include bed races, the Shady Lady Fancy Dress Ball, arts and crafts, a golf tournament, pancake feed, tall-tales contest, and best-beard contest. From mid-May to mid-June, pull out your fishing pole for the **King Salmon Derby**—top prize is $6,000. The main summer event is the town's **July 4th** celebration, with a parade, logging show, log rolling contests, tug of war, tugboat races, street dance, and fireworks. All this is funded by a handful of teenagers and their families who run downtown food booths in June.

Information and Services

The small **Wrangell Visitor Center** (on Front St., 907/874-3901 or 800/367-9745, www.wrangell .com) is housed inside the Stikine Inn. It's open Monday–Friday 10 A.M.–2 P.M. year-round, and whenever cruise ships are in port. If it's closed, get information from the museum.

The Forest Service's **Wrangell Ranger District Office** (on Bennett St., 907/874-2323) is three-quarters of a mile from town on the left side of the road. It has information on local hiking trails, the Stikine River, and nearby recreation cabins.

Adjacent to the Stikine Inn is **River's Edge Fine Arts and Gifts** (907/874-3593), which sells locally made clothing, carved wooden bowls, pottery, and jewelry, plus the distinctive marine art of owner Brenda Schwartz.

The **library** (124 2nd Ave., 907/674-3535) has a good collection of books about Alaska and a couple of petroglyphs out front, along with computers for Internet access. **B.B. Brock's Bookstore** (on Front St., 907/874-3185), next to the city dock, has Alaskan titles.

Located out Airport Road, the **Wrangell Medical Center** (907/874-3356, www.wrangellmedicalcenter.com), has physicians on staff.

Transportation

Wrangell's **ferry terminal** (907/874-2021; 907/874-3711 for departure times) is right in town. Alaska Marine Highway ferries head both north and south almost daily during the summer months. The terminal is open only for vessel arrivals and departures. Reservations and information available at 907/465-3941 or 800/642-0066; www.ferryalaska.com.

The airport is 1.5 miles from town on Bennett Street. **Alaska Airlines** (800/426-0333, www.alaskaair.com) has daily flights from Wrangell to Juneau, Ketchikan, Petersburg, and Sitka. **Sunrise Aviation** (907/874-2319 or 800/874-2311, www.sunriseflights.com) provides charter flights to nearby Forest Service cabins and Anan Creek; 45-minute Le Conte Glacier and Stikine River flightseeing trips cost $100 per person (minimum three people).

Rent cars at the airport from **Practical Rent-A-Car** (907/874-3975). Both **Northern Lights**

Taxi (907/874-4646) and **Star Cab** (907/874-3622) charge $5 to campsites at City Park, or from the airport to town.

THE STIKINE RIVER

Seven miles north of Wrangell is the Stikine River, one of the top 10 wild rivers of Canada, and the fastest navigable river in North America. The river begins its 330-mile journey to the sea high inside British Columbia's Spatsizi Wilderness Park. The 55-mile-long **Grand Canyon of the Stikine,** just above Telegraph Creek, B.C., has thousand-foot walls enclosing fierce white water. River travel is easier below Telegraph Creek all the way to Wrangell, between high peaks of the coast range, past glaciers and forested hills. At one spot on the river, 21 different glaciers are visible! These glaciers dump tons of silt into the river, coloring it a milky gray; at the mouth of the Stikine, the sea takes on this color for miles in all directions. So much for the advertisements about glacially pure water!

Each spring upward of 1,500 bald eagles flock to the river mouth to eat hooligan (eulachon), an oily fish that spawns here from late March to early May. The fish also attract hundreds of thousands of gulls and kittiwakes, plus harbor seals, Steller sea lions, and even killer whales.

Tours from Wrangell

Several charter boat operators in Wrangell provide day trips or longer voyages by jetboat up the Stikine River and to surrounding areas, including Anan Creek, Le Conte Glacier, and Shakes Glacier. Recommended is **Breakaway Adventures** (907/874-3455 or 888/385-2488; www.breakawayadventures.com). All-day trips up the Stikine to Shakes Glacier are $135 per person, and these also include time at the garnet ledge and Chief Shakes Hot Springs. **Alaska Waters** (907/874-2378 or 800/347-4462, www.alaskawaters.com) also runs jetboat trips up the Stikine.

Running the River

The Stikine River is a popular destination for kayakers, canoeists, and river rafters. (It's even more popular with local jetboaters, so don't expect peace and quiet in the lower reaches.) Most folks choose to float down the river, after being transported up from Wrangell by boat or plane. You will need to go through Customs (907/874-3415) at the Wrangell airport if you cross the border. In addition, a Canadian agent is frequently stationed along the river just across the border. The Forest Service publishes a helpful guide to canoeing or kayaking the Stikine River; it's available from the Wrangell Ranger District (907/874-2323).

Stikine Riversong Lodge (250/235-3196, www.kermode.net/stikine) in Telegraph Creek 160 miles upriver from Wrangell, has lodging, supplies, and a pleasant café. The owners also offer river tours, canoe and kayak rentals, and will help you set up trips down the Stikine.

In Wrangell, rent kayaks and canoes from **Rain Walker Expeditions** (907/874-2549, www.rainwalkerexpeditions.com); they can also set up jetboat transportation to Telegraph Creek. **Alaska Vistas** (907/874-3006 or 866/874-3006, www.alaskavistas.com), leads nine-day raft trips down the Stikine River twice each summer.

Camping and Cabins

The lower Stikine is a multi-channeled, silt-laden river nearly a mile wide in places. The route is spectacular, wildlife crowds the banks, campsites are numerous, and 13 Forest Service cabins (reservations: 518/885-3639 or 877/444-6777, www.reserveusa.com, $35) are available. One of the finest is the **Mount Rynda Cabin** along crystal-clear Andrew Creek, a spawning area for king salmon. You may also want to stay in one of the two extremely popular cabins near **Chief Shakes Hot Springs.** At the springs you'll discover beautifully maintained wooden hot tubs (one enclosed to protect you from the mosquitoes); these are great places to soak those aching muscles. The area gets mighty busy on summer weekends, so you probably won't have it to yourself, and things can get rowdy after the locals pop a few beers. Escape the crowds at the main hot springs by finding your own undeveloped springs nearby.

The upper portion of the Stikine is a vastly different river, with less noise and development than on the U.S. side of the border, and a drier, colder climate. The vegetation reflects this. The historic settlement of **Telegraph Creek** is accessible by road from the rest of British Columbia, or you can charter a small plane or jetboat from Wrangell. The upper river above here is some of the wildest white water anywhere; canoeists and kayakers intent on running the river would do best to begin at Telegraph Creek.

Petersburg

Southeast Alaska's picture-postcard town, Petersburg (pop. 3,200) sits at the northern tip of Mitkof Island along Wrangell Narrows. Great white walls of snow and ice serve as a dramatic backdrop for the town. "Peter's Burg" was named after Peter Buschmann, who built a sawmill here in 1897, followed by a cannery three years later. With ample supplies of fish, timber, and glacial ice, the cannery proved an immediate success— 32,750 cases of salmon were shipped that first season. Unlike boom-and-bust Wrangell, the planned community of Petersburg has kept pace with its expanding fishing base. A number of the present inhabitants are descended from Norwegian fishermen, who found that the place reminded them of their native land. The language

is still occasionally heard on Petersburg's streets, and Norwegian rosemaling (floral painting) can be found on shutters of the older homes.

Petersburg is a prosperous and squeaky-clean town with green lawns, tidy homes, and a hardworking heritage that may appear a bit cliquish to outsiders. The country around Petersburg is filled with opportunities for exploration by those who love the outdoors, but this off-the-beaten-path community still views tourism with a degree of skepticism. Although Petersburg has a lumber mill, fishing remains the main activity, with salmon, halibut, herring, crab, and shrimp all landed. The odor of fish hangs in the air, and bumper stickers proclaim "Friends don't let friends eat farmed salmon." Petersburg has the most canneries in Southeast Alaska (four) and is home to a large halibut fleet.

Wrangell Narrows

Between Wrangell and Petersburg the ferry passes through tortuous Wrangell Narrows, a 46-turn nautical obstacle course that resembles a pinball game played by ship. This is one of the highlights of the Inside Passage trip and is even more exciting at night when the zigzag course is lit up like a Christmas tree. Be up front to see it. The larger cruise ships are too big to negotiate these shallow waters between Kupreanof and Mitkof Islands,

thus sparing Petersburg from the tourist blitz and glitz that most other Southeast towns endure.

SIGHTS

In Town

Petersburg's main attraction is its gorgeous harbor and spectacular setting. The sharply pointed peak visible behind Petersburg is **Devil's Thumb,** a 9,077-foot mountain 30 miles away on the U.S.-Canadian border. Built in 1912, the large **Sons of Norway Hall** (907/772-4575), stands on pilings over scenic Hammer Slough, and is adorned with traditional Norwegian rosemaling designs.

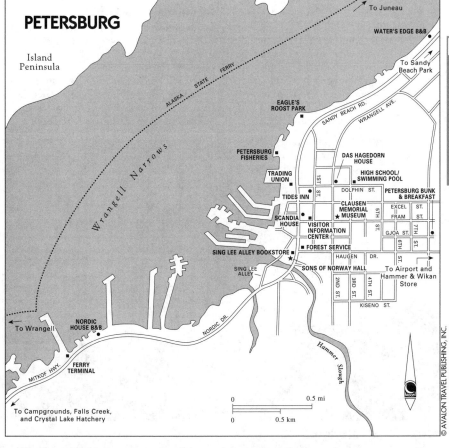

Next to Sons of Norway is the surprisingly small *Valhalla,* a replica of the original Viking boat. It was built in 1976 and sailed in the parade of ships bicentennial celebration in New York Harbor. A memorial to fishermen lost at sea stands next to the Sons of Norway Hall. Walk up the wooden street along **Hammer Slough** to see old homes hanging over this tidal creek.

The boat harbors usually have several Steller sea lions cruising around. And keep your eyes open for Lloyd Pederson's 1963 Rambler station wagon, decorated with fishing buoys and other paraphernalia; it's pretty hard to miss.

Clausen Memorial Museum (2nd and Fram streets, 907/772-3598, www.clausenmuseum .alaska.net, $2) is open Monday–Friday 10 A.M.–5 P.M. and Sat. 10 A.M.–4:30 P.M. May to early September. Call for winter hours. Inside are exhibits on commercial fishing—including the world's largest king salmon (a 126-pound monster) and chum salmon (36 pounds)—plus the Cape Decision lighthouse lens, a 200-year-old Tlingit dugout canoe, bentwood box, and other historical exhibits. Outside is *The Fisk,* a fishy sculpture and fountain by Carson Boysen.

Nearby

A good place to watch for America's national bird is **Eagle's Roost Park,** north of the Petersburg Fisheries cannery. Upward of 30 eagles can be seen along here when the tide is low. Whales, seals, and sea lions are frequent sights in Frederick Sound near **Sandy Beach Park** north of town. Covered picnic tables and a playground add to the allure, and by late summer, pink salmon spawn in the tiny creek that flows through the park. Hike to the west side of Sandy Beach Park to discover ancient petroglyphs on the rocks. Icebergs from Le Conte Glacier are common along the north side of Frederick Sound and sometimes drift across to Petersburg, especially in winter.

Heading out the Road

South of town, the main road is paved for 18 miles, with a gravel road continuing another 16 miles to the southeast end of Mitkof Island. From this point you have excellent views of the nearby Stikine River mouth and the white-capped peaks of the Coast Range. Canoeists or kayakers (with transportation) may want to start their trip up the Stikine from here rather than at Wrangell.

Hammer Slough, Petersburg

Approximately eight miles out is a small turnoff to **Falls Creek,** a pleasant picnic spot. Stop here to look at the fish ladder (built in 1959) used by coho and pink salmon, as well as steelhead.

Located 15 miles south of town, the **Blind River Rapids Trail** is an easy half-mile boardwalk that leads through the muskeg to a three-sided shelter overlooking the saltwater rapids. Bring your fishing pole. The trail loops back through the muskeg for a total distance of nearly a mile.

A **trumpeter swan observatory** is set up on Blind Slough 16 miles south of Petersburg. A dozen or so of these majestic birds overwinter here and other waterfowl abound during spring and fall migrations. The state-run **Crystal Lake Fish Hatchery** (907/772-4772), 18 miles south of Petersburg, produces king and coho salmon. The kings return in June and July, while the coho come back to spawn from mid-August through September. Blind Slough flows away from the hatchery and is a great place to explore by canoe or kayak. The water gets swimmably warm by mid-summer, and picnic tables sit in the trees. The Forest Service's Ohmer Creek Campground is three miles farther down the road.

LE CONTE GLACIER

Le Conte Glacier, the southernmost tidewater glacier in North America, dips into Le Conte Bay on the mainland, 25 miles east of Petersburg. Part of the vast Stikine Icefield, its glacial ice was once used by local fishermen to keep their catches cold on the way to market in Seattle. Today, locals use it to cool their drinks. Le Conte Bay is home to 2,000 harbor seals. The entire area is included within the 448,841-acre **Stikine–Le Conte Wilderness.**

There are no Forest Service cabins in Le Conte Bay, but an excellent one is on **Mallard Slough** (reservations: 518/885-3639 or 877/444-6777, www.reserveusa.com, $35), near its entrance. A 1.5-mile trail connects the cabin and Le Conte Bay, where you're likely to find icebergs high and dry at low tide. A fine trip for experienced sea kayakers is to head up the Stikine River from Wrangell and then into Le Conte Bay, 10 miles north, before crossing Frederick Sound and continuing on to Petersburg. Total distance is approximately 50 miles (longer if you explore the Stikine River or Le Conte Bay).

Getting There

The visitor center has a complete listing of boat charters for sightseeing and fishing around the area. Good companies include **Kaleidoscope Cruises** (907/772-3736 or 800/868-4373, www.alaska.net/~bbsea), **Petersburg Creek Charters** (907/772-2425, www.alaska.net/~psgcreek), **Alaskan Escapes** (907/772-2782, www.alaskanescapes.com), **Hook & Eye Adventures** (907/772-3400, www.alaska.net/~hookeye), and **Whale Song Cruises** (907/772-9393, www.whalesongcruises.com).

A number of local companies rent skiffs, but be forewarned that weather conditions across Frederick Sound can sometimes change abruptly, so don't go out unless you have considerable experience in small boats. Also be sure to stay well away from the face of Le Conte Glacier. There are other hazards near the glacier—including hidden ice below the water that suddenly breaks loose and rises to the surface—so it really isn't a good idea to do this without a guide.

Kupreanof Flying Service (907/772-3396, www.kupreanof.com), **Nordic Air** (907/772-3535), and **Pacific Wing** (907/772-4258, www.pacificwing.com) all charge around $250 for a 45-minute flightseeing trip over the glacier (up to three people). **Temsco Helicopters** (907/772-4780 or 877/789-9501, www.temscoair.com) also offers flightseeing tours.

SEA KAYAKING TOURS

Contact **Tongass Kayak Adventures** (907/772-4600, www.tongasskayak.com) for sea kayaking around the harbor and up Petersburg Creek. Four-hour trips with guide are $70. The company also runs multiday kayaking tours to Le Conte Glacier, the Stikine River, and Tebenkof Bay, and rent kayaks for do-it-yourselfers.

HIKING AND CABINS

Stop by the **Forest Service district office** at Nordic and Haugen for detailed maps of local hiking trails and 25 nearby cabins (reservations: 518/885-3639 or 877/444-6777, www.reserveusa.com, $35). A pleasant walk takes off from Nordic Drive, three miles from town and just beyond Sandy Beach, and continues down a mile-long boardwalk to **Frederick Point.** Along the way, you get a taste of muskeg, rainforest, and a creek that's packed with salmon in August. You can return to town along the beach.

A short in-town boardwalk leads through the muskeg from the top of Excel Street to the senior center on 12th Street. The center is crowded with flowers outside, along with a menagerie of ducks, rabbits, geese, turkeys, and chickens. Right across the street is the Forest Service's area office. In addition, the half-mile **Hungry Point Trail** traverses the muskeg from Hungry Point to the ball field.

Ravens Roost Cabin

Petersburg has one of the few Forest Service cabins in Southeast Alaska that can be reached by hiking from town. The Ravens Roost cabin lies 1,600 feet above sea level at the end of a four-mile trail that starts near the airport. The trail crosses muskeg for the first mile and becomes very steep (and often mucky) for the next mile through the forest before breaking into open muskeg again along a ridge. Here the trail is in better condition and you are treated to grand views of Devil's Thumb and the surrounding country. The path ends at a two-level Forest Service cabin with space for up to eight people. Allow three hours for the hike up and be sure to make advance reservations for the cabin through the Forest Service.

Three Lakes Recreation Area

Very popular with locals for picnicking, fishing, and berry picking is the beautiful Three Lakes Recreation Area along Forest Service Road 6235, 22 miles southeast of town. You can hitch there, but it's a long hike back to town if your thumb is numb. Each lake has a rowboat and picnic table and you may want to camp nearby at the old three-sided shelter built by the CCC along tiny **Shelter Lake.** An easy three-mile boardwalk loop trail connects the lakes, and a boardwalk trail continues from Sand Lake to nearby Ideal Cove, a mile and a half away. The three main lakes (Sand, Hill, and Crane) are named after the sandhill cranes that announce each spring.

Kupreanof Trails and Cabins

On nearby Kupreanof Island, the Petersburg Mountain and Petersburg Lake trails provide good hiking and great views. Both paths begin at Bayou Point directly across Wrangell Narrows. Contact **Petersburg Creek Charters** (907/772-2425, www.alaska.net/~psgcreek) for a water taxi from town. A number of Forest Service cabins are available on Kupreanof.

For **Petersburg Mountain Trail,** walk north (right) up the road 1.5 miles to the trail marker. Be prepared for a very steep, muddy, and brushy path, rising 3,000 feet in a distance of only 2.5 miles. From the top, however, you'll be rewarded with outstanding views of the entire Petersburg area.

Petersburg Lake Trail provides an easy 6.5-mile hike to a Forest Service cabin on Petersburg Lake within the 46,777-acre **Petersburg Creek–Duncan Salt Chuck Wilderness.** Check with the Forest Service for current conditions on both of these trails. From Petersburg Lake it's possible to continue another 10.5 miles along a primitive trail to the Forest Service's Salt Chuck East Cabin. The trail is nearly level the entire distance and offers spectacular views of Portage Mountain.

On the south end of Kupreanof Island is **Kah Sheets Lake,** where the Forest Service has a very popular A-frame cabin. It's a 30-minute flight from Petersburg. A three-mile trail leads from the lake to Kah Sheets Bay, where you can fish for coho and sockeye salmon. A second Forest Service cabin sits along the bay.

West Point Cabin, in Portage Bay on the north end of Kupreanof Island, is a great spot to watch for whales, and the beach makes for good hiking.

Thomas Bay Area

Several of the most popular local Forest Service cabins are in the country around Thomas Bay, on the mainland approximately 20 miles from Petersburg. Spectacular Baird and Patterson Glaciers feed into this bay. Reserve months ahead to ensure a spot. **Cascade Creek Cabin** is on the saltwater and is accessible by either air or charter boat. Backpackers will love **Cascade Creek Trail,** one of the best (and steepest) paths in the Southeast. This three-mile path climbs 3,000 feet from the cabin to Falls Lake, passing cascading water much of the way. A three-sided shelter (free) sits along the shore of Falls Lake, and there's good fishing for rainbow trout. Hikers can continue two more miles up the trail beyond Falls Lake to Swan Lake. **Swan Lake Cabin** is on the opposite end of the lake from the trailhead and offers great views of the rocky mountain country. Contact the Petersburg Forest Service office for details on trail conditions and access.

ACCOMMODATIONS

For a complete list of local lodging choices, see the Petersburg Chamber of Commerce website (www.petersburg.org) or try www.petersburg alaska.com.

Petersburg Bunk & Breakfast (805 Gjoa St., 907/772-3632, www.bunkandbreakfast.com) is a friendly home hostel where $25 gets you a bunk in a four-person dorm, including kitchen access and self-serve breakfast. Reservations required for winter stays.

Tides Inn (307 N. 1st., 907/772-4288 or 800/665-8433, www.tidesinnalaska.com, $70 s, $85 d) is Petersburg's largest lodging place, with clean and well maintained rooms, some with fridges and microwaves. Very friendly owners too.

Yurtsville Retreat (907/772-2921, www.alaska .net/~yurts, $88 d) is Petersburg's most unique lodging choice. Two large and nicely furnished yurts are set in trees and muskeg four miles south of town. Each contains a kitchen, gas fireplace, and queen bed; $10 per person for extra guests. An outhouse and showers are a few steps away. Guests will love the outdoor hot tub and lov-

ingly landscaped grounds. One of the owners is from Chile, making this a good place to practice your Spanish.

Scandia House (110 Nordic Dr., 907/772-4281 or 800/722-5006), is a modern building with well-maintained and brightly furnished rooms. Standard rooms (some with kitchenettes) go for $90–130 s or $100–140 d. Full suites with in-room hot tubs and king beds cost $185 d. A courtesy van is available.

A number of fishing lodges line the Wrangell Narrows, offering multinight stays, but the nicest is **Rocky Point Resort** (907/772-4420, www.rocky ptresort.com), midway along the channel.

Bed-and-Breakfasts

Water's Edge B&B, (705 Sandy Beach Rd., 907/772-3736 or 800/868-4373, www.alaska .net/~bbsea, $90 s, $100 d) is a fine place if you want peace and quiet, with a beachfront room facing Frederick Sound. The two guest rooms have private baths, and a light breakfast is served. A canoe, bikes, and courtesy van are available for guests, and the owners also run Kaleidoscope Cruises.

One of Petersburg's older homes (built in the 1920s), **Broom Hus B&B** (411 S. Nordic, 907/772-3459, www.aptalaska.net/~broomhus, closed Feb.–April) has a downstairs apartment for $70 s or $85 d, plus $15 per person (max six people). The kitchen is stocked for a make-it-yourself breakfast.

Das Hagedorn Haus—The Hawthorne House (400 2nd St., 907/772-3775, www .alaska.net/~trask, $80 s, $90 d)—is similar, an attractive basement apartment with a full kitchen, including a light breakfast.

Another good local place is **Nordic House B&B** (1106 Nordic Dr., 907/772-3620, www.nordichouse.net, $77 s, $88 d). This comfortable home has four guest rooms with private or shared baths, plus a light breakfast; $99 for the apartment. A glassed-in deck overlooks the harbor.

Built in 1997, **Waterfront B&B** (1004 S. Nordic Dr., 907/772-9300, www.alaska.nte /~h20frbnb, $95–105 d) stands on pilings along the shore just north of the ferry terminal. Three guest rooms have private baths and share a sitting room and large waterside deck; continental breakfast included.

Other places to check out include **Feathered Nest B&B** (907/772-3090, www.featherednest-bandb.com), **Heather & Rose Guest Hus** (907/772-4675, www.alaska.net/~hrosehus), and **A Lille Hus B&B** (907/772-4810).

Camping
Those with a vehicle or willing to try hitching should head south 22 miles to the Forest Service's **Ohmer Creek Campground** ($6). This is a quiet place in a flower-filled meadow along Blind Slough, with tap water available. Not far away is the quarter-mile-long, wheelchair-accessible **Ohmer Creek Trail,** complete with interpretive signs. This is a beautiful old-growth rainforest walk, with steelhead fishing in the spring.

Le Conte RV Park (4th and Haugen, 907/772-4680) has tent and RV spaces in town, and **Tonka RV Park** (907/772-4814) is right on the water south of town, but is basically a parking lot (no bathhouse).

FOOD
Drop by **AlasKafe** (907/772-5282), upstairs on the corner of Nordic and Excel, for an espresso and pastry in the morning, lunchtime panini, or Friday and Saturday night seafood dinners. **Helse Cafe** (on Sing Lee Alley, 907/772-3444), serves inexpensive and earthy sandwiches, burgers, salads, and chai lattes, plus ice cream and shakes.

Given the importance of fishing in the local economy, it comes as no surprise that Petersburg has a number of places offering fresh seafood. Budget watchers should try the docks to buy fresh-caught crab, halibut, or shrimp. **Coastal Cold Storage Fish Market** (306 N. Nordic Dr., 907/772-4177) serves tasty halibut beer bits, shrimp baskets, reubens, wraps, and other lunch fare, plus omelets for breakfast. You can also buy fresh fish, scallops, crab (cooked if you like), and other seafood.

Tonka Seafoods (907/772-3662 or 888/560-3662, www.tonkaseafoods.com) specializes in premium smoked, canned, or fresh salmon and halibut. The retail store, across from the Sons of Norway Hall on Sing Lee Alley, is open weekdays, with hour-long tours ($5) at 1:30 P.M.; minimum of six.

For some of the better pizzas in the Southeast, head to **Papa Bear's Pizzeria** (907/772-3727), a small shop across from the ferry terminal. In addition to whole pizzas and pizza slices, they serve burritos, wraps, calzones, ice cream, and espresso.

Next door is **Joan Mei Chinese Restaurant** (907/772-4222), serving breakfast, American grub, and Chinese food, including a surprisingly good wonton soup.

Located inside Kito's Kave on Sing Lee Alley, **El Rincon** (907/772-3207) is worth a visit for fast Mexican lunches.

Prices for food and other items are higher in Petersburg than in other Southeast towns. Two local grocers have all the supplies: **Hammer & Wikan** (1300 Haugen Dr., 907/772-4246, www.hammerandwikan.com), with a full deli and bakery, and the downtown **Trading Union** (907/772-3881).

ENTERTAINMENT AND EVENTS
Petersburg's **Little Norway Festival,** held each year on the weekend nearest Norwegian Independence Day (May 17), is the town's biggest event. The three-day festivities include a parade, crafts, pageant, and a big seafood feast. The **American Independence Day** (July 4) is another time for fun and games, and the annual king salmon derby in late May is always popular with locals.

The annual **Petersburg Canned Salmon Classic** is a contest to guess the number of cans of salmon packed by local canneries each year; $2,500 goes to the person who comes closest. It's awarded in mid-August.

Live music, booze, cigarette smoke, and a clientele of local toughs make for good fights in **Kito's Kave** (on Sing Lee Alley, 907/772-3207). The nautically themed **Harbor Bar** (on Nordic Dr., 907/772-4526) is a good place to meet local fishermen over a beer.

INFORMATION AND SERVICES

The **Petersburg Visitor Information Center** (corner of 1st and Fram streets, 907/772-4636 or 866/484-4700, www.petersburg.org) has travel brochures only. Hours are Sunday noon–4 P.M., Monday–Saturday 9 A.M.–5 P.M., May–September; and Monday–Friday 10 A.M.–2 P.M. the rest of the year.

The Forest Service (907/772-3871) publishes a map of the Petersburg area, *Mitkof Island Road Guide,* available from the visitor center or its office on Main Street. The map is a must if you're planning to ride a mountain bike around the island.

Get cash 24 hours a day from ATMs at First Bank and Wells Fargo. The post office (907/772-3121) is out near the airport on Haugen Drive, and the **Petersburg Library** (907/772-3349, www.ci.petersburg.ak.us) is upstairs in the municipal building on Nordic Drive. Stop by here to check your email. For additional Internet access, plug into **System Overload** (110 Harbor Way, 907/772-2343).

Coin-op showers are downtown at the harbormaster's office, and at **Glacier Laundry** on Nordic Drive. For a better deal, paddle over to the Petersburg High School swimming pool (907/772-3304). A fine community gym is nearby, complete with weight room and racquetball courts. **Petersburg Medical Center** (on 2nd and Fram, 907/772-4299) is the local hospital.

Shopping

Sing Lee Alley Books (907/772-4440), next to the Sons of Norway Hall, has an excellent collection of Alaskan books and other choice reading material. **CubbyHole** (102 S. 2nd St., 907/772-2717) sells Norwegian-style handicrafts decorated with rosemaling designs.

Petersburg has two notable galleries: **The Framers Loft Gallery** (on Sing Lee Alley, 907/772-2471) and **Seaport Gallery & Gifts** (on Main St., 907/772-3015). Get beautiful Norwegian and Icelandic sweaters at **Lee's Clothing** (207 Nordic Dr., 907/772-4229).

TRANSPORTATION

Petersburg is strung out along Wrangell Narrows, with the **ferry terminal** (907/772-3855) a mile south of the town center. During the summer, ferries run almost daily both northbound and southbound from Petersburg. They usually stop for an hour or two, long enough to walk into town or at least check out the nearby harbor. The ferry terminal opens two hours before ship arrivals and generally stays open a half-hour after it departs. For reservations and schedules, contact the Alaska Marine Highway (907/465-3941 or 800/642-0066, www.ferryalaska.com).

City Cab (907/772-3003) and **Maine Cab** (907/772-6969) both charge $4 for transport from the ferry to town.

Rent cars from **Allstar Rent-A-Car** (907/772-4281 or 800/722-5006) at Scandia House, or **Avis** (907/772-4716 or 800/331-1212, www.tidesinnalaska.com) in Tides Inn.

Petersburg Airport is a mile southeast of town on Haugen Drive. **Alaska Airlines** (907/772-4255 or 800/426-0333, www.alaskaair.com), has daily service to other Southeast towns and the Lower 48. **L.A.B. Flying Service** (907/772-4300 or 800/426-0543, www.labflying.com) also has air taxi service to Kake and Juneau. **Pacific Wing** (907/772-9258, www.pacificwing.com), **Kupreanof Flying Service** (907/772-3396, www.kupreanof.com), and **Nordic Air** (907/772-3535) all provide air charter service to Forest Service cabins. **Temsco Helicopters** (907/772-4780 or 877/789-9501, www.temscoair.com) offers helicopter service.

KAKE

The small Tlingit village of Kake (pop. 700) lies along the northwest shore of Kupreanof Island, halfway between Petersburg and Sitka. Kake's claim to fame is the **world's tallest totem pole,** exhibited at the 1970 World's Fair in Osaka, Japan. This 132-foot pole is unique in that it contains figures representing all the Tlingit clans on a single pole. Kake is also the starting point for sea kayak trips into two large wilderness areas on nearby Kuiu Island.

History

During the 1800s the Kake tribe had a reputation as one of the fiercest in the Southeast. Richard Meade (1871) recorded the following incident: "In 1855 a party of Kakes, on a visit south to Puget Sound, became involved in some trouble there, which caused a United States vessel to open fire on them, and during the affair one of the Kake chiefs was killed. This took place over 800 miles from the Kake settlements on Kupreanof Island. The very next year the tribe sent a canoe-load of fighting men all the way from Clarence Straits in Russian America to Whidby's Island in Washington Territory, and attacked and beheaded an ex-collector—not of internal revenue, for that might have been pardonable—but of customs, and returned safely with his skull and scalp to their villages. Such people are, therefore, not to be despised, and are quite capable of giving much trouble in the future unless wisely and firmly governed." John Muir later described a visit to a Kake village where human bones were scattered all over the ground, reminders of previous battles: "Chief Yana Taowk seemed to take pleasure in kicking the Sitka bones that lay in his way, and neither old nor young showed the slightest trace of superstitious fear of the dead at any time." Needless to say, the people of Kake treat outsiders in a friendlier manner today.

Recreation

If you have the time, equipment, and skill, nearby **Kuiu Island** (pronounced Q-U) provides excellent kayaking and canoeing opportunities. The area is filled with an enjoyable network of islands and waterways. The Forest Service has cleared four portages ranging 1–4 miles in length, making it possible to do a variety of loop trips. Plan on at least a week and be sure to check with the Forest Service on current trail conditions, especially the Alecks Creek Portage. Be cautious along portions of Kuiu Island exposed to ocean swells, particularly near Point Ellis. Three Forest Service cabins are along the route. Also of interest are the protected waters of scenic **Rocky Pass** separating Kupreanof and Kuiu Islands. Because of the numerous reefs, the pass is treacherous for

boats, but can be run in a kayak if you traverse with the tidal flows.

Two wilderness areas encompass the south and west sides of Kuiu Island; other parts have been heavily logged. Dozens of interesting islands, islets, and coves crowd the west side of Kuiu in the 67,000-acre **Tebenkof Bay Wilderness,** while the south end includes the 60,000-acre **Kuiu Wilderness.** The Forest Service publishes a detailed map of Kuiu Island, with descriptions of all portages and routes. Get a copy of *Kuiu Island/Tebenkof Bay Canoe/Kayak Routes* from Petersburg Ranger District (907/772-3871). Experienced kayakers will enjoy the paddle between Kake and Petersburg around the south end of Kupreanof Island. There is open water in places, but a good portion of the route is protected and the state ferry makes it easy to get between Kake and Petersburg. Contact Tongass Kayak Adventures for sea kayak tours within Tebenkof Bay Wilderness.

Practicalities

Nugget Inn (907/785-6469, $39 s, $49 d) has a few rooms with bath down the hall. **Waterfront Lodge** (907/785-3472, www.waterfront-lodgekake.com, $75 s, $95 d) has attractive rooms, one with a kitchenette. Another good place is **Keex' Kwaan Lodge** (907/785-3434, www.kakealaska.com, $85 s, $95 d).

Both Keex' Kwaan and Nugget Inn have restaurants. Get groceries from **SOS Value-Mart** (907/785-6444). Kake has a laundromat and liquor store, but no bank. For local information, contact the **City of Kake** (907/785-3804).

Camping facilities are not available and much of the land around Kake is privately owned, but camping is permitted on Forest Service land, two miles south of town. Kake is one of the drier towns in the Southeast, with only 50 inches per year of precipitation. The town has a fish hatchery and cold-storage plant but no Forest Service office. Ask at the Forest Service office in Petersburg about the Cathedral Falls, Goose Lake, and Hamilton River Trails. **Big John Cabin** on Big John Bay is accessible via the road network from Kake.

The **Alaska Marine Highway** (800/642-0066, www.ferryalaska.com) ferry *Le Conte* visits

Kake twice a week, heading both east to Petersburg and west to Sitka. It docks a mile and a half from the center of town. There is a covered shelter area, but no phone. The ferry usually stops just long enough to load and unload cars (a half-hour or so).

L.A.B. Flying Service (907/785-6435 or 800/426-0543, www.labflying.com) has daily service from Kake to Petersburg and Juneau. **Harris Aircraft Services** (907/966-3050 or 877/966-3050, www.harrisaircraft.com) has service several times a week between Sitka and Kake.

Sitka

With its gemlike, island-dotted setting, Sitka (pop. 8,800) is everybody's favorite Southeast Alaska town. On a typical summer day you'll see fishing boats heading out to sea from the four harbors around Sitka Sound, and cruise ships steaming by, their decks crowded with tourists as they pass Mt. Edgecumbe, the Fuji-like snowcapped volcano that adorns Sitka's outer waters. Back in town, other visitors glance inside the Russian church that dominates Sitka's center, wander along totem-pole-lined paths in peaceful Sitka National Historical Park, and climb the sharply rising wooded peaks behind town. The people who make this their home are similarly diverse, ranging from back-to-the-land ecofreaks to beer-guzzling fishermen. This surprising diversity and the gorgeous setting make Sitka a detour well worth the effort. Be forewarned, however, to expect rain—the town soaks in 94 inches a year. By the way, Sitka lays claim to being the "biggest city in America"; its boundaries encircle Baranof Island, fully 4,710 square miles! (New York City covers only 301 square miles.)

Once labeled the "Paris of the North Pacific," New Archangel quickly became the Northwest's most cosmopolitan port. The wealthier citizens lived in elaborate homes filled with crystal and fine lace, but as in czarist Russia itself, the opulence of Sitka did not extend beyond a select few.

Peril Strait

Located on the western shore of Baranof Island, "Sitka-by-the-Sea" is Southeast Alaska's most remote ferry stop, and the only major Inside Passage town to front on the Pacific Ocean. Getting to Sitka by ferry requires a long detour through the scenic but treacherous Peril Strait that separates Baranof and Chichagof Islands—a great

place to watch for eagles perched on trees along the shore. During larger tides, fierce currents prevent ferries from going through, and the ships must time their passage to coincide with a high or low slack tide. The passage narrows to only 300 feet in one spot (24 feet deep). When the tide is really cooking, the buoys are often bent far over by the wild currents. This has one side benefit: The ferry is forced to stay for three hours or so in Sitka, long enough for you to get a taste of this fascinating town. But to see this pretty place better, be sure to stay awhile.

HISTORY
Russian America

First established as a base for collecting sea otter pelts, Sitka has a long and compelling history. In 1799, Alexander Baranof—head of the Russian American Company—founded the settlement under a charter from the czar. Baranof built his original fort, Redoubt St. Michael, near the present Alaska ferry terminal, only to see it destroyed by a Tlingit attack in 1802. (There is evidence that the British, long enemies of the Russians, assisted the Tlingits in the fort's destruction.) Two years later, Baranof returned with 120 soldiers and 800 Aleuts in 300 *baidarkas*, defeating the Tlingits in what was to become the last major resistance by any Northwest Coast Indians. The Russians rebuilt the town, then called New Archangel, on the present site and constructed a stockade enclosing

SITKA

Baranof Island

To Indian
River Trail

To Sawmill Creek
Campground

ALASKA RAPTOR
REHABILITATION
CENTER

*Sitka National
Historical Park*

Indian River

INDIAN RIVER RD.

VISITOR &
CULTURAL CENTER

SHELDON
JACKSON
MUSEUM

SHELDON
JACKSON
COLLEGE

SHELDON JACKSON
HATCHERY

SITKA NATIONAL
CEMETERY

JEFF DAVIS ST.

PARK ST.

ETOLIN ST.

LINCOLN ST.

Crescent Harbor

SAWMILL CREEK BLVD.

Gavan Hill Trail

DEGROFF ST.

BIORKA ST.

BARANOF ST.

SEE DETAIL

Crescent Bay

MONASTERY ST.

SUPER 8
MOTEL

LAKE ST.

LAKE ST.

VERSTOVIA ST.

LAKE ST.

Swan Lake

LAKEVIEW DR.

HALIBUT POINT RD.

ERLER ST.

SEWARD ST.

HARBOR DR.

LINCOLN ST.

Crescent Bay

MARINE ST.

OSPREY ST.

NEW ARCHANGEL ST.

KOGWANTAN ST.

KATLIAN ST.

O'CONNELL
BRIDGE

YOUTH HOSTEL/
METHODIST CHURCH

KIMSHAM ST.

WARSHAM ST.

PETERSON AVE.

EDGECUMBE DR.

LAKESIDE
GROCERIES

JUNIOR HIGH/
SWIMMING POOL

KATLIAN ST.

FRESH FISH CO.

FOREST SERVICE
REGIONAL OFFICE

Thomsen
Harbor

Sitka Channel

SEWARD AVE.

Turning
Island

To Ferry Terminal and
Starrigen Campground

MT. EDGECUMBE
HIGH SCHOOL

Japonski
Island

TONGASS ST.

HARBOR DR.

AIRPORT
TERMINAL

AIRPORT

Whiting Harbor

Detail

Crescent Bay

RUSSIAN
BISHOP'S
HOUSE

MONASTERY ST.

Crescent
Harbor

SHEE ATIKA
LODGE

LAKE ST.

CENTENNIAL HALL/
ISABEL MILLER
MUSEUM

SEWARD ST.

HARBOR DR.

LIBRARY

SITKA
CONVENTION
& VISITORS
BUREAU

OBSERVA-
TORY ST.

AMERICAN ST.

ST. MICHAEL'S
CATHEDRAL

RUSSIAN
GRAVES

BARRACKS
ST.

OLD
HARBOR
BOOKS

MARINE ST.

BLOCKHOUSE

LINCOLN ST.

Castle Hill

KOGWANTAN ST.

PIONEERS
HOME

SITKA HOTEL

KATLIAN ST.

NAA KAHIDI
COMMUNITY
HOUSE

O'CONNELL
BRIDGE

0.25 mi

0.25 km

© AVALON TRAVEL PUBLISHING, INC.

what is now downtown Sitka. New Archangel soon became the capital of Russian America and a vital center for the sea otter and fur seal trade with China. Although the Tlingits were invited back in 1821 (Native leaders say the Russians begged them to return), the groups coexisted uneasily. Tlingits built their houses just outside the stockade, facing a battery of eight Russian cannons.

Once labeled the "Paris of the North Pacific," New Archangel quickly became the Northwest's most cosmopolitan port. By 1840, it was already home to a library of several thousand volumes, a museum, a meteorological observatory, two schools, a hospital, an armory, two orphanages, and dozens of other buildings. The wealthier citizens lived in elaborate homes filled with crystal and fine lace, but as in czarist Russia itself, the opulence of Sitka did not extend beyond a select few. Slavelike working and living conditions were forced upon the Aleut sea otter hunters.

America Takes Over

An emotional ceremony at Sitka in 1867 marked the passage of Alaska from Russian to American hands, and most of the Russians returned to their motherland, including many third-generation Sitkans. Even today, there are locals who speak Russian. Although the town served as Alaska's first capital city for three decades, its importance declined rapidly under the Americans, and it was almost a ghost town by the turn of the century. The territorial government was moved to the then-booming mining town of Juneau in 1900.

During World War II, Sitka became a major link in the defense of Alaska against Japan. Hangars remain from the large amphibious air base just across the bridge on Japonski Island (Fort Ray), and the barracks that once housed 3,500 soldiers were turned into Mt. Edgecumbe High School, Alaska's only boarding high school for Natives. The boarding school is now fully integrated.

Sitka's largest employer until 1993 was a Japanese-owned pulp mill five miles east of town. The mill closed mainly because of the high cost of production and competition from mills elsewhere. Before it closed, the mill gained national attention for dumping large quantities of can-

cer-causing dioxin into nearby Silver Bay, and for being one of the primary forces behind the clear-cut logging of Tongass National Forest. Many Sitkans still work in the fishing and tourism industries, or for the government. The mill's closure did not have nearly the devastating effect the prophets of doom had predicted; in fact Sitka seems to be doing just fine, fueled by tourism and the arrival of retirees. Large cruise ships are in port most summer days, but things aren't nearly as bad (yet) as in Juneau, Ketchikan, or Skagway.

SIGHTS
St. Michael's Cathedral

The most striking symbol of Russian influence in Sitka is St. Michael's Cathedral (907/747-8120), right in the center of town. Built in 1848, the building burned in 1966 but was replaced by a replica a decade later. The original Russian artifacts and icons, including the Sitka Madonna (purportedly a miraculous healer), were saved from the fire and have been returned to their original setting in this, the mother church for

St. Michael's Cathedral

all of Alaska's 20,000 Russian Orthodox. During the summer, the church ($2 donation) is open Monday–Friday 9 A.M.–4 P.M., or whenever cruise ships are in port. It's open by appointment at other times, but is not open to tourists during religious services.

Isabel Miller Museum

This small museum (330 Harbor Dr., 907/747-6455, www.sitka.org/historicalmuseum, donation requested) is tucked away inside Centennial Hall. It's open daily 8 A.M.–5 P.M. in summer; Tuesday–Saturday 10 A.M.–4 P.M. in winter. The museum houses local artifacts and an interesting scale-model of Sitka in 1867 (the year Alaska became a U.S. territory). Out front is a 50-foot carved and painted replica of a **Tlingit war canoe.**

Other Downtown Sights

One of the finest views of Sitka is from the walkway along the distinctive cable-stayed, girder-span bridge that connects Sitka with Japonski Island. On a clear day, you'll have a hard time deciding which direction to look: The mountains of Baranof Island rise up behind the town, while the perfect volcanic cone of **Mt. Edgecumbe** (3,000 feet) on Kruzof Island dominates the opposite vista. Beside the old post office on Lincoln Street a stairway leads up to **Castle Hill,** a tiny state park commemorating the spot where the ceremony transferring Alaska to the United States was held on October 18, 1867. The Kiksadi Indian clan inhabited this hill for many generations before the Russians' arrival. After defeating the Indians, Alexander Baranof built his castlelike house here, but the building burned in 1894. The splendid view makes Castle Hill a must.

The most prominent downtown feature is the large yellow **Alaska Pioneers Home** (built in 1934), housing elderly Alaskans with 15 or more years of state residence. The *Prospector* statue out front was based upon William "Skagway Bill" Fonda, an Alaskan pioneer. Across the road is a **totem pole** bearing the Russian coat of arms, three old English anchors, and a couple of Indian petroglyphs. Adjacent to the Pioneers Home is **Sheet'Ka Kwaan Naa Kahidi Community House,** based upon traditional longhouse designs,

offering Native dance performances in summer. Two tall housescreens dominate the interior.

Atop a small hill just west of the Pioneer Home stands a reconstructed **Russian blockhouse** from the stockade that kept the Indians restricted to the area along Katlian Street. It's open Sunday afternoons during the summer. **Kogwantan and Katlian streets,** directly below the blockhouse, are a picturesque mixture of docks, fish canneries, shops, and old houses, one with its exterior entirely covered in Tlingit designs. The main **Finnish Lutheran Cemetery** (400 graves dating from 1848) is behind the blockhouse at the end of Princess Street. The grave of the Russian **Princess Maksoutoff** is here, and nearby are more Russian graves, including that of Iahov Netsvetov, a Russian Orthodox saint. Cemetery buffs might also be interested in the small **Sitka National Cemetery,** accessible via Jeff Davis Street beside Sheldon Jackson College. It's the oldest national cemetery west of the Mississippi.

Russian Bishop's House

Administered by the National Park Service, the Russian Bishop's House (907/747-6281, www.nps.gov/sitk, daily 9 A.M.–5 P.M. in summer, by reservation the rest of the year) is Sitka's oldest building and one of just four Russian structures still standing in North America. Built in 1842, it was home to Ivan Veniaminov, bishop of Alaska and later head of the entire Russian Orthodox church hierarchy in Moscow. The first floor houses exhibits describing the building and its occupants, as well as the exploits of Russia's American colony. The second floor has been fully restored to its 1853 appearance and is filled with original furnishings and artifacts. Access to the second floor is part of a half-hour tour ($3) led by park interpreters.

Sheldon Jackson Museum

Farther along the waterfront is **Sheldon Jackson College,** with its distinctive brown and white buildings. Established in 1878 as a place to train Alaska's Natives, this is the oldest educational institution in the state. The outstanding Sheldon Jackson Museum (907/747-8981, www.museums.state.ak.us, daily 9 A.M.–5 P.M. mid-

May–mid-Sept., Tues.–Sat. 10 A.M.–4 P.M. rest of year; $4, or free for students) is the state's oldest museum. Dr. Sheldon Jackson (1834–1909) worked as both a Presbyterian missionary and as the first General Agent for Education in Alaska. His extensive travels throughout the territory between 1888 and 1898 allowed him to acquire thousands of Eskimo, Athabascan, Tlingit, Haida, and Aleut artifacts. To protect this priceless collection, a fireproof museum (the first concrete structure in Alaska) was built here in 1895. The museum houses a remarkable selection of kayaks, hunting tools, dogsleds, baskets, bentwood boxes, Eskimo masks, and other artifacts. Be sure to check out the drawers of artifacts beneath the display cases. Also here is a small gift shop selling quality Alaskan jewelry, crafts, and note cards. Native artisans are often at work inside the museum during the summer. A small **salmon hatchery** (907/747-5254) is across the street.

Sitka National Historical Park

For many, the highlight of a visit to Sitka is Sitka National Historical Park, at the mouth of Indian River where the Tlingits and Russians fought their final battle in 1804. The Indians kept the invaders at bay for a week, but with their ammunition exhausted and resupply efforts thwarted, they abandoned the fortress and silently withdrew to Peril Strait. The visitor and Native cultural center (907/747-6281, www.nps.gov/sitk, $3) includes a small museum of Tlingit culture. It's open daily 8 A.M.–5 P.M. in the summer, and Monday–Friday 8 A.M.–5 P.M. the rest of the year. In summertime, Native craft workers can be seen producing bead blankets, jewelry, and woodcarving in the workshop. The 10-minute historical slide show, "Battle of Sitka," is very informative, and rangers offer historical walks four days a week in the summer.

Quite a few historical totems are housed in one large room, and outside are 15 more totems, most of which were carved for the 1904 St. Louis World's Fair. The totems line a one-mile trail through the lush second-growth spruce forest, with outstanding views of Sitka Sound along the way. You'll find spawning pink salmon in Indian River (near the 1804 battleground) late in the summer. The park is a peaceful place, with mysterious in-the-trees totems, strident calls of ravens and eagles, and the lapping of waves combining to enhance the beauty.

Alaska Raptor Center

Located off Sawmill Creek Road, this impressive facility (907/747-8662 or 800/643-9425, www.alaskaraptor.org, $12 adults, $6 kids under 12) has two dozen or so bald eagles and other birds of prey—including owls, hawks, falcons, and ravens—at any given time. Most are recovering from gunshots, car accidents, or encounters with power lines. Of the birds brought in, a third recover sufficiently to be released back into the wild. Most of the others end up in captive breeding or educational programs in the Lower 48. Get to the center by walking out of town along Sawmill Creek Road a couple hundred feet beyond the Indian River bridge. The access road takes off to your left a short distance beyond this. A more scenic route is to follow the trails through Sitka National Historical Park or along the Indian River behind Sheldon Jackson College. It's an easy 10-minute walk from Sitka National Historical Park, or 20 minutes from the center of town. The Community Ride Bus ($2) takes you within two blocks of the center.

A focal point is the 20,000-square-foot flight-training center that replicates the rainforest environment outside; visitors watch the eagles through one-way glass. Staff use the enclosure to teach eagles survival skills prior to their release. Out back is a deck overlooking a large enclosure (mew) where eagles unable to survive in the wild are kept. Additional mews with hawks, owls, and other birds are along a rain forest path. The gift shop sells all sorts of eagle paraphernalia.

Visitors get the chance to meet one of the birds up-close, and are given a half-hour tour and video. The center is open Sunday–Friday 8 A.M.–4 P.M. May–September, and there's always someone on hand whenever a cruise ship or ferry is in town. No winter tours.

Farther out Sawmill Creek Rd. (at Mile 6) is **Whale Park,** consisting of a roadside turnout with interpretive signs and a boardwalk to an overlook where there's a good chance of seeing whales during the fall and winter months.

SOUTHEAST ALASKA

Tours

The ferry terminal is seven miles from town, but despite the distance you'll have time for a quick "ferry stopover tour," even if you don't stay. Many folks ride the **Sitka Tours** buses (907/747-8443, round-trip $12 adults, $6 kids) that meet the ferries and stop at the cathedral and Sitka National Historical Park. If you have more time in Sitka, you may want to join the three-hour narrated tour ($25 adults, $13 kids) that takes in most of the local sights and emphasizes Russian history. They also offer 2.5-hour guided historic and nature walks ($28 adults or $14 kids).

Tribal Tours (907/747-3770 or 888/270-8687, www.sitkatours.com, $42 adults, $32 children), offers a Tlingit slant to tours of Sitka's sights. The 2.5-hour bus tours include a traditional dance performance at the Tribal Community House, plus visits to most local sights.

Harbor Mountain Tours (907/747-8294, $30 adults, $20 kids) takes visitors to the summit of Harbor Mountain and out to Starrigavan River.

St. Lazaria Islands National Wildlife Refuge is a great place to see tufted puffins, storm petrels, auklets, whales, seals, and Steller sea lions. Two recommended companies with a strong biological orientation are **Raven's Fire** (907/747-5777 or 888/747-4789, www.ravensfire.com) and **Sitka's Secrets** (907/747-5089, www.sitkasecret.com). Both offer cruises to the refuge and to other parts of Sitka Sound, including **Goddard Hot Springs,** a favorite locals' relaxation place accessible only by boat or floatplane.

Allen Marine Tours (907/747-8100 or 888/747-8101, www.allenmarine.com) offers a two-hour "Wildlife Quest" Tuesday and Thursday evenings, plus Saturday and Sunday mornings. If sea conditions aren't too rough, these include time at St. Lazaria Island and Salisbury Sound. Two-hour tours cost $49 adults, $30 kids.

For something completely different, **Sea Life Discovery Tours** (907/966-2301 or 877/966-2301, www.sealifediscoverytours.com, May–Sept.), operates the only semi-submersible vessel in Alaska, with large underwater windows and an underwater camera for close-up views on the video monitor. It's a fun way to view kelp forests, fish, crab, sea urchins, anemones, starfish, and other creatures without getting wet. Two-hour tours cost $79 adults, $59 kids, and a 1.5-hour tour is available on weekends for $50 adults, $38 kids.

HIKING AND CABINS

The Forest Service's **Sitka Ranger District Office** (204 Siginaka Way, 907/747-4220) has up-to-date information on the more than 40 miles of local trails, ranging from gentle nature walks to treks that take you high up onto nearby peaks. Contact **Sitka Bike & Hike** (907/747-4821 or 877/292-5325, www.sitkaadventures.com) for guided hikes and bike rides.

Indian River Trail

One of the finest of Sitka's trails, this is an easy valley hike within walking distance of town. The route follows a clear salmon stream through the rainforest, with a chance to see brown bear and deer. Begin by heading out Sawmill Creek Road and turning left onto Indian River Road. Continue past the gate about a half-mile to the city water pumphouse. The gentle trail leads from here up along the Indian River and a tributary to the right as far as a lovely 80-foot waterfall in a V-shaped valley. The last mile of the trail is not well maintained. Allow six hours round-trip to cover the 5.5-mile trail.

Gaven Hill Trail

This "stairway to heaven" walkway starts at the end of Baranof Street and climbs three miles to the top of 2,650-foot Gaven Hill. (Bear right at the junction with Cross Trail just under a mile up.) Gaven Hill Trail then switchbacks to a long ridge that opens onto subalpine meadows before a steep final climb up the last 200 feet of elevation. From here, it's relatively easy to follow rock cairns on through the alpine, connecting to the Harbor Mountain Trail. This makes an outstanding loop hike with impressive vistas of Sitka Sound.

Harbor Mountain Trail

One of the easiest and most scenic ways to get into the alpine is via Harbor Mountain Trail. Built by the Army during World War II, the road originally provided access to a lookout post for invading Japanese ships and submarines (none were ever seen, though a whale was once mistakenly bombed). Head four miles out Halibut Point Road and turn right onto Harbor Mountain Road. The gravel road climbs five miles up the mountain to an elevation of 2,000 feet, but snow blocks the way until June. On sunny days the view over Sitka Sound is breathtaking. Those without a car or mountain bike should be able to hitch a ride up with locals. You could also join a tour to the top from **Harbor Mountain Tours** (907/747-8294, $25 for 2.5 hours).

A trail begins at the parking area on top and switchbacks up a side hill before leveling out in the subalpine meadows. A spur trail heads to an overlook here, but the main trail turns right and continues past the ruins of wartime lookout buildings. Beyond this, rock cairns follow the ridge, and the path eventually connects with the Gaven Hill Trail back to town. A small hut (no stove) provides a camping place approximately three miles in.

Mt. Verstovia Trail

On a clear day get spectacular views of Sitka Sound and Mt. Edgecumbe from the Mt. Verstovia Trail, a strenuous climb to this pointy peak overlooking Sitka. The steep 2.5-mile trail begins on the west side of the Kiksadi Club, two miles east of town on Sawmill Creek Road. The trail is brushy and poorly maintained, and inexperienced hikers have gotten lost. You'll pass some old Russian charcoal pits (signposted) only a quarter-mile from the trailhead. The route switchbacks to a ridge, which you follow to the shoulder of Mt. Verstovia. The true summit is farther northeast along the ridge. Allow four hours for the return trip as far as the "shoulder" (2,000 feet), six hours round-trip to the top (2,550 feet).

Beaver Lake Trail

This excellent mile-long trail begins at the bridge in Sawmill Creek Campground seven miles east of town. The path gains 250 feet in elevation as it climbs through the forest and out onto a boardwalk over the muskeg to Beaver Lake. The lake has been stocked with grayling and is one of the

only places to catch these fish in the Southeast. There are fishing platforms along the lakeshore.

Mt. Edgecumbe

Mt. Edgecumbe, a 3,000-foot volcanic cone that looks like Mt. Fuji, can be climbed via a 6.5-mile trail that starts on the southeast shore of Kruzof Island. The last mile is above timberline through red volcanic ash. The island is 10 miles west of Sitka and can be reached by kayak (beware of ocean swells) or by arranging for a skiff drop-off. Stay in Fred's Creek Cabin at the trailhead or in the free three-sided shelter halfway up. Panoramic views can be had from atop this dormant volcano.

Cabins

The Forest Service has 24 cabins (reservations: 518/885-3639 or 877/444-6777, www.reserveusa.com, $35) in the Sitka area, most accessed by floatplane or water taxi from Sitka.

Redoubt Lake Cabin is at the end of a six-mile trail that starts in Silver Bay (10 miles southeast of Sitka). The cabin is also accessible by sea kayak from town, and a short portage takes you to Redoubt Lake.

The wheelchair-accessible **Lake Eva Cabin** is 27 miles northeast of Sitka on Baranof Island. **Plotnikof Lake Cabin** sits in the heart of the spectacularly rugged South Baranof Wilderness Area, a 45-minute flight from Sitka.

Baranof Lake Cabin looks across this blue-green lake to a waterfall. A trail at the end of the lake leads a half-mile to the little settlement of **Baranof Warm Springs,** where a privately owned hot springs is available.

Brent's Beach Cabin is on the eastern shore of Kruzof Island, 15 miles northwest of Sitka. There's a white-sand beach out front (rare in the Southeast), and interesting caves and lava domes just up the shore.

The **Allan Point Cabin,** 16 miles north of Sitka, is an impressive, two-story log cabin that commands a fine view across Nakwasina Sound from its location on the northeast end of Halleck Island. The equally spacious **Samsing Cove Cabin** sleeps 10 folks comfortably and is just six miles south of Sitka.

OTHER RECREATION

The protected waters near Sitka provide excellent kayak access to many Forest Service cabins and trails. **Baidarka Boats** (201 Lincoln St., 907/747-8996, www.kayaksite.com), above Old Harbor Books, rents fiberglass and folding sea kayaks, and offers instruction at all levels. Baidarka also offers half-day and all-day guided kayak trips.

Sitka Sound Ocean Adventures (907/747-6375, www.ssoceanadventures.com) offers guided kayak day trips ($55 for two hours) and rents kayaks. They also have a floathouse ($150–170 for six or more) at Coogan Bay that makes a good base for soft-adventure kayaking. The ubiquitous **Alaska Travel Adventures** (907/789-0052 or 800/478-0052, www.alaskaadventures.com) also leads sea kayak trips for $85, but these are geared to the cruise ship crowd.

Local water taxis will do kayaker and hiker drop-offs; **Sitka Water Taxi** (907/747-5970, www.sitkawatertaxi.com) and **EZC Transfer** (907/747-5044) are good choices.

Many visitors to Sitka come to fish in these pristine waters. The visitors bureau has a handout describing 45 or so local charter boat operators, and provides the same information online.

Scuba divers are increasingly discovering the beauty of local waters during the winter months (when the sea is clearer). **Southeast Diving and Sports** (105 Monastery, 907/747-8279) has scuba gear for rent, and can direct you to local charter boat operators willing to take you out.

Rent quality mountain bikes from **Yellow Jersey Cycle Shop** (329 Harbor Dr., 907/747-6317) downtown. Jeff Budd of **Sitka Bike & Hike** (907/747-4821 or 877/292-5325, www.sitkaadventures.com) leads biking and hiking tours.

ACCOMMODATIONS

The Sitka Convention & Visitors Bureau produces a pamphlet and website that detail hotels, motels, B&Bs, fishing lodges, wilderness lodges, private apartments, and houses.

Hostel

The **Sitka Youth Hostel** (303 Kimsham Rd.,

907/747-8661, $10 for AYH members, $13 for nonmembers) is in the Methodist church. If you're arriving by ferry, the shuttle bus will drop you at the door. The hostel is open 6 P.M.–9:30 A.M., with an 11 P.M. curfew. It has cooking facilities and a friendly staff that accommodates travelers arriving at any hour; call ahead to make sure they'll be open for you. There's usually space, and the hostel is open June–August; sleeping bag required.

Hotels and Motels

Built in 1939, **Sitka Hotel** (118 Lincoln St., 907/747-3288, www.sitkahotel.com) has been beautifully restored to a Victorian splendor that it probably never had even when new. Rooms with private baths are a reasonable $75 s or $80 d, and most of these have small fridges. Those with a bath down the hall are an even better bargain: $55 s or $60 d.

Cascade Inn (2035 Halibut Point Rd., 907/747-6804 or 800/532-0908, www.cascadeinnsitka.com) has standard rooms for $115–125 d, and kitchenettes for $140 d. The building is two miles out of town, and all rooms include private balconies facing the water. Guests also have access to a sauna, and bikes are available for rent.

Super 8 Motel (404 Sawmill Creek Rd., 907/747-8804 or 800/800-8000, $116–128 s or d) has predictable rooms, including a jacuzzi and continental breakfast.

Westmark Shee Atika Lodge (330 Seward St., 907/747-6241 or 800/544-0970, www.westmarkhotels.com, $159 d) is Sitka's largest lodging place, with a couple of suites for $199–235 d.

Sitka's most distinctive lodging option is **Rockwell Lighthouse** (907/747-3056), a modern three-bedroom home built in the shape of a lighthouse on an island less than a mile from town. Access is by skiff (provided). With its nautical decor, curving interior staircase up into the lighthouse, and picture-perfect setting, you'll be signing up for lighthouse duty after a night or two here. The entire house rents for $150 d or $200 for four people, plus $35/day if you want use of the hot tub. This place fills up fast in the summer, so call a year ahead for reservations in mid-summer. No credit cards.

Bed-and-Breakfasts

The Sitka Convention and Visitors Bureau has links to two-dozen local B&Bs, and you can also try www.accommodations-alaska.com.

Angler's Landing B&B (206 Lance Dr., 907/747-6055, www.anglerslanding.com, $70 d) has reasonably priced rooms with continental breakfast and shared bath. They're close to the Raptor Center.

Helga's B&B (907/747-5497, $75 d) is a large beachside home three miles out Halibut Point Road. The five guest rooms have private baths, and a continental breakfast is served.

Within walking distance of downtown, **Ann's Gavan Hill B&B** (415 Arrowhead St., 907/747-8023, www.annsgavanhill.com, $70 s, $80 d) features three guest rooms with a hot tub, full breakfasts, disabled access, and relaxed Alaskan atmosphere.

Biorka B&B (611 Biorka St., 907/747-3111, $85 d) is a quaint in-town home with two guest rooms with private baths and entrances, plus a continental breakfast.

At **Baranof Island B&B** (401 Charteris St., 907/747-8306, www.baranofislandbandb.com, $85 d) two guest rooms share a bath on a private level of this comfortable home. A full breakfast is included.

Annahootz B&B (907/747-6498 or 800/746-6498, www.sitka.org/annahootz, $95 d) has two suites with private baths and kitchenettes, including a make-it-yourself breakfast.

Alaska Ocean View B&B (1101 Edgecumbe Dr., 907/747-8310 or 888/811-6870, www.sitka-alaska-lodging.com, $109–159 s, $119–189 d) is a shoreside home with fabulous Sitka Sound vistas. Two guest rooms and a suite have private baths, and include a big breakfast. Other amenities include in-room fireplaces and a hot tub.

Crescent Harbor Hideaway (709 Lincoln St., 907/747-4900, www.sitkabedandbreakfast.com) is housed in one of Sitka's oldest homes, dating from the late 1800s. It has been lovingly restored, and includes a guest room ($120 d) and private apartment with a full kitchen ($150 d). The location is hard to beat, right on the boat harbor. A light breakfast is included.

Other B&Bs worth a look include **Alaska Swan Lake Guest Cottage** (907/747-5746, www.sitka.org/swanlake, $85 d), **Seaview B&B** (907/747-3908, $65 d), **Sitka Woodside Lodging** (907/747-8287, $85 d), and **Where Eagles Roost** (2713 Halibut Point Rd., 907/747-4545, $70 d).

Vacation Rentals and Lodges

Sitka has a number of homes, apartments, and cabins that are rented out to travelers, including **The Dacha** (304 Monastery, 907/747-4872, www.thedacha.com, $150 d), **An Abode** (407 Degroff St., 907/747-4932, www.alaskamexico.com, $145 d), **Frank & Gloria's Place** (907/747-8711, www.sitkadream.com, $105 d), **Chocolate Moose** (907/747-5159, $125 for four people), and **Salmonberry House** (907/966-2504, www.salmonberryhouse.com, $125 d).

A number of Sitka-area lodges provide all-inclusive fishing, meals, and lodging packages. These include **Baranof Wilderness Lodge** (800/613-6551, www.flyfishalaska.com), **Dove Island Resort** (907/747-5660 or 888/318-3474, www.aksitkasportfishing.com), and **Quest Alaska Lodges** (605/229-8685, www.questalaskalodges.com).

Camping

No campgrounds are near downtown Sitka, but the Forest Service provides camping at each end of the road. The outstanding **Starrigavan Campground** ($12–16, reservations $9 extra) is seven miles northwest of town and three-quarters of a mile beyond the ferry terminal. Open all year, but no services October–April. All sites are wheelchair accessible. Campsites to the left of the road face onto a rocky beach, while those to the right border Starrigavan Creek, where you can watch spawning coho salmon in late summer. Starrigavan fills up with RVs in July and August, but there are six walk-in sites on the ocean side of the campground. Starrigavan also has an **artesian well** with wonderfully fresh spring water. Sitkans often drive out to fill big bottles for themselves.

The .25-mile boardwalk **Estuary Life Trail** (wheelchair accessible) leads along the edge of the marsh from the campground, and connects with a .75-mile **Forest and Muskeg Trail.** Placards describe points along this easy trail. On the road between the ferry and campground are interpretive display signs marking the site of **Old Sitka**—burned by the Tlingits in 1802.

The little-used **Sawmill Creek Campground** (free, but no water) is up Blue Lake Road, six miles east of town. The campground is a bit remote, making it hard to reach on foot; not recommended for RVs. Park RVs at the city-run **Sealing Cove RV Park** (907/747-3439, $21) on Japonski Island, with hookups. **Sitka Sportsman's RV Park** (907/747-6033, $18) has RV spaces with hookups near the ferry terminal.

FOOD

Breakfast and Lunch

A great place to spend time is **Backdoor Cafe** (907/747-8856), an espresso shop behind Old Harbor Books on Lincoln Street. The Backdoor is the literary/greenie hangout, and also serves tasty bagels and pastries. The same folks run **MoJo Cafe** (907/747-0667), next door, serving inexpensive, home-style sandwiches, soups, and salads, along with light breakfasts. Lunch specials are mostly vegetarian.

Victoria's (118 Lincoln St., 907/747-9301), in the Sitka Hotel is a favorite breakfast spot, but also serves lunchtime sandwiches, soups, and salads, plus a full dinner menu. A few doors up the street is the pharmacy, which houses **Harry's Soda Shop** (907/747-8006), for malts, shakes, and banana splits.

All-American

Popular with tourists and families, **Bayview Restaurant** (407 Lincoln St., 907/747-5440), upstairs in Bayview Trading, serves every possible type of burger (16 at last count), plus Wednesday and Friday night prime rib. Big windows provide a view of the harbor.

Get great burgers, milk shakes, and other fast food—plus hearty breakfasts—at **Lane 7 Snack Bar** (236 Katlian St., 907/747-6310). **Subway** probably has the cheapest meal-deal in town; it's behind the Westmark on Seward Street. Of course, there's always the **McDonald's** a mile out on Halibut Point Road for industrial-strength junk food. With the harbor-and-mountains view,

this McD's certainly has one of the most impressive vistas in the entire corporate chain.

While waiting for your flight be sure to stop by the airport's **Nugget Restaurant** (907/966-2480), where the fresh-baked pies and Friday night prime rib are locally acclaimed.

Seafood

Van Winkle & Sons (205 Harbor Dr., 907/747-7652), near the bridge, has seafood, pasta, prime rib, and pizzas, but is famous for its halibut fish and chips. This is the real thing, Alaskan style.

The **Channel Club** (907/747-9916) three miles out Halibut Point Road, broils up seafood and top sirloin steaks, or you can do some grazing at Sitka's best salad bar.

Ethnic Food

Sitka's culinary gem, **Ludvig's Bistro** (256 Katlian St., 907/966-3663, closed Sun. and Mon.), easily ranks among the top cafés in Alaska. It's stylish and noisy, but prices are reasonable and the artfully prepared food is simply wonderful. Mediterranean fare fills the menu, which changes weekly. You'll always find Caesar salads, daily chowders, seafood specials, and pasta. Ludvig's is two blocks down Katlian, which, fortunately, is too far for most of the cruise ship folks to walk. Dinner reservations are advised, but singles will usually find space at the wine bar. Highly recommended.

For Chinese food, head to **Twin Dragon Restaurant** (907/747-5711), next to the Pioneer Bar on Katlian Street. A bit heavy on the MSG for some folks. **Pizza Express** (236 Lincoln St., 907/966-2428) serves Mexican food and pizzas.

Groceries

Sea Mart (907/747-6266, www.seamart.com), two miles from town along Halibut Point Road, has a salad bar, deli, bakery, food court, and Sitka's most complete selection of groceries. Closer to town is **Lakeside Grocery** (705 Halibut Point Rd., 907/747-3317).

The **Fresh Fish Company** (907/747-5565 or 888/747-5565), behind Murray Pacific on Katlian Street, sells fresh local salmon, halibut, shrimp, snapper, and smoked salmon. They'll also smoke fish that you bring in.

ENTERTAINMENT AND EVENTS
Cultural Performances
When cruise ships are in town, Herrigan Centennial Hall auditorium comes alive with half-hour performances of traditional Russian, Ukrainian, Armenian, and Moldavian dance by the 35-member, all-female **New Archangel Dancers** (907/747-5516, www.newarchangel-dancers.com, $7). The troupe has toured extensively, including visits to Japan, Russia, Canada, and Mexico.

For a very different form of dance, the **Sheet'Ka Kwaan Naa Kahidi Dancers** ($6 adults, $4 kids) give Tlingit performances in full regalia through the summer months. These excellent half-hour productions are offered when cruise ships are in port. Most folks see them as part of a bus tour given by Tribal Tours. Performances take place in the imposing Sheet'Ka Kwaan Naa Kahidi Community House, next to the Pioneers Home on Katlian Street.

Nightlife
Fishermen and would-be crew members hang out at the sometimes-rowdy **Pioneer Bar** (on Katlian St., 907/747-3456). The P-Bar's walls are crowded with hundreds of photos of local fishing boats, and the blackboard often has "crew wanted" ads.

Events
For three weeks in June, the renowned **Sitka Summer Music Festival** (907/747-6774, www.sitkamusicfestival.org) attracts musicians from all over the world. Chamber music concerts are given several evenings a week in Centennial Hall, but the most fun is the annual BoatParty Concert. Reserve early. Concert tickets may be hard to come by, but you can always visit rehearsals for free. Another cultural event, the **Sitka Symposium** (www.home.gci.net/~island) in mid-June, attracts nationally known poets and writers.

In late May, visitors can join locals in the **Sitka Salmon Derby,** where the top fish is often a 60-pound-plus king salmon. **July 4th** features a parade, races, softball tournament, live music, dancing, and fireworks. On Labor Day weekend, the **Mudball Classic Softball Tournament** attracts teams from around the nation for fun in the muck.

As the town where Alaska was officially transferred from Russian to American hands, Sitka is also the place to be on **Alaska Day.** A celebration of "Seward's Folly" is held each October 18 with dances (including a remarkable performance by the New Archangel Dancers), traditional Russian costumes, a parade, and a reenactment of the brief transfer ceremony.

In early November, the **Sitka Whalefest** (907/747-7964, www.sitkawhalefest.org) attracts biologists and those who love whales and other marine mammals to a series of scientific seminars, whale-watching tours, concerts, crafts, and exhibits.

INFORMATION AND SERVICES
The Centennial Building houses a small information desk and brochure rack, or stop by the **Sitka Convention & Visitors Bureau** (upstairs at 303 Lincoln St., 907/747-5940, www.sitka.org, Mon.–Fri. 8 A.M.–5 P.M.). In addition to the Sitka CVB's website, you may want to also check out www.travelsitka.com.

The Forest Service office is in the orange-red building at 204 Siginaka Way, 907/747-6671. Call 907/747-6685 for recorded info.

Get showers from **Baranof Laundromat** (1211 Sawmill Creek Rd.) and **Duds and Suds,** across from McDonald's on Halibut Point Road. A better deal is the public **swimming pool** (601 Halibut Point Rd., 907/747-8670) in Blatchley Middle School, where you can swim, sauna, and shower. The pool at Sheldon Jackson College is also open to the public daily.

Sitka's main post office is on Sawmill Creek Road, 1.5 miles south of town, but a substation is downtown at 338 Lincoln Street. ATMs can be found at the Wells Fargo downtown, and First Bank at Lake and Seward streets. For medical emergencies, head to **Sitka Community Hospital** (209 Moller Ave., 907/747-3241, www.sitkahospital.org).

Shopping

Sitka's specialty is Russian art, especially the colorful nesting eggs, painted icons, and other traditional works. Several shops sell Russian crafts downtown; walk around until you find something you like. More noteworthy is **Sitka Rose Gallery** (907/747-3030 or 888/236-1536, www.sitkarosegallery.com), in a historic century-old home next to the Russian Bishop's House on Lincoln Street. Inside, find a mix of quality Native art and Alaskan paintings, sculpture, and jewelry. The same building houses **WinterSong Soap Company** (907/747-8949 or 888/819-8949, www.wintersongsoap.com), where colorful and scented soaps are handcrafted on the premises.

Fairweather Prints (209 Lincoln St., 907/747-8677, www.fairweatherprints.com) is a fine place to buy "wearable art" in the form of exquisite hand-painted dresses, tops, and scarves. It has the most unique T-shirts in town, plus a backroom art gallery. Just up the street is **Fishermen's Eye Gallery** (907/747-5502 or 888/747-5502), selling prints from well-known Alaskan artists. The Sheldon Jackson Museum is a great place to go for Native crafts.

Books

Old Harbor Books (201 Lincoln St., 907/747-8808, www.oldharborbooks.com) has an outstanding collection of books on Alaska (and beyond), along with a pleasant coffee shop in the back.

The **Sitka public library** (907/747-8708, www.cityofsitka.com), next to Centennial Hall downtown, has a free paperback exchange with plenty of titles, plus a phone for free local calls. Check your email on the computers here, or borrow the binoculars to watch whales, seals, and porpoises from the library windows that overlook the bay. The curved benches out back make a pleasant lunch spot when it isn't raining.

TRANSPORTATION

Ferry

State ferries reach Sitka up to five times a week during the summer. The larger ferries often stop for three hours; the Saturday "turnaround" runs put the *Le Conte* in Sitka for six hours. The ferry terminal (907/747-8737), is open two hours before ship arrivals. Make reservations through Alaska Marine Highway (907/465-3941 or 800/642-0066, www.ferryalaska.com). A new high-speed ferry, the *Fairweather,* began service between Juneau and Sitka in 2004, cutting the travel time dramatically.

Because of the difficult tidal conditions in Peril Straits, a small mechanical problem can lead to a six-hour delay since ferries must hit the straits at just the right time, or wait for the next tide. Be sure to confirm the ferry departure time so you don't end up sitting in the ferry terminal for six hours.

The ferry terminal is seven miles north of town, and ferry **shuttle buses** are available for $5 each way or $7 round-trip. A taxi runs around $10–12 each way. Other options include tours and hitching—easy and often faster than the buses, both into and out of town.

Air

The airport is on Japonski Island, just under a mile from town by road. **Alaska Airlines** (907/966-2926 or 800/426-0333, www.alaskaair.com) flies to Juneau twice a day, and then onward to other cities in Alaska and the Lower 48. Note that these flights can be canceled or delayed when the weather gets particularly adverse, a common winter experience. **Harris Aircraft Services** (907/966-3050 or 877/966-3050, www.harrisaircraft.com) has scheduled service several times a week to Angoon, Kake, and Port Alexander, plus flightseeing and charters.

For transit into town, **Airport shuttles** (907/747-8443, $7 round trip) meet Alaska Airlines flights, or get a ride with **Floyd's Taxi** (907/747-8141) or **Sitka Cab** (907/747-5001).

Getting Around

The city's **Community Ride Bus** (907/747-7103), has hourly service on weekdays, taking you from downtown out Halibut Point Road and Sawmill Creek Road for $2 one-way or $3 round-trip.

Transit Shuttle (907/747-7290, $7 day pass) buses cruise around Sitka, stopping at all the major sightseeing destinations. The bus operates weekdays and when cruise ships are in port.

Rent cars at the airport from **North Star Rent-A-Car** (907/966-2552 or 800/722-6927) or **Avis** (907/966-2404 or 800/478-2847). Book ahead for the busy summer months.

Chichagof Island

HOONAH

The largest Tlingit village in the Southeast, Hoonah (pop. 900) nestles in Port Frederick, 20 miles south of Glacier Bay. Port Frederick has served as a home for the Tlingits since the last ice age drove them out of Glacier Bay and across Icy Strait to the north coast of Chichagof Island. There they found a protected bay they called Huna, meaning "place where the north wind doesn't blow." The Northwest Trading Company opened a store here in 1880 and missionaries added a church and school the following year. A cannery opened in 1912, operating until 1953. The attractively restored old cannery still stands a mile north of town on the entrance to Port Frederick, but the old village and many priceless Tlingit cultural items were destroyed by a fire in 1944. The people rebuilt their village on the ashes.

Today Hoonah is far from being the prettiest town in Alaska. The weathered clapboard houses are unpainted, and junk cars pile up in the yards. It's the sort of town where the eagle calls blend with the sounds of motorboats and mufflerless dump trucks. There are dogs in almost every house and children playing on every porch. Life in Hoonah follows a slow pace: Residents half-complain that they are unable to go anywhere without meeting someone who wants to talk the hours away. Hoonah's economy is a blend of commercial fishing, a bit of logging, and traditional activities such as deer hunting, fishing, and berry picking.

The impressive cliff faces of **Elephant Mountain** (2,775 feet) guard the southern flank of Hoonah. Unfortunately, two Native corporations, Huna Totem and Sealaska, have logged much of their land near town, selling off their centuries-old heritage for short-term gain. Hoonah is now surrounded by a spider web of logging roads on both Native and Forest Service land, making this a good place to explore by mountain bike if you're ready for clearcuts.

In 2004 Hoonah took the plunge into cruise ship tourism in a big way. The picturesque cannery building at Port Frederick (Icy Strait Point) has been nicely restored, and cruise ship passengers get a look at the way canneries operated in the 1930s, along with cultural presentations, a salmon bake, Native crafts, whale- and bear-watching excursions, charter fishing, mountain biking, and other "soft" adventures. These are really for cruise passengers only, but contact Huna Totem (907/789-1773, www.hunatotem.com) for access by independent travelers.

Recreation

The Hoonah area offers little in the way of developed trails or other recreation facilities for independent travelers. If you have a car, the quarter-mile **Bear Paw Lake Trail,** 18 miles south of town on Road 8508, leads to a good lake where you can catch trout or coho salmon. Kayakers and canoeists may want to paddle the 40 miles from Hoonah to Tenakee Springs. The route goes to the head of Port Frederick, where there is a 100-yard portage into Tenakee Inlet. Neka Estuary in Port Frederick is a good place to see bears. A Forest Service cabin is available at nearby **Salt Lake Bay,** but a considerable amount of logging has beaten you there. Ask at the **Forest Service Hoonah District Office** (907/945-3631) for details on these and other possible kayak trips in the area, including to **Neka Hot Spring,** 16 miles west of Hoonah.

Accommodations and Food

Icy Strait Lodge (907/945-3636, www.icystraitlodge.com, $85 s, $95 d) is the main place in town, with 23 rooms, plus a full-service restaurant and bar. **Mary's Inn Restaurant** (907/945-3228) is a reasonable place to get burgers or more substantial meals.

Wind 'N Sea Inn (907/945-3438 or 877/945-3438, $65 s, $75 d) is a very nice lodging choice, with seven guest rooms that share two baths and two kitchens, and include a continental breakfast.

Information and Services
The **Hoonah Cultural Center** (907/945-3545) has a few local artifacts. Hoonah has two small grocery stores, and a laundromat with coin-operated showers. Showers are also available in the harbor building or at the **swimming pool** (907/945-9911) next to the high school. In addition, Hoonah has a bank, tavern, variety store, and liquor store. A few miles southwest of town is the only agricultural commune in Southeast, Mt. Bether Bible Center.

Transportation
Hoonah's **ferry terminal** (907/945-3293) is a half-mile from town. Across from the ferry terminal is a tiny but interesting old cemetery. Ferries arrive six days a week, stopping for approximately an hour, long enough for a quick jog into town and back. Make reservations through Alaska Marine Highway (907/465-3941 or 800/642-0066, www.ferryalaska.com).

Wings of Alaska (907/789-0790, www.wingsofalaska.com) and **L.A.B. Flying Service** (907/945-3661 or 800/426-0543, www.labflying.com) have scheduled daily flights between Juneau and Hoonah.

PELICAN AND VICINITY

If you're looking for a place to get away from it all, it's hard to get more remote than the tiny, picturesque fishing village of Pelican (pop. 150) inside narrow Lisianski Inlet on the western shore of Chichagof Island. During the summer, Pelican's population doubles with the arrival of fishermen and cold-storage workers. The town received its name from *The Pelican,* a fishing boat owned by the town's founder; there are no pelicans in Alaska.

A boardwalk connects Pelican's primary businesses: restaurants, bars, a general store, laundromat, and the large cold-storage plant operated by Pelican Seafoods. Showers are available at the laundromat, or try the steam baths at the liquor store (no joke). The **Pelican Visitors Association** (907/735-2460, www.pelican.net) has info on local businesses.

Tiny Pelican has achieved notoriety as a party town, particularly when festivities reach their peak each **July 4th.** Featured attractions include a beer-can-throwing contest, a parade, barbecue, log-rolling contests, and fireworks. Also popular is the **Boardwalk Boogie** at the end of May, with two days of live music and partying.

Accommodations
Boardwalk Bed & Boat (907/735-2476, www.boardwalkbandb.com) has a variety of lodging options, starting with $70 d rustic cabins, up to a nicely furnished apartment for $140 d, and a three-bedroom apartment that sleeps six for $300.

Lisianski Inlet Wilderness Lodge (907/735-2266 or 800/962-8441, www.alaskaecoadventures.com, May–mid-September), two miles west of Pelican, offers a pricey but idyllic setting for a splurge. Package trips are $2,250 per person for four nights, including lodging, meals, fishing, and guide service.

Food
Infamous **Rosie's Bar and Grill** (907/735-2288) no longer stars Rosie (she retired), but is still a good place for drinking and pub grub, including burgers, chicken dinners, oysters, and BLTs. **Lisianski Inlet Cafe** (907/735-2282) is open for breakfast in the summer with big omelets, soup, sandwiches, and homemade cookies. Its bar is a hopping place.

On the Water
Several local folks run fishing and sightseeing boat charters, and will be happy to run you and your kayak out to such local destinations as White Sulfur Springs. **Howard Charters** (907/735-2207 or 877/254-8433, www.howardcharters.com) has kayak rentals, drop-offs, and guided excursions.

Transportation

Ferry service to Pelican arrives only once or twice a month. The *Le Conte* usually stays for two hours and then turns around for the return trip to Juneau. Get details from Alaska Marine Highway (800/642-0066, www.ferryalaska.com).

Alaska Seaplane Service (907/735-2244 or 800/478-3360, www.akseaplanes.com) has daily flights to Pelican from Juneau.

West Chichagof–Yakobi Wilderness

On the northwestern shore of Chichagof Island is the wildly rugged 264,747-acre West Chichagof–Yakobi Wilderness. Brown bears, marten, and deer are common, with sea otters and Steller sea lions in the waters. The coast is deeply indented with many small bays, lagoons, and inlets. It also supports areas of distinctive open spruce forest with grassy glades. Except for White Sulfur Springs, this wilderness gets little recreational use because of its remoteness and the storms that frequently make it a dangerous place for small boats and kayaks.

One of the most popular Forest Service cabins in Southeast (make reservations well in advance) is at **White Sulfur Springs,** accessible by boat, sea kayak, helicopter, or floatplane. The springs are a 20-mile kayak trip from Pelican. Much of the trip is through the protected waters of Lisianski Inlet and Strait, but the last five miles are exposed to the open ocean and require great care. The cabin has a wonderful hot springs bathhouse overlooking Bertha Bay just 50 feet away. Note, however, that the springs are free and open to the public, so fishermen, kayakers, and others from nearby Pelican will probably disturb your solitude.

Elfin Cove

This tiny fishing settlement (pop. 50 year-round, but 200 in the summer) tops the north end of Chichagof Island, and is considered one of Alaska's prettiest towns. The setting is hard to beat: right on the edge of the wild waters of Cross Sound, yet protected within a narrow harbor. Elfin Cove has two general stores, lodging facilities, plus showers and a sauna during the summer.

The waters of Cross Sound and Icy Strait separate Chichagof Island from Glacier Bay National Park. This is one of the best areas to see whales in Southeast Alaska, especially near Point Adolphus. Charter boats offer day trips from Glacier Bay to Elfin Cove during the summer months. Also nearby is the 23,000-acre **Pleasant-Lemesurier-Inian Islands Wilderness.**

Several fishing lodges in Elfin Cove offer multinight accommodations: **Tanaku Lodge** (907/239-2205 or 800/482-6258, www.tanaku.com), **Elfin Cove Sport Fishing Lodge** (907/239-2212 or 800/422-2824, www.elfincove.com), and **Inner Harbor Lodge** (907/239-2245 or 800/424-0801, www.innerharborlodge.com).

The state ferry does not go to Elfin Cove, but **Alaska Seaplane Service** (907/789-3331 or 800/478-3360, www.akseaplanes.com) has scheduled flights from Juneau.

TENAKEE SPRINGS

Residents of the tiny hamlet of Tenakee Springs (pop. 100) include retirees, counterculture devotees, and a handful of fishermen. Many Juneau folks have second homes here. Tenakee's houses stand on stilts along the shoreline; some have "long-drop" outhouses over the water. The town has only one street, a dirt path barely wide enough for Tenakee's three vehicles (its oil truck, fire truck, and dump truck). Everyone else walks or uses four-wheelers and bicycles. This simplicity is by choice—when rumors arose that the Forest Service would complete a road to Hoonah, locals successfully blocked the idea. And when the cruise ship *World Discoverer* made a visit in 1998, the residents gave it such a cold shoulder (along with more than a few four-letter words) that it decided to not return. Locals aren't opposed to travelers—in fact they're downright friendly—but they don't want big groups of gawkers.

Tenakee is best known for its hot (106 degrees) **mineral springs,** housed in a building right beside the dock. The springs feed a small concrete pool with an adjacent changing room. There are separate hours for men (2–6 P.M. and 10 P.M.–9 A.M.) and women (6–10 P.M. and 9 A.M.–2 P.M.), but after midnight the rules tend to relax a bit. If the ferry is in town for more than a half-hour, be sure to take a quick dip in the pool.

Practicalities

You can pitch your tent two miles east of town along Indian River, but be sure to hang your food, since brown bears are sometimes a problem. Trails extend out of town for several miles in both directions along the shore. The trail south of town reaches eight miles to an old cannery and a homestead at Coffee Cove.

Beside the dock is **Snyder Mercantile Co.** (907/736-2205), a classic bush Alaska store with groceries, supplies, and the latest gossip. Great folks. They rent six cabins ($55–65 d) and a minilodge ($80 for up to six people), all with kitchens, but you'll need to bring sleeping bags since they don't provide bedding! These are at a premium in November and December, when Juneau folks book them a year ahead for deer-hunting season. There's a private bath (no showers) in the minilodge, but the other cabins have outhouses. Head to the hot springs for showers. Make advance reservations since the ferry often arrives late at night when the Merc is closed.

The other main feature of town is the Shamrock building, which houses **The Bakery** (907/736-2366), for pastries, coffee, light breakfasts and lunches, plus the **Artist Co-op,** displaying pieces by local artists. Next door is **Rosie's Blue Moon Cafe** serving lunch and dinner daily: cheeseburgers (with freshly cut fries), chicken, and steaks. A laundromat is in the back. There are local fishing charter boats, a small library, a grade school, and two bars.

Tenakee Hot Springs Lodge (907/736-2400 or 760/641-8252, www.tenakee.com) is an upscale fishing lodge on the edge of town.

Transportation

Tenakee is a popular weekend vacation spot for both Juneauites and travelers. The ferry *Le Conte* arrives in Tenakee four times a week with a schedule that makes it possible to stop over for a Friday night before returning to Juneau the following evening. There is no ferry terminal and cars cannot be off-loaded. The ferry usually stays in town briefly, sometimes not even long enough to get off the boat for a walk around. Get details from Alaska Marine Highway (800/642-0066, www.ferryalaska.com).

Both **Wings of Alaska** (907/789-0790, www.wingsofalaska.com) and **Alaska Seaplane Service** (907/789-3331 or 800/478-3360, www.akseaplanes.com) have flights most days between Tenakee Springs and Juneau. Wings also connects Tenakee with Angoon.

Juneau

America's most beautiful state capital, Juneau (pop. 30,000) is a thriving slice of civilization surrounded by rugged Inside Passage scenery. The city perches on a thin strip of land at the mouth of Gold Creek, and behind it rise the precipitous summits of Mt. Juneau and Mt. Roberts. Out front, Gastineau Channel separates it from Douglas Island and the town of Douglas. The city abounds with cultural and artistic attractions, and the adjacent wild country provides a broad sampling of Southeast Alaska, from glacially capped mountains to protected coves where sea kayakers relax.

Juneau is the only state capital with no roads leading in or out. A government town, nearly half the local jobs are at state, federal, or city agencies. Tourism provides another mainstay for the local economy, fed by an annual influx of more than 700,000 visitors, primarily aboard luxury cruise ships. On summer days, up to five different ships tie up simultaneously, disgorging thousands of passengers. (To avoid the worst of the rush, get here before July or after August.) Juneau has a small fishing fleet and provides workers for a silver mine on nearby Admiralty Island.

Juneau may be small in population, but its boundaries extend to the Canadian border, covering 3,100 square miles. Less than half of Juneau's population actually lives downtown. The rest are spread into Douglas (across the channel),

JUNEAU

SOUTHEAST ALASKA

© AVALON TRAVEL PUBLISHING, INC.

Map labels:

To Last Chance Basin, Perseverance Trail, and Silverbow Basin

Mt. Roberts Trail

To Mt. Roberts

To Thane Ore House

SUMMIT RESTAURANT

TWISTED FISH CO./ TAKU SMOKERIES

CRUISE SHIP TERMINAL

CRUISE SHIP DOCK

MT. ROBERTS TRAMWAY

PUBLIC LIBRARY

RED DOG SALOON

HERITAGE COFFEE COMPANY

ALASKAN HOTEL

HEARTHSIDE BOOKS

BARANOF HOTEL

CASHEN QUARTERS

ST. NICHOLAS RUSSIAN CHURCH

SILVERBOW INN

BACAR'S

GOLDBELT HOTEL

MERCHANT'S WHARF MALL/ THE HANGAR

Marine Park

North Park

YOUTH HOSTEL

SEACC

HOUSE OF WICKERSHAM

ALASKA STATE CAPITOL

JUNEAU-DOUGLAS CITY MUSEUM

STATE OFFICE BUILDING

CENTENNIAL HALL VISITOR CENTER

GOVERNOR'S MANSION

DRIFTWOOD LODGE

FIDDLEHEAD RESTAURANT

ALASKA STATE MUSEUM

PROSPECTOR HOTEL

ALASKAN & PROUD MARKET

FEDERAL BUILDING/ POST OFFICE

EVERGREEN CEMETERY

SWIMMING POOL

To Ferry, Airport, and Mendenhall Valley

To Douglas

Harris Harbor

JUNEAU-DOUGLAS BRIDGE

Gastineau Channel

Cope Park

Evergreen Bowl

Gold Creek

Street names:
PARK ST., KENNEDY ST., 6TH ST., EAST ST., HARRIS, BASIN RD., 4TH ST., GOLD ST., 2ND ST., 3RD ST., NORTH FRANKLIN ST., SHATTUCK ST., 2ND, FRONT ST., MAIN ST., SEWARD ST., 5TH, 6TH, MAIN ST., DIXON ST., CALHOUN, DISTIN ST., W. 9TH ST., WEST, WHITTIER ST., WILLOUGHBY AVE., EGAN AVE., EGAN DR., MARINE DR., ADMIRAL AVE., SOUTH FRANKLIN ST., GASTINEAU AVE., FRANKLIN ST.

GOLDBELT AVE.

EVERGREEN AVE., MARTIN RD., IRWIN ST., HEMLOCK ST., ALDER ST., SEATER ST., SPRUCE ST., GLACIER ST., BEHRENDS AVE.

A ST., B ST., C ST., D ST., F ST., GLACIER AVE., 9TH ST., 10TH ST., 11TH ST., 12TH ST., W. 8TH ST., HWY., EGAN DR.

Stairs

0.25 km

0.25 mi

N

Mendenhall Valley (10 miles northwest), and other surrounding areas. As might be expected, these areas exhibit diverse personalities. Even the weather varies, with an average of 92 inches of rain each year downtown, but only 55 inches in Mendenhall Valley.

Downtown Juneau is marked by a mix of modern government offices and older wooden structures, many dating from the early 1900s. Across the bridge is Douglas Island and its bedroom community of Douglas. The town now consists of a few shops, but at its peak in 1915, when the Treadwell Gold Mine was operating, Douglas housed 15,000 miners. The road north from downtown Juneau is the Southeast's only divided highway. Heading north, you first reach Mendenhall Valley, Juneau's version of suburbia: three shopping malls, a slew of fast fooderies, and hundreds of pseudo-rustic, split-level homes and condos. But you can also see something most suburbs don't have: a drive-up glacier spilling out from the massive Juneau Icefield. The road continues north from Mendenhall Valley for another 30 miles, passing Auke Lake, the ferry terminal, and scattered homes along the way, ending at scenic Echo Cove.

HISTORY
Gold in the Hills
In October 1880, two prospectors—Joe Juneau and Richard Harris—arrived at what would later be called Gold Creek. Along its banks was a small Tlingit fishing camp of the Auke tribe. Chief Kowee showed the prospectors gold flakes in the creek, and the resulting discovery turned out to be one of the largest gold deposits ever found. Harris and Juneau quickly staked a 160-acre town site. The first boatloads of prospectors arrived the next month, and almost overnight a town sprouted along the shores of Gastineau Channel. Three giant hard-rock gold mines were developed in the area, eventually producing some seven million ounces of gold, worth nearly *$3 billion* at today's prices! Compare that to the $7.2 million the United States paid Russia for Alaska only 13 years before the discovery.

The **Alaska Juneau (AJ) Mine** proved the most successful, operating for more than 50 years. Built in Last Chance Basin behind Juneau, its three tunnels connected the ore source to the crushing and recovery mill site on Gastineau Channel. Inside the mine itself was a maze of tunnels that eventually reached over 100 miles in length. Because the ore was low grade—it could take 28 tons of ore to yield one ounce of gold— enormous quantities of rock had to be removed. At its peak, the mill (still visible just south of town) employed 1,000 men to process 12,000 tons of ore a day. Tailings from the mill were used as the fill upon which much of downtown Juneau was constructed. (Franklin St. was originally built on pilings along the shore.) The AJ closed down in 1944 because of wartime labor shortages and never reopened.

The **Perseverance Mine** operated between 1885 and 1921, with a two-mile tunnel carrying ore from Gold Creek to the mill four miles south of Juneau. It eventually ran into low-grade ore and was forced to close.

The best known Juneau-area mine was the **Treadwell,** on Douglas Island. The Treadwell Complex consisted of four mines and five stamping mills to process the ore. It employed some 2,000 men who were paid $100 a month, some of the highest wages anywhere in the world at the time. The men enjoyed such amenities as a swimming pool, Turkish baths, tennis courts, bowling alley, gymnasium, and 15,000-volume library. The giant Treadwell stamping mills where the ore was pulverized made so much noise that people in downtown Douglas had to shout to be heard. Everything changed on April 21, 1917, when the ground atop the mines suddenly began to collapse, swallowing first the gymnasium and swimming pool, then the fire hall. Sea water rushed in, filling the tunnels as the miners ran for their lives. Amazingly, all apparently escaped alive. (The only missing miner was reportedly later seen in a nearby tavern before he skipped town.) Only one of the four mines was not destroyed in the collapse, and that one closed five years later.

Later Years
Juneau became the capital of Alaska in 1906 as a result of its rapid growth and the simultaneous

decline of Sitka. Several attempts have been made to move the capital closer to the state's present power center, Anchorage. In 1976, Alaskan voters approved a new site just north of Anchorage, but six years later, when expectations for petro-billions had subsided into reality, voters thought better of the move and refused to fund it. Juneauites breathed a sigh of relief and went on a building spree that only ended with the sudden drop in state oil revenue from the 1986 oil-price plummet. Recent years have seen ever-increasing cruise ship tourism. Locals are starting to tire of the influx and its impact on the town; in 1999 they slapped a head tax on every cruise passenger who steps off in Juneau. By the way, Fridays are usually a light day for cruise ship traffic, so time your downtown visits accordingly.

SIGHTS

Juneau is jam-packed with things to see and do, from glaciers to salmon bakes and tram rides. It's the sort of place that travelers love. Many interesting places are right downtown—including two museums, numerous historic buildings, unusual shops, and even a library-with-a-view. Farther afield are dozens of hiking trails, several easily accessible glaciers, and such attractions as an informative fish hatchery, a brewery, old mining buildings, a stone church, and much more. Even on a rainy day, you'll find something fun in Juneau.

Alaska State Museum

Anyone new to town should not miss the Alaska State Museum (395 Whittier St., 907/465-2901; www.museums.state.ak.us, admission $5, under 18 free). Inside, you'll find an impressive collection of Native artifacts (including wildly creative Yup'ik Eskimo spirit masks) and exhibits relating to the Russian-American period and other aspects of Alaskan history. The museum also houses a gallery of contemporary fine arts, and brings in special exhibits each summer. But the highlight is the circular stairwell, which houses a full-size bald eagle nest and other Alaskan wildlife. The museum is open daily 8:30 A.M.–5:30 P.M. mid-May–mid-September, and Tuesday–Saturday 10 A.M.–4 P.M. the rest of the year.

Franklin Street in downtown Juneau

Juneau-Douglas City Museum

The fine Juneau-Douglas City Museum (4th and Main, 907/586-3572, www.juneau.org/parksrec/museum,$3) houses an interesting collection of maps, artifacts, photos, and videos from Juneau's rich gold-mining history. Be sure to check out the three-dimensional model of Perseverance Mine with its intricate maze of tunnels. Other features include a 19th-century store, a hands-on history room that's popular with kids, and a small gift shop, as well as brochures describing **walking tours** of historic Juneau—60 remaining downtown buildings were built before 1904! The museum is open Monday–Friday 9 A.M.–5 P.M. and Saturday–Sunday 10 A.M.–5 P.M. mid-May–September; Thursday–Saturday noon–4 P.M. the rest of the year.

Mt. Roberts Tramway

The Mt. Roberts Tramway (907/463-3412 or 888/461-8726, www.goldbelttours.com, daily

9 A.M.–9 P.M., May–Sept.) provides a fast way into the high country above Juneau. The tram starts at the cruise ship dock on the south end of town and climbs 1,800 feet up the mountain, providing panoramic views of the surrounding land and water. The six-minute ride ends at an observation deck surrounded by tall Sitka spruce trees. Facilities here include a nature center, restaurant, gift shops, and theater where you can watch an award-wining 20-minute film about Tlingit culture. The tram costs $22 adults, $13 for kids ages 7–12, and is free for children under seven. If you hike up (see "Climbing Mt. Roberts"), the ride down is only $5. Tickets are good all day, but the lines can get very long in late afternoon as cruise ship passengers rush back down to avoid missing their ship departures.

Gastineau Guiding (907/586-2666, www.stepintoalaska.com) leads hikes from the nature center, including special "earlybird" treks that depart at 8 A.M. to avoid the cruise ship hordes. A 4.5-hour version encompasses a long hike up the ridge and an all-you-can-eat crab feed for $85 with tram ride ($49 kids). Or you can save your cash and simply strike out on your own along scenic alpine trails.

House of Wickersham

Built in 1889, the House of Wickersham (213 7th St., 907/586-9001, $2) offers a good view of Juneau and the surrounding country. The house is open daily (except Wednesday) 10 A.M.–noon and 1–5 P.M. mid-May–September. Off-season hours are by appointment only. Your admission includes a fine tour, plus sourdough cookies and Russian tea. This was the home of Judge James Wickersham (1857–1939), a man who had a major impact upon Alaskan history. As Alaska's longtime delegate to Congress he introduced the first statehood bill in 1916—43 years before it passed—and was instrumental in the establishment of the territorial legislature, McKinley National Park, the University of Alaska, and the Alaska Railroad. Be sure to take a gander at the Native ivory carvings that Judge Wickersham collected from around the state.

State Office Building

Enter the State Office Building (SOB; a term many Alaskans also use for their current governor) from Willoughby Avenue and take the elevator up to the 8th floor. Here you'll discover a 1928 Kimball organ, a lovingly preserved totem pole from the 1880s, the Alaska State Library, and an incredible panoramic view from the big **observation deck** (great for bag lunches). The airy lobby is also a pleasant place to stay dry on a rainy day; Friday at noon you'll enjoy the added bonus of an organ recital.

Governor's Mansion

Just up Calhoun Avenue from the SOB is the large, white Governor's Mansion. Built in 1912 in the New England Colonial style, it overlooks much of Juneau from its hilltop location. The mansion is not open to the public. Out front is a **totem pole** carved in 1939–1940. Near its base are the figures of a mosquito and a man, representing the Tlingit tale of the cannibalistic giant, Guteel, and his capture by hunters in a pit. The hunters built a fire to kill him, but just before he died he warned, "Even though you kill me, I'll continue to bite you." His ashes swirled into the air, becoming the mosquitoes that fulfill Guteel's promise.

More than 20 other totems are scattered around downtown. Most are recent carvings, but some date to the 19th century. Pick up the "Totem Pole Walking Tour" brochure from the Juneau-Douglas City Museum to find them all.

State Capitol

Back on 4th Street is the marble Alaska State Capitol. Completed in 1931, it was originally the federal office building and post office. The building is not at all like a traditional state capitol, and from the outside it could easily be mistaken for an aging Midwestern bank, complete with wide steps and marble columns. Free tours of the bank—oops, Capitol are every half-hour Monday–Saturday 9 A.M.–4:30 P.M. June–mid-September; call 907/465-3800 for reservations. Historical photos line the 2nd floor. You may sit in on the legislature when it's in session January–May. The antics of the legislature are always a hoot.

Last Chance Mining Museum
Behind town, Basin Road climbs 1.5 miles to the old AJ Gold Mine. The former compressor building here has been turned into the Last Chance Mining Museum (907/586-5338, daily 9:30 A.M.–12:30 P.M. and 3:30–6:30 P.M. mid-May–late September, $4, free for kids), which houses mining paraphernalia and a 3-D map of the ore body.

Historic Downtown
Dozens of historic buildings fill the heart of downtown Juneau. Get a brochure describing them from the Juneau-Douglas City Museum. One of Juneau's most photographed sights is the onion-domed **St. Nicholas Russian Orthodox Church** (5th and Gold, 907/586-6790, Mon.–Fri. 9 A.M.–5 P.M. mid-May–Sept., no winter tours, $2 donation), built in 1894. Inside are icons and artwork, some dating from the 1700s. For a more evocative experience, attend a service (Sat. 6 P.M., Sun. 10 A.M.).

Marine Park, along Shattuck Way, with its lively mix of people and picturesque views, is a good place to relax after your tour of downtown. Directly across the street a bright mural depicts the Haida creation legend.

Evergreen Cemetery, between 12th and Seater streets on the north side of town, has the graves of Juneau's founders, Joe Juneau and Richard Harris, along with a marker near the spot where Chief Kowee was cremated.

Macaulay Salmon Hatchery
The impressive Douglas Island Pink and Chum (DIPAC) salmon hatchery (2697 Channel Dr., 907/463-4810 or 877/463-2486, www.dipac.net, $3 adults, $1 kids) is three miles north of town. Here you can learn about salmon spawning and commercial fishing, watch fish moving up one of the state's largest fish ladders, and check out the saltwater aquariums and underwater viewing windows. The facility includes shops and a visitor center where tours are offered. It's a fascinating place, and well worth the entrance fee. Open Monday–Friday 10 A.M.–6 P.M. and Saturday–Sunday 10–5 P.M. May–September, or by appointment the rest of the year. The salmon return

July–September, and during that time you can try your hand at fishing by renting poles and lures from the **Ketch-A-Bunch** tackle shack nearby.

Glacier Gardens
This unique private botanical garden (7600 Glacier Hwy., 907/790-3377, www.glaciergardens.com, daily 9 A.M.–6 P.M. May–Sept., $18 adults, $13 ages 6–12, under 6 free) is eight miles north of downtown Juneau. The gardens are spread over 50 acres of hillside forest and include hiking trails, waterfalls, ponds, and "flower tower" cascades of blooms from upside down trees. Motorized carts (some set up to carry wheelchairs) transport visitors along four miles of paved paths to an overlook 500 feet up the mountainside, with views across the Mendenhall Wetlands. The atrium at Glacier Gardens is a popular spot for summer weddings. The city bus stops out front.

Alaskan Brewing Company
For something completely different, take the city bus to Anka Street in Lemon Creek and walk two blocks to Shaune Drive. Follow it a block to the Alaskan Brewing Company building (907/780-5866, www.alaskanbeer.com, tours every half-hour Mon.–Sat. 11 A.M.–4:30 P.M. free). You're given a sample of various beers at the end of the tour. The brewery has developed into one of America's finest, with its beers winning top prizes at national and international festivals. The brewery gift shop sells T-shirts, hats, and other items.

Mendenhall Glacier
The Southeast's best-known drive-up ice cube, Mendenhall Glacier is without a doubt Juneau's most impressive sight. This moving river of ice pushes down from the 1,200-square-mile Juneau Icefield and is 12 miles long and up to 1.5 miles wide. Since 1750, the glacier has been receding, and is now several miles farther up Mendenhall Valley. It is retreating at about 150 feet each year, but still calving icebergs into Mendenhall Lake. The **Mendenhall Glacier Visitor Center** (907/789-0097, www.fs.fed.us, $3; free for kids) provides panoramic views of the glacier from the floor-to-ceiling windows. Use the spotting scopes

© DON PITCHER

Mendenhall Glacier

to check the slopes of nearby Bullard Mountain for mountain goats. Walk through the interpretive exhibits, slip into the theater for an excellent 11-minute film on the glacier, or buy a couple of glacier postcards in the bookstore. The center is open daily 8 a.m.–6:30 p.m. May–September, and Thursday–Friday 10 a.m.–4 p.m., Saturday–Sunday 9 a.m.–4 p.m. the rest of the year. Forest Service naturalists lead walks on nearby trails and can answer your questions. Walk up at least one of these excellent paths if you want to come away with a deeper appreciation of Mendenhall Glacier.

Although it's 13 miles northwest of town, the glacier is easily accessible by city bus. Have the driver let you off when the bus turns left a mile up Mendenhall Loop Road. It's a one-mile walk up the road from here to the glacier. Buses run both directions around Mendenhall Loop Road. On the way back you can catch a bus heading either direction since both eventually drop you off downtown.

Mighty Great Trips (907/789-5460, www .mightygreattrips.com) provides transportation from town to the glacier for $5 each way, and offers a 2.5-hour tour that includes time at the glac-

ier for $20. Most other tour companies also offer tours to Mendenhall (see "Bus Transportation" for details).

For a much more intensive exploration of Mendenhall and other glaciers, the University of Idaho's Glaciological & Arctic Sciences Institute (208/882-1237, www.mines.uidaho.edu /glacier), conducts research on the Juneau Icefield in July and August.

University and Auke Lake

The campus of the University of Alaska Southeast (2,600 students) is a dozen miles northwest of Juneau on beautiful Auke Lake. The view across the lake to Mendenhall Glacier makes it one of the most attractive campuses anywhere. City buses reach the university hourly Monday–Saturday. Also here is **Chapel By the Lake,** a popular place for weddings, with a dramatic backdrop of mountains and the Mendenhall Glacier. Across the highway, **Auke Bay Fisheries Lab** (Mon.–Fri. 8 A.M.–4:30 P.M.) has a small saltwater aquarium and fisheries displays.

Out Glacier Highway

If you have a vehicle, the 40-mile drive north

from Juneau provides a wonderful escape. Twenty-three miles out is a quaint Catholic chapel built in 1939, the **Shrine of St. Therese** (907/780-6112, www.shrineofsainttherese.org). The cobblestone chapel is hidden away on a small, bucolic, wooded island connected to the mainland by a 400-foot causeway. Named for Alaska's patron saint, St. Therese of Lisieux, the chapel is open all the time, with Sunday service at 1 P.M. This is a nice, quiet place to soak up the scenery or to try your hand at fishing for salmon from the shore. The trail to Peterson Lake is nearby, and cabins are available for rent.

Eagle Beach (at Mile 28, $5/car) is a popular day-use area with picnic tables and panoramic vistas of the snowcapped Chilkat Range. Pull out your binoculars to look for whales in Lynn Canal. Stop at **Point Bridget State Park** (Mile 38) for a pleasant hike. The road ends at scenic **Echo Cove,** a launching point for boats and kayaks.

Taku Glacier Lodge

Historic Taku Glacier Lodge (907/586-6275, www.takuglacierlodge.com, mid-May–Sept.) sits just across Taku Inlet from the glacier of the same name. This classic log structure was built in 1923, and short nature trails lead into the surrounding country. Black bears and eagles are frequent visitors (the bears were Juneau garbage bears that would have been shot if they had not been brought here). Three-hour visits to the lodge cost $199 adults or $156 kids, and include a half-hour scenic flight over Taku Glacier, along with a big salmon lunch or dinner. Flights depart the Juneau waterfront up to five times a day between 9 A.M. and 5 P.M.

Taku Glacier Lodge is primarily oriented to the cruise-ship crowd, so expect to see lots of other folks if you go on a day when several ships are docked. No overnight visits in the summer.

Tours

Mighty Great Trips (907/789-5460, www.mightygreattrips.com) runs two-hour summertime tours that include Juneau and Mendenhall Glacier for $20. Other bus tour companies include **Gray Line of Alaska** (907/586-3773 or 800/544-2206, www.graylineofalaska.com), **Last** **Frontier Tours** (907/789-0742, www.lastfrontiertours.com), **Princess Tours** (907/463-3900 or 800/774-6237, www.princess.com), and **Juneau Limousine** (907/463-5466, www.juneaulimousine.com). Keith Carpenter of **AKcess Eco-Tours** (907/789-2090, www.akcess.org) specializes in wheelchair-accessible natural history tours around Juneau.

HIKING AND CABINS

The Juneau area has an amazing wealth of hiking paths leading into the surrounding mountains. For a complete listing, pick up a copy of *Juneau Trails* from the Centennial Hall Visitor Center (101 Egan Dr., 907/586-8751). This is also the place to go for hiking and cabin information in Juneau. Rubber boots are recommended for all these trails, though you could get by with leather boots on some of the paths when the weather is dry.

Guided Hikes

The **City Parks and Recreation Department** (155 S. Seward St., 907/586-5226 or 24-hour line 907/586-0428, www.juneau.lib.ak.us/parksrec,) offers guided summertime day hikes into areas around Juneau every Wednesday and Saturday 9:30 A.M.–4 P.M. The Wednesday outings are for adults only (no, they are not X-rated). Pick up a schedule from its office at

Gastineau Guiding (907/586-2666, www.stepintoalaska.com) leads hikes in the Juneau area, including early-morning treks that avoid the cruise ship crowds, three-hour rainforest nature walk on Douglas Island ($64 adults, $40 kids), and a four-hour "guide's choice" hike ($73 adults with tram ride, $45 kids). Or you can join the blue-haired throngs for an easy hike that includes a 20-minute bus tour of town, a tram ride up Mt. Roberts, and a one-hour hike for $48 ($32 kids).

Mendenhall Glacier Trails

The Mendenhall area is laced with trails, including a couple of paved interpretive paths that swarm with visitors all summer. The relatively easy **East Glacier Loop Trail** (3.5 miles), also

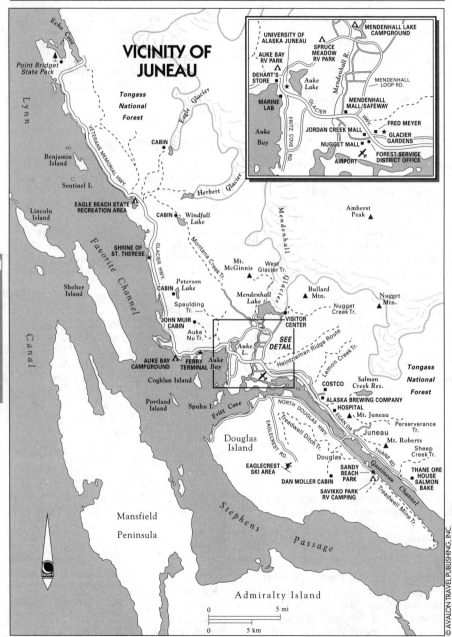

VICINITY OF JUNEAU

Point Bridget State Park

Echo Cove

Lynn

Tongass National Forest

Eagle Glacier

CABIN

VETERANS MEMORIAL HWY.

Benjamin Island

Sentinel I.

Herbert Glacier

Lincoln Island

EAGLE BEACH STATE RECREATION AREA

CABIN

Windfall Lake

Favorite Channel

Shelter Island

SHRINE OF ST. THERESE

GLACIER HWY.

Montana Creek Tr.

Mt. McGinnis

West Glacier Tr.

Amherst Peak

Mendenhall Glacier

Peterson Lake

CABIN

Spaulding Tr.

Mendenhall Lake

Bullard Mtn.

Nugget Mtn.

Canal

JOHN MUIR CABIN

Auke Nu Tr.

Nugget Creek Tr.

VISITOR CENTER

SEE DETAIL

AUKE BAY CAMPGROUND

FERRY TERMINAL

Auke Bay

Auke L.

Heintzleman Ridge Route

Lemon Creek Tr.

Tongass National Forest

Coghlan Island

Portland Island

Spuhn I.

Fritz Cove

COSTCO

Salmon Creek Res.

ALASKA BREWING COMPANY

HOSPITAL

Mt. Juneau

Perserverance Tr.

NORTH DOUGLAS HWY.

EGAN DR.

Juneau

Douglas Island

Treadwell Ditch Tr.

EAGLECREST RD.

Mt. Roberts

Sheep Creek Tr.

EAGLECREST SKI AREA

Douglas

DAN MOLLER CABIN

SANDY BEACH PARK

Gastineau Channel

THANE RD.

THANE ORE HOUSE SALMON BAKE

SAVIKKO PARK RV CAMPING

Treadwell Mine Tr.

Mansfield Peninsula

Stephens

Passage

MOON

Admiralty Island

Detail inset

UNIVERSITY OF ALASKA JUNEAU

MENDENHALL LAKE CAMPGROUND

AUKE BAY RV PARK

SPRUCE MEADOW RV PARK

DEHART'S STORE

Auke Lake

Mendenhall R.

MENDENHALL LOOP RD.

MARINE LAB

Auke Bay

FRITZ COVE RD.

GLACIER HWY.

MENDENHALL MALL/SAFEWAY

JORDAN CREEK MALL

FRED MEYER

GLACIER GARDENS

NUGGET MALL

AIRPORT

FOREST SERVICE DISTRICT OFFICE

SOUTHEAST ALASKA

0   5 mi

0   5 km

begins near the center and provides good views of the glacier. A more challenging hike splits off from this trail and follows Nugget Creek uphill to an Adirondack shelter. Vegetation along the East Glacier Trail consists of brush and trees established since the glacier's recent retreat, while trees along the Nugget Creek Trail are much older.

My favorite Mendenhall trail is the **West Glacier Trail** (seven miles round-trip), which begins from the end of Montana Creek Road, just beyond the Mendenhall Lake Campground: incredible views of the glacier and icefalls en route. Experienced ice-climbers use the path to access the glacier itself. Finally, for the really ambitious there's a primitive route up 3,228-foot **Mt. McGinnis** from the end of the West Glacier Trail, an additional four miles (six hours) round-trip. This trail is generally covered with snow until late summer, but offers panoramic vistas of the entire Juneau area—on clear days.

Douglas

The remains of the **Treadwell Mine,** destroyed by the collapse and flood of 1917, offer a fascinating peek into the past. Pick up the "Treadwell Mine Historic Trail" brochure from the Juneau-Douglas City Museum for a description of the area. The trail starts from the south end of St. Ann's Avenue in Douglas and passes the crumbling remains of old buildings. Get there by catching the hourly Douglas bus ($1.50) in Juneau and riding it to the end of the line at Sandy Beach. Keep right on the main trail to reach the **Treadwell Glory Hole,** once the entrance to a network of shafts under Gastineau Channel, but now full of water and wrecked cars. A waterfall drops into the hole. Return to the fork in the trail and continue down to the shore to see remains of more buildings and pieces of old mining machinery. Mine tailings dumped into Gastineau Channel created an attractive sandy beach along the shore here (Sandy Beach Park). Just to the south is a steep-sided pit where the mine collapsed in 1917. Walk back along the beach and past the Small Boat Harbor to Douglas Post Office, where you can catch a bus back to Juneau.

Climbing Mt. Roberts

The most convenient way to get a panoramic view of Juneau and Gastineau Channel is by taking the tram ($22 round-trip) to the summit of Mt. Roberts, directly behind town. A more aerobic way is to take the 2.5-mile rainforest trail that begins at the east end of 6th Street. This enjoyable climb attracts many locals, especially on summer weekends, when you'll even encounter ironman-type joggers. After a strenuous hike you're suddenly surrounded by hundreds of folks—some barely ambulatory—who have ridden the tram from their cruise ships to commune with nature in the gift shop, restaurant, espresso stand, and theater. It's a bit disconcerting, but that's the new *Alaskan Wilderness Experience,* made easy for everyone. Beyond the tram station, well-maintained trails climb uphill past Native-carved trees to spectacular viewpoints and a large wooden cross just above the timberline at 2,030 feet. There may be snow above this point until late July.

Once you get beyond the cross, the crowds quickly thin and then virtually disappear. The trail continues up to 3,666-foot **Gastineau Peak,** six miles from town, then on along the ridge to the summit of **Roberts Peak** (3,819 feet), nine miles from your starting point. Experienced hikers with a map and compass may want to continue along the ridge, eventually connecting up with other trails in the area. Weather conditions change rapidly on these ridge tops, so be aware of incoming clouds and never hike into fog.

Up Gold Creek

Some of the finest hiking around Juneau is found in the old gold mining areas up beyond the end of Basin Road, a pleasant half-hour walk from town. You could easily spend several days exploring this scenic area. In Last Chance Basin, 1.5 miles up Basin Road, are the fascinating remains of the **AJ Mine.** A number of paths lead around the compressor building (which houses the Last Chance Mining Museum), a locomotive repair shop, and a variety of remains from the heyday of gold mining. For more details of the area, pick up the "Last Chance Basin Walking Tour" brochure from the Juneau-Douglas City Museum. **Princess Tours** (907/463-3900 $59), has a three-hour tour that includes time inside the mines and lots of historical info.

Perseverance Trail leads past Last Chance Basin to Silverbow Basin, site of the Perseverance Mine, three miles away. The **Mt. Juneau Trail** branches off from Perseverance Trail a half-mile up. It's very steep and only suitable for experienced hikers, but offers unparalleled vistas across Gastineau Channel. Plan on seven hours round-trip. Directly across from the Mt. Juneau trailhead is a short path down to Ebner Falls. Continue another mile out Perseverance Trail to the **Granite Creek Trail** (1.5 miles each way), which follows the creek up past several waterfalls into the alpine. Just before Silverbow Basin yet another side trail leads right to the Glory Hole, which is connected to the AJ Mine by a tunnel. Old mining ruins are at the end of the trail, but signs warn of potential hazards from toxic tailings at the mine site.

Point Bridget State Park

Point Bridget is a delightful park along the edge of Lynn Canal, 38 miles north of Juneau, and near Echo Cove. It's a great place to hike if you have the wheels to get there. Several paths lace this 2,850-acre park, including the **Point Bridget Trail** (seven miles round-trip) which takes hikers out to a fine vantage point across Lynn Canal to the Chilkat Mountains. Sea lions, harbor seals, and humpback whales are often seen from here. Before heading out, pick up a park map from the Department of Natural Resources (400 Willoughby Ave., 907/465-4563, www.alaskastateparks.org). Two cozy public-use cabins ($35) each sleep eight.

Cabins

The Juneau area has four popular Forest Service cabins that can be reached by hiking trails or on skis in winter. Some of these book up six months in advance.

Located on a scenic alpine ridge, the **John Muir Cabin** overlooks Auke Bay and the surrounding islands. Get there by following the **Spaulding Trail** a half-mile, turning left onto the **Auk Nu Trail,** and continuing another 2.5 miles to the cabin. The trail starts from a parking

area on the right side of the road 12 miles northwest of town and just beyond the Auke Bay Post Office.

The **Peterson Lake Cabin** lies at the end of a 4.5-mile trail. Although it's mostly boardwalk, rubber boots are highly recommended. The trailhead is on the right, 24 miles northwest of town, and just beyond the Shrine of St. Therese. Experienced hikers or cross-country skiers with a map and compass may want to cross the alpine ridges from Peterson Lake to the John Muir Cabin (2.5 miles away), where they can head back along the Auke Nu and Spaulding Trails.

The **Dan Moller Cabin** on Douglas Island lies at the end of a three-mile trail. Get there by taking the Douglas bus to West Juneau. Get off the bus on Cordova Street and hike three blocks up the street. Turn left onto Pioneer Avenue; the trail begins from a small parking lot next to 3185 Pioneer Avenue. One of the most popular wintertime skiing trails in the area, it leads up to the beautiful alpine country of central Douglas Island.

Eagle Glacier Cabin faces this magnificent glacier, and is accessed via the **Amalga (Eagle Glacier) Trail** that begins 28 miles north of town. The path is relatively easy to hike, passes the cabin at the 5.5-mile point, and ends at the Eagle Glacier, 7.5 miles from the trailhead. The cabin faces across a lake to the glacier, offering some of the most dramatic vistas anywhere. Wear rubber boots for the oft-muddy trail.

Windfall Lake Cabin is a modern cabin with a gorgeous setting on this lake north of Juneau. It's accessible via a three-mile trail from Herbert River Road.

Two trail-accessible cabins (reservations: 907/465-4563, www.alaskastateparks.org, $35) are in Point Bridget State Park, at Mile 39 of Glacier Highway. The 12-person **Cowee Meadows Cabin,** is a three-mile hike (or wintertime ski) from the road, and the **Blue Mussel Beach Cabin** is four miles with a wonderful bay vista.

In addition to these hike-in cabins, there are five other Forest Service cabins on the mainland around Juneau, plus another 15 on nearby Admiralty Island. Access to these cabins is by floatplane or sometimes by sea kayak. For more details on all Forest Service cabins in the area, contact the Forest Service Information Center downtown or the district office near Nugget Mall. The **Berners Bay Cabin** is just eight kayak miles from the north end of Glacier Highway. The location is grand, with fine vistas across the bay, good fishing, a beautiful waterfall, and lots to explore on the two-mile-wide river delta just north of here. But book early for this cabin.

Two close and extremely popular cabins (they fill up several months in advance) are on **Turner Lake,** 20 miles east of Juneau. Great fishing for cutthroat trout and incredible waterfall-draped rock faces on all sides. The flight in takes you near the enormous Taku Glacier, an added bonus.

RECREATION

Sea Kayaking

In business since 1972, **Alaska Discovery** (5310 Glacier Hwy., 907/780-6226 or 800/586-1911, www.akdiscovery.com) is one of Alaska's oldest and most respected wilderness expedition companies. Emphasizing low-impact travel and camping, Alaska Disco guides lead groups of 6–12 people throughout the state. Examples include an eight-day Glacier Bay sea kayaking trip ($2,500 from Gustavus), a nine-day Tatshenshini River rafting trip ($2,900 from Haines), and an Arctic National Wildlife Refuge 10-day trip ($4,200 from Fairbanks). In addition to these long voyages, Disco has guided kayaking day trips in Glacier Bay ($125 from Bartlett Cove), as well as bear-watching/canoeing day trips to Pack Creek ($500, including round-trip airfare from Juneau).

Alaska Travel Adventures (907/789-0052 or 800/478-0052, www.alaskaadventures.com) leads sea kayak day trips from Auke Bay ($76 for 3 hours); these are geared to cruise ship tourists.

Rent kayaks from **Alaska Boat & Kayak Rental** (907/789-6886, www.juneaukayak.com) at Auke Bay boat harbor 12 miles north of Juneau. Guided trips are also available.

Auk Nu Tours (907/586-8687 or 800/820-2628, www.goldbelttours.com) provides kayak drop-offs to Gustavus ($69 one-way plus $40 extra for the kayak), but make reservations to be sure there is space on board. **Auke Bay Landing**

© DON PITCHER

sea kayakers in Auke Bay, near Juneau

Craft (907/790-4591, www.aukebaylandingcraft.com), operates a helpful kayak drop-off service to Oliver's Inlet and other points in the Juneau area. **Adventure Bound Alaska** (907/463-2509 or 800/228-3875, www.adventureboundalaska.com), does kayak drop-offs in the Tracy Arm area.

Floating Mendenhall River

Experienced rafters and canoeists sometimes float the Mendenhall River, but be sure to ask the Forest Service for the details. The river is not particularly treacherous, but a number of people have died in independent boating accidents. For a guided float, join the cruise ship folks on a raft from **Auk Ta Shaa Discovery** (907/586-8687 or 800/820-2628; www.goldbelttours.com). These four-hour summertime raft floats cost $95 adults, $63 kids, including lunch and transportation from town. A canoe trip across Mendenhall Lake is also offered.

A second company, **Alaska Travel Adventures** (907/789-0052 or 800/478-0052, www.alaskaadventures.com), also has Mendenhall River raft trips for $95 adults, $63 kids.

Fishing and Whale-Watching

The visitor center offers a listing of Juneau's many **charter boat** operators. All sorts of options are available, from half-day fishing and whale-watching ventures to two-week cruises around Southeast. If you want to do it on your own, rent a skiff and fishing gear from Alaska Boat & Kayak Rental at Auke Bay.

A number of companies specialize in whale-watching day trips out of Juneau, including Auk Nu Tours, **Orca Enterprises** (907/789-6801 or 888/733-6722, www.alaskawhalewatching.com), **Dolphin Whale Watch Tours** (907/463-3422, www.dolphintours.com), **Four Seasons Marine** (907/790-6671, www.4seasonsmarine.com) and **Juneau Sportfishing & Sightseeing** (907/586-1887, www.juneausportfishing.com).

Skiing and Snowboarding

Come wintertime, the **Eaglecrest Ski Area** (907/586-5284 or 907/790-2000, www.juneau.org/ecrestftp, Thurs.–Mon. from early Dec.–March) on Douglas Island provides excellent skiing opportunities, including night skiing on Fridays. Thirty ski trails are available, with a vertical drop of 1,400 feet. Adult lift tickets cost $26, and cross-country skiers can get a special two-ride pass for $10 that takes them into the alpine meadows. Call 907/586-5330 for current snow conditions. A bus provides weekend-only transport to Eaglecrest for $3 each way.

The City Parks and Recreation Department (907/586-5226, www.juneau.lib.ak.us/parksrec), leads **guided cross-country ski tours** in the winter if there's enough snow. These take place every Wednesday and Saturday 9:30 A.M.–4 P.M.; Wednesday outings are only for adults.

Flightseeing

Flightseeing and charter flights are available from **Ward Air** (907/789-9150, www.wardair.com), a long-established company with a good safety record. For charter flights, expect to pay around $480/hour for a Beaver (seats six people or four with gear) or $330/hour for a Cessna 180 (seats three). A 45-minute flight over the Juneau Icefield is $135 per person. Glacier Bay flightseeing can also be booked, but they're expensive due to the distance. Wait till you visit Haines, Skagway, or Gustavus where the cost and flying time to the park are less.

A number of companies offer helicopter glacier tours to the spectacular Juneau Icefield, with landings on crevasse-free portions of the glaciers. Despite their popularity with tourists, the helicopters are controversial in Juneau, primarily because of the constant din they create in Mendenhall Valley. Juneauites have become increasingly annoyed with the noise, and there are efforts to reduce the hours and numbers of helicopters that are allowed to fly. What started as a fun adventure for well-heeled travelers has mushroomed into a huge summertime business for cruise ship passengers. Flights operate May–September, but trips that include dogsledding may end earlier due to snow conditions. All prices are per person.

Era Helicopters (907/586-2030 or 800/843-1947, www.flightseeingtours.com) lands on Norris Glacier. A one-hour trip with a 15-minute walk is $215. It also offers a longer two-hour flight ($365) that includes a dogsled ride.

Temsco Helicopters (907/789-9501 or 877/789-9501, www.temscoair.com) has a one-hour flight ($189) that spends 25 minutes on Mendenhall Glacier. Other flight options, include a "pilot's choice" 90-minute flight ($269) with two glacier landings, and a tour that allows two hours of hiking time on a glacier ($299).

Coastal Helicopters (907/789-5600 or 800/789-5610, www.coastalhelicopters.com) charges $173 for a 60-minute trip, or $290 for a 90-minute trip; both include 15 minutes on a glacier. Also popular are dogsled tours on Herbert Glacier. These include an hour on the ice with the dogs and 30 minutes of flying time for $366.

Northstar Trekking (907/790-4530, www.glaciertrekking.com) specializes in Mendenhall Glacier hikes of varying lengths, starting with a flight plus one-hour hike for $249, up to a trek that includes more technical climbing and four hours on the ice for $439. Clients are fully outfitted with mountaineering gear and crampons for these adventures.

All four of these companies include transportation from downtown to their landing pads and also provide chartered flights to the glaciers for heli-hiking or skiing. Warning: Helicopters can be dangerous, and a number of fatal crashes have taken place around Juneau. Be sure to ask about safety procedures before stepping onboard.

Other Recreation

Rent mountain bikes from **Driftwood Lodge** (435 W. Willoughby, 907/586-2280 or 800/544-2239, www.driftwoodalaska.com).

The **Augustus Brown Swimming Pool** (1619 Glacier Ave., 907/586-5325) at the high school has an excellent pool, coed sauna, and workout equipment.

Rock climbers will enjoy a visit to the **Rock Dump** (1310 Eastaugh Way, 907/586-4982, www.rockdump.com, $10 day pass), a indoor climbing facility south of Juneau off Thane Road. **Juneau Racquet Club/Alaska Club** (2841 Riverside Dr., 907/789-2181, www.thealaskaclub.com) features exercise equipment, indoor racquetball and tennis courts, a sauna, and hot tub. A second downtown location (641 W. Willoughby Ave., 907/586-5773) has more limited facilities. Non-members pay $9 per day.

Golfers should head to **Mendenhall Golf Course** (907/789-1221), a nine-hole course near the airport, where $25 gets you the full package. Not quite up to Arizona standards, but where else would you have a glacier backdrop?

ACCOMMODATIONS

A full range of options is available to travelers staying in Juneau, but you should make reservations well in advance for arrivals in July and August when everything in town is sometimes booked. See the Juneau Convention and Visitors Bureau website (www.traveljuneau.com) for links to many local hotels, motels, B&Bs, lodges, and resorts. If you aren't bringing a vehicle up on the ferry, be sure to ask about if your lodging place offers a free pickup; it could save you the $18 taxi fare.

Hostel

One of the finest hostels in Alaska, Juneau International Hostel (614 Harris St., 907/586-9559, www.juneauhostel.org) is in a lovely old home just a few blocks uphill from downtown. In addition to dorm space for 46 people, the hostel has a comfortable community room, kitchen facilities, washer, and dryer. It does not have a TV (hooray!). The hostel is open year-round, but is closed daily 9 A.M.–5 P.M. The doors are locked at midnight (10:30 P.M. in winter), putting a damper on your nightlife. Lodging costs just $10, with a maximum stay of three nights. Rooms are clean and the managers are friendly, but things are often crowded. Be sure to reserve ahead in summer, or get here early to be sure of a place.

In-Town Hotels and Motels

The **Alaskan Hotel** (167 S. Franklin St., 907/586-1000 or 800/327-9347, www.pti alaska.net/~akhotel) has reasonably priced downtown Juneau lodging in a historic setting. Built in 1913, this is Juneau's oldest lodging place, with small, but surprisingly charming rooms. Those with a shared bath and no TV cost $60 s or d; nicer ones with private baths and TVs are $80 s or d, and some have fridges and microwaves. Larger kitchenette units sleep four for $90. Try to get a room away from the bar and not on the second floor since these can get noisy when bands are playing. During the Folk Festival each April the Alaskan is the heart of the music scene, with impromptu jams in the halls and downstairs at all hours.

Driftwood Lodge (435 W. Willoughby, 907/586-2280 or 800/544-2239, www.driftwoodalaska.com), is convenient to town, with dated rooms (some with kitchenettes) for $79 s or d; one-bedroom units with kitchens for $93 d, and two-bedroom units that sleep four for $115. The Driftwood provides a courtesy van to the airport or ferry terminal.

Prospector Hotel (375 Whittier St., 907/586-3737 or 800/331-2711, www.prospectorhotel.com), has spacious in-town rooms, most of which contain kitchenettes. Rates are $107–137 d in standard rooms, up to $155 d in suites.

Baranof Hotel (127 N. Franklin St., 907/586-2660 or 800/544-0970, www.westmarkhotels.com) is a nine-story downtown classic with a dark lobby and a romantic restaurant. It's a favorite haunt of state legislators and lobbyists in the winter, and 20 of the rooms have kitchenettes. Several smaller and older rooms have twin beds for just $79 d, but nicer rooms are $159 d, with suites for $209–229 d. The higher levels have the best views and least street noise.

The seven-story **Goldbelt Hotel Juneau** (51 W. Egan Dr., 907/586-6900 or 888/478-6909, www.goldbelt.com), has a convenient downtown location, modern rooms, a decent restaurant, and a free airport shuttle. Lodging costs $169–179 d or $195 d for the suite.

Mendenhall Valley/Airport Hotels and Motels

Most of Juneau's newest hotels are clustered around the airport in Mendenhall Valley. These lack the charm of the historic downtown places, and you will probably want a rental car to get around. Of course, they are also close to Mendenhall Glacier, and offer the predictability of corporate lodging.

Super 8 Motel (2295 Trout St., 907/789-4858 or 800/800-8000, $85–105 s or d) has reasonable rates, including a continental breakfast and courtesy van. Some rooms have fridges and microwaves.

A good family place is **Frontier Suites Airport Hotel** (9400 Glacier Hwy., 907/790-6600 or 800/544-2250; www.frontiersuites.com, $109–149 d). It has a wide variety of rooms, all with full kitchens (including dishes), and some with jetted tubs. Two even have bunk beds.

Also near the airport is **Grandma's Feather Bed** (2358 Mendenhall Loop Rd., 907/789-5566, www.gramdmasfeatherbed.com, $160 d) a 14-unit motel with spacious rooms, jacuzzi tubs, and a hot breakfast. Nearby (same owners) is **Best Western Country Lane Inn** (9300 Glacier Hwy., 907/789-5005 or 888/781-5005, www.countrylaneinn.com, $99–139 d) with standard motel rooms and a continental breakfast. Both places have a courtesy shuttle van to downtown, the ferry, or the airport.

The same neighborhood contains **Airport Travelodge** (9200 Glacier Hwy., 907/789-9700 or 800/255-3050, www.travelodge.com,

$105–135 d) a south-of-the-border style building that also houses a popular Mexican restaurant, **Mi Casa.** Nothing special at the motel, though it does have a postage-stamp-size indoor pool and a courtesy van; continental breakfast included.

Aspen Hotel (1800 Shell Simmons Dr., 907/790-6435 or 866/483-7848, www.aspenhotelsak.com), is just a block away from the airport, and nine miles from downtown. Juneau's newest lodging place has all the amenities travelers have come to expect, including an indoor swimming pool, hot tub, exercise room, microwaves and fridges in all rooms, continental breakfast, and free shuttle service to town and the ferry. Most rooms go for $149 d and have either two queens or a king bed, but a few rooms ($169 d) also feature private whirlpool tubs.

Lighthouses and Cabins

Nonprofit preservation groups are renovating three historic lighthouses in the Juneau area. **Sentinel Island Lighthouse** (907/586-5338, $50 per person) is a few miles north of Juneau and right across from a Steller sea lion haulout. You'll need to get there by kayak, skiff, or helicopter.

Point Retreat Lighthouse (907/364-2410, www.aklighthouse.org), on the northern tip of Admiralty Island west of Juneau, should be open to the public by 2005, with a small maritime museum and B&B lodging.

Five Fingers Lighthouse (907/364-3632, www.5fingerlighthouse.com), 75 miles south of Juneau on Stephens Passage, is another work in progress, but overnight stays may be available.

Located 23 miles north of Juneau, the **Shrine of St. Therese** has a delightful collection of cabins for rent. Two rustic cabins with wood stoves are just $30 s or $35 d; no kitchen, and you'll need to use the nearby bathrooms. A historic 1938 log cabin has two bedrooms, plus a kitchenette and private bath for $40 s or $70 d. Three larger places are available, including a lodge that can sleep 22 guests! The St. Therese cabins are popular with groups, but are also open to families and couples. You don't have to attend Catholic mass, but guests must abide by the contemplative spirit of this unique and peaceful place.

Bed-and-Breakfasts

Couples may want to spend the extra money to stay at one of more than 40 Juneau B&Bs. Accommodations run the gamut from old miner's cabins to gorgeous log hillside homes. Pick up the "Juneau Visitors Guide" brochure at the visitor center for a listing of local places, or check out its rack for flyers from many B&Bs. Two good Web resources for Juneau B&Bs are the Juneau Convention and Visitors Bureau (www.traveljuneau.com) and the B&B Association of Alaska INNside Passage Chapter (www.accommodations-alaska.com).

Downtown B&Bs

Cashen Quarters B&B (907/586-9863 or 888/543-5701, www.cashenquarters.com, open May–Sept., $95–110 d) has simple but clean accommodations in a historic downtown rooming house. The five rooms have private entrances and baths, and include a continental breakfast.

Best known for its bagels and other baked goods, **Silverbow Inn** (120 2nd St., 907/586-9866 or 800/586-4146, www.silverbowinn.com, $128–138 s or d) also has six small but bright guest rooms, each with private bath, phone, and TV. Includes a breakfast from the bakery and evening cheese and wine. A two-night minimum is required in mid-summer.

Built in 1906, and now restored to its foursquare glory, **Alaska's Capital Inn** (113 W. 5th St., 907/586-6507 or 888/588-6507, www.alaskacapitalinn.com, $150–219 d) offers sumptuous heart-of-Juneau lodging. The rooms of this four-story home are filled with period antiques (including an 1879 pump organ and maplewood floors from a 1920s YMCA), and the entire top level has been transformed into a very private suite ($275 d) with a gas fireplace, jetted tub, and king-size sleigh bed. Two smaller basement rooms ($124–144 d) are more contemporary, with private entrances—making them popular with families. All have private baths, and most also feature clawfoot tubs. The flower-filled yard has a gazebo-enclosed hot tub, and a wonderful Alaskan breakfast is served each morning.

Farther Afield B&Bs

Located on the north end of Douglas Island, **Blueberry Lodge B&B** (907/463-5886, www.blueberrylodge.com, $95 s, $105 d) features an attractive log lodge with five guest rooms and a big country breakfast. An active eagle's nest is visible from the picture windows, and the Mendenhall Wetlands are nearby.

A Cozy Log B&B (8668 Dudley St., 907/789-2582, www.cozylog.net, $95 d) has two guest rooms with a shared bath in a quiet Mendenhall Valley log home; hearty breakfast included. Trivia note: Novelist Sidney Sheldon based parts of his novel, *The Sky Is Falling,* in this B&B; the owners even appear as characters.

Alaska Wolf House B&B (1900 Wickersham Dr., 907/586-2422 or 888/586-9053, www.alaskawolfhouse.com, $95–115 d), two miles north of Juneau, is a 4,000-square-foot in-the-trees cedar home with three guest rooms and two comfortable suites ($155 d). A gourmet breakfast is served.

Auke Lake B&B (11595 Mendenhall Loop Rd., 907/790-3253, www.admiraltytours.com) occupies a prime piece of shoreline on this picturesque lake where you can borrow the kayak for a paddle. The striking 5,000-square-foot home has a big deck with a hot tub for relaxing, two luxury suites ($135 d), and a guest room ($115 d), all with private baths, fridges, and a light breakfast. Recommended.

Serenity Inn (10495 Ann Coleman Rd., 907/789-2330 or 800/877-5369, www.ptialaska.net/~serenity, $119–139 d) in Auke Bay is a contemporary A-frame cedar home with vaulted ceilings, outdoor decks, and wonderful Auke Bay views. The three rooms, include a big breakfast, and a hot tub awaits on the deck.

Glacier Trail B&B (907/789-5646, www.juneaulodging.com), is right on Mendenhall Lake across from Mendenhall Glacier. Two guest rooms have kitchenettes and jacuzzi baths for $120 d, and an apartment has a full kitchen for $145 d ($20 for each additional guests up to six). The hosts are wilderness guides and have kayaks ($30/day) for use on Mendenhall Lake.

Aurora View Inn (2917 Jackson Rd., 907/586-3036 or 888/580-8439, www.ptialaska.net/~auroravu) offers luxurious accommodations in a recently built Douglas home. Two guest rooms ($129–139 d) and a suite ($199 d) are available, all with private baths, a light breakfast, sauna, and outdoor hot tub. You'll find great views of Juneau, and the B&B borders Tongass National Forest.

Located on the north end of Douglas Island, six miles from Juneau and close to the Eaglecrest Ski Area, **Fireweed House B&B** (907/586-3885 or 800/586- 3885, www.fireweedhouse.com), has a scenic and peaceful setting. Accommodations include two rooms in the main house ($129–149 d), an apartment with kitchen and jacuzzi bath ($169 d), and a separate two-bedroom guesthouse with hot tub ($299 for four; three-night stay required). Delicious breakfasts too, and kids are welcome.

Pearson's Pond Luxury Inn and Garden Spa (907/789-3772 or 888/658-6328, www.pearsonspond.com, $219 s, $249 d) is a comfortable lakeshore home with two hot tubs, a three-level deck, three guest rooms, and Mendenhall Glacier vistas. Borrow a kayak to paddle around the small pond, join in a morning yoga session, or just enjoy the beautiful gardens. Two separate condos are $160 d with a five-night minimum.

Other fine B&Bs worth investigating include **A Red Tin Roof B&B** (907/790-4873, www.aredtinroof.com), **Gill's Horizon** (907/586-2829, www.gillshorizon.com) **Gould's B&B** (907/463-1546), **Rainforest B&B** (907/790-6644, www.rainforestbnb.com), and **The Highlands B&B** (907/463-5404 or 877/463-5404, www.juneauhighlands.com).

CAMPING

The Forest Service maintains two campgrounds in the Juneau area, but neither is close to town, and both are only open in the summer. No reservations, but call 907/586-8800 for details. **Mendenhall Lake Campground** hugs the shore of Mendenhall Lake, with glacier views and access to several hiking trails. Here you will find backpacker units and vehicle sites for $10, along with RV sites with full hookups for $26. From the ferry terminal, turn right and go two miles to De Hart's Store, then left onto Loop Road. Follow it three miles to Montana Creek Road, then an-

other three-quarters of a mile to the campground. From Juneau by foot, take the city bus to where Montana Creek Road intersects Mendenhall Loop Road. Walk up Montana Creek Road, bear right at the Y after a half-mile, then continue another half-mile to the campground (well marked).

Auke Village Campground ($8) is 16 miles north on Glacier Highway and another two miles out Point Louisa. The area is secluded, with a nice beach and views of nearby islands. If you lack a vehicle, the nearest city bus stop is four miles away.

Eagle Beach State Recreation Area (Mile 28, 907/465-4563, mid-May–mid-Sept., $10) has rustic campsites. Nearby is a picnic area with all-encompassing views of the Chilkat Range.

RV Campgrounds

The city of Juneau has four RV spaces at **Savikko Park** (907/586-5255) on Douglas Island. Free, but no hookups, no tents, and stays are limited to three days.

Auke Bay RV Park (907/789-9467, open year-round, $24 with full hookups) is a mile and a half southeast of the ferry terminal. Reservations are recommended here, no tent camping, and a two-night minimum stay.

Spruce Meadow RV Park (10200 Back Loop Rd., 907/789-1990, www.juneaurv.com, $26 for full hookups) is four miles from the ferry terminal. In addition, recreational vehicles can generally overnight at Nugget Mall near the airport for free, but no facilities, of course.

FOOD

One of Juneau's strong points is a variety of quality restaurants and reasonable prices. There's quite a bit of turnover, so some of these may be gone when you visit, but you certainly won't be disappointed.

Coffee Shops and Bakeries

Heritage Coffee (174 S. Franklin St., 907/586-1087 or 800/478-5282, www.heritagecoffee.com) is easily the most popular and crowded Juneau espresso-and-pastries shop, and remains open until 11 most summer nights. It's a great place to meet tie-and-sportcoat politicians, ring-nosed teens, plaid-shirted fishermen, and GoreTexed vacationers. Walk down the halls of this building to view over-sized historic photos of Juneau. **Valentine's Coffee House & Bakery** (111 Seward, 907/463-5144) is smaller and away from the action, but also popular.

Silverbow Inn Bakery (120 2nd St., 907/586-9866) is a fine spot for a hot bagel and latte or a lunchtime sandwich and soup. The atmosphere is homespun and funky, and the side-street location keeps the crowds at bay. Saturday dinners are more substantial, with fresh halibut or salmon, burgers on house-made buns, and other treats served while movies show in the back room. Silverbow is said to be the oldest operating bakery in Alaska.

Get an ice cream to go at **Chilkat Cone Kitchen** (inside the Merchant's Wharf on Marine Way, 907/463-2663), where the waffle cones are decorated with traditional Native designs.

Breakfast and Lunch
Hungry for a filling all-American breakfast or lunch? You certainly won't go wrong at **BaCar's** (230 Seward St., 907/463-4202), where the bread is fresh from the oven, and the home-style meals are filling and delicious. Featured are French toast on homemade bread, biscuits and gravy, pineapple fritters, omelets, and corned beef hash. Lunchtime clam chowder, burgers, pork chops, and sandwiches attract state workers.

Rainbow Foods (224 4th St., 907/586-6476) is the local natural foods market, but also has a buffet with healthy hot meals to go; it's great for a fast lunch without a lot of fat—the opposite of BaCar's.

For a Mendenhall Valley lunch, head to **Heritage Glacier Cafe** (9112 Mendenhall Mall Rd., 907/789-0692, www.glaciercafe.com), where favorites include a rockfish wrap, turkey and bacon panini, and Philly cheese steak. Or just get today's soup with focaccia for $4. Well off the tourist path, and worth the side trip. They also have a breakfast menu.

Downtown Juneau has a couple of **street vendors** who sell quick, cheap, and tasty lunchtime food such as salads, bagels, burgers, chicken, and tacos. Sure beats the local McD's!

Locals' Favorites
The Hangar (2 Marine Way in Merchant's Wharf, 907/586-5018, dinner entrées $10–25) is an extremely popular waterfront pub with seafood, steaks, pasta, burgers, sandwiches, and salads. Fresh sushi is available Thurs.–Sat. nights. Historic photos line the walls, and you can head upstairs for a game of pool. It's a great place to watch the sun go down while enjoying one of its 24 brews on draught. Loud, energetic, and fun are the operative terms here.

Most airport eateries are the pits, but **Glacier Restaurant** (907/789-7538) is a real exception. Stop by before your flight for a reasonably priced menu that covers all the basics three meals a day, or for their biggest-in-town salad bar.

Even farther afield is **Hot Bite** (907/790-2483) at Auke Bay Harbor. The menu includes halibut and chips, Portobello grilled mushroom sandwiches, buffalo burgers, and other fast but good-tasting bites. It's especially popular with boaters after a day on the water.

Pizza and Italian
Juneau's best-known pizza joint is **Bullwinkle's** (907/586-2400), directly across from the State Office Building on Willoughby Avenue and also in Mendenhall Valley next to Super Bear Market. Daily lunch pizza specials start around $6, and the popcorn is always free. Good salad bar, too.

You'll get better and more authentic pizza (including by the slice) at **Pizzeria Roma** (2 Marine Way in Merchant's Wharf, 907/463-5020). **Vito 'N Nick's Pizzeria** (9342 Glacier Hwy., 907/789-7070) makes tasty deep-dish pizzas, along with sandwiches, Italian dinners, and monstrous homemade cinnamon rolls.

International Meals
Olivia's de Mexico (222 Seward St. downstairs, 907/586-6870) serves traditional Mexican food, with fair prices and big portions.

Out in Auke Bay, **Chan's Thai Kitchen** (907/789-9777) is popular with locals looking for a little spice in their lives. It's justifiably busy most nights, so you may need to wait. For Japanese sushi and Chinese take-out head to the Korean-American owned **Seong's Sushi Bar** (740 W. 9th St., 907/586-4778) across from the Federal Building.

Dragon Inn (213 Front St., 907/586-4888) has a convenient downtown location and an upscale setting. The menu includes such specialties as Mandarin scallops, mo shu pork, seafood with pan-fried noodles, and sautéed eggplant in hot garlic sauce. But no alcohol, and you can't bring any in. For Chinese meals in the Valley, head to **Canton House** (8585 Old Dairy Rd., 907/789-5075).

Pel' Meni (on Marine Way in Merchant's Wharf, 907/463-2630) is a tiny Russian eatery, where the house specialty is dumplings made with sirloin steak and topped with a spicy curry and cilantro sauce. This late-night hangout is popular with teens.

Salmon Bakes

Juneau has two excellent salmon bakes with all-you-can-eat dinners and free bus transport from town. Both are open only in the summertime. **Thane Ore House Salmon Bake** (907/586-3442), four miles south of town, charges $20 for a dinner of salmon, halibut, BBQ ribs, salad, baked beans, and corn bread.

In Last Chance Basin behind town, **Gold Creek Salmon Bake** (907/789-0052 or 800/323-5757, www.alaskaadventures.com) charges $29 (kids $19) for similar food served on the site of an old gold mine.

Four Seasons Tours (907/790-6671, www.4seasonsmarine.com) combines a three-hour whale-watching trip with an hour at Orca Point Lodge on Colt Island where guests are served grilled salmon, rice pilaf, corn on the cob, and dessert. The total cost is $99 adults, $49 kids under 13. The boat departs from Auke Bay, with a free shuttle from downtown. Taku Glacier Lodgeis another unique spot for a salmon bake—this time with fly-in access.

Seafood

Get high-quality freshly smoked salmon at **Taku Smokeries** (550 S. Franklin St., 907/463-3474 or 800/582-5122, www.takusmokeries.com), a few blocks south of town. Drop by for a sam-

ple or to watch through the windows as they process the fish.

On the water side of the Taku Smokeries building is **Twisted Fish Co.** (907/463-5033, open May–Sept., dinner entrées $16–25), where the decor is playful and the food is contemporary. Big windows face Gastineau Channel, where floatplanes and cruise ships create a busy scene all summer. Watch the crew in the open kitchen as they prepare grilled halibut burgers, sirloin kabobs, eight-inch pizzas, cedar plank salmon, and a tasty clam chowder.

Alaska Seafood Co. (5434 Shaune Dr., 907/780-5111 or 800/451-1400, www.alaskaseafoodcompany.com), across from the Alaskan Brewery, makes smoked salmon and halibut, plus smoked salmon caviar and jerky. Although primarily a wholesale operation, it has a retail counter. You might also try walking the docks to buy fresh fish or crab.

Gourmet Meals

Juneau's most famous eating place is the **Fiddlehead Restaurant and Bakery** (429 W. Willoughby Ave., 907/586-3150, www.thefiddlehead.com). In business since 1978, the Fiddlehead has a loyal following. There are actually two restaurants in the same building. Downstairs is a casual eatery where the menu rambles through an intriguing mix of pastas, seafood, salads, burgers, focaccia sandwiches, and inspired vegetarian dishes. Be sure to check out today's fish specials, along with the fresh sourdough breads and delectable desserts. Breakfasts and lunches are also great. Upstairs at Di Sopra, the setting is classy, with a Mediterranean-inspired menu that includes daily fresh raviolis. Piano or guitar tunes accompany your weekend meals, and entrées run $15–28.

Another upscale Juneau restaurant is the **Gold Room** (127 N. Franklin St., 907/586-2660, dinner entrées $15–25) inside the Baranof Hotel. House specialties include roast breast of pheasant, prime rib, garlic prawns, and other treats served in a formal setting. Open for lunch and dinner with Juneau's most complete wine list.

The **Summit Restaurant** (455 S. Franklin St., 907/586-2050, entrées $15–35) is right across from the main cruise ship dock. The building has been here since 1889, and served for many years as a brothel. Today it houses a romantic little restaurant where menu offerings include filet mignon, pan-seared duck, and pecan-crusted halibut; delicious desserts, too. Reservations are essential.

Groceries

You'll find no-frills grocery shopping at the big **Fred Meyer** (907/789-6503), nine miles northwest of town along Glacier Highway. Nearby, notice the old hip-roofed barn that was once home to the Juneau Dairy. Other grocers out in Mendenhall Valley are **Safeway** (3033 Vintage Blvd., 907/790-5500) and **Super Bear Supermarket** (in Mendenhall Mall, 907/789-0173).

In town, head to friendly **Alaskan & Proud Market** (615 Willoughby Ave., 907/586-3101 or 800/478-2118)—better known as A&P, but not to be confused with the East Coast chain—for a complete selection of fresh produce and meats. Safeway, A&P, and Fred Meyer are all open 24 hours a day. You might also try the somewhat-downsized **Costco** (5225 Commercial Way, 907/780-6740) in Lemon Creek, though most visitors won't find much need for cases of tuna fish or 50-pound bags of charcoal.

The local natural foods market downtown, **Rainbow Foods** (224 4th St.), has a good lunchtime buffet.

ENTERTAINMENT AND EVENTS

The Bar Scene

Juneau has an active night life, with plenty of live music almost every evening. The famous **Red Dog Saloon** (on South Franklin St., 907/463-3658, www.reddogsaloon.cc) has sawdust on the floor and honky-tonk music in the air every day and night during the summer, starting at 2 P.M. Be sure to look for Wyatt Earp's gun; he checked it in when passing through on June 17, 1900, but his ship left for Nome before the Marshall's office reopened, so it remained unclaimed in Juneau. This is where cruise ship tourists and crewmembers drink.

A block up the street, inside the Alaskan Hotel, is the **Alaskan Bar** (167 S. Franklin, 907/586-1000), a quieter place with blues or folk music on weekends, and Thursday night jam sessions. It's always packed with locals, who head here in summer to escape the Red Dog crowds. The Alaskan has a Victorian decor and you can hear lawyers and lobbyists talk shop from any seat in the place during the legislative session.

Billiards aficionados fill the half-dozen tables upstairs at the **Viking Bar** (218 Front St., 907/586-2159). Downstairs in the back is a classy disco with occasional live music and the best dance floor in Juneau. Across the street is **Imperial Bar** (907/586-1960), popular with the young crowd on weekends, when live bands perform. Thursday is jam night. More music around the corner at the **Rendezvous** (184 S. Franklin, 907/586-1270); very loud rock and a lowlife crowd.

The Hangar (2 Marine Way, 907/586-5018), on the wharf, has music to kick up your rain boots on Friday and Saturday nights, and is especially popular with state government workers on weeknights. It has more than 100 brews on tap or in bottles. Get here early for the window seats facing the waterfront.

Out near the airport, **The Sandbar** (2525 Industrial Blvd., 907/789-3411) has a large dance floor and rock or country music on weekends. Also out in Mendenhall Valley is **Marlintini's Lounge** (9121 Glacier Hwy., 907/789-0799), which mixes Karaoke on weeknights with rock bands Thursday–Saturday nights.

For something more romantic, the **Fiddlehead Restaurant and Bakery** (429 W. Willoughby Ave., 907/586-3150) has piano music or jazz upstairs on summer weekends.

Performing Arts and Music

On Friday evenings 7–8:30 P.M. in the summer, Marine Park in downtown Juneau comes alive with free **Concerts in the Park** (907/586-2787), ranging from classical to Middle Eastern folk. The **Juneau Symphony** (907/586-4676, www.juneau.com/symphony) has monthly concerts October–April at the various local venues. **Perseverance Theatre** (907/364-2421, www.perserverancetheatre.org) is a respected

Douglas-based group that puts on plays September–May.

Movies

Local movie houses are **20th Century Twin Theatre** (222 Front St., 907/586-4055) downtown and **Glacier Cinemas** (9091 Cinema Dr., 907/789-9191) in Mendenhall Valley. **Silverbow Inn** (120 2nd St., 907/586-9866 or 800/586-4146, www.silverbowinn.com, $3) screens classic flicks on Saturdays in the back room, and serves meals for the Saturday evening shows.

Events

Call 907/586-5866 for a recording of upcoming events and activities in Juneau. If you're around in April, don't miss the free weeklong **Alaska Folk Festival** (907/463-3316, www.juneau.com/aff), which attracts musicians from Alaska and the Northwest. You can attend workshops and dance to some of the hottest folk and bluegrass bands. Lots of fun.

In late May, culture comes to town with the **Juneau Jazz and Classics** (907/463-3378, www.jazzandclassics.org), a 10-day series of performances and workshops by local musicians and nationally acclaimed guest artists.

On even-numbered years (2004 and 2006), Juneau is home to a big **Native Celebration** (907/463-4844) that attracts hundreds of participants from throughout the state. This is primarily a conference, but there are also performances, crafts, and a grand procession. Celebration takes place on the first weekend of June.

As in most every Alaskan town, June 21, the **summer solstice** is a time for celebration in Juneau; there's always some sort of party that long day and short night. **July 4th** is Juneau's day to play. Parades and a big fireworks show (see them from Douglas Island for the most impressive backdrop) are joined by dog Frisbee-catching and watermelon-eating contests, along with a sand castle contest at Sandy Beach Park.

Those who like to fish should throw in their lines at the annual **Golden North Salmon Derby** in early August. A top prize of $15,000 in cash and prizes makes it *the* big summer event for locals.

ARTS AND CRAFTS
Galleries

Wm. Spear Designs (174 S. Franklin St. upstairs, 907/586-2209, www.wmspear.com) has the complete collection of colorful enameled pins by this local artisan with an international reputation. A former lawyer, Spear's work covers the spectrum from UFOs to dinosaurs. Definately worth a stop.

Rie Muñoz Gallery (2101 Jordan Ave., 907/789-7411, www.riemunoz.com), near the airport, features works by several of Alaska's best-known artists. Muñoz's works are famous for their bold colors and fanciful designs of Alaskans at work and play. Her prints can also be found downtown at **Decker Gallery** (233 S. Franklin St., 907/463-5536 or 800/463-5536).

The cooperatively run **Juneau Artists Gallery** (175 S. Franklin St., 907/586-9891, www.juneau artistsgallery.com) features a wide range of artwork, including paintings, pottery, jewelry, and photography.

Annie Kaill's Fine Art and Craft Gallery (244 Front St., 907/586-2880) is packed with whimsical gifts, pottery, jewelry, and fine art.

Native Arts

Juneau is a good place to purchase Native Alaskan artwork, and one of the best is downstairs at the airport: **Hummingbird Hollow Gift Shop** (907/789-4672, www.hummingbirdhollow.net). Fair prices and authentic Alaskan work, with a big choice of Tlingit, Haida, Yup'ik, and Eskimo pieces.

Raven's Journey (439 S. Franklin St., 907/463-4686), across from the tram, is another reputable shop with authentic Native Alaskan and Canadian art. Beware that some other shops in Juneau sell "Native Alaskan" items made in Bali factories. When asked about the origins, sales clerks have been known to claim that they "got them in Anchorage"—which means they took them off the plane there!

Scads of other galleries and gift shops sell artwork and trinkets. The quality varies widely, but much of it is overpriced, particularly anything by a Native artisan. Unfortunately, the romanticized paintings, carvings, and sculpture depicting these original Alaskans hunting seals in kayaks or carving totem poles meets head-on a much sadder picture of inebriated Natives leaning against the windows of downtown Juneau bars.

The Literary Scene

Juneauites enjoy several fine public libraries. The award-winning **Juneau Main Library** (907/586-5249, www.juneau.lib.ak.us/library), is on the top floor of the parking garage on South Franklin Street. There's a wonderful view of all the activity in Gastineau Channel from the outside walkway. Visitors may want to stop by the freebie shelves near the entrance for a trashy novel to read. Located on the 8th floor of the State Office Building, the **Alaska State Library** (907/465-2921, www.library.state.ak.us), is a good place to track down historical documents and photos.

Hearthside Books (907/586-1760 or 800/478-1000, www.hearthsidebooks.com) is a packed downtown bookshop; it also has a larger store (907/789-2750) in the Nugget Mall near the airport. **The Observatory** (235 2nd St., 907/586-9676, www.observatorybooks.com) sells used books—including the largest collection of out-of-print Alaskana—plus first editions and antiquarian maps. Also worthy of a visit is **Rainy Day Books** (113 Seward St., 907/463-2665), with over 10,000 used and rare titles.

INFORMATION AND SERVICES

Juneau's info spot is the **Centennial Hall Visitor Center** (101 Egan Dr., 907/586-2201 or 888/581-2201, www.traveljuneau.com). Hours are Monday–Friday 8:30 A.M.–5 P.M. and Saturday–Sunday 9 A.M.–5 P.M. May–September,Monday–Friday 9 A.M.–4 P.M. the rest of the year. Ask for the "Juneau Walking Tour" map on a nice day, or pick out a video for a rainy-day diversion. You can make ferry reservations here, and there's usually a Forest Service volunteer available to answer your questions.

Three other information kiosks in Juneau have brochures and may be staffed in the summer. Find them at Marine Park, the airport, and the Cruise Ship Terminal on South Franklin Street.

Other useful online info sources for Juneau include www.juneaualska.com, www.juneau.com, and the city site www.juneau.org.

Services

The main post office is in the downtown Federal Building at 9th and Willoughby, and a branch post office is on Seward and 2nd streets. **Bartlett Regional Hospital** (907/796-8900, www.bartletthospital.org), halfway between Juneau and Mendenhall Valley, is the largest medical facility in Southeast Alaska. For non-emergencies, contact **Juneau Urgent Care** (8505 Old Dairy Rd., 907/790-4111).

A number of local places have computers where you can check your email. The Juneau Public Library has free computers. Or pay to view downtown at **Uncle Artie's** (on S. Franklin St. in the Tram Building, 907/463-2543) **Seaport Cyber Station** (170 S. Franklin St., 907/586-8676), or **Copy Express** (223 Seward St., 907/586-2174).

Shopping

Most locals do their shopping out the road at Nugget Mall in Mendenhall Valley, Fred Meyer (near the airport), or Costco (in Lemon Creek).

Foggy Mountain Shop (134 N. Franklin St., 907/586-6780, www.foggymountainshop.com) sells camping gear, topographic maps, and sports equipment. It also rents skis and rollerblades. The best place for rugged raingear, boots, and outdoor clothes is **Nugget Alaskan Outfitter** (Nugget Mall, 907/789-9785 or 800/478-0770, www.outdoorhq.com). While there, check out the mall's nine-foot-tall stuffed brown bear.

If you're in the market for hand-tailored Alaskan-tough coats, step into **Kodiak Coat** (174 S. Franklin St., 907/463-4986, www.kodiakcoat.com) at the back of the Emporium Mall behind Heritage Coffee. The owner sews coats, mittens, hats, and other gear that are waterproof, windproof, and breathable. Recommended.

Cleaning Up

Coin-operated showers can be found at **Harbor Washboard** (1114 Glacier Ave., 907/586-1133), **Zach Gordon Youth Center** (396 Whittier St.,

907/586-2635), the **Alaskan Hotel** (167 S. Franklin St., 907/586-1000), and out of town at **Auke Bay Boat Harbor** (907/789-0819). A better deal is the high school **swimming pool** (1619 Glacier Ave., 907/586-5325), where your entrance buys access to a shower, pool, sauna, and weight-lifting equipment. Plus, you get to check out the pallid-skin Juneauites. Launderettes include the above-mentioned Harbor Wash Board, along with **The Dungeon** (4th and Franklin, 907/586-2805) and **Mendenhall Laundromat** (Mendenhall Mall, 907/789-9781).

SEACC

The Southeast Alaska Conservation Council, or SEACC (419 6th St., Suite 328, 907/586-6942, www.seacc.org), has material on regional environmental issues, plus activist T-shirts. This is the primary environmental group in the Southeast and has a reputation as a highly effective organization both locally and in Washington, D.C. Members receive a quarterly newsletter and periodic notices of important environmental issues. You can join for $50 per year.

TRANSPORTATION
Ferry

Juneau's Alaska Marine Highway **ferry terminal** (907/465-3940) is 14 miles northwest of town at Auke Bay. Ferries arrive and depart daily during the summer, headed north to both Haines and Skagway, southwest to Sitka, and south to other Alaskan towns. Arrivals are sometimes very late at night, so be ready to stumble off in a daze. Ferries generally stay one to two hours in Auke Bay. New in 2004, the *Fairweather* is a high-speed passenger and vehicle ferry with frequent service from Juneau to Sitka, Haines, and Skagway. The other state ferries are larger and slower. Several covered picnic tables are behind the terminal where you can crash if you have an early-morning departure. Make ferry reservations through Alaska Marine Highway (907/465-3941 or 800/642-0066, www.ferryalaska.com).

A cab ride to town will set you back $25–30, but hitching to town is relatively easy during the day. You can also walk the two miles from the

ferry terminal to De Hart's Store, where hourly city buses ($1.50) will pick you up Monday–Saturday 7 A.M.–11:30 P.M.

There is no state ferry service to Glacier Bay, but **Auk Nu Tours** (907/586-8687 or 800/820-2628, www.goldbelttours.com) operates a daily passenger ferry between downtown Juneau and Gustavus in the summer. The fare is $69 ($32 kids) each way, and bikes are $10, while kayaks cost $40. A wildlife- and whale-watching tour around Pleasant Island is $79 ($60 kids), or combine these for a round-trip to Gustavus and whale-watching trip for $195 round-trip ($105 kids).

Chilkat Cruises (907/766-2100 or 888/766-2103, www.chilkatcruises.com) offers high-speed catamaran service on weekends between Auke Bay in Juneau and Haines for $69 roundtrip, $39 one-way. Bring your own food along.

Air

Juneau airport is nine miles northwest of downtown. Express **city buses** ($1.50) arrive hourly in front of the airport between 8 A.M.–5 P.M. On weekends or later hours (until 11:15 P.M.) you can catch the regular city bus behind Nugget Mall, a half-mile away. Taxis cost $18 to downtown.

Inside the terminal, take a look at the glass cases with various stuffed critters, including a huge polar bear (upstairs). The upstairs Glacier Restaurant offers impressive vistas out across Mendenhall Glacier, along with surprisingly good and reasonable meals; locals actually come here to eat!

A good place to see waterfowl and eagles is the **Mendenhall Wetlands** that surround the airport. An overlook provides a view from Egan Highway on the way into Juneau.

Alaska Airlines (800/426-0333, www.alaskaair.com) has daily flights into Juneau from Seattle, and on to Anchorage. Alaska's jets also connect Juneau with other Southeast towns and points south all the way to Mexico.

Air North (867/668-2228, 800/764-0407 U.S. or 800/661-0407 Canada, www.flyairnorth.com) flies between Juneau and Whitehorse, Yukon, and onward to Dawson and Fairbanks.

Options abound for small-plane service to communities around Juneau. **Wings of Alaska** (907/789-0790, www.wingsofalaska.com), has daily flights to Angoon, Gustavus, Haines, Hoonah, Skagway, and Tenakee Springs. **Alaska Seaplane Service** (907/789-3331 or 800/478-3360, www.akseaplanes.com) offers daily service to Angoon, Elfin Cove, Pack Creek, Pelican, and Tenakee. **Skagway Air** (907/789-2006, www.skagwayair.com) flies to Haines and Skagway daily. **L.A.B. Flying Service** (907/789-9160 or 800/426-0543, www.labflying.com) has daily service to Gustavus, Haines, Hoonah, Kake, Petersburg, and Skagway. **Air Excursions** (907/697-2375 or 800/354-2479, www.airexcursions.com), offers the cheapest flights to Gustavus from Juneau. Flightseeing and charter flights are also available from the above-listed companies.

City Buses

Capital Transit buses (907/789-6901, $1.50) operate daily, connecting Juneau, Douglas, and Mendenhall Valley. Buses to and from Mendenhall Valley run every half-hour 7 A.M.–10:30 P.M. (9 A.M.–5:30 P.M. on Sunday), with both regular and express service (weekdays only). Bus service to Douglas is hourly. For details, call or pick up route maps and schedules from the various visitor centers or at the ferry terminal or airport.

Trolley

The **Juneau Trolley Car Company** (907/586-7433, www.juneautrolley.com, daily May–Sept. 8 A.M.–6 P.M.) covers most of downtown. Fares are $12 ($8.50 kids) for all day. This red trolley features a narrated tour, and you can get on and off at various points along the way.

Taxis

The local taxi companies are **Alaska Taxi & Tours** (907/780-6400), **Capital Cab** (907/586-2772), **Juneau Taxi & Tours** (907/790-4511), and **Metro Taxi** (907/586-2121). From the airport to downtown the charge is typically around $18. A cab ride from downtown to the ferry terminal (14 miles) will cost upward of $30, but might be worth it if you get several people together. Taxi tours are $55 per hour.

Car Rentals

With nearly 100 miles of roads in the Juneau area, renting a car is a smart idea. Be sure to call two or three weeks ahead of mid-summer arrivals, or you may find every car already rented. Three national chains have offices at the airport: **Avis** (907/789-9450 or 800/478-2847), **Hertz** (907/789-9494 or 800/654-3131), and **National** (907/789-9814 or 800/478-2847). The other companies are all within a few blocks, and will pick you up during business hours: **Allstar/Practical** (907/790-2414 or 800/722-0741), **Payless** (907/780-6004 or 800/729-5377), **Rent-A-Wreck** (907/789-4111, www.juneaualaska.com/rent-a-wreck), **Mendenhall Auto Center** (907/789-1386 or 800/478-1386), and **Evergreen Ford** (907/789-9386, www.evergreenmotorsjuneau.com). The best rates are typically with Mendenhall Auto, starting around $37 per day for a compact.

TRACY ARM–FORDS TERROR WILDERNESS

Located 50 miles southeast of Juneau, the 653,000-acre Tracy Arm–Fords Terror Wilderness contains country that rivals Glacier Bay National Park, but costs half as much to reach. The wilderness consists of a broad bay that splits into two long glacially carved arms—Tracy Arm and Endicott Arm. (Fords Terror splits off as a separate channel halfway up Endicott Arm.) Within Tracy Arm, steep-walled granite canyons plummet 2,000 feet into incredibly deep and narrow fjords. We're talking rocks-to-the-waterline here. The fjords wind past waterfalls to massive glaciers, their icebergs dotted with hundreds of harbor seals. Humpback whales are a common sight, as are killer whales. Look closely on the mountain slopes and you're bound to see mountain goats, especially near North Sawyer Glacier. John Muir noted that the fjord was "shut in by sublime Yosemite cliffs, nobly sculptured, and adorned with waterfalls and fringes of trees, bushes, and patches of flowers, but amid so crowded a display of novel beauty it was not easy to concentrate the attention long enough on any portion of it without giving more days and years than our lives can afford." Modern-day visitors come away equally impressed.

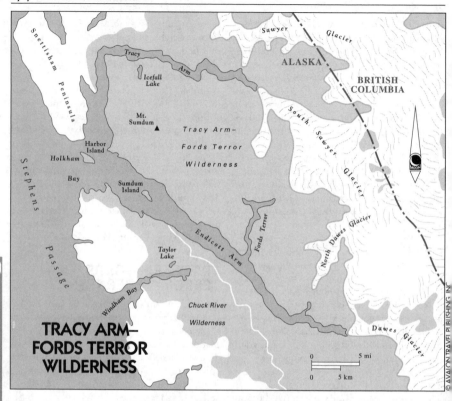

TRACY ARM–
FORDS TERROR
WILDERNESS

Two glaciers—Sawyer and South Sawyer—cap the end of Tracy Arm. Sawyer Glacier is retreating up bay at 85 feet per year, while South Sawyer is heading up at over 300 feet per year. Contact the Forest Service Information Center in Juneau (907/586-8751) for details on Tracy Arm.

Boat Trips

Visitors to Tracy Arm have three different all-day boat tour options. The fast 87-foot catamaran operated by **Auk Nu Tours** (907/586-8687 or 800/820-2628, www.goldbelttours.com, $119 adults, $72 kids) offers a full-day round-trip cruise to Tracy Arm, including a light lunch. These run three days a week in the summer. No kayaker drop-offs.

For a more personalized (and slower) boat trip into Tracy Arm, contact **Adventure Bound Alaska** (907/463-2509 or 800/228-3875; www.adven-tureboundalaska.com). All-day cruises on a 56-foot boat are $105 adults, $65 kids; food is extra.

Tantallon Tours (907/364-3989 or 888/673-4527, www.tantallon.com), runs the 16-passenger *Noble Lady* to Tracy Arm, charging $140 per person, including lunch.

On Your Own

There are no trails in the Tracy Arm–Fords Terror Wilderness, but experienced sea kayakers discover spectacular country to explore. Unfortunately, kayakers in Tracy Arm should be prepared for a constant parade of giant cruise ships, leaving large wakes and plenty of engine noise to contend with. (Sound travels a long way over the water. Wilderness rangers report being startled to suddenly hear loudspeakers announcing, "Margaritas will be served at 1630 in the aft lounge.") You can, however, escape the boats by hiking up the ravines into the high country, or by heading into the less-congested waters of Endicott Arm where the big cruise ships and power boats rarely stray. Adventure Bound Alaska provides kayaker drop-offs.

If you plan to go into Tracy Arm in a kayak, check ahead with the Forest Service's Juneau Ranger District for the good campsites. As you approach the glaciers at the upper end of Tracy, these become harder to find. Many boaters anchor in No Name Cove near the entrance to Tracy Arm. Kayakers will probably prefer to head to the middle part of the fjord and away from the motorboats. Ambitious folks (with a topo map) may want to try the steep half-mile cross-country climb up to **Icefall Lake** (1,469 feet above sea level).

Massive **Dawes Glacier** jams the top of Endicott Arm with thousands of bergs of all sizes and shapes, making it tough to get close to the face of the glacier. **Fords Terror** is a turbulent but spectacular inlet that angles away from Endicott Arm. Tidal changes create wild water conditions near the entrance, so kayakers and boaters need to take special precautions. Only run the narrows at slack tides, when the water is relatively calm. (The narrows are named for the terror felt by H.R. Ford, who rowed into the inlet one day in 1889 when the water was calm, but nearly died while fighting the currents, whirlpools, and icebergs on the way back out.) Fords Terror has no tidewater glaciers, but numerous hanging glaciers and craggy peaks are visible.

Chuck River Wilderness

Twelve miles south of Tracy Arm is **Windham Bay,** entrance to the Chuck River Wilderness. This small wild area receives very little use, but offers good fishing for salmon and a chance to explore the ruins of the Southeast's oldest mining community, Windham Bay. You can hike up the mile-long **Taylor Creek Trail** from Windham Bay to Taylor Lake.

Endicott River Wilderness

Although it encompasses 94,000 acres, this is one of the least-visited wilderness areas in America. Located some 60 miles northwest of Juneau, the wilderness borders on Glacier Bay National Park and includes the Endicott River watershed along the eastern slope of the Chilkat Range. The country is spruce and hemlock forests, mixed with alders. Trails are nonexistent, and access from Lynn Canal is virtually impossible. Visit the Forest Service's Juneau Ranger District office for more on this decidedly off-the-beaten-track area.

Admiralty Island

Just 20 miles west of Juneau lies the northern end of Admiralty Island National Monument, and the massive Kootznahoo Wilderness. At nearly a million acres, the wilderness covers 90 percent of Admiralty, making it the only large island in the Southeast that has not been extensively logged or developed. The Tlingit name for Admiralty is Kootznahoo (Bear Fortress). The island is aptly named: It has perhaps 1,500 brown bears, giving it one of the highest bear densities anywhere on earth. Eagles are extraordinarily abundant along the shoreline, and the cries of loons haunt Admiralty's lakes. This is truly one of the gemstones of Southeast Alaska.

ANGOON

Located along Admiralty's southwestern shore, the Tlingit village of Angoon (pop. 600) is the island's lone settlement. It sits astride a peninsula guarding the entrance to Kootznahoo Inlet, an incredible wonderland of small islands and saltwater passages. Tourism is not encouraged in Angoon, but people are friendly. Locals have cable TVs and microwave ovens, but smokehouses sit in front of many homes and you'll hear older people speaking Tlingit. Angoon weather generally lives up to its reputation as Southeast Alaska's "Banana Belt"; yearly rainfall averages only 38 inches, compared to three times that in Sitka, only 40 miles away. By the way, the word *hootch* originated from the potent whiskey distilled by the "Hoosenoo" Indians of Admiralty in the 19th century. Today, Angoon is a dry town with a reputation as a place where traditional ways are encouraged. As with most other bush towns, it is far from attractive, with lots of trash strewn about.

History

The village of Angoon still commemorates an infamous incident that took place more than a century ago. While working for the Northwest Trading Company, a local shaman was killed in a seal-hunting accident. The villagers demanded 200 blankets as compensation and two days off to honor and bury the dead man. To ensure payment, they seized two hostages. Unaware of Tlingit traditions, the company manager fled to Sitka and persuaded a U.S. Navy boat to "punish them severely." On October 26, 1882, the town was shelled, destroying most of the houses. All the villagers' canoes were smashed and sunk, and all their winter supplies burned. Six children died from the smoke and the people nearly starved that winter. In a U.S. Congressional investigation two years later, the shelling was called "the greatest outrage ever committed in the United States upon any Indian tribe." Finally, in 1973, the government paid $90,000 in compensation for the shelling, but the Navy has never formally apologized.

Unlike most other villages in the Southeast, the people of Angoon have fought hard to preserve their island from logging and development. Unfortunately, they were unable to stop logging by Atikon Forest Products, a Native-owned corporation that logged right down to the water around beautiful Lake Florence. This is what happens when money talks. Fortunately, nearly all the rest of Admiralty remains a pristine wilderness.

Sights

Even if you don't stay overnight in Angoon, get off the ferry and walk across the road and down to the beach. From there you can look up to a small **cemetery** with old gravestones and fenced-in graves. Another interesting cemetery is near the

end of the peninsula a half-mile behind the **Russian Orthodox church** in town. A number of rustic old houses line the shore, one with killer whales painted on the front. A hundred feet uphill from the post office are five memorial **totems** topped by representations of different local clans. Near Angoon Trading you get a great view of the narrow passage leading into **Kootznahoo Inlet,** where tides create dangerous rapids.

Accommodations and Food

Built in 1937, **Favorite Bay Inn** (907/788-3123 or 800/423-3123, www.whalerscovelodge.com, all year, $99 s, $129 d) is on the edge of town near the boat harbor. Five guest rooms share three baths; full breakfast included. The owners also run **Whaler's Cove Sportfishing Lodge** (open June–Sept.) with packages for anglers in search of salmon and halibut. Guests of Favorite Bay Inn can also eat other meals at Whaler's Cove, and canoe and skiff rentals are available.

Kootznahoo Inlet Lodge (907/788-3501, $65 s, $75 d) a few hundred feet closer to town, has rooms and efficiency apartments, some with kitchenettes. They rent skiffs and can provide meals to guests upon request. Owner Albert Kookesh is one of the state's best-known Native legislators.

Angoon's newest lodging place is **Favorite Bay Sportfishing Lodge** (907/788-3344 or 866/788-3344, www.favoritebay.com, open May–Sept.). This isn't your dad's boots-on-the-table fishing lodge, but a luxurious place with an extraordinary setting and such amenities as floor-to-ceiling windows facing on the bay, and elegant rooms with handcrafted rugs, top-end beds, and soaking tubs, plus a French chef who crafts four-course gourmet dinners. Package fishing and lodging trips start at $2,200 per person for four nights, including air transport from Juneau. Guided kayaking and hiking trips are extra.

Angoon has no official camping facilities, but people sometimes pitch tents at the trashed-out picnic area just to the right of the ferry terminal along the beach. It's 2.5 miles to town along the road or a pleasant 1.5-mile walk north along the rocky beach.

Angoon Trading (907/788-3111) sells a limited and rather expensive selection of groceries and supplies. Both Whaler's Cove Sportfishing Lodge and Favorite Bay Sportfishing Lodge serve meals during the summer, but you'll need to make reservations if you aren't a guest.

Transportation

The ferry *Le Conte* visits Angoon six times a week, staying just long enough to unload and load vehicles. The dock (no ferry terminal) is 2.5 miles out of town, so you won't get to see Angoon up close unless you disembark. Get details from the Alaska Marine Highway (800/642-0066, www.ferryalaska.com).

"Taxis" meet most ferries, or you can hitch or walk the dirt road to town. **Wings of Alaska** (907/789-0790, www.wingsofalaska.com) and **Alaska Seaplane Service** (907/789-3331 or 800/478-3360, www.akseaplanes.com) have floatplane service between Angoon and Juneau. Wings also flies between Angoon and Tenakee Springs. **Harris Aircraft Services** (907/966-3050 or 877/966-3050, www.harrisaircraft.com) has service several times a week to Sitka.

PACK CREEK

Located a short flight from Juneau along the west side of Seymour Canal, Pack Creek is one of Alaska's premier brown bear-viewing areas. The creek fills with spawning humpback and chum salmon during July and August, and they attract the bears, which in turn attract the people. Most visitors arrive on day trips from Juneau on the local air taxis. Others come aboard kayaks and boats, or with commercially guided groups. Pack Creek is jointly managed and staffed by the U.S. Forest Service and the Alaska Department of Fish and Game. Special regulations apply to travel and camping in the area, and it's only open for visitation 9 A.M.–9 P.M.

Bear-Watching

The number of bears varies greatly through the summer, but most visitors see at least one bear, and often several. Plan to spend a full day—or longer—to increase your odds and to soak in the beauty of the area. Binoculars or a spotting scope are helpful, and photographers should be sure to bring plenty of film and long lenses. Rubber boots and raingear are highly recommended for anyone visiting Pack Creek. Food and drinks must be stowed in a special bear-resistant box, and neither is allowed in the viewing areas.

There are two primary bear-viewing areas along Pack Creek. The most accessible is a sandy spit of land right at the mouth of the creek and a short beach hike from where floatplanes land and boats tie up. A bit more challenging is a beautiful one-mile trail that leads through an old-growth rainforest to a viewing tower. The tower has room for eight people, and is an excellent place to watch bears as they pass directly below you.

Forest Service and Fish and Game rangers at Pack Creek will be happy to answer your questions, so it isn't necessary to come with a guide (unless you can't get in otherwise). They will not, however, accompany you to the observation tower.

Rules and Regulations

If you travel independently, you will need to obtain a permit and set up a charter with a local air taxi. Guided visitors are provided with transportation and permits, but the fee is much higher. Because of its popularity with both bears and people—and the potential for conflicts between the two—Pack Creek has stringent and rather confusing rules. Permits are required June 1–September 10, and only 24 people per day are allowed during the peak of the bear-viewing season (July 5–Aug. 25).

Reservations cost $50, and can be postmarked as early as February 20 for the following summer. Apply early to be sure of getting a permit for the peak season. Of the 24 permits, 4 are held for late arrivals, and are available three days in advance of your visit. These are in high demand, however, and are chosen by lottery from the applicants who show up. An unlimited number of shoulder-season permits (June 1–July 9 and Aug. 26–Sept. 10, $20) are available, but bear activity is lower. Get additional details from the Forest Service.

Getting to Pack Creek

Most visitors to Pack Creek arrive by floatplane on day trips from Juneau, landing next to the south sandspit. The following companies fly to Pack Creek: **Alaska Fly 'N Fish Charters**

(907/790-2120, www.alaskabyair.com), **Alaska Seaplane Service** (907/789-3331 or 800/478-3360, www.akseaplanes.com), **Ward Air** (907/789-9150, www.wardair.com), and **Wings of Alaska** (907/789-0790, www.wingso-falaska.com). The costs vary depending upon how many people are on the flight, but with three or more people in a group the price drops to around $175 per person round-trip (but you'll need to get your own permit).

Guided Trips

Several guide companies offer trips to Pack Creek, and are likely to have space available at the last minute. They're a good option if you can't get a permit—and if you have the cash. **Alaska Discovery** (907/780-6226 or 800/586-1911, www.akdiscovery.com) has $500 day trips to Pack Creek that include charter air service, an experienced guide, lunch, rubber boots, and raingear. They also have three-day kayak trips to Pack Creek for $950, including airfare from Juneau.

Alaska Fly 'N Fish Charters (907/790-2120, www.alaskabyair.com) offers guided day trips to Pack Creek; $475 for a five-hour tour that includes air transport from Juneau. Two companies have multiday boat trips that include a day at Pack Creek: **All Aboard Yacht Charters** (360/898-7300 or 800/767-1024, www.alaskacharters.com) and **Dolphin Charters** (510/527-9622 or 800/472-9942, www.dolphincharters.com).

Camping

Camping is not allowed on Admiralty Island near the mouth of Pack Creek, but is permitted on Windfall Island, where you're far less likely to have encounters with the bears. The island is a quarter-mile from Pack Creek. Independent travelers can rent a sea kayak on Windfall from Alaska Discovery (advance reservation required) to reach Pack Creek.

Seymour Canal

The bear-viewing area along Pack Creek is only a tiny portion of Seymour Canal. This is a wonderful place to explore by sea kayak, with beautiful country, relatively protected waters, and the chance to see eagles, brown bears, and other wildlife. Most kayakers head south from Juneau, crossing the often-rough Stephens Passage and entering Oliver Inlet. **Auke Bay Landing Craft** (907/790-4591, www.aukebaylandingcraft.com) can deliver you to Oliver's Inlet. An ingenious boat tramway makes it easy to bring kayaks across from Oliver Inlet to upper Seymour Canal, a mile away. Alaska State Parks maintains the **Oliver Inlet Cabin** ($25) at the northern tip of Seymour Canal.

In Seymour you'll find many coves and islands to explore, and have a chance to observe bears that are protected from hunting. If you're adventurous, take a climb up the nearby peaks for fantastic views of the entire area. A three-sided shelter (free) is available in **Windfall Harbor.** Bears can be a real problem in Seymour Canal so be sure to select your camping spots very carefully (preferably on a small island) and hang all food.

CROSS-ADMIRALTY CANOE ROUTE

Admiralty Island is ideally suited for people who enjoy canoeing or sea kayaking. Kootznahoo Inlet reaches back behind Angoon through a labyrinth of islands and narrow passages, before opening into expansive Mitchell Bay. From there you can continue to Salt Lake or Kanalku Bay, or begin the Cross-Admiralty Canoe Route—a chain of scenic lakes connected by portages, one of which is over three miles long. Using this 42-mile route you should reach Seymour Canal in four to six days (the record is 12 hours). Along the way are six Forest Service cabins ($35) and six Adirondack shelters (free), so you won't have to sleep out in the rain all the time.

Kootznahoo Inlet

Twice each day, tidal fluctuations push water through the narrow passages of Kootznahoo Inlet into Mitchell Bay and Salt Lake. At full flood or ebb tide, the water becomes a torrent that creates some of the fastest-flowing stretches of salt water in the world (13 knots). These strong tidal currents create eddies, whirlpools, standing waves, and even falls, depending upon the tides and the stage. To avoid these Class III white-water conditions, be sure you reach the narrow passages at slack tide. Use a tide chart, adding approximately two hours to the Juneau times for the passage through the inappropriately named Stillwater Narrows. Inside Mitchell Bay and at Salt Lake the tides are delayed even longer, up to three hours beyond Juneau tides. If you aren't sure how to read the tide charts or need more information on running Kootznahoo Inlet, talk to folks at the monument office in Juneau.

Practicalities

Be sure to make Admiralty cabin reservations well in advance. The **Centennial Hall Information Center** (907/586-8751) in Juneau has maps of the canoe route that include details on navigating Kootznahoo Narrows and crossing the island. Trail conditions may vary along the canoe route. The Distin Lake–Thayer Lake trail may be in poor condition, but other trails on the route are in better shape, with long stretches of puncheon or boardwalk.

Guided canoe treks are not offered across Admiralty. Most canoeists and kayakers bring their own boats along on the ferry, but you can rent canoes in Angoon from Favorite Bay Inn. For more specific canoe-route information, contact the office of **Admiralty Island National Monument** (907/586-8790) in Juneau.

Thayer Lake Lodge (907/225-3343 winter or 907/789-5646 summer, www.alaskabearviewing.com) is a great place to escape civilization. The facilities—a main lodge and two cabins—are comfortably rustic and you get three big meals a day as well as use of the lodge's boats, canoes, and fishing gear. Besides, you get to meet some real old-time Alaskans. Highly recommended if you have the cash. Two-night packages that include lodging, meals, transportation from Juneau, and a stop to see the bears at Pack Creek, cost $1,400 for two people.

If you're really ambitious (and experienced) it's possible to cross Admiralty Island and then continue up Seymour Canal, eventually reaching Juneau. Only a few hardy souls try this, however, because the canoes that work so well on the lakes can be dangerous in the open water of Seymour Canal, and sea kayaks are impractical for the long canoe-route portages.

Glacier Bay National Park and Preserve

America's national parks are this country's version of Mecca, places where hordes of pilgrims are drawn in search of a fulfillment that seems to come from experiencing these shrines of the natural world. Since Glacier Bay's discovery by John Muir in 1879, the spectacles of stark rocky walls, deep fjords, and giant rivers of ice calving massive icebergs into the sea have never ceased to inspire and humble visitors.

Established as a national park in 1925, Glacier Bay received major additions in the Alaska National Interest Lands Conservation Act of 1980. The park and preserve now cover more than 3.3 million acres and contain half a dozen glaciers that reach the ocean, making this one of the largest concentrations of tidewater glaciers on earth. These glaciers originate in the massive snowcapped Fairweather Range, sliding down the slopes and carving out giant troughs that become fjords when the glaciers retreat. **Mt. Fair-**

weather, rising 15,320 feet, is Southeast Alaska's tallest peak. On a clear day, it is prominently visible from park headquarters, 72 miles away. The vegetation of Glacier Bay varies from a 200-year-old spruce and hemlock forest at Bartlett Cove to freshly exposed moraine where tenacious plant life is just starting to take hold. Wildlife is abundant in the park: Humpback whales, harbor porpoises, harbor seals, and bird rookeries can be seen from the excursion boats and kayaks. Black bears are fairly common.

HISTORY

Glacier Bay has not always looked as it does today. When Captain George Vancouver sailed through Icy Strait in 1794, he found a wall of ice more than 4,000 feet thick and 20 miles wide. Less than 100 years later (1879) when Hoonah Indian guides led John Muir into the area, he

SOUTHEAST ALASKA

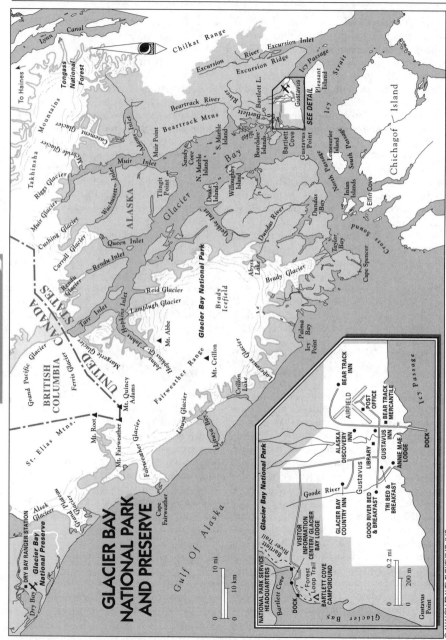

GLACIER BAY NATIONAL PARK AND PRESERVE

SEE DETAIL

NATIONAL PARK SERVICE HEADQUARTERS
VISITOR INFORMATION CENTER / GLACIER BAY LODGE
Bartlett River Trail
Forest Loop Trail
BARTLETT COVE CAMPGROUND
DOCK
Bartlett Cove

Glacier Bay National Park

GLACIER BAY COUNTRY INN
Goode River
GOOD RIVER BED & BREAKFAST
TRI BED & BREAKFAST

ALASKA DISCOVERY INN
Gustavus
LIBRARY
GUSTAVUS INN
ANNIE MAE LODGE

BEAR TRACK INN
AIRFIELD
POST OFFICE
BEAR TRACK MERCANTILE
DOCK

Icy Passage

Glacier Bay
Gustavus Point

© AVALON TRAVEL PUBLISHING, INC.

discovered that the glaciers had retreated nearly 50 miles, creating a new land and a giant bay splitting into two deep fjords on its upper end. The bay was shrouded by low clouds, but Muir, anxious to see farther into the country, climbed a peak on its western shore: "All the landscape was smothered in clouds and I began to fear that as far as wide views were concerned I had climbed in vain. But at length the clouds lifted a little, and beneath their gray fringes I saw the berg-filled expanse of the bay, and the feet of the mountains that stand about it, and the imposing fronts of five huge glaciers, the nearest being immediately beneath me. This was my first general view of Glacier Bay, a solitude of ice and snow and newborn rocks, dim, dreary, mysterious. I held the ground I had so dearly won for an hour or two, sheltering myself from the blast as best I could, while with benumbed fingers I sketched what I could see of the landscape, and wrote a few lines in my notebook. Then, breasting the snow again, crossing the shifting avalanche slopes and torrents, I reached camp about dark, wet and weary and glad." Today's traveler is less likely to take such pains to see this grand place.

The rapid retreat of the glaciers over the last 200 years has caused the land to rebound, much like a sponge that has been squeezed and then reforms. The process is astoundingly rapid by geological standards; around Bartlett Cove it is rising nearly two inches a year and even faster farther up the bay. Ask the park rangers to point out some of the changes in vegetation because of this rebound effect.

VISITING GLACIER BAY

The vast majority of the over 400,000 visitors who come to Glacier Bay each year arrive aboard cruise ships, two of which are allowed in each day; they're given a talk by a Park Service naturalist as the ship heads up the west arm of the bay and never set foot on the land itself. Most other visitors stay in Glacier Bay Lodge at Bartlett Cove or in nearby luxury lodges in the town of Gustavus, venturing out only to cruise past the glaciers on a tour boat. The tiny percentage who come to actually see and touch their national park—rather

than view it in a naturalist's slide show—are often prevented from doing so by prohibitive costs. It is somewhat ironic that the park is most accessible to those who would rather look out on its glaciers from their stateroom windows.

The nearest tidewater glacier is 40 miles from park headquarters in Bartlett Cove. To see these glaciers, expect to spend at least $400 from Juneau for a fast two-day trip. A visit to Glacier Bay is a wonderful experience, but there are few options for the budget traveler, and you should probably make other plans if you're pinched for cash.

Park Information

The Park Service maintains a visitor center upstairs in the Glacier Bay Lodge at Bartlett Cove, open daily 12:30–9 P.M. in the summer. A small museum here contains natural history and geology exhibits. Naturalists lead interpretive walks every day, and also put on evening talks and slide shows in the auditorium. The park's **back country office** is near the boat dock, a short hike from the lodge, and is open daily

© DON PITCHER

Glacier Bay National Park

8 A.M.–7 P.M. during the summer. Stop here before heading into the park on an overnight trip. For additional details, contact Glacier Bay National Park (907/697-2230, www.nps.gov/glba).

Getting to the Glaciers

The park concessionaire—Native-owned Goldbelt Tours—operates the *Baranof Wind* which heads up the west arm of Glacier Bay daily in the summer, departing at 7:30 A.M. and returning at 3:30 P.M. Tours on this high-speed catamaran cost $159 for adults or $80 for kids under 13. A light lunch is served, and a Park Service naturalist and a Native guide are on board to provide information on wildlife, geology, and cultural history along the route. Another *Baranof Wind* option is to pay $358 for a day-long trip that includes a flight from Juneau to Gustavus followed by a trip up the bay and another flight back to Juneau that evening. (You could book your own Alaska Airlines flights and do the same thing for less.) You can also ride the *Auk Nu Keet* ferry from Juneau to Gustavus, take a trip up the bay on the *Baranof Wind,* return for a night at Glacier Bay Lodge, then fly back to Juneau for a very full two days at a total cost of $400 per person.

Another Goldbelt-owned company, **Glacier Bay Cruiseline** (206/623-2417 or 800/451-5952, www.glacierbaytours.com), operates the luxurious *Wilderness Explorer* in the bay, and guests have access to sea kayaks for exploring on their own when the boat is anchored. This 112-foot boat accommodates 34 guests who take part in a six-day, five-night trip, starting around $3,600 for two people. These trips begin and end in Gustavus.

BARTLETT COVE HIKING TRAILS

There are several enjoyable walks in the Bartlett Cove area. The mile-long **Forest Loop Trail** connects the lodge, boat dock, and campground, providing an excellent introduction to the area. **Bartlett River Trail** (four miles round-trip) leads from park headquarters to the mouth of the river, with opportunities to observe wildlife. Salmon

can be seen moving up the river in August. For a satisfying beach walk, head south along the shore from the campground. If you're ambitious, it is possible to walk to **Point Gustavus** (six miles) or on to **Goode River** (13 miles). Follow the river upstream a mile to Gustavus, where you can walk or hitch back along the road. Beach walking is easiest at low tide; the backcountry office has tide charts. Note that none of these trails goes anywhere near the tidewater glaciers for which the park is famous, and there are no developed trails anywhere in the park's backcountry.

CAMPING

An excellent free **campground** at Bartlett Cove comes complete with bear-proof food storage caches, outhouses, and a three-sided shelter with a woodstove (great for drying your gear after a kayak trip up the bay). The campground is only a half-mile from Glacier Bay Lodge and usually has space. Running water is available next to the backcountry office. All cooking must be done below the high-tide line (where the odors are washed away every six hours) to reduce the chance of bear problems. You can store things for free in the shed next to the backcountry office.

Backcountry Camping

No trails exist anywhere in Glacier Bay's backcountry, but Park Service rangers can provide details on hiking and camping up the bay. Camping is allowed in most park areas. Exceptions are the Marble Islands—closed because of their importance for nesting seabirds—and a few other areas closed because of the potential for bear incidents. A gas stove is a necessity for camping, since wood is often unavailable.

Free permits (available at the backcountry office) are recommended before you head out. Park naturalists provide camper orientations each evening, including information on how and where to go, bear safety, and minimum-impact camping procedures. Bears have killed two people within the park in the past decade or so, and to lessen the chance of this happening, free bear-proof containers are loaned to all kayakers and hikers. A small storage shed beside the back-

SOUTHEAST ALASKA

country office is a good place to store unneeded gear while you're up the bay. Firearms are not allowed in Glacier Bay.

SEA KAYAKING

Guided Trips

Alaska Discovery (907/780-6226 or 800/586-1911, www.akdiscovery.com) has six-hour kayak trips from the Bartlett Cove dock in the summer. These are a good way to learn the basics of sea kayaking, and include kayak and gear, guide, food, and boots for $125. Alaska Discovery also offers several excellent but pricey longer trips into Glacier Bay National Park. Kayak trips up the bay cost $1,900 for a six-day trip, or $2,200 for eight days, plus airfare from Juneau. The company also has 10-day trips to beautiful Icy Bay for $2,450. These trips are based out of Yakutat.

Spirit Walker Expeditions (907/697-2266 or 800/478-9255, www.seakayakalaska.com) runs excellent sea kayak tours, including overnight trips to nearby Pleasant Island. All sorts of longer voyages are available, all the way up to eight-day trips to remote islands off Chichagof Island. It does not tour within Glacier Bay National Park itself.

On Your Own

An increasingly popular way to visit Glacier Bay is by sea kayak. Some folks bring their own folding kayaks on the plane, or pay $40 to carry them from Juneau aboard the *Auk Nu Keet* ferry, but most people rent them from the friendly proprietors of **Glacier Bay Sea Kayaks** (907/697-2257, www.glacierbayseakayaks.com) in Bartlett Cove. Kayak rentals include a two-person boat, paddles, life vests, spray skirts, flotation bags, and a brief lesson. Reservations are a must during midsummer. They also rent raingear and rubber boots, and will help set up your trip, including making the all-important boat reservations. In addition, you can rent kayaks in Gustavus from **Sea Otter Kayak** (907/697-3007, www.he.net/~seaotter).

Several focal points attract kayakers within Glacier Bay. The **Beardslee Islands,** in relatively protected waters near Bartlett Cove, make an ex-

cellent two- or three-day kayak trip and do not require any additional expenses. Beyond the Beardslees, Glacier Bay becomes much less protected and you should plan on spending at least a week up bay if you paddle there. (It is 50 miles or more to the glaciers.) Rather than attempting to cross this open water, most kayakers opt for a drop-off. The locations change periodically, so ask at the backcountry office in Bartlett Cove for specifics.

Muir Inlet (the east arm of Glacier Bay) is preferred by many kayakers because it is a bit more protected and is not used by the cruise ships or most tour boats. The **West Arm** is more spectacular—especially iceberg-filled Johns Hopkins Inlet—but you'll have to put up with a constant stream of large and small cruise ships. If the boat operators have their way, even more ships can be expected in future years.

The *Baranof Wind* does camper and sea kayaker drop-offs in Glacier Bay; $95 each way. For details, contact **Glacier Bay Cruiselines** (907/586-8687 or 800/820-2628, www.goldbelttours.com).

Talk with Park Service personnel in Bartlett Cove before heading out on any hiking or kayaking trip. You'll need to be in Gustavus airport by 3 P.M. the day before to go through all the hoops (getting to Bartlett Cove, renting the kayak, going through the Park Service camping and bear safety session, and getting your kayak onboard the *Baranof Wind*). This means you cannot take the evening Alaska flight; it arrives too late in the day.

TATSHENSHINI AND ALSEK RIVERS

Along the western edge of Glacier Bay National Park flows the Tatshenshini River, considered one of the world's premier wilderness-rafting routes. Bears, moose, mountain goats, and Dall sheep are all visible along the way. The river rolls through Class III white water and spectacular canyons along its way to the juncture with the Alsek River. **Alaska Discovery** (907/780-6226 or 800/586-1911, www.akdiscovery.com) has several trips each summer down this spectacular route, as well as down the more remote Alsek. A 12-day river-rafting trip isn't cheap at $3,300, but the price includes a van ride from Haines to the put-in point at Dalton Post in the Yukon, and a spectacular helicopter portage around the Class VI rapids of Turnback Canyon. One of the real treats of this trip is paddling past the seven-mile-wide Alsek Glacier. The trip begins in Juneau and ends in Yakutat.

Other good companies offering Alsek and Tatshenshini trips include **Chilkat Guides** (907/766-2491, www.raftalaska.com) and **O.A.R.S** (209/736-4677 or 800/346-6277, www.oars.com). Many other American and Canadian companies feature float trips down the "Tat" and Alsek Rivers. For their addresses or information on running the rivers on your own (permit required), contact Glacier Bay National Park and Preserve (907/697-2230, www.nps.gov/glba). Only one launch is allowed per day, with half of these set aside for commercial guides.

GUSTAVUS AND VICINITY

There are two basic centers for visitors to Glacier Bay. **Bartlett Cove,** inside the park, has Park Service Headquarters, a campground, Glacier Bay Lodge (with bar, restaurant, and park service visitor center), and boat dock. Ten miles away (a $10 shuttle bus ride) and outside the park boundaries is the community of **Gustavus** (pop. 370). Here you will find the airport, main boat dock, a general store, B&Bs, and luxury lodges.

The town of Gustavus consists of equal parts park employees, fishermen, and folks dependent upon the tourism trade. It's one of the only places in Southeast Alaska that has enough flat country to raise cows, and the only Southeast town of any size without service from the state ferry system. Be sure to check out the historic—and still working—gas pumps decorated with the old Mobil flying horse at **Gustavus Dray** (907/697-2481), which also sells antiques and gifts. **Smokehouse Gallery** (907/697-2336) is a seasonal cooperative gallery along the river, with paintings, woodwork, drawings, watercolors, and pottery by local artisans. Gustavus is also home to the nine-hole **Mt. Fairweather Golf Course** (907/697-2214).

The **Gustavus Visitors Association** website (www.gustavusalaska.org) has information and links to local lodging and other businesses; also try www.gustavus.com for info. Based in Gustavus, **Glacier Bay Travel Cruises and Tours** (907/697-2475, www.glacierbaytravel.com) can help you find local lodging and book trips into the park.

Fishing and Whale-Watching
Fishing, primarily for halibut and salmon, is a big attraction for many visitors, and most of the lodges offer package deals for anglers. Get a list of charter boat operators from the Park Service or at www.gustavusalaska.org. Most of these companies also run whale-watching trips, and some can carry sea kayaks onboard.

Flightseeing
Air Excursions (907/697-2375 or 800/354-2479, www.airexcursions.com) and **L.A.B. Flying Service** 907/789-9160 or 800/426-0543, www.labflying.com) both provide flightseeing trips over the park. Five people will pay around $390 for a 1.25-hour tour. Flightseeing over Glacier Bay are also available from Juneau, Haines, and Skagway, but prices are generally higher since you'll need to fly farther.

Accommodations
Located within Glacier Bay National Park is **Glacier Bay Lodge** (206/623-2417 or 800/451-5952, 907/697-2226 summers only, www.glacierbaytours.com, open May–Sept., $149 s, $180 d). The lodge sits in the forest at Bartlett Cove (park headquarters), and has a restaurant, informal deck dining, a pleasant bar, plus a big stone fireplace that makes a cozy place to sit on a rainy evening, even if you're not a guest. Laundry facilities, coin-operated showers, and gear storage are available. The lodge rents mountain bikes and fishing poles, and has a gift shop with quality Native handicrafts.

Glacier Bay Lodge provides the only in-park accommodations, but many options are available in nearby Gustavus. Most places provide free transport to and from the Gustavus airport or boat dock, along with clunker bikes to ride on the roads. With a few exceptions, these places are only open mid-May–mid-September. All of these will also help set up tours, fishing, sea kayaking, and other activities within the park.

Honeymooners or others looking to splurge will love a visit to **Gustavus Inn** (907/697-2254 or 800/649-5220, www.gustavusinn.com, open mid-May–mid-Sept.), the most famous local lodging place. Built in 1928 as the centerpiece for a homestead, the farmhouse was transformed into Gustavus Inn in 1965. Owners David and Jo Ann Lesh have created a delightful country place with a picturesque garden that provides fresh vegetables all summer. Gourmet meals are served family style. Lodging and meals cost $320 d with private baths. Highly recommended.

Annie Mae Lodge (907/697-2346 or 800/478-2346, www.anniemae.com) is a quiet two-story lodge in a meadow-and-forest setting along the Goode River. The 11 guest rooms are $135 s or $215 d with shared bath, and $145–155 s or $240–260 d with private bath, including three big meals and round-trip transportation from Juneau.

Glacier Bay Country Inn (907/697-2288 or 800/628-0912, www.glacierbayalaska.com) combines a rambling log structure with modern amenities. Guests stay in five well-appointed cabins ($390 d) or the main lodge ($370 d) and are treated to three gourmet meals a day. The lodge is open mid-May–mid-September. The owners also operate **Whalesong Lodge** (www.whalesonglodge.com, $75 s, $100 d) with five small and simple rooms, all with private bath. It's in "downtown" Gustavus. No phones, TVs, or meals, but you can eat dinners at the inn for $30.

Modern **Bear Track Inn** (907/697-3017 or 888/697-2284, www.beartrackinn.com, open Feb.–Sept.) occupies a 57-acre spread six miles from Gustavus. This luxuriously furnished 15,000-square-foot log inn has a central lobby with fireplace, large windows fronting on Icy Strait, a big deck and grassy front lawn, plus 14 spacious guest rooms. A number of packages are available for stays of one ($908 d) to seven nights ($3,930 d). These rates include transportation from Juneau, lodging, and sumptuous meals; activities are extra.

TRI Bed & Breakfast (907/697-2425,

www.glacierbaylodging.com, $120–125 s or d) has three cabins with private baths, including a full breakfast.

Bear's Nest Cabins (907/697-2440, www.gustavus.com/bearsnest) charges $99 d for a distinctive round cedar cabin, or $85 d for a simple A-frame cabin. Both have private baths and kitchens.

Good River Bed & Breakfast (907/697-2241, www.glacier-bay.us, open June–late Aug.) has rooms for $80 s or $95 d in an attractive three-story log home, or $85 d in a rustic log cabin with an outhouse. A full breakfast is included.

Alaska Discovery Inn (907/780-6505 or 800/586-1911, www.akdiscovery.com, open June–early Sept.) has five rooms for $110 d with a shared bath or $125 d with a private bath. A full breakfast is served. They're often filled up by Alaska Discovery clients.

Food and Supplies

Bear's Nest (907/697-2440, www.gustavus.com/bearsnest) serves lunch and dinner in the summer, specializing in locally caught salmon, halibut, and crab, along with salads and daily specials. Save room for a slice of their rhubarb-strawberry pie. Friday night is pizza night. Open daily in the summer.

If you have a rental car, you may want to drive the 10 miles to **Glacier Bay Lodge** (907/697-2225) in Bartlett Cove. The food is good and reasonable; try the baked halibut. The outside deck is open for casual evening dining.

Located six miles from town, **Bear Track Inn** (907/697-3017 or 888/697-2284, www.beartrackinn.com, open May–Sept., $35) has a full-service restaurant serving seafood, steaks, and other dinners.

For outstanding gourmet dinners, make reservations at **Gustavus Inn** (907/697-2255 or 800/649-5220, www.gustavusinn.com, $30), where a few spots are held for those who aren't overnighting.

Open daily in the summer, the small grocery store at Gustavus, **Beartrack Mercantile** (907/697-2358), has a deli and sells essentials for a price, but it's better to bring all your own food from Juneau. **Pep's Packing** (907/697-2295) sells locally caught salmon if you have access to a BBQ.

Nobody in Gustavus sells alcohol, but Glacier Bay Lodge has a full bar.

TRANSPORTATION

Glacier Bay National Park and Preserve transportation—including tours and sea kayaking—is described in *Getting to the Glaciers*.

Ferry

There is no state ferry service to either Glacier Bay or Gustavus. Locals have kept the ferry out, fearing—correctly, I'm sure—that it would inundate the area with RVs and lead to major development. Residents receive most of their supplies by barge every two weeks.

Auk Nu Tours (907/586-8687 or 800/820-2628, www.auknutours.com, mid-May–mid-Sept.) operates a passenger-only ferry between Juneau and Gustavus. The fare is $69 ($60 kids) each way, and it runs four days a week. The boat also transports bikes for $10, and kayaks for $40 each way. A wildlife and whale-watching tour around Pleasant Island is $79 ($60 kids), or combine these for a round-trip to Gustavus and whale-watching trip for $195 round-trip ($105 kids).

Air

Many visitors fly by jet from Juneau to Gustavus on **Alaska Airlines** (800/426-0333, www.alaskaair.com); but book ahead to be sure of getting on these popular flights. The trip takes only 15 minutes in the air, so the flight attendants don't even have time to throw bags of pretzels at you.

More rewarding are flights by **Skagway Air** (907/789-2006, www.skagwayair.com), **Wings of Alaska** (907/789-0790, www.wingsofalaska.com), and **L.A.B. Flying Service** (907/789-9160 or 800/426-0543, www.labflying.com). They offer more personal service and the small planes fly lower, providing excellent on-the-way sightseeing for around $130 round-trip. **Air Excursions** (907/697-2375 or 800/354-2479,

www.airexcursions.com) doesn't have scheduled service, but usually flies to Juneau several times a day. L.A.B. also connects Gustavus with Skagway and Haines.

Note that it's illegal to transport white gas and other potentially explosive fuels in any commercial aircraft, so be sure your gas stove and fuel bottles are empty before you reach the airport. You can buy white gas in Bartlett Cove next to the visitor center or in Gustavus at Beartrack Mercantile. Also, you can't carry "bear mace" on the jets, though the floatplanes will sometimes carry it in their floats.

Rentals

Bud's Rent-A-Car (907/697-2403) has a dozen beater rental cars for $60 per day, and you don't even need to fill up the tank at the end. Of course, it's also pretty hard to put many miles on around here! Check out his nonexistent license plates; in their place it simply says "Bud's Rent-A-Car" in big red letters. Apparently the state doesn't require license plates in Gustavus because it's so difficult to get in or out of here.

Most local lodging places have loaner bikes, but if you want something more dependable, rent one from **Wolf Track Expeditions** (907/697-2326, www.wolftrackexpeditions.com). The owners also lead mountain bike tours of the area. Glacier Bay Lodge in Bartlett Cove also rents bikes.

Getting Around

The airport in Gustavus is 10 miles from Bartlett Cove/Park Headquarters. A **shuttle bus** meets all Alaska Airlines flights, transporting you to Bartlett Cove for $10 each direction (free if you have a room reservation for Glacier Bay Lodge). Hitching eliminates this, but traffic can be downright scarce in tiny Gustavus. **TLC Taxi** (907/697-2239), provides passenger and kayak transport in the Gustavus area, and meets Alaska Airlines jets, air taxis, and the *Auk Nu Keet* ferry.

Yakutat

The friendly town of Yakutat (pop. 800) is in a protected harbor on Yakutat Bay—halfway between Juneau and Cordova along the Gulf of Alaska. This out-of-the-way settlement was named for the Eyak *Yak-tat,* (lagoon behind the breakers). Behind Yakutat soars the pyramidal 18,008-foot summit of **Mt. St. Elias,** second-tallest in the United States. Across the bay is **Malaspina Glacier,** the largest piedmont glacier on the continent (it's bigger than Rhode Island). Both of these lie within mighty Wrangell–St. Elias National Park.

Yakutat is a famous fishing destination, particularly for steelhead on the Situk River, but also for king, silver, and sockeye salmon, plus halibut. But it isn't just fish that attracts visitors; in recent years Yakutat has drawn cold-water surfers who come to ride the big ones on the 70 miles of sandy beaches that stretch southeast from town. These beaches are also great places for bird-watching, beachcombing, or simply relaxing. Head out to **Ocean Cape** (just west of town) on a clear day for spectacular views of Mt. St. Elias and the Gulf of Alaska.

The weather in Yakutat can be summed up on one word: wet. Summers are rainy and winters are snowy. The town gets over 130 inches of precipitation annually, so visitors can plan on seeing their share of that. All this precipitation feeds the enormous glaciers and productive salmon and trout streams for which the area is famous.

Yakutat is Alaska's surfing capital, with mile after mile of sandy beaches, virtually no competition for waves, and great swells rolling off the Gulf of Alaska. On a warm summer day you might see as many as 15 surfers riding the waves.

History

The area around Yakutut served for centuries as a winter village for the Eyaks, a people with links to both the Tlingits to the east and Athabascans to the north. In 1805, the Russian-American Company built a fort at Yakutat, using it as a base for the harvesting of sea otters. The post was later destroyed by the Eyaks. Gold seekers came to the area in the 1860s, mining the black-sand beaches, followed by missionaries, loggers, and fishermen. During World War II, Yakutat was home to an aviation base, and the long paved runway that was developed now serves as the local airport. Quite a few military bunkers and other signs of the war are still visible. Today, commercial and sportfishing provide most of the local jobs. More than half of the people who live in Yakutat are Native Alaskans.

Surfing Safari

Yakutat is Alaska's surfing capital, with mile after mile of sandy beaches, virtually no competition for waves, and great swells rolling off the Gulf of Alaska. On a warm summer day you might see as many as 15 surfers—typically a mix of locals and wandering California beach bums—riding the waves at **Cannon Beach** (named for a World War II cannon here) and other spots. Because of all the rainfall, the ocean around Yakutat is less saline than in California or Hawaii, so the boards need to be thicker and more buoyant to keep surfers from sinking. Owned by local surfer Jack Endicott, **Icy Waves Surf Shop** (907/784-3253, www.icywaves.com) sells surfboards (the big ones), wetsuits, booties, hoods, and other gear, along with very popular T-shirts. No rentals, but he may be able to lease gear.

Russell Fiord Wilderness

This beautiful 348,701-acre wilderness is 15 miles northeast of Yakutat. It centers around Russell and Nanatak Fiords, where hanging glaciers fill the rugged mountains and valley glaciers pour icebergs into the water. The area made headlines in 1986 when the advancing **Hubbard Glacier** (largest tidewater glacier in North America) temporarily dammed Russell Fiord, trapping sea mammals and threatening to change river courses as the water level rose 75 feet behind the ice dam. The ice gave way six months later, freeing the animals and reconnecting the fjord to the ocean, but a similar situation occurred in 2002. Because of all the icebergs from this glacier, access into Russell Fiord is difficult by boat, though floatplanes or wheeled planes fly into the area from Yakutat. The Hubbard Glacier is still an amazing sight, 6 miles wide by 70 miles long, and rising 400 feet out of the water at its snout. It is a prime stopping point for cruise ships heading between Southeast Alaska and Seward. Visit the U.S. Geological Survey (http://ak.water.usgs.gov) for more on the Hubbard.

On the southeastern edge of the wilderness is the five-mile-long **Harlequin Lake,** dotted with ice from the enormous Yakutat Glacier. A 26-mile gravel road leads from Yakutat to just across the "bridge to nowhere" over the Dangerous River (which drains from the lake). A .75-mile trail leads to Harlequin Lake from here, and charter boats are available for trips to the face of the glacier.

The Forest Service's **Situk Lake Cabin** ($35) is inside the wilderness, and accessible by trail (often flooded) or floatplane. Eleven other cabins are scattered along the **Yakutat Forelands,** the relatively flat and forested area that stretches for 50 miles east of town. Especially popular with anglers are three cabins along the Situk River ($35).

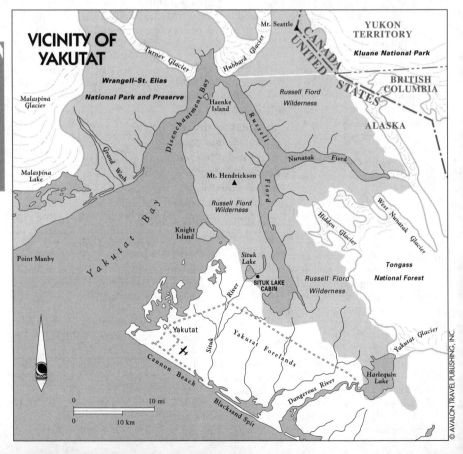

SOUTHEAST ALASKA

© AVALON TRAVEL PUBLISHING, INC.

PRACTICALITIES

Accommodations

Leonard's Landing Lodge (907/784-3245 or 877/925-3474, www.leonardslanding.com, $75–100 s, $100–160 d) is a large fishing lodge where most guests stay for multiple nights. Package rates with meals and a fishing guide are also available, along with boat rentals. There's a restaurant on the premises, and the lodge is open mid-April–mid-October.

Mooring Lodge (907/784-3300 or 888/551-2836, www.mooringlodge.com, open all year) rents out six two-bedroom apartment units that can sleep six, and have full kitchens, a sauna, and views across Monti Bay to the St. Elias Mountains. Rates are $315 for up to four people.

Yakutat Lodge (907/784-3232 or 800/925-8828, www.yakutat-lodge.com, open mid-April–Sept.) has a variety of fishing packages, starting with a three-night package for $1,900 d, including food, lodging, rental vehicle, and a day of guided fishing.

Red Roof B&B (907/784-3131, www.yakutatlodging.com, $75 s, $150 d) has three comfortable guest rooms with a full breakfast

Blue Heron Inn B&B (907/784-3287, www.johnlatham.com, $150 s or d) is a fine place to stay, with a hunting and fishing decor and two guest rooms, both with private entrances and baths. The home overlooks the bay, and rooms come with a full breakfast.

Other local bed-and-breakfasts include **Copperhouse B&B** (907/784-3598) and **Yakutat B&B** (907/784-3414, www.yakutat.net/ybb).

Camping

A couple of simple campsites are along Cannon Beach. In addition, much of the land surrounding Yakutat is within Tongass National Forest, and is open to camping. Above the tide line on Cannon Beach is a fun (but exposed) place to pitch a tent.

Food

Several places serve meals in Yakutat, but **Leonard's Landing Lodge** is your best bet, with good food three meals a day and a waterfront setting.

Get groceries and supplies from **Mallott's General Store** (907/784-3355). **Raven's Table Smokery** (907/784-3497 or 888/784-3497) sells freshly smoked fish. Yakutat's **Glass Door Bar** (907/784-3331), has a pool table and big-screen television for sports.

Information and Services

The **Yakutat Chamber of Commerce** (907/784-3933, www.yakutatalaska.com) will send you a brochure on the area, or call the **City of Yakutat** (907/784-3323) for additional information. The best local Internet site is www.yakutat.net, with links to local businesses. Alaska Pacific Bank has an ATM. A number of local folks run fishing charters; contact any of the lodging places above for recommendations.

Wrangell–St. Elias National Park and Preserve has a **district office** (907/784-3295, www.nps.gov/wrst) in Yakutat, where you can get information on Malaspina Glacier and other incredible sights northeast of Yakutat. The office also exhibits Native artifacts, and the staff leads interpretive programs in the summer.

Stop by Tongass National Forest's **Yakutat Ranger District** (907/784-3359) for details on the Russell Fiord Wilderness, public-use cabins, and other recreation opportunities. Looking for wildlife? Head out to the dump, where the brown bears often forage.

Fairweather Days each August at Cannon Beach is a good time to camp out and party with the surfers.

Transportation

Yakutat is said to be the smallest community in the world served by year-round commercial jet service. **Alaska Airlines** (800/426-0333, www.alaskaair.com) connects Yakutat with the outside world, with two flights daily: one northbound flight to Cordova and Anchorage, and the other southbound to Juneau.

The state ferry *Kennicott* has a "whistle-stop" in Yakutat, but this is only when you're transporting a vehicle. The ferry does the run between Juneau and Valdez twice a month in each direction in the summer; less often in winter. For details, contact the Alaska Marine Highway (907/465-3941 or 800/642-0066, www.ferryalaska.com).

SOUTHEAST ALASKA

Haines

The pleasant and friendly town of Haines (pop. 1,400) provides a transition point between the lush greenery of the Southeast and the more rugged beauty of the Yukon and Alaska's Interior. As the ferry sails north to Haines on the Lynn Canal—at 1,600 feet deep it's the longest and deepest fjord in North America—the Inside Passage gets narrower, and you sense that this unique waterway, and your passage on it, are coming to an end. To the east, waterfalls tumble off the mountainsides, while to the west, glaciers lumber down from the icefields of the Chilkat Range. The long river of ice you see 40 minutes before Haines is **Davidson Glacier. Rainbow Glacier,** also on the left, hangs from a cliff just beyond. Both originate from the same icefield that forms part of Glacier Bay National Park.

Haines lies 90 miles north of Juneau, straddling a narrow peninsula between Chilkoot and Chilkat Inlets. Its mountain-ringed setting seems to define the word *spectacular:* from the ferry you catch a glimpse of the white Victorian buildings of Fort Seward backdropped by the 6,500-foot tall Cathedral Peaks. Haines has a wealth of outdoor experiences, almost as many for those without cash as for those with. Plenty of hiking trails run up surrounding peaks, camping is right next to town, and travelers will discover a pleasant mixture of working stiffs, fishermen, and artisans.

Unlike nearby Skagway where a tidal wave of tourists inundates the town daily, Haines only sees a single large cruise ship each week during the summer. Most Haines visitors arrive by ferry and head on up the highway (or vice versa), but Haines is also becoming a popular weekend getaway for Canadians from Whitehorse. With "only" 60 inches of precipitation a year, the weather here is decidedly drier than points farther south.

HISTORY

Long before the arrival of whites to the Haines area, the Tlingit people of the Chilkoot and Chilkat tribes established villages nearby. Fish were plentiful, as were game animals and berries.

The area's "mother village" was Klukwan, 20 miles up the Chilkat River, but another large Chilkoot village nestled near Chilkoot Lake, and a summer camp squatted just northwest of present-day Haines. The Chilkat people were renowned for their beautiful blankets woven from mountain-goat wool and dyed with an inventive mixture of copper nuggets, urine, lichen, and spruce roots. The blankets were (and are) worn during dance ceremonies. Today they are also exceedingly valuable.

In 1879, the naturalist John Muir and the Presbyterian minister Samuel Hall Young reached the end of Lynn Canal. The Reverend Dr. Young was looking for potential mission sites to convert the Natives to Christianity. Muir was along for the canoe ride, wanting a chance to explore this remote territory. While there, they met with members of the Chilkat tribe at a settlement called Yendestakyeh. Both men gave speeches before the people, but the Chilkats were considerably more interested in Muir's "brotherhood of man" message than Dr. Young's proselytizing. Muir wrote: "Later, when the sending of a missionary and teacher was being considered, the chief said they wanted me, and, as an inducement, promised that if I would come to them they would always do as I directed, follow my councils, give me as many wives as I liked, build a church and school, and pick all the stones out of the paths and make them smooth for my feet." Two years later the mission was established by two Presbyterian missionaries (Muir had other plans) and the village was renamed Haines, in honor of Mrs. F. E. H. Haines of the Presbyterian Home Missions Board. She never visited her namesake.

During the Klondike gold rush, an adventurer and shrewd businessman named Jack Dalton developed a 305-mile toll road that began across the river from Haines and followed an old Indian trade route into the Yukon. He charged miners $150 each to use his Dalton Trail; armed men never failed to collect. To maintain order among the thousands of miners, the U.S. Army

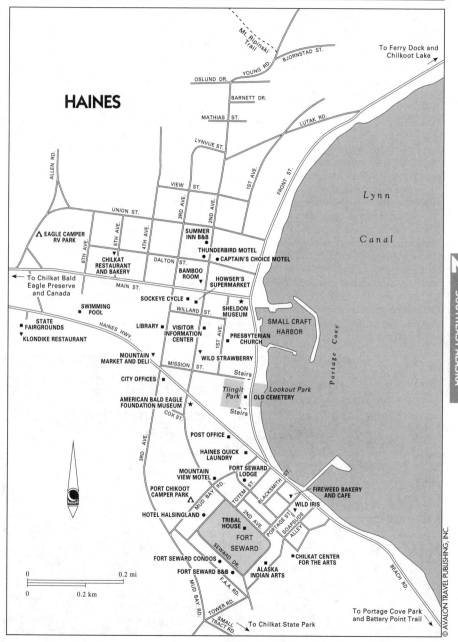

HAINES

To Ferry Dock and
Chilkoot Lake

Mt. Ripinski Trail

BJORNSTAD ST.

YOUNG RD.

OSLUND DR.

BARNETT DR.

MATHIAS ST.

LUTAK RD.

LYNVUE ST.

ALLEN RD.

VIEW ST.

3RD AVE.

2ND AVE.

1ST AVE.

FRONT ST.

UNION ST.

5TH AVE.

4TH AVE.

6TH AVE.

△ EAGLE CAMPER RV PARK

SUMMER INN B&B

THUNDERBIRD MOTEL

CAPTAIN'S CHOICE MOTEL

CHILKAT RESTAURANT AND BAKERY

DALTON ST.

BAMBOO ROOM

HOWSER'S SUPERMARKET

MAIN ST.

← To Chilkat Bald Eagle Preserve and Canada

SOCKEYE CYCLE

WILLARD ST.

SHELDON MUSEUM

SMALL CRAFT HARBOR

SWIMMING POOL

LIBRARY

VISITOR INFORMATION CENTER

HAINES HWY.

1ST AVE.

PRESBYTERIAN CHURCH

STATE FAIRGROUNDS

KLONDIKE RESTAURANT

MOUNTAIN MARKET AND DELI

MISSION ST.

WILD STRAWBERRY

Stairs

CITY OFFICES

AMERICAN BALD EAGLE FOUNDATION MUSEUM

COX ST.

Tlingit Park

Lookout Park

OLD CEMETERY

Stairs

POST OFFICE

3RD AVE.

HAINES QUICK LAUNDRY

MOUNTAIN VIEW MOTEL

FORT SEWARD LODGE

PORT CHIKOOT CAMPER PARK

MUD BAY RD.

TOTEM ST.

BLACKSMITH ST.

FIREWEED BAKERY AND CAFE

HOTEL HALSINGLAND

2ND AVE.

PORTAGE ST.

SOAPSUDS ALLEY

WILD IRIS

TRIBAL HOUSE

FORT SEWARD

SEWARD DR.

FORT SEWARD CONDOS

CHILKAT CENTER FOR THE ARTS

FORT SEWARD B&B

F.A.A. RD.

ALASKA INDIAN ARTS

BEACH RD.

Lynn Canal

Portage Cove

MUD BAY RD.

TOWER RD.

SMALL TRACT RD.

To Chilkat State Park

To Portage Cove Park and Battery Point Trail

0   0.2 mi

0   0.2 km

MOON

SOUTHEAST ALASKA

© AVALON TRAVEL PUBLISHING, INC.

established Fort William H. Seward at Haines. Named for Alaska's "patron saint," it was built between 1900 and 1904 on 100 acres of land deeded to the government by the Haines mission. Renamed Chilkoot Barracks in 1923 (in commemoration of Chilkoot Pass), it was the only military base in all of Alaska until 1940.

In 1942–1943 the Army built the 150-mile Haines Highway from Haines to Haines Junction as an emergency evacuation route from Alaska in case of invasion by the Japanese. After World War II, the post was declared excess government property and sold to a veterans' group that hoped to form a business cooperative. The venture failed, but many stayed on, making homes in the stately old officers' quarters. The site became a National Historic Landmark in 1978 and its name was changed back to Fort Seward.

Today the town of Haines has a diversified economy that includes fishing (no canneries, however), tourism, and government jobs. Haines has also recently become something of a center for the arts, attracting artists and crafts workers of all types, from creators of stained glass to weavers of Chilkat blankets.

SIGHTS

Museums

Located on Main Street in the center of town, the **Sheldon Museum** (907/766-2366, www.sheldonmuseum.org, $3 adults, under 12 free) houses a fine collection of items from the gold rush, such as Jack Dalton's sawed-off shotgun, and Tlingit artifacts—including Chilkat blankets, a gorgeous carved ceremonial hat from the Murrelet clan, and a model of a tribal house. Upstairs, you can watch the excellent Audubon Society video about the Chilkat Bald Eagle Preserve, or see a slide show about local history. The museum is open Monday–Friday 11 A.M.–6 P.M. and Saturday–Sunday 2–6 P.M. mid-May–mid-September, and whenever cruise ships are in port. Winter hours are Monday–Friday 1–4 P.M.

The strangest sight in Haines has to be the **Hammer Museum** (108 Main St., 907/766-2374, Mon.–Fri. 10 A.M.–5 P.M. summer, $2, under 13 free). Collector—and hammer expert—Dave Pahl displays some 1,200 types of hammers here, from cobbler's hammers to ones used by 19th-century

Officers' Row homes, Fort Seward

© DON PITCHER

bankers. The little museum is enough to make you break out in song: "If I had a hammer . . ."

Fort Seward

The well-preserved buildings of Fort Seward make an excellent place to explore. Inside the central parade ground is a **Tlingit tribal house** decorated inside and out with colorful carvings.

The nonprofit **Alaska Indian Arts** (907/766-2160, www.alaskaindianarts.com, Mon.–Fri. 9 A.M.–5 P.M. year-round) operates from the old hospital building on the southeast side of Fort Seward. Inside you'll find master woodcarvers, silversmiths, blanket weavers, and other crafts workers, plus a gallery.

Along the top of the hill is **"Officers' Row,"** the attractive white century-old homes that once housed captains, lieutenants, and their families. A couple of them have been transformed into bed-and-breakfasts, while others are residences. Stop by the Haines visitor bureau for a free, detailed historical guide and walking tour of Fort Seward.

American Bald Eagle Foundation

The Bald Eagle Foundation (907/766-3094; www.baldeagles.org) sits at the intersection of Haines Highway and 2nd Avenue. Inside, you'll find a collection of dead, stuffed critters, more dead eagles overhead, and a video about live eagles in the back room. More interesting are talks by founder Dave Olerud, who provides an introduction to eagles and their role in the web of life. Entrance costs $3 adults, $1 ages 8–12, and free for younger kids. It's open Monday–Friday 9 A.M.–5 P.M., Saturday–Sunday 1–4 P.M. May–August, and Monday, Wednesday, and Friday 1–4 P.M. in the fall, plus whenever cruise ships are in port. Winter hours are by appointment only.

Other Sights

Lookout Park (next to the harbor) is a great place to watch the fishing boats, eagles, and scenery. Bring a lunch. Behind it is a small cemetery with Tlingit graves dating from the 1880s. An old building, all that remains of **Yendestakyeh,** is just beyond the airport, 3.5 miles from town. The mission bell (1880) that once

called the Tlingit people to worship now sits out front of the Presbyterian church on 2nd Avenue.

Tsirku Canning Company (5th and Main, 907/766-3474, www.cannerytour.com), has recreated an old salmon-canning line with reconditioned antique equipment. The 45-minute tours, with a video, are $10, free for kids under 12. No fish guts here; for that you'll need to get a job at a salmon cannery to see how it's done today.

Walt Disney's *White Fang* was filmed next to Haines in 1990, and the **Dalton City** gold rush town created for the movie is at the Southeast Alaska State Fairgrounds. Wander around the buildings or poke your head inside Alaska's smallest brewery, **Haines Brewing Company** (907/766-3823), for a sample of IPA, pale ale, amber, and seasonal beers. Haines bars have them on draught. Locals especially rave about the stout.

Great Land Wines (on Small Tracts Rd., 907/766-2698, www.greatlandwines.com) crafts wines from an offbeat collection of sources, including rhubarb, dandelion, onion (!), rose hip, blueberry, and fireweed. Last I knew they hadn't tried crab-flavored wines—yet. Local stores and restaurants sell the wines.

HIKING

The Haines area has a number of excellent hikes, ranging from the easy (Battery Point) to the strenuous (Mt. Ripinski). For more details, pick up the "Haines is for Hikers" pamphlet from the visitors center.

Mt. Riley

Three trails lead to the top of 1,760-foot Mt. Riley, from which you get a panoramic view of Lynn Canal, Davidson and Rainbow Glaciers, the Chilkat River, Taiya Inlet, and 360 degrees of snowcapped peaks. The shortest and steepest route (two miles) starts three miles southeast of Haines on Mud Bay Road. A small parking area is opposite the trailhead. You can also follow FAA Road from behind Fort Seward to another trail. This one is four miles long and follows the city water supply route for two miles before splitting off to join the more direct trail.

Battery Point

An easy and relatively level four-mile path starts from the end of the road at Portage Cove and follows the shore to a campsite at Kelgaya Point and across pebbly beaches to Battery Point.

Mt. Ripinski

The full-day hike up and down Mt. Ripinski (3,900 feet) offers unparalleled views of mountains and inland waterways, but it's strenuous and long (10 miles round-trip). You may want to camp in the alpine country and make this a two-day hike. From Haines, take Young Road north until it intersects with a jeep road that follows a buried pipeline around the mountain. The trail begins about a mile along this dirt road and climbs through a spruce/hemlock forest to muskeg and finally alpine at 2,500 feet. You can continue along the ridge to the north summit (3,160 feet), or on to the main peak. Return the same way, or via a steep path that takes you down to a saddle and then to the Haines Highway,

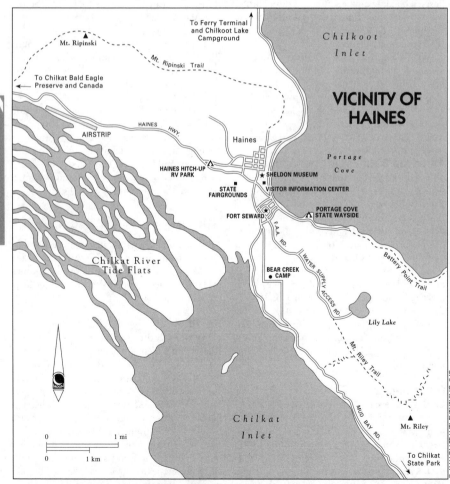

VICINITY OF HAINES

To Ferry Terminal and Chilkoot Lake Campground

Chilkoot Inlet

Mt. Ripinski

Mt. Ripinski Trail

To Chilkat Bald Eagle Preserve and Canada

AIRSTRIP

HAINES HWY.

Haines

Portage Cove

HAINES HITCH-UP RV PARK

SHELDON MUSEUM

STATE FAIRGROUNDS

VISITOR INFORMATION CENTER

FORT SEWARD

PORTAGE COVE STATE WAYSIDE

F.A.A. RD.

Battery Point Trail

Chilkat River Tide Flats

WATER SUPPLY ACCESS RD.

BEAR CREEK CAMP

Lily Lake

Mt. Riley Trail

MUD BAY RD.

Mt. Riley

Chilkat Inlet

0   1 mi

0   1 km

To Chilkat State Park

seven miles northwest of Haines. Mt. Ripinski is covered with snow until mid-summer, so be prepared. Don't go in bad weather and do stay on the trail in the alpine areas.

Seduction Point

For a gentle, long, and very scenic beach walk, head to Chilkat State Park campground, seven miles southeast of Haines on Mud Bay Road. Seduction Point is on the end of the peninsula separating Chilkoot and Chilkat Inlets, a five-mile hike from the campground. The trail alternates between the forest and the beach, and it's a good idea to check the tides to make sure that you're able to hike the last beach stretch at low tide. This hike also makes a fine overnight camping trip.

TOURS

The visitor center has a complete listing of local guide companies and charter boat operators. **Keet Gooshi Tours** (907/766-2168 or 877/776-2168, www.keetgooshi.com, $71 adults, $44 kids) is a Native-owned company with van tours that take in the Bald Eagle Preserve, the village of Klukwan, and the Bald Eagle Museum. **Yeshua Guided Tours** (907/766-2334 or 800/765-2556, www.yeshuaguidedtours.com) leads van tours in the Haines area, including a two-hour tour of Haines and the Chilkoot River area for $30.

River and Lake Trips

Chilkat Guides (907/766-2491, www.rafta-laska.com, $79, $62 for kids) offers an excellent four-hour float trip down the Chilkat River. This is a leisurely raft trip (no white water) with good views of the Chilkat Mountains, glaciers, and roosting eagles. They also guide longer adventures, including a 10-day float down the Tatshenshini River, and a 13-day Alsek River adventure. **Eco Orca Raft Trips & Tours** (907/766-3933 or 866/298-6287, www.alaskafloattrips.com) has similar prices for their Chilkat river float trip. **Chilkoot Lake Tours** (907/766-2891, www.alaskaeaglecruise.wytbear.com) offers two-hour pontoon boat tours of this turquoise lake. **River Adventures** (907/766-2050 or 800/478-

9827, www.jetboatalaska.com) runs half-day jet-boat tours up the Chilkat River. The company recently got in trouble for filling herring with compressed air and using them to draw bald eagles closer to their boat!

Nature Treks

Alaska Nature Tours (210 Main St., 907/766-2876, www.alaskanaturetours.net), leads educational three-hour bus-and-hiking trips to the eagle-viewing area along the Chilkat River, charging $55 for adults, $40 for kids. Other treks include a twilight hike where you're likely to see brown bears (2.5 hours; $45), and a four-hour rainforest hike ($65 with lunch). Wintertime ski trips are also available, and their outdoor shop rents skis, snowboards, and snowshoes.

Glacier Valley Wilderness Adventures (907/767-5522, www.glaciervalleyadventures.com) offers a variety of trips that include a flight into a gold mine basecamp at the base of DeBlondeau Glacier followed by a rafting or jetboat trip down the Tsirku River, and then past the Chilkat Bald Eagle Preserve to Haines. These cost $275–399, with the more expensive options including a helicopter glacier landing. Overnight accommodations are also available in a cabin or tent at the basecamp. In the winter months, they offer backcountry ski trips along the upper Tsirku. **Alaska Mountain Guides & Climbing School** (907/766-3366 or 800/766-3396, www.alaskamountainguides.com), leads a multitude of trips, from half-day hikes to week-long adventures.

Sea Kayaking

Deishu Expeditions (907/766-2427 or 800/552-9257, www.seakayaks.com) guides sea kayak trips around Haines, including half-day trips for $85, all day for $125, and an overnight guided trip to Davidson Glacier for $320. Kayak rentals are available for experienced kayakers.

ACCOMMODATIONS

The Haines Convention and Visitors Bureau website (www.haines.ak.us) has detailed info and links to local lodging places.

SOUTHEAST ALASKA

Hostel

The youth hostel in Haines, **Bear Creek Camp** (907/766-2259, www.kcd.com/hostel, open May–Sept.) is a mile south of town on Small Tract Road. Dorm spaces are $18 and the six private cabins run $44 d. Bear Creek has kitchen facilities, and rents bikes. The hostel is a clean and friendly place to stay, but reservations are advised in the summer. If it's full, pitch a tent out front for $10. They'll pick you up at the ferry terminal of in town for $3.

Hotels and Motels

Hotel Halsingland (907/766-2000 or 800/542-6363, www.hotelhalsingland.com, open April–mid-Nov.) is a beautiful old Victorian hotel that originally served as the commanding officer's quarters at Fort Seward. In addition to the standard rooms ($109 s or d), it has a few small but inexpensive shared-bath rooms ($69 s or d). All rooms have been recently updated with new furnishing, but retain the original charm; it's like a step back in time to a quieter era.

Fort Seward Lodge (907/766-2009 or 800/478-7772, www.ftsewardlodge.com) is located in another of the Fort Seward structures: This one once housed the fort's PX, bowling alley, and gym. Rooms are simple but clean. Those with private baths are $70 s or $80 d. Tiny rooms with a bath down the hall and no television or phone cost $50 s or $60 d. Also available are a couple of rooms with kitchenettes for $85 s or $95 d.

Beach Roadhouse (907/766-3060, www.beachroadhouse.com, $85–95 d) is a mile out Beach Road near the Battery Point trailhead. The five kitchenette units have nice views, too.

Mountain View Motel (Mud Bay Rd. near Ft. Seward, 907/766-2900 or 800/478-2902, www.mtnviewmotel.com, $78 s, $88 d) has large rooms, some with kitchenettes.

Thunderbird Motel (Dalton St., 907/766-2131 or 800/327-2556, www.thunderbird-motel.com), has both standard rooms with fridges and microwaves ($70 s or $80 d) and kitchenettes ($115 for up to four).

Eagle's Nest Motel (907/766-2891 or 800/354-6009, www.eaglesnest.wytbear.com,

$77 s, $87–97 d) on Haines Highway has kitchenettes for $15 extra.

Housed within a historic officer's row building, **Fort Seward Condos** (907/766-2425, www.fortsewardcondos.com, $110 d) are one- and two-bedroom apartments with full kitchens; two-night minimum stay.

The nicest local motel, **Captain's Choice Motel** (108 2nd St., 907/766-3111 or 800/478-2345, www.capchoice.com) has standard rooms for $100 s or $110 d, and suites (these sleep six) for $125–165. All rooms contain small fridges, and a courtesy van is available.

Bed-and-Breakfasts

Mountain Home Retreat (907/767-5681, open seasonally) is 18 miles out of town—in the heart of Chilkat Bald Eagle Preserve. The modern home is quiet and secluded, with decks and cozy, small rooms ($55–75 s, $65–85 d) and a suite ($125 d) with kitchenette. A gourmet breakfast is included.

Chilkat Eagle B&B (907/766-2763, www.kcd.com/eaglebb, $70 s, $80 d) is in one of the less ostentatious Fort Seward buildings, with three comfortable guest rooms and two baths. A full breakfast is included.

Summer Inn B&B (2nd and Main, 907/766-2970, www.summerinn.wytbear.com, $70 s, $80 d) is a five-bedroom home near the center of town. Built in 1912 by a member of Soapy Smith's gang, the charming home has rooms with a full breakfast.

Fort Seward B&B (907/766-2856 or 800/615-6676, www.fortsewardbnb.com), is a beautifully maintained historic home that once housed the fort's chief surgeon. Rates are $85–105 d, or $135 d for second-floor suites, including a full breakfast. Recommended.

Other places to check out include **Little Crooked House B&B** (907/766-3933 or 866/298-6287, www.alaska-b-and-b.com) and **Tanani Bay Luxury Suite** (907/766-3936, www.taninibay.com).

Resort

Weeping Trout Sports Resort (907/766-2827, www.weepingtrout.com, open mid-May–Sept.) is a small lodge along the shores of remote

Chilkat Lake, 20 miles northwest of Haines. Access is by van and jetboat (or floatplane) from Haines. The wilderness setting is grand and the lodge itself is modern and comfortable. Most guests come to play on the nine-hole golf course and to fish for salmon and trout. Four cabins are available, with packages—including transportation—starting at $740 d for a complete two-day/one-night stay. Longer stays or day visits are also available.

CAMPING

The best campsite near Haines is at **Portage Cove State Wayside** ($5), just three-quarters of a mile from town. Water and outhouses are available, but there is no overnight parking; the site is for hikers and cyclists only. The location is quiet and attractive, and eagles hang around nearby.

If you have a vehicle, stay at one of the two other excellent state-run campgrounds, both with drinking water, toilets, and picnic shelters. **Chilkat State Park** ($5), seven miles southeast of Haines, has a fine hiking trail to Seduction Point; and **Chilkoot Lake State Recreation Site** ($10), five miles northwest of the ferry, has good fishing and a lovely view over this turquoise-blue lake. More camping at **Mosquito Lake State Park,** ($5), 27 miles north of Haines.

RV Parks

Most local RV parks are open May–September. Located behind Hotel Halsingland, **Port Chilkoot Camper Park** 907/766-2000 or 800/542-6363, www.hotelhalsingland.com, $16 tents, $23 full hookups) has attractively wooded campsites, showers, and a laundromat.

Salmon Run Adventures RV Campground (907/766-3240, www.salmonrunadventures.com, $14 for RVs or tents, no hookups), seven miles out Lutak Road, also offers showers for $2. **Haines Hitch-Up RV Park** (851 Main St., 907/766-2882, www.hitchuprv.com) is $24–32 with full hookups; no tents. RVers also park at the gravel lot on Main Street named **Oceanside RV Park** (907/766-2437). **Swan's Rest RV Park** (907/767-5662, $18 full hookups, $5 tents) is near Mosquito Lake, 27 miles north of Haines.

FOOD

For a town of this size, Haines has surprisingly good food, and the prices won't ruin your credit rating. Get filling meals, friendly service, and an unpretentious setting at the **Bamboo Room** (on 2nd Ave., 907/766-2800, www.kcd.com/bamboo, entrées run $10–25). Breakfasts are a standout, but the Bamboo also fills up at lunch and dinner when the menu features burgers, fried chicken, halibut fish and chips, and other greasy fare. Be sure to check the board for today's specials.

Chilkat Restaurant and Bakery (5th and Dalton, 907/766-3653), bakes pastries, bagels, and croissants daily, and serves up tasty breakfasts and lunches (including homemade soups, burgers, and sandwiches). The atmosphere is relaxing.

The Wild Strawberry (on 2nd Ave., 907/766-3608, closed Oct.–April, entrées $14–22) is just down from the visitors center, with delicious smoked salmon chowder, a crab and artichoke melt, halibut tacos, and other seafood. It also has a small salad bar, panini sandwiches, espresso, ice cream, and breakfast specials. Everything is made from scratch, so you don't come here in a hurry. The outside deck is great on a sunny afternoon.

Mountain Market & Deli (3rd and Haines Hwy., 907/766-3340, closes 7 P.M. most evenings) makes whole-grain baked goods daily, along with homemade soups, deli sandwiches, wraps, salads, and espresso. They even roast their own coffee beans, and serve pizzas on Friday nights. It's a center for the longhair and peasant-dress crowd, but also for cops and other locals. A natural foods market here sells organic produce.

Get groceries from **Howser's Supermarket** (on Main St., 907/766-2040). Ask around the boat harbor to see who's selling fresh fish, crab, or prawns if you want to cook your own.

Weeping Trout Sports Resort (907/766-2827 or 877/948-7688; www.weepingtrout.com) offers Saturday dinners that include a van and jetboat ride from Haines, plus a family-style meal for $48 per person. It's a remote and beautiful spot along Chilkat Lake.

Fort Seward Eateries

Housed in one of Fort Seward's historic buildings,

Fireweed Bakery and Cafe (on Portage St., 907/766-3838, open May–early Sept.) serves good food in a classy setting. There's a deck with a couple of tables outside, plus an earthy interior where the scents of freshly baked bagels, breads, and sweets fill the air. Breakfast includes a grilled halibut eggs benedict, while lunches and dinners feature organic salads, sandwiches, pasta, pizzas, and more. Get there early for a full selection of breads and sweets; they tend to sell out by the afternoon. Highly recommended, but service can be slow.

The restaurant at **Hotel Halsingland** (907/766-2000 or 800/542-6363, www.hotel-halsingland.com, $13–30 entrées) is a pleasant place for an evening out, with a fine-dining menu that stars Caesar salads, braised lamb shank, filet mignon, and salmon with fire-roasted red peppers. The bar menu has simpler meals. The hotel also offers a delicious all-you-can-eat lunchtime **salmon bake** for $25 ($35 when combined with the Chilkat Dancers performance). These take place when cruise ships are in port and are held at the tribal house; call for the schedule.

Not far away at **Fort Seward Lodge** (907/766-2009 or 800/478-7772, $23), all-you-can-eat Dungeness crab dinners are served nightly. The halibut burgers and salad bar are also popular with locals, and deserts include an "ice screaming pie."

Dejon Delights Smokery (on Portage Rd., 907/766-2505 or 800/539-3608, www.alaska smokery.com) at Fort Seward has freshly smoked salmon for sale or will smoke fish that you catch.

ENTERTAINMENT AND EVENTS

Entertainment

Chilkat Dancers' Storytelling Theater (907/766-2540, www.tresham.com/show, $10 adults, $5 kids) brings ancient Tlingit legends to life with theatrical performances and magnificent costumes and masks. Hour-long shows—timed for cruise ship arrivals—take place in the tribal house at Fort Seward throughout the summer.

If you hit the bar at **Fort Seward Lodge** (907/766-2009), be sure to ask for a Roadkill, the flaming house drink that's guaranteed to set your innards on fire. It also has live music on some

weekends, as does the downtown, **Fogcutter Bar** (907/766-2555). Fishermen school up at the **Harbor Bar** (on Front St., 907/766-2444).

Events

The **Great Alaska Craftbeer & Homebrew Festival** in mid-May is a fine opportunity to taste regional microbrews. Around the summer solstice in June, the **Kluane to Chilkat International Bike Relay** (www.kcibr.org) attracts more than 1,100 cyclists for an exciting 160-mile relay race that ends in Haines. Other solstice events include live music and dancing at the fairgrounds. **July 4th** brings a parade, barbecue, pie-eating contest, soapbox derby races, a race up Mt. Ripinski, and other fun events.

Every year during the third week in August thousands of visitors from all over Alaska and the Yukon flock to Haines for the five-day-long **Southeast Alaska State Fair** (www.seafair.org). Events include a logging show, farmers' market, parade, pig races, dog show, exhibits, and evening concerts by nationally known artists. Don't miss this one!

The **Alaska Bald Eagle Festival** (www.baldeaglefest.org) in mid-November features scientific talks, photography workshops, live birds, and evening entertainment.

Galleries and Gifts

Haines is an excellent place to buy arts and crafts. Alaska Indian Arts is described above under Fort Seward. One of the best local galleries is **Wild Iris Shop** (on Portage St., 907/766-2300), run by Fred and Madeleine Shields, who act as a comedy tag-team. Fred will be happy to give you a dose of his "retail therapy," complete with a German accent stolen from old TV shows. Oh yes, the gallery is great too, with jewelry, trade beads, carved ivory, and photos. Find it a block up from the Port Chilkoot Dock and just down from the fort. The garden out front is full of flowers all summer.

Extreme Dreams (907/766-2097, www.extremedreams.com) has the unusual watercolors, block prints, and textiles of John and Sharon Svenson, in a gorgeous setting, seven miles out Mud Bay Road. Another interesting Mud Bay Road gallery is nearby, **Catotti & Goldberg Stu-**

dio (907/766-2707, www.artstudioalaska.com), where you can see the paintings of Donna Catotti and Rob Goldberg.

Although he is not Native, Tresham Gregg makes distinctive woodcarvings and prints using Tlingit-inspired designs. Find them in his **Sea Wolf Gallery** (907/766-2540, www.tresham.com) near the center of Ft. Seward.

For quality outdoor gear, head to **Backcountry Outfitters** (210 Main St. upstairs, 907/766-2876, www.alaskanaturetours.net). Get Alaskan and other books from **The Babbling Book** (907/766-3356), on Main Street next to Howser's.

Haines is home to one of several birch syrup producers in Alaska—**Birch Boy Products** (907/767-5660, www.birchboy.com). The syrup is sold locally in gift shops. Don't expect the smoothness of maple syrup; birch syrup has a bit of a bite to it, but is quite good on ice cream and when blended with sugar syrup.

INFORMATION AND SERVICES

The **Haines Visitor Information Center** (907/766-2234 or 800/458-3579, www.haines .ak.us), on 2nd Avenue near Willard Street. Mid-May–mid-September, it open Monday–Friday 8 A.M.–7 P.M., Saturday–Sunday 9 A.M.–6 P.M. The rest of the year, hours are Monday–Friday 8 A.M.–5 P.M. Packs can generally be left here while you walk around town. Stop here for a listing of local charter fishing boats if you want to catch salmon or halibut.

Check your email at **Internet Lounge** (715 Main St., 907/766-2337), or for free at the brand new **Haines Public Library** (111 3rd Ave., 907/766-2545, www.haineslibrary.org). The **post office** is on Haines Highway near Fort Seward. Get cash from ATMs inside Howser's Supermarket and the First National Bank of Alaska. Buy topographic maps from **Chilkoot Gardens** (2nd Ave. and Main St.).

Showers are available at **Port Chilkoot Camper Park,** behind Hotel Halsingland, and **Haines Quick Laundry,** across from Fort Seward Lodge. Another option is the fine **swimming pool** (907/766-2666), next to the high school, where entrance gets you a shower and swim.

For something completely different, check out the nine-hole golf course at **Weeping Trout Sports Resort** (907/766-2827 or 877/948-7688, www.weepingtrout.com) on Chilkat Lake. The owners claim that local golfers are so inept that the trout weep. Access is only by jetboat or floatplane; all-day golf and fishing packages (including transportation from Haines) are $185.

TRANSPORTATION
Ferry
The Haines **ferry terminal** (907/766-2111) is 3.5 miles north of town on Lutak Highway. Ferries arrive in Haines almost every day during the summer, heading both north to Skagway and south to Juneau. They generally stop for an hour and a half. Call Alaska Marine Highway for information (907/465-3941 or 800/642-0066, www.ferryalaska.com).

Alaska Fjordlines (907/766-3395 or 800/320-0146, www.alaskafjordlines.com) operates a high-speed catamaran with daily summertime runs from Skagway to Haines and then on to Auke Bay in Juneau. The boat leaves Haines at 9 A.M., arrives in Juneau at 11:30 A.M., and then heads back at 5 P.M., returning to Haines at 7:30 P.M. The cost is $99 roundtrip, or $119 if you add a Juneau bus tour. Breakfast and dinner are included, and the skipper stops for wildlife and photo opportunities. One-way trips and overnight stays in Juneau are allowed; reservations recommended.

Chilkat Cruises (907/766-2100 or 888/766-2103, www.chilkatcruises.com, $44 round-trip, $22 for kids) offers high-speed catamaran service between Skagway and Haines, with several departures a day mid-May–mid-September.

Taxis
Haines Shuttle & Tours (907/766-3138) and **24/7 Taxi Service** (907/766-2676) both charge $8 to town from the ferry terminal, and also offer town tours and trips up to Chilkat Bald Eagle Preserve.

Rentals
Rent cars from **Captain's Choice Motel** (907/766-3111 or 800/478-2345, www.capchoice.com) and

Eagle's Nest Car Rental (907/766-2891 or 800/354-6009, www.eaglesnest.wytbear.com). Eagle's Nest allows Skagway drop-offs, and has the cheapest rates, starting at $45/day with 100 free miles.

Rent mountain bikes from **Sockeye Cycle** (907/766-2869, www.cyclealaska.com) at Fort Seward. A variety of bike tours are also offered. **Deishu Expeditions** (907/766-2427 or 800/552-9257, www.seakayaks.com) rents sea kayaks.

Air

The airport is 3.5 miles west of town on the Haines Highway. The flight between Juneau and Haines is pretty spectacular; on clear days you'll be treated to views of glaciers along both sides of Lynn Canal. Several companies have scheduled daily service to Juneau and Skagway: **Wings of Alaska** (907/766-2030, www.wingsofalaska.com), **Skagway Air** (907/789-2006, www.skagwayair.com), and **L.A.B. Flying Service** (907/766-2222 or 800/426-0543, www.labflying.com). L.A.B. also flies between Haines and Gustavus.

Mountain Flying Service (907/766-3007 or 800/766-4007, www.flyglacierbay.com), a few doors up from the visitor center, is a good company that offers charters and flightseeing trips over Glacier Bay starting for $115 per person for one hour. A longer trip ($259) includes two hours in the air and a beach landing within the park that gives you the chance to see bears and other wildlife. L.A.B. also offers hour-long Glacier Bay flightseeing trips.

Heading North

The paved highway north from Haines is the most direct route to Fairbanks (665 miles) and Anchorage (775 miles). For cyclists it's much easier than the Klondike Highway out of Skagway. If you're thinking of driving to Skagway from Haines, think again. It's only 15 water or air miles away, but 359 road miles. Take the ferry!

In the summer, **Alaska Direct Bus Line** (907/277-6652 or 800/770-6652, www.home .gci.net/~akdirectbus) has service several times a week from Haines to Whitehorse, Anchorage, and Fairbanks. The buses stop overnight in Tok, so you'll have to pay for lodging or camping. It's also possible to hitch north from Haines, but traffic depends upon ferry arrivals.

Crossing the Border

The Canadian border is 42 miles north of Haines. Both Canadian and U.S. Customs are open 7 A.M.–11 P.M. Alaska Time (8 A.M.–midnight Pacific Time). Be prepared for lots of questions if you're traveling on the cheap. No handguns are allowed across the Canadian border.

CHILKAT BALD EAGLE PRESERVE

Each fall on the Bald Eagle Council Grounds, the Chilkat River north of Haines becomes home to the largest eagle gathering on earth. Because of upwellings of warm water near the Tsirku River alluvial fan, the lower Chilkat River doesn't freeze over, and a late run of up to 100,000 chum salmon arrive to spawn. The dying salmon attract bears, wolves, gulls, magpies, ravens, and up to 3,500 bald eagles along a four-mile stretch of river just below the Tlingit village of **Klukwan** (pop. 140). The 48,000-acre Chilkat Bald Eagle Preserve protects this unique gathering of eagles.

During the peak of the salmon run (Nov.–Jan.), black cottonwoods along the river are filled with hundreds of birds, and many more line the braided riverbanks. The area is very popular with photographers, but be sure to stay off the flats to avoid disturbing these majestic birds. During the summer, local eagle populations are much lower, but, with 80 active nests and up to 400 resident eagles on the river, you're guaranteed to see some eagles.

A state campground ($5) is at **Mosquito Lake,** five miles north of Klukwan and three miles off the highway. Tours by van or boat go through the bald eagle preserve. For information contact the state parks (907/766-2292, www.dnr.state.ak.us).

Skagway

Occupying a narrow plain along the mouth of the Skagway River at the head of Lynn Canal, Skagway (year-round pop. 800; twice that in the summer) is a triangle-shaped town that seems to drive a wedge into the sheer slopes that lead to White Pass. Northern terminus of the Inside Passage, Skagway is derived from an Indian word meaning "home of the North Wind." During the Klondike gold rush, the town was the gateway to both the Chilkoot and White Pass Trails, a funnel through which thousands of frenzied fortune-seekers passed. Today, the boardwalks, frontier storefronts, restored interiors, gift shops, historic films and slide shows, and old-time cars and costumes all in the six-block town center give it the flavor for which it has been famous for nearly a century. Skagway survives on the thousands of visitors and adventurers who come each summer to continue on the trail that led to gold. This is the most popular cruise port in Alaska, and the Skagwegians are inundated with over 5,000 cruise ship visitors on a typical mid-summer day; up to five ships can dock at once. Today, 700,000 travelers spend time in Skagway each year, the vast majority stepping off these mega-ships.

Independent travelers often leave Skagway with mixed feelings, and some regard it as a schmaltzy shadow of its former self, sort of a Disneyland version of the gold rush. To some extent this is true, but the town also has genuine charm, and when the cruise ships sail away each night, the locals come out to play. Skagway is compact enough to walk around easily, and is filled with all sorts of characters. Besides, if the downtown scene isn't to your taste, it's easy to escape into the surrounding mountains or to head up the Chilkoot Trail where only the hardy stray. One way to avoid most of the crowds is to get here before mid-May or after mid-September. Come in the winter and you'll have it almost to yourself!

Skagway's weather is considerably drier than other parts of the Southeast. It gets only 22 inches of precipitation a year, and alder, willow, and cottonwood carpet the adjacent hillsides. It is especially colorful in mid-September when the leaves are turning. The driest time is before July; after that rain is more likely.

HISTORY
Klondike Gold

An enormous amount of Alaskan history was collapsed into the final decade of the 19th century at Skagway. In August 1896, on the day that George Carmack struck it rich on Bonanza Creek, Skagway consisted of a single cabin, constructed eight years previously by Captain William Moore, but only occupied sporadically by the transient pioneer. News of the Klondike strike hit Seattle in July 1897; within a month 4,000 people huddled in a haphazard tent city surrounding Moore's lone cabin, and "craft of every description, from ocean-going steamers to little more than floating coffins, were dumping into the makeshift village a crazily mixed mass of humanity." Almost immediately, Frank Reid surveyed and plotted the town site, and the stampeders grabbed 1,000 lots, many within Moore's homestead. There was no law to back up either claims or counterclaims, and reports from the time describe Skagway as "the most outrageously lawless quarter" on the globe.

Into this breach stepped Jefferson Randall "Soapy" Smith, Alaska's great bad man. A notorious con artist from Colorado, Soapy Smith oversaw a mind-bogglingly extensive system of fraud, theft, armed robbery, prostitution, gambling, and even murder. He had his own spy network, secret police, and army to enforce the strong-arm tactics. Finally, a vigilance committee held a meeting to oppose Soapy. Frank Reid, the surveyor, stood guard. Soapy approached. Guns blazed. Smith, shot in the chest, died instantly, at age 38. Of Soapy, the newspaper reported, "At 9:30 o'clock Friday night the checkered career of 'Soapy' Smith was brought to a sudden end by a 38 caliber bullet from a revolver in the unerring right hand of City surveyor Frank H. Reid . . . ."

SOUTHEAST ALASKA

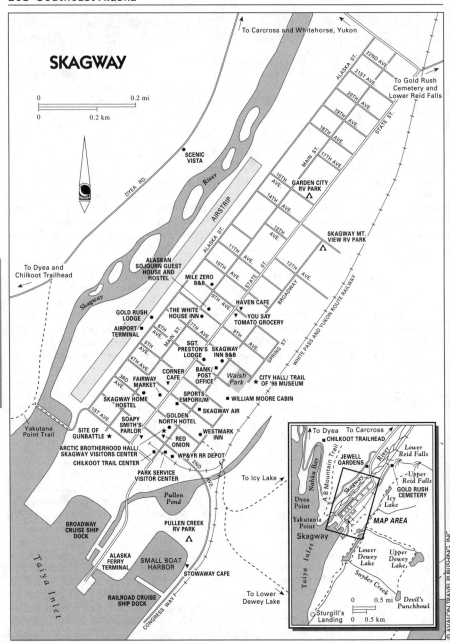

SKAGWAY

SOUTHEAST ALASKA

To Carcross and Whitehorse, Yukon

To Gold Rush Cemetery and Lower Reid Falls

SCENIC VISTA

DYEA RD.

River

AIRSTRIP

ALASKA ST.

STATE ST.

22ND AVE.
21ST AVE.
20TH AVE.
19TH AVE.
18TH AVE.
17TH AVE.
15TH AVE.
14TH AVE.
13TH AVE.
12TH AVE.
11TH AVE.
10TH AVE.
9TH AVE.

GARDEN CITY RV PARK

SKAGWAY MT. VIEW RV PARK

MAIN ST.

BROADWAY

WHITE PASS AND YUKON ROUTE RAILWAY

To Dyea and Chilkoot Trailhead

Skagway

ALASKAN SOJOURN GUEST HOUSE AND HOSTEL

MILE ZERO B&B

HAVEN CAFE

YOU SAY TOMATO GROCERY

GOLD RUSH LODGE

AIRPORT TERMINAL

THE WHITE HOUSE INN

SGT. PRESTON'S LODGE

SKAGWAY INN B&B

SPRING ST.

6TH AVE.
5TH AVE.
4TH AVE.
3RD AVE.
1ST AVE.

8TH AVE.

7TH AVE.

CORNER CAFE

BANK/ POST OFFICE

Walsh Park

CITY HALL/ TRAIL OF '98 MUSEUM

FAIRWAY MARKET

SPORTS EMPORIUM

WILLIAM MOORE CABIN

SKAGWAY HOME HOSTEL

SOAPY SMITH'S PARLOR

GOLDEN NORTH HOTEL

SKAGWAY AIR

Yakutania Point Trail

SITE OF GUNBATTLE ★

RED ONION

WESTMARK INN

ARCTIC BROTHERHOOD HALL/ SKAGWAY VISITORS CENTER

CHILKOOT TRAIL CENTER

WP&YR RR DEPOT

2ND AVE.

To Icy Lake

PARK SERVICE VISITOR CENTER

Pullen Pond

BROADWAY CRUISE SHIP DOCK

PULLEN CREEK RV PARK

ALASKA FERRY TERMINAL

SMALL BOAT HARBOR

STOWAWAY CAFE

CONGRESS WAY

RAILROAD CRUISE SHIP DOCK

To Lower Dewey Lake

Taiya Inlet

0   0.2 mi
0   0.2 km

MOON

Inset map

To Dyea   To Carcross

CHILKOOT TRAILHEAD

JEWELL GARDENS

A/B Mountain Trail

Nahku Bay

Skagway

River

Lower Reid Falls

Upper Reid Falls

GOLD RUSH CEMETERY

Dyea Point

Icy Lake

MAP AREA

Yakutania Point

Skagway

Lower Dewey Lake

Upper Dewey Lake

Taiya Inlet

Snyder Creek

Devil's Punchbowl

Sturgill's Landing

0   0.5 mi
0   0.5 km

© AVALON TRAVEL PUBLISHING, INC.

Reid was shot in the groin, and died in agony a week later. His gravestone reads, "He gave his life for the honor of Skagway." More recent evidence has been less kind to Frank Reid's reputation. It turns out that he had been a prime suspect in an Oregon murder, and as a surveyor for the railroad was deeply involved in the theft of William Moore's homestead lands. Some locals say both men got what they deserved.

Over the Top

Skagway was the jumping-off point for **White Pass,** which crossed the Coastal Range to Lake Bennett and the Yukon headwaters. This trail, billed as the "horse route," was the choice of prosperous prospectors who could afford pack animals to carry the requisite "ton of goods." But it was false advertising at best, and death-defying at worst. The mountains were so precipitous, the trail so narrow and rough, and the weather so wild, that the men turned merciless; all 3,000 horses and mules that stepped onto the trail in 1897–1898 were doomed to a proverbial fate worse than death. Indeed, men swore that horses leaped off the cliffs on purpose, committing suicide on the "Dead Horse Trail."

The famous **Chilkoot Trail,** which started in Dyea (die-EE), 15 miles from Skagway, was the "poor-man's route." Stampeders had to backpack their year's worth of supplies 33 miles to Lake Lindeman, which included 40 trips up and down the 45-degree "Golden Stairs" to the 3,550-foot pass. This scene, recorded in black and white, is one of the most dramatic and enduring photographs of the Days of 1898. At Lindeman, the men built wooden boats for the sometimes-treacherous journey to the gold fields at Dawson.

Building the Railroad

The late 19th century was a time when the railroad was king, and the sudden rush of men to the gold fields attracted entrepreneurs intent upon figuring a way to build a railroad from Skagway over White Pass. Into this breach stepped Michael J. Heney, an Irish-Canadian contractor with a genius for vision, fund-raising, management, and commanding the loyalty of his workers. Heney punched through the 110-mile narrow-gauge White Pass & Yukon Route Railway to Lake Bennett by July of 1899, and then on to Whitehorse a year later. The route, so treacherous to pack animals, was no less malevolent to railroaders. They worked suspended from the steep slopes by ropes, often in 50-below temperatures and raging Arctic blizzards, for $3 a day. Completion of the railroad ensured the constant flow of passengers and freight to the gold fields—as well as Skagway's survival. For the next four decades, the railroad was virtually the only way into the Yukon.

During World War II, the White Pass & Yukon Route hauled much of the construction equipment and personnel to build the Alaska Highway. In the 1970s, the railroad shifted to hauling lead, zinc, and silver ore concentrate from a big mine in the Yukon. The concentrate was shipped from Skagway for processing in Asia. When metal prices plummeted in 1982, the mine closed and train traffic halted. (One legacy of this mine is the presence of lead and other toxins in the waters off Skagway.) But just as mining was ending, Alaska's current gold rush arrived in the form of cruise ships. The WP&YR reopened for excursion travel in 1988, and it is once again not only Skagway's favorite attraction, but one of the only operating narrow-gauge railroads in North America. Today, nearly 300,000 passengers ride the train each summer.

SIGHTS

Downtown Skagway is made up of seven blocks on Broadway, along which are most of the sights. The ferry terminal is at the bottom of Broadway: A three-minute hike and you're in the heart of beautiful downtown Skagway. More than a dozen historic downtown buildings are owned and managed by the National Park Service as **Klondike Gold Rush National Historical Park** in commemoration of the 1898 stampede of miners to Canada's Yukon. Most of the restored structures are leased to private businesses. (The park is actually split into two pieces, with one visitors center in Skagway, and another in Seattle, where nearly all the miners began their journey.)

Park Service Visitor Center

The old White Pass & Yukon administration building houses the Klondike Gold Rush National Historical Park Visitor Center (907/983-2921, www.nps.gov/klgo). It's open daily 8 A.M.–6 P.M. early May–late September, and Monday–Friday 8 A.M.–5 P.M. the rest of the year. Don't miss "Days of Adventure, Dreams of Gold," a 30-minute film shown hourly. Ranger talks typically take place at 10 A.M. and 3 P.M., and 45-minute walking tours of old Skagway are offered five times a day. Additional programs and tours to Dyea are also offered; see the day's event schedule for details. There's no charge for any of these talks. Personnel behind the desk have the latest weather and transportation information, and can probably answer that burning question you've been carrying around all day.

Across Broadway and next to the tracks, the historic **Martin Itjen House** contains the Chilkoot Trail Center, where rangers can provide details on hiking in the footsteps of the miners. This 32-mile trail starts from the old Dyea town site, nine miles from Skagway, and climbs over Chilkoot Pass (3,535 feet) before dropping down to Bennett, British Columbia. (See *Chilkoot Trail* later in this chapter for the full story.)

Just up 2nd Street is **Soapy Smith's Parlor,** the saloon from which the infamous blackguard supervised his various nefarious offenses. The building is not open to the public.

White Pass & Yukon Route Railroad

Adjacent to the Park Visitor Center is the **White Pass & Yukon Route Depot** (on 2nd St. 907/983-2217 or 800/343-7373, www.wpyr.com) built in the 1990s to closely resemble the town's many historic structures. Narrow gauge WP&YR trains depart from the depot several times a day from mid-May until the third week of Sept.; no winter service.

White Pass Summit Excursion trains leave Skagway at 8:30 A.M. and 1 P.M. (plus at 4:30 P.M. on Tuesdays and Wednesdays in mid-summer). These go to the summit of White Pass and back, a round-trip of 56 miles that takes three hours. The tracks follow along the east side of the Skagway River, with vistas that get better and better as

the train climbs. Tour guides point out the sights and explain the railroad's history. Be sure to sit on the left side from Skagway (right side returning) for the best views. The diesel smoke is less toward the rear of the train. These excursions cost $89 adults, $45 ages 3–12, and free for tots.

The WP&YR has two photogenic old **steam engines**—one built in 1920, the other from 1947—that huff and puff out of town each day, with video cameras rolling in all directions. For most runs the steam engine is replaced by a diesel engine on the edge of town to save it from wear and tear on the strenuous climb. The railroad's special **Lake Bennett Steam Adventure** is a real treat for train lovers. Pulled by a steam engine, these trains leave at 8 A.M., and stop in the mountains to let passengers out for a chance to photograph as the engine rolls by with steam billowing. They then climb back aboard for the ride to Lake Bennett where a lunch is served in the restored 1903 train station, before returning back down the mountain to Skagway at 4:30 P.M. These delightful Saturday runs cost $160 for adults, $80

White Pass & Yukon Route Railroad

for kids, include a lunch, and operate mid-June–August only.

Also available is a **Skagway–Whitehorse rail-and-bus connection** that costs $95 adults, or $48 kids each way. Trains depart Skagway daily at 8 A.M., with passengers transferring to buses at Fraser, British Columbia, before continuing on to Whitehorse, arriving at 1 P.M. The buses leave Whitehorse daily at 1:30 P.M., connect with the train in Fraser, and reach Skagway at 4:30 P.M. You can also take the train one-way from Skagway to Fraser for $67 adults, $34 kids; several bus companies use this as part of a train-up and bus-back trip.

The **Chilkoot Trail Hikers Special** provides a daily shuttle from Lake Bennett (the end of the trail) to Fraser ($30) or Skagway ($65 adults or $33 kids).

Arctic Brotherhood Hall

You can't miss Arctic Brotherhood (AB) Hall between 2nd and 3rd streets—the only example of turn-of-the-century Alaska driftwood stick architecture, and probably the most-photographed building in Alaska. Thousands of pieces of wood—8,841 to be exact—decorate the exterior. The brotherhood was organized aboard the vessel *City of Seattle,* which waited out the winter of 1899 in Skagway Harbor. The order spread, and local chapters were established in most Alaskan towns, with dues paid solely in nuggets.

The AB Hall now houses the **Skagway Visitor Information Center** (907/983-2854 or 888/762-1898 message, www.skagway.org). It's open daily 8 A.M.–6 P.M. May–September, and Monday–Friday 8 A.M.–5 P.M. the rest of the year. It has the standard brochures, plus a good hiking map. Stop in and take Buckwheat out to lunch, but be sure to ask about his travels with Martha Stewart. Tell him I sent you.

Skagway Museum

This excellent collection is housed in the beautifully restored City Hall (700 Spring St., 907/983-2420, www.skagwaymuseum.org), a block off Broadway. It's open Monday–Friday 9 A.M.–5 P.M. and Saturday–Sunday 1–5 P.M. in the summer, with variable off-season hours. Check out the old

gambling equipment, the "Moorish queen" from the Chicago World's Fair of 1893, the Native artifacts (including a 19th-century Tlingit canoe), and the July 15, 1898, edition of the *Skagway News* with the story of the killing of Soapy. Also here are an amazing salmon-skin parka and an Eskimo mask from Anaktuvuk Pass. Several videos are available if you want to know more about the characters in Skagway's past. Entrance costs $2 adults, $1 students, and free for under age 13.

Other Sights

The National Park Service has restored the historic **Mascot Saloon** (3rd and Broadway, open daily in summer, no charge) with exhibits depicting the saloon and life in the days of '98. Across the street is another structure from that era, **Golden North Hotel,** with its distinctive gold-colored cupola. The hotel closed in 2002, and is now used as housing for workers. Duck into the abundant gift shops in the next few blocks of Broadway. Many of the furnishings, display cases, and even a smidgen of the stuff for sale are worth a look.

The original **Captain William Moore cabin** (5th and Spring), which was moved under pressure from the early stampeders to its present location, has been completely refurbished by the Park Service. Its interior walls are papered with newspapers from the 1880s.

Corrington's Museum of Alaskan History (5th and Broadway, 907/983-2637 or 800/943-2637) is a combination gift shop and free scrimshaw museum. The collection includes 40 or so exquisitely carved pieces that tell the history of Alaska on walrus ivory. It's well worth a visit. The building is flanked by a colorful flower garden.

Be sure to poke your head into **Skagway Hardware Company** (Broadway at 4th Ave., 907/983-2233), one of the few old-time hardware stores left in Alaska. The wooden floors creak, and items of all types (even washers and dryers) are crammed into the shelves.

Broadway has more than its share of soak-the-tourists gift shops staffed by folks whose only connection to Skagway is a paycheck. The most egregious examples are the Caribbean, Colombian, British, and Swiss jewelry shops that barely make an effort to sell anything remotely connected with Alaska. Despite this, do step inside the Little Switzerland Store (Broadway and 5th Ave.), where you'll discover both the world's largest and smallest gold nugget watch chains. Local people do run many of the other shops in town. Recommended are **Inside Passage Arts** (Broadway near 5th, 907/983-2585) for Native arts and crafts and **Hunter Art Studio** (7th and Broadway, 888/877-5841), featuring the works of Robert Hunter and other Alaskan artists.

North of Town

The historic Gold Rush Cemetery sits right beside the railroad tracks two miles north of town. The largest monument is Frank Reid's, while Soapy Smith only rates a wooden plank. While you're here, be sure to follow the short trail above the cemetery to scenic **Lower Reid Falls.** City-run SMART buses will take you as far as 23rd Avenue for $3 each way; from there it's an almost-level stroll to the cemetery.

Continue out the Klondike Highway and cross the bridge over Skagway River. On the left is **Jewell Gardens** (907/983-2111, www.jewell-gardens.com, open early May–Sept.), with a very impressive collection of flowers and vegetables plus a garden railroad for model train enthusiasts. Tours cost $13, and a tour-and-tea (with quiche, carrot cake, rhubarb bars, and nasturtium sandwiches) is $28, or pay $8 to just walk around on your own. Farther up the road at Mile 3 is **Liarsville** (907/983-3000), with sled dogs and gold panning for the cruise ship masses.

Dyea

Located nine miles northwest of Skagway, the ghost town of Dyea is the starting point for the famed Chilkoot Trail. The old town site sits at the head of Taiya Inlet. During the Klondike gold rush of 1898, Dyea was where miners began the long trek into the Yukon Territory, and at its peak, the town provided a temporary home to some 10,000 people. Two factors caused Dyea to disappear: a devastating avalanche on Chilkoot Pass in April of 1898, and the completion of the White Pass & Yukon Route Railroad in 1899. Just four years later, only a half-dozen people lived in Dyea.

Little remains to be seen at Dyea except for the **Slide Cemetery,** where 45 men and women who died in the Palm Sunday avalanche of 1898 are buried. Walk through the forests that now cover old Dyea to find a few crumbling buildings and wharf pilings extending into the bay. Hard to imagine that this was once Alaska's largest city! The town site is now part of Klondike Gold Rush National Historical Park, and not far from old Dyea is the trailhead for the Chilkoot Trail and the free **Dyea Campground.**

The Park Service leads free 1.5-hour walking tours (907/983-2921) of the old Dyea town site Wednesday–Sunday at 2 P.M. in the summer, but you'll need to find your own transportation from Skagway.

Tours

Given the influx of tourists to Skagway, it's no surprise to find a multitude of tour options. The most unique local tours are aboard the canary-yellow 1920s vintage White Motor Company cars run by **Skagway Street Car Company** (907/983-2908, www.skagwaystreetcar.com). The complete two-hour trip costs $39 ($20 kids), but most seats are presold to cruise ship passengers. To be sure of a spot, book a week in advance. This is one of the few Alaskan guided tours that I'd actually recommend.

A number of other companies also offer van tours around the area. These typically cost $35 for a 2.5-hour trip that includes the town of Skagway and White Pass Summit; some take an alternate route to the Chilkoot Trailhead and Dyea, or a longer trip into the Yukon. Try the following: **Frontier Excursions** (907/983-2512 or 877/983-2512, www.frontierexcursions.com), **Dyea Dave's** (907/983-2731), **Klondike Tours** (907/983-2075), **Discover Skagway Tours** (907/983-2134 or 866/983-8687), **Southeast Tours** (907/983-2990 or 800/478-2990, www.southeasttours.com). The corporate operators—Gray Line of Alaska and Princess Tours—also lead bus tours in Skagway, but these really aren't of much interest to independent travelers.

Skagway Carriage Company (907/723-3117) provides a completely different sort of tour: horse-drawn carriage rides around town. Just look for the carriages on Broadway.

RECREATION

Nearby Hiking

A network of well-marked trails on the slopes just east of town offers excellent day hikes and a place to warm up for the Chilkoot Trail. Cross the small footbridge and railroad tracks beyond the end of 3rd and 4th Avenues, then follow the pipeline up the hill. **Lower Dewey Lake** is a 20-minute climb that gains 500 feet in elevation. A trail right around the lake branches at the south end off to **Sturgill's Landing** (3.5 miles) on Taiya Inlet. **Upper Dewey Lake** and the **Devil's Punchbowl** are a steep 2.5-mile climb from the north end of the lower lake. Icy Lake is a relatively level two miles from the lower lake, but the trail to **Upper Reid Falls** is steep and hard to follow. A number of clearings with picnic tables surround the lower lake where camping is possible; more are at the other lakes and Sturgill's Landing.

At 2nd Avenue and Alaska Street, go around the airport and take the footbridge over Skagway River. A short hike goes left to beautiful **Yakutania Point,** with views down Taiya Inlet. Go right and head steeply up to the Dyea Road; you'll see the trailhead in a mile for **A.B. Mountain,** named for the Arctic Brotherhood—the letters *AB* are supposedly visible in snow patches each spring. This five-mile hike is steep and strenuous; the summit is 5,100 feet above your starting point (sea level).

The Forest Service maintains a refurbished rail car as the **Denver Caboose Cabin** ($35). This attractive old caboose is six miles north of Skagway near where the railroad crosses the East Fork of the Skagway River. Access is by foot, or the WP&YR train will drop you off for $54 round-trip. Take your binoculars to scan nearby slopes for mountain goats. The **Denver Glacier Trail** begins right beside the caboose, and climbs five miles and 1,200 feet to Denver Glacier. It's a beautiful hike through subalpine fir, paper birch, cottonwood, spruce, and other trees.

Another excellent hiking option begins at Glacier Station (14 miles north of Skagway). Have the WP&YR train drop you off here, and then hike up the easy two-mile trail that leads to a Forest Service cabin near **Laughton Glacier** ($35). Flag down the train to return. Make cabin reservations for either the caboose or cabin at 518/885-3639 or 877/444-6777.

Located at the Mountain Shop in Skagway, **Packer Expeditions** (907/983-2544, www.packerexpeditions.com), leads guided hikes in the Skagway area, including day trips and multiday hikes over Chilkoot Pass. Its most popular trip combines a helicopter flight over the Juneau Icefield with a four-mile hike to Laughton Glacier, followed by a train ride back to town. The cost is $250 for this 5.5-hour trip that is mainly for cruise shippies.

On the Water

A number of companies offer charter fishing out of Skagway; get their brochures in the downtown visitor center or find them at www.skagway.org.

Skagway Float Tours (907/983-3688, www.skagwayfloat.com) has easy three-hour float trips down the Taiya River for $65 ($45 kids). A combination trip that includes a one-hour hike up the first part of the Chilkoot Trail followed by a float down the river is $75 adults or $55 kids. The company also has a variety of other hiking, floating, and tour options.

Flightseeing

Skagway Air (907/983-2218, www.skagwayair.com) does 90-minute Glacier Bay flightseeing trips for $130, and 45-minute gold rush tours to Lake Bennett for $70 per person. **Temsco Helicopter** (907/983-2900 or 877/789-9501, www.temscoair.com) offers 50-minute flights over the Chilkoot Trail for $189, including a 25-minute glacier landing. Other options are a longer "pilot's choice" tour (1.5 hours and two glacier landings for $269), and a tour that includes an hour on the Denver Glacier where you get to do some dogsledding ($349).

Biking, Horseback-Riding, and Dog Mushing

Rent a quality mountain bike from **Sockeye Cycle** (5th Ave. near Broadway, 907/983-2851, www.cyclealaska.com), which also offers a speedy ride down White Pass: Sockeye drives you up and you roll back down on the bikes for $72. Another popular option includes a train ride up to Fraser, followed by a downhill ride to town for $158. A 2.5-hour Dyea bike tour is $72. **Sourdough Car Rental** (6th Ave. and Broadway, 907/983-2523) also rents bikes, including tandems.

Chilkoot Horseback Adventures (907/983-3990, www.chilkoothorseback.com) has 3.5-hour horseback rides up historic Dyea Valley for $119. The same folks also offer sleddog cart rides at Dyea for $89.

ACCOMMODATIONS AND CAMPING

If you're heading here in midsummer, try to make reservations at least two weeks ahead of time to be sure of a room. Visit www.skagway.org for links to local lodging places.

Hostels

The delightful **Skagway Home Hostel** (3rd and Main, 907/983-2131, www.skagwayhostel.com) is right in town. Built more than a century ago, the home was once owned by the marshall who arrested the Soapy Smith gang after the shoot-out. An 11 P.M. curfew may put a crimp in your social life, but the owners are very friendly and the hostel is open year-round. There's space for only 12, so reserve ahead. Registration is 5–9 P.M., but late ferry arrivals are accommodated. The hostel has a kitchen, commons area, showers, laundry, and bag storage. Bunks are $15, and a couple's room costs $40 d. The owners offer family-style, shared lunches, and mostly vegetarian dinners for a small charge.

Skagway's other hostel is the immaculate **Alaskan Sojourn Guest House and Hostel** (488 8th Ave., 907/983-2030, www.alaskansojourn.com). Guests stay in a new building with separate floors for the men's and women's dorms. The kitchen and commons room (with Internet access) are in a beautifully furnished and historic home. The cost is $20 (with linen and towel), or $50 d for a private room in the main house; book far ahead for the latter. Alaskan Sojourn is open year-round, and the owner picks ferry

travelers up in her classic 1977 Oldsmobile station wagon (think Chevy Chase in *Vacation*). Credit cards are accepted, and no curfew or lockout times.

Hotels and Motels

Sgt. Preston's Lodge (6th and State, 907/983-2521, $75–85 s, $80–90 d) is a tidy 30-room motel right in town, with attractive rooms. **Gold Rush Lodge** (6th and Alaska, 907/983-2831, www.goldrushlodge.com, $95–115 d) has nicely appointed rooms with fridges and microwaves.

Skagway's largest lodging place is the seasonally open **Westmark Inn** (3rd and Broadway, 907/983-2291 or 800/544-0970, www.westmarkhotels.com, $119 d) with all the charm of a retirement home; you might feel you were in one given the cruise ship folks. Grossly overpriced.

Bed-and-Breakfasts

Hosted by longtime Alaskans Howard and Judy Mallory, **Mile Zero B&B** (9th Ave. at Main St., 907/983-3045, www.mile-zero.com, $105 d) is a modern seven-room B&B with large rooms, private entrances and baths, a cozy parlor, and a continental breakfast.

Located within one of the town's oldest buildings, **Skagway Inn B&B** (7th and Broadway, 907/983-2289 or 888/752-4929, www.skagwayinn.com, open mid-May–mid-Sept., $109–129 d) served through the years as a bordello, a residence, a boarding house, and now as a delightful inn. Five guest rooms have private baths, and the other five share three baths. Hot breakfast served downstairs.

Built in 1902 and completely rebuilt after a fire, **The White House Inn** (8th Ave. and Main St., 907/983-9000, www.atthewhitehouse.com, $108–125 d) is a large plantation-style home with 10 guest rooms, one of which is wheelchair accessible. All rooms feature a country Victorian decor, with private baths, quilts on the beds, phones, and TVs. Full breakfast included.

Chilkoot Trail Outpost (907/983-3799, www.chilkoottrailoutpost.com) is a newly built lodge eight miles out Dyea Road. Eight cabins are available, all with private baths and kitchenettes; $50 s or 70 d in cabins with bunks, or

$125 d for deluxe cabins with queen beds. Breakfast is included, but you'll need to find your own transport from town. Guests can use the screened-in gazebo cooking area for other meals, or pay $15 for dinner. Because of its location, this lodge is very popular with hikers setting out for the Chilkoot Trail; the trailhead is just a half-mile away.

Cabins

Two miles from town out Dyea Road, **Cindy's Place** (907/983-2674 or 800/831-8095, www.alaska.net/~croland, open May–Sept.) includes two modern cabins with private baths and kitchenette for $105 d. Also available is a tiny cabin with no running water for $35 s or $49 d. Mountain bikes and breakfast fixin's are provided, and guests will appreciate the hot tub.

Another place with cabins on the way to Dyea is **Skagway Bungalows** (907/983-2986, www.aptalaska.net/~saldi, open April–Oct., $99 d). It's a mile from town, and two in-the-woods cabins have private baths.

Camping

The Park Service maintains a peaceful, free campground at **Dyea,** northeast of Skagway. It is especially popular with hikers along the Chilkoot Trail. You'll need to bring water or filter it from the river. For those without wheels, hitching is possible, or contact one of the local taxi companies for a ride. Showers are available from local RV parks or at the small boat harbor.

Skagway's three private campgrounds are all priced around $14 for tents and $25 for RVs, and are open seasonally. **Skagway Mountain View RV Park** (14th and Broadway, 907/983-3333 or 888/778-7700, www.alaskarv.com) is the in-town tenters' campground, with wooded sites, flush toilets, and showers. The narrow-gauge tracks border the grounds, making this a good place for photo opportunities. **Pullen Creek RV Park** (907/983-2768 or 800/936-3731, www.pullencreekrv.com) is next to the harbor and cruise ship dock. This is great if you like being in the heart of the action, with steam engines, cruise ships, and shopping, but not so great if you're looking for a more natural setting.

Garden City RV Park (16th Ave. and State St., 907/983-2378, www.gardencityrv.com) is little more than a parking lot with bathhouse.

FOOD

With so many visitors flashing the cash, Skagway's high meal prices should come as no surprise. But at least the variety and quality are considerably higher than what you'll find in Wrangell!

Breakfast and Lunch

Corner Cafe (4th Ave. and State St., 907/983-2155) is the local greasy spoon, with burgers and pizzas, plus reasonable breakfasts and fast service. A better bet is probably **Sweet Tooth Cafe** (3rd and Broadway, 907/983-2405, daily 6 A.M.–3 P.M.), with good all-American breakfasts and lunches. Both Corner Cafe and the Sweet Tooth stay open year-round; most other eateries close when the cruise ships flee to the Caribbean. Unfortunately, both places can also get quite smoky at times.

You'll find espresso, along with fresh-baked muffins and cookies, at **Mabel G. Smith's** (5th Ave. between Broadway and State, 907/983-2609).

Haven Cafe (9th Ave. and State St., 907/983-3554) is far enough off the tourist path to be mainly for locals, and they like it that way. It's a great place for breakfast sandwiches, yogurt shakes, panini sandwiches, salads, soups, and espresso. Recommended.

Sabrosa (6th and Broadway, 907/9842469), is a hidden gem, with homemade musli, espresso, good sandwiches, fat burritos, fresh soups and salads, and outstanding halibut chowder. This is a fine spot for a quick breakfast or lunch. Find them behind Legacy Jewelers; open seasonally.

Dinner

Skagway Fish Company (907/983-3474, daily May–Sept.) is a tent-like structure near the cruise ship dock and facing the small boat harbor. The menu includes T-bone steaks, pork chops, BBQ ribs, oysters, and fresh salmon or halibut, but I recommend the halibut fish and chips. The fish is locally caught, and it comes with a pile of fries and homemade coleslaw. Good cheesecake too.

Skagway Inn (7th Ave. at Broadway, 907/983-2289 or 888/752-4929, www.skagwayinn.com) is home to a pair of summer-only dining choices: **Greg's Bistro** is an espresso and bakery spot, while **Olivia's** serves reasonably priced Alaskan seafood dinners. Outdoor seating is available on the deck adjacent to the big organic garden.

Stowaway Cafe (907/983-3463) is where locals (and tourists) go for good food in a harborside setting. There's even a big deck for sunny days. The café specializes in seafood of all types, but also serves everything from smoked ribs to Thai curry. Be sure to check the daily specials. Reservations are advised for dinner at this seasonal cafe.

Groceries

Fairway Market (4th Ave. and State St., 907/983-2220), is Skagway's grocery store. Locals buy most of their groceries a hundred miles away in Whitehorse, where prices are better (especially with the favorable exchange rate). **The Pill Box** (3rd Ave. near Broadway) convenience store is the only place that's open 24 hours a day year-round. It sells most of the junk-food essentials.

You Say Tomato (9th Ave. at State St., 907/983-2784), is a little natural-foods market, and even has some locally grown produce for reasonable prices.

ENTERTAINMENT AND EVENTS

Entertainment

Skagway's best-known boozing establishment, the **Red Onion** (2nd Ave. and Broadway, 907/983-2222), delivers live tunes most summer afternoons courtesy of musicians off the cruise ships. The bar, mirrors, and stove are from the time it served as both a saloon and brothel. But don't believe any tall tales about ghosts; they're all made up for the tourists. If you want to get down and dirty and start drinking with the locals at 10 A.M., head across the street and up the block to **Moe's Frontier Bar. Bonanza Bar & Grill** (3rd Ave. and Broadway, 907/983-6214) has pool tables, microbrews, and sports on the TVs.

The most fun thing to do at night is to attend the **Days of '98 Show** (6th Ave. and Broadway, 907/983-2545, www.alaskan.com/daysof98) in the Fraternal Order of Eagles building. The great-granddaddy of them all, this production is the oldest running theater in Alaska—over 75 years! Matinees are offered most summer days at 10:30 A.M. and 2 P.M., and full evening performances start at 7 P.M. Warm-up gambling with "Soapy money" comes first, then the show goes on at 8. The cost is $16 adults, $8 for kids under 16. Splurge on this one—it's worth the cash.

"Buckwheat" Donahue, a memorable local character (and head of the Skagway Convention and Visitors Bureau), occasionally recites "The Cremation of Sam McGee," "The Shooting of Dan McGrew," and other Robert Service ballads at the Park Service building on Broadway. It's a first-rate show, and Buckwheat always knows how to make people laugh. Free, and worth every penny. Highly recommended.

Events

Skagway's first July 4th in 1898 was celebrated with the outlaw Soapy Smith leading the parade on a white horse; he was dead four days later. **July 4th** is still a big day, with a huge parade (locals call it the best in Alaska) and other events. **Soapy Smith's Wake** on July 8th toasts the conman's life and death at the Eagles Hall. The less savory aspects of the wake have been (officially at least) deleted from the program, but certain individuals may still join in after massive consumption of cheap champagne.

The **Klondike Trail of '98 International Road Relay** (www.sportyukon.com) takes place every September, with more than a 150 teams composed of 10 runners each competing over a grueling 110-mile course from Skagway to Whitehorse.

Certainly the strangest event in a town where odd is normal, is **Abduct and Release—A Skagway Paranormal Symposium** which takes place one weekend before Halloween. Call the Visitors Bureau for the full story (907/983-2854 or 888/762-1898), or contact them psychically.

The main winter event is the **Buckwheat Classic,** a cross-country ski race that attracts both serious competitors and rank amateurs (including the "lazy and infirm") each March.

INFORMATION AND SERVICES

Both the Park Service Visitor Center and the Skagway Visitor Information Center are described in *Sights*. The small **town library** (8th Ave. and State St., 907/983-2665) offers free reading material on the paperback racks inside, and you can check your email on its computers. Rent computer time from **Alaska Cruiseship Services** (2nd Ave. between Broadway and State, 907/983-3398).

Mountain Shop (4th Ave. between Broadway and State, 907/983-2544, www.packerexpeditions) is the outfitter in town, and also sells supplies for the trail. Books are available at **Skagway News Depot** (Broadway, 907/983-3354).

One of Alaska's oldest bank buildings, **Wells Fargo** (6th Ave. and Broadway), changes green dollars into multicolored Canadian dollars, and has an ATM. Other cash machines are inside the White Pass & Yukon Route depot and the Trail Bench Gift Shop.

There is no swimming pool in Skagway, but cellular phone service has finally arrived. For medical emergencies, **Skagway Medical Clinic** (11th Ave. and Broadway, 907/983-2255) has a physician's assistant on staff.

TRANSPORTATION

On the Water

Skagway is the northern terminus of the ferry system, and ferries arrive daily during the summer, stopping at the **ferry terminal** (907/983-2941), just a block from downtown. Get details from the Alaska Marine Highway (907/465-3941 or 800/642-0066, www.ferryalaska.com).

Alaska Fjordlines (907/766-3395 or 800/320-0146, www.alaskafjordlines.com) operates the *Fjord Express*, a large and stable high-speed catamaran with daily summertime runs from Skagway to Haines and then on to Auke Bay in Juneau. The boat leaves Skagway at 8 A.M., arrives in Juneau at 11:30 A.M., and then heads back at 5 P.M., returning to Skagway at 8:15 P.M.

The cost is $109 roundtrip, or $129 if you add a Juneau bus tour. Breakfast and dinner are included, and the skipper stops for wildlife and photo opportunities. This passenger-only ferry is very popular with RVers who want to see Juneau in a day. One-way trips and overnight stays in Juneau are allowed; reservations recommended. This is an efficiently run and friendly operation.

Chilkat Cruises (907/766-2100 or 888/766-2103, www.chilkatcruises.com) offers high-speed catamaran service between Haines and Skagway, with several departures a day mid-May–mid-September. The cost is $44 roundtrip ($22 for kids). On weekends, they also run between Juneau and Haines for $69 roundtrip/$39 one-way. The boat does not stop on any of these trips for wildlife viewing or photos, and no food is on board.

Air

Three companies have daily flights connecting Skagway with Juneau and Haines: **Skagway Air** (907/983-2218, www.skagwayair.com), **Wings of Alaska** (907/789-0790, www.wingsofalaska.com), or **L.A.B. Flying Service** (907/983-2471 or 800/426-0543, www.labflying.com). L.A.B. also flies to Gustavus from Skagway.

Car Rentals

Rent new cars from **Avis** (907/983-2247 or 800/331-1212) at the Westmark Hotel, or used vehicles from **PB Cruisers** (326 3rd Ave., 907/983-3385) in the Pill Box or **Sourdough Car Rental** (6th Ave. and Broadway, 907/983-2523). If you're driving to Whitehorse, stick with Avis or PB Cruisers since Sourdough hits you with 25 cents per mile after 100 miles.

Long-Distance Buses

In the summer, **Alaska Direct Bus Line** (800/770-6652 or 867/668-4833 in Whitehorse, www.home.gci.net/~akdirectbus), has service several times a week from Skagway to Whitehorse, Anchorage, and Fairbanks. Buses overnight in Tok.

Getting Around

City-run **SMART** (Skagway Municipal and Regional Transit) buses (907/983-2743) run daily, shuttling from the cruise dock into town out to 23rd Avenue (access to the gold rush cemetery). The one-way cost is $1.50 up to 10th Avenue, or $3 beyond that. Buses run continuously 7:30 A.M.–9 P.M. May–September.

Several local tour outfits offer drop-off services ($10) for hikers heading up the Chilkoot Trail and for campers staying at Dyea: **Dyea Dave's** (907/983-2731), **Frontier Excursions** (907/983-2512 or 877/983-2512, www.frontierexcursions.com), and **Skagway Float Tours** (907/983-3688, www.skagwayfloat.com).

CHILKOOT TRAIL

One of the best reasons for coming to Skagway is the historic and surprisingly scenic 33-mile Chilkoot Trail. During the gold rush of 1897–1898, what had once been an Indian route from the tidewater at Dyea to the headwaters of the Yukon River became a trail for thousands of men and women. Today, the trail is hiked by several thousand hardy souls each summer, along with a few insane wintertime trekkers. The western portion of this route lies within **Klondike Gold Rush National Historical Park,** while the eastern half is managed by Parks Canada as **Chilkoot Trail National Historic Park.** All hikers crossing the border must clear Canadian Customs.

A minimum of three days and nights (but preferably four or five) is needed to hike from Dyea to Bennett over 3,246-foot-high Chilkoot Pass. This is no easy Sunday outing: You must be fit and well prepared. It is best to hike north from Dyea rather than south from Bennett since this is the historic route, and a descent down the "Golden Stairs" can be dangerous.

You will be above the treeline and totally exposed to the elements during the 11 miles from Sheep Camp to Deep Lake (the hardest stretch). Weather conditions can change quickly along the trail, and hikers need to be prepared for strong winds, cold, low fog, rain, and snow, even in mid-summer. Because of the rain-shadow effect, the Canadian side is considerably drier than the Alaskan side. Mosquitoes and other insects are an annoyance, and snowfields linger between Sheep Camp

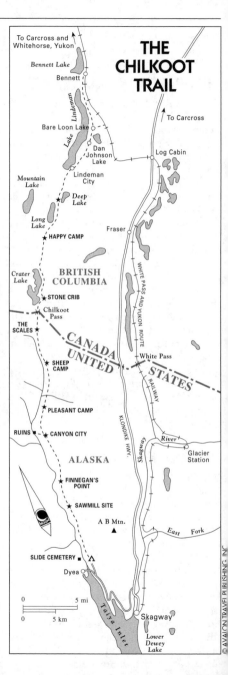

and Happy Camp well into the summer. Despite these challenges, for scenery and historical value the Chilkoot Trail is unsurpassed in Alaska and western Canada.

Flora and Fauna

The vegetation changes from coastal rainforest up the Taiya Valley to alpine tundra as you approach the pass and rise above the 2,700-foot level. On the drier Canadian side you'll find an open boreal forest of alpine fir and lodgepole pine. Although black bears are often seen along the trail, there has never been an attack on a hiker. Help keep it this way by storing food and garbage properly.

History

It took each would-be miner an average of three months and dozens of trips back and forth from cache to cache to pack his required ton of supplies into Canada. By the spring of 1898, three aerial tramways were operating on the Chilkoot. The thousands of stampeders stopped at Lindeman and Bennett, built boats and rafts, and waited for spring break-up, which would allow them to sail the 900 km to Dawson City along a series of lakes and rivers. When the ice broke up in May 1898, some 7,124 boats and rafts sailed from the shores of Lakes Lindeman and Bennett. Mounted Police records show 28,000 people traveling from Bennett to Dawson in 1898. Ironically, by the time they got to Dawson every claim in the Klondike was already staked. By 1900, the railway had opened from Skagway to Whitehorse, and Dyea and the Chilkoot Trail became ghost towns.

The Route

The Chilkoot Trail begins just before the bridge over the Taiya River at Dyea, nine miles northwest of Skagway. The first section of the trail traverses lush rainforests along the Taiya River. Artifacts from the gold rush litter parts of the path here, including bits of clothing, rusting stoves, pulleys, cables, and old wagons. At **Canyon City,** 7.5 miles from the trailhead, a short side trail and a suspension bridge across the Taiya River provide access to the remains of one of the settlements that sprang up during the rush to the Klondike. You'll find

a number of artifacts here, including a boiler that powered tramways to haul supplies over the summit. Beyond this, the trail climbs steeply to another long-abandoned settlement, **Sheep Camp** (Mile 13), where a ranger is in residence all summer.

Beyond Sheep Camp, the trek becomes far more challenging as the route takes hikers through a narrow valley before heading above tree line. Artifacts—including metal telegraph poles and pieces from an old tramway used to haul goods up the mountain—become more common as you climb past "The Scales" (Mile 16), where packers reweighed their loads and increased their fee for the difficult final climb. Modern-day hikers start to wonder about their sanity at this point, since the infamous "Golden Stairs" lie ahead; the name came from the steps carved in the ice and the snow by the miners. During the winter of 1897–1898 thousands of prospectors carried their heavy loads to the 3,535-foot summit of **Chilkoot Pass.** Photos of men going up here in single file are still the best-known images of the gold rush. Today, hikers struggle up this 45-degree slope with full backpacks. Snow generally covers the pass until mid-July, and can be waist-deep early in the summer. A warming hut provides protection from the weather once you cross into British Columbia; Parks Canada rangers here check to make sure you have a permit.

After the challenging summit climb, hikers are rewarded with easier hiking and spectacular vistas (when weather permits), but it's still a long distance to the end of the trail. Many hikers camp at **Deep Lake** (Mile 23), while others continue on to **Lindeman Lake** (Mile 26) for the night. A Canada Parks warden station and warming huts are at Lindeman. During the stampede, thousands of miners halted along the shores of this lake, quickly forming the town of Lindeman City. Here they built boats for the journey down the Yukon River to the Klondike gold fields. Reminders of the gold rush can be found in the countryside here, and a small cemetery marks the final stop for those who never made it to the Klondike.

Beyond Lindeman, the trail climbs a ridge overlooking the lake and then splits, with one path turning south to meet the Klondike Highway at **Log Cabin,** where you can catch a bus back to Skagway or Whitehorse. Those who continue straight at the junction will reach a pretty place called **Bennett** on the shores of Lake Bennett. Only one family lives here today, but hikers will enjoy exploring the log church built by the miners and a grand White Pass & Yukon Route Railroad depot. Most hikers end their trip here, catching the train back to Skagway.

Practicalities

Official campgrounds—most with outhouses, cooking shelters, and bear-proof food storage—are at nine sites along the Chilkoot Trail in addition to the one at the Dyea Trailhead; most popular are those at Canyon City (Mile 7.5), Sheep Camp (Mile 12), Happy Camp (Mile 21), Lindeman City (Mile 26), and Bennett (Mile 33). Campfires are permitted only at Canyon City and Sheep Camp. There are shelters with woodstoves at Canyon City, Sheep Camp, and Lindeman, but these are for drying out only (not overnighting). Everything along the trail dating from the gold rush (even a rusty old tin can) is protected by law, and there are severe penalties for those who damage or remove items.

The first section of the Chilkoot Trail traverses lush rainforests along the Taiya River. Artifacts from the gold rush litter parts of the path here, including bits of clothing, rusting stoves, pulleys, cables, and old wagons.

Everyone entering Canada must clear Canadian Customs. If you come in along the Chilkoot Trail and do not speak to an official at either Whitehorse or Fraser, you should report at the first opportunity to either the RCMP in Carcross or the Immigration Office (open Mon.–Fri.) at the Federal Building in Whitehorse.

Hiking Permits

Backcountry permits are required of hikers on the Chilkoot, and the number of hikers is limited. The U.S. permit is free, but permits for the Canadian side cost C$50. For trail information, maps (including an excellent *Hiker's Guide to the Chilkoot Trail*), and backcountry permits, contact the Park Service's **Chilkoot Trail Center** (907/983-9234, www.nps.gov/klgo, daily June–Aug. 8 A.M.–4:30 P.M.) in the historic Martin Itjen house in Skagway. You can also buy trail permits through Parks Canada in Whitehorse (867/667-3910 or 800/661-0486, http://parkscan .harbour.com/ct).

Most permits are reserved months ahead of time, but eight permits are reserved for walkins each day at 1 P.M. Much of the time you won't have a problem getting onto the trail even at the last minute, but call the Trail Center for the latest situation. In July and August, folks without permits start lining up at the Trail Center by 11 A.M. to be sure of a spot.

Transportation

Several Skagway companies offer drop-off services ($10) from town for hikers heading up the Chilkoot Trail. Best known is **Dyea Dave's** (907/983-2731), but similar services are available from **Frontier Excursions** (907/983-2512 or 877/983-2512, www.frontierexcursions.com) and **Skagway Float Tours** (907/983-3688, www.skagwayfloat.com). All three will also pick you up from Log Cabin or Fraser for an additional $15, but call ahead for reservations.

The WP&YR's **Chilkoot Trail Hikers Special** train (907/983-2217 or 800/343-7373, www.ypyr.com, Mon.–Thurs. and Sat. at 1 P.M.), provides a shuttle (usually a rail bus) from Bennett to Fraser ($30) or Skagway ($65 adults, $33 kids). Make advance reservations since space is limited.

Although most hikers choose the train, some prefer (or have no option because the rail bus is full) to hike out along the railroad tracks from the Lindeman area to Log Cabin, where they catch a bus or hitch. **Alaska Direct Bus Line** (800/770-6652 or 867/668-4833 in Whitehorse, www.home.gci.net/~akdirectbus) will do a flag stop at Log Cabin and take you to Skagway or Whitehorse, but call ahead for their schedule.

THE KLONDIKE HIGHWAY

This 98-mile road from Skagway to the Alaska Highway 21 miles south of Whitehorse closely follows the White Pass & Yukon Route rail line built at the turn of the century. The 65-mile stretch north to Carcross was opened in 1981, completing the route started by the U.S. Army in 1942 from the Alaska Highway south to Carcross. The road ascends quickly from sea level at Skagway to White Pass at 3,290 feet in 14 miles. Many turnouts provide views across the canyon of the narrow-gauge White Pass & Yukon Route track, waterfalls, gorges, and long drop-offs—if you're lucky and the weather cooperates. At the summit, **Canadian Customs** welcomes you to British Columbia, and is open 8 A.M.–midnight year-round; set your watch ahead an hour to Pacific Time on the Canadian side.

Anchorage and Vicinity

Texas always seemed so big, but you know you're in the largest State in the Union when you're anchored down in Anchorage . . . .

from "Anchored Down in Anchorage"
by Michelle Shocked

It's hard to arrive in Anchorage (pop. 260,000) without some strong preconceived notions of what to expect—especially if you've been traveling around the state for a while. Generally, Alaskans either love or hate Anchorage, and their degree of affection or distaste is usually revealed by their chosen proximity to the city.

You'll certainly have heard of Anchorage's urban sprawl, its traffic jams, sprouting trailer parks and condos, corporate skyscrapers, mall mania, fast-food frenzy, and crime; in other words, that it's the antithesis of every virtue and value that God-fearing, law-abiding, and patriotic Alaskans hold sacred. And you've probably also heard the old joke about being "able to see Alaska from Anchorage." You might also have been told that Anchorage has nothing to offer travelers, and that if you're looking for a true *Alaskan* experience, you should avoid the city al-

together. Don't believe everything you hear; Anchorage is an attraction of its own and definitely worth some time.

Anchorage can be an eminently enjoyable *and* affordable place in which to hang out. It certainly has one of the most flower-filled downtowns of any American city; visitors are always impressed with the summertime bounty of blooms. You can easily fill a whole day touring downtown, another exploring its far-flung corners, another researching the many places to go from Anchorage and the best ways to get there, and another just lying around a downtown park for the one day in four that the sun shines.

Anchorage's highlights include its outstanding Museum of History and Art (arguably the state's best), the Alaska Native Heritage Center, the Alaska Heritage Library and Museum, along with an abundance of good restaurants, hip coffeehouses, hopping bars, and two minor league baseball teams—all that you might expect from the state's largest city. But with the natural beauty of Mt. McKinley and the Alaska Range visible beyond the city skyline on clear days, it's hard to forget that you're in Alaska. And there are also attractions you would only find in an Alaskan city: a wonderful coastal trail that starts right downtown, great day-hiking in the nearby Chugach Mountains, fascinating Cook Inlet with its enormous tides and beluga whales, and places to outfit yourself for any adventure in the Alaskan outdoors. Anchorage is within easy striking distance of some of the most exciting and extensive hiking, climbing, fishing, kayaking, river rafting, flightseeing, and wilderness areas. Budget travelers will enjoy reasonable food prices, inexpensive flights to the Lower 48, several hostels, and a good bus system.

Of course, if you can't overcome the idea that "Alaska population center" is a contradiction in terms, you can simply breeze into town, make your connection, and quickly "get back to Alaska." But if you want a fully rounded experience of the 49th state, get to know Anchorage, *urban* Alaska, and come to your own conclusions.

CLIMATE

Two of the deciding factors in choosing Anchorage as a main construction camp for the Alaska Railroad were mild winters and comparatively low precipitation. The towering Alaska Range shelters Cook Inlet Basin from the frigid winter breath of the Arctic northerlies; the Kenai and Chugach Mountains cast a rain shadow over the basin, allowing only 15–20 percent of the annual precipitation in communities on the windward side of the ranges. Anchorage receives around 20 inches of annual precipitation (10–12 inches of rain, 60–70 inches of snow), while Whittier, 40 miles away on the Gulf side of the Chugach, gets 175 inches. Anchorage's winter temperatures rarely drop much below 0°F, with only an occasional cold streak, compared with Fairbanks' frequent -40°F; its summer temperatures rarely rise above 65°F, compared with Fairbanks' 80s and 90s.

HISTORY

In June 1778, Captain James Cook sailed up what's now Turnagain Arm in Cook Inlet, reaching another dead end on his amazing search for the Northwest Passage. But he did dispatch William Bligh (of HMS *Bounty* fame) to explore, and he saw some Tanaina Indians in rich otter skins. George Vancouver, who'd also been on Cook's ship, returned in 1794 and noted Russian settlers in the area. A century later, prospectors began landing in the area and heading north to Southcentral Alaska's gold country, and in 1902 Alfred Brooks began mapping the Cook Inlet for the U.S. Geological Survey. In 1913, five settlers occupied Ship Creek, the point on the inlet where Anchorage now stands.

A year later, Congress passed the Alaska Railroad Act and in April 1915, the route for the federally financed railroad from Seward to Fairbanks was made official: It would pass through Ship Creek, where a major staging area for workers and supplies would be located. This news traveled fast, and within a month a ramshackle tent city of nearly 2,000 railroad job seekers had sprung up. Things developed so quickly that in July, the U.S. Land Office auctioned off 650

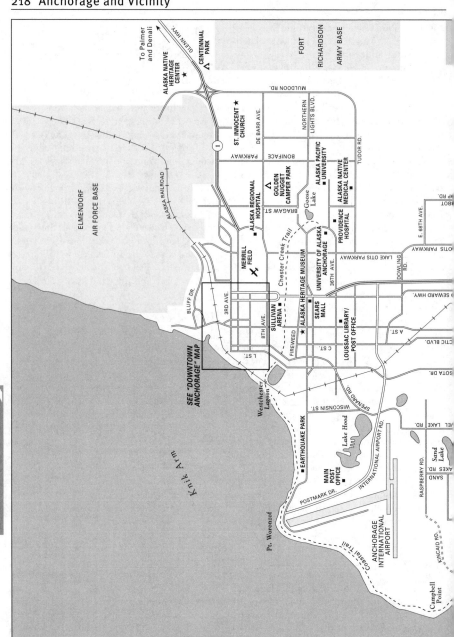

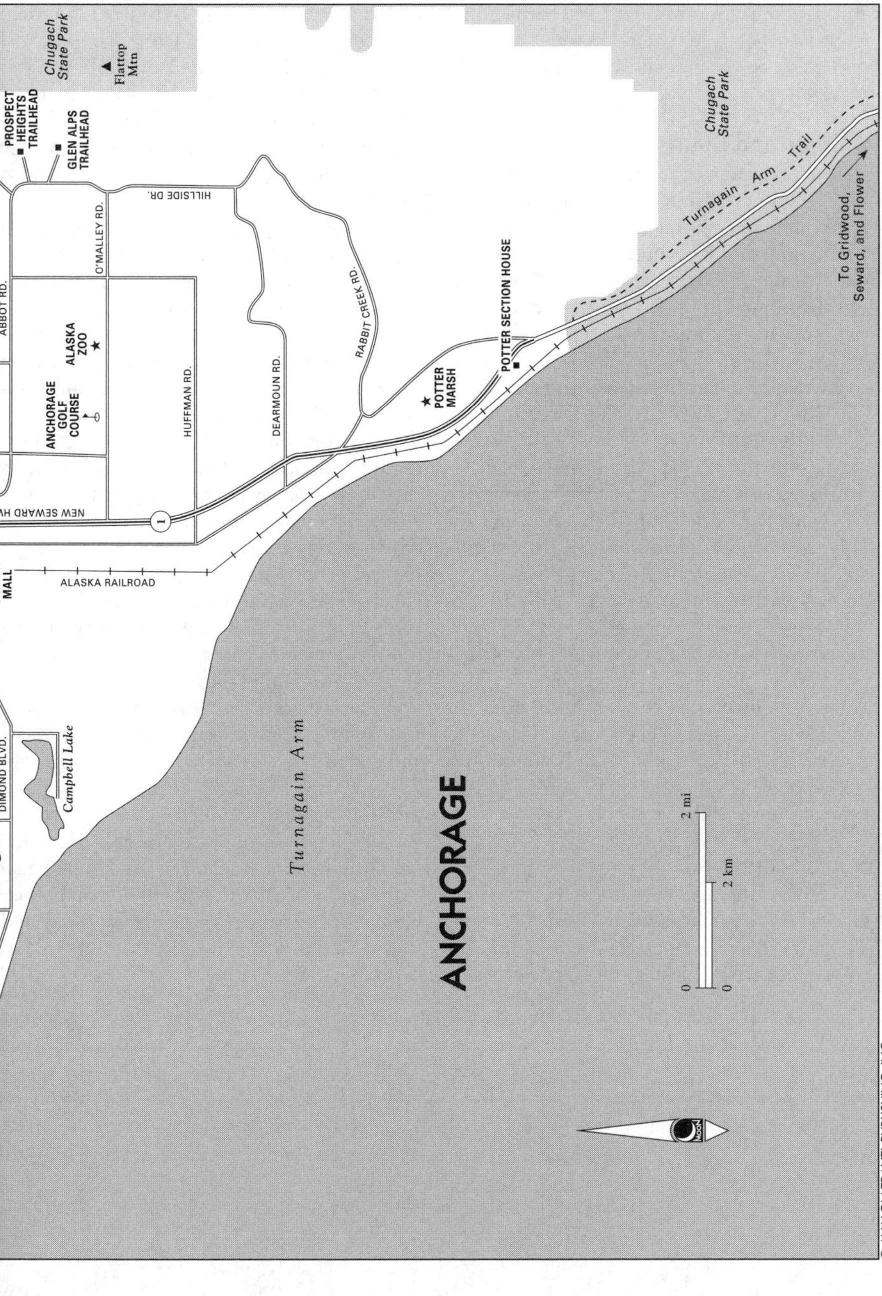

Chugach
State Park

▲ Flattop
Mtn

PROSPECT
HEIGHTS
TRAILHEAD ■

GLEN ALPS
TRAILHEAD ■

HILLSIDE DR.

Chugach
State Park

O'MALLEY RD.

Turnagain Arm Trail

ABBOT RD.

RABBIT CREEK RD.

POTTER SECTION HOUSE

To Gridwood,
Seward, and Flower

ALASKA
ZOO ★

ANCHORAGE
GOLF
COURSE

HUFFMAN RD.

DEARMOUN RD.

★ POTTER
MARSH

NEW SEWARD HWY

① 1

MALL

ALASKA RAILROAD

DIMOND BLVD.

Campbell Lake

Turnagain Arm

ANCHORAGE

0   2 mi

0   2 km

ANCHORAGE AND VICINITY

parcels at the new town site. The settlement, renamed Anchorage, grew quickly, with water, telephone and power lines, sidewalks, and schools in place within a year.

Slumps and Spurts

Railroad laborers, earning 37 cents an hour (low for Alaska), struck in 1916, after which the minimum wage was raised to 45 cents an hour. The population continued to boom, topping out at around 7,000 in 1917. With World War I and completion of the southern portion of the railroad, the number of people dropped below 2,000 in 1920, when the town incorporated, electing its first mayor and city council. Through the 1930s, Anchorage held steady at 3,000–4,000 people, but World War II changed that in a hurry. The town's strategic location led to a huge influx of military personnel, when the Army's Fort Richardson and Air Force's Elmendorf Field were constructed outside of town. By 1950, Anchorage was a prosperous small city of over 11,000. In the following decade Anchorage also experienced the postwar boom, with the attending shortages of housing and modern conveniences, which created its own construction miniboom. In 1957, when Richfield Oil discovered black gold on the Kenai Peninsula, the oil companies started opening office buildings in the city, and the economy stabilized.

Since Statehood

Much of Anchorage collapsed in the incredible **Good Friday earthquake** of March 27, 1964, which lasted an interminable five minutes, registering 9.2 on the Richter Scale. The north side of 4th Avenue wound up 8–10 feet lower than the south side of the street. A very rich residential section on the bluff overlooking Knik Arm was destroyed. Nine people were killed and upward of $300 million in damages were recorded. Anchorage was rebuilt, and because only a few large buildings survived the quake, nearly everything in the city was put up after 1964.

Though the pipeline doesn't come within 300 miles of Anchorage, oil money towers over the city in the form the tall office buildings scattered around town. The military still plays an important role in the local economy, with Elmendorf Air Force Base and Fort Richardson right on the margins of town, and military jets and surveillance planes a common presence in the sky. Tourism also affects Anchorage enormously, especially in the summer months when the city is a way point for many travelers. Anchorage fancies itself quite the cosmopolitan city, boasting dozens of arts organizations, a modern performing arts center, a 16-theater cinema with stadium seating, plus many fancy hotels, restaurants, cafés, and bars catering to the thousands of suits who fill the skyscrapers that gleam in the light of the midnight sun. Indeed, if Juneau is bureaucratic Alaska, and Fairbanks is rank-and-file Alaska, then Anchorage is corporate and commercial Alaska.

If you can't find it at an Anchorage store, it probably isn't sold anywhere in the state. And if you find it elsewhere, you'll probably pay more. For bush dwellers, Anchorage is a shopping trip disguised as a city. Put people from Bethel, Nome, or Homer in Anchorage for a day and they're likely to spend most of their time at Costco and Wal-Mart!

Sights

It doesn't take long to get the hang of downtown Anchorage. The blocks are square, with the lettered streets (A through L) going north–south and the numbered avenues (starting at 2nd Ave. just up the hill from the tracks) running east–west. Once you get east of the lettered streets they start over again using alphabetized names (Barrow, Cordova, Denali, Eagle, Fairbanks).

Beyond downtown, the city of Anchorage sprawls across the Anchorage Bowl, with hillside homes peering down on the masses below. A number of neighborhoods are scattered around Anchorage, but most travelers are likely to spend their time in downtown and **Midtown.** The latter is a nondescript Anytown, USA, collection of malls, shopping centers, supermarkets, fast food joints, bars, movie theaters, discount stores, gas stations, and other businesses just a 20-minute walk or a 10-minute bus ride south of downtown. Midtown is encompassed by Northern Lights and Benson Boulevards between Minnesota Drive and Old Seward Highway. It isn't exactly a tourist attraction, but this, along with shopping malls on the south and east end of town, is where locals—and others looking to save money—spend their cash. Another large shopping district is along Dimond Boulevard in South Anchorage; here are all the stalwarts: Best Buy, Wal-Mart, Costco, Borders, CompUSA, and more.

DOWNTOWN
Visitor Center
Start your tour of downtown at the **Anchorage Convention and Visitors Bureau** (ACVB), a sod-roofed log cabin on the corner of 4th Avenue and F Street. The cabin isn't actually the main place for information; go out the back door to a more spacious visitor center, where you'll find a plethora of brochures from around the state and a helpful staff. Be sure to pick up a copy of the fat *Anchorage Visitors Guide* which includes a downtown walking tour and an Anchorage-area driving tour, plus details on sights, attractions, activities, lodging, restaurants, and more.

The ACVB office is open daily 7:30 A.M.–7 P.M. June–August; daily 8 A.M.–6 P.M. in May and September; and daily 9 A.M.–4 P.M. the rest of the year. Details at 907/274-3531, www.anchorage.net; the website is packed with information on the city and links to local businesses. Call 907/276-3200 for a recording of forthcoming events.

Free city buses (907/343-6543; www.peoplemover.org) run around downtown daily if you get tired of walking. They stop right in front of the ACVB.

The nonprofit **Anchorage Historic Properties** (907/274-3600, www.anchoragehistoricproperties.org) leads informative walking tours of downtown for $5 ($1 kids). These last an hour, and begin Monday–Friday at 1 P.M. from old city hall (524 W. 4th Ave.), June–August.

Public Lands Center
Kitty-corner from the ACVB is the old Federal Building, which now houses the **Alaska Public Lands Information Center** (907/271-2737; www.nps.gov/aplic, daily 9 A.M.–5:30 P.M. Memorial Day–Labor Day, Mon.–Fri. 10 A.M.–5:30 P.M. the rest of the year). This is a great starting point to learn about federal lands in Alaska, including national parks and forests, wildlife refuges, and Bureau of Land Management areas. Displays introduce you to Alaska's wildlife and wild places, the bookstore has a good selection of Alaskan titles, and the auditorium is used for nature videos and talks. Daily historical walks are offered throughout the summer. You can even create customized waterproof topographic maps and make reservations for state ferries or cabins in Kenai Fjords National Park.

State Information Center
A few blocks away is the **Department of Natural Resources Public Information Center** (550 W. 7th Ave., 907/269-8400, www.alaskastateparks.org, open weekdays). Located on the 12th floor, the information center has a helpful staff, and details on state parks, public-use cab-

DOWNTOWN ANCHORAGE

Knik Arm

Ship Creek

0.25 mi
0.25 km

Tony Knowles Coastal Trail

LOOP RD.

ALASKA RAILROAD

ALASKA RAILROAD

OCEAN DOCK RD.

SALMON VIEWING PLATFORM ★

COMFORT INN ●

RAILWAY STATION ■

RESOLUTION PARK

COPPERWHALE INN ●
OSCAR ANDERSON HOUSE ★

CAPTAIN COOK HOTEL ●

MARX BROS CAFE ●

ALASKA PUBLIC LANDS INFO CENTER ■

IMAGINARIUM ★

WESTMARK HOTEL ●

BUS TRANSIT CENTER ■

YOUTH HOSTEL ●

HAWTHORN SUITES ●

HILTON HOTEL ●

SATURDAY MARKET ★

POST OFFICE ■

ANCHORAGE HOTEL ●

VISITOR CENTER ■
CONVENTION CENTER ■

PERFORMING ARTS CENTER ★

5TH AVE. MALL ●

ANCHORAGE MARRIOTT HOTEL ●

WESTMARK INN ●

ANCHORAGE UPTOWN SUITES ●

HOLIDAY INN ●

DAYS INN ●

ANCHORAGE MUSEUM OF HISTORY AND ART ★

CLARION SUITES ●

FEDERAL BUILDING ■

SHERATON HOTEL ●

ASPEN HOTEL ●

Delaney Park

W. 2ND AVE.
W. 5TH AVE.
W. 5TH AVE.
W. 8TH AVE.
W. 9TH AVE.
W. 8TH AVE.
W. 9TH AVE.

L ST.
M ST.
N ST.
O ST.
I ST.
H ST.
G ST.
F ST.
E ST.
D ST.
C ST.
B ST.
A ST.
BARROW ST.
CORDOVA ST.
DENALI ST.
EAGLE ST.
FAIRBANKS ST.
GAMBELL ST.

E. 3RD AVE.
W. 3RD AVE.
E. 4TH AVE.
E. 5TH AVE.
E. 6TH AVE.
E. 7TH AVE.
E. 8TH AVE.
E. 9TH AVE.
E. 10TH AVE.

JUNEAU ST.
INGRA ST.

1

ins, where to look for gold, state land sales, and much more.

Anchorage Museum of History and Art

This museum (7th Ave. at A St., 907/343-6173, www.anchoragemuseum.org) is a downtown Anchorage highlight. Plan to linger a while in the permanent wing downstairs; the Cook Inlet collection is outstanding. The historical art section is fascinating, especially the paintings by Sydney Laurence, one of Alaska's most famous and prolific artists; his 6- by 10-foot oil of Mt. McKinley is the centerpiece. Upstairs is the extraordinary Alaska Gallery, with Alaska-size dioramas chronicling a spectacular journey from prehistoric archaeology all the way up to the present. Informative documentary films and 45-minute tours are offered several times a day throughout the summer, and the library houses thousands of historical photographs. The museum is open daily 9 A.M.–6 P.M. (Thurs. until 9 P.M.) mid-May–mid-September, Tuesday–Saturday 10 A.M.–6 P.M. and Sunday 1–5 P.M. the rest of the year. Entrance costs $6.50 for adults, $6 for seniors, free for kids under 18.

Also inside is **Marx Bros. Cafe at the Museum** (907/343-6190, www.marxcafe.com), with delicious light lunches; it's worth a visit even if you don't plan to explore the museum! A major museum expansion is in the works here, providing space for additional Native exhibits and a science center, but it probably won't be completed till 2008.

Performing Arts Center

Anchorage's central focal point is the Alaska Center for the Performing Arts (better known as the "Pac"—short for Performing Arts Center), an unusual brick and glass building with colorful Olympic-like rings of light around the top. Find it at 5th Avenue and G Street. Inside are three auditoriums with wonderful acoustics and horrific carpeting; wags say it looks like a pepperoni pizza. Hold the anchovies! Free tours of the center are offered Wednesdays at 1 P.M., and two IMAX films are also screened throughout the summer: one on wolves and the other on the Great Land.

the Performing Arts Center

© DON PITCHER

The latter is narrated by Charlton Heston, so check your NRA pistols at the door. In addition, the center has an interesting slide show on the northern lights. Get the full scoop at 907/563-9171, www.alaskapac.org.

The spacious front lawn of the Performing Arts Center comprises **Town Square,** a fine, flower-filled field of fecundity. It's a wonderful place to meet up with friends or just relax on a sunny summer day. **Egan Civic & Convention Center** is right across 5th Avenue.

Kids' Play

The **Imaginarium** (5th Ave. and G St., 907/276-3179, www.imaginarium.org, Mon.–Sat. 10 A.M.–6 P.M., and Sun. noon–5 P.M.) is a fun place if you've got young ones in tow. Learn all about northern lights in the planetarium, hold a starfish, stand inside a mega-bubble, or see the world through the eyes of a grasshopper at Alaska's only science discovery center. The exhibits change all the time, and the Imaginarium is open all year. Entrance costs $5 for adults, $4.50 for ages 2–12 or seniors, and free for toddlers.

Other Downtown Sights

A block from the museum, is **Wolf Song of Alaska** (corner of 6th Ave. and C St., 907/274-9653, www.wolfsongalaska.org), a nonprofit organization dedicated to educating the public about wolves. It houses a small but interesting museum with exhibits and a gift shop.

Across the street from the old Federal Building is the refurbished **4th Avenue Theater,** built in 1947, and one of the few structures to survive the 1964 earthquake. It's now used as a forgettable gift shop, but be sure to look overhead to see the twinkling big dipper on the ceiling. Right next to the log cabin visitor center is **Old City Hall,** which houses the offices of the ACVB. Step inside the lobby to view a few exhibits and historic photos from early Anchorage.

Historic Buildings

Anchorage is pretty short on historical buildings since much of the city was destroyed in the 1964 quake and most of the city's development and growth has taken place since the 1970s. The neighborhood around 2nd Avenue at F Street includes several of the original town site homes constructed in the early 1900s, and historical panels describe the city's early days.

A few other structures survive from quieter times, including the **Oscar Anderson House Museum** (420 M St., 907/274-2336, www.anchoragehistoricproperties.org, open for 45-minute tours Mon.–Fri. noon–5 P.M. June–mid-Sept., $3 adults, $1 kids). This refurbished little bungalow—built in 1915 by Anchorage's first butcher—is the oldest frame residence in this young city. It reopens during the first two weekends of December, when it is festooned with traditional Swedish Christmas decorations. The Tony Knowles Coastal Trail passes right in front of the Oscar Anderson House, and adjacent is tiny **Elderberry Park,** a pleasant place to relax on a sunny afternoon, with picnic and playground facilities.

Ship Creek Area

Immediately north of downtown on West 1st Avenue is the **Alaska Railroad Depot,** where you can book train travel or check out the 1907 train engine out front. Behind it is **Ship Creek,** a favorite place to cast for king or silver salmon all summer long—it's probably the only place where you can catch kings within sight of office high-rises. But watch out for the quicksand-like mud at the mouth of the creek; it can trap unwary anglers.

The **Elmendorf State Fish Hatchery** (Reeve Blvd. and Post Rd., 907/274-0065), has a salmon viewing area where you'll see king salmon late May–July and silver salmon August–mid-September. The viewing area is open daily 8 A.M.–10 P.M. from late May through September.

Delaney Park

Enjoyable Delaney Park runs between 9th and 10th Avenues from L Street to Barrow. Known as the "park strip," early in Anchorage's history it marked the boundary where the town stopped and the wilderness started, and in 1923 the strip where the park is today was cleared as a firebreak. Since then it has served as a golf course, an airstrip, and now hosts half a dozen softball games every night of summer, tennis and basketball courts, and large grassy sections for Frisbee, hackey sack, tai chi, sunbathing, or people-watching.

Resolution Park

A very popular stop for tour buses, visitors on foot, and the occasional (probably drunk) local is Resolution Park, on the west end of 3rd Avenue at L Street. This tiny city park consists of a viewing platform centered around a statue of Captain James Cook, who discovered what is now called Cook Inlet in 1778. The park is named for his ship, the *Resolution*. On clear days you'll delight to the mountainscape vistas. **Mt. McKinley** (many locals call it Denali) rises 125 miles to the north, and the low mountain just northwest across Cook Inlet is aptly named **Sleeping Lady** (the maps call it Mt. Susitna). Behind it, and just a bit south, stands a chain of active volcanoes that dump ash on Anchorage every few years, including **Mt. Spurr** and **Mt. Redoubt.** If you have eagle eyes and crystalline weather, you might pick out a third volcano, **Mt. Iliamna,** far to the southwest. Out of sight is yet a fourth volcano, **Mt. Augustine,** which last spewed ash in 1986.

Tony Knowles Coastal Trail

This is one of Anchorage's highlights, a wonderful 11-mile asphalt track that wends its way along the shore from downtown past the airport to Kincaid Park at Point Campbell, where the Knik and Turnagain Arms meet. From downtown, the trail is accessible from the west ends of 2nd, 5th, and 9th Avenues, with additional access at Westchester Lagoon, Earthquake Park, Point Woronzof, and Kincaid. Stroll the trail a ways, at least through the tunnel, beyond which you leave downtown behind and emerge into a new world: the grand sweep of the Arm, tidal flats, railroad tracks, and a residential neighborhood. On warm summer evenings this trail is more like a freeway, with people on every kind of wheels imaginable: bike riders, inline skaters, skateboarders, and babies in carriages. In winter, they trade the wheels for skis. The Coastal Trail gets especially crowded around duck-filled **Westchester Lagoon,** a mile south of downtown, and the city's favorite wintertime ice skating rink.

A second paved path intersects the Coastal Trail at Westchester Lagoon, the **Chester Creek Trail,** which creates another greenbelt across Anchorage. This one heads east along the creek, continuing for five miles to the University of Alaska at Anchorage campus.

BEYOND DOWNTOWN
Alaska Native Heritage Center

Located on a 26-acre site facing the Chugach Mountains, the Alaska Native Heritage Center (907/330-8000 or 800/315-6608, www.alaskanative.net) provides an excellent introduction to Native culture in the state. The central "Welcome House" has a variety of exhibits and is used for concerts and demonstrations. Outside, five traditional village settings have been recreated around a small lake, and Native guides explain Alaska's various cultures. The center is open daily 9 A.M.–6 P.M. mid-May–September, and admission costs $21 for adults, $19 for seniors, $16 for ages 7–16, and free for kids under seven. The remainder of the year, the main building (but not the village settings around the lake) is open Saturdays only, noon–5 P.M., and costs $9 for adults, $6 for kids. The Heritage Center is east of downtown near the intersection of the Glenn Highway and Muldoon Road. Get there on the free summertime shuttle from the visitor center downtown.

feeding ducks at Westchester Lagoon

Heritage Museum

Housed in the lobby of the Wells Fargo bank in Midtown, the Alaska Heritage Library and Museum (Northern Lights Blvd. and C St., 907/265-2834, www.wellsfargohistory.com/museums, free admission) is one of the state's largest privately owned collections of Alaskan artifacts and books. Open Monday–Friday noon–5 P.M. from late May to early September, and Monday–Friday noon–4 P.M. the rest of the year, it will keep you spellbound for hours, if you have the time. Only a handful of the highlights—many Native baskets, parkas made from bird skins and walrus intestines, Sydney Laurence's paintings, Nome and Fairbanks newspapers from the early 1900s, and bookcases filled with rare books and maps. This little gem of a museum is not to be missed.

Up in the Air

The **Alaska Aviation Heritage Museum** (4721 Aircraft Dr., 907/248-5325, www.alaskaairmuseum.com) is off the Lake Hood exit from International Airport Road. June through mid-September, it's open Wednesday–Monday 10 A.M.–6 P.M., and for groups only the rest of the year. Entrance costs $5 for adults, $4 for seniors, $3 for ages 4–12, and free for kids under four. This unusual museum displays 25 vintage aircraft—including a 1936 Stinson A Trimotor—as well as Japanese artifacts from the World War II Aleutian Island battles and historical photos. The theater shows videos on early aviation in Alaska. The museum fronts on **Lake Hood,** the world's largest seaplane base, where floatplanes take off and land almost constantly in the summer.

One of the nation's busiest airfields is **Merrill Field,** on the east side of town along the Glenn Highway. There are more than 230,000 takeoffs and landings each year here; overall, Alaska has 16 times as many aircraft per capita as the Lower 48 states! (But it also has a far higher airplane accident rate.)

Other Sights

Earthquake Park, out West Northern Lights Boulevard near the airport, has interpretive signs about the Big One on Good Friday 1964, and a view of the skyline and the Chugach Mountains.

But the views are even more dramatic from **Point Woronzof,** another mile or so out. Tony Knowles Coastal Trail parallels the coast along Earthquake Park and Point Woronzof; it continues from downtown all the way south to **Kincaid Park.** And speaking of Kincaid, the trails here are a destination for hikers and mountain bikers all summer, and cross-country skiers when the snow flies.

The **Alaska Botanical Garden** (907/770-3692, www.alaskabg.org, no charge) covers 11 acres of land at Campbell Airstrip Road off Tudor Road. You'll find more than 480 varieties of plants spread across perennial, rock, and herb gardens that create an extraordinary variety of flowering plants. An information kiosk is at the entrance, and a pleasant one-mile nature trail leads through the grounds.

The **St. Innocent Russian Orthodox Church** (6724 E. 4th Ave.) is one of the most dramatic churches in Alaska. Check out the 12 onion-shaped domes, or attend a Sunday service to view the interior. Russian Orthodoxy is not just history, but a living, breathing, dynamic religious organization, with over 90 parishes and roughly 20,000 members in Alaska. Based in Sitka, the Alaskan Orthodox Church is the mother diocese of the church in the Western Hemisphere.

Alaska Zoo

Located two miles east of New Seward Highway, the zoo (4731 O'Malley Rd., 907/346-3242, www.alaskazoo.com, daily 9 A.M.–6 P.M. summer, daily 10 A.M.–5 P.M. rest of the year) is connected by a special hourly bus from the Transit Center. Entrance is $8 for adults, $7 for seniors, $5 for ages 13–18, $4 for ages 3–11, and free for tots. The zoo is not too bad from a human standpoint—nice grounds, enjoyable shady paths, bridges over creeks, and all the Alaskan animals, plus a number of other critters (including, inexplicably, an elephant). From the animals' perspective, however, this—like many zoos—is a pretty sad place. A cage is a cage is a cage. If you have kids, they'll enjoy it, especially the star attractions: Oreo the brown bear and Ahpun the polar bear. Personally, I'd skip the zoo and continue out O'Malley Road to nearby Chugach State Park, where you can see wildlife in the wild.

Recreation

SUMMER

Hiking

One of the most popular hiking trails in Alaska is the 1.5-mile path to the summit of **Flattop Mountain** within Chugach State Park. The trailhead is on the southeastern edge of Anchorage, so you'll need a car to get there. For a description of this and other hiking trails around Anchorage, see *Chugach State Park.*

The **Alaska Mountaineering Club** (907/272-1811, www.mcak.org) holds meetings at 7:30 P.M. on the third Wednesday of each month at the Pioneer Schoolhouse (3rd Ave. and Eagle St.). Visitors are welcome to enjoy the presentations, and it only costs $10 to join the club and go along on any of their frequent outings.

The University of Alaska Anchorage's **Alaska Outdoor & Experimental Education** (907/786-4083, www.uaa.edu/aoee) offers reasonably priced classes in camping, backpacking, natural history, skiing, and many other subjects throughout the year. Most of these involve expeditions to various parts of Alaska, some right next door, others as far away as the Brooks Range. Unfortunately, the program has a huge black mark against it: a horrific 1997 climbing accident that killed two students and seriously injured several others. A close friend of mine—Mary Ellen Fogarty—died because of disastrous mistakes by the instructors; this book is dedicated to her memory.

Biking

Anchorage has 200 miles of urban cycling/jogging trails; pick up bike trail maps at the downtown visitor center. A delightfully easy ride—it's all paved—goes 11 miles from the west end of 2nd Avenue along the Tony Knowles Coastal Trail, past Westchester Lagoon, Earthquake Park, and Point Woronzof, and then all the way to Kincaid Park at Point Campbell, out on the western tip of the city. The Chester Creek Trail meets the Coastal Trail at Westchester Lagoon and takes you almost five miles to Goose Lake, where you can take a dip if you're hot. Or just bomb around

to wherever the wind blows you. Note, however, that the major Anchorage arteries are not especially bike-friendly, so you may want to stick to the side streets to avoid contending with exhaust fumes and speeding pickup trucks. Dirt biking/hiking trails abound within Kincaid Park, Hillside Park, and Far North Bicentennial Park, or you can head up Powerline Pass Trail inside Chugach State Park, Eklutna Lake (bike rentals available onsite), or out the 40-mile Resurrection Pass from the town of Hope.

Based in Anchorage, the **Arctic Bicycle Club** (907/566-0177, www.arcticbike.org) organizes races and tours, and has a very helpful website. For mountain bike rentals, try **The Bicycle Shop** (1035 W. Northern Lights Blvd., 907/272-5219), **The Bike Exchange** (211 E. 4th Ave., 907/276-2453), **Downtown Bicycle Rental** (245 W. 5th Ave., 907/279-5293, www.alaska-bike-rentals.com), and **Sunshine Sports** (1231 W. Northern Lights Blvd., 907/272-6444).

Mountain Bike Alaska (907/746-5018 or 866/354-2453, www.mountainbikealaska.com, $95–119) guides all-day bike trips into backcountry areas around Anchorage.

River Rafting

Two companies lead white-water trips down the wild Sixmile Creek near Hope: **Chugach Outdoor Center** (907/277-7238 or 866/277-7238, www.chugachoutdoorcenter.com) and **Nova Riverrunners** (907/745-5753 or 800/746-5753, www.novalaska.com). The latter also has trips on the Matanuska River east of Palmer.

Rock-Climbing

Climbing walls are at **Alaska Rock Gym** (4840 Fairbanks St., 907/562-7265, www.alaskarock-gym.com), with a considerably smaller version at **Alaska Pacific University** (907/564-8308, www.alaskapacific.edu). The Rock Gym has classes, a pro shop, locker rooms, and a weight room. Quite impressive. For the real thing, most folks head south to Turnagain Arm or north to Hatcher Pass. For specifics, check with folks at

AMH or REI. Turnagain Arm is also extremely popular with ice-climbers in the winter months.

Bird-Watching

Anchorage is home to a surprising diversity of bird species in the summer. The **Anchorage Audubon Society** (907-276-7034, www.anchorageaudubon.org), offers bird-watching field trips and a bird hotline (907/338-2473) with the latest unusual sightings. Experts at **Bird Watching Tours of Anchorage** 907/248-7282 or 888/334-7282, www.anchoragebirding.com, 4 hours $75) guide birders to local hot spots where you're likely to see Pacific loons, alder flycatchers, red necked phalaropes, bald eagles, and other species.

Flightseeing

The best way to get a bird's-eye view of the Anchorage area is from a bird's-eye vantage point: in an airplane. Anchorage has a large number of companies offering flightseeing; see the Yellow Pages under "Aircraft Charter" for the full list. Two respected Lake Hood operations have been around for many years: **Rust's Flying Service** (907/243-1595 or 800/544-2299, www.flyrusts.com) and **Regal Air** (907/243-8535, www.alaska.net/~regalair). The following long-established companies fly out of Merrill Field: **Jayhawk Air** (907/276-4404), **Spernak Airways** (907/272-9475, www.spernakairways.com), and **VernAir** (907/258-7822, www.alaskavernair.com). **Era Helicopters** (907/266-8351 or 800/843-1947, www.flightseeingtours.com) is based at the airport.

Typical flights include a 90-minute flight over the Chugach Mountains and Knik Glacier for $180 per person; a three-hour flight over Prince William Sound and Columbia Glacier for $240 (including a remote water landing); and a three-hour flight over Mt. McKinley for $300 (including a glacier landing). The air taxis also feature fly-in fishing trips, primarily to the Susitna River area, where Rust's has rental cabins available. Also popular are bear-viewing day trips out of Anchorage; these generally run around $570 per person. Charter service may be the way to go if you have a group of four or more people and a

specific destination, such as a public cabin in Chugach National Forest.

Fishing

Although Anchorage sits along Cook Inlet, wild tides and strong winds create notoriously treacherous conditions. As a result, there are no charter boat fishing operations out of Anchorage. A popular salmon-fishing stream, **Ship Creek,** flows right through downtown, and has good runs of king salmon (late May–July) and silver salmon (Aug.–mid-Sept.). You can also rub shoulders with fellow anglers in mid-summer at **Bird Creek,** 25 miles south of town on the Seward Highway.

The downtown visitor center has brochures for many sportfishing options on the Kenai Peninsula, just a couple of hours by car from Anchorage. To figure out where the fish are running, or what the local regulations are, call Fish and Game (907/344-0541, recorded message 907/349-4687) or visit the Public Lands Information Center downtown for a copy of the fishing regulations. Both the *Anchorage Daily News* (www.adn.com/outdoors) and the *Anchorage Press* publish weekly fishing reports for the Anchorage area.

Increasingly popular are fly-in fishing trips. All the local air-taxi services offer guided or unguided trips to nearby rivers and lakes for world-class salmon fishing.

Swimming

The big news in Anchorage is **H2Oasis Indoor Waterpark** (907/522-4420, www.h2oasiswaterpark.com), which opened in 2003. On busy weekends half the kids in town seem to be there, splashing in the wave pool, shooting jets of water at each other from the pirate ship, gliding down "Lazy River," and riding the roller-coaster-like Master Blaster water ride. Hot tubs are reserved for the over-16 set. Entrance is $20 for ages 13 and up, $15 for ages 2–12, and free for tots.

If you're lucky enough to be in Anchorage during a hot spell and want to cool off under the bright blue sky, head out to **Lake Spenard/Lake Hood** (the two are actually one connected lake) down Spenard Road toward the airport, then right on Lakeshore Drive. **Jewel**

Lake also has swimming on Dimond Boulevard between Jewel Lake and Sand Lake Roads in the southwest corner of the city. The most developed outdoor swimming is at **Goose Lake,** out Northern Lights between Lake Otis and Bragaw near the University of Alaska Anchorage, on the bike trail, with basketball courts, changing room and toilets, and a snack bar.

If you're in the mood for a swim anytime, Anchorage is a good place to experience Alaska's love affair with Olympic-size indoor pools. There are seven to choose from–five at the various high schools; call 907/343-4474 for locations and times. Other pools are at Alaska Pacific University (APU) and the University of Alaska Anchorage (UAA). With its high ceiling, taut diving boards, and hard-body swimmers, the **UAA pool** (907/786-1231), is easily the finest in Alaska. The cost is $5 for adults, $3 for kids under 12. For the same price you also get access to the other facilities here, including a fine ice rink, weight room, saunas, racquetball courts, and gym.

Ice-Skating

Anchorage is wild about ice-skating and hockey. The **UAA Seawolves** (907/786-1293, www.uaa.alaska.edu) and the semipro **Alaska Aces** (907/258-2237, www.alaskaaces.com) attract crowds all season, and the area has five indoor rinks. All are open year-round and offer skate rentals as well as instruction: **Ben Boeke Ice Arena** (334 E. 16th, 907/274-5715) in the Sullivan Arena, **Dempsey Anderson Ice Arena** (1741 W. Northern Lights Blvd., 907/277-7571), **Fire Lake Recreation Center** (Eagle River, 907/688-4641), **UAA Sports Center** (2801 Providence Dr., 907/786-1233), and **Dimond Ice Chalet** (800 E. Dimond, 907/344-1212) in the Dimond Mall. Two of these—Ben Boeke and Fire Lake—are Olympic-size hockey rinks.

Golf

There are four Anchorage-area public golf courses: **Anchorage Golf Course** (907/522-3363) on lower hillside in South Anchorage, **Russian Jack Springs** (5200 DeBarr Rd., 907/343-6992), **Tanglewood Lakes Golf Club** (11701 Brayton Dr., 907/345-4600), and **Moose**

Run (27000 Arctic Valley Rd., 907/428-0056). The last two are on military bases, but are open to the general public as well.

WINTER

Contrary to popular belief, Alaska—and Anchorage in particular—does not go into hibernation for the long months of winter. Instead, many locals look forward to the cold and snow because of the wonderful outdoor activities they bring. Anchorage is a national center for cross-country skiing, dogsledding, skijoring (skiing behind a dog), hockey, and all sorts of other winter fun.

Visitors soon discover what the residents already know—the city is blessed with excellent facilities for all of these. There are dogsled race tracks; dozens of miles of free, groomed ski trails; several excellent ice rinks; and three downhill ski areas, including the state's best resort—Alyeska. Add in such events as the Iditarod and Fur Rendezvous, the college and semipro hockey games, and it's easy to see why more and more visitors are coming to Anchorage in the winter.

Downhill Skiing

Alpine skiers and snowboarders head 37 miles south of Anchorage to **Alyeska Resort** (907/754-1111 or 800/880-3880; www.alyeskaresort.com) for the finest skiing to be found, and some of the deepest snow at any American resort. (See the *Girdwood* section later in this chapter for details.)

Hilltop Ski Area (907/346-1407 or 907/346-1446, www.hilltopskiarea.org, daily until 10 P.M.) is right on the edge of town at Abbott Road near Hillside Drive, and consists of a small chairlift and a rope tow. It has lights for night skiing, and is a favorite place to learn skiing or to play around without having to suffer the 45-minute drive to Alyeska. Tickets cost $24 for adults, $22 for students, free for kids under eight skiing with an adult.

A bit farther afield is **Alpenglow at Arctic Valley** (907/428-1208 or 907/569-4754; www.skialpenglow.com). Rates are $18 for adults, $10 for ages 7–18, $9 for seniors, and free for kids under seven. There are two chairlifts, a T-bar,

snowboarder at Alyeska Resort

and a rope tow, providing a wide range of slopes and conditions. More adventurous skiers turn left from the uppermost lift and ski into often-untracked powder in the upper bowls. Arctic Valley is only open weekends and holidays, generally from early November to mid-April.

Downhill skis and snowboards can be rented from REI (907/272-4565) and the various ski areas.

Sledders of all ages play on the steep powerline slope that cuts along the road up to Arctic Valley, with parents taking kids back uphill in their cars. Another great sledding hill (600-foot run) is in Centennial Park. Popular short sledding hills are at Kincaid Park and Service High School.

Cross-Country Skiing

Any Anchorageite over the age of four seems to be involved in cross-country skiing in one form or another. The city is laced with trails that serve as summertime cycling and jogging paths and wintertime ski routes. Most of these are groomed, with set tracks for traditional cross-country skiers and a wider surface for the skate-skiing crowd. Skate-skiing is getting more popular each year, and skijorers are also often seen on the Coastal Trail in this dog-happy town (dogs aren't allowed on most ski trails).

The **Nordic Skiing Association of Anchorage** (907/276-7609, www.anchoragenordicski.com) is Alaska's largest cross-country association, and its website has all sorts of information on the sport. Pick up *The Alaska Nordic Skier* at local ski shops and newsstands; it's published October–April each year.

The best-known cross-country area is **Kincaid Park,** where a convoluted maze of paths cover the rolling terrain, offering fun for all levels of ability. Kincaid is considered one of the top three competitive ski venues in America. You can warm up inside the Kincaid chalet and enjoy the vistas of Sleeping Lady and Mt. McKinley.

Russian Jack Springs Park, near Debarr Road and Boniface Parkway, has many more groomed ski trails, as well as a small rope tow and a warming house.

Several more miles of groomed trails await at **Hillside Park** off Abbot Road next to Hilltop Ski Area; watch out for the moose here. All these trails are groomed for both traditional cross-country and the faster skate skis, which are becoming increasingly popular. Rent cross-country skis from REI (907/272-4565) or AMH (907/272-1811).

SAFETY IN AVALANCHE COUNTRY

Skiing and snowmobiling are becoming increasingly popular in Alaska's limitless backcountry. Unfortunately, many of these winter outdoor enthusiasts fail to take necessary precautions before heading out. Given the heavy snowfalls that occur, the steep slopes the snow piles up on, and the high winds that accompany many storms, it should come as no surprise that avalanches are a real danger in Alaska. Nearly all avalanches are triggered by the victims. This is particularly true for snowmobilers who often attempt such dangerous practices as "high-marking"—riding as high as they can up steep slopes—and are killed in avalanches that result.

If you really want to avoid avalanches, ski only on groomed trails or "bombproof" slopes that, because of aspect, shape, and slope angle, never seem to slide. Unfortunately, this isn't always possible, so backcountry skiers (and snowmobilers) need to understand the conditions that lead to avalanches. The best way to learn is from a class such as the avalanche safety programs taught by the **Alaska Mountain Safety Center** (907/345-3566, www.alaskaavalanche.com) in Anchorage, or Juneau's **Southeast Alaska Avalanche Center** (907/586-5699, www.avalanche.org/~seaac). Learn more at www.avalanche.org, including information on avalanches and course offerings around the nation.

Heading Out
An avalanche safety course is extremely valuable, but you can also help protect yourself by following these precautions when you head into the backcountry:

• Before leaving, get up-to-date avalanche information. On the Web, you can visit www.avalanche.org for links to avalanche-forecasting sites throughout the western states. The **Chugach National Forest Avalanche Information Center** (907/754-2369, www.fs.fed.us) has current snow conditions for the Kenai Peninsula; it's updated twice a week in the winter.

• Be sure to carry extra warm clothes, water, high-energy snacks, a dual-frequency avalanche transceiver (make sure it's turned on and that you know how to use it!), a lightweight snow shovel (for digging snow pits, or emergency snow shelters, or for excavating avalanche victims), first-aid supplies, a Leatherman knife, topographic map, extra plastic ski tip, flashlight, matches, and compass. Many skiers also carry that cure-all, duct tape, wrapped around a ski pole. Let someone know exactly where you are going and when you expect to return. It's also a wise idea to carry special ski poles that extend into probes in case of an avalanche.

• Check the angle of an area before you ski through it; slopes of 30–45 degrees are the most dangerous, while lesser slopes do not slide as frequently.

• Watch the weather; winds over 15 mph can pile snow much more deeply on lee slopes, causing dangerous loading on the snowpack. Especially avoid skiing on or below cornices.

• Avoid skiing on the leeward side (the side facing into the wind) of ridges, where snow loading can be greatest.

• Be aware of gullies and bowls; they're more likely to slip than flat open slopes or ridgetops. Stay out of gullies at the bottom of wide bowls; these are natural avalanche chutes.

• Look out for cracks in the snow, and listen for hollow snow underfoot. These are strong signs of dangerous conditions.

• Look at the trees. Smaller trees may indicate that avalanches rip through an area frequently, knocking over the larger trees. Avalanches can, however, also run through forested areas.

• Know how much new snow has fallen recently. Heavy new snow over older, weak snow layers is a sure sign of extreme danger on potential avalanche slopes. Most avalanches slip during or immediately after a storm.

• Learn how to dig a snow pit and how to read the various snow layers. Particularly important are the very weak layers of depth hoar or surface hoar that have been buried under heavy new snow.

Backcountry Skiing

If you're more ambitious—and have the wheels to get there—you'll find incredible backcountry skiing all around Anchorage. The Chugach Mountains offer an endless choice of skiing options that last from mid-October all the way into late June in some places. Note, however, that these areas are *not* for novices, so don't head out without knowing about and being prepared for such dangers as avalanches and hypothermia. Quite a number of skiers (and more snowmobilers) have died in the mountain avalanches near Anchorage. Even such favorites as the nearby summit of Flattop Mountain have taken a high human toll over the years.

The best-known backcountry areas are in Chugach State Park and at Turnagain Pass and Hatcher Pass. Access to **Chugach State Park** is the same as in the summer; pick up a winter routes map from the state park office. **Turnagain Pass** is 60 miles southwest of Anchorage on the way to Seward. The west side of the road is open to snowmachiners, but tele-skiers avoid them by heading to the east side. There's a big parking lot, and from here you can continue into the open meadows or high into the mountains for deep, untracked powder.

Located 70 miles northeast of Anchorage, **Hatcher Pass** is a favorite backcountry area, and serves as a training area for the U.S. National Cross-Country Ski Team. The road can sometimes be a bit treacherous if you don't have studded tires, so be sure to call the park for road conditions (907/745-2827).

REI in Anchorage offers cross-country and telemark clinics.

Dog Mushing

There are all sorts of dogsled races in Anchorage each winter, from teens' competitions all the way up to the world-famous Iditarod. If you want to try it on your own, several local operators offer tours. A few even let you drive a small team of dogs; trying to control a full team of eight or more huskies requires a pro. Anchorage-area mushers to contact include **Alaska's Trails and Tails** (907/373-1408 or 888/300-6874, www.dogsledtours.com) in Wasilla, **Chugach Express Dog Sled Tours** (907/786-2266, www.alaskasnowdogs.com) in Girdwood, **Susitna Dog Tours** (907/495-6324, www.susitnadogtours.com), and **Plettner Sled Dog Kennels** (907/892-6944 or 877/892-6944, www.plettner-kennels.com) in Wasilla.

Accommodations and Camping

As might be expected in a city of more than a quarter-million people, Anchorage has a wide range of lodging options. Unfortunately, most of these also have Alaskan-sized prices. A good one-stop place to begin your search for local lodging is the Anchorage Convention & Visitors Bureau website (www.anchorage.net). Be sure to make Anchorage lodging reservations far ahead for July and August, or try bidding at www.priceline.com for last-minute deals.

UNDER $50

A tolerable option for shoestring travelers is the **Anchorage Youth Hostel** (700 H St., 907/276-3635, www.alaska.net/~hianch). This 100-bed facility is open for check-in 7:30 A.M.–noon and

2 P.M.–midnight, but the rooms are closed between 10 A.M. and 5 P.M. (though the lobby and kitchen remain open). At $20 for AYH members and $23 for nonmembers, it fills up *fast* in the summer. A few private couple's rooms are available at $40 d for members, $46 d for nonmembers. Reservations are strongly advised for the summer. There's a four-night maximum stay in summer, and you must be out by noon. Curfew is 1 A.M. The hostel has a kitchen, common rooms, washers, dryers, and baggage storage. Bed linen is provided. The hostel also provides reasonable wintertime long-term lodging rates.

Another cheap and popular option is **Spenard Hostel International** (2845 W. 42nd Pl., 907/248-5036, www.alaskahostel.org, $16), where 42 dorm spaces are spread through four apartments. Things are less restrictive than at the youth hostel, and there's no curfew. Spenard Hostel has three kitchens, and weekly rates are available. They rent bikes, have space for tents, plus potluck dinners on Sunday and Wednesday nights. Sheets and blankets provided.

The managers at **International Backpackers Hostel** (3601 Peterkin St., Unit A, 907/274-3870), maintain houses on the northeast side of Anchorage in the Mountain View area. These contain 30 beds in coed or same-sex dorm rooms for $15, including a full kitchen. No curfew, private rooms, or alcohol. Tent spaces are $12, and short-term bag storage is available. The location is not as central as the AYH hostel, but is an easy bus ride from downtown. One major drawback is that Mountain View is the most crime-ridden section of Anchorage, though the Backpackers Inn is in one of the better parts of that neighborhood. Not everyone is comfortable staying in Mountain View, but the inn is well maintained and open all day.

Popular with outdoor enthusiasts, **Anchorage Guesthouse** (2001 Hillcrest Dr., 907/274-0408, www.akhouse.com) has a fine location above Westchester Lagoon and near the Coastal Trail. Inside are two private rooms ($74 d), and three bunk rooms ($28 per person) with shared baths. A make-it-yourself breakfast is available, and all guests can use the living room, dining room, kitchen, and sunroom. Bike rentals and internet access are available, along with a big garage to store your kayak, camping gear, bikes, and more. Owner Andy Baker is an accomplished singer/songwriter. Highly recommended.

$50–100

Located in Midtown, **Qupqugiaq Inn** (640 W. 36th Ave., 907/562-5681, www.qupq.com) occupies the upstairs of a boxy building. Accommodations are cramped and Spartan, but everything is well maintained and guests have access to the communal kitchen. This is a good place for couples on a budget. Rooms with shared bath are $50 s, $62 d; add $20 for a private bath.

Hillside Motel (2150 Gambell St., 907/258-6006 or 800/478-6008, www.hillside-alaska.com) is a modest Midtown place with a mix of reasonably priced rooms: $95–109 d for standard rooms with microwaves and fridges, $129 for a kitchenette that sleeps four, $139 for a six-person suite, and $159 for a four-person cabin.

A number of Anchorage B&Bs also have rooms (with breakfast) for under $100 d.

$100–150

Merrill Field Inn (420 Sitka St., 907/276-4547 or 800/898-4547, www.merrillfieldinn.com, $110–126 d) has large and modern rooms including continental breakfast, fridges, microwaves, and free airport and downtown transport in the summer. A suite ($145 d) includes a king bed and jacuzzi tub. Recommended.

Far from the center of town at New Seward Highway and Tudor Street in South Anchorage, **Parkwood Inn** (907/563-3590 or 800/478-3590, www.home.gci.net/~sncparkwood) is a fine option for families. All of the apartment-style rooms include full kitchens with dishes. Standard rooms are $130–140 d, and apartment suites cost $150 d.

Lakeshore Motor Inn (3009 Lakeshore Dr., 907/248-3485 or 800/770-3000, www.lakeshore-motorinn.com) is a quiet motel near the airport with standard rooms for $129–139 s or d, rooms with kitchenettes for $149 d, and one-bedroom suites at $169 d. Free airport transport, too. All rooms contain fridges.

Out near the airport, **Microtel Inn & Suites** (5205 Northwood Dr., 907/245-5002 or 888/680-4500, www.microtelinn.com) charges $120–140 d in standard rooms, or $150 d in minisuites with fridges and microwaves. A continental breakfast is included, and an airport shuttle is provided. Off-season rates are very reasonable, and guests will appreciate the indoor Jacuzzis and large rooms.

Copper Whale Inn (440 L St., 907/258-7999, www.copperwhale.com) is downtown along "lawyer row" next to Simon and Seafort's. This nicely appointed 15-room inn/B&B has a couple of rooms that share a bath for $125 d, but most have private baths and run $185 d.

There are good views across Cook Inlet from the sitting room, and a light breakfast is included.

The **Anchorage Grand Hotel** (505 W 2nd Ave., 907/929-8888 or 888/800-0640, www.anchoragegrandhotel.com, $139 for up to four) is a cozy all-suites hotel with reasonable prices, including a continental breakfast.

Another moderately priced option is **Anchorage Uptown Suites** (234 E. 2nd Ave., 907/279-4232 or 800/478-4232, www.alaskan.com/anchorageuptownsuites), with standard rooms for $139, one-bedroom apartments with kitchens for $149 d, and deluxe suites with fireplace, king bed, and jacuzzi tub for $189 d. German spoken.

Long House Alaskan Hotel (4335 Wisconsin St., 907/243-2133 or 888/243-2133, www.longhousehotel.com) is a large log-sided building near the airport where spacious rooms are $149–160 d, and suites go for $189 d. Free airport shuttle and continental breakfast.

Other mid-range places worth a look include **Puffin Place Suites** (1058 W. 27th Ave., 907/279-1058 or 800/478-3346, www.puffininn.net), **Sourdough Lodge** (801 Erickson St., 907/279-4148 or 800/478-3030, www.alaskasourdoughlodge.com), and **Executive Suite Hotel** (4360 Spenard Rd., 907/243-6366 or 800/770-6366, www.executivesuitehotel.com).

OVER $150

Built in 1953 but newly remodeled, **Inlet Tower Suites** (1200 L St., 907/276-0110 or 800/544-0786, www.inlettower.com) is a 14-story tower atop a hill halfway between downtown and Midtown. Rooms are nicely furnished and spacious, and with great views of the mountains or Cook Inlet from higher floors. Rooms with microwaves and fridges are $169–199 d; suites cost $259 d. Free airport or railroad transportation is included.

Anchorage Hotel (330 E St., 907/272-4553 or 800/544-0988, www.historicanchoragehotel.com) is a classy little 26-room hotel that was built in 1916, and is now on the National Register of Historic Places. The rooms have been brought up to date, and all have stocked mini-

bars. Standard rooms cost $199 d suites $239 d; including continental breakfast.

Sheraton Anchorage Hotel (401 E. 6th Ave., 907/276-8700 or 800/325-3535, www.sheraton.com, $240 d) is a 16-story downtown hotel with comfortable rooms (better views as you go higher), a sauna, jacuzzi, and exercise equipment. The lobby houses Ptarmigan Bar & Grill, with gourmet buffets for breakfast ($11) and dinner ($30).

The **Anchorage Marriott Downtown Hotel** (820 W. 7th Ave., 907/279-8000 or 800/228-9290, www.marriott.com) has nearly 400 rooms spread over 20 floors. Spacious rooms have big windows and a bright decor, and amenities include a fitness center, an indoor pool, hot tub, and business center. Rates are $259 d for standard rooms, $299 d with breakfast and evening snacks for nicer rooms with access to the concierge lounge, and $425–675 for suites.

Hotel Captain Cook (5th Ave. and K St., 907/276-6000 or 800/843-1950, www.captaincook.com), occupies an entire block, with three towers and three restaurants. The hotel is owned by the family of former governor Wally Hickel, who also served as President Nixon's Secretary of Interior in the 1970s. The hotel's 550 rooms follow a nautical theme (befitting the name), and the building has an old-money feeling with dark woods and lots of suits and power ties. Hotel amenities include concierge service and a full athletic club with hot tub, sauna, and indoor pool. Rates start at $245 d for a standard room or $275 for junior suites, and rise to $610 d for a two-bedroom suite. For those really looking to splurge, the $1,500-a-night Crow's Nest Suite covers almost 1,700 square feet, and features a stunning 19th-floor view.

Alaska's largest hotel (almost 600 rooms), the **Anchorage Hilton Hotel** (500 W. 3rd Ave., 907/272-7411 or 800/445-8667, www.anchoragehilton.com, $284 s, $304 d) is another downtown skyscraper (of sorts). The hotel is a major stop on the cruise ship travel circuit, and has a big lobby that stars a shockingly large stuffed grizzly and up-to-date rooms with equally shocking rates. Other features include an indoor pool, sauna, hot tub, health club, and free airport shuttle. Ask for an upper level north-side room for in-your-face views of the F-15 jets landing at Elmendorf Air Force Base (not to mention Mt. McKinley on a clear day).

Millennium Alaskan Hotel (4800 Spenard Rd., 907/243-2300 or 800/544-0553, www.millennium-hotels.com) sits along Anchorage's floatplane headquarters, Lake Hood, and has very comfortable rooms and an Alaskan decor. The lobby is decked out in trophy heads and fish, with a stone fireplace in the center. Rooms are modern and stylish, $260–300 s or $280–320 d; jacuzzi suites for $350–375 s or $370–400 d. Also offered are an exercise facility, jacuzzi, sauna, and free airport and downtown shuttle. The restaurant has a deck right on the water, and serves a popular Sunday brunch. It's a ways from town, but the Millennium has a cozier feeling than most other large Anchorage hotels.

ALL-SUITES HOTELS

Anchorage's newest corporate boxes are geared to business travelers and families looking for more space who don't mind the inevitable this-could-be-Tacoma atmosphere. These places typically have one room with two queen beds and a separate sitting room with pull-out sofa, plus a microwave and fridge. All also include indoor pools, hot tubs, exercise facilities, a breakfast buffet, and free airport shuttle. Summer rates average $210 d.

Downtown places are **Aspen Hotel** (108 E. 8th Ave., 907/868-1605 or 866/483-7848, www.aspenhotelsak.com); **Hawthorn Suites** (1110 W. 8th Ave., 907/222-5005 or 888/469-6575, www.hawthorn.com) and **Clarion Suites** (325 W. 8th Ave., 907/274-1000 or 888/389-6675, www.clarioninn.com). Five Midtown places have similar facilities and prices: **Dimond Center Hotel** (700 E Dimond Blvd., 907/770-5000 or 866/770-5002, www.dimondcenterhotel.com), **Hilton Garden Inn** (4540 A St., 907/562-7000 or 800/445-8667, www.hilton.com), **SpringHill Suites by Marriott** (3401 A St., 907/562-3247 or 888/287-9400, www.springhillsuites.com), **Residence Inn by Marriott** (1025 35th Ave., 907/563-9844 or 888/331-3131, www.residenceinn.com), and **Hampton Inn** (4301 Credit Union Dr., 907/550-7000 or 800/426-7866, www.hamptoninn.com).

BED-AND-BREAKFASTS

Anchorage had over 175 B&Bs at last count, including luxurious hillside homes with spectacular vistas, cozy older downtown places, and rent-out-the-spare-room suburban houses. An excellent starting point when looking for a local B&B is the **Anchorage Alaska B&B Association** (907/272-5909 or 888/584-5147, www.anchorage-bnb.com). Its website has links to 60 or so B&Bs, with location and price details. See the *Anchorage Visitors Guide* (available from ACVB's Visitor Information Center downtown or on the web at www.anchorage.net) for a fairly complete listing of local B&Bs, or take a look at the blizzard of B&B brochures filling visitors center racks. If the task seems too daunting on your own, contact **Alaska Private Lodgings/Stay With a Friend** (907/235-2148 or 888/235-2148, www.alaskabandb.com) or **Alaska Sourdough B&B Association** (907/563-6244).

The following are a few recommended B&Bs in the under–$120 d price range: **Aurora B&B** (907/562-2411), **Earth B&B** (907/279-9862, www.alaskaone.com/earthbb), **Gallery B&B** (907/274-2567), **K Street B&B** (907/279-1443), **Oscar Gill House B&B** (907/279-1344, www.oscargill.com), **Susitna Place B&B** (907/274-3344, www.susitnaplace.com), **12th and L B&B** (907/276-1225, www.anchorage-lodging.com), and **Wandering Moose B&B** (907/522-3780, www.alaskawanderingmoose.com).

Recommended finer B&Bs (most over $120 d) with additional amenities include **Alaskan Frontier Gardens B&B** (907/345-655, www.alaskafrontiergardens.com), **All the Comforts of Home B&B** (907/345-4279, www.alaska.net/~comforts), **Aurora Winds B&B** (907/346-2533, www.aurorawinds.com), **B&B on the Park** (907/277-0878 or 800/353-0878, www.bedandbreakfastonthepark.com), **Camai B&B** (907/333-2219 or 800/659-8763, www.camaibnb.com), **Claddagh Cottage B&B** (907/248-7104, www.claddaghcottage.com),

15 Chandeliers B&B Inn (14020 Sabine St., 907/345-3032, www.15chandeliers.com), Sleeping Lady B&B (545 M St., 907/258-4455, www.anchsleepingladybnb.com), Mahogany Manor (907/278-1111 or 888/777-0346, www.mahoganymanor.com), and North County Castle B&B (14600 Joanne Ct., 907/345-7296, www.castlealaska.com).

CAMPING

The city-run Centennial Park (907/343-6986, www.ci.anchorage.ak.us/parks) has space for both tents and RVs (no hookups), and costs $15, plus $2 for showers. Take Muldoon Road south from the Glenn, hang your first left onto Boundary, then the next left onto the highway frontage road for a half-mile to the campground. It's open late May–September.

Anchorage RV Park (1200 N. Muldoon Rd., 907/338-7275 or 800/400-7275, www.anchrvpark.com) has one of the better RV park locations, a quiet, wooded area on the eastern edge of town near the Alaska Native Heritage Center. Other RV campgrounds are primarily parking lots: Anchorage Ship Creek Landings RV Park (907/277-0877 or 888/778-7700, www.alaskarv.com), Golden Nugget Camper Park (4100 DeBarr Rd., 907/333-5311 or 800/449-2012), Hillside Motel & RV Park (2150 Gambell, 907/258-6006 or 800/478-6008, www.hillside-alaska.com), and John's Motel and RV Park (3543 Mountain View Dr., 907/277-4332 or 800/278-4332, www.johnsmotel.com). Expect to pay around $26–28 with full hookups. Many travelers also park RVs for free in the Wal-Mart and Fred Meyer parking lots; the store managers don't care.

Food

If you can't find a good meal in Anchorage you aren't trying. The city's size and diverse population are mirrored in a wide range of eating places, from grab-a-bite fast-food joints to high-class (and high-priced) gourmet restaurants. To reach many of the best places, you'll need a vehicle or knowledge of the bus schedule, but there are a number of fine restaurants right downtown. Two useful free dining publications are available from racks around town: *Cuisine Scene* and the *Restaurant and Entertainment Guide.* Both are filled with restaurant ads (often with menus) and brief descriptions.

BREAKFAST

Looking for a great downtown breakfast in an unpretentious setting? Head to Snow City Cafe (1034 W. 4th Ave., 907/272-2489), where meals are ample, reasonably priced, and always good. Breakfast is available until the 4 P.M. closing time; try the Mediterranean scramble or huevos rancheros. But get here early on weekends to avoid a wait. Recommended.

Gwennie's Old Alaska Restaurant (4333 Spenard Rd., 907/243-2090) makes the best sourdough pancakes and reindeer sausage in town, with breakfast all day. Meals are Alaska-size, so those with small appetites may want to split an order. Memorabilia crowds the walls on this sprawling two-story place, and big tables fill with families filling up. Dinner specials include all-you-can-eat BBQ for $16.

Hogg Bros. Cafe (1049 W. Northern Lights Blvd., 907/276-9649) serves gigantic breakfasts and burgers, and has a rather impressive collection of pig trinkets. Not surprisingly, the menu is heavy on the fat, featuring 20 different omelets and other artery-cloggers. It's very noisy and crowded on weekends as Alaskans and tourists make pigs of themselves.

Three very good places for a Sunday splurge are Sacks Cafe (328 G St., 907/276-3546, www.sackscafe.com) downtown, Millennium Hotel (4800 Spenard Rd., 907/243-2300 or 800/544-0553, www.millennium-hotels.com), and Josephines (401 E. 6th Ave., 907/276-8700) on the 15th floor of Sheraton Anchorage Hotel. The Millennium's outside deck faces scenic Lake Hood, where you can watch floatplanes take off.

Both Millennium and Josephine's charge $30, while Sacks is à la carte.

BAKERIES AND SWEETS

Some of the best Anchorage breads and pastries come from **Europa Bakery** (601 W. 36th, 907/563-5704), where the rustic, thick-crusted artisan breads compare favorably to anything you might find in Europe. Similarly noteworthy breads and sweets can be found at **L'Aroma Bakeries,** inside both New Sagaya stores.

Great Harvest Bread Co. (570 E. Benson Blvd., 907/274-3331), across from Sears in Midtown, cranks out hefty two-pound loaves for an equally hefty price. Stop by for a free sample slice of the day's best.

Crazy Croissants (1406 W. 31st, 907/278-8787) has a stupid name, but the French pastries are authentic, right down to the French owners. Another notable European-style bakery (wonderful sweets) is **French Oven** (2917 Spenard Rd., 907/563-8989). **The Bagel Factory** (136 W. 34th, 907/561-8871) makes the city's best bagels.

Alaska Wild Berry Products (907/562-8858 or 800/280-2927, www.alaskawildberryproduct.com) has a large chocolate factory and gift shop on Juneau St. near the corner of Old Seward Highway and International Airport Road. This is a fun place for chocoholics; there's even a 20-foot melted-chocolate waterfall. Free taste samples, too. Fifteen-minute tours are given throughout the day, and this is a very popular stop on the Anchorage tour-bus circuit. The big gift shop offers all the standard tourist junk, and then some.

Cold Stone Creamery serves rich ice cream and "add-in" flavors of all types. Its shop at 9001 Jewel Lake Road (907/248-2644), on the south end of town, fills to overflowing on warm summer afternoons.

COFFEE AND TEA

Anchorageites love strong coffee, and the town is packed with espresso stands and cafés of all types. Tucked away in a Midtown shopping mall, **Cafe del Mundo** (341 E. Benson, 907/274-0026, www.cafedelmundo.com) is a favorite of the lawyer/Volvo crowd, and a fine place to while away a morning. Another upscale place is **Cafe Fonte,** with several Anchorage locations; the one in Dover Center (36th Ave. and C St., 907/562-1702) has free Internet access. Tucked inside a shopping mall next to REI, **Middle Way Cafe** (1200 W. Northern Lights Blvd., 907/272-6433) is a surprising little coffeehouse with delicious, mostly vegetarian lunches. Downtown **Side Street Espresso** (412 G St., 907/258-9055) is where the greenie art crowd hangs out.

A personal favorite is the local chain of seven **Kaladi Brothers** espresso shops (www.kaladi.com), including ones inside the New Sagaya groceries and Titlewave Books. The latter, located in the best Anchorage bookstore—at 1360 W. Northern Lights Boulevard next to REI—includes an internet cafe. Many other Alaskan coffee shops buy their espresso beans from Kaladi Brothers.

LUNCH

An Anchorage institution, **Downtown Deli and Cafe** (525 W. 4th Ave., 907/278-7314) opens with sourdough pancakes, omelets, and cheese blintzes, and rolls through the lunch crunch with a wide range of sandwiches (chicken teriyaki to Italian sausage), salads, and seafood. Owner Tony Knowles is a former governor of Alaska. A block away is **Sweet Basil Cafe** (335 E St., 907/274-2434), with cold or hot sandwiches on their freshly baked basil bread, along with juice bar specials, light breakfasts, and lattes.

Sacks Cafe (328 G St., 907/276-3546, www.sackscafe.com), crafts Anchorage's finest lunches (and dinners), and is especially popular with the business crowd. You'll find an arty decor, creative cooking, and heady talk. The menu changes frequently, but typically includes fresh halibut or salmon, baked penne pasta, chipotle sirloin burgers, and chicken curry. Great desserts, too. Reservations are essential for dinner, though they aren't taken for the wine bar.

Marx Bros. Cafe (121 W. 7th Ave., 907/343-6193, www.marxcafe.com) has a wonderful lunch spot inside the Anchorage Museum of History and Art. The setting is hard to beat, an open atrium surrounded by works of art, and the food is equally fine, with homemade soups, fresh salads, and creative sandwiches.

Middle Way Cafe (1200 W. Northern Lights Blvd., 907/272-6433) hides out next to the REI store, but always manages to fill up when lunch arrives. Check out today's specials on the board, order at the counter, and wait for your name to be called. The menu includes vegetarian sandwiches and wraps, soy burgers, salads, and fruit smoothies. The lip-ringed barista will make a mocha while you wait, or serve a big piece of carrot cake. Sundays espresso only.

Don't miss the perpetually crowded **L'Aroma Bakeries** at both New Sagaya stores (in Midtown at 3700 Old Seward Hwy., and near downtown at 900 W. 13th Ave.; www.newsagaya.com) for sandwiches, small pizzas baked in wood-fired ovens, and delightful pastries. Both New Sagayas also house Kaladi Brothers Coffee shops and very good delis that include everything from meatloaf to Chinese specials. You're guaranteed to find something that appeals. Recommended.

Several other Midtown eateries offer quick lunch meal deals. **Atlasta Deli** (701 W. 36th Ave., 907/563-3354) is a good place for sandwiches. **The Bagel Factory** (136 W. 34th, 907/561-8871) has fresh bagel sandwiches and other light meals, and is popular with nearby office workers. **Crazy Croissants** (1406 W. 31st, 907/278-8787) can be a bit hard to find since 31st Avenue is really just an alleyway off Minnesota Drive, but inside you'll find authentic from-scratch French baked goods and lunches.

CHEAP EATS

Several vendors have downtown carts in front of the old Federal Building on 4th Ave. in the summer. The best of these—look for the queue—is the vendor of reindeer sausage and grilled onions. For more downtown fast food, head to the **food court** on the 4th floor of the 5th Avenue Mall at 5th Avenue and C Street. Inside are fast-food eateries of all persuasions, offering Thai, Chinese, deli sandwiches, seafood, frozen yogurt, burritos, and pizza. A few blocks away at 8th and D is the **Federal Building,** where the reasonably priced cafeteria is open weekdays till 3:30 P.M. On summertime Saturdays, get great fast meals at the downtown **Saturday Market.**

You'll find the national grease pits (McD's, Burger King, Wendy's, and Pizza Hut) strung out the east end of town along 6th Avenue, and in Midtown along Benson and Northern Lights. For far better burgers—at reasonable prices—head to **Arctic Roadrunner** (2477 Arctic Blvd., 907/279-7311) or **Tommy's Burger Stop** (W. Benson at Spenard Ave., 907/561-5696).

PIZZA, ITALIAN, AND MEDITERRANEAN

Anchorage has all the pizza chains—Chuck E. Cheese, Domino's, Godfather's, Pizza Hut, and Round Table—and the "Pizza" listing in the Yellow Pages includes some 60 different places. Out of these, **Pizza Olympia** (2809 Spenard Rd., across from REI, 907/561-5264) is a personal favorite. Four generations of the Maroudas family run this place with authentic affection, rolling out such unique offerings as garlic and feta cheese pizzas and Greek specialties.

Two excellent pizza options are **Moose's Tooth Pub and Pizzeria** and **L'Aroma Bakery & Deli.** Other good pizza places include **Sorrento's** (610 E. Fireweed, 907/278-3439), with the best southern Italian food in Anchorage; and **Fletcher's** (in Hotel Captain Cook at 5th Ave. and K St., 907/276-6000), where Anchorage waiters and cooks go after work.

For delicious northern Italian dinners with an Alaskan twist, visit the small **CampoBello Bistro** (601 W. 36th Ave., 907/563-2040, $15–25). This is a relaxing and romantic spot, though the entrées are a bit pricey, and salads are extra. Lunches are a better bargain.

For creative Tuscany-inspired food in the heart of town, you won't go wrong at **Ristorante Orso** (737 W. 5th Ave., www.orsoalaska.com, 907/222-3232, $13–33). This popular restaurant exudes energy, and the menu includes wild mushroom ravioli, osso bucco lamb, and seafood gemelli, along with a dessert selection that stars molten chocolate cake. Open for lunch and dinner.

Aladdin's (4240 Old Seward Hwy. at Tudor, 907/561-2373, www.aladdinsak.com) serves traditional Mediterranean dishes from North Africa and the Middle East, including mousaka, lamb couscous, seafood kebab, and various vegetarian specialties for $11–16. The restaurant has a big local following, with wonderfully different flavors.

ASIAN

Chinese and Korean

Many of Anchorage's Chinese restaurants are actually run by Korean-Americans, who make up a surprisingly large ethnic community in the city. For good and inexpensive Korean kimchee and noodle dishes, take a visit to **Noodle House** (3301 Spenard Rd., 907/563-9880).

Twin Dragon Mongolian Bar-B-Que (612 E. 15th Ave., 907/276-7535) is a fun place where you fill a plate with veggies and meat and watch the chefs do their show. Great fun, and reasonable too; $12 for the dinner buffet.

Golden Pond Restaurant (300 W. 36th, 907/563-5525) has a good all-you-can-eat Chinese buffet for lunch or dinner, as does **Yen King Restaurant** (3501 Old Seward Hwy., 907/563-2627). The latter also offers free delivery around town. **Chinese Kitchen** (2904 Spenard Rd., 907/279-2222) is a tiny family eatery with lunch specials and friendly owners. If you're adventurous, ask about the menu items listed only in Chinese.

A personal favorite is **Fu Du** (2600 E. Tudor Rd., 907/561-6610), where service is efficient and friendly, the setting is cozy, and servings are enormous. Entrees come with soup, Chinese kimchee, rice, eggroll, and tea. Lunch specials are an even better deal, and they offer free delivery.

Thai and South Asian

Anchorage has quite a few Thai restaurants—seven at last count. None of these measures up to what you'd find in Thailand (or Berkeley for that matter), but several are well worth a visit. Hip locals know that the most authentic Thai food is **Thai Kitchen** (3405 E. Tudor, 907/561-0082, www.thaikitchenalaska.com) tucked away in a strip mall on Tudor near Bragaw. Be sure to try the Popeye chicken or any of the spicy soups. The restaurant is open for lunch and dinner on

weekdays, but dinners only on weekends. Get there early since it closes at 9 P.M.

A good lunchtime choice is **Sawaddi Thai** (300 W. 36th Ave., 907/563-8335), where the big Thai lunch buffet (served weekdays) is $8, including salad and dessert. At dinner, try the roast duck special or fresh papaya salad. The owners are Laotian, and also offer specialties from their home country.

Another fun place (housed in an old Dairy Queen) is **Thai House Restaurant** (860 E. 36th Ave., 907/563-8616). Excellent service, and everything is made fresh while you wait. Also recommended is **Thai Orchid Restaurant** (219 E. Dimond Ave., 907/868-5226), with the best pad Thai in town and a diverse and inexpensive menu that includes many vegetarian choices.

Get Vietnamese meals from **Saigon Restaurant** (3561 E. Tudor Rd., 907/563-2515). One of the only Indian restaurants in Alaska, **Bombay Deluxe** (555 W. Northern Lights Blvd., 907/277-1200), has an ample weekday lunch buffet.

Japanese

Get fresh sushi, tempura, and teriyaki from **Peter's Sushi Spot** (3337 Fairbanks St., 907/276-5188) or **Yamato Ya** (3700 Old Seward Hwy. next to New Sagaya, 907/561-2128). Another good place is **Ichiban** (2488 E. Tudor Rd., 907/563-6333), a Japanese restaurant and sushi bar. There's also a **Benihana Restaurant** (8th Ave. and L St., 907/222-5212) franchise where the Japanese chefs show off their cutlery skills; it's inside Hawthorn Suites.

Kumagoro (533 W. 4th Ave., 907/272-9905) is a plant-bedecked downtown restaurant with house-made udon noodle soups, and an evening-only sushi bar. The restaurant fills up for lunch with the business crowd. Local Carrs, Fred Meyer, and New Sagaya supermarkets also have fresh sushi in their delis.

MEXICAN

A longtime favorite—it's the oldest Mexican restaurant in Alaska—is **La Cabaña** (312 E. 4th Ave., 907/272-0135). This is a good place for lunch, with notable halibut fajitas. Three **La Mex** restaurants (900 W. 6th, 907/274-7678; 2552 Spenard Rd., 907/274-7511; and 8330 King St., 907/344-6399), are very popular places for evening nachos and margaritas, or for full meals. Fast service, and the steaks aren't bad, either.

In business since 1972, **Mexico in Alaska** (7305 Old Seward Hwy., 907/349-1528), is one of the best and most authentic south-of-the-border spots in Alaska, but it's a long way out if you don't have a car.

If you're looking for the quick version, **Taco King** (112 W. Northern Lights Blvd., 907/276-7387) serves fat burritos and tacos, as does **Taco del Mar** (343 Benson Blvd., 907/563-9097). A great family option for nachos, burritos, and pizzas is **Bear Tooth Theatre pub** (1230 W. 27th Ave., 907/276-4200, www.beartooththeatre.net), where you can take in a $3 movie while you eat.

VEGETARIAN

Organic Oasis (2610 Spenard Rd., 907/277-7882), in the heart of "beautiful" Spenard , delivers tasty organic sandwiches (even a few with meat), fresh-squeezed juices, smoothies, and other lunch and dinner cuisine. The enjoyable, airy setting is right next to a yoga studio.

Natural Pantry (601 E. Dimond Blvd., 907/522-4330), is across from Dimond Mall on the south end of town, with groceries, organic smoothies, fresh juices, and light lunches. More adventurous types may want to risk a shot of their wheatgrass juice; it's sort of like drinking liquefied lawn clippings.

All the places listed in *Lunch* have vegetarian specials of one sort or another; Middle Way Cafe is particularly notable. Also try Snow City Cafe, Aladdins, and any of the aforementioned Thai restaurants for vegetarian specialties.

SEAFOOD

Countless Anchorage restaurants serve fresh seafood in season, and some of the best are described above (Sacks Cafe and Ristorante Orso) and below (Simon & Seaforts, Marx Bros. Cafe, Jens', and F Street Station). **Sourdough Mining Co.** (907/563-2272, www.alaskaone.com/ak-

sourdough) is a favorite for busloads of cruise ship tourists, with a faux-millhouse setting (500 seats) and Alaskan seafood.

The best places to find fresh fish, clams, crab, and other Alaskan specialties are **Tenth & M Seafoods** (1020 M St., 907/272-6013 or 800/770-2722, www.10thandmseafoods.com) and **New Sagaya** (900 W. 13th Ave., 907/274-6173, www.newsagaya.com). For smoked salmon (and reindeer sausage), drop by **Alaska Sausage & Seafood** (2914 Arctic Blvd., 907/562-3636 or 800/798-3636, www.alaskasausage.com).

STEAK AND RIBS

As you might guess, Anchorage has several of the meat-lover chain restaurants, including Black Angus Steak House, Cattle Company, Lone Star Steakhouse, Wayne's Texas Bar-B-Q, and Outback Steakhouse. More upscale is **Sullivan's** (ins Fifth Ave. Mall at C St., 907/258-2882, www.sullivansteakhouse.com), where two-inch-thick steaks are seared at high temperatures and cooked to perfection, and the dessert soufflés are to die for.

Just a block away is Anchorage's old-time steakhouse, **Club Paris** (417 W. 5th Ave., 907/277-6332, www.clubparisrestaurant.com), a fixture on the downtown scene since 1957. The atmosphere is dark and one wall is lined with the famous and infamous visitors who've eaten here over the decades. Super-tender filet mignon is the house specialty, $26 and worth it, but other items are somewhat cheaper, including fresh seafood, burgers, and salads.

BREWPUBS

Anchorage's food-and-booze scene is thriving, with several quite-different options from which to choose. Right downtown, **Glacier Brew-House** (737 W. 5th Ave., 907/274-2739, www.glacierbrewhouse.com) is a lively and noisy place that overflows most evenings; reservations recommended. Chefs work furiously in the open kitchen, sending out delicious meals of salmon, steak, ribs, and thin-crusted pizzas, while the bar pours beers made in the behind-the-glass brewery. Most dinner entrées run $16–36, though you can get small pizzas for $11.

A few blocks away is **Snow Goose Restaurant** (717 W. 3rd Ave., 907/277-7727, www.alaskabeers.com), featuring sandwiches, pasta, and pizza for lunch, and seafood, poultry, and beef for dinner. The real treat is an upstairs pub where the outdoor patio overlooks Cook Inlet, with Mt. McKinley in the distance. Snow Goose always has a half-dozen homebrews on tap from its Sleeping Lady Brewery (on the premises), along with a substantial wine selection.

Moose's Tooth Pub and Pizzeria (3300 Old Seward Hwy., 907/258-2537, www.moosestooth.net) is the most laid-back of the city's brewpubs, with a pizza and salad menu and a convivial atmosphere. It's a bit out of the way on the edge of Midtown, but that doesn't keep folks away. Get there early (especially on a weekend evening) or be ready to wait. Its distinctive pizzas-try the "brewhouse favorite" with chorizo sausage, sundried tomatoes, red onions, sauce and cheese-are all made from scratch and baked in a stone oven. Medium pizzas cost $12–20. Highly recommended, and the beers are great too. Same owners for the equally popular Bear Tooth Theatre pub.

You won't go wrong by eating at tiny **F Street Station** (325 F St., 907/272-5196) where there are always reasonably priced seafood specials, fast service, and a convivial, white-collar atmosphere. Try the perfectly cooked beer-batter halibut for $10, or the $11 New York steak and fries. Be sure to ask the bartender the story behind the huge hunk of cheddar that's always on the counter. Highly recommended, but smoke can be a problem, and this isn't a place for kids.

Humpy's Great Alaskan Alehouse (610 W. 6th Ave., 907/276-2337, www.humpys.com) attracts a 20-something crowd with more than 40 microbrews on tap and a pub menu of halibut burgers, salads, pastas, nachos, and other crunchy fare. Live bands play nightly in this always-packed hangout.

Another place with good beer bites is the **Peanut Farm** (5227 Old Seward Hwy., 907/563-3283), where the draft beer and bulging burgers (served on an outdoor deck in the summer) attract both locals and visitors.

Harry's Restaurant & Bar (101 W. Benson Blvd., 907/561-5317, www.harrysalaskanrestaurant.com) in Midtown specializes in fresh seafood, and has an more than 20 microbrews on tap at any time.

FINE DINING

Several of Anchorage's fine-dining establishments are described above, including Ristorante Orso, Sacks Cafe, and Club Paris.

Simon & Seaforts (420 L St., 907/274-3502, www.r-u-i.com/sim), has an eclectic menu, efficient service, and splendid views. Simon's serves daily fresh fish specials and aged prime rib; wonderful cracked wheat sourdough bread comes with each meal. Expect to pay $30 for dinner, though lunch is considerably less expensive. If you don't have restaurant dinner reservations, head to the more relaxed bar, where the menu is more limited, but still diverse enough to satisfy. If you're in the bar, check out the collection of single-malt Scotch whiskies, said to be one of the largest in the nation.

A much smaller and quieter place than Simon's, the elegant **Marx Bros. Cafe** (627 W. 3rd Ave., 907/278-2133, www.marxcafe.com) has been in business since 1979, and is open Tuesday–Saturday. Hors d'oeuvres cost $12–15 and dinner entrées $38–50. The Caesar salad—made at your table—is especially notable. The menu changes daily, but it's always innovative, and the big wine list and good dessert selection complement the meal. Highly recommended, but reservations are essential at this dinner-only café; call well ahead of your visit to be assured of a table. For an option that won't wound your credit card as much, take in a lunch at the Marx Bros. Cafe in the museum.

Crow's Nest (907/343-2217 or 800/478-3100, www.captaincook.com) sits atop the Hotel Captain Cook at 4th and K, 20 floors above masses. Fine dining, with prices (and a view) to match. You can either order off the sky-high menu or choose a five-course spectacular for $60 or $90 with matched wines from the 10,000-bottle wine cellar. This is one of the only places in Alaska where you can't eat in Carhartts; not only would you stand out from the rest of the crowd, but there's also a dress code. Reservations required.

Don't let the strip-mall setting for **Jens'** (701 W. 36th Ave., 907/561-5367, www.jensrestaurant.com), throw you off—this is a great European-style bistro with an Alaskan twist. The atmosphere is art-filled, and the food is equally beautiful, from the rockfish filets to the tenderloin of veal. Attentive service, a nice wine list, and delectable desserts complete the picture. Reservations recommended.

GROCERIES

Those new to Alaska may be surprised that the major grocery stores look pretty much like those in the Lower 48. True, the prices are somewhat higher, but not nearly as high as out in the bush. You'll find good delis, fresh sushi, and big salad bars at **Carrs Supermarkets,** with 10 stores scattered around Anchorage, including one at the Sears Mall in Midtown. Unfortunately, Safeway bought out Carrs several years ago and the stores have since taken a noticeable nosedive. Grocery prices are generally a bit lower at the four big **Fred Meyer** stores, including one at Northern Lights and New Seward.

A distinctive gourmet grocer is **New Sagaya** (stores at 3700 Old Seward Hwy., 907/561-5173; and 900 W. 13th Ave., 907/274-6173, www.newsagaya.com). Featured attractions include exotic produce and Asian foods, outstanding delis and bakeries, live crab and oysters, and fresh-from-the-sea seafood.

Many Alaskans buy groceries at the two **Costcos** (on Dimond Ave. at C St., and Muldoon at 15th Ave.) where you need to be a member and most things come in sizes meant to feed whole villages (or a family of teenagers). Their pizza-by-the-slice and polish dogs are a fattening bargain, once you've finished your shopping ordeal.

FARMERS MARKETS

Anchorage's finest and freshest produce can be found at the **Saturday Market** (907/272-5634, www.anchoragemarkets.com), held at the downtown parking lot on 3rd Avenue and E Street every Saturday 10 A.M.–6 P.M. from mid-May to mid-September. In addition to produce, arts, and crafts, the market stars a diverse mix of finger food—everything from salmon quesadillas to sweet funnel cakes. Be sure to stop by **Kahiltna Birchworks** (907/733-1309, www.alaskabirchsyrup.com), where you'll find Michael and Dulce East's distinctive and flavorful birch syrups and caramels created from their home in the Alaskan bush.

A smaller **Wednesday Market** takes place at Northway Mall mid-June to late August 11 A.M.–5 P.M., along with a produce-only **Anchorage Farmers Market** on Saturdays 9 A.M.–2 P.M. until early October at the *Anchorage Daily News* parking lot on Bragaw Street across from Costco.

Entertainment and Events

PERFORMING ARTS

Anchorage's active cultural scene centers on the **Alaska Center for the Performing Arts** (907/263-2900, www.alaskapac.org), downtown at 5th Avenue and G Street. There are events throughout the year, including modern dance, ballet, Broadway musicals, comedy troupes, opera, and concerts by nationally known artists, along with winter performances by the **Anchorage Symphony Orchestra** (907/274-8668 or 800/478-7328, www.anchoragesymphony.org), the **Anchorage**

Concert Chorus (907/274-7464, www.anchorageconcertchorus.org), and the **Anchorage Opera** (907/279-2557, www.anchorageopera.org).

Call 907/566-2787 for a recording of upcoming events at the PAC and elsewhere. Tickets are available at the PAC box office, in all Carrs stores, and at 800/478-7328 or www.tickets.com. Also check Friday's "8" section of the *Anchorage Daily News* (www.adn.com/weekend) for upcoming events.

Anchorage is a city that showers appreciation on traveling musicians who come out of their way to visit the city, particularly those with a folk-rock or

Celtic bent. Many of Anchorage's best folksy performances arrive courtesy of **Whistling Swan Productions** (www.whistlingswan.net); visit their website for upcoming shows.

For theatrical productions, contact **Anchorage Community Theatre** (1133 E. 70th Ave., 907/344-4713), **Cyrano's Off Center Playhouse** (413 D St., 907/274-2599, www.cyranos.org), and **Out North Contemporary Art House** (1325 Primrose St., 907/279-8200, www.out-north.org), which puts on a wide range of multidisclipinary arts—from storytelling to avant-garde videos.

DRINKING AND DANCING

The best source for Anchortown action is the Friday **"8" section** of the *Anchorage Daily News* (www.adn.com/weekend). With dozens of listings from coffeehouse folk guitarists to the Young at Heart big band that livens up the senior center on Friday nights, there's something to satiate even the most bored visitor. The newspaper's pithy descriptions of Anchorage's nightclubs and coffeehouses are a big help in making your evening plans.

The *Anchorage Press* (www.anchoragepress.com) is a free weekly newspaper available in racks all over town. There's always some sort of muckracking article here, and its coverage of the night life scene is strong.

Neighborhood Bars

Anchorage is a *Cheers*-type town, with lots of corner bars and local pubs tucked away. Downtown, a popular place is **F Street Station** (4th and F Streets), which also serves good-value lunches and dinners. **Darwin's Theory** (426 G St., 907/277-5322), attracts a fun after-work crowd. Free hot pepper schnapps—if you can stomach it—when the bartender rings the bell (quite often some evenings).

A friendly neighborhood pub in Midtown is the **Cheechako Bar** (317 W. Fireweed, 907/276-9490). The owner is Irish, so the crowd packs in here on St. Patrick's Day. It also has a great jukebox. **Harry's Restaurant & Bar** (101 W. Benson Blvd., 907/561-5317, www.harry salaskanrestaurant.com) in Midtown has more than 20 draught beers on tap.

Popular Anchorage sports bars include **Peanut Farm** (5227 Old Seward Hwy., 907/563-3283), **Crossroads Lounge** (1402 Gambell, 907/276-9014), and **Eddie's Sports Bar** (6300 Old Seward Hwy., 907/563-3970).

Rockin' Out

Anchorage's favorite downtown bar is **Humpy's Great Alaskan Alehouse** (610 W. 6th Ave., 907/276-2337, www.humpys.com). Drop by on any night of the week to rub shoulders (arms, legs, and other body parts—it gets mighty crowded) with a hip, raucous, and youthful crowd. The bar has dozens of microbrews on tap, the kitchen cranks out pub fare, and bands play nightly. Humpy's is a must-see place if you're staying downtown, especially if you're single.

Chilkoot Charlie's (2435 Spenard Rd. at Fireweed, 907/272-1010, www.koots.com) is a ramshackle building where you can do some serious jumping up and down to real rock 'n' roll and generally have a night of good raunchy fun—so long as you don't ask the wrong guy's girl (or the wrong girl's guy) to dance. There are three separate dance floors and eight (!) bars inside. It's big enough to get lost in. The main stage has loud and very live rock, while the other two dance floors are filled with folks dancing to DJ Top 40 or swing tunes. 'Koots is a love-it or hate-it sort of place; if you aren't into the bar cruisin' and pickup scene, try elsewhere. The motto should give you fair warning, "We cheat the *other* guy and pass the savings on to *you!* But you should at least go here to say you didn't miss the most famous place in town. 'Koots gets extremely crowded on weekend nights, so you may have to wait quite a while to get in if you come after 10 P.M. There's a cover charge on weekends. You can't miss Chilkoot's, just look for the tall, lighted windmill.

A dressier crowd heads to **Hot Rods** (4848 Old Seward Hwy., 907/562-5701), where the decor is what you might expect, with '50s and '60s cars as the centerpiece. No live bands, but lots of dancing to old rock 'n' roll discs; cover charge on weekends. Downstairs, you'll find a fine billiards room with 16 antique tables, certainly the classiest pool joint in the state; it's been ranked one of the best billiard rooms in the nation.

Bernie's Bungalow Lounge (626 D St., 907/276-8909, www.berniesbungalow lounge.com) is a little downtown place with live music several nights a week, from Latin jazz to funk. The back patio and lawn are open all summer.

Chef's Inn (825 W. Northern Lights Blvd., 907/272-1341) is Anchorage's "Blues Central," with live blues bands nightly ($3–5 cover). The bar attracts leather-clad, chain-smoking bikers and others. Good food and great blues, but bring a gas mask.

Downtown's **Rumrunners** (415 E St., 907/278-4493) is a spacious no-cover DJ club Tuesday–Saturday nights.

Club Soraya (333 W. 4th Ave., 907/276-0670) is a fun downtown place where Latin dance bands fill the air with salsa and merengue on weekends. Free Latin dance lessons on Saturday nights; there's a $10 cover.

Try **Club Millennium** (420 W. 3rd Ave., 907/277-1428) for DJ raves with an $8 cover; no alcohol. A number of other teen places have rave or techno tunes; see the Friday newspaper for the current scene. **Snow City Cafe** (1034 W. 4th Ave., 907/272-2489) has Wednesday-night Irish jam sessions.

Gay and Lesbian

If your boyfriend or girlfriend happens to be of the same sex as you, pop into **Mad Myrna's** (530 E. 5th Ave., 907/276-9762, www.alaska.net/~mad-myrna) or **The Raven** (708 E. 4th Ave., 907/276-9672). Myrna's has drag shows on Fridays, karaoke Wednesday–Thursday, and DJ tunes on other nights; Raven is a pool-shootin' joint. **PrideFest** (www.anchoragepride.com) in mid-June is Alaska's big coming-out party, so to speak.

Twisted Fun

Don't miss Anchorage's most distinctive bar: Mr. Whitekey's **Fly By Night Club** (3300 Spenard Rd., 907/279-SPAM or 907/279-7726, www.fly-bynightclub.com). The "Gormay Kweezeen" menu explains the phone number: It features del-

icacies such as Spam with Nachos and Cajun Spam. (In case you didn't know, Spam is an old Alaskan bush standby, and remains popular today.) Mr. Whitekey's **"Whale Fat Follies"**—put on most weeknights in the summer—is a hilarious send-up of everything Alaskan, including spawning salmon, duct tape, and Skinny Dick's Halfway Inn. Not to mention the tap-dancing outhouse. Newcomers to Alaska may be a bit baffled by the political humor and inside jokes, but the more time you've spent here, the funnier it is. Beware, however, that the humor gets pretty raunchy at times. Aunt Norma from Salt Lake City will be mortified. The show costs $13–20; consider it money well spent! (They also have $5 cheap seats, if you don't mind looking around a post!) No-smoking show Tuesday–Thursday nights. Shows start at 8 P.M. and, after the Follies, Mr. Whitekeys and his Fabulous Spamtones return to the stage with "Sleazy jazz." No cover if you just come for the tunes. Fly By Night is closed January–March.

Date Bars

Several Anchorage bars offer a quiet and romantic atmosphere. If you luck into a clear evening, have packed something a little dressy, and don't mind blowing two-days' budget on a beer, head up to the **Crow's Nest** (4th and K, 907/276-6000) atop the Captain Cook Hotel—the view is worth the effort. The **Millennium Hotel** (4800 Spenard Rd., 907/243-2300 or 800/544-0553) has an upscale bar with outdoor seating overlooking Lake Hood.

MOVIES

Free documentary flicks are shown several times a day at the **Public Lands Information Center** and the **Museum of History and Art.** For something more dramatic, the downtown Alaska Center for the Performing Arts (907/263-2900, www.alaskapac.org) offers summer-only **IMAX shows** on Alaska and wolves, plus slide shows on the northern lights. The **Alaska Experience Theatre** (705 W. 6th Avenue, 907/276-3730, www.alaskaexperiencetheatre.com), has a wraparound visual show and earthquake shaker for the tourists.

Bear Tooth Theatrepub (1230 W. 27th Ave., 907/276-4200, www.beartooththeatre.net) has a winning combination: inexpensive second-run movies ($3), tasty light meals (including nachos, salads, burritos, stone-baked pizzas), and brewery-fresh draught beer. It's a great place with a family atmosphere, and is run by the same folks who bring you Moose's Tooth Pub & Pizzeria. You can eat downstairs and drink while watching the movie; upstairs is reserved for underage kids. It also has a restaurant area (very noisy) in the lobby for those who just want a meal in a family setting, and an upscale grill with seafood, steaks, and margaritas. Highly recommended.

Anchorage's main theater action is the huge **Century 16** (36th Ave. and A St., 907/929-3456), where all 16 theaters have stadium seating and reclining chairs. Other Anchorage multiplexes include **Totem 8** (3131 Muldoon Rd., 907/566-3329), **Fireweed 7** (Fireweed and New Seward, 907/566-3328), and **Dimond Center 9** (in Dimond Mall at Dimond and Old Seward, 907/566-3327). See what's showing at all local theaters by visiting www.anchoragemovies.com.

EVENTS

Winter is the time for Anchorage's best-known events (the Iditarod and Fur Rendezvous), but the city is certainly full of life in the summer. Check the Anchorage Convention and Visitors Bureau website (www.anchorage.net) for a complete listing of events.

Summer

Anchorage's most popular ongoing event is the **Saturday Market** (907/272-5634, www.anchoragemarkets.com), which takes place at the parking lot on 3rd Ave. and E St. on Saturday 10 A.M.–6 P.M. from mid-May to mid-September. It features over 300 vendors selling fresh produce, quality arts and crafts, and great food. Don't miss it! A smaller market takes place Wednesday afternoons at Northway Mall.

Every Wednesday and Friday at noon, head downtown to 4th Ave. and E St. for free **Music in the Park** (907/279-5650, www.ancdp.com) next to the visitor center.

Anchorage has not just one, but two different semipro baseball teams—the **Anchorage Bucs** (907/561-2827, www.anchoragebucs.com) and the **Glacier Pilots** (907/274-3627, www.glacierpilots.com)—so there's usually a game worth watching between June and early August. Past players have included such pro stars as Reggie Jackson, Dave Winfield, Mark McGuire, and Randy Johnson. Games take place at Mulcahy Stadium at East 16th and Cordova.

Even if you're only in Anchorage for two nights, drop $20 to see **"Whale Fat Follies"** at Mr. Whitekey's Fly By Night Club (3300 Spenard Rd., 907/279-7726, www.flybynightclub.com).

The **Arctic Thunder Air Show** (907/552-7469, www.elmendorf.af.mil) at Elmendorf Air Force Base comes around each June, and includes a stunning performance by the Air Force's Thunderbirds.

Three Barons Renaissance Faire (907/868-8012, www.3barons.org) takes place in early June at Hilltop Ski Area, and the crowd gets into the act by pelting rotten acting with rotten tomatoes. The **Spenard Solstice Street Party** (www.awaic.org) brings an offbeat parade, live music, and food booths to Spenard, while the serious athletes race in the big **Mayor's Midnight Sun Marathon** (www.mayorsmarathon.com).

Held at Kincaid Park in June, **Blues on the Green** (907/272-1341) attracts such acclaimed artists as Otis Rush and Bo Diddley. There's a **July Fourth** parade downtown, but when the fireworks show starts at midnight the sky still isn't very dark!

Also in early July, the **Bear Paw Festival** (907/694-4702, www.cer.org) comes to nearby Eagle River, with family fun, a beauty pageant, races, a chili cook-off, carnival rides, and the state's biggest parade.

Several of the biggest "local" events—the State Fair in Palmer, the Girdwood Forest Fair, the Talkeetna Bluegrass Festival, the Mountain Marathon in Seward, and the KBBI Concert on the Lawn in Homer—are not in Anchorage. But, if you're around when any of these are happening, get out of town to where the fun really is!

Winter

In recent years, tourism to Alaska has increased in the winter months as visitors discover what Alaskans already know—that winter opens up a panoply of outdoor options. Several companies specialize in winter tours and activities; see the visitor center for brochures.

The **Anchorage Folk Festival** (907/566-2334, www.anchoragefolkfestival.org) is a major winter diversion, with free concerts that fill two consecutive weekends in late January. Concerts take place on the campus of the University of Alaska Anchorage.

In mid-February **Fur Rendezvous** (907/274-1177, www.furrondy.net) is one the city's biggest annual events, with all sorts of fun activities during this 10-day-long festival. A carnival packs a downtown lot, and there are car races, fireworks, snow sculpture and ice carving contests, dress balls, concerts, ski races, dog-pulling contests, and-most exciting of all-the world championship sled dog race.

The one Alaskan event that always attracts national attention is the **Iditarod Trail Sled Dog Race** (907/376-5155 or 800/545-6874, www.iditarod.com) from Anchorage to Nome. The start is in downtown Anchorage in early March.

Another very popular event is the **Great Alaska Shootout** (907/786-1250, www.goseawolves.com/shootout) basketball tournament that takes place in Sullivan Arena each November, and features seven top college teams and the lowly University of Alaska Seawolves. This one gets national media attention because it's so early in the year.

The **Nordic Skiing Association of Anchorage** (907/276-7609, www.anchoragenordicski.com) keeps dozens of miles of local trails groomed, and puts on such events as the **Tour of Anchorage** (www.tourofanchorage.com) in early March. The **Ski for Women** (907/279-9581, www.alaskaskiforwomen.org) in early February is the largest North American ski event for women, attracting more than 1,500 participants.

Spring Carnival and Slush Cup in mid-April, is a wet and wild event for skiers as they try to cross a slushy pond at Alyeska Resort (907/754-1111, www.alyeskaresort.com).

Shopping

Although big-city folks sometimes complain that Anchorage doesn't have the fancy boutiques they're accustomed to finding, it *does* have just about every other sort of place—from Sam's Club to Nordstrom. The city is a car haven, so many of these stores are scattered in the various shopping malls that help give Anchorage its "charming" urban sprawl.

Downtown Anchorage's **5th Avenue Mall** includes two big stores—JCPenny and Nordstrom—along with several dozen storefronts on four levels. The city's largest mall is **Dimond Center** on the south side at Dimond Boulevard and Old Seward Highway. Other malls include **The Mall at Sears** (Northern Lights and Seward Highway) and **Northway Mall** (Airport Heights and Glenn Highway). Anchorage has all the mega-stores, including Wal-Mart, Fred Meyer, Costco, Home Depot, Toys 'R' Us, Barnes & Noble, ad nauseam.

GIFTS AND NATIVE ART

Much of downtown is given over to shops selling tourist doo-dads, particularly along 3rd and 4th Avenues, where you'll find everything from $2 made-in-China trinkets to $20,000 sculptures.

One People (425 D St., 907/274-4063), has a fine selection of Native Alaskan art in a convenient downtown location. One of the best places to buy Native crafts is the out-of-the-way **Alaska Native Medical Center Gift Shop** (4315 Diplomacy Dr. off East Tudor Rd., 907/729-1122). Excellent grass baskets, dolls, masks, yo-yos, and more are sold on consignment here. Another recommended place is the gift shop at the **Alaska Native Heritage Center** (Glenn Highway and Muldoon Rd., 907/330-8000 or 800/315-6608, www.alaskanative.net).

Anyone looking for a traditional Alaskan parka should stop by Moose Hollow Gifts at 720 D Street for **Laura Wright's Alaskan Parkys** (907/274-4215; www.alaskan.com/parkys). They're also available at the Saturday Market.

An unusual (and very expensive) purchase to consider is *qiviut:* caps, scarves, shawls, sweaters, or baby booties, hand-knitted by Natives from the wool of domestic musk ox (the musk ox farm is outside of Palmer). Many times warmer and lighter than wool, these fine knits can be seen and salivated over at **Oomingmak Co-op** (609 H St., 907/272-9225 or 888/360-9665; www .qiviut.com).

GALLERIES

On the **First Friday** of each month Anchorage's art scene comes alive with openings, hors d'oeuvres, and the chance to meet regional artists at a dozen or so galleries. Check the Friday *Anchorage Daily News* or the weekly *Anchorage Press* for details.

Anchorage's premier gallery is **International Gallery of Contemporary Art** (427 D St., 907/258-0307, www.igcaalaska.org), where you'll find something new each month from top regional artists.

Three good places to buy original artwork in Anchorage are **Artique, Ltd.** (314 G St., 907/277-1663, www.artiqueltd.com), **Arctic Rose Gallery** (420 L St., 907/279-3911), and **Aurora Fine Arts Gallery** (737 W. 5th Ave., 907/274-0234). A fun shop for wearable art is **Tracy Anna Bader Design Studio & Gallery** (416 G St., 907/278-9327).

A great option is the **Saturday Market** (907/272-5634, www.anchoragemarkets.com) held at the parking lot on 3rd and E every summer Saturday. The market has works by Alaskan painters, photographers, potters, and others.

OUTDOOR OUTFITTERS

Anchorage is an excellent place to stock up on outdoor gear before heading into the bush. The biggest place to shop—and one of the best—is **REI (907/272-4565, www.rei.com)**, on the corner of Northern Lights and Spenard Road. REI stands for Recreation Equipment Inc. This Seattle-based cooperative where members get an end-of-the-year dividend on their purchases has a knowledgeable staff, and they offer free clinics and talks throughout the year. You can also rent canoes, kayaks, tents, backpacks, skis, snowshoes, and other outdoor equipment from REI.

Another excellent outdoor store with a technically adept staff is **Alaska Mountaineering & Hiking** (2633 Spenard Rd., 907/272-1811, www.alaskamountaineering.com)—better known as AMH—just a block away from REI. Though much smaller, AMH often has equipment unavailable elsewhere. This is where the hard-core climbers and backcountry skiers go. Check the bulletin boards here and at REI for used gear and travel partners. Across the street is **Play it Again Sports** (907/278-7529), where used equipment of all sorts is available, from backpacks and tents to baseball gloves and fishing poles. They also buy used equipment if you need a little cash on your way out of town.

Downtown shoppers head to the **Army Navy Store** (320 W. 4th Ave., 907/279-2401) for more traditional Alaskan outdoor clothing and boots. **B&J Commercial** (2749 C St., 907/274-6113) has a downstairs packed with sport and commercial fishing supplies. This is where you'll find the really heavy-duty clothing and equipment at fair prices.

BOOKS AND MUSIC

Alaska's largest independent bookstore is **Title Wave Books** (1360 W. Northern Lights Blvd., next to REI, 907/278-9283 or 888/598-9283, www.wavebooks.com). Offering both new and used titles, this is a great hangout spot, with a literate crowd and an adjacent Kaladi Brothers espresso shop to surf the internet.

Also in Midtown is **Metro Music and Books** (530 E. Benson Blvd., 907/279-8622), with a huge selection of CDs, any of which you can listen to before deciding to buy.

A fine downtown bookstore, **Cook Inlet Book Company** (415 W. 5th Ave., 907/258-4544 or

800/240-4148, www.cookinlet.com) specializes in Alaskan titles.

Borders Books & Music (1100 E. Dimond Blvd., 907/344-4099) features books and CDs, plus an espresso café. Even bigger (and more centrally located) is **Barnes & Noble Bookseller** (200 E. Northern Lights Blvd., 907/279-7323 or 888/279-7323). In addition to books and CDs, you'll find an impressive magazine selection, plus a Starbucks café.

Information and Services

VISITOR CENTERS

One of the best things about Anchorage is how easy it is to collect all the information you could possibly need, not just for the city, but also for much of the state. Two stops near the corner of 4th Ave. and F St. downtown can supply you with a ton of fliers, brochures, booklets, guides, schedules, and maps, plus the synthesizing expertise of the knowledgeable staffs who can help you make sense of it all. The **Anchorage Convention and Visitors Bureau** (ACVB) is the place to go for every possible Anchorage brochure, handout, or free newspaper. Across the intersection is the **Alaska Public Lands Information Center** where you can learn about national parks, forests, wildlife refuges, and much more. Both of these places, and the nearby **Department of Natural Resources Information Center,** are described in detail under Sights above.

The ACVB also maintains two **Airport Visitor Centers:** one near the baggage area in the domestic terminal (907/248-4979) and the other in the international terminal (907/266-2657). Both are staffed daily 9 A.M.–4 P.M. in the summer.

LIBRARIES

The **Z.J. Loussac Library** (36th and Denali, 907/261-2975, http://lexicon.ci.anchorage.ak.us, Mon.–Thurs. 10 A.M.–8 P.M., Fri.–Sat. 10 A.M.–6 P.M.) is a spacious facility out in Midtown. You could easily lose an afternoon just wandering among the stacks, enjoying the cozy sitting room on Level 3, studying the huge relief map of the state, browsing among the paintings hanging on the walls, or picking a book at random from the large Alaskana collection. Getting to the Alaskana section is an adventure in its own right-the architects did everything they could to make it difficult to reach: up two flights of stairs, across a long connecting walkway, and then back down two levels. And it's back out the same way, since there is no exit here! The library has computers for free internet access, but you may have to wait awhile.

Two other good places to track down info are the **University Library** (907/786-1871) on the UAA campus, and the **Alaska Resources Library** (3150 C St., 907/272-7547, www.arlis.org), which covers Federal lands in Alaska.

BANKING

As might be expected in a city of this size, ATMs can now be found practically anywhere, including most banks and grocery stores. Wells Fargo (630 E. 5th Ave., 907/267-5700) offices will exchange traveler's checks or bills in Canadian dollars, Japanese yen, Euros, and other currency for greenbacks.

MEDICAL SERVICES

Alaska's three largest hospitals are in Anchorage. Of the first two, **Alaska Regional Hospital** (2801 DeBarr Rd., 907/276-1131, www.alaskaregional.com) and **Providence Alaska Medical Center** (3200 Providence Dr., 907/562-2211, www.providence.org), Providence has a better reputation and is a nonprofit. The modern **Alaska Native Medical Center** (4315 Diplomacy Dr., 907/257-1150) is perhaps the finest facility in Alaska, but is only for Native people.

To find a doctor, call the **physician referral services** offered by Providence (907/261-4900) and Alaska Regional (907/264-1722 or 800/265-8624). You'll find a 24-hour pharmacy inside the **Carrs** (907/297-0560) store at West Northern Lights Boulevard. and Minnesota Drive.

Several "Doc-in-a-box" offices are scattered around Anchorage, but you're likely to see a physi-cian's assistant rather than a doctor. Try **FirstCare** (3710 Woodland Dr., 907/248-1122) or **Urgent Care** (5437 E. Northern Lights Blvd., 907/333-8561). **Primary Care Associates** (3500 LaTouche St., 907/562-1234) is a recommended place to find a real doctor, but you'll need an appointment.

Transportation

ANCHORAGE INTERNATIONAL AIRPORT

Almost everybody who flies into Alaska from the Lower 48 lands at Anchorage, even if just to connect to other carriers around the state. While waiting for your luggage, take a look at the collection of stuffed Alaskan animals and fish on the upper level. The city skyline and Chugach Mountains are visible from up here; go out, breathe the air, dig the view, and indulge in a private smile—you finally made it to Alaska. You, and the other five million people (honest) who pass through the airport annually.

Anchorage International Airport (907/266-2525, www.anchorageairport.com) is six miles southwest of downtown. (Officially, it is Ted Stevens Anchorage International Airport, in honor of the U.S. senator who continues to bring home the pork to fund all sorts of Alaskan projects, including the airport.) An information booth—open daily 9 A.M.–5 P.M. in the summer—is near the baggage area; if it's closed, check the racks for free brochures. You can store luggage (even frozen fish) nearby, 907/248-0373.

The **People Mover** bus ($1.25, 907/343-6543, www.peoplemover.org) runs from the lower level into downtown Anchorage hourly, seven days a week. Taxi fare is approximately $16 to or from downtown, and there's always a line of cabs waiting out front as you exit the baggage claim area.

The Alaska Railroad has a terminal at the airport that is used by cruise ship companies, with passengers flying into Anchorage and riding the train to Seward where they disembark for their cruise to Southeast Alaska (or vice versa). Additional train connections to the airport may be available in the future.

In addition to passengers, the airport serves a vital link for air cargo companies. Both Federal Express and UPS have major international terminals, and hundreds of cargo flights land and refuel each week.

Domestic Airlines

Many of the big domestic carriers fly into and out of Anchorage from the Lower 48, including **Alaska Airlines** (800/426-0333, www.alaskaair.com), **American** (800/433-7300, www.aa.com), **Continental** (800/523-3273, www.continental.com), **Delta** (800/221-1212, www.delta.com), **Frontier** (800/432-1359, www.frontierairlines.com), **Northwest** (800/225-2525, www.nwa.com), and **United** (800/241-6522, www.ual.com).

Most of these flights arrive via Seattle, but Alaska also has year-round nonstop flights to Chicago, Los Angeles, and Portland, Oregon, with connecting service via Seattle to most Western cities and all the way to Boston, Denver, Washington D.C., Miami, Newark, Orlando, and a number of Mexican cities. Northwest has year-round nonstop service to Minneapolis-St. Paul and Detroit, while Delta flies nonstop year-round to Salt Lake City and Cincinnati. In addition, **Hawaiian Vacations** (907/261-2700 or 800/770-2700, www.hawaiianvacations.com) offers charter flights several times a week between Anchorage and Honolulu (plus nonstop flights to Maui in the winter), while **Sun Country Airlines** (800/359-6786, www.suncountry.com) has seasonal charters between Anchorage and Minneapolis.

Summer-only nonstop Anchorage flights arrive from Atlanta (Delta), Chicago (United), Cleveland (Continental), Dallas (American), Denver (United, Alaska, and Frontier), Los Angeles (Continental), Houston (Continental),

Portland (Continental), Newark (Continental), and San Francisco (Alaska and United), St. Louis (American).

International Flights

Anchorage has what may be the best connections to international destinations of any city its size in America. The following companies offer nonstop service into Anchorage: Alaska Air and **Air Canada** (888/247-2262, www.aircanada.ca) from Vancouver; **Korean Air** (800/438-5000, www.koreanair.com) from Seoul; **China Airlines** (800/227-5118, www.china-airlines.com) from Taipei; and **Thomas Cook Airlines** (800/524-6975, www.thomascook.us) from Frankfurt. **Magadan Airlines** (907/248-2994) has weekly summertime service from Anchorage to Petropavlovsk on Russia's Kamchatka Peninsula using old Aeroflot jets. Two companies offer seasonal flights to Tokyo in the summer: **Japan Airlines** (800/525-3663, www.jal.com) and **Alaskan Vacations** (907/261-2700 or 800/770-2700, www.hawaiianvacations.com, a subsidiary of Hawaiian Vacations.

Regional Airlines and Air Taxis

Anchorage's largest regional airlines are **Era Aviation** (907/266-8394 or 800/866-8394, www.fly-era.com), with daily flights to Cordova, Homer, Kenai, Kodiak, and Valdez; and **PenAir** (907/243-2323 or 800/448-4226, www.penair.com), with flights to Aniak, Cold Bay, Dillingham, Dutch Harbor, Iliamna, King Salmon, McGrath, Pribilof Islands, Sand Point, and Unalakleet. **Hageland Aviation** (907/245-0119 or 866/239-0119, www.hageland.com) serves northern and western Alaska towns and villages, including Aniak, Barrow, Bethel, Dillingham, and Nome. **Frontier Flying Service** (907/450-7200 or 800/478-6779, www.frontierflying.com) flies from Anchorage to Fairbanks, Aniak, Bethel, Dillingham, and many bush villages.

ALASKA RAILROAD

Anchorage is a major stop for the Alaska Railroad, with service north all the way to Fairbanks, and south to Seward and Whittier. The Alaska Rail-road train depot (411 W. 1st Ave., 907/265-2494 or 800/544-0552, www.alaskarailroad.com) is just down the hill from the center of Anchorage. Its daily express to Fairbanks has prices comparable to those of the tour buses but is a much more comfortable, historical, enjoyable, and leisurely ride. The express departs Anchorage mid-May to mid-September at 8:15 A.M. for **Denali** (arriving around 4 P.M., $125 one-way) and **Fairbanks** (arriving 8:15 P.M., $175 one-way). The express also stops in Wasilla and Talkeetna, where you can hop off, but you're not allowed to check any luggage—only what you can carry on.

The local service (self-propelled rail diesel car) departs Anchorage Thursday–Sunday in the summer for Hurricane Gulch (south side of Broad Pass *before* Denali). This is flag-stop service; a good way to meet rural Alaskans; $70 round-trip. A variety of possible rail/lodging and rail/lodging/boat tour options are listed in Alaska Railroad's brochure or online. Winter service is twice a week in each direction.

Take the Alaska Railroad south to **Seward** for a fantastic over-the-top voyage across the Kenai Peninsula. The route diverges from the highway near Portage, and then winds steeply into the Kenai Mountains past several glaciers. Daily train service costs $59 one-way or $98 round-trip. The Anchorage to **Whittier** train departs at 10 A.M., arriving 2.5 hours later; $55 round-trip. Service to both Whittier and Seward is from mid-May to mid-September only. Both of these trains also stop in Girdwood, but only hand-carry baggage is allowed from there.

Princess Tours (206/336-6000 or 800/835-8907, www.princesslodges.com) and **Holland America Tours-Gray Line of Alaska** (907/277-5581 or 800/544-2206, www.graylineo-falaska.com) hook their superdome cars to the back of the express for an old-fashioned luxury rail experience to Denali. These are mostly for the cruise ship crowd, but they also sell seats to independent travelers. Be ready to plunk down $800 d for an Anchorage-Denali-Anchorage trip that includes one nights at a hotel near the park; or $640 d from Anchorage to Fairbanks for a trip that includes an overnight near Denali.

BUSES

A number of bus companies head out from Anchorage to other parts of the state, and most will carry bikes for an extra charge. Try a city bus for a cheaper option if you're just heading to Palmer or Wasilla from Anchorage.

In the summer **Alaska Direct Bus Line** (907/277-6652 or 800/770-6652, www.home .gci.net/~akdirectbus) has service several times a week connecting Anchorage with Whitehorse, Haines, and Skagway. Winter service is less frequent.

Alaska Trails (907/479-3065 or 888/600-6001, www.alaskashuttle.com) has a daily Anchorage–Talkeetna–Denali–Fairbanks run in the summer, and five times a week the rest of the year.

Talkeetna Shuttle Service (907/733-2222 or 888/288-6008, www.denalicentral.com) connects Anchorage with Talkeetna daily May to mid-July, less often the rest of the summer, and on request at other times.

Denali Overland Transportation (907/733-2384 or 800/651-5221, www.denalioverland.com) offers charter service to Talkeetna and Denali on a regular basis.

Alaska Park Connection (907/245-0200 or 800/208-0200, www.alaskacoach.com) connects Anchorage with Seward, Talkeetna, and Denali.

Homer Stage Line (907/883-3914, www.homerstageline.com) has service to Soldotna, Kenai, Cooper Landing, and Homer. Service is daily in the summer, and once a week the rest of the year.

Seward Bus Lines (907/563-0800, www.sewardbuslines.com) runs daily vans year-round to Seward.

GETTING AROUND

City Bus

People Mover (907/343-6543 www.peoplemover.org), Anchorage's public bus system, covers the entire Anchorage Basin. Weekday service is extensive, with all routes operating 6 A.M.–10 P.M. On Saturday, most lines run 8 A.M.–8 P.M., but Sunday service is only offered on certain routes 9:30 A.M.–6:30 P.M. Visit the

Transit Center at 6th and G, where you can pick up a "Ride Guide" timetable of all routes. It's open Monday–Friday 7 A.M.–6 P.M. Exact fare ($1.25 adults, 75 cents for children) is required, and transfers are valid only on a different bus traveling in the same direction within two hours of the time of receipt. People Mover buses are free all day in the downtown area; just get on board and ride. A $2.50 day pass—good for unlimited rides—is sold on all buses.

All People Mover buses can transport wheelchairs, or call the **Anchor Ride** program (907/562-8444) for special transportation needs. You'll need to call at least a day in advance.

People Mover service takes you as far as Eagle River (25 miles north of Anchorage), where you can hop on a Mat-Su Community Transit bus, better known as **MASCOT** (907/376-5000, www.matsutransit.com), for Monday–Friday runs to Palmer, Wasilla, and even Big Lake. Using this combination of public transit, you can get to the Mat-Su Valley for $4! **Downtown Connection** (907/373-8014 or 866/344-6667, www.akdowntownconnection.com) has scheduled service from Anchorage to Wasilla for $9 each way.

Taxis

Taxis are expensive: Most charge $2 per flag drop, plus $2/mile thereafter. The companies include **Alaska Cab** (907/563-5353), **Yellow Cab** (907/272-2422), and **Anchorage Checker Cab** (907/276-1234). There's always a line of waiting cabs outside the airport if you are just arriving and need a way into Anchorage; the fare is $15–18. Disabled travelers should contact Alaska Cab; it has wheelchair lifts on some vehicles. **Shuttleman** (907/677-8537) is cheaper from the airport: $10 for the first person, plus $2 for additional folks heading to the same downtown destination.

Car Rentals

Anchorage is car-happy, so rental cars can be very hard to come by. Make car reservations as much as two months ahead to be sure of a car in the peak season. All the major companies (Alamo, Avis, Budget, Dollar, Hertz, National, Payless, Rent A Wreck, and Thrifty, and U-Save) operate from the Anchorage airport, offering rates starting around $47/day for an economy car with unlimited mileage. Many of these companies also rent 4WD vehicles and vans. Don't even think of renting a car in Anchorage and leaving it elsewhere in Alaska; the charges are sky-high for this luxury.

Check www.travelocity.com to see who currently has the cheapest Anchorage rentals. The best rates are frequently through **Payless** (907/243-3616 or 800/729-5377, www.paylesscarrental.com), **Budget** (907/243-0150 or 800/248-0150, www.budget.com), and **Dollar** (907/248-5338 or 800/800-4000, www.dollar.com). **Denali Car Rental** (907/276-1230 or 800/757-1230) has lower rates (starting at $35/day), but its cars are older.

Most car rental companies prohibit driving on the McCarthy Road; one exception is **Affordable New Car Rental** (907/243-3370 or 800/248-3765, www.ancr.com). If you're traveling in the winter, ask for a car with studded tires, which are—surprisingly—not on many Anchorage rental cars. Companies with studded tires include Affordable, Denali Car Rental, and U-Save.

When making a reservation, be sure to mention if you have an AAA card; you can often save substantially on the rates. Most of the national companies have car rental desks at the airport, but if you rent one there you'll have to add on an extra 10 percent airport concession fee, plus an 8 percent municipal tax to these rates. Especially for long rentals, it's always best to *not* get a rental car from the airport.

RV Rentals

Quite a few places let you rent honkin' Alaska-size RV land yachts-the ones you sit behind for miles as they waddle down the road at 30 mph and four miles to the gallon. Recreational vehicles may be of some value for groups of six or more, but are completely unnecessary for smaller groups.

The following Anchorage companies rent RVs: **Great Alaskan Holidays** (907/248-7777 or 888/225-2752, www.greatalaskanholidays.com), recommended; **Clippership Motorhome Rentals** (907/562-7051 or 800/421-3456, www.clippershiprv.com); **ABC Motorhome Rentals**

(907/279-2000 or 800/421-7456, www.abcmotorhome.com); **Alaska Economy RVs** (907/561-7723 or 800/764-4625, www.goalaska.com); **Alaska Panorama RV Rentals** (907/562-1401 or 800/478-1401, www.alaskapanorama.com); **Sweet Retreat** (907/344-9155 or 800/759-4861, www.sweetretreat.com); and **Alaska Motorhome Rentals** (907/258-7109 or 800/254-9929, www.alaskarv.com). RVs rent for $165–195/day in mid-summer. A better option may be to rent a pickup-truck-based camper from **GoNorth RV Camper Rental** (907/479-7272 or 866/236-7272, www.gonorthalaska.net); these are much better if you plan any trips out the state's gravel roads.

Bus

At least a half-dozen tour companies are happy to sell you bus tours of Anchorage and the surrounding area; get their brochures from the visitor center. The larger companies—**Gray Line of Alaska** (907/277-5581 or 800/544-2206, www.graylineofalaska.com), **Alaska Sightseeing/Cruise West** (907/441-9571 or 800/426-7702, www.cruisewest.com), and **Princess Tours** (800/835-8907 or 800/774-6237, www.princess.com)—also offer a wide range of other package trips on land, sea, or air throughout Alaska.

Boat

Although there are no boat tours out of Anchorage, it *is* a good place to check out boat trips across Prince William Sound and out of Seward. Several tour companies offer trips that include a bus from Anchorage to Whittier, boat across the Sound, and flight or bus ride back to Anchorage. Or get to Whittier on your own and hop on one of these tour boats.

Alaska Marine Highway's southwest ferry routes do not reach Anchorage, but you can connect up with the system in Whittier or Seward via the Alaska Railroad or one of the bus companies. The ferry has an office inside the Alaska Public Lands Information Center at 4th and F, 907/272-7116 (general), or 907/272-4482 (arrival and departure times). You can also get ferry schedules at 800/642-0066, www.ferryalaska.com.

Vicinity of Anchorage

CHUGACH STATE PARK

Alaska's second-largest chunk of state-owned land, Chugach State Park (907/345-5014, www.alaskastateparks.org) encompasses nearly half a million acres—half the size of Delaware. The park covers the entire Chugach Range from Eagle River, 25 miles north of Anchorage, to Girdwood, 35 miles south. It could take a committed hiker years to explore all its trails, ridges, peaks, and passes. From the short but steep 1.5-mile trail up Flattop Mountain in Anchorage, to the 25-mile trek from the Eagle River Nature Center over Crow Pass down to Girdwood, you have a wide range of trails to choose from, each varying in length, elevation, difficulty, access, and congestion.

Pick up hiking brochures at the Alaska Public Lands Information Center in Anchorage, decide on a trail, then dress for rain! The clouds often sit down on these city—surrounding mountaintops and when it's sunny and hot in Anchorage, it could be hailing only a few minutes away on the trails. But don't let that stop you. This whole park is within a few miles of where half of Alaska's population huddles, but up in these mountains it's easy to pretend you're a hundred years behind the crowds, and all the hustle and bustle on the Inlet flats is far in the future.

Jenny Zimmerman's *A Naturalist's Guide to Chugach State Park, Alaska* tells the full story on the park.

Camping and Cabins

Developed state park campgrounds are found at **Eklutna Lake** ($10) and **Eagle River** ($15) north of Anchorage, and at **Bird Creek** ($10) to the south. All three have four-day limits, outhouses, and water, and are generally open May–September. Located just off the Hiland Road exit a dozen miles north of Anchorage, the often-full Eagle River Campground can be reserved by calling 907/694-7982 or 800/952-8624.

A wonderful cabin ($40) can be rented on the shore of Eklutna Lake, and two yurts and an eight-person cabin ($55) are available near the Eagle River Nature Center. Details at 907/269-8400, www.alaskastateparks.org.

Hillside Trails

Two trailheads on the city's southeastern outskirts give access to a network of crisscrossing and connecting trails in the section of the range that hems in Anchorage Bowl. They're all off Hillside Dr., which skirts a suburb of sparkling glass houses and gorgeous views of the skyline, inlet, and Mt. Susitna to the west. City buses do not reach the park in this area, so you'll really need a vehicle to get to the Hillside trailheads. Day use parking costs $5/vehicle.

For the **Glen Alps Trailhead** drive south on New Seward Highway, and turn east toward the mountains on O'Malley Road. Follow it to Hillside Dr., where you turn right, then left on Upper Huffman Road. In a half-mile, go right again onto aptly named Toilsome Hill Drive. Toil steeply uphill for 2.5 miles to reach the Glen Alps parking lot ($5 day-use fee). On warm summer weekends every space in the lot fills with cars, so get there early. Take a look from the nearby overlook, and then head up the **Flattop Mountain Trail** for even better looks. This extremely popular 1.5-mile trail gains 1,500 feet and is very steep near the top as you scramble through the boulders.

Also from the Glen Alps Trailhead are several moderate and very scenic hikes: **Little O'Malley Peak,** 7.5 miles round-trip; the **Ramp and Wedge,** 11 miles round-trip; and **Williwaw Lakes,** 13 miles round-trip. A great mountain bike route is the 11-mile (one-way) **Powerline Trail** that also takes off from the Glen Alps Trailhead and goes over 3,550-foot Powerline Pass all the way to the Indian Creek Trailhead on Turnagain Arm.

Continue north on Hillside past Upper Huffman Rd. and take a right on Upper O'Malley Road. The second left leads to **Prospect Heights Trailhead,** where the **Wolverine Peak Trail** leads to the top of this 4,455-foot mountain (11 miles round-trip). You'll discover great views of the

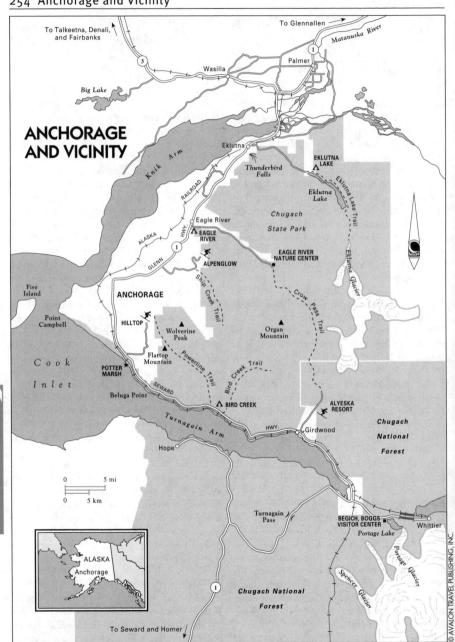

ANCHORAGE AND VICINITY

To Talkeetna, Denali, and Fairbanks

To Glennallen

Matanuska River

Wasilla

Palmer

Big Lake

ANCHORAGE AND VICINITY

Knik Arm

Eklutna

Thunderbird Falls

EKLUTNA LAKE

Eklutna Lake

Eklutna Lake Trail

RAILROAD

Chugach State Park

Eagle River

EAGLE RIVER

ALASKA

ALPENGLOW

EAGLE RIVER NATURE CENTER

GLENN HWY

Eklutna Glacier

Crow Pass Trail

Fire Island

ANCHORAGE

Ship Creek Trail

MOON

Point Campbell

HILLTOP

Wolverine Peak

Organ Mountain

Cook Inlet

Flattop Mountain

Powerline Trail

POTTER MARSH

Bird Creek Trail

Beluga Point

SEWARD

Turnagain Arm

BIRD CREEK

ALYESKA RESORT

Chugach National Forest

HWY

Girdwood

Hope

0   5 mi
0   5 km

Turnagain Pass

BEGICH, BOGGS VISITOR CENTER

Whittier

Portage Lake

Portage Glacier

ALASKA
Anchorage

Spencer Glacier

1

Chugach National Forest

To Seward and Homer

© AVALON TRAVEL PUBLISHING, INC.

Alaska Range and Anchorage, but go in late summer when the snow has melted.

Eagle River Area

Take the Eagle River exit 13 miles north of Anchorage on the Glenn Highway, then your first right onto Eagle River Road, a dazzling, paved, 11-mile ride right into the heart of Chugach State Park. Rafters and kayakers on the Class II Eagle River can put in at two access points (Miles 7.5 and 9) along this road. The road ends at the **Eagle River Nature Center** (907/694-2108, www.ernc.org), which features a "close-up corner" with furs and a track book, as well as an aurora display, and gift shop. The center is open daily 10 A.M.–8 P.M. from mid-June–mid-August, and Tuesday–Sunday 10 A.M.–5 P.M. May–mid-June and mid-August–October; closed the rest of the year. Park rangers offer daily hikes at 1 P.M. in mid-summer. Parking is $5. The **Rodak Nature Trail** is a wide gravel route, a half-mile round-trip, with informative signs on snow, glaciers, forest, and the sun. It's 15 minutes well spent. For a longer walk, take the seven-mile **River Trail** along the Eagle River.

Eklutna Lake Area

Twenty-six miles north of Anchorage on the Glenn Highway is the exit for Eklutna Lake, a favorite weekend destination. Narrow and winding Eklutna Rd. follows the Eklutna River 10 miles to the lake, where you'll find a pleasant, small campground ($10) with outhouses and a large picnic area. The 14-mile **Lakeside Trail-Eklutna Glacier Trail** starts nearby, skirting the west side of Eklutna Lake and then climbing to this very scenic glacier. Three side trails lead off the main route to Twin Peaks, Bold Ridge, and East Fork of Eklutna River. This is an outstanding mountain biking area in summer, and a popular wintertime ski/snowmachine trail. Most of the route is also open to ATVs Sunday–Wednesday, so you may not have peace and quiet. Experienced skiers may want to continue beyond Eklutna Glacier via a multiglacier traverse that takes them 31 miles to Crow Pass. The Alaska Mountaineering Club

(907/272-1811, www.mcak.com) has three huts along the way.

Kayak and bike rentals are available near the Eklutna Campground from **Lifetime Adventures** (907/746-4644 or 800/952-8624, www.lifetimeadventures.net), along with a popular paddle-and-peddle option ($70): you kayak across the lake and ride a mountain bike back.

Also from the Eklutna exit, you can follow the access road a mile south to scenic **Thunderbird Falls** (if you're heading north from Anchorage, there's a marked Thunderbird Falls exit before you reach the Eklutna exit). The trail takes you on an easy one-mile hike up Thunderbird Creek. Follow your ears to the falls.

Crow Pass

For one of the longest and most scenic hikes in the park, head out the 25-mile **Crow Pass Trail.** This trail (also known as the Historic Iditarod Trail) provided a turn-of-the-century overland route from Seward through the Chugach to the Interior gold mining town of Iditarod. The gradual climb to Crow Pass fords several streams, including Eagle River midway along the trail. It might be wise to camp overnight and cross the river in the morning, when the glacial runoff is lower. Raven Glacier and Crystal Lake are scenic highlights near Crow Pass, where you leave Chugach State Park and continue in immense Chugach National Forest. The Forest Service has a popular A-frame **cabin** (reservations: 518/885-3639 or 877/444-6777, www.reserveusa.com, $35) on the summit that you can rent. From the cabin it's four miles down to the trailhead on rough Crow Creek Road, then another five miles to the Alyeska Ski Resort access road. Experienced skiers sometimes use the Iditarod/Crow Pass Trails for a winter traverse of the mountains, but be aware that avalanche danger can be very high.

Additional Trails

The Turnagain Arm Trail and several other popular Chugach State Park hiking paths are described in the *Turnagain Arm* section, along with the Potter Section House, where park headquarters is located.

NORTH OF ANCHORAGE

Chugach State Park includes several popular destinations north of Anchorage around Eklutna Lake and Eagle River.

Arctic Valley

Six miles north from Anchorage along the Glenn Highway is the exit to Arctic Valley Road, which climbs seven steep miles to the parking lot at the Alpenglow ski area (see Downhill Skiing under Winter Recreation in the Anchorage section). A trailhead about a mile before road's end leads to long **Ship Creek Trail,** which with a little cross-country hiking hooks up with Bird Creek and Indian Creek Trails via the passes of the same names. It's 22 miles from Arctic Valley to Indian Creek Trailhead. Plan on two or three days to do this traverse. From the Alpenglow parking lot a two-mile trail goes up to **Rendezvous Peak,** an easy hike with great views of the city, inlet, and even Mt. McKinley if you're lucky.

Eklutna Historical Park

This is one of those surprising discoveries just off the Glenn Highway. Take the Eklutna Road exit (26 miles northeast of Anchorage), and cross back over the highway to Eklutna Village. From this point, at the site of the first Tanaina (a branch of the Athabascans) settlement on the Inlet, down through the western Kenai Peninsula, Kodiak, and the Aleutians, Russian Orthodoxy is strongly overlaid on the Native culture. The ancestors of most of these Indians were converted by Russian missionaries, and **St. Nicholas Russian Orthodox Church**—a miniature log chapel that dates from the 1830s and was reconstructed in the 1970s-is the oldest building in the Anchorage area. Nearby is a newer and larger church. Both are set against a backdrop of 80 or so colorful above-ground **spirit houses** that sit atop Native graves. Informative half-hour tours (907/688-6026, www.eklutna.com, $5 adults, $2.50 seniors and ages 10–15, free for kids under 10) are offered Mon.–Fri. 10 A.M.–5:30 P.M., Sat. 10–4:30, and Sun. 1–4, mid-May to mid-September; the rest of the year you'll have to look in from the picket fence. There's also a small gift shop that sells Native crafts.

TURNAGAIN ARM

The Seward Highway heads south from Anchorage, curving around Turnagain Arm, past the town of Girdwood and the turnoff to Portage Glacier and Whittier, and finally over the Kenai Mountains to Seward, 127 miles away. The Turnagain Arm stretch is exceptionally scenic, but traffic is usually heavy, so drive carefully and keep your lights on at all times.

Potter Marsh Area

Potter Marsh is on the south edge of Anchorage, with a boardwalk along the edge of the marsh. This is a good spot to look for waterfowl, including Canada geese, trumpeter swans, and even the flyin'-fool Arctic terns. Bring binoculars and a light jacket for the often-breezy conditions. This marsh was created when the railroad builders installed an embankment to protect the track from Turnagain Arm's giant tides, which dammed the freshwater drainage from the mountains.

A mile south on the other side of the highway is the **Potter Section House** (907/345-5014, Mon.–Fri. 8 A.M.–4:30 P.M. year-round), a small railroad museum of interpretive displays and signs outside, and inside, the restored original "section" house. This is also headquarters for Chugach State Park; get brochures on local trails here. Check out the nine-foot rotary snowplow once used to clear avalanches. A small gift shop sells railroad memorabilia and books.

Turnagain Arm Trail

Across the highway from Potter Section House is the parking lot for **Potter Creek Trailhead,** the first access to the Turnagain Arm Trail, which parallels the highway for over nine miles, with good opportunities to see Dall sheep, moose, and spruce grouse. The trail began as a turn-of-the-century wagon road built to transport railroad workers and supplies. This is a very popular early-summer path since its south-facing slopes lose the snow early. In three miles is **McHugh Creek,** an always-crowded day-use area and trailhead for the seven-mile hike up to **Rabbit Lake.** You can continue south along the Turnagain Arm Trail past three more trailheads all the way to **Windy Corner Trailhead** nine miles from your starting point, and not far from Beluga Point.

Beluga Point

Twenty miles south of Anchorage is Beluga Point, a good place to see the small white **beluga whales** cavorting in Turnagain Arm in late May and late August; they follow salmon into these shallow waters. Unfortunately, over-hunting by Natives caused the population of belugas to plummet in the 1990s, and it may take many years for them to recover. Look behind you for the **Dall sheep** that often wander close to the highway in this area. Or just have a picnic and wait for the Cook Inlet's famous **bore tides.** The tides here, at 30 feet, are among the world's highest, and the lead breaker can be up to eight feet high, a half-mile across, and can move at over 10 miles per hour. This is the only bore tide in the U.S., created when a large body of water (Cook Inlet) is forced by strong tidal action into a narrow, shallow one (Turnagain Arm). Look for a series of small swells (two to three feet high, larger depending on the wind) that crash against the rocks and send up a mighty spray. You won't soon forget the roar of the bore, which goes by Beluga Point roughly two hours after low tide in Anchorage-check the tide tables in the daily newspapers. One warning: Never go out on the Turnagain Arm mudflats at any time. The mixture of glacial silt and mud creates quicksand; people have drowned after getting their feet stuck in the mud and being inundated by the incoming tide. Don't take a chance!

Indian and Bird Creeks

Twenty-five miles south of Anchorage, and right before Turnagain House Restaurant in Indian, take a left on the gravel road and head 1.5 miles to the **Indian Valley Trailhead.** This trail, which follows Indian Creek over Indian Pass (especially rewarding during Indian summer), is five miles of easy walking on a well-maintained path. You can then continue for several miles of undeveloped hiking until you hook up with the Ship Creek Trail, which runs 22 miles to Arctic Valley north of Anchorage. The Powerline Pass Trail (see above) goes 11 miles from the Glenn Alps trailhead to Indian Creek Trail; look for the signed turnoff 100 yards up the Indian Valley Trail. Historic **Indian Valley Mine** (907/653-1120, www.indianvalleymine.com) has gold panning, a little museum, and a gift shop.

Two miles down the highway from Indian is the Bird Creek area, where dozens of cars line the roadside on July and August afternoons. They're all here trying to hook a silver salmon in this very productive creek. A half-mile north of the creek is a parking area for **Bird Ridge Trail,** which climbs straight up this 3,500-foot promontory in less than two miles.

Also nearby is the **Bird Creek Campground** ($10), a surprisingly pretty place just off the busy Seward Highway. Campsites are just a few feet from Cook Inlet. This thickly forested campground is often full of anglers working Bird Creek. The **Bird to Gird Bike Trail** runs right through the middle of the campground, continuing north for three miles to Indian and south three miles to Girdwood along the old highway.

GIRDWOOD

The town of Girdwood is officially part of the hectic Anchorage municipality, but feels a world away. Located 37 miles south via the Seward Highway, the original town was leveled by the 1964 earthquake. A cluster of businesses stands along the highway, providing a rest stop for travelers, but new Girdwood and the Alyeska Resort sit at the end of a three-mile access road (Alyeska Highway). This winter resort is a favorite destination for locals, package tourists, unsuspecting travelers, and the occasional backpacker who likes a quick ride to the alpine tundra in the summer.

ANCHORAGE AND VICINITY

Girdwood doesn't have a visitor center, but you'll find information on the web at www.girdwoodalaska.com. In addition to the resort, the town has several restaurants, a grocery store, post office, and a laundromat with showers.

Alyeska

First check out **Alyeska Resort,** and the impressive lobby of the enormous Alyeska Prince Hotel. Next, fork over $16 to catch a ride 2,300 feet up Mt. Alyeska on the **tram** (907/754-2275). On top are two restaurants. The two 60-passenger tram cars are entirely wheelchair accessible. Follow the well-marked trail to the alpine overlook onto cute Alyeska Glacier. If you have reservations to dine at Seven Glaciers restaurant, the tram ride is free. A tram-and-lunch special to Glacier Express Cafe costs $20. The tram office has more information.

Skiing

Owned by a Japanese corporation, Alyeska Resort (907/754-1111 or 800/880-3880, www.alyeskaresort.com) is at the center of winter activity in Southcentral Alaska, with an elaborate complex that encompasses the ski area, a hotel, and several restaurants. The resort covers 500 skiable acres and has 60 trails, a 60-passenger tram, eight chairlifts, and two pony lifts. Most of the ski runs are at the intermediate or advanced level. In addition to abundant natural snowfall (depths generally exceed 10 feet), there is snowmaking capability on the lower slopes.

Alyeska Resort generally opens for skiing in mid-November and closes the end of April. Hours are daily 10:30 A.M.–5:30 P.M., with night skiing Friday–Saturday until 9:30 P.M.; reduced hours early and late in the season. A shuttle bus connects the main ski area with the Alyeska Prince Hotel (where the tram departs). If you're coming from Anchorage, the resort also has a wintertime shuttle bus on weekends and school holidays for $12 round-trip. It's a good way to let someone else do the driving.

Adult lift tickets cost $40–46 full day, $33 half-day; on Friday and Saturday there's night skiing for $10–19 extra. A half-day ticket plus night skiing will run you $40–45. There are discounts for chil-

Crow Creek Mine

dren, students, and multiday passes. Skis, snowshoes, snowboards, and ice skates (for use on the skating pond) can be rented in the day lodge, where you can also get expensive cafeteria food. More cafeteria fare, along with an elaborate restaurant and lounge, is on top of the mountain. Ski and snowboarding classes at all levels are available. Traffic between Anchorage and Girdwood can back up on winter weekends, so head out early if you're driving. Call 907/754-7669 for a recording of the latest snow conditions.

Crow Creek Mine

The gravel Crow Creek Road leads from Girdwood three miles to Crow Creek Mine (907/278-8060, www.crowcreekgoldmine.com), one of the earliest gold strikes in Alaska (1896), and Southcentral Alaska's richest mine. The area was actively mined until World War II, producing over 45,000 ounces of gold. There's still a lot of gold to be found, and the creek attracts both casual panners looking for a flake of gold and those who come with metal detectors and large suction dredges. Eight of the original mine buildings have been restored by the Toohey family and are open daily 9 A.M.–6 P.M. mid-May to mid-September. Entrance is $3, or plunk down another $8 to pan for gold (including a lesson from a pro in the panning shed). There's a gift shop on-site, panning equipment rental, and overnight campsites ($5). It's a pretty place with a rich history, and a *must* stop in the Girdwood area.

Continue another four miles out Crow Creek Road beyond Crow Creek Mine to the **Crow Pass Trailhead.** It's an invigorating and beautiful 3.5 miles to the pass, with a 2,000-foot elevation gain. The trail is in the alpine much of the route, and passes old mining ruins and a Forest Service cabin ($35). A half-mile beyond the pass is Raven Glacier, where you enter Chugach State Park.

Other Sights

The six-mile paved **Bird to Gird Bike Trail** starts from the Alyeska Prince Hotel, and continues north all the way to Bird Creek, following Turnagain Arm much of the way.

Girdwood Center for Visual Arts (907/783-3209, www.girdwood.org) is across from the post office on Hightower Road. It's open daily in the summer, with quilts, pottery, paintings, glasswork, jewelry, and other locally crafted pieces for sale.

The Forest Service's **Glacier Ranger District office** (907/783-3242) is on the left as you drive into town from the Seward Highway, and is open weekdays. It can provide details and maps for hikers, anglers, sea kayakers, and other recreation enthusiasts heading into Chugach National Forest.

Stop off at the **Alaska Candle Factory** (907/783-2354) on the access road a half-mile from Seward Highway. Their candles are not only unique and inexpensive souvenirs or gift items, but they also burn until the cows come home.

Accommodations

Heading toward the resort on the access road, go right on Timberline, pass gorgeous ski chalets, then turn right again on Alpina. Around a couple of curves is the **Alyeska Hostel** (907/783-2099, www.alyeskahostel.com). This is a great place, with a sleeping loft for women and a downstairs men's dorm, plus a kitchen and bath, and a

wood-burning sauna out back; $13 per person, or $40 d in a private room.

The **Girdwood Bed-and-Breakfast Association** (907/222-4858, www.gbba.org) has a B&B hot line for referrals to eight local places.

The luxurious 307-room **Alyeska Prince Hotel** (907/754-1111 or 800/880-3880, www.alyeskaresort.com) offers some of the fanciest lodging in Alaska. This eight-story, 307-room hotel features nicely appointed rooms with heated towel racks, ski-boot storage boxes, and safes. The rooms are, however, a bit small. Other in-hotel amenities include three restaurants, a fitness center, indoor swimming pool, sauna, and hot tub. There's even a virtual golf course where you can play a round without leaving the room. The tram to the top of Mt. Alyeska is right out the back door; guests get a discounted rate of $16. Rooms start at $195 d, up to $1,500 d for a top-level suite. If you aren't staying here, plunk down $5 for access to the pool, sauna, and hot tub at the Prince—it's a great deal for campers who get all the amenities for the price of a shower.

Food and Entertainment

At the intersection of the Girdwood Spur Road and Seward Highway is a little strip mall with a variety of services, including a gas station/convenience store, laundromat, video store, and restaurant. Travelers heading south to Seward or north to Anchorage stop here before pushing back out on the highway. The **Alpine Diner & Bakery** (907/783-2550_, serves breakfast, lunch, and dinner, but is best known for enormous pastries. There's always a queue on winter mornings as the preski gang comes in to inject sugar and caffeine into their veins.

In business since 1962, the famous **Double Musky Inn** (907/783-2822, www.doublemuskyinn.com) is a quarter-mile up Crow Creek Road on the left, closed Mondays. The restaurant is crowded and loud, with long waits, a tacky New Orleans-meets-Alaska decor, and brief visits from your server. No reservations, either. Despite these drawbacks, the food is dependably good, if not stellar. Featured attractions are Cajun shrimp, garlic seafood pasta, rack of lamb, and the house specialty, French Pepper Steak; entrées run

$18–30. Save space for the ultra-rich Double Musky pie.

At the Alyeska resort is **The Bake Shop** (907/783-2831, www.thebakeshop.com), a fine spot for lunch or an after-ski warmup. Homemade sourdough bread, hearty soups, sandwiches, big breakfasts, and pizza fill out the menu. The Bake Shop is open daily until 7 P.M. in the summer, and the boardwalk out front has hanging baskets of flowers.

Not far away on Arlberg Street is **Jack Sprat Restaurant** (907/783-5225, www.jacksprat.net), with "fat and lean world cuisine" in a relaxed atmosphere. Dinners include everything from BBQ ribs to Thai shrimp wraps and smoked salmon pasta, plus several vegetarian choices. Brunch is served on weekends, with all the usuals, along with eggs benedict, tofu scramble, and crepes.

Located next to the post office on Hightower Road, **Chair 5 Restaurant** (907/783-2500, www.chairfive.com) is a townie spot for very good pizzas, halibut burgers, and fresh salmon. The bar has a great choice of single malt scotches and microbrews. Après-ski partiers head to the **Sitzmark Bar & Grill** at Alyeska Resort for a pitcher of beer and the chance to dance the night away to live bands on winter weekends. Unfortunately, the bar is closed in the summer.

On top of the mountain, **Seven Glaciers Restaurant** (907/754-2237, www.alyeskaresort.com) offers excellent food with one of the best views you're ever likely to get while dining. Reservations required. Sitting on a crag at 2,303 feet above sea level, you can see the valley below, across to the Crow Pass area, and up Turnagain Arm. Main courses run $25–49, or you can splurge on a $70 pp four-course menu with wine. *Très élégant,* but not at all stuffy or pretentious. The seven-minute tram ride gives you the chance to survey the area, and if you've got dinner reservations, the tram ride is free.

Events

The big summertime event is **Girdwood Forest Fair** (907/566-3039, www.girdwoodforestfair.com) held in early July for over a quarter century. Hundreds of folks show up to buy arts and crafts, graze through the food booths, and listen to bands cranking out the tunes from two separate stages. It's a two-day party that seems to attract every free-spirited hippie left in Alaska. No dogs, politicians, or religious orders allowed.

Skiing and snowboarding events fill the winter calendar at Alyeska Resort (907/754-1111, www.alyeskaresort.com) but the most fun for spectators is the **Spring Carnival and Slush Cup** in mid-April, when costumed skiers blast downhill and attempt to ski across a slushy pond. Lots of cold, wet folks on this one!

Transportation

The **Alaska Railroad** (907/265-2494 or 800/544-0552, www.alaskarailroad.com) connects Girdwood with Anchorage daily in the summer, but the trains stop at a small shelter out near the Seward Highway. You'll need to make advance reservations for a pickup in Girdwood, and only carry-on luggage is allowed.

Alpine Air (907/783-2360, www.alaska.net/~alpineair) offers a one-hour flight with a glacier landing, plus floatplane tours of Prince William Sound, drop-off fishing flights, and charters. For a very different form of flying, hook up with **Chugach Tandem Paragliding** (907/754-2400, www.alyeskaadventure.com). They take novices on exciting tandem paragliding rides from the top of the tram.

PORTAGE GLACIER

Fifty miles south of Anchorage on the Seward Highway is the turnoff to Portage Glacier and Whittier. A six-mile access road takes you through Portage Valley to Portage Glacier. A town that stood on this corner was destroyed when the 1964 earthquake dropped the land 6–10 feet. Saltwater from Turnagain Arm inundated the area, killing the still-standing trees, and the remaining buildings are gradually disintegrating. Portage Glacier is one of the more popular tourist attractions in Southcentral Alaska, so be ready to share the ride with busloads of cruise ship travelers.

An info booth along the Seward Highway has details on Whittier, and sells tickets for various tour options, including the Alaska Railroad's scenic trips to Grandview.

Visitor Center

The Forest Service's **Begich, Boggs Visitor Center** (907/783-2326, www.fs.fed.us) is a named after Nicholas Begich (U.S. representative from Alaska and father of Anchorage mayor Mark Begich) and Hale Boggs (majority leader of the U.S. Senate and father of journalist Cokie Roberts), whose plane disappeared in the area in 1972. They were never found. The center, is open daily 9 A.M.–6 P.M. from late May–September, and Saturday–Sunday 10 A.M.–5 P.M. the rest of the year. A large picture window overlooks the narrow outlet of Portage Lake. When the visitor center first opened, the glacier was readily visible, but it is now out of sight around a corner, and in recent years the number of icebergs entering the lake has decreased greatly as it continues to shrink.

The visitor center boasts an amazing array of displays, including an ice cave, a small iceberg hauled in from the lake, an engrossing relief map of local icefields, and everything you ever wanted to know about glaciers, including displays on glacial motion and crevasses. Don't miss the vial of tiny iceworms, which inhabit the surfaces of glaciers, feeding on pollen grains and red algae and surviving within a delicate, near-freezing temperature range. There's also good footage on iceworms in the 20-minute movie, *Voices from the Ice,* shown every hour, $1.

During the summer, Forest Service naturalists lead half-mile nature walks. The **observation platform** near Williwaw Campground is a good place to see spawning red and chum salmon in late summer.

Seeing the Glacier

To see Portage Glacier, you'll need to hop onboard the 200-passenger *Ptarmigan* tour boat; catch it at the dock near the visitor center. Operated by Gray Line of Alaska (907/277-5581 or 800/544-2206, www.graylineofalaska.com), these one-hour cruises across Portage Lake cost $25 and start at 10:30 A.M., with the last tour at 4:30 P.M. This boat tour, plus round-trip bus transportation from Anchorage (includes a stop at Alyeska) costs $59 on Gray Line.

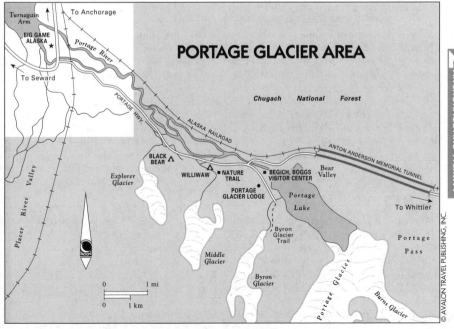

Hiking

Two hikes are within walking distance of the visitor center. The **Moraine Loop Trail,** accessible from the path to the lodge, is a five-minute stroll through typical moraine vegetation; Portage Glacier occupied this ground only 100 years ago. Follow the access road past the visitor center (south) just under a mile. At the back of the parking lot starts the **Byron Glacier Trail,** an easy three-quarter-mile walk along the runoff stream to below this hanging glacier.

Practicalities

Two Forest Service **campgrounds** near Portage contain woodsy sites: **Black Bear Campground** is $10, and the larger **Williwaw Creek Campground** costs $12. The latter has summertime campfire programs on Saturday evenings and a wheelchair-accessible observation platform where spawning salmon are visible in the summer. Williwaw's sites can be reserved ($9 extra) at 518/885-3639 or 877/444-6777, www.reserveusa.com. **Portage Glacier Lodge,** across from the visitor center (907/783-3117) has a cafeteria with reasonable prices; try the cross-cut fries for your crunch craving. Open daily year-round.

Big Game Alaska

This 140-acre game farm (907/783-2025, www.biggamealaska.com) sits along Turnagain Arm just across the Seward Highway from the turnoff to Portage Glacier. Owner Mike Miller raises buffalo, elk, moose, musk ox, deer, and caribou for this drive-through wildlife park. Entrance is $5 adults, $3 kids and seniors, or a maximum $20 per vehicle.

Mat-Su Valley and Beyond

The Parks Highway heads north from Anchorage to Denali and Fairbanks, but before you're even close to either of these, the road takes you through the heart of the Matanuska-Susitna Valley, named for the two rivers that drain this part of Alaska. Originally established as an agricultural center, the Mat-Su is now primarily a bedroom community for Anchorage, with reasonably priced homes and fast-spreading semi-urban sprawl. Two towns dominate the valley. The old farming settlement of Palmer is along the Glenn Highway 42 miles from Anchorage, while Wasilla rears its ugly face 40 miles north of Anchorage along the Parks Highway.

PALMER

For its first 20 years, Palmer (pop. 4,100) was little more than a railway depot for Alaska Railroad's Matanuska branch. Then in May 1935, during the height of both the Depression and a severe drought in the Midwest, the Federal Emergency Relief Administration of President Franklin D. Roosevelt's New Deal selected 200 farming families from the relief rolls of northern Michigan, Minnesota, and Wisconsin, and shipped them here to colonize the Matanuska Valley. Starting out in tent cabins, the colonists cleared the dense virgin forest, built houses and barns, and planted crops pioneered at the University of Alaska's Agricultural Experimental Station. These hardy transplanted farmers endured the inevitable first-year hardships, including disease, homesickness, mismanagement, floods, and just plain bad luck. But by the fall of 1936, the misfits had been weeded out, 120 babies had been born in the colony, fertile fields and long summer days were filling barns with crops, and the colonists celebrated with a three-day harvest festival, the forerunner of the big state fair. In a few more years, Palmer had become not only a flourishing town, but also the center of a bucolic and beautiful agricultural valley that was and still remains unique in Alaska.

Driving into Palmer from Wasilla along the Palmer–Wasilla Highway is a lot like driving into Wasilla from the bush on the Parks Highway–time warp. The contrast between Palmer, an old farming community, and Wasilla, with its spontaneous combustion of helter-skelter development,

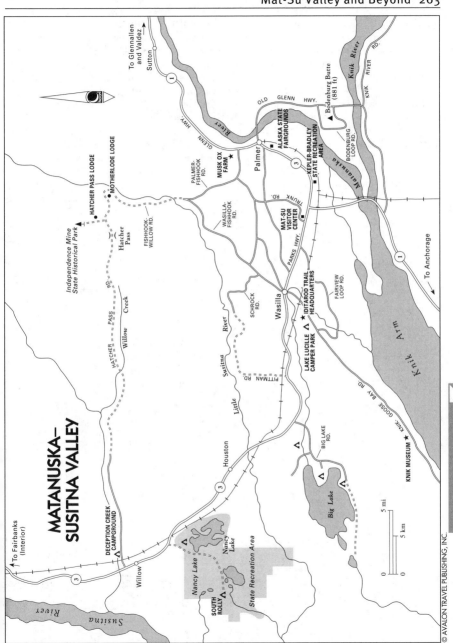

MATANUSKA–SUSITNA VALLEY

To Fairbanks (Interior)

To Glennallen and Valdez

Sutton

Susitna River

Willow

Nancy Lake

Nancy Lake State Recreation Area

SOUTH ROLLY

DECEPTION CREEK CAMPGROUND

Houston

Willow Creek

Little Susitna River

HATCHER PASS RD.

Hatcher Pass

Independence Mine State Historical Park

HATCHER PASS LODGE

MOTHERLODE LODGE

FISHHOOK-WILLOW RD.

PALMER-FISHHOOK RD.

WASILLA-FISHHOOK RD.

SCHROCK RD.

PITTMAN RD.

Wasilla

IDITAROD TRAIL HEADQUARTERS

LAKE LUCILLE CAMPER PARK

MAT-SU VISITOR CENTER

PARKS HWY.

TRUNK RD.

GLENN HWY.

Matanuska River

Palmer

MUSK OX FARM

OLD GLENN HWY.

ALASKA STATE FAIRGROUNDS

KEPLER-BRADLEY STATE RECREATION AREA

Bodenburg Butte (881 ft)

BODENBURG LOOP RD.

Knik River

KNIK RIVER RD.

FAIRVIEW LOOP RD.

BIG LAKE RD.

Big Lake

KNIK-GOOSE BAY RD.

KNIK MUSEUM

Knik Arm

To Anchorage

5 mi

5 km

N

ANCHORAGE AND VICINITY

© AVALON TRAVEL PUBLISHING, INC.

is startling. Suffice it to say, Palmer is more conducive to sightseeing. I actually know people whose home is in Wasilla, but they keep a post office box in Palmer for their business to avoid the stigma of being labeled from Wasilla!

Today, downtown Palmer is a blend of the old and new, with Klondike Mike's Saloon right next to Sisters of Essence Holistic Center. Palmer is also home to the **National Outdoor Leadership School's** Alaska campus (907/745-4047, www.nols.edu). From this base, NOLS offers a range of courses that involve backpacking, sea kayaking, and mountaineering in remote parts of Alaska.

Downtown Sights

Start your visit at the **Palmer Visitor Information Center** (723 S. Valley Way, 907/745-2880, www.palmerchamber.org). Open daily 8 A.M.–6 P.M. mid-May to mid-Sept., and Mon.–Fri. 10 A.M.–4 P.M. the rest of the year. Outside is a phone with direct connections to local lodging places, and an adjacent garden with elephantine-size produce by late summer. Inside, load up with brochures, check out the gift shop, and visit the small **Colony Museum** downstairs depicting the colonists' lifestyle. Don't miss the framed front page of the June 30, 1958, *Anchorage Daily Times* fea-

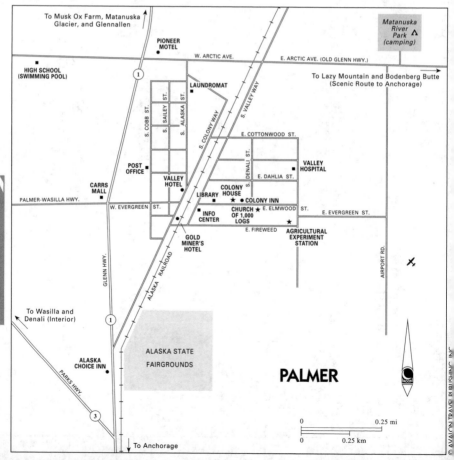

turing the story of Alaska being voted into the Union.

Colony House (316 E. Elmwood Ave., 907/745-1935, Mon.–Sat. noon–4 P.M. summers only, $2 adults, $1 kids) is just up the block from the visitor center. This home was originally built by the Beylund family who moved here in 1935 from Wisconsin. It has been restored and filled with period furnishings to provide a window on life for the Matanuska Colonists.

Continue another block east on East Elmwood to visit the appropriately named **Church of a Thousand Logs,** built by the colonists in 1936-37, and still in use. And one more block east lies the **Agricultural Experimental Station** headquarters, where you can walk through the greenhouses and arboretum across the street.

Fairgrounds, Farms, and Glaciers

Heading north through downtown, take a right on Arctic Avenue, which turns into the Old Glenn Highway. About a mile south of town down the Glenn Highway is the **Alaska State Fairgrounds.** At the fairgrounds is **Colony Village** (Mon.–Sat. 10 A.M.–4 P.M., free), which preserves some of Palmer's early buildings, including houses (one built in 1917 in Anchorage), several barns, a church, and a post office.

Continue another three miles beyond the fairgrounds to **Bodenberg Loop Rd.,** a five-mile drive through some of the most gorgeous valley farmland, with 6,400-foot **Pioneer Peak** towering behind. To see some of the original colony farms, head east out the Glenn Highway nine miles to **Farm Loop Road.** Matanuska Valley's best-known crop isn't mentioned in any of the tourism brochures: marijuana. The local version (Matanuska Thunder) has a reputation as big as Alaska and is some of the most potent in the nation. It was formerly grown outside, but today nearly all grow operations are indoors under lights.

Knik River Road splits off the Old Glenn Highway at Mile 9. Turn here and drive four miles to the trailhead for the **Pioneer Ridge–Knik River Trail,** which climbs a staggering 5,100 feet in less than six miles. Beyond this alpine ridge, only experienced rock climbers should consider heading to the twin summits of Pioneer Peak.

Knik Glacier is visible approximately seven miles up the Knik River Road, and several companies offer air/boat trips to the face of this unusual riverside glacier. **Mountain View Boat Tours** (907/745-5747 or 800/264-4582) leads tours throughout the summer from mile six of the Knik River Rd. for $65 per person; best and quietest boat on the river. Other companies with similar services are **Hunter Creek Outfitters** (907/745-1577, www.huntercreekoutfitters.com) and **Knik Glacier Outfitters** (907/746-5133). Hunter Creek Outfitters also has raft and kayak rentals, while Knik Glacier Outfitters offers llama treks.

Musk Ox Farm

While in Palmer, take the opportunity to visit the world's only domestic musk-ox farm (907/745-4151, www.muskoxfarm.org) and see 50 or so of these fascinating prehistoric Arctic creatures up close. During the half-hour tour you learn that, among other things, these exotic animals were hunted nearly to extinction in the early 1900s, but have been reestablished in northwestern and Arctic Alaska. The musk ox wool is collected here, shipped back east to be spun, then distributed to Native villages to be woven into *qiviut* wool products. *Qiviut* is eight times warmer than sheep's wool and much softer and finer than even cashmere. Scarves, stoles, caps, and tunics are sold in the showroom; don't miss the display of little squares of *qiviut,* cashmere, alpaca, and wool from sheep, camel, and llama to compare the softness. The farm opens on Mothers Day in May (a great time to see the calves), and remains open daily 10 A.M.–6 P.M. through September. Winter visits by appointment only. Get there by taking the Glenn Highway north of town to Mile 50 and following the signs. Admission to this nonprofit facility is $9 adults, $7 seniors and ages 13–18, $6 for ages 6–12, and free for younger tots. This includes an interesting half-hour tour. They also offer a $4 entrance that provides access to a viewing area and the museum, but no tour.

a Matanuska Valley farm, near Palmer

Hiking

Two excellent hikes are accessible off the Old Glenn Highway east of Palmer. Heading north from downtown, go right on Arctic Avenue, which becomes the Old Glenn. Just beyond the bridge across the Matanuska River, go left onto Clark-Wolverine Road, then continue about a mile until the next junction. Take a right on Huntley Road, go about a mile and bear right at the fork, then drive a quarter mile to the trailhead for **Lazy Mountain.** It's a two-mile hike to the summit of this 3,270-foot mountain with views of the Matanuska Valley.

A better view and shorter hike are to the top of **Bodenberg Butte** (881 feet). Keep going south on the Old Glenn, pass the first right onto the Loop Road, and take the second right. A parking lot ($3) is a quarter-mile up, and a 40-minute huff rewards you with a 360-degree view of the farm-filled valley, Chugach, Talkeetnas, Knik Glacier, and some of the uncleared forest, which graphically illustrates what the colonists confronted in "clearing the land." Nearby is a raindeer farm that may be open to the public.

Motels and Hotels

Lodging is surprisingly reasonable in Palmer—at least by Alaska standards. Located downtown, **Pioneer Motel** (124 W. Arctic, 907/745-3425, $50–70 d) has the cheapest rooms around. Also in the heart of town is **Valley Hotel** (606 S. Alaska St., 907/745-3330 or 800/478-7666). Built in 1948, it has 43 remodeled rooms for $75 d, and a few larger ones with two queen beds for $100. Downstairs you'll find a 24-hour coffee shop, plus a lounge and a liquor store.

The **Colony Inn** (325 E. Elmwood Ave., $80–100 d) is one of the older buildings in the valley, built in 1935 as a teachers' dormitory for the Matanuska Valley Colony. Today this historic structure has been transformed into a 12-room hotel with a central sitting room containing a fireplace and wingback chairs. Most rooms contain antiques, quilts, and jacuzzi tubs; all are nonsmoking. It's managed by the Valley Hotel, where you register.

Alaska Choice Inn (907/745-1505 or 800/745-1505, $65–85 d) is directly across from the fairgrounds at Mile 40 of the Glenn Highway. Request one of the newer rooms, some of which have kitchenettes.

Gold Miner's Hotel (918 S. Colony Way, 907/745-6160 or 800/725-2752, www.gold-minershotel.com, $79–99 d) across from the visitor center downtown, has upstairs rooms with fridges and microwaves; some also have kitchenettes or deck access.

B&Bs and Cabins

Visit the **Mat-Su Bed & Breakfast Association's** website (www.alaskabnbhosts.com) for links to Palmer B&Bs, including a daily vacancy listing in the summer. **River Crest Manor B&B** (907/746-6214, www.rivercrestmanor.com, $85–95 d) is a quiet, colonial-style bed-and-breakfast with an extraordinary view of Pioneer Peak and the Chugach Mountains; private bath and full breakfast included.

Another home with fine mountain vistas is **Iditarod House B&B** (907/745-4348; www.iditarodhouse.com). This contemporary country home belongs to former Iditarod musher Donna Massay. The two rooms ($60–70 d) and an apartment ($95 d) have private baths, and guests are served a filling breakfast.

Alaska Gold Rush B&B (907/745-5312 or 877/745-5312, www.alaskagoldrush.com) features two rooms ($85–95 d) and three lovely cabins ($95 d), all with a full breakfast. They're in the country six miles north of Palmer.

Other local places worth a look include **Active Alaska B&B** (907/745-0747 or 877/745-0747, www.activealaska.com), **Alaska's Caribou Cabins** (907/746-6881 or 888/408-2246, www.akcariboucabins.com), **A-Lazy Acres B&B** (907/745-6340), **Alaska's Harvest B&B** (907/745-4263, www.alaskasharvest.com), and **Moose Wallow B&B** (907/745-7777, www.moosewallow.com).

Camping

Palmer has one of the most luxurious city campgrounds in Alaska. **Matanuska River Park,** on East Arctic Ave. about a half-mile east of town, occupies a lush site full of big old cottonwoods and wild roses. There's lots of space between the 80 campsites, which are usually uncrowded except at state fair time, $10 for tents, $15 for RV hookups. Surrounding the campground is a day-use area, complete with picnic tables, softball and volleyball, horseshoe pits, and a nature trail around the ponds. The park also has coin-operated showers, firewood, trails, river access, and an observation deck. Contact Mat-Su Parks and Recreation (907/745-9631, www.co.mat-su.ak.us) for more information. Open late May to early October.

Local RV parks include **Homestead RV Park** (907/745-6005 or 800/478-3570) six miles east of Palmer, **Town & Country RV Park** (907/746-6642) near the fairgrounds, and **Mountain View RV Park** (907/745-5747 or 800/264-4582) three miles south of town.

Food

Palmer's **Vagabond Blues** (642 S. Alaska St., 907/745-2233) is a surprise in this bacon-and-eggs town. The espresso and pastries are fine, the atmosphere is heady, and the food is prepared with panache. You won't go wrong ordering a big hunk of freshly baked bread and an enormous bowl of today's soup (served in hand-painted pottery).

If you just want a good down-home halibut sandwich or dinner of chicken, pork, steak, scallop, or pasta, head to **Round House Cafe** (606 S. Alaska St., 907/745-3330) at the Valley Hotel. It's open 24 hours and non-smoking. More all-American fare (steaks and BBQ ribs) at **Denali Steakhouse** (918 S. Colony Way, 907/357-9444); it's famous for floats made with home-brewed root beer. Get authentic and reasonably priced Mexican food downtown at **La Fiesta** (132 W. Evergreen, 907/746-3335).

Palmer has a 24-hour **Carrs** grocery store (907/745-7505) on the corner of the Glenn Highway and Palmer–Wasilla Highway. Treat your sweet tooth at **Slack's Sugar Shack Bakery** (340 W. Evergreen Ave., 907/745-4777).

In late summer, keep an eye out for roadside produce stands to sample some of the valley's harvest. Check the following places for the U-Pick version: **Northern Fruits** (907/745-1070), **Palmer Produce** (907/746-2885), and **Pyrah's Pioneer Peak Farms** (907/745-4511).

Entertainment

Klondike Mike's Dance Hall & Saloon (820 S. Colony Way, 907/745-2676) has live rock 'n' roll most nights in a rustic Alaskan setting. Also check the lineup at **Vagabond Blues** (642 S. Alaska St., 907/745-2233), which comes alive on weekends when folk musicians pack the house.

Alaska State Fair

Don't miss Alaska's biggest summertime event, an 11-day party to bring down the curtain on summer that draws 300,000 visitors annually. The state fair (907/745-4827 or 800/850-3247, www.alaskastatefair.org) cranks up the fourth Friday of August, and continues through Labor Day. On a weekend day it may seem as though half of Anchorage has driven up to the fair. Long lines of cars wait to turn into the open field parking lots around the grounds, and crowds throng the 4-H displays, livestock auctions, horse shows, and carnival rides. There's live music daily, a rodeo, demolition derby, three nights of fireworks, and lots of food and craft booths. Favorites always include the roasted corn on the cob, sickly sweet elephant ears, supersized turkey legs, and finger-lickin' halibut tacos. One big attraction is the gargantuan vegetables, including 125-pound pumpkins, 10-pound onions, and two-pound radishes. The cabbage weigh-off makes front-page news in Alaska each year; an American record was set in 2000 when a Wasilla woman grew a 105-pound cabbage! Entrance is $8 adults, $5 seniors and youths, and free for kids under six.

One big attraction at the Alaska State Fair is the gargantuan vegetables, including 125-pound pumpkins, 10-pound onions, and two-pound radishes. The cabbage weigh-off makes front-page news in Alaska each year; an American record was set in 2000 when a Wasilla woman grew a 105-pound cabbage!

The **Alaska Railroad** (907/265-2494 or 800/544-0552, www.alaskarailroad.com) has direct train service from Anchorage to the fair grounds during the state fair; it's a great way to avoid the traffic jams and parking hassles. The round-trip cost is $45 adults, $42 seniors, or $23 ages 6–12, and $18 ages 2–5, free for tots. Prices include your entrance to the fair grounds—an excellent bargain.

Other Events

Colony Days takes place the third weekend of June, and includes a downtown parade, shopping cart races, arts and crafts booths, foot races, and games. The main wintertime event is the **Colony Christmas Celebration,** with a lighted parade held on the second Friday and Saturday of December, along with reindeer sled rides, caroling, arts and crafts, visits with Santa, and fireworks.

Recreation and Services

Swim at Palmer High School's **indoor pool** (1170 W. Arctic Ave., 907/745-5091). The **Palmer Golf Course** (907/745-4653) is an 18-hole course on Lepak Avenue along the Matanuska River.

The **Mat-Su Miners** (907/745-6401, www.matanuska.com/miners) play semiprofessional baseball on the Alaska State Fair Grounds throughout the summer. They're part of the Alaska Baseball League.

The **Palmer Library** (655 S. Valley Way, 907/745-4690), has public-use computers. Palmer's **Valley Hospital** (907/746-8600, www.valley-hosp.com) is at 515 E. Dahlia.

Transportation

Mat-Su Community Transit, better known as **MASCOT** (907/376-5000, www.matsutransit.com) has weekday service throughout the valley ($2) and commuter runs to Eagle River ($2.50) that can be combined with the People Mover bus system into Anchorage.

Alaska Direct Bus Line (907/277-6652 or 800/770-6652, www.home.gci.net/~akdirectbus) stops in Palmer en route to Whitehorse, Haines, or Skagway from Anchorage. The **Alaska Railroad** offers special trips from Anchorage to Palmer during the state fair.

WASILLA

In 1977, Wasilla consisted of a landing strip and a grocery store, which advertised the convenience of flying in from the bush, buying Matanuska Valley produce, and flying out again—without the hassles of Anchorage. Then, when the capital looked like it might be moved to Willow, 25 miles up the highway, Anchoragites began to discover Wasilla's quiet, beauty, and affordable land, and contractors took advantage of the town's lax restrictions on development. And develop it did, with a vengeance. During 1980–1982, the town's population of 1,200 doubled, then doubled again 1982–1984. Stores, malls, and fast-food chains popped up faster than you could say, "We do chicken right." Teeland's General Store was jacked up, moved from the corner it had sat on for over 60 years, and unceremoniously dumped in a parking lot around the block to make way for a 7-Eleven. The original airstrip, which had kept Wasilla on the map for so long, was moved out from the middle of all the hustle and bustle of town.

The unbridled growth continues today, as low real estate prices and good roads make the area a favorite of Anchorage commuters wanting a piece of the suburban lifestyle. In the 1990s, Wasilla's Wal-Mart proved so popular that after just a few years Wal-Mart built a new and much larger version across the highway. Dozens of strip-type buildings line the highway, with more added all the time in this fast-growing part of Alaska. Driving south into and through Wasilla on the Parks Highway is like passing through a space warp and reemerging in any southern California suburb. Because of its total lack of style and reputation for hick politics, Wasilla is the butt of jokes; visit Anchorage's Fly By Night Club for a particularly scathing version. By the way, Wasilla spelled backward is "All I Saw." Scary.

Historical Sights

Make sure to visit **Dorothy Page Museum and Historical Park** (907/373-9071, www.cityofwasilla.com/museum, Tues.–Sat. 9 A.M.–5 P.M. April–Sept. only) on Main Street just off the Parks Highway. Entrance is $3 adults, $2.50 seniors, free for kids under 13. The museum's hundreds of artifacts include a collection of old lenses, a 1920s radio, and an excellent relief map. Downstairs through the "mining tunnel" are more displays, including an entire early dentist's office. Walk out the back door to the old town site park settle-

ment with a schoolhouse, bunkhouse, smokehouse, steam bath, blacksmith shop, and cache.

Right across the street from the Dorothy Page Museum is the historic Teeland's Store, one of the oldest buildings in Alaska. Today the beautifully restored structure houses **Valley Bistro** (907/357-5633), the hippest place in Wasilla. Good pastries and espresso to start your day, followed by lunchtime salads, sandwiches, and smoothies, and evening burgers, appetizers, and other fare. Check out the building's amazing acoustics when musicians perform on Friday and Saturday nights. This a delightful place to write letters, meet friends, check your email on their computers, or enjoy a leisurely meal.

About four miles north of town (Mile 47), take a left at the sign and head .75 miles down to the **Museum of Alaska Transportation and Industry** (907/376-1211, www.museumofalaska.org). This museum houses an extensive collection of antiques relating to Alaskan aviation, railroading, fishing, mining, and road transportation. Take a gander at the "Chitina auto railer" an old car built to run on rail tracks. Outside are wooden boats, farm machinery (much of it still running), ancient snowmobiles, and several rail cars. The museum is open daily 10 A.M.–5 P.M. May–September, and Saturday 10 A.M.–5 P.M. and Sunday 1–5 P.M. the rest of the year. Admission is $8 adults, $5 seniors and youths, and free for kids under three.

Next to the museum is **Alaska Live Steamers,** a delightful scale model railroad that takes families through the forest, over bridges, and through tunnels on summer weekends. It's a good place to meet men living out their model railroad dreams. Rides cost $2. Trains run on weekends June–September; call 907/373-6412 for hours.

Knik Museum (907/376-7755, June–Aug. Fri.–Sun. noon–6 P.M., admission $2) is 14 miles out Knik Road from Wasilla. Housed in a century-old building, it exhibits items from the Knik gold rush of 1897–1917 and the Iditarod Trail.

Other Nearby Sights

Wasilla is the headquarters for the 1,049-mile **Iditarod Trail Sled Dog Race** from Anchorage to Nome. The headquarters (907/376-5155 or

800/545-6874, www.iditarod.com) includes a log museum containing race memorabilia, Native artifacts, videos, and dog-mushing equipment. It's two miles out Knik Road, open daily 8 A.M.–7 P.M. Memorial Day to mid-Sept., and Mon.–Fri. 8 A.M.–5 P.M. the rest of the year. Admission is free, though a $5 fee is charged to go for a ride on a wheeled dogsled. Next door is a gift shop selling products from **Alaska Birch Syrup Company** (907/357-4884, www.birchforests.com).

Lakeshore Park at Wasilla Lake right off the highway has swimming (not too cold), picnic tables, and a view of the craggy Chugach Mountains—great place to set up your tripod. A less crowded day-use lake area is at **Kepler-Bradley Lakes** just beyond the junction of the Parks and Glenn Highways, on the Glenn toward Palmer.

Seven miles south of Wasilla on the Parks Highway, and immediately north of the intersection with the Glenn Highway, turn onto Trunk Road and climb the hill to the University of Alaska's **Agricultural Experimental Station** (907/746-9481). Founded in 1917 by the U.S. Department of Agriculture, this 960-acre farm was deeded to the university in 1931. Agricultural information collected here was the contributing factor in colonizing this valley with Midwestern farmers in 1935. Come here late in the summer to see large cabbages, giant begonias, and scores of flowers. You can tour the demonstration garden on your own at any time.

Motels

Several motels are strung along the Parks Highway. On the south end of Wasilla is **Windbreak Hotel** (907/376-4484, www.windbreakalaska.com, $65 d) rebuilt following a 2002 fire, with 10 reasonably priced rooms. **Valley Country Motel** (907/357-7878, $70 for up to four) has clean rooms in an older building at Mountain Village Plaza.

Alaskan View Motel (2650 E. Parks Hwy., 907/376-6787, www.alaskanviewmotel.com, $109–115 d) is a modern two-story log building across from Nye Ford.

Best Western Lake Lucille Inn (1300 W. Lake Lucille Dr., 907/373-1776 or 800/528-1234, www.bestwestern.com/lakelucilleinn, $134–169 d) has 54 roomy rooms, half with

private balconies overlooking the lake. Guests will also appreciate the fitness center, sauna, hot tub, and outside dining in the restaurant. Paddle boats and canoes are available for rent.

Agate Inn (907/373-2290 or 800/770-2290, www.agateinn.com), is three miles from Wasilla on the Palmer–Wasilla Highway, and has a variety of lodging options, from motel-type rooms with king beds in the main house ($95 d) to apartments with kitchens ($125 d) and a two-bedroom cottage ($205 for four people).

Kozey Cabins (351 E. Spruce Ave., 907/376-3190, www.alaskaone.com/kozeycabins, $129 d) has modern cabins with kitchenettes a mile off Parks Highway.

Mat-Su Resort (1850 Bogard Rd., 907/376-3228, www.alaskan.com/matsuresort) charges $95 d for standard rooms and $105 d for larger rooms with king beds. The resort sits on the quiet north side of Lake Wasilla.

Bed-and-Breakfasts

Visit the **Mat-Su Bed & Breakfast Association's,** website (www.alaskabnbhosts.com) for links to local B&Bs, including a daily vacancy listing throughout the summer.

Lake Lucille B&B (907/357-0353 or 888/353-0352, www.alaskaslakelucillebnb.com) is a large new home on the shore of Lake Lucille, just a short distance from Wasilla. The four guest rooms (shared baths) are a reasonable $69 s or $79 d; a family suite is $135. A light breakfast starts each day.

For something more traditionally Alaskan, stay at **Pioneer Ridge B&B** (1830 E. Parks Hwy., 907/376-7472 or 800/478-7472, www.pioneerridge.net). This distinctive 10,000-square-foot home sits on a hill in the country south of Wasilla. Seven guest rooms with shared or private baths are available ($100–155 d), along with a separate homestead cabin ($100 d). A light breakfast is served in the common room, where you can also play a game of pool, watch a video, listen to the player piano, or simply relax. On top of the house is a unique glass-enclosed room with a fireplace and 360-degree views.

Wasilla Lake B&B (961 N. Shore Dr., 907/376-5985, www.wasillalake.com) has a pretty lakeside location surrounded by trees, and the friendly owners have been welcoming guests since 1987. Lodging options include three bedrooms ($85 d) with a shared bath, a spacious apartment with a full kitchen ($150 d). A full breakfast is included.

Tollers' Timbers (907/746-1438 or 800/795-1438, www.alaskavacationcabins.com, $105–135 d) consists of five cabins and apartments. One even has a private hot tub. The buildings are on a 14-acre spread in the country halfway between Wasilla and Palmer.

Alaskan Sampler B&B (907/745-7829 or 877/228-7829, www.alaskansampler.com, $95–150 d) is a luxurious place to bed down just a mile from the Parks Highway. The two suites come with full breakfast and jetted tubs.

Other places ($80–95 d) worth checking out include **Harrington Gardens B&B** (907/357-0357, www.harringtongardens.com), **Gate House B&B** (907/376-5960 or 888/866-9326, www.gatehousealaska.com), and **Shady Acres Inn B&B** (907/376-3113 or 800/360-3113, www.shadyacresbnb.com).

Camping

Lake Lucille Park (907/745-9631, www.co.mat-su.ak.us) is an 80-acre natural area with trails and campsites two miles south of Wasilla off Knik–Goose Bay Road. This Mat-Su Borough campground has sites for $10 (no hookups). There's also a public campground ($10) at **Finger Lake State Recreation Site**, six miles east of Wasilla on Bogard Road.

Best View RV Park (907/745-7400 or 800/478-6600) has RV hookups near the Mat-Su Visitor Center, Mile 36 of the Parks Highway, but it may be closed by the time you visit since a new hospital will open on the site by 2006. Many RVers park for free in local shopping mall lots.

Food

Perhaps because of all the early-morning commuters to Anchorage, Wasilla seems to have an espresso stand on almost every corner—along with an equal number of gun shops. Sounds like a dangerous combination, especially with all those folks listening to Rush Limbaugh each

morning. A better bet for a jolt is the delightfully old fashioned **Valley Bistro** (907/357-5633), with good pastries and espresso to start your day, followed by lunchtime salads, sandwiches, and bagels.

Windbreak Cafe (907/376-4484) is a good choice for home-cooked meals, prime rib, and seafood. Breakfast is served all day. **Chepo's Fiesta** (731 W. Parks Hwy., 907/373-5656) serves authentic Mexican food in a fun setting.

Evangelo's Trattoria (907/376-1212) is, like most Wasilla businesses, in a strip mall along the Parks Highway. The interior is surprisingly classy, and locals rave about the food: lasagna, calzones, scampi, pizzas, and an excellent Italian sausage sandwich. Dinner entrées are $15–23.

Great Bear Brewing Co. (238 N. Boundary St., 907/373-4782, www.greatbearbrewing.com, daily until midnight) has fresh beers and huge portions of pub fare, including seafood, pasta, steaks, and burgers. Rock bands on weekends. Recommended.

Schwabenhof Bavarian Restaurant and Beer Garden (907/357-2739) is halfway between Wasilla and Palmer on the Palmer–Wasilla Highway. One of Alaska's only German restaurants, the Schwab serves a different special nightly, but typically includes schnitzel, sausages, sauerkraut, potato salad, and German pastries. Don't expect fine dining; your meal is served on a paper plate. The interior of this *very* smoky bar may not be exactly romantic, but it's fun and friendly. Ornate steins line the log walls of this octagonal hilltop cabin.

Mat-Su Resort (1850 Bogard Rd., 907/376-3228) has a good lakeside dining room that specializes in Angus steaks; open for lunch and dinner daily, and breakfast on weekends.

The **Best Western Lake Lucille Inn** (1300 W. Lake Lucille Dr., 907/373-1776) has best-in-the-valley steak and seafood dining, plus a soup and salad bar. This is one of the priciest places in the Valley, but the good food and great views from the lakeside windows help to soften the blow to your wallet. It also serves a popular Sunday brunch.

Wasilla has all the standard generic grease glop; just keep driving until your favorite chain shows its predictable exterior. A better bet is to head to the deli at **Carrs** grocery store; they're open 24 hours. Wasilla's **Farmers Market** (907/376-5679, Wednesday evenings 3–6 P.M.) takes place mid-June to mid-September at the old Wasilla town site. **Cold Stone Creamery** (1830 Parks Hwy., 907/357-2653) is a destination for ice cream, smoothies, and cut-in flavors.

Entertainment and Events

Wasilla's big event comes in early March, as the **Iditarod Trail Sled Dog Race** slides through town. The race officially begins in Anchorage, but after a 25-mile run to Eagle River, the dogs are trucked north for the "restart" at the Wasilla Airport. Just west of here the teams move completely away from the road system, and are in wilderness all the way to Nome. The **Wasilla Water Festival** on the 4th of July features parades, competitions, and a fireworks display around midnight (when it gets dark enough to be almost visible).

Borealis Beach Club (907/376-5350, www.borealisbeachclub.com) calls itself "an Alaskan tradition since 1962." Located at Mile 49, it's Mat-Su's place where men go to check out the latest in skimpy female attire (or the lack thereof). Try Great Bear Brewing Co. for a less risqué entertainment option.

Information and Services

The **Matanuska-Susitna Convention and Visitors Bureau** (907/746-5000, www.alaskavisit.com) has a large visitors center just north of the junction of the Parks and Glenn Highway, and six miles south of Wasilla. It's open daily 8:30 A.M.–6:30 P.M. mid-May to mid-September; closed the rest of the year. You can also get info from the **Wasilla Chamber of Commerce** (415 E. Railroad Ave., 907/376-1299, www.wasillachamber.org), housed in the historic railroad depot. It's open Monday–Friday 9 A.M.–5 P.M. year-round.

The **Wasilla Public Library** (391 N. Main St., 907/376-5913) is a good place to stop and check your email or play on the Web. If you don't want to wait, head to **The Digital Cup** (1451 E. Parks Hwy., 907/373-2727) next to Fred Meyer at, or **Valley Bistro.**

Swim at Wasilla High School's **swimming pool** (701 W. Bogard Rd., 907/376-4222).

Transportation

Mat-Su Community Transit, better known as **MASCOT** (907/376-5000, www.matsutransit.com) has weekday service throughout the valley ($2) and commuter runs to Eagle River ($2.50) that can be combined with the People Mover bus system into Anchorage.

Downtown Connection (907/373-8014 or 866/344-6667, www.akdowntownconnection.com) has scheduled Anchorage runs for $9 each way. A number of bus companies pass through Wasilla on their way between Anchorage and Denali, and can pick you up with prior arrangement.

Based at Lake Lucille Inn, **Bear Air** (907/373-3373 or 888/430-3373, www.alaska.net/~bearair) takes passengers on flightseeing trips over Mt. McKinley.

HATCHER PASS

This is one of the most beautiful parts of the Mat-Su Valley region, and a wonderful side trip from either the Parks Highway north of Wasilla, or the Glenn Highway at Palmer. It's a 49-mile drive, starting in Palmer and ending at Mile 71 of the Parks (30 miles north of Wasilla).

Most folks get to Hatcher Pass from the Palmer end. Hatcher Pass Road (also called Fishhook–Willow Rd.) begins in rolling forest-and-farm country and then climbs along the beautiful Little Susitna River—popular with experienced kayakers who enjoy Class V white water. After passing Motherlode Lodge (open only for groups), the road climbs steeply uphill to Independence Mine State Historical Park at Mile 17 (where the pavement ends) before topping out at 3,886-foot Hatcher Pass and Summit Lake in an area of vast vistas, high tundra, excellent hiking, and backcountry camping. Then it's downhill through pretty forests along Willow Creek all the way to the Parks Highway; this route was originally a wagon road built to service the gold mines. The road is paved from Palmer all the way to Independence Mine, and for 10 miles from the Willow

Independence Mine State Historical Park

side; the rest is gravel. A bike path follows the road along the Little Susitna River section, and campsites can be found at Deception Creek, two miles from the Parks Highway.

Independence Mine State Historical Park

It's hard to imagine a park that better combines the elements of the Alaska experience: scenery, history and lore, and that noble yellow metal, gold. This mine is very different from the panning, sluicing, deep-placer, and dredging operations seen in Interior Alaska. This was "hard-rock" mining, with an intricate 21-mile network of tunnels under Granite Mountain. The miners drilled into the rock, inserted explosives (which they set off at the end of shifts to give the fumes time to dissipate before the next crew went in), then "mucked" the debris out by hand, to be sorted, crushed, amalgamated, and assayed.

Hard-rock or "lode" mining is often preceded by panning and placer mining. Prospectors who first took gold from Grubstake Gulch, a tributary of Willow Creek, in 1897 noticed the gold's rough, unweathered nature, which indicated a possible lode of unexposed gold nearby.

In 1906, Robert Lee Hatcher staked the first lode claim, and his Alaska Free Gold Mine operated until 1924. In 1908, the Independence Mine opened on the mountain's east slope, and over the next 25 years it produced several million dollars' worth. In 1937, the two mines merged into the Alaska Pacific Consolidated Mining Company, which operated Independence Mine at peak production through 1942, when World War II shut it down. A series of private sales, and public deals with the Alaska Division of Parks, culminated in 1980, leaving the state with 271 acres, including the whole mining camp, and deeding 1,000 acres to the Coronado Mining Corporation, which has active operations in the area.

A couple of dozen camp buildings are in various stages of ruin and refurbishing. Start at the visitor center in the rehabilitated house of the camp manager. Take some time to enjoy the excellent displays: historic charts, gold-mining overview, "touch tunnel" complete with sound effects, and wage summaries of workers and management. Guided tours are given daily at 1 and 3 P.M. (plus 4:30 P.M. on weekends) by park personnel. Tours cost $3 adults, $2 seniors. At other times, just wander the site on your own; interpretive signs describe the various buildings. Independence Mine State Historical Park is a must-see on any Alaskan itinerary.

The visitor center (907/745-2827 summer only or 907/745-3975, www.alaskastateparks.org) is open daily 10 A.M.–7 P.M. from late May to early September; closed the rest of the year. Parking is $5.

Accommodations

A number of B&Bs are scattered along the southern section of Hatcher Pass Road near Palmer. **Hatcher Pass B&B** (907/745-6788, www.hatcherpassbb.com, $70 s, $80 d) has delightful log cabins. **Rose Ridge B&B** (907/745-8604 or 877/827-7673, www.roseridgebnb.com) has rooms for $75 s or $85 d.

Just downhill from Independence Mine is **Hatcher Pass Lodge** (907/745-5897, www.hatcherpasslodge.com). This A-frame lodge is a great spot for sandwiches, fondues, pizza, steaks, and halibut ($14–23 dinner entrées), with a sunset view to die for. Nine cozy cabins cost $115 d, and three tiny upstairs rooms are $95 d each. Also on the grounds is a creekside sauna, $5 extra (guests only). The lodge is open daily all year. Speaking from personal experience, this is the perfect place for a summer wedding. The lodge also maintains 10 km of groomed ski trails (donation) in the winter, and more adventurous backcountry skiers and snowboarders head up the steep (and avalanche-prone) slopes that rise on three sides. In winter the road isn't plowed beyond Independence Mine State Park but you can park here to play; it's a special favorite of snowmobilers.

NORTH TO DENALI

It's a long 195-mile drive from Wasilla (and 237 miles from Anchorage) to Denali National Park on the Parks Highway. After the first few miles, the developments peter out and roadside attractions shift from fast food, gun shops, and video stores to the real Alaska of forests and mountains. The land is a seemingly endless birch and spruce forest, with a smattering of half-finished plywood homesteads covered in blue tarps, their yards piled high with firewood. The road follows a gradual climb toward the magnificent Alaska Range that seems to grow in magnitude the farther north you get. Mile after mile of pink fireweed flowers brighten the roadside in mid-summer.

Big Lake

The Big Lake area is a popular recreation destination, especially on summer weekends when many Anchorageites head to summer homes here. Access is via nine-mile-long Big Lake Road which splits off the Parks Highway at Mile 52 (10 miles north of Wasilla). Don't expect quiet along this large and scenic lake. In summer, Big Lake is jet-ski central 24 hours a day, and when winter arrives the snowmobile crowd comes out for more motorized mayhem. For local information, contact the **Big Lake Chamber of Commerce** (907/892-6109, www.biglake-ak.com).

Big Lake was near the center of the 1996 Miller's Reach Fire that blackened 37,500 acres and destroyed over 400 buildings. Three state park campgrounds ($10–15) are in the area: **Rocky Lake State Recreation Site, Big Lake North State Recreation Site,** and **Big Lake South State Recreation Site.**

Lodging is available at **Klondike Inn** (907/892-6261, www.klondikeinn.com) and **Big Lake Motel** (907/892-7976). **Sunset View B&B** (907/892-8885, www.sunsetviewbb.com, $125–165 d) is an elegant, three-story lakeside home where the four guest rooms all have private entrances and hot tubs. Also here is a pool table and exercise room.

Houston

This podunk gathering of 900 or so souls 58 miles from Anchorage includes the usual lineup of suspects: gas, groceries, café, lodging, RV park, laundromat, and air taxi operators, but it is best known for its fireworks stands. Four of these giant eyesores—it's especially hard to miss Gorilla Fireworks—sit on the edges of town, pulling families from Anchorage looking for fun on the Fourth of July. Fireworks are illegal to shoot off almost anywhere in Alaska. Of course, this is one of those legal niceties that is widely ignored. It's a bit ironic that the devastating 1996 Miller's Reach

Fire that threatened Houston was probably started by fireworks purchased in Houston. **Little Susitna River Campground** ($8) is a Mat-Su Borough facility on the south side of Houston.

Nancy Lake State Recreation Area
Access to Nancy Lake is from Mile 67 of the Parks Highway, just south of Willow, and 25 miles north of Wasilla. This flat, heavily forested terrain is dotted with over 100 lakes, some interconnected by creeks. As you might imagine, the popular activities here are fishing, boating, and canoeing, plus a comfortable campground and a couple of hiking trails. As you might also imagine, the skeeters here are thick in early summer.

Follow the Nancy Lake Road a little more than a mile to **Nancy Lake State Recreation Site Campground** ($5). A half-mile past the kiosk is the trailhead to several **public-use cabins** (reservations: 907/745-3975, www.alaskastateparks.org). The cost is $35–50, but reserve well ahead to be sure of getting one of these exceptionally popular cabins. Just under a mile beyond this trailhead is the **Tulik Nature Trail,** an easy walk that takes about an hour. Keep an eye out for loons, beavers, and terns, and watch for that prickly devil's club!

The **Tanaina Lake Canoe Route** begins at Mile 4.5, Nancy Lakes Road. This leisurely, 12-mile, two-day trip hits 14 lakes, between most of which are well-marked portages, some upgraded with boardwalks over the muskeg. Hunker down for the night at any one of 10 primitive campsites (campfires in fireplaces only). Another possibility, though requiring a long portage, is to put into the Little Susitna River at Mile 57 on the Parks Highway and portage to Skeetna Lake, where you connect up to the southern leg of the loop trail. **Tippecanoe** (907/495-6688, www.paddlealaska.com), at South Rolly Campground, rents canoes for the Nancy Lake canoe trails, has rafts for nearby streams, and guides canoe tours within the park. **Nancy Lake Resort** (Mile 65, 907/495-6284, $45 d), has very rustic cabins (bring your bedding; separate showerhouse) with kitchenettes. The campground has sites for $15, with coin-op showers but no hookups.

At the end of Big Lake road is the scenic **South**

Rolly Lake Campground ($10). An easy three-mile round-trip trail leads to an overlook above Red Shirt Lake. Continue on this trail all the way to the lake.

Willow
At Mile 69 is Willow (pop. 400), a roadside town with gas, grocery, hardware, café, and air service that you'll miss if you sneeze. Back in 1980, however, Alaskans voted to move the state capital here. A multibillion-dollar city was planned, and real estate speculation went wild. However, when a second election was held in 1982 to decide whether to actually *spend* the billions, the plan was soundly defeated.

Stay at **Pioneer Lodge** (907/495-1000), right on the creek with rustic lodging ($80 d), camping ($22 for RVs, $12 for tents), and good pizzas. **Willow Island Resort** (907/495-6343), has an RV park on the opposite bank.

Both **Willow Air Service** (907/495-6370 or 800/478-6370, www.matnet.com/~wilair) and **Denali Flying Service** (907/495-5899, www.denaliflying.com) offer scenic flights over Knik Glacier, Hatcher Pass, and Mt. McKinley from Willow. **Willow Creek Resort** (907/495-7238, www.willowcreekresort.com) rents rafts and outdoor gear.

North to Talkeetna
At Mile 71 of the Parks is the turnoff to **Willow Creek State Recreation Area,** four miles down the Susitna River access road. Sites are $10, but don't expect a quiet night's repose in the wilderness here if the salmon are running, which they do for most of the summer. The boat launch attracts fishing parties at all hours of the day and night, as well as lots of RVs with their inevitable generator noise. Still, it's a pretty and handy place to spend the night if it's getting late and you plan to travel over the exceptionally scenic Hatcher Pass to Independence Mine State Historical Park. More camping along nearby Deception Creek, two miles up Hatcher Pass Road.

In the 45 miles from Willow to the Talkeetna cutoff are scattered lodging places, restaurants, and gas stations. The most notable place is **Sheep Creek Lodge** (Mile 89, 907/495-6227, www.sheepcreeklodge.com). This classic log Alaskan roadhouse was rebuilt in 1986 after a fire destroyed the previous incarnation. Its restaurant serves meals year-round. Modern hotel rooms with private baths are $100 d. Rustic cabins are $52 d, with a bathhouse nearby. There's also an RV park ($23 with full hookups) and tent spaces ($3).

Gigglewood Lakeside Inn (907/495-1014 or 800/574-2555, www.gigglewood.com) is a remote and lovingly designed log home on a small lake several miles off the Parks Highway at Mile 88. The home contains a suite with private bath and kitchenette for $120 d, and two guest rooms that share a bath for $95 d each. A full breakfast is served in the common room overlooking the lake. You can relax in the sauna or try out the paddleboat and mountain bikes.

Additional lodging, with breakfast, is available at **Susitna Dog Tours B&B** (Mile 92, 907/495-6324, www.susitnadogtours.com, $60 s or $85 d) which also offers wintertime dog mushing tours.

The privately run **Montana Creek Campgrounds** (Mile 97, 907/566-2267) have wooded sites on both sides of this popular salmon fishing creek.

The Kenai Peninsula

The Kenai Peninsula is like a mini-Alaska, compressing all of the state's features into an area roughly one-thirty-fifth the size of the state. You'll find mountains, icefields and glaciers, fjords and offshore islands, large fish-filled rivers and lakes, swampy plains, varied climate and precipitation, a few scattered port towns and a sprawling population center. The Kenai is the major playground for both Anchorage residents and travelers from Outside, and it's possibly the most popular all-around destination for all Alaskans. The outdoor recreational opportunities are practically inexhaustible, with innumerable choices of every pedestrian, pedaled, paddled, piloted, port-holed, piscatory, predatory, and picaresque particular you could ever ponder—just you and 300,000 other folks from the neighborhood. But don't let the possibility of crowds deter you. The resources are abundant, well developed, and often isolated. And besides, what's wrong with a little company along the trail or under sail?

The Land

At 16,056 square miles, Kenai Peninsula is a little smaller than Vermont and New Hampshire combined. The Kenai Mountains form the peninsula's backbone, with massive Harding Icefield dominating the lower lumbar. The east side,

sailboats on Kachemak Bay

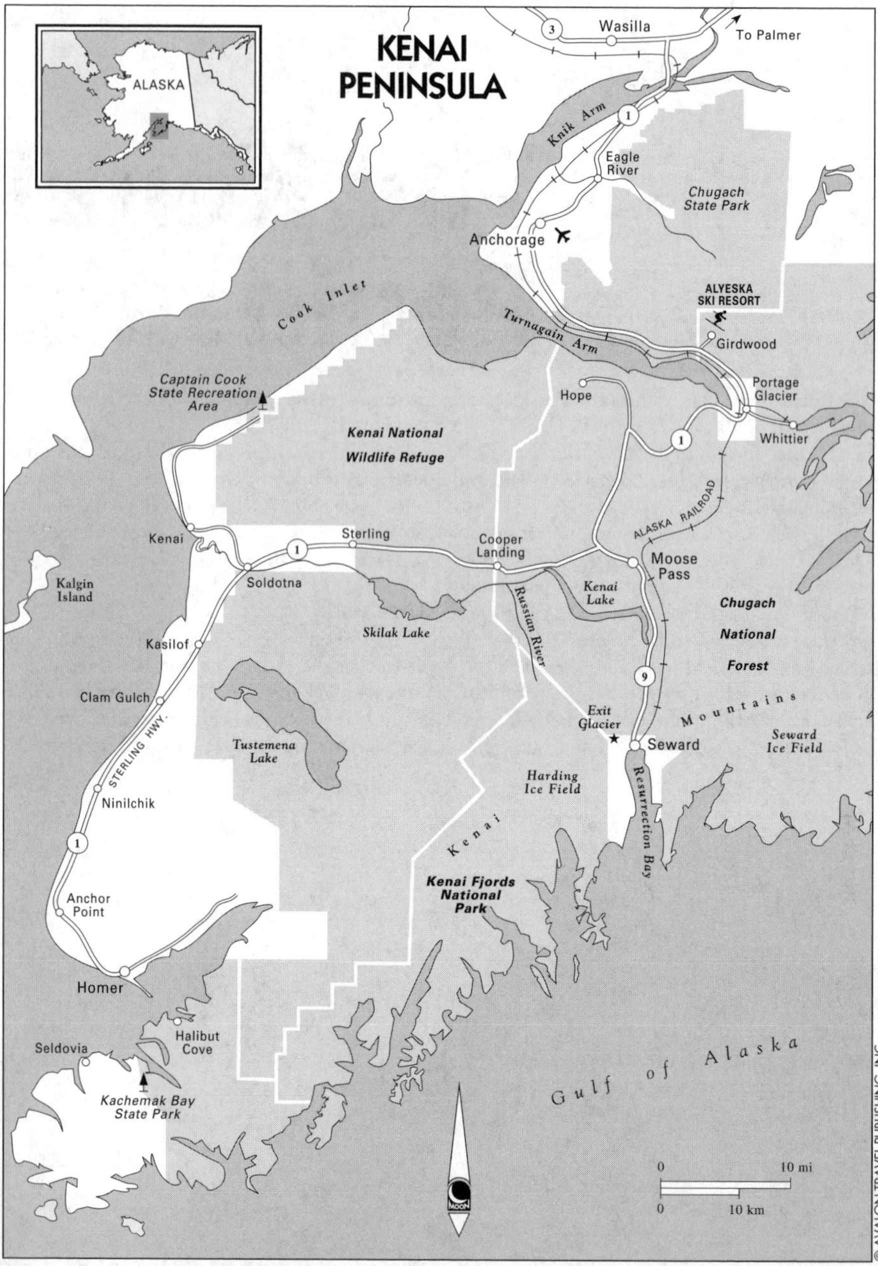

KENAI PENINSULA

ALASKA

To Palmer

Wasilla

Knik Arm

Eagle River

Chugach State Park

Anchorage

ALYESKA SKI RESORT

Turnagain Arm

Girdwood

Cook Inlet

Portage Glacier

Captain Cook State Recreation Area

Hope

Whittier

Kenai National Wildlife Refuge

ALASKA RAILROAD

Kenai

Sterling

Cooper Landing

Moose Pass

Kalgin Island

Soldotna

Kenai Lake

Chugach

Kasilof

Skilak Lake

Russian River

National

Forest

Clam Gulch

STERLING HWY.

Tustemena Lake

Exit Glacier

Mountains

Seward Ice Field

Ninilchik

Harding Ice Field

Seward

Resurrection Bay

Anchor Point

Kenai

Kenai Fjords National Park

Homer

Seldovia

Halibut Cove

Gulf of Alaska

Kachemak Bay State Park

0   10 mi

0   10 km

© AVALON TRAVEL PUBLISHING, INC.

MOON

THE KENAI PENINSULA

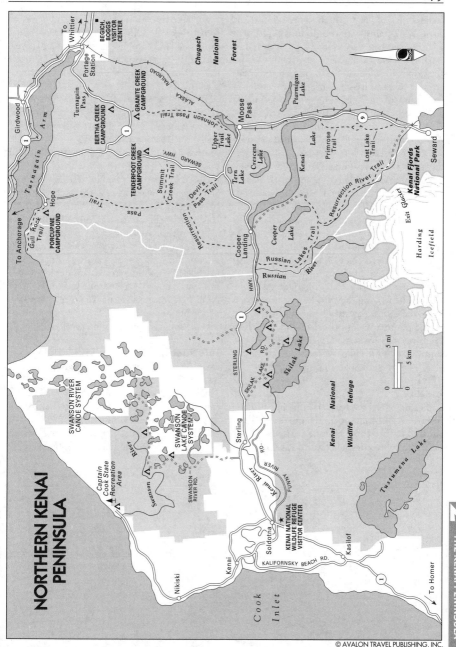

NORTHERN KENAI PENINSULA

© AVALON TRAVEL PUBLISHING, INC.

facing Prince William Sound, hosts a spur of the Kenai Mountains, with the glimmering Sargent Icefields; the west side, facing Cook Inlet, is outwash plain, sparkling with low-lying swamp, lakes, and rivers. The icefields, glaciers, and plains are all a result of ice sculpting over the million-year course of the Pleistocene, with its five major glacial periods. During the last, the Wisconsin Period, Portage Glacier filled the entire Turnagain Arm, 50 miles long and a half-mile high. Portage stopped just short—10,000 years ago—of carving a fjord between Prince William Sound and Turnagain Arm; otherwise, Kenai Peninsula would've been Kenai Island. Still, this peninsula is so digitated with peninsulettes that it has more than 1,000 miles of coastline. The land is almost completely controlled by the feds; Chugach National Forest, Kenai National Wildlife Refuge, and Kenai Fjords National Park account for nearly 85 percent of the peninsula.

Two roads provide the primary access to the Kenai. The 127-mile **Seward Highway** connects Anchorage with Seward on the southwest end of the peninsula, and the 143-mile **Sterling Highway** cuts across the Kenai, leading west and south from Tern Lake (where it meets the Seward Highway) to Soldotna and Homer.

History

You begin to feel the Russian influence strongly in this neck of the woods. Baranov's first shipyard was somewhere along Resurrection Bay down from present-day Seward. Russians built a stockade near Kasilof in 1786 and a fort at Kenai in 1791. Other than these brief incursions, the land belonged to the Kenai Natives, part of the great Athabascan tribe on the north half of the peninsula, while the Alutiiqs occupied the southern half.

During the gold rush, color was uncovered around Hope and Sunrise on Turnagain Arm, and at Moose Creek halfway to Seward. First trails ran between the mining communities, then wagon roads and finally the railroad pushed from Seward through Anchorage to Fairbanks in the early 1920s. The Seward and Sterling Highways were completed in 1952, opening the Kenai's western frontier. When Atlantic Richfield tapped into oil (1957) and gas (1962) off the west coast, the peninsula's economic star began to twinkle. Oil and gas production have dropped steadily since the peak in the 1970s as the reserves are depleted, but new gas deposits are being developed near Ninilchik. Today, the Kenai Peninsula Borough's nearly 50,000 residents are occupied with fishing, oil and gas, tourism, and services.

Information

Every Kenai Peninsula town of any size has its own chamber of commerce and website; they're listed under the individual towns. A good overall information source is the **Kenai Peninsula Tourism Marketing Council** (907/283-3850 or 800/535-3624, www.kenaipeninsula.org), which produces a detailed annual travel publication.

Eastern Kenai Peninsula

CHUGACH NATIONAL FOREST

Much of the eastern Kenai Peninsula lies within Chugach National Forest, the second largest national forest in America after the Tongass. Covering 5.5 million acres—bigger than Massachusetts—the Chugach encompass not just this part of the Kenai, but also continues eastward across all of Prince William Sound, to well beyond the Copper River. Developments and logging are relatively minor on the Chugach, but all this wild country provides incredible opportunities for recreation, with good fishing, hiking, mountain biking, river-rafting, skiing, kayaking, wildlife-watching, glacier-gazing, and a host of other outdoor adventures. Forest headquarters is in Anchorage (3301 C. St., 907/743-9500, www.fs.fed.us), with district offices in Seward (907/224-3374), Girdwood (907/783-3242), and Cordova (907/424-7661).

Cabins

The Kenai Peninsula has 18 Forest Service public-use cabins available for $35–45 per night. These are mostly Pan-Abode log structures that sleep four and have wood or oil stoves. Most of these are along hiking trails—including eight cabins on the Resurrection Pass Trail—but a few are accessible only by floatplane. The Chugach website has cabin details, or you can get brochures from the Alaska Public Lands Information Center in Anchorage. Because of their high popularity, it's a wise to reserve cabins well ahead of your visit by contacting **ReserveUSA** (518/885-3639 or 877/444-6777, www.reserveusa.com). Additional public cabins can be found within Kenai Fjords National Park and Kachemak Bay State Park.

Camping and Hiking

Six Forest Service campgrounds are located along the Seward Highway south of Portage, with another four along the Sterling Highway, and two more off the Hope Highway; all are described below. A number of very popular hiking trails cover the eastern half of the Kenai Peninsula, and it's possible to hike (or mountain bike) all the way from the town of Hope to Exit Glacier near Seward, a distance of 74 miles. Several of these trails are described below. Contact the Forest Service for details on various camping and hiking options within the Chugach.

THE SEWARD HIGHWAY

The 127-mile Seward Highway—a National Scenic Byway—connects Anchorage with Seward on the Kenai Peninsula. Mileposts are numbered from the Seward end; subtract these numbers from 127 for the distance to Anchorage. (See the *Anchorage and Vicinity* chapter for details on the first 48 miles of the road south from Anchorage—including Girdwood and Portage Glacier.) The Seward Highway has passing lanes, wide shoulders, and a 65 mph speed limit much of the way, but take the time to enjoy the scenery. Keep your headlights on at all times, and watch for moose.

Near Portage at Mile 48, the Seward Highway banks sharply to the west along Turnagain Arm before turning again southward as it climbs into the Kenai Mountains. At **Turnagain Pass** (Mile 69, elevation 988 feet), the west side of the road has a big pullout with port-a-potties. Stop and stretch in this pretty alpine area where the snow remains until late June. In the winter the snow is often 10 feet deep. The west side is popular with snowmobilers, while the east side is reserved for those on skis or snowshoes. Turnagain Pass can be deadly at certain times of the winter, and a number of snowmobilers have died in avalanches here while riding on the dangerous upper slopes.

At Mile 64 is the northern trailhead for the **Johnson Pass Trail,** which goes 23 miles over relatively level terrain and emerges at Mile 33 of the Seward Highway. Two in-the-trees Forest Service campgrounds ($9) are nearby: **Bertha Creek Campground** (Mile 65) and **Granite Creek Campground** (Mile 63). The paved **Sixmile Bike Trail** parallels the highway from the Johnson Pass Trailhead south to the junction with the Hope Highway.

Sixmile Creek

At Mile 59 the highway crosses a staging area along Granite Creek for rafters and kayakers down Granite Creek and on to Sixmile Creek, where some sections are Class V. This is one of Alaska's premier white-water areas. Check out the action from the footbridge that crosses Sixmile Creek, accessible via a short path from the parking area just east of the Canyon Creek bridge. **Nova River-runners** (907/745-5753 or 800/746-5753, www.novalaska.com) and **Chugach Outdoor Center** (907/277-7238 or 866/277-7238, www.chugachoutdoorcenter.com) guide white-water trips down both Sixmile Creek and Granite Creek in the summer.

HOPE

The Hope Highway begins at Mile 56 of the Seward Highway, just west of the towering bridge over Canyon Creek. This sparsely trafficked road follows Sixmile Creek north back up to Turnagain Arm; pan for gold along the first five miles of the crick. The entire 17 miles to Hope is paved.

© DON PITCHER

downtown Hope

Gold was discovered on Resurrection Creek in 1888, and by 1896 3,000 people inhabited this boom neighborhood, between Hope and Sunrise on Sixmile Creek. Many came by way of the Passage Canal where Whittier now squats, portaging their watercraft over the Chugach glacial pass to Turnagain Arm, which is how Portage Glacier got its name. Large-scale mining prospered into the 1940s, but then Sunrise was abandoned and left to the ghosts. Hope (www.advenalaska.com/hope) hangs on today primarily as a place where recreation and tourism support the town's 135 people.

Sights

"Downtown" Hope is marked by a cluster of old buildings, some over a century old. Stop here to walk the dirt street past photogenic **Social Hall**—the original Alaska Commercial Co. store—and down to the tidal flats (caused by the earth sinking seven feet in the 1964 quake); they're dangerous—don't walk on them! Go back and turn left for new Hope, with its post office, its red schoolhouse, and beautiful new and old log cabins. The old one-room school (built in 1938) now serves as a **library**. Next door is **Hope Chest** (907/782-3311), selling locally made crafts.

Hope & Sunrise Historical and Mining Museum (907/782-3740, summer Fri., Sat., and Mon. noon–4 P.M., Sun. noon–2 P.M., free admission) is a log museum housing historical photos and artifacts from the Turnagain Arm gold rush of 1894–-1899. The grounds contain the original Canyon Creek Mining buildings.

Accommodations and Food

Seaview Cafe (907/782-3300) has tent sites, RV hookups, and simple cabins ($45 d; outhouses and no running water). The century-old café is open for lunch and dinner daily May–September. Food is also available from **Tito's Discovery Cafe** (907/782-3274), a popular meeting place for locals.

Get a taste of pioneer life with a night at **Hope Gold Rush B&B** (907/782-3436). This lov-

FOLLOWING THE RESURRECTION PASS TRAIL

The Resurrection Pass Trail covers 38 miles between the towns of Hope and Cooper Landing, with two side routes leading off to trailheads along the Seward Highway. You'll gain and lose 2,000 feet in elevation along the way. A series of Forest Service cabins make this one of the most popular hiking destinations in Southcentral Alaska. The trail winds through spruce forests and tops out in tundra, affording opportunities to see a variety of habitats. Wildlife, wildflowers, and wild fish in the lakes and streams add to the trail's appeal.

The trail begins four rough miles from Hope up Resurrection Pass Road, where a trailhead has parking, an information signboard, and a fun bridge across the crick. Eight cabins along the trail, one of which can only be reached via a floatplane, provide a welcome respite from the often-inclement weather. They're basic, each consisting of wooden bunks, a table and benches, a countertop for cooking, an outhouse, and a heating stove for warmth, but without running water, cooking utensils, or bedding. These very popular cabins cost $35–45 per night, and the farther in advance you can make plans, the more likely you are to secure a reservation. Make reservations through ReserveUSA.

If you can't secure cabins, there are plenty of spots to camp for the night. Be very careful with campfires or, better yet, use a camp stove for cooking. Also filter or boil all drinking water.

Local wildlife includes moose, black and brown bears, wolves, mountain goats, Dall sheep, and even a local caribou herd. The caribou are scattered and often hard to spot in the summer, but if you look up high in the Resurrection Pass and Devil's Pass areas, maybe you'll get lucky. They often like to bed down in snow patches during the heat of the day, so look for dark spots in the snow near ridgelines.

Loop trips are possible, and you can do the Devil's Pass trailhead–Devil's Pass cabin–Cooper Landing trip (27 miles) in three or four days, though hard-core mountain bikers often do it in one day. Hitchhiking to pick up your car is possible, but the Hope trailhead is well off the beaten path for most car traffic.

The high point of the main trail is Resurrection Pass at 2,600 feet. However, even at this comparatively low elevation, the snows of winter can linger well into June. Postholing through thigh-deep snow can dampen the enthusiasm of even the jolliest of hikers. If you're thinking of an early-season hike, check with the Forest Service office in Anchorage (907/271-2500) or the Seward Ranger District (907/224-3374) for trail conditions.

At the southern end of the Resurrection Pass Trail at Cooper Landing, you can continue south on the 16-mile **Russian Lakes Trail** which connects with the 16-mile **Resurrection River Trail** all the way to Exit Glacier near Seward. Together, these three trails make it possible to hike 74 miles, a 12-day trek that covers the Peninsula from head to toe.

---

ingly remodeled cabin was built in 1940, and has a bedroom, woodstove, living room with day bed, and that rare Hope luxury, an indoor bathroom. Guests enjoy breakfast in the owner's 1916 cabin next door. Rates are $95 d, plus $10 extra for additional people.

Bear Creek Lodge (Mile 16 of Hope Highway, 907/782-3141, www.bearcreeklodgen-cafe.com) has a restaurant and five log cabins clustered around a pond, complete with wood-stoves and a shared bath for $85–105 d.

Discovery Cabins (907/782-3730 or 800/365-7057, www.adventurealaskatours.com, $75 d) has five modern cabins in the trees on the edge of Bear Creek in Hope. The cabins share a bathhouse and an outdoor hot tub, and are open summers only.

Eagle Rising (907/782-3222 or 888/313-2453) has it all: hostel beds in a historic cabin for $15, small motel rooms for $75–85 d, newly built cabins—each with a private hot tub and covered porch—for $125 d (plus $8 for each additional guests up to six), RV sites ($20), tent spaces ($5–10), showers for campers ($3), a laundromat, a small grocery store, espresso, and Native arts gift shop where you'll find local artisans at work on summer weekends. Eagle Rising is open all year.

Camping and Hiking

At the end of Hope Highway is the Forest Service's **Porcupine Campground** ($12), featuring fine views across Turnagain Arm, and red raspberry hors d'oeuvres in late summer.

Gull Rock Trail begins from the campground and parallels the shoreline of Turnagain Arm. It's a fairly easy stroll out to Gull Rock (five miles), making this a popular family day hike or overnight camping trip. The **Hope Point Trail** starts at the campground and climbs a steep knob into the alpine. From here you can hike forever along the ridgeline.

Resurrection Pass Trail

A half-mile east of Hope on the Hope Highway is the junction with Palmer Creek Road. Follow it three-quarters of a mile to a fork: Go straight for seven long miles to **Coeur D'Alene Campground** (free), or go right on Resurrection Pass Road. In just under four rough miles is the Resurrection Pass trailhead with parking, an information signboard, and a fun bridge across the crick. This popular backpack or mountain bike trip leads 38 miles down to Cooper Landing on the Sterling Highway, or you can cut across on **Devil's Pass Trail** to Mile 39 on the Seward.

SOUTH TO SEWARD

Beyond the Hope Highway junction, the Seward Highway climbs to scenic Summit Lake. At Mile 46 is **Tenderfoot Creek Campground** ($10) in a beautiful area on the shores of this alpine water. Next to it is **Summit Lake Lodge** (907/244-2031, www.summitlakelodge.com, open year-round). Cozy and well placed, it has consistently recommendable food. Breakfast is served until 2 P.M., after which you have your choice of burgers, salads, and other entrées. There's also a small motel ($80 d) and a gift/ice cream/espresso shop. The original lodge was built in 1953, but the big fireplace and chimney are the only parts of the building that survived the '64 quake. The newer building is constructed of local logs.

Just after Mile 40 and a mile before the Seward–Sterling junction is **Devil's Pass Trailhead;** this trail leads nine miles to the pass, then another

mile to where it joins the Resurrection Pass Trail. An alpine cabin ($35) sits on the pass. Devil's Pass Trailhead is very poorly marked—be prepared.

The **Carter Lake Trail** leaves the highway at Mile 33, climbs 1,000 feet in just over two miles to Carter Lake, and continues another mile around Carter Lake to Crescent Lake. This route gets you into the alpine fast and can be used to loop back to the highway on the Crescent Lake and Crescent Creek Trails. There's a Forest Service cabin ($45) on the south shore of Crescent Lake.

A half-mile beyond the Carter Lake Trailhead is the southern trailhead to **Johnson Pass Trail** (whose northern trailhead is at Mile 64). And just beyond that is **Trail Lakes Fish Hatchery** (8 A.M.–4:30 P.M.), which has a fascinating display about spawning and stocking salmon.

Moose Pass

At Mile 30 you slow down for tiny Moose Pass (pop. 200), where the classic **Estes Brothers Grocery** (907/288-3151), has been updated with a deli and espresso. The main event here comes on the summer solstice in June, when the town springs to life with music, food, and games. Learn more about Moose Pass on the web at www.moosepassalaska.com.

Trail Lake Lodge (907/288-3103 or 800/865-0201, www.traillakelodge.com, $89–104 s or d) is the main place to stay at Moose Pass, with comfortable motel rooms.

Other local places ($110–135 d) include **Alpenglow Cottage** (907/288-3142, www.alpenglowcottage.com), **Cranberry Creek Guest House** (907/288-3150, www.cranberrycreekguesthouse.com), **Jewel of the North B&B** (907/288-3166 or 877/317-7378, www.jewelofthenorth.net), **Midnight Sun Log Cabins** (907/288-3627, www.midnightsunlogcabins.com), **Teddy's Inn to the Woods B&B** (907/288-3126, www.seward.net/teddys), **Wolf Trail Log Cabins** (907/288-3117, www.bnb-web.com/wolfcabins), and **Spruce Moose B&B** (907/288-3667, www.seward.net/sprucemoose). The last of these is definitely worth checking out.

Scenic Mountain Air (907/288-3646 or 800/478-1449, www.scenicmountainair.com)

offers one-hour floatplane trips from Trail Lake. If it's a clear day, the views are stunning.

South from Moose Pass

Six miles south of Moose Pass is the turnoff for **Trail River Campground** ($10), a quiet wooded campground just over a mile off the highway,with some choice sites on the lakeshore loop. Next up on the left at Mile 23 is **Ptarmigan Creek Campground** ($10). Both Trail River and Ptarmigan Creek campgrounds can be reserved ($9 extra) through ReserveUSA (877/444-6777, www.reserveusa.com). The **Ptarmigan Creek Trail** climbs from the campground of the same name for 3.5 miles along the creek to Ptarmigan Lake, where there's good fishing for grayling.

Magnificent **Kenai Lake** comes into view just south of here: huge, beautiful, blue-green, with snowcapped peaks all around. Breathe deeply. Three-mile **Victor Creek Trail** starts at Mile 20; in three miles is the turnoff to the small **Primrose Campground** ($10), a mile from the Seward Highway along Kenai Lake.

Primrose Trail climbs 1,500 feet in eight miles to Lost Lake, where you can hook up to **Lost Lake Trail** and come out at Mile 5 near Seward. This is one of the most popular loop trails in the area. If you planned far enough ahead and made a reservation, you can stay at the Clemens cabin ($45). On clear days, you get a magnificent view of Resurrection Bay and on out to the Gulf of Alaska.

Beautiful **Porcupine Creek Falls** is three miles in on the Primrose Trail and a favorite day hike destination. Above the lake are dramatic alpine views and the chance to explore this high and mighty landscape.

Seward

Seward (907/224-8051, www.sewardak.org) is a pocket-size (pop. 3,000) port town on a sparkling bay surrounded by snowcapped peaks, and the only large settlement on the east side of the Kenai Peninsula. It's hooked up by bus, ferry, and plane, and has a maritime climate and a seafood industry, just like a half-dozen other places you've visited so far—but with a difference: Seward is right on the doorstep of Kenai Fjords National Park. This park contains some of the most inhospitable visitable country in the state. Harding Icefield—a prehistoric frozen giant with three dozen frigid digits—rivals Glacier Bay for scenery and wildlife but is decidedly less expensive to visit. Combine this with Seward's Alaska SeaLife Center, convenient camping, good food, and excellent access by public transportation, and you've got all the elements for a great time in this old town.

HISTORY

In 1791, Baranov, on a return voyage to Kodiak from around his Alaskan domain, waited out a storm in this bay on Sunday of Resurrection, a Russian holiday. The sheltered waters of Resurrection Bay prompted Baranov to install a small shipyard. In 1903, surveyors for the Alaska Central Railroad laid out the town site for their port. This private enterprise, financed by Seattle businessmen, established Seward, laid 50 miles of track, and went broke. In 1911, Alaska Northern Railroad extended the track almost to present-day Girdwood. In 1912, the U.S. government began financing the completion of this line, which reached Fairbanks, 470 miles north, in 1923. From then, Seward's history parallels Valdez's as one of the two year-round ice-free ports with shipping access to Interior—Seward's by rail, Valdez's by road. And like Valdez, Seward was almost completely destroyed by 1964's Good Friday earthquake.

Today, Seward has a diverse economy supported by tourism, commercial and sport fishing, fish processing, and other activities. The Alaska SeaLife Center is the main focal point for travelers, with excellent exhibits. The Alaska Vocational Technical Center trains 1,600 students each year, and a maximum security prison on the east side of Resurrection Bay houses another 450 folks under less academic conditions.

A towering coal-shipping facility dominates the harbor; the Alaska Railroad hauls coal here

SEWARD

To Exit Glacier and Anchorage

9

CHAMBER OF COMMERCE
INFORMATION CENTER

SEWARD
AIRPORT

BUS
STATION

EAGLE
CENTER

ALASKA
RAILROAD

MARINA MOTEL

RAILROAD DEPOT

BENNY BENSON
MEMORIAL

FERRY &
CRUISE SHIP
DOCK

TOUR BOAT
COMPANIES

HARBORMASTER

SUNEEL
COAL DOCK

BREEZE INN
MOTEL

KENAI FJORDS
NATIONAL PARK
VISITOR CENTER

2 Lakes Trail

FOURTH AVE.

Resurrection Bay

D ST.

MURPHY'S MOTEL

C ST.

HARBORVIEW
INN

B ST.

A ST.

MONROE ST.

POST OFFICE

CAMPING
AREA

FIRST AVE.

SECOND AVE.

THIRD AVE.

FOURTH AVE.

MADISON AVE.

FIFTH AVE.

SIXTH AVE.

BALLANTINE BLVD.

HOSPITAL

ST.

SEWARD VISITOR
INFORMATION CENTER

JEFFERSON ST.

SEWARD
MUSEUM

FOREST
SERVICE
OFFICE

VAN GILDEN HOTEL

ADAMS ST.

PUBLIC LIBRARY

TAROKA INN

HOTEL SEWARD

NEW SEWARD HOTEL

HOTEL EDGEWATER

WASHINGTON ST.

To Mt. Marathon

Waterfall

ALASKA
SEALIFE
CENTER

To Lowell Point and
Caines Head State Park

N

0   0.2 mi

0   0.2 km

© AVALON TRAVEL PUBLISHING, INC.

THE KENAI PENINSULA

© DON PITCHER

Alaska SeaLife Center

from the Usibelli Coal Mine in Healy for shipment to Korea. Quite a few cruise ships also dock in Seward, but most of these cruisers don't cruise around town long—passengers are typically herded onto a train or bus for Anchorage shortly after arrival. Too bad for them, since they miss one of the most enjoyable towns in Southcentral Alaska.

SIGHTS

Parking is often a problem in Seward, particularly near the harbor, where you'll need to pay $5 per day. (The boat tour companies have free lots with shuttle buses back to the harbor.) It's easy to see the local sights even if you don't have a vehicle. Simply hop on the **Seward's Trolley** (907/224-8051 daily 10 A.M.–7 P.M. in summer) that cruises through by every half hour, connecting downtown, the boat harbor, and the cruise ship dock; $2 one way or $5 for all day.

Alaska SeaLife Center

Seward's most fun attraction, the SeaLife Center (907/224-6300 or 800/224-2525, www .alaskasealife.org) sits on the south edge of town facing Resurrection Bay. This impressive facility provides visitors a wonderful way to learn about marine wildlife up-close. There are exhibits, aquariums filled with crabs and octopus, and a tidepool touch tank, plus videos, a Subway shop, and gift shop. The main attractions are three gigantic tanks, each with big windows where visitors can watch puffins and other seabirds, seals, and sea lions swimming. The playful 1,500-pound Steller sea lions are especially fun; they always come up to check out children. For visitors, the SeaLife Center is a place to learn about the marine environment, but this is also an important center for marine research and the rehabilitation of wildlife, including with pigeon guillemots and endangered Steller sea lions. Admission is $13 adults, $10 ages 7–12, and free for younger children. If you want to learn about research here, plunk down an extra $5 for a detailed behind-the-scenes tour, offered most afternoons. It's open daily May–Labor Day 8 A.M.–8 P.M.; daily 9 A.M.–6 P.M. the rest of September and in April; and daily 10 A.M.–5 P.M. in the winter.

Seward Museum

The Seward Museum (336 3rd Ave., 907/224-3902) houses a fine collection of Native baskets and carved ivory, equipment from the original Brown and Hawkins store, the cross-section of a 350-year-old Sitka spruce, and an impressive display of photographs from the 1964 earthquake that dropped parts of this country six feet. Entrance is $3 adults, 50 cents kids, and the museum is open daily 9 A.M.–5 P.M. May to mid-October, weekends noon–4 P.M. the rest of the year.

Information and Services

Seward Library (5th and Adams, 907/224-3646), houses the original Alaska flag, designed by a local boy in 1927. The **Benny Benson Memorial** on the north end of the lagoon memorializes this bit of trivia.

THE KENAI PENINSULA

Downtown's **Brown & Hawkins Store** (205 4th Ave., 907/224-7313), is Alaska's oldest family-owned business. It's been here since 1900, and still houses the old bank vault and cash register.

RECREATION
Day Hikes

For an enjoyable one-mile walk on a winding trail through the forest and around the creatively named First Lake and Second Lake, look for the **Two Lakes Trail** behind Alaska Vocational Tech Center at 2nd and C. There's a picnic area at the trailhead.

The high, bare slope hanging over Seward is **Mt. Marathon,** featured attraction for the 4th of July Mountain Marathon Race. It generally takes non-runners at least four hours to get up and back. Follow Jefferson Street due west up Lowell Canyon and look for the trailhead to the right just beyond a pair of large water tanks. You can run all the way back down the mountain on a steep gravel incline if your legs and nerves are good, but beware of slipping on the solid rock face near the bottom. The trail does not actually reach the summit of Mt. Marathon (4,560 feet), but rather the broad east shoulder (3,022 feet), which offers a spectacular view of Seward and the entire surrounding country.

Public Lands

Two popular state parks (907/262-5581, www.alaskastateparks.org) are close to Seward on the shores of Resurrection Bay: Caines Head State Recreation Area and Thumb Cove State Marine Park. (See the *Kenai Fjords National Park* and *South to Seward* sections for other local hiking paths.)

Caines Head State Recreation Area was the site of a World War II military base, Fort McGilvray, and the old command post still stands atop a massive 650-foot headland. There are dramatic views of Resurrection Bay and the surrounding country. The 4.5-mile Coastal Trail leads to the old fort from **Lowell Point State Recreation Site,** three miles south of Seward. Parts of the trail follow the shoreline and can only be hiked at low tide; be sure to check the

tide charts before heading out. Take a flashlight to explore the maze of underground passages and rooms at Fort McGilvray. Also here are ammunition magazines and firing platforms for the six-inch guns that guarded Seward. This area makes a fine overnight trip, and a walk-in campground complete with three-sided shelter is available at Tonsina Point, a mile in. Caines Head is very popular with sea kayakers who paddle here from Seward to hang out with the sea otters and seals. Also within the park are often-booked hike-in public use cabins (reservations: 907/269-8400, $50) at Derby Cove and Callisto Canyon.

Thumb Cove State Marine Park is on the east side of Resurrection Bay, seven miles from Seward, and accessibly only by boat. The park includes a long sandy beach, forested uplands, and the waters of Thumb Cove. Porcupine Glacier towers behind. Thumb Cove is a favorite stop for recreational boaters, and camping is popular along its beaches. Two cozy cabins are in the park, each sleeping up to eight people for $50 per night. Get there by water taxi from Miller's Landing (907/224-5739 or 866/541-5739).

Fishing

Fishing is one of Seward's most popular activities, and in midsummer dozens of boats dot the waters while hundreds of anglers cast from the shore. Salmon are the main attraction, made all the more enticing by a summer-long fishing derby. Your odds of catching one increase if you can get away from the shore, and many charter boats are available. Halibut fishing is another favorite, but you'll need to get quite far out—sometimes all the way to Montague Island in Prince William Sound—to catch one.

Get a complete list of charter operators from the Visitor Information Center, or contact a booking agency. Oldest and largest (it represents 30 or so boats) is **The Fish House** (907/224-3674 or 800/257-7760, www.thefishhouse.net), across from the harbor master's office. Also try **Charter Option** (907/224-2026 or 800/224-2026, www.charteroption.com). If you aren't fishing, drop by the harbor in the late afternoon when charter operators hang today's catch up for photos. It's quite a sight.

Sea Kayaking

Most Resurrection Bay sea kayaking originates from the scenic Lowell Point area, three miles south of Seward. There are three companies that guide from here: **Sunny Cove Sea Kayaking** (907/224-8810 or 800/770-9119, www.sunnycove.com), **Alaska Kayak Camping Company** (907/224-6056, www.seward.net/kayakcamp), and **Kayak & Custom Adventures Worldwide** 907 224-3960 or 800/288-3134, www.kayakak.com). All three offer similar paddling trips: a half-day (or sunset) paddle for $59, and an all-day trip for $99. The latter trip typically takes you to Caines Head or up Tonsina River to watch the spawning salmon. In addition, all three companies offer more expensive trips into Kenai Fjords National Park, including various multinight options. Sunny Cove offers day trips ($149–169) to Fox Island aboard a Kenai Fjords tour boat followed by a paddle, salmon bake, and wildlife cruise back to town. Another choice includes a boat tour to Aialik Bay within Kenai Fjords National Park, followed by a glacier paddle and return to town for $325.

Miller's Landing (907/224-5739 or 866/541-5739, www.millerslandingak.com) rents kayaks for do-it-yourselfers, and offers kayaking instruction. It's also at Lowell Point.

Kayakers Cove (907/224-8662) is a unique operation a dozen miles from Seward. Reasonably priced lodging and kayak rentals are available, with access by water taxi from Millers Landing.

Sailing

Sailors say Resurrection Bay contains some of the finest sailing waters north of San Francisco Bay, with windy conditions almost every day. Because of this, there are three local yacht clubs and dozens of sailboats berthed in the Small Boat Harbor. A local school, **Sailing, Inc.** (907/224-3160, www.sailinginc.com), has classes for both novices and experts, and does bareboat chartering.

Dog Mushing, Horseback-Riding, and Biking

Godwin Glacier Dog Sled Tours (907/224-8239 or 888/989-8239, www.alaskadogsled.com)

has the only on-the-snow summertime dog sledding in Southcentral Alaska. The action begins from Seward Airport, where you climb aboard a helicopter for a 15-minute flight to a world of snow, ice, and rocky peaks on crevice-free Godwin Glacier. The base camp here has 90 dogs and their handlers. Guests are given a tour of the operation, an introduction to mushing, and a fun ride behind a team of eight dogs. The entire trip lasts an hour and a half, and costs $365 adults, $325 kids. Glacier trekking and technical climbing may also be available. This is a first-rate operation, and definitely recommended if you have the money.

Veteran Iditarod musher Mitch Seavey operates **IdidaRide Sled Dog Tours** (907/224-8607 or 800/478-3139, www.ididaride.com) from his home along Old Exit Glacier Road. Summertime visitors are pulled on a wheeled cart along a two-mile route. The cost is $39 adults, or $19 kids, including an introduction to the Iditarod and a chance to play with husky puppies.

Bardy's Trail Rides (907/224-7863, www.sewardhorses.com) leads two-hour horseback rides twice daily throughout the summer for $65. This is a fun way to explore the scenic country at the head of Resurrection Bay, with good chances to see bald eagles, moose, and spawning salmon.

You can rent mountain bikes and baby joggers from **Seward Mt. Bike Shop** (907/224-2448) across from the boat harbor.

ACCOMMODATIONS

Seward has plenty of indoor lodging options, but be sure to book ahead in the summer, especially any weekend in August when the Silver Salmon Derby attracts throngs of visitors and every room for miles around. The city of Seward hits travelers with a 10 percent lodging tax.

A great first stop when looking for lodging is **Connections** (907/224-2323 or 888/227-2424, www.alaskasview.com), where owner Debra Hafemeister makes bookings (no extra charge) for more than 100 local places at a wide range of prices. Her website has links to many of these places, or call 800/844-2424 for recorded information on Seward.

Hostels

There's a quiet and lovely **Snow River Hostel** (907/440-1907) 16 miles north of Seward. It's convenient to hikers coming off the Lost Lake Trail. Inside are four rooms with two baths, a kitchen, and common room. Rates are $15, or $40 d for a private room. Reservations recommended in mid-summer.

Moby Dick Hostel (432 3rd Ave., 907/224-7072, www.mobydickhostel.com) has 30 beds in dorm-style rooms ($17), with kitchen facilities and showers. Private rooms cost $45 d (one of these is large enough for families), while rooms with kitchenettes run $60 per night. The hostel is open April–October.

Adventurous travelers should check out **Kayakers Cove** (907/224-8662), on a small bay near Fox Island, 12 water miles from Seward. Rustic lodging is $20 per person, or $60 d in a private cabin. No showers and you'll need a sleeping bag, but a kitchen and wood-fired sauna are on the grounds. Kayakers Cove is accessible by water taxi ($45 round-trip), and has kayak rentals for $30/day.

Hotels and Motels

The **Hotel Seward** (221 5th Ave., 907/224-2378 or 888/656-2723, www.alaskaone.com/hotelseward) is one of the better places in town, with economy rooms for $135 d, and larger ones for $199–224 d. They also own the adjacent **New Seward Hotel** with basement rooms and down-the-hall baths for only $66 d.

Just two blocks from the boat harbor, **Murphy's Motel** (909 4th Ave., 907/224-8090 or 800/686-8191, www.murphysmotel.com) has a mixture of older rooms ($99–115 d) and new units ($130–150 d), some with balconies. All rooms contain fridges and microwaves.

Taroka Inn (233 3rd Ave., 907/224-8975, www.alaskaone.com/tarokainn, $85 d), is an older nine-unit hotel with kitchenette units. **Marina Motel** (1603 Seward Hwy., 907/224-5518, www.sewardmotel.com, $105–130 d) rooms all have fridges, and the newer and larger units contain microwaves.

Opened in 1916, and now on the National Register of Historical Places, the **Van Gilder Hotel** (308 Adams St., 907/224-3079 or 800/204-6835, www.landsendvangilder.com) has rooms for $135–155 d, and two-bedroom suites for $185 d. Furnishings include period antiques, and rooms are impeccably clean.

Breeze Inn Motel (1306 3rd Ave., 907/224-5237 or 888/224-5237, www.breezeinn.com) has an edge-of-the-harbor location and 86 rooms for $130–188 d, or $218 d for a whirlpool-bath suite.

Harborview Inn (804 3rd Ave., 907/224-3217 or 888/324-3217, www.sewardhotel.com) is an attractive place with standard units for $129 d, while deluxe units have log furniture, king beds, fireplaces, and whirlpool baths for $179 d. It's often full throughout the summer, but the name is a bit of a misnomer since the harbor views are pretty marginal from Harborview. It also has beachfront apartments in a separate building for $139–149 d.

Hotel Edgewater (Railway and 5th Ave., 907/224-2700 or 888/793-6800, www.hoteledgewater.com, $110–245 d) is Seward's newest lodging place. Amenities include a hot tub, sauna, exercise room, and continental breakfast.

Out of town on the road to Exit Glacier is **Seward Windsong Lodge** (907/224-7116 or 888/959-9590, www.sewardwindsong.com), a modern lodge that's mostly booked with cruise ship folks. Rooms with two queen beds go for $189 d, suites for $239 d. It's open May to mid-September.

Bed-and-Breakfasts

Seward has dozens of bed-and-breakfasts. The Visitor Information Center has rack cards from many of these, or give Connections a call to book a good one.

Two Korean-American women own comfortable in-town B&Bs. **Morning Calm B&B** (218 Bluefield Dr., 907/224-3049, www.seward.net/~morningcalm, $70 d) is a great deal for people on a budget. Kim Martin's cozy home has two guest rooms that share a bath; a hot tub sits on the back deck and a full breakfast is served. **Soo's B&B** (810 2nd Ave., 907/224-3207 or 888/967-7667, $110 d) was designed by her architect son, and blends Asian and Scandinavian sensibilities. The four bright rooms are reasonable, and include a full breakfast and private baths. Across the street, Soo Kang has a second home (same rate) where guests have access to the kitchen.

Alaska Saltwater Lodge (907/224-5271, www.alaskasaltwaterlodge.com), is right on Resurrection Bay two miles south of Seward. There are stunning vistas from the common room, and just out the door is a quiet sandy beach. Rates run $85 d for standard rooms with private baths, or $129–159 for the spacious upstairs suites. A continental breakfast is included. Also on the beach at Lowell Point is **Ocean Front B&B** (907/224-5699, www.seward.net/~ocean, $120 d), with continental breakfasts.

Kim's Forest B&B (907/224-7632 or 888/512-7632, www.sewardalaskabnb.com) is a luxurious modern home with six guest rooms ($100 d with shared bath, $120–130 d with private baths), a very friendly owner, and full breakfasts. No children allowed. The home is six miles north of Seward along Bear Lake, with impressive glacier vistas. Floatplanes take off from the lake on flightseeing trips.

Castle on the Rock (1302 Chamberlain Rd., 907/362-1621) is a popular in-town B&B. Two rooms with twin beds ($125 d) share a bath, and the suite ($200 d) has a private bath and sauna. A full breakfast is included.

Located six miles north of Seward, **Bell-in-the-Woods B&B** (907/224-7271, www.bellinthewoodsbnb.com) has two large suites ($150–170 d; $25 for additional guests), and five rooms ($109–125 d), all with private baths and full breakfasts.

Alaska's Point of View Suites (318 1st Ave., 907/224-2323, www.alaskasview.com, $110 d) has two small suites, each with a private entrance. One of these has a two-person whirlpool bath, the other includes a separate bedroom that works well for families. Continental breakfast included.

Falls Inn B&B (1103 2nd Ave., 907/224-5790, www.fallsinnalaska.com) is a large edge-of-town B&B with a quiet backyard accented by a small waterfall. The home has a comfortable living room and two suites for $159 d, and a two-bedroom unit that sleeps four for $259.

Cabins

Renfro's Lakeside Retreat (907/288-5059 or 877/288-5059, www.seward-alaska.com/renfros) is 20 miles north of Seward along the shore of Kenai Lake. Here you'll find eight cabins, all with private baths and kitchenettes. Five are right on the lake ($125 d) and two are back in the woods ($100–115 d).

Located on Fox Island and accessible only by boat, **Kenai Fjords Wilderness Lodge** (907/224-8068 or 800/478-8068, www.kenaifjords.com) sits in the heart of Resurrection Bay. Guests stay in modern private cabins (but no electricity or phones), and enjoy hearty family-style meals at the lodge. Get there onboard a Kenai Fjords Tours boat, and spend a night and two days on the island for $329 per person ($165 kids), including meals, lodging, and a boat tour.

Other recommended Seward-area cabins include **Box Canyon Cabins** (907/224-5046, www.boxcanyoncabin.com), **River Valley Cabins** (907/224-5740, www.alaskan.com/sewardcabins), **Salmon Creek Cabins** (907/224-2323), **Moosewood Guest Cabins** (907/224-2323 or 888/227-2424, www.moosewoodcabin.com), and **Victorian Serenity by the Sea** (907/224-3635, www.seward-alaska.com/cabin).

CAMPING

City officials provide a fine stretch of year-round camping along the shore on Ballaine Boulevard, with toilets, showers, picnic shelters, beautiful views, and lots of company (450 sites!). It costs $8 for tents, $12 for RVs ($17 with hookups). You can also camp at the other city campground at Mile 2 out the Seward Highway—large trees, some highway noise, $8. Details for both at 907/224-4055, www.cityofseward.net.

Those with wheels can head out to Exit Glacier (13 miles from town) to pitch a tent in the small **Kenai Fjords National Park Campground.** It has only 10 sites and a small parking lot. There's water at the entrance; otherwise, this is minimalist camping on a strange moraine terrain.

RVers looking for full hookups head to **Kenai Fjords RV Park** (907/224-8779) at the Small Boat Harbor, **Miller's Landing** (907/224-5739 or 866/541-5739, www.millerslandingak.com) three miles south at Lowell Point, **Fjords RV Park** (907/224-9134, www.fjorsrv.com) one mile out Exit Glacier Road, **Bear Creek RV Park** (907/224-5725 or 877/923-5725, www.bearcreekrv.com) seven miles north, **Creekside RV Park** (907/224-3647) seven miles north of town, or **Stoney Creek RV Park** (907/224-4760 or 877/437-6366, www.stoneycreekrvpark.com) five miles north.

FOOD

Get a fast taco, burrito, or quesadilla from **Railway Cantina** (1401 4th Ave., 907/224-8226), directly across from the boat harbor. Everything's under $8.

Christo's Palace (133 4th Ave., 907/224-5255) is highly recommended, offering creative pizzas and pasta, along with Mexican dinners, steaks, and seafood. The 150-year-old back bar is particularly impressive, and it's noisy enough that your kids won't even be heard.

In business since 1958, **Harbor Dinner Club** (220 5th Ave., 907/224-3012, entrées $17–24) is popular with locals who rave about the prime rib, halibut, salmon, and scallop dinners. Lunch brings the usual array of sandwiches and burgers, and an outdoor deck for sunny days.

Two places serve Chinese food in town, both with $8 lunchtime buffets and Korean-American owners: **Peking Chinese Cuisine** (338 4th Ave., 907/224-5444) and **Oriental Garden** (907/224-7677), right across the street.

Located at Seward Windsong Lodge on the road to Exit Glacier four miles north of town, **Resurrection Roadhouse** (907/224-7116 or 800/208-0200, www.sewardwindsong.com) has big windows facing the mountains. The menu covers all the Alaskan seafood favorites, along with a big variety of other choices, from pizza to roast duck. Dinner entrées run $21–30. On

Every July 4th the Mt. Marathon Race attracts more than 800 runners who race up and back down the steep slopes of this 3,022-foot summit that rises behind Seward. Many do it in under an hour, but end up with bruises and bloody knees to show for the torture.

tap are 16 different microbrews. Open three meals a day late April to mid-September.

Seafood

Seward is the fish and chips capital of Alaska, with at least a half-dozen options in the harbor area alone. One of the best is **Northern Latitudes Seafood Grill** (907/224-4458), on the south end of the harbor, with beer batter halibut and chips for $11. A few outside tables face the water.

Ray's Waterfront (907/224-5606, www.alaskaone.com/waterfront), at the Small Boat Harbor, is especially convenient for grabbing a bite while you wait for your tour boat (or for a hot toddy when you get back). The walls of Ray's are lined with all sorts of trophy fish, and picture windows look out over the harbor. It also serves big breakfasts. The main problem with Ray's is its popularity; reservations are a wise idea for dinner if you don't want to wait an hour on summer weekends. Dinner entrées at Ray's run $20–23. Winter visitors will be disappointed; it's only open April–September.

Just up the street is **Chinooks Waterfront Grill** (907/224-2207, www.chinookswaterfront.com), with two levels fronting the harbor and a menu of pasta (try the halibut cheek linguine for $20), seafood (of course), and steaks.

Coffee, Bakeries, and Groceries

On summer mornings, the fishing crowd crowds into **Bakery at the Harbor** (907/224-6091) across from the Small Boat Harbor for coffee and fresh-baked pastries. Good lunch soups, too.

Get groceries and deli sandwiches at **Eagle Quality Center** (907/224-3698), the Safeway on the north end of town along the Seward Highway.

Housed in an old Lutheran church, **Resurrect Art Coffeehouse Gallery** (320 3rd Ave., 907/224-7161), is a wonderful place to hang out over an espresso on a rainy day, play a game of chess, or listen to local musicians most evenings. It's also one of the best Seward spots to buy Alaskan art, pottery, and jewelry.

ENTERTAINMENT AND EVENTS
Events
The year kicks off in Seward with the **Polar Bear Jump-Off,** a leap of faith into the frigid 39°F water of Resurrection Bay on the third weekend in January. All sorts of goofy costumed jumpers join the fray.

Every July 4th the **Mt. Marathon Race** attracts more than 800 runners who race up and back down the steep slopes of this 3,022-foot summit that rises behind Seward. Many do it in under an hour, but end up with bruises and bloody knees to show for the torture—the record is 43 minutes and 23 seconds. It has been run annually since 1915. This event is a major Alaskan institution, filling the bars and campgrounds with runners and spectators.

August brings another event that draws the crowds, the **Silver Salmon Derby,** where the top prize is $10,000, and over $150,000 in prizes are available. This is one of Alaska's richest fishing derbies. Entry costs $10 daily or $50 for the entire derby.

Nightlife
If you're looking for nightlife, virtually every other storefront on 4th is a bar. There's the **Yukon, Tony's,** and **DJ's Wheelhouse**—take your pick. Yukon and Tony's both have rock 'n' roll on some weekends; DJ's features an unusual right-angled billiard table that makes for strange bounces. **Liberty Theater** (305 Adams, 907/224-5418) shows movies.

INFORMATION AND SERVICES
Visitor Centers
For Seward maps and brochures, start out at the **Seward Chamber of Commerce** (907/224-8051, www.sewardak.org), located two miles north of town. It's one of the first places you pass as you're driving into Seward from Anchorage. The chamber office is open Monday–Friday 8 A.M.–6 P.M.

and Saturday–Sunday 9 A.M.–5 P.M. mid-May to mid-September, and Monday–Friday 9 A.M.–5 P.M. the rest of the year.

The **Chugach National Forest Seward Ranger District** office (907/224-3374, www.fs.fed.us, Mon.–Fri. 8 A.M.–5 P.M.) is on 4th near Jefferson. Staffers can tell you about all the hikes and cabins, but they can't make up your mind which of the dozen and a half to choose.

Kenai Fjords National Park visitors center is also in Seward, located along the boat harbor at 1212 4th Avenue.

Shopping
Seward has a number of interesting studios scattered around town, including the Resurrect Art Coffeehouse Gallery. **Resurrection Bay Galerie** (500 4th Ave., 907/224-3212) is a small place with big, colorful oil paintings. Also worth a look is **Starbird Studio** (221 4th Ave., 907/224-8770, www.starbirdstudio.com).

Services
Soap and rinse your entire naked body at the **Harbormaster Building** (907/224-3138), or head to **Seward Laundry** (804 4th Ave., 907/224-5727). Additional showers are in the city campground at the foot of Madison Street. There's a **swimming pool** (907/224-3900) at the high school where they throw in a free swim with your shower; call for hours. The **Seward library** (5th and Adams) houses computers where you can check email.

For medical emergencies, head to **Providence Seward Medical Center** (417 1st Ave., 907/224-5205, www.providence.org).

TRANSPORTATION
Railroad
An **Alaska Railroad** (907/265-2494 or 800/544-0552, www.alaskarailroad.com) train leaves Anchorage daily during the summer at 6:45 A.M. and arrives in Seward at 11 A.M., then returns to Anchorage at 6 P.M., arriving at 10:30 P.M.; $59 one-way or $98 round-trip. Passenger service to Seward is only available between mid-May and mid-September.

Ferry

The **Alaska Marine Highway's** (907/224-5485 or 800/642-0066, www.ferryalaska.com) trusty MV *Tustumena* calls in at its home port of Seward several times a week, at all different hours of the day and night, on its way to and from Homer, Seldovia, Kodiak, and Dutch Harbor. The MV *Kennicott* also does a twice-a-month run from Seward to Juneau in the summertime.

Air

Bear Lake Air & Guide Service (907/224-5985, or 800/224-5985, www.seward-alaska.com/bearlakeair) offers flightseeing trips over the Harding Icefield and courtesy van service to Bear Lake, seven miles north of Seward. Both **Scenic Mountain Air** (907/224-9152 or 800/478-1449, www.scenicmountainair.com) and **Era Helicopters** (907/224-8012 or 800/843-1947, www.flightseeingtours.com) offer flightseeing trips from Seward Airport.

On the Road

A **Seward's Trolley** runs around town every half hour in the summer; $2/ride or $5 for all day.

Seward Bus Lines (907/224-3608, www.sewardbuslines.com) has daily year-round bus service to and from Anchorage. **Homer Stage Line** (907/224-3608, www.homerstageline.com) has daily service mid-May to mid-September to Cooper Landing, Soldotna, Kenai, and Homer, but no winter runs. **Alaska Park Connection** (907/245-0200 or 888/277-2757, www.alaskacoach.com) connects Seward with Anchorage, Talkeetna, and Denali.

Rent a car from **Hertz** (907/224-4378 or 800/654-3131, www.hertz.com) or catch a ride from **PJ's Taxi** (907/224-5555) or **Glacier Taxi** (907/224-5678).

Rent bikes from **Seward Mt. Bike Shop** (907/224-2448), across from the boat harbor.

Kenai Fjords National Park

Kenai Fjords National Park covers 580,000 acres of ice, rock, and rugged coastline on the southern end of Kenai Peninsula. The centerpiece of this magnificent national park is the Harding Icefield, a massive expanse of ice and snow broken only by "nunataks"—the peaks of high, rocky mountains. The icefield pushes out in all directions in the form of more than 30 named glaciers. Along the coast, eight of these glaciers reach the sea, creating a thundering display of calving icebergs. Kenai Fjords has only been a national park since 1980, but today is one of the most popular attractions in Alaska. Many visitors come to ride the tour boats past teeming bird colonies or up to tidewater glaciers; many others hike to scenic Exit Glacier or up a steep path to the edge of Harding Icefield itself.

Kenai Fjords National Park Visitor Center (1212 4th Ave., 907/224-3175, www.nps.gov/kefj) is in Seward next to the harbor and is open daily 9 A.M.–6 P.M. Memorial Day–Labor Day, Monday–Friday 9 A.M.–5 P.M. in the spring and fall,

and closed November–February. Inside are excellent exhibits on Harding Icefield and little-known sights within the park. The center also has videos of the park, along with maps and publications of local interest.

EXIT GLACIER AREA

This is the only part of the park that is accessible by road. Get to Exit Glacier by heading four miles north from Seward and turning left at the sign. The road ends nine miles later at a parking lot; $5 day use, $3 for bikes or walk-ins. If you don't have a vehicle, PJ's Taxi (907/224-5555) charges $40 for a drop-off and later pick-up, and their van holds seven for this price.

Exit Glacier Nature Center—the only fuel-cell powered one in Alaska—houses interpretive displays and a natural history bookstore. Rangers give programs and lead one-hour nature walks several times daily, with a longer all-day trip to the icefield on Saturdays in July and August.

© DON PITCHER

Exit Glacier, Kenai Fjords National Park

Hikes

A three-quarter-mile round-trip **nature trail** provides an easy, quiet forest walk. The **Lower Loop Trail** goes a half-mile, crosses a creek, then climbs a steep quarter-mile up to the 150-foot face of Exit Glacier. The steep and winding **Upper Trail** continues another quarter-mile, offering views across the glacier and of several ice caves (don't go into these).

Harding Icefield Trail, seven miles round-trip, forks off just after the bridge over the creek and climbs to 3,500 feet and the icefield. Plan on at least six hours for this far more difficult hike, and check at the ranger station for current trail conditions since deep snow may block this route until midsummer. Skilled skiers may want to carry cross-country skis and slide around on the relatively crevasse-free icefield. In the winter, the road into Exit Glacier is not plowed but is very popular with skiers and snowmobilers.

The 16-mile **Resurrection River Trail** starts at Mile 8 of the Exit Glacier Road. This is the southern end of the 74-mile, three-trail system from Kenai's top to bottom. Resurrection River Trail leads to the 16-mile Russian Lakes Trail, which hooks up near Cooper Landing to the 38-mile Resurrection Pass Trail to Hope. A Forest Service cabin ($35) is six miles from the trailhead; reserve it through ReserveUSA. Note that the Resurrection River Trail can become quite a quagmire when it rains, and it may be poorly maintained beyond the cabin; most folks simply hike to the cabin and then turn around. The trail is popular with cross-country skiers in wintertime because of its relatively low avalanche danger.

CAMPING AND CABINS

The **Exit Glacier Campground** has a dozen walk-in tent sites just a short distance from the glacier; no charge and no reservations. There's also a bear-proof food locker and cooking shelter.

The Park Service maintains four popular public-use cabins within Kenai Fjords. Three of these are along the coast, and the fourth is a winter-only cabin at Exit Glacier. The coastal cabins are open June–Labor Day and cost $35/night. Each has its own treat—a pleasant beach walk at **Aialik Bay,** thunderous calving glaciers at **Holgate Arm,** and an old-growth rainforest at **North Arm** in remote Nuka Bay. Access to the Aialik Bay and Holgate Arm cabins is primarily by charter boat from Seward, but because of the distance involved, it's cheaper to take a floatplane to North Arm from Homer (the closest town). Contact the Park Service for detailed access info. Be sure to reserve far ahead of time for these extremely popular cabins by contacting the Alaska Public Lands Information Center in Anchorage (907/271-2737). Bookings are available in early January for the summer season, and nearly all the spaces fill up by the end of April.

During the winter, the park rents the **Willow Cabin** near Exit Glacier ($35/night). Ski to this cabin the eight easy miles from the highway along unplowed Exit Glacier Road. There is also a second enclosed winter-use structure nearby that is used as a warming shelter. Make reservations for this cabin with the Park Service in Seward (907/227-3175).

THE KENAI PENINSULA

BOAT TOURS

The most exciting thing to do in Seward is to get on a tour boat out into Resurrection Bay or into some nearby fjords. This is *the* cruise for seeing marine wildlife. On a good day, you could see three kinds of whales—including humpbacks and orcas—plus porpoises, seals, sea otters, sea lions, hundreds of puffins, kittiwakes, auklets, and the occasional bald eagle and oystercatcher. A number of tour companies offer cruises with knowledgeable guides. Half-day trips take you around nearby Resurrection Bay and out as far as Rugged Island, while longer voyages include Aialik Bay, Holgate Glacier (calving icebergs), and the Chiswell Islands (a Steller sea lion rookery and nesting seabirds—most notably puffins). The latter is a far more interesting trip and actually goes inside the park rather than to its edge, but the waters are often rough, so take your seasickness pills.

Seward's largest tour company, **Kenai Fjords Tours** (907/224-8068 or 800/478-8068, www.kenaifjords.com), offers a variety of cruises into the park, ranging from a three-hour Resurrection Bay tour ($56 adults, $28 kids) up to a nine-hour Northwestern Fjord Tour ($149 adults, $74 kids). Their most popular voyage is an eight-hour trip that includes an hour-long stop on Fox Island for a salmon lunch at Kenai Fjords Wilderness Lodge ($125 adults). Overnight stays at the lodge are $329 per person. Kenai Fjords Tours operates large boats that hold up to 150 people.

For a more intimate sailing, book a tour aboard the two small boats of **Mariah Tours,** also owned by CIRI, an Anchorage-based Native corpora-

> *The most exciting thing to do in Seward is to get on a tour boat out into Resurrection Bay or into some nearby fjords. This is the cruise for seeing marine wildlife. On a good day, you could see three kinds of whales—including humpbacks and orcas.*

tion. Mariah boats hold a maximum of 16 passengers and charge $135 for a 10-hour cruise to Northwestern Fjord, or $145 for the "captain's choice" 10-hour tours that focus on wildlife. Rates for kids under 12 are half the adult rate for all Kenai Fjords and Mariah trips.

Major Marine Tours (907/224-8030 or 800/764-7300, www.majormarine.com) offers a half-day dinner cruise to Resurrection Bay for $69 ($34 kids), and an all-day trip to Aialik Bay for $109 ($54 kids). Guests are treated to an all-you-can-eat salmon and prime rib buffet for $12 extra. The boat is large and stable, helpful when seas are rough.

Renown Charters and Tours (907/224-3806 or 800/653-3806, www.renowncharters.com) is a locally owned company with a smaller boat that allows for more personalized trips. Its 2.5-hour Resurrection Bay tour ($45 adults, $25 kids) departs several times a day; seven-hour cruises are $90 adults, $35 kids. Box lunches are $5 extra.

Most of these tour boats operate between mid-April and mid-September only, though Renown Charters runs tours daily all year. If you get here early or late in the season, you're likely to find lower prices and fewer people on board. All the tour companies have booths on the dock behind the harbor master's office on 4th Avenue. Binoculars and telephoto lenses are handy, and a light jacket is wise. This trip is guaranteed to be one of the highlights of your Alaskan visit, but if you get seasick easy, take along medication, especially on the all-day voyages that go into more exposed waters. You may want to wait if the marine weather report predicts rough seas.

Northwestern Kenai Peninsula

The northwestern end of the Kenai Peninsula is accessible via the **Sterling Highway** which joins the Seward Highway 37 miles north of Seward and 90 miles south of Anchorage. The mileposts along the Sterling also start counting at 37 from this point. The Sterling Highway heads west through Cooper Landing and Soldotna, then south all the way to Homer, a total of 143 miles.

Between the junction and Cooper Landing (Mile 49) are two USFS campgrounds along Quartz Creek Road. **Quartz Creek Campground** ($13) is in a beautiful setting right on Kenai Lake. Reserve a space through ReserveUSA. **Crescent Creek Campground** ($10) is three miles down Quartz Creek Road. A 6.5-mile trail climbs 1,000 feet from the Crescent Creek parking lot to Crescent Lake.

COOPER LANDING

Located a dozen miles west of the junction with the Seward Highway, this is the first of the service centers that cling to both sides of the Sterling Highway. Clumped together in central Cooper Landing (907/595-8888, www.cooperlandingchamber.com) are three motels, a couple of restaurants, a gas station, and tackle shops. A little visitor cabin (unstaffed) next to the boat launch on the south side of the Kenai River bridge is open daily in the summer.

Recreation

The main attractions in Cooper Landing are Kenai River float trips and fishing. Several raft companies offer a 14-mile ride to Jim's Landing, which includes some Class II rapids at Schooner Bend. Four-hour float trips cost around $45, and all-day Kenai trips run $100 or so from **Alaska River Adventures** (907/595-2000 or 888/836-9027, www.alaskariveradventures.com), **Alaska Rivers Co.** (907/595-1226 or 888/595-1226, www.alaskariversccompany.com), **Alaska Wildland Adventures** (907/595-1279 or 800/478-4100, www.alaskarivertrips.com), and **Whitewater Expeditions of Alaska** (888/350-

7238, www.weraftalaska.com). Many other companies have guided fishing trips aboard drift boats for around $170–200 for all day (including lunch), or $100–125/half-day.

Alaskan Horsemen Trail Adventures (907/595-1806 or 800/595-1806, www.alaskahorsemen.com) leads trail rides into the scenic country around Coopers Landing.

Kenai Lake Sea Kayak Adventures (907/595-3441) offers guided sea kayaking on the lake ($52 for three hours) and rents quality mountain bikes for rides up Resurrection Pass Trail.

Combat Fishing

The **Resurrection Pass Trail** crosses the Sterling Highway just west of Cooper Landing, and is accessible from a trailhead at Mile 53. A half-mile farther is Alaska's most famous salmon-fishing area, near the junction of the Russian and Kenai rivers. The U.S. Fish & Wildlife Service has a big parking lot here ($6 for day use) with a few tent spaces for those who arrive early enough.

© DON PITCHER

Kenai River anglers, near Cooper Landing

THE KENAI PENINSULA

The **Russian River Ferry** is a cable-guided, current-powered ferry ($5 adults, $2.50 kids) that shuttles anglers across the Kenai River to the sockeye-rich opposite bank. Come here in July to learn the true meaning of "combat fishing" as hundreds of folks fight for space, hooking both sockeye salmon and fellow anglers in the process. You'll need hip waders, and can only use flies, not lures. Local fishing shops have the correct flies, and often rent poles and boots. A real fly fisherman wouldn't be caught dead here, but this is all about killing fish, not enjoying a wilderness or purist experience!

Accommodations and Food

Cooper Landing spreads out over a seven-mile stretch that centers around Mile 50 of the Sterling Highway. Lodging options are listed from east to west. On the eastern end of Cooper Landing at Mile 45, **Sunrise Inn** (907/595-1222, www.alaskasunriseinn.com) has a café, bar, RV park, gas station, and motel ($90 d). The lakeside location is especially pleasant, and they're open all year.

At Mile 47, **Kenai Lake Cabins** (907/595-1802) is a friendly and inexpensive place to stay. The half-dozen simple cabins ($55 d, no kitchens, shared baths) sit on a hill overlooking Kenai Lake. Motel-type units with private baths are $75 d. Canoes and fishing gear can also be rented.

Kenai Princess Lodge (907/595-1425 or 800/426-0500, www.princessalaskalodges.com), near the Kenai River bridge at Mile 48, overlooks the roiling turquoise water of the Kenai River, and features a restaurant, lounge, half-mile nature trail, and gift shop. Most summertime guests arrive from Princess cruise ships. Bungalow-style rooms have naturally finished wood walls, a sitting area, wood-burning stove, TV, phone and small private deck. Two large hot tubs and saunas add to the appeal. The lodge is open year-round; summer rates are $239 for standard rooms or $269 d with a king bed. Reasonable off-season rates make the lodge a popular winter destination for Alaskans.

TroutFitters Alpine Motel (907/595-1212, www.aktroutfitters.com), at Mile 48, has a dozen cozy kitchenette units for $95–115 d. In addition, they offer fly-fishing instruction, a fly shop,

and rentals. Nearby is **Cooper Landing Grocery** (907/595-1677), and a short distance up the road is **Drifters Lodge** (907/595-5555 or 866/595-5959, www.drifterslodge.com), with seven modern chalet-cabins for $269 d, plus $25 for each additional guest. All of these include fridges and microwaves. Open all year.

Alaska Wildland Adventures (www.alaskawildland.com) operates two Kenai Peninsula lodges. Located in Cooper Landing, **Kenai River Sportfishing Lodge** (907/595-1279 or 800/478-4100) has a variety of all-inclusive fishing, food, and lodging packages; a three-night stay is $1,350 per person. More unique is **Kenai Backcountry Lodge** (907/783-2928 or 800/334-8730), hidden away on Skilak Lake and accessible only by boat. Accommodations are comfortably rustic tent cabins and log cabins, with a central bathhouse and lodge. All-inclusive stays start at $925 per person for two nights.

Located on the western edge of "town" at Mile 52, **Gwin's Lodge** (907/595-1266, www.gwinslodge.com) is a classic Alaskan eatery and a great place to pick up tips from the anglers while enjoying down-home cooking. Be sure to save space for the famous pies. Gwin's rents no-frills duplex cabins ($109), nicely appointed log cabins ($129–139), and deluxe cottages ($159). The store sells groceries, sodas, beer, and fishing licenses, and you can also buy or rent fishing gear, including poles and hip waders. Closed weekdays in the winter.

For delicious food in a funky and friendly waterside setting, head to **Sackett's Kenai Grill** (907/595-1827), where the menu includes ribs, seafood pasta, Caesar salads, and prime rib; $14–21 dinner entrées. Portions are enormous, so come hungry or split an order. They're open year-round. Recommended.

Upper Kenai River Inn (907/595-3333, www.upperkenairiverinn.com, $150 d) is a spacious and modern riverside home with four guest rooms, including a big breakfast. Other Cooper Landing B&Bs include **Kenai River B&B** (907/595-1712, www.kenairiverbandb.com), **Alaskan Sourdough B&B** (907/595-1541, www.alaskansourdoughbb.com), and **The Hutch B&B** (907/595-1270, www.arctic.net/~hutch).

Camping

Just west of Cooper Landing is the Forest Service's **Cooper Creek Campground,** with sites ($15) on both sides of the road. A mile and a half farther is the large **Russian River Campground,** one of the best places in the state to catch sockeye salmon when they're running (generally mid-June and mid-July). Campsites are strung along the two-mile paved road; $13 tents, $20 RVs for one of these large, well-spaced sites. Make campground reservations for Cooper Creek or Russian River (highly recommended for July; $9 extra) through ReserveUSA (877/444-6777, www.reserveusa.com). Park in the lot if you just want to hike on the 21-mile **Russian Lakes Trail** or take the "fisherman's path" along the river to **Russian River Falls,** where salmon leap. The Russian River runs into the Kenai River near the entrance station.

Located at Kenai Princess Lodge, **Kenai Princess RV Park** (907/595-1425 or 800/426-0500, www.princessalaskalodges.com) charges $30 for full hookups (no tents), and is open mid-May to mid-September.

Transportation

Homer Stage Line (907/235-2252, www.homerstageline.com) runs to Anchorage, Homer, and Seward. Service is daily to Anchorage in the summer, and twice week in winter. Seward runs are daily, but only in summer. **Wildman's** (907/595-1456 or 866/595-1456) has a laundry with showers, and offers a shuttle service and car rentals at Mile 48. Gwin's Lodge also has a shuttle service for folks floating the river.

KENAI NATIONAL WILDLIFE REFUGE

This large habitat supports so many moose, Dall sheep, bear, salmon, and other wildlife that it was designated a refuge by President Roosevelt in 1941. The Alaska National Interest Lands Act (1980) changed the name from Kenai National Moose Range and expanded the refuge to its present two million acres, managed by the federal Fish & Wildlife Service (http://kenai.fws.gov).

An information cabin is at Mile 58, right at the junction of the Sterling and the rough and dusty 19-mile **Skilak Lake Loop Road.** Stop here to pick up a copy of *Reflections,* the refuge's annual newspaper, with details on day hikes, wildlife viewing, fishing, canoeing, picnicking, and camping. The big action in this neck of the woods is along the Loop Road, where you'll find five different campgrounds (free–$10); **Hidden Lake Campground** features campfire programs and guided walks on summer weekends. In addition to those along Skilak Lake, three other F&WS campgrounds are on the Sterling Highway between Cooper Landing and Sterling.

Oil was discovered in 1957 in the northern wilderness near the Swanson River, and an 18-mile gravel road built to the oilfields also opened up this lake-studded lowlands. Approximately 13 miles in on Swanson River Road is **Dolly Varden Lake Campground:** free, uncrowded, nice views, right on the lake, with frequent moose visits. For additional information about the campgrounds, more than a dozen trails, and hundreds of miles of boating and fishing waterways, inquire at the USF&WS greeting cabin or their headquarters in Soldotna.

Canoeing

Two canoe routes—Swanson River Route and Swan Lake Route—are accessible by Swanson River Road, a right turn off the Sterling at Mile 84. Both offer a wonderful way to explore the refuge. Pick up the USF&WS brochure *Canoeing in the Kenai National Wildlife Refuge* for detailed information. Two companies rent canoes and offer guided canoe trips: **Alaska Canoe & Campground** (907/262-3583, www.alaskacanoetrips.com), and **Weigner's Backcountry Guiding** (907/262-7840, www .alaska.net/~weigner). *Kenai Canoe Trails* by Daniel L. Quick is a useful guidebook for anyone heading out on the refuge's lakes.

Located on the northern Kenai Peninsula, **Swan Lake Canoe Route** is the most popular canoeing area within Kenai National Wildlife Refuge. This 60-mile route encompasses 30 lakes that are connected by fairly short portages (longest is under a mile). The entire 60-mile route can be traversed in less than a week. In addition, the route provides access to a 17-mile float down the gentle Moose River. Canoeing on this system offers not only scenic beauty, but also excellent wildlife viewing and good rainbow trout fishing.

The **Swanson River Canoe Route** links 40 small lakes on the northern Kenai Peninsula, and also includes a 46-mile stretch of the Swanson River. The lakes are connected by portages of varying lengths and conditions, but they are more difficult than those on the nearby Swan Lake Canoe Route. Traveling from the Paddle Lake entrance (at mile 12 on Swan Lake Rd.), trips can stretch from a long weekend to over a week. In remote lake areas of the Swanson River Route east of Pepper Lake, travel is difficult and the routes and portages are often indistinct. This is true wilderness and can be challenging. Bring a compass, an accurate map, a pair of hip waders, and a lot of patience.

STERLING TO SOLDOTNA

The unincorporated settlement of **Sterling** (pop. 6,000 spread over a wide area) around Mile 83 is mainly notable for the four-lane highway that cuts across this part of the northern Kenai Peninsula; it seems totally out of place in such a po-dunk spot. The Sterling Highway crosses the Moose River in Sterling, where it joins the widening Kenai River, and the fish-hook frenzy pervades all your senses. The **Izaak Walton State Recreation Site** (907/262-5581, $10) on the east side of the river is a pretty campground with 38 sites, toilets, and water. Archaeological excavations conducted here indicate that Natives occupied this fish-rich confluence up to 2,000 years ago.

The 13-mile stretch of highway from Sterling to Soldotna bristles with guides and outfitters, fish camps, bait and tackle shops, charters, fish smokeries, boat and canoe rentals, boat engine sales and repairs, and so forth—essential infrastructure in the eternal struggle between sportsmen and salmon.

An excellent local lodging choice is **Alaska Mountain View Cabins** (907/262-4827 or 888/388-4827, www.alaskamountainview.com, $100–175 d). The cabins and guest house con-

tain kitchens and private baths; one features an impressive view from the deck. Other local places worth a look are **Angler's Lodge** (907/262-1747 or 888/262-1747, www.anglerslodge.com) and the inexpensive **Alaska Cozy Cabins** (907/262-2401, www.alaska.net/~dbarber).

SOLDOTNA

Soldotna was established in the late 1940s, as World War II veterans filed for homestead lands along Soldotna Creek. Today this town of 4,000 is the seat of the Kenai Borough government, and serves as a busy stopping point for travelers, anglers, and locals. "Slowdotna" has all the charm of Wasilla, another place disparaged by anyone not living there. Fast-food joints, strip malls, fishing supply stores, shopping centers, and a jumble of signs greet your arrival in this sprawling suburban burgh with no real downtown—unless you count the big **Fred Meyer** store. Its parking lot also serves as a de facto free RV campground all summer.

Sights

The **Soldotna Visitor Information Center** (907/262-9814; www.soldotnachamber.com) is on Sterling Highway just south of the bridge over the Kenai River. The center is open daily 9 A.M.–7 P.M. May–September, and Monday–Friday 9 A.M.–5 P.M. the rest of the year. Stop by to sift through several hundred pamphlets describing B&Bs, fishing charters, RV parks, restaurants, and other businesses. The walls are lined with photos, and be sure to see the 94-pound king salmon that was caught nearby in 1984; it's one of the largest ever caught by a sport fisherman. Just out the door, a short path leads to the Kenai River, where the **Kenai River Fish Walk** provides a spot to try your luck at catching an even bigger one.

For the **Kenai National Wildlife Refuge Visitor Center** (907/262-7021, http://kenai.fws.gov), take a left at Kalifornsky (named for a prominent Native family), then an immediate right, and go a mile up Ski Hill Road. The center is open Monday–Friday 8 A.M.–5 P.M. and Saturday–Sunday 9 A.M.–6 P.M. in the summer; Monday–Friday 8 A.M.–4:30 P.M. and Saturday–Sunday 10 A.M.–5 P.M. the rest of the year. Buy books and posters, and see the free wildlife videos, stroll the mile-long nature trail, and climb the observation tower.

Soldotna Homestead Museum (www.geocities.com/soldotnamuseum) is a collection of a half-dozen log cabins on the way into Centennial Park; it's open Tuesday–Saturday 10 A.M.–4 P.M. and Sunday noon–4 P.M. from mid-May to mid-September. No charge. Inside are the usual settlers' items, stuffed critters, and Native artifacts. The real treat is that this surprisingly quiet spot is just a short distance from the bustling Sterling Highway.

Motels

Dozens of lodging options crowd the Sterling-Soldotna-Kenai area, from rustic cabins to riverside wilderness lodges. Visitor centers racks are crammed with descriptive flyers, and their website (www.soldotnachamber.com) has links to most of these.

Aspen Hotel (326 Binkey Circle, 907/260-7736 or 866/483-7848, www.aspenhotelsak.com) is a big, modern place with an indoor pool, jacuzzi, and continental breakfast. Rooms with fridges and microwaves go for $149 d.

Not far away is another large motel, **Kenai River Lodge** (393 Riverside Dr., 907/262-4292, www.kenairiverlodge.com), where rooms facing the river cost $140 s or d, including a continental breakfast.

Best Western King Salmon Motel (35545 Kenai Spur Hwy., 907/262-5857 or 888/262-5857, www.bestwestern.com) has large rooms for $89 s or d; $99 for kitchenettes.

Bed-and-Breakfasts

The website of the **Kenai Peninsula B&B Association** (www.kenaipeninsulabba.com) offers links to a dozen Soldotna B&Bs. Recommended places include **Longmere Lake Lodge B&B** (907/262-9799, www.longmerelakelodge.com), **Moose Hollow B&B** 907/262-7526 or 800/262-7548, www.alaskaone.com/moosehollow), **Kenai River Raven B&B** (907/262-5818 or 888/262-5818, www.kenairiverraven.com),

and **Alaskan Dream B&B** (907/260-3147 or 888/326-3147, www.ptialaska.net/~akdream).

Fishing Lodges

Kenai Riverbend Resort (907/283-9489 or 800/625-2324, www.kenairiverbend.com) has fishing and lodging packages in attractive riverfront log cabins, starting at $1,300 per person for four nights lodging and three days of charter salmon and halibut fishing.

Soldotna B&B Lodge (399 Lovers Lane, 907/262-4779 or 877/262-4779, www.soldotnalodge.com) is a 16-room lodge where fishing packages are the feature attraction, starting with three nights lodging and two days fishing for $639 per person, including breakfast.

Camping

Get to **Centennial Park City Campground** (907/262-9107, www.ci.soldotna.ak.us, $11) by crossing the bridge on the Sterling, taking a right at the light onto Kalifornsky, then another immediate right into the campground. This is a big city park with nice wooded sites (some right on the river), picnic tables, fire pits, water, boardwalks, fishing walkways, and a boat-launching ramp. Identical rates apply at **Swiftwater Campground,** also run by the city of Soldotna, on East Redoubt Street. No reservations at either place.

Local RV parks include **Across the River RV Park** (907/262-0458 or 800/276-2434, www.acrosstheriver.com), **Edgewater RV Park** (907/262-7733), **Kenai Riverbend Resort Campground** (907/283-9489 or 800/625-2324, www.kenairiverbend.com), and **River Terrace RV Park** (907/262-5593). Free RV parking in the Fred Meyer parking lot.

Food

When I asked a longtime Soldotna resident for recommendations on local restaurants, I was told something that should perhaps come as a warning: "I'd rather eat at home." Most Soldotna dining comes courtesy of McDonald's, Subway, Dairy Queen, Taco Bell, Burger King, Arby's, and Godfather's Pizza, but the town does have a number of homegrown options.

Klondike City is a little shopping center that features a bowling alley and the 24-hour **Sal's Klondike Diner** (907/262-2220), where you can get typical truck-stop food and big pieces of pie. It's *the* place for breakfast in Soldotna, served anytime.

Grand Burrito (907/262-2228) will fill you up with its combination burritos, but the owners show their true heritage by also serving tasty Armenian/Russian food and pastries.

For East Coast–style subs (with Alaskan-size prices), stop by **Jersey Subs** (907/260-3343). Best Philly cheesesteak in these parts.

Don't expect much from Soldotna's Asian restaurants, but the **Golden International** (907/262-7862) is worth a visit. It also has a weekday Chinese buffet lunch and Sunday brunch.

Mykel's Restaurant & Lounge (907/262-4305, www.mykels.com) is just up Kenai Spur Highway from the Sterling Highway. This is Soldotna's fine-dining establishment, with fresh local salads, pasta, seafood, steaks, and fine wines. Dinner entrées run $18–22.

Located at the Soldotna Y, **Charlotte's at River City Books and Cafe** (907/260-7722) provides a pleasant escape from the ubiquitous fast-food joints and anglers in hip waders. You'll find both a fair selection of new books and a café serving sandwiches, soups, and espresso.

For fresh veggies and fruits, head to the **Soldotna Farmers' Market** on Saturdays from 10 A.M. to 2 P.M. June–September; it's held next to the Peninsula Center Mall.

Recreation and Services

Rent bikes or take a guided mountain bike ride from **Mackey Lake Re-Bike** (907/262-7192) in Soldotna. **Birch Ridge Golf Course** (907/262-5270, www.birchridgegolf.com) is a nine-hole private course three miles from town.

Grab a shower at **Alpine Laundromat** on the highway right next door to Dairy Queen.

Central Peninsula General Hospital (250 Hospital Place, 907/262-4404) is especially adept at removing fish hooks from all parts of the body; in a typical year they pull out 100 of them! Be sure to wear shatterproof eyewear to protect your eyes while rubbing shoulders with the Kenai River fishing crowds.

Transportation

Air taxis offering charters and flightseeing from the Soldotna Airport include **Talon Air Service** (907/262-8899, www.talonair.com), **Clearwater Air** (907/262-5022, www.clearwaterair.com), **Natron Air** (907/262-8440, www.natronair.com), and **High Adventure Air** (907/262-5237, www.highadventureair.com).

Local taxi companies are **Alaska Cab** (907/262-1555) and **Yellow Cab** (907/260-1900).

Homer Stage Line (907/235-2252, www.homerstageline.com) runs from Soldotna to Anchorage, Homer, and Seward. Service is daily to Anchorage and Homer in the summer, and twice weekly in winter. Seward service is daily, but only in the summer.

KENAI

The town of Kenai sits on a bluff above the mouth of the Kenai River overlooking Cook Inlet. With over 7,000 residents, it's the largest town on the Kenai Peninsula. Across the inlet to the southwest rise Redoubt and Iliamna, active volcanoes at the head of the Aleutian Range. The Alaska Range is visible to the northwest. Beluga whales sometimes enter the mouth of the river on the incoming tides to look for fish.

History

Kenai is the second-oldest permanent settlement in Alaska, founded by Russian fur traders who built St. Nicholas Redoubt in 1791. The U.S. Army built its own fort, Kenay, in 1869, two years after the Great Land changed hands. Oil was discovered in 1957 offshore, followed by natural gas two years later, and now Kenai is the largest and most industrialized city on the peninsula. Several of the 15 Cook Inlet platforms are visible from shore. The oil and gas are processed at two petroleum refineries, a liquefied natural gas plant, and a fertilizer plant, all in nearby Nikiski.

To Captain Cook State Recreation Area

KENAI MUNICIPAL AIRPORT

KENAI SPUR RD.

BEAVER LOOP RD.

KALIFORNSKY BEACH RD.

Kaliforski Beach

Kenai

CANNERIES

Cook Inlet

To Captain Cook State Recreation Area

Kenai River

Soldotna

KENAI NATIONAL WILDLIFE REFUGE HEADQUARTERS

To Sterling, Seward, and Anchorage

To Kasilof

To Homer

0   2 mi

0   2 km

MOON

KENAI

AIRPORT WAY

WILLOW ST.

COOK INLET AIRPARK

To Soldotna

NORTH KENAI HWY.

1ST AVE.

POST OFFICE

FIDALGO WAY

CORAL RD.

SPRUCE ST.

FOREST DR.

CITY PARK

KENAI COMMUNITY LIBRARY

KENAI SPUR RD.

MAIN ST. LOOP

VISITORS AND CULTURAL CENTER

KENAI MALL

To Kalifornsky Beach Rd.

NIKOLAI RD.

FORT KENAY

OVERLAND

UPLAND

HIGHLAND

OUTLAND WALK

BROADWAY

RUSSIAN CHURCH

CHAPEL OF ST. NICHOLAS

ALASKA WY.

MISSION RD.

PENINSULA CT.

PENINSULA

COOK DR.

BELUGA WHALE LOOKOUT

RIVERVIEW RD.

Cook Inlet

Beach

Kenai River

0   0.25 mi

0   0.25 km

© AVALON TRAVEL PUBLISHING, INC.

Sights

Most of the sights of Kenai are in one small area, which you can tour on foot in 90 minutes. Start at the **Kenai Visitors and Cultural Center** (right at the corner of Main St. and Kenai Spur Rd., 907/283-1991, www.visitkenai.com). The center is open weekdays 8 A.M.–7 P.M., Saturday–Sunday 10 A.M.–6 P.M. from Memorial Day to Labor Day, and Monday–Friday 9 A.M.–5 P.M. the rest of the year. Here you'll find a complete and well-organized selection of brochures and flyers about the area. Its museum collection ($3 in the summer, free in winter and for kids) is impressive, with gorgeous cultural artifacts from the Native peoples, a permanent exhibit of local historical lore and natural history, and temporary exhibits. There's even a detailed scale model of one of the oil drilling platforms that stand a few miles offshore. Various interpretive programs

are taught several times a week; check the schedule for upcoming events.

Next, walk down toward the bluff on Overland Avenue to the replica of **Fort Kenay,** built in 1967 for the Alaska Centennial. It isn't open to the public. Next door is **Holy Assumption of the Virgin Mary Orthodox Church,** built in 1895 and the second-oldest Russian Orthodox Church in the state (the oldest is on Kodiak). It's a working church with regular services; tours are available on request, or peek through the windows at the painted altar and brass chandelier. The **Chapel of Saint Nicholas** (1906) nearby, built over the grave of Kenai's first priest, also reflects the traditional Russian Orthodox architectural style. Walk east on Mission Road for two viewpoints over the bluff; from the first, look out over the riverside canneries, with the Kenai Mountains

THE KENAI PENINSULA

behind and the Aleutian and Alaska Ranges strung out across the inlet. The second has an interpretive sign about beluga whales.

Recreation

My favorite Kenai destination is the wonderful **beach** near the mouth of the Kenai River; it's one of the best, easily accessible beaches in Alaska! Find it at the end of Spruce St. on the north side of the river. A line of low dunes backs the fine sand.

Captain Cook State Recreation Area (907/262-5581, www.alaskastateparks.org) is 25 miles from Kenai at the end of the North Kenai Road. This is a delightful place to camp, hike the rocky shoreline, look for agates, enjoy the views across Cook Inlet, or simply relax. On summer weekends locals come here to swim in the surprisingly warm waters of Stormy Lake.

Families will love spending an afternoon at the North Peninsula Recreation Area's **Nikiski Pool** (907/776-8472), where the featured attractions are 136-foot waterslide, a "rain umbrella," hot tub, and a large pool for lap swimming. Open daily. Another public pool is at Kenai High School.

The **Kenai Peninsula Oilers** (907/283-7133, www.oilersbaseball.com) play semiprofessional baseball at Coral Seymour Memorial Park in Kenai. The team has won several National Baseball Congress World Series championships over the years and is always fun to watch. **Kenai Golf Course** (1420 Lawton Dr., 907/283-7500) is an 18-hole public course. In the winter, cross-country ski trails are maintained here; call 907/283-3855 for specifics.

Accommodations

The Kenai Visitors and Cultural Center has a complete listing of local lodging places, along with brochures their brochures. In the middle of Kenai town, **Uptown Motel** (on the Spur Rd., 907/283-3660 or 800/777-3650, $135–145 d) has rooms all with fridges and microwaves. Check out the 100-year-old gold-plated cash register behind the front desk.

Kings Inn (907/283-6060 or 877/883-6060, www.alaskakingsinn.com) is on the Soldotna side of the Spur Road near the airport. Rates are $105–120 d; some rooms include fridges and microwaves. **Kenai Merit Inn** (260 S. Willow St., 907/283-6131 or 800/227-6131, www.kenaimeritinn.com) is a bit less expensive: $90–100 d, including a continental breakfast.

Recommended Kenai B&Bs include **Daniels Lake Lodge B&B** (907/776-5578 or 800/774-5578, www.danielslakelodge.com, $95–250 d), **Diamond M Ranch B&B** (907/283-9424 or 866/283-9424, www.diamondmranch.com, $80–130 d), and **Harborside Cottages** (907/283-6162 or 888/283-6162, www.harborsidecottages.com, $125–150 d).

Camping

The nearest public camping places are in Soldotna. Twenty-five miles north of Kenai is quiet **Captain Cook State Recreation Area** (907/262-5581, www.alaskastateparks.org), which contains **Bishop Creek Campground,** a popular tent-only area where you can see spawning salmon in late summer, and **Discovery Campground** with fireside programs on summer weekends. Both campgrounds cost $10.

Beluga Lookout RV Park (929 Mission Ave., 907/283-5999 or 800/745-5999) has full hookups overlooking Cook Inlet, and **Diamond M Ranch** (907/283-9424 or 866/283-9424, www.diamondmranch.com) has RV sites at Mile 17 on Kalifornsky Beach Road.

Food

A classy place to eat in Kenai is **Paradisos Restaurant** (907/283-2222) on Kenai Spur Road a block east of the visitors center. They've been serving lunch and dinner to locals and visitors since 1971. The big menu features Italian, Mexican, and Greek food. Free local pizza deliveries, too.

Veronica's (907/283-2725), is a popular espresso and dessert café across the street from the Russian Orthodox Church in Old Kenai. Housed in an historic log cabin, it's a hangout for locals.

Transportation

Era Aviation (907/283-3028 or 800/866-8394, www.flyera.com) flies to Kenai Airport from Anchorage at least 15 times a day. Local air taxis include **Mavrik Aire** (907/262-6790 or 888/628-7457, www.mavrikaire.com), and **Alaska West Air** (907/776-5147, www.alaskawestair.com). Call **Alaska Cab** (907/283-6000) or **Inlet Taxi** (907/283-4711) for rides into town.

A number of companies rent cars and vans at the Kenai Airport: **Avis** (907/283-7900 or 800/331-1212), **Budget** (907/283-4506 or 800/527-0770), **Great Alaska Car Company** (907/283-3469, www.greatalaskacar.com), **Hertz** (907/283-7979 or 800/478-7980), or **Payless** (907/283-6428 or 800/729-5377).

Homer Stage Line (907/262-4584, www.homerstageline.com) runs to Homer and Seward daily mid-May to mid-September. For Anchorage, you'll need to catch their year-round bus that stops in Soldotna.

SOUTH TO HOMER

South of Soldotna, the Sterling Highway hugs the coastline all the way to Homer, a distance of 75 miles. The view across the Cook Inlet is of the Aleutian volcanic crown, **Mt. Redoubt** (10,197 feet) to the north and **Mt. Iliamna** (10,016 feet) to the south—both within rhyming Lake Clark National Park. On a very clear day you can also see active **Mt. Augustine,** a solitary volcanic island with a well-defined cone at the bottom of the Inlet.

Travelers will be dismayed to find that nearly all the larger spruce trees in this area have been killed by **spruce bark beetles** over the last decade, leaving behind the brown skeletons of a once-healthy forest. Many areas of spruce have been logged, but others are simply a mass of standing dead trees. Fortunately, the youngest spruce trees have generally survived the onslaught, and other species, such as birch and alder, are unaffected. The dead spruce forests extend well south of Homer, and across Kachemak Bay through Kachemak Bay State Park. It's a sad sight and one that is not likely to change for decades to come. Unfortunately, the infestation continues to spread to the east across the Kenai Peninsula and all the way to the Wrangell Mountains on the east side of Alaska.

Kasilof and Clam Gulch

From Kenai, backtrack on Kalifornsky over the Kenai River and go right at the fork to the coast; this spur road joins the Sterling at Mile 109 in Kasilof (ka-SEE-loff), gateway to huge Tustumena Lake, whose turnoff is at Mile 110.

At Mile 117 is the turnoff for **Clam Gulch State Recreation Area,** a two-mile gravel road down to the campground and clamming grounds. Campsites go for $10, and day use is $5 per vehicle. Make sure you have a sportfishing license (required for clam diggers over age 16), a shovel, a bucket, and gloves before you dig in the cold sand for the razor-sharp clams; best during a low tide in early summer, but possible anytime April–September. Watch how the pros first spot the small hole in the sand, then dig a few shovels full and reach fast for the escaping clams. Contact the Alaska Department of Fish and Game for regulations.

Clam Gulch Lodge (907/260-3778 or 800/700-9555, www.clamgulch.com) is a modern place with rooms for $95 d, including a full breakfast. Some rooms have shared baths. The lodge is open May–August, with fishing packages available.

Tustumena Lodge (907/262-4216) also has fishing packages; rooms start at $45. The exterior is bush-Alaska ugly, but the lodge is famous for its collection of hats, with nearly 20,000—said to be one of the largest in the world. Want more minutiae? It claims to also have the world's largest razor clam on display.

Several B&Bs and cabin rentals dot the Kasilof area. Especially nice is **Ingrid's Inn** (907/262-1510 or 888/422-1510, www.alaskaone.com/ingrids, $85–95 d). Also well worth a look is **Deal's Den B&B** (907/262-2643). Rent cabins from **Kasilof River Cabins** (907/262-6348, www.kasilofriverlodge.com), **Crooked Creek Cabins** (907/262-2729 or 877/302-2729, www.ak-cabins.com), or **Tustumena Ridge Cabins** (907/262-7050, www.trcabins.com).

Park RVs at **Crooked Creek RV Park** (907/262-1299) or **Kasilof RV Park** (907/262-0418 or 800/264-0418).

Kasilof Mercantile (907/262-4809) has a café, groceries, and espresso.

Ninilchik

This small town of 700, located where the
Ninilchik River empties into the Inlet, has a long
history. Settled in the early 1800s by retired Russ-
ian-America Company workers who took Native wives, the old village is down a short side
road off Sterling Highway. In old downtown are
some classic water's-edge houses, a few businesses
and weathered structures. Follow the road that
parallels the Ninilchik River around toward the
"spit"; you wind up on the other side of the river
and village on the hardpan inlet beach. A dozen
historical buildings and signs are along the way; a
short footpath leads up to the beautiful **Russian
Orthodox Church,** built on an overlook in 1900.
The church is also accessible by road; look for
Coal Street on the left side of the highway as you
head north from town. Ninilchik hosts the small-
town **Kenai Peninsula Fair** the third weekend in
August, with games, livestock, and craft booths.

A little **Visitor Kiosk** (907/567-3571) on the
west end of town has local brochures. Most businesses are strung along the highway above the
main town and include Ninilchik General Store
(907/567-3378), restaurants, and charter fishing companies. Don't miss **Boardwalk Cafe**
(907/567-3388) for great clam chowder, fresh
seafood, espresso, and homemade pies.

Many charter boats put in at nearby Deep
Creek State Recreation Area, using large tractors
to get the boat trailers out beyond the waves on
the beach. It's quite the scene on a summer weekend morning, with the action generally taking
place an hour or two before high tide. Trivial
celebrity connection enthusiasts may want to stop
at Chihuly's Charters (907/567-3374, www.pita-
laska.net/~chihuly) to talk with Mike, the cousin
of world-renowned glass artist Dale Chihuly. All-
day halibut charters cost $150. **Deep Creek Cus-
tom Packing** (907/567-3395 or 800/764-0078,
www.deepcreekcustompacking.com) sells quality fresh and smoked fish, and is open for tours.

The Ninilchik Chamber of Commerce's website (www.ninilchickchamber.com) has links to a
dozen or so local lodging places. Budget travelers
should check out **Ninilchik Hostel/The Eagle
Watch** (907/567-3905), a summer-only place
with dorm beds for $13 ($10 for members of

the old Russian Orthodox Church in Ninilchik

Hostelling International). A full kitchen is available, along with two private rooms. The hostel is
closed 10 A.M.–5 P.M.

Two places with great vistas across Cook Inlet
are **Bluff House B&B** (907/567-3605,
www.alaska.net/~bluffbb) and **Kennedy's Lookout B&B** (907/567-3482 or 877/547-4005,
www.charters.bizland.com). **Meander In B&B**
(907/567-1050, www.meanderin.net) is a new
hilltop home overlooking the Ninilchik River.

Three very popular state campgrounds
(907/235-7024, www.alaskastateparks.org) are
scattered around town: **Ninilchik River Campground** (big, woodsy, and uncrowded; $10),
Ninilchik View Campground (atop a high
bluff; $10), and **Ninilchik Beach Campground**
(undeveloped sites; $5). **Deep Creek State
Recreation Area** ($10) is just two miles to the
south, with undeveloped campsites. Day use
parking is $5.

Park RVs at **Heavenly Sights Camping**
(907/567-7371 or 800/479-7371, www.heav-
enlysights.com) on the bluff just north of

Ninilchik, or **Scenic View RV Park** (907/567-3909, www.scenicviewrv.com). Other Ninilchik area RV parks include **Alaskan Angler RV Resort** (907/567-3393 or 800/347-4114, www.afishunt.com), **Country Boy Camp Grounds** (907/567-3396), and **D&M RV Park** (907/567-4368 or 800/479-7357, www.dnmrvpark.com).

Anchor Point

This small town of 1,100 people is another sportfishing destination, with the Anchor River attracting anglers in pursuit of king salmon, silver salmon, Dolly Varden, and steelhead. Anchor Point is the most westerly highway point in North America (or more precisely, the most westerly town on a road system connected with the Lower 48).

Stay at **Anchor River Inn** (907/235-8531 or 800/435-8531, www.xyz.net/~jjclutts), where the rooms include aging and tiny "fishermen's special" (no TVs) for $54–60 d. Standard motel rooms with fridges and microwaves are $89 d. A better bet is probably **Sleepy Bear Cabins** (907/235-5625 or 866/235-5630, www.sleepybearalaska.com), where three modern cabins all have microwaves, fridges, and private baths for $95 d or $115 for four people. Also worth a look is **Northwood Cabins** (907/235-5142 or 888/972-2246, www.northwoodcabins.com).

Anchor River State Recreation Area covers five campgrounds with campsites ($10) scattered along the Anchor River Beach Road just downhill from town. **Stariski State Recreation Site** ($10) four miles north of Anchor Point, has one of the best views of any state campground. Day use parking is $5.

The Anchor Point Chamber of Commerce (907/235-2600, www.anchorpointalaska.info) maintains a **Visitor Information Center** that houses historical photos and memorabilia. It's generally open daily 8 A.M.–4 P.M. in the summer, and Monday–Friday 8 A.M.–noon the rest of the year.

Nikolaevsk

The Russian Old Believer village of Nikolaevsk is nine miles east of Anchor Point via North Fork Rd. and Nikolaevsk Road. This isolated community is one of several on the Kenai Peninsula where these traditional Russian Orthodox people live; nearly all speak both Russian and English. There's a picturesque church, and the women and girls wear scarves and ankle-length dresses. But they also have all the modern conveniences, including big pickup trucks, satellite dishes, and computers. Villagers are not particularly accepting of outsiders, so don't go around pointing your camera at folks.

One exceptionally open local is Nina Fefelov, owner of the delightful **Samovar Cafe** (907/235-6867, www.russiangiftsnina.com), which serves such traditional dishes as borsch, pelmeni, piroshki, and Russian tea, and sells traditional Russian gifts. Overnight stays at her B&B are just $50 d.

Homer

Homer has a dazzling reputation for some of the finest scenery, the mildest climate, heaviest halibut, biggest bays, longest spits, coolest people (wearing the most tie-dye), and best quality of life in the state. And the truth is, Homer is one of Alaska's peerless towns. It has an undeniably beautiful setting, with the unruly coastline, lingualate fjords, and cavalcading Kenai Mountains across magnificent Kachemak Bay. The temperatures are generally mild—for Alaska. The halibut sometimes tip the scales at over 200 pounds, and you can try your luck at salmon fishing for the cost of a fishing license. An abundance of fine artists and craftspeople call Homer home, selling their wares at small galleries full of rare and tempting stuff. And some of the state's best fishing, boating, hiking, kayaking, natural history, wildlife, and photo ops revolve around Homer in Kachemak Bay. So the bottom line is: Homer distinctly deserves its reputation. Welcome to Homer, Cosmic Hamlet by the Sea. You might even run into a travel writer or two here.

HISTORY

The Russians knew of the limitless coal in this area in the early 1800s, and Americans were mining the seams only a decade after the Alaska Purchase. The gold rush began delivering men and supplies to the small port at the end of the sandy spit on their way to the gold fields at Hope and Sunrise up the Inlet in the mid-1890s. One of the most flamboyant prospectors to pass through, Homer Pennock left his name on the settlement. Mining the hundreds of millions of tons of accessible bituminous fuel continued until 1907, when a combination of fire in Homer, federal policy, and falling prices burned out the market. Slowly, the inevitable fishermen and homesteaders began settling in during the 1920s, and they found a lifetime supply of home-heating fuel free for the taking right on the beach; it's still collected by some locals.

Homer remained a small fishing and canning port until the early 1950s, when the Sterling Highway finally connected the town with the rest of the continent. Since then, the population has grown to over 4,000 today, with commercial fishing and tourism the primary economic pillars. Homer has an interesting mix of people. Drop by the docks and you'll encounter both the longhair Rasta crowd and Russian Old Believers whose women wear prim and proper long dresses while the men sport long beards.

SIGHTS

The Homer Spit

This four-mile finger of real estate juts boldly into Kachemak Bay hosting the Small Boat Harbor, touristy boardwalks, a famous Fishing Hole, the infamous Salty Dawg Saloon, Land's End Resort, public camping, charter halibut and salmon fishing, a ferry terminal, and lazy beachcombing with an incomparable view. It is Homer's main attraction, and a wonderfully busy place in midsummer. You could easily spend several days just exploring the shops, walking the beaches, flying kites, fishing for salmon in the Hole, renting a sea kayak to paddle around, soaking up the mountain vistas, and sitting around a campfire as the mid-summer sun heads down around midnight. No wonder so many folks love Homer!

A paved two-mile **bike path** starts at the base of the Spit and continues to the Fishing Hole; it's great for bikes and inline skates, but the traffic is constant and noisy. Come out early in the morning before the cars and wind pick up. Bike rentals are available from Sportsman's Supply (907/235-2617) across from the boat launch, and at Lands End Resort (907/235-2500).

In the winter, Homer Spit is home to hundreds of **bald eagles.** Every winter morning octogenarian Jean Keene feeds herring to the eagles from her trailer near the end of the Spit. You can watch, but will need to remain in your vehicle. The eagles attract photographers from around the globe; most of the close-up, in-flight eagle photos that you see in print were shot here—including those in *National Geographic.*

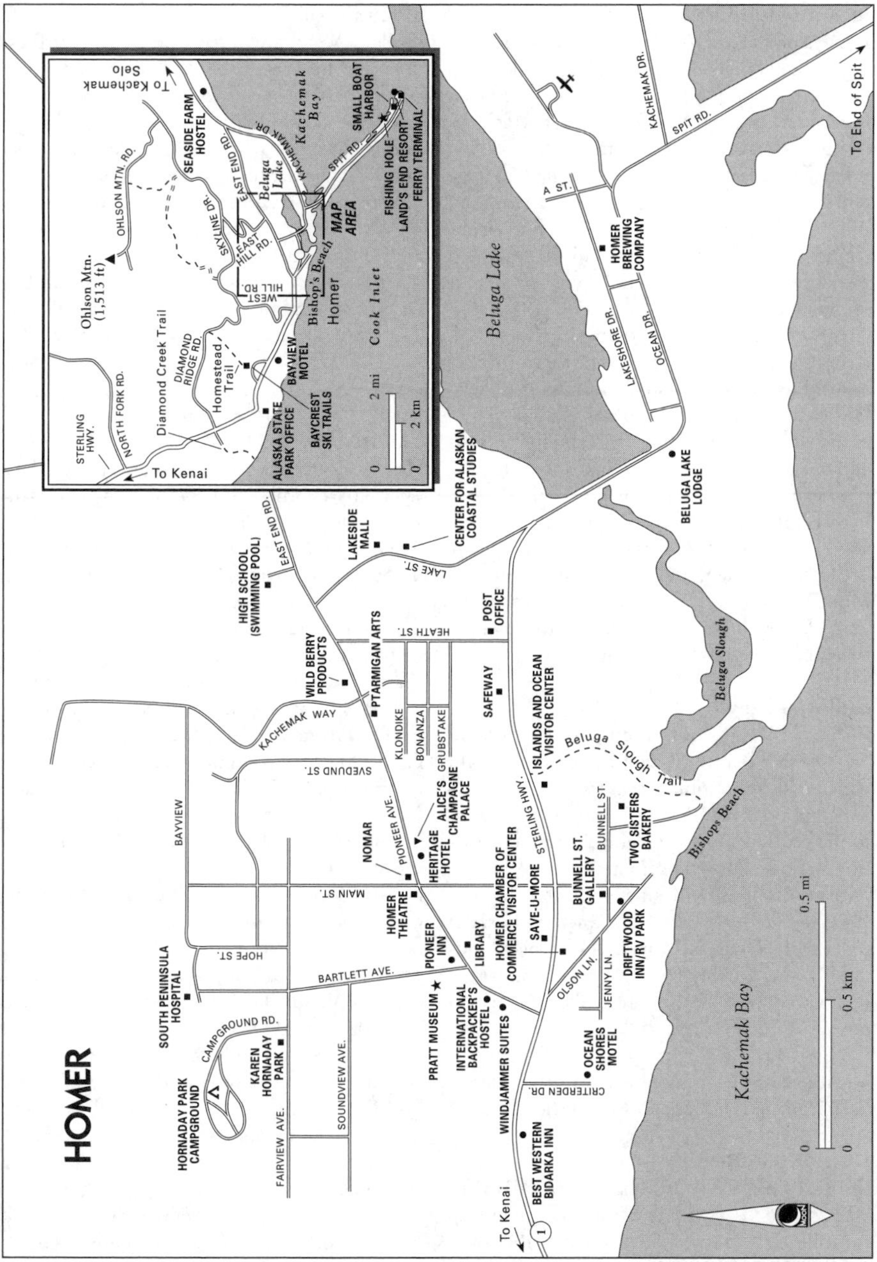

HOMER

© AVALON TRAVEL PUBLISHING, INC.

Map inset (MAP AREA):

To Kachemak Selo
SEASIDE FARM HOSTEL
Kachemak Bay
SMALL BOAT HARBOR
FISHING HOLE
LAND'S END RESORT
FERRY TERMINAL
OHLSON MTN. RD.
Beluga Lake
EAST END RD.
KACHEMAK DR.
SPIT RD.
SKYLINE DR.
EAST HILL RD.
WEST HILL RD.
Bishop's Beach
Homer
MAP AREA
Cook Inlet
Ohlson Mtn. (1,513 ft)
Diamond Creek Trail
DIAMOND RIDGE RD.
Homestead Trail
NORTH FORK RD.
STERLING HWY.
BAYVIEW MOTEL
ALASKA STATE PARK OFFICE
BAYCREST SKI TRAILS
To Kenai
0 2 mi
0 2 km

Main map labels:

To End of Spit
SPIT RD.
KACHEMAK DR.
A ST.
HOMER BREWING COMPANY
OCEAN DR.
LAKESHORE DR.
Beluga Lake
BELUGA LAKE LODGE
EAST END RD.
CENTER FOR ALASKAN COASTAL STUDIES
LAKESIDE MALL
LAKE ST.
HIGH SCHOOL (SWIMMING POOL)
POST OFFICE
HEATH ST.
WILD BERRY PRODUCTS
PTARMIGAN ARTS
Beluga Slough Trail
Beluga Slough
KACHEMAK WAY
KLONDIKE
BONANZA
GRUBSTAKE
SAFEWAY
ISLANDS AND OCEAN VISITOR CENTER
SVEDRUP ST.
ALICE'S CHAMPAGNE PALACE
HERITAGE HOTEL
NOMAR
STERLING HWY.
BAYVIEW
PIONEER AVE.
BUNNELL ST.
TWO SISTERS BAKERY
MAIN ST.
HOMER THEATRE
HOMER CHAMBER OF COMMERCE VISITOR CENTER
BUNNELL ST. GALLERY
Bishop's Beach
HOPE ST.
PIONEER INN
LIBRARY
SAVE-U-MORE
DRIFTWOOD INN/RV PARK
BARTLETT AVE.
OLSON LN.
JENNY LN.
SOUTH PENINSULA HOSPITAL
PRATT MUSEUM
INTERNATIONAL BACKPACKER'S HOSTEL
WINDJAMMER SUITES
CAMPGROUND RD.
OCEAN SHORES MOTEL
KAREN HORNADAY PARK
HORNADAY PARK CAMPGROUND
SOUNDVIEW AVE.
CRITTENDEN DR.
Kachemak Bay
FAIRVIEW AVE.
BEST WESTERN BIDARKA INN
To Kenai
1

0 0.5 mi
0 0.5 km

Islands and Ocean Center

Located on the edge of Homer, this extraordinary $19-million facility opened in 2003. Inside, you'll find interactive exhibits that detail the **Alaska Maritime National Wildlife Refuge** which encompasses 4.9 million acres sprawled across 2,500 Alaskan islands. Millions of seabirds nest on these remote islands—the largest seabird refuge in America. The Alaska Islands and Ocean Visitor Center opens a window into this little-visited world, and has quickly become a required stop for Homer visitors.

A grand two-story glass lobby faces Kachemak Bay, and visitors can step into a room that re-creates the sounds (and smells!) of a bird rookery, take a stunning voyage to the islands via an award-winning film, and learn about the birds and marine mammals that inhabit these remote places and the researchers that work there. This free visitor center (95 Sterling Hwy., 907/235-6961, www.islandsandocean.org) is open daily 9 A.M.–6 P.M. Memorial Day to Labor Day, and Monday–Saturday 9 A.M.–5 P.M. the rest of the year. During the summer, guided bird-watching treks and beach walks are offered.

Bishops Beach

A short trail leads from the Islands and Ocean Center past Beluga Slough to Bishops Beach, which is also accessible by car from Bunnell Avenue; turn right on Beluga Avenue, and follow it to the beach. This is a delightful spot for a low-tide walk, with extraordinary views of mountains, volcanoes, and glaciers lining the bay. Intrepid hikers can follow the beach north seven miles to the **Diamond Creek Trail**, which heads uphill to the Sterling Highway; leave a car at the trailhead off the highway to make your return easier. (Diamond Creek trailhead is directly across the Sterling Hwy. from Diamond Ridge Rd.) You'll need to time this hike with the tides to keep from getting trapped against the cliffs.

Pratt Museum

Be sure to visit the Pratt Museum (3779 Bartlett, 907/235-8635, www.prattmuseum.org), just up from Pioneer Avenue. This is one of the finest small museums in Alaska, with interesting his-torical and cultural pieces, artwork, and wildlife displays. Watch them feed the sea critters Tuesdays and Fridays at 4 P.M. The beaked whale skeleton extends nearly the length of one room; follow the story of how it was shot and washed up onto a Homer beach, then was taken apart and put back together piece by piece. A gift shop features Alaskan-made crafts. The museum website also features webcams from McNeil River and Gull Island. The museum is open daily 10 A.M.–6 P.M. from mid-May to mid-September, and Tuesday–Sunday noon–5 P.M. the rest of the year (closed January). Entrance costs $6 adults, $5.50 seniors, or $3 ages 6–18, free for younger kids.

Scenic Drives and Hikes

Head back out the Sterling Highway and take a right on West Hill Road; just after the pavement ends, go right at the fork (a left puts you on Diamond Ridge Rd., which drops you back down to the Sterling) onto **Skyline Drive.** You climb along a high ridge among expensive homes and B&Bs, until you see the famous view of the Spit, the bay, and the march of mountains on the southern coast, all framed by fireweed late in the summer.

Continue on Skyline Drive to the turnoff for **East Hill Road,** which takes you steeply downhill to Homer, or continue out East Skyline Drive (a gravel road) 1.5 miles to **Carl E. Wynn Nature Center** (907/235-6667, www.akcoastalstudies.org). Here you'll find nature trails and a learning center that's open daily 10 A.M.–6 P.M. mid-June to Labor Day. Guided walks are offered; $5 adults, $4 seniors, or $3 for anyone under 18. Keep going out E. Skyline, and turn left on remote Ohlson Mountain Road until it ends at **Ohlson Peak** (1,513 feet). Return to town via East Hill Road, which meets East End Road on—you guessed it—the east side of town.

Pioneer Avenue through town turns into **East End Road,** which also has beautiful homes and great views of the Spit and the bay. Nine miles out are the down-home Fritz Creek General Store and the Homestead Restaurant, along with increasingly jaw-dropping views of the Kachemak Bay and the glaciers. The road ends 20 miles from town, but you can walk down a steep dirt road from here to the shore and past the Russian Old Believer village of **Kachemak Selo** along the beach at the head of Kachemak Bay. Not many folks get this far from Homer, but those who do are well rewarded for the effort. If you don't want to drive all that way, take a hard right onto Kachemak Drive three miles out, and head back down to the Spit. But watch your speed on this road; local cops enforce the 35 mph limit with a vengeance.

Galleries

Homer has a statewide reputation as an arts center, and a few local showcases are must-sees on any Homer itinerary. If you're around on the first Friday of the month, don't miss the aptly named **First Friday,** when new exhibitions open and the hors d'oeuvres come out. A number of galleries are scattered around town, most notably **Bunnell Street Gallery** (907/235-2662, www.xyz.net/~bunnell). This nonprofit gallery is in the old Inlet Trading Post, built in 1937, and just up from Bishop's Beach. Although small, Bunnell Gallery attracts nationally known artists, with new exhibitions monthly. In the back are pieces for sale in a variety of media.

Ptarmigan Arts (471 E. Pioneer Ave., 907 /235-5345, www.artinhomer.com) has a diversity of artists, all of whom also work one day a month at this pseudo-cooperative. Here you'll find everything from handmade hats to ceramics, beaded jewelry, wildlife and landscape photos (including those of the author), and watercolors. Next door is **Fireweed Gallery** (907/235-3411, www.xyz.net/~homerart), and **Picture Alaska** (907/235-2300, www.xyz.net/~akartgal) is across the street.

Head out the Spit for several seasonal galleries, including **Sea Lion Gallery** (907/235-3400), **High Tide Arts** (907/226-2600), and **Homer Clay Works** (907/235-6118).

Shopping

Alaska Wild Berry Products (528 E. Pioneer Ave., 907/235-8858 or 800/280-2927, www .alaskawildberryproduct.com) specializes in Alaska-made wild berry jams, jellies, chocolates, and sauces, some of which are fashioned on the premises. The counter usually has free samples, but it's hard to resist buying some before you leave.

Nomar (downtown at 104 E. Pioneer Ave., 907/235-8363 or 800/478-8364, www.nomar-alaska.com) sells high-quality handmade clothing and outdoor gear. Some of its most popular items are specifically designed for commercial fishermen, but Nomar also has warm and windproof outerwear, kids' garb, hats, raingear, purses, duffel bags, and more. Next door is **Main Street Mercantile** (907/235-9102), a beautifully restored 1936 building filled with outdoor gear and home accessories.

Head three miles out East End Road to **Kachemak Gear Shed** (907/235-8612 or 800/478-8612), which sells quality clothing and other gear for anyone heading out on the water. It's a great place to check out the commercial fishing supplies too.

The Bookstore (332 E. Pioneer, 907/235-7496) has all of Tom Bodett's books, along with works of other local authors, a big Alaskana section, field guides, and lots more. (Tom Bodett is known to most Americans as the folksy "We'll leave the light on for you" voice in the Motel 6 commercials, but he is also the author of several humor books. Like fellow Homerite celebrity Jewel, Bodett no longer lives in Homer.) **Old Inlet Bookshop** (3984 Main St., 907/235-7984) is a great used bookstore. It's housed in a cabin that was originally part of a 1905 fox farm on Yukon Island.

RECREATION

See the *Across Kachemak Bay* section for details on the popular boat trips from Homer to Seldovia, Halibut Cove, and Kachemak Bay State Park.

Sea Kayaking

A number of local companies lead guided sea kayak trips within Kachemak Bay, or rent kayaks to do it on your own. Based on protected Yukon Island near Kachemak Bay State Park, **True North Kayak Adventures** (907/235-0708, www.true northkayak.com) offers a range of trips, from six-hour paddles to Elephant Rock ($115) to two-night/three-day packages ($450). Especially popular are their guided all-day trips from Homer that include a round-trip water taxi ride to Yukon Island, sea kayaks, guide, and lunch for $135. Kayak rentals are available if you want to head out on your own.

Across the Bay Tent & Breakfast Adventure Company (907/235-3633 summer or 907/345-2571 winter, www.tentandbreakfastalaska.com) has a distinctive operation that's perfect for adventurous travelers on a budget. Guests stay in furnished, canvas wall-tents set atop wooden platforms along Kasitsna Bay (near Seldovia), with showers, a sauna, and "two of the most beautiful outhouses in Alaska." Tent and all meals are $95/day/person; tent and breakfast only are $63/day. You can rent a mountain bike, take a sea kayak tour, or join one of their summertime workshops.

Other companies offering sea kayak tours include **Homer Ocean Charters** (907/235-6212 or 800/426-6212, www.homerocean.com), **St. Augustine's Kayak & Tours** (907/235-6126 or 800/770-6126, www.homerkayaking.com), **Seaside Adventures** (907/235-6672, www.seasideadventure.com). **Isis Alaskan Adventures** (907/399-8071, www.isisalaskanadventures.com), and **Alaska Canoe & Kayak Base** (907/235-2090, www.alaskakayakschool.com). The last of these operates year-round, with dry suits when winter hits. Homer Ocean Charters also rents kayaks on the Spit, as does **Mako's Water Taxi** (907/235-9055, www.makoswatertaxi.com).

Charter Fishing

Homer calls itself the halibut fishing capital of the world, with commercial fishermen often landing more halibut here than any other port. Sport fishing attracts droves of enthusiasts every day of the summer, not only for halibut, but also for king and silver salmon. Charters run around $175 pp for an all-day trip, including tackle and bait supplied. When comparing prices, make sure that cleaning and processing your catch is included, unless you plan to do it yourself. Some companies charge extra (by the pound) for the service, and the fees can get hefty if you catch a "barn-door" halibut. Wear warm, layered clothing topped by raingear, and wear soft-soled shoes. Binoculars

Homer's boat harbor, with the Kenai Mountains in the background

are a definite plus, since seabirds and marine mammals are usually viewable. You can have your catch vacuum-packed, frozen, and shipped home for additional fees, but they add up quickly.

Whatever you do, don't forget to enter the summer-long **Homer Jackpot Halibut Derby** (www.homerhalibutderby.com) if you go fishing. First prize is more than $40,000, with additional monthly prizes. Every year sob stories abound of people who saved $10 by not entering, then caught potential prize-winning sea monsters. Don't let this happen to you!

Homer has dozens of fishing charter boats to help you go out and bag a big halibut. An easy way to find one is through **Central Charter Booking Agency** (907/235-7847 or 800/478-7847, www.centralcharter.com), **Homer Ocean Charters** (907/235-6212 or 800/426-6212, www.homerocean.com), **Inlet Charters** (907/235-6126 or 800/7700-6126, www.halibutcharters.com), or **North Country Charters** (907/235-7620 or 800/770-7620, www.northcountycharters.com). In addition to charter fishing, all of these can set up sea kayaking, water taxi service, flightseeing, bear-viewing, and lodging for the area.

Once you do catch a big halibut or salmon, how do you get it back home? Several companies on the Spit will flash-freeze your fish and FedEx it to you; **Coal Point Seafood** (907/235-3877 or 800/325-3877, www.welovefish.com) is a good one. And if you don't catch anything, they'll sell you frozen seafood of all types. If you're going to be flying out and can take the fish with you, be sure to get the specially coated cardboard box (sold in grocery stores and at Kachemak Gear Shed) and pack it with blue ice. There are freezers at the Homer and Anchorage airports that charge a daily rental fee.

The Fishing Hole

If you just want to simply drive into town and cast a line in the water, head out to the famous Fishing Hole on the Spit, across from Glacier Drive-In and Sportsman's Supply. The Alaska Department of Fish & Game stocks this little bight with king and silver salmon smolt, and their return draws crowds of anglers all summer long. It's a classic roadside fishing stop for RVers, kids, lazy locals, and the like. On a busy weekend, you might be able to squeeze in at water's edge.

Get fishing licenses or rent a pole from **Sport Shed** (907/235-5562) across from the Hole or **Sportsman's Supply** (907/235-2617) near the boat launch.

Bear-Watching and Flightseeing

Homer is a popular base for bear-viewing trips to coastal Katmai National Park in the summer, primarily the stretch between Geographic Harbor and Swikshak Lagoon. The destination depends upon the bears' seasonal activity. All-day trips costing $525 pp are offered by **Emerald Air Service** (907/235-6993, www.emeraldairservice.com, recommended), **Kenai Fjords Outfitters** (907/235-6066 or 888/536-6066, www.seaplanealaska.com), **Bald Mountain Air Service** (907/235-7969 or 800/478-7969, www.baldmountainair.com), **Beluga Air** (907/235-8256), **Hallo Bay Wilderness** (907/235-2237, www.hal-

lobay.com), **Homer Air** (907/235-8591 or 800/478-8591, www.homerair.com), and **Smokey Bay Air** (907/235-1511 or 888/482-1511). Hallo Bay is particularly notable, with a unique camp setting in the heart of Katmai National Park; it's described in the *Southwest Alaska* chapter. All of these companies also offer exceptionally scenic flightseeing trips, typically around $130 for a 1.5-hour flight.

Kachemak Air Service (907/235-8924, www.alaskaseaplanes.com) has a lovingly restored 1929 Travel Air floatplane for one-hour scenic flights; $120 per person with a two-person minimum.

Maritime Helicopters (907/235-7771, www.maritimehelicopters.com) guides eagle's-eye tours of the region's glaciers, islands, and mountains on a charter basis from the Homer Airport.

Sea Bear Charters (907/235-0123 or 888/825-1828, www.seabearcharters.com) provides 12-hour bear-viewing to coastal Lake Clark National Park in June and July. They take a maximum of six passengers onboard a 36-foot boat at $395 per person. These trips don't go every day due to the tides and wind conditions, but are a unique way to see brown bears without flying.

Winter Sports

Homer doesn't entirely shut down in the winter, though many of the tourists (and some residents) flee for warmer and drier climes. The town itself is just above sea level, and it may rain even in January, but surrounding hills often pile high with snow. **Kachemak Nordic Ski Club** (907/235-6018, www.xyz.net/~watson/knsc.html) maintains 35 kilometers of groomed cross-country trails near McNeil Canyon (13 miles east of town), at Baycrest (just west of town off Sterling Hwy.), and at Lookout Mountain (out Ohlson Mountain Road). Also popular in the winter are snowmobiling, ice skating on Beluga Lake, and eagle-watching on the Spit.

Other Recreation

Homer High School houses the local **swimming pool** (907/235-7416), open daily for lap swimming. The **Bay Club** (2395 Kachemak Dr., 907/235-2582) is an excellent private facility with a small pool, racquetball court, workout equipment, yoga classes, and climbing wall. Entrance costs $14 for visitors, with free childcare available while you work out.

Rent **mountain bikes** from Homer Saw and Cycle (1532 Ocean Dr., 907/235-8406) or on the Spit from Sportsman's Supply (907/235-2617) and Lands End Resort (907/235-2500). **Trails End Horse Adventures** (907/235-6393) offers horseback rides in the Fox River area at the head of Kachemak Bay.

If you have kids in tow, drive uphill on Bartlett Avenue, then left on Fairview to **Karen Hornaday Park,** where the playground has all sorts of fun adventures.

ACCOMMODATIONS

The Homer Chamber of Commerce website (www.homeralaska.org) has links to most local lodging places.

Hostels

Homer's old-time favorite is **Seaside Farm Hostel** (907/235-7850, www.xyz.net/~seaside), five miles out East End Road from town. It's a great country location with horses in the pasture below, bike rentals, beach access, and views across Kachemak Bay. Beds in the coed dorm cost $15, including cooking facilities and showers. Private rooms are $40 d in the lodge, and simple cabins run $55 d; showers are in the lodge. Scenic tent spaces are $6. Open May–September. (Seaside Farm is owned by the Kilcher family, whose internationally known offspring is the singer Jewel Kilcher, better known as simply Jewel. Homer's most famous former resident now lives in Washington.)

The **Homer Hostel** (304 W. Pioneer Avenue, 907/235-1463, www.homerhostel.com) is housed within the historic Pratt House (built in 1939). Three dorm-style rooms sleep up to four at $21 per person. Private rooms are $45 s or $58 d, and a full kitchen, laundry, and showers are available. The hostel has a convenient downtown location, a friendly owner, and no curfew. Guests can rent bikes and fishing poles. Open all year.

A few blocks away is **Bunkhouse** (4030 Bartlett) with two dorm rooms, a kitchen, and common area, and a big front porch. Beds are $20, and they're open all year.

Motels and Hotels

Driftwood Inn (907/235-8019 or 800/478-8019, www.thedriftwoodinn.com), a simple place near Bishop's Beach, charges $55–69 s or $65–78 d for tiny older rooms; pricier rooms face the water and cost $100–120 s or $110–130 d.

Pioneer Inn (244 W. Pioneer Ave., 907/235-5670 or 800/782-9655, www.xyz.net/~abc) is a cozy downtown motel with standard rooms for $89 d, and five apartment-style units with full kitchens for $109 d.

It's hard to miss the **Heritage Hotel** (147 E. Pioneer Ave., 907/235-7787 or 800/380-7787, www.alaskaheritagehotel.com). Built in 1948, this rambling log hotel has rooms for $99 s or $109 d, and one deluxe whirlpool-bath suite for $150 d. This is a love-it or hate-it place; some folks rave about the classic rooms, while others prefer something more modern.

Ocean Shores Motel (451 Sterling Hwy., 907/235-7775 or 800/770-7775, www.akoceanshores.com) has large rooms, all with balconies facing Kachemak Bay. Most also include fridges and microwaves. The motel actually consists of four buildings, with prices matching your proximity to the water: $99–179 d.

Located on a high hill as you drive into Homer, **Bay View Inn** (907/235-8485 or 800/478-8485, www.bayviewalaska.com) has standard rooms and kitchenettes ($84 s or $89–99 d), or suites and cottages ($124 s or $149 d). All but the least expensive of these face the water, with panoramic vistas. Recommended.

Windjammer Suites (412 E. Pioneer, 907/235-9761 or 888/730-2770, www.alaskan.com/windjammersuites) has large in-town suites with full kitchens for a reasonable $95 d. **Beluga Lake Lodge** (984 Ocean Dr., 907/235-5995, www.belugalakelodge.com) charges $89 s or d in standard rooms, $139 for up to four people in its kitchenette units.

Popular with fishermen are three units over the **Sport Shed** (907/235-5562), a fishing shop. These comfortable rooms—all with full kitchens and water views—are $100 d ($85 d for multiple nights), plus $5 each for extra guests. They're right across from the Fishing Hole, and are open May–September.

Land's End Resort (907/235-0400 or 800/478-0400, www.lands-end-resort.com) occupies the very tip of Homer Spit, with bay-and-mountain views from some rooms, a waterside hot tub, and a jetted lap pool. The 80 rooms range greatly in price ($124–197 s or $135–207 d), and in size and amenities. The nicest are suites with private decks facing the bay; the cheapest are tiny boxes facing the parking lot. Also on the premises is one of the better local restaurants.

Most rooms at **Best Western Bidarka Inn** (575 Sterling Hwy., 907/235-8148 or 800/528-1234, www.bestwestern.com) go for $144 d, though they do have rooms with private whirlpool baths for $174.

Alaskan Suites (907/235-1972 or 888/239-1972, www.alaskansuites.com) consists of five modern cabins on the west side of Homer, each containing two queen beds, a fridge and microwave, and private bath. The panoramic views include Kachemak Bay and several volcanoes. Cabins rent for $195, and can sleep up to five guests. Also available is a private two-story cottage for $245.

Homer Floatplane Lodge (907/235-4160 or 877/235-9600, www.floatplanelodge.com) has a variety of multinight packages based in modern log cabins on the shore of Beluga Lake.

Bed-and-Breakfasts

Typically, more than 100 (!) bed-and-breakfasts are at your disposal in Homer. A couple of local bed-and-breakfast organizations provide one-stop shopping: **Homer's Finest B&B Network** (907/235-4983 or 800/764-3211, www.homer-accommodations.com) and the larger **Homer B&B Association** (907/235-0518 or 800/473-3092, www.homerbedbreakfast.com).

Old Town B&B (106 W. Bunnell St., 907/235-7558, www.xyz.net/~oldtown) is owned by Asia Freeman and Kurt Marquardt, who run Bunnell Street Gallery, downstairs. The four rooms have period pieces in this lovingly renovated 1936 building, and are priced at a re-

markable $75–85 d, including a light breakfast. Unique and definitely recommended.

In business for more than 20 years, **Magic Canyon Ranch** (907/235-6077, www.magic-canyonranch.com) has one of the largest spreads in the area, a 75-acre homestead set against the bluffs five miles out East End Road. The comfortable home contains four guest rooms ($85–100 d), great views, knowledgeable owners, and filling country breakfasts. There's even a 1915 Model T parked out in the barn. Highly recommended.

The aptly named **Majestic View B&B** (907/235-6413 or 888/246-6413, www.majesticviewbb.com) offers four modern rooms, a large deck with unobstructed bay vistas, and full breakfasts for $85–125 d. The deluxe suite has a whirlpool tub.

A B&B on the Green (907/235-0606 or 800/295-5969, www.alaskagolfandfishing.com) is seven miles out East End Road, at the site of a par-three golf course (the most westerly course in North America). Five rooms are in the main house, with two more over the clubhouse; rates are $85–125 d, including private baths, a continental breakfast, and unlimited golf.

A Room with a View (62252 Rosebud Court, 907/235-3706, www.aroomwith-aviewhomer.com) is a large hillside home with two guest rooms ($90 d), private baths, and filling breakfasts. The owners speak German, and their decades as florists show in the immaculately landscaped grounds. No kids.

Victorian Heights B&B (61495 Race Rd., 907/235-6357, www.victorianheightsbedand-breakfast.com) is a hilltop mansion with four spacious guest rooms; $95–135 d, with private baths. A full breakfast is included, and a two-night minimum stay is required. Guests love the big deck with a hot tub overlooking the bay.

Kachemak Kiana B&B (907/235-8824 or 866/235-8824, www.akms.com/kiana) is five miles out East End Road, with bay vistas from the picture windows. Rates are $95–115 d for the four rooms in the main house, or $130 d for the separate cottage; all have private baths and access to a glass-enclosed hot tub and gazebo. A full breakfast is served. No kids under 10.

Aloha B&B (62209 Glacier View Court, 907/235-0607 or 877/355-0607, www.alohabb.com) has one of Homer's famous "million-dollar" views—a 180-degree panorama of bay, mountains, and glacier. The owners are natives of Hawaii, and a Hawaiian theme carries through all four guest rooms. Two share a bath, and the others have private baths. Rates are $105–120 d, with a full breakfast.

Chocolate Drop Inn (907/235-3668 or 800/530-6015, www.chocolatedropinn.com) is six miles out East End Road, and offers outstanding views of Grewingk Glacier and a peak locally known as Chocolate Drop. The 8,000-square-foot log home has a hot tub on the back deck, a sauna, private baths and entrances for most of the six guest rooms, plus a filling breakfast. Rates are $115–165 d in the rooms, or $165–185 for four guests in the two-bedroom suites. The Chocolate Drop isn't really set up for kids. Be sure to ask about the B&B's neighbors; you might know them.

Ocean House Inn (907/235-3294 or 888/353-3294, www.homeroceanhouse.com) sits atop a low cliff, with guest rooms ($100 d), suites with kitchens ($120 d), and full condos ($175–205 d). Breakfast is $8 extra. Relax in the hot tub facing the Spit.

Good Karma Inn (907/235-4728 or 866/435-2762, www.goodkarmainn.com) is a recently completed log home six miles east of Homer, with complete accessibility for handicapped travelers. Rates are $135 d, including a continental breakfast.

Honey's Place B&B (907/235-8232 or 907/279-5055, www.honeysbeachhouse.com) is one of the only private homes on Homer Spit. The location is perfect for bird-watchers and folks wanting to be close to the fishing action. Guests get exclusive use of the three-bedroom beachfront home, plus a make-it-yourself breakfast each morning; $195 d, plus $50 pp to a maximum of six. Open May–September.

Cabins and Guest Houses

Start your cabin search at **Homer Cabins & Cottage Network** (907/235-0191 or 888/364-

0191, www.cabinsinhomer.com), with nearly 20 rental cabins in the Homer area.

One place worth a mention is **Lighthouse Village Cabins** (907/235-7007, www.lighthousecabins.com). Located at the base of the Homer Spit, these cute cabins include private baths, kitchens, phones, and TVs. This is an especially good spot for shorebird enthusiasts, with the tideflats right out the door. One unit has been built in the shape of a lighthouse; reserve well ahead for this! Rates are $100–150 d, plus $15 for each additional guest.

Near the end of Homer Spit, **Sea Lion Cove** (907/235-3400 (summers) or 907/235-8767, www.alaskaone.com/sealion) is operated by artist Gary Lion, whose gallery is downstairs. The two rooms are right in the heart of the summertime fishing action. Each has a kitchenette, TV, phone, and shared deck delivering wonderful bay vistas; $110–120 d, plus $10 pp for additional guests.

Homer Seaside Cottages (907/235-2716 or 877/374-2716, www.homerseasidecottages.com) has several reasonably priced cottages for rent, one of which is just a block from Bishops Beach; rates are $125–140 d.

Shorebird Guest House (907/235-2107 or 888/934-2377, www.shorebirdcabin.com), sits atop a low cliff overlooking Kachemak Bay, with a stairway leading to the beach. This is a good place for honeymooners or small families wanting a private place. It rents for $120 d, plus $20 pp for additional guests (up to six). Two-night minimum stay, and they're open May through Labor Day.

Located on the west side of Homer, **Alaska Adventure Cabins** (907/223-6681, www.alaskaadventurecabins.com) has two newly built cabins, a restored caboose, and a landlocked boat. Each contains full kitchens, large decks facing the bay, and space for four at $215–255. Check their website for details on these immaculate and unique lodging choices.

CAMPING

Camping on the Spit is what most budget travelers, RVers, and backpackers do, though it's no picnic. It's within spitting distance of the noisy road, and it's barren, windy, and high-density.

The city maintains camping areas along the Spit; $6 tents or $10 RVs (no hookups). Self-register at the sites or pay at the camping fee office (907/235-1583) near the Fishing Hole. Campsites are open April–October, with a few free sites for hardy winter campers. A quieter and more protected campground is at **Hornaday Park** (907/235-3170, www.ci.homer.ak.us) near the hospital on Fairview; same rates.

In addition to the city campsites, the Spit is home to three privately run RV parks with hookups for $23–25. **Homer Spit Campground** (907/235-8206) is near the tip of the Spit, but is not to be confused with the city campground. **Sportsman's Supply** (907/235-2617) has a few spots right across from the boat launch. **Heritage RV Park** (907/235-8350) has all the latest amenities, including satellite TV and phone lines, and is close to the Fishing Hole.

Other private RV parks ($25) are scattered around town: **Driftwood Inn RV Park** (907/235-8019 or 800/478-8019, www.thedriftwoodinn.com) near Bishops Beach; **Oceanview RV Park** (907/235-3591, www.oceanview-rv.com), a crowded RV lot on the west edge of town; and **Village Barabara RV Park** (907/235-1203), just west of Homer on a high bluff over Kachemak Bay

If you're staying in the city campgrounds, showers ($5) are available at Sportsman's Supply or Homer Spit Campground. Local launderettes also have shower facilities; a good bet is **The Washboard** (1204 Ocean Dr., 907/235-6781), where you can even get an espresso drink while watching the clothes spin or after showering. And even better deal is the high school pool, where they throw in a free swim for the cost of a shower.

FOOD

Homer's dining-out options are varied, with several excellent choices. Unfortunately, some of the town's best restaurants are only open seasonally, so winter visitors may be a bit disappointed.

In addition to its reputation as a halibut fishing center, Homer is famous for oysters, and you'll find **Kachemak Bay oysters** in local restaurants and regional seafood shops. Get excellent halibut, salmon, shrimp, and other seafood on the Spit at **Coal Point Trading Company** (907/235-3877; www.welovefish.com). It'll even package the fish with blue ice and FedEx it out for you. But don't expect low prices. Mobile vendors often sell fresh fish and other seafood (including Kachemak Bay Oysters) for a better price at the base of the Spit.

Breakfast

You can't miss **Cafe Cups** (162 W. Pioneer Dr., 907/235-8330)—four Alaska-size teacups hang atop the front of the converted house. Try eggs Benedict, or bagels and lox for breakfast. Cups also serves unusual lunch and dinner dishes, and sports big art on the walls. Dinners ($16–19) include prime rib, fresh oysters, tofu coconut curry, and other inspired dishes.

Duncan House (125 E. Pioneer Ave., 907/235-5344) is a family place with substantial all-American meals three times a day; it's often crowded on weekend mornings, but can get smoky.

Also good for big breakfasts and lunches is the seasonal **Fresh Sourdough Express Bakery** (1316 Ocean Dr., 907/235-7571, www.fresh-sourdoughexpress.com). It serves hotcakes, scrambles, granola, muffins, and pastries for breakfast; sandwiches, homemade soups, and salads for lunch; and some vegetarian meals for dinner, but also plenty of protein acceptable to carnivores.

Quick Meals

Yes, Homer does have McDonald's, Arby's, and Subway, but you're much better off heading out the Spit to **Boardwalk Fish and Chips** (907/235-7749), across from the harbor master and Salty Dawg. It's open daily May–September, and the halibut fish-on-a-stick and chips will have you smackin' your chops. **Finn's Pizza** (907/235-2840) has thin-crust wood-fired pizza by the slice a few doors down, and across the street a few hundred feet farther out the Spit is another tiny seasonal eatery, **Fishwifes Galley** (907/235-4951). Head here in the morning for an espresso and pastry, and return at lunch for handmade tamales, salmon burgers, and sandwiches using its own breads.

Far from the hubbub on the Spit is **Fritz Creek General Store** (907/235-6753), eight miles out East End Road. The store has a small selection of groceries, a little post office, and a bigger choice of videos and booze. The real attraction here is the food, including freshly baked bread, sandwiches, burritos, bagels, pizza by the slice, ribs, and espresso. Fritz Creek is a great place to hang out in an old-time country setting.

Downtown's **Cosmic Kitchen** (510 E. Pioneer Ave., 907/235-6355) serves quick-Mex food such as burritos, tacos, and enchiladas, plus burgers, sandwiches, and homemade soups. Good and tasty. They're also open for breakfast.

Drop by **Frosty Bear** on the Spit and in town at 639 E. Pioneer Avenue, for ice cream and hot dogs; the downtown one has a 1943 Wurlitzer jukebox. Also on the Spit is **Glacier Drive-In** (907/235-7148) for greasy all-American burgers.

Coffeehouses and Bakeries

Two popular espresso stops are Cafe Cups and Fritz Creek General Store. **Two Sisters Espresso and Bakery** (907/235-2280, www.twosisters.com) is a great place to meet the locals any time of year. It's always warm and fragrant with the smell of fresh baked goods, including pastries, breads, and savories, along with sandwiches, focaccia, and deep-dish pizza by the slice. A bit pricey, but highly recommended, and open year-round. They're within a block of Bishops Beach, and the covered deck is a relaxing place to while away the hours.

Inside historic Old Town B&B building a block away is **Panarelli's** (907/235-1555), with a small and high-quality deli, along with a chalkboard full of today's sandwiches, soups, and salads. Excellent food.

Captain's Coffee Roasting Co. (528 E. Pioneer Ave., 907/235-4970) is the only local coffee roaster.

A real surprise is **K Bay Caffe** (907/235-1551, www.homercafe.com), three miles out East End Road. This one is actually little more than a drive-up window and outside deck, with enough space inside for a couple of people to read the newspaper and talk politics. Michael McGuire (the guy in dreadlocks) is one of the best baristas anywhere; he even won top prize at a national espresso-making contest!

International Foods

Two restaurants have Chinese meals and buffets for lunch and dinner: **Young's** (565 E. Pioneer Ave., 907/235-4002) and **China Grill Restaurant** (3798 Lake St., 907/235-3662). Those desperate for something with a slight resemblance to Mexican food could try **Don Jose's** (127 Pioneer Ave., 907/235-7963).

Though it's on the Spit, **Las Pampas Restaurant** (907/235-4328 or 877/750-8294) is a quiet spot away from the crowds, with unusual Argentinean fare, including a tasty asado a la criolla (BBQ ribs with a special sauce). Big portions too. Dinner entrées cost $11–17.

Get very good Thai food to go at **Sockeye Thai,** in a little trailer behind Mako's Water Taxi on the Spit. It offers such favorites as pad Thai, tom yum soup, and vegetable curry. Open seasonally. There's even a seasonal place with spicy Malaysian food in Homer: **Tidewater Cafe** on Olson Lane near Bunnell Street Gallery.

On-the-Town Restaurants

At the very tip of the Spit is **Land's End Resort** (907/235-0400 or 800/478-0400, www.lands-end-resort.com), where panoramic views are the main attraction. The restaurant serves somewhat predictable seafood, steaks, prime rib, and daily specials ($16–24), but the bar is less expensive (not smoke free, however). Land's End is also open for breakfast and lunch, and their large deck is delightful on a sunny summer afternoon.

The Homestead Restaurant (907/235-8723), eight miles out East End Road, is Homer's gourmet dinner-only restaurant, with some of the finest meals on the Kenai Peninsula. The menu specializes—not surprisingly—in fresh Alaskan seafood, but also includes pasta, steaks, and melt-in-your-mouth prime rib. There's a bar in the middle, and two somewhat noisy rooms on either side of this log building right across from the Fritz Creek Store. Homestead is open for dinners only ($18–29 entrées) April–September. Reservations advised.

Another place that gets high marks is **Fat Olives Restaurant** (276 Olson Lane, 907/235-8488). The setting evokes a trendy Italian bistro, and the menu stars wood-fired pizzas, calzones, fresh salmon, beef tenderloin, oven-roasted chicken, and delicious appetizers. It's noisy and fun, perfect for kids. Fat Olives is just off the Homer Bypass as you enter town. In a hurry? Get a giant pizza slice to go for $2.75.

Groceries

Safeway (on Homer Bypass heading toward the Spit, 907/235-2408), is the main grocery store in town, and is open 24 hours. The selection rivals that in Anchorage, but be ready for prices almost 50 percent higher. Better deals can be found at the warehouse-style **Save-U-More** (on Homer Bypass, 907/235-8661). There's also a fun and popular **Farmers Market** on Saturday mornings July to mid-September (plus Wed. afternoons in August) along Ocean Drive.

ENTERTAINMENT AND EVENTS

Alice's Champagne Palace (downtown on Pioneer Ave., 907/235-7650), rocks all night, and is the main venue for visiting singer/songwriters of all types. Check out Hobo Jim on Wednesday nights for some folksy Alaskan nostalgia. The bar has eight or so draught beers, including several from **Homer Brewing Company** (907/235-3626). Or get your own directly from the brewery (1411 Lakeshore Dr.), where you can sample before buying a half-gallon growler to go. Recommended.

The **Salty Dawg Saloon** out near the end of the Spit is Homer's most famous landmark. The original building dates from 1897, the second building from 1909, and the tower from the mid-'60s. Each building housed different companies in eight different locations before settling down here on the Spit. Open from 11 A.M. until the last patron staggers out the door; have a beer for the experience, and leave your business card or signed bra with the thousands of others. The Dawg is closed Nov.–March.

Duggan's Waterfront Pub (907/235-9949) is another longtime local's hangout with bands most weekend, two pool tables, sports on the TVs, and smoke in the air.

Homer has a high proportion of talent, and some of the performers have gotten together to do **Pier One Theater** (on the Spit, 907/235-7333, www.pieronetheatre.org). Whatever is playing, this is guaranteed to be one of the finest theater experiences in the state. It's typically open on weekends May–August only.

For a different kind of theatrical event, catch a flick at little **Homer Theatre** (Pioneer and Main, 907/235-6728). Get there early to snag one of the comfy couches.

Events

The first weekend of May brings the **Kachemak Bay Shorebird Festival** to Homer, with birdwalks, bay tours, an arts fair, speakers, and other activities, all in celebration of the great northward migration of shorebirds. Also on the calendar that same weekend is the **Wooden Boat Festival,** a fun chance to learn how these handcrafted boats are built and to see examples by local boat builders. Fun for all ages.

Public radio station KBBI's **Concerts on the Lawn** (907/235-7721, www.kbbi.org) is the biggest summer event, attracting musicians from around the state. It takes place in late July. This is one of Alaska's best and most eclectic radio stations; find it at 890 AM.

INFORMATION AND SERVICES

Stop by the Homer Chamber of Commerce **Visitor Information Center** (on the Homer Bypass at Main St., 907/235-7740, www.homer-alaska.org), for local details and a plethora of brochures. It's open Monday–Friday 9 A.M.–7 P.M. and Saturday–Sunday 10 A.M.–6 P.M. Memorial Day to Labor Day; Monday–Friday 9 A.M.–6 P.M. and Saturday 10 A.M.–6 P.M. the rest of September, and Monday–Friday 9 A.M.–5 P.M. the rest of the year.

Homer has some of Alaska's best schools, along with a surprising number of writers and would-be authors, so you might expect an admirable local library. Wrong! Instead, you'll discover that the **Homer Public Library** (141 Pioneer Ave., 907/235-3180, http://library.ci.homer.ak.us) is pathetically tiny. Use their always-busy computers to check email or to surf the Web.

The post office (907/235-6129) is on the

Homer Bypass, and **South Peninsula Hospital** (4300 Bartlett St., 907/235-8101) is a fully staffed facility.

TRANSPORTATION
Air
Homer Airport is out East Kachemak Road, which forks off from the Spit Road. **Era Aviation** (907/235-5205 or 800/866-8394, www.fly-era.com) flies to Homer from Anchorage six times a day. Their best rates are with a seven-day advance purchase or by buying a "commuter coupon" book of eight one-way tickets. (These can also be sold to other folks.)

Two local companies offer daily flights from the airport to nearby towns: **Homer Air** (907/235-8591 or 800/478-8591 in Alaska, www.homerair.com) and **Smokey Bay Air** (907/235-1511 or 888/482-1511). These include Seldovia ($25 one-way), along with the Native villages of Nanwalek and Port Graham.

Ferry
The **Alaska Marine Highway** ferry terminal (907/235-8449 or 800/382-9229, www.ferry alaska.com) is out near the end of the Homer Spit. From here, you can catch the *Tustumena* to Seldovia twice a week, Kodiak three times weekly, and once a week around the Peninsula to Seward, Valdez, and Cordova. Once a month it runs all the way out to Dutch Harbor in the Aleutians.

See the *Across Kachemak Bay* and *Kachemak*

Bay State Park sections for other water-travel options in the Homer area.

On the Road
Homer Stage Line (907/235-2252, www.homer-stageline.com) runs to Anchorage, Soldotna, Cooper Landing, and Seward. Service is daily to Anchorage in the summer, and twice a week in the winter; to Seward it runs daily from mid-May to mid-September.

Rent cars at the airport from **Hertz** (907/235-0734 or 800/654-3131), **Polar Car Rental** (907/235-5998 or 800/876-6417, www.polar-carrental.com), or **Jeeps 4 You** (907/235-8640, www.homercarrental.com). **Adventure Alaska Car Rental** (907/235-4022 or 800/882-2808, www.adventurealaskacars.com) has somewhat lower rates for used cars (starting at $50), and will pick you up from the airport. Call **Chux Cab** (907/235-2489) or **Kache Cab** (907/235-1950) for a taxi ride.

Tours
The Pratt Museum operates excellent one-and-a-half-hour **walking tours of Homer Spit** and the harbor for $5. These depart Thursday–Saturday at 3 P.M. throughout the summer, and include local history and lots of detail on commercial and sport fishing. Get tickets at the Pratt or in the little booth next to the Salty Dawg Saloon on the Spit. Shelly Erickson of **Homer Tours** (907/235-6200, www.ptialaska.net/~ericson) leads custom van tours of the Homer area.

Across Kachemak Bay

BAY TOURS
If you have three days in Homer, spend one of them on beautiful Kachemak Bay. A great way to do this is through a **Natural History Tour** (907/235-6667, www.akcoastalstudies.com) with naturalists from the nonprofit Center for Alaskan Coastal Studies. You'll spend time at bird rookeries, tidepools, rainforest trails, and prehistoric sites, and will gain an appreciation for the marine world that you'll carry for life. The eight-hour ex-

perience costs $90 ($60 for ages 6–12, free for younger kids), a bargain, which includes a visit to Gull Island during your ride across to Peterson Bay on the *Mainstay* or *Beowulf.* Bring your own lunch, raingear, rubber boots, binoculars, and camera. Overnight stays and kayak trips are also available at the Peterson Bay field station. For reservations, contact the Center, or drop by Central Charters on the Spit. Trips operate Memorial Day to Labor Day.

St. Augustine's Kayak & Tours (907/235-

6126 or 800/770-6126, www.homerkayaking.com) also offers wildlife day tours and kayak trips from the 14-passenger MV *Seabird*.

Central Charters (907/235-7847 or 800/478-7847, www.centralcharter.com) books two other boats that spend time at Gull Island: the *Danny J* on its runs to Halibut Cove, and the *Dena'ina* as it heads to Seldovia. Water taxis are listed below under Kachemak Bay State Park. Watch the Gull Island action in real-time through the "birdcam" on the web at www.prattmuseum.com.

HALIBUT COVE

Even if you only have two days in Homer, spend half of one visiting this enchanted village (pop. 75) across Kachemak Bay on Ismailof Island. At one time Halibut Cove was the center for a thriving herring fishery, with 36 saltries operating. The fishery collapsed in 1928, and today the town is a small center for artists and fishermen. Halibut Cove has long been known for its picturesque harbor ringed by dense green forests; unfortunately, most of the trees were killed by a devastating spruce bark beetle infestation in the 1990s, so the land is in recovery mode now. The town consists of a long boardwalk that connects shorefront businesses and homes.

Sights

Halibut Cove's boardwalks head out in both directions from the boat dock. Straight ahead, stairs climb steeply to the studio of Diana Tillion (907/296-2207), known for her subtle octopus-ink watercolors. Head right on the boardwalk past Clem and Diana Tillion's classic Alaskan home (a resident for over 50 years, Clem is jokingly called "the king of Halibut Cove") to a sandy spit of land that leads to galleries exhibiting pottery and expensive opal jewelry. Head left on the boardwalk for a 20-minute walk to the Saltry Restaurant. Along the way, you pass a tiny visitor center that makes a good place to escape the rain, before continuing past a large boat-building shop to **Halibut Cove Experience Gallery** (907/296-2215), an excellent cooperative. The boardwalk ends near the Saltry; a working pottery studio is directly behind. A hiking path leads from the boardwalk to a hilltop viewpoint over Halibut Cove.

Accommodations

The Cove Country Cabins (907/296-2257 or 888/353-2683, www.halibutcovealaska.com) has three attractive timber-frame cabins, each with a kitchenette and running water. No toilets, but it does have a central shower and outhouses. Cabins range from a cute little unit ($95 d) to a small two-story house ($150 d) with a fine view. The owner picks up guests at the boat dock.

Halibut Cove Lodge (907/235-6891, www.halibutcovelodge.com) has four waterside cabins—each with room for four—at the entrance to Halibut Cove Lagoon. These go for $350 pp/night including three meals a day, and the owners will be happy to book sea kayaking, bear-viewing, fishing charters, and other activities. Kids are half-price. Open May–September.

Food

Halibut Cove does not have a grocery store, so bring your own food from Homer if you're spending time in the area. The town's famous **Saltry Restaurant** (907/296-2223) serves daily specials featuring pasta, chowders, fresh mussels, and locally caught fish. Everything is homemade, from the plates to the fresh breads, pies, and chocolate cheesecake. There's a waterfront deck for al fresco dining on a sunny afternoon, a clamshell-shaped aquarium filled with tidepool creatures, along with a blazing fire in the fire pit. The Saltry is open for lunch and dinner; reservations recommended. Dinner entrées run $14–25.

Transportation

The *Danny J* is a classic wooden boat that has been transporting passengers from Homer Spit to Halibut Cove for decades. It does the run twice daily between Memorial Day and Labor Day. The noon sailing costs $45 adults, $38 seniors, or $22 kids, and includes a tour of the Gull Island bird sanctuary, which Alfred Hitchcock should've known about; wear a hat and breathe through your mouth! After three hours onshore in Halibut Cove, the boat returns to Homer. Its second trip ($22) leaves Homer at 5 P.M., and is only for Halibut Cove residents or visitors with dinner or lodging reservations. For details, contact **Central Charters** (907/235-7847 or 800/478-7847, www.centralcharter.com).

SELDOVIA

Another sleepy fishing village (pop. 400), Seldovia (from the Russian for "herring") was once the bustling metropolis that Homer is now. The road, the earthquake, and fate exchanged their roles. On the same latitude as Oslo, Norway, Seldovia was first settled by Russians in the early 1800s and became an active fur-trading post. Through the years, Seldovia has had many ocean-oriented industries, from the short-lived herring boom to salmon, king crab, and tanner.

Seldovia is a convenient place for really getting away from it all. Catch a ride over from Homer on the state ferry once a week, or on the tour boats; the tour boats give you two hours to visit, just enough time to wander around town and maybe get to the Otterbahn Trailhead.

Sights and Recreation

Start out by strolling along Main Street. Interpretive signs describe Alaska's Russian history, commercial fishing, the earthquake, and more. The picturesque **Russian Orthodox Church** sits atop a small hill overlooking town like a proud parent. Walk along the last remaining section of original boardwalk—the rest was wiped out in the 1964 earthquake—just up from the small-boat harbor. The Seldovia Tribe's small **Museum and Visitor Center** (907/234-7898, www.seldovia.com) is across from the boat harbor.

One of the most fun things to do in Seldovia is to pedal out the road to beautiful Outside Beach and Jakalof Bay where you can savor the great views across Kachemak Bay; Main Street Market (907/234-7631) rents mountain bikes. The **Rocky River Road Trail** at the end of Jakalof Bay Road is a locals' favorite. The well-marked **Otterbahn Trail** leads 1.5 miles from the school grounds around the headland to Outside Beach.

homes built on pilings, along Seldovia Slough

For on-the-water fun, rent a kayak or take a guided tour from **Kayak 'Atak** (907/234-7425, www.alaska.net/~kayaks); three-hour trips are $80.

Seldovia's big party comes on the **4th of July** when the sleepy town comes alive with a parade, canoe jousting, log rolling, an egg toss, foot race, and food booths.

Accommodations

Seldovia has many B&Bs and a number of other lodging choices. The Seldovia Chamber of Commerce's website (www.xyz.net/~seldovia) has links to most of these. Kachemak Bay State Park is another nearby option.

Dancing Eagles B&B (907/234-7627 summer or 907/278-0288 winter, www.dancingeagles.com) has perhaps the finest location in Seldovia, with a big deck perched on the water at the entrance to Seldovia Slough. Rooms are $110 d, including a gourmet breakfast and private baths. A cabin ($175 d; $50 pp for extra guests) sleeps six and includes a kitchen and bath. Open Memorial Day to Labor Day.

Seldovia Seaport Cottages (907/234-7483, www.xyz.net/~chap) has four homey cottages

along Seldovia Slough, all with kitchens and baths, plus free bikes to tool around town. Three of these go for $80 d, and a larger cottage sleeps six for $110.

Seldovia Rowing Club B&B (907/234-7614, www.ptialaska.net/~rowing) is another right-on-the-water place where the suites ($110 d) feature a "nautical Victorian" decor, along with private baths and decks. A big breakfast is served each morning. Owner/artist Susan Mumma sells watercolors in her downstairs gallery.

Seldovia Bayview Suites (907/234-7631 or

800/478-7898, www.alaskaadventurelodge.com) has spacious three-bed suites for $109–139, and a four-room apartment with full kitchen and living room for $250.

Boardwalk Hotel (907/234-7816 or 800/238-7862, www.alaskaone.com/boardwalkhotel) is right on the boat harbor; the back patio is a great place to hang out. Small rooms with double beds are $89 d, but a better bet is the larger waterside rooms with two queen beds for $130 d. Just down the street is **Seldovia Harbor Inn** (907/234-1414, www.seldoviaharborinn.com), with three

THE KENAI PENINSULA

new waterside units, each with a kitchen and deck for $115–130 d.

Swan House B&B (907/234-8888 or 800/921-1900, www.alaska.net/~swan1) is a distinctive modern home with its own dock. One guest room ($139 d) and four suites ($169–199 d) are available, along with a private boathouse cottage ($259 d) popular with honeymooners. A big breakfast is included. Open May–September.

Bridgekeeper's Inn (907/234-7535) overlooks the bridge across Seldovia Slough, and has two nicely furnished guest rooms, each with queen beds and private baths. A full breakfast is served; $125–135 d.

Camping

Pitch a tent for $5 ($8 RVs) at **Wilderness Park** (907/234-7643) along Outside Beach. It's 1.5 miles out Jakalof Bay Road, and has running water and outhouses. Take showers in town at the launderette across from the boat harbor.

Food

The Buzz (907/234-7479) has light breakfasts pastries, soups, and espresso in the summer. **Tide Pool Cafe** (907/234-7502) is a great lunch spot, with sandwiches, salads, burgers, and more. Their deck overlooks the boat harbor. Get ice cream from **Sweet N Clean Ice Cream & Laundry** (907/234-7420), but be ready to pay $5 for a milkshake!

Mad Fish Restaurant (907/234-7676, www.madfishalaska.com) has the finest lunches and dinners in Seldovia, with creative sandwiches, homemade soups, big salads (try the Szechuan seafood noodle salad), and a dinner menu that focuses on pasta, seafood, and steaks; $19–23 dinner entrées. Recommended.

Get groceries and supplies from **Main Street Market** (907/234-7631).

Transportation

The **State Ferry** (907/235-8449 or 800/382-9229, www.ferryalaska.com) *Tustumena* sails over to Seldovia from Homer twice a week, taking 90 minutes and laying over for an hour or two before returning to Homer, $22 each way.

Two companies offer summertime trips be-tween the Spit and Seldovia. The *Dena'ina* departs at 11 A.M., stopping to watch the puffins and gulls at Gull Island and the sea otters near Sixty Foot Rock. They dock in Seldovia for three hours before heading back across Kachemak Bay. Tours are $45 adults, $40 seniors, or $25 kids. Make reservations at **Central Charters** (907/235-7847 or 800/478-7847, www.centralcharter.com). The **Rainbow Tours** (907/235-7272, www.rainbowtours.net) shuttle boat leaves Homer at 10 A.M. returning at 5 P.M. No stops along the way, but the round-trip fare is just $35 adults, $30 seniors, or $25 kids. They also offer all-day whale-watching from Seldovia for $75.

Both **Homer Air** (907/235-8591 or 800/478-8591, www.homerair.com) and **Smokey Bay Air** (907/235-1511 or 888/482-1511) fly the short 15-minute trip from Homer ($25 one-way), and also to the Native villages of Port Graham and Nanwalek on a daily basis. **Great Northern Airlines** (907/243-1968 or 800/243-1968, www.gnair.com) flies between Anchorage and Seldovia several times a week.

KACHEMAK BAY STATE PARK

One of the largest coastal parks in the nation, Kachemak Bay State Park reaches for 200 miles along the southwestern edge of the Kenai Peninsula. Within the park's 400,000 acres are glaciers, high mountains, lakes, islands, beaches, and a scenic rocky shoreline. Highlighted by constantly changing weather patterns, the park's outstanding scenery is a backdrop for high quality recreation. Hiking and camping along the shoreline and in the surrounding forests and mountains are excellent. Above timberline, skiers and hikers will find glaciers and snow fields stretching for miles.

Almost three-quarters of the land here is wilderness; it's officially called Kachemak Bay Wilderness State Park. Land mammals include moose, black bear, mountain goats, coyotes and wolves. Kachemak Bay supports a rich diversity of marine life and is famous for its halibut and salmon fishing, plus the chance to view sea otters, seals, porpoise, and whales. Five very popular public-use cabins are available ($50–65), along with over 80 miles of hiking trails. Unfortunately, a major spruce bark beetle outbreak in the 1990s left massive stretches of dead forest within Kachemak Bay State Park (and in many other parts of the Kenai Peninsula).

The Kachemak Bay State Park office (907/235-7024, www.alaskastateparks.org) is four miles northwest of Homer along the Sterling Highway. **Alaskan Yurt Rentals** (907/235-0132, www.nomadshelter.com) has cozy yurts ($65) located at six trailheads around the park, including China Poot Bay and Tutka Bay. Each includes five bunks and a wood stove.

Grewingk Glacier

For an outstanding day (or multinight) hike, have the water taxi drop you at the Glacier Spit Trailhead, where an easy and very scenic two-mile hike leads to a lake in front of picture-perfect **Grewingk Glacier.** You can camp nearby, and return via the one-mile **Saddle Trail** which takes you over a small ridge to Halibut Cove, where you can get a ride back to Homer. Water taxis cost $45 per person round-trip. A multitude of side trips are available along this route, including ones that take you high into the alpine over the glacier, and a delightful beach walk. Contact the park for many other hiking options.

Guided sea kayak tours to Grewingk are available through **Three Moose Meadow Guide Service** (907/235-0755 or 888/777-0930, www.threemoose.com). These cost $145, including a water taxi from Homer, a hike to the lake, and kayaking. Fly-in trips are also offered.

Access

In addition to the daily summertime boat tours of Kachemak Bay, several Homer companies provide water taxi service and sea kayaker drop-offs within park waters, for $45 round-trip: **Smoke Wagon Water Taxi** (907/399-3455, www.homerwatertaxi.com), **Mako's Water Taxi** (907/235-9055, www.makoswatertaxi.com), **Bay Excursions** (907/235-7525, www.bayexcursions.com), **Jakolof Ferry Service** (907/235-6384, www.jakolofferryservice.com), **Triton Water Taxi** (907/235-7630, www.xyz.net/~fogg), and **Tutka Bay Taxi** (907/235-7166 or 907/399-1723, www.tutkabaytaxi.com).

Remote Cabins and Lodges

Porter's Alaskan Adventures (907/776-3626 or 907/399-7256, www.portersak.com) has three modern cabins on the shore of Hesketh Island near the mouth of Tutka Bay, seven miles from Homer. All cabins contain full kitchens, decks, and waterfront views, but you'll need to bring sleeping bags. There's a sauna and bathhouse on the beach, and an outhouse in the back. Rates are $125 for up to four people, plus $45 per person for the water taxi from Homer. Sea kayak rentals are available.

Sadie Cove Wilderness Lodge (907/235-2350 or 888/283-7234, www.sadiecove.com) is a wilderness retreat in the heart of Kachemak Bay State Park. Guests stay in very comfortable but rustic cabins built by Keith and Randi Iverson, who have lived here since the 1970s. Amenities include uniquely crafted cabins, a sauna and creekside bathhouse, communal lounge, and professional chef. Lodging and meals cost $250 pp/day, plus $65 for a boat ride from Homer.

Tutka Bay Wilderness Lodge (907/235-3905 or 800/606-3909, www.tutkabaylodge.com) occupies the south shore of Kachemak Bay between Halibut Cove and Seldovia, nine water miles from the Spit. The lodge caters to nature lovers, photographers, bird-watchers, and anglers with an appreciation for the finer things in life, and a willingness to pay dearly. Two-night minimum stays will set you back $1,160 for two people, but this does include round-trip transportation from Homer and delicious family-style meals. Activities include boat tours, guided walks, beachcombing, clam digging, and wildlife viewing (all included), plus mountain biking, sea kayaking, sportfishing, and flightseeing (extra fee). Accommodations are luxurious; no roughing-it here.

Otter Cove Resort (907/235-7770 or 800/426-6212, www.ottercoveresort.com) sits along Eldred Passage, five miles by boat from the end of Homer Spit. Two duplex cabins provide rustic accommodations with bunk beds, electricity, and showers for a reasonable $80 s or d, but you'll need to bring sleeping bags (or rent linen). Kayak rentals and tours are available and hiking trails lead up to the alpine. This is also a popular destination for day-guests who come to dine in the

Rookery Restaurant or to enjoy a drink on the waterside deck. The restaurant specializes in seafood, and it is open for lunch and dinner ($18–24 entrées); overnight guests can use the cook shack to prepare their own breakfasts. Otter Cove is owned by Homer Ocean Charters, which has a variety of options for visitors who come for the day. Especially popular is a four-hour trip that include a wildlife boat tour from the Homer Spit and lunch at the restaurant for $55. Otter Cove is open late May to mid-September.

Sailwood Adventures (907/235-6126, www.sailwood.com) is an attractive and fully furnished home on peaceful Sadie Cove. Nightly rentals are $120 d, plus $55 pp roundtrip for the water taxi from Homer. The friendly and knowledgeable owners, Marcee Gray and Willie Condon, also offer sea kayak trips or rentals, along with weeklong wilderness camping trips for teens and women.

Peterson Bay Lodge (907/235-7156 or 866/899-7156, www.petersonbaylodge.com) occupies the head of this remote bay where the owners raise the famous Kachemak Bay oysters and rent out four tent cabins with a sauna. Guests get transportation from Homer, kayaking, and breakfast for $145 per person.

Kachemak Bay Wilderness Lodge (907/235-8910, www.alaskaildernesslodge.com) lies within China Poot Bay in the heart of the state park. Guests stay in cozy artistic cabins, each with a cedar bath, picture window, and homemade quilts, and are served gourmet organic meals. All-inclusive rates are $2,800 pp for five days.

The Wrangells and Prince William Sound

This sprawling region includes several mountain ranges and gorgeous Prince William Sound. The Wrangell Mountains and St. Elias Mountains form the backbone of massive Wrangell–St. Elias National Park and Preserve, home to the second highest peak in the United States (18,008-foot Mt. St. Elias), a glacier larger than Rhode Island, towering volcanoes, and country that seems to define the word spectacular. The park is located on the eastern margin of Alaska and is bordered by Canada's Kluane National Park and Tatshenshini-Alsek Park, and Southeast Alaska's Glacier Bay National Park. Together they include more than 24 million acres—the largest protected area on planet earth. The equally impressive Copper River drains much of the Wrangells, reaching the Gulf of Alaska east of Cordova. Given the grandeur of this country, the settlements seem minor in this part of Alaska; largest are Glennallen, Copper Center, and Chitina. Two primary roads cut through this country: the east–west Glenn Highway and the north–south Richardson Highway.

© DON PITCHER

Wrangell–St. Elias National Park and Preserve

Prince William Sound arcs around the Gulf of Alaska, encompassing a multitude of densely forested islands, dissected bays, and rugged coastlines, with the Chugach Mountains forming a glacier-topped northern border. Virtually all of this wild county lies within Chugach National Forest, the nation's second largest national forest. Within the Sound are three towns: Whittier on the west is connected by tunnel and road to Anchorage, Valdez on the north serves as the terminus of the Alyeska Pipeline, and the fishing town of Cordova on the east provides a gateway to the Copper River.

Copper River Valley

GLENN HIGHWAY

Named for Captain Edwin Glenn, an early Army explorer of the area, the **Glenn Highway** (Route 1) stretches 328 miles from downtown Anchorage to Tok, where it joins the Alaska Highway. Most of the Glenn was built during the corridor-construction craze of 1942, first from Tok to Gulkana, where it joins the Richardson Highway, then from Glennallen, where it leaves the Richardson, and finally to Palmer. Palmer was already connected to Anchorage by rail; the final 42 miles of road were completed a few years later.

Twenty miles east of Palmer is the tiny settlement of **Sutton** (pop. 470). Of interest here is the nonprofit **Alpine Historical Park** (907/745-7000), with its collection of historical buildings, coal mining relics, and Athabascan Indian artifacts, open daily 9 A.M.–7 P.M. from Memorial Day to Labor Day.

At Mile 72, **Castle Mountain B&B** (907/745-7818, www.castlemountainb-b.com) is a large and modern log home with a big deck and two guest rooms: $65 s or $85 d with a big breakfast. Four miles up the road is **King Mountain State Recreation Area,** a large, beautiful campground with water, outhouses, and choice spots right on the Matanuska River (though the interior loop might be less windy) for $10. The site faces King Mountain across the river—a perfect triangular peak. **King Mountain Lodge** (907/745-4280) is nearby, and is the oldest lodge on the Glenn Highway. The café has burgers, pizzas, and espresso. You could easily spend an idyllic day and night simply enjoying the King Mountain area.

Based in Chickaloon at Mile 77, **Nova Riverrunners** (907/745-5753 or 800/746-5753, www.novalaska.com) guides daily raft trips. Two options are a white-water ride along the Matanuska River past dramatic Lion Head (Class IV) for $80, or an easy float trip along lower reaches of the river for $70 ($36 kids).

A few miles up is **Long Lake State Recreation Area,** Mile 85, where you can stretch your legs. A handful of free campsites are available; no water.

Matanuska Glacier

Located at Mile 102 of the Glenn Highway, Matanuska Glacier is a don't-miss highlight. Today, this glacier is 27 miles long and four miles wide; 18,000 years ago it occupied Palmer, but it hasn't done much in the last 400 years. Much of the land in front of the glacier is owned by Jack Kimball, who spent decades developing a road and bridges to a bluff overlooking the ice. Access to **Glacier Park** (907/745-2534 or 888/253-4480, www.matanuskaglacier.com) costs $8 adults, $6 seniors, $4 ages 6–12, and free for younger kids. You can hike on the easier sections with tennis shoes, but will need a guide for the steeper parts of the glacier. **MICA Guides** (800/956-6522, www.micaguides.com) offers glacier hiking and ice climbing adventures. Glacier Park is open April–October, and also has a snack bar and close-to-the glacier campsites for $6 (plus your admission); no water.

Out along the highway is **Matanuska Glacier State Recreation Site** ($10), on a hillside overlooking the ice giant. Nearby is **Long Rifle Lodge** (907/745-5151 or 800/770-5151), with homemade meals, a lounge, and motel rooms ($75 d). However, the real reason to stop here is the view from the dining room of the nearby glacier and

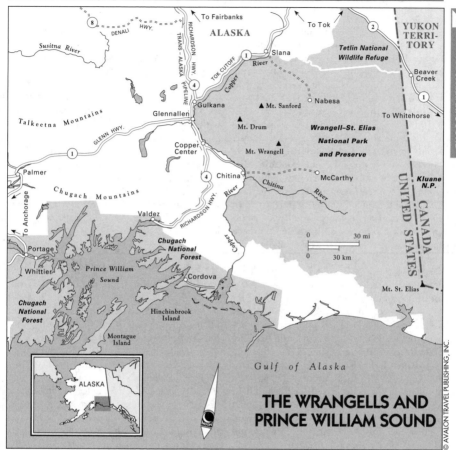

THE WRANGELLS AND
PRINCE WILLIAM SOUND

© AVALON TRAVEL PUBLISHING, INC.

valleys—it's hard to keep your eyes on your plate with this mountain panorama in front of you.

Over Eureka Summit

It's another 85 miles eastward to Glennallen and the intersection of the Glenn and Richardson Highways. If you have a chance to make this drive in September, by all means, do it. The acres of aspen trees along this route turn a brilliant gold, and the contrasting dark green spruce, combined with the backdrop of glaciers and snowcapped peaks, make for some extraordinary photo ops. You'll be tempted to pull off at every twist in the road to burn film and take in the surroundings.

At Mile 98, pull out your binoculars and glass slopes to the north for scattered bunches of white dots—Dall sheep like to congregate here, apparently for a mineral lick on the hillside.

Sheep Mountain Lodge (907/745-5121 or 877/645-5121, www.sheepmountain.com) at Mile 113 is a rustic summer and winter destination. Its greenhouses and flower gardens add to the gorgeous mountain-backed setting in the summer, and the lodge serves home-cooked meals year-round. Ten cabins all have private baths and wonderful views; $125 d. Hostel-style dorm rooms with a shared bath are a great bargain: $60 for four people. The glassed-in hot tub is a great place to relax after a winter day of skiing on its 10 miles of groomed trails. Highly recommended.

Two miles away is **Majestic Valley Wilderness Lodge** (907/746-2930, www.majesticvalley-lodge.com), another place with a country setting and grand vistas. Guests stay in motel rooms ($80 s or $90 d), or cabins ($105 s or $115 d).

Slide Mountain Cabins (at Mile 118, 907/822-5864, www.slidemountaincabins.com) has modern cabins that share a shower house; $65 d, plus $10 for each additional guest.

When you get past **Eureka Summit** (Mile 130), you're in caribou country, so scan the open ground everywhere for members of the Nelchina herd. From Eureka to Glennallen, and then north on the Richardson Highway toward Tok, it's possible to spot caribou almost anywhere. Slow down and keep your eyes open to avoid colliding with one. Lodging, RV spots, and meals are available near the summit at **Eureka Lodge** (907/822-3808, www.eurekalodge.com); $70 s or $80 d for motel rooms with private baths, $70 d for bring-your-sleeping-bag cabins with a shower house. In the winter, this is a popular snowmobiling destination. Pitch a tent at **Little Nelchina State Recreation Site** at Mile 138; no charge.

Tolsona Lake Resort (907/822-3433 or 800/245-3342, www.akfish.com) is 17 miles west of Glennallen at Mile 170 of the Glen Highway, with a motel, cabins, RV hookups, and a restaurant and bar. Three miles up the road toward Glennallen is **Tolsona Wilderness Campground** (907/822-3865, www.tolsona.com), with additional tent sites.

Lake Louise

At Mile 160 of the Glenn Highway (27 miles west of Glennallen), the Lake Louise Rd. turns north, continuing 19 miles to this popular summer fishing and winter snowmobiling destination.

The **Lake Louise State Recreation Area** has campsites ($5–10) and a swimming area for those who can brave the water. Stay at **Lake Louise Lodge** (907/822-3311 or 877/878-3311, www.lakelouiselodge.com), where the log lodge overlooks the lake. Modern rooms cost $79–119 d, including private baths, a hot tub and sauna, plus use of canoes and paddleboats. Simple cab-

ins are $59 d ($15 for additional guests), with shared bath. A restaurant is here, and motorboat rentals are also available. Open year-round.

The Point Lodge at Lake Louise (907/822-5566 or 800/808-2018, www.alaskapoint-lodge.com) has comfortable rooms with panoramic views from a wraparound deck. Rates are $85 s or $95 d in the lodge, including private baths and a sauna. Five cabins are $75 d; no plumbing, so guests bathe at the lodge. Family style meals are available for guests. The lodge is open by reservation only in the winter.

Other Lake Louise area accommodations include **Wolverine Lodge** (907/822-3988, www.wolverinelodgeak.com) and **Evergreen Lodge** (907/822-3250, www.alaskaevergreen-lodge.com).

GLENNALLEN AND VICINITY

At Mile 187 of the Glenn, just before the junction with the Richardson Highway, is this small service town, named for both Edwin Glenn and Henry Allen, leader of the first expedition up the Copper River. Strung along both sides of the road, Glennallen (pop. 900) is the gateway to the big Copper River Valley country and Wrangell–St. Elias National Park.

Glennallen is an odd amalgamation of businesses, including the standard gas stations, motels, and food stops, along with seven churches and three liquor stores. This is the heart of right-wing Christian Alaska, as you will quickly discover with a spin of the radio dial; KCAM 790 AM dominates the air waves with stirring messages of conversion along with its "Caribou Clatters" for those without phone service. The station beams out from the small campus of the Alaska Bible College in Glennallen (www.akbible.edu). (Fortunately, the area now also has a repeater for the public radio station out of Valdez.)

The best thing about Glennallen is its setting. As you approach Glennallen from the west—if the weather's clear—there's a stunning view of the Wrangell Mountains: Mt. Drum is the beautiful snowcapped peak right in the middle at 12,010 feet elevation, Mt. Sanford is just to the north (left) of it at 16,237 feet, and Mt. Wrangell is to the south at 14,163 feet. It's an incredible backdrop for a very ordinary junction town.

The **Greater Copper River Valley Visitor Center** (907/822-5555, www.traveltoalaska.com) occupies the highway junction at the Hub gas station, and is open daily 8 A.M.–7 P.M. Memorial Day to Labor Day, plus reduced hours in mid-May and early September. You'll find exhibits on local attractions and details about every place between Tok and Cordova. The Wells Fargo Bank has an ATM for cash.

Accommodations

Caribou Hotel (907/822-3302 or 800/478-3302, www.caribouhotel.com) is the largest place in town, and has budget rooms in the old pipeline Atco unit for $59 s or $69 d. The main building is considerably nicer at $139 d, and suites are $195 d. The owners also operate **Cranberry Hill B&B,** with attractive guest rooms $125–139 d), and cabins ($65–139 d) with a breakfast at the hotel restaurant.

Located 11 miles north of Glennallen, **Fiddler's Green on Bear Creek** (907/822-5852 or 888/822-1178, www.bearcreekalaska.com) has a spectacular view of the Wrangells. Rooms in the house are $70–80 d, and the cabin goes for $100. A full breakfast is included.

Historic **Gakona Lodge** (907/822-3482) sits along the Gakona and Copper rivers, 18 miles north of Glennallen. Built in the 1920s, the picturesque log building includes a dinner-only restaurant (steaks, burgers, and chicken), bar, and gift shop with locally made Native crafts. Old-fashioned rooms are sometimes available for $75 s or $90 d with shared baths. Open mid-May through September.

Other local lodging options include **Carol's B&B** (907/822-3594, www.alaska.net/~neeley), **Little Cabin in the Woods** (907/822-4007), **Fireweed Hill B&B** (907/822-3627, www.alaska.net/~dmbowler), and **Sourdough Lodge** (907/822-7122).

Camping

The state's **Dry Creek Campground** ($12) is five miles north of the Glenn-Richardson junction and has pit toilets and too-friendly mosqui-

toes. Local RV parks include **Cabins on the Glenn** (907/822-5833 or 877/822-5833), **Moose Horn RV Park** (907/822-3953), and **Northern Nights Campground & RV Park** (907/822-3199). Northern Nights is easily the nicest of these. **Gakona RV Park** (907/822-3550, www.alaskarvpark.netfirms.com) is four miles north from the junction on the Tok Cutoff.

Food

New Caribou Restaurant (907/822-3302 or 800/462-3221) at the Caribou Hotel is open 24 hours a day in the summer, with all the seafood, steaks, and all the standard American basics. Get groceries or deli items from the **Park's Place** market (907/822-3334).

Brown Bear Rhodehouse (907/822-3663), three miles west of the junction at Mile 184 of the Glenn Highway, is famous for its hunting lodge atmosphere where dead critters stare from the walls. The filet mignon is great, and they also serve sandwiches, seafood, and roasted chicken. Even if you aren't hungry, stop by to take a gander at the photos or to talk with the locals about those damn Outside environmeddlers (unless you are one).

Transportation

In the summer, **Alaska Direct Bus Line** (907/277-6652 or 800/770-6652, www.home.gci .net/~akdirectbus) has service several times a week from Glennallen to Whitehorse, Anchorage, and Fairbanks.

Alaska Trails (907/479-3065 or 888/600-6001, www.alaskashuttle.com) has a reservation-only summertime van service connecting Glennallen with Valdez and Fairbanks.

Glennallen's airport is just north of town, but for some reason it's officially called the Gakona Airport. **Ellis Air Taxi** (907/822-3368 or 800/478-3368, www.ellisair.com) will fly you from Glennallen to McCarthy for $80, or from Anchorage to McCarthy for $235. Other air taxis include **Alaskan AirVentures** (907/822-3905), **Copper Valley Air Service** (907/822-4200, www.coppervalleyair.com), and **Lee's Air Taxi** (907/822-3343). Rent mountain bikes from **Tez Lende Treks and Adventures** (907/822-4141).

Wrangell–St. Elias National Park and Preserve

Though somewhat less accessible than Denali, this park is an excellent alternative to the crowds, clouds, wows, and crying-out-louds. The mountains (Chugach, Wrangells, and St. Elias) are incredible, and Mt. Wrangell—highest volcano in Alaska at 14,163 feet—sometimes puffs away on earth's crustal cigar. In fact, of the 16 tallest mountains in North America, nine are in this park! The icefields are world class, and their glacial tentacles rival any in the state. The Copper River can provide weeks-long raft or canoe rides, with all the fish you can stand. The wildlife is abundant, and this park even has beaches on the Gulf of Alaska. Two roads plunge deep into the park's wildlands, and bus and plane service are available.

This is the largest national park in the country (larger than southern New England), with over 12 million acres; along with Kluane National Park across the Canadian border, the whole area was the first designated U.N. World Heritage Site. Finally, you don't need backcountry permits to traipse around or camp on this federal land—just pick a direction and backpack until you crack.

INFORMATION AND ACCESS

The large **Wrangell–St. Elias National Park and Preserve Visitor Center** (907/822-7261, www.nps.gov/wrst) is at Mile 107 on the Richardson, seven miles south of Glennallen. Hours are daily 8 A.M.–6 P.M. in the summer, and Monday–Friday 8 A.M.–4:30 P.M. the rest of the year. Rangers can help with trip planning, sell you books and topographic maps, or show an acclaimed film about the park. Seasonal ranger stations are in Kennicott, Chitina, and Yakutat.

Air taxis and charter services can drop you off anywhere inside the park, with most flights departing from Glennallen/Gulkana, Cordova, Chitina, or McCarthy.

Nabesna Road

Ground access to the park is via the Edgerton Highway and McCarthy Road in the center, and the Nabesna Road on the north side. The 42-mile Nabesna Road turns off at Mile 65 of the Tok Cutoff, and leads to the abandoned gold mining town of Nabesna. The Park Service maintains the **Nabesna Visitor Center** (907/822-5238), just up Nabesna Road from the junction, open daily 8 A.M.–6 P.M. in the summer and weekdays 8 A.M.–4:30 P.M. the rest of the year.

Nabesna area lodging and RV options include **Hart D Ranch** (907/822-3973), **Nabesna House B&B** (907/822-4284, www.nabesna-house.com), and **Huck Hobbit's Homestead** (907/822-3196).

RIVER RUNNING

Cordova-based **Alaska River Rafters** (907/424-7238 or 800/776-1864, www.alaskarafters.com) leads a variety of rafting trips inside the park, including a five-day float ($1,350) on the powerful Copper River, and 10-day trips ($2,150) begin in McCarthy and continue all the way to the Million Dollar Bridge near Cordova. All trips start with a scenic floatplane flight into the park.

Operating from McCarthy, in the heart of the park, **Copper Oar** (907/554-4453 or 800/523-4453, www.copperoar.com) offers a paddle-and-peddle daytrip that includes a float down the Kennicott River followed by a mountain bike ride back to McCarthy for $70. Longer float trips are also available.

River Wrangellers (907/822-3967 or 888/822-3967, www.alaskariverwrangellers.com) is a Gakona-based company with trips down major rivers in the area, including the Kennicott River from McCarthy (Class III and IV; $750 for three days), the great-for-fishing Gulkana River (starting at just $75 for a three-hour run), the raging Tana River (Class IV+; $1,275 for five days), the remote Tazlina River (Class III; $750 for three days), and the accessible Tonsina River (Class III and IV; $100 day trip). They also rent out rafts and other river gear, and provide shuttles for do-it-yourselfers.

© DON PITCHER

Kennicott Glacier in Wrangell–St. Elias National Park and Preserve

Based in Copper Center, **Osprey Expeditions** (907/822-5422, www.ospreyexpeditions.com) offers river trips of varying lengths, from a six-day float on the Tana River ($1,860) to a leisurely 15-day raft trip from McCarthy to the Million Dollar Bridge near Cordova ($3,900).

St. Elias Guides (907/345-9048 or 888/933-5427, www.steliasguides.com) offers raft trips in the Wrangells, including a fly-in trip on the Nizina River ($245 for one day).

McCARTHY AND KENNICOTT

The McCarthy-Kennicott area is a mostly private island surrounded by the vast Wrangell–St. Elias National Park. This was once an incredibly important copper mining area, but today it contains Alaska's most famous almost-ghost town. Access to the area is via the McCarthy Road, which leads from the town of Chitina to the Kennicott River. Located within Wrangell–St. Elias National Park and Preserve, the historic Kennecott Mine contains picturesque old buildings right alongside Kennicott Glacier, with the pinnacles of snowcapped mountains ringing the horizon.

McCarthy Road

This could be the longest 60-mile road in the Alaska—plan on three hours from Chitina, several more if it's clear and you stop for the views of the Wrangells. The road is in fairly good shape, but gets rutted by late summer, and can be very dusty if it hasn't rained recently. There are tire repair and towing services in Chitina and McCarthy, along with various lodging options as you approach McCarthy. You may be tempted to speed on the road at times, but try to keep around 30 mph since you never know what's around the next bend. It's also a good idea to have a full-size spare tire, though many folks drive out without one. Note that many car rental companies will not allow their vehicles on the McCarthy Road; Affordable Car Rentals in Anchorage is one exception.

At Mile 16, get ready for an adrenaline-pumping drive across the **Kuskulana River** on a narrow three-span bridge built in 1910 by the railroad and improved in 1988 (when guardrails were added). The bridge is nearly 600 feet long and sits almost 400 feet above the water—perfect, in other words, for bungee jumping, which does take place here. Another attraction is the aban-

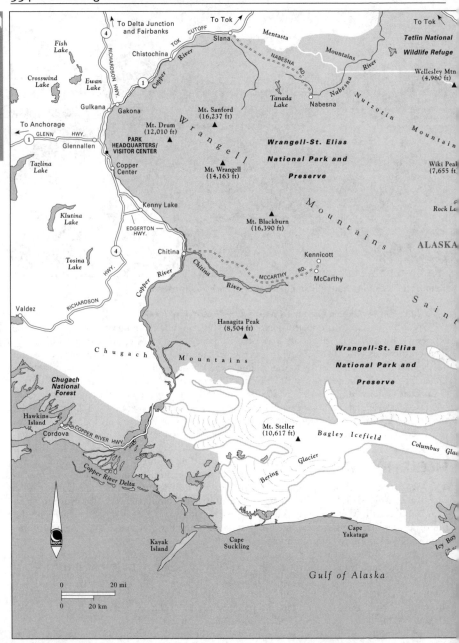

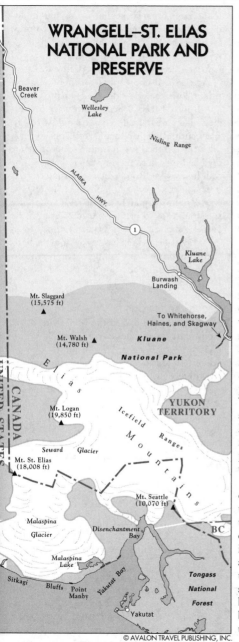

WRANGELL–ST. ELIAS NATIONAL PARK AND PRESERVE

Beaver Creek

Wellesley Lake

Nisling Range

ALASKA HWY.

1

Kluane Lake

Burwash Landing

Mt. Slaggard (15,575 ft) ▲

To Whitehorse, Haines, and Skagway

Mt. Walsh ▲ (14,780 ft)

Kluane

National Park

E l i a s

Mt. Logan (19,850 ft) ▲

YUKON TERRITORY

Icefield Ranges

M o u n t a i n s

Seward Glacier

Mt. St. Elias (18,008 ft) ▲

CANADA

UNITED STATES

Mt. Seattle (10,070 ft) ▲

Malaspina Glacier

Disenchantment Bay

BC

Malaspina Lake

Sitkagi Bluffs Point Manby

Yakutat Bay

Tongass National Forest

Yakutat

doned railroad trestle across the Gilahina River at Mile 28. Just before the end of the road is a spectacular overlook of the town of McCarthy, the surrounding mountains, and the Kennicott and Root glaciers.

The road ends on the west side of the Kennicott River, and parking is available ($5–10/day) on nearby private land. Footbridges cross the river and a smaller tributary. Once across, walk up the road; the right fork takes you a mile to McCarthy, the left fork nearly five miles to Kennicott. Shuttle buses ($5 each way) transport visitors from McCarthy to Kennicott, and mountain bikes are available to rent nearby. Backcountry Connection (see Transportation and Tours below) provides van service to McCarthy from Glennallen or Chitina.

History

Prospectors discovered rich copper deposits at Kennecott Mine in 1900, and at its peak the mine employed some 600 workers. (Note: Because of a typographic error when the mine was established, the mine's name is spelled Kennecott, while the town, glacier, river, and vicinity are generally spelled Kennicott.) The mines, in their nearly 30 years of operation, extracted $220 million in rich ore, nearly 70 percent copper, with a little silver and gold on the side. The Alaska Syndicate—owned by J.P. Morgan and Daniel Guggenheim—held the controlling interest. They also owned the CR&NW railroad, which freighted the ore to tidewater, plus the Alaska Steamship Co., which shipped the ore to Tacoma, Washington.

The mines shut down in 1938 when world copper prices dropped and the cost of production became prohibitive. After the mine's closure, the buildings were abandoned and gradually deteriorated. Today, these dark red buildings are in varying states of disrepair. They—and 3,000 acres of surrounding land—were purchased by the Park Service in 1998, and the agency is spending millions of dollars to stabilize and rebuild the buildings. You can walk through the beautifully restored structures, or take a guided tour through ones still being worked on.

McCarthy

The quaint little settlement of McCarthy (pop. 25) was a boomtown from the early 1900s to 1939, serving the copper workers at Kennecott mines and the railroad workers on the Copper River and Northwestern. At its peak, the town was full of hotels, restaurants, bars, and pool halls, along with the obligatory red light district. Today it's a busy base for outdoor enthusiasts to explore nearby mine buildings and spectacular mountain country. The little **McCarthy-Kennicott Museum** is open daily in the summertime; find it just as you arrive in McCarthy from the footbridge. Inside are interesting photos, maps, and artifacts. A model of the Bonanza mine occupies the adjacent boxcar.

Kennicott Area

The semi–ghost town of Kennicott and the mines of Kennecott are five miles from McCarthy on a dirt road. It's a pleasant (but all uphill) mountain bike ride, or pay $5 each way to **Copper Point Shuttle Bus Service** (907/554-4411) or **Wrangell Mountain Air** (907/554-4411 or 800/478-1160, www.wrangellmountainair.com). Their vans run back and forth daily in the summer.

The Park Service's **Kennicott Visitor Center** (907/554-4417) is open daily 8 A.M.–6 P.M. from Memorial Day to Labor Day. Rangers offer daily nature and history hikes, and a Sunday night speaker series brings glaciologists and other scientists. Most historic Kennicott Mine buildings are open only for guided tours, but you can visit the restored recreation hall. Visitors are welcome to explore the building exteriors, but watch for nails, glass, and metal scraps underfoot, and don't try to walk on decks or stairs alongside the buildings since the boards may be unsafe. **St. Elias Guides** (907/345-9048 or 888/933-5427, www.steliasguides.com) leads two-hour tours ($25 pp) of the historic mine buildings, along with a variety of glacier and alpine hikes and fly-in adventures. A half-day trip on the Root Glacier is $50.

Kennicott Wilderness Guides (907/554-4444 or 800/664-4537, www.kennicottguides.com) leads a variety of hikes in the Kennicott area, including mine tours ($35 for three hours), glacier treks ($50 for four hours), ice climbing ($100/day), fly-in backcountry trips, plus multiday mountaineering and glacier skills courses. **Copper Oar** (907/554-4453 or 800/523-4453, www.copperoar.com) also offers guided hikes and natural history tours in the McCarthy area.

An easy and popular hike or mountain bike ride follows the east side of Kennicott Glacier and Root Glacier. When the weather cooperates, hikers are treated to gorgeous views of Mt. Blackburn, Regal Mountain, and Donaho Peak. Take the old road north from Kennecott Mine for a half-mile, turning left when it diverges. The trail follows the Root Glacier, crossing bridges over Bonanza Creek and Jumbo Creek along the way. At approximately a mile and a quarter a side trail leads to primitive campsites near the glacier. An outhouse is nearby, and storage lockers are available to keep food away from the bears that sometimes roam through. The Kennicott Visitor Center has additional details on this and other local hikes.

Accommodations

Located near the end of the McCarthy Road, **Kennicott River Lodge & Hostel** (907/554-4441, www.kennicottriverlodge.com) has a variety of pleasant lodging choices in the summer, all with access to a full kitchen, common area (satellite TV and Internet access), shower house, and large sauna. Budget options include a tent cabin for $20 and hostel bunks for $28 pp; bring a sleeping bag. Private cabins cost $100 d, lodge rooms are $90 d, and the family suite is $150 d.

Wrangell St. Elias News B&B (907/554-4454, www.mccarthy-kennicott.com/WSENBB) is two miles from McCarthy. Two cozy cabins share a bathhouse; $75–85 s or d, including breakfast.

In McCarthy, stay at the historic—built in 1916—**McCarthy Lodge** (907/554-4402, www.mccarthylodge.com), the true heart and soul of the area. They offer two divergent lodging choices. **Lancaster's Backpacking Hotel** has simple rooms with twin beds, shared baths, and a common area for $40 s or $60 d. Considerably more upscale is **Ma Johnson's Hotel,** where the six bedrooms share three baths. All rooms are furnished in period antiques, and the rooms cost $99 s or $149 d, including a full breakfast. Recommended and open year-round.

The modern **Swift Creek Cabins** (907/554-1234, www.swiftcreekalaska.com) are three miles before the end of the McCarthy Road. No running water, but front porches face the Chitina River Valley and the Chugach Mountains. Rates are $100 d, plus $20 each for additional guests.

Kennicott Glacier Lodge (907/554-4477 or 800/582-5128, www.kennicottlodge.com) is a sprawling and spotlessly clean modern lodge five miles from McCarthy. The setting is graceful, with a long covered porch facing Root Glacier and the colorful mine buildings. Vacation package rates for rooms-which include three meals, transportation to and from McCarthy, and a tour of the ghost town-are $265 d per day, $75 more for each additional person, half-price for children. All rooms have shared baths. The à la carte rate (rooms, transportation, and a tour only) is $179 s or $209 d. Be sure to request a room facing the glacier. Open mid-May to mid-September.

Moose in the Spruce B&B (907/554-4420) has an inexpensive cabins three miles from McCarthy; $40 s or $50 d with a stocked kitchen.

The Park Service maintains 11 public-use cabins within Wrangell–St. Elias, with most accessible only by air. These rent for $25 per night; get details at www.nps.gov/wrst.

Camping

There are no Park Service campsites in McCarthy or Kennicott, but hike-in campsites are located at Root Glacier out of Kennicott.

The privately owned **Glacier View Campground** (907/554-4490) has tent and RV spaces for $12 a half-mile from the end of the McCarthy Road. **West McCarthy Wayside Park** (907/746-0606) occupies the end of the road next to the McCarthy bridge, and has camping for $15. Both are open late May to mid-September, and showers are available for a fee if you're camping elsewhere. Kennicott River Lodge & Hostel, provides showers and a sauna for $10.

Food

Food options are limited in the Kennicott and McCarthy area, and anyone on a budget should

bring groceries from Chitina. The restaurant at **Kennicott Glacier Lodge** (907/554-4477 or 800/582-5128, www.kennicottlodge.com) serves excellent "wilderness gourmet" meals three times a day, including lunch specials and filling family-style dinners for $25–30. It is open to both lodge guests and the general public.

McCarthy Lodge (907/554-4402) serves an all-you-can-eat buffet breakfast ($10) and a three-course dinner menu that often includes famous Copper River red salmon. Their bar, New Golden Saloon, features occasional bands in the summer.

The seasonal **Glacier View Campground** (907/554-4490) near the end of the McCarthy Road, has a tasty barbecue menu for lunch and dinner, plus half-pound Glacier Burgers.

For inexpensive meals in downtown McCarthy, **The Potato** (907/554-4432) is open for breakfast and lunch, with potato and egg burritos, burgers, fresh-cut fries, and the only espresso in the area.

Tailor-Made Pizza (907/554-1155), in McCarthy, has a big deck out front for al fresco dining, and a tasty menu of pizzas, sandwiches, pastas, baked goods, and ice cream, plus beer on tap.

Information and Services

The Park Service maintains a small **visitor kiosk** a half-mile from the McCarthy bridge that is open daily 8 A.M.–6 P.M. Memorial Day to Labor Day, plus a seasonal visitor center in Kennicott.

Regional visitors centers have a useful free visitor's guide to the area, or find the same information online (www.mccarthy-kennicott.com/vg). Also check out the **Wrangell Mountains Center** (www.wrangells.org), a McCarthy-based organization dedicated to environmental education and research.

McCarthy Lodge has a computer with Internet access for a fee. Pay phones are located at the bridge and next to the McCarthy Lodge. Cell phones generally work in the McCarthy area, though it depends upon your service provider.

For artwork, visit **Mountain Arts** at McCarthy Lodge or **Fireweed Mountain Arts & Crafts** (907/554-4420), three miles from the end of McCarthy Road.

PRINCE WILLIAM SOUND

Transportation

It's a rough ride to McCarthy, but you can save wear and tear on your car with a van ride from **Backcountry Connection** (907/822-5292 or 866/582-5292, www.alaska-backcountry-tours.com). The round-trip cost is $115 from Glennallen or $100 from Chitina.

Wrangell Mountain Air (907/554-4411 or 800/478-1160, www.wrangellmountainair.com) has scheduled service connecting Chitina with McCarthy, plus a variety of flightseeing trips from McCarthy, starting with a $60 half-hour glacier tour. **Ellis Air Taxi** (907/822-3368 or 800/478-3368, www.ellisair.com) will fly you from Glennallen to McCarthy for $80 one-way, or from Anchorage to McCarthy for $235 one-way. **McCarthy Air** (907/554-4440 or 800/245-6909, www.mccarthyair.com) does flightseeing and backcountry drop-offs.

Glacier View Campground (907/554-4490), near the end of the road, has a few beat-up mountain bikes for rent ($15 for a half-day), but you should call ahead to reserve one on a mid-summer weekend. For horseback rides ($35 for an hour), contact **McCarthy Trail Rides** (907/632-4631).

Richardson Highway South

The 366-mile Richardson Highway provides a north–south connection between Fairbanks and Valdez, passing through the towns of North Pole, Delta Junction, Glennallen, and Copper Center along the way. The 115 mile stretch between Glennallen and Valdez cuts between the rugged Chugach Mountains to the west and the massive Wrangell Mountains to the east. This route—the oldest road in Alaska—was blazed during the stampede of 1898 and has since been used as a footpath, a telegraph right-of-way, a wagon trail, and an auto thoroughfare. The last 25 miles to Valdez is one of the most spectacular drives in Alaska.

COPPER CENTER

Copper Center (pop. 500) is 15 miles south of Glennallen on a side road (the Old Richardson Highway) that splits off at Mile 106 of the Richardson Highway. Settled in 1896, this was the first non-Native town in the interior of Southcentral, opened up by all the explorations on the mighty Copper River. This was also the point where the perilous trail over Valdez Glacier came down from the mountains. When the stampeders arrived, they found a score of tents, several log cabins, a post office, and the Blix Roadhouse, which opened in 1898 for $15,000, with spring beds and a modern bath. Today the settlement has a handful of businesses and a mixed popula-

tion, including Athabascans in the neighboring village of Kluti Kaah.

Practicalities

The Blix was replaced in 1932 by beautiful **Copper Center Lodge** (907/822-3245 or 888/822-3245, www.coppercenterlodge.com). Comfortable rooms (some with private baths) cost $109 s or d. The restaurant serves sourdough pancakes (using a century-old sourdough starter), burgers, sandwiches, shrimp, halibut, and steaks; dinner entrées run $20–24. Great homemade blueberry and rhubarb pies, too. The lodge is open year-round.

Right next door are two small cabins that comprise the **George Ashby Museum.** Exhibits trace the history of the Copper River Valley, including Athabascan Indian and early-settler artifacts. Gold rush and pioneer days are remembered with photographs, tools used to develop the area, and old Sears catalogs, the only way the local inhabitants could procure many necessary supplies from Outside. The museum is open June–August Monday–Satday 1–5 P.M. Across the highway, **Chapel on the Hill,** the oldest log chapel in the Copper River Basin, was built by Army volunteers in 1942. It's open all summer.

The modern 85-room **Copper River Princess Lodge** (907/822-4000 or 800/426-0500, www.princesslodges.com) is at mile 102 of Richardson Highway, and features with hilltop

old roadhouse remains near Copper Center

views of Mt. Drum, upscale lodging ($199 s or d), and a restaurant. Most of the guests are cruise ship passengers, but independent travelers are welcome.

Park RVs at two campgrounds on opposite sides of the Klutina River: **Klutina Salmon Charters** (907/822-3991, www.klutinacharters.com) and **Grove's Klutina Charters** (907/822-5822 or 800/770-5822, www.alaskan.com/groves).

Wrangell–St. Elias National Park and Preserve Visitor Center (907/822-7261, www.nps.gov/wrst) is just north of town at Mile 107, and is open daily in the summer. **Tonsina Native Arts and Crafts** (907/822-3852) sells locally made crafts.

EDGERTON HIGHWAY AND CHITINA

The turnoff for the Edgerton Highway is at Mile 82 of the Richardson (18 miles south of Copper Center). This paved 34-mile road leads past the disperse farming community of Kenny Lake and on to the town of Chitina (CHIT-nuh, from the Athabascan *chiti,* "copper," and *na,* "river"). The

Chitina Indians used copper tools to hammer copper nuggets into plates, which they traded with the Tlingits; someone who owned five or six plates was considered very rich. Chitina became an important junction in 1909, when the Copper River and Northwest Railroad arrived; a spur road connected the track to the original Richardson wagon trail to Fairbanks. The town began its decline in 1938 when the railroad shut down, and its future was further eroded by the Good Friday earthquake of 1964, which knocked out several bridges on the Copper River Highway. The highway project to link Cordova and Chitina was abandoned at that time.

Chitina

This town of less than 100 people is famous for its dip-netting season in June, when Alaskan residents converge on the confluence of the Copper and Chitina Rivers, "dip" 35-gallon nets on 10-foot-long aluminum poles into the water, and lift out 8-pound reds and 25-pound kings by the score. In addition, a number of fish wheels can be seen above the bridge. The dip-net fishery is only open to Alaskans. The rest of the year, Chitina serves primarily as a way station for folks heading out the McCarthy road. Chitina is decidedly rustic, with aging log cabins in various stages of collapse lining the dusty dirt roads. Poke around a bit more to find antique vehicles, an abandoned railcar, and even an old-fashioned gas pump. Chitina is also a very windy spot, with winds funneling through the narrow mountains along the Copper River.

Chitina House B&B (907/823-2298, www.chitinahouse.com) is an attractive and historic home that once served as a railroad bunkhouse. Two rooms share a bath, and a continental breakfast is included for $85. Open summers only.

A number of people rent out cabins in the Chitina vicinity, including the recommended **Chitina Guest Cabins** (907/823-2266), **Tonsina River Retreat** (907/822-3078), and **Chitina Lake Cabins** (907/823-2223).

A little downtown trailer serves burgers and other greasy fare in Chitina. **Chitina Trading Post** (907/823-2211) sells food for those who want to cook their own meals. You'll also find everything from videos to dip nets, not to mention gas for your car. **Uncle Tom's Tavern** (907/823-2253) is the local drinking establishment for the "nip and dip" crowd.

Housed within an historic cabin, the National Park Service's **Chitina Ranger Station** (907/823-2205) has information and videos on the park and the McCarthy Road. Open daily 10 A.M.–6 P.M. Memorial Day to Labor Day; closed the remainder of the year.

For quality Alaskan art in a historic setting, drop by **Spirit Mountain Artworks** (907/823-2222).

Wrangell Mountain Air (907/554-4411 or 800/478-1160, www.wrangellmountainair.com) has scheduled service connecting Chitina with McCarthy. See the Copper River by jetboat with **Copper River Tours** (907/822-3017, www.copperrivertours.com).

> *This town of less than 100 people is famous for its dip-netting season in June, when Alaskan residents converge on the confluence of the Copper and Chitina Rivers, "dip" 35-gallon nets on 10-foot-long aluminum poles into the water, and lift out 8-pound reds and 25-pound kings by the score.*

Kenny Lake Area

Kenny Lake Mercantile (907/822-3313, www.kennylake.com) has groceries and gas, a café, austere lodging, wooded RV park and tent sites, laundromat, and showers. It's at Mile 7 of the Edgerton Highway, 26 miles west of Chitina. Nicer accommodations can be found in the Kenny Lake area at **Golden Spruce Cabins** (907/822-5556), which also has an espresso stand and hot showers, and **Wellwood Center B&B** (907/822-3418, www.wellwoodcenter.com), where three guest rooms go for $75 s or d.

Pippin Lake B&B (907/822-3046), on Richardson Highway near the Edgerton turnoff has a cozy lakeside cabin that sleeps five for $100. The kitchen is stocked for a make-it-yourself breakfast, and a canoe and paddleboat add to the allure.

Camping

Two free camping areas are near Chitina: **Copper River State Campground** is just across the bridge one mile east of town, while **O'Brien Creek State Campground** is three miles to the south along the old Copper River Road. **Liberty Falls State Recreation Site** has several free sites 10 miles west of Chitina along the Edgerton Highway. It's a beautiful spot.

OVER THOMPSON PASS

From the Edgerton Highway junction to Valdez is 82 beautiful miles through green forested hillsides along surging creeks with countless waterfalls emanating from ice patches and small glaciers atop the jagged Chugach. If you're terminally enchanted by this stretch of road and want to linger, two state recreation sites offer camping: **Squirrel Creek** at Mile 79 and **Little Tonsina** at Mile 65. The Tonsina site is a bit noisy, located a half-mile from pipeline pump station number 12, which, run by jet aircraft turbines, sounds like a plane perpetually taking off. Signboards across the highway from the pump station (Mile 65) describe pipeline history, oil spills, communications, the turbines, and the pump station. At Mile 56, the **Tiekel River Lodge** (907/822-3259) has food, gas, rooms, campsites, and a gift shop.

Worthington Glacier

Near Mile 33, you come around a bend, unsuspecting, and the Worthington Glacier looms into view, its three fingers creeping out of Girls Mountain like a grotesque hand in a horror movie. In another few miles is the turnoff to this state recreation site, on a short road that leads to the overlook parking lot. There's no established campground here, only a small visitor center staffed by State Parks folks in the summer. Trails cover the short distance to the glacier, and a one-mile path climbs the lateral moraine for even more dramatic vistas.

Topping Out

A mere three miles down (or more accurately, *up*) the road from Worthington Glacier is **Thompson Pass,** elevation 2,771 feet. A long row of serrated peaks, like a cosmic cross-cut saw with only a few dull or missing teeth, lines the high horizon. Blueberry and Summit Lakes are accessible by a loop road about a mile on the Valdez side of the pass; the small campground at Blueberry is beautiful—though it's exposed, especially if Thompson Pass is in the process of maintaining its record-setting precipitation levels. Confirming that this is one of the snowiest spots on earth are 15-foot-tall, right-angle, orange poles that show snowplow drivers the edge of the road.

Thompson Pass Mt. Chalet (907/835-4817, www.alaska.net/~chalet) is a modern cabin at Mile 19 with space for four people, a private bath, and continental breakfast. Rates are $120 s or d. The owners live in a nearby cabin and guide summertime hikes and wintertime ski trips.

Keystone Canyon

About seven miles south of Thompson Pass, you drop to Keystone Canyon, one of the most gorgeous sights in Alaska, even in the rain. This four-mile section is steeped in gold rush and copper-frenzy history. At the height of Klondicitis, accounts of the heavy tax and strict regulations that Canadian authorities imposed on the stampeders (which saved countless lives) were passed down the coast, and rumors of an old Indian-Russian trail from Valdez to the Yukon circulated simultaneously. The vague story of an "all-American route" to the gold sent 4,000 would-be prospectors headlong to Valdez—a measure of the madness that gripped the land. Suicidally unprepared, like lemmings they attempted to cross the brutal Valdez Glacier. Also responding to the rumors, the U.S. Army dispatched Captain William Abercrombie in 1898 to find or blaze a route from Valdez to the Interior. Abercrombie had been on the original American expedition to Copper River country in 1884. He *knew* the land and the conditions; when he crossed Valdez Glacier in 1898, he postponed his trail-blazing assignment in order to deal with the horror that he found. Abercrombie returned in 1899 and thoroughly explored and mapped the whole area, locating and naming the Lowe River, Keystone Canyon, and the Thompson Pass route to the Interior.

Then in 1906, during the often violent race to build a railroad from tidewater to the Kennecott copper mines, two of the competing construction companies clashed over the right-of-way through Keystone Canyon; one man was killed. The ensuing murder trial further fanned the flames, and the "Shoot-out at Keystone Canyon" became a great issue between the opposing sides. All this is highly dramatized in Rex Beach's novel, *The Iron Trail.*

Today, you drive along the raging Lowe River, at the bottom of nearly perpendicular 300-foot cliffs. The entire canyon is a psychedelic green; every crack and crevice in the sheer walls is overgrown with bright lime moss. Waterfalls tumble over the walls to the river below, spraying the road with a fine mist. **Bridal Veil Falls** and **Horsetail Falls** live up to their names. And now you're ready to enter Valdez.

Valdez

At the end of Valdez Arm and completely surrounded by snowcapped peaks, Valdez (val-DEEZ, *never* val-DEZ, pop. 4,000) occupies one of the most picturesque settings in Southcentral Alaska. The prosperous town has wide streets, and year-round access by land and sea; it's the northernmost ice-free port in America. Because of the latter, Valdez was chosen as the terminus for the 800-mile Trans-Alaska Pipeline. And because of this, the town always seems to prosper.

HISTORY

Captain James Cook sailed into and named Prince William Sound in 1778; Spanish explorer Don Salvador Fidalgo entered "Puerto de Valdez" in 1790, naming it after Spain's Marine Minister. In 1898, Valdez was a tent city of stampeders similar to Skagway—except for one critical detail: no trail to the Interior. Still, between 4,000 and 6,000 death-defying cheechakos crossed the Valdez Glacier that year. Army Captain William Abercrombie described the foolhardy newcomers as "terrifyingly incompetent . . . wholly unprepared physically and morally for what they would face." They barely knew how to strap packs on their backs, and few thought to carry the two basic necessities: water and wood. Many were blinded by the sun's reflection off the ice. Many got lost in howling storms, in which it was impossible to see or hear the man ahead. Of those who managed to reach the summit, many lost their loads and lives on slick downhill slides into oblivion. And those who actually got off the glacier intact had to contend with the fast cold waters of the runoff. Many men with heavy packs lost their footing and drowned in knee-deep water. Some attempted to build boats and float down the Klutina River to Copper Center; few made it. And those stuck between the glacier and the river had nothing.

In the final count, all but 300 (and the countless dead) of those who'd set out from Valdez during the spring and summer of '98 returned to Valdez the way they came by fall. Abercrombie found them destitute and broken. Many had gone mad, most had scurvy and frostbitten hands, feet, and faces. Facilities were squalid. And there was no food. Abercrombie postponed his orders to blaze a trail into the Interior for six months to feed, clothe, house, and arrange transportation home for the survivors. Eventually, the army built a road through Keystone Canyon—providing access to the Interior—and a military base across the bay from Valdez called Fort Liscum; it lasted until 1923.

The 20th Century

In the early 1900s a corporate copper rush kicked off a fierce competition among Valdez, Cordova, and a town called Katalla, all vying to be selected as the tidewater terminus of the proposed railway to the copper mines of what's now Kennecott. A dozen projects were conceived, and one was even begun out of Valdez, but Cordova won out in the end. For the next 60 years, Valdez was a sleepy fishing and shipping port, competing with Seward, and later Whittier, to provide access for freight to the Interior. Then in 1964 the Good Friday earthquake struck, wiping out the entire town, which was rebuilt four miles inland on property donated by a local. Finally, in 1974, civic leaders sold the virtues of Valdez—its ice-free port, 800-foot-deep harbor, and proximity to the Interior—to the pipeline planners, who chose the town as their terminus.

Everything went along without serious incident until March 29, 1989 (Good Friday once again), when the *Exxon Valdez* ran aground on Bligh Reef a few hours after leaving the pipeline terminal in Valdez, dumping 11 million gallons of North Slope crude into Prince William Sound. The unthinkable had happened. In the mad summer of 1989, Valdez was turned on its head by the "Exxon Economy." The waters of Port Valdez escaped the spill, and the town's residents are back to normal, but Prince William Sound is still a long way from returning to the way it was before the spill.

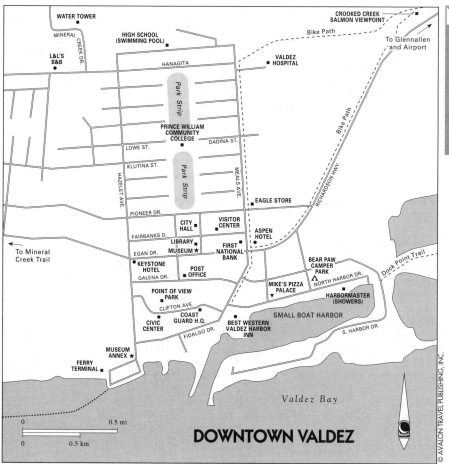

DOWNTOWN VALDEZ

0   0.5 mi

0   0.5 km

Valdez Bay

© AVALON TRAVEL PUBLISHING, INC.

SIGHTS

Downtown

For its size, **Valdez Museum** (217 Egan Dr., 907/835-2764, www.alaska.net/~vldzmuse) right in the middle of town, has an extraordinary amount of comprehensive displays. Check out the fascinating photo display on the pipeline's impact, and the early black-and-whites, especially one of a steamship at Columbia Glacier in 1928. Some rare early maps and charts include a Russian one from 1737; look for the beautiful engraving by Webber, Cook's prolific

ship's artist. Informative displays illustrate Native, mining, and military history, but two beautifully restored fire pumpers—one from 1886—are the striking centerpieces. There's a small section from the hull of the *Exxon Valdez,* but surprisingly little information on this disaster. From May to mid-September the museum is open daily 9 A.M.–6 P.M., the rest of the year Monday–Friday 1–5 P.M. and Saturday noon–4 P.M. Entrance costs $3 adults, $2.50 seniors, $2 ages 14–18, and free for children.

The **Valdez Museum Annex** (436 S. Hazelet St., 907/835-5407) houses a warehouse full of earthquake exhibits, including a sprawling 1:20 scale replica of Valdez as it appeared before the big one hit in 1964. You can also watch a video on the quake, try out the computer programs, and check the seismograph for recent activity. There's even a 1950s Civil Defense Jeep on display. Entrance is $1.50; free for kids under 18. The Annex is open daily 10 A.M.–4 P.M. May to mid-September, or by appointment the rest of the year.

Down Meals Avenue by the harbor, bear left onto Clifton and go up past Coast Guard HQ to the **Civic Center,** where a viewing pavilion has an interpretive signboard describing the pipeline terminal across the bay. Climb the steep stairs up to **Point of View Park** for the panorama of town.

Out of Town

The **Whitney Museum** (907/834-1690, www.uaa.alaska.edu/pwscc) occupies a warehouse-type building next to the airport terminal, five miles from town. The location is odd, but the collection is well worth the drive. Housed here are items collected over several decades by Jeese and Maxine Whitney, including trophy big game mounts, an Eskimo kayak and umiak, and a wide range of Native parkas, baskets, and beautiful, carved ivory pieces. Of particular interest is a large and elaborate model ship built of ivory. Entrance is $5 adults, seniors $4, and $3 ages 3–12. Open daily 9 A.M.–8 P.M. May to mid-September, or by appointment the rest of the year.

The Forest Service's **Crooked Creek Information Site** (907/835-4680) is out the Richardson about a mile from town. It's open daily 9 A.M.–6 P.M. from Memorial Day to Labor Day. In late summer, walk out on the boardwalk to see salmon go through the final act of their incredible life cycle. The TV inside the information center is wired to a video camera that provides a live underwater view of the spawning action for salmon voyeurs. A four-mile paved **bike path** leads north from town past Crooked Creek.

Continue out the Richardson about three and a half miles to where a historical sign points to **Old Valdez.** The only thing left of the old town site besides the post office foundation and memorial plaque are the mileposts on the Rich: zero

still starts here. In another three miles, turn right onto Dayville Road. In several miles you come to the hydroelectric plant and **Solomon Gulch Hatchery** (907/835-4874). Pause here to see the powerful small falls and to take a self-guided tour around this private pink and coho salmon hatchery. The staff is generally around to answer questions. Black bears sometimes emerge from the nearby forest to catch salmon in late summer.

The **Alyeska Pipeline Terminal** is farther out Dayville Road, but is no longer open to the public due to security concerns. Prince William Sound Community College (303 Lowe St.) shows an interesting 90-minute video about the pipeline, the terminal, double-hull oil tankers, and the Valdez area during the summer. Tickets cost $5 ($4 seniors; $15 families).

TOURING PRINCE WILLIAM SOUND
Columbia Glacier

Prince William Sound has the greatest concentration of tidewater glaciers in Alaska, including Columbia Glacier, the stunning grandfather of glaciers in the Sound. Covering about 440 square miles, Columbia Glacier is 40 miles long and more than three miles wide at its face, which rises up to 250 feet above the water and plunges an incredible 2,000 feet below. Although it's the second largest of its kind in Alaska and still extends 15 miles out into its ancestral fjord, Columbia Glacier is but a minor remnant of the vast glacier that only a few thousand years ago filled Prince William Sound; its face reached a height of 4,000 feet.

Since 1982 the glacier has been in rapid retreat, at a rate averaging a half-mile per year. This retreat has filled Columbia Bay with icebergs, and tour boats can no longer get within six miles of the face. Ice in the bay has also caused navigational hazards in Prince William Sound, and it was to avoid ice that the *Exxon Valdez* took its fateful shortcut near, and onto, Bligh Reef. Scientists speculate that by the time the glacier stops its current rate of backward movement, a new fjord 25 miles long will be exposed, into which several calving glaciers will flow.

icebergs from Columbia Glacier

Seeing the Glacier

The state ferry pauses on its trip between Valdez and Whittier to view the Columbia Glacier.

Two companies offer boat tours of the Sound out of Valdez, and several others operate out of Whittier. Because of the glacier's recent movement back up the bay, boats can only get to within about six miles of the face. This changes, but does not diminish, the experience, as the boats cruise through and over the fields of drifting ice towering above the deck to see the glacier as more huge chunks shear off and drop into the bay. Beyond the glaciers, the main attraction for Prince William Sound is wildlife, including the chance to see humpback and killer (orca) whales, Dall's porpoises, sea otters, Steller sea lions, and other marine mammals. These animals are most often seen on the southern end of the Sound, an all-day boat ride from Whittier or Valdez.

The *Lu-Lu Belle* (907/835-5141 or 800/411-0090, www.lulubelletours.com) is a comfortable 60-passenger boat with daily Columbia Glacier and wildlife tours in the summer; $80 for a five-hour. A snack bar is on board.

Stan Stephens Glacier & Wildlife Cruises (907/835-4731 or 866/867-1297, www.stan

stephenscruises.com) has a 5.5-hour Columbia Glacier tour ($85 adults, $42 kids), and an all-day trip that encompasses Columbia and Meares glaciers, plus the sea lions of Glacier Island for $119 adults, $59 kids.

State Parks

Three state marine parks (www.alaskas-tateparks.org) offer a variety of recreational opportunities within an hour's boat ride from Valdez. The serene, forest-ringed **Sawmill Bay State Marine Park** has protected anchorage and good camping. For island camping and a fair-weather anchorage, visit **Jack Bay State Marine Park** on the east side of Valdez Narrows. At **Shoup Bay Marine Park** the Shoup Glacier spills into an iceberg-filled saltwater lagoon accessible on most high tides by sea kayaks and small boats. Visitors will enjoy this pretty bay with lots of icebergs and thousands of nesting kittiwakes.

RECREATION
Hiking

Get complete details on local hikes from the Forest Service's Crooked Creek visitor center. The easiest local path, the **Dock Point Trail,** starts from Kobuk Dr. across from the boat ramp. This three-quarter-mile trail (partially boardwalk) has a grassy meadow and good viewpoints across Valdez Bay. **Mineral Creek Valley** is a beautiful canyon accessible from the north end of town via Mineral Creek Drive. A bumpy gravel road—great for mountain bikes—crosses the creek and then parallels it for the next 5.5 miles, ending at a locked gate. From here it's a one-mile walk to the abandoned W.L. Smith Stamp Mill (1913), which crushed ore from mines up the mountain. A number of beautiful waterfalls crowd the slopes of Mineral Creek Valley, so be sure to bring your camera.

The **Keystone Canyon Pack Trail** (a.k.a. Goat Trail or Trans-Alaska Military Trail) begins from a trailhead at Mile 14 of the Richardson Highway, climbing gradually 2.5 miles. The trail was built in 1899 by the Army to provide an "All-American" route to the gold fields, and this short portion was restored almost a century later.

For an excellent overnight trip, hike the **Shoup Bay Trail,** which begins from the west end of Egan Street. This trail affords views of Valdez and Valdez Bay, and passes a fine camping area along Gold Creek at three miles. It ends at Shoup Bay (across from majestic Shoup Glacier), 10 miles from town.

Sea Kayaking

If you've always wanted to learn how to kayak, or if you know how and want to explore Prince William Sound around Valdez in style, contact Hedy Sarney of **Anadyr Adventures** (225 N. Harbor Dr., 907/835-2814 or 800/865-2925, www.anadyradventures.com). Trips range from a three-hour natural history tour for $55, to customized mothership multinight tours. Especially popular are eight-hour Shoup Glacier trips ($145), and 10-hour Columbia Glacier paddles ($185), both of which include an open water crossing by charter boat. Anadyr's most popular multinight trip is a five-day paddle that encompasses Columbia Glacier, Sawmill Bay, and Shoup Glacier for $795 ($1,025 with meals). Anadyr

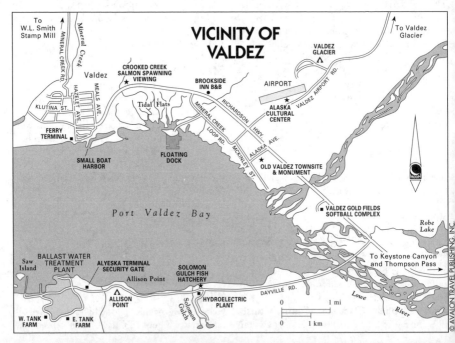

conducts other excursions of varying lengths, including boat-based and cabin-based trips, along with a remote drop-off and pickup service. They also rent kayaks, bikes, and camping gear, and the Alaskan arts and crafts sold here make it worth a visit even if you aren't planning a paddle.

Pangaea Adventures (101 N. Harbor Dr., 907/835-8442 or 800/660-9637, www.alaskasummer.com) also leads a wide range of sea kayaking trips. Least expensive ($55) is a three-hour paddle around the duck flats, but more challenging are day trips to Gold Creek ($75), Shoup Glacier ($145), and Columbia Glacier ($189). The last of these lasts 10 hours and includes a water taxi ride to and from the Columbia, along with time to explore this magnificent glacier. Longer trips start with an overnight trip to Shoup Glacier, a six-day "mothership" tour ($1,050) that takes sea kayakers around Prince William Sound aboard a sailboat, and a 15-day trip ($3,600) that combines sea kayaking, backpacking, and river rafting. Kayak rentals are available if you just want to head out on your own.

Rafting

Keystone Raft and Kayak Adventures (907/835-2606 or 800/328-8460, www.alaskawhitewater.com) offers an exciting two-hour raft trip ($35) down the Class III Lowe River through Keystone Canyon. Other choices include a half-day trip on the Tsaina River (Class-IV; $70) near Thompson Pass, and all-day Tonsina River trips (Class III-IV; $85), 80 miles from town. Trips depart from their office at Mile 17 of the Richardson Highway; transport from Valdez is $10 extra. Also ask about longer trips throughout the Copper River Valley.

Fishing and Biking

Valdez has three dozen charter fishing and cruising boats. Contact the visitor center for a listing, or visit their website (www.valdezalaska.org). **Fish Central** (907/835-5090 or 888/835-5002, www.fishcentral.net) books fishing charters, boat rentals, and sightseeing trips. Find them next to the boat harbor.

Rent mountain bikes from Anadyr Adventures, or **Beaver Sports** (316 Galena, 907/835-4727).

Flightseeing

Era Helicopters (907/835-2595 or 800/843-1947, www.eraaviation.com) offers a one-hour flight ($229) that includes time over Columbia Glacier and a dramatic landing near Shoup Glacier.

Winter Sports

When winter comes, Keystone Canyon's waterfalls freeze, making them destinations for ice climbers, particularly during the Ice Climbing Festival in early March. Valdez itself gets some of the heaviest snowfalls anywhere in Alaska, averaging 25 feet per year; the record came the winter of 1989–1990: 47 feet! It isn't uncommon to arrive in March to find the town buried to the rooftops in snow. More snow falls here than at any other sea-level location in North America. Because of all this snow, the area can be a winter-lovers' paradise, especially since the temperature rarely drops below 20 degrees. Groomed cross-country ski trails are maintained in Mineral Creek Valley.

Two companies offer heli-skiing at Thompson Pass for the ultimate mountain skiing adventure: **Valdez Heli-Ski Guides** (907/835-4528, www.valdezheliskiguides.com) and **Valdez Heli-Camps** (907/783-3243, www.alaska.net/~heliski). Skis and snowboards are available for rent at Thompson Pass from **Phatz Ski Rental** (907/835-5377, www.alaska.net/~pcprice).

ACCOMMODATIONS

Hotels and Motels

Valdez has seven hotels, but book a room well ahead for July and August when nearly most rooms get taken early. For quick and easy reservations at B&Bs, hotels, charter-boat fishing companies, rafting, and sea kayaking, call Cathy at **One Call Does It All** reservation service (907/835-4988 or 888/304-4988, www.ocdia.com). She can describe all the B&Bs in town and provide a map to the place when you reserve through her service, all at no charge.

The 31-room **Downtown B&B Inn** (113 Galena Dr., 907/835-2791 or 800/478-2791, www.alaskan.com/downinn) charges $85 with a shared bath or $100 with a private bath. Rates

THE EXXON VALDEZ OIL SPILL

On March 23, 1989 (Good Friday), at 11 P.M., Captain Joseph Hazelwood turned the 987-foot *Exxon Valdez* supertanker, just a few hours after leaving the pipeline terminal loaded with over 20 million barrels of Prudhoe Bay crude, out of the normal shipping lanes of Prince William Sound to avoid icebergs from Columbia Glacier. Through a series of mistakes and misunderstandings, and ignoring standard procedure, at 12:01 A.M. on March 24 the *Valdez* ran up hard aground on Bligh Reef, opening a tractor trailer-size hole in the ship, which began to leak oil at a rapid rate. It took 3 hours for the Coast Guard to be notified, and 12 hours for the spill-response team to arrive at the scene. It was a full 72 hours after the oil began to spill before a containment boom was installed to surround the tanker. But as the rest of the oil was off-loaded onto the *Exxon Baton Rouge,* the fate of more than 1,000 miles of Southcentral coastline had already been sealed. The oil began its inexorable spread.

The Cleanup

In the following weeks, the technology available to clean up an environmental disaster of such magnitude proved grossly inadequate. To begin with, Alyeska Pipeline Company's emergency procedures and equipment had atrophied over the years. The use of chemical dispersants, a major part of the plan, was not only ineffective, but controversial as well: Later in the summer workers who'd handled them began to show symptoms of toxic poisoning. Of the few skimmers that could be deployed (a dozen after a week), those that worked were able to clean up 500 gallons of oil an hour—in the face of millions. And then there were no support facilities for unloading the skimmed crude.

Local fishermen mobilized to try to contain the oil with booms, keeping it away from some of the most bountiful fisheries on earth at the peak of their seasons. As the oil washed up on the wildlife-rich shorelines of Prince William Sound, crews were sent to attack the thickening, hardening sludge with shovels, buckets, and plastic bags. As early as the first week in June, 24,000 birds and 1,000 sea otters, killed by the oil, had been counted—some so covered with crude that they were impossible to identify. At the height of the summer clean-up, 10,000 workers were engaged in a somewhat futile effort to return the beaches of Prince William Sound, the Kenai and Alaska Peninsulas, Kodiak Island, and all the way down to the Shumagin Islands in the Aleutians to their previously pristine state. Garbage clean-up crews were cleaning up after the oil clean-up crews. It's estimated that Exxon spent $1.25 billion on the effort.

The Aftermath

Well over a decade after the spill, oil can still be found on some Prince William Sound beaches, particularly under rocks on the worst-hit beaches. Many species of birds and mammals are far below their prespill populations, including killer whales, sea otters, loons, cormorants, harbor seals, pigeon guillemots, and harlequin ducks. In addition, research shows that even tiny concentrations of crude oil can harm the eggs of pink salmon and herring. Herring fishermen have been especially hard hit, and the value of commercial salmon fishing permits has plummeted.

Shortly after the spill, Exxon renamed all its ships, replacing the "Exxon" with "Sea River"; if there's ever another Exxon-caused spill its name won't be so indelibly etched in the news accounts. The 1989 spill led to enactment the following year of the Oil Pollution Act which requires double-hulled tankers in Prince William Sound by 2015. Unfortunately, the aging single-hulled tankers are still used today. Many other measures have been taken to prevent a repeat, however, including the addition of large ocean-going tugs and response vessels (containing spill equipment) to escort all tankers.

In a 1991 out-of-court settlement, Exxon agreed to a $900 million payout that has been used to buy land, to reimburse cleanup expenses, and to fund environmental research and restoration. More contentious was a 1994 case in which a jury awarded 40,000 commercial fishermen and others damaged by the spill $5 billion in punitive damages. It was one of the biggest damage awards ever. Exxon has been dragging out the appeals process since then, with no end in sight, but if they ever have to pay, it will cost them the $5 billion plus an interest of 5.9 percent, around $2 million more per day! And what of Captain Hazelwood? He was convicted in 1990 of a misdemeanor charge of negligent discharge of oil. After nine years of appeals, Hazelwood was finally sentenced to 1,000 hours of community service, including working in an Anchorage soup kitchen. He now lives in New York state.

For the latest on the spill, visit the *Exxon Valdez* Oil Spill Trustee Council website (www.oilspill.state.ak.us).

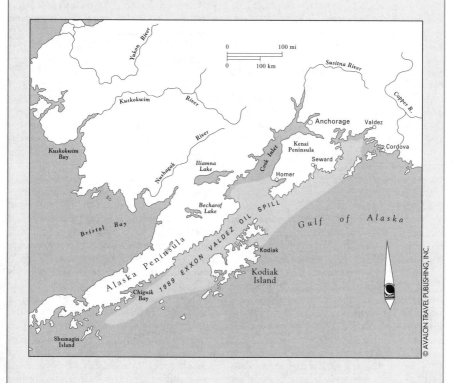

include a light breakfast. **Glacier Sound Inn** (210 Egan Dr., 907/835-4485 or 888/835-4485) has motel rooms for $100 s or d.

Keystone Hotel (at Hazelet and Egan Drives, 907/835-3851 or 888/835-0665, www.alaskan.com/keystonehotel) has cramped little rooms for $85 s or $95 d. Larger ones with two double beds cost $105 for up to three people. The hotel is clean and well maintained, and a continental breakfast is included. Keystone is open late May to early September.

The **Best Western Valdez Harbor Inn** (100 Fidalgo Dr., 907/835-4391 or 888/222-3440, www.valdezharborinn.com) faces the small boat harbor, with standard rooms for $129–139 s or d.

Totem Inn (144 E. Egan Dr., 907/835-4443, www.toteminn.com) has a variety of lodging options, including standard rooms with fridges and microwaves ($144 d), cottages with kitchenettes ($159 d), and full suites ($199 d).

Aspen Hotel (100 Meals Ave., 907/835-4445 or 800/478-4445, www.aspenhotelsak.com) is the town's nicest hotel with rooms for $149–179 s or d, and such amenities as indoor pool, whirlpool tub, exercise room, and breakfast. The more expensive rooms have king beds, in-room fridges, and microwaves.

Bed-and-Breakfasts

Visit the Valdez Convention and Visitors Bureau website (www.valdezalaska.org) for links to most local B&Bs. **Kansas North B&B** (413 W. Klutina, 907/835-3576) is a contemporary suburban home with two private rooms downstairs. They are small and share a bath, but include fridges and microwaves for a make-it-yourself breakfast, for a bargain rate of $60 d. Kids are welcome, and there's a porch with wicker rocking chairs.

L&L's B&B (533 W. Hanagita St., 907/835-4447, www.lnlalaska.com) is a large and modern home with five immaculate guest rooms, three baths, and continental breakfasts. Rates are $70–80 d.

Brookside Inn B&B (907/835-9130, www.brooksideinnbb.com) is a quaint home with a long history. Constructed in 1898, it survived the earthquake and was moved to new Valdez.

The four guest rooms are $115 d, and two suites cost $140–160 d, all with private baths. A full breakfast is served, and kids are welcome. The front porch and deck are good places to relax.

Located 1.5 miles from town, **Wild Roses by the Sea B&B** (907/835-2930, www.bytheseaalaska.com) sits atop a bluff overlooking Port Valdez. The home features a mix of Chinese and Alaskan décor, plus a delicious continental breakfast. Rates are $125–140 d, and one room includes a king bed and jacuzzi bath.

Also well worth a look are **Anna's Ptarmigan B&B** (907/835-2202), **Eagle B&B** (907/835-3831, www.eaglebb.com), **Gussie's Lowe Street B&B** (907/835-4448, www.alaskaone.com /gussiesbb), **Headhunters B&B** (907/835-2900), and **Lake House B&B** (907/835-4752, www.geocitties.com/lakehousevaldez).

Camping

The closest official campground is five miles away. Go back out the Richardson Highway, turn left toward the airport, and continue another mile past it to the **Valdez Glacier Campground** (907/835-2282, www.valdezcampgrounds.com, $10). This large and scenic campground has picnic and barbecue areas, outhouses, and water. **Allison Point Campground** (907/835-2282) is on Dayville Road near the Alyeska oil terminal, and has toilets and water; $10 for tents. There's good fishing from shore nearby. The closest state park campsites ($12) are at **Blueberry Lake Campground,** 27 miles up the Richardson Highway on Thompson Pass.

Find **public showers** at the harbor master's office, corner of Meals Avenue and Harbor Drive across from the chamber of commerce. Showers are also available from **Like Home Laundromat** on Egan Drive near Meals. A better deal is the **swimming pool** at Valdez High School (907/835-3200), where the showers are free with a swim.

Large RV parks abound right in Valdez: **Bear Paw Camper Park** (907/835-2530, www.bearpawrvpark.com), **Bayside RV Park** (907/835-4425 or 888/835-4425, www.baysiderv-park.com), **Sea Otter RV Park** (907/835-2787 or 800/831-2787), and **Eagle's Rest RV Park**

(907/835-2373 or 800/553-7275, www.eaglesrestrv.com). Tent prices are around $17; RV hookups cost $22. Bear Paw and Sea Otter RV parks are right along the waterfront.

FOOD

Mike's Palace (201 Harbor Dr., 907/835-2365) has a harborside location and wide-ranging menu with excellent pizzas ($19 for a medium combo), pasta, and Mexican meals. Open for lunch and dinner; call for takeout orders. Recommended.

Alaska Halibut House (Meals Ave. at Egan Dr., 907/835-2788) has fast-food fish, such as a halibut sandwich and halibut basket, as well as burgers and sandwiches. **Ernesto's** (326 Egan St., 907/835-2519) serves authentic, reasonable, and tasty Mexican meals.

Fu Kung (907/835-5255) occupies a Quonset hut at 207 Kobuk. In addition to the expected Chinese favorites, the restaurant also has seafood, including mu shu shrimp. Lunch specials are a deal at $8. Fu Kung is open until 11 P.M. daily.

The **Pipeline Club** (112 Egan Dr., 907/835-4332) is an old-time, smoke-filled place where Captain Hazelwood had a number of drinks before climbing on board the *Exxon Valdez* that fateful night in 1989. It lays claim to the best filet mignon, prime rib, char-broiled steaks, and seafood in town. But don't drink and drive (or boat).

Get groceries at **Eagle** (907/835-2100), the Safeway-owned market near Egan. Several spots sell espresso in town, including **Latte Dah** (130 S. Meals, 907/835-3720), which uses Kaladi Brothers coffees.

EVENTS

The **Valdez Ice Climbing Festival** (www.alaskagold.com/ice) in early March attracts some of the top climbers to the frozen waterfalls of Keystone Canyon.

Two events crown the early April calendar: **King of the Hill Extreme Snowboard Competition** for extreme snowboarders, and the **World Free Skiing Championship/Chugach Mountain Festival** (907/835-2108, www.xonet.org). Both attract an amazing group of hard-core downhillers who are ferried into the Chugach Mountains by helicopter for death-defying runs off near-vertical faces.

The acclaimed **Edward Albee Theatre Conference** (www.uaa.alaska.edu/pwscc) takes place in June at the Prince William Sound Community College. It's a weeklong theatrical event with performances and seminars by nationally known playwrights and actors including, of course, Edward Albee.

Valdez has two popular summertime fishing derbies (907/835-2330): the **Halibut Derby** all summer and **Silver Salmon Derby** in August. Other popular summer events are the **4th of July** celebration and **Valdez Gold Rush Days** in early August. The latter is a weeklong celebration complete with cancan girls, a hoosegow, parade, and fish fry.

INFORMATION AND SERVICES

The **Valdez Visitor Information Center** (200 Chenega St., 907/835-2984 or 800/770-5954, www.valdezalaska.org) is across from City Hall. It's open daily 8 A.M.–7 P.M. from April–September, and Monday–Friday 8 A.M.–5 P.M. the rest of the year. Out front are phones with direct lines to local businesses, including several B&Bs.

The **Valdez Consortium Library** (Fairbanks St., 907/835-4632) has computers for checking your email and shows a 30-minute video on Valdez on request. **Anadyr Adventures** (225 N. Harbor Dr., 907/835-2814 or 800/865-2925) also has a computer for Internet access (as do RV parks and hotels), and their gift shop sells Alaskan arts and crafts.

TRANSPORTATION

Valdez is 366 miles from Fairbanks on the Richardson Highway; from Anchorage it's 189 miles on the Glenn Highway to Glennallen, then another 115 on the Richardson Highway. **Valdez U-Drive** (907/835-4402 or 800/478-4402, www.valdezudrive.com) has rental cars at the airport, but reserve ahead since they go fast in the summer. Compacts cost $50 a day with 100 free miles.

Valdez Tours (907/835-2686) leads 1.5-hour van tours of the area in the summer.

Alaska Trails (907/479-3065 or 888/600-6001, www.alaskashuttle.com) has a summertime van service connecting Valdez with Glennallen, Delta Junction, and Fairbanks, but reservations are required, and they need a minimum of four people.

Era Aviation (800/866-8394, www.flyera.com), flies turboprop airplanes between Valdez and Anchorage several times a day. Its best rates are with a seven-day advance purchase or by buying a "commuter coupon" book of eight one-way tickets. (These can be sold to other folks.)

The airport is four miles outside town; calling a **Yellow Cab** (907/835-2500) will get you a ride into town.

Ferry

The Alaska Marine Highway (907/465-3941 or 800/642-0066, www.ferryalaska.com) has frequent passenger and vehicle ferry service connecting Valdez, Whittier, and Cordova, with the high-speed *Chenega* starting service on this route in 2005. A Forest Service naturalist is on board for summer sailings, and the trip to Whittier includes time among the icebergs near Columbia Glacier. The *Tustumena* departs from Valdez a couple days a week on its way around Prince William Sound and over to Seward, Homer, and Kodiak.

Cordova

Cordova (pop. 2,000) is noticeably less populated, less prosperous, and less accessible than its big-sister city Valdez—and most people like it that way. Though only a ferry ride away, its setting is its own, its climate is milder and wetter, and its vibration is nothing like Valdez's. Cordova might feel more at home somewhere between Petersburg and Juneau: connected only by boat and plane, with a large commercial fishing fleet, lush forests, small islands, and snowcapped peaks.

But Cordova is more than just the coast; it's also Chugach National Forest, Prince William Sound, and their abundant outdoor recreation; the Copper River and its wild rides and massive delta; spectacular Childs Glacier; railroad history and the Million Dollar Bridge. Amid all of this is a bustling little community bursting at its seams during the summer fishing season, but also glued together by the magic of the fishing lifestyle. Drift over to Cordova and spend a couple of days exploring this special corner of Alaska—you'll be glad you did.

HISTORY

In 1884, Army Captain William Abercrombie surveyed the Copper River delta, which made the area known to a few hardy prospectors. The crazed stampede of 1897-98 opened up the area to settlement. Still, in 1905, Cordova was little more than a couple of canneries processing the pinks and silvers from the Sound. Then Michael J. Heney showed up.

After years of surveying rights-of-way, watching railroad ventures to the rich coal and copper mines nearby start and fold, and failing to convince the Morgan-Guggenheim Alaska Syndicate not to start its road from Katalla, Heney invested his entire savings and in 1907 began laying track from Cordova toward Kennecott Mines. After the Katalla facilities were destroyed by a storm, the Syndicate bought the Copper River and Northwest line from Heney and completed it in 1911 at a total cost of $23 million; by 1917 it had hauled over $100 million in ore to Cordova for transshipment to smelters. Cordova was a boomtown until the Kennecott Mines closed in 1938.

The 1964 earthquake caused extensive damage to the town, and uplifted the sea floor six feet. Since then the town's economy has reverted to fishing and canning. The year-round population doubles in the summer, and in good years there's plenty of work. The town's fishing fleet tops 800 vessels at the peak of the sockeye salmon season.

Copper River red and king salmon have attained an almost mythical status, and always garner a high price. They're the first major run of

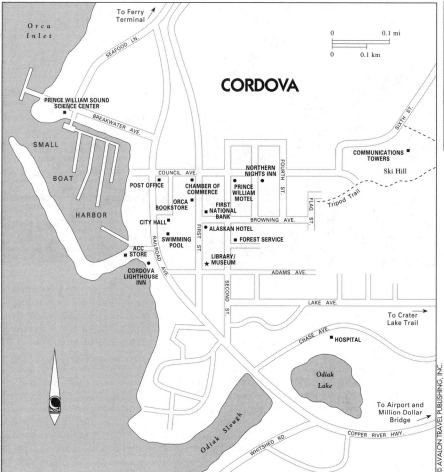

CORDOVA

Orca Inlet

SEAFOOD LN.

To Ferry Terminal

0   0.1 mi
0   0.1 km

PRINCE WILLIAM SOUND SCIENCE CENTER

BREAKWATER AVE.

SMALL

BOAT

HARBOR

SIXTH ST.

COMMUNICATIONS TOWERS

Ski Hill

COUNCIL AVE.

NORTHERN NIGHTS INN

FOURTH ST.

POST OFFICE

CHAMBER OF COMMERCE

PRINCE WILLIAM MOTEL

ORCA BOOKSTORE

FIRST NATIONAL BANK

FLAG ST.

Tripod Trail

CITY HALL

FIRST ST.

BROWNING AVE.

SWIMMING POOL

ALASKAN HOTEL

FOREST SERVICE

ACC STORE

CORDOVA LIGHTHOUSE INN

RAILROAD AVE.

LIBRARY/ MUSEUM

SECOND ST.

ADAMS AVE.

LAKE AVE.

To Crater Lake Trail

CHASE AVE.

HOSPITAL

Odiak Lake

To Airport and Million Dollar Bridge

Odiak Slough

WHITSHED RD.

COPPER RIVER HWY.

MOON

© AVALON TRAVEL PUBLISHING, INC.

Alaska salmon each summer, and are prized for their rich flavor and deep red color. Anchorage restaurants often compete to get the first shipment of these salmon, and others are shipped by air directly to markets and restaurants throughout the United States. Find out more from the **Copper River Salmon Producers Association** (907/424-3115, www.copperriver.com).

SIGHTS

The **Cordova Historical Museum** (622 1st St., 907/424-6665, Tues.–Sat. 1–5 P.M. all year, $1) is in the Centennial Building. This museum is small but packed with artifacts, including an old Linotype, an ancient slot machine, a three-seat *baidarka,* and an amusing exhibit on Cordova's famous Iceworm Festival. Look for the aerial views of earthquake damage to the Million Dollar Bridge. The 30-minute *Cordova Story* is shown daily. Next door is the **Cordova Library** (907/424-6667) a good place to read, rest, check your email, and meet fellow travelers while waiting for the ferry.

hillside homes in Cordova

Many buildings around town were built during Cordova's original construction in 1908, including (all on 1st St.) the Alaskan Hotel and Cordova House, and the Red Dragon, oldest building in town, which served weekdays as a rowdy clubhouse but on Sundays turned into a church when the altar was let down by ropes from the beams. Pick up the historic walking-tour map at the museum for a complete list of the old buildings.

Located at the harbor entrance, the **Prince William Sound Science Center** (907/424-5800, www.pwssc.gen.ak.us) is a scientific base for research on the regional ecosystem. No exhibits to speak of, but you may want to stop by with questions about the *Exxon Valdez* spill and how it has affected Prince William Sound, or to just enjoy the view from the waterfront deck. The center is open weekdays 9 A.M.–5 P.M.

COPPER RIVER HIGHWAY

There aren't enough superlatives in the English language to describe adequately the 50-mile ride out the Copper River Highway from Cordova to the famous Million Dollar Bridge. The scenery—mountains, glaciers, river, and delta—rivals any 50 miles on the continent, let alone the state. The wildlife—thousands of shorebirds and ducks, Canada geese, trumpeter swans, bald eagles, moose, bears, and spawning salmon—gives Denali a run for its money. The history encompasses punching an early-20th-century railroad 200 miles into the Interior and starting a road in the 1960s on its right-of-way, only to be destroyed by the largest earthquake ever recorded in North America. The crowning glory of the trip, as visible in rain or fog as in bright sunshine, built at great expense and great danger in 1910 between the faces of two moving glaciers and left mostly standing by the earthquake, is the Million Dollar Bridge, the vista from which is unsurpassed in a land of unsurpassed vistas.

Just outside of town, the Copper River Highway passes beautiful **Eyak Lake** at the base of Eyak Mountain. Notice how the lake is two colors, deep blue and light green, which don't merge. From around Mile 6 at the bridge over Eyak River to Mile 12 where the pavement ends, keep a sharp eye out for waterfowl and wildlife in the runoff sloughs from nearby Scott Glacier. Take a left at Mile 13 (across from the airport road) and follow a two-mile gravel road up to **Cabin Lake,** with trout fishing, picnic tables, and trails to three other lakes.

At Mile 14, another left and another four miles of gravel bring you to the **Mt. Sheridan** trailhead; hike a mile on the 4WD extension spur and scramble up on the ridge to look out over the two-finger **Sheridan Glacier** flowing down either side of the mountain, and the iceberg-clogged lake at its face. A side road to the right at Mile 17 goes off to **Alaganik Slough;** the three rough miles are excellent for viewing shorebirds. Picnic tables and an information plaque occupy the end of the road, and you can pitch a tent anywhere along here.

The **Haystack Trail** at mile 19 is a little under a mile, mostly uphill over boardwalks and through second-growth forest. It terminates at a wonderful overlook spot, affording sweeping views of the delta, well worth the short trek. This is a good place to find moose and bears. At Mile 21, the **Pipeline Lakes Trail** leads to the south on a marshy two-mile path. The Forest Service's **McKinley Trail Cabin** is just off the highway at Mile 22. From here, it's an easy two-mile saunter along **McKinley Lake Trail** to McKinley Lake where you can fish for trout or stay in a second cabin.

Across the River

At Mile 27, you cross the first of nearly a dozen bridges and causeways to the other "side" of the Copper River, more than 10 miles distant—it might remind you of the south Florida Keys. Long Island, from Mile 28 to Mile 34, sits smack in the middle of the mighty river delta. Good canoeing in the ponds along here, which connect up with a minimum of portage. Out here you can understand why, out of 196 miles of track from Cordova to Kennicott, 96 miles were built over bridges or trestles.

Finally, at Mile 48, you arrive at **Million Dollar Bridge.** This bridge, which cost a little over a million dollars to build in 1910, was the culmination of Michael Heney's vision, faith, and employee loyalty—not to mention the uncanny abilities of his civil engineers. It had to be built entirely in winter, when the two glaciers that sandwiched it were dormant. The working conditions were unbearable at best and the danger was extreme, especially as the builders raced to finish the final span even as its supports were being washed away by break-up. But it *was* completed, and Heney sold the whole show to the Syndicate and, according to Rex Beach in *The Iron Trail,* married the girl of his dreams and lived happily ever after.

The north span collapsed in the 1964 earthquake, but the state jury-rigged a ramp down to the abutment, and it's a fun little joyride to the other side. On the bridge, look to your left at the massive face of the **Childs Glacier;** look right about three miles across Miles Lake to the **Miles Glacier,** which has receded two miles since 1910. A short side road on the left just before the bridge leads past a small concrete shack, used by Fish and Game while counting the salmon escapement, down to a viewing pavilion set up on a small bluff over the river. From here you can safely view the face of Childs Glacier, under cover from the often-inclement weather. Informative displays give you something to read while you wait for huge chunks of ice to fall into the river. Plan to spend all afternoon here as the glacier creaks, groans, and cracks, dropping calves into the narrow river channel. Be careful of particularly big calves, whose waves can splash all the way up the embankment.

RECREATION

Close-in Hikes

Two trails climb **Mt. Eyak**—one through the forest, the other up the ski slope. The unmarked **Tripod Trail** is a little hard to find, but if you cut to the right between a cabin and a driveway near the end of 5th Street, you'll see the trailhead. This is a pretty hike through forest primeval, with salmonberries ripe for the picking in August. Otherwise, head straight up Council Avenue, bear left onto 6th, and follow it around the communications apparatus. You can start right up the mountain from there, and you don't have to go far to get a great view of the town and harbor.

The excellent **Crater Lake Trail** begins opposite Skaters Cabin on Eyak Lake, two miles from town beyond the old cemetery, the seaplane base, and the municipal airstrip. The trail climbs 1,500 feet in two miles through a beautiful forest, with panoramic views near the top of Eyak Lake and the Heney Range. The terrain around Crater Lake is fairly open and it would be easy to scale the surrounding summits, if you have the time and energy. Allow a minimum of two hours round-trip from the road to the lake. The trail is solid and very easy to follow; even if a wet wind is blowing, it will be relatively still in the forest, but be careful not to slip. Don't miss this one.

At the end of Power Creek Road, six miles from town, a trail leads about a mile up to Ohman Falls—and when you see it you'll definitely say, "Oh man!" Continue another three miles on **Power Creek Trail** to the Power Creek Cabin.

The Forest Service maintains a number of trails along the Copper River Highway. Pick up a handout on these hikes at the Forest Service office in Cordova (907/424-7661).

Cabins

Ten Forest Service cabins are available for rent ($35) in the Cordova area; all but three are accessible only by plane or boat. There are cabins at both ends of the McKinley Lake Trail. If you've never seen one, hike for 75 yards up the McKinley Lake Trail (Mile 20) and peer in the windows. Staying here is quiet (except for the spawning salmon), secluded, and beautiful. The other foot-accessible cabin (Power Creek Cabin) is four miles north of Cordova via the Power Creek Trail. Make reservations through ReserveUSA (877/444-6777, www.reserveusa.com).

On the Water

Alaska River Rafters (907/424-7238 or 800/776-1864, www.alaskarafters.com) has a wide variety of rafting trips in the Cordova area, including a half-day run that includes iceberg-filled waters at the head of Sheridan Glacier and a rolling trip down the rapids of the Sheridan River ($75), all the way up to 10-day raft trips ($2,150) from headwaters of the Copper River to the Million Dollar Bridge. Longer floats all include a floatplane flight into Wrangell–St. Elias National Park. Good folks.

kayaking on Prince William Sound

The MV **Auklet** (907/424-3428, www.auklet.com) is a classic wooden boat that has been used as a fisheries research vessel. Captain Dave Janka leads overnight or multinight adventure cruises around Prince William Sound.

Cordova Coastal Outfitters (907/424-7424 or 800/357-5145, www.cdvcoastal.com) is a one-stop operation with sea kayak day trips and overnight tours, wildlife cruises in Orca Inlet, and shorebird jet boat trips of the Copper River Delta. In addition, they rent gear, including kayaks, canoes, small boats, inflatables, mountain bikes, fishing poles, and camping supplies. they even provide drop-off and pick-ups by van or boat.

Cordova's Olympic-size **swimming pool** (907/424-7282) is on Railroad Avenue.

Tours

Becky Chapek of **Copper River & Northwest Tours** (907/424-5356, www.northernnightsinn.com) runs excellent six-hour bus tours out to the Million Dollar Bridge and back for $40 per person (minimum six), snack included. In addition, she provides river pick-ups for rafters (from

38 mile $30, $25 per person from Flag Point, or $35 from the Million Dollar Bridge) and trail drop-offs for hikers and mountain bikers.

ACCOMMODATIONS

The Cordova Chamber's website (www.cordovachamber.com) has links for most local lodging places.

Hotels and Lodges

The **Alaskan Hotel** (in the heart of town on 1st St., 907/424-3299), is an old-time place with eight clean and well-maintained rooms over the Alaska Bar. Noise and smoke may carry up from below on weekends, but it's inexpensive and authentic. Simple rooms with a bath down the hall are only $39 s or d; those with a private bath cost $61 s or d.

Northern Nights Inn (907/424-5356, www.northernnightsinn.com) has four rooms with private baths and entrances, full kitchens, and more in a beautiful old downtown home facing the harbor. Rooms cost just $60 s or d. Owner Becky Chapek will help you find a spot if her place is full, and also runs Copper River & Northwest Tours.

The **Prince William Motel** (501 2nd St., 907/424-3201 or 888/796-6835, www.akbiz.com/princewilliammotel) has 16 attractive rooms for $90 s or $100 d. All include fridges and microwaves; kitchenettes are $20 extra.

Cordova Lighthouse Inn (Nicholoff Way at the harbor, 907/424-7080 or 888/424-7080, www.cordovalighthouseinn.com) houses four homey rooms (ask for one overlooking the harbor) for a reasonable $90 d.

An old cannery just north of Cordova has been transformed into **Orca Adventure Lodge** (907/424-7249 or 866/424-6722, www.orcaadventurelodge.com). The rambling buildings sit right on the water, and are decorated with historical items. The bunkhouse was transformed into a charming lodge where the attractive rooms all have private baths and ocean vistas. Lodging-only rates are $125 d or $150 for four in a two-bedroom suite. Add in three meals (served family style), kayaks, bikes, and airport transportation

for a popular package rate of $135 per person, half-price for kids. A wide range of other activities can be booked, including sea kayaking, fishing, flightseeing, and white-water rafting. For budget travelers, they also offer simple bunkhouse rooms for $50, with a bath down the hall.

Bed-and-Breakfasts and More

The Udder Inn (601 Lake Ave., 907/424-3895) has four rooms with private baths for $75 d, including continental breakfast. In a past life the building was a barn, hence the name. Other local B&Bs include **Johnson's Downtown B&B** (519 2nd St., 907/424-7773), **Enchanted Garden Lodging** (401 1st St., 907/424-5455), **The King's Chamber B&B** (907/424-3373, www.thekingschamber.com), and **Harbor View B&B** (907/424-7829).

Bear's Den Cabins (907/424-7168, www.bearsdencabins.com) consists of three delightful cabins located along the Eyak River six miles from town; $150 s or $170–250 d.

Cordova Rose Lodge (1315 Whitshed, 907/424-7673, www.cordovarose.com) has rooms in a converted landlocked barge surrounded by inlet waters. The private lighthouse acts as a navigation aid for ships. Rates are $100–125 d, including a full breakfast and a sauna.

Bear Country Lodge (907/424-5901, www.bearcountrylodge.net) is a private one-bedroom home with loft, full kitchen, and bath. It's three miles out of Cordova along Eyak Lake. The house rents for $100 s or $115 d.

Lighthouse Lodging

For something totally out of the ordinary, spend time at **Cape St. Elias Lighthouse** on Kayak Island in the wild Gulf of Alaska 60 air miles southeast of Cordova. This 22-mile long and two-mile wide island was the first place that Europeans landed on the Northwest coast of North America. Captain Vitus Bering set foot here in 1741, and the island remains virtually unchanged more than two and a half centuries later.

The nonprofit **Cape St. Elias Lightkeepers Association** (907/424-5182, www.alaskalighthouse.org) works with the Coast Guard to preserve the lighthouse at the southern end of the island. The old lightkeeper's house still needs work, but you can stay in a comfortable cabin with kitchen, woodstove, and space for 10 people; $70 d. No electricity or running water, and you'll need to hike an hour and a half from where the plane lands on the beach. It costs around $700 round-trip to fly from Cordova to Kayak Island. The lighthouse (built in 1916) is of interest, a Steller sea lion haulout and seabird rookery are nearby, and the beachcombing is some of the best in Alaska (lots of glass balls).

Camping

The city-run **Odiak Camper Park** (907/424-7282) is a half-mile out Whitshed Road. Camping on this gravel-surfaced area overlooking Orca Inlet is $5 for tents (with showers); RV sites are $18 (reservations required for these). It's open mid-April through September. Showers are also at the harbormaster's office.

Plopping down your tent close to town is a problem, since almost all of the land is owned by individuals or by a Native corporation. If you've got wheels, head out of town toward the Million Dollar Bridge, and as soon as you pass Mile 17, you're on Forest Service land. You can theoretically camp anywhere after this point, but the most comfortable places are at the roadside picnic area at Mile 22, or at the parking area of Alaganik Slough.

FOOD

A great place to eat brunch or lunch is the **Killer Whale Cafe** in the Orca Bookstore (507 1st Ave., 907/424-7733). The big breakfast menu includes all the standards, and lunchtime features sandwiches, homemade soups, and salads, along with baked goods and espresso coffees; sit upstairs for the view of the harbor. Closed Sundays.

Cordova Lighthouse Inn (907/424-7080, www.cordovalighthouseinn.com) faces the boat harbor, with artisan breads and pastries from their wood-fired oven. The café is open for healthy from-scratch breakfasts and lunches, with pizzas Thursday–Saturday nights. Closed Mondays.

Head two miles out the Copper River Highway to **Powder House Bar and Restaurant** (907/424-3529), where a deck overlooks pretty Lake Eyak. (Motto: "I got blasted at the Powder House.") Soups and sandwiches are featured, but it also has daily lunch specials, along with steak, shrimp, and salmon dinners on weekends. Open year-round.

Alaska Commercial Co. (on Nickoloff Rd., 907/424-7141) is the large supermarket in town. Nearby is **Baha Taco** (907/424-5599), which serves up fish tacos, burritos, breakfast burritos, espresso and other fast food all summer, but they wing south to Mexico for the winter months.

ENTERTAINMENT AND EVENTS

Cordova's **Iceworm Festival** (www.iceworm.org) comes to town the first full week of February. A 140-foot "iceworm" parades through the streets during this offbeat festival. Other events include a fun fair, talent show, crowning of Miss Iceworm, and various wacky contests.

The big springtime event is the **Copper River Delta Shorebird Festival** in early May. Held as the first shorebirds appear, it includes workshops, educational seminars, a seafood dinner, and guided field trips to witness the migration of millions of shorebirds.

The arrival of the justly famous Copper River reds (sockeye salmon) is cause for celebration in this fishing town, The **Wild Salmon Festival** in early June includes a community salmon feed, street dance, and marathon race up the Copper River Highway.

Don't come to Cordova for the night life; other than drinking with the seafood folks, it's strictly make-your-own. The **Alaskan** and **Cordova** bars, next to each other on 1st Avenue, and the **Anchor Bar** on Breakwater Avenue, are hard-core. The Alaskan often has live bands on summer weekends. At the **Powder House** a mile out the Copper River Highway, you can have a drink on the deck along Eyak Lake.

INFORMATION AND SERVICES

Anything you want to know about Cordova you can find out at the **Cordova Chamber of Commerce** (401 1st St., 907/424-7260, www.cordovachamber.com). It's open Tuesday–Friday

10 A.M.–5 P.M., Saturday and Monday 10 A.M.–2 P.M. in the summer, and weekdays the rest of the year. Also stop by the Chugach National Forest **Cordova Ranger District office** (2nd Ave., 907/424-7667, www.fs.fed.us, Mon.–Fri. 8 A.M.–5 P.M.) for local maps, handouts, and info on cabins and trails. **Cordova Community Medical Center** (907/424-8000) is the local hospital.

Jenny Parks of **Copper River Fleece** (907/424-4304) crafts hand-sewn outerwear using wind-stop material. A bit pricey, but the designs are beautiful, warm, and durable. Her shop is in the old harbor area on Breakwater Avenue. Recommended.

TRANSPORTATION

Ferry

The Alaska Marine Highway (907/465-3941 or 800/642-0066, www.ferryalaska.com) has frequent passenger and vehicle ferry service between Cordova and Valdez in the summer, with the high-speed **MV Chenega** beginning service in 2005. It's a 20-minute walk from the Cordova ferry terminal to town; take a right at the fork onto Railroad Avenue to avoid the 1st Avenue hill, then walk up Council Avenue.

Air

The airport is 13 miles from town out the Copper River Highway. **Alaska Airlines** (800/426-0333, www.alaskaair.com) provides daily connections to Anchorage and Juneau. **Era Aviation** (800/866-8394, www.flyera.com) flies turboprops two or three times a day between Cordova and Anchorage. **Cordova Air Service** (907/424-3289) has charter flights throughout the Prince William Sound.

Getting Around

If you want to get out to the glaciers or Million Dollar Bridge, you have a number of options. You can ferry your own car across from Valdez, but advance reservations are needed. **Cordova Auto Rental** (907/424-5982, www.ctcak.net/~cars) rents cars, pickups, and vans for $70 a day.

Catch a cab ($18 to town from the airport, or $4 within the downtown area) from **Wild Hare Taxi** (907/424-3939) or **Cordova Taxicab** (907/424-5151). Half-hour town tours are $15 per person.

Whittier

Named for poet John Greenleaf Whittier, this town of 300 friendly people has a picturesque mountains-and-bay setting. Unfortunately, the town itself is anything but poetic, and several other less flattering words come more quickly to mind. Thousands of tourists pass through this settlement every week, but very few choose to spend much time in this strange place where the entire population lives in concrete high-rises and the wind never seems to stop. Ask an Alaskan about Whittier and you're likely to hear the little ditty, "nothing could be shittier than a day in Whittier." Okay, perhaps I'm too harsh, since Whittier *does* have a gorgeous setting and lots of great outdoorsy things to do in nearby Prince William Sound. So come here for the surrounding land, but don't expect to fall in love with the town.

HISTORY

While less well known than the Alaska Highway, the construction of the railway to Whittier was one of the great engineering feats of World War II. Two tunnels, one mile and 2.5 miles long, were carved through the Chugach Mountains to link the military bases in Anchorage and Fairbanks to a secret saltwater port. Seward, the main ice-free port in Southcentral Alaska at that time, was considered too vulnerable to Japanese attack, so from 1941 to 1943 the Army blasted through the mountains and laid the tracks that would ensure the flow of supplies for the defense of Alaska. After the defeat of Japan, the military pulled out of Whittier, but a year later they were back as the Cold War began with the Soviet Union. Whittier became a permanent base, and large concrete buildings were built at that time. The 14-story Begich Tower (completed in 1954), an unlikely skyscraper in this small village, is near another anomaly, the "City Under One Roof," which once housed 1,000 men and was the largest building in Alaska. Why build high-rises? To lessen the need for snow removal in a place where the snow sometimes tops 14 feet.

The base was deactivated in 1960 and the buildings were heavily damaged in the 1964 earthquake. One of them is still vacant, but Begich Tower has been restored and converted into condos. A third high-rise, Whittier Manor, was privately built in the 1950s and later turned into more condos. The military presence today is limited to an oil pipeline that supplies military installations in Anchorage. Princess Cruises stops in Whittier, but most of their passengers quickly depart the town.

For nearly half a century the town of Whittier was connected to the road system only via the Alaska Railroad. This changed in 2000, when an $80 million project made it possible for cars to drive in directly from the Seward Highway through two tunnels, one of which is shared with the railroad.

SIGHTS

Most travelers never get farther than the tourist action on the waterfront, where boats of all sizes bob in the picturesque harbor.

Follow the signs for Whittier down past the dry dock, then go left across the tracks onto Whittier Street. Take a right on Glacier Avenue to the **Begich Tower.** In its 198 condos live most of the town's population; the rest reside in the 70 condos at **Whittier Manor.** Many are owned by Anchoragites who use them for weekend and summer getaways, boosting Whittier's summer population to nearly 1,000. The little **Whittier Museum** (907/472-2667, open daily in summer) houses exhibits on local history in a new building adjacent to Anchor Inn. Admission is $3 adults, $1.50 ages 7–12, or free for younger kids.

Continue a quarter-mile out Eastern Avenue to quiet, scenic **Smitty's Cove,** where one of Whittier's few private residences sits. You'll get a great view across Passage Canal of waterfalls, a kittiwake rookery, and Billing's Glacier.

UP PORTAGE PASS

The most popular Whittier trail is up to Portage Pass. In the early days when gold was discovered around Hope on the Kenai Peninsula, Hope-bound hopefuls would boat to this harbor, portage their supplies over the glacier pass, and float down Turnagain Arm to their destination. This highly recommended day hike from Whittier affords splendid views of Passage Canal, Portage Glacier, and the Chugach Mountains. On a clear day, the views of the glacier from the Portage Pass area are far superior to those from the Portage Visitor Center.

This trail starts near the oil tanks and tunnel entrance at the foot of Maynard Mountain. Cross the tracks on the dirt road to the left. Take the road to the right and climb southwest along the flank of the mountain up a wide, easy track. If you walk briskly, you can be at Portage Pass (elevation 700 feet) in less than an hour. There are places to camp or picnic beside Divide Lake, but beware of strong winds at the pass. From the lake follow the stream down toward the glacier, then find a way via a tributary on the right up onto one of the bluffs for a view of Portage Lake. Deep crevasses in the blue glacial ice are clearly visible from here. **Portage Glacier** has receded far enough that the gold-rush route is no longer traversable, because of the lake. You must go back the way you came. This hike is highly recommended; allow a minimum of three hours roundtrip. Note that there is no clear trail beyond Divide Lake; you must find your own way. Do not attempt to walk on the glacier itself, as the crevasses can be deadly.

BOAT TOURS

Whittier is a popular departure point for day trips to the glaciers of Prince William Sound. **Phillips Tours and Cruises** (907/276-8023 or 800/544-0529, www.26glaciers.com) operates the 4.5-hour, 26-Glacier Cruise for $129 ($69 kids). The trip aboard its 340-passenger *Klondike Express*—

a high-speed (45-knot!), three-deck catamaran-covers a lot of ground but still allows plenty of time to linger at the faces of several glaciers. A hot lunch is included, there's a bar on board, and the lounges provide plenty of room inside should the weather be less than perfect.

Prince William Sound Cruises and Tours (907/835-4731 or 800/992-1297, www.princewilliamsound.com), runs a 5.5-hour "Wilderness Explorer" tour that includes Barry Arm (Barry and Cox Glaciers) and Esther Passage; $109 adults, $54 kids under 12. Their four-hour trip to Blackstone Glacier is $79 adults, $39 kids.

Major Marine Tours (907/274-7300 or 800/764-7300, www.majormarine.com) takes visitors on a leisurely 5.5-hour voyage into stunning Blackstone Bay daily. Rates are $99 adults, $50 for ages 2–11, free for tots. The cruise includes a filling salmon and prime rib buffet for an extra $12 adults, $6 kids.

In addition to these large operators, a number of locals offer small-boat trips into Prince William Sound. The prices may be a bit higher, but you get a more personal journey. Recommended companies for sightseeing, fishing, and kayak drop-offs are **Honey Charters** (907/472-2493 or 888/477-2493, www.honeycharters.com), **Lazy Otter Charters** (907/345-1175 or 800/587-6887, www.lazyotter.com), and **Sound Eco Adventures** (907/472-2312 or 888/471-2312, www.soundecoadventure.com).

SEA KAYAKING

Although it is possible to paddle from Whittier to the heart of Prince William Sound, most people prefer to get a boat ride out so they can spend more time near the glaciers and wild country that make this such a special place. A number of local water taxis provide these services, transporting sea kayaks, paddlers, and their gear, and picking them up several days later.

Prince William Sound Kayak Center (907/472-2452 or 877/472-2452, www.pwskayakcenter.com) mainly rents kayaks but also offers instruction and guided tours.

Two other companies offer guided day trips (starting with a $70 three-hour paddle to the kit-

tiwake colony): **Alaska Outdoor Adventures** (907/783-7669, www.akadventures.com) and **Alaska Sea Kayakers** (907/472-2534 or 877/472-2534, www.alaskaseakayakers.com). Both also lead multinight tours and rent sea kayaks.

ACCOMMODATIONS AND CAMPING

New in 2004, **The Inn at Whittier** (907/472-7000 or 866/858-7549, www.innatwhittier.com) is an impressive luxury lodge right on Whittier's harbor. Rooms start at $199 d facing the mountains, or $249 d on the water side. Townhouse suites with two levels, a jacuzzi tub, and other luxuries will set you back $799 d.

June's Whittier B&B (907/472-2396 or 888/472-2396, www.breadnbuttercharters.com) consists of 10 condo suites on the 14th and 15th floors of Begich Tower, starting for $98 d in a one-bedroom apartment, up to $300 for a three-bedroom unit that sleeps six. A continental breakfast is included.

Soundview Getaway B&B (907/472-2358 or 800/515-2358, www.soundviewalaska.com) features waterside condo units for $100 d or $125 for four people, including a continental breakfast.

Anchor Inn (907/472-2354 or 877/870-8787, www.whittierhotel.us) has basic rooms for $80 s or $85 d, but noise from the bar can keep you awak. Also here is a restaurant, grocery store, gift shop, and launderette.

Camping beside **Begich Tower** (907/472-2670, $10) is plentiful, with secluded spots for tents and RVs, and a shelter for cooking and socializing in the rain. No hookups or running water, but you can use bathrooms on the first floor of Begich Tower, and showers are available at the harbormaster's office.

FOOD

Rolling Pin Bakery (907/472-2562), serves pastries, homemade bread, and breakfast fare in Begich Tower. In addition to espresso, breakfast burritos, sandwiches, and salads, **Cafe Orca** has a pleasant waterside deck with picnic tables for sunny mornings.

Swiftwater Cafe (907/472-2550) is a popular spot for fish and chips, halibut burgers, and seafood chowder; nothing over $11. **Hobo Bay Trading Company** (907/472-2374), is open for lunch and dinner: fresh fish, burgers, burritos, and good pies.

China Sea Restaurant (907/472-2222) has a $9 lunch buffet with soup and salad bar, and **Lisa's Ice Cream Parlor** (907/472-2459) is especially popular on those rare sunny days in summer.

The Inn at Whittier (907/472-7000, www.innatwhittier.com) serves Alaska and New England fare in a gorgeous waterside setting, with prices to match.

INFORMATION AND SERVICES

Anchor Inn has a small grocery store, but don't miss the classic **Harbor Store,** a combination grocery/dry goods/clothing/sporting goods/laundromat/hardware/bait-and-tackle/supermarket/department store—all in an ATCO trailer. The post office is on the first floor of Begich Tower; the **library** is in the firehall. Get **showered** at the Harbor Office, next to Hobo Bay.

Log Cabin Gifts (907/472-2501) features arts and crafts items, ivory, and watercolors by the owner, Wilma Buethe Wilcox. You can pet, photograph, and even feed the two pet **reindeer** next door.

The main Whittier events—other than the rain in summer, snow in winter, and year-round wind—is the **Fourth of July** celebration featuring a parade, picnic, kid's games, and fireworks. Also check out the **sailing regatta** in early May.

TRANSPORTATION

Whittier is accessible by boat, ferry, train, or car. Drivers get here by turning from Seward Highway at Mile 79 (50 miles south of Anchorage) onto Portage Glacier Highway. The road to Whittier splits off near the Begich, Boggs Visitor Center, heading through a 400-foot tunnel before emerging into Bear Valley. Here you'll find a staging area for access to the 2.5-mile **Anton Anderson Memorial Tunnel** that is shared by both trains and cars. It's the longest auto tunnel in North America, and perhaps the only tunnel in the world where the same roadbed is used by both rail and auto traffic. The tunnel is open to one-way travel throughout the day; get a schedule at 907/472-2584 or 877/611-2586, www.dot.state.ak.us. The east-bound toll is $12 for autos; no charge heading west. The tunnel is not recommended for anyone with claustrophobia, and you will be driving on an odd roadbed over the railroad tracks. There are pullouts for emergency use, and enormous fans to clean the air after freight trains pass through.

Alaska Heritage Tours (907/265-4500 or 877/258-6877, www.ahtours.com) operates a summertime shuttle between Anchorage and Whittier for $26 each way.

Railroad

The **Alaska Railroad** (907/265-2494 or 800/544-0552, www.akrr.com) train connects Whittier with Anchorage daily in the summer, departing Anchorage at 10 A.M. and arriving in Whittier at 12:30 P.M. The northbound train leaves Whittier at 6:45 P.M. and arrives in Anchorage at 9:15 P.M.; $55 round-trip. This makes an excellent day trip from the city. A trivia note: The route to Whittier was used in scenes from the 1986 film *Runaway Train.*

Ferry

The Alaska Marine Highway (907/465-3941 or 800/642-0066, www.ferryalaska.com) has frequent passenger and vehicle ferry service between Whittier and Valdez in the summer, with the high-speed **MV *Chenega*** starting service in 2005.

The Interior

Interior Alaska is a great tilted plateau between the crests of two long mountain ranges, the Alaska Range and the Brooks Range. The mighty Yukon and Tanana rivers are the main features of this region, but vast expanses of rolling hills are usually in view. Interior Alaska has one medium-sized city, Fairbanks, several small towns, and a number of bush villages, the most interesting along the rivers but some beside the highways. Much of the region is expensive or inaccessible to visit without your own vehicle, but great adventures await on the many wild and scenic rivers, in the wildlife refuges, and in the national parks, especially spectacular Denali National Park.

riverboat *Discovery* on the Chena River near Fairbanks

Talkeetna

The outdoorsy and youthful town of Talkeetna (pop. 360) lies at the end of a 14-mile side road that splits away from the Parks Highway 98 miles north of Anchorage and 111 miles south of Fairbanks. Two closely related phenomena dominate this small bush community: The Mountain, and flying to and climbing on The Mountain. On a clear day, from the overlook a mile out on the Spur Road, Mt. McKinley and the accompanying Alaska Range scrape the sky like a jagged white wall. Though still 60 miles northwest, you actually have to crane your neck to see the summit of the highest peak in North America.

Also on a clear day, local flightseeing and air-taxi companies take off in a continuous parade to circle Mt. McKinley, buzz up long glaciers or even land on them for a champagne lunch, then return to Talkeetna's busy airport to drop off passengers whose wide eyes, broad smiles, and shaky knees attest to the excitement of this once-in-a-lifetime thrill. From late April to early July, these same special "wheel-and-ski" planes might be delivering an American, European, Japanese, or Russian climbing expedition to the Kahiltna Glacier (elevation 7,000 feet), from where—if they're lucky—they inch their way up the popular West Buttress route 13,000 feet to the peak. On a clear day, if you're anywhere within striking distance, make a beeline for Talkeetna and be whisked away to some of the most stunning and alien scenery you'll ever see.

If you visit Talkeetna early in the summer you'll find a peculiar mixing of people: the earthy locals with their beards and rusty pickups, the mountaineers—mostly male—decked in color-coordinated Gore-Tex, and the busloads of cruise ship passengers who unload on the south side of town and wander through in a dazed blur of gawks and photo-ops.

Talkeetna (Where the Rivers Meet), nesting at the confluence of the Talkeetna, Chulitna, and Susitna Rivers, was originally settled by trappers and prospectors who paddled up the Susitna River to gain access to rich silver, coal, and fur country around the Talkeetna Mountains. The settlement got a boost when the railroad was pushed through in the early 1920s and still remains a popular stop on the route. In 1965 the Spur Road from the Parks Highway to Talkeetna was completed, providing further access to the town.

At the intersection of the Parks Highway and the Talkeetna Spur Road is a helpful visitor center. Covering the area from Willow (south) to Healy (north), the **Talkeetna/Denali Visitor Center** (907/733-2688 or 800/660-2688, www.alaskan .com/talkeetnadenali, daily 10 A.M.–6 P.M. mid-May to mid-Sept.) is staffed by friendly and informative local residents. The rest of the year, the visitor center is above Talkeetna Air Taxi at the airport. Folks here can book flightseeing trips, fishing expeditions, guided hikes, and rooms at hotels and B&Bs, or just supply brochures and information on the area. The Talkeetna Chamber of Commerce (907/733-2330, www.talkeetna-chamber.com) has a useful website, and can send out brochures.

SIGHTS

Talkeetna is a wonderful walk-around town, with most of the action within a couple of blocks from Nagley's Store and Fairview Inn. This is one of the few Alaskan towns that still looks the way people imagine Alaskan towns should look, with rustic log buildings lining main street and a local population that encompasses grizzled redneck miners and back-to-the-earth tree-huggers. Local bumper stickers proclaim "Talkeetna, where the road ends and life begins." If you ever saw *Northern Exposure* on TV, this is the place it must have been modeled upon.

For a graphic and detailed look at the history of the town and its connection to The Mountain, check out the excellent **Talkeetna Historical Museum** (907/733-2487, $3). Take a left after Nagley's Store, which you can read all about in the museum; the museum is a half-block down the side street on the right in an old red schoolhouse, open daily 10:30 A.M.–6:30 P.M. May–September, and Friday–Sunday 10:30 A.M.–6:30 P.M. the rest of the year.

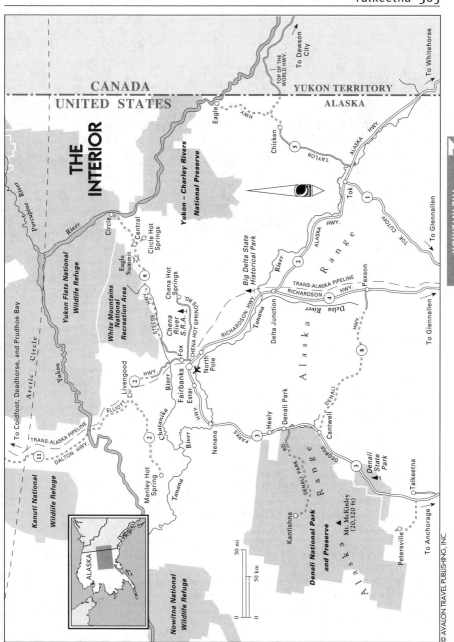

THE INTERIOR

CANADA
UNITED STATES

YUKON TERRITORY
ALASKA

THE INTERIOR

To Dawson City
To Whitehorse
TOP OF THE WORLD HWY.

Eagle
HWY
Chicken
5
TAYLOR
ALASKA HWY.
Tok
1
TOK CUTOFF
To Glennallen

Yukon – Charley Rivers National Preserve

Circle
Central
Circle Hot Springs
Eagle Summit
6
Chena Hot Springs
STEESE HWY.
Chena River S.R.A.
Fox
CHENA HOT SPRINGS RD.
Fairbanks
Ester
PARKS HWY.
North Pole

Big Delta State Historical Park
RICHARDSON HWY.
TRANS-ALASKA PIPELINE
RICHARDSON HWY.
Delta Junction
Tanana River
4
Paxson
Delta River
8
HWY.
To Glennallen

Alaska Range

Porcupine River
River
Yukon Flats National Wildlife Refuge
Arctic Circle
Yukon
To Coldfoot, Deadhorse, and Prudhoe Bay
TRANS-ALASKA PIPELINE
ELLIOTT HWY.
DALTON HWY.
11
Kanuti National Wildlife Refuge

White Mountains National Recreation Area

Livengood
2 HWY
Chatanika River
2
Manley Hot Spring
Tanana River
Nenana
Healy
Denali Park
3
DENALI PARK RD.
GEORGE PARKS HWY.
Cantwell
DENALI HWY.
3
Denali State Park
Talkeetna

Kantishna
Mt. McKinley (20,320 ft)
Denali National Park and Preserve
Alaska Range
Petersville
To Anchorage

Nowitna National Wildlife Refuge

ALASKA

0   50 mi
0   50 km

© AVALON TRAVEL PUBLISHING, INC.

In business since 1921, Nagley's Store is a classic frontier general store.

Housing hundreds of historical articles, including an eclectic library in the back room with eyebrow-raising old magazines and scrapbooks of newspaper clippings, the museum is dedicated to Don Sheldon and Ray Genet, hometown boys who were two of Alaska's most heroic figures. Sheldon was the honorary guiding light of Alaska's elite fraternity of bush pilots until his untimely death from cancer in 1975 at the age of 56; Genet was the all-time recordholder for climbs on McKinley and other Alaska Range peaks until his untimely death at 27,000 feet on Mt. Everest in 1979 at the age of 48. Separately and together, they pulled off some of the most daredevil rescues imaginable, and Sheldon's exploits have been immortalized in *Wager with the Wind*. Reading the displays devoted to these giants of northern lore will give you an idea of the kind of people who gravitate to Talkeetna. Also check out the original railroad depot with its restored ticket office, Ole Dahl's trapper cabin, and an old railroad section house with an impressive 3-D map of the region, along with photos and stories on local adventurers.

The Park Service's attractive log **Talkeetna Ranger Station** (B St., 907/733-2231) is open daily 8 A.M.–6 P.M. mid-April to early September, and Monday–Friday 8 A.M.–4:30 P.M. the rest of the year. It's a pleasant place to watch a video or look over the mountaineering books. Rangers give programs daily in the summer at the museum and Talkeetna Alaskan Lodge.

You might also glance at the **Museum of Northern Adventure** (Main St., 907/733-3999), a combination gift shop and private collection with north country dioramas; $2 adults or $1 kids.

RECREATION
Flightseeing

Talkeetna is famous as a launching point for flights over Mt. McKinley, and on a clear summer day a constant parade of planes takes off from the airport on the edge of town. The flight services in town offer a bewildering array of possibilities, including short scenic flights, glacier landings, drop-off hiking or fishing, wildlife viewing, overnight trips, and flights to, around, or over the top of The Mountain. Rates vary according to the type of airplane, length of the flight, and how many people there are in your group. Most out-fits will try to match you up with other folks to maximize your flightseeing dollar. Be flexible in your plans, since weather is infinitely variable and is always the most important consideration when it comes to flying you safely. Prices start around $135 pp for a one-hour ride; tack on $50 for a glacier landing. A flight to the summit of Mt. McKinley (good chance to see the climbers) is $195.

As always, reservations are recommended, but not always necessary. Note that the climbing season on Mt. McKinley runs from early spring until mid or late June, and the flight services are busiest then. As always with bush flying, risks are involved, and fatalities have taken the lives of some of the best local pilots and climbers over the years. Your odds are probably better (not to mention the vistas) if you wait until a clear day to fly.

A number of charter companies provide service to Mt. McKinley: **Hudson Air Service** (907/733-2321 or 800/478-2321, www.hudsonair.com), **Doug Geeting Aviation** (907/733-2366 or 800/770-2366, www.alaskaairtours.com), **K2 Aviation** (907/733-2291 or 800/764-2291, www.flyk2.com), **Talkeetna Aero Service** (907/733-2899 or 800/660-2688, www.talkeetnaaero.com), **Talkeetna Air Taxi** (907/733-2218 or 800/533-2219, www.talkeetnaair.com), and **Fly Denali** (907/733-7768 or 866/733-7768, www.flydenali.net). Owned by Rust's Flying Service of Anchorage, K2 Aviation is the largest of the five air taxi operators. Doug Geeting (of Doug Geeting Aviation, of course) is a world-famous bush pilot who has more experience on Denali than anyone—over 25 years.

Era Helicopters (907/683-2574 or 800/843-1947, www.flightseeingtours.com) also flies from Talkeetna; $315 for a 75-minute trip that includes a glacier landing in the park.

Rafting and Boating
Denali View Raft Adventures (907/733-2778 or 877/533-2778, www.denaliview.com) has three-hour Susitna River trips for $75 ($50 kids) and two-hour floats for $55 ($30 kids). **Talkeetna River Guides** (907/733-2677 or 800/353-2677,

www.talkeetnariverguides.com) offers two-hour Talkeetna River floats for $54, four-hour Chulitna River trips for $84, and the "Grand Slam" that includes a one-hour flight to Denali, lunch, a float down the Nenana River, and return flight to Talkeetna for $379.

Mahay's Riverboat Service (907/733-2223 or 800/736-2210, www.mahaysriverboat.com) has a very popular jetboat tour up the Susitna River: two hours for $50 ($25 kids). **Jet Boat Odyssey** (907/733-2511) offers a four-hour river trip into Denali National Park for $95.

Nenana Raft Adventures (907/683-7238 or 800/789-7238, www.raftdenali.com) runs multiday river trips, including a three-day expedition ($950) that begins in the Talkeetna River headwaters and floats all the way to Talkeetna.

Fishing
The fishing in Talkeetna is excellent all summer long; rainbow trout, grayling, Dolly Varden, and all five species of Pacific salmon are there for the catching. Local riverboat services can supply you with a fishing guide or drop you off along the river for the day or overnight. Contact Mahay's Riverboat Service, **Denali Anglers** (907/733-1505 or 866/733-1505, www.denalianglers.com), **Sandfish Tackle** (907/733-7263, www.sandfishtackle.com, for fly-fishing), or **Tri-River Charters** (907/733-2400, www.tririvercharters.com).

D&S Alaskan Trail Rides (907/733-2205, www.alaskantrailrides.com) has wagon rides and guided horseback rides into the country around Talkeetna.

Biking
A paved bike path parallels the Spur Road all the way to Talkeetna. Turn off onto gravel roads at Miles 3 and 12 for out-of-the-way lakes and camping spots. At Mile 13 is the big turnout with an interpretive sign on the Alaska Range and heart-stopping views—if the clouds are co-operating. **Talkeetna Alaskan Lodge** is on the opposite side of the road; stop in for the Mt. McKinley view from its Great Room even if you aren't overnighting here.

ACCOMMODATIONS

Hostel

Talkeetna Hostel International (907/733-4678, www.talkeetnahostel.com) is a good option for budget travelers. The beds are comfortable, the location—a few blocks east of downtown on I St.—is convenient, and the rate is just $25 per person in a dorm room or $60 d for a private room. There are showers, a full kitchen, mountain bike rentals, internet access, TV room, and no curfew. Additional hostel beds can be found at Talkeetna Roadhouse, below.

Hotels

Talkeetna Roadhouse (907/733-1351, www.talkeetnaroadhouse.com) has simple but clean rooms for $47 s or $63–89 d, and a four-bed coed hostel for $21 per bed. All rooms have shared baths in this classic Alaskan lodge, in business since 1944.

Historic **Fairview Inn** (907/733-2423, www.mtdenali.com, $50 s, $60 d), built in 1923, has reasonable rates, but its six rooms over the bar fill up fast. Take your chances and register at the bar, or reserve ahead. There's music most nights, so don't come here for a restful night.

Latitude 62 Motel (907/733-2262, www.latitude62.com), is a two-story log building with a 10 standard rooms for $60 s or $70 d. **Talkeetna Motel** (907/733-2323), charges $80 d for modern economy rooms, up to $145 for four guests in a larger ones.

Swiss-Alaska Inn (907/733-2424, www.swissalaska.com) has 20 motel rooms with private baths for $90 s or $110 d.

Eye of Denali Inn (907/733-2655, www.eyeofdenali.com) is a beautiful log home along the Susitna River, with four guest rooms ($80–120 d), a kitchen, and shared baths.

Talkeetna Alaskan Lodge (907/733-9500 or 888/959-9590, www.talkeetnalodge.com) sits atop a hill a mile south of Talkeetna, with spacious, modern rooms for $225 d ($350 d for those that face Mt. McKinley). Luxury suites are $399–499 d, and all guests have access to the whirlpool tub and fine-dining restaurant. The grand lobby includes a stone fireplace and towering windows framing The Mountain. This 200-room Native-owned lodge serves up a million-dollar views for an upscale clientele. It's pretty much the opposite of most Talkeetna lodging places.

Cabins

Chinook Wind Cabins (907/733-1899 or 800/643-1899, www.talkeetna-alaska.net) has six modern cabins ($130 d), each with kitchenette and private bath; two have upstairs lofts. Bed-and-breakfast rooms in the main house are $70 s or $80 d.

Paradise Lodge & Cabins (907/733-1471, www.paradiselodge.net) is aptly named, with a delightful location along Fish Lake south of Talkeetna. Rustic cabins rent for $125 d with a shared bathhouse. Breakfast is served in the lodge.

Talkeetna Cabins (907/733-2227 or 888/733-9933, www.alaska.net/~talcabin) has recently built cabins with full kitchens, private baths, and continental breakfasts; $125 d or $155 for four people.

Susitna River Lodging (907/733-1505 or 866/733-1505, www.susitna-river-lodging.com) has modern cedar cabins ($189 d) and lodge rooms ($149–169 d) just a few minutes walk from downtown Talkeetna. All rooms have private baths and kitchenettes.

Bed-and-Breakfasts

Denali View B&B (907/733-2778 or 877/533-2778, www.denaliview.com) is one of the most elaborate homes in the area. Located three miles up the Spur Road (11 miles south of Talkeetna), the home has commanding views of Mt. McKinley and the upper Susitna Valley. Two rooms are available in the house for $135 d, with queen beds, antiques, private baths, and a full breakfast.

Trapper John's B&B (907/733-2353 or 800/735-2354, www.alaska.net/~trapperj) is the real thing, a cozy red-roofed log cabin built in the 1920s, with a full kitchen and "the finest outhouse in town." The cabin goes for $95 d or $125 for four people, including a sourdough pancake breakfast.

Five miles east of town, **Traleika B&B** (907/733-2711, www.traleika.com) has a mountaintop location facing Denali. The guesthouse rents for $160 d, and a smaller cottage is $130 d. Both have full baths and kitchens.

Built in 1946 and beautifully maintained **Fireweed Station** (907/733-1457 or 888/647-1457, www.fireweedstation.com) is a gorgeous log home at Mile 2 of Talkeetna Spur Road. The entire upstairs is a spacious suite ($200 d), and downstairs are three guest rooms ($150–175). A restored 1930s log cabin is $125 d; all rates include a full breakfast.

Owned by wildlife photographer Steve Gilroy, **Denali Overlook Inn** (907/733-3555, www.denalioverlook.com) is a memorable home where the view really does meet up with your expectations. On a clear day you can't miss Mt. McKinley and the rest of the Alaska Range. Five bedrooms have private baths, and guests love the great room and the outdoor hot tub. Rates are $175 d in standard rooms, or $225 for the master suite, including a big breakfast. It doesn't get much better than this!

Other local B&Bs worth a look include **Talkeetna Landings B&B** (907/733-8500), **Freedom Hills B&B** (907/733-3444), and **Beverly's B&B** (907/354-7472 or 800/733-9025).

CAMPING

Find free camping at shady **River Park** at the end of Main Street, but no running water. **Talkeetna Camper Park** (907/733-2693, www.talkeetnacamper.com) is just up from the railroad depot, and charges $26 for full hookups.

Take showers or wash your clothes at **Washi-Washi** or **Three Rivers Tesoro** (907/733-2621).

FOOD AND ENTERTAINMENT

Talkeetna has turned into quite the spot for good, inexpensive food, a definite rarity on the Alaska road system.

At **Talkeetna Roadhouse** (907/733-1351, www.talkeetnaroadhouse.com) breakfast starts at 7 A.M. and late risers can still get a filling breakfast until 3 P.M. (when it closes). Their cinnamon rolls are legendary, and for lunch the Roadhouse cranks out homemade soups, salads, and sandwiches with its freshly baked breads.

Nagley's Store (907/733-3663, www.nagleys generalstore.com) opened in the 1920s, and is still the main place for groceries in town, but it's also added such staples of 21st-century life as an ATM and espresso.

Behind Nagley's is **West Rib Deli and Pub** (907/733-3663, www.westribpub.com), with steaks, seafood, ribs, sandwiches, salads (try the grilled salmon salad), and Alaskan brews on draught. Best deal? Meet the locals at the Friday night burger-and-beer for just $5. There's an outside deck for sunny days.

Housed in a modern log building, **Main Street Cafe** (907/733-1275) is popular for a cheeseburger and fries, cheesesteak sandwich, chicken salad, or veggie burger. They also have nightly dinner specials.

Mt. High Pizza Pie (907/733-1234), in the purple log cabin, is a busy spot for great pizzas, along with salads and subs. A "super slice" is $3.50.

Swiss-Alaska Inn (907/733-2424) serves fresh halibut and salmon dinners, and has a cocktail lounge. German spoken.

One place really stands out in Talkeetna, **Cafe Michele** (907/733-5300, www.cafemichele.com), where the bistro atmosphere is decidedly classy and the menu includes such treats as venison flank steak, soy-ginger king salmon, or basil-walnut pasta. Entrées run $17–25. Open for lunch and dinner and highly recommended.

The classic **Fairview Inn** (907/733-2423, www.mtdenali.com) has live bands nightly in the summer, and is a great place to soak up the atmosphere (not to mention the smoke).

Events

Talkeetna likes to party. The **Talkeetna Moose Dropping Festival** takes place the second weekend of July, with a parade, mountain mother contest, food and craft booths, and the infamous moose nugget toss and moose nugget dropping contests. If you don't know what moose nuggets are, just ask any Alaskan.

The other big event in these parts is the **Talkeetna Bluegrass Festival** (907/495-6718, www.talkeetnabluegrass.com), held the first weekend of August at Mile 102 of the Parks Highway. "Alaska's greatest campout," this is a great chance to get in touch with your earthy side, hang out with the Deadheads, and see what mind-altering substances are in fashion. The music rarely strays to bluegrass; more often it's rock, folk, or blues. Great fun, even if it rains.

When winter arrives with a vengeance, **Talkeetna Winterfest** comes to town to brighten the December spirits, especially those of the many local bachelors. The main events are a Wilderness Woman Contest that includes all sorts of wacky activities, followed later that evening by a Bachelor Society Ball during which local bachelors are bid upon by single women, many of whom drive up from Anchorage for the chance. It has all the sexual energy of a male stripper night, except that some of the men are considerably less fit and keep their clothes on (at least during the bidding). This is one of Alaska's most authentic winter events.

INFORMATION AND SERVICES

Several local shops are worth a visit, including **Talkeetna Chocolate Corner** (733-2457), in a historic log cabin on the west end of Main Street. **Talkeetna Artisans** (907/733-4222) is upstairs over the gas station, with photography, watercolor, and more. Across the street find Steve Gilroy's fine wildlife and nature photos at **Denali Images Art Gallery** (907/733-2026, www.stevegilroy.com).

Keep in touch with the outside world via the internet at the library. Other spots to check your email are Talkeetna Natural Foods Cafe and Talkeetna Travel.

For outdoor gear, topo maps, and climbing supplies, head to **Talkeetna Outdoor Center** (on Main St., 907/733-4444). They rent gear, and this is also a good place to set up backcountry hikes, glacier treks, and other adventures. Check their bulletin board for used items. The same folks run **Alaska Wilderness Journeys** (907/733-2230 or 800/349-0064, www.alaska-journeys.com), with a big range of wilderness treks throughout Interior Alaska.

GETTING THERE

The turnoff to Talkeetna is 100 miles north of Anchorage on the George Parks Highway, and the town is another 14 miles out Talkeetna Spur Road.

Bus Service

Several companies provide van transportation to Talkeetna; one-way rates are around $55 to Anchorage, $55 to Denali, or $75 to Fairbanks.

Alaska Trails (907/479-3065 or 888/600-6001, www.alaskashuttle.com) has a daily Anchorage–Talkeetna–Denali–Fairbanks run in the summer, and five times a week service the rest of the year.

Talkeetna Shuttle Service (907/733-2222 or 888/288-6008, www.denalicentral.com) connects Anchorage with Talkeetna daily during the climbing season (May–mid-July), less often the rest of the summer, and on request at other times.

Denali Overland Transportation (907/733-2384 or 800/651-5221, www.denalioverland.com) has charter service to Talkeetna and Denali on a regular basis.

Alaska Park Connection (907/245-0200 or 800/208-0200, www.alaskacoach.com) connects Talkeetna with Seward, Anchorage, and Denali.

Railroad

The Alaska Railroad (907/265-2494 or 800/544-0552, www.alaskarailroad.com) charges $78 one-way to Talkeetna. The train leaves Anchorage every morning at 8:15, arrives in Talkeetna at 11:25, and a second train leaves for the return trip at 4:40 P.M. A local "flag-stop" train runs the 50 miles from Talkeetna north to Hurricane Thursday–Sunday in the summer. It's a great way to see the countryside with locals for $33 each way.

North from Talkeetna

TRAPPER CREEK AND PETERSVILLE ROAD

The minuscule settlement of Trapper Creek (pop. 350) is at Mile 115 of the Parks Highway, and 16 miles north of the junction with Talkeetna Spur Road. Petersville Road splits off at Trapper Creek, providing access to the western end of Denali State Park, and offering some of the finest views of Mt. McKinley. A half-mile out Petersville Road is **Trapper Creek Museum** (907/733-2555), a collection of local historical items and local crafts in a log cabin built in 1959. The museum is on Spruce Lane Farms, which raises miniature horses.

A number of rural subdivisions and homesteads are found along Petersville Rd., and this is a popular winter destination for dog mushers and hordes of snowmobilers. The road continues all the way to old mining developments in the Petersville mining camp, 30 miles in, though the last section may not be passable without a high-clearance vehicle. The National Park Service is planning a new visitor center near Petersville, but don't look for it till 2006 or so. By the time it opens, the road will probably be paved the entire distance, and there's even talk of a train or tram to the site. Visit this wonderful area before the crowds get there!

Accommodations

Located at Mile 114 of the Parks Highway, **Trapper Creek Inn and General Store** (907/733-2302, www.alaskan.com/trappercreekinn) has rooms for $65–95 d. It also sells groceries and has a deli, laundromat with showers, and RV park.

Trapper Creek B&B (907/733-2234, www.trappercreekbedandbreakfast.com) has three rooms with a shared bath and full breakfast for a reasonable $50 s or $80 d. They're just off the Parks Highway on Petersville Road.

Nestled on a small lake with a spectacular Mt. McKinley view, **North Country B&B** (907/733-3981) is three miles out Petersville Road. Five guest rooms go for $70 s or $85 d with a continental breakfast and private baths.

Denali View Chalets (907/733-1333, www.denaliviewchalets.com) is two miles out Petersville Road; the cottages ($89 d) have kitchenettes and bathrooms, and can sleep up to 10 people.

Gate Creek Cabins (907/733-1393, www.gatecreekcabins.com) is 11 miles out the road, with six modern log cabins (the largest has four bedrooms) and a sauna; $121 d.

Happy Hearts of Denali (907/529-1695) has rental cabins ($65 d) 18 miles out the Petersville Road. Great views of Mt. McKinley from here.

Forks Roadhouse (907/733-1851), 19 miles in, is a classic Alaskan bush roadhouse with a genuine sense of history. Rooms upstairs above the bar are $45 d (bath down the hall), and basic cabins cost $70 for four people (bath inside the lodge). Breakfast, burgers, and sandwiches are served in the roadhouse, or you can shoot a game of pool and tip a brew in the bar.

McKinley Foothills B&B (907/733-1454, www.matnet.com/~mckinley) is near the Forks, with three rustic Alaskan cabins (with outhouse) for $60–70 d, or $75–90 d with breakfast.

DENALI STATE PARK

This 325,240-acre state park lies just southeast of Denali National Park and Preserve, and is bisected by the Parks Highway from Mile 132 to Mile 169. Situated between the Talkeetna Mountains to the east and the Alaska Range to the west, the landscape of Denali State Park varies from wide, glaciated valleys to alpine tundra. The Chulitna and Tokositna rivers flow through western sections of the park, while the eastern half is dominated by Curry Ridge and Kesugi Ridge, a 35 mile-long section of alpine country.

Denali State Park provides an excellent alternative wilderness experience to the crowds and hassles of its federal next-door neighbor. The Mountain is visible from all over the park, bears are abundant, and you won't need to stand in line for a permit to hike or camp while you wait for Mt. McKinley's mighty south face to show itself. Several trails offer a variety of hiking experiences and spectacular views. Trailhead parking is $5/day.

Sights

Denali State Park is best known for its breathtaking **views of Mt. McKinley** and the Alaska Range from pullouts along the Parks Highway. If The Mountain or even "just" some of the lower peaks of the Alaska Range are out, you won't need to read the next sentence to know what or where the sights are. The best viewpoint along the highway in the park, and the most popular, is at mile 135, where you will find an interpretive signboard and crowds of fellow travelers on a clear day. Set up your tripod and shoot, shoot, shoot. Other unforgettable viewpoints are at Miles 147, 158, and 162.

The **Alaska Veterans Memorial** at Mile 147 (within walking distance of Byers Lake Campground) consists of five monumental concrete blocks with stars carved out. Turn your back to the monument, and if you're lucky, there's blue-white McKinley, perfectly framed by tall spruce trees.

The western section of Denali State Park lies within the remote Peters Hills, an area known for its pristine Mt. McKinley vistas and open country. This section is accessed via the Petersville Road, described above.

Hiking

Little Coal Creek trailhead is at Mile 164, five miles south of the park's northern boundary. This is the park's gentlest climb to the alpine tundra—five miles east up the trail by Little Coal Creek, then you cut southwest along Kesugi Ridge with amazing views of the Range and glaciers; flags and cairns delineate the trail. Watch for bears! The trail goes 27 miles until it hooks up with Troublesome Creek Trail just up from Byers Lake Campground. About halfway there, **Ermine Lake Trail** cuts back down to the highway, an escape route in case of really foul weather.

Troublesome Creek Trail is so named because of frequent bear encounters; in fact, Troublesome Creek Trail is frequently closed in late summer and early fall because of the abundance of bears. It has two trailheads, one at the northeast tip of

Byers Lake (Mile 147), the other at Mile 138. The park brochure describes this 15-mile hike along Troublesome Creek as moderate. It connects with Kesugi Ridge Trail just up from Byers Lake or descends to the easy five-mile **Byers Lake Loop Trail,** which brings you around to both campgrounds. Just down and across the road from the Byers Lake turnoff is a family day hike along Lower Troublesome Creek—a gentle mile.

Camping and Cabins

Byers Lake Campground ($10) has large and uncrowded sites, water, outhouses, interpretive signs, and beautiful Byers Lake a stone's throw down the road. **Susitna Expeditions** (907/892-7727 or 800/891-6916, www.susitnaexpeditions.com) offers kayak rentals and tours, backcountry hikes, and nature walks from their base in the campground.

Just under two miles along the Loop Trail from the campground or across the lake by boat is **Lakeshore Campground,** with six primitive sites, outhouses, no running water, but unimpeded views of The Mountain and Range from your tent flap. Across the road and a quarter-mile south, **Lower Troublesome Creek Campground** ($5) has 20 sites and all the amenities of Byers Lake.

Also at Byers Lake is a popular **public-use cabin** (907/745-3975, www.alaskastateparks.org, $50/night).

Accommodations

Turn off the highway at Mile 133 for a one-mile side road into **McKinley Princess Lodge** (907/733-2900 or 800/426-0500, www.princessalaskalodges.com). This stylish 334-room retreat is famous for its riverside location and picture-perfect vistas of the Alaska Range and Mt. McKinley. Most rooms are filled with Princess cruise passengers, but anyone can stay or eat here. The lodge itself centers around a "great room" with a stone fireplace, a pianist at the grand piano most evenings, and enormous windows fronting the mountain. Lodging is $200 d in smaller buildings scattered around the grounds; ask for one of the new rooms with a king bed. There's also a small fitness center and two outdoor hot tubs. Get formal meals in the restaurant ($20–35 dinner entrées) or lighter fare in the café and pizza parlor. The lodge is open mid-May to mid-September.

Located at the southern edge of Denali State Park near Mile 134, **Mary's McKinley View Lodge** (907/733-1555, www.mckinleyview lodge.com) has a restaurant, great views of The Mountain out the big picture windows, and guest rooms ($75 d) with private baths. This is the home of Mary Carey, one of the most prolific Alaskan authors. You can buy auto-graphed copies of her dozen books, including her best known, *Alaska, Not for a Woman.* The lodge is run by Mary and her daughter, Jean Richardson, who writes children's books.

At Mile 144, **Byers Creek Station** (907/457-2333, www.byerscreek.com) has a general store, restaurant, gas, tent and RV sites, and showers, plus bunkhouse beds for $30 s or $50 d, and private cabins for $85 d.

DENALI HIGHWAY AND VICINITY

The Denali Highway, which stretches 136 miles east-west across the waist of mainland Alaska from Cantwell, 30 miles south of Denali Park to Paxson at Mile 122 of the Richardson High-

way, may be the best-kept secret in Alaska. Orig-inally the only road into Denali National Park, this beautiful side trip has been largely ignored by visitors since the opening of the George Parks Highway in 1971. Denali Highway is paved for 21 miles on the east end of the road (from Paxson to Tangle Lakes), and for three miles on the west-ern end, but the rest is well-maintained gravel, which has received an undeserved bad rap—usu-ally from folks hoping to set world land-speed records on their Alaska vacation.

The Denali Highway offers a varied selection of outstanding scenery and wildlife-viewing oppor-tunities. Much of the route punches through the foothills of the magnificent Alaska Range. This area is part of the home range of the huge Nelchina caribou herd (30,000 strong). In the fall they begin to group in the greatest numbers—sightings of several hundred caribou are not unusual.

The Denali Highway is closed from October through mid-May, but in the winter it becomes a popular trail for snowmobilers, dog mushers, and cross-country skiers. Die-hard Alaskans also use this trail in the winter for access to unparalleled ice fishing and caribou and ptarmigan hunting.

As always, travelers on the Denali Highway should be prepared for emergencies. Always carry a spare tire and tire-changing tools, water, some

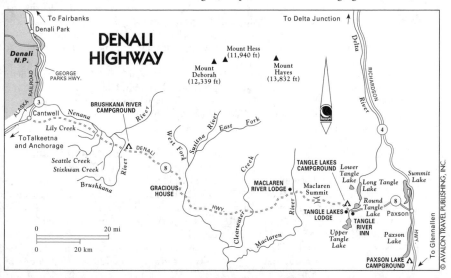

snacks, and warm clothing. Towing is available from Paxson, Gracious House, and Cantwell. But it ain't cheap, so take your time and be safe.

History
The Denali Highway began as a "cat" track in the early 1950s when a man named Earl Butcher first established a hunting camp at Tangle Lakes. Known for years as Butcher's Camp, it's now the site of Tangle Lakes Lodge. About the same time, Chalmer Johnson established a camp at Round Tangle Lake. Now known as the Tangle River Inn, this lodge is still operated by the Johnson family. The oldest known structure in the area is probably Whitey's Cabin at the Maclaren River Lodge. Built during the mid-1940s as a private residence, this old cabin serves as a rental unit at the lodge.

Cantwell
Cantwell is a minuscule settlement (pop. 160) at the junction of the Parks Highway and Denali Highway. The town began as a railroad settlement, and most of the decrepit buildings are along the tracks two miles west of the highway junction. Cantwell is less than 30 miles south of Denali National Park, and a couple of businesses provide the staples: fuel, food, lodging, and booze. Most folks stop to fill up on the expensive gas, get a soda, and tool on up the highway. There aren't a lot of reasons to stay in Cantwell itself, though the surrounding country is grand.

Cantwell Lodge (907/768-2300 or 800/768-5522) is the main action, though it's little more than a plywood box. Here you'll find motel units for $65 s or $75 d, a café, bar, liquor store, RV parking ($15), camping ($10), laundry, and showers ($2).

Backwoods Lodge (907/768-2232 or 800/292-2232, www.backwoodslodge.com) has modern motel rooms with fridges and microwaves for $120–130 d. **Denali Manor B&B** (907/768-2223 or 800/378-5990, www.denali-manor.com) charges $95 d, including a full breakfast. **Lazy J Cabins** (907/768-2414) has cozy log cabins with private baths. There's also a café, lounge, and even a hair salon.

Park RVs at **Cantwell RV Park** (907/768-2210 or 800/940-2210), an open lot just west of the junction with the Parks Highway.

Denali Sightseeing Safaris (907/240-0357, www.denalisights.com) operates from the igloo-on-steroids at Mile 188 of the Parks Highway (22 miles south of Cantwell). These unique tours are in customized big-tired trucks to allow them to cross glacial rivers and take you up old mining roads into the spectacular alpine. Seven-hour treks are $100 adults, $50 kids under 14.

EAST ON DENALI HIGHWAY
About three miles east of the Denali Highway/Parks Highway junction is a turnout with a view of Cantwell and Mt. McKinley, if it's out. There's another potential view of the mountain at Mile 13, then in another five miles the highway runs parallel to the Nenana River. The headwaters of the Nenana emanate from a western digit of the icefields atop the Alaska Range trio of Peaks: **Mt. Deborah** on the left at 12,339 feet, **Mt. Hess** in the middle at 11,940 feet, and **Mt. Hayes** on the right at 13,832 feet.

Over the next 10 miles the road crosses Lily Creek, Seattle Creek, and Stixkwan Creek; throw in a line and pull up some grayling or Dolly Varden. At Mile 31 you come to the **Brushkana River,** where the Bureau of Land Management (BLM) has a good campground ($6) right on the river, and over the next 10 miles you get some great views of the three prominent peaks, along with the West Fork Glacier. The southern glaciers off Deborah, Hess, and Hayes feed the Susitna River, which travels west (to the Parks Highway), then south, and empties into the Cook Inlet across from Anchorage.

Gracious House Lodge and Beyond
Fifty-four miles east of the junction of the Parks and Denali Highways is **Gracious House Lodge** (907/259-1111, www.alaskaone.com/gracious), with lodge has cabins and motel rooms: $70 s or $90 d with shared bath, or $105 d with private bath. Tent sites ($5) and RV spaces ($12) are also available, along with minor tire and mechanical repairs and towing. The café serves home-style

Alaskan meals, and will set up air taxi and guide services. Open June to mid-September.

Five miles farther you cross the single-lane, 1,000-foot-long Susitna River bridge. Farther south, the Susitna is a popular river to float, but passage between here and there is considered impossible because of the impassable Devil's Canyon just downriver from the bridge.

At Mile 79, the highway crosses Clearwater Creek; there are pit toilets at a rest stop/camping area here. In six miles is a turnout with a view of numerous lakes and ponds that provide a staging area for waterfowl; look for ducks, cranes, geese, trumpeter swans, and migrating shorebirds.

Maclaren

At Mile 93 out of Cantwell, the road crosses the Maclaren River, a tributary of the Susitna, flowing from the southern icefields of mighty Mt. Hayes. From here to the other end of Denali Highway, you get occasional views of the three Alaska Range peaks. A mile west of the bridge is Maclaren River Road, which leads 12 miles north to Maclaren Glacier.

Just before the bridge crossing is **Maclaren River Lodge** (907/322-3670 or 888/880-4264, www.maclarenriver.com). This year-round facility caters to hikers, hunters, anglers, and sightseers in the summer, and snowmobilers and dog mushers in the winter. You can stay overnight in motel rooms, cabins, or the bunkhouse. All of these run around $35 per person/night and share bath facilities and a sauna. The lodge has a restaurant and bar with a pretty good selection of beer, a pool table, satellite TV, and gas.

In another seven miles is Maclaren Summit, at 4,080 feet the second highest road pass in Alaska. It provides breathtaking views of Mt. Hayes and the Maclaren Glacier. Peer through binoculars at the plains below to spot wildlife. Up at the summit you might see rock ptarmigan.

East End

At Mile 113—just a mile from the pavement— is **Tangle Lakes Lodge** (907/822-4202, www.tanglelakeslodge.com). In addition to serving some of the best meals in the area, the lodge offers comfortable log cabins ($75 d; $200 for up to eight in a spacious cabin), canoes, fishing charters and gear, a bar, showers, and a sauna. Fly-fishing is spoken fluently here; the "Tangle Lakes Teaser" dry fly is a grayling-getter. This is also a good place to get a look at some of the Nelchina caribou herd, and it's one of the best places in Interior Alaska for bird-watching.

The BLM's **Tangle Lakes Campground** (907/822-3217, www.ak.blm.gov, free) is just up the road, with water pumps, pit toilets, blueberries in season, and a boat launch for extended canoe trips into the "tangle" (or maze) of lakes and ponds and creeks in the neighborhood. Get info from the BLM office in Glennallen.

Two miles east of the campground is **Tangle River Inn** (907/822-7304; www.tangleriverinn.com). Jack and Naidine Johnson have owned this place for over three decades. The Johnsons sell gas, liquor, and gifts, and offer good home-cooking, a lively bar, lodging ($60–100 d; $28 for bunkhouse beds), RV hookups, camping sites, canoes, and fishing gear.

The **Tangle Lakes Archaeological District** begins at Mile 119 and extends back to Crazy Notch at Mile 90. A short hike from the highway to any given promontory along this 30-mile stretch could have you standing at an ancient Athabascan hunting camp where no human footprints have been made for hundreds of years.

At Mile 122, there's a viewpoint from the summit that looks south over a great tundra plain. The three most prominent peaks of the Wrangell Mountains are visible from here: Mt. Sanford on the left, Mt. Drum on the right, and Mt. Wrangell in the middle.

At Mile 125 is a paved turnout with a view of **Ten Mile Lake.** A short trail leads down to the lake, where you can catch grayling and trout. A turnout at Mile 129 affords a spectacular view of the Alaska Range to the north. The Gulkana and Gakona Glaciers can be seen from this point. The Denali Highway joins the Richardson Highway at Paxson.

Paxson and Points North

This tiny settlement at Mile 186 of the Richardson Highway and Mile 136 (from Cantwell) of the Denali Highway has a 3,000-foot airstrip and two lodging options. **Paxson Lodge** (907/822-3330), offers gas, gifts, food, lodging ($60 s or $70 d), and a liquor store. There's a big deck for summertime dining.

Also at the highway junction is **Paxson Alpine Tours and Cabins** (907/822-5972, www.denali-hwy.com), which provides wildlife float trips on the Gulkana and Delta rivers ($45 for three hours) and other adventures. They also have modern log cabins with private baths for $135–165 d, and rooms in a guest house for $165 d.

For one of Alaska's most memorable drives, head north from Paxson along the Richardson Highway. The pipeline parallels the route as it climbs through a grand landscape of tundra, mountains, and rivers. Comfortable lodging is available at pretty Summit Lake, 10 miles north of Paxson: **Waters Edge Cottages** (907/822-4443, www.summit-connection.com). Another 30 miles north is the century-old **Black Rapids Roadhouse** (www.blackrapids.org), now being restored after years of neglect.

The BLM's **Paxson Lake campgrounds** ($6) is at Mile 175 of the Richardson, 10 miles south of the junction with Denali Highway.

Denali National Park and Preserve

Denali National Park is Alaska's most famous tourist attraction, drawing over 300,000 visitors during its brief summer season. Most travelers come to see Mt. McKinley, highest peak in North America (20,320 feet), which towers above the surrounding lowlands and 14,000- to 17,000-foot peaks. Although it's visible only one day in three, and often shrouded for a week or more at a time, those who get lucky and see the mountain experience a thrill equivalent to its majesty and grandeur. Those who don't are usually consoled by lower snowcapped mountains and attending glaciers, high passes and adrenaline-pumping drops off the road, tundra vistas and "drunken forests," and an incredible abundance of wildlife, including caribou, moose, sheep, and bear. But even if the mountain's socked in, the grizzlies are hiding, and the shuttle-bus windows are fogged up, you're still smack in the middle of some of the most spectacular and accessible wilderness in the world. It was the call of the wild that brought you out here in the first place. And all you have to do is step outside and answer.

THE LAND

The Alaska Range is a U-shaped chain that extends roughly 600 miles from the top of the Alaska Peninsula (at the head of the Aleutians) up through the park and down below Tok. It's only a small part, however, of the coastal mountains that include California's Sierra Nevada, the Northwest's Cascades, the Coast Mountains of British Columbia, Yukon's St. Elias Range, and eastern Alaska's Wrangell Range. The Park Road starts out a bit north of the Alaska Range and follows the "U" 90 miles southwest toward its heart—Mt. McKinley. One thing that makes the mountain so spectacular is that the surrounding lowlands are so low: The entrance is at 1,700 feet, and the highest point on the road, Thoroughfare Pass, is just under 4,000. The base of Mt. McKinley is at 2,000 feet, and the north face rises at a 60-degree angle straight up to 20,000 feet—the highest vertical rise in the world.

Weather patterns here differ between the south side of the range (wetter and cooler) and the north. During the summer, the prevailing winds come from the south, carrying warm moisture from the Pacific. When they run smack into the icy rock wall of the Alaska Range, they climb, the moisture condenses, and depending on the amount of moisture and altitude, it either rains or snows. A lot. On top of that whole system sits mighty Mt. McKinley—high, cold, and alone. So alone that the mountain has its own relationship to the weather. The combination of wind, wet, cold, and height creates weather extremely localized—and often violent—around Mt. McKinley. Storms can blow in within an hour and last a week or more, dumping 10 feet of snow. Winds

caribou along the roadside in Denali National Park

scream in at up to 80 mph. The mercury drops below zero in mid-July. Some of the worst weather in the world swirl around up there. But when the mountain emerges bright white against bright blue, and you're craning your neck to see the top, it's an unforgettable sight worth waiting around for—even in the rain.

Flora and Fauna

From sea level to around 2,300 feet is the habitat for the **boreal forest,** in which the black spruce, with its somber foliage and clusters of tawny cones, is the climax tree. Younger white spruce, along with deciduous aspen, birch, and cotton-wood, grow near the streams and the road and in recently burned areas.

Climbing out of the forest above 2,300 feet you enter the **taiga,** a Russian word meaning "land of twigs." This transition zone (between the forest below and tundra above) accommodates no deciduous trees; the spruce are thinned out and runty (though they can be over 60 years old), and a green shag carpet of bush, mostly dwarf willow, layers the floor. Sitka spruce is the state tree because of its size, grandeur, and commercial value, but it's the willow that vegetates

Alaska. And it has endless uses. Before synthetics like nylon, the bark was stripped, split, and braided and made into rope, bows, wicker baskets, snowshoes, fishnets, and small game and bird snares and traps. The inner bark is sweet; the sap is very sweet. Young buds and shoots are edible and nourishing, and willows are the nearly exclusive staple of the moose diet. The taiga also hosts a variety of berries: blueberries and low bush cranberries by the ton, crowberries, bearberries, soap and salmon berries, and raspberries.

Above 2,500 feet is the **tundra,** its name a Lapp word meaning "vast, rolling, treeless plain." There are two types of tundra: the moist, or Alaskan, tundra is characterized by the taiga's dwarf shrubbery, high grasses, and berries, but no trees; the alpine tundra, the highest zone, has grasses, moss, lichens, and small, hardy wildflowers, including the stunning forget-me-not, Alaska's state flower.

The animal life varies with the vegetation. In the forest, look for moose, porcupine, snowshoe hare, marten, lynx, two kinds of weasels, red or tree squirrels, and several varieties of small rodents. On the taiga—or in both the forest and the tundra—you might see coyote, wolf, fox, grizzly, and ground squirrel. In the tundra, keep an eye out for caribou, wolverine, Dall sheep, marmot, vole, lemming, and shrew.

HISTORY

In 1896, a prospector named Bill Dickey was tramping around interior Alaska looking for gold. Like everyone who sees it, Dickey was captivated by the size and magnificence of the mountain that was then variously known as Tenada, Denali, Densmore's Mountain, Traleika, and Bulshaia. Dickey was from Ohio, William McKinley's home state, and a Princeton graduate in economics. When he came out of the bush and heard that McKinley had been nominated for president, he promptly renamed the mountain "McKinley," wrote numerous articles for stateside magazines, and lobbied in Washington, D.C., in support of adoption of the name, which finally caught on after President McKinley was assassinated in 1901. The name has been something of a sore point with Alaskans ever since, for McKinley had absolutely nothing to do with the mountain, and the more lyrical Native names were completely ignored. Many in Alaska support renaming the peak Denali (The High One), a term used by Natives in the lower Yukon and Kuskokwim rivers. Unfortunately, any move to eliminate "McKinley" from maps is inevitably met by howls of protest from Ohio's congressional delegation.

Creating a Park

Karstens reached the Klondike in 1898 when he was 19, bored by Chicago and attracted by adventure and gold. Within a year he'd crossed over into American territory and wound up at Seventymile, 20 miles south of Eagle. When the local mail carrier lost everything one night in a card game and committed suicide, Karstens took his place. He became proficient in dog mushing and trail blazing and within a few years was delivering mail on a primitive trail between Eagle and Valdez, a 900-mile round-trip every month (the Richardson Highway follows the same route). Later he moved on to Fairbanks and began delivering mail to Kantishna, the mining

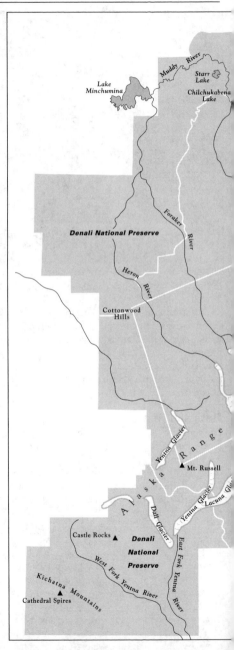

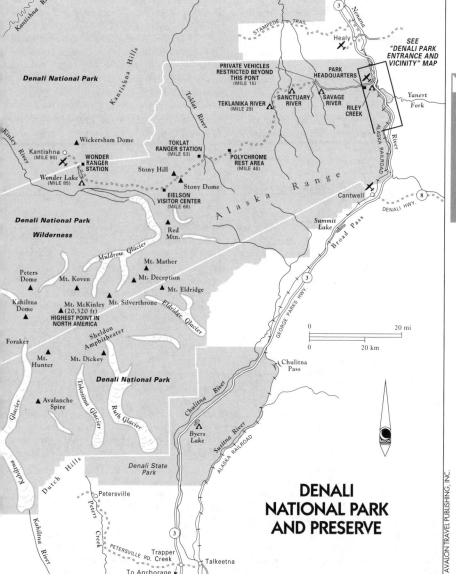

DENALI NATIONAL PARK AND PRESERVE

town on what is now the west end of the Park, growing very fond of and familiar with the north side of the Alaska Range. So when a naturalist from the East Coast, Charles Sheldon, arrived in 1906 to study Dall sheep in the area, Karstens guided him around Mt. McKinley's northern foothills, delineating the habitat of the sheep. Karstens was also the co-leader of the four-man expedition that was the first party to successfully climb the true peak of Mt. McKinley, the south summit, in 1913.

Meanwhile, Charles Sheldon was back in Washington, lobbying for national-park status for the Dall sheep habitat, and when Mt. McKinley National Park was created in 1917, Karstens was the obvious choice to become the first park superintendent. He held that post from 1921 to 1928, patrolling the park boundaries by dog sled.

Woodrow Wilson signed the bill that created Mt. McKinley National Park, Alaska's first, in 1917. The Park Road, begun five years later, was completed to Kantishna in 1940. In 1980, with the passage of the Alaska National Interest Lands Conservation Act, McKinley Park was renamed Denali National Park and Preserve and expanded to nearly six million acres, roughly the size of Vermont.

Pioneer Climbs

Many pioneers and prospectors had seen the mountain and approached it, but Alfred Brooks, a member of the first U.S. Geological Survey expedition in Alaska (1902), first set foot on it. He approached it from the south and reached an elevation of 7,500 feet before running out of time. He published an article in the January 1903 issue of *National Geographic,* in which he recommended approaching the mountain from the north. Following that suggestion, the next attempt was from the north, led by James Wickersham, U.S. district judge for Alaska. Judge Wickersham was sent from Seattle to bring law and order to Eagle in 1900; he moved to Fairbanks in 1903. That summer, he had a spare couple of months and set out to climb the mountain, traveling more than 100 miles overland and reaching the 7,000-foot level of the north face, later named Wickersham Wall in honor of His Honor.

That same summer, Dr. Frederick Cook, who'd been with Peary's first party to attempt the North Pole (1891) and Amundsen's Antarctic expedition (1897), also attempted to climb the mountain from the north and reached 11,300 feet. In 1906, Cook returned to attempt Mt. McKinley from the south but failed to get near it. His party broke up and went their separate directions, and a month later, Cook sent a telegram to New York claiming he'd reached the peak. This was immediately doubted by the members of his party, who challenged his photographic and cartographic "evidence." But through public lectures and articles, Cook's reputation as the first man to reach the peak grew. Two years later, he claimed to have reached the North Pole several months ahead of another Peary expedition, and Cook began to enjoy a cult status in the public consciousness. Simultaneously, however, his credibility among fellow explorers rapidly declined, and Cook vanished from sight. This further fueled the controversy and led to the Sourdough Expedition of 1910.

Four sourdoughs in Fairbanks simply decided to climb the mountain to validate or eviscerate Cook's published description of his route. They left town in December and climbed to the north peak in early April. Then the three members who'd actually reached the peak stayed in Kantishna to take care of business, while the fourth member, Tom Lloyd, who hadn't reached the peak, returned to Fairbanks and lied that he had. By the time the other three returned to town in June, Lloyd's story had already been published and widely discredited. So nobody believed the other three—*especially* when they claimed they'd climbed up to the north peak and down to their base camp at 11,000 feet in 18 hours, with a thermos of hot chocolate, four doughnuts, and dragging a 14-foot spruce log that they planted up top and claimed was still there! Finally, in 1913, the Hudson Stuck/Harry Karstens expedition reached the true summit, the south peak, and could prove that they'd done so beyond a shadow of a doubt. Only then was the Sourdough Expedition vindicated: All four members of the Stuck party saw the spruce pole still standing on the north peak!

Today more than a thousand mountaineers attempt the summit of Mt. McKinley each year, and approximately half of them actually reach the top. The youngest climbers ever to summit (a girl and a boy) were 12; the oldest man was 71, and the oldest woman 62.

PARK ENTRANCE

Park admission is $5/person or $10/family, or buy a National Park Pass—good for all national parks—for $50 a year. A Golden Age Passport for all national parks is available to anyone over 62 for a one-time fee of $10, and people with disabilities can get a free Golden Access Passport that covers all the parks. Get additional park information at 907/683-2294, www.nps.gov/dena.

Visitor Access Center

This busy center just a short distance off the Parks Highway focuses on getting around the park, with areas to book park shuttle buses, campgrounds, and backcountry trips, along with a gift shop that has maps and natural history books.

A 12-minute slide show on the park and orientation programs take place regularly throughout the day. Pick up a copy of *Denali Alpenglow*, the park newspaper, and check the bulletin board for a schedule of daily naturalist programs—guided walks, talks, slide shows, and kids' programs.

From late May to mid-September the visitor center is open daily 7 A.M.–8 P.M. For the first three weeks of May, and from mid-September to late September it is open daily 10 A.M.–4 P.M. It's closed the rest of the year, but you can get information up the road at park headquarters; open Monday–Friday 8 A.M.–4:30 P.M. all year. A new Denali Science and Learning Center complex opened in 2004, and will serve as a wintertime visitor center for the park.

As this was written, the Park Service was building a new visitor center near the rail depot. When completed in 2005 this center will contain interpretive displays, an auditorium, gift shop, and food court. The current Visitor Access Center will continue as a place to book bus trips, make

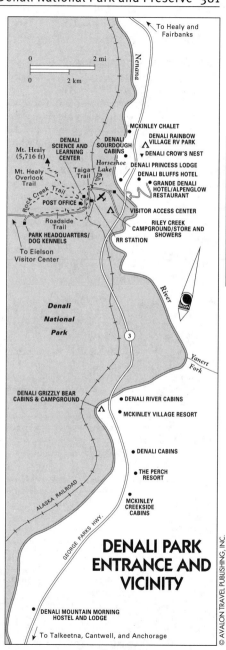

THE INTERIOR

DENALI PARK
ENTRANCE AND
VICINITY

© AVALON TRAVEL PUBLISHING, INC.

campground reservations, and obtain backcountry permits.

Sled Dog Demonstrations

One of the highlights of the park is the sled dog demonstration at the kennels behind headquarters. The dogs are beautiful and accessible (the ones not behind fences are chosen for friendliness and patience with people), and the anxious collective howl they orchestrate when the lucky six dogs are selected to run is something to hear. Naturalists give a talk about the current and historical uses of dogs in the park, their breeding and training, different commands for controlling them, and sometimes the fascinating statistics of maintaining a working kennel in a national park. Then certain dogs, according to a rotating schedule, are taken from their cages or houses, hitched up to a wheel sled, and run around a gravel track. The enthusiasm of the dogs to get off the chain and into the harness is an eyebrow-raising glimpse into the consciousness of Alaskan sled dogs—they live to run.

Demonstrations are given daily at 10 A.M. and 2 and 4 P.M. A free shuttle bus leaves the Visitor Access Center and the Riley Creek bus shelter 30 minutes before the demos. Don't miss this one!

When to Visit

Denali National Park is open year-round, though most facilities only operate mid-May to mid-September. Plowing of the Park Road generally starts in early May, but only the first 30 miles are open before late May, when the shuttle buses begin running. Those who arrive before this date will not be able to reach the best vantage points for Mt. McKinley.

The wildflowers peak around summer solstice—as do the mosquitoes. The berries, rose

COEXISTING WITH BEARS

Bears seem to bring out conflicting emotions in people. The first is an almost gut reaction of fear and trepidation: What if the bear attacks me? But then comes that other urge: What will my friends say when they see these *incredible* bear photos? Both of these reactions can lead to problems in bear country. "Bearanoia" is a justifiable fear, but can easily be taken to such an extreme that one avoids going outdoors at all for fear of running into a bear. The "I want to get close-up shots of that bear and her cubs" attitude can provoke a bear attack. The middle ground incorporates a knowledge of and respect for bears with a sense of caution that keeps you alert for danger without letting fear rule your wilderness travels. Nothing is ever completely safe in this world, but with care you can avoid most of the common pitfalls that lead to bear encounters.

Brown bears occur throughout Alaska, except on islands in southern Southeast Alaska, in the Bering Sea, and out most of the Aleutian Chain. Black bears are found in forested area across most of the state, but not on several islands in northern Southeast Alaska. Old-timers joke that bears are easy to differentiate: a black bear climbs up the tree after you, while a grizzly snaps the tree off at the base. Both grizzlies and black bears pose potential threats to backcountry travelers; polar bears are potentially the most dangerous of the three species, but are almost never encountered by summertime visitors, since they only occur in remote northern and western parts of the state.

Enter bear country with respect but not fear. Bears rarely attack humans; you're a thousand times more likely to be injured in a highway accident than by a bear. In fact, more people in Alaska are hurt each year by moose or dogs than by bears. Contrary to the stories you often hear, bears have good eyesight, but they depend more upon their excellent senses of smell and hearing. A bear can tell who has walked through an area, and how recently, with just a quick sniff of the air. Most bears hear or smell you long before you realize their presence, and hightail it away.

Bears are beautiful, eminently fascinating, and surprisingly intelligent animals. They can be funny, playful and inquisitive, vicious or protective, and unpredictable. The more you watch bears in the wild, the more complex their lives seem, and the more they become individual animals, not simply the big and bad.

hips, and mushrooms are best in mid-August—as are the no-see-ums. The fall colors on the tundra are gorgeous around Labor Day weekend, when the crowds start to thin out and the northern lights start to appear, but it can get very cold. A skeleton winter Park Service crew patrols the park by dog sled. After the first heavy snowfall, the Park Road is plowed only to headquarters.

GETTING AROUND DENALI

In 1971, before the George Parks Highway connected McKinley National Park to Fairbanks (125 miles) and Anchorage (245 miles), you had to take the train, or from Fairbanks you had to drive down to Delta Junction, take the Richardson Highway to Paxson, the Denali Highway to Cantwell, then the Parks Highway up to the park entrance, for a grand total of 340 miles. From Anchorage you had to drive to Glennallen, then up the Richardson to Paxson, over to Cantwell and beyond, for 440 miles. That year, nearly 45,000 visitors passed through the park. In 1972, when the George Parks Highway radically reduced driving times from both main urban centers, almost 90,000 visitors came. In anticipation of the huge jump in tourism, the Park Service initiated the shuttle system of school buses running a regularly scheduled service along the Park Road. Today, the park sees well over a million visitors annually.

There's no question that the shuttle system is highly beneficial to the park experience: the road is tricky and dangerous, crowds are much more easily controlled, there's much less impact on the wildlife (which take the buses for granted), and it's much easier to see wildlife when 40 passengers have eyeballs, binoculars, spotting scopes, and telephotos trained on the tundra. The excellent *Denali Road Guide,* available in park bookstores, has detailed information on sights along the road.

Shuttle Buses into the Park

Green buses depart from the Visitor Access Center daily mid-May to mid-September, with some continuing all the way to the Kantishna, an exhausting 89-mile, 13-hour ride round-trip. Most visitors don't go that far (or certainly not in one day), turning around instead at Polychrome Pass, Eielson, Wonder Lake, or other places along the way. Buses for Eielson begin departing from the Visitor Access Center at 5 A.M. and continue roughly every 30 minutes through 3:30 P.M. Other buses depart during the day for Polychrome/Toklat and Wonder Lake.

You can reserve tickets in advance (907/272-7275 or 800/622-7275, www.nps.gov/dena), starting on the last Monday in February and up to the day before you travel. Sixty-five percent of the available tickets go on sale December 1; the other 35 percent are made available just two days ahead of the travel date. Adults pay $18 to Polychrome/Toklat (six hours round-trip), $23 to Eielson (eight hours round-trip), $31 to Wonder Lake (11 hours round-trip), and $34 to Kantishna (12 hours round-trip). Kids under 15 ride free, and fares are half-price for ages 15–17. Fares do not include park entrance fees ($5). Wheelchair-accessible shuttle buses are available. Backpackers pay $23 to anywhere in the park on the special **camper shuttle bus.**

It's recommended that you try to get on an early-morning bus into the park: better chance to see wildlife and the mountain in the cool of the morning, and more time to get off the bus and fool around in the backcountry.

Schedules are readily available at the visitor centers and hotels. Take everything you need, as nothing (except books and postcards) is for sale once you get into the park. You can get off the bus and flag it down to get back on (if there's room; the buses leave with a few seats empty to pick up day-hikers in the park) anywhere along the road. Many riders never get off the bus at all and just stay on for the entire, exhausting round-trip.

Local Shuttles

A free **Riley Creek Loop Bus** provides service connecting the Riley Creek Campground, Visitor Access Center, and train depot every half hour 5:30 A.M.–9:30 P.M. In addition, a free bus connects the Visitor Access Center with the dog sled demonstrations at park headquarters. The **Savage River Shuttle** also provides a free shuttle service from the visitor center to Savage River

Bridge. Private shuttle buses run between the visitor center and Denali Bluffs Hotel, Princess Lodge, and McKinley Village.

Tour Buses

The park's **tan nature tour buses** leave from the Visitor Access Center throughout the day. You can take a three-hour natural history tour ($41 adults or $23 kids) to Primrose Ridge (17 miles each way), where you walk around with the driver/naturalist; or take the seven-hour wildlife tour ($76 adults or $40 kids; includes a box lunch) to Toklat (53 miles each way). These wildlife tours are extremely popular and they fill up fast with package travelers, so you need to make your reservations (907/276-7234 or 800/276-7234) as far in advance as possible.

Katnishna Wilderness Trails (907/479-2436 or 800/230-7275 www.seedenali.com) provides private all-day bus tours ($115) that leave Denali Park hotels at 6:30 A.M. These take you to Kantishna Roadhouse near the end of the road for a lunch, gold panning, and sled dog demonstration, before heading back out, arriving at the hotels by 8 P.M.

Drive it Yourself

For most of the summer, only the first 15 miles (to Savage River) of the Park Road are open to private vehicles. This portion is paved, and makes for an excellent day trip. From early May (when the road is plowed) to late May (when the shuttle buses start running), it is possible to drive as far as the Teklanika River rest area at Mile 30. The road beyond this doesn't open until late May, so early park arrivals will not be able to see many of the sights for which it is famous.

At the end of summer, the Park Road is opened to auto traffic for four days in mid-September. Only 400 vehicles are allowed per day, and passes are selected by a lottery. In a typical year, you may be competing with 10,000 other entries for these passes! You'll need to apply during July, but contact the Park Service (907/683-2294, www.nps.gov/dena) for details. A handful of professional photographers are allowed vehicular access to the park during the summer, but these slots are highly sought after, and may involve giving up your first-born child and opening your home as a lodging place for all Park Service employees who might be passing through.

AVOIDING BEAR HUGS

Surprising a bear—especially a sow with cubs—is the last thing you want to do in the backcountry. Before heading out, check at a local ranger station or visitor center to see whether there have been recent bear problems. If you discover an animal carcass, be extremely alert since a bear may be nearby and might attack anything that appears to threaten its food. Get away from such areas! Do not hike at night or dusk, when bears can be especially active. There's safety in numbers: The more of you hiking together, the more likely a bear is to sense you and stay away.

Be especially wary when traveling through thick brush or high grass, into the wind, or along streams where salmon are spawning. If you're unable to see everything around you for at least 50 yards, warn any hidden animals by talking, singing, clapping your hands, tapping a cup, or rattling a can of pebbles. Some people tie bells to their packs for this purpose, while others regard this as an annoyance to fellow hikers. In general, bells are probably of little value since the sound does not carry far, and it might even attract inquisitive bears.

Don't be shy—make a lot of noise! It might seem a bit foolish, but yelling may prevent an encounter of the furry kind. Unfortunately, it will probably scare off other animals, and other hikers may not appreciate the noise. Personally, I reserve yelling "Hey Bear!" for situations where I'm walking in brushy bear country with low visibility and have to contend with other noises such as a nearby creek.

Hunters and photographers are the main recipients of bear hugs. Never under any circumstances approach a bear, even if it appears to be asleep. Move away if you see cubs, especially if one comes toward you—mom is usually close by. Dogs create dangerous situations by barking and exciting bears—leave yours at home. And, of course, never leave food around for bears. Not

HEADING OUT THE PARK ROAD

A few miles beyond headquarters the road climbs out of the boreal forest, levels off, and travels due west through a good example of taiga. The ridgeline to the north (right) of the road is known as the **Outer Range,** foothills of the massive Alaska Range to the south (left). The Outer Range is much older, of different geological origins, and much more rounded and eroded than the jagged Alaska Range. First view of the mountain comes up at Mile 9; look southwest. The day has to be nearly perfectly clear to see Mt. McKinley from here: you're at around 2,400 feet and the mountain is at 20,000 feet, which leaves nearly 18 grand spread over 70-odd miles of potential cloud cover. That's a lot of potential.

Next you pass the **Savage River Campground,** then wind down to the river valley and cross the bridge which marks the end of road access for those in private vehicles. The "Checkpoint Charlie" kiosk at Mile 15 has a park employee to turn back private vehicles; they're prohibited beyond this point. From the bridge, look upriver (left) and notice the broad, U-shaped, glacial valley with large gravel deposits forming braids or channels, then look right to compare the V-shaped valley obviously cut by running water. The Savage Glacier petered out right where the bridge is now around 15,000 years ago during the last Ice Age. Here you also kiss the pavement good-bye, then start climbing Primrose Ridge, which offers excellent hiking, especially in June and early July when the wildflowers are in full bloom. Turn around and look back at the Savage Bridge; the stark rock outcropping just up from it has a distinct resemblance to an Indian's facial bone structure, which is how the Savage got its politically incorrect name. Just up the road is a pullout—if the mountain's out, the driver should stop for the clear shot.

Savage River to Igloo Canyon

Mt. McKinley disappears behind jagged lower peaks as the road descends into the broad, glacial **Sanctuary River** valley at Mile 23. Watch for moose, caribou, fox, lynx, waterfowl, and eagles along here. Right on the other side of the Sanctuary is a good view down at a "drunken forest," one effect that permafrost has on the vegetation.

THE INTERIOR

only is this illegal, but it also trains the bears to associate people with free food. Fed bears become garbage bears, and that almost inevitably means that the bear gets killed. Remember, bears are dangerous wild animals. This is *their* country, not a zoo. By going in you accept the risk—and thrill—of meeting a bear.

When choosing a campsite, avoid places like salmon streams, ground-squirrel mounds, berry patches, or game trails. Before camping, take a look around the area to see if there are recent bear tracks, scat, or diggings. Keep your campsite clean! If possible, avoid smelly foods such as fish, fresh meat, cheese, sausage, or bacon; freeze-dried food is light and relatively odorless. Keep food in airtight containers or several layers of plastic bags. Some national parks—including Denali and Glacier Bay—require and provide bear-resistant food containers. Your cooking, eating, and food-storage area should be at least

50 yards away from your tent. Wash up after eating. Burying garbage is useless, as animals soon dig it up. Instead, burn what garbage you can, and wash and flatten tin cans. Store unburnable garbage, and the clothes you were wearing while cooking, in the same place.

Put your food, toothpaste, deodorant, and soap in a plastic bag inside a stuff sack and suspend it from a branch or between two trees, at least 12 feet off the ground and four feet from tree trunks; bring 50 feet of rope for this purpose. Tie two cups or pots to it so you will hear if it's moved. In the absence of trees, store food well downwind of your tent.

Researchers have found no evidence that either sexual activity or menstrual odors precipitate bear attacks, despite reports to the contrary. It is, however, wise for menstruating women to use tampons instead of pads and to store soiled tampons in double ziplock bags above the reach of bears.

Notice how many of the trees are leaning at bizarre and precarious angles, with some of them down entirely. As an adaptation to the permafrost, these spruce trees have evolved a root system that spreads horizontally across the surface soil; there's no tap root to speak of. So the taller a tree grows around here, the less support it maintains, and the more susceptible it is to falling over. When the surface soil becomes saturated (because of lack of absorption over the permafrost), it sometimes shifts, either spontaneously or because of slight tremors (a major fault runs through here), taking the trees with it.

Next you descend into the broad **Teklanika River** valley, with a good view across the river of the three vegetation zones on the mountain slopes: forest, taiga, and tundra. You pass a number of small ponds in this area, known as "kettles," usually formed when a retreating glacier drops off a large block of ice, which melts, leaves a depression, and fills with rainwater. The stagnant water is rich in nutrients and provides excellent hatching grounds for Alaska's famous mosquitoes, and as such the ponds are good feeding spots for ducks and shorebirds. Look for mergansers, goldeneyes, sandpipers, buffleheads, and phalaropes in these ponds. And in some of the higher, smaller, more private kettles, look for hikers and park employees with no clothes on . . . maybe even join them, if you care to brave the skeeters, which have been known to show up on Park Service radar screens.

PROTECTING YOURSELF DURING A BEAR ENCOUNTER

If you do happen to suddenly encounter a bear and it sees you, try to stay calm and not make any sudden moves. Do not run, since you could not possibly outrun a bear; they can exceed 40 mph for short distances. Bear researchers now suggest that quickly climbing a tree is also not a wise way to escape bears, and may actually incite an attack. Instead, make yourself visible by moving into the open so the bear will (hopefully) identify you as a human and not something to eat. Never stare directly at a bear. Sometimes dropping an item such as a hat or jacket will distract the bear, and talking calmly (easier said than done) also seems to have some value in convincing bears that you're a human. If the bear sniffs the air or stands on its hind legs, it is probably trying to identify you. When it does, it will usually run away. If a bear woofs and postures, don't imitate—this is a challenge. Keep retreating. Most bear charges are also bluffs, and the bear will often stop short and amble off.

If a **grizzly bear** actually attacks, hold your ground and freeze. It may well be a bluff charge, with the bear halting at the last second. If the bear does not stop its attack, curl up face-down on the ground in a fetal position with your hands wrapped behind your neck and your elbows tucked over your face. Your backpack may help protect you somewhat. Remain as still as possible even if you are attacked, since sudden movements may incite further attacks. It takes an enormous amount of courage to do this, but often a bear will only sniff or nip you and leave. The injury you might sustain would be far less than if you tried to resist. After the attack, prevent further attacks by staying down on the ground until the grizzly has left the area.

Bear authorities now recommend against dropping to the ground if you are attacked by a **black bear,** since they tend to be more aggressive in such situations and are more likely to prey on humans. If a black bear attacks, fight back with whatever weapons are at hand; large rocks and branches can be surprisingly effective deterrents, as can yelling and shouting. (This, of course, assumes you can tell black bears from brown bears. If you can't, have someone who knows—such as a park ranger—explain the differences before you head into the backcountry.)

Nighttime bear attacks are perhaps the most frightening kind, and could happen to even the most seasoned adventurer. In 1996, one of Alaska's best known wildlife photographers, Michio Hoshino, was sleeping in his tent on Russia's Kamchatka Peninsula when a brown bear attacked and killed him. In the rare event of a night attack in your tent, defend yourself *very* aggressively. Never

Cross the river and enter **Igloo Canyon,** where you turn almost due south. The mountain on the right is Igloo (4,800 feet); the one on the left is Cathedral (4,905 feet). Igloo is in the Outer Range, Cathedral in the Alaska Range. Closest distance between the two ranges, the canyon is right on the migration route of the Dall sheep and a great place to view the white dots on the slopes. Or climb either mountain to get close.

Sable Pass is next at Mile 38, at 3,900 feet the second-highest point on the road. This area is closed to hiking and photography because of the large grizzly population. Keep your eyes peeled. Also, the next good views of the mountain are from these highlands.

Over Polychrome Pass to Eielson

Once you cross the **East Fork River** at Mile 44 (great hiking out onto the flats from here), you begin your ascent of Polychrome Pass, one of the most spectacular and sphincter-clamping sections of the road. If you're scared of heights or become frightened at the 1,000-foot drop-offs, just do what the driver does—close your eyes. These rocks have a high iron content; the rate of oxidation and the combination of the iron with other minerals determine the different shades of rust, orange, red, and purple. Look and listen for hoary marmots in the nearby rocks, and from here almost the rest of the way to Eielson Visitor Center, watch for caribou and wolves; these are the Murie flats,

play dead under such circumstances, since the bear probably views you as prey, and may give up if you make it a fight. Before you go to bed, try to plan escape routes should you be attacked in the night, and be sure to have a flashlight and pepper spray handy. Keeping your sleeping bag partly unzipped also allows the chance to escape should a bear attempt to drag you away. If someone is attacked in a tent near you, yelling and throwing rocks or sticks may drive the bear away.

Many Alaskan guides, government employees, and others working in wild places carry weapons of some sort; 12-gauge shotguns are a common choice. Visitors to Alaska are unlikely to carry such weapons, and even less likely to know when to use them. Don't endanger the lives of bears by heading out into the wilderness with a gun but without an understanding of bear behavior. You have plenty of alternative places to go; the bears do not. Far too many bears die unnecessarily in Alaska following encounters with humans. Guns are not allowed in several Alaskan national parks, including Denali, Katmai, Glacier Bay, Sitka, and Klondike Gold Rush.

Cayenne pepper sprays such as "Counter Assault" (800/695-3394, www.counterassault.com) have proven useful in fending off bear attacks in some situations; they're sold in most Alaskan camping supply stores. These "bear mace" sprays are effective only at close range, particularly in tundra areas, where winds quickly disperse the spray or may blow it back in your own face. Another real problem with bear mace is that you cannot carry it aboard commercial jets, and most air taxis do not allow it inside an aircraft, because of the obvious dangers should a canister explode. Many floatplane pilots will, however, carry it in the storage compartments of the floats. But be sure to let the pilot know that you have it with you on the flight.

If you do carry a pepper spray on a hike, make sure it is readily available by carrying it in a holster on your belt or across your chest. Also be sure to test-fire it to see how the spray carries. Though they *are* better than nothing, pepper sprays are certainly not a cure-all or a replacement for caution in bear country. It's far better to avoid bear confrontations in the first place.

Detailed bear safety brochures are available at Alaska Public Lands Information Centers in Ketchikan, Tok, Anchorage, and Fairbanks, or on the Alaska Department of Fish and Game's website (www.state.ak.us/adfg). Two good bear safety books are *Bear Attacks: Their Causes and Avoidance* by Stephen Herrero, and *Bear Aware: Hiking and Camping in Bear Country* by Bill Schneider.

where wildlife biologist Adolph Murie studied the lifestyle of *Canis lupus.*

Descend to the **Toklat River** at Mile 53, the last and largest you cross before Eielson. This is the terminus of the wildlife tour, but the shuttle buses continue on to Eielson and Wonder Lake. The Toklat's source is the Sunrise Glacier, just around the bend upriver (left). You can see from the size of the river how big the glacier was 20,000 years ago. Great hiking up into the Alaska Range from here. Next you climb up **Stony Hill** and, if the weather is cooperating, when you crest the ridge you're in for the thrill of a lifetime: Denali, The Great One, in all its immense, majestic glory. You can't believe that the mountain is still 40 miles away! But wait, you get another five miles closer, crossing **Thorofare Pass,** highest elevation on the road (3,950 feet; Mile 62). A few miles up the road you finally arrive at Eielson Visitor Center.

Eielson Visitor Center

Open daily 9 A.M.–7 P.M. from June to mid-September (reduced hours after Labor Day and closed for the winter), Eielson is four hours and 66 miles from the park entrance. The view from here—weather cooperating—is unforgettable. Even if you can only see the bottom 12,000 or 14,000 feet, have a naturalist or your driver point to where the top of Mt. McKinley is, and visualize it in your mind's eye. Also, things change fast around here, so keep an eye out for the peak popping out of the clouds as a surprise just for you.

The visitor center has running water and flush toilets; sells film, maps, and books; and has a nice display delineating the peaks and features in the cloudless view. Naturalists lead 30-minute "Tundra Walks" daily at 1:30 P.M. The excellent backpacking zones in this area are usually the first to fill up. No food is available at Eielson. A spectacular new visitor center is in the works for Eielson, but don't look for it until 2007.

To Wonder Lake

Half the buses turn around at Eielson and travel back the same 66 miles; the other half go on another 25 miles to beautiful Wonder Lake. The road comes within 25 miles of the mountain, passing **Muldrow Glacier,** which is covered by a thick black layer of glacial till and vegetation. From Wonder Lake, the **Wickersham Wall** rises magnificently above the intervening plains, with the whole Alaska Range stretching out on each side. In addition, the reflection from the lake doubles your pleasure and doubles your fun, from which even the mosquitoes here, some of the most savage, bloodthirsty, insatiable beasts of the realm, cannot detract.

HIKING

Note: Guns are not permitted within Denali National Park, but many hikers carry Counter Assault or other pepper-based sprays for protection. There has never been a fatal bear attack in the park, but bears certainly are a potential hazard. Obey all park regulations and follow safety tips from the rangers.

Entrance Area Day Hikes

Horseshoe Lake Trail starts at the shuttle bus stop and then descends to the lake, where you might see waterfowl and beaver. It's three miles round-trip. Ranger-led hikes to the lake are offered daily in the summer; see the visitor center for today's schedule.

Hiking the five-mile round-trip **Mt. Healy Overlook Trail** is a great way to get the lay of the land, see the mountain if it's out, quickly leave the crowds behind, and get your heart pumping. Once at the overlook (a mile in), keep climbing the ridges for another several hours to get to the peak of Mt. Healy (5,200 feet).

The 2.3-mile **Rock Creek Trail** starts near the post office and climbs to park headquarters, gaining 400 feet along the way. You can then loop back along the road via the 1.8-mile **Roadside Trail. Taiga Trail** is an easy 1.3-mile loop that also begins near the post office.

Pick up *The Nature of Denali* by Sheri Forbes in the visitor center for additional day-hiking options.

Backpacking Trips

Ask at the backcountry desk at the Visitor Access

Center (www.nps.gov/dena) where the best hiking is found. Popular backpacking areas include up the Savage River toward Fang Mountain; down the far side of Cathedral Mountain toward Calico Creek (get off the bus just before the Sable Pass closure); up Tatler Creek a little past Igloo Mountain; anywhere on the East Fork flats below Polychrome toward the Alaska Range; anywhere around Stony Hill; and the circumnavigation of Mt. Eielson (get off five to six miles past the visitor center, cross the hundred braids of the Thorofare River, and walk around the mountain, coming back up to the visitor center). There are backcountry description guides at the backcountry desk, or you can find the same info online, with photos. For additional details and hiking tips, purchase a copy of *Backcountry Companion* in the park visitor center.

On all these hikes, you can get off the outbound bus, explore to your heart's content, then get back on an inbound bus, if space is available. Consult with the driver and study the bus schedule closely; the camper buses usually have space coming back.

Large as it is, it's hard to get lost in Denali—you're either north or south of the road. And since the road travels mostly through open alpine tundra, there aren't any man-made trails to follow—just pick a direction and book. Usually you'll want to make for higher ground in order to: a) get out of the knee- to hip-high dwarf shrubbery of the moist tundra and onto the easy hiking of the alpine, b) get to where the breeze will keep the skeeters at bay, and c) see more. Or walk along the gravel riverbars into the mountains, though depending on the size of the gravel, it can be ankle-twisting. Hiking boots are a must, and carry food, water, compass, binoculars, maps, raingear, and litter bag. And keep your eyes and ears wide open for wildlife that you don't want to get close to, sneak up on, or be surprised by.

Backcountry Permits
You need a free permit to spend the night in the backcountry. Permits are issued one day in advance from the visitor center and reservations are not accepted. Check the big maps at the backcountry desk; you'll see 43 units, where a limited number of backpackers are allowed; the same info can be found online. Now check the board to find the vacancies in the units. Make sure the unit is open (some are always closed; others periodically close because of overcrowding or bears) and that there are enough vacancies to accommodate your whole party. Watch the 30-minute backcountry video that describe bear safety, river crossings, minimum impact camping, emergencies, and other topics, and finally get a permit from the ranger. You might have to wait a few days for openings in your chosen area, or have a plan B or C in mind. The park loans out bear-proof food storage containers; be sure to get one for your hike. Finally, reserve a seat on one of the camper buses ($23) to get you and your gear into the park.

OTHER RECREATION
Mountain Biking
An excellent way to explore Denali at your own pace is by mountain bike. Bikes are allowed on the Park Road, and can be transported aboard the camper shuttle bus, but be sure to mention the bike when you make a reservation. Note that only the camper buses carry bikes and that they only carry two at a time, so it is possible to get far out the Park Road and then find yourself unable to catch a bus back. Be sure to pick up a "rules of the road" handout at the visitor center before heading out. **Denali Outdoor Center** (907/683-1925 or 888/303-1925, www.denalioutdoorcenter.com) has mountain bike rentals and tours from its office next to the Denali Princess Lodge.

Rafting
Three raft companies run the Nenana along the eastern margin of the park, including two-hour whitewater or float trips ($65), four-hour trips that include both the rapids and easy sections of the river ($90), and all-day river floats ($155). All provide raingear, boots, and life jackets, plus transportation to and from the hotels. The companies are **Denali Outdoor Center** (907/683-1925 or 888/303-1925, www.denalioutdoorcenter.com), **Denali Raft Adventures** (907/683-2234 or 888/683-2234,

www.denaliraft.com), and **Nenana Raft Adventures** (907/683-7238 or 800/789-7238, www.raftdenali.com). Denali Outdoor Center also has inflatable kayak tours for those who want to paddle on their own.

Flightseeing

If the mountain is out and there's room on the plane, this is the time to pull out the credit card. These one-hour flights around Mt. McKinley will leave you flying high for days.

Denali Air (907/683-2261, www.denaliair.com) operates from a private airstrip at Mile 229 of the Parks Highway (eight miles south of the park entrance). Their one-hour trip over the mountain is $220 in a twin-engine plane.

Based in Kantishna at the center of the park, **Kantishna Air Taxi** (907/683-1223, www.katair.com) provides charter air service to end-of-the-road Kantishna lodges, and flightseeing trips within the park. Quite a few other flightseeing companies operate out of Talkeetna and Anchorage.

You can go for a helicopter ride on **Era Helicopters** (907/683-2574 or 800/843-1947, www.flightseeingtours.com), based along the river in Denali Park. Tour options include a 50-minute flight over the park ($245), or a 75-minute trip that includes a glacier landing ($339).

Mountaineering

Mt. McKinley—tallest peak in North America—is a major destination for mountaineers. Over a thousand climbers attempt to summit Mt. McKinley each year, with three-quarters of these attempts via the West Buttress. The primary climbing season is May–July. From the south side of Mt. McKinley, the usual approach is by ski plane from Talkeetna to the Southeast Fork of the Kahiltna Glacier or to the Ruth Glacier in the Don Sheldon Amphitheater. From the north, the approach for Denali and other peaks is by foot, ski, or dog sled. Specific route information can be obtained from the Talkeetna Ranger Station. Climbers on Mt. McKinley and Mt. Foraker are charged a special use fee of $150 per climber. Call the ranger in Talkeetna (907/733-2231), or visit the Park Service website

(www.nps.gov/dena) for additional mountaineering information.

Six companies are authorized to lead guided mountaineering climbs of Mt. McKinley and other peaks in the Alaska Range; contact the Park Service for specifics. Two of the best are **Alaska Mountaineering School** (907/733-1016, www.climbalaska.org) in Talkeetna and **N.O.L.S.** (907/745-4047, www.nols.edu) in Palmer.

Dog Mushing

Visitors whose appetite is whetted by the daily dogsledding demonstrations at park headquarters may want to return when the snow flies for the real thing. **Earth Song Lodge** (907/683-2863, www.earthsonglodge.com) offers wintertime dogsled adventure tours into Denali National Park. These range from an easy overnight trip to ones lasting 10 days.

Three-time Iditarod winner Jeff King lives with his family at Goose Lake near Denali, and offers summertime tours of his state-of-the-art **Husky Homestead** (907/683-2904, www.huskyhomestead.com) kennels and training area. One-and-a-half hour tours depart from his wife's Goose Lake Gallery (next to Princess Hotel), and cost $39 adults, $19 kids.

ACCOMMODATIONS

Most of the local lodging action centers around busy Denali Park, though other lodges and B&Bs are a few miles south of the park entrance, or 10 miles north in the town of Healy. Denali area lodging options are expensive, so those on a budget will need to either camp or head to the hostel 13 miles south at Carlo Creek.

Denali Park Lodging

If you've been driving the Parks Highway north from Anchorage, soaking up the wild Alaskan wilderness, you're in for a rude awakening when you reach the unincorporated settlement called Denali Park. Just a mile north of the Denali National Park turnoff, it's impossible to miss: an ugly hodgepodge of hotels, restaurants, RV parks, rafting companies, and gift shops crammed between the highway and the Nenana River to the west, and climbing the steep hillside to the east. The area is packed with tour buses, tottering tourists, and rumbling RVs. It's enough to make Wasilla look good.

The cheapest place to stay in Denali Park is the **McKinley/Denali Cabins** (907/683-2733, www.denalipark.com). The aging and very basic tent cabins ($65 s or d) have wooden walls, screened windows, electric heat, and a shared bathhouse. Slightly better are small cabins ($105 s or d) with fridges, private baths, and two double beds. Definitely not for everyone, but they're right there in the thick of things near the park entrance. Open mid-May to mid-September.

Denali Sourdough Cabins (907/683-2773 or 800/544-0970, www.denalisourdoughcabins.com) charges $145 d for little boxes down the bluff below Princess Lodge. All have either two double beds or a queen bed, and full baths. Open mid-May to mid-September; they're owned by Westmark Hotels.

Denali Crow's Nest (907/683-2723 or 888/917-8130, www.denalicrowsnest.com), is one of the best local places, with 39 attractive hillside cabins away from the noise and highway traffic for $139 d. The outdoor hot tub is relaxing after a day of exploring, and they provide a free shuttle for the railroad depot and park visitor center.

Denali Bluffs Hotel is a hillside place where the rooms all contain two double beds and fridges; $175 s or $185 d. Request one with a private balcony. High atop the bluff is **Grande Denali Lodge,** a new 154-room hotel accessed by a steep, switchback road. Spacious rooms and family style cabins cost $189 s or $199 d. Both Denali Bluffs and Grande Denali have the same management and contact info (907/683-8500 or 866/683-8500, www.denalialaska.com). They provide free shuttles from the rail depot and park visitor center, and are open mid-May to mid-September.

Though primarily for cruise ship passengers, the sprawling **Denali Princess Lodge** (907/683-2282 or 800/426-0500, www.princessalaskalodges.com) is also open to independent travelers if they don't mind the corporate feeling and tour bus queues. Mid-summer rates are $179 d for a standard room, and amenities include outdoor hot tubs overlooking the Nenana

River, a fitness center, restaurants and cafes, a dinner theatre, and bar. Open mid-May to mid-September.

Denali River View Inn (907/683-2663 or 866/683-2663, www.denaliriverviewinn.com) is just down from Princess Lodge, with a dozen nicely furnished, large rooms, all with one double and one queen bed; $139 d. Open mid-May to mid-September.

Managed by Denali Park Resorts (Aramark), the park concessionaire, **McKinley Chalet Resort** (907/276-7234 or 800/276-7234, www.denaliparkresorts.com) is a modern 345-room hotel along the Nenana River. Rooms go for $210 d. You've got to call and book amazingly early to get one; most rooms are set aside for Holland America passengers. They're open mid-May to mid-September.

Carlo Creek Area Lodging

A number of lodging places are in the Carlo Creek area near Mile 224 of the Parks Highway, 14 miles south of the park entrance. Least expensive is the friendly **Denali Mountain Morning Hostel and Lodge** (907/683-7503 or 866/346-7835, www.hostelalaska.com), with rustic accommodations. Coed bunk cabins are $23 per person, and private rooms cost $65 d. Cabins ($75–100 d) are also available. Amenities include a shared kitchen, internet access, hot showers, gear storage, and a lounge. Open mid-May to mid-September. They offer a $3 shuttle to the park visitors center and rail station that's available to anyone.

The Perch Resort (907/683-2523 or 888/322-2523, www.denaliperchresort.com) has 20 very small cabins for $65 d with a shared bathhouse, or $95 d with tiny private baths. They're open year-round. Nearby are **Carlo Creek Lodge** (907/683-2576, www.alaskaone.com/carlocreek), with cabins and a shared bath ($75 d) or private bath ($95–125 d), wooded campsites (tents $12; RVs $15), and showers ($4); and **McKinley Creekside Cabins** (907/683-2277 or 888/533-6254, www.mckinleycabins.com), with cabins ($79–149 d), a great café, and espresso.

At Mile 231 (eight miles south of the park turnoff), you'll find **Denali River Cabins**

(907/683-2500 or 800/230-7275, www.denalirivercabins.com), in a fine location right on the Nenana River. These panabode cabins include private baths and access to a large riverfront deck with hot tub and sauna. Cabins on the river are $169 d, while those back from the water cost $139 d.

Across the highway is **Denali Grizzly Bear Cabins & Campground** (907/683-2696, www.denaligrizzlybear.com), with a range of lodging choices that include canvas tent cabins ($30 d), crowded simple cabins ($49–60 d), kitchen cabins with a central shower house ($75 for four), and attractive log cabins with private bath and kitchens ($120–128 for four people). Open mid-May to mid-September.

A little south of there at Mile 229 is **Denali Cabins** (907/683-2595 or 888/560-2489, www.denali-cabins.com), with cedar cabins and two outdoor hot tubs. Duplex units are $99 d, and larger cabins cost $159 for up to four. Two-room suites sleep six for $199. Open mid-May to mid-September.

McKinley Village Resort (907/276-7234 or 800/276-7234, www.denaliparkresorts.com) is along the Nenana River at Mile 231. Here you'll find 150 comfortable hotel rooms ($199 d), a café, and lounge. It is run by Denali Park Resorts (Aramark), the park concessionaire.

Kantishna Lodges

The town of Kantishna, 91 miles from the park entrance at the western end of the Park Road, has four roadhouses. The area was first settled in 1905, when several thousand miners rushed to the foothills just north of Mt. McKinley to mine gold, silver, lead, zinc, and antimony. After 1980 and the Alaska National Interest Lands Conservation Act, which expanded Denali National Park's boundaries, Kantishna found itself inside the park, and in 1985, mining was halted by court order. A number of the property owners have moved into the tourism business, and the area is a popular destination for people wanting to escape to the heart of the park. These upscale lodges are definitely not for budget travelers, and it's a long bus ride to Kantishna, so most guests stay at least three nights in this very scenic area. All four of the lodges are open only from early June to mid-September. Private buses transport visitors to the lodges at Kantishna, or you can fly out on Kantishna Air Taxi (907/683-1223, www.katair.com).

Kantishna Roadhouse (907/683-1475 summers or 800/942-7420, www.kantishnaroadhouse.com) is highly recommended for comfort, service, and friendliness. The all-inclusive rate of $670 d per day includes lodging in cabins or duplex rooms, meals, bus transportation from the park entrance, wagon rides, dog sled demonstrations, mountain bikes, gold panning, guided hikes, and interpretive programs. A bar and restaurant are on the premises.

Denali Backcountry Lodge (907/644-9980 or 800/841-0692, www.denalilodge.com) has a spacious central lodge with dining and lounge areas, along with 30 panabode log cabins, all containing private baths. Rates are $680 d per night, including meals, bus transportation from the park entrance, mountain bikes, gold panning, guided hikes, and interpretive programs.

Two wonderful Kantishna lodges—Camp Denali and North Face Lodge—have the same management and contacts (907/683-2290, www.campdenali.com). At both places, the emphasis is on the natural world, with guided hikes, mountain biking, canoeing, fishing, and evening programs. **Camp Denali** has spectacular views of Mt. McKinley, and is operated as a low-key wilderness retreat for a maximum of 40 guests. Special programs are offered throughout the summer, focusing on such topics as bird conservation, nature photography, and environmental issues. Lodging is in cozy cabins with woodstoves, propane lights, an outhouse, and shower building.

One mile from Camp Denali is **North Face Lodge,** which is operated more like a country inn, with 15 guest rooms, all containing private baths. All-inclusive rates at either Camp Denali or North Face Lodge start at $1,200 pp for three nights ($900 for kids under 12). The price includes lodging, food, bus transportation to and from Kantishna, and all activities. Guests must stay at least three nights, with fixed arrival and departure dates. Definitely recommended.

Remote Lodges

Located on the northeastern margin of the park along Lake Minchumina, **Denali West Lodge** (907/674-3112 or 888/607-5566, www.denaliwest.com) is as remote as you can get. Five immaculate log cabins are available with a central shower house and sauna, and all guests have their own private guide for canoeing, hiking, boating, and nature walks. In winter, the action shifts to dog mushing, with multiday trips February–April. All this pampering doesn't come cheap: $2,900 d for three nights in the summer, plus air transpiration ($500 pp from Anchorage).

Tokosha Mountain Lodge (907/733-2821, www.wildsidedenali.com) sits within Denali National Park close to the terminus of Ruth Glacier. This remote homestead has simple cabins for $150 per person/day including lodging and meals. Access is by boat or floatplane.

CAMPING

Park Campgrounds

Inside Denali National Park are seven campgrounds, four of which have evening nature programs throughout the summer.

Riley Creek Campground is the largest and most accessible campground, located just a quarter-mile off the Parks Highway. Rates are $18 for pull-in sites, $12 for walk-in sites. It's open year-round, but with limited facilities September–May. This campground is very popular with RVers and car campers. Adjacent is **Riley Creek Mercantile** with a few supplies (including firewood), a dump station, and $4 showers.

Savage River, Teklanika River, and **Wonder Lake campgrounds** all have water and flush toilets, and go for $16–18 a night. **Sanctuary River Campground** has chemical toilets, and costs $9. Savage River, Sanctuary River, and Teklanika River campgrounds are open May–September, but Wonder Lake Campground doesn't open until June, and may close early because of snow.

All but the Sanctuary River Campground can be reserved in advance (907/272-7275 or 800/622-7275, highly recommended; $4 fee) starting in mid-February. You can also reserve campsites for any of these at the visitor center if they aren't already full.

You can drive to Riley Creek, Savage River, and Teklanika River campgrounds, so they fill up fast. There's a three-night minimum stay for vehicular campers at Teklanika River, and only hard-sided campers are allowed. Otherwise, campground access is via the camper buses ($23 pp). The Wonder Lake Campground is also extremely popular for hiking and the potential to see the mountain, especially around sunset and sunrise, when the alpenglow turns it purple and pink and you'll expose every frame of film you have, plus make a permanent imprint on your retina. Reserve well ahead of your trip.

RV Parks

Denali Rainbow Village (907/683-7275, www.denalirvrvpark.com) is in the heart of the Denali Park action, with a big lot behind the row of log buildings on the east side of the road. Tents cost $15, full hookups for RVs are $34, and showers are $2 if you aren't camping here.

Denali Riverside RV Park (907/388-1748 or 888/778-8800, www.alaskarv.com) is a gravel lot two miles north of the park entrance. It charges $14 for tents or $29–34 for RVs. Open May–September.

Eight miles south of the park entrance is **Denali Grizzly Bear Cabins & Campground** (907/683-2696, www.denaligrizzlybear.com). Tent sites are $18, RV hookups cost $24. Showers and laundry are also available. Additional RV parks are in Healy.

FOOD

A number of places offer pricey summertime eats just north of the park entrance at the development called Denali Park; most are shuttered when the tourists flee south. Start your day at **Black Bear Coffee House** (907/683-1656) with eggy breakfasts, bagels, espresso, sandwiches, salads, ice cream, and even computers to check your email.

Bub's Subs (907/683-7827), has great sandwiches (including Philly cheesesteak), soups, salads, and other favorites. They're the little shop just down from Princess Lodge.

Overlook Bar & Grill (907/683-2723) occupies a hillside location above the frenzy at Denali Park. Big windows a deck face the park, and the menu specializes in burgers (including halibut burgers) and other munchies. They claim to offer Alaska's best choice of beers.

All the big hotels at Denali Park have fine in-house restaurants. **Denali Princess Lodge** has an enclosed riverside deck and serves such favorites as roasted tomato and gorgonzola pasta and Thai chicken satay, along with all the standards: salmon, steak, and salads. The lounge here serves reasonably priced seafood nachos and Alaskan crab pot.

Nenana View Bar & Grill, at McKinley Chalet Resort serves wood-fired pizzas and a range of dinner entrées, including seafood, pasta, lamb, and more for $18–27. Since being taken over by Princess, **Lynx Creek Pizza** (907/683-2547) has lost most of its charm, and the pizzas are now made using frozen crust, but they'll do if you're desperate for a slice of pizza or an ice cream cone.

Located high atop the bluff at Denali Park, **Alpenglow Restaurant** (907/683-8500 or 866/683-8500, www.denalialaska.com) has the most impressive vistas in the area. Wraparound windows face Denali National Park and the high ceilings are accented by an open timber-frame design. Try their buffet for breakfast or lunch; dinner entrées start at $24.

One of the best restaurants in the Denali area is 11 miles south of the park entrance: **McKinley Creekside Cafe** (907/683-2277 or 888/533-6254, www.mckinleycabins.com). You'll find great breakfasts, homemade soups, sandwiches, and chili for lunch, plus filet mignon and fresh Alaskan halibut in the evening. Dinner entrées are $18–22.

The **Fruit Lady,** a step van outfitted like a catering truck, stops at various points around Denali Park and Healy on Wednesdays and Thursdays in the summer.

ENTERTAINMENT

Alaska Cabin Nite Dinner Theater at the McKinley Chalet Resort (907/276-7234 or 800/276-7234, www.denaliparkresorts.com) is an all-you-can-eat affair, with salmon and other Alaskan favorites. Dinner and a rip-roaring half-hour musical comedy are $48. It's corny but fun; seatings are at 5:30 and 8:30 P.M.

Not to be outdone, Princess puts on its own production at the Denali Princess Lodge: the **Music of Denali Dinner Theater,** with a professional cast and shows at 5:30 and 8:30 P.M. The cost is $42 adults, $21 kids with a big dinner that includes ribs and salmon.

Park Service rangers give talks, walks, slide shows, movies, and kids' programs. For specifics, check the bulletin boards at the Visitor Access Center, or the free park newspaper, *Denali Alpenglow.*

You can catch the a summertime aurora show at **Northern Lights Theatre** (907/683-4000, www.alaskan.com/northernlights) in Denali Park. The cost is $7 adults, $5 kids.

A good place to hang out with the locals is the Burgermeister Bar at **McKinley Village Lodge** at the south entrance to the park, eight miles south of the Park Road. It's low-key and congenial, with pool tables and Alaskan Beer on tap. Most of the Denali Park hotels also have lounges.

TRANSPORTATION AND SERVICES

Alaska Railroad

The Alaska Railroad (907/265-2494 or 800/544-0552, www.alaskarailroad.com) passenger train leaves Fairbanks at 8:15 A.M. and arrives at Denali at noon, $50 each way; it departs Anchorage at 8:15 A.M., arriving Denali at 3:45 P.M., $125. Inside the park depot is a railroad gift shop, storage lockers, and a big rack of brochures.

Buses

Several companies provide van transportation to Denali, with one-way rates to the park at around $60 from Anchorage, $50 from Talkeetna, or $40 from Fairbanks.

Alaska Park Connection (907/245-0200 or 800/208-0200, www.alaskacoach.com) connects Denali with Talkeetna, Seward, and Anchorage.

Denali Overland Transportation (907/733-2384 or 800/651-5221, www.denalioverland.com) has charter service from Anchorage to Talkeetna and Denali on a regular basis.

Alaska Trails (907/479-3065 or 888/600-6001, www.alaskashuttle.com) connects Denali with Anchorage or Fairbanks. Van service is daily in the summer, five times a week in winter.

Caribou Cab (907/683-5000) operates a shuttle van in the Denali Park area.

Air Taxis

Local air taxis include **Denali Air** (907/683-2261, www.denaliair.com), which operates from Mile 229 of the Parks Highway; **Kantishna Air Taxi** (907/683-1223, www.katair.com from Kantishna); and five companies based in Talkeetna: **Hudson Air Service** (907/733-2321 or 800/478-2321, www.hudsonair.com), **Doug Geeting Aviation** (907/733-2366 or 800/770-2366, www.alaskaairtours.com), **K2 Aviation** (907/733-2291 or 800/764-2291, www.flyk2.com), **Talkeetna Aero Service** (907/733-2899 or 800/660-2688, www.talkeetna-aero.com), **Talkeetna Air Taxi** (907/733-2218 or 800/533-2219, www.talkeetnaair.com).

Era Helicopters (907/683-2574 or 800/843-1947, www.flightseeingtours.com) is based along the river in Denali Park.

Medical Help

The closest medical aid is a physician's assistant (907/683-2211) in Healy, 11 miles north of the park. For a physician or hospital, you'll need to head to Fairbanks.

North to Fairbanks

HEALY AND VICINITY

Located 11 miles north of the turnoff to Denali National Park at Mile 249 of the Parks Highway, the town of Healy (pop. 640) has most of the necessities of life, including gas stations (considerably cheaper than at Denali Park), convenience stores, restaurants, a laundromat, and medical clinic. Healy has grown up around the coal mining that has operated here since the 1930s. Usibelli Coal Mine (907/683-2226, www.usibelli.com) is the largest in Alaska, which isn't saying much, since it's Alaska's *only* commercial coal mine. However, its one million tons of coal mined a year *does* say something: a four-million-pound "walking dragline" digs 1,000 cubic yards of overburden every hour, exposing the seams. The coal is shipped to Korea or used at an adjacent power plant that supplies the Tanana Valley and Fairbanks. Healy also benefits from tourism to nearby Denali National Park.

Motels and Lodges

On the west side of the Parks Highway is sprawling **Denali North Star Inn** (907/683-1560 or 800/684-1560, www.denalinorthstarinn.com). Built as a camp for pipeline workers in the 1970s, it's not much to look at outside, just a long building with a range of rooms, starting with budget boxes with twin beds ($65 s or d) and bath down the hall. Nicer are the standard rooms ($75 d) with private baths, and suites ($125 for up to four guests). Amenities include an exercise room and sauna, large-screen TV, and restaurant.

Three miles south of Healy is **Denali RV Park and Motel** (907/683-1500 or 800/478-1501, www.denalirvpark.com), where motel rooms with shared bath are $54 d; $74 d with a private bath. Family units with kitchens run $119 for four people. Open late May to early September.

Earth Song Lodge (907/683-2863, www.earthsonglodge.com) rents 10 cozy cabins, all with private baths. It's four miles down Stampede Rd., off the Parks Highway at Mile 251. Rates are $115–135 d. Earth Song is open all year, with a nightly slide show, dog cart rides in summer, winter dogsledding into Denali National Park, and a summertime coffeehouse for breakfast, sack lunches, and light dinners.

White Moose Lodge (907/683-1231 or 800/481-1232, www.whitemooselodge.com) has a dozen clean and reasonably priced motel rooms: $85 s or $95 d. **Park's Edge Log Cabin Accommodations** (907/683-4343, www.parksedge.com) has simple cabins for $99 d, and a larger one for $119 d.

Denali Park Hotel (907/683-1800 or 866/683-1800, www.denaliparkhotel.com) a mile south of Healy, features modern rooms for $109–129 d. The hotel's lobby is an old Alaska Railroad car.

Other local motels include **Totem Inn** (on Healy Spur Rd., 907/683-2384 or 800/478-2384, www.thetoteminn.com, $110 d) and **Motel Nord Haven** (907/683-4500 or 800/683-4500, www.alaskaone.com/nordhaven, $115 s, or $125–140 d).

Bed-and-Breakfasts

Denali Dome Home B&B (907/683-1239 or 800/683-1239, www.denalidomehome.com) has year-round lodging in a unique dome-shaped house with rock fireplaces and seven guest rooms, all with private baths. The cost is $115 d with a full breakfast.

Touch of Wilderness B&B (907/683-2459 or 800/683-2459, www.touchofwildernessbb.com) is another large home in a quiet location five miles north of Healy along Stampede Road. The nine guest rooms are $120–130 d, all with private baths and full breakfasts.

Alaskan Chateau B&B (907/683-1377, www.alaskachateau.com) is an attractive modern log home with suites containing private entrances and baths, queen beds, fridges, and microwaves. They rent for $100 d, including a make-yourself breakfast. Open summer only.

Denali Lakeview Inn (907/683-4035, www.denalilakeviewinn.com) is a nice place right on Otto Lake. The nine bright guest rooms are $125–160 s or d, including breakfast. Also on

Otto Lake is **Denali Lakeside Lodging** (907/683-2511, www.denalilakesidelodging.com), with family friendly cabins and suites for $110–120 d; plus $10 pp for additional guests. Borrow the canoe to paddle around this pretty lake.

Camping

McKinley RV and Chevron (907/683-2379 or 800/478-2562) charges $17 for tents or $29 for RVs in a somewhat wooded area right next to the gas station. Also here are a convenience store, deli, espresso bar, laundry, and showers ($3). Open May–September.

Denali RV Park and Motel (907/683-1500 or 800/478-1501, www.denalirvpark.com) has tent sites ($15) and RV spaces ($28); showers cost $2 extra. It's three miles south of Healy. Open late May to early September.

Food

Denali North Star Inn (907/683-1560 or 800/684-1560) serves reasonably priced all-you-can-eat buffet style dining three meals a day, year-round. There's a lounge and 24-hour restaurant at **Totem Inn** (907/683-2384 or 800/478-2384, www.thetoteminn.com). **Earth Song Lodge** has a coffeehouse with bagels, baked goods, soups, sandwiches, salads, pizzas, and espresso. They're open for breakfast and dinner in the summer.

Play a round of golf at the nine-hole **Black Diamond Golf Course** (907/683-4653, www.blackdiamondgolf.com) two miles south of town on Otto Lake Road. For food, the **Black Diamond Grill** serves a menu of creative breakfasts, prime rib sandwiches, steaks, halibut, and a big Sunday brunch. Covered wagon tours (www.denalihorsetours.com) are also offered here.

Information and Services

The **Greater Healy/Denali Chamber of Commerce** (907/683-4636, www.denalichamber.com) will send you local brochures, and has a log visitor center that is open occasionally. For medical care head to **Interior Community Health Center** (907/683-2211), open Monday–Friday; a physician's assistant and nurse are on call at other times.

Denali Car Rentals (907/683-1377, www.denalicarrental.com) is useful if you arrive in Denali by bus or rail and need wheels to get around.

Clear and Anderson

At Mile 283 of the Parks Highway—45 miles north of Healy and 21 miles south of Nenana—is the turnoff to Clear and Anderson. Clear is a military early-warning station for ballistic missiles, and not surprisingly, entry is prohibited. Six miles down the Clear road is the little settlement of Anderson along the Tanana River. The town is best known for the popular **Anderson Bluegrass Festival,** held the last weekend of July. You'll hear country and bluegrass tunes by musicians from all over Alaska.

Run by the town of Anderson, 600-acre **Riverside Park** (907/582-2500) has tent and RV sites, toilets, and showers along the Nenana River. Gas, groceries, and food are also in town.

At Mile 280 is **Clear Sky Lodge** (907/582-2251), with gas, a steakhouse, and lounge. Four miles south of there is the popular **Tatlanika Trading Company** (Mile 276, 907/582-2341), with a major selection of Alaskan-made arts and crafts. It's worth a stop to browse. They also have RV and tent sites along the Nenana River.

NENANA

Nenana (nee-NA-na), pop. 370, sits at the junction of the Nenana River and Tanana River (TAN-na-naw); a large steel bridge crosses the Tanana here. Nenana was an Athabascan village at the confluence of the two rivers (*na* in Athabascan means "river"; Nenana means "Camping Spot at Two Rivers") until it mushroomed into a town of 5,000 in 1916 as a base for construction on the northern leg of the Alaska Railroad. The town is 300 miles north of Anchorage, and 57 miles south of Fairbanks.

At the north end of the 700-foot railroad bridge spanning the Tanana, Warren G. Harding, first president to visit Alaska, drove in the golden spike, marking the completion of the line on July 15, 1923. Harding's visit was the culmination of a long train tour across the country, on which he attempted to rally support for his flagging administration, which was dogged by suspicions of high-level corruption. Before his trip, Harding had supported exploitation of Alaska's resources, but the firsthand experience changed his mind. Returning from Alaska to Seattle, he made a speech calling for more roads and agriculture, and conservation of lumber, fish, and mineral resources. "We must regard life in lovely, wonderful Alaska as an end and not a means, and reject the policy of turning Alaska over to the exploiters." Unfortunately, Harding died a week later, under extremely mysterious circumstances; his new vision was buried with him.

Ice Classic

Nenana is famous for its yearly Ice Classic, "Alaska's Biggest Guessing Game" (www.nenanaakiceclassic.com). It all began in 1917, when Alaska Railroad workers started a pool for the exact time the ice on the Tanana River would break up; the payoff was $800. Today, the prize

Nenana Ice Classic tripod

has grown to over $300,000, which is 50 percent of the gross. The rest goes to taxes, salaries, promotion, and the town till. Tens of thousands of Alaskans and Outsiders place $2.50 bets on the day, hour, and minute of the break-up. A four-legged tripod (the town's symbol) is set up on the river ice in February, with a cable running to a clock tower on the river bank. When the ice moves, the cable stops the clock, recording the official time. Earliest break-up was April 20, in 1940; latest was May 20, in 1964. Pick up entry forms at the visitor center or the Tripod Gift Shop and enter before the April 1 deadline. They're also available at most Carrs stores.

The Ice Classic and the town's active waterfront, where freight and supplies are loaded onto barges for bush towns strung along the Tanana and Yukon Rivers, make Nenana a prosperous, photogenic, and friendly little place—great for a leisurely stroll to break up (sorry) the trip from Fairbanks to Denali.

Sights

Stop off at the log-and-sod **visitor center** at the bottom of the bridge (corner of the Parks Highway and A St., 907/832-5435, daily 8 A.M.–6 P.M. late May–early Sept.). Behind the cabin is the *Taku Chief*, the last commercial wooden tugboat to ply the Yukon and Tanana Rivers, until it was condemned in 1978 in Nenana, where it still sits. Unfortunately, you can't climb on it.

Walk up A Street toward the river. Go right on Front St. and enter the old depot. Inside is the **Alaska State Railroad Museum** (907/832-5500, daily 8 A.M.–6 P.M. mid-May–Sept., free). Built in 1922 as a depot, this is a wonderful little museum, full of information, photographs, and artifacts from planning, construction, and maintenance of the Alaska Railroad. Be sure to read the railroad bridge-building history, and flip through the logbooks on the stationmaster's counter. The gift shop inside is worth a few minutes, and sells the fine historical video on the railroad.

Outside there's a monument with a memorial plaque and the once-golden spike. A block over at Front Street and B is **St. Mark's Mission Church,** established in 1904 to educate Native children from around the Interior. The inside of this beautiful log building is equally impressive, with a big stained glass window and an alter covered with Athabascan moosehide beadwook. Keep heading down toward the big single-span bridge, then go left into the heavy-equipment parking lot on the waterfront. Here is the **Ice Classic tower;** next to it is a building with the clock. Information signs about riverboats and railroads stand in the center of the parking lot.

The **Alfred Starr Cultural Center** (907/832-5520, daily 9 A.M.–7 P.M. Memorial Day–Labor Day; closed rest of year) houses displays on the Yukon 800 boat race, fish wheels, the Episcopal mission, and dog mushing. Also here is a gift shop with locally made crafts. Out front are two old railcars. The **Nenana Public Library** (907/832-5812) has computers you can use to check your email.

The white markers across the river on the hillside are Native headstones in a hillside cemetery. A second graveyard just south of town contains the bodies of those who died during the railroad's construction and in a deadly influenza epidemic in 1920. And on the way out of town, don't miss the oft-photographed log-cabin bank on the left. Fish wheels are visible on both sides of the river.

Five miles north of town is **Woodland Farms** (907/832-5233, $7.50 adults, $5.50 kids), a combination tree farm and reindeer ranch that's open for informative tours in the summer.

Accommodations and Camping

Bed and Maybe Breakfast (907/832-5272) is upstairs from the Railroad Museum at the depot; this could be the most historic B&B in the state, with hardwood floors, braided rugs, brass beds, and a railroad theme; $65 d. Four rooms share one bath. Request the engineer's room. Breakfast ($7) is served across street at Two Choice Cafe (same owner), hence the "maybe breakfast" part of the name. Open mid-May to mid-September.

Other Nenana lodging options include **Rough Woods Inn** (2nd and A Streets, 907/832-5299) and the rather basic **Tripod Motel** (along the highway, 907/832-5590).

Nenana Valley RV Park (4th and B Streets, 907/832-5230), has tent and RV sites, plus a laundry.

Food

Have a bite at **Two Choice Cafe** (907/832-1010) on Main Street, a classic bush diner. Breakfast is served anytime. (By the way, rumor has it that the two choices are "take it or leave it.") Five miles north of town is **Monderosa Bar & Grill** (907/832-5243), whose "best burger in Alaska" is in fact a great deal—one fills up two. Great fries too.

Have a cold one with the locals—who are often there by early afternoon—at the **Corner Bar** on the west corner of A and Front Streets. The bar on the east corner is *not* called the Corner Bar, though it is on the corner; the Corner Bar got to the name first. (It's called Moocher's Bar).

Coghill's General Store (907/832-5422, open Mon.–Sat. 9 A.M.–6 P.M.) has been selling groceries, fresh meat and produce, hardware, guns, and fishing and hunting licenses to Nenanans and travelers since 1917. The building is starting to show its age, as evidenced by the slanting wooden floors. The Coghills are a six-generation Alaskan family, well-known throughout the state for their conservative politics.

Transportation

Nenana is 67 miles north of the entrance to Denali National Park, and 54 miles south of Fairbanks. The Alaska Railroad passes through, but it's not a scheduled stop. You can get off there if you want to, but can't check any baggage.

Alaska Trails (907/479-3065 or 888/600-6001, www.alaskashuttle.com) has daily bus service connecting Nenana with Fairbanks or Anchorage. In the winter, the run is five times a week.

North to Fairbanks

North of Nenana, the highway begins a gradual climb into the wooded Tanana Hills with a multitude of vista points featuring the Alaska Range to the east. Much of this country lies within **Tanana Valley State Forest.**

At Mile 328 you pass **Skinny Dick's Halfway Inn**; it *is* halfway between Fairbanks and Nenana, which makes it an even better pun. If it's tasteless, Skinny Dick's has it, including a chef's apron, complete with a small towel covering the "skinny dick." Call 907/452-0304 for the naked truth on this goofy tourist trap.

Fairbanks

Arguably no city in the North is closer to the Edge than Fairbanks. With several hundred miles of subarctic bush Alaska surrounding it, the frontier feeling is pervasive: haphazard layout, constant infrastructure improvements, two military bases, dozens of churches overflowing with large families on Sunday mornings, and a colorful core of hard-drinking, hard-living "pioneers." Second-largest town in the state, it's still less than an eighth the size of Anchorage, with a compact, convenient, and hospitable hominess that Anchorage has long since forgotten. But it's still one of the largest population centers this far north on earth.

The town itself isn't pretty—barely scenic—but for such an outback, plain, boxy place, Fairbanks, like the rest of Alaska, takes extrovert pride in itself; it has a lot to offer the visitors who stagger in from the bush and want to kick

back or live it up for a few days. Plan on at least a couple of days here to dust off from the road and relax in comfort without abandoning the Edge—one of the best places in Alaska to combine all three.

Climate

Fairbanks has one of the widest temperature ranges of any city in the world. The mercury can plummet to -66°F in January and soar to 99°F in July, for a whopping 165-degree differential. In addition, one day in July could be 90°and cloudless, while the next day could be 40°and rainy. Visitors are often taken aback by Fairbanks' occasional sizzling summer days, and scramble for the few air-conditioned hotel rooms. During the mild days, the 21 hours and 47 minutes (on solstice, to be exact) of direct sunlight are a novelty to travelers, but that hot sun beating

THE INTERIOR

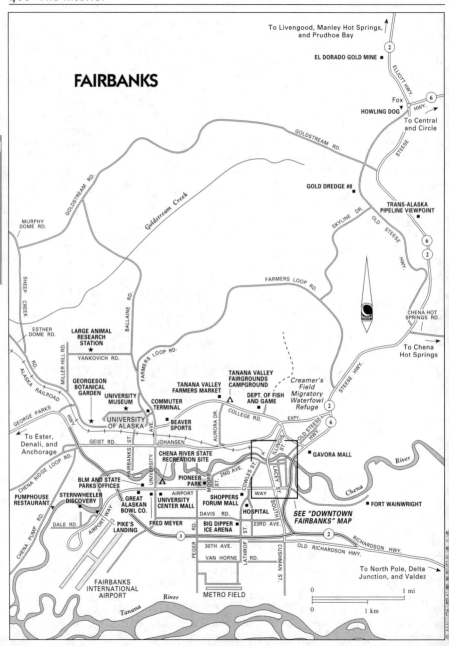

FAIRBANKS

To Livengood, Manley Hot Springs, and Prudhoe Bay

EL DORADO GOLD MINE ■

ELLIOTT HWY.

Fox

HOWLING DOG ▼

To Central and Circle

GOLDSTREAM RD.

GOLD DREDGE #8 ■

TRANS-ALASKA PIPELINE VIEWPOINT ■

GOLDSTREAM RD.

MURPHY DOME RD.

Goldstream Creek

SKYLINE DR.

OLD STEESE

MURPHY DOME RD.

SHEEP CREEK

BALLAINE RD.

FARMERS LOOP RD.

CHENA HOT SPRINGS RD.

ESTHER DOME RD.

LARGE ANIMAL RESEARCH STATION ★

YANKOVICH RD.

MILLER HILL RD.

FARMERS LOOP RD.

To Chena Hot Springs

ALASKA RAILROAD

GEORGESON BOTANICAL GARDEN

UNIVERSITY MUSEUM

Creamer's Field Migratory Waterfowl Refuge

STEESE HWY.

GEORGE PARKS HWY.

UNIVERSITY OF ALASKA

COMMUTER TERMINAL

TANANA VALLEY FARMERS MARKET

TANANA VALLEY FAIRGROUNDS CAMPGROUND

DEPT. OF FISH AND GAME

COLLEGE RD.

To Ester, Denali, and Anchorage

BEAVER SPORTS

AURORA DR.

EXPY.

GAVORA MALL ■

GEIST RD.

JOHANSEN

CHENA RIVER STATE RECREATION SITE

ILLINOIS ST.

OLD STEESE HWY.

River

CHENA RIDGE LOOP RD.

BLM AND STATE PARKS OFFICES

PIONEER PARK

2ND AVE.

COWLES ST.

LACEY ST.

Chena

PUMPHOUSE RESTAURANT

STERNWHEELER DISCOVERY

AIRPORT

GREAT ALASKAN BOWL CO.

UNIVERSITY CENTER MALL

SHOPPERS FORUM MALL

MOORE ST.

WAY

SOUTH

FORT WAINWRIGHT ■

CHENA PUMP RD.

DALE RD.

AIRPORT WAY

PIKE'S LANDING

FRED MEYER

DAVIS RD.

HOSPITAL ■

SEE "DOWNTOWN FAIRBANKS" MAP

BIG DIPPER ICE ARENA ■

23RD AVE.

LATHROP ST.

CUSHMAN ST.

RICHARDSON HWY.

FAIRBANKS INTERNATIONAL AIRPORT

PEGER RD.

30TH AVE.

VAN HORNE RD.

OLD RICHARDSON HWY.

To North Pole, Delta Junction, and Valdez

METRO FIELD

Tanana River

0   1 mi

0   1 km

relentlessly down on residents *all summer long* can make you just as crazy as 18 hours of darkness in December.

The seasons here are pronounced. Spring generally occurs around Memorial Day weekend, sometimes over a single day! During the 90-day summer the foliage changes from green to yellow, orange, and red. It generally goes brown in early September, sometimes over Labor Day weekend! It can snow and drop into the teens anytime in September, when the first official day of winter is still more than three months away. Winter solstice sees a few hours of daylight, and then there's five more months until spring.

A visit to Fairbanks in the throes of winter provides a harsh lesson in bitter cold, darkness, and ice fog—caused mainly by auto exhaust and made worse when folks leave their cars running while they shop for groceries. By 40 or 50 degrees below zero, car tires go hard as a rock and can explode if you drive too fast before they warm up. Fan belts snap in the cold, and vehicles need block heaters or they will never start (electrical outlets are in front of many businesses). Even with the warmest clothing, you'll find yourself wanting to be back inside soon. Fairbanks folks adapt to the harsh winters, and you'll even find them out skiing, dog sledding, or snowmobiling when the mercury hides out at the bottom of the thermometer. But they also have a beautiful central library with indoor trees where they can pretend it's spring when it's months away.

HISTORY

E. T. Barnette

In August 1901, E. T. Barnette was traveling up the Tanana River on the *Lavelle Young* with a boatload of supplies bound for Tanacross to set up a trading center on a well-used gold-rush trail. Unable to negotiate some rapids, Captain Charles Adams turned into the Chena River to try to bypass them but got stuck on the Chena's silt-laden sandbars. Adams refused to go any farther, and Barnette refused to turn back, leaving the two men as stuck as the boat.

Peering through field glasses from a distant hill, Felice Pedroni (Felix Pedro, as he's remembered) watched the boat's progress—or lack thereof—by the smoke from its stacks. A mountain man and prospector, Pedro had been looking for gold in the huge wilderness north of the Tanana and Chena Rivers for several years and had found signs of color on some creeks near where he stood watching the steamer. However, running low on provisions, he was facing a several-hundred-mile round-trip to Circle to restock, unless . . . .

Meanwhile, Captain Adams was unceremoniously dumping Barnette, his wife, and their goods on the shore. "We cut some spruce and helped him get his freight off," Adams recalled 30 years later. "We left Barnette furious. His wife was weeping on the bank." They were standing directly in front of the present site of downtown Fairbanks. That's when Pedro showed up, quietly informed Barnette of his prospect, and bought a winter's worth of supplies. Back at his promising creek, Pedro finally hit pay dirt.

News of the strike traveled far and fast. Miners abandoned played-out Klondike and Nome and headed for the tiny outpost on the Chena River, named after Illinois Senator Charles Fairbanks, who soon became vice president under Teddy Roosevelt. Unfortunately, Barnette wasn't content with his good fortune of owning most of the town site of rich little Fairbanks. In 1911, he was tried for embezzling funds from his own Washington-Alaska Bank. Though he was acquitted, he left town with his family, never to return. His wife divorced him in 1920 in San Francisco; where he went from there, and when or how he died, are complete mysteries. Only one clear photograph of his face survives today: Barnette standing in a line with several other early Fairbanks bankers. But when the photo was found, old-timers were hard-pressed to identify which one was the town father. In fact, a discrepancy even exists over his first name. In *E. T. Barnette,* Terrence Cole calls him "Elbridge," while *The $200 Million Gold Rush Town,* by Jo Anne Wold, remembers him as "Eldridge," and the city fathers commemorated him by naming an elementary school Ebenezer T. Barnette. Whatever his name, possibly no man embodies the boom-bust character of Fairbanks better than its founder, E. T. Barnette.

Gold

The Fairbanks strike differed markedly from the shiny shores of the Klondike and the golden sands of Nome—this gold was buried under frozen muck anywhere from eight to 200 feet deep. Fortune hunters quickly became discouraged and left, which rendered Fairbanks's boom much less explosive than Dawson's or Nome's.

Even determined miners eventually reached the limits of both their endurance and the primitive placer-mining technology. After fires and floods, by 1913, when the road from Valdez to Fairbanks was completed, the town was in the midst of a serious bust cycle. But in 1923 the Alaska Railroad reached Fairbanks from Seward and Anchorage, which inaugurated the real Golden Age. Major mining corporations freighted up and installed the mechanical monsters required to uncover the gold, and eventually $200 million worth was dredged from the surrounding area. When the Alcan was pushed through to Delta from Canada in 1942, connecting the Richardson Highway to the outside world, the city's future was assured.

News of the strike traveled far and fast. Miners abandoned played-out Klondike and Nome and headed for the tiny outpost on the Chena River, named after Illinois Senator Charles Fairbanks, who soon became vice president under Teddy Roosevelt.

From the Pipeline to Today

A massive flood in the summer of 1967 nearly drowned the town, and the future looked bleak for a while, but in early 1968 the Prudhoe Bay strike promised to drown the town *in oil* and Fairbanks' prospects looked bright again. Many local people invested heavily on speculation of a boom around the proposed pipeline; most went bust in the six years it took to start the project. But pipeline construction finally began in 1974, and Fairbanks boomed yet again. Of the 22,000 total pipeline workers, 16,000 were dispatched from Fairbanks' union halls. Suddenly demand far exceeded supply, making it a seller's market for everything from canned food to cocaine, from housing to hookers. In fact, there were so many hookers, and the unions grew so strong, that the hookers themselves sought union representation to get the city council and cops off their backs, so to speak.

So many people poured in with dreams of big bucks that officials took out ads in Lower 48 newspapers telling everyone to stay away. Only half the job seekers ever got hired, and the lines at the bank were only exceeded in length by those at the unemployment office. For three years you could barely utter or hear a sentence in Fairbanks that didn't contain the word "pipeline." The word itself eventually reached mythical status, with the locals blaming the exploding population, rampant crime, deteriorating social services, long separations from home and family, and every other local problem on it, while the oil companies and workers hailed it as the best thing since J. Edgar Hoover invented the vacuum cleaner. For better or for worse, the locals mined this vein for three years, and those with enough brains and self-control set themselves up for the bust that was sure to follow. And did. E. T. Barnette would've been proud. Those were the days.

Like the rest of the state, the town has surfed the oil wave and has survived the peaks and valleys of oil prices. Meanwhile, Fairbanks (31,000 town residents, 84,000 in the borough) prospers on the military payroll, on the summer tourist season, as a supply center for the bush, and on the Fort Knox gold mine up in suburban Fox, which will keep the area flush with gold for years to come.

DOWNTOWN SIGHTS

The smoothest sight around hard-edged Fairbanks may be the rounded hills that surround the bowl at the bottom of which Fairbanks sits, flat as a mackerel. It's not a particularly colorful town, but the residents do their bit to beautify, and the profusion of potted, planted, and painted flowers really spruces up the place. Walk around downtown to get the frontier flavor, and be sure to wander through the nearby residential neigh-

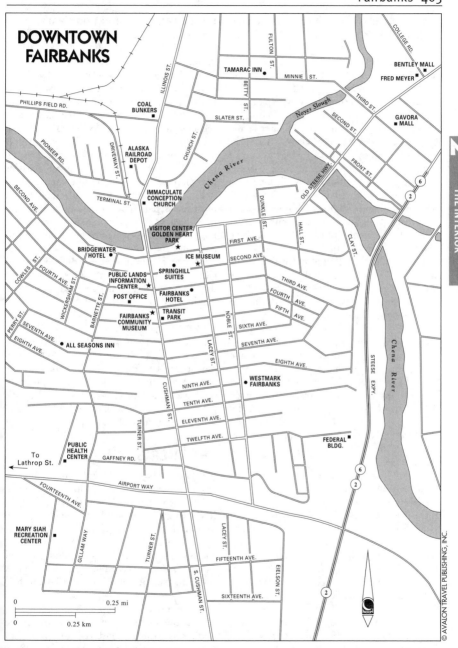

DOWNTOWN FAIRBANKS

FULTON ST.

COLLEGE RD.

TAMARAC INN

BENTLEY MALL

MINNIE ST.

BETTY ST.

FRED MEYER

ILLINOIS ST.

Noyes Slough

THIRD ST.

PHILLIPS FIELD RD.

COAL BUNKERS

SLATER ST.

SECOND ST.

GAVORA MALL

CHURCH ST.

Chena River

PIONEER RD.

DRIVEWAY ST.

ALASKA RAILROAD DEPOT

OLD STEESE HWY.

FRONT ST.

SECOND AVE.

TERMINAL ST.

IMMACULATE CONCEPTION CHURCH

DUNKLE ST.

HALL ST.

CLAY ST.

2
6

COWLES ST.

FOURTH AVE.

VISITOR CENTER/ GOLDEN HEART PARK

FIRST AVE.

BRIDGEWATER HOTEL

ICE MUSEUM

SECOND AVE.

WICKERSHAM ST.

PUBLIC LANDS INFORMATION CENTER

SPRINGHILL SUITES

THIRD AVE.

BARNETTE ST.

POST OFFICE

FAIRBANKS HOTEL

FOURTH AVE.

PERRY ST.

SEVENTH AVE.

FAIRBANKS COMMUNITY MUSEUM

TRANSIT PARK

FIFTH AVE.

EIGHTH AVE.

ALL SEASONS INN

NOBLE ST.

SIXTH AVE.

LACEY ST.

SEVENTH AVE.

EIGHTH AVE.

CUSHMAN ST.

NINTH AVE.

WESTMARK FAIRBANKS

STEESE EXPY.

Chena River

TURNER ST.

TENTH AVE.

ELEVENTH AVE.

TWELFTH AVE.

FEDERAL BLDG.

To Lathrop St.

PUBLIC HEALTH CENTER

GAFFNEY RD.

6
2

FOURTEENTH AVE.

AIRPORT WAY

GILLAM WAY

TURNER ST.

MARY SIAH RECREATION CENTER

LACEY ST.

S. CUSHMAN ST.

FIFTEENTH AVE.

EIELSON ST.

SIXTEENTH AVE.

2

0   0.25 mi

0   0.25 km

MOON

borhoods for the flowers, log cabins, and huge heads of cabbage.

Visitor Center

Start out at the Log Cabin Visitor Information Center (1st Ave. near Cushman, 907/456-5774 or 800/327-5774 recording, www.explorefairbanks.com), a sod-roofed structure along the Chena River. The building is open daily 8 A.M.–8 P.M. from Memorial Day to Labor Day, and Monday–Friday 8 A.M.–5 P.M. the rest of the year. You can access the infoline with the day's events at 907/456-4636. While here, load yourself down with a few pounds of publications, including the *Fairbanks Visitors Guide,* a comprehensive listing of local practicalities; as well as the *Fairbanks Walking Tour,* describing many downtown historical sites.

Just outside the log cabin is **Golden Heart Park,** a flower-packed plaza centered around a large heroic sculpture of *The First Unknown Family,* representing those who first crossed into Alaska over the Bering Land Bridge. Free concerts (907/456-1984) take place on Wednesdays, weather permitting, at 7 P.M. in June and July.

On the opposite side of the visitor center, the Cushman Street Bridge crosses the Chena River. The flags of all 50 states line the bridge. Visit the **Immaculate Conception Church** (1904), just across the river, for its beautiful stained-glass windows. Farther north along Illinois Street are the old wooden **coal bunkers** erected in the 1930s to supply fuel to steam locomotives.

Ice Museum

At the corner of 2nd Avenue and Lacey Street in the historic Lacey Street Theater is the Fairbanks Ice Museum (907/451-8222, www.icemuseum.com, daily 10 A.M.–9 P.M. June–Aug.; $10 adults, $5 ages 6–12, free for younger kids). This is the "coolest show in town," with a 25-minute film about the process of creating ice art at the International Ice Sculpting Competition in Fairbanks each March. There's also glass-walled walk-in freezer that displays intricate pieces of sculpted ice, and you can often watch artisans demonstrate their craft.

Public Lands Information Center

The Alaska Public Lands Information Center (3rd Ave. at Cushman, 907/456-0527, www.nps.gov/aplic) is open daily 9 A.M. to 6 P.M. Memorial Day to Labor Day; Tuesday–Saturday 10 A.M.–6 P.M. the rest of the year. A combination museum and information bureau, this excellent facility represents eight state and federal agencies, from the Alaska Division of Tourism to the U.S. Geological Survey. You can easily spend an hour here looking and playing: interesting aerial and relief maps hang on the walls, videos give thumbnail sketches on different aspects of Alaska; an aquarium is filled with Alaskan fish; old-time stereoscopic viewers show three-dimensional views of historic Alaska; a trip-planning computer is programmed with public-land sites throughout the state; and a variety of tasteful displays. You can view scheduled films and videos in the comfortable theater several times a day, or buy books, prints, postcards, and topographic maps.

Community Museum

The Fairbanks Community Museum (551 2nd Ave., 907/452-8671, daily 10 A.M.–6 P.M. Memorial Day–Labor Day, closed rest of year; free admission) is housed within historic City Hall. Inside are displays and photos on dog mushing, the gold rush, and the growth of Fairbanks. My personal favorite is the collection of old bar napkins.

CREAMER'S FIELD

Head north about a mile on Illinois and take a left at College Road. In another mile is the 1,800-acre **Creamer's Field Migratory Waterfowl Refuge** where you might observe migratory birds and most of the common vegetation of the Interior. Early in the year, the field is plowed and tons of barley are spread around. Sandhill cranes, Canada geese, and many species of ducks stop off at the field in April and May on their migratory route north—a local herald for the arrival of spring.

Take the long gravel driveway between the Alaska Department of Fish & Game office and the Creamer's Field parking lot to the gate at the

sandhill cranes in Creamer's Field Migratory Waterfowl Refuge

dairy, where you can pick up a free trail guide. The dairy was the first in Alaska (1904) and the northernmost in the Western Hemisphere. Charles Creamer owned it from 1928 to 1966, when he sold it to Fish & Game for use as a migratory-waterfowl refuge. Volunteer-led nature walks (907/459-7307, free) depart from the **Farmhouse Visitor Center** (daily 10 A.M.–5 P.M., June–Aug.) several times a week; call for upcoming walks.

At other times, you can head out on the two-mile nature path to explore forest, shrub, muskeg, and riparian areas. The high point of the trail, literally, is a 20-foot observation platform, from which you are supposed to be able to spot wildlife—if you can see anything through the mass of skeeters buzzing around your head. The trail is mostly boardwalk over swamp, with the predictable insectoid results. Either wear lots of clothes and headgear, or wear just shorts and a T-shirt and come here to jog, but you'd better be fast. Pretty good jogging trail, actually, with fun ups and downs. Even though mosquitoes flap their wings 1,000 times a minute, you can outrun them!

Alaska Bird Observatory

Located upstairs in the visitor center at Creamer's Field, this nonprofit organization (907/451-7059, www.alaskabird.org) conducts long-term research on Interior Alaska birds, and works to protect their habitat. It's the only organization of its kind in the state. Visitors can watch banding demonstrations in July and August, and the staff lead bird walks throughout the summer.

UNIVERSITY OF ALASKA

Continue west on College Road to the University of Alaska, Fairbanks (UAF), Alaska's primary educational facility (Admissions Office 907/474-7500 or 800/478-1823, www.uaf.edu). When it opened in 1922 as Alaska Agricultural College and School of Mines, there were six students and as many faculty; today 9,000 students attend the 2,500-acre campus. This facility is highly regarded for its Arctic research and Alaska Native studies. Smaller University of Alaska campuses are in Anchorage and Juneau. Ask any student to direct you to the **Wood Campus Center,** where you can pick up a free map of the grounds, check the ride board, and grab a cheap breakfast, a slice of pizza, an espresso, a cafeteria lunch, or a beer in the pub. A free shuttle bus runs every 15 minutes around campus.

Free two-hour **walking tours** (907/474-7581) of the campus take place Mon.–Fri. at 10 A.M. June–August. Led by UAF students, these start from the museum and end at the campus center. No reservations are needed, but the tours may be canceled if it is raining; call to confirm.

University Museum

This is one of Alaska's finest museums (907/474-7505, www.uaf.edu/museum), and an important stop for anyone visiting Fairbanks. The collection is divided according to the state's five geographical areas, and includes hands-on objects, dioramas, and videos. The wildlife and gold exhibits are mind-boggling; the Russian artifacts and the permafrost display are exceptional. So is an exhibit dealing with the incarceration of Japanese-Americans during World War II; read the heartbreaking personal letters from the families pleading for compassion. Other highlights include Blue Babe, a mummified 36,000-year-old steppe bison discovered in 1979 at a placer mine, a 1,250-pound brown bear, a video on whaling, fist-sized gold nuggets, ancient ivory carvings, dinosaur bones from the North Slope, and lots more. The gift shop sells the usual books, prints, and cards, plus Native dolls, baskets, and ivory carvings. On a clear day, Mt. McKinley—across the broad Tanana Valley—can be seen in all its awesome eminence from the museum hill.

In addition, they offer daily talks by experts on wolves, bears, Native art, or history. The one drawback of the University Museum is that all the exhibits are jammed into a tiny space. Fortunately a major addition opens in 2005, with an art gallery, learning center, auditorium, cafe, and more.

The museum is open daily 9 A.M.–7 P.M. mid-May to mid-Sept., and Mon.–Fri. 9 A.M.–5 P.M., Sat.–Sun. noon–5 P.M. the rest of the year. Admission costs $5 adults, $4.50 seniors, $3 ages 7–17, and free for younger kids.

Large Animal Research Station

This Arctic biology research center (907/474-7207, www.uaf.edu/lars) houses more than 100 musk ox, caribou, and reindeer, mostly tame animals used for nutritional, physiological, and behavioral studies. Find the 150-acre research station north of the campus on Yankovich Road, 1.5 miles off Ballaine Road. This unique facility is open for guided tours daily at 1:30 P.M. June–August; and Tuesday and Saturday at 1:30 P.M. in May and September. A free viewing stand here is open at any time. Admission is $10 adults, $9 seniors, $6 students, and free for kids under seven.

Georgeson Botanical Garden

This five-acre garden (907/474-7627, daily 7 A.M.–8 P.M. summer, no charge) is on the grounds of the Agricultural and Forestry Experimental Station downhill from the museum on the west end of campus. It's the northernmost botanical garden in the Western Hemisphere, and contains flowers, vegetables, fruits, herbs, and perennials that can withstand the northern

rigors. Giant cabbages and other veggies are the star attractions.

Other University Sights

Learn about the northern lights, earthquakes, and more in a tour of the **Geophysical Institute** on Wednesdays at 2:30 P.M. June–August. This building (the tall one with the satellite dishes on top) also houses a Map Office, where you can buy topographic maps. The **International Arctic Research Center** is open for tours on Wednesdays at 3:30 P.M. June–August; it's adjacent to the Geophysical Institute. Call 907/474-7558 for details on either of these tours. Visit one of the world's fastest supercomputers (yet another example of the largess created by Alaska's powerful congressional delegation) at the Butrovich Building, below the museum. Tours (907/474-6935) are given June–Aug. on Wednesdays at 1 P.M.

Poker Flat Research Range (907/474-7558, www.pfrr.alaska.edu)—the only university-operated sounding rocket range anywhere—is 33 miles north of Fairbanks on the Steese Highway. Tours are offered some Thursdays in the summer.

PIONEER PARK

This enjoyable 44-acre theme park (907/459-1087, www.co.fairbanks.ak.us/parks&rec, 11 A.M.–9 P.M., grounds open year-round, shops and rides Memorial Day–Labor Day, no charge)—the only one of its kind in the state—occupies the site of the 1967 state centennial celebration. Many of the original buildings from the early days of Fairbanks and various locations around Alaska have been moved here and assembled into a gold-rush-era town. Park headquarters is in one such restored building just inside the entrance off Airport Way between Nome and Peger Roads. Pick up a map of the park and spend a few hours exploring the grounds of this free open-air museum.

The big (227-foot-long) 1933 sternwheeler *Nenana* has been beautifully restored, and sits just inside the entrance. It's the second-largest wooden-hull vessel in existence, and now houses a fascinating and detailed diorama of towns along the Yukon and Tanana rivers. Entrance is $5 adults, $4 kids.

To your right inside the entrance is the **Harding Car,** a railcar used by Warren G. Harding when he came to Alaska on his ill-fated trip in 1923, just before his death under questionable circumstances.

Continue to **Gold Rush Town,** a collection of 29 colorful and historic buildings that includes the interesting home of Alaska's first Territorial Governor, James Wickersham. The **Palace Theatre & Saloon** has a musical-comedy revue nightly, while the **Pioneer Museum** is a free collection of mining and other memorabilia. The same building houses **The Big Stampede Show,** a 45-minute look at the lives of early pioneers; $4 adults, $2 kids.

Pioneer Air Museum (907/451-0037, daily 11 A.M.–9 P.M. in the summer, $2) is housed in a dome-shaped building near the center of Pioneer Park. Inside are a number of historic and modern aircraft, from a 1933 Stinson SR-5 to a 1966 Bell UH1 helicopter.

The narrow-gauge **Crooked Creek and Whiskey Island Railroad** ($2 adults, $1 kids, free for seniors and toddlers) circles Pioneer Park throughout the day. Kids will also love a vintage 1915 carousel ride ($1) and miniature golf course. Browse around the replica **Mining Valley** with its antique mining equipment, and the **Native Village** where you will find historic artifacts. Also at Pioneer Park is an excellent **salmon bake.**

RIVERBOAT TOURS

The Binkley family, now in its fourth generation of riverboat pilots, runs **Discovery Riverboat Cruises** (907/479-6673 or 866/479-6673, www.riverboatdiscovery.com). This four-hour, 20-mile cruise on the Chena and Tanana Rivers—a bargain at $45 adults, $30 for ages 3–12, free for tots—includes the chance to view an Athabascan-style camp and to watch Iditarod champion Susan Butcher's dog team in action (from the boat). The boat docks at a recreated Alaskan bush village with log cabins and giant cabbages. Reservations are necessary.

Cruises depart from the dock at the end of Dale Road out by the airport at 8:45 A.M. and 2 P.M. A large gift shop awaits if you get there early.

Tanana Chief (907/452-8687 or 866/452-8687), is a smaller paddlewheel boat with two-hour summertime sightseeing trips ($25), along with prime rib dinner cruises for $50, and Sunday brunch cruises for $37.

The *Tanana Queen* (907/456-5134 or 800/770-7275) is a pontoon boat that departs twice daily in the summer from both Golden Heart Plaza and Pioneer Park. You'll get a narrated historical tour with a box lunch or ice cream and cookies for $20 adults, $15 kids.

Alexander's River Tours (907/474-3924, home.gci.net/~alexriveradv) takes folks on a four-hour jetboat ride down the Chena and Tanana rivers that includes time at a remote fish camp. Owner Wes Alexander is five-time winner of the grueling Yukon 800 Riverboat Race.

RECREATION
Hiking

For local trails, try Creamer's Field and Chena River State Recreation Area. Farther afield, find hiking and backpacking opportunities in the White Mountains and in the Pinnell Mountains.

Biking

Fairbanks has an excellent series of connecting bike routes: from downtown along the river to Pioneer Park; from University and Airport out on Chena Pump Road; and a great up-and-down route on Farmers Loop Road from the Steese Highway to the university. **Alaska Outdoor Rentals & Guides** (907/457-2453, www.akbike.com) has bike rentals at three places in town: Pioneer Park, Fairbanks Hotel (517 3rd Ave.), and Pike's Riverfront Lodge (1850 Hoselton). The cost is $18 for a half-day or $27 for all day. The company also offers guided bike excursions around town. You can also rent mountain bikes from **GoNorth Adventure Travel Center** (3500 Davis Rd., 907/479-7272 or 866/236-7272, www.go northalaska.net).

THE INTERIOR

Swimming

Three indoor pools are open to the public: **Hamme Pool** (Airport and Cowles, 907/456-2969) at Lathrop High School, **Mary Siah Recreation Center** (1025 14th Ave., 907/456-6119), and **Patty Gym Pool** (at UAF, 907/474-7205).

Floating the River

The peaceful Chena River is a favorite destination for canoeists. **GoNorth Adventure Travel Center** (3500 Davis Rd., 907/479-7272 or 866/236-7272, www.gonorthalaska.net) rents canoes, and can provide equipment and transportation up the Chena River, and a pickup once you return to Fairbanks three days later. **Alaska Outdoor Rentals & Guides** (at Pioneer Park, 907/457-2453, www.2paddle1.com) has canoe and kayak rentals and transportation, guided excursions, and paddling classes.

Alaska Fishing & Raft Adventures (907/388-4193 or 888/890-3229, www.aktours.net) takes guests on six-hour raft trips down the upper Chena River. These easy floats cost $95 per person, including transportation from Fairbanks and a lunch or dinner.

Ice-Skating

No need to wait for winter freeze-up in this town. **Big Dipper Ice Arena** (19th and Lathrop, 907/456-6683) is open all year. If you do come in winter, you'll find ideal ice conditions at many local ponds.

Fishing

A number of local companies provide Chena River fishing trips; get their brochures at the visitors center. Fishing in the Chena for grayling is fair, but better grayling fishing is found at the Chatanika River, between miles 30 and 40 on the Steese Highway toward Circle. Chum, silver, and a few kings run up here from mid-July. Chena Lakes Recreation Area has good rainbow-trout fishing. Fish & Game provides a recorded hot line (907/459-7385) of fishing tips. The *Fairbanks Daily News-Miner* carries fishing updates every Friday.

Dog Mushing

Fairbanks is a major center for dog mushing. Well-known musher and author **Mary Shields** was the first woman to finish the Iditarod. She offers two-hour summer visits (907/457-1117, www.maryshields.com) that include time with the dogs and a sledding demonstration for $25 adults, or $20 kids. She also leads wintertime sled dog tours.

Other dogsledding tours or rides (depending upon the season) are available from **Chena Dog Sled Adventures** (907/488-5845), **Chena Hot Springs Resort** (907/452-7867 or 800/478-4681, www.chenahotsprings.com), **Northern Sky Kennel** (907/388-9954, www.northernskylodge.com), **Paws for Adventure** (907/378-3630 or 800/890-3229, www.pawsforadventure.com), **Sled Dog Adventures** (907/479-5090, www.sleddogadventures.com), and **Sun Dog Express** (907/479-6983, www.mosquitonet.com/~sleddog).

Skiing

Moose Mountain (907/479-8362, www.shredthemoose.com) is 20 minutes north of Fairbanks near Murphy Dome. It has 1,250 feet of vertical drop, and an unusual lift system: a "variable capacity terrestrial tram," more commonly called a bus with ski racks. Ski here at $25 adults, $20 college students, and $15 ages 7–12. Get the snow report at 907/459-8132. Fortunately, temperatures are typically 20–30 degrees warmer here than in Fairbanks (because of an inversion). The ski area is open Thursday–Sunday 10 A.M.–5 P.M. in the winter.

Cross-country skiing is very popular around Fairbanks; the nicest place is **Birch Hill Ski Area,** with 33 km of groomed trails, 6 km of which are lighted. Contact the **Nordic Ski Club of Fairbanks** (907/474-4242, www.nscfairbanks.org) for details.

Northern Lights Viewing

The Fairbanks area has some of the finest aurora displays anywhere on the planet. The clear winter nights and proximity to the North Pole create ideal viewing conditions (once you get away from the city lights and ice fog). For predictions of upcoming activity, visit the website

for UAF's Geophysical Institute (www.gi.alaska
.edu). A number of lodges in the Fairbanks area
have geared their winter season for people who
come to view and photograph the northern
lights. These include Chena Hot Springs Resort, A Cloudberry Lookout B&B, and Mt. Au-
rora/Skiland. In addition, many Fairbanks hotels
provide aurora wake-up calls upon request.

Other Recreation

Midnight Sun Balloon Tours (907/456-3028,
www.mosquitonet.com/~sracina) has flights for
$150 adults or $125 kids. These
last an hour or so and depart
early in the morning when wind
conditions are mild.

Play a midnight round of
summertime golf at **Fairbanks
Golf & Country Club** (1735
Farmers Loop Rd., 907/479-
6555), where 24-hour tee times
are available on the nine-hole
course in June and July! **North
Star Golf Club** (330 Golf Club
Dr., 907/457-4653, www.north-
stargolf.com),"America's northernmost," is the other local
nine-hole club.

Saddle Horse Trail Rides
(907/457-3601), offer guided horseback rides
from their farm off Chena Hot Springs Road.

ACCOMMODATIONS

Fairbanks has the complete lodging spectrum,
from backpacker hostel beds and questionable
motels to newly opened hotels with top-end features and amenities. Start your exploration by
looking over the descriptions in the Fairbanks
Visitors Guide from the CVB, or their online
version at www.explorefairbanks.com.

Under $50

Fairbanks is blessed with some of Alaska's best
hostels. For **Billie's Backpackers Hostel** (2895
Mack Rd., 907/479-2034, www.alaskahos-
tel.com) head north on College Road, take a
right on Westwood, and look for the house with

international flags. You can stay in four-person
dorms for $22 per person, or pay $15 per person for a tent space. Private rooms are $44 d,
but these go fast. The hostel provides a kitchen,
showers, internet access, travel information,
and has the added bonus of a sun deck, barbecue, volleyball, and basketball. Bikes are available
for rent. Open year-round.

GoNorth Base Camp Hostel (near the airport
at 3500 Davis Rd., 907/479-7272 or 866/236-
7272, www.gonorthalaska.net) has a mix of lodging choices, including bunks in surprisingly nice
wall tents for $20 pp, beds in cab-
ins for $30 pp ($56 d for a private cabin), and tent spaces for
$12. Kids love the tipi, and other
facilities include coin-op showers,
internet access, outdoor equipment rentals (from canoes to satellite phones), and trip planning.
The Swiss-born owners also speak
German and French. The hostel is
open mid-May to late September.

Boyle's Hostel (310 18th Ave.,
907/456-4944) has rooms with
two bunks each for $17 per per-
son, and private rooms for $30
d. Tent spaces are $12, and all
guests have access to the kitchens
and showers. Linen is provided.

Backpackers' Adventure In & Hostel (1221
9th Ave., 907/374-9287) has a central location
and reasonable rates for bunk rooms: $15 per
person, with a full kitchen, showers, and laundry.

$50-100

College Inn (700 Fairbanks St., 907/474-3666
or 800/770-2177, www.college-inn.com), on
the west side of town near the university, is an
aging dorm-style hotel with down-the-hall
baths and a communal kitchen. Not the least
bit fancy, but clean and reasonably priced at
$59 s or $69 d.

Ten miles south of Fairbanks is another inexpensive option, the **Ester Gold Camp**
(907/479-2500 or 800/676-6925, www.alaskas-
best.com/ester), where basic rooms start at $60
s or $70 d.

*The Fairbanks area
has some of the finest
aurora displays
anywhere on the
planet. The clear
winter nights and
proximity to the North
Pole create ideal view-
ing conditions. Many
Fairbanks hotels
provide aurora wake-
up calls upon request.*

The art aeco–style **Fairbanks Hotel** (517 3rd Ave., 907/456-6440 or 888/329-4685, www.fbxhotl.com) is the oldest in town (1941) and the rooms are small but remodeled with brass headboards, antique dressers, and pedestal sinks. Rates are $55–69 s or $85–89 d with bath down the hall, or $85–89 s or $105–109 d with a private bath. Their shuttle will fetch you from the airport or train station, and they rent bikes and storage lockers in the summer and winter clothes (!) when the temperature drops well below zero. The nicest rooms (recently remodeled) are on the first floor.

Alaska Motel (1546 Cushman St., 907/456-6393, www.ak-motel.com) is another older motel with renovated rooms—most with kitchenettes—for $65–85 s or d.

Golden North Motel (4888 Airport Way, 907/479-6201 or 800/447-1910, www.golden northmotel.com) is near the airport, and its courtesy van is available 24 hours. Rooms are small but reasonable, and include a continental breakfast; $69 d for one bed, $99 d for two beds.

Ranch Motel (2223 S. Cushman St., 907/452-4783 or 888/452-4783, www.ex-page.com/ranchmotel) is a small motel with clean rooms for $85–95 s or d.

$100–150

All Seasons Inn (downtown at 763 7th Ave., 907/451-6649 or 888/451-6649, www.allsea-sonsinn.com) is a cross between a motel and B&B, with eight elegant modern rooms and full breakfasts. Two rooms with single beds share a bath and are just $85 d, but the others have private baths and cost $135–160 d. Recommended.

The exterior of **Golden Nugget Hotel** (900 Noble St., 907/452-5141, www.golden-nuggeth-otel.com) is dated, but the rooms are spacious and have air-conditioning; $95 d.

Captain Bartlett Inn (1411 Airport Way, 907/452-1888, 800/544-7528 outside Alaska, or 800/478-7900 in Alaska, www.captain-bartlettinn.com), is one of the largest places in town, with nicely appointed rooms following an Alaskan theme, plus a fun saloon and restaurant. Rates are $145 d.

Over $150

Fountainhead Development (907/452-6661 or 800/528-4916, www.fountainheadhotels.com) owns three Fairbanks lodging places: Bridge-water Hotel, Sophie Station Hotel, and Wedge-wood Resort. Just a block from the downtown visitor center, the entirely non-smoking **Bridge-water Hotel** (723 1st Ave.) has attractive rooms for $140 d. Ask for a corner room overlooking the river. Open mid-May to mid-September. Catering to business travelers, luxurious **Sophie Station Hotel** (1717 University Ave.) has very attractive suites—all with full kitchens—for $180 s or d. **Wedgewood Resort** (on the north side of town at 212 Wedgewood Dr.) has homey apartments, all with full kitchens, living rooms, and dining rooms. One-bedroom units are $150 d or $170 for four, and two-bedroom units run $185 d or $225 for six people. Free airport shuttle, too. Also on the resort grounds is the seasonal **Bear Lodge,** with small rooms for $185 d, but they're typically filled with Princess cruise folks.

Comfort Inn (1908 Chena Landings Loop, 907/479-8080 or 800/228-5150, www.com-fortinn.com) has an indoor pool and hot tub, plus a free airport shuttle. Rates are $149–169 d, including a light breakfast.

Regency Fairbanks (95 10th Ave., 907/452-3200, 800/478-1320, or 800/348-1340 outside Alaska, www.regencyfairbankshotel.com) is a large, centrally located hotel where the rooms all have full kitchens. Standard rooms cost $149 d; those with jacuzzi tubs are $169 d. Free airport and railroad shuttle.

The recently built **Aspen Hotel** (4580 Old Airport Rd., 907457-2288 or 888/595-2151, www.aspenhotelsak.com) has all the amenities travelers have come to expect: indoor pool, jacuzzi, exercise room, business center, in-room fridges, microwaves and VCRs, and a continental breakfast. Standard rooms go for $159 d, or pay $179 d for family suites, jacuzzi suites, or suites with full kitchens and king beds.

River's Edge Resort (4200 Boat St., 907/474-0286 or 800/770-3343, www.rivers edge.net) features 90 modern cottages crowded together along the Chena River. Each is charm-ingly decorated, and includes two queen beds; $175 d. A restaurant and pub are on the premises.

The **Westmark Fairbanks Hotel** (813 Noble St., 907/456-7722 or 800/544-0970, www.westmarkhotels.com) has 400 large rooms-many of them brand new-for $171 d in standard rooms or $200 d for suites. Rates include a summertime airport shuttle, fitness center, business center, and valet service.

SpringHill Suites (575 1st Ave., 907/451-6552 or 877/729-0197, www.springhillsuites.com) is a recently opened six-story hotel in the center of Fairbanks, just across the street from the Chena River. Rooms are large, and guests appreciate the indoor pool, exercise room, jacuzzi, sauna, minifridges, microwaves, and continental breakfast. Rooms cost $179–189 d.

Pike's Waterfront Lodge (907/456-4500 or 877/774-2400, www.pikeslodge.com) is one of Fairbanks' newest lodgings. This 180-room motel on Airport Way next to Pike's Landing Restaurant has attractively furnished rooms and suites for $190–375 d. Some rooms include river views and in-room jacuzzis, and all guests have access to the fitness center, sauna, and steam room.

Fairbanks Princess Riverside Lodge (4477 Pikes Landing near the airport, 907/455-4477 or 800/426-0500, www.princessalaskalodges.com) has 325 rooms, a terraced deck right on the river, three restaurants, and a health spa. Rates are $200 d for (ask for a riverfront room with a king bed), up to $500 d for a two-bedroom suite. Not surprisingly, the Princess is typically filled with cruise ship passengers.

Bed-and-Breakfasts

For many travelers, B&Bs are the best deal in Fairbanks, with most places charging around $100 d, including a full breakfast. The downtown visitor center has racks of cards from local B&Bs, or find links on their website (www.explorefairbanks.com) or that of the **Fairbanks Association of B&Bs** (www .ptialaska.net/~fabb).

Ah, Rose Marie B&B (302 Cowles St., 907/456-2040, www.akpub.com/akbbrv/ah rose.html) is a small historic home a few blocks

from downtown with reasonable rates ($60 s or $75 d) and a full breakfast. Other good downtown places with rooms for $100 d or less include **Fairbanks Downtown B&B** (1461 Gillam Way, 907/452-7700, www.alaska.net /~balty), **Eleanor's Northern Lights B&B** (360 State St., 907/452-2598 or 800/467-4167, www.eagle.ptialaska.net), and **Downtown Log Cabin Hideaway** (9304 Badger St., 907/452-1100).

Also reasonable is **Richter House B&B** (501 Summer Ave., 907/457-3924, www.mosquitonet.com/~richter, $55 s, $70 d) six miles north of town. The private guest cabin is cozy, but you'll need to use the bath in the main house.

Midge's Birch Lane B&B (4335 Birch Lane, 907/388-8084, www.alaskaone.com/midgebb) is an inviting home near the university with four guest rooms ($100 d), a friendly hostess, and excellent breakfasts.

Located atop a knoll near the university, **A Cloudberry Lookout B&B** (907/479-7334, www.mosquitonet.com/~cloudberry) is a grand home with a central aurora viewing tower and rooftop walkway that's accessed via a spiral staircase. The four rooms include an $95 d room with a king bed, up to a $115 d two-room suite; all have private baths and antique furnishings. A full breakfast is served each morning. The house isn't really kid-friendly.

The **7 Gables Inn** (4312 Birch Lane, 907/479-0751, www.7gablesinn.com) is one of the largest B&Bs in Alaska. Originally a university frat house, the 7 Gables is a 7,000-square-foot custom Tudor house beside the river, complete with seven-foot stained-glass windows, an indoor waterfall, and a two-story greenhouse. Rates start at $90 d for regular rooms up to $130 d for the bridal suite with jacuzzi tub. All have full baths, and a gourmet breakfast is served.

Minnie Street B&B Inn (345 Minnie St., 907/456-1802 or 888/456-1849, www.minniestreetbandb.com) is a large and modern downtown place with eight rooms ($100–130 d) and suites ($110–150 d), all including a big breakfast.

A Taste of Alaska Lodge (907/488-7855, www.atasteofalaska.com), is a 7,000-square-foot log home off Chena Hot Springs Road.

Amenities include private baths, an indoor jacuzzi and exercise room, and full breakfasts. The hilltop location provides fine mountain (and wintertime aurora) views. Guests stay in the main lodge for $175–195 d, or in two cabins for $195–225 d.

Fairbanks' most unique lodging is—without a doubt—**Aurora Express** (907/474-0949 or 800/221-0073, www.aurora-express.com). Susan and Mike Wilson have assembled a nostalgic collection of Alaska Railroad cars (the oldest dates from 1924) and decorated the interiors with playful themes, including a 19th-century bordello with antiques and crystal chandeliers! Rates are $ 100–125 d or $115–135 d. Families will love the restored Pullman sleeper with two baths; it sleeps five for $225. A big breakfast is served in the dining car each morning. Be sure to ask Susan about her time as the only woman on a pipeline construction crew in the 1970s. Aurora Express is definitely recommended, especially if you're a train enthusiast.

CAMPING
Public Campgrounds
The **Pioneer Park** parking lot is open to motor homes for $10. No hook-ups or showers, but potable water, restrooms, and a disposal station. Register in the cabin just inside the entrance. Many other folks park RVs for free at several of the larger malls around Fairbanks.

Tanana Valley Campground (at the fairgrounds on College Rd. at Aurora Dr., 907/456-7956, www.tananavalleyfair.org) is close to hiking and biking trails, and near Creamer's Field. Sites cost $9 tents, $16 RVs, showers are free, and campfires are allowed in this natural setting. open mid-May to mid-September.

Chena River State Recreation Area (907/451-2695, www.alaskastateparks.org, $10–15) is a state campground on University Avenue just north of Airport Way. It has running water, fireplaces, boat launch, and fishing—a bit high density, but not bad for city camping, if you arrive early enough to get a site. No showers here, so you'll need to find one at a local laundromat. Another fine public

campground ($10) is **Chena Lakes Recreation Area,** near North Pole.

Private Campgrounds and RV Parks
Norlite Campground (on Peger Rd. near Pioneer Park, 907/474-0206, www.norlite.com) has been here since 1968; the city has grown up around it. Tent sites cost $15; $25 for RVs. Open mid-May to mid-September.

River's Edge RV Park (on Boat St. off Airport Way near University Ave., 907/474-0286 or 800/770-3343, www.riversedge.net) is a large handy campground on the banks of the Chena River. This campground is right on the river bike trail and has a private boat launch; $16 tents, $28 RVs.

Chena Marina RV Park (1145 Shypoke Dr., 907/479-4653, www.chenarvpark.com) sits next to a floatplane pond out Chena Pump Road; $23 tents, $29–32 RVs, including a continental breakfast, free carwash, and cable TV hookups.

Riverview RV Park (1316 Badger Rd., 907/488-6281 or 888/488-6392, www.alaskaone.com/riverview) is three miles east of town and right along the Chena River; $26 for RVs, $17 for tents.

FOOD
Fairbanks has a fine diversity of food choices, including not just places with down-home meals (and prices), but also those offering gourmet meals (and prices).

Breakfast
The Diner (244 Illinois St., 907/451-0613) serves breakfast anytime. Gigantic portions, efficient service, and reasonable prices; nothing is over $10—even their dinners. It opens daily at 6:30 A.M.

The Bakery Restaurant (on College Rd. near Illinois, 907/456-8600) is a smoke-free family place where the booths create a relaxed atmosphere. It's especially popular for breakfast, but also serves all-American lunches and dinners. Pies and other freshly baked desserts are always on the menu.

Co-Op Diner (535 2nd Ave., 907/451-9128)

in the center of town is a delightfully old-fashioned 1950s-style diner with omelets, French toast, and blueberry pancakes for breakfast, along with burgers, sandwiches, and grilled chicken for lunch. Great shakes too.

The same building (Co-Op Plaza) houses **Two Street Station** (907/456-6242), a popular stop for an espresso and pastry. Other notable espresso joints include **Alaska Coffee Roasting Company** (4001 Geist Rd., 907/457-5282) and **Java.com** (in Northgate Square at 334 Old Steese Hwy., 907/456-1150). Befitting the name, the last of these also has computers where you can check your email.

Lunch and Quick Meals

Looking for lunch in a hurry? You certainly won't go wrong at **Bun on the Run,** a little trailer parked out front of Beaver Sports at 3480 College Rd. near the university. Sandwiches are made to order; check the board for today's specials and then wait at one of the cable-spool tables in the parking lot. Open for lunch Mon.–Sat., May–September. Recommended.

L'Assiette da Pomegranate (414 2nd Ave., 907/451-7505) is a delightful downtown lunch spot with creative sandwiches, salads, and soups; most entrées run $9. Outstanding desserts too.

Second Story Cafe (on College Rd. at University Ave., 907/474-9574) is upstairs inside Gulliver's Books. The menu covers the latest trends in wraps, espresso, homemade soups, salads, and other light fare. Free Internet access, too. Not to mention all the great books.

Satisfy your sweet tooth at **Hot Licks** (near UAF on College Rd. at Hess Ave., 907/479-7813). There's often a line out front on a summer afternoon as folks wait for a scoop of the 20-plus flavors of homemade ice cream. Also on the menu are banana splits, Hawaiian shaved ice, and frappuccinos.

Fast-food row is on Airport Way between Lathrop and Wilbur: Wendy's, McDonald's, Denny's, Pizza Hut, Burger King, ad nauseam. A better bet is **College Town Pizzeria** (3549 College Rd., 907/457-2200) next to Gulliver's, with pizza by the slice or pie, eggplant parmesan calzones, and "heart attack in a tube" strombolis. Also good

for pizza (including one packed with garlic) is **Geraldo's** (701 College Rd., 907/452-2299).

Riverside Juice Bar (907/474-1035, www.rivesidejuicebar.com) is far off the beaten track, but fun if you're looking for a quiet setting, wholesome sandwiches, and organic juices. Head four miles out Chena Pump Road, and follow the signs out a dirt road to this simple spot right on the Tanana River.

Tourists love **Fudge Pot** (515 1st Ave., 907/456-3834, www.thefudgepot.com), just up from the downtown visitor center, where you'll find 30 types of fudge, plus soups, sandwiches, and espresso.

International

Thai House Restaurant (526 Fifth Ave., 907/452-6123) is a wonderful Fairbanks option, especially on a bitterly cold winter day. The food is spicy and fresh, service is attentive, and even the Thai tea is a delight at this little family-run café in the heart of town. Highly recommended.

Out near the university across from the Farmers Market is **Little Saigon** (1753 College Rd., 907/452-4399). This tiny hole-in-the-wall eatery serves authentic Vietnamese meals, including pho bo vein (beef soup with rice noodles).

A number of Mexican-style places are found around Fairbanks; you might try **Hot Tamale** (112 Turner St., 907/457-8350), with a big lunch and dinner buffet, or **El Mariachi** (541 3rd Ave., 907/457-2698).

Biscotti (364 Chena Pump Rd., 907/479-0670) serves Mediterranean lunches and dinners. Gambardella's Pasta Bella has good Italian.

Salmon Bake

Don't miss the **Alaska Salmon Bake** (907/452-7274 or 800/354-7274, www.akvisit.com) at Pioneer Park. For $24 you get all-you-can-eat king salmon (caught near Sitka and flown in fresh daily), halibut, ribs, or porterhouse steaks ($26), plus a big salad bar and desserts. The owner grew up in Juneau where his father was a commercial fisherman, so he knows his fish. This may be the best salmon bake in Alaska. It's open daily 5–9 P.M. from mid-May to mid-September, and a free salmon-bake shuttle bus runs 4–10 P.M., stopping at the major hotels and RV parks around town.

Riverfront Dining

For some alfresco Chena River dining, head to **Pike's Landing** (out Airport Rd., 907/479-6500, www.pikeslanding.com, open daily). Lloyd Pike opened his log bar at this site in 1969; since then, the Landing has expanded greatly, with a dining room and a sports bar, an 11,000-square-foot wood deck that accommodates over 400 diners, and a dock for boaters who pull up for a meal. Pike's serves burgers, clam linguine, crab-stuffed chicken, king salmon, king crab, plus great desserts (including Key-lime pie and baked Alaska). On the expensive side; most dinner entrées run $23–40. Save a few bucks by coming for lunch or eating in the bar or on the deck. Pike's is where the locals take their guests for a fun and noisy meal.

For a more old-time atmosphere on the river, head out to the **Pump House** (1.3 Mile Chena Pump Rd., 907/479-8452, www.pump-house.com). A National Historical Monument, the Pump House was built in 1933 to pump water up Chena Ridge to provide pressure for the hydraulic "giants" used in gold dredging. The restaurant/bar has a fascinating interior of mining and pumping artifacts. Good food, too, especially the big lunch buffet (summers only; $12). Dinner entrées run $15–35, and include the usual Alaskan favorites: steak, chicken, burgers, salmon, pepper steak, and king crab. The Sunday brunch ($17) is especially popular.

Out in Fox (10 miles out Old Steese Highway), the **Turtle Club** (907/457-3883, www.alaskanturtle.com) is a fine dining establishment with prime rib, jumbo prawns, lobster, halibut, and BBQ rib dinners.

Chena's Fine Dining (at River's Edge Resort, 4200 Boat St., 907/474-3644, www.riversedge.net) is another pleasant riverside option, with Alaskan halibut and salmon, prime rib, steaks, and pasta, available on the covered veranda or sun deck in the summer, or inside year-round.

Downtown Dinners

Just a block from the downtown visitor center,

Gambardella's Pasta Bella (706 2nd Ave., 907/457-2992) is popular for pasta, homemade bread, gourmet pizzas, calzones, and subs. The atmosphere is warm and inviting, and there's an enclosed back patio.

One of Alaska's only wine bars, **Cafe Alex** (310 1st Ave., 907/452-2539) has a playful but relaxed atmosphere, with finger food in small portions-perfect for sharing with your sweetie. You can get a light gourmet meal without spending a ton of money-most items are $8–10, and wine is available the glass. Highly recommended.

Lavelle's Bistro (inside Springhill Suites at 575 1st Ave., 907/450-0555, www.lavelles-bistro.com) has a setting that seems out of place in jeans-and-bunny-boots Fairbanks. It's modern and trendy, with a 2,000-bottle wall of wine, an open kitchen where you can watch the chefs at work, and upscale dining for $15–30. Unfortunately, the food and service get mixed reviews.

Groceries and Farmers Market

Fairbanks lacks a downtown grocery store, but you'll find **Safeways** at University Center on Airport Way and in the Bentley Mall on College Road, and two big **Fred Meyer** shopping centers at 3755 Airport Way and 19 College Road.

The **Tanana Valley Farmers Market** (corner of College Rd. and Aurora, 907/456-3276, www.tvfmarket.com) is *the* place to buy locally grown produce, flowers, baked goods, arts, and crafts. The market is open Wednesday 11 A.M.–4 P.M. and Saturday 9 A.M.–4 P.M. early May to late September. This is a wonderful place to get a taste of Alaska (literally).

ENTERTAINMENT
Drinking and Dancing

Blue Loon (on the Parks Hwy. three miles south of town, 907/457-5666, www.theblueloon.com), is Fairbanks' party place with hot bands (including nationally known acts), art house movies, dancing, 15 beers on tap, and good pub meals till midnight on Friday and Saturday nights. Don't miss their Jerry Garcia pig roast each August. Closed Sundays and Mondays.

Other dance-'til-2 places are **The Marlin**

(3412 College Rd., 907/479-4646), **Castle Restaurant and Lounge** (4510 Airport Way, 907/474-2165), and **Silverspur Nightclub** (285 Old Richardson Hwy., 907/456-6300).

For a nice riverside drink and hors d'oeuvres in an historic setting, head out to the **Pump House** (1.3 Mile Chena Pump Rd., 907/479-8452). Good meals, too. **College Coffeehouse** (3677 College Rd., 907/374-0468) has Friday night folk music.

Silver Gulch Brewery (at the Fox Roadhouse, 907/452-2739, www.silvergulch.com) brews four beers: a porter, two lagers, and amber ale. Free tours and tastings on Fridays 5–7 P.M. Locals call it the best beer in Alaska.

Movies and Plays

Goldstream Cinema (on Airport Way at Lathrop, 907/456-5113) has comfortable seating and 16 movie screens. The Blue Loon sometimes shows films, too. **Fairbanks Shakespeare Theatre** (907/457-1114, www.fairbanks-shakespeare.org), performs at Birch Hill Recreation Area (off Chena Hot Springs Rd.) in July and August.

Saloon Theaters

The **Palace Theatre & Saloon** (at Pioneer Park, 907/456-5960, www.akvisit.com) offers a musical-comedy revue nightly mid-May to mid-September. The show, *Golden Heart Revue,* goes on at 8:15 P.M. It's professionally produced, and worth the admission: $15 adults or $8 kids.

The **Malemute Saloon** (10 miles south of Fairbanks, 907/479-2500, www.akvisit.com), in Ester, has been a local institution since 1958, putting on a musical revue and Robert Service recitations nightly at 9 P.M., with additional shows at 7 P.M. Wed.–Sat. evenings; $15 adults or $8 ages 3–12. You sit at plywood and beer-barrel tables; the pitchers keep coming and the peanut shells mingle with the two-inch-deep sawdust.

Baseball

One local "rookie" team, the **Alaska Goldpanners** (907/451-0095, www.goldpanners.com) plays against teams in the Alaska Baseball League. The games are played at Growden Field (2nd and Wilbur, behind Pioneer Park), starting at 7 P.M. The famous Midnight Sun game, played around the summer solstice, starts at 10:30 P.M. and goes nine innings without using the field's artificial lights. The Goldpanners are composed of college players, dozens of whom have gone on to play in the major leagues, including Dave Winfield, Graig Nettles, and Tom Seaver.

EVENTS
Summer
Locals have roughly 90 days a year to get their fill of outdoor extravaganzas—without having to worry about frostbite, that is—and they go at it with a vengeance. The first big event of the season is the **Midnight Sun Festival,** held on summer solstice (June 21), with live music (30 bands), food, a car show, and the famous Alaska Goldpanners **Midnight Sun baseball game** that continues past midnight without lights. Details at www.downtownfairbanks.com.

Next comes **Golden Days,** between the second and third weekends in July—a weeklong party culminating in a fun parade. The whole town turns out, and if you happen to be there, even without your camera, you won't forget it.

Next comes the **World Eskimo-Indian Olympics** (907/452-6646, www.weio.org), featuring Alaska Native athletic games, dance, and art. This three-day mid-July event, includes such unusual competitions as the Ear Pull, Greased Pole Walk, Kneel Jump, Knuckle Hop, Seal Skin, Toe Kick, and Blanket Toss. There's even a Native baby contest. It could be one of the most exotic and memorable events in Alaska.

The **Fairbanks Summer Arts Festival** (907/474-8869, www.fsaf.org) is a two-week-long series of workshops, performances, and concerts, encompassing classical music, opera, dance, theatre, figure skating (!), and visual arts. It takes place from late July to early August, and attracts hundreds of students and instructors.

The big **Tanana Valley State Fair** (907/452-3750, www.tananavalleyfair.org) is at the Fairgrounds on College Road, the second and third weeks of August, with rides, music, food booths, and craft booths.

Winter

Things don't entirely shut down when winter arrives in Fairbanks. The biggest event is the **Yukon Quest International Sled Dog Race** (907/452-7954, www.yukonquest.com), held in February. Other sled dog races include the **Limited North American Sled Dog Championships** in early March followed by the **Open North American Championship Sled Dog Races** in mid-March. Details on both from the Alaska Dog Mushers Association (907/457-6874, www.sleddog.org).

The **World Ice Art Championship** (907/451-8250, www.icealaska.com) is an early March event that attracts international sculptors who create truly amazing works of art. This isn't your standard fancy restaurant art; some of these pieces may stand 20 feet tall and contain incredibly intricate work. Just getting the 1,500 tons of clear ice is a challenge.

SHOPPING

On Wednesdays and Saturdays in the summer, the **Tanana Valley Farmers Market** (corner of College Rd. and Aurora, 907/456-3276, www.tvfmarket.com) is *the* place to find locally grown or crafted items, from asparagus and berry pies to Native beadwork and polar fleece booties.

Great Alaskan Bowl Company (4630 Old Airport Rd., 907/474-9663 or 800/770-4222, www.woodbowl.com), sells a variety of nesting birch hardwood bowls, all fashioned from a single split log (take a left off Airport onto Sportsman between the Castle Restaurant and Fred Meyer and follow it around to the right). This is a good made-in-Alaska product to take home with you. A window overlooks the wood shop; the wood shavings are used for packing material and decoration in the showroom.

YUKON QUEST

The Yukon Quest International Sled Dog Race began in February 1984 with 26 teams in competition. The race has close ties to the past of the Yukon and Interior Alaska, taking place along trails that once carried fur traders and missionaries, gold-hungry pilgrims and determined mail carriers. In the days before airplanes and automobiles, the dog team was often the only method of transportation in the great North. The Yukon Quest has been called the "toughest race on earth." For good reason.

The race, which takes place in early February, runs from Fairbanks to Whitehorse in even-numbered years and from Whitehorse to Fairbanks in odd-numbered years. It's named for the mighty Yukon River, "the Highway of the North," and travels across some of the wildest and most sparsely populated country in the world. Terrain, trail conditions, and temperatures vary wildly along the trail, from steep hills to miles of flat frozen lake, from hard-packed snow and frozen rivers to rough gravel, from -60– +30°F.

Although most of the media focus is on the mushers, the real stars of this or any sled dog race are the canine athletes. Since the teams are limited to 14 dogs, the Quest is musher-friendly to those with smaller kennels. And a smaller team ensures better care for individual dogs.

Depending on weather and trail conditions, the race takes 10–14 days. There is a mandatory 36-hour layover in Dawson City, Yukon. This is the only stop where dog handlers can feed and care for the teams while the mushers get some much-needed rest. A large veterinarian tent is set up in the dog camp, which lies across the frozen Yukon River from Dawson.

If a dog exhibits signs of fatigue or illness at a checkpoint, the animal is dropped from the race and turned over to the handlers. If dropped at a remote spot, the dog is transported by one of the many volunteer pilots to a point where it can be met by the handlers.

Unlike other long-distance races, the Quest is easily accessible to onlookers. Race fans may follow the mushers' progress by driving to many of the checkpoints along the way. Photo opportunities are plentiful from start to finish. For further information, contact Quest headquarters (600 3rd St. in Fairbanks at 907/452-7954, www.yukonquest.org).

Galleries and Gifts

Fairbanks' best and largest art stop is **New Horizons Gallery** (519 1st Ave., 907/456-2063 or 888/456-2063, www.newhorizonsgallery.com) across from the visitors center. Also of note are **Alaska House Art Gallery** (at 10th and Cushman, 907/456-6449, www.thealaskahouse.com) and **The Artworks** (near the university at 3677 College Rd., 907/479-2563).

Gift shops abound downtown; **Arctic Travelers** (at 201 Cushman, 907/456-7080, www.arctictravelers.com) is the biggest. Next door is **Alaska Rare Coins** (907/452-6461) selling rare coins, old license plates, and out-of-print books about the North—a classic old store. Native-owned **Beads and Things** (537 2nd Ave., 907/456-2323) sells handmade gifts and curios. **The Craft Market** (on the corner of 5th and Noble, 907/452-5495) has a good collection of carved ivory, woven baskets, masks, dolls, and other Native arts and crafts.

Alaska Rag Co. (603 Lacey St., 907/451-4401, www.alaskaragco.com) is a unique shop with hand-woven rag rugs made on the premises, plus jewelry, stained glass, and other gifts. (The rugs are woven from locally recycled cloth, and many of the workers are mentally disabled individuals who could not otherwise find work.) **The Spinning Room** (516 2nd Ave., Studio 220, 907/458-7610, www.spinning-room.com) sells handspun fabrics, including those made from musk ox wool.

If you're looking for gold nuggets fresh from Alaskan streams at "spot" prices, go to **Oxford Assaying** (748 Gaffney Rd., 907/456-3967); it has all sizes of nuggets at all prices—great to take home as authentic souvenirs or to bring to a jeweler to be made into rings, necklaces, or earrings.

Outdoor Gear

Beaver Sports (3480 College Rd., 907/479-2494, www.beaversports.com) is *the* place for outdoor gear of all types in Fairbanks, and has the largest selection of canoes in Alaska. They also rent canoes, mountain bikes, skis, and snowshoes.

Go North (3820 University Ave., 907/479-7272, www.gonorthalaska.net) acts as a one-stop place for travelers, with hostel space, tent sites, trip planning, and rental canoes, mountain bikes, tents, sleeping bags, cooking utensils, and all sorts of other gear, including GPS units and satellite phones!

Get hand-sewn outdoor creations, along with fast repairs on tents, backpacks, sleeping bags, and other gear from **Apocalypse Design** (101 College Rd., 907/451-7555 or 866/451-7555, www.akgear.com).

INFORMATION AND SERVICES

In addition to the **Fairbanks Visitors Bureau** and the **Alaska Public Lands Information Center,** go to the State of Alaska's **Department of Natural Resources Public Information Center** (3700 Airport Way, 907/451-2705, www.alaskastateparks.org, Mon.–Fri. 9 A.M.–5 P.M.), across the street from Fred Meyer. Stop here to get brochures on state parks and trails, reserve a state park cabin, or to learn about mining claims and state land sales.

Topographical maps of Alaska are sold in Room 126 of the Federal Building (101 12th Ave.), and at the Map Office in UAF's International Arctic Research Center (907/474-6960).

Useful **Fairbanks websites** include the Fairbanks Visitors and Convention Bureau (www.explorefairbanks.com), the *Fairbanks News-Miner* (www.newsminer.com), and the aurora forecast at the Geophysical Institute (www.gi.alaska.edu). How cold (or hot) is it in Fairbanks? Visit the National Weather Service (www.arh.noaa.gov).

Books and Internet

The **Noel Wien Library** (corner of Airport Way and Cowles, 907/452-5177, http://library.fnsb.lib.ak.us) is a comfortable and complete facility (indoor trees, even). One look inside tells you a lot about Fairbanks' nine months of winter. Over 60 percent of borough residents hold library cards, compared to an average of 20 percent nationally. Noel Wien was a pioneer bush pilot who, with his two brothers, founded Wien Airlines. The library was built on the site of Weeks Field, the first airport in Fairbanks. You can surf the Web for free in the library, or rent computer time at

College Coffeehouse (3677 College Rd., 907/374-0468).

Gulliver's Books (on College Rd. at University Ave., 907/474-9574 or 800/390-8999, www.gullivers-books.com) is a great little two-story place with both new and used titles. More books at the **University Bookstore** (in Constitution Hall, 907/474-7348, www.uaf.edu/bookstore) on campus.

Services

Two local launderettes have showers: **B&C Laundromat** (College Rd. at University Ave., 907/479-2696) and **Plaza Cleaners and Laundry** (3417 Airport Way, 907/479-0791). Or shower and then swim at **Mary Siah Recreation Center** (1025 14th Ave., 907/459-1082). **Fairbanks Hotel** (517 3rd Ave., 907/456-6440 or 888/329-4685, www.fbxhotl.com) has lockers for gear storage. The post office is downtown between 3rd and 4th Avenues.

If you need a doctor, try **Fairbanks Urgent Care** (1867 Airport Way, 907/452-2178), and for emergencies, drag yourself to **Fairbanks Memorial Hospital** (1650 Cowles, 907/452-8181, www.fairbanksmemorial.com).

TRANSPORTATION

Getting There By Air

Fairbanks International Airport is six miles southwest of downtown. The second floor houses a gift shop, snack shop, and lounge. On the first floor are an unstaffed information booth with a bunch of brochures, a few stuffed animals, and the Curtiss JN-4D "Jenny" biplane used by Carl Ben Eielson, one of the earliest and most famous bush pilots from the area.

Alaska Airlines (907/452-1661 or 800/426-0333, www.alaskaair.com) has multiple daily flights between Fairbanks and Anchorage, plus once-a-day nonstop service to Seattle. Both options are available year-round.

Air North (867/668-2228 or 800/764-0407 U.S. and 800/661-0407 Canada, www.flyairnorth.com), flies to Dawson and Whitehorse several times a week from Fairbanks. **Hawaiian Vacations** (907/261-2700 or 800/770-2700, www.hawaiianvacations.com), has charter flights between Fairbanks and Maui during the winter, providing an escape to the sun for frigid Fairbanksians.

Seasonal service includes nonstop flights from Minneapolis-St. Paul on **Northwest Airlines** (800/225-2525, www.nwa.com), and from Frankfurt to Fairbanks (with a stop in Whitehorse, Yukon) aboard **Thomas Cook Airlines** (800/524-6975, www.thomascook.us).

There is no city bus out to the airport, but **Airlink Shuttle** (907/452-3337) offers inexpensive service to town: $7 for two people. Taxis are another airport option.

Regional Air Carriers

In business since 1950, **Frontier Flying Service** (907/474-0014 or 800/478-6779, www.frontierflying.com) is the largest regional carrier, with daily flights between Fairbanks and Anchorage, plus scheduled service to most of Interior Alaska.

Warbelow's Air Ventures (907/474-0518 or 800/478-0812, www.warbelows.com) is another long-established air taxi with extensive connections throughout the Interior.

Both **Larry's Flying Service** (907/474-9169, www.larrysflying.com) and **Everts Air Alaska** (907/450-2350, www.evertsair.com) also have scheduled regional service. Warbelow's, Larry's, and Everts all offer charter air taxi service, as do **Wright Air** (907/474-0502 or 800478-0502) and **Alaska Flying Tours** (907/457-4424 or 888/326-4424, www.alaskaflyingtours.com).

Train

The train depot (280 N. Cushman, 907/456-4155) is only a five-minute walk to downtown. A new inter-modal facility for trains and buses opens here in 2005. The **Alaska Railroad** (907/265-2494 or 800/544-0552, www.alaskarailroad.com) departs Fairbanks daily mid-May to mid-September at 8:15 A.M., arriving in Denali National Park at noon ($50), and Anchorage at 8:15 P.M. ($175). Tour-bus fares to Denali and Anchorage are comparable to those of the train, though minivan fares are much cheaper. But the train is a more comfortable, enjoyable, and historical way to see this part of Alaska.

If you want to go in luxury, however, buy a ticket for the superdome vista cruisers hooked onto the end of the train, run by Princess Tours and Holland America.

Bus

During the summer, **Alaska Direct Bus Line** (907/277-6652 or 800/770-6652, www.home .gci.net/~akdirectbus) has service several times a week connecting Fairbanks with Whitehorse, Skagway, and Haines. The buses stop overnight in Tok, where you'll have to pay for lodging or camping.

Alaska Trails (907/479-3065 or 888/600-6001, www.alaskashuttle.com) runs a daily Fairbanks–Denali–Talkeetna–Anchorage van in the summer, and five times a week the rest of the year. In addition, summer-only vans connect Fairbanks with Delta Junction, Tok, Chicken, and Dawson City, and they also offer a reservation-only service between Fairbanks and Valdez (four person minimum).

RC Shuttles (907/479-0079 or 877/479-0079, www.rcshuttles.com) provides personalized transportation practically anywhere from their Fairbanks base; to Haines it's $150 per person with a two-person minimum.

Local Bus Service

Fairbanks' public bus system, **Metropolitan Area Commuter Service** (907/459-1011, www.co.fairbanks.ak.us/transportation), known as "MACS," operates Monday–Friday 7 A.M.–7 P.M. and Saturday 9:30–6:30 P.M. Pick up timetables at the information center. All routes stop at **Transit Park** on Cushman and Fifth Avenue. The fare is $1.50, or $3 for an all-day pass.

Taxi

There are 20 or so local cab companies; find them in the Yellow Pages. Taxis charge around $15 to get downtown from the airport. You may be a bit better off with **Airlink Shuttle** (907/452-3337), which charges $10 d for rides to the university, or $7 d to the airport.

Car and RV Rentals

Several companies have reasonable prices, late model cars, and will pick you up at the airport: **Affordable Car Rental** (907/452-7341 or 800/471-3101), **Aurora Rentals** (907/459-7033 or 800/849-7033), **National** (907/451-7368 or 800/227-7368), and **U-Save Auto Rental** (907/479-7060 or 877/979-7060). Also try **Rent-A-Wreck** (907/452-1606 or 800/478-1606), for deals on not-too-badly beat-up cars, vans, and trucks.

The following companies all have airport counters: **Arctic Rent-A-Car** (907/479-8044 or 800/478-8696, www.arcticrentacar.com), **Avis** (907/474-0900 or 800/478-2847), **Budget** (907/474-0855 or 800/474-0855), **Dollar** (907/451-4360 or 800/800-4000), **Hertz** (907/452-444 or 800/654-3131), and **Payless** (907/474-0177 or 800/729-5377). Most rental car companies do not allow their cars north of the Arctic Circle on the Dalton Highway, and other road restrictions are often imposed.

If you feel the urge to tool around in a gas-guzzling RV, try **Alaska Motorhome Rentals** (800/254-9929, www.alaskarv.com), **Alaskan Motor-Home Rentals** (907/488-9650 or 888/442-5764), **Denali RV** (907/479-3764), **Diamond Willow RV Rentals** (907/457-2814 or 888/724-7373), or **Tanana Motorhome Rentals** (907/452-2477, www.tmhrentals.com). Rent pickup-truck-based campers from **GoNorth RV Camper Rental** (3500 Davis Rd., 907/479-7272 or 866/236-7272, www.gonorthalaska.net).

Bus Tours

Gray Line of Alaska (907/451-6835 or 800/544-2206, www.graylineofalaska.com) leads regional bus tours, but you can do all of these on your own for less if you have a vehicle. Several other companies offer less corporate versions: try **River's Edge Resort** (907/474-0286 or 800/770-3343, www.riversedge.net) for $20 historical city tours. (See the *Dalton Highway* section later in this chapter for details on bus tours to the Arctic Circle and Prudhoe Bay.)

Airlink Shuttle (907/452-3337) has a two-hour city tour for $25, and a variety of shared-ride shuttles around town.

Vicinity of Fairbanks

NORTH POLE

In 1949, Con Miller was cleaning out the Fairbanks trading post he'd just bought and found a Santa Claus suit. He liked it so much that he took to wearing it during his trips to the Interior to buy furs and sell supplies. The costume made a big impression on the Native children. A few years later, when he moved 12 miles southeast of Fairbanks near Eielsen Air Force Base, he built a new trading post and called it Santa Claus House. Miller and his neighbors chose the name North Pole for their new town, reportedly to attract a toy manufacturer to the area. It never arrived, but the name stuck.

Today, North Pole (pop. 1,600) is a suburb of Fairbanks, but the business he established has become the town's primary attraction. The town is dotted with more Xmas fever: street names like St. Nicholas and Kris Kringle Drives and Santa Claus and Mistletoe Lanes, business names such as Santaland RV Park, Santa's Pull Tabs, and Elf's Den Diner, along with a 50,000-watt Christian radio station, KJNP (King Jesus of North Pole). There are 23 churches in the area, including, of course, St. Nicholas Church. But, as if to counteract all the religion, there's also Fantasy Video just north of town, where the fantasies certainly aren't about sugarplums.

Sights

Santa Claus House (907/488-2200 or 800/588-4078, www.santaclaushouse.com) right along the Richardson Highway, is the largest and tackiest gift shop in the state, and probably the biggest one this side of Las Vegas. Out front stands a 40-foot Santa figure ("the world's tallest"), and inside you'll find Santa in the flesh eight hours a day, any day of the year. When I last visited (a May afternoon), he was obviously bored and eager to talk about his real life away from the red clothes and hat. But when a child showed up, he turned on the charm. And yes, it is a real beard. Outside, two of Santa's reindeer are housed in a pen.

It's Christmas 365 nights a year in North Pole, Alaska.

Santa Claus House is open 8 A.M.–8 P.M. in the summer, with variable hours the rest of the year. Buy a "holiday message from Santa," mailed in December from North Pole to anyone in the world for $7.50. For an extra $10 they'll send you a deed to one square inch of the Santa Claus subdivision in town. There's even a free summertime shuttle bus to Santa Claus House from hotels and RV parks in Fairbanks.

One of the attractions in town is getting your letters postmarked from "North Pole, Alaska." Mail them at the Santa Claus House or the post office on Fifth Avenue. Throughout December, this post office is deluged with letters and cards from people wanting a North Pole postmark—the stacks can be piled 10 feet high. And that's *not* including the estimated 10,000 letters to Santa

THE INTERIOR

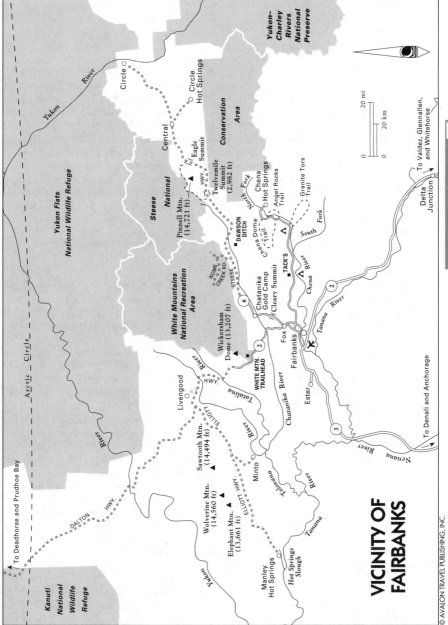

VICINITY OF FAIRBANKS

Yukon-Charley Rivers National Preserve

Circle

Circle Hot Springs

Central

Conservation Area

Steese National

Eagle Summit

Twelvemile Summit (2,982 ft)

Chena Hot Springs

Granite Tors Trail

Angel Rocks Trail

Pinnell Mtn. (14,721 ft)

HWY. 9

North Fork

Chena Dome Trail

DAWSON DITCH

South Fork

Chena River

Yukon Flats National Wildlife Refuge

Yukon River

Kanuti National Wildlife Refuge

To Deadhorse and Prudhoe Bay

Arctic Circle

White Mountains National Recreation Area

NOME CREEK RD.

STEESE

Chatanika Gold Camp

Cleary Summit

TACK'S

Wickersham Dome (13,207 ft)

6

2

Fox

WHITE MTN. TRAILHEAD

Chatanika River

Fairbanks

Ester

Tanana River

Chena River

2

Delta Junction

To Valdez, Glennallen, and Whitehorse

3

To Denali and Anchorage

Nenana River

Livengood

ELLIOTT HWY.

Tatalina River

River

Sawtooth Mtn. (14,494 ft)

Wolverine Mtn. (14,560 ft)

Elephant Mtn. (13,661 ft)

Minto

Tolovana River

Tanana River

Manley Hot Springs

Hot Springs Slough

Tanana

DALTON HWY.

Yukon River

20 mi

20 km

0

© AVALON TRAVEL PUBLISHING, INC.

Claus himself, which are all answered by students at North Pole Middle School.

Not everything is about Christmas here. North Pole is also home to two oil refineries (they tap into the Trans-Alaska Pipeline), along with **Eielson Air Force Base** (12 miles south of town, 907/377-2116, www.eielson.af.mil). The base has a variety of aircraft, including F-16s, A-10s, and KC-135 air tankers, but is closed to the public.

Located on the Richardson Highway at Mission Road, the North Pole **Visitor Log Cabin** (907/488-2242, www.fairnet.org/npcc) is open daily 10 A.M.–6 P.M. mid-May to mid-September.

Accommodations and Food

Jolly Acres Motel (907/488-9339) charges $80 d for suites with full kitchens. **Beaver Lake Resort Motel** (2555 Mission Rd., 907/488-9600, www.beaverlakeresort.com) has rooms for $60 d, and lakeside suites with full kitchens for $105–140 d, with a two-night minimum stay.

North Pole Cabins (907/490-6400, www.northpolecabins.com) rents modern cabins with baths for $119 d.

Santaland RV Park (907/488-9123 or 888/488-9123, www.santalandrv.com) is right next door to Santa Claus House, with tent and RV sites. Camping is also available at nearby Chena Lakes Recreation Area. **Forbes Laundry** (on St. Nicholas Dr., 907/488-2141) has showers and is open 24 hours.

Elf Den (907/488-8788), next to the visitor center, is popular for Sunday brunch, and serves all the standards at other times. North Pole also has a mix of eateries, including Chinese, Mexican, fast food, and even **Thai Cuisine Restaurant** (907/488-8260).

Chena Lakes Recreation Area

In August, 1967, it rained seven inches in seven days, and the Chena River overflowed, inundating low-lying Fairbanks under five feet of floodwaters. Half the town's residents were evacuated, and damage neared $200 million. The task of preventing a similar disaster in the future fell to the Army Corps of Engineers, which mucked around for 15 years, building a dam at Moose Creek, a levee and spillway into the Tanana River, and this 2,000-acre park of man-made lakes and recreational facilities. The recreation area contains the nearest beach to Fairbanks, and on hot weekends the exodus is not unlike that of Bostonians fleeing to Cape Cod—you might be able to wedge a dishtowel onto some sand and swim in place.

Most of the season, though, Chena Lakes (907/488-1655) is a delightful place to picnic, stroll (self-guided nature trail), bike (seven-mile trail), play volleyball and horseshoes, pick berries, camp, fish, and rent canoes, paddleboats, and sailboats. In the winter, the trails are groomed for cross-country skiing. Camp at either the Lakes campground or the river park. From Fairbanks, go five miles south of North Pole on the Richardson Highway (Mile 347), take a left on Laurance Road, and follow the signs. Fees are $3 for day use, $10 for camping.

FOX

In 1901, Felice Pedroni (a.k.a. Felix Pedro) found color on what is now Pedro Creek and was credited with the discovery of the Cleary and Goldstream veins, which touched off the rush from the Klondike and Nome to the Fairbanks area. However, the gold here was anything but easy for the taking: This gold-laden bedrock was normally 80–100 feet under gravel, muck, and permafrost. Within 20 years of the find, the rich creeks were worked out, the shallow, low-grade ground was exhausted, and most miners couldn't afford the expense of working the deep claims. In 1923, however, the railroad was finished from Seward to Fairbanks and brought with it the feasibility of large-scale gold production. Hydraulic giants, monster dredges, miles of tailings, and businessmen in three-piece suits replaced the lone prospector with his hammer and bucket. This second—corporate—gold rush to Fairbanks eventually produced almost $200 million worth of the precious heavy metal.

A ride 10 miles up the Steese Highway from Fairbanks to and around Fox clearly reveals the impact of this second boom. Huge cleared fields and stripped hillsides trace the progress of the giants and dredges, and the tailings lie in the snaking mounds they were spit into 50 years ago. Marble, gravel, and sand are for sale along the roadside. Heavy machinery dots the land with the bovine patience of metal and rubber.

Fox boasts the **Fox Roadhouse** (907/457-7461), one of the most popular local steak-and-seafood houses, and best prime rib in the Interior. Call for reservations. **Silver Gulch Brewery**—a locals' favorite—is housed in the same building. Up the road a hair is the **Turtle Club** (907/457-3883, www.alaskanturtle.com), with prime rib, halibut, prawns, lobster, and king crab.

Continue another five miles past Fox on the Steese Highway for the monument to **Felice Pedroni,** who started it all rolling in 1902. Across the road is Pedro Creek; try your hand at panning for a little dust, and note the unnatural look of a creek played for gold for most of a century.

Pipe Dreams

Eight miles out the Steese Highway on the way to Fox is a **Trans-Alaska Pipeline Viewpoint,** a favorite pose-for-a-photo stop. Interpretive displays describe the site, and Alyeska Pipeline Services runs a visitor center here (907/456-9391, daily mid-May–mid-Sept.). The viewing area itself is open year-round.

Gold Dredge No. 8

Local placer gold derives from ancient quartz veins once exposed in creek beds, now buried up to 100 feet below the surface. To get to it, first you hose off the surface layer down to two feet with hydraulic cannons or "giants," then down another few feet as the exposed frozen gravel thaws on its own. The deeper frozen muck and rock is thawed over a year or so by water pumped through pipes from the surface to bedrock, supplied by monumental aqueducts such as the Davidson Ditch. Once the earth down to bedrock is diggable, a gold dredge is brought in.

The dredge dwarfs even the largest machines in this land of giant machines. It's a true Alaska-size contraption that looks like a cartoon cross between a houseboat and a crane. An endless circular conveyor of up to 100 steel buckets scoops up the gravel, conveys it to the top end of a revolving screen, and dumps it. The screen separates the larger rocks, shunting them off to the

tailing piles, from the golden gravel, which is sifted from the screen to riffles, where quicksilver (mercury) gleans the gold, forming an amalgam. The riffles are cleaned every couple of weeks, then the gold is further processed and assayed. In the old days during the height of production, the gold would next be shipped to the mint, where it earned $35 per troy ounce.

Gold Dredge No. 8 (907/457-6058, www.golddredgeno8.com, open daily), the only National Historic Mechanical Engineering Landmark in Alaska, is just a little larger than its official designation. One of Alaska's first steel-hulled bucketline dredges, it was installed in 1928—five stories tall, 250 feet long, weighing over 1,000 tons. The dredge stopped operating in 1959, but it was bought by Holland America in 1996 and completely restored. Tours—including a 20-minute video on gold mining—are offered seven times a day, with the first at 9:30 A.M. and the last at 3:30 P.M. Admission is $23 adults, or $14 kids; add $10 for lunch. After the tour you can pan for gold—and keep what you find—for as long as you like. The grounds also contain a restaurant, bar, a small hotel, and gift shop. To get there, drive eight miles up the Steese Highway toward Fox, take a left on Goldstream Road and another left on the Old Steese Highway.

El Dorado Gold Mine

Located a mile north of Fox on the Elliott Highway, this active placer mine (907/479-7613 or 866/479-6673, www.eldoradogoldmine.com) is another tourist draw. Here, you climb onboard a small-scale railroad to view the mine, walk into a tunnel in the permafrost, and get a chance to try your hand at panning for a flake or two. Two-hour tours start take place mid-May to mid-September, and cost $28 adults, $20 kids. A free shuttle is provided from Fairbanks.

Fort Knox Gold Mine

Alaska's largest gold mine—it produces over 1,000 ounces a day—has fascinating tours that include a chance to watch the open pit excavation, crushing of the rock, and milling. Guests get to hold a 21-pound gold bar (worth $100,000) and buy your own gold from the gift shop. Two-hour tours

(907/488-4653 ext. 2800, www.kinross.com) are $21 and generally take place on Tuesday and Thursday, but call for reservations. The mine is 25 miles northeast of Fairbanks.

ESTER

Like Fox, Ester had a two-boom gold rush: panning and placer mining in the early 1900s, then dredging by the Fairbanks Exploration Co. from the mid-1920s to the late 1950s. Today, Ester, which is 10 miles south of Fairbanks on the Parks Highway, has a few buildings that remain from the once-booming mining days, now housing a hotel, gift shop, gallery, and the famous Malemute Saloon. By car, head down the George Parks Highway toward Denali 10 miles, then follow the signs for Ester and Ester Gold Camp.

Since 1958, the Hotel Cripple Creek, now **Ester Gold Camp** (907/479-2500 or 800/676-6925, www.akvisit.com) has been in operation in a refurbished bunkhouse. The rooms are plain but functional (no TVs or phones) and a bar-gain at $60 s or $70 d with shared bath—making Ester Gold Camp an attractive alternative to pricey Fairbanks if you have a car. A campground here has tent ($10) and RV sites ($15). Ester Gold Camp is open late May to early September.

The restaurant at Ester Gold Camp spreads out an all-you-can-eat dinner buffet with broasted chicken, reindeer stew, and halibut daily 5–9 P.M., $18. You can also partake of all-you-can-eat Dungeness crab for an extra $12.

Top off the evening with the Robert Service musical extravaganza in the **Malemute Saloon** at 9 P.M. nightly, plus 7 P.M. Wednesday–Saturday evenings; $15 adults, $8 kids. All the tour companies offer packages with round-trip transportation and the saloon show.

Just up the road in the Firehouse Theater is the **Northern Lights PhotoSymphony** (www.photosymphony.com), a 45-minute musically accompanied slide show with panoramic northern lights photos on a curved screen. The cost is $8 adults, $4 kids and shows are daily at 6:45 and 7:45 P.M.

Heading out from Fairbanks

The country around Fairbanks offers outstanding opportunities to explore and experience the land and waterways, and then to luxuriate in hot springs that have soothed and refreshed travelers for well over a century. With the Interior's predictable good weather, the long days and low lighting, and the humbling power of this vast humanless wilderness, you'll return from any of these trips knowing a lot more about Alaska, and yourself.

Chena Hot Springs Road boasts three exciting hiking trails, two campgrounds, a cozy public cabin, a choice of canoe routes and fishing spots, and a large pool resort, all within an hour's drive of town on a good paved road. The **Steese Highway** has five campgrounds, abundant canoeing and fishing, a high-country backpack that rivals much of Denali National Park, and the fascinating evidence of gold fever—past and present. The **Elliott Highway** is the longest, roughest, and most primitive ride of the three. Along it is one long trail close to Fairbanks, no campgrounds to speak of, and no facilities of any kind, all of which make the small pool and hot tubs at the road's end in friendly Manley all the more rewarding.

And for a real road adventure, you can head up the **Dalton Highway,** which begins at Mile 73 on the Elliott Highway and continues 414 miles all the way to Deadhorse, a few miles south of Prudhoe Bay.

CHENA HOT SPRINGS ROAD

Depending on whom you believe, either Felix Pedro (1903) or the U.S. Geological Survey (1907) discovered the hot springs off the north fork of the Chena River. Shortly after, the land was homesteaded by George Wilson, who built a lodge and cabins and enclosed the springs in a pool. The 55-mile road from Fairbanks was completed in 1967, only to be wiped out a few weeks later by the great flood. It was finally rebuilt and completely paved by 1983. From Mile 26 to Mile 51 is Chena River State Recreation Area, a well-developed and beautiful playground in Fairbanks' backyard, where numerous trails, river access, picnic areas, and two campgrounds are within an easy hour's drive from town. You could easily fill up three or four days camping, hiking, backpacking, and canoeing (all free), and then satisfy the creature-comfort yearnings you accumulated in the backcountry with a soak in the pool and a drink at the resort at the end of the road. (Note: Don't mix up three confusingly named recreation areas around Fairbanks—the Chena River State Recreation Area along Chena Hot Springs Road, the Chena Lakes Recreation Area near North Pole, and the Chena River State Recreation Site in Fairbanks!)

By car, take the Steese Highway just north of town to the exit to Chena Hot Springs Road. The road starts out somewhat rollercoasterish from frost heaves, but the scenery is pleasing—rolling green hills dotted by small verdant farms.

Nestled along a small lake at Mile 16, **Two Rivers Lodge** (907/488-6815, www.tworiverslodge.com) serves gourmet seafood, pasta, and chicken, but their specialty is all-you-can-eat BBQ ribs. You'll probably pay around $30 per person. Just up the road a mile, **Earthtone Huskies B&B** (907/488-8074, www.earthtonehuskies.com) has comfortably rustic log cabins (no running water) for $40 s or $50 d, including a light breakfast. Owner Judy Cooper leads dogsled treks in the winter.

Not far away is **Paw Print Bed & Sled** (907/488-5788, www.lara-kesiberians.com), where three rooms ($65 d with breakfast) in the post-and-beam lodge share a bath. Iditarod mushers Devan and Judy Currier breed Siberian huskies, and also offer sled dog tours.

Chandalar Ranch (at 18.5 Mile, 907/488-8402, www.chandalarranchalaska.com), offers rustic bush-style accommodations—including hostel beds and a cabin—along with horseback rides, wagon rides, and pack trips.

In the summer months Chena Hot Springs attracts a mixed American and European crowd, but in winter it's even busier with Japanese travelers who come to experience the spectacular northern lights shows.

Chena River State Recreation Area

Covering 254,000 acres, Chena River State Recreation Area boasts luxurious campgrounds, excellent outdoor recreational opportunities, lush greenery, towering trees (for Interior Alaska), rolling hills, the curvy Chena River, and best of all, no crowds. When town becomes oppressive, head a half-hour east to some of the best that Interior has to offer. For the complete story, contact the Alaska Department of Natural Resources in Fairbanks (907/451-2700, www.alaskastateparks.org).

Numerous well-marked pullouts give easy river access and your choice of the length of a canoe trip. A good place to put in is at the Mile 44 bridge—a little faster and more fun than downriver. Watch for sweepers, deadheads, shallows, and especially the many impassable sloughs—stagnant, stinking, and mosquito-ridden. Get details from local canoe rental companies or state park folks before heading out.

Rosehip Campground (Mile 27, $10) right at the entrance to the recreation area, is as big and lush a campground as you could ever want, only a half-hour from town. The river is never more than a two-minute walk away. There are 25 sites, pit toilets, water pumps, and numerous signboards with information about trails, wildlife, and canoe routes.

The road parallels the river all the way to the hot springs and crosses it four times, at Miles 37, 40, 44, and 49. After heavy rains, the road often floods, especially around Mile 37. Grayling fishing is great on this river, especially in July and August. You'll throw most back in, but you'll usually keep a half-dozen 12- to 15-inchers. If you see salmon migrating upriver, enjoy the view; you're not allowed to catch them in the state recreation area. Four small lakes (Miles 30, 43, 46, and 48) are also well stocked with grayling and trout.

The **Chena River Cabin** is an easily accessed and attractive log cabin right on the river at Mile 32, with a porch and space for nine people; $25–40 per night. Make reservations in the Department of Natural Resources Information

© DON PITCHER

Chena Hot Springs

Center (3700 Airport Way in Fairbanks, 907/451-2705, www.alaskastateparks.org). **Granite Tors** loop trail starts across the road from the campground, and just before the bridge. This well-maintained path is a 15-mile, six-hour round-trip. The first mile or so is on boardwalk over muskeg; the first tors (strange granite sculptures thrust near the surface, then exposed when the surrounding earth eroded away) are around six miles from the trailhead on both the north and south forks of the trail.

Angel Rocks trail begins at Mile 49 just beyond a pullout and right before the fourth bridge over the Chena River. It's only three miles or so, though the first couple are uphill. The rock outcroppings in the high country are worth the huff. Allow three to four hours.

For the **Chena Dome Trail,** take the northern trailhead, which starts at Mile 51, a half-mile past Angel Creek on the left side of the road; it's a three-day, 29-mile loop trail mostly along ridgetops marked by cairns—great views. A quarter-mile up the trail is the sign for Chena Dome (nine miles); after a short boardwalk you start to climb and leave the mosquitoes and heat behind. One mile up the trail is a good viewpoint.

Chena Hot Springs Resort

At Mile 57, the road ends at a sprawling resort (907/452-7867 or 800/478-4681, www.chenahotsprings.com) that seems to always be adding something new. Along with the hot-spring-fed swimming pools and hot tub, it offers hotel rooms and suites ($105–170 d in summer; $135–200 d in winter), rustic cabins ($65–200 d with outhouses), bring-your-sleeping-bag yurts ($65 d), along with tent and RV sites ($23 with showers). The cabins are particularly popular with families, and the largest one sleeps six guests. Call for additional information and reservations.

All sorts of activities are available at the 440-acre resort (for an extra fee), including rafting, canoe trips, fishing, mountain bike rentals, flightseeing, and gold panning in the summer, along with dog sled rides, a dog mushing school, snowmobiling, horse-drawn sleigh rides, cross-country skiing (eight miles of groomed trails), and ice skating in the winter. And if that isn't enough, the resort has free activities such as volleyball, badminton, hiking, horseshoes, and basketball. In the summer months Chena Hot Springs attracts a mixed American and European crowd, but in winter it's even busier with Japanese travelers who come to experience the spectacular northern lights shows. You'll see aurora displays 90 percent of the winter nights here.

The featured attraction at Chena, of course, is the hot springs, first discovered by Anglos in 1905. The water comes out of the spring at nearly 160°F, and is a little under 110°in the pools. There's an indoor pool and hot tub, plus a second outdoor hot tub, redwood deck, and large sandy-bottom pond that is best experienced when the stars are obscured by the aurora borealis. It's all first-rate. Guests (except campers and RVers) get free access to the springs, but if you aren't staying here a day pass costs $10 adults, $7 seniors and ages 6–12, or free for younger children.

The lodge is worth exploring for its neat little dining rooms, beautiful woodwork and furniture, and relaxing couches and library. Prices at the restaurant are reasonable (considering where you are): $8–14 for burgers, fish & chips, and sandwiches in the lounge, or $16–32 in the Victorian-style dining room for steaks, prime rib, chicken, pasta, and seafood prepared with a European flair.

During the winter, famed ice artist Steve Brice builds a 30-foot-high gothic style **ice hotel** (open mid-Nov.–March) here, with intricately carved pieces, including chandeliers, knights, gargoyles, and winged lions. Six guest rooms are available, and guests snuggle in sleeping bags on reindeer hides atop their ice beds. The room temperature averages 28°F. This is the only ice hotel in America, so don't be surprised at the pricetag. A three-night package, including one night in the ice room and two nights in other rooms at the lodge, plus transport from Fairbanks, costs $878 d.

STEESE HIGHWAY

Gold is the color of this country: The precious metal wrested with brute force from the reluctant earth, the golden-green panoramas of the alpine tundra, the golden light sparkling through the plumes of dust-fog along the road, and the pot of gold of the hot springs at the end of its own rainbow.

Other than the drive itself and the unlimited fishing and canoeing on the Chatanika River and Birch Creek, the excitement on the Steese can be found at the **Davidson Ditch** and on the challenging **Pinnell Mountain Trail**. The Davidson Ditch was one of the first miracle-of-engineering pipelines in this country and, unlike the oil pipeline, you can play on it! The Pinnell Trail is a three-day stroll along the windswept ridges of the White Mountains, with distant jagged horizons for the long-eyed, and stunning alpine wildflowers for the short. And after you've reached the limits of backcountry endurance, only 20 miles up the road is the biggest, deepest, hottest pool in Alaska, with not only all the conveniences and sociability you've been missing, but budget accommodations as well.

The Road

Named for Army general James G. Steese, president of the Alaska Road Commission 1920–1927 who oversaw its entire construction, the Steese Highway parallels the original Fairbanks–Circle Trail. Thousands of fortune seekers floated up and down the Yukon to Circle, hit the trail after news of Felix Pedro's strike spread, and helped open up the Interior in the early 20th century. The road was completed in 1928, and is paved for the first 44 miles.

Starting from Fairbanks, the highway immediately climbs into the gold-bearing hills, with a great viewpoint overlooking the Tanana Valley on the left at Hagelbarger Road. On a clear day, turn around to see if the Alaska Range is "out"—a stunning panorama from Mt. McKinley to the eastern peaks of Deborah, Hess, and Hayes. Just up the road is a pullout to view the **Trans-Alaska Pipeline**—which runs aboveground here—and an informative sign. In a few miles you come to the town of Fox, where you'll note the extensive placer mine tailings from **Gold Dredge No. 8** which operated from 1927 to 1959.

At the junction with the Elliott Highway (Route 2), take a right for the Steese (Route 6). At Mile 16 is a turnout with a plaque mounted on a stone monument to Felix Pedro; walk across the road to Pedro Creek, whose golden sands infected the stampeders with Fairbanks fever.

Cleary Summit

From Pedro Creek the frost-heaved pavement climbs quickly to Cleary Summit (elevation 2,233 feet), home to **Mt. Aurora Skiland** (907/389-2314, www.skiland.org), where you can downhill ski or snowboard December to early April. The area has a double chairlift, day lodge, and snack bar, plus ski and snowboard rentals. Lift rates are $28 adults, $24 college students, and $10–20 for younger kids. Call 907/456-7669 for the snow report. Nearby is **Fairbanks Creek Lodge** (907/389-2000, www.mt-aurora.com), a 12-room lodge that was once a bunkhouse for miners; $100 s or $110 d in twin beds. This is a great place to view and photograph the northern lights.

Fairbanks Exploration Company

Beyond the summit, the road twists and turns down to **Chatanika;** at Mile 28, take a hard right and climb to the site of the Fairbanks Exploration Company Gold Camp. After the completion of the Alaska Railroad in 1923, the U.S. Smelting, Refining, and Mining Co. began acquiring and consolidating many of the placer properties around Fairbanks. By 1938, the subsidiary F. E. Co. had three dredges operating between Chatanika and Ester, had installed the Davidson Ditch (see below), and fueled the entire operation with its own power plant in Fairbanks. In its 30 years of production, F. E. Co. took out nearly $100 million in gold—and that was at no more than $35 per troy ounce. The grounds are covered with vintage equipment and 15 restored buildings that are still maintained by machinery used during the 1940s. Gold Dredge No. 3 is visible near Mile 29 amid tailings on the north side of the road.

The **Chatanika Old F. E. Gold Camp** resort (907/389-2414, www.fegoldcamp.com) is open year-round, and is chock-full of early Alaska memorabilia and mining artifacts. Rooms start at $55 s or d with shared baths in the main building, or $75 d for larger rooms that share a bath containing a jacuzzi tub. The restaurant is particularly notable, with gourmet meals ($16–22 entrées), including a locally famous rack of lamb, plus a great Sunday champagne brunch.

A mile up the road is the **Chatanika Lodge** (907/389-2164), with hearty meals and simple bath-down-the-hall rooms for $50 s or $60 d. They host **Chatanika Days Outhouse Races** on the second weekend of March. Five-person outhouse teams race a one-mile course, with four pushing and one riding in the specially built "racing outhouses."

Poker Flat

At **Poker Flat Research Range** (907/474-7558 for times, www.pfrr.alaska.edu), two miles up the Steese from Chatanika, the Geophysical Institute of UAF studies the aurora and upper atmosphere. When it was constructed in the late 1960s, Poker Flat took its name from a Bret Harte short story,"The Outcasts of Poker Flat," about a gambler and a prostitute who were banished from a mythical California gold-rush town in the winter and eventually froze to death. The construction crew building the rocket range for the Geophysical Institute considered themselves similarly outcast. This is the only rocket range owned by a university in the world, and is used for the launching of suborbital rockets. Poker Flats is open some Thursdays in the summer for tours.

Upper Chatanika River Recreation Site

Located at Mile 39, this excellent state campground ($10) has 25 sites, pit toilets, a water pump, and plentiful river access for fishing (grayling) and boating. Head around to the back of the grounds and try for a campsite right on the river. Bring an inner tube and ride from the bridge down to your tent.

Davidson Ditch

The pavement ends at Mile 44, and the next 15 miles are rough—washboard shaky and deep gravel—slippery when dry. Take heart, though; it gets much smoother along the way. At Mile 57, the U.S. Creek Road leads seven miles to two BLM campgrounds, a recreational gold panning area along Nome Creek, and a put-in point for floating Beaver Creek, all within the White Mountains Recreation Area).

Also at Mile 57 is a highway pullout for a long stretch of pipe, a remnant of the Davidson Ditch, the amazing engineering feat (1925) that slaked the F. E. Co. dredges' enormous thirst for water; the dredges floated on man-made ponds so they could be moved. Starting at a dam on the upper Chatanika River, the 12-foot-wide, 4-foot-deep, 83-mile-long ditch, along with nearly seven miles of 48-inch pipe and a combined mile of tunnels, crossed 90 miles of hilly wilderness, directing 56,000 gallons of water per minute to the gold fields. Notice the expansion or "slip" joint in the middle of the level section of the pipe here, and the wooden saddle below it. The pipe was drained in the winter but the cold still took its toll: Note the bulge in the pipe where it cuts uphill, and the repair job on the joint.

This is one of several views of the ditch in the next 10 miles, standing in mute testimony to the struggle of rugged miners against rugged terrain and harsh elements in the quest for gold. You can't help but be amazed by this project, especially when you consider that the road was barely built, the machinery was primitive, and the land unyielding. F. E. Co.'s contract did not require the removal of the pipe when gold production ceased, so here it still sits—either a blight on the landscape or evidence of the colorful history of this land, depending on your perspective. Whichever it is, watch your footing if you monkey around on the pipe.

Cripple Creek Campground and Beyond

This BLM facility (Mile 60, 907/474-2200, www.ak.blm.gov) consists of an inner loop for cars and RVs and a walk-in section. Either take a site with the RV crowd or park in the walk-in lot by the toilets, head to the back of the campground, and pitch your tent right by the river. The mosquitoes are fierce in mosquito season. Camping costs $6. A public-use cabin is also nearby.

The road out here gets smoother, wider, and less slippery. From the back of a large pullout at Mile 62 is another view of the pipe disappearing into a tunnel. At Mile 81, natural spring water gushes cold and delicious from an open spigot, about five gallons a minute. While you've got the Davidson Ditch on your mind, multiply the pressure of the water from the spigot by a factor

of 10,000 for an idea of the force with which the ditch moved its H20.

Steese National Conservation Area

The BLM's Steese National Conservation Area encompasses 1.2 million acres of land just north of the Steese Highway. This area protects important caribou calving grounds and Dall sheep habitat, and includes the 23-mile **Pinnell Mountain National Recreation Trail.** This trail provides access to alpine tundra, with excellent views of nearby mountain ranges.

The first trailhead for Pinnell Mountain leaves the Steese near Mile 85 at **Twelvemile Summit** (elevation 2,982 feet); the second rejoins the highway near Eagle Summit (Mile 107). A short access road (right) at the first trailhead leads past a signposted section of the Fairbanks–Circle Trail to a small mountain pond—nice spot for a picnic. The Pinnell Mountain Trail follows a boardwalk for the first quarter-mile, then climbs steadily for a long time. Most hikers prefer to start at the second trailhead, 700 feet higher, which has a great signboard full of fascinating information. This beautiful 27-mile, three-day trail through alpine tundra along White Mountain ridgelines is famous for its views of the Alaska and Brooks Ranges and the midnight sun on solstice, plus the incomparable wildflowers (especially the state flower, forget-me-not, with its striking blue dots on the tundra), which also peak in mid-June. Small emergency shelters are at miles 10 and 18 along the trail. This rolling, treeless high country, with long-distance views in all directions, makes you want to stop, get out, and book all the way to the Edge. But be prepared for wind! Get information and a trail map at the Public Lands Information Center in Fairbanks or at the BLM website (www.ak.blm.gov).

Eagle Summit and Beyond

At Mile 94 a road to the right leads to undeveloped camping and the launching point for the popular **Birchcreek Canoe Trail.** Eagle Summit, 13 miles farther out the Steese, is the third of three summits that the highway tops (others are at Cleary and Twelvemile). At 3,624 feet,

Eagle Summit is the highest point on the road, and a popular destination for locals and travelers around solstice time to watch the sun skirt the horizon, never setting. If the sun is *shining,* that is. It's been known to snow up here on solstice, or you could be socked in by clouds or fog. In fact, you might wish for a nice blizzard to hold down the skeeters, so thick and ferocious that they've been rumored to pick up men—large men—and carry them off. The mile-long access road to the summit is particularly steep and rocky; alternatively, walk up or drive a couple of miles past the turnoff just past Mile 109 and hike up the back side to save wear and tear on your vehicle. If you drive up and down the access road, though, when you get back to the Steese it feels like pavement!

Coming down from the summit, there are gorgeous views of the current gold-mining activities on the valley floor, along Mammoth and Mastodon Creeks, so named for the frozen remains of large Alaskan mammals uncovered by strip mining. The tusks on display at the UAF Museum came from here. Make sure to stop at 101 Gas to check out the ancient gas pump, which pumped its last gas(p) in the past. Take a left at Mile 119 and go straight at the fork for Bedrock Creek, a good spot to camp if you can handle the skeeters.

Central

Nine miles farther is Central, whose year-round population of 60 souls triples in the summer because of the influx of miners. **The Circle District Museum** in the log cabin in town has mining and mushing artifacts from the early days and a good wildflower photo display. Free and open daily noon–5 P.M. in the summer. Walk around back to see the wagon-wheel camper. **Mills Junction** (907/520-5599) has everything in one place: motel rooms, convenience store, gas, RV parking, a restaurant, laundromat, and bar. It's open year-round.

Eight miles out Hot Springs Road is the historic and famous **Circle Hot Springs Resort,** with its buildings from 1905. Unfortunately, it closed in 2002, and is not expected to reopen anytime soon.

Circle

Erroneously named by miners who thought the town site was close to the Arctic Circle—it's actually 50 miles north—Circle is a long 34 miles beyond Central. The road is in good condition, just quite winding, particularly the last 11 miles. Gold was discovered on nearby Birch Creek in 1893, and Circle was a boomtown with two dozen saloons, a library, a hospital, and even an opera house, long before anyone had heard of the Klondike. When the miners did hear of the Klondike a few weeks after the strike, Circle immediately lost half its population. The town gradually declined as a supply center for the big Circle Mining District, largest in Alaska, after the Steese Highway hooked up to Fairbanks.

Today, with a population of just under 100, Circle is typical of end-of-the-road Alaska—a couple of streets, lots of cars (mostly junked). The main attraction is the mighty Yukon. Pitch your tent at the denuded campground (free) on the banks and watch the river flow. **Yukon Trading Post** (907/773-1217) has a café, a bar, gasoline, motel rooms, a post office, and free camping. **H. C. Company Store** (907/773-1222), sells gas, repairs tires, and has groceries, gold pans, and gifts. Get directions here to the **Pioneer Cemetery.**

Warbelow's Air Ventures (907/474-0518 or 800/478-0812, www.warbelows.com) flies to Central and Circle. **Circle Air** (907/520-5223, www.circleair.com) has air charters out of Central, and rents rafting equipment.

THE ELLIOTT HIGHWAY

The Elliott Highway, named after Major Malcolm Elliott, president of the Alaska Railroad Commission 1927–1932 (following George Steese), begins at the junction with the Steese Highway in Fox, 11 miles north of Fairbanks. The road is paved to Mile 28 (but watch for frost heaves), then turns into a very wide, occasionally smooth, two-lane gravel road until the junction with the Dalton, when it narrows to a one-and-a-half-lane, rough, hard-dirt ribbon through total wilderness.

Other than the BLM White Mountain Trail at Mile 28, and gorgeous views in several spots on the road (especially Miles 95–96), there's little on the way to Manley Hot Springs, a small town at the end of the highway, 152 long miles from Fox. In fact, there's only one facility between the Hilltop Truck Stop (just outside of Fox, 907/389-7600) and Manley: It's the Arctic Circle Trading Post at Mile 49. Most of the road is in the 40–50 mph range, with a few 20–30 mph stretches, totaling four to five hours one-way from Fairbanks.

Between Fox and the Dalton Highway junction, huge supply trucks to and from Prudhoe Bay barrel along, raising blinding clouds of dust; by the time you get back to Fairbanks from Manley, a fine layer of dust will have settled over everything you've got, including your entire respiratory tract. It's essential to have *plenty* of water along for this ride. Also take food, as there's no Denny's at the next exit, since there aren't any exits. And don't forget your bathing suit.

The road climbs quickly out of Fox, with good views of the Interior's rolling hills. One mile north of the abandoned railroad and mining town of **Olnes,** just before the Mile 11 bridge over the Chatanika River, a large gravel road on the left goes a mile in to Chatanika Pond, part of the **Lower Chatanika River State Recreation Site:** no facilities, but fair fishing and primitive camping. On the other side of the Mile 11 bridge is the rest of the recreation site: camping ($10), picnicking, pit toilets, fishing for grayling in the summer, and for whitefish in the fall.

White Mountains National Recreation Area

The BLM's White Mountains National Recreation Area covers a million acres of forests, rivers, and mountains approximately 30 miles north of Fairbanks. It is the largest national recreation area in the U.S., and a favorite weekend escape for locals who enjoy the 200 miles of backcountry trails.

At Mile 28 of the Elliott Highway are trailheads for myriad paths through the White Mountains. Read the information board carefully. Most trails are for winter use and are not maintained during the summer for hiking. The **Summit Trail**

starts from the trailhead on the left and is designated for summer use. This 21-mile trail (one-way), mostly along alpine ridge tops through the foothills of the White Mountains, ends at Beaver Creek. This trail starts out high up to begin with, and the first mile or so of the Wickersham Creek Trail takes you out of the taiga and onto a ridge top, with a beautiful 300-degree view of the Tanana Valley, Alaska Range, and gigantic sky. Even if you're not hiking all the way, it's worth it to day hike this mile for the view.

During the winter, 10 public-use cabins—each a day's ski apart—are available to rent in the White Mountains. Each cabin has a cookstove and lantern, woodstove, table and benches, bunk beds, and outhouse. In the summer only two of these cabins are readily accessible; the others are difficult to reach because of wet and muddy trail conditions. Cabins rent for $20–25. Contact the BLM (907/474-2251 or 800/437-7021, http://aurora.ak.blm.gov) for details. Also check out **Trailhead Cabins** (907/374-0717, www.trailheadcabins.com, $65), road-accessible three-person cabins on the south side of the mountains.

Bye Bye Pavement

The pavement ends 100 yards north of the White Mountains trailhead. Enjoy this wide gravel stretch while you've got it! Nice views of the oil pipeline here—shining in the sunlight, twisting through the tundra, suddenly disappearing underground and surfacing again. At Mile 49 is **Arctic Circle Trading Post** (907/474-4565)—a.k.a. Wildwood General Store—where you can get snacks, drinks, fresh sandwiches, and Arctic Circle gifts. No gas or lodging, and it's only open mid-May to mid-September.

At Mile 71 is the two-mile access road to **Livengood,** a tiny mining center that flourished briefly as a pipeline construction camp. It now has a population of 30. Two miles farther is Mile 0 of the Dalton Highway. Take a left to stay on the Elliott Highway.

To Manley

A bit past the junction with the Dalton, and right after the bridge over the Tolovana River, is a little pullout (left), a nice spot for a picnic, camping, fishing, or even swimming (no facilities). Here the road narrows considerably, and you follow the two tire-packed stripes down the middle of it, hoping nobody is coming in the other direction. At Mile 96 is a fantastic view overlooking the Minto Flats, the Tanana River, and the foothills of the Alaska Range. If you're very lucky and have charmed cloud karma, you'll get a breathtaking view of Mt. McKinley and the accompanying snowcapped peaks to its right and left, jutting straight up like a big militant fist from the lowlands. Even though the range is more than 100 miles due south, the possibility of seeing it is worth the whole ride—even the dust. From here to Manley are some fun roller-coaster humps and curves; watch for porcupines, foxes, snowshoe hares, squirrels, hawks, and other cars.

Manley Hot Springs

This relaxing and friendly town (pop. 70) is a couple of miles this side of the end of the Elliott at the Tanana River. Like many Interior villages, Manley Hot Springs had its heyday in the early 1900s during the peak activity of nearby mines. The U.S. Army Signal Corps set up a telegraph station here in 1903, and Frank Manley built the town's first resort in 1907. Because of the geothermal activity, Manley boasts agricultural features uncommon for Interior—rich warm soil, a long growing season, even earthworms—and is known for its abundant produce. Manley also has a roadhouse, a popular landing strip, and more ATVs than cars. A lot more. Best of all, the hot springs have no sulfur, so you can enjoy the soak without the stench.

Open since 1906, the **Manley Roadhouse** (907/672-3161) is a popular meeting place for local miners, trappers, and dog mushers. It has many prehistoric and historic artifacts on display, collected from around the area, along with the usual bar, restaurant with down-home food, friendly atmosphere, and rooms with a bath down the hall for $65 d. Modern motel-type rooms are $90–120 d, and cabins with outhouses cost $95 (shower in the lodge). Showers for campers are $3. Open May to mid-October.

Right on the edge of town are the **Manley Hot Springs** (907/672-3171), on private property belonging to Chuck and Gladys Dart. These long-time Manley residents—the school is named after Gladys—are friendly Alaskan farmers who use the hot springs bubbling up on their property to grow flowers and grapes in greenhouses. Inside the first greenhouse are three concrete soaking tubs with 108°spring water; $5 per person.

Keep going toward town and park by the bridge over Hot Springs Slough. Go right just before the bridge and walk a half-mile to the first road to the right. The first part of the trail past the cabins is private property. Then it's three miles to the tower, and two more up to Bean Ridge. Great views and camping up there.

The public campground below the bridge on the other side of **Hot Springs Slough** in the middle of town has toilets, picnic tables, and barbecues for $5.

The Elliott Highway continues past the landing strip and trading post 2.5 miles to the end of the road at the mighty Tanana River. Here it's scenic and breezy, and you could camp here in a pinch.

DALTON HIGHWAY TO DEADHORSE

Before pipeline days, the Elliott Highway ran from just outside of Fairbanks to Livengood, where a 56-mile spur road cut north to the Yukon River. The Dalton Highway began as the "Haul Road" in 1974, constructed to run parallel to the **Trans-Alaska Pipeline** from the Yukon River to Deadhorse, a small oil settlement on Prudhoe Bay. In 1981, the spur road and the Haul Road, a total of 414 miles, were renamed the Dalton Highway after James Dalton, who pioneered early oil exploration efforts on the North Slope. This long road traverses some of the most spectacular and remote land accessible by road in Alaska (and therefore in the country), through taiga and tundra, over the Arctic Circle, past towering snowcapped peaks, through the Brooks Range, and within a mile of Gates of the Arctic National Park. Wildlife is abundant: caribou, Dall sheep, and wolves can be seen if you look closely. For additional information on the Dalton Highway, contact the BLM (907/474-2200 or 800/437-7021, http://aurora.ak.blm.gov/dal-

THE INTERIOR

Dalton Highway with the Trans-Alaska Pipeline in the background

ton) or request their very helpful "Discover the Dalton" publication.

Driving It Yourself

The Dalton Highway is still primarily a truck-supply route and is fairly wide, but it can become very dusty or slippery depending on recent weather. The road is open all the way to Deadhorse, but make no mistake: this is a somewhat excruciating seven to 11 hours on a tire-eating, bone-jarring, teeth-grinding, anus-clenching "highway." A trip up the Dalton is not to be taken lightly!

There are only a few service stations/supply stops along the way: at Yukon River crossing (Mile 56), Coldfoot (Mile 175), Wiseman (Mile 189), and the end of the line in Deadhorse (Mile 414). You'll be maxing out your Visa card if you get towed very far, so extended towing coverage (such as AAA's Plus policy) is highly recommended! Always travel with plenty of water, keep your headlights on, carry two spare tires, and *watch for trucks.* The trucks do not slow down for oncoming traffic, but in most cases you can see them coming thanks to the dust trails they raise. Be prepared for all that dust to come your way, along with a hail of flying gravel that sometimes shatters windshields.

Once you reach Deadhorse, don't expect to simply drive around the oilfields; all access is tightly controlled and only authorized tour operators can pass through the checkpoints. Tours and lodging are available through the Arctic Caribou Inn (907/659-2368 or 877/659-2368, www.arcticcaribouinn.com).

Arctic Outfitters (907/474-3530 or 800/474-1986, www.daltonhighway.com) in Fairbanks rents cars for travel on the Dalton at $79/day. These include two full-size spare tires, a CB radio, first aid kit, and other useful items.

Transportation and Tours

Alaska Airlines (800/426-0333, www.alaskaair.com) has daily flights from Anchorage to Prudhoe Bay/Deadhorse. Several companies offer tours up the Dalton Highway to the Arctic Circle and beyond if you want to save the wear and tear on yourself and your vehicle. There are all sorts of variations on the theme, starting with one-day-to-the-Circle-and-back tours ($130), up to multinight trips to Prudhoe Bay or the Brooks Range. One popular choice includes a flight from Fairbanks to Prudhoe where you tour the oilfield and overnight before taking a butt-bustin bus excursions down the Dalton, stopping in Coldfoot for a night, reaching Fairbanks the third evening. This one costs around $800 s or $1,500 d.

Tour companies include **Northern Alaska Tour Company** (907/474-8600 or 800/474-1986, www.northernalaska.com), **Trans Arctic Circle Treks** (907/479-5451 or 800/479-8908, www.arctictreks.com), and **Alaskan Arctic Turtle Tours** (907/457-1798 or 888/456-1798, www.polarnet.com/~wlodgejw). Both **Princess Tours** (907/276-7711 or 800/835-8907, www.princesstours.com) and **Gray Line of Alaska** (907/835-2357 or 800/544-2206, www.graylineofalaska.com) offer more expensive bus and air tours from Fairbanks up the Dalton Highway.

Dalton Highway Express (907/452-2031, www.daltonhighwayexpress.com) has scheduled summertime bus service up the Dalton Highway; $50 to the Arctic Circle, $65 to Coldfoot or Wiseman, $125 to Prudhoe Bay.

To the Arctic Circle

Mile 0 of the Dalton is 73 miles north of Fairbanks, accessed by the Elliott. From here it's 56 miles to the Yukon River, with sweeping views of the undulating landscape and good glimpses of the pipeline. Only one developed campground is maintained along the Dalton, but the first of many undeveloped areas is at **Hess Creek,** Mile 24.

A 2,290-foot wooden-deck bridge crosses the mighty Yukon at Mile 56. On the northern side is **Yukon Ventures Alaska** (907/655-9001), the only service facility before Coldfoot, with a small mercantile, gift shop, gas, tire and minor auto repairs, and motel rooms with two twin beds and shared bath facilities for $89 d. The restaurant here serves excellent food—from burgers and homemade chili to steaks and fresh seafood. They're open May–October.

An interesting pipeline interpretive display is near the bridge, and the BLM's **Yukon Crossing Visitor Station** is open seven days a week June–August. Cross the road and drive under the pipeline for an undeveloped camping area. In-

formative one-hour boat tours are offered June–August by **Yukon River Tours** (907/452-7162, www.mosquitonet.com/~dlacey, $25 adults, $15 kids under 12).

Isolated granite tors are visible to the northeast at Mile 86, and at Mile 98 are excellent views of the mountains across the tundra before the road descends again to travel along the valley floor. At Mile 115 is the **Arctic Circle:** latitude 66°, 33 minutes. A huge sign proclaims the location, and nearly everyone stops to pose for a photo. A road behind the sign leads a half-mile to camping.

Coldfoot

At Mile 132 are **Gobbler's Knob** and the first views of the Brooks Range on the distant northern horizon. The road winds past Pump Station 5, over numerous rivers and creeks, and by great fishing; at Mile 175 it rolls into Coldfoot. Gold was discovered at Tramway Bar in the upper reaches of the Koyukuk River in 1893, attracting enough prospectors and miners to found the town of Coldfoot. Still, the town reportedly received its sobriquet when most of them got cold feet at the onset of the first winter and left the country. Two of the original mining cabins are still in the bush at the northern end of the airstrip.

It's no wonder the old miners' feet became frosty. In January 1989, Coldfoot recorded a temperature of -82°F, and for 17 days the mercury refused to rise above 62°below. Then, that summer, it got up to 97°above—the 179-degree differential broke all North American records.

The spacious **Arctic Interagency Visitor Center** (907/678-5209, http://aurora.ak.blm.gov/arcticinfo, daily 10 A.M.–10 P.M. Memorial Day–mid-Sept., closed winters) is staffed by BLM, Park Service, and FWS personnel. Stop here for travel information, wildlife films, natural history publications, and nightly natural history programs.

Sourdough Fuel (907/678-5201, www.sourdoughfuel.com) has meals at Coldfoot Cafe, expensive gas, and lodging. The Coldfoot post office and a gift shop are also here. Top off your tank; the next gas is 239 miles away at Deadhorse.

Coldfoot Camp (907/474-3400 or 866/474-3400, www.coldfootcamp.com) has an always-open restaurant, plus gas, repairs, and rooms in pipeline-era Atco trailers: two twin beds for $165 s or d. No TVs or phones in the rooms. For flights into the Brooks Range or Arctic National Wildlife Refuge, contact **Coyote Air Service** (907/678-5995 or 800/252-0603, www.flycoyote.com).

Camp at the BLM's beautifully situated **Marion Creek Campground** (five miles north of Coldfoot, open June–mid-Sept.; $8).

Wiseman

A mining village that dates back to 1910, Wiseman is home to 20 or so folks. The settlement is three miles out a spur road off the Dalton Highway at Mile 185, and 12 miles north of Coldfoot. A number of picturesque log cabins are scattered around, beneath a fantastic mountain setting, including the **Wiseman Museum** housed in the

old Carl Frank cabin. Inside are historical photos and various mining items from the Koyukuk River gold rush, along with gifts. **Arctic Getaway B&B** (907/678-4456, www.arcticgetaway.com) offers lodging with breakfast for $90 d in cozy log cabins. **Boreal Lodging** (907/678-4566) also has cabins.

To the Slope

North of Wiseman the Dalton Highway parallels the Koyukuk River for 20 miles or so. The edge of Gates of the Arctic National Park is high up on the slopes west of Wiseman (see the *Arctic* chapter for more on this grand area). At Mile 194 are the first views of 4,000-foot **Sukakpak Mountain.** The road passes along the base of this rugged peak, and a trail at Mile 203 leads a half-mile right to the base. The strange-looking mounds

THE INTERIOR

JURASSIC PARK ALASKA

Dinosaurs in Alaska? Unlikely as it may sound, dinosaurs did live here during the Triassic, Jurassic, and Cretaceous periods (66 million to 248 million years ago). The first discovery of dinosaur bones came in 1961 when a Shell Oil geologist happened upon strange bones along the Colville River. Thinking they were just mammoth bones from the last ice age, the company shelved them for two decades. When government scientists finally took a look, they were stunned to discover that these were instead the bones of dinosaurs. This discovery is now regarded as one of the most important dinosaur finds of the last several decades, and one of the greatest Cretaceous vertebrate deposits anywhere on earth.

Over the last two decades, scientists have come to the Colville site—right along the Arctic Ocean—to discover how the supposedly cold-blooded dinosaurs could survive such a harsh northern climate. Their findings threw several scientific theories into question, and most paleontologists now believe the dinosaurs were warm-blooded and could move fast enough to migrate long distances, much as the caribou do on today's North Slope. In 1998, dinosaur tracks were discovered at more than a dozen sites along the Colville River, providing evidence that these animals were not only present, but actually common 100 million years ago.

Temperate Times

The world the dinosaurs inhabited was vastly different from that of northern Alaska today. A warm inland sea ran from the tropics to the polar regions east of Alaska. The Arctic land was covered with dense, fern-filled redwood forests, and winter temperatures rarely dropped below freezing. This moderate climate and abundant food source allowed the dinosaurs to survive for millions of years. The largest animals were the four-ton horned pachyrinosaurs and the three-ton duck-billed hadrosaurs, both of which were vegetarians. They were preyed upon by such meat-eaters as the tyrannosaurs. Why the dinosaurs disappeared is one of the ongoing mysteries in science, though the prevailing theory is that a giant comet slammed into the earth some 65 million years ago, causing the planet to cool so rapidly that the dinosaurs could not survive.

And what of the possibility of a "Jurassic Park" in Alaska? The dinosaur discoveries along the Colville River are unique in that some of the bones were never mineralized (turned into stone). Some of these are still the original bones, and it is even possible that a bit of the original DNA is present. Don't expect to see mutant dinosaurs roaming around Alaska anytime soon, but the bones could potentially provide information on what the dinosaurs ate and whether or not they were cold-blooded.

between the road and the mountain are "palsas" formed by ice beneath the soil pushing upward.

Above Disaster Creek at Mile 211, the road climbs quickly up to Chandalar Shelf, a huge basin with a healthy population of grizzlies, then over **Atigun Pass** at Mile 244, the highest highway pass in Alaska (4,800 feet). The road winds quickly down through the Atigun Valley and onto the North Slope. At Mile 414 is the town of Deadhorse.

Prudhoe Bay/Deadhorse

This is the place that makes Alaska run, home to the massive Prudhoe Bay Oilfield (largest in North America and 18th largest in the world), and starting point for the Trans-Alaska Pipeline that carries oil to Valdez, 800 miles to the south. The oilfield encompasses a 250-square-mile area, though the wells, roads, and facilities actually cover just 2 percent of this land. Keep your eyes open for the caribou that graze amid the small city of buildings, pump stations, and other equipment. Some 3,500 well-paid oilfield and related workers stay around Deadhorse, working on a rotating basis that is typically two weeks on followed by two weeks off. The oil companies fly them home for their days off.

The developed areas are called Deadhorse, but the entire area is commonly called Prudhoe Bay

or even more generically, the North Slope or in local parlance, simply the Slope. It is just a few miles from Deadhorse to Prudhoe Bay on the Beaufort Sea (Arctic Ocean). Are you confused yet? If so, try the Prudhoe website (www.prudhoebay.com). Alaska Airlines has flights to Deadhorse, but the only way to get to the Arctic Ocean or into the oilfields is on a tour.

Arctic Caribou Inn (907/659-2368 or 877/659-2368, www.arcticcaribouinn.com) charges $130 for a room with two single beds. RV parking is available, and meals—served in all-you-can-eat buffet-are reasonable. Open late May to early September. The same folks run **Prudhoe Bay Hotel** (www.prudhoebayhotel.com), open year-round, but primarily for workers. Lodging and three meals a day costs $90 s or $150 d with a bath down the hall, or $110 s or $180 d for nicer rooms with private baths and TVs. Arctic Caribou Inn and **Tour Arctic** (907/442-3441 or 800/523-7405, www.tourarctic.com) both offer tours that include the Oilfield Visitor Center and a stop at the Arctic Ocean.

Prudhoe Bay General Store (907/659-2412) has supplies, a post office, and the Deadhorse Museum (of sorts). Auto and RV parts and repairs are available, and the NANA Gas station provides RV parking with hookups.

Eastern Interior Alaska

DELTA JUNCTION

This town of 900 people is 100 miles south of Fairbanks on the Richardson Highway at its junction with the Alaska Highway. Delta Junction marks the official ending point for the Alaska Highway, and Milepost 1,422 stands in front of the visitor center. The World War II road designers specifically aimed the Alcan to join at Delta, connecting it to both Interior Alaska and tidewater at Valdez (266 miles to the south).

History

Alaska's first road, the **Richardson Highway** was originally envisioned as an "all-American route"

to the Yukon gold fields in the late 1890s, and a trail was constructed in conjunction with the WAMCATS telegraph cable all the way to Eagle. But with the shift of attention to the Fairbanks area in the early 1900s, the trail was redirected there and upgraded to a wagon road in 1907 under the auspices of Wilds P. Richardson, first president of the Alaska Road Commission.

Delta began as one of the numerous roadhouses along the trail, which were spaced a day's journey apart (roughly 30 miles). Bate's Landing was opened in 1906 at the confluence of the Delta and Tanana Rivers, where travelers crossed the Tanana on a government-operated ferry that utilized the current for propulsion.

Delta hit the big time, however, with the construction of the Alcan, and when Allen Army Airbase (later Fort Greely) was established nearby as one of the many military installations along the highway. Delta received another boost when a pipeline-construction camp was located here; the pipe crosses the Tanana right next to the highway—a spectacular first view of it for overland travelers. Fort Greely is a major center for the Missile Defense System, and a $2.4-billion project here includes the construction of a half-dozen interceptor missile silos as part of the "Star Wars" anti-missile program.

Delta services the largest agricultural area in the state, including thousands of acres of grain and potato farms and smaller farms. Delta is also home to a herd of nearly 500 bison, a species that once outnumbered caribou in Alaska before being driven into extinction. In 1920, the Delta area was stocked with 23 bison from Montana, and the 70,000-acre Delta Bison Range was created in 1980. Ask locally to find the bison since they are often not visible from the highway. In addition to wild bison, local ranchers raise other bison for meat, along with such exotics as reindeer, elk, and even yak.

Big Delta State Historical Park

If you only do one thing in Delta, take an enjoyable and educational stroll through history at Big Delta State Historical Park (8 miles north of town, daily 8 A.M.–8 P.M.). Set in a scenic spot along the banks of the Tanana just below the pipeline crossing, this lush 10-acre piece of property centers around **Rika's Roadhouse** (www.rikas.com), a longtime travelers' stop on the Richardson Road between Valdez and Fairbanks. Restored and expanded in the mid-1980s, the park now features a museum, barns, flourishing gardens, cabins, signboards, outhouses new and old, and displays on mining, trapping, clothing, and more. Guided tours are given several times a day. The Roadhouse itself now houses a fine gift shop with Alaskan-made items, and you can grab a bite at the **Packhouse Pavillion Restaurant** (907/895-4201), known for dependably good sandwiches, home-made soups, salads, and delicious pies and bearclaws. Big Delta is one of only two historical parks in the state (the other is Independence Mine near Wasilla). Highly recommended.

Information and Other Sights

The **Delta Junction Visitor Center** (907/895-5069 or 877/895-5068, www.deltachamber.org) is right at the junction of the Alaska Highway and Richardson Highway. It's open daily 8 A.M.–8 P.M. Memorial Day to Labor Day, daily 9 A.M.–4:30 P.M. for the rest of May and September, and closed the remainder of the year.

Adjacent to the visitor center is **Sullivan Roadhouse Historical Museum** (907/895-5068, daily 9 A.M.–5 P.M. late May to mid-Sept.; free). The oldest roadhouse in Interior Alaska (built in 1905), this log building is packed with memorabilia and old photos from the Valdez-Fairbanks Trail and the roadhouses that operated along its route.

You can take a short loop through Delta's rich **agricultural area** by heading eight miles east down the Alaska Highway; take a left at Sawmill Creek Rd., another left on Bailey Way, again a left on Hansen Rd., and one more left on Clearwater, which delivers you back to the highway. Good views of the eastern peaks of the Alaska Range from the Clearwater area, if it's clear.

To get the total 360 degrees, though, head to **Donnelly Dome,** 23 miles south of town on the Richardson Highway. Go right on the gravel road at Mile 248, continue for a quarter-mile past the second sharp bend; an obvious though unmarked trailhead is at the car park there. Allow a half-day to the dome and back.

Ten miles north of Delta Junction, get a dose of Alaskan kitsch at **The Fur Shack** (907/895-1950, www.alaskarafts.com), home to Ethel, a mannequin decked out in a white fur bikini. You'd think you'd stumbled upon an artifact from *Planet of the Apes.*

A dozen miles north of town at Mile 278 is **Quartz Lake State Recreation Area,** known for excellent rainbow trout and silver salmon fishing. Several day hiking trails head out from the campgrounds, past a homestead cabin from the 1950s and archaeological sites to hilltop vistas.

Accommodations

Alaskan Steak House & Motel (907/895-5175, www.wildak.net/~akstkhse) charges $60 d for rooms with shared baths and $80 d for those with private baths. Head four north miles up the Richardson for **Alaska 7 Motel** (907/895-4848, www.alaska7motel.com) a big older place with large rooms for $75 d.

Back in town, **Kelly's Alaska Country Inn** (907/895-4667, www.kellysalaskacountryinn.com) charges $89 s and $94 d, including some kitchenettes.

Other options are **Morning Star B&B** (907/895-4129, www.wildak.net/~rgsparks), **True North B&B** (907/895-4963), and **Bald Eagle Ranch B&B** (907/895-5270 or 877/895-5270, www.deltaalaska.com).

Camping

You'll find many camping options in the Delta Junction area, including several pleasant state campgrounds. Pitch your tent at **Delta State Recreation Site** ($10), just a half-mile west of town near the airport. There's a good view across the flats of the eastern Alaska Range. In the morning, grab a shower at the **Delta Laundry** (907/895-4561), another half-mile west. **Clearwater State Recreation Site** is 11 miles from town on Jack Warren Road, with 16 campsites ($10) and a picnic area along Clearwater Lake. **Big Delta State Historical Park** ($5), eight miles north of town, has parking for RVs (no tents) in its lot. **Quartz Lake State Recreation Area,** 12 miles north of town, has campsites for $10.

Farther afield in the opposite direction are two more state campgrounds. **Donnelly Creek State Recreation Site** ($10), 32 miles south of Delta on the Richardson, is an uncrowded area with stunning Alaska Range vistas and a good chance to see wild bison. **Fielding Lake State Recreation Site** is near Mile 201 of the Richardson Highway (65 miles south of Delta), at 3,000-feet in elevation. It's a rustic seven-site campground (free), right on the lake. A public-use cabin here is $25 (907/451-2705, www.alaskastateparks.org).

Right in town, **Green Acres RV Park** (907/895-4369 or 800/895-4369, www.greenacresrv-park.com) has attractive RV and tent spaces. Just east of town along the Alcan is **Bergstad's RV Park** (907/895-4856), open all year. Both of these have showers that can be used by folks who aren't staying there.

Food and Events

Across from the visitor center on the Richardson is **Pizza Bella** (907/895-4841), where pizzas, pastas, seafood, steaks, and sandwiches fill the menu.

Buffalo Center Drive In (907/895-5089), has buffalo burgers made from locally raised bison. Get steaks and other meaty fare at **Alaskan Steak House & Motel** (907/895-5175). **Clearwater Lodge** (907/895-5152) also serves meals, with specials on Friday and Saturday nights, when it sometimes has live bands in the lounge. **IGA Food Cache** (907/895-4653) has a deli and decent bakery, or head to the Wednesday and Saturday **Farmer's Market** all summer long next to the visitor center.

Delta's big annual event is **Deltana Fair,** a three-day festival of farming exhibits, a rodeo, carnival, parade, mud bog races, and outhouse races. It takes place the last weekend of July.

Transportation

In the summer, **Alaska Direct Bus Line** (907/277-6652 or 800/770-6652, www.home.gci.net/~akdirectbus) has service several times a week from Delta Junction to Whitehorse, Anchorage, Fairbanks, Haines, and Skagway. The buses stop overnight in Tok, so you'll have to pay for lodging or camping.

Alaska Trails (907/479-3065 or 888/600-6001, www.alaskashuttle.com) has summer service connecting Delta Junction with Fairbanks and Dawson City several times a week. Service to Valdez is by reservation only.

TOK

The Alaska Highway leads east from Delta Junction toward the border with Canada and then continues south all the way to Dawson Creek, British Columbia. One hundred and eight miles east of Delta Junction—and 96 miles from the border—is the town of Tok (pop. 1,200; rhymes with "joke"). Tok considers itself the "gateway to Alaska" and acts as the service center for several Native villages in the upper Tanana Valley. The Tok Cutoff of the Glenn Highway heads south from Tok, providing connections to Anchorage, 326 miles away.

The town of Tok grew from a mid-1940s highway-construction camp, and is still unincorporated. Where the Tok River empties into the Tanana, the Athabascan tribes once gathered to affirm peace, and Tok is usually translated to mean "Peace Crossing." (Other folks say the name came from "Tokyo Camp"—a term used during construction of the Alcan Highway in 1942. There is, however, no evidence that the town was named by potheads, though more than a few folks have posed next to the town's entrance sign with a joint in hand.)

Much of the land around Tok was burned in a massive 100,000-acre fire in 1990, but the winds abruptly shifted, sparing the town itself.

Sights

The main Tok attractions are restaurants, motels, gas stations, and information centers. The modern Civic Center houses **Tok Mainstreet Visitors Center** (907/883-5775, www.tokinfoalaska.com, daily 8 A.M.–7 P.M. May–mid-Sept., closed rest of year). Next door in the State of Alaska building is the tiny **Alaska Public Lands Information Center** (907/883-5667, www.nps.gov/aplic, open 8 A.M.–8 P.M. mid-May–Sept., Mon.–Fri. 8 A.M.–4:30 P.M. rest of year).

Mukluk Land (907/883-2571) is a little amusement park with a kids' igloo for bouncing, skee-ball machines, minigolf, dog sled rides, Alaska's largest "mosquito," gold panning, gardens, videos, a museum of sorts. This peculiar collection of bush Alaska humor costs $5 adults or $2 kids. Open June–August.

Tetlin National Wildlife Refuge

This 730,000-acre refuge occupies much of the land east of Tok and south of the Alaska Highway. It borders on Wrangell–St. Elias National Park and Canada's Kluane National Park. The refuge gets very little use by travelers, but is an important home for trumpeter swans, moose, black and grizzly bears, caribou, wolves, and other animals. Marshes here contain some of the highest densities of waterfowl in Alaska, not to mention mosquitoes. Two refuge campgrounds are accessible from the Alaska Highway. The **Tetlin National Wildlife Refuge Visitor Center** (907/883-5312, http://tetlin.fws.gov, daily 8 A.M.–4:30 P.M. mid-May–mid-Sept.) is 85 miles east of Tok. The staff offers nature talks here daily in the summer, plus evening programs at Deadman Lake Campground (Mile 1249). A three-quarter-mile nature trail is at the campground.

Accommodations

Tok has a good choice of reasonably priced places to spend the night. Cheapest is **Cozy Cabins and Hostel** (907/883-3602, www.tokhostel.com), where hostel bunks are $25 ($30 if they provide bedding), and private rooms start at $44 s or $56 d ($6 extra for bedding). Rates includes a big breakfast, access to the kitchen and common area, and evening snacks. Tent spaces (no breakfast) are $15 s or $22 d. Open year-round.

Tok Lodge (907/883-2851) has older upstairs rooms for $60 s $65 d. Next door are considerably nicer rooms at **Tok Motel** (907/883-2852 or 800/883-3007, www.alaskan.com/toklodge) for $80 s or $85 d.

Snowshoe Motel (907/883-4511 or 800/478-4511, www.alaskaone.com/snowshoe) charges $68 s or $72 d for modern two-room units, including a continental breakfast. **Young's Motel** (907/883-4411) is right next to Fast Eddy's Restaurant, with clean rooms containing two beds for $74 s or $19 d. **Golden Bear Motel** (907/883-5950 or 888/252-2123) has well-maintained motel rooms; $90–100 s or $95–105 d.

Westmark Tok (907/883-5174 or 800/544-0970, www.westmarkhotels.com) is the largest place in town, and charges a too-high $129 s or d for plain rooms.

Burnt Paw Cabins (907/883-2121, www.burntpawcabins.com) has four modern log cabins for $99 d including breakfast. They're next to the post office and open mid-April to mid-October. **Cleft of the Rock B&B** (907/883-4219 or 800/478-5646, www.cleftoftherock.net) has cabins and guest rooms; $85–125 with breakfast.

Other options include **Off the Road House B&B** (907/883-5600), **Tok Line Camp B&B** (907/883-5506), and **Discovery Inn B&B** (907/883-5559, www.discoveryinnalaska.com).

Camping

Pitch your tent at the pleasant **Tok River State Recreation Site** ($10), five miles east of Tok on the Alaska Highway. The site is too close to the highway for a quiet night, but a short trail follows the river and climbs stairs up the hillside. Across the river is part of the area that was burned in the 1990 fires. Other nearby state campgrounds ($10) include **Eagle Trail State Recreation Site,** 16 miles south of Tok on the Tok Cutoff, and **Moon Lake State Recreation Site,** 15 miles northwest of Tok on the Alaska Highway.

Tok offers plenty of parking choices for RVers: **Golden Bear Motel and RV Park** (907/883-2561 or 888/252-2123), **Sourdough Campground** (907/883-5543 or 800/789-5543), **Tok RV Center** (907/883-5877 or 800/478-5878), **Tok RV Village** (907/883-5877 or 800/478-5878), and **Tundra Lodge & RV Park** (907/883-7875).

Food

Although a number of places serve food in Tok, you only need to know two: Fast Eddy's and Gateway Salmon Bake. **Fast Eddy's** (907/883-4411, 6 A.M.–11 P.M. year-round) is Tok's main restaurant action, a clean and classy family place with good food, fair prices, and long hours. The menu covers most standards: pizzas, halibut burgers, salad bar, sandwiches, ribs, and steaks.

A fine alternative is the **Gateway Salmon Bake** (907/883-5555). Cleta Allen takes your order and your money at the check-in booth, and her husband Dave barbecues your buffalo or salmon burger, king salmon or halibut slab, ribs, or reindeer sausage, then calls you by name to pick up your chow. The meal includes a big salad bar, baked beans, sourdough rolls, and lemonade. For a lighter option, pig-out at the chowder and salad bar.

Transportation

Alaska Trails (907/479-3065 or 888/600-6001, www.alaskashuttle.com) has summertime service connecting Tok with Fairbanks and Dawson City several times a week, plus reservation-only trips to Valdez.

During the summer **Alaska Direct Bus Line** (907/277-6652 or 800/770-6652, www.home.gci .net/~akdirectbus) connects Tok with Whitehorse, Anchorage, Fairbanks, Skagway, and Haines.

40-Mile Air (907/883-5191, www.40-mileair.com) has flightseeing trips from the Tok Airport.

The Alaska Highway crosses into the Yukon Territory 124 miles east of Tok. Both U.S. and Canadian customs are open 24 hours a day, year-round. Be sure to reset your watches since the time is an hour earlier in Alaska.

TAYLOR HIGHWAY

This is the scenic shortcut to Dawson City from Alaska, a 160-mile gravel-and-pavement road through wild and undeveloped country. The road starts at Tetlin Junction (Mile 1302 Alaska Highway), 11 miles east of Tok, and is paved for the first 50 miles. The road is typically open to traffic May to mid-October, but closed the rest of the year by heavy snows. The first portion of the Taylor Highway cuts through the 1.8-million acre **Tanana Valley State Forest,** with periodic hilltop vistas over the rolling green countryside, particularly near the road summit on the slopes of 5,541-foot **Mt. Fairplay.** Keep your eyes open for the Fortymile caribou herd along the highway. Beyond Mt. Fairplay the road descends to the Fortymile River country, reaching the little settlement of Chicken at Mile 66.

Chicken

With barely 20 people, you wouldn't think this wide spot in the road would be worthy of mention, but it is actually a favorite stopping point for travelers. The town was originally named "Ptarmigan," for the chicken-like bird that inhabits the country here. The spelling of "Ptarmigan" proved a problem for the miners who were mucking for gold around here in 1895, so the name was switched to something they could handle: "Chicken." Anyone who's read *Tisha* by Ann Purdy, the story of a young teacher who overcame enormous local resistance to teach in this neck of the tundra, will be interested to know that the author made her home here.

Be sure to stop at **Chicken Mercantile** in "downtown Chicken" for copies of *Tisha,* funny T-shirts, and a taste of Sue Wiren's enormous cinnamon rolls and great pies, along with homemade chicken soup (of course), reindeer bratwurst, sandwiches, and a daily salmon bake in the summer. Tenters and RVs can park for free at the Mercantile; or pay to park behind the **Goldpanner,** just up the road, where you can also buy groceries and gas, or try your luck at panning for the yellow stuff.

Behind the Goldpanner is **Gold Dredge No. 4,** in use from 1959 to 1967, and moved here from Pedro Creek. The original town of Chicken, an abandoned mining camp, is now on private property. Hour-long tours are given in the summer; ask at the Goldpanner.

During the summer, **Alaska Trails** (907/479-3065 or 888/600-6001, www.alaskashuttle.com) has van service connecting Chicken with Fairbanks and Dawson City several times a week.

To Jack Wade Junction

It's another 30 miles from Chicken to Jack Wade Junction on the Taylor Highway. This section is the most challenging part of the drive: narrow, winding, and often rough as it passes through the forested **Fortymile Country** with its dramatic vistas and tailings from past and present mining operations. Stop for a break at the BLM's **Walker Fork Campground** (Mile 82; $8) to stretch your legs—and maybe soak your feet if it's real hot. The campground is on a beautiful site where the South and Walker Forks of the Fortymile meet. A footbridge across the creek leads to a three-minute trail to the top of the limestone wall—nice view of the valley, one of innumerable similar valleys in the immense Interior of Alaska. Four miles ahead is the gotta-take-a-photo **Jack Wade Dredge No. 1,** abandoned in 1942, and a few miles beyond this are active placer mining operations and the old **Jack Wade** mining camp—take care not to trespass.

To Dawson City

From Jack Wade Junction (Mile 96) the Taylor Highway heads north to Eagle, while the **Top of the World Highway** (the main road) continues east to Dawson, Yukon Territory, 79 miles away. From the junction it is only 13 miles to the U.S.–Canada border, the northernmost border crossing on the continent. The road is wide and well-maintained gravel on the U.S. side, and paved on the Canadian side. The name Top of the World says it all; this is a grand exit from (or entrance into) Alaska, with vistas in all directions on a clear day. The border crossing is at **Poker Creek** on the U.S. side, and Canadian customs are at **Little Gold Creek.** Both American and Canadian Customs operate mid-May to mid-September, 8 A.M.–8 P.M. Alaska Time (9 A.M.–9 P.M. Pacific Time). **Boundary Lodge** on the American side has gas and other emergency supplies—for a price.

To Eagle

From Jack Wade Junction, the Taylor Highway continues north to Eagle, 65 miles away. This stretch is almost more trail than road: very narrow and winding, with steep grades, rough surface, endless hairpin turns, and little traffic—30 mph max. For the same reasons, it's one of the most fun roads in the state. Lots of twists and turns, ups and downs, and not many cars. The scenery is the same Interior hills and spruce trees you've been accustomed to, so it's not a loss to keep your eyes glued to this road at all times; one glance away and you're driving into a ditch or off a 300-foot cliff. Expect to spend at least two hours for these 65 miles, two hours of white-knuckled, bug-eyed, teeth-chattering thrills and chills—hopefully without the spills.

EAGLE

It takes a strong desire and a serious commitment to get to Eagle—more than 160 miles from Tetlin Junction and 145 miles from Dawson. Even if you're on the way from Dawson into Alaska, it's 130 miles, at least five hard hours of driving, from the junction of Top of the World and Taylor Highways to Eagle and back. Is it worth it? Consider this. Eagle is a total history lesson. The small photogenic town of 150 may have more square feet of museum space than anywhere else in the state, and the moving-right-along walking tour can take up to three hours! Add to that a beautiful free campground, great showers, good food, friendly people, and Yukon River scenery, and Eagle is without hesitation worth the extra time, effort, and expense. This is one friendly, peaceful, close-knit community.

History

In 1881, Francis Mercier, a French-Canadian trader, established a trading post at the site of Eagle to compete with Fort Yukon and Fort Reliance, two Hudson's Bay Co. posts along this eastern stretch of the Yukon River. It was a shrewd choice of location. Just inside the American border, stampeders fed up with Canada's heavy-handed laws and taxes organized a supply town here in spring 1898, naming it Eagle for the profusion of the majestic birds in the area. Also, sitting at the southernmost point on the Yukon in eastern Alaska, Eagle occupied a strate-

gic spot for transportation, communication, and supply routes to the Interior from Valdez at tidewater. Within six months, three large trading companies had developed Eagle into a major Yukon port. In 1899, the Army began building Fort Egbert next to the town site. In 1900, Judge James Wickersham arrived to install Interior's first federal court, with jurisdiction over half the state. And by 1902, the WAMCATS telegraph line was completed between Eagle and Valdez, inaugurating the first "all-American" communication system to the Lower 48.

The biggest event in Eagle's history happened in 1905, when a Norwegian Arctic explorer appeared out of the icy fog and somehow communicated to the townspeople (he spoke no English) who he was and what he'd done. The man was Roald Amundsen, and he had just navigated the Northwest Passage (for the first time in more than 350 years of attempts) and had crossed over 500 miles of uncharted country by dogsled in the deepest Arctic winter from his ice-locked ship off the north coast of Alaska to announce his

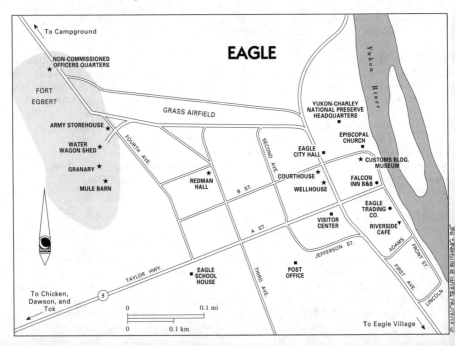

feat to the world. The message, going out over the telegraph line, was the news story of the decade.

By then, however, Eagle's star had faded. The stampeders had moved on to Nome and Fairbanks, followed by Judge Wickersham and his court. The importance of Fort Egbert declined, until it was abandoned in 1911. WAMCATS was replaced, seven years after it was installed, by wireless communication. Eagle's population continually dwindled, to a low of 13 in 1959. Fortunately, the remoteness of the town made it almost impossible to haul out the antiques that had accumulated over the decades, so they stayed in Eagle where they remain today. Since then, with a small resurgence of gold activity in the area, the establishment of the Yukon–Charley Rivers National Preserve, and increased tourism, Eagle has become a revitalized community, proud of its past and present, and optimistic about its future. The 150 or so residents proudly note that "visiting Eagle is like opening a 100-year-old time capsule."

Sights

In Eagle (907/547-2325,www.eagleak.org), it's almost impossible to find a resident who isn't something of a historian (and a cheerleader) for the area. The Eagle Historical Society is one of, if not the, most successful and well-organized groups in the state. It was founded in 1961 after someone showed up at the old mule barn with a truck and made off with the entire collection of saddles.

The care, devotion, and thoroughness with which they display Eagle's awe-inspiring array of artifacts is something to see. And their guided summertime tours ($5), which leaves from Judge Wickersham's courthouse steps at 9 A.M., is really the only way to see it; it's a fun, hands-on outing, during which you're encouraged to operate an old peanut-warming machine or tickle the keys of an ancient pump organ. While waiting in the morning, fill up your water containers at the wellhouse next door to the court. The well, dug 60 feet deep by hand in 1910, still pumps cold H2O—delicious; three out of four residents still haul water from this source. Struggle through the three heavy doors and either fill your bottle

at the faucet or stretch the gas-pump-type handle to the jugs in your vehicle.

The tour begins appropriately inside the **courthouse,** built in 1901 by Judge Wickersham for $5,000. All four rooms plus the hallway on the ground floor are covered with displays of the Han Natives, geology and archaeology, early pioneers, the telegraph story, and more. Be sure to check out the front page of the December 7, 1905, issue of *The New York Times,* with Amundsen's story, plus the map of the Northwest Passage in the hallway. (A romantic footnote: The intrepid Suzan Amundsen, Roald's great-granddaughter, continues a family tradition by taking a rest at the popular Eagle checkpoint during the Yukon Quest Sled Dog Race.) Don't miss the amazing Nimrod's false teeth (homemade from caribou and bear teeth) and his remarkably accurate relief map of the vicinity—a newspaper papier-mâché printed with moose blood. Upstairs in Wickersham's courtroom is a small gift shop run by the Historical Society.

Then you mosey down to the **Customs House** on the Yukon waterfront, another two-story museum brimming with history. Study the six dated shots of the freezing of the Yukon River from October 13, 1899, to January 12, 1900, plus the photos upstairs of "wild" animals—Fred Ferwilliger's wolf pups, Mae Collins's pet black bear, and some bewildered-looking moose hitched to wagons and carriages. Sign the original U.S. Customs entry book.

A walk along the town's grassy airstrip leads to **Fort Egbert.** The huge old mule barn, at 150 feet long and 30 feet wide one of the largest restored buildings in Alaska, is full of relics from Eagle's past: tools, weapons, uniforms, wagons and tack, dog sleds, boats, a prototype Sears chain saw, an old outboard motor that looks like a cross between an early sewing machine and a Weedwacker, and much more. Upstairs is the gold-mining exhibit with its own collection of Rube Goldberg equipment. The water wagon shed houses historic vehicles, including a Model A pickup and Model B dump truck.

The newest acquisition on the tour is the **Improved Order of Redmen Building,** a wilderness version of a lodge/benevolent society, ostensibly dedicated to the preservation of the ways and traditions of the area's Native people. Of course, only white guys were allowed to be members.

For more on the town and its rich history, pick up a copy of *Jewel on the Yukon: Eagle City* by Elva Scott; it's sold in the courthouse.

Out 1st Avenue (take a right coming into town) two and a half miles is **Eagle Village,** a picturesque Native settlement that predates the white settlers. Fish wheels operate just offshore, and racks of salmon dry under the clouds. The residents are friendly, but please respect their privacy.

Practicalities

Follow the signs from town left to the free **campground** just beyond the cemetery (a few old markers; Nimrod's grave is here): big, uncrowded, nice wooded sites, firewood, vault toilets. There's an easy nature walk between the campground and the airstrip. **Eagle Trading Co.** (907/547-2220, www.eagletrading.com), on the riverfront, has rooms with river views for $60 s or $70 d, groceries, showers, RV hookups ($20), gas, and tire repairs. Next door is **Riverside Café,** open seasonally. A couple of gift shops are in Eagle, and locals set up booths selling handicrafts across from the courthouse when the *Yukon Queen II* is in town.

Falcon Inn B&B (907/547-2254, www.aptalaska.net/~falconin) is an attractive three-story log structure with dormers and a lookout tower right on the Yukon. Rooms are $65–75 s or $75–85 d with a full breakfast.

Transportation

The *Yukon Queen II* (206/281-3535 or 800/544-2206, www.graylineofalaska.com) is a high-speed, 120-passenger riverboat with daily summertime runs between Dawson City in the Yukon and Eagle. Most passengers are part of a Holland America/Gray Line of Alaska trek, but independent travelers can ride for $192 each way, including a meal. If you're entering the U.S. on the *Yukon Queen II,* be sure to stop by Customs at the post office. No buses run to Eagle, and it's a good four hours by car from Dawson, and at least another five down to Tetlin Junction.

Everts Air Alaska (907/450-2350, www.everetsair.com) and **Warbelow's Air Ventures** (907/474-0518 or 800/478-0812, www.warbelows.com) offer daily flights from Fairbanks. This is a real bush-pilot trip, the daily mail and supply run.

YUKON–CHARLEY RIVERS NATIONAL PRESERVE

Eagle itself is pretty far out there, but if you really want to disappear, you can explore Yukon–Charley Rivers National Preserve. This huge, 2.5 million-acre park is primitive, with virtually no facilities or established transportation and only a skeleton Park Service staff. The park protects 115 miles of the Yukon River and the entire Charley River basin.

The park's **Visitor Center** (corner of 1st and Fort Egbert Ave. in Eagle, open Mon.–Fri. 8 A.M.–5 P.M., 907/547-2233, www.nps.gov/yuch) has a selection of books and maps on the preserve, and the staff will plug in a video on request and can provide advice for those contemplating a trip.

Most park visitors float the Yukon by raft, kayak, or canoe, starting in Eagle (on the eastern margin) and taking out in Circle (on the western edge of the park). The float takes 5–10 days. Within the park are four public use cabins available on a first-come, no-cost basis.

You can also charter a bush plane to drop you and a kayak or raft way up around the Charley headwaters and float down to the Yukon. You must be highly experienced, entirely self-sufficient, and have at least a tolerance for, if not a love of, mosquitoes. Check in at headquarters for advice and conditions, and to leave your intended itinerary.

Eagle Canoe Rentals (907/547-2203, www.aptalaska.net/~paddleak) rents canoes to paddle the Yukon from Eagle to Circle City; $175 for five days. You leave the canoe in Circle and they return it upriver. You can also pick up canoes in Dawson City and float downriver to Eagle for $110. Experienced paddlers only.

Southwest Alaska

Southwest Alaska includes Kodiak Island, the Alaska Peninsula, and the barren, windswept Aleutian and Pribilof Islands—all told, an incredible sweep of wild and stormy coastline. This part of the state contains world-famous brown bear-viewing opportunities in Kodiak Island National Wildlife Refuge, Katmai National Park, and McNeil River State Game Sanctuary. In addition, it encompasses less-visited Lake Clark National Park, the remote Aniakchak National Monument, and four national wildlife refuges, one of which reaches all the way out the Aleutian chain. Fur seals, sea otters, walrus, and other marine animals are common around the Aleutians and Pribilofs, and the islands are also a bird-watcher's paradise. Because of climatic conditions there are no forests west of northern Kodiak Island and the adjacent mainland; most of the Alaska Peninsula and all the Aleutians are open tundra.

The largest settlements in Southwest Alaska are Kodiak and Unalaska/Dutch Harbor, but many smaller fishing towns and Native villages are sprinkled over this remote landscape. Only Kodiak is fairly reasonable to visit; other places will require considerable outlays of cash. A very useful regional website is run by the **Southwest**

the town of Kodiak on Kodiak Island

SOUTHWEST ALASKA

Anchorage

Lake Clark National Park and Preserve

Kenai

Kenai Peninsula

Yukon Delta National Wildlife Refuge

Bethel

Wood-Tikchik State Park

Iliamna Lake

Homer

Nunivak Island

Togiak National Wildlife Refuge

Dillingham

Cook Inlet

McNeil River State Game Sanctuary

Afognak Island

B e r i n g   S e a

King Salmon

Katmai N.P. and Preserve

Port Lions

Kodiak Island

Kodiak

Becharof National Wildlife Refuge

Kodiak National Wildlife Refuge

St. Paul Island

0   100 mi

0   100 km

Aniachak National Monument and Preserve

Pribilof Islands

St. George Island

Chignik

Alaska Peninsula National Wildlife Refuge

Izembek National Wildlife Refuge

Cold Bay

Sand Point

Shishaldin Volcano ▲

King Cove

False Pass

Unga Island

Shumagin Islands

SEE MAP BELOW FOR CONTINUATION

Akutan

Unimak Island

Unalaska/ Dutch Harbor

Umnak Island

P A C I F I C

Unalaska Island

O C E A N

Nikolski

ALASKA

Yunaska Island

Alaska Maritime National Wildlife Refuge

Attu Island

Attu

Shemya Island

Umnak Island

Agattu Island

B e r i n g   S e a

Nikolski

Kiska Island

Alaska Maritime National Wildlife Refuge

Tanaga Island

Adak

Atka

Seguam Island

Yunaska Island

Amchitka Island

Adak Island

Atka Island

Kanaga Island

SEE MAIN MAP

P A C I F I C   O C E A N

Alaska Municipal Conference (www.south-westalaska.com).

The Land

From Denali National Park the Alaska Range swings southwest to become the Aleutian Range, marching right into the North Pacific as the Alaska Peninsula and Aleutian Islands. This 1,100-mile arc from the northern end of the Alaska Peninsula to the western tip of the Aleutians is an area of extraordinary volcanic and seismic activity, accounting for an amazing 10 percent of the world's recorded earthquakes. Tremors of all sizes—some too small to feel—are a daily occurrence, and three of the four largest earthquakes ever recorded in the United States occurred in the Aleutians; all three had a magnitude of 8.2 or greater. Only the massive Good Friday quake of 1964 that hit Southcentral Alaska was larger.

Kodiak Island sits uneasily on the edge of the Aleutian Trench; Kodiak is nonvolcanic, yet bears the brunt of its fiery neighbors. Great collapsed craters at Katmai and Aniakchak are now administered by the National Park Service, and the 50–60 volcanoes along the archipelago comprise the longest and straightest line of smoke-belchers and ash-spewers anywhere on earth.

The vegetation of Southwest Alaska is a thick, luxurious shag carpet of grass and brush; you can travel for hundreds of miles here without seeing a single tree. The climate, however, is particularly disagreeable—fog, rain, snow, and wind.

Getting There

With ferry service from Homer and Seward three times a week, Kodiak is the only easily accessible place in Southwest Alaska. The trusty *Tustumena* sails out as far as Dutch Harbor once a month, but only in summer. Alaska Air flies from Anchorage to Kodiak, Dutch Harbor/Unalaska, and Adak, and PenAir serves King Salmon, Iliamna, Sand Point, Dutch Harbor/Unalaska, and the Pribilofs. Access to remote backcountry areas is by small floatplanes that land on the myriad of lakes and ponds.

Kodiak Island

Kodiak Island is an unlikely land of superlatives. At 60 by 100 miles, it is the largest island in Alaska, and second-largest in the United States (after Hawaii's Big Island). Kodiak has the world's biggest brown bears, Alaska's longest history, and one of the largest fishing fleets, along with the country's largest Coast Guard station and weirdest golf tournament. Besides, what other town has chewing tobacco named for it, and a dump once voted the nation's "most scenic"?

Kodiak Island is home to nearly 14,000 people, 9,000 of whom live in and around the city of Kodiak. Only 250 air miles from Anchorage or 84 nautical miles from Homer, Kodiak is a highly accessible and pleasurable place to visit. The city of Kodiak sits on the island's northeast side along St. Paul Harbor, protected from the wild Gulf of Alaska by wooded islands in Chiniak Bay. Visitors will quickly learn that the town runs on commercial fishing; it's hard to escape not only the sights but also the smell of fish.

THE LAND

The Kodiak Island group, an extension of the Chugach-Kenai Ranges, was once possibly connected to the mainland but is now separated by the "entrances" to Cook Inlet and Shelikof Strait. The group perches on the continental shelf, right on the edge of the Aleutian Trench. This makes it highly susceptible to the after-effects of volcanic and seismic activity, such as the ash of Novarupta and the tsunamis of the 1964 earthquake. However, glaciation, not volcanism, has been the primary agent in the shaping of Kodiak's geologic features. Snow and ice almost completely covered the group during the last ice age, and the alpine is chiseled roughly steep slopes, short fast runoff streams, and rounded kettles. In addition, Kodiak's coastline is so characterized by long fjords that even with a maximum width of 60 miles, no point on the island is over 20 miles from tidewater.

Dense Sitka spruce forests cover the northwest corner of Kodiak Island, along with nearby Afognak and Shuyak islands. The trees are slowly spreading southward, but most of Kodiak is a open mix of tundra, tall grass, bushes, alder, and other plants that turn florescent green in the too-brief peak of summer. Visit in July to see why they call this "The Emerald Isle."

Climate

Expect cool, wet, and windy weather on Kodiak. The average temperature in August, the "hottest" month, is 54°F. Kodiak's record high is 86°F, but most years only half a dozen summer days even exceed 70. Kodiak receives 75 inches of rain a year, of which 12 inches fall June–September. Locals claim that some sun shines one out of every three days—but it can be clear or partly clear for three glorious days, then soupy for nine in a row! Dress warm, and if you intend to explore the backcountry, bring raingear and rubber boots.

HISTORY

Russian America

Russian fur trader Glotoff "discovered" Kodiak in 1763 and told Grigori Sheilikhov (Shelikof) about the abundant sea otters there. The island's second-highest peak (4,450 feet) was named for Glotoff. Shelikof is remembered as the founder of the Russian America Company and the first European settlement in Alaska, at Three Saints Bay, Kodiak, in 1784. This is the site of present-day Old Harbor and had long been an important Alutiiq (also called Koniag) village. To gain the site, Shelikof ordered his men to massacre hundreds of the Alutiiq on the rock where they had taken refuge. Native leaders refer to the battle as "Wounded Knee of Alaska." This slaughter broke the back of Native resistance to Russian rule.

Alexander Baranof arrived in 1791 to manage the company and colony; he promptly relocated the whole settlement to St. Paul's Harbor (present-day Kodiak town) after a tsunami nearly wiped out the previous town. The Eskimo-related Alutiiq population wasn't sorry to see the Russians and their Aleut slaves move again, in

The Ascension of the Lord Russian Orthodox Church in Karluk is a visible sign of the Russian heritage of the Kodiak villages.

1800, to New Archangel (Sitka)—except that the sea otters in the vicinity had been almost completely eradicated and, as happened in the Queen Charlottes, the 20,000 Native inhabitants were decimated to 1,500 in a couple of decades because of war and introduced diseases such as smallpox.

Later Years

Kodiak survived the 19th century by fur trading, whaling, fishing, and even ice-making (Russian die-hards began producing ice in the 1850s to supply California gold rush boom towns; they introduced the first horses and built the first roads in Alaska). Salmon fishing really caught on in the early 1900s, and the living was easy until the awesome explosion of Novarupta on Katmai across the strait in 1912. It showered ash down on the town, blanketing fields and villages, crushing roofs, and changing the green island into a gray-brown desert overnight. After 48 hours of total blackness and gasping for air, 450 residents were evacuated by a U.S. revenue cutter in a daring rescue. It took over two years for life to return to normal, and the deep ash layer can still be seen on stream-cut banks around the island.

Kodiak, like the rest of Alaska, was mobilized during World War II, but the fortifications here had a more urgent quality: Forts, gun emplacements, submarine bases, and command centers were installed to protect the island from Japanese invasion and to manage the Aleutian campaign. Thousands of servicemen left a large economic legacy as well. The major economic boom for the island came later, in the form of the famous Kodiak king crab, harvested by the hundreds of millions of pounds in the early 1960s. Then the Good Friday earthquake struck in 1964, quaking the earth for over five minutes, then flooding the town for the next 12 hours with several "waves," that first sucked the tidewater out, exposing the harbor bottom, then swept half the town from its moorings with swells up to 35 feet high. For a gripping description of that terrible night—and a fascinating first-hand look at Kodiak fishing life—read *Highliners,* by William B. McKloskey.

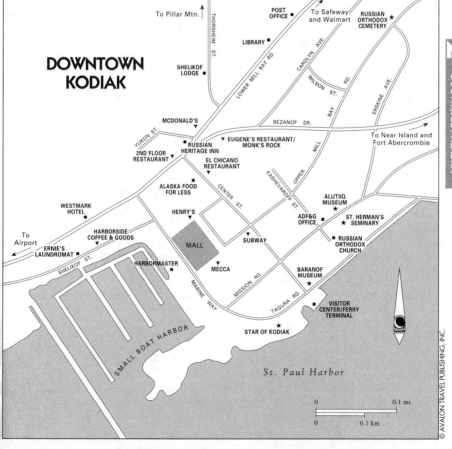

Kodiak Today

Since the earthquake, Kodiak has rebuilt and re-tooled for the harvesting of salmon, halibut, shrimp, herring, and bottom fish (king crab were nearly fished out by 1983). The bottom-fishing industry—especially for pollock—grew dramatically in the 1990s; these "junk fish" are processed into surimi: imitation crab and shrimp meat. Today, Kodiak consistently ranks near the top of U.S. ports in value of fish landed, and there are eight different canneries around the city.

A 1993 *National Geographic* article noted that "Kodiak's the kind of town where you think the municipal emblem ought to be a red pickup hauling a golden retriever, with the truck shaking to a country tune like 'Achy Breaky Heart.'" Despite this impression, visitors to modern-day Kodiak may be surprised to see how diverse the population actually is. Many of the taxi drivers, cannery workers, and other blue-collar employees are of Filipino, Mexican, or Latin American heritage. You'll hear more Spanish spoken here than almost anywhere else in Alaska. A controversial Korean church has a significant presence in the local economy, and the island even has the only state-owned missile spaceport anywhere.

SIGHTS

Baranof Museum

Several downtown buildings are reminders of Kodiak's deep Russian heritage. The Baranof Museum (907/486-5920, www.ptialaska.net /~baranov), housed in the oldest Russian building in North America, was built around 1808 as a storehouse for sea otter pelts. It's open Monday–Saturday 10 A.M.–4 P.M., late May to early September; and Monday–Wednesday and Friday–Saturday 10 A.M.–3 P.M. the rest of the year (closed February). Admission is $3, free for kids under 13.

Displays include an impressive Russian samovar and china collection, along with other artifacts such as a 10-kopek note printed on sealskin; it's from Alexander Baranof's time. Also here are Alutiiq and Aleut items, including a remarkable three-person kayak, an impressive collection of historic grass baskets, and a bear-muzzle carving found in 1956 on Cape Douglas. The photos from the 1964 tsunami are hard to believe: Boats were strewn throughout downtown. The small **gift shop**—one of the most unusual in Alaska—sells painted Ukrainian Easter eggs, lacquered boxes, Father Frost carvings, and Russian nesting dolls ($6–600). If you have the money, take a look at the gorgeous antique Russian samovars that start around $600. This is the only place in Alaska where you can buy them. Out front are several large whalebones.

Orthodox Church and Seminary

Just across the green on Mission Road and Kashevaroff Street is Holy Resurrection Orthodox Church, under the distinctive blue onion domes. This is the third church in which Kodiak's Orthodox faithful have worshipped since the parish was founded in 1794. It shelters the earthly remains of St. Herman of Spruce Island, the only Russian Orthodox saint in the Western Hemisphere; he was canonized in 1970. The interior contains colorful icons and religious paraphernalia, with a good view of the room from the balcony. To get inside, either put on clean clothes and attend a service (Thurs. at 7:30 P.M., Sat. at 6:30 P.M., or Sun. at 9:30 A.M.) or take a tour (weekdays at 1 P.M. in the summer). Call the parish priest (907/486-3854) for details.

Walk up toward the bridge overpass to the **St. Herman's Theological Seminary,** one of three Orthodox seminaries in the United States. The beautiful seminary chapel is open all the time, and is worth a visit. A brochure provides details on the chapel and the Orthodox religion.

Alutiiq Museum

The Alutiiq Museum (215 Mission Rd., 907/486-7004, www.alutiiqmuseum.com) is open Monday–Friday 9 A.M.–5 P.M. and Saturday 10 A.M.–5 P.M. June–August, and Tuesday–Friday 9 A.M.–5 P.M. and Saturday 10:30 A.M.–4:30 P.M. the rest of the year. Entrance costs $2, free for kids under 12. This collection features a tiny sampling of the thousands of artifacts found during archaeological digs at the village of Karluk (masks, wooden spoons, stone oil lamps, knives, *ulus,* and more), along with a diorama of a prehistoric village, kayak replicas, and other items such as spruce baskets and seal pokes. The museum store sells Native crafts.

Other Downtown Sights

The **Kodiak Alutiiq Dancers** (312 W. Marine Way, 907/486-4449, $12) perform several times weekly in the summer. Half-hour productions include singing, dancing, and a talk about Alutiiq culture and history. Call for details.

Wander along the shore to Kodiak's **Small Boat Harbor,** one of the state's most crowded. When the fleet is in, all the masts, rigging, and fishing equipment make the harbor an almost impenetrable thicket. The danger in a seafarer's life is revealed by the small monument in front of the harbormaster's office. The plaque lists the names of more than 150 men and women lost at sea.

A high bridge links Kodiak with nearby Near Island, home to a second boat harbor and float-plane dock, and the **Kodiak Fisheries Research Center** (907/481-1700, www.afsc.noaa.gov/kodiak, open weekdays)—which houses a small info center, along with a fascinating large aquarium and touch tank.

Continue left down Shelikof Street to "cannery row," where Steller sea lions are sometimes just off the docks. Additional canneries line the shore on either side of the ferry terminal. Certainly the hardest cannery to miss is the ship-ashore *Star of Kodiak.* Originally christened the *Albert M. Boe,* this was the last Liberty Ship built. It was launched in 1945 as a troop ship, but was towed up from the "mothball" fleet after the 1964 tsunami wiped out other canneries in Kodiak. Today it's owned by Trident Seafoods. One of the other plants—International Seafoods—is owned by the controversial Unification Church (otherwise known as the "Moonies"). They also own several commercial fishing boats, a group house/day care center in town, and a lodge along the Ayakulik River. Reverend Moon himself has come here several summers—along with hundreds of followers—to sportfish for salmon.

Kodiak Tours (907/486-3920, www.kodiaktours) leads van tours of Kodiak sights and history.

OUT-OF-TOWN SIGHTS

Fort Abercrombie State Park

This evocative historical and recreational site (907/486-6339, www.alaskastateparks.org) is five miles northeast of town out East Rezanof Drive. The peninsula supports a lush rainforest of huge Sitka spruce thriving on the volcanic ash from Novarupta. Thick chartreuse moss clings to these stately trees. Check out the gun emplacements on the cliff above the bay-ancient cannons that could never have hit the broad side of any Japanese (floating) barn. From this overlook, watch for puffins (one of the few places in Alaska where they can readily be seen from the shore), whales, sea otters, sea lions, and cormorants. The trails are all well maintained, and one takes you past Lake Gertrude to a beautiful beach. The park also has a campground and some fascinating tidepools.

The **Kodiak Military History Museum** (907/486-7015; www.kadiak.org, open Sat.–Sun.

© DON PITCHER

moss-covered rainforest, Fort Abercrombie State Park

1–4 P.M. in summer) is within a World War II ammunition bunker at Miller Point. Inside is a 1944 Ford jeep and other items from that era. A self-guided tour takes you past other structures from the war; pick up a free brochure at the museum.

To Monashka Bay

Monashka Bay Road begins at Fort Abercrombie State Park and skirts around this bay north of town, passing the Pillar Creek Hatchery, and a black sand beach at the mouth of Pillar Creek, before terminating 11 miles from Kodiak at **Monashka Bay,** with its shallow bay and delightful sandy beach. Follow the coast north along the beach, and head into the trees to find a trail that continues three miles to a scenic bluff called **Termination Point.**

Pillar Mountain

A good road climbs right up to the top of **Pillar Mountain,** from which all the overviews of Kodiak town are photographed. Start out at Thorsheim Street and go as far as Maple, where you turn left and go up Pillar Mountain Road. Hikers can scramble up the front of the mountain from Rezanof Drive (west of town)—steep, but much faster than walking up the road.

Exploring Kodiak Roads

All told, Kodiak Island has nearly 100 miles of fun-to-explore roads, making a rental car a wise investment for visitors. A detailed mileage guide for all the roads is found in the "Kodiak Island Visitors Guide."

The longest road—**Chiniak Road**—heads south from town all the way to Cape Chiniak (43 miles). The drive is worth the time, even if it's foggy or raining, to see this part of the Emerald Isle. The first 12 miles are paved. Four miles out is the **Kodiak National Wildlife Refuge** visitor center, and **Buskin River**

State Recreation Site, with campsites and great fishing in late summer for Dolly Varden and coho.

Another mile down Chiniak Road is the unmarked turnoff to **Anton Larsen Bay,** on the island's northwest tip. This winding 12-mile, mostly-gravel road goes by Coast Guard communications towers, a golf course, trailheads to pointy Pyramid Peak and Cascade Lake, and finally the boat launching area on this scenic and protected fjord.

Back on Chiniak Road, cruise by the airport (Mile 5) and the trail to Barometer Mountain

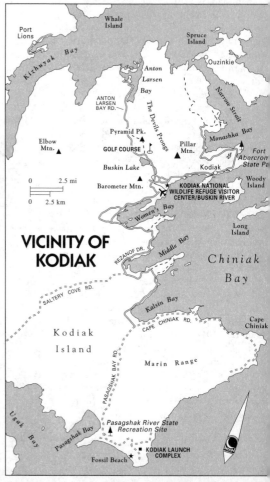

(see Hiking below) to the overlook of the **U.S. Coast Guard Station** at Mile 6. Largest in the nation (21,000 acres), this support center is home to four large cutters and more than 1,100 personnel. Main activities include patrolling the 200-mile fishing zone for illegal fishing (offenders are mostly Japanese and Russian trawlers), as well as search and rescue for commercial fishing boats.

Beyond the Coast Guard Station, the road continues around scenic Women's Bay and on to Kalsin Bay (Mile 30), where you'll find the **Kalsin Bay Inn** (907/486-2659), with food, booze, and lodging. Several pretty beaches are located over the next 10 miles, including **Roslyn Bay Beach** at Mile 37. Not far away is **Kodiak Island Winery** (907/486-4848, www.chiniak.net/winery), where they make berry and rhubarb wines. The wine-tasting room sits on the second floor of a converted barn, and is open daily 1–6 P.M. in the summer. The road ends at Mile 43 near Chiniak Point on the island's eastern tip, and a trail leads to the point itself. **Roads End Lounge** (907/486-2885) has reasonably priced lunches and dinners.

A side route, **Pasagshak Bay Road,** turns south off Chiniak Road in Kalsin Bay and leads nine miles to **Pasagshak River State Recreation Site** with free camping and a great beach. Beyond this, the road continues to Narrow Cape (16 miles from Kalsin Bay) where you're treated to all-encompassing views. Be sure to take the rather steep side road (not for RVs) to **Fossil Beach,** a fascinating and remote place to look for rocks containing fossilized shells. The beach is also a favorite of local surfers. Several of Kodiak's large cattle ranches are visible along the Chiniak and Pasagshak Bay roads, and near Narrow Cape you're likely to see grazing buffalo—part of a herd of 400 that wander freely here. It's a 47-mile drive from Kodiak to the end of the road.

Kodiak Island's unlikeliest surprise is also at Narrow Cape, the **Kodiak Launch Complex** (907/273-1582). The first rocket launch here took place in 1998, and the site will continue to be used to blast military satellites into low polar orbits, and as a major base for the testing of "Star Wars" interceptor missiles. See www.akaerospace.com for information on upcoming launches.

Shuyak Island State Park

Shuyak Island is 50 miles and a 40-minute floatplane trip north from Kodiak (or south from Homer); a flight that takes you to another world. This 47,000-acre park contains virgin Sitka spruce forests and a gorgeous coastline pockmarked with small islands and protected waterways. It's perfect for sea kayaking and wildlife watching. Kayak rentals are available within the park from **Mythos Expeditions** (907/486-5536, www.thewildcoast.com), but reserve early.

The state maintains four excellent public-use cabins at Shuyak for $65. Each can sleep up to eight people, and includes a propane cookstove, woodstove, water system, outhouse, and shower. Two of these—**Eagle's Nest Cabin** and **Salmon Cove Cabin**—are within Big Bay, and the other two are **Deer Haven Cabin** in Carry Inlet and **Mulcahy View Cabin** in Neketa Bay. There are only a few hiking trails on Shuyak, and the dense devil's club makes bushwhacking very difficult; it is possible to hike along the shore at low tide if you don't have a kayak.

Request a brochure on Shuyak sea kayaking, or make cabin reservations by contacting Alaska State Parks (907/486-6339, www.alaskastateparks.org). The cabins are generally available, but reserve well ahead during the silver salmon run in September.

Afognak Island

This large island lies 30 miles north of Kodiak Island, but is vastly different from its neighbor. Afognak is—or rather was—covered with a luxuriant, dense spruce forest. Unfortunately, much of this spectacular country was logged in the 1990s by the local Native corporation. Much of what remains is within the 49,000-acre **Afognak Island State Park** on the east side of the island, where the land is covered with a mix of forested areas and alpine country. A public use cabin at **Pillar Lake** (907/486-6339, www.alaskastateparks.org, $35) has space for up to six people. The cabin is used as a base for backcountry hiking, fishing, and hunting. A raft or kayak is useful for getting around on Pillar Lake, and you can reach the alpine in approximately an hour of hiking. When making flight arrangements for the

Pillar Lake Cabin, make sure the air taxi service can land on wheels at Izhut Bay beach near the cabin. In addition, the U.S. Fish & Wildlife Service (907/487-2600, http://kodiak.fws.gov, $30) has a wheelchair-accessible cabin in remote **Blue Fox Bay** on Afognak Island.

Another area that managed to escape the chainsaw is the property that surrounds **Afognak Wilderness Lodge** (907/486-6442 or 800/478-6442, www.afognaklodge.com). Anyone willing to part with $550 per day (including three meals) will find some of the finest old-time accommodations in Alaska.

Afognak Native Corporation are the folks behind the wholesale clear-cutting of Afognak's forests, but they have four rental cabins ($150–200) in unlogged sections. Reservations are through **Andrew Airways** (907/487-2566, www.andrewairways.com).

Port Lions

This community of 250 people came into existence after the 1964 earthquake and tsunami destroyed the nearby village of Afognak. It was named to honor the funding and support from the Lions International Club that led to its establishment. The town has a commercial fishing base and also has a handful of lodges, eating places, and stores. The state ferry stops here, and there is air taxi service to the surrounding country.

Settlers Cove B&B (907/454-2573) has nightly lodging, and **Port Lions Lodge** (907/454-2264 or 800/808-8447, www.portlionslodge.com) offers fishing packages. **Pete Squartsoff** (907/454-2333 or 888/357-6616, www.petestrophykings.com) has a cabin on nearby Whale Island, where visitors will be able to see whales, sea otters, and a kittiwake bird rookery.

RECREATION
Hiking

Many hikes are available around Kodiak, in addition to those at Pillar Mountain, Fort Abercrombie, and the Termination Point Trail; see the visitor center for a handout ($5) that details the more popular routes.

Pyramid Peak has two trailheads off Anton Larsen Bay Road that climb this precipitous, 2,400-foot mountain just west of town. Start near the ski lift 1.5 miles past the golf course. Great vistas from the summit of Kodiak's mountainous interior. **Barometer Mountain Trail** is a steep five-mile hike to the 2,500-foot peak. It starts at an unmarked (but recognizable) trailhead on the first road to the right past the airport runway out Rezanof Drive West. This is one of the most popular local hikes.

Sea Kayaking

Kodiak Kayak Tours (907/486-2722) guides four-hour paddling around Near Island for $60. Wendy Eskew of **Alaskan Wilderness Adventures** (907/487-2397) has a similar operation, and also leads a variety of other half- and full-day kayak trips.

Fishing and Boating

Kodiak is world famous as a fishing destination, with remote fishing lodges, charter halibut and salmon fishing boats, and surprisingly good road-accessible fishing. Pick up the informative sport fishing brochure from the visitor information center, which also has a listing of more than 30 charter operators. The same info is online at www.kodiak.org. The **Kodiak Charter Association** (907/486-6363 or 888/972-6363, www.kodiakcharterassn.net) books for a number of these companies. Find their booking desk inside Best Western Kodiak Inn. An all-day halibut or salmon trip costs around $185.

Chef and author-photographer Marion Owen runs **Galley Gourmet** (907/486-5079 of 800/253-6331, www.kodiak-alaska-dinner-cruises.com), with three-hour evening cruises aboard a 42-foot motor yacht; the price depends upon the number of guests, and the menu features creative seafood entrees, organic salads, and desserts

Kodiak Sailing Charters (907/486-1732 or 866/486-1732, www.kodiaksailingcharters.com) offers dinner cruises and multiday trips aboard the 49-foot *Kirsten Anne*. The visitor center offers a complete listing of local fishing and sightseeing charter boats.

Horseback-Riding and Biking

Horseback rides are available from two ranches south of town near Pasagshak Bay: **Burton's Ranch** (907/486-3705) and **Northland Ranch Resort** (907/486-5578).

Rent a mountain bike from **58° North** (1231 Mill Bay Rd., 907/486-6249). This is also a good place to buy outdoor gear, snowboards, clothes, and even sea kayaks. Just up the street is **Orion's Mountain Sports** (907/486-8380), with more backcountry supplies, including surfboards and wetsuits.

ACCOMMODATIONS

Kodiak has a half-dozen motels and more than two dozen B&Bs. This is a working-class town, so don't expect Ritz-Carlton quality here. The chamber of commerce website (www.kodiak.org) has links to many local places, and is a good place to start when looking over the lodging options.

Motels

Inlet Guest Rooms (1315 Mill Bay Rd., 907/486-4004 or 800/423-4004) has a half-dozen rooms a mile from town for $55–65 s or d. **Shelikof Lodge** (211 Thorsheim Ave., 907/486-4141, www.ptialaska.net/~kyle) offers comfortable and well-maintained rooms near downtown for only $70 s or $75 d.

Russian Heritage Inn (119 Yukon St., 907/486-5657, www.ak-biz.com/russianheritage) is a modest downtown motel with a mix of well-maintained rooms, all with fridges and microwaves. Standard rooms are $65–75 d, kitchenettes are $85 d, and two-room suites are $110–120 d.

Best Western Kodiak Inn (236 Rezanof W., 907/486-5712 or 888/563-4254, www.kodiakinn.com) is one of the better local motels, with microwaves and fridges in all rooms, plus a hot tub; $139–149 s or d.

Buskin River Inn (1395 Airport Way, 907/487-2700 or 800/544-2202, www.kodiakadventure.com) is a 50-room motel close to the airport (five miles from town). Standard rooms (with fridges and microwaves) are $135–145 d, and suites cost $155–170 d.

B&Bs and Guest Houses

Berry Patch B&B (1616 Selief Lane, 907/486-6593, www.berrypatchbb.com) provides inexpensive accommodations in two guest rooms: $60 s or $70 d with a full breakfast.

Shahafka Cove B&B (1812 Mission Rd., 907/486-2409 or 888/688-6565, www.ptialaska.net/~rwoitel) has a big deck that provides panoramic waterfront views. Four guest rooms: a small one with a twin bed ($55 s), two others with shared bath ($75 d), and a master bedroom with private entrance and sauna ($95 d). A full breakfast is included.

Wintel's B&B (907/486-6935, www.wintels.com) has a fine waterside location at 1723 Mission Road. Two guest rooms ($75 s or $90 d) share a bath, and the very comfortable suite ($110 d) has a private bath. Guests will appreciate the sauna, indoor whirlpool tub, and full breakfasts. Big windows in the dining room face Chiniak Bay.

On the Cape B&B (3476 Spruce Cape Rd., 907/486-4185, www.onthecape.net) is a contemporary home close to town with two guest rooms, a large deck with hot tub, and spectacular ocean views. Rates are $75 s or $95 d with a light breakfast. Highly recommended.

Kodiak B&B (308 Cope St., 907/486-5367, www.ptialaska.net/~monroe) has two guest rooms and is near the boat harbor; $85 s or $105 d with a full breakfast. This is the oldest B&B on Kodiak Island.

Emerald Isle B&B (1214 Madsen St., 907/486-4893 or 866/486-4893, www.kodiaklodging.com) has three bedrooms with private baths, a patio, and continental breakfasts; $85 s or $95 d. Open March–September.

Other recommended Kodiak B&Bs include **Eider House B&B** (907/487-4315, www.eiderhouse.com), **A Smiling Bear B&B** (907/481-6390, www.ptialaska.net/~djturner), **Sea Otter B&B** (907/486-3682, www.ptialaska.net/~seaotter), **Harborview B&B** (907/486-2464 or 888/283-2464, www.kodiakfishkonnection.com), and **The Teal House B&B** (907/486-3369, www.tealhouse.com). Teal House has a handicap-accessible room.

Several guesthouses are available for families or

couples looking for their own place. Two nice ones are **Parkside Guesthouse** (907/486-9446, www.parksideguesthouse.com), near Fort Abercrombie State Park, and **Distant Loon Guest House** (907/486-1789, www.chiniak.net/distantloon), in the rainforest 37 miles south of town.

Wilderness Lodges

Kodiak is home to more than 30 remote lodges, most focused on fishing, bear-viewing, and hunting, with all-inclusive rates, and access by floatplane. Visit www.kodiak.org, for links to most of these. A few of the more established lodges are **Kodiak Lodge** (907/847-2322 or 888/556-3425, www.kodiaklodge.com), **Larsen Bay Lodge** (907/847-2238 or 800/748-2238, www.larsenbaylodge.com), **Munsey's Bear Camp** (907/847-2203), **Raspberry Island Remote Camps** (907/486-1781, www.raspberryisland.com), **Uyak Bay Lodge** (907/847-2350, www.uyakbaylodge.com), and **Zachar Bay Lodge** (907/486-4120 or 800/693-2333, www.zacharbay.com).

Kodiak is home to more than 30 remote lodges, most focused on fishing, bear-viewing, and hunting, with all-inclusive rates and access by floatplane.

Aleut Island Lodge (907/487-2122, www.kodiaktreks.com) offers overnight lodging and meals, bear-viewing hikes, and multiday hiking trips from the lodge in Uyak Bay on the west side of Kodiak Island.

CAMPING

The closest official campground, **Buskin River State Recreation Site** (campsites $10), is four miles south of town on Buskin Beach Road next to the airport. This is an OK site on the water, with shelters, pit toilets, trails, and runways in your ear. A better option is **Fort Abercrombie State Park** ($10) on the eastern tip of town, five miles away. It's worth the hitch, bike ride, or extra miles on the rental car—this is a magical place to pass your nights on Kodiak.

Pasagshak River State Recreation Site, 45 miles south of town at the very end of the road, also has good camping (no charge). It's illegal to camp in town, but in a pinch you could probably

walk across the bridge to Near Island and lose yourself in the woods.

Park RVs for $20 at **VFW RV Park** (907/486-3195, www.vfw7056.org), seven miles north of town out Monashka Bay Road.

FOOD

Coffeehouses

Kodiak's favorite hangout is **Harborside Coffee & Goods** (216 Shelikof, 907/486-5862), with lattes, pastries, fresh soups, bagels, and rich espresso shakes. It's a wonderful place to relax on a rainy day.

Monk's Rock Coffee House (202 E. Rezanof Dr., 907/486-0905), is undoubtedly Kodiak's most distinctive gathering place, run by a splinter group of the Russian Orthodox Church. There's a back room chapel, icons lining the walls, a bookstore, coffees and Russian tea to soothe the soul, plus ice cream, fresh-squeezed juices, and smoothies.

Don't miss Kodiak's legendary **Mill Bay Coffee & Pastry** (3833 E. Rezanof Dr., 907/486-4411, www.millbaycoffee.com), where baker Joel Chanet once served as head chef for the president of France! When you taste the chocolate éclairs you'll know why; I've never tasted better anywhere. Delectable pastries and cakes fill the cases, but the café also serves quiche, French onion soup, salads, sandwiches, and a Kodiak salmon burger. The shop is out near Fort Abercrombie, making this a fine lunch stop. Five stars.

All-American

Locals looking for the best burgers and other dense American grub head to **King's Diner** (beside Lilly Lake at 1941 Mill Bay Rd., 907/486-4100). It's open for breakfast and lunch daily, but for dinners only on Friday (seafood) and Saturday (prime rib). Noisy, family friendly, and recommended.

Get very good pub grub at **Henry's Great Alaskan Restaurant** (512 Marine Way, 907/486-8844), where the menu covers the spectrum of pasta, burgers, seafood, fish & chips, along with nightly specials—including a Wednesday crawfish pie. This lively (and somewhat smoky) sports bar is right downtown across from the harbor.

Eagle's Nest Restaurant (907/487-2700), in the Buskin River Inn near the airport, serves good meals three times a day, including prime rib and seafood. Another upscale place is **The Chart Room** (236 W. Rezanof Dr., 907/486-5712) inside the Best Western.

Cactus Flats (338 Mission Rd., 907/486-4677) has organic foods, plus freshly squeezed juices and smoothies.

Subway (326 Center, 907/486-7676) is open until 11 P.M. in the summer. Also in town are Kentucky Fried Chicken and Pizza Hut, both near Safeway on Mill Bay Road, and a downtown McDonald's with an indoor playground that's great if your kids need a rainy-day break. **Big Al's Pizzeria** (2161 Mill Bay Rd., 907/486-0044), inside Cost-Savers, makes the best local pizzas, and also sells by the slice.

International

El Chicano (103 Center St., 907/486-6116), has unexpectedly authentic Mexican food, with chiles rellenos, tasty homemade tamales, *chorizo con huevos,* and even a little *menudo* for your hangover. Big servings, a pleasant atmospheres, fair prices, and great margaritas. For the fast version, look for the **Martha's Place** (907/496-0752), a taco truck that can be spotted in various parts of town.

Several places serve Chinese meals in town, including **Kodiak Mongolian Barbecue** (1247 Mill Bay Rd., 907/486-2900), an all-you-can-stuff-in place where the chef cooks your spicy meal while you watch. **Eugene's Restaurant** (202 E. Rezanof Dr., 907/486-2625) has reasonable prices, a downtown location, and a Chinese lunch buffet. Across the street is **2nd Floor** (907/486-8555), with a more formal setting and good—but expensive—Japanese food, including tempura and sushi.

Groceries and Seafood

Many visitors to Kodiak buy their groceries at the downtown **Alaska Food for Less** (907/486-

5761), but the best selection can be found at **Safeway** (two miles out Mill Bay Rd., 907/486-6811). It's said to be the largest Safeway in the western United States, but prices are equally inflated. **Cost-Savers** (2161 Mill Bay Rd., 907/486-2408) is the bare-bones market with lower prices and good produce. **Asian Groceries** (1410 Mill Bay Rd., 907/486-1947) has more exotic fare.

Island Seafoods (330 Shelikof Ave., 907/486-8575 or 800/355-8575, www.islandseafoods.com), next to the harbor, has a retail shop with salmon, scallops, halibut, shrimp, and king crab, and will process your sport-caught fish. They'll ship anywhere in the world.

ENTERTAINMENT AND EVENTS

You'd expect a town whose inhabitants live close to the "Edge" to party hearty, and Kodiak definitely won't disappoint you. You don't even have to venture any farther than downtown, whose many storefronts are half occupied by bars, big bars. After a big salmon opener, a beer can thrown in any direction would hit a drunk fisherman.

The **Mecca** (907/486-3364) has a popular dance floor; this place competes with the ocean for rockin' and rollin'! For hard drinking with the highliners, sit down at **The Village** or **Tony's.** Tony's advertises itself as the "biggest navigational hazard on Kodiak" and simultaneously "a friendly neighborhood bar with over 3,000,000 drinks spilled." **Tropic Lounge** is a huge bar where some people go bowling. For TV sports, a big choice of draught beers, and good pub grub, head to **Henry's** (512 Marine Way, 907/486-3313), where the decor includes a gorgeous Chilkat robe and other Alaskan pieces of the past. Otherwise, take in a flick at **Orpheum Theater** (on Center St., 907/486-5449).

If you're heading out to Pasagshak Bay, stop at **Kalsin Bay Inn** (907/486-2659), an old-time place with an impressive collection of military caps from Navy and Coast Guard ships, signed dollar bills, and big bear photos. It's 30 miles south of Kodiak.

Events

The new year begins with a masquerade ball and celebration of **Russian New Year** in mid-January. Shortly before this is the **Starring ceremony,** during which a choir follows a twirling star to the home of the Russian Orthodox faithful.

The infamous **Pillar Mountain Golf Classic,** on at the end of March, is a deranged, par-70, one-hole tournament up the side of this 1,400-foot mountain behind town. The course, cleared by spotters with machetes, runs all the way to the peak, where a bucket in the snow serves as the hole and lime Jello as the green. No power tools allowed, so leave your chainsaw at home.

In mid-April, **Whalefest** celebrates the return of migrating whales with tours, performances, and other productions. The big summertime event on Kodiak is the **Crab Festival,** held on Memorial Day weekend. There's a parade, survival suit races, a foot race, blessing of the fleet, and various concerts. Lots of fun. In mid-July, the **Kodiak Bear Country Music Festival** brings a mix of sounds—country, rock, blues, and bluegrass—to Kodiak. **St. Herman's Day** in early August honors the canonization of the only Russian Orthodox saint from the Americas with a pilgrimage to Monks Lagoon on Spruce Island.

The **Kodiak State Fair and Rodeo** comes around on Labor Day weekend, and features everything from craft demonstrations and live music to stock car races and a small-town rodeo with bull riders.

INFORMATION

The **Visitor Information Center** (907/486-4070 or 800/789-4782, www.kodiak.org) shares the same building with the ferry office on Marine Way and Center Street, and is open summers Monday–Saturday 8 A.M.–5 P.M., Sunday 10:30 A.M.–3 P.M. and 6:30–9 P.M., plus evenings when the ferry is in port. The rest of the year, it's open Monday–Friday 8 A.M.–5 P.M. Pick up the Kodiak Island map and the excellent visitor's guide, and take a gander at the nine-and-a-half-foot bearskin on the wall. They'll also hold your backpack if you want to scout around a little. The other local visi-

tor center is Kodiak National Wildlife Refuge, out by the airport.

SHOPPING AND SERVICES

Budget shoppers head to Kodiak's **Wal-Mart** (907/486-1670); it's three miles north of town on Mill Bay Road.

The Treasury (104 Center St., 907/486-0373) is a good place to pick up *Highliners* and immerse yourself in local lore. The **library** (319 Lower Mill Bay Rd., 907/486-8680, www.city.kodiak.ak.us) downtown has an big collection of books on Alaskan history, plus computers for surfing the Web.

For an indoor shower, head straight to **Ernie's Laundromat,** across the street from the Small Boat Harbor on Shelikof, or **Dillard's Stop or Drop Laundromat** (216 Shelikof St., 907/486-2345).

Providence Kodiak Island Medical Center (1915 E. Rezanof, 907/486-3281) is the local hospital.

TRANSPORTATION
On the Water

If you have time and want to save a bundle on transportation, catch the trusty *Tustumena* in Homer, arriving in Kodiak 12 hours later. This is a great, relaxing way to reach Kodiak, but take seasickness pills upon boarding—you'll need them! The downtown Kodiak **ferry terminal** (907/486-3800) is open Monday–Friday 8 A.M.–5 P.M. The Alaska Marine Highway ferry (800/642-0066, www.ferryalaska.com) often stops in the Kodiak Island community of Port Lions along the way.

Air

Era Aviation (800/866-8394, www.eraaviation.com) and **Alaska Airlines** (800/426-0333, www.alaskaair.com), both have daily flights from Anchorage. If you're a little short on time and don't want to ride the ferry, this is the way to experience Kodiak. On the way down, if you're very lucky and it's clear, sit on the right side of the plane for a view of Mounts McKinley and Foraker, down to Mounts Spurr, Redoubt, Il-

the *Tustumena* docked at Kodiak's ferry terminal

Iiamna, and even Augustine—nearly 500 miles of spectacular peaks with just a slight twist of your head. You'll also see enormous swaths of clear-cut Native land on Afognak Island. On the way back, also sit on the right to see the vast Harding Icefield and Kenai Mountains. The airport is five miles from Kodiak town. Hitching is fairly easy, or catch a cab if you're willing to spend $15.

Air Taxis

A number of companies have floatplane flights to various parts of Kodiak from the dock on Near Island (across the bridge). They include **Sea Hawk Air** (907/486-8282 or 800/770-4295, www.seahawkair.com), **Island Air** (907/486-6196 or 800/478-6196, www.kodiakislandair.com), **Andrew Airways** (907/487-2566, www.andrewairways.com), **Harvey Flying Service** (907/487-2621, www.harveyflyingservice.com), and **Kodiak Air Service** (907/486-4446, www.kodiakair.com).

Island Air has daily service to Akhiok, Karluk, Larsen Bay, Old Harbor, Ouzinkie, and Port Lions.

Harvey Flying Service uses a classic Grumman Widgeon—one of the few still flying in Alaska. If you want to fly with one of the finest pilots in Alaska, ask for Rolan Ruoss at Sea Hawk Air.

Most air taxis offer **bear-viewing** flights around Kodiak or to the Alaska Peninsula. Expect to pay around $420 per person for a four-hour flight that includes an hour or more on the ground watching the bears.

Car Rentals and Taxis

Avis (907/487-2264 or 800/478-2847) and **Budget** (907/487-2220 or 800/248-0150) both have cars at the airport for around $60/day with unlimited miles. Cheaper deals from **Rent-A-Heap** (907/486-4001), downtown, but you'll pay extra for every mile you drive, and these can add up fast on Kodiak. **A&B Taxicabs** (907/486-4343) charges Kodiak-size rates: $15 north to Fort Abercrombie or south to the airport.

KODIAK NATIONAL WILDLIFE REFUGE

The 1.9 million-acre Kodiak National Wildlife Refuge was established in 1941 to preserve brown bear habitat on Kodiak. It covers the southwestern two-thirds of the island, along with Uganik Island, Ban Island, and a small portion of Afognak Island. Located south of Kodiak town near the Buskin River, the **U.S. Fish & Wildlife Service Visitor Center** (907/487-2600, http://kodiak.fws.gov) is open Monday–Friday 8 A.M.–4:30 P.M. and Saturday–Sunday noon–4:30 P.M. mid-June to mid-September, Monday–Friday 8–4:30 P.M. the rest of the year. Inside the center, find a fine relief map of the island, exhibits, and a 15-minute video about bears and the incredible life cycle of salmon-stunning footage, don't miss it. Every Saturday in the summer it also has special family programs; check with the center for what's coming up. Buy nature books here, or pick up handouts on animals, birds, and cabins in the refuge. The easy quarter-mile **Audubon Buskin View Trail** takes off out back.

Kodiak National Wildlife Refuge itself begins 25 miles southwest of headquarters and is accessible only by floatplane (unless you have a boat or are willing to do some Olympic-class hiking). Most visitors to the refuge fly to one of the lakes and camp or stay in a Fish & Wildlife Service cabin. Many others stay at one of the expensive wilderness fishing lodges around the island.

Bear-Watching

Kodiak is world renowned for its enormous brown bears. The largest reach 10 feet tall when standing and approach 1,500 pounds, and most adult males (boars) average 800 pounds, with adult females (sows) averaging 550 pounds. Eight out of the 10 largest brown bears ever killed were taken on Kodiak Island. There are some 2,500 bears on the island, or an average of one for every 1.5 square miles! Visitors often come to watch or photograph these magnificent animals. Unfortunately, quite a few hunters come to kill them as well. Anyone who has spent time around Kodiak bears quickly gains an appreciation for their beauty, and a respect for their intelligence. Hunting for food is justifiable; how someone could kill such an animal to just mount as a trophy—often in a ludicrously menacing position—is beyond me.

Assuming that you're on Kodiak to see—rather than kill—the bears, several local air taxi operators will fly you on four-hour bear-viewing trips for around $420 per person. This includes at least an hour on the ground watching the bears. Depending upon the weather and what the bears are doing, these floatplanes land either within Kodiak National Wildlife Refuge (the fishpass at Frazer Lake is a popular destination) or to the west on the coast of Katmai National Park and Preserve. The companies include **Sea Hawk Air** (907/486-8282 or 800/770-4295, www.seahawkair.com, highly recommended), **Andrew Airways** (907/487-2566, www.andrewairways.com), and **Kodiak Air Service** (907/486-4446, www.kodiakair.com).

These bear-viewing flights are not, of course, the only way to see brown bears. They are present along all of Kodiak's salmon streams in midsummer (best time is July), especially where there are major runs of sockeye or king salmon. Ask at the visitor center for your best viewing opportunities. In late summer the bears tend to move up to the smaller spawning streams and into berry patches where they are less visible. You aren't likely to see a brown bear from the Kodiak road sys-

BEAR-WATCHING

In the last decade or so a very hopeful trend has begun in Alaska: More and more people come to watch living bears than to kill them for trophies. Bear-viewing is a booming business in some parts of the state, and visitors never forget their first sighting. There are plenty of bears to see in Alaska if you know where to look and are willing to take the time, effort, and money to get there. Most folks, however, choose a package trip to one of the better-known viewing areas where the bears have become habituated to the presence of humans.

See the sidebars *Avoiding Bear Hugs* and *Protecting Yourself During a Bear Encounter* in the *Interior* chapter for tips on safe travel in bear country. These recommendations especially apply to photographers who sometimes get so distracted that they put themselves in dangerous situations. Bear photographers should arrive with relatively fast film (at least ISO 100 or 200), and lots of it. Professional digital cameras also have the ability to provide high quality images at faster ISO settings. Long lenses (300 mm or greater) are useful for those full-face shots at McNeil or Brooks Camp, but bring a range of lenses or zooms to get more variety in your photos. A tripod is highly recommended if you're shooting with a telephoto. Be sure to use a fast enough shutter speed to stop the action, generally at least 1/250 second (or faster).

The **Alaska Public Information Center** in Anchorage (907/271-2737, www.nps.gov/aplic) has a free publication on bear-viewing in Alaska. See the appropriate chapters of this book for details on the bear-viewing areas listed below.

Brown Bears

The most famous places to see and photograph brown bears are **Denali National Park** (www.nps.gov/dena) in Interior Alaska, **Brooks Camp** within Katmai National Park and Preserve (www.nps.gov/katm), and at nearby **McNeil River**

tem; most of the bears were shot long ago, and the rest tend to stay out of sight in the day.

Operated by Konaig Native corporation, **Karluk Wilderness Adventures** (866/686-2527, www.thekarluk.com) has a bear-viewing camp at Karluk Lake; $2,000 for four nights, plus airfare. Day trips are also available.

Cabins

The wildlife refuge maintains rustic public-use cabins ($30) at seven different locations around Kodiak and Afognak islands. These provide a wonderful way to see the wilderness up-close and personal. You will need to bring fuel oil for the heater, plus all the standard camping supplies. And don't forget insect repellent and headnets for the abundant and pesky no-see-ums. Because of their popularity, mail-in lotteries are held for the cabins on the first days of January, April, July, and October. Apply before January for the months of April–June, and before April for the months of July–September. The most popular time is July. Because of cancellations, the cabins sometimes become open; call the refuge at 907/487-2600 if you decide to go at the last minute.

Anyone interested in bear-viewing may want to check out the cabins at **South Frazer Lake** or **Uganik Lake.** It's very helpful to have an inflatable boat or folding kayak to get around these lakes; air-taxi operators have them for rent. It is also possible to camp out anywhere on the refuge without a permit. The abundance of both bears and rain can make this a less enjoyable experience, but experienced backcountry travelers will enjoy the chance to savor an untouched landscape.

Hiking

The vast Kodiak National Wildlife Refuge is undeveloped country with few trails (other than those created by bears and deer). Despite this, it is relatively easy to hike since there are almost no trees on the southern three-fourths of the island. The best time is early in summer after the snow is gone and before the grass and brush get too dense; by mid-August hiking can be a struggle. Besides, it's a bit more risky crawling through bear country when the willow thickets are too dense to see the bears! Be sure to make noise while hiking to alert bears of your presence. Once you get above the brush line (approximately 2,000 feet in eleva-

State Game Sanctuary (www.wc.adfg.state.ak.us/mcneil). Some boats and planes also offer bear-viewing day trips to coastal **Lake Clark National Park** (www.nps.gov/lacl). On Kodiak Island, bear-viewing centers around **Frazer Lake** within the Kodiak National Wildlife Refuge (http://kodiak.fws.gov). In Southeast Alaska, the most popular area is **Pack Creek** (www.fs.fed.us/r10/chatham/anm) on Admiralty Island, though you will also see brown bears at Anan Creek and Fish Creek.

In addition to the official bear-viewing areas, quite a few air taxi operators fly out of Anchorage, Homer, Kodiak, Soldotna, and King Salmon on day-long trips in search of brown bears. Most of these head to the outer coast of Katmai National Park and Preserve, for $450–550 per person.

Black Bears

The best Alaskan places to see black bears (and

some brownies) are **Anan Creek** near Wrangell and **Fish Creek** near Hyder, both within Tongass National Forest (www.fs.fed.us/r10/tongass).

Polar Bears

In Alaska, polar bears are most abundant within Arctic National Wildlife Refuge (http://arctic.fws.gov), but they are occasional visitors to **Barrow** and the village of **Kaktovik,** particularly during the fall whaling season when the carcasses attract bears. Local taxis may be able to take visitors to places where the bears are seen, but there is no guarantee of seeing a polar bear. These are powerful and dangerous creatures, and passenger vehicles do not really provide protection from a bear attack.

If you're really looking for polar bears, head to Churchill in Manitoba, Canada, where special tundra buggy vehicles provide safe platforms for viewing and photography.

tion) the hiking gets very easy even in late summer. Much of Kodiak Island is marshy, so rubber boots are highly advised for any hiking.

Floating Karluk River

The Karluk and Ayakulik rivers are world famous for their king, sockeye, and silver salmon runs, but also have impressive runs of pink and chum salmon, along with Dolly Varden, steelhead, and rainbow trout. At the turn of the century—before seven local canneries wiped the salmon out and then went out of business—the Karluk River had runs of up to 10 million red salmon! It has taken decades of careful Fish and Game management for the populations to recover, but today this is some of the finest fishing anywhere on the planet.

The most popular time to float the 25-mile-long Karluk River is at peak of the king salmon run in July. Kodiak air taxis can drop you off either at the Karluk Lake outlet or Portage, halfway downriver. Most of these companies also rent rafts, or get one from **Kodiak Kamps** (907/486-5333). If you fly in to Portage, expect to pay around $1,000 round-trip for a charter flight with room for two people and gear; service to nearby Larson Bay is just $90 per person (though you're limited to 70 pounds of gear). A four-mile trail connects Larsen Bay with the Karluk River. **Andrew Airways** (907/487-2566, www.andrewairways.com) manages five cabins along the river; $100–200/day for up to six people.

A free **public-use permit** from the F&WS (907/487-2600, http://kodiak.fws.gov) is required for the Karluk River, and just 28 permits are allowed per day. Because of their popularity, these are on a lottery system.

The Karluk River enters the waters of Shelikof Straits near the tiny village of **Karluk** (pop. 30), where you'll find a picturesque old Russian Orthodox church (built in 1888), along with a spectacular cliff-and-ocean backdrop. There is also a small store and a couple of fishing lodges. Daily plane service takes you back to Kodiak.

Alaska Peninsula

LAKE CLARK NATIONAL PARK

This 3.6-million-acre national park reaches from the western shore of Cook Inlet and across the Chigmit Mountains to enclose 50-mile-long Lake Clark. The park was established in 1980. Although there are a few lodges and cabins, the only developed site within the park is **Port Alsworth** (pop. 60) on the east side Lake Clark. Despite the name, Port Alsworth is *not* a port, since the ocean is 50 miles away.

Because of the park's ocean-to-mountaintop coverage, it includes a diversity of ecosystems, from dense spruce forests along the coast to active volcanoes (Iliamna and Redoubt). The western flank of the Chigmit Mountains is covered with tundra and boreal forests. Just south of the park is huge Iliamna Lake, Alaska's largest lake. The settlement of **Iliamna** (pop. 100) sits on the shore of this lake and has a store selling limited supplies.

Once you get away from the scattering of lodges, Lake Clark National Park is a vast, undeveloped wilderness without roads, trails, or other facilities. Those not staying in the lodges come here to boat and fish on the lake, or to backpack in the mountains. The western foothills have open, dry tundra that's perfect for hiking. Floating down the various rivers that lead westward from the park is another popular activity. Wildlife viewing can be impressive, since you can find caribou, moose, wolves, brown and black bears, and Dall sheep, among other mammals.

Practicalities

Lake Clark National Park headquarters is in Anchorage (4230 University Dr., 907/271-3751, www.nps.gov/lacl). The **Port Alsworth Visitor Center** (907/781-2218) is open year-round, and offers short hikes, slide shows, and videos. There are no stores in Port Alsworth, but boats can be rented from local lodges. There is a pretty waterfall on the Tanalian River near town, and if you keep your eyes open you might meet former Republican governor Jay Hammond—easily the most respected politician the state has seen for many decades. (He and his wife live in a log cabin along Lake Clark.)

Expensive accommodations are available from more than a dozen fishing lodges on Lake Clark or within the park boundaries along Cook Inlet. These include **Silver Salmon Creek Lodge** (907/252-5504 or 888/872-5666, www.silver-salmoncreek.com), **Lake Creek Lodge** (907/733-2718 or 907/240-0101, www.lakecreeklodge alaska.com), **Redoubt Bay Lodge** (907/274-2710, www.withinthewild.com), **Lake Clark Bear Lodge** (800/544-2261, www.greatalaska.com), and **The Farm Lodge** (907/781-2208 or 888/440-2281, www.lakeclarkair.com). In addition to fishing, guests at these lodges also enjoy bear-watching, kayaking, and other activities.

Sea Bear Charters (907/235-0123 or 888/825-1828, www.seabearcharters.com) provides boat-based bear-watching to Lake Clark National Park, visiting Tuxedni Bay on Cook Inlet during June and July. They take a maximum of six passengers for $395 per person on these all-day trips. You'll get around six hours to explore this large bay by skiff and foot, with an equal amount of time in transit on the water.

Getting There

Lake Clark Air (907/278-2054 or 888/440-2281, www.lakeclarkair.com) has daily service between Anchorage and Port Alsworth, plus flightseeing trips. Several Kenai and Homer air taxis fly to the Lake Clark shoreline for bear-viewing; contact the Park Service for specifics.

KATMAI NATIONAL PARK

Katmai National Park occupies a large chunk of the northern Alaska Peninsula, over four million acres (roughly the size of Connecticut and Rhode Island), just northwest of Kodiak Island across Shelikof Strait. Several features attract visitors to Katmai: its wild volcanic landscape, outstanding salmon fishing in a world-class setting, and the opportunity to see brown bears up close. The bears are the big attraction nowadays; they're big, they're bad, and they're ubiquitous, thanks to the million or so salmon that run up the Naknek

River drainage system from Bristol Bay each year. Dozens of other mammal, bird, and fish species thrive in the park.

The primary starting point for trips into Katmai is the town of King Salmon, which is accessible by jet from Anchorage. From King Salmon, most visitors fly into Naknek Lake to either stay at Brooks Lodge or camp at the nearby park campground. The Valley of Ten Thousand Smokes is accessible by a park bus from Brooks Lodge.

Novarupta Erupts

In June 1912, one of the great cataclysms of modern history took place here as Mt. Novarupta blew its top, violently spewing volcanic glass, ash, and sulfurous fumes for three days. One of the explosions was heard in Ketchikan, 860 miles away. The fallout choked Kodiak, whose 450 inhabitants were evacuated in a daring marine rescue, but nobody is known to have been killed. Hot ash and pumice piled up 700 feet deep over a 40-square-mile area, and acid rain destroyed clothing hanging on clotheslines in Vancouver. Massive amounts of dust cloaked the vicinity in pitch darkness for 60 hours and circulated in the upper atmosphere for two years, changing weather patterns worldwide. Scientists say this was the second largest blast in recorded history, exceeded only by the eruption of Greece's Santorini in 1650 B.C. By way of comparison, the 1883 eruption of Krakatoa in Indonesia was only half as large (though it killed 35,000 people).

Robert Griggs, a botanist sent by the National Geographic Society, discovered in 1916 the nearby **Valley of Ten Thousand Smokes,** where hot gases surfaced through tens of thousands of holes and cracks when the hot ash contacted buried rivers and springs. He reported, "The whole valley as far as the eye could reach was full of hundreds, no thousands—literally, tens of thousands—of smokes curling up from its fissured floor." The area has gradually cooled, and only a few fumaroles remain today. A national monument was created here in 1918; it has since been expanded five times to encompass the large brown bear and salmon habitat. In 1980, under the Alaska National Interest Lands

Conservation Act (ANILCA), it was declared a national park.

It's been more than 90 years since the "Noveruption," but volcanologists are still studying this unique phenomenon—a young, intact volcano created by a single event—to determine the hazards from future eruptions. Novarupta, however, is only one of 15 active volcanoes monitored within Katmai National Park. The last to spew was Trident Volcano in 1968, but steam plumes occasionally rise from Megeik and Martin Volcanos as well.

The Valley

Be sure to take the guided, eight-hour, 46-mile (round-trip) bus tour from Brooks Camp to a viewpoint over the Valley of Ten Thousand Smokes. From Three Forks Overlook, you can join a three-mile hike (round-trip) to the valley floor and back. The bus leaves Brooks Lodge daily 9 A.M. in June to mid-September, and costs $89 round-trip, including a sack lunch. Take warm clothing and raingear, along with your binoculars and camera. Advance reservations for the bus are highly recommended in July and Au-

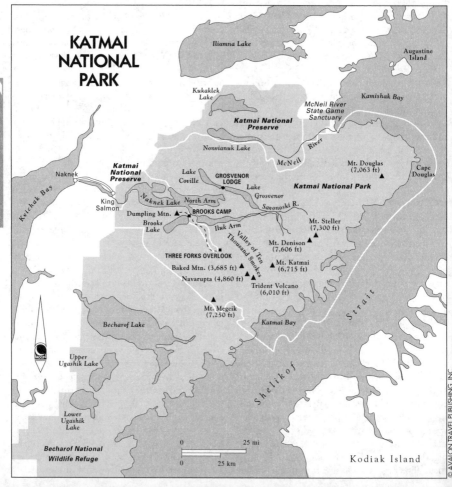

SOUTHWEST ALASKA

© AVALON TRAVEL PUBLISHING, INC.

gust; contact Katmailand (907/243-5448 or 800/544-0551, www.katmailand.com).

Hikers use this bus to access the valley, catching a later bus for the return trip ($48 each way). Two of the most popular hiking destinations are **Megeik Lake** (15 miles away) and **Baked Mountain** (12 miles away). There are no trails across the valley, and the rivers make for hazardous crossings, but the barren country is relatively easy to hike through. A USGS research cabin at Baked Mountain offers protection from the sometimes harrowing wind conditions that can create fierce dust storms, but check at the visitor center to be sure it is available. Bring ski goggles for your eyes and a bandanna to protect your mouth and nose from the flying ash. Don't let this dissuade you from hiking here, however. This is spectacular country, with a lunar landscape cut through by deep and colorful canyons. Before heading out, stop by the Park Service visitor center in Brooks Camp for a map, a backcountry permit, and more information. Jean Bodeau's *Katmai National Park and Preserve* (available at the visitor centers) provides detailed hiking information.

> *Several features attract visitors to Katmai: its wild volcanic landscape, outstanding salmon fishing in a world-class setting, and the opportunity to see brown bears up close. The bears are the big attraction nowadays; they're big, they're bad, and they're ubiquitous.*

If you can get a bike to Brooks Camp, the 23-mile dirt road to the Valley of Ten Thousand Smokes is a fine place to ride bikes; the views get more dramatic as you go. **Lifetime Adventures** (907/746-4644 or 800/952-8624, www.lifetimeadventures.net) guides seven-day hike-bike-kayak trips in the park for $3,000 d.

Brooks Camp

Katmai has gained worldwide fame for its brown bears, and is one of the few places where large numbers of visitors can see wild bears throughout the summer. Bear activity centers on the Brooks River, which flows into Naknek Lake just a half-mile from the campground. A floating bridge crosses the river to an elevated viewing platform where you can watch the bears. **Brooks Falls** are a half-mile hike from here. An extremely popular viewing platform at the falls gets crowded during the peak of the season. In fact, it's so popular that park rangers limit use to one hour at a time, and there's often a long wait to get to the Brooks Falls platform.

Added to this is the other reason people come here: fishing. Brooks River is open to sportfishing—mainly for sockeye salmon—and is often lined with anglers. When bears wander by, and this is often, anglers are required to immediately release any fish, and park rangers will even cut your line if you don't act fast enough. Unfortunately, some bears are starting to equate anglers with free fish; sometimes the park has been forced to close the river to fishing to keep the bears from becoming more aggressive toward humans.

The **Dumpling Mountain Trail** leaves from Brooks Camp and climbs four miles to the top of this 2,440-foot peak. You'll discover outstanding panoramic vistas from the summit across the surrounding lake-filled, volcano-crowned country.

Coastal Bear-Viewing

Bear-viewing is becoming increasingly popular on the eastern side of Katmai along Shelikof Strait, where brown bears dig for clams, eat grass and sedges, catch salmon, and scavenge for carcasses that wash ashore. A number of air taxi operators out of Homer, Kodiak, Soldotna, and Anchorage take clients there on day trips for $450–525 per person. Note that many of these fly-in trips have big groups, and a number of planes can be in one area at once, reducing your wilderness experience.

Hallo Bay Bear Viewing (907/235-2237, www.hallobay.com) is a unique wilderness camp on a wild and beautiful stretch of the Katmai coast. It is entirely surrounded by national park land, and includes a half-dozen cabin-like structures (Weatherports) with a central building for dining and relaxing. Bear guides lead hikes to viewing areas around the camp with a maximum of four guests per guide. Extended backpacking trips and professional photography workshops are also offered. Meals are filling and delicious, and other amenities include hot showers, heated cabins, a satellite phone, computer to burn digital photo CDs, stereo microscope, and solar-powered electricity to charge your batteries. Most guests stay 4–7 days for $350 per person/day. Guests fly to Hallo Bay from Homer, a one-hour trip from Homer that adds $400 roundtrip to the cost. Shorter trips are also available, including bear-viewing day trips from Homer for $550.

Located in a private inholding on Kukak Bay, **Katmai Wilderness Lodge** (907/486-8767 or 800/488-8767, www.katmai-wilderness.com) is a modern log-cabin-style lodge on Kukak Bay, where the guest rooms have private baths and hot showers. Guests come here to fish, hike, or watch bears. It's a beautiful spot, but the weather can make it difficult for flights to get in or out. A variety of package trips are offered, starting at three nights for $4,800 d; this includes float plane travel from Kodiak, lodging, guided bear-viewing, home-style meals, kayaking, and fishing.

Katmai Coastal Bear Tours (907/235-8337 or 800/532-8338, www.katmaibears.com) operates from a sturdy 73-foot wooden tug, *The Waters.* The boat acts as a floating lodge for photographers and others who use skiffs to go ashore along the Katmai coast, mainly from Geographic Harbor (a gorgeous and protected place) north to Hallo Bay. Meals are great, and the guides are highly knowledgeable naturalists. The boat goes where the bears are, providing a mobility lacking in shore-based operations, but the quarters are cramped and the boat rolls somewhat—so bring Dramamine. A two-night trip costs $3,000 per person, and three nights is $3,250 per person. Access is by floatplane from Kodiak (included in the cost).

Mythos Expeditions (907/486-5536, www.thewildcoast.com) also leads boat-based bear-viewing trips to the Katmai Coast in June and August on the fishing vessel *Mythos.*

On the Water

Savonoski Loop is a favorite backcountry canoe or kayak trip. Boaters start in Brooks Camp, head up the north arm of Naknek Lake, portage a mile to Lake Grosvenor, float down the Grosvenor and Savonoski Rivers, and paddle across the Iluk Arm of Naknek Lake back to Brooks Camp. Be ready for a 4–10-day trip, and be sure to talk with Park Service rangers for precautions and backcountry permits before heading out. Canoes and kayaks can be rented from Brooks Lake Lodge. **Lifetime Adventures** (907/746-4644 or 800/952-8624, www.lifetimeadventures.net) sets up do-it-yourself folding kayak trips; for $1,500 d, you get airfare from Anchorage to King Salmon, charter flights to and from the park, and folding kayaks. They can also provide camping equipment for an extra charge, and offer guided kayak trips on the Savonski Loop (seven days for $3,000 d).

Several companies rent motorboats on Naknek Lake; see the King Salmon Visitor Center (907/246-4250) for a listing. The visitor center can also provide a list of guided sportfishing outfitters and boat tours.

Park Accommodations

If you want to stay the night at famous **Brooks Lodge** (907/243-5448 or 800/544-0551, www.katmailand.com), be prepared to shell out wads of cash. During July (peak season), a package trip that includes round-trip airfare from Anchorage to Brooks Lodge plus three nights of lodging will set you back $2,500 for two people. Stuff-yourself buffet meals are extra. If you're willing to share a cabin with another couple or arrive sometime other than July, your overall cost will be somewhat lower. Brooks Lodge fills up fast, so make reservations in January to be assured of a place in midsummer.

A tiny gift shop at the lodge sells snacks, film, and tourist trinkets, and rents canoes, fishing poles, and hip waders. Two other fishing lodges are on other lakes within the park. They're even more expensive than Brooks Lodge, but are far from the hubbub. **Grosvenor Lodge** charges $4,250 d for three nights lodging and airfare; **Kulik Lodge** charges $4,900 d for the same. Brooks, Kulik, and Grosvenor lodges are all owned by Katmailand, and share the same contact information. Note that the three lodges, along with services such as the bus tours, operate only June–September. Before or after that, you're on your own.

King Salmon and Naknek

The town of King Salmon is the main gateway to Katmai National Park. Travelers who are unable to get a lodge or campground space at Brooks Camp often stay here and make day trips by floatplane into the park. The village of Naknek, 15 miles west of King Salmon by road, is an important commercial fishing port. Both towns have food and lodging, and taxi service connects the two. The towns represent an odd clash between the upscale tourists out to see Katmai bears and grubby commercial fishermen out to make a buck (or several thousand bucks).

Several places in King Salmon offer lodging, but most are only open seasonally. **King Ko Inn** (907/246-3377 or 866/234-3474, www.kingko .com) has comfortable and modern cabins (some with kitchenettes) for $175–190 d.

Antlers Inn (907/246-8525 or 888/735-8525)

gillnet fishermen at the mouth of Naknek River, near Naknek

has two rooms for $100 s or $120 d, and three apartments with full kitchens for $160 s or $180 d. The in-town location can be a bit noisy.

A mile out of town is **Ponderosa Inn** (907/246-3444 246-3360 or 888/224-7648, www.ponderosa-inn.com). Simple but clean rooms with two twin beds are $110 s or $160 d, including transport from King Salmon. Most clients are fishermen who get room, meals, and boat rental packages starting at $752 d for two nights.

The fanciest local place is **Quinnat Landing Hotel** (907/246-3000 or 800/770-3474, www.quinnat.com), with attractive riverside rooms for $234 s or $259 d.

Lodging prices are lower in Naknek, but you'll need to pay $15 each way for the taxi fare, so this may wipe out any savings. **Naknek Hotel** (907/246-4430) is pretty basic, but so are the prices: $55 s or $65 d with a bath down the hall. **Red Dog Inn** (907/246-4213 or 907/246-4215, www.reddoginn.net) has rooms with private baths for $66 s or $76 d. Other Naknek options include **Al-Lou's B&B** (907/246-4270, $70 s or d), **Apple Haus B&B** (907/299-6777, www.applehaus.com, $125 s or d), and **A Little House B&B** (907/246-4486, $75 s or d).

Visit www.southwestalaska.com for links to a multitude of fishing lodges in the area. **Bear Trail Lodge** (907/246-2327, www.beartrail-lodge.com) has a two-night package that includes lodging, meals, a day of guided fishing and a day of bear-viewing at Brooks Camp for $3,000 d. Six miles upriver from Naknek, **Rainbow Bend Charter Adventures** (907/246-3750 or 888/575-4249, www.bristolbayfishing.com) is a fishing lodge with two-night minimum stays; $1,150 d for a cabin, meals, and a motorboat.

Food

Brooks Lodge (907/243-5448 or 800/544-0551, www.katmailand.com) serves filling buffet meals and is open to both guests and the general public: $12 for breakfast, $18 for lunch, or $26 for dinner. The bar serves mixed drinks.

Arctic Fox (907/246-3377, www.kingko.com), at King Ko Inn in King Salmon, has dependably good food three times a day in the summer, with fresh seafood, pizzas, burgers, and other faves. It has a big bar with live music some summer weekends. Across the way is **Eddie's Fireplace Inn** (907/246-3435), with lower prices and great burgers. They're open three meals a day, year-round. Meals are also available in the summer at **Quinnat Landing Hotel,** and you'll find pizzas and Italian food at **D&D Restaurant** (907/246-4430) in Naknek. Get groceries, sporting goods, and even espresso at **Alaska Commercial Company** (907/246-6109) in King Salmon.

Camping

A short distance from the Brooks Lodge, the 60-person campground at **Brooks Camp** has potable water and costs $8 per person/night. It's extremely popular and the spaces fill fast. Reservations are required far ahead of your visit; contact the **National Park Reservation Service** (301/722-1257 or 800/365-2267, http://reservations.nps.gov). The campground often gets booked for the month of July within a few hours after reservations open in late January!

Don't bring your kitchen sink along on this trip; you'll have to carry it a quarter-mile from the floatplane dock to the campground, and the bear-proof caches don't have room for a sink anyway. (The Park Service provides carts to make transportation easier.) This is the only developed campground in Katmai, and backcountry camping is not allowed within five miles of Brooks Camp, so don't come here without a reservation unless you're willing to hike. No-shows sometimes

McNEIL RIVER STATE GAME SANCTUARY

Wedged above the northeast corner of Katmai and 100 air miles west of Homer, this state sanctuary is where many of the famous photographs of brown bears were taken. At the peak of the season (late July to early August), visitors may see 40 or more bruins as they catch chum salmon at McNeil River falls. More brown bears congregate here than in any other single site on earth; up to 130 have been counted in a single day! The sanctuary is managed by the Alaska Department of Fish and Game (ADF&G), which allows only 10 people per day into the viewing area. Because of all these bears, the department has stringent rules, and visitors must remain within small viewing areas throughout the 6–8 hour day. A permit system and user fees are required of all visitors.

National Geographic photographer Cecil Rhode first published frames of McNeil River—without identifying it—in 1954, after which the federal government closed the area to hunters. It became a state game sanctuary in 1967, and the limited permit system was installed in 1973. And in 1979, the river was completely closed to sportfishing. Since ADF&G instituted these restrictive use policies, there have been no casualties to either humans or bears. This is particularly amazing given how close the bears often come.

Getting In

Each year, more than 2,500 people apply to visit McNeil River and nearby Mikfik Creek; only 250 or so permits are granted (including standby permits). **Non-transferable permits** are required for all visitors between June 7 and August 25. Only 10 of these are available per day, and a $25 per person non-refundable application fee is required. The ADF&G (907/267-2182, www.wc.adfg.state.ak.us /mcneil) can provide you with details and a downloadable application form. Forms must be postmarked or emailed no later than March 1. The best time to find bears at McNeil is mid-July to early August, when the chum salmon are running, but it's also the time that most people apply to visit. Second choice is as close to peak as possible on the earlier side; later the excitement tapers off.

Because of McNeil's immense popularity, a lottery system is used to decide who gets the available time slots. Winners are given a four-day period at McNeil, and pay (in addition to the application) $350 per person ($150 for Alaskan residents) to visit the sanctuary. As a backup, many people also apply for a **standby permit** to get into McNeil in case they're not among the lucky applicants for the regular permits. Only three of these are available each day. A separate standby lottery is held, and those chosen pay $175 ($75 for Alaskan residents) and wait for slots to open up when regular

create openings at the campground even when it was officially full, but it's pretty risky to arrive in Brooks Camp without a place reserved. Campers can buy meals at Brooks Lodge or take showers there for $5. Katmai experiences weather similar to that of the rest of the Aleutian arc—cool, wet, and wildly windy; so come prepared to get wet!

No camping in the town of King Salmon, but **Dave's World** (907/246-3353), has sites ($10) right across the river; he takes you over by skiff. He has a tackle shop and also rents motorboats, canoes, and camping equipment.

Information and Services

The very helpful **King Salmon Visitor Center** (907/246-4250) at King Salmon airport is open daily 8 A.M.–5 P.M. June–September, Monday–Saturday 8 A.M.–5 P.M. the rest of the year. Stop here for details on Katmai National Park, Aniakchak National Monument, Alaska Peninsula National Wildlife Refuge, and Bacherof National Wildlife Refuge. There's a big selection of books and cards too. Need cash? The Wells Fargo in King Salmon has an ATM.

The Park Service's **Brooks Camp Visitor Center** inside the park is open daily June to mid-September. All visitors must check in here upon arrival to learn about bear safety and to get a park orientation. Rangers lead free afternoon **cultural and nature walks,** plus evening slide shows at Brooks Camp daily throughout the summer, plus guided hikes up Dumpling

permit holders decide to stay in camp rather than going out that day (typically when the weather is bad). People who visit on a standby basis usually get to spend at least one day at the falls, but bears are also visible around the campground and along the nearby beach.

Seeing the Bears

People come from around the world to see and photograph bears within McNeil River State Game Sanctuary. Visitors actually have the chance to view bears at two seasonal locations. In June, several dozen bears (primarily females with cubs) can be found feeding on a small run of sockeye salmon in **Mikfik Creek.** This area provides a great opportunity to see bears in a lush and intimate setting—they're all around you. Also, the weather is generally better than later in the summer.

The big show takes place on the nearby **McNeil River** between early July and mid-August, when a major run of chum salmon head up this much larger river. The activity peaks around July 15, when dozens of bears (including many large males) come to a low waterfall—McNeil Falls—where the fish are easier to catch. Visitors have opportunities to see and photograph bears 75–200 feet away, though the bears may occasionally come within 30 feet. Be sure to bring plenty of film! A note to professional photographers: Because so many people have photographed bears at McNeil for so long, the market for bear pics from here is flooded. Try somewhere else if you want a shot that stands out from the crowd.

Practicalities

Visitors to McNeil overnight in a camping area and hike two miles to the viewing areas overlooking McNeil Falls (in June they head to areas along Mikfik Creek where you're more likely to see females with cubs than at McNeil). The campground has a cabin for food storage and cooking, a sauna, outhouses, and staff cabins, but no other developments or services.

ADF&G employees carry shotguns and stay with the visitors at all times when they are away from the campground. Visitors need to be in good physical condition for the hike to the falls, and if the weather is bad (a common situation) it's easy to get cold while sitting in the rain and wind for hours. Hip boots are essential, along with heavy-duty raingear, wind-resistant clothes, and gloves. People typically remain at McNeil Falls for a 6–8 hour period.

Quite a few air taxis provide transport to McNeil from Homer (the primary departure point), King Salmon, Kodiak, or Anchorage. Homer-based **Beluga Air** (907/235-8256) charges $450 round-trip.

Mountain. Check the bulletin boards at the visitor center, campground, and lodge for today's events.

For more on Katmai, contact the National Park Service in King Salmon (907/246-3305, www.nps.gov/katm). You can also pick up a map of the park and a copy of the informative park paper, *The Novarupta,* at the Alaska Public Lands Information Center in Anchorage.

Getting There

Getting to Katmai isn't cheap. First, fly from Anchorage to King Salmon ($325 round-trip) on **Alaska Airlines** (800/426-0333, www.alaskaair.com) or **PenAir** (907/246-3373 or 800/448-4226, www.penair.com). From King Salmon it will cost another $152 round-trip to get out to Brooks Camp. **Katmai Air** (907/246-3079 or 800/544-0551, www.bear-viewing.com), has scheduled service. Other local air-taxi operators that fly daily include **Egli Air Haul** (907/246-3554), **Birchwood Air** (907/776-5147), and **Branch River Air Service** (907/248-3539, www.branchriverair.com). All of these also offer flightseeing and trips to nearby McNeil River. One warning: The weather in King Salmon is often bad, so weather-related flight cancellations are not uncommon. People get stuck here often.

A more leisurely option is to take the boat service to Brooks Camp from **Quinnat Landing Hotel** (907/246-3000 or 800/770-3474, www.quinnat.com) in King Salmon. This is primarily for those staying at the hotel, but is available to the general public for $154 roundtrip.

Day Trips

A number of companies offer quick day trips to either the Katmai coast or Brooks Camp to watch bears. From Homer ($525 pp) the air-taxi operators are **Bald Mountain Air Service** (907/235-7969 or 800/478-7969, www.baldmountainair.com), **Beluga Air** (907/235-8256), **Emerald Air Service** (907/235-6993, www.emeraldairservice.com), **Homer Air** (907/235-8591 or 800/478-8591, www.homerair.com), **Kenai Fjords Outfitters** (907/235-6066 or 888/536-6066, www.seaplanealaska.com), and **Smokey Bay Air** (907/235-1511 or 888/482-1511,

www.andrewairways.com). From Anchorage ($579 per person) try **Rust's Flying Service** (907/243-1595 or 800/544-2299, www.flyrusts.com). From Kodiak ($420 per person), operators include **Sea Hawk Air** (907/486-8282 or 800/770-4295, www.seahawkair.com), **Harvey Flying Service** (907/487-2621, www.harveyflyingservice.com), **Kodiak Air Service** (907/486-4446, www.kodiakair.com), and **Andrew Airways** (907/487-2566).

ANIAKCHAK NATIONAL MONUMENT

This remote and rarely visited park covers over 600,000 acres, and is approximately 400 miles southwest of Anchorage on the Alaska Peninsula. The park centers around the six-mile-wide **Aniakchak Caldera,** which last erupted in 1931. Located in the volcanically active Aleutian Range, the crater contains lava flows, cinder cones, and explosion pits. Dominating the crater is 3,350-foot-high Vent Mountain, with a volcanic cone that occasionally sends up plumes of smoke. On the northwest inner edge is a large eruption crater covered with patterned lava that presents an otherworldly appearance from the air. **Surprise Lake,** on the northeast side of the caldera, is the source of the Aniakchak River, which cascades through a 1,500-foot gorge cut in the caldera wall. The river is a wild whitewater trip for the experienced.

Getting There

Aniakchak Monument is infamous for bad weather, and it's an expensive flight from Homer, King Salmon, or Kodiak (the closest towns of any size). There are no developed facilities, but floatplanes can land in Surprise Lake, and the northern portion of the park is smooth enough for wheeled landings. For additional information, contact the Aniakchak National Monument office in King Salmon (907/246-4286, www.nps.gov/ania).

NATIONAL WILDLIFE REFUGES

Much of the land on the lower Alaska Peninsula and out the Aleutian Island chain lies within four national wildlife refuges. These are rarely visited by human travelers, but provide vital habitat for many species of animals.

The **Alaska Maritime National Wildlife Refuge** covers 3.5 million acres, encompassing 2,500 islands that stretch from Forrester Island in southern Southeast all the way out the Aleutians, and on scattered places up the mainland to Barrow. Headquarters is in Homer (907/235-6961, http://alaskamaritime.fws.gov), where their elaborate Islands and Ocean Center opened in 2004.

The **Alaska Peninsula National Wildlife Refuge** covers 3.5 million acres on the peninsula, and includes a chain of volcanoes dominated by 8,400 foot Mt. Veniaminof. This massive volcano has a base almost 30 miles across, larger than any active volcano on record. And the summit crater contains the most extensive crater glacier in North America. The refuge is based in King Salmon (907/246-3339, http://alaskapeninsula.fws.gov).

Also based in King Salmon is **Becharof National Wildlife Refuge** (907/246-3339, http://becharof.fws.gov), sandwiched between Katmai National Park and Preserve and Alaska Peninsula National Wildlife Refuge. The refuge is dominated by Becharof Lake, the second largest lake in Alaska. The lake is surrounded by low rolling hills, tundra wetlands, volcanic peaks and to the east, and the 477,000 acre Becharof Wilderness. Some 10,000 caribou migrate through the refuge each spring and fall, and other wildlife—from seabirds to salmon—abound.

Izembek National Wildlife Refuge spans the tip of the Alaska Peninsula, and protects the watershed of Izembek Lagoon, a State Game Refuge containing one of the largest eelgrass beds in the world. The state and federal refuges act as an international crossroad to many thousands of migrating waterfowl and shorebirds, including the world's entire population of Pacific brant and emperor geese. For migrating shorebirds, this is the last stop before their unbelievable over-water flights to wintering areas as far away as South America, Polynesia, and New Zealand. The refuge is based in Cold Bay (907/532-2445, http://izembek.fws.gov).

The Aleutian Islands

From the tip of the Alaska Peninsula, an arc of 200 islands curves more than a thousand miles southwest to Attu Island, separating the North Pacific Ocean from the Bering Sea. The Aleutian Islands are part of the circum-Pacific "Ring of Fire," one of the most geologically unsettled regions on earth. The titanic tectonic forces clash as the Pacific plate pushes under the North American plate at the deep Aleutian Trench, making the earth rumble, quake, and spew. Of the 79 named Aleutian Islands, only eight are occupied by humans. The 14 large and 65 smaller islands (plus countless tiny islets) are all windswept northern Pacific outposts. The meeting of the mild Japanese Current with the icy Bering Sea causes a climate of much fog, rain, and wind, but little sun. Compounding this is a meteorological phenomenon known as the "Aleutian low," a low-pressure atmospheric valley that funnels a number of intense storms east into North America. In short—it's not the greatest place to get a tan.

High peaks drop abruptly to the sea. There is no permafrost, but the constant strong winds inhibit tree growth; only tundra and brushy vegetation survive. Frequent storms blow through (Unalaska experiences almost 250 rainy days a year), but because of the warm currents the sea never freezes. Given these harsh climatic conditions, it's perhaps surprising that, before the arrival of the Russians, every island was inhabited by Aleut peoples. On the other hand, given the abundance of the ocean, the Aleut were skillful hunters who lived in balance with the fish, marine mammals, and birds of their islands. The Russians enslaved and slaughtered the Aleut, and their numbers plummeted from around 25,000 in 1741 to 2,000 a century later. The Russians also hunted the sea otters and fur seals of the islands to near extinction, and the single-minded exploitation of the islands' resources continues even today. Get the latest on the status of sea lions at www.stellersealions.noaa.gov, and on sea otters at www.ry.fws.gov/mmm.

WAR IN THE ALEUTIANS

The Japanese Challenge

During the spring of 1942, Japan was sweeping triumphantly across the Pacific to the gates of Australia and Hawaii. However, the strength of the U.S. aircraft carriers—none of which had been lost at Pearl Harbor—worried Fleet Admiral Isoroku Yamamoto, commander-in-chief of the Japanese navy. He knew that time was on the side of the United States. To win, he would have to draw the American carriers into a great naval battle where his superior forces could crush them and end the war. His target was Midway, a tiny island west of the Hawaiian chain, where the United States had recently built a base. But to first split the American forces, Yamamoto ordered a diversionary thrust at the Aleutians. In June 1942, Japanese carrier-based planes struck twice at Dutch Harbor, a large new U.S. naval base in Unalaska Bay, but inflicted only slight damage; the base continued to function. Meanwhile, at Midway, the United States had broken the Japanese naval code, and Yamamoto's plans were falling apart. Their own strength divided, one Japanese carrier after another sank before American momentum. As a face-saving move, the retiring Japanese occupied undefended Attu and Kiska at the west end of the Aleutians in the hope that bases on these islands would shield northern Japan and drive a wedge between the United States and Russia.

The Struggle for the Islands

In August 1942, the U.S. Navy occupied Adak Island and built an airfield from which to attack nearby Attu and Kiska. In January 1943, the Navy leapfrogged to Amchitka Island, right next door to Kiska, to provide an advance base. Continuous bombing and a naval blockade weakened Japanese resistance and on May 11, 1943, 16,000 U.S. troops landed on Attu. Of these, 549 Americans were killed before the 2,650 Japanese troops entrenched in the mountains were overcome. On May 29 about 800 remaining Japanese staged a banzai charge. At first they overran the American lines, but their thrust was finally quelled by reserve forces. Only 28 Japanese pris-

oners were taken, and the 6,000 Japanese on Kiska seemed to face a similar fate.

Late in July, however, Japanese destroyers slipped through the U.S. blockade in dense fog and evacuated their soldiers. On August 15 some 34,000 U.S. and Canadian troops landed, unopposed, on Kiska. Though there was no one to attack and rout, incredibly, they suffered a shocking 99 dead and 74 wounded through landing mishaps, "friendly fire," and other accidents. The Japanese had also booby-trapped all the structures. With their masterful evacuation, the Japanese had ended the Aleutian campaign.

UNALASKA ON DUTCH HARBOR

Located about 800 miles southwest of Anchorage, Unalaska Bay cuts into the north side of mountainous Unalaska Island, creating the finest and most sheltered ice-free harbor in the Aleutians. On a clear day you can see the sometimes-smoking 6,680-foot cone of **Makushin Volcano** rising to the west. The city of Unalaska spreads across both Unalaska Island and the much smaller Amaknak Island. A 500-foot bridge officially named "Bridge from the Other Side" links the two islands.

Although often called Dutch Harbor, this name actually refers to the protected harbor rather than the town itself. Longtime Unalaskans take umbrage at the suggestion that they live in Dutch Harbor; to them it's sort of like saying "Frisco" instead of San Francisco. That doesn't stop most folks—especially the transient fishermen and cannery workers—from calling it Dutch Harbor, or simply "Dutch." The folks who live in Unalaska take pride in their small city, but many others just view it as a place to get rich quick and get out. This is perhaps best symbolized by a T-shirt seen around town. On the front is a hand filled with hundred dollar bills, and below the picture it simply says, "Dutch Harbor."

Dutch Harbor today is an extremely busy place, often ranking as the nation's number-one port in both pounds of seafood caught and total dollar value. At any given time you're likely to see a dozen or more cargo ships waiting to load fish, surimi, or crab destined for Japan, Korea, the

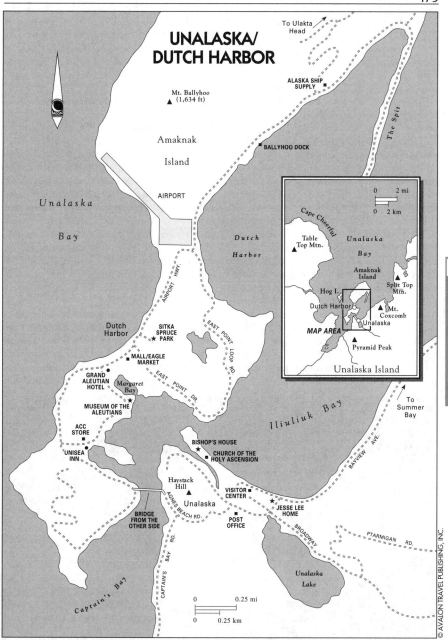

UNALASKA/
DUTCH HARBOR

To Ulakta
Head

ALASKA SHIP
SUPPLY

Mt. Ballyhoo
▲ (1,634 ft)

The Spit

Amaknak

Island

BALLYHOO DOCK

AIRPORT

Unalaska

Bay

Dutch

Harbor

AIRPORT HWY.

EAST POINT LOOP RD.

Dutch
Harbor

SITKA
SPRUCE
PARK

MALL/EAGLE
MARKET

EAST POINT DR.

GRAND
ALEUTIAN
HOTEL

Margaret
Bay

MUSEUM OF THE
ALEUTIANS

ACC
STORE

UNISEA
INN

Iliuliuk Bay

To
Summer
Bay

BISHOP'S HOUSE

CHURCH OF THE
HOLY ASCENSION

BAYVIEW AVE.

Haystack
Hill

VISITOR
CENTER

Unalaska

JESSE LEE
HOME

AGNES BEACH RD.

BRIDGE
FROM THE
OTHER SIDE

POST
OFFICE

BROADWAY

PTARMIGAN RD.

CAPTAIN'S BAY RD.

Unalaska
Lake

Captain's Bay

0   0.25 mi

0   0.25 km

Inset map:

0   2 mi

0   2 km

Cape Cheerful

Table
Top Mtn. ▲

Unalaska

Bay

Amaknak
Island

Split Top
Mtn. ▲

Hog I.

Dutch Harbor

Mt.
Coxcomb ▲

MAP AREA

Unalaska

Pyramid Peak ▲

Unalaska Island

SOUTHWEST ALASKA

Lower 48, or elsewhere. Most impressive of all is the huge container crane at the American President Lines dock where truck-size loads are dropped onto ships. Crab pots and nets line the roads, and seven different seafood processing plants are scattered around the harbors, processing pollock, crab, salmon, halibut, cod, herring roe, and other seafood. Most of the catch is processed during the hectic winter fishing season, November–April. Despite this rowdy make-a-million-bucks present, Unalaska/Dutch Harbor is filled with history, and visitors will find a number of places worth exploring.

History

When the first Russians "discovered" Unalaska in 1759, it was already home to more than 1,000 Aleut people scattered in 24 settlements. Over the next century the Russians decimated the Aleut, enslaving many of them to harvest fur seals and sea otters. The first permanent Russian settlement of Unalaska began in 1772, and Captain Cook spent three weeks here six years later. Under the Russians, Unalaska quickly became the main trading center in the Aleutians. After America took over in 1867, the focus gradually shifted, and it became an important coal and supply station for the Nome gold rush.

In the 1940s, the U.S. Navy appropriated Dutch Harbor. After the city was bombed by the Japanese in June 1942, all the Aleuts were shipped off to relocation camps in Southeast Alaska. Ten percent of them died in these refugee camps (generally abandoned canneries) due in part to unsanitary conditions and overcrowding. Once World War II ended, they returned to a vastly different place filled with military facilities. Many of their homes had been ransacked.

The boom in bottom fishing for pollock led to rapid growth in Unalaska/Dutch Harbor. The population now tops 4,200—double that of 25 years earlier—plus another 2,500 transient workers. Boom times have come to the Aleutians, and right now there are lots of blue-collar jobs paying relatively high wages. The island is also starting to see a handful of cruise ships each summer, but this is a long ways from anywhere else and the Gulf of Alaska can get mighty rough.

Sights

The most interesting attraction in Unalaska is the beautiful **Russian Orthodox Church of the Holy Ascension.** Built 1824–1827 and restored in the 1990s, this is the oldest Russian church still standing in Alaska, and a National Historic Landmark. Out front is a small graveyard, and not

Russian Orthodox Church of the Holy Ascension

far away is the **Bishop's House,** built in 1882. Another historic site is the **Jesse Lee Home** near the cemetery. It was constructed by Methodist missionaries in 1890.

The excellent **Museum of the Aleutians** (907/581-5150, www.aleutians.org) is a large and modern facility with the only archaeological collection in the Aleutians. On exhibit are artifacts from original Native cultures, the Russian era, and World War II. Hours are Monday–Saturday 11 A.M.–4 P.M. and Sunday noon–5 P.M. June–September, and Tuesday–Saturday 11 A.M.–4 P.M. the rest of the year. Admission costs $4. The museum runs an archaeological field school each summer with month-long sessions for college credit, but they're happy to take volunteers even for a day or two.

Not far from the airport is **Sitka Spruce Park,** where you'll find four scraggly stolid spruce trees planted by Russian settlers in 1805. At their base lies a plethora of stunted, struggling, younger spruce. These, plus a couple of other clusters of trees around town, make up the only "forest" in this otherwise treeless country. The park is a National Historic Landmark.

Although often called Dutch Harbor, this name actually refers to the protected harbor rather than the town itself. Longtime Unalaskans take umbrage at the suggestion that they live in Dutch Harbor; to them it's sort of like saying "Frisco" instead of San Francisco.

Exploring the Country

The countryside around Unalaska is pockmarked with all sorts of evidence from World War II, including underground bunkers, gun emplacements, buildings of all types, and various flotsam and jetsam from the military. The best places to find these are on the northeast end of Amaknak Island near Ulakta Head, and in the Summer Bay area on Unalaska Island.

A popular hiking place is 1,634-foot tall **Mt. Ballyhoo,** just northeast of the airport on Amaknak Island. The easiest way to the top is to drive or mountain bike up the steep and very rough dirt road (4WD recommended, unless you have a rental car that needs a workout) that ends at Ulakta Head. This area is packed with decaying military structures of all sorts, but the open country is very pretty in late summer, with flowers galore, plus Arctic ground squirrels and bald eagles. (Red foxes are the only other wild mammal found on these islands, though some of the fishermen could fall into the "wild mammal" category.)

Climb up the ridge from the end of the road for more dramatic vistas out to sea and back to the mountain-rimmed harbors. The west side of Amaknak Island consists of a harrowing series of cliffs that plummet to the sea 1,500 feet below, so stay away from the edge. In the winter months Mt. Ballyhoo is a popular walk-up, ski-down summit.

For a good view of town, climb **Haystack Hill** on the south side of Iliuliuk River (filled with spawning pink salmon in late summer). More panoramic vistas (and military bunkers) are atop the 421-foot Bunker Hill. A road up this hill veers west of the bridge.

Get to **Summer Bay** by heading northeast out of town on Summer Bay Rd. past the dump, a good place to see eagles. Five miles out is a lagoon where you can swim on a sunny day or practice your long-jumping form on the tall sand dunes. Nice place for a picnic. Continue out the progressively rougher road past bunkers, Quonset huts, and a gun emplacement that guarded Iliuliuk Bay. Keep your eyes open for the two horses—the only ones on Unalaska—that graze here.

Recreation

Sportfishing is increasingly popular out of Unalaska, and several charter fishing operators take you out in search of the monster halibut. The world's largest sport-caught halibut—a 459-pound fish—was caught nearby in 1996, and the city runs a "World Record Halibut Derby" with a $100,000 prize if you break that record! Contact the information center for a list of charter boats. Grand Aleutian Hotel (907/581-1325

SOUTHWEST ALASKA

or 800/891-1194, www.grandaleutian.com) specializes in sportfishing vacations.

Aleutian Adventure Sports (907/581-4489, www.aleutianadventure.com) rents mountain bikes and sea kayaks in the summer, and snowboards and snowshoes when the snow flies. They also lead backcountry, mountaineering, and kayaking trips.

Accommodations

Walashek Bunkhouse (907/581-4357) has small but clean rooms in Dutch Harbor for only $55 s or d.

Carl's Bayview Inn (907/581-1230 or 800/581-1230) has rooms for $90 s or $110 d, studios with kitchenettes for $125 s or $145 d, and suites for $150–175 s or $170–195 d. This is the only place in downtown Unalaska; the others are away from town center. Carl's also has a restaurant, grocery, and hardware store as well as Carl's Lounge, a popular place for live music and dancing.

The elaborate 112-room **Grand Aleutian Hotel** (907/581-1325 or 800/891-1194; www.grandaleutian.com) is the place to stay if you've got the bucks to go in style. Standard rooms are $159 s or $179 d. Same owners and contact information for the **UniSea Inn,** where the 42 clean rooms have TVs, phones, and private baths and cost $99 s or $110 d.

Camping

Contact Ounalashka Corporation office (907/581-1276, www.ounalashka.com) for camping permits ($11/day). The wind and rain make camping an uncomfortable proposition.

Food

Amelia's (907/581-2800) serves hearty breakfasts. Best place for burgers? Try the restaurant at the airport. **Nicky's Place** (907/581-1570) in downtown Unalaska sells books, music, and posters, along with the best espresso coffee in town. The walls are lined with works by local artists. **UniSea Inn** (907/581-1325) has fresh seafood specials nightly.

By far the fanciest local eating places—and the best spots for fresh fish—are inside the Grand Aleutian Hotel. Downstairs find **Margaret Bay Cafe** with reasonably priced breakfast and lunches, including an all-you-can-eat soup, salad, and dessert bar. Upstairs is the fine-dining **Chart Room,** with a reasonable lunch buffet on weekdays, a Wednesday night seafood buffet, and a Sunday brunch. There's an impressive wine selection; not at all what you might expect in this blue-collar fishing town.

Get groceries at **Alaska Commercial Co.** (ACC) or **Eagle Quality Centers** (907/581-4040). Both have in-store delis and bakeries.

Entertainment

Given the nature of the population—especially the young, transient, and sometimes-wealthy fishermen—it should come as no surprise that bars are the main attraction in Unalaska. (There are only half as many churches as places with liquor licenses.) In the 1970s, *Playboy* labeled Unalaska's **Elbow Room** (907/581-1271) America's most notorious bar, the sort of place where drunken brawls were the norm. Things have calmed down in recent years, but you'll be rubbing elbows with lots of other folks—including some tough cookies—at the Elbow. When the crews are in from the crab fleet, things quickly start to resemble the *Star Wars* bar scene, with characters who might just as well have crawled off a different planet. It's the kind of place where the matchbooks have condoms. The Elbow has live rock music on weekends, as does **Unisea Sports Bar,** a bright, glitzy place, the opposite of the Elbow. **Carl's Bayview Lounge** is a lively downtown Unalaska bar with dart boards, pool tables, karaoke, live music, and dancing.

Information and Services

The **Unalaska/Port of Dutch Harbor Convention and Visitors Bureau** (on Broadway at 5th St., 907/581-2612 or 877/581-2612, www.unalaska.info, Mon.–Fri. 9 A.M.–5 P.M., Sat. noon–5 P.M.) is in the old World War II Army chapel in Unalaska.

Take a shower—and they throw in a free swim—at the fine **Community Center** (907/581-1297), which also houses an indoor track, weight room, and basketball court. Get fast cash from ATMs inside the Eagle store and Key Bank.

Transportation

Unalaska has not traditionally been a place for tourists, and most everyone comes here to make money, not to vacation. The high costs of transportation and accommodations will continue to keep most tourists away, though a few cruise ships visit during the summer. If you decide on a quick visit by air, try to schedule it around a period of good weather. On a clear day the countryside is stunning, but much more common are the rainy and windy periods when the place doesn't look so great and you start to wonder why you spent so much cash to get here. Besides, you may find yourself stuck for days waiting for the weather to lift enough for planes to land.

The state ferry *Tustemena* (907/465-3941 or 800/642-0066, www.ferryalaska.com) heads out once a month (April–Oct.) to Dutch Harbor, by way of Homer, Kodiak, Chignik, Sand Point, King Cove, and Cold Bay. The trip takes three and a half days one-way and can be somewhat rough, so bring lots of Dramamine. The ferry docks near the airport on Amaknak Island.

The other way to reach Unalaska is by air from Anchorage on **Alaska Airlines** (800/426-0333, www.alaskaair.com). Try to get a seat on the right side of the plane when you fly out of Anchorage. The flight passes near the dramatic and volcanic summits of Mt. Iliamna and Mt. Redoubt. Landing or taking off is always an adventure since the runway is only 3,900 feet long—about 2,000 feet shorter than jet pilots (and passengers) would like. Nearly everyone who has flown into or out of Dutch has a hair-raising story to tell. During the winter fishing season many flights are booked up far in advance. Weather delays and cancellations are not unusual—the airport had one of the worst schedule reliability rates in the nation. It isn't uncommon for a jet to almost reach Dutch and still turn back due to bad weather.

PenAir (800/448-4226, www.penair.com) also flies from Unalaska to Anchorage (freight only from Anchorage to Unalaska) daily, but three hours in a little plane gets old fast.

Getting Around

The settlements of Dutch Harbor and Unalaska are spread over two islands, and the distances mean some sort of transport is needed. Mountain bikes offer the most enjoyable way to explore the many dirt roads leading into the hills. They are not, however, nearly as much fun in the rain. Rent bikes from **Aleutian Adventure Sports** (907/581-4489, www.aleutianadventure.com).

Most folks don't have cars in Unalaska, so there's a thriving **taxi** business. The companies all cruise around town, so it's very easy to get a ride to the airport or other places. Expect to pay $10 for most points.

Car rentals are high and gas is expensive; get the specifics at **BC Vehicle Rental** (907/581-6777) or **North Port Rentals** (907/581-3880, www.northportrentals.net). Unlimited miles, but there are only 38 miles of roads to drive anyway!

OTHER ALEUTIAN ISLANDS

The main tourist attraction for Alaska's far-flung Aleutians is probably birds; the islands get quite a few Asian species.

Akutan (pop. 400), a small island 35 miles northeast of Dutch Harbor, is a minor fishing center, with a general store, restaurant, and hotel, but not much else.

Tiny Aleut villages exist at **Atka** (on Atka Island; pop. 100) and **Nikolski** (on Umnak Island; pop. 35). Despite its fragile geological situation and frequent earthquakes, the remote volcanic island of Atka was used by the United States for underground nuclear testing until as late as 1971. In its first public action, Greenpeace sent a protest vessel into the area, and the resulting controversy led to cancellation of the tests.

Adak

This 28-mile-long island is midway out the Aleutian chain, 500 miles west of Dutch Harbor. **Alaska Airlines** (800/426-0333, www.alaskaair.com) provides twice-weekly service to the island from Anchorage, and cruise ships visit once or twice a summer. There's a general store with expensive supplies, a restaurant, plus **Hotel Adak** (907/592-2384), where rooms are $150. Ask around for folks with beater cars for rent. Anyone planning on exploring the island should drop by the Alaska Maritime National Wildlife Refuge's summer office to see a video on avoiding the unexploded ordinance on parts of the Adak. Get details from the U.S. Fish & Wildlife Service (year-round 907/235-6961, in summer 907/592-2406).

The Navy had a major base on Adak from 1943 to 2000, when they left following the end of the Cold War. Suddenly Alaska's sixth-largest city became a virtual ghost town, with just 100 or so year-round residents. The now-abandoned city would make a great setting for a post-apocalypse movie, with the incessant wind blowing through empty houses, schools, and businesses. Amazingly the Olympic-size swimming pool remains open.

As this was written, the Native-owned Aleut Corporation was negotiating to acquire the old Navy facility on Adak; learn more at www.adak-island.com.

Attu

At the far western end of the Aleutians lies the sur-

prisingly beautiful island of Attu, less than 200 miles from Siberia. The Aleut villagers of Attu were deported to Japan in 1942 by the Japanese, and more than 2,500 Japanese and Americans died in battles here. After the war, the U.S. government refused to allow the Aleuts to resettle on their island, and today the only inhabitants are the staff of the Coast Guard Loran station. Bird-watchers visit Attu to look for Asian species that have strayed into the Aleutians, and this is also the only place in America where the white-tailed eagle breeds. Visit www.attu.com for info on the island's birds. Access is by charter flight only.

Shemya

Minuscule Shemya Island—so small that the airport covers half of its four-mile length—is 40 miles east of Attu, near the end of the Aleutians. The Missile Defense Agency is upgrading an early-warning radar base here, and a security clearance is required to visit. Also in the works is a massive $900 million floating radar station that will operate in the area.

Pribilof Islands

The remote, volcanic Pribilofs sit in the middle of the Bering Sea 250 miles north of the Aleutians, 300 miles west of the mainland, and a thousand miles from Anchorage. The two main islands—**St. Paul** (pop. 760; world's largest Aleut community) and **St. George** (pop. 150)—host what may be the largest concentration of mammals and seabirds anywhere on earth. Although both islands have abundant wildlife of all sorts, St. Paul is best known for its fur seal colonies, and St. George for its seabird rookeries. Tiny Walrus and Otter Islands also support thousands of seals and birds.

St. Paul is the largest of the islands: 14 miles long and eight miles wide, with hills reaching 500 feet in elevation. St. George has a sheer wall rising from the sea to almost 1,000 feet, with millions of waterfowl breeding in its nooks and crannies. There are no trees on either island, but the rolling tundra becomes a dense rainbow of flowers in mid-July. The weather is similar to that of the Aleutians-cool, damp, foggy, and

windy; summer temperatures average 47°F, with an occasional 60°F day in July. Useful websites for information on the Pribilofs are www.southwestalaska.com and www.beringsea.com.

WILDLIFE

Each summer thousands of northern fur seals return to the Pribilofs (the majority to St. Paul) to breed and give birth. The "beachmasters" are first to arrive at the haul-out sites and rookeries (late May), with the females coming ashore in June to give birth. At 90–130 pounds, the females are far smaller than the largest males, which can reach 600 pounds. Harbor seals, sea otters, Steller sea lions, and long-tusked walruses round out this brawling, bawling, and caterwauling marine mammalian gumbo. Nowhere else in North America, and arguably the world, is wildlife so easily seen in such numbers. If you're set on doing something really wild (and expensive) during your trip north, this would be it.

In addition to the sea mammals, over 220 species of birds have been identified on the Pribilofs, including millions of murres and thousands of puffins, cormorants, kittiwakes, and fulmars. The late birder and artist Rodger Tory Peterson called one of St. George's rookeries "probably the greatest single bird cliff anywhere in North America." (Note, however, that only a dozen or so bird species actually breed on the islands; the rest are migrants.) Bird-watchers interested in adding to their life list may want to come early (mid-May to early June) for accidental Asian species that sometimes wander over from Siberia. Don't forget your bird book and binoculars!

HISTORY

Soon after Russian fur finder Gerassim Pribylov discovered the uninhabited islands in June 1786—and named them for himself—his fur company brought Aleut slaves to harvest the seals. Accounts vary, one claiming that the Russians slaughtered the seals here nearly to extinction; the other that in 1867 the population had regenerated to record numbers and that it was the Americans who trimmed their skins by the millions (these fur seal rookeries were a prime reason the U.S. government bought Alaska from the Russians). In either case, by 1911 the seal population had dwindled to fewer than 150,000 animals (10 percent of what it had been). That same year, the United States, Russia, England, and Japan signed a treaty banning ocean hunting and limiting the number allowed to be taken on land. But it wasn't until 1985 that commercial seal harvesting was finally halted, in large part because of pressure from environmental groups. The Aleut people were not given full control of their islands until 1983.

Today, the economy of St. Paul depends upon seafood processing plants and floating processing ships. There are increasing concerns of overfishing and the impact upon sea lion and seal populations, both of which declined sharply in recent years. Get the latest on the status of sea lions at www.stellersealions.noaa.gov, and on walrus and sea otters at www.ry.fws.gov/mmm.

PRACTICALITIES

St. Paul

The old **St. Peter and Paul Church** is a focal point of life on St. Paul. This plain Russian Orthodox church has a lavishly ornate interior.

Stay in the rough-at-the-edges **King Eider Hotel** (907/546-2477), where $125 s or d gets you a room with a bath down the hall. Camping is not allowed on the island.

Meals are available from **St. Paul Cafe** (907/546-2660), but your best bet is to bring food with you. There is also a small general store with limited and expensive supplies, plus **Zees Cab Service** (907/546-2352) and **North Star Truck Rental** (907/546-2420).

The vast majority of the 3,000 or so annual visitors to St. Paul arrive through **St. Paul Island Tours** (907/278-2318 or 877/424-5637, www.stpaulislandtour.com). These trips include roundtrip air transportation from Anchorage, lodging, transport around the island, and an experienced guide. Meals will add $40/day extra, or bring your own food and use the microwaves and fridges at the hotel. These trips start at $1,360 per person for three days and two nights, up to $2,375 for eight days and seven nights. Be sure to schedule a buffer of several days since foggy weather sometimes prevents flights from landing for up to a week. The tours are offered mid-May through August.

St. George

St. George the Martyr Russian Orthodox Church is the most distinctive local structure, though the **St. George Tanaq Hotel** (907/859-2255, www.stgeorgetanaq.com) is also a National Historic Landmark. Lodging here costs $99 pp with a shared bath. Reserve ahead to be certain of a space, since there are only nine rooms. No restaurants on the island, but you can buy food locally and cook it at the hotel kitchen. **St. George Island Canteen** has limited groceries at bush prices; better to bring your own from Anchorage. The hotel also offers van transportation from the airport. Camping is not allowed on St. George Island.

GETTING THERE

PenAir (800/448-4226, www.penair.com) has flights to both St. Paul and St. George four or five times a week. If you're going all the way out to one of the Pribilofs on your own, why not do a two-for-one deal? PenAir lets you fly to one of the islands, hop over to the other one, and then fly back to Anchorage for the same fare as a round-trip to either island, plus $70 for the inter-island flight. Getting on these may be tricky because of the weather, and you'll have to set up all your own hotel and other arrangements, but this can save money over the package tours.

Western Alaska

This is Alaska's true outback: far, far, from the reach of civilization. The scattered settlements—Dillingham, Bethel, and Nome—are really more like pinpricks on the map. The vast distances between the towns make them difficult and expensive to reach, but also exotic and fascinating to visit.

Bristol Bay, on the southern end of the Bering Sea, is considered the world's most productive red salmon fishery. Dillingham, the main port town, is home to hundreds of salmon fishing boats and a multitude of sportfishing lodges. It's also the gateway to remote Wood-Tikchik State Park, America's largest state park. Also nearby are the Walrus Islands, with an extraordinary walrus haul-out on Round Island. The village of Bethel occupies a low-lying, lake-filled delta where the Kuskokwim and Yukon Rivers spread and finally empty into the Bering Sea. Yup'ik villages are scattered across the stark, treeless plain. Farther north is Nome, a gold rush town with an abundance of history and a network of roads across the beautiful rolling country.

Brown Slough and fishing skiffs, Bethel

WESTERN ALASKA

RUSSIA

Big Diomede Island

Bering *Strait*

UNITED STATES

St. Lawrence Island

Bering Sea

Nunivak Island

Cape Krusenstern National Monument

Noatak River

Noatak National Preserve

Kobuk Valley National Park

Kotzebue Sound

Kotzebue

Kobuk

Kobuk River

Selawik

Arctic Circle

ALASKA

Bering Land Bridge National Preserve

Seward Peninsula

Teller

Taylor

Council

Nome

Norton Bay

Norton Sound

Selawik National Wildlife Refuge

Koyukuk River

Koyukuk National Wildlife Refuge

Galena

Innoko National Wildlife Refuge

Innoko National Wildlife Refuge

Yukon River

Holy Cross

Kuskokwim River

River

Yukon Delta National Wildlife Refuge

Bethel

Wood–Tikchik State Park

Iliamna Lake

Nushagak River

0   200 mi
0   200 km

Kuskokwim Bay

Togiak National Wildlife Refuge

Dillingham

Walrus Islands

King Salmon

Katmai National Park and Preserve

Becharof Lake

Bristol Bay

MOON

ALASKA

WESTERN ALASKA

© AVALON TRAVEL PUBLISHING, INC.

Dillingham and Vicinity

Dillingham (pop. 2,300) is the regional center for Bristol Bay, Alaska's largest sockeye salmon fishery. A large portion of the world's *wild* salmon catch comes from this enormous bay on the southern end of the Bering Sea. During the peak of the season, set nets line Dillingham beaches while gillnetters catch fish just offshore, and the town's four canneries run full blast. You won't, however, see the big fishing boats found elsewhere in Alaska, since commercial boats are limited to a maximum of 32 feet in length throughout Bristol Bay.

HISTORY

Dillingham's origins came from the first Russian fur traders who established a fort (Alexandrovski Redoubt) on the other side of Nushagak Bay in 1822. After the Americans took over, canneries were established in the area to process the enormous runs of red (sockeye) salmon up the Nushagak and Wood Rivers. When an influenza epidemic decimated the Native villages around Nushagak Bay in the winter of 1918–1919, many of the survivors moved to Dillingham. The result is a place composed of Yup'iks, Aleuts, Russians, and Americans. The local radio station, KDLG, still has Yup'ik-language broadcasts. Today, the town is almost wholly dependent upon the rich salmon fisheries of Bristol Bay. Unfortunately, with low prices and a market flooded by farmed salmon from Chile and British Columbia, the value of Bristol Bay fish has plummeted in recent years. Still, you're likely to see 500 boats crowded into Dillingham's harbor.

SIGHTS

Although there are many sportfishing lodges in the area, Dillingham is not much of a tourist town; most people come here to work. For a one-stop visit to town, head to Seward and D streets, where under one roof you'll find the **Sam Fox Museum** (907/842-5610, open Mon.–Fri. noon–4 P.M.), the **Dillingham Visitor Center**

(907/842-5115, www.dillinghamak.com, open Mon.–Fri. 10 A.M.–4 P.M.), and the **library** (907/842- 5610), with computers for Internet access. The city website is www.ci.dillingham.ak.us.

The main attractions for visitors—if they aren't fishermen—are Wood-Tikchik State Park and Walrus Islands State Game Sanctuary. **Togiak National Wildlife Refuge** begins just three miles west of Dillingham and covers 4.3 million acres. It is a vital staging area for migrating waterfowl, especially brant, emperor geese, common eiders, and Steller's eiders. Stop by the refuge office in Dillingham (907/842-1063, http://togiak.fws.gov) before heading out.

An enjoyable 24-mile dirt road leads out of Dillingham to the village of **Aleknagik** (pop. 200) where the state has a boat ramp on Lake Aleknagik. Wood-Tikchik Park begins at the upper end of this lake. Dillingham's main event is the **Beaver Round-Up,** a five-day winter party that features a championship dog sled race, dances, and the locally heralded Miss Dillingham pageant. There's also a **Silver Salmon Derby** in the summer.

ACCOMMODATIONS AND FOOD

Bristol Inn (104 Main St., 907/842-2240 or 800/764-9704, www.alaskaoutdoors.com/bristolinn), charges $105 s or $115 d; kitchenettes are $10 more.

Hillside Haven (907/842-3523) is two miles out of town atop Kleetuk Hill, with vistas in all directions. This large home has four nicely furnished guest rooms and three baths; rates are $140–168 d including a three meals a day.

The Overlook B&B (907/842-4524) sits atop a cliff overlooking Nushagak Bay, and is open mid-May to mid-September. Rooms are $80–100 d, with a full breakfast.

Dillingham's most unusual lodging place, **Thai Inn** (907/842-7378 or 877/510-8424, www.thaiamerican.com), is a huge nine-bedroom downtown hilltop home. Several rooms are decorated with hand-carved Thai pieces, giving it a decidedly un-Alaskan look. Two guest rooms ($85 s or $125 d) include private baths, and the large suite ($95 d) has a whirlpool tub. Breakfast is self-serve, and a more basic room ($50 d) may be available.

Beaver Creek B&B (907/842-7335 or 866/252-7335, www.dillinghamalaska.com) has several houses and cabins in the area. All rooms include access to full kitchens and laundry facilities; $125 s or $160 d with a make-it-yourself breakfast.

No camping in Dillingham, and much of the land out the road is in Native corporation or private hands. Showers are available at the boat harbor.

Ricardos' of Dillingham (907/842-1205) is the best bet overall for meals, with Mexican food and surprisingly good pizzas. Get groceries at **N&N Market** (907/842-5283) or the larger **Alaska Commercial Company** (907/842-5444).

TRANSPORTATION

The airport is a bit over two miles from Dillingham; get into town on **Ernie's Cab** (907/842-2606) or **Nushagak Cab Company** (907/842-4403). A car is useful if you plan to

WALRUS ISLANDS STATE GAME SANCTUARY

The Walrus Islands are a cluster of seven small rocky points of land in northern Bristol Bay. One of them—Round Island—is famous as a haul-out spot for thousands of walrus during the summer; only the bulls come ashore here. The walrus masses form what author Tom Kizzia called "a writhing mat of wrinkled, rust-colored leather" on the rocky beach where they rest. There are also hundreds of thousands of nesting seabirds-black-legged kittiwakes, common murres, cormorants, and parakeet auklets-as well as tufted and horned puffins. Also on the island are inquisitive red foxes. Steller sea lions come ashore on one beach.

Getting There

Contact the Alaska Department of Fish & Game (907/842-1013, www.state.ak.us/adfg) for an information packet and permit application. You can apply as early as January 1, and it's a good idea to get your application in early to be sure of a place at the peak time (mid-June through July). To keep human impacts to a minimum, only 12 permits ($50 pp) are issued for each five-day period, so you won't have a lot of neighbors, other than the birds and bulls. Two of the 12 permits are held open for those who apply within 10 days before a given time slot, so you might be able to get in at the last minute. Access to Round Island is difficult and equally expensive. Because of rough seas, there is no air access.

Two companies offer boat access to Round Island, with the permit included in the price, but you'll first need to fly to Dillingham from Anchorage (around $450 RT). Peter Andrew of **Ayungsi Charters** (907/442-4392) can take six people from Dillingham to the island for $2,400 round-trip; that's $400 per person if you find five others to go along.

Terry Johnson of **Walrus Islands Expeditions** (907/235-9349, www.alaskawalrusisland.com) has a variety of cruises, starting with an overnight trip for $550 per person that includes a berth in the boat, meals, and a guide. In addition to the nightly costs, you'll need to fly from Dillingham to Nunavachak Bay (where he's based) for around $350 per person. He also does one-day trips and drop-offs to Round Island for $450 per person out of the more-accessible Togiak; scheduled flights from Dillingham to Togiak are around $120 per person round-trip.

You'll have to bring all your own camping gear, food, and supplies. The weather can be pretty wild— 60-knot winds and pelting rain—so don't skimp on your tent and raingear. Be sure to take long tent stakes—and some extras—to hold everything down. Also bring enough food to last a week longer than you'd expected, since the weather can occasionally close in for long periods, making it impossible to leave. Trails lead from the camping area to outstanding cliffs where you can look down on the walrus or across to nesting seabirds. Fish & Game has two research technicians on the island who will answer your questions; they aren't guides, however.

spend any time in the Dillingham area or want to head up the road to Aleknagik; rent one from **D & J Rentals** (907/842-2222).

Alaska Airlines (800/426-0333, www.alaska air.com), **PenAir** (800/448-4226, www.penair .com), and **Frontier Flying Service** (907/450-7200 or 800/478-6779, www.frontierflying.com) have daily flights between Anchorage and Dillingham all year. PenAir also services many surrounding villages and towns. Local air taxis include **Arctic Circle Air** (907/842-3870 or 888/214-2364, www.arctic-circle-air.com), **Bay Air** (907/842-2570, www.bayair-alaska.com), **Grant Aviation** (907/842-2955, www.flygrant.com), **Shannon's Air Taxi** (907/842-5509), **Tikchik AirVentures** (907/842-5841), and **Tucker Aviation** (907/842-1023).

WOOD-TIKCHIK STATE PARK

This 1.6-million-acre state facility—the largest state park in the country—is 300 miles southwest of Anchorage, and a half-hour floatplane flight from Dillingham. The park preserves a vast system of rivers and lakes, including two long chains of interconnected waterways. There are eight different lakes at least 20 miles long, plus countless smaller ponds. These lakes offer some of the most awesome sportfishing to be found: trophy salmon, trout, Arctic char, northern pike.

The east side of Wood-Tikchik is almost flat, wooded terrain, but to the west the rugged Wood River Mountains rise, some topping 5,000 feet. Canoeists or kayakers may want to float down such rivers as the Nuyakuk or Tikchik, where

the unsurpassed scenery is untouched by development. You could easily spend several weeks exploring this area, but be forewarned that there's lots of big open water and storms can blow up. Also come prepared to battle the mosquitoes and other flying menaces.

Practicalities

For complete details on this remote park, contact Wood-Tikchik State Park headquarters in Anchorage (907/269-8698, www.alaskastate parks.org, year-round) or the Dillingham office (907/842-2375, late May–late Sept.).

Access is primarily by floatplane from Dillingham, but it's also possible to drive the 24 miles from Dillingham to the village of Aleknagik on Aleknagik Lake, and then boat through a long series of connected lakes. There are no trails or other developed facilities within the park itself, but camping and hiking opportunities abound if you have the right gear and a boat to get around. **Tikchik State Park Tours** (907/243-1416 or 888/345-2445, www.tikchik.com) leads kayaking trips within the park on Tikchik, Chaukaktuli, and Chikuminuk lakes, along with Tikchik River and Salmon River float trips. They also rent kayaks for do-it-yourselfers.

Most visitors to Wood-Tikchik stay at local fishing and hunting lodges, including **Wood River Lodge** (612/618-9999 or 800/842-5205 www.woodriverlodge.com), **Bearclaw Fishing Lodge** (907/232-7568 or 888/353-4748, www.bearclawlodge.com), and **Tikchik Narrows Lodge** (907/243-8450, www.tikchik-lodge.com). Tikchik Narrows is recommended.

Bethel

Flying to Bethel (pop. 5,000) from Anchorage hammers home an appreciation of how vast this country is. The Alaska Range and Kuskokwim Mountains serve up a seemingly impenetrable set of summits for over 300 miles. Then, it terminates abruptly in a range of hills that flattens into an enormous coastal plain. Far below, the land is pockmarked with thousands of ponds of all sizes, and the Kuskokwim River meanders its way toward the sea, past oxbows and brush-lined shores. The mixed Native and immigrant town of Bethel sprawls along the wide Kuskokwim River some 80 miles from its mouth.

Bethel is one of the largest settlements in the Alaskan bush. It serves as a supply center, as well as a transportation and communication hub, for dozens of outlying villages. You're likely to meet many people fluent in both English and Yup'ik (the nightly TV news is in both languages) along with a surprising number of recent emigrants from Eastern Europe and Korea. The country here is essentially flat tundra with willows along the river banks and thin black spruce forests farther upriver. In the summer, the Kuskokwim provides boat access to villages all along the river; when winter comes, it becomes an ice road for settlements hundreds of miles upriver. This is certainly one of the most unique roads in America. Each spring all commerce shuts down for a couple of weeks, when the river is too thin to drive on and the ice has not yet floated away in the big breakup.

Bethel is built on permafrost, so all buildings are constructed on stilts to prevent heat from thawing the ground and causing them to sink into a quagmire. Permafrost makes it very difficult to lay water lines, so water is trucked to holding tanks outside each home and business. This means you won't have a lot of water to waste on showers, and in some places the water is nearly undrinkable (this depends upon the source). This undrinkable water might partly explain the high sales of soda pop at local grocery stores, and makes a good excuse for the abundance of vodka in a town where alcohol can not be legally sold.

SIGHTS

A trading post was established along the Kuskokwim River in the 1870s, and was followed a decade later by a Moravian Church mission. The town of Bethel—named for the scriptural directive "Arise, go to Bethel, and dwell there"—grew up around this mission and trading post. The old **Moravian Church,** built around 1885, is the most interesting and photogenic local structure.

The **Yupik Cultural Center** (907/543-1819), in the same building as the University of Alaska's Kuskokwim campus, contains a fascinating collection of old Yup'ik clothing and tools, along with photographic exhibits. There are seal-gut parkas, dolls, baskets, and beautiful carved ivory pieces.

Other than this, the primary sights are the town itself and the wild country that reaches for an eternity in all directions from Bethel. The **Yukon-Kuskokwin Delta Regional Hospital** is that strange yellow building you pass on the way into town from the airport. It looks like the old drawings of space stations once planned for Mars.

Hang around the Alaska Commercial Co. store for that most Bethel of all Bethel attractions, the legion of local taxi cabs—all waiting outside with their engines running while the Slavic, Albanian, and Korean drivers smoke cigarettes and talk. Imagine it as a scene from an old Western, except that the horses tied up out front have been replaced by taxis, and the cowboys speak with an Eastern European or Asian accent.

Bethel lacks a visitor center, but for info you might try the **Bethel Chamber of Commerce** (907/543-2911, www.bethelchamber.com) or two private websites: www.kusko.net and www.deltadiscovery.com.

YUKON DELTA NATIONAL WILDLIFE REFUGE

The town of Bethel is encircled by this 20-million-acre wildlife refuge, largest in America. The refuge covers the widely spreading mouths of both the Yukon and Kuskokwim Rivers (The Y-K Delta), plus nearby Nunivak Island. Nearly all this land is a potholed mélange of tundra marshes, lakes, and streams. Yukon Delta National Wildlife Refuge is a vital area for waterfowl. The numbers are staggering: More than two million ducks, 750,000 geese and swans, plus another 100 million shorebirds nest here each summer. Most outsiders come to the refuge to see the birds and other animals; most Yup'ik people come here to hunt and fish as they have for time immemorial.

Access to the refuge is by boat or floatplane. Hiking is difficult on this marshy terrain. The **visitor center** at refuge headquarters in Bethel (907/543-3151, http://yukondelta.fws.gov) has wildlife displays and photographs. It occasionally offers guided bird-watching tours in the summer.

Kuskokwim Wilderness Adventures (907/543-3856, www.kuskofish.com) leads camping and rafting trips in the Bethel area.

ACCOMMODATIONS

Pacifica Guest House (907/543-4305) has comfortable rooms for $105 s or $125 d with shared baths, and suites for $165 s or $180 d s with private baths. Free airport transport, and unlimited water for long showers (it's on a well system; a real luxury in Bethel).

Bethel's newest and largest lodging place is **Long House Bethel Inn** (907/543-4612 or 866/543-4613, www.longhousehotel.com; $129–139 s or d). Don't confuse this with the Bethel Inn, a place that should be avoided!

Bentley's Porterhouse B&B (907/543-3552) has 30 attractive rooms spread over five buildings; $103–113 s or $128–139 d with breakfast.

Brown Slough B&B (907/543-4334 or 888/543-4334, www.bethelhotel.com) has two large and comfortable across-the-street homes along the slough. One of these is a beautiful two-story log structure. Most of the eight guest rooms share baths, and are $95 s or $115 d, but one room has its own bath; $116 s or $126 d. All include a continental breakfast. Recommended.

FOOD

Get pizza, calzones, and Greek specialties (including gyros, shish kebab, and baklava) at **Dimitri's Restaurant** (907/543-3434). **Datu's Place** (907/543-2216) has Chinese food. Open weekdays, **Diane's Cafe** (907/543-4305) at Pacifica Guest House, has the most expensive meals in town. It's the on-the-town place. Several other Bethel places also offer the standard burgers and fries menu.

Get groceries and supplies from **Alaska Commercial Company** (907/543-2661) or **Swanson's** (907/543-3221).

Bethel is a "damp" town where booze cannot be sold, but can be brought in for "personal use." This creates a situation ripe for bootlegging. More than a few locals import booze—especially vodka—to sell for a high markup ($50 a fifth!) to others desperate for a drink. A few years back a man was caught with 108 bottles in his possession, but he managed to convince a jury that they were for the wedding of a long-lost daughter.

© DON PITCHER

Dried salmon is one of the primary staples for those who live in the Kuskokwim.

EVENTS

Bethel's primary winter event is the **Kusko-kwim-300 Sled Dog Race** (907/543-3300, www.k300.org) held each January. It's a three-day mad dash up the frozen ice that attracts some of the fastest teams in the nation and even a few international entries. The **Cama'i Festival** (907/543-1977, www.bethelarts.com) in April is a three-day Native dance event with performers from all over Alaska and even Russia. This is a great time to buy Native crafts.

LOCAL CRAFTS

Adjacent to the Moravian church, the **Moravian Book Store** (907/543-2474) sells books, postcards from all the surrounding villages, church pamphlets, locally made jewelry, and a dose of the religious radio station. **Sourdough Trading Post** (907/543-3400) also sells Native handicrafts. Ask around and you might find someone to sew one of the beautiful and distinctive parkas worn by Native women, or to knit a garment out of musk ox wool, but be ready to part with a large amount of cash for either of these one-of-a-kind items. The finest

Alaskan baskets come from the village of Hooper Bay, 100 miles northwest of Bethel.

TRANSPORTATION

Bethel serves as the transportation hub for much of western Alaska, and has the third-busiest flight service station in the state. **Alaska Airlines** (800/426-0333, www.alaskaair.com), **Era Aviation** (907/266-8394 or 800/866-8394, www.flyera.com), and **Frontier Flying Service** (907/450-7200 or 800/478-6779, www.frontierflying.com) all have daily year-round service between Anchorage and Bethel.

Several air-taxi companies offer scheduled flights or charters from Bethel to other bush villages: Era Aviation, **Grant Aviation** (907/543-2000, www.flygrant.com), **Arctic Circle Air** (907/543-5906 or 888/214-2364, www.arctic-circle-air.com), and **Kusko Aviation** (907/543-3279), **Craig Air** (907/543-2575), **Village Aviation** (907/543-4040), and **Yukon Aviation** (907/543-3280).

Rent cars from **Payless Car Rental** (907/543-3058 or 800/729-5377). Oh yes—if you want a cab, just look around; one is bound to be within a couple hundred feet of any place in town.

Nome and Vicinity

If you make only one long flight to see bush Alaska, make it to fascinating Nome (pop. 3,500, of whom nearly 1,900 are Native). The town sits on the Seward Peninsula on the edge of Norton Sound facing the Bering Sea, only 190 miles east of Siberia, and 2,300 miles north of Seattle. Flying time is 90 minutes from Anchorage.

Nome was named when a cartographer marked its unnamed location on a map as "? Name," and a second mapmaker misread it as "C. [for Cape] Nome." One hundred fifty miles south of the Arctic Circle, Nome is on roughly the same latitude as Fairbanks, and shares similar hours of daylight, as well as warmer temperatures than its Arctic coast cousins, Kotzebue and Barrow—though the mercury rests around

0°F in January, and soars to a sizzling 60°F in the long days of July! Local motels advertise: "Visit picturesque Nome this summer. Three days—no nights."

Like other bush Alaska settlements, Nome is far from pretty, with piles of junk strewn about the yards and more than a few drunks stumbling from the town's eight saloons. But it has more of a small-city feeling than Bethel or Kotzebue, with historic buildings, paved streets (some of them), and a real downtown. Although there are almost no trees in Nome, each winter the "Nome National Forest" sprouts as locals plant their former Christmas trees in the offshore pack ice. (People cut the trees near Teller each fall before the road closes for the winter.)

NOME

0.1 mi

0.1 km

To Teller

To Airport

SEPPALA DR.

BERING ST.

NORTON SOUND
REGIONAL HOSPITAL

RECREATION CENTER

NOME BYPASS

FIFTH AVE

HANSON'S
SAFEWAY

OLD ST.
JOSEPH'S
CHURCH

NUGGET INN

CITY HALL/
IDITAROD
ARCH

VISITOR
CENTER

MUSEUM/
LIBRARY

POLARIS
HOTEL

NANUAQ
MANOR
HOTEL

PONDEROSA
INN

METTLER

MOORE

OCEAN VIEW
B&B

AURORA
INN HOTEL

CAMPBELL

CARSTENS
ST.

FRONT ST.

BETTY'S
IGLOO

CHATEAU DE
CAPE NOME

SWANBERG'S
DREDGE

BEACH GOLD
DREDGES

To Council
and Taylor

Bering Sea

WEST D ST

WEST C ST.

WEST
SECOND AVE

FIRST AVE

FIFTH AVE

FOURTH
AVE.

THIRD
AVE.

DIVISION ST.

STEADMAN ST.

EAST FIFTH AVE.

EAST FOURTH AVE.

EAST THIRD AVE.

EAST G ST.

EAST H ST.

EAST I ST.

EAST SIXTH AVE.

EAST K ST.

EAST L ST.

EAST M ST.

EAST N ST.

EAST FIRST AVE.

HISTORY

In 1898, the "three lucky Swedes," Jafet Lindberg, Erik Lindblom, and John Brynteson, discovered fabulous deposits of gold in Anvil Creek above present-day Nome. Word reached Dawson the next spring, and by fall, 10,000 stampeders had arrived and set up tents on the beach, only to have them blown away by a fierce September storm that prompted a migration inland. There, more gold was found; in fact, placer deposits were carried by most streams that emptied into the Bering Sea. By 1900, 20,000 prospectors crowded the coast, fully a third of the white population in Alaska at the time. For a time it was the territory's largest city. A railroad had been built to Anvil Creek, which produced several dozen million-dollar claims. Some became rich, but many men who had bought one-way passage to the gold fields found themselves destitute, and the Army had to be brought in to get them home before the winter of 1901. Judge James Wickersham brought law and order to Nome in 1902, after the first judge was convicted of corruption. Several devastating fires and storms have destroyed most of Nome's historic downtown buildings, but a few of the original buildings survive.

In 1925, a diphtheria epidemic required emergency delivery of serum from Nenana 650 miles overland by dog sled. Through the heroic efforts of mushers and dogs, the serum arrived in time to save many lives. This event is commemorated today in the famous Iditarod Sled Dog Race from Anchorage to Nome. The race takes place every March and turns Nome into a late winter carnival.

During World War II, Nome was a major transfer point for lend-lease aircraft being sent to Russia from the United States. The planes were flown up to Alaska from the lower 48 states, transferred to Russian pilots in Fairbanks, and then flown on to Nome and the Soviet Union. Almost 8,000 planes came through Nome between 1942 and 1945, with most making it to the front for use in the war against Germany.

Today, Nome survives on small-scale gold mining, tourism, and as a regional center for the Seward Peninsula. Many visitors try their luck by panning for gold along the beaches here. The Native people maintain subsistence fishing and hunting traditions, along with the herding of some 30,000 reindeer. The antlers are sold for medicinal use (aphrodisiacs) in Asia, and the meat is available in local stores. Nome is a good place to buy ivory and other artwork in the various gift shops, along with imported crafts from Russia. Of course, the Iditarod Race focuses international attention on Nome every March.

IN-TOWN SIGHTS

Start out at the helpful **Nome Visitor Center** on Front St. in the center of town, run by the Nome Convention and Visitors Bureau (907/443-6624 or 800/478-1901, www.nomealaska.org). The knowledgeable staff will point you in the right direction, and the scrapbooks, photo albums, and amazingly detailed handouts provide an excellent introduction to the area. Pick up the walking-tour brochure, mostly focusing on historical attractions, such as the nearby dredges. The center is open daily 9 A.M.–9 P.M. in from late May to mid-September, and Monday–Friday 9 A.M.–6 P.M. the rest of the year.

Step across the street to **city hall,** with its Victorian exterior. During the Iditarod Race, the massive **burled wooden arch** out front is moved over Front Street to mark the finish line.

The **Carrie McLain Museum** (907/443-6630), in the basement of the library, a few doors east on Front Street, is open daily 9 A.M.–5:30 P.M. June to early September, and Tuesday–Saturday noon–6 P.M. the rest of the year. It houses a fascinating collection of historical photos from the gold rush era, along with exhibits on Native culture, sled dog racing, and the discovery of gold in 1898, the arrival of Wyatt Earp, and the rush of

Today, Nome survives on small-scale gold mining, tourism, and as a regional center for the Seward Peninsula. Many visitors try their luck by panning for gold along the beaches here.

40,000 miners to Nome in 1900. The **Kegoayah Kozga Library** (907/443-6628) houses an interesting rare books section, plus computers you can use to check your email.

The National Park Service's **Information Center** (179 Front St., 907/443-2522 or 800/471-2352, www.nps.gov/bela) is open Monday–Friday 9 A.M.–5 P.M. all year. Step inside to view the exhibits and videos or to talk with the staff about nearby Bering Land Bridge National Preserve and other national parks in the vicinity, including Cape Krusenstern, Noatak, and Kobuk Valley.

Over on Division Street at 3rd Avenue is **Old St. Joseph's Catholic Church,** built in 1901, but closed in 1945. The building has been lovingly restored and is now used for local events. It's open Monday–Friday 10 A.M.–2 P.M. in the summer. Take your photo at "America's largest gold pan," next to the church.

If you have a car or bike (or want a nice day hike), take the 4.5-mile road to the 1,062-foot summit of **Anvil Mountain** behind Nome. World War II gun emplacements and an abandoned Cold War–era distant early warning station are on top, and on a clear day you'll be treated to views of the city, the Bering Sea, the Kigluaik Mountains, and the surrounding tundra.

Gold Fever

Gold dredges were once sprinkled all across the Seward Peninsula, and the last of these operated until 1995, when low gold prices and rising costs forced the last one to shut down. With a little exploration, you're sure to find some of the more than 100 old dredges that remain in the surrounding country. A number of these are within walking distance of Nome, but don't climb on them since they're unsafe. Closest is the **Swanberg Dredge** just east of town. Nearby is a small park with old mining equipment, including a steam shovel. Far more impressive is **Dredge No. 5** a couple of miles north of town off the Teller Road. Offshore to the north of

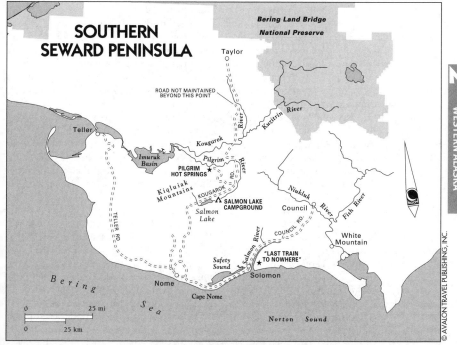

WESTERN ALASKA

town is an enormous 14-story-tall dredge; it was the largest ever built.

Across the road from the Swanberg Dredge is a public beach where anyone can try a hand at panning for gold. The beach attracts an annual gathering of ambitious recreational miners who operate dredges throughout the summer months. It's hard work that involves a dry-suited diver operating a suction dredge atop a raft several hundred feet offshore. They're a pretty tightlipped group, but must be finding something since many return each summer.

SEEING THE COUNTRY

The real treat in Nome is the opportunity to explore this expansive, far-as-the-eye-can-see landscape. Over 250 miles of gravel roads fan out from town, taking you across the subarctic countryside around Seward Peninsula. Wildlife-including musk ox, red foxes, wolves, moose, reindeer, and even a few grizzlies-can be seen, and the fishing is good for salmon, pike, grayling, whitefish, and Dolly Varden. Anglers will want to pick up the free "Nome Roadside Fishing Guide" from the visitor center before heading out.

Bird-watchers come from all over the nation to track down unusual bird species in the Nome area, including some that wander across the Bering Strait from Russia. The visitor center posts unusual sightings, and has a bird checklist and brochure listing companies offering bird-watching trips. Also available at the visitor center is a brochure describing hiking routes.

In midsummer, the roads are lined with verdant tundra plants and a massive display of 200 species of flowers. Some have likened it to driving through Denali National Park, but without anyone else there. The roads lead to the tiny settlements of Teller, Council, and Taylor, taking you past remnants from the gold rush—dredges, miners' cabins, and even an old train.

Air taxis from Nome provide flights to Bering Land Bridge National Preserve, where you will find popular Serpentine Hot Springs. (See *The Arctic* chapter for details.)

Kougarok Road

Also known as the Taylor Road, this exceptionally scenic route leads north along Nome River into the beautiful **Kigluaik Mountains,** a great place to explore on foot. The road parallels part of the historic Wild Goose Pipeline, built of metal hoops and redwood slats between 1905 and 1909 to carry water to Nome gold mines. The pipeline was never completed, but is still intact in places. There's a free Bureau of Land Management campground and picnic area at **Salmon Lake,** 40 miles out, and a hike-in shelter cabin in the Mosquito Pass area. Contact the BLM office in Nome (907/443-2177) for the access route. A side trip to the old Catholic church and orphanage at **Pilgrim Hot Springs** is another option. The orphanage opened after the 1918 influenza epidemic killed many Eskimo parents in the area. The springs are not open to the public. Kougarok Rd. is not maintained beyond the Kougarok River bridge (mile 85), though a trail continues to the village of Taylor.

Council Road

This gravel road heads east from Nome, following the shoreline of the Bering Sea for the first 30 miles, before turning northeast. Eskimo fishing and hunting camps are all along this route. Bird-watchers flock to Safety Sound, a great place to watch for unusual species of ducks, swans, geese, and shorebirds.

At mile 33, the road passes a favorite photographic stop, the rusting hulk of the **"Last Train to Nowhere."** The train consists of three locomotive engines and several cars from the Council City and Solomon River Railroad, begun in 1881. The engines originally served on the New York Elevated Railroad Company before they were shipped north in 1903, and are the only such engines still in existence. The railroad was originally envisioned as part of a system that would connect Nome's gold fields with the Lower 48, but the vision died because of financial problems and wild storms that destroyed the tracks along the Bering Sea in 1907. At its maximum, the tracks only extended a distance of 35 miles.

The road ends at the Niukluk River (good fishing) near **Council,** 72 miles from Nome.

"Last Train to Nowhere," the old Council City and Solomon River Railroad

It is possible to drive across the river at a fording point, but don't do so without help from locals. An alternative would be to have someone take you across by boat. One unusual aspect of the country around Council is the presence of trees, a real treat after all the open tundra elsewhere on the Seward Peninsula. The settlement of Council still has remnants of log cabins from the gold rush era when the town was home to 10,000 people. Now it's a summer home area for folks from Nome. Simple cabins are available at **Camp Bendelben** (907/443-2880).

Teller Road

It's a beautiful two-hour drive on this 73-mile gravel road that leads from Nome to the Eskimo village of **Teller** (pop. 250). Along the way, you're likely to see reindeer herded by locals, along with musk ox and unusual bird species. Two stores have limited supplies.

TOURS

Most visitors to Nome arrive as part of a see-the-Arctic package from **Tour Arctic** (907/442-3441 or 800/523-7405, www.tourarctic.com). You can also book these same trips through **Alaska Airlines**

Vacations (800/4468-2248, www.alaskair.com). Tour options include an overnight in Kotzebue and a day in Nome for $585 s or $1,000 d, or a trip that includes one night in Kotzebue and a second night in Nome $680 s or $1,100 d. Both of these options also include local tours and round-trip air transportation from Anchorage.

For amusing and personalized tours of the Nome area, contact Richard Beneville of **Nome Discovery Tours** (907/443-2814). His background as an actor, dancer, and singer in New York may seem a bit out of place, but he's been in Alaska for many years and has good knowledge of Nome and its history. Half-day trips start at $45. **Nome Tour and Marketing** (907/443-2651) also offers local tours. Both companies include the chance to pan for gold.

Naturalists Lee and Regina Zimmerman of **Sub-Arctic Wilderness Tours** (907/443-4895, www.subarctictours.com) lead one-week tours of the area that emphasize birding, plants, and photography.

Circumpolar Expeditions (907/272-9299 or 888/567-7165, www.arctictravel.net) has three-day tours from Nome to Provideniya, Russia, for $1,400. The price includes transportation, visas, lodging, meals, tours, and English-speaking guides.

Iditarod musher Jerry Austin operates **Austin's Alaska Adventures** (877/923-2419, www.alaskaadventures.net) with one-week sled dog tours from the remote village of St. Michael.

ACCOMMODATIONS
Hotels
Ponderosa Inn (907/443-5737) has rooms for $75–85 s or $85–95 d, and suites with full kitchens for $120 d.

Nome's best-known hotel, **Nugget Inn** (907/443-2323 or 877/443-2323, www.nome nuggetinn.com) has small older rooms ($129 s or $149–159 d) but the exterior, lobby, and bar are full of character. Be sure to check out the "doll house" out front that was originally built during the gold rush.

The newest and finest lodging in town is **Aurora Inn & Suites** (907/443-3838 or 800/354-4606, www.aurorainnome.com), where bright and spacious rooms go for $130 d. Kitchenettes cost $140, and studio apartments and suites (these sleep four) are $185–225.

Another good place for families is **Nanuaq Manor Hotel** (199 E. King Place, 907/443-5296), where two- and three-bedroom apartments with full kitchens are $95 s or $125 d.

Bed-and-Breakfasts
Chateau de Cape Nome (907/443-2083) has four guest rooms sharing two baths for $75 s or d, including a light breakfast. Owner Cussy Kauer is from a longtime Nome family; her grandmother was Carrie McClain (for whom the museum is named). The house is packed with historical items from the area, and you'll even find a pet reindeer (Mr. Moses) in the yard.

An Oceanview B&B (907/443-2133, www.nomebb.com) has three guest rooms with shared or private baths and a continental breakfast for $75–120 d.

Other Nome B&Bs are **Arctic Lodge B&B** (907/443-3515, $75 d), **Mai's Guest House** (907/443-4113, $55 s, $60 d), **No Place Like Nome B&B** (907/443-2451, $75 s, $85 d), and **Sweet Dreams B&B** (907/443-2919, $75 s, $85 d). During the Iditarod each March many locals open their homes for out-of-towners. The Convention and Visitors Bureau (907/443-6624 or 800/478-1901) keeps a list.

Camping
Anyone can camp for free on the beach on the east side of Nome, but you'll need to get water from the visitor center and take showers at the recreation center. The abundant beach driftwood makes for great campfires. There's also a free BLM campground at **Salmon Lake,** 40 miles out the Kougarok Road. Located in the mountains, it's worth the drive if you can afford a rental vehicle. Good fishing for grayling, whitefish, and Dolly Varden, too. It is also possible to camp on open tundra along the road system fanning out from Nome, but check first with the visitor center for a map of public lands since much of this is Native-owned.

FOOD
Eat at the popular **Fat Freddie's** (behind the Nugget Inn on Front St., 907/443-5899), for breakfast or a big lunch. The food is reasonable and dependably good. They're also open evenings with steaks, fried chicken, and halibut.

Despite the name, **Milano's Pizzeria** (907/443-2924) is not owned by an Italian. Like many other bush Alaska restaurants, it is run by Korean-Americans. To add to the confusion, it also serves Japanese food! Pizzas start at $10 for a small cheese.

You won't go wrong with authentic Vietnamese cuisine prepared by Thu Lan at **Gold Rush Food to Go** (inside Gold Rush Video, 108 Front St., 907/443-5111). Stop here for surprisingly flavorful pho (Vietnamese soup), egg rolls, stir-fried noodles, and other specialties, along with various grilled specialties.

Get groceries in town from **Hanson's Safeway** (4th and Bering, 907/443-5454) or **Alaska Commercial Company** (on the north edge of Nome, 907/443-2243). Several places have espresso in town, including **Northern Delights** (245 Front St., 907/443-5200) and **Arctic Trading Post** (907/443-2686), across from the visitor center. The latter also has regional books for sale.

ENTERTAINMENT

Nome is a hard-drinking town with four liquor stores and eight bars, including the surprisingly capacious **Board of Trade** (on Front St., 907/443-2611). There's live music here most summer nights and during the Iditarod. The Board of Trade opened as the Dexter Saloon in 1901 under the proprietorship of gunslinger Wyatt Earp. Selling liquor and running gambling tables helped make Earp a very rich man; by the time he left Nome later that year, he had pocketed $80,000 in profits. Today, the gambling comes in the form of pull tabs and nightly bingo games.

Picturesque **Gold Dust Lounge** inside the Nugget Inn is a great place to soak up the ambiance while enjoying the picture-window views of Norton Sound. Residents from outlying villages (all of which are dry) come to Nome to drink, and do a very thorough job of it, as you will quickly see. Things can get pretty bad sometimes as the alcohol pours and the drunks get drunker. It could be worse though—in the town's early days three-foot-thick urine glaciers were reported outside some saloons.

EVENTS

Nome's main attraction is the famous **Iditarod Trail Sled Dog Race** (www.iditarod.com). Beginning in Anchorage on the first Saturday in March, the race covers 1,049 miles to the finish point in Nome. It generally takes 10–12 days for the first team to reach Nome. Reserve far ahead to be sure of a motel room for the hectic finish. Everyone comes out to cheer the winning mushers and also-rans. The race ends under the burled arch that stands along Front Street.

Other March events include the **Iditarod Basketball Tournament.** With over 50 different high school boys' and girls' teams, this is said to be the largest in the nation. And, of course, there's the infamous **Bering Sea Ice Golf Classic.** The golf classic is played on the frozen sea off Nome, a place with hazards not common to most courses. It uses orange golf balls and green-dyed ice for the "greens." Another goofball event is the annual **Summer Solstice Polar Bear Swim** in the Bering Sea—assuming the ice is out! If you aren't so foolhardy, there's always the indoor swimming pool at the high school. The Nome Convention and Visitors Bureau (907/443-6624 or 800/478-1901, www.nomealaska.org) has details on all these (and other) events.

SHOPPING

Check out Nome's gift shops for Eskimo dolls, carved ivory and soapstone, grass baskets, mukluks, and sealskin slippers. Good places to start are **Arctic Trading Post** (907/443-2686) and **Chukotka-Alaska** (907/443-4128 or 800/416-4128). The latter also sells handicrafts from Provideniya, Russia, just across the Bering Strait from Nome. Also worth a peek is the **XYZ Senior Center** (907/443-5238), on Hunter St. near the visitor center, where you may meet the elders who create these pieces if you stop by during lunch.

Get camping gear and other outdoor supplies from **Nome Outfitters** (235 E. 1st Ave., 907/443-2880 or 800/680-6663).

INFORMATION AND SERVICES

Nome's visitor centers are described in Sights above. Find an ATM in the Wells Fargo on Front Street. The **Recreation Center** (907/443-5432) is three miles east of town next to the high school, and includes a swimming pool, racquetball courts, weight room, sauna, and even a bowling alley. It's open daily.

For emergencies, head to **Norton Sound Regional Hospital** (at Bering and 5th, 907/443-3311, www.nortonsoundhealth.org).

TRANSPORTATION

Alaska Airlines (907/443-2288 or 800/426-0333, www.alaskaair.com) has two or three daily flights into Nome from Anchorage and Kotzebue. **Bering Air** (907/443-5464 or 800/478-5422, www.beringair.com), **Flight Alaska** (907/443-3073 or 866/347-6432), and **Hageland Aviation** (907/443-7595 or 866/239-0119, www.hageland.com) offer scheduled flights to surrounding villages and St. Lawrence Island.

Bering Air also offers charter service to Provideniya, Russia. **Cape Smythe Air** (907/443-2414 or 800/478-5125, www.capesmythe.com) also has scheduled flights, but its safety record is far from stellar. Other air taxis include **Baker Aviation** (907/443-3081) and **Grant Aviation** (907/443-4650, www.flygrant.com).

The Nome airport is 1.5 miles from town, or a $5 taxi ride. It costs $3 for in-town rides from **Louie's Taxi** (907/443-6000), **Checker Cab** (907/443-5211), or **Village Taxi** (907/443-2333).

Rent pickups, vans, or SUVs from **Stampede Rent-a-Car** (907/443-5252 or 800/354-4606, www.aurorainn.com) or **Alaska Cab Garage** (907/443-2939). Rates at both companies start around $80/day, but Stampede has newer vehicles. Reserve ahead to be sure of finding a vehicle when you arrive. Gas prices in Nome are often twice those in Anchorage.

ST. LAWRENCE ISLAND

This hundred-mile-long island is about 160 miles southwest of Nome and just 36 miles from the Chukotsk Peninsula in Siberia. On a clear day, residents can see across the Bering Sea to the mountains of Siberia. The village of **Gambell** (pop. 550) is the primary settlement, and is home to Siberian Eskimos who have lived here for centuries. Most people speak Siberian Yup'ik as their primary language (though they also know English) and depend upon subsistence hunting of bowhead and gray whales, seal, walrus, fish, birds, and even polar bears. This is one place where walrus-hide umiak boats are still used. Because of its location, St. Lawrence Island is a good place to find unusual bird species. Beautifully carved ivory and other crafts are available locally, but visitors should refuse to buy any Eskimo artifacts. Many of these priceless cultural relics have been looted from ancient village sites around the island.

Bering Air (907/443-5464 or 800/478-5422, www.beringair.com) has daily service to St. Lawrence from Nome. There is a well-stocked general store in Gambell, thanks to daily flights from Nome. **Sivuqaq Native Corporation** (907/985-5826) sets up local tours, and runs the Sivuqaq Inn and deli in Gambell. Limited lodging is also available in the island's other village, **Savoonga** (pop. 630). Anyone wanting to camp should contact the Native corporation for permission to go outside the city limits ($50 fee). There are no cars on St. Lawrence Island; folks get around by foot or on four-wheelers.

Find additional information about St. Lawrence Island on the web at www.okvik.com.

The Arctic

In Arctic Alaska, settlements are far, far apart, and the land predominates. Geographically, it is a relatively simple area. The rugged Brooks Range parallels the Arctic Circle in a long arc across the state, descending on its northern margin to the treeless tundra of the North Slope. On the tundra are thousands of lakes and ponds, creating a vital nesting area for ducks, geese, swans, and shorebirds. Polar bear, grizzly bear, arctic fox, musk ox, and other mammals are found in the Arctic, and vast herds of caribou make this their summer home, notably within the Arctic National Wildlife Refuge, which holds down the far northeast corner, bordered by the Arctic Ocean and Yukon Territory.

The Brooks Range encompasses both Noatak National Preserve and Gates of the Arctic National Park and Preserve, while other large public lands border the southern margins of these mountains: Kobuk Valley National Park, Cape Krusenstern National Preserve, and Selawik National Wildlife Refuge. Only one road connects the Arctic with the outside world: The **Dalton Highway,** which parallels the Trans-Alaska Pipeline from Livengood (north of Fairbanks) all the way to Deadhorse/Prudhoe Bay. It's almost 500 miles by car from Fairbanks to the Beufort Sea/Arctic Ocean. This route and the developments at **Prudhoe Bay** are detailed in the *Interior Alaska* chapter.

The extremes of the Arctic make it hard to imagine how life survives. The too-brief summers can be gloriously beautiful, with a sun that never sets and luxuriant vegetation stretching in all directions, but winter brings a cold so bitter that even stepping outside for a few moments

whalebone arch, Barrow

THE ARCTIC

THE ARCTIC

ARCTIC OCEAN

Beaufort Sea

Chukchi Sea

Cape Lisburne

Point Hope
Point Hope

Point Lay

Wainwright

Barrow

North Slope

Nuiqsut

Colville River

Prudhoe Bay
Deadhorse

Kaktovik

Arctic National Wildlife Refuge

Brooks Range

Anaktuvuk Pass

Gates Of The Arctic National Park and Preserve

Noatak National Preserve

Ambler

Kobuk River

Kobuk Valley National Park

GREAT KOBUK SAND DUNES

Kiana

Kotzebue

Kotzebue Sound

Cape Krusenstern National Monument

Cape Krusenstern

Bering Land Bridge National Preserve

Seward Peninsula

Nome

Iditarod

Selawik

Selawik National Wildlife Refuge

Koyukuk

Koyukuk National Wildlife Refuge

Huslia

Galena

Yukon River

Bettles

Kanuti National Wildlife Refuge

Arctic Circle

Wiseman
Coldfoot

TRANS-ALASKA PIPELINE

DALTON HWY.

Arctic Village

Fort Yukon

Yukon River

Circle

Yukon-Charley Rivers National Preserve

Yukon Flats National Wildlife Refuge

White Mts Nat. Rec. Area

Livengood

Manley Hot Springs

Nowitna National Wildlife Refuge

CANADA

YUKON TERRITORY

Ivvavik National Park

INTERNATIONAL DATELINE

ALASKA

100 km
100 mi

© AVALON TRAVEL PUBLISHING, INC.

without proper protective clothing can be life-threatening. Visitors need to be well prepared before venturing away from the settlements. This is not a landscape to take lightly.

The People

Only two towns of any size are found in Arctic Alaska: Kotzebue and Barrow. Both are predominately Inupiat Eskimo in population. Several national parks surround Kotzebue, and more parks and refuges encompass the Brooks Range, offering exciting possibilities for hikers and river runners in search of adventure. At the top of the continent on the Arctic Ocean lies Barrow, famous as the summertime land of the midnight sun, but also as the land where the sun does not rise for two straight months in winter. Prudhoe Bay, the source of Alaska's oil wealth, is also here, providing a temporary home for several thousand oilfield employees.

The Eskimo people who have made the Arctic their home for centuries have seen their culture undergo massive changes since their initial contact with whites 200 years ago. Christian missionaries brought new religions, attempted to obliterate all traces of their "pagan" beliefs, and forced them to take Anglicized names. Other newcomers decimated the whales, seals, walrus, and other animals that were food for the Eskimos, and brought deadly diseases for which they had no immunity. Entire villages were killed by measles and influenza. In addition, the American culture of materialism and self-accomplishment contrasted sharply with traditions that emphasized getting along and working together. But perhaps the worst scourge whites brought was alcohol. Even today, alcohol is a major factor in Alaska's high rate of suicide, drowning, and accidental deaths, particularly in the Arctic, where life is so challenging already. Visitors need to treat local people with sensitivity and respect, realizing that this is their land, not yours. If you show a genuine interest in people and their culture you'll be rewarded with a far deeper understanding of their world. For an excellent introduction to the culture from an Eskimo perspective, see *The Epic of Qayaq: The Longest Story Ever Told by My People* by Lela Kiana Oman.

Kotzebue

The state's largest Native settlement, Kotzebue (pop. 3,000) serves as a commercial hub for northwestern Alaska. The town covers a three-mile-long sandy spit at the tip of Baldwin Peninsula that has been occupied by Inupiat Eskimos for the last six centuries. Originally called Kikiktagruk (Almost An Island), today's name comes from Otto von Kotzebue, a Russian sailor who happened upon the village in 1816. Surrounding Kotzebue are the shallow waters of Kotzebue Sound, and nearby are the mouths of the Noatak, Kobuk, and Selawik rivers.

The Natives of Kotzebue lead a traditional lifestyle (with all the amenities, including snowmobiles and VCRs). It has the feeling of a large village, with a single paved road, a few attractions, rolling tundra, and open water. There are no trees, though the brush gets over your head in places. Just 30 miles north of the Arctic Circle,

Kotzebue experiences endless sunlight for 36 days starting on June 3, but then suffers through an almost equal period of darkness around the winter solstice.

Red Dog Mine

Kotzebue's economy is dependent upon the giant Red Dog Mine (907/426-2170, www.teckcominco.com), largest zinc mine in the world, and the employer of nearly 400 workers (many of them Native). Located 100 miles north of town, Red Dog is owned by Teck Cominco, but the land belongs to the Northwest Alaska Native Association (NANA); both profit handsomely from the venture. Recent discoveries have added to the mine's life, and it will be producing zinc and lead for decades to come. The ore concentrate is trucked 45 miles from the mine to a port on the Chukchi Sea, where it is stored in an enormous warehouse (the largest building north of the Arctic Circle). Although mining takes place year-round, ore can only be shipped during the three-month summer, when the sea is ice-free.

SIGHTS

Stroll around to absorb a bit of Kotzebue's Native flavor. An interesting **cemetery** occupies several blocks in the center of town, and includes colorfully decorated graves. Unfortunately, too many of these are from young people killed in alcohol-related accidents or from suicide. Another cemetery occupies a hill overlooking town, and the same road continues out a couple of miles over the tundra to the town's water source. Walk south of Kotzebue past the airport to find a fish camp where several dozen structures are used for the drying and smoking of fish, seal, and walrus meat.

Museum

Located on 2nd Avenue near the airport, **NANA Museum of the Arctic** (907/442-3747, www.tour-arctic.com, daily 9 A.M.–6 P.M. May–August, by appointment rest of year; no charge) houses a small but interesting collection of wildlife and cultural items, including kayaks, parkas, ivory and stone tools, and mukluks. A special program is given several times daily in the summer, and includes Native drumming and dancing, an impressive slide show on the region, an introduction to local wildlife, and a blanket toss. All of this takes place indoors, and lasts around an hour; $20. Most visitors join in these events as part of a package tour that includes time in Kotzebue and Nome.

Park Information

The National Park Service's Visitor Information Center (907/442-3890 or 800/478-7252, www.nps.gov/nwak, daily 9 A.M.–6 P.M. late May–Aug.) for Kobuk Valley National Park, Cape Krusenstern National Monument, and Noatak National Preserve is at 154 2nd Avenue. Drop by to learn about the parks through displays, videos, and occasional programs.

TOURS

Tour Arctic (907/442-3441 or 800/523-7405, www.tourarctic.com) is a Native-owned company (part of NANA Regional Corporation) that provides tours around Kotzebue year-round. Most popular is its all-day trip ($100) that includes a bus tour, tundra walk, visit to the museum, and an introduction to Eskimo culture through singing, dancing, demonstrations, and a multimedia show. Most people join these as part of a see-the-Arctic package booked through Tour Arctic. You can also book the same trips through **Alaska Airlines Vacations** (800/468-2248, www.alaskaair.com).

Package tour options include a one-day trip from Anchorage to Kotzebue and back ($369), an overnight trip to Kotzebue with a second day in Nome ($585 s or $1,000 d), or a trip that includes one night in Kotzebue and a second night in Nome ($680 s or $1,100 d). All of these

tundra pond near Kotzebue

include local tours and round-trip transportation from Anchorage on Alaska Airlines.

Noatak Tours (907/442-2747) has boat trips from Kotzebue to 870-foot-high Yugo's Mountain north of town along the Noatak River; $100 per person with a minimum of two for this five-hour jaunt. Various other scenic tours and dropoffs are also available.

ACCOMMODATIONS

Kotzebue's primary lodging place is the modern **Nullagvik Hotel** (907/442-3331, www.nullagvik.com), where rooms are $149 d. Reserve ahead, since tour groups sometimes book it solid in the middle of summer.

A much better bet is **Lagoon B&B** (907/442-3723), where Sue and LeRoy White have three rooms available for $85–100 d, and a studio apartment for $120, all with breakfast. Guests share a comfortable central space and can relax on the back deck.

Guests stay in modest cabins at **LaVonne's Fish Camp** (907/272-9299 or 888/567-7165, www.fishcamp.org) five miles out of town along the beach. Rates start at $250 pp/day, including lodging, three meals a day, guided tours, and the chance to fish, learn about Native culture, or simply relax.

No camping in Kotzebue, but you may be able to pitch a tent south of town past the airport along the beach. Many local people have summertime fish camps here, so ask around to make sure you aren't on someone's private space.

FOOD

The seasonal **Nullagvik Hotel** restaurant (907/442-3331) features fresh fish and reindeer stew, but is pricey and serves small portions. **Bayside Restaurant** (907/442-3600) has decent

Chinese food, along with sandwiches, steak, and halibut; it's probably your best choice.

Groceries are available from both **Alaska Commercial** (907/442-3285) and **Hanson's** (907/442-3101). Kotzebue is a "damp" town that doesn't allow alcohol sales, so bring your own from Anchorage.

ARTS AND SERVICES

Native arts and crafts—especially carved ivory pieces and Eskimo dolls—are sold in the NANA Museum, the Nullagvik Hotel, and other gift shops. The city of Kotzebue website (www.cityofkotzebue.com) has local info and links. An ATM is located at the Wells Fargo building (907/442-3258).

Manillaq Health Center (907/442-3321, www.maniilaq.org) is a modern hospital with physicians on staff.

TRANSPORTATION

Alaska Airlines (800/426-0333, www.alaskaair.com) has daily service to Kotzebue from Anchorage or Fairbanks. Local taxi companies charge $5 from the airport.

Scheduled flights to surrounding communities and air charters are available from **Baker Aviation** (907/442-3108), **Bering Air** (907/442-3943 or 800/478-5422, www.beringair.com), and **Cape Smythe Air** (907/442-3020 or 800/478-5125, www.capesmythe.com). (But Cape Smythe Air had five crashes between 1995 and 2000, some of them with multiple fatalities.) You can also book air charters with **Arctic Air Guides** (907/442-3030), **Northwestern Aviation** (907/442-3525), **Hageland Aviation** (907/442-2936 or 866/239-0119, www.hageland.com), and **Yute Air** (907/442-3330). Recommended are Arctic Air Guides and Northwestern; both have pilots with many years of Arctic flying experience.

Arctic Parks and Refuges

Four little-known national parks are found within a 100-mile radius of Kotzebue: Bering Land Bridge National Preserve, Cape Krusenstern National Monument, Kobuk Valley National Park, and Noatak National Preserve. Noatak and Kobuk abut Gates of the Arctic National Park, and the three combine to create a massive 16 million-acre wilderness, with another 2 million acres of wild country within Selawik National Wildlife Refuge, immediately south of Kobuk Valley.

BERING LAND BRIDGE AND KRUSENSTERN

The 2.8 million-acre Bering Land Bridge National Preserve covers the northern Seward Peninsula 90 miles north of Nome and 50 miles south of Kotzebue. The area is considered a remnant of the land bridge that connected Siberia with Alaska during the last ice age. It served as a migratory corridor for people as well as animals, and the preserve has many archaeological sites, some of which date back 10,000 years or more.

Bering Land Bridge is vast; there are no roads that lead directly into it, and summer access is by small plane or boat. The preserve contains no trails and very few developed facilities, although six shelter cabins are available, along with a bunkhouse-style cabin at **Serpentine Hot Springs.** Next to the cabin is a bathhouse where you can soak in the mineral-laden waters. Unimproved trails lead up nearby ridges and to distinctive granite spires called tors. Other attractions include interesting lava flows near Imuruk Lake and volcanic craters. Get additional information from the Park Service office in Nome (907/443-2522 or 800/471-2352, www.nps.gov/bela).

Cape Krusenstern
The 660,000-acre Cape Krusenstern National Monument is northwest of Kotzebue, with access by boat or air charter. It contains significant archaeological sites on a series of 114 beach ridges that were formed over a period of 6,000 years. There are no developed facilities or trails within

the national monument, but hikers enjoy the chance to look for a wide variety of waterfowl along with grizzlies, Dall sheep, and caribou. Park headquarters is in Kotzebue (907/442-3890 or 800/478-7252, www.nps.gov/cakr).

KOBUK VALLEY NATIONAL PARK

The 1.7 million-acre Kobuk Valley National Park lies on the south side of the Baird Mountains 80 miles east of Kotzebue. The park is best known for the **Great Kobuk Sand Dunes** that cover 25 square miles near the Kobuk River, with some reaching to 250 feet in height. The dunes are a one-hour hike from the river, but the route can be obscure in places so be sure to get directions from the Park Service in Kotzebue (907/442-3890 or 800/478-7252, www.nps.gov/kova) before heading out.

Kiana Lodge (907/333-5866, www.alaskaoutdoors.com/kiana) has river trips into the park

Great Kobuk Sand Dunes

from the village of Kiana. You can also fly directly to the dunes from Ambler or Kotzebue; contact **Ambler Air** (907/445-2121), **Arctic Air Guides** (907/442-3030), or **Northwestern Aviation** (907/442-3525).

Two smaller areas of dunes dot the park, and the mountain passes are traversed by massive herds of caribou each spring and fall. In addition to the dunes, Kobuk Valley National Park offers pristine mountains and rivers, making it a destination for kayakers and canoeists. Most arrive by floatplane, flying from Bettles or Ambler into Walker Lake within Gates of the Arctic National Park. The 125-mile float trip to the village of Kobuk generally takes six days, or you can continue downriver all the way to Kiana. Contact the Park Service for more on running the river, and for a list of outfitters offering guided float trips.

There are no developed facilities within Kobuk Valley National Park itself, though several Native villages dot the banks of the wide, slow-moving, and clear Kobuk River. *The Alaska River Guide* by Karen Jettmar provides details on floating its more challenging upper reaches. Accommodations are available at **Kiana Lodge** (907/333-5866, www.alaskaoutdoors.com/kiana). Both **Ambler Air** (907/445-2121) and **Warbelows** (907/474-0518, www.warbelows.com) offer scheduled service between Fairbanks and Ambler.

NOATAK NATIONAL PRESERVE

The 6.6 million-acre Noatak National Preserve covers the enormous Noatak River drainage northeast of Kotzebue. Gates of the Arctic National Park is immediately east of Noatak National Preserve. Its northern edge is the crest of the DeLong Mountains, while to the south lie the Baird Mountains and Kobuk Valley National Park.

There are no developed trails or other facilities within the preserve. Most visitors float the river in kayaks or rafts, with the put-in point on the upper reaches. Fly in from Bettles and get picked up in the village of Noatak, approximately 350 miles away. Expect to take at least two weeks for this extraordinary and memorable trip. Contact the Park Service in Kotzebue (907/442-3890 or 800/478-7252, www.nps.gov/noat) for additional

information. Karen Jettmar's *The Alaska River Guide* has details on floating the Noatak River.

GATES OF THE ARCTIC NATIONAL PARK

The central section of the Brooks Range is included within Gates of the Arctic National Park and Preserve, an 8.4 million-acre slice of majestic mountainous terrain. The park is famous for its deeply glaciated valleys, rugged summits—including the much-photographed **Arrigetch Peaks**—and abundant wildlife.

Park headquarters is in Fairbanks (201 1st Ave., 907/456-0281, www.nps.gov/gaar). Field offices include the **Arctic Visitor Center** in Coldfoot (907/678-5209, open daily in the summer), **Bettles Ranger Station** (907/692-5494), and **Anaktuvuk Pass Ranger Station** (907/661-3520).

There are no roads or established trails within Gates of the Arctic, and the remote location and extreme climate of the Brooks Range require travelers to have strong wilderness skills. Before visiting the park, you will need to attend a backcountry orientation program at one of these ranger stations or at park headquarters.

Lodging facilities can be found on the park margins in Anaktuvuk Pass, Bettles, Coldfoot, and Wiseman. Of particular note is **Bettles Lodge** (907/692-5111 or 800/770-5111, www.bettleslodge.com), built in 1948, and open year-round. It even offers wintertime dogsledding trips into the park.

Access to Gates is primarily by air out of Fairbanks, Bettles, Anaktuvuk Pass, or Coldfoot. **Brooks Range Aviation** (907/692-5444 or 800/692-5443, www.brooksrange.com) has air charter service from Bettles, and **Coyote Air Service** (907/678-5995 or 800/252-0603, www.flycoyote.com) flies out of Coldfoot. **Northern Alaska Tour Company** (907/474-8600 or 800/474-1986, www.northernalaska.com) and **Trans Arctic Circle Treks** (907/479-5451 or 800/479-8908, www.arctictreks.com) offer one-day tours to Anaktuvuk Pass from Fairbanks. A small museum (907/661-3413) in Anaktuvuk Pass has exhibits on Native traditions and handicrafts.

ARCTIC NATIONAL WILDLIFE REFUGE

It doesn't get any wilder or more remote than this. The Arctic National Wildlife Refuge (ANWR; pronounced ANN-war) covers almost 20 million acres in the far northeastern part of Alaska, a landscape of flat and marshy coastal tundra, rolling hills, and tall, glaciated peaks topping 8,000 feet. Other than a few summertime travelers in search of the ultimate wilderness experience, this treeless country has almost no human presence. There has, however, been intense pressure from the oil companies and their allies (including virtually all Alaskan politicians from both parties) to "unlock" this wilderness. The oil wealth that lies beneath ANWR is undoubtedly great, but the loss of this last great wilderness would be greater. As of this writing, conservationists and their Democratic allies in the Senate have been able to block development schemes, but there is no guarantee that the oil companies won't finally win out. The battle has pitched Native people against each other—the Inupiat-owned Arctic Slope Regional Corporation is a big proponent of development (it stands to gain many millions of dollars in oil revenue)—but the Gwich'in people are adamantly opposed, fearing that development would destroy the vital caribou herds upon which they depend.

The main reason people come to ANWR—other than to experience the stunning beauty of this place—is the wildlife. During the long and fierce winter, only the hardiest animals venture out of their dens, but in summer, the refuge erupts with life. (The ubiquitous mosquitoes are the best example of this; bring headnets and insect repellents.) Best-known are the annual migrations of the 150,000-strong **Porcupine caribou herd**—they are the reason the reserve was established—but also here are millions of nesting ducks, geese, swans, loons, and other birds. Large mammals include musk ox, wolves, polar and grizzly bears, moose, and Dall sheep. Several major rivers drain ANWR on both sides

of the Phillip Smith Mountains that split the refuge. The Sheenjek and Wind Rivers are favorites of experienced kayakers and rafters.

Visiting ANWR

Access to ANWR is by floatplane out of the surrounding settlements of Fort Yukon, Kaktovik, and Deadhorse. There are no developed facilities or trails within the refuge. Several companies offer expensive wilderness treks into ANWR, but one of the best is **Alaska Discovery** (907/780-6226 or 800/586-1911, www.akdiscovery.com). A 10-day Sheenjek River trip out of Fairbanks is $3,500.

For more on this magnificent wild place, contact the U.S. Fish & Wildlife Service in Fairbanks (907/456-0250, http://arctic.fws.gov). And email your members of Congress to help protect ANWR from development!

OTHER ARCTIC REFUGES

In addition to ANWR, three other national wildlife refuges are at least partly inside the Arctic Circle. These include **Selawik, Yukon Flats, and Kanuti National Wildlife Refuges.** For details, contact the U.S. Fish & Wildlife Service in Anchorage (907/786-3542, www.r7.fws.gov).

Selawik National Wildlife Refuge

This large wetland covers more than two million acres along the Selawik River and its tributaries, and provides important habitat for caribou and other animals. The refuge is used by local people for subsistence hunting, fishing, and trapping, and sees only a handful of visitors. Selawik River—a National Wild and Scenic River—is a class I float trip from the headwaters to the village of Selawik. The Waring Mountains lie on the northern border of the refuge, and the Selawik Hills border the southern margin, providing hiking opportunities. Contact the refuge office in Kotzebue (907/442-3799, http://selawik.fws.gov) for details.

Barrow

Located 350 miles north of the Arctic Circle, at 71° latitude, and 800 miles northeast of Nome, the small city of Barrow (pop. 4,400) is filled with paradoxes. Barrow has an $80 million high school with room for 2,000 students, plus a swimming pool, indoor track, and weight room. The grade school's indoor playground is useful in the winter, when typical temperatures often drop below -30°F outside, and the town also has a first-rate hospital. Despite this, all the streets are unpaved, and yards are cluttered with old snow-machines, barking sled dogs, four-wheelers, skin boats, polar bear hides, and racks hung with dead ducks, caribou, and seal meat.

Barrow's population is predominantly Inupiat Eskimo, and many people still speak their native tongue, but the taxi drivers are Filipinos, and many restaurants are owned by Koreans. One Native woman I met sews gorgeous traditional Eskimo parkas and has dead eider ducks on her front porch, but she also spends a month or two lying on the beach in Hawaii each year!

Barrow receives 84 days of uninterrupted sunlight in summer, 67 days of darkness in winter. It sits on the edge of the Arctic Ocean, which remains virtually frozen 10 months of the year—an amazing sight in itself. Wintertime temperatures plummet far below zero, and the wind chill can push them as low as -80°F! Even in the summer, the weather is often chilly, wet, and windy. By mid-August it can be downright cold; be sure to bring warm clothes no matter when you visit. The dirt roads and wind also make for dusty conditions much of the summer.

Most visitors to Barrow arrive as part of a summertime package tour, some staying just a few hours, and others overnight. Few independent travelers visit the town since the cost of airfare alone is often higher than the tour price. Even fewer visitors get to see the events that are so important to Barrow—the whale hunts during the spring and the fall bowhead migrations. When a whale is brought in, the entire community comes out to help. Many assist in the butchering process, and the whale's fatty meat is shared. Afterward, the carcasses are dragged far out along Point Barrow to keep polar bears from wandering into town.

HISTORY

This stretch of coast was first mapped in 1826 by Captain Beech of the British Navy, who named it after Sir John Barrow, an English nobleman who encouraged and outfitted numerous Northwest Passage and polar expeditions. Whalers began arriving in the 1870s, and many of their ships became trapped in the ice; relief expeditions helped survey the North Slope. The first plane reached Barrow in 1926, and famous bush pilot Wiley Post and humorist Will Rogers crashed and died there in 1935. Today, Barrow is the seat of the vast 88,000-square-mile North Slope Borough, and has profited greatly from the oil pipeline—as can be seen in the modern buildings, services, and high wages. The average North Slope teacher earns over $55,000 per year.

One of the early white settlers was Charles D. Brower, who established a trading post at Barrow in 1884, and later married two Native women. Their 14 children became important leaders in Barrow, and the big Brower family is still a vital part of the community. One part of town is even called Browerville.

SIGHTS

This must-see **Inupiat Heritage Center** (907/852-4594, www.nps.gov/inup) is a good place to learn about Inupiat Eskimo culture, particularly as it relates to whaling. Run by Ilisagvik College in coordination with the National Park Service, the heritage center houses artifacts, carved ivory, masks, dolls, sealskin boots, and a skin-covered boat. It's open Monday–Friday 8:30 A.M.–5 P.M. year-round, and entry is $5 adults, $2 ages 15–17, $1 for ages 7–14, and free for seniors and kids. Dance and blanket-toss performances take place each afternoon in the summer, and are an additional $10.

Surprisingly, this facility is affiliated with the

BARROW

Chukchi Sea

ARCTIC OCEAN

To Pt. Barrow, Gas Line Rd., and NARL

INUPIAT HERITAGE CENTER

ACC STORE

ST.

AHKOVAK ST.

TAHAK ST.

Isatkoak Lagoon

WHALEBONE ARCH

BROWER'S CAFE

SIMMONDS

ST.

STEVENSON

Tasigarook Lagoon

HOSPITAL

UTQIAGVIK PRESBYTERIAN CHURCH

NORTH SLOPE BOROUGH OFFICE

CEMETERY

HIGH SCHOOL

KING EIDER INN

AHKOVAK ST.

TOP OF THE WORLD HOTEL

PEPE'S

AGVIK ST.

AIRPORT INN

INFO CENTER/WILL ROGERS MONUMENT

MOMEGANA ST.

ALASKA AIRLINES

BUS STATION

CAPE SMYTHE AIR

AIRPORT

SAM AND LEE'S RESTAURANT

EGASAK ST.

STEVENSON

STEVENSON

SOD HOUSE SITES

ARCTIC PIZZA

ARCTIC GROCERY

0   300 yds
0   200 m

© AVALON TRAVEL PUBLISHING, INC.

New Bedford Whaling National Historical Park in New Bedford, Massachusetts. More than 2,000 whaling voyages left New Bedford for Arctic waters during the late 19th and early 20th century, and many Inupiat Eskimo people participated in these commercial whaling ventures. In the winter, the center hosts today's whaling crews as they prepare their skin boats for the hunt.

A shop here sells quality Inupiat Eskimo arts and crafts. Other places to find them include gift shops at the Top of the World Hotel and King Eider Inn, and the North Slope Borough Office. The heritage center building also houses the **Barrow Public Library,** where you can check your email.

Other than the Inupiat Heritage Center, Barrow's main attraction is simply the place and its people. Located on the Arctic Ocean (technically the town is on the Chukchi Sea; the Beaufort Sea lies just east of Point Barrow), it has long been occupied by the Inupiat. The remains of old whale-bone-and-sod houses are visible on the shore at the west end of town, and are fascinating to explore—but do not disturb any artifacts. Walk the eroding shoreline to the east past skin-covered wooden boats and a pair of arched whale bones at Brower's Cafe. More bones, along with a "milepost" sign, can be found outside historic **Utqiagvik Presbyterian Church,** established in 1898, and rebuilt after a fire in 1909. The **North Slope Borough Office** has a big bowhead whale skull out front, and an impressive collection of artifacts—including parkas and carved walrus tusks—inside. It also sells carved ivory, garments, and other items.

Wander around Barrow and you're bound to find something of interest. There's always a dead animal hanging in somebody's yard, and the sophisticated above-ground piping system is distinctively Arctic. (Barrow's gas comes from nearby fields and is very cheap, but water must be desalinated from brackish ponds, and costs a typical household $200 a month.) East of town is a mostly inactive Distant Early Warning (D.E.W.) site and Naval Arctic Research Lab (N.A.R.L.), now used as a community college. A bowhead whale skull also sits outside the college. Listen to the local radio station (KBRW 630 AM) for a touch of North Slope reality. Last time I tuned in, the announcer was warning residents of Browerville to keep on the lookout for wandering polar bears!

The small **Barrow Visitor Center,** across from Cape Smythe Air terminal, is open daily in the summer. For local information at other times, you might try the **City of Barrow** (907/852-5211). Outside the visitor center stands a monument to **Wiley Post and Will Rogers,** who died nearby in 1935. Another monument is at the actual crash site, 16 miles away and accessible only by foot or four-wheeler. Gas Line Road extends 10 miles into the tundra from Barrow, providing good access for folks who want to wander or watch for birds. Barrow's excellent indoor **swimming pool** and recreation center are at the high school.

ACCOMMODATIONS

Barrow has several places to stay. Largest and best-known is the **Top of the World Hotel** (907/852-3900 or 800/478-8520, www.alaska one.com/topworld), where standard motel rooms run a budget-busting $140 s or d.

The **Airport Inn** (907/852-2525), has clean and comfortable rooms with microwaves and fridges for $115 s or d, including a continental breakfast.

The least expensive local place is **Narl Hotel** (907/852-7800, $75 s, $90 d), where dorm-style rooms in an Atco trailer have shared baths. This is primarily used by construction workers and scientists, and is three miles out of town, so you'll need to pay for a taxi ride. Eat next door at Ilsigavik College cafeteria, with lots of food for the buck.

Barrow's newest and nicest place, **King Eider Inn** (907/852-4700 or 888/303-4337, www.kingeider.net), is right across from the airport, with standard rooms for $170 s or $195 d, kitchenettes for $180 s or $205 d, and a luxury suite for $275 s or $300 d. A sauna is available for all guests.

FOOD

For the most expensive Mexican food you could ever imagine, eat at **Pepe's North of the Border** (907/852-8200)—a taco-enchilada combination plate is $16, and worth it! Or just order a bean burrito for $5 and fill up on chips and salsa. In business since 1978, Pepe's is run by Fran Tate, who has filled this big, fun place with the trappings of Mexico. And yes, the chefs really are from south of the border.

Another unexpected find in Barrow is **Osaka Sushi Bar** (907/852-4100), directly across from the Top of the World Hotel.

Sam & Lee's Restaurant (907/852-5555) has a filling lunchtime buffet, and is open until 2 A.M. Also try **Brower's Cafe** on the other side of town in Browerville. Outside you'll see two arched whalebones and several skin boats.

Arctic Pizza (907/852-4222) bakes surprisingly good pizzas for fair prices, and serves up prime rib on Sunday nights, plus a mix of Italian, American, and Mexican food at other times. There's a big-screen TV to watch sports or CNN, and an upstairs with windows facing the Arctic Ocean.

For do-it-yourself meals, head to the **Alaska Commercial (A.C.) Store** (907/852-6711), where you'll find everything from ice cream to sofas. (And yes, they do sell refrigerators, even at the top of the world.) The AC also has a deli with espresso coffee and an ATM. But hold onto your wallet: Food prices are sky-high. Many of these items arrive by air—which explains the high prices—but anything that won't spoil comes in aboard the barges that arrive during the brief ice-free period each August.

TRANSPORTATION AND TOURS

Alaska Airlines (800/426-0333, www.alaskaair.com) has daily jet service between Barrow and Fairbanks year-round. They also offer excursions from Fairbanks that include a tour and an overnight in Barrow at Top of the World Hotel for $525 s or $910 d. The same trip from Anchorage is $695 s or $1,250 d. If you're really in a hurry—and have tons of cash—take a 12-hour quick trip from Fairbanks to Barrow and back with a tour of the town for $400 ($560 from Anchorage).

Tours of Barrow are offered by **Tundra Tours** (907/852-3900 or 800/478-8520, www.alaskaone.com/topworld), and cost $70 if taken independently. All-day tours start with a visit to the Inupiat Heritage Center for an introduction to the culture through dancing, drumming, and singing, followed by demonstrations of how traditional items are made and the opportunity to buy pieces from local artisans. The indoor blanket toss is always a highlight, but get your photos fast since they generally do just a couple of tosses. After a lunch break, you step aboard a bus for a very informative cruise around town and out to the end of the road near Point Barrow; the point itself is several more miles away. Tundra Tours can also book the full-blown excursion from Fairbanks or Anchorage offered by Alaska Airlines.

For scheduled flights to remote North Slope villages, plus air charters and flightseeing, contact **Frontier Flying Service** (907/474-0014 or 800/478-6779, www.frontierflying.com), **Hageland Aviation** (907/442-2936 or 866/239-0119, www.hageland.com), or **Cape Smythe Air** (907/852-8333 or 800/478-5125, www.capesmythe.com). Unfortunately, Cape Smythe Air had five crashes between 1995 and 2000, some of them with multiple fatalities, and Hageland had a fatal crash near Barrow in 2003.

One of the big surprises in Barrow is the excellent borough-run **public bus** service that transports folks throughout the area. Buses are frequent Monday–Saturday, and provide a cheap way to get around this surprisingly sprawling town. Taxis are also available, or rent used cars and pickups from **King Eider Inn** (907/852-4700 or 888/303-4337, www.kingeider.net).

Resources

Suggested Reading

An excellent place to find Alaskan books is through the **Alaska Natural History Association,** (907/274-8440, www.alaskanha.org). You can order several hundred nature books, maps, calendars, guides, and other titles online or through their print catalog. Another fine source for Alaskan titles is the Anchorage-based **Cook Inlet Book Company** (907/258-4544 or 800/240-4148, www.cookinlet.com).

A number of the books listed below are out of print, but you can find many of them in regional libraries, or check the web for special orders or rare book auctions. Amazon.com, barnesandnoble.com, and other online sites will also search used bookstores for out-of-print titles. Two recommended sources for rare and out-of-print Alaskan books are Anchorage's **Title Wave Books** (907/278-9283 or 888/598-9283, www.wavebooks.com) and Juneau's **The Observatory,** (907/586-9676, www.observatorybooks.com).

Description and Travel

Alaska Almanac. Anchorage: Alaska Northwest Books, www.gacpc.com; published annually. A rich source of useful information about the state, all in one compact volume.

Alaska Atlas & Gazetteer. Freeport, ME: DeLorme Mapping, www.delorme.com, 2001. This large book of up-to-date topographic maps is a wise investment if you plan to explore the more remote parts of Alaska. Very easy to use,

Alaska Wilderness Guide. Augusta, GA: Morris Communications, www.morris.com, 2001. A good source for general information on all of Alaska's villages and cities, as well as it's many wild places.

Bodeau, Jean. *Katmai National Park and Preserve.* Anchorage: Alaska Natural History Associa-

tion, www.alaskanha.org, 1995. Describes the park's history, sights, access, hiking, bears, etc.

Colby, Merle. *A Guide to Alaska.* New York: MacMillan, 1939. Written over half a century ago, this Federal Writers' Project guide to Alaska has never been surpassed. Out of print, but can be found in a good library.

Hempstead, Andrew. *Moon Handbooks British Columbia.* Emeryville, CA: Avalon Travel Publishing, www.moon.com, 2002. Like this book, Andrew Hempstead's titles are part of the Moon Handbooks series. He provides excellent advice for travelers in Canada, Alaska's neighbor to the east.

Hempstead, Andrew. *Moon Handbooks Alberta.* Emeryville, CA: Avalon Travel Publishing, www.moon.com, 2004.

Hempstead, Andrew. *Moon Handbooks Canadian Rockies.* Emeryville, CA: Avalon Travel Publishing, www.moon.com, 2003.

Hempstead, Andrew. *Moon Handbooks Western Canada.* Emeryville, CA: Avalon Travel Publishing, www.moon.com, 2004.

Howard, Jim. *Guide to Sea Kayaking in Southeast Alaska: The Best Trips and Tours from Misty Fjords to Glacier Bay.* Old Saybrook, CT: Globe Pequot Press, www.globepequot.com, 1999. This book describes 41 Southeast Alaska kayak trips.

Jettmar, Karen. *Alaska's Glacier Bay.* Anchorage: Alaska Northwest Books, www.gacpc.com, 1997. A good little sourcebook for park information.

Jettmar, Karen. *The Alaska River Guide.* Anchorage: Alaska Northwest Books, www.gacpc.com, 1998. Filled with vital information for anyone planning to float more than 100 Alaska rivers.

Kelley, Mark. *Glacier Bay National Park Alaska.* Juneau: Mark Kelley Photography, www.markkelley.com, 2000. A beautiful coffee table book by Southeast Alaska's foremost photographer.

Larson, Richard. *Mountain Bike Alaska—49 Trails in the 49th State.* Anchorage: Glacier House Publications, 1991. A reasonably complete look at mountain biking in Alaska.

The Milepost. Augusta, GA: Morris Communications, www.themilepost.com; published annually. For motorists, this publication—in existence for more than 55 years—is the best guidebook to Alaska. The highway maps and description make it a must if you're driving north. Although the information is accurate and comprehensive, specific listings of hotels, bars, and restaurants are limited to advertisers, and the ads don't exactly tell the whole story.

Moore, Terris. *Mt. McKinley: The Pioneer Climbs.* Seattle: The Mountaineers, www.mountaineers.org, 1981. An exciting history of the challenge to climb North America's highest mountain.

Nienhueser, Helen, and John Wolfe Jr. *55 Ways to the Wilderness in Southcentral Alaska.* Seattle: The Mountaineers, www.mountaineers.org, 2002. A compact trail guide, complete with maps, photos, and descriptions of the best the region has to offer.

Praetorius, Pete and Alys Culhane. *Alaska Bicycle Touring Guide.* Juneau: Denali Press, 1992. The best source for cyclists planning a trip around Alaska and the Yukon.

Quick, Daniel L. *Kenai Canoe Trails.* Anchorage: Todd Publications, 1997. A very helpful guide to canoe routes within Kenai National Wildlife Refuge.

Romano-Lax, Andromeda. *How to Rent a Public Cabin in Southcentral Alaska.* Berkeley: Wilderness Press, www.wildernesspress.com, 2003. An enjoyable and detailed guide to dozens of Forest Service and state park cabins.

Shepherd, Shane and Owen Wozniak. *50 Hikes in Alaska's Chugach State Park.* Seattle: The Mountaineers, www.mountaineers.org, 2001. An informative guide to hiking in the second-largest state park in America.

Skillman, Don. *Adventure Kayaking: Trips in Glacier Bay.* Berkeley: Wilderness Press, www.wildernesspress.com, 1998. A helpful guide to sea kayaking around Glacier Bay.

Wayburn, Peggy. *Adventuring in Alaska.* San Francisco: Sierra Club Books, www.sierraclub.org/books, 1998. A guide to the remote wilderness regions of Alaska and how to get there.

Zimmerman, Jenny. *A Naturalist's Guide to Chugach State Park, Alaska.* Anchorage: AT Publishing, 1997. Everything you ever wanted to know about Anchorage's wonderful next-door neighbor, from history to hikes to ski treks. Out of print.

Natural History

Hulten, Eric. *Flora of Alaska and Neighboring Territories.* Stanford: Stanford University Press, www.sup.org, 1968. A huge manual of the vascular plants—highly technical, but easy to consult.

Matsen, Brad. *Ray Troll's Shocking Fish Tales.* Anchorage: Alaska Northwest Books, www.gacpc.com, 1993. Illustrated by Ray Troll, outrageous fish artist par excellence, this book offers a mix of scientific and philosophic ramblings about creatures of the sea. Great fun.

Murie, Adolph. *A Naturalist in Alaska.* Tucson: University of Arizona Press, www.uapress.arizona.edu, 1990. This reprint of a 1961 classic still offers excellent insight into the fauna of Alaska.

Murie, Adolph. *The Wolves of Mount McKinley.* Seattle: University of Washington Press, www.washington.edu/uwpress, 1985. Another of Murie classic, originally published in 1944.

O'Clair, Rita M., Robert H. Armstrong, and Richard Carstensen. *The Nature of Southeast Alaska.* Anchorage: Alaska Northwest Books, www.gacpc.com, 2003. See the world through the naturalists' eyes in this beautifully illustrated guide to the lives of animals and plants in Southeast Alaska.

Sydeman, Michelle and Annabel Lund. *Alaska Wildlife Viewing Guide.* Old Saybrook, CT: Globe Pequot Press, www.globepequot.com, 1996. A small, helpful guide to the state's animals.

Walker, Tom. *River of Bears.* Stillwater, Minnesota: Voyageur Press, 1993. The story of McNeil River and the bears that have made it a favorite of photographers. Photos by Larry Aumiller, the Fish and Game employee who guides hundreds of visitors here each summer. Out of print.

Wynne, Kate. *Guide to Marine Mammals of Alaska.* Fairbanks: University of Alaska, 1997. An outstanding, easy-to-use guide to the whales, seals, porpoises, sea lions, and other sea mammals around Alaska. Perfect for anyone riding the ferry boats or heading out on a wildlife tour. Out of print.

History

Adney, Tappan. *Klondike Stampede.* Vancouver: University of British Columbia Press, www.ubcpress.ubc.ca, 1995. The best and most readable book on Alaska's gold rush.

Berton, Pierre. *The Klondike Fever.* New York: Carroll & Graf, www.carrollandgraf.com, 2003. Originally published in 1958, this remains the definitive account of the gold rush.

Chevigny, Hector. *Lord of Alaska.* Portland, OR: Binford & Mort, 1971. Biography of Alexander Baranof, manager of the Russian American Company from 1791 to 1817. Out of print.

Cohen, Stan. *The Forgotten War.* Missoula, MT: Pictorial Histories Publishing Co., 1993. A pictorial history of World War II in Alaska and northwestern Canada.

Greiner, James. *Wager with the Wind: The Don Sheldon Story.* New York: St. Martin's Press, www.stmartins.com, 1982. The true story of one of the state's most famous bush pilots.

Heller, Herbert L. *Sourdough Sagas.* Cleveland: World Publishing Co., 1967. Colorful tales of mishap and adventure among Alaska's prospecting pioneers. Out of print.

Morgan, Murray. *One Man's Gold Rush: A Klondike Album.* Seattle: University of Washington Press, www.washington.edu/uwpress, 1995. A feast of gold-rush photography.

Muir, John. *Travels in Alaska.* Written in 1915, this is Muir's classic narration of his experiences on the Stikine River and at Glacier Bay during 1879, 1880, and 1890. Several publishers offer reprints.

Neufeld, David and Frank Norris. *Chilkoot Trail, Heritage Route to the Klondike.* Whitehorse, Yukon: Lost Moose Publishing, 1996. A fascinating book about the gold rush, filled with black and white photos.

Okun, S.B. *The Russian-American Company.* Cambridge: Harvard University Press, 1951. This translation from the Russian gives a different view of Alaska in the period up to 1867. Out of print.

Oman, Lela Kiana. *The Epic of Qayaq: The Longest Story Ever Told by My People.* Seattle: University of Washington Press, www.washington.edu/uwpress, 1995. The story of the Inupiat people of the Kobuk Valley as told in stories passed down though the generations. Beautifully illustrated. The author is a respected elder in Nome.

Sherwood, Morgan B. *Exploration of Alaska, 1865-1900.* Fairbanks: University of Alaska Press, www.uaf.edu/uapress, 1992. This reprint of the 1965 book details the opening of the Interior.

Wilson, Graham and Clelie Rich (editors). *The Klondike Gold Rush: Photographs from 1896-1899.* Whitehorse, Yukon: Wolf Creek Books, 2003. An excellent collection of historical photos from the Klondike gold rush.

Art and Literature

Bancroft-Hunt, Norman. *People of the Totem: The Indians of the Pacific Northwest.* New York: Peter Bedrick Books, 1989. A beautifully illustrated history of the art of Tlingit and other Northwest peoples. Out of print.

Bodett, Tom. *As Far As You Can Go Without a Passport.* New York: Perseus Publishing, 1986. A collection of wry, bring-a-smile-to-your-face Alaska tales. Bodett's other books include *The End of the Road* and *Small Comforts.* Out of print.

Jans, Nick. *The Last Light Breaking.* Anchorage: Alaska Northwest Books, www.gacpc.com, 1993. A beautifully written collection of essays about life in the Eskimo village of Ambler.

Jans, Nick. *A Place Beyond.* Anchorage: Alaska Northwest Books, www.gacpc.com, 1996. Another fine collection of stories by one of Alaska's most observant writers.

Kizzia, Tom. *The Wake of the Unseen Object.* Lincoln, NE: University of Nebraska Press, www.nebraskapress.unl.edu, 1998. A lovingly written journey through the wild heart of today's Alaskan Bush. Filled with insights into the clashing cultures of Native and white America.

London, Jack. *The Call of the Wild.* This gripping tale of a sled dog's experience along the gold rush trail was Jack London's most successful rendering of the spirit of the North. Reprint editions are available from several publishers.

Lopez, Barry. *Arctic Dreams.* New York: Random House, www.randomhouse.com, 2001. A wonderful exploration of the Arctic, with a mixture of scientific information and environmental thinking. Get this book!

Lopez, Barry. *Of Wolves and Men.* New York: Scribner, www.galegroup.com/scribners, 1982. An excellent discussion of the hunter/hunted dynamic.

Marshall, Robert. *Alaska Wilderness: Exploring the Central Brooks Range.* Berkeley: University of California Press, www.uscpress.edu, 1983. A thrilling account of the author's exploration of the Central Brooks Range.

McGinniss, Joe. *Going to Extremes.* New York: Plume, 1989. One man's journey to Alaska leads him to a series of characters as diverse as the state itself. This reissue of a 1980 book, though quite dated, is still popular with travelers.

McPhee, John. *Coming into the Country.* New York: Noonday Press, 2003. Even though it was actually written in the 1970s, this remains perhaps the best portrayal of Alaskan lifestyles ever written. It's the book you'll see folks reading on the long ferry ride north.

Muir, John. *Stikeen.* Berkeley: Heyday Books, www.heydaybooks.com, 1990. Originally published almost a century ago, this classic short dog story offers a vastly different take on Glacier Bay than that seen by the cruise ship tourists.

Schooler, Lynn. *Blue Bear: A True Story of Friendship, Tragedy and Survival in the Alaskan Wilderness.* New York: Harper-Collins Publishers, www.harpercollins.com, 2002. This beautifully crafted memoir chronicles Lynn's life and how it was changed by Michio Hoshino, the renowned wildlife photographer killed by a grizzly in 1996.

Service, Robert. *Collected Poems.* New York: Putnam Publishing, www.penguinputnam.com, 1989. No one has ever better captured the flavor of northern life than the poet Robert Service.

Stewart, Hilary. *Looking at Indian Art of the Northwest Coast.* Seattle; University of Washington Press, www.washington.edu/uwpress, 2003. A concise analysis of the art forms of this powerful culture.

Stewart, Hilary. *Looking at Totem Poles.* Seattle: University of Washington Press, www.washington.edu/uwpress, 2003. Details on the history and art of more than 100 totem poles in Alaska and British Columbia.

Walker, Spike. *Working on the Edge.* New York: St. Martin's Press, www.stmartins.com, 2003. Harrowing tales from the edge of the abyss—working the king-crab boats of the Bering Sea in the boom years of the 1970s and early '80s, when the financial stakes were almost as high as the risks to life. Read it before you even consider working on a crab boat!

Internet Resources

The Internet is a great source of information on Alaska. The following is a tiny sample; a quick Google search will turn up a multitude of additional websites for your area of interest.

www.travelalaska.com
This is the homepage of the Alaska Travel Industry Association, which distributes the official Alaska State Vacation Planner.

www.state.ak.us
This is the State of Alaska homepage, with links to state agencies and tourism sites.

www.alaskachamber.com
Links to all Alaskan chambers of commerce are featured here.

www.alaskastateparks.org
Find details on Alaska's state parks and recreation areas on this useful site.

www.wildlife.alaska.gov
The Alaska Department of Fish & Game's site is a good starting place for details on sport fishing and wildlife viewing around Alaska.

www.firstgov.com
The federal government's primary web portal offers links to all of its various agencies.

www.nps.gov/aplic
Four Alaska Public Lands Information Centers are scattered around the state; this is their homepage, which offers an overview of federal lands in Alaska.

www.r7.fws.gov
Head here for details on the U.S. Fish & Wildlife Service, which manages 16 refuges across the state, including Kodiak National Wildlife Refuge and Arctic National Wildlife Refuge.

www.nps.gov
The National Park Service's homepage has details on Denali, Glacier Bay, Wrangell–St. Elias, Katmai, and other national parks in Alaska.

www.ferryalaska.com
Visit this website for current Alaska Marine Highway ferry schedules and fares.

www.511.alaska.gov
Especially useful for winter travel in Alaska, this site has details on road conditions, ferry arrival times, highway construction updates, and more. Get the same info by dialing 511 toll-free anywhere in Alaska.

www.ak.blm.gov
Alaska's largest land management agency, the Bureau of Land Management has over 90 million acres in the state, including popular recreation areas near Fairbanks.

www.fs.fed.us/r10
The U.S. Forest Service homepage for Alaska covers the nation's two largest national forests: Tongass and Chugach.

www.reserveusa.com
A private company, ReserveUSA, books all Forest Service cabins in Alaska, plus a handful of campgrounds around the state.

www.usgs.gov
Head to the U.S. Geological Survey website for downloadable topographic maps.

http://climate.gi.alaska.edu
This site includes climatic data, current weather conditions, and Alaskan forecasts.

www.arh.noaa.gov
The National Weather Service site features up-to-date forecasts for Alaska.

www.adn.com/visitors
The excellent online Alaska visitor guide, produced by the *Anchorage Daily News*.

www.alaska.net/~jrc/alaska.html
Find a complete listing of Alaskan environmental groups here, with links to their homepages.

www.alaskaecotourism.org
Operated by the Alaska Wilderness Recreation and Tourism Association, this site provides links to more than 300 wilderness travel businesses.

www.alaska.com
This website is a great resource, with tons of links. It's operated by the *Anchorage Daily News*, whose website, www.adn.com has current Alaska news, fishing info, and much

more, including a trivia page with all sorts of useless factoids.

www.inalaska.com
Maintained by Anchorage's KTUU television, this is a good general site for state info.

www.alaskaone.com
This is another fairly comprehensive website for Alaska information.

www.everythingalaska.com
Yet another good place to explore Alaska on the web.

www.dced.state.ak.us/dca
The Alaska Community Database offers trivia on 350 cities and towns around the state. Maps and photos are also featured.

Index

Index

Canoeing/Kayaking

Index

Index

Index

Hiking

Index

Index

Index

Index

Acknowledgments

Now in its eighth edition, *Moon Handbooks Alaska* has evolved substantially from the book that first emerged from the primordial ooze. It would be impossible to thank all of the people who helped me with this update, but a number of individuals deserve appreciation.

A heartfelt thank you goes to the following people who helped open doors to their hometowns or reviewed my manuscript for problems: Karen Hofstad in Petersburg, Gloria Ohmer of Tides Inn in Petersburg, Jeff Butcher of Hotel Halsingland in Haines, Buckwheat Donahue at the Skagway Visitor Information Center, Pam Foreman of the Kodiak Island Convention and Visitors Bureau, the staff at the Russian Heritage Inn in Kodiak, Karen Lundquist and Nicholas Jacobs of the Fairbanks Convention and Visitors Bureau, Susan Wilson of Aurora Express in Fairbanks, and Leslie Seamon at the Nome Convention and Visitors Bureau. A tip of the hat also goes to the friendly folks at New York Hotel, Gilmore Hotel, and Alaska Cruises, all in Ketchikan, along with Echo Sutton of the Ketchikan Visitors Bureau, and the Forest Service's Julie Rowe and Vernon Keller. Thanks also to two travelers who provided tips: Elizabeth Webb and Janet N. Moran. I wish to especially thank Elizabeth Dahl for her assistance in Juneau—from transportation to lodging to editing. This book was shepherded through the production process by my editor, Kevin McLain. Thanks to him and the rest of the gang at Avalon Travel Publishing for getting this book into your hands.

I offer a very special thanks to my sweet wife, Karen Shemet, and our two live-wire children, Aziza and Rio, for keeping my priorities straight and adding a bit of levity.

U.S.~Metric Conversion

1 inch = 2.54 centimeters (cm)
1 foot = .304 meters (m)
1 yard = 0.914 meters
1 mile = 1.6093 kilometers (km)
1 km = .6214 miles
1 fathom = 1.8288 m
1 chain = 20.1168 m
1 furlong = 201.168 m
1 acre = .4047 hectares
1 sq km = 100 hectares
1 sq mile = 2.59 square km
1 ounce = 28.35 grams
1 pound = .4536 kilograms
1 short ton = .90718 metric ton
1 short ton = 2000 pounds
1 long ton = 1.016 metric tons
1 long ton = 2240 pounds
1 metric ton = 1000 kilograms
1 quart = .94635 liters
1 US gallon = 3.7854 liters
1 Imperial gallon = 4.5459 liters
1 nautical mile = 1.852 km

To compute Celsius temperatures, subtract 32 from Fahrenheit and divide by 1.8. To go the other way, multiply Celsius by 1.8 and add 32.

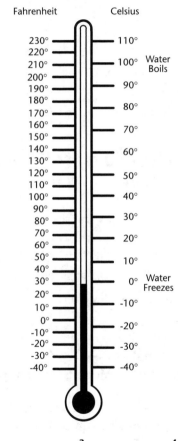

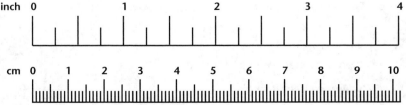

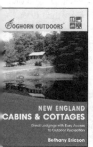

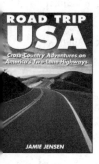

Keeping Current

Although we strive to produce the most up-to-date guidebook humanly possible, change is unavoidable. Between the time this book goes to print and the moment you read it, a handful of the businesses noted in these pages will undoubtedly change prices, move, or even close their doors forever. Other worthy attractions will open for the first time. If you have a favorite gem you'd like to see included in the next edition, or see anything that needs updating, clarification, or correction, please drop us a line. Send your comments via email to atpfeedback@avalonpub.com, or use the address below.

Moon Handbooks Alaska
Avalon Travel Publishing
1400 65th Street, Suite 250
Emeryville, CA 94608, USA
www.moon.com

Editor and Series Manager: Kevin McLain
Copy Editor: Kate McKinley
Graphics and Production Coordinator: Justin Marler
Cover Designer: Kari Gim
Interior Designers: Amber Pirker, Alvaro Villanueva, Kelly Pendragon
Map Editor: Naomi Adler Dancis
Cartographers: Kat Kalamaras, Mike Morgenfeld
Indexer: Deana Shields

ISBN: 1-56691-591-0
ISSN: 1547-0261

Printing History
1st Edition—1983
8th Edition—April 2004
5 4 3 2 1

Text © 2004 by Don Pitcher
Maps © 2004 by Avalon Travel Publishing, Inc.
All rights reserved.

Avalon Travel Publishing is a division of Avalon Publishing Group, Inc.